The Oxford Encyclopedia of the Reformation

The Oxford Encyclopedia of the Reformation

HANS J. HILLERBRAND

EDITOR IN CHIEF

Volume 3

New York Oxford

OXFORD UNIVERSITY PRESS

1996

Oxford University Press

Oxford New York
Athens Auckland Bangkok Bombay
Calcutta Cape Town Dar es Salaam Delhi
Florence Hong Kong Istanbul Karachi
Kuala Lumpur Madras Madrid Melbourne
Mexico City Nairobi Paris Singapore
Taipei Tokyo Toronto

and associated companies in
Berlin Ibadan

Published by Oxford University Press, Inc.,
198 Madison Avenue, New York, New York 10016

Library of Congress Cataloging-in-Publication Data
The Oxford encyclopedia of the Reformation / Hans J. Hillerbrand, editor in chief
p. cm.
Includes bibliographical references and index.
ISBN 0-19-506493-3 (set : alk. paper)
1. Reformation—Encyclopedias. 2. Reformation—Biography—Encyclopedias.
3. Theology, Doctrinal—Europe—History—16th century—Encyclopedias.
4. Europe—Church history—16th century—Encyclopedias.
I. Hillerbrand, Hans J.
BR302.8.093 1996 270.6'03—dc20 95-24520 CIP

ISBN-13-978-0-19-506493-3
ISBN 0-19-506493-3 (set)
ISBN 0-19-510364-5 (vol. 3)

Printing (last digit): 9 8 7 6 5 4 3

Printed in the United States of America
on acid-free paper

M

CONTINUED

MARBACH, Johannes (1521–1581), president of the Compagnie des Pasteurs in Strasbourg, Lutheran controversialist, and theologian. Born in Lindau as the son of a furrier, Marbach likely received his secondary education at Strasbourg's academy and then was sent to Wittenberg in the aftermath of the Wittenberg Concord (1536). Luther himself chaired Marbach's doctoral disputation in 1543 on the episcopal office. Marbach returned to Lindau for a few years as a pastor but was called to Strasbourg by 1546 to serve as pastor of Saint Nicholas and a professor in the academy's fledgling theology faculty. He became the city's theologian in the negotiations that produced the Württemberg Confession and the representative of Lutheran theologians to the second session of the Council of Trent. On the death of Caspar Hedio late in 1552, he was chosen as president of the Compagnie des Pasteurs in Strasbourg and held the post until his death on 17 March 1581.

His successor described him as "a teacher of the true faith and student of the great Luther." As such, Marbach was not an original theologian and did not intend to be one. Rather, he was a defender of the Augsburg Confession and sought to be in close accord with like-minded churchmen (with whom he corresponded extensively) throughout Germany. He was such an intentional Lutheran that, when the debate began around Mathias Flaccius Illyricus over original sin and human nature, he carefully determined the tide of orthodox opinion on the matter and then went with it.

It was no accident, therefore, that Marbach's published theological works concerned solely matters of current controversy and practical applications to church life and teachings at the moment. He thus wrote on the real presence in the Lord's Supper, the proper way to elect a bishop, and at great length against the miracles that Jesuits in the area alleged to be associated with devotions at a Marian shrine near Freiburg im Breisgau. His commitment to Lutheranism showed through above all in a controversy (1561–1563) with Girolamo Zanchi, a professor at the academy, in which Marbach anticipated the contents of article 11 (predestination) in the Formula of Concord and, with respect to the Lord's Supper, repeatedly replied, "Augsburg Confession! Augsburg Confession!" For Zanchi, Luther had begun a theological investigation; for Marbach, he had ended it.

Marbach's chief contribution to the Lutheran Reformation was therefore as a churchman. Within less than a year after becoming president of the Compagnie des Pasteurs, he produced an "agenda" that proposed a substantial alteration (chiefly in the area of worship practices) to the rudimentary church order of 1534. At the same time, he convened the city's pastors every other week to discuss the business of the church and, with the support of the civil authorities, began to carry out visitations chiefly in the rural parishes. He also used the theology faculty, of which he was the longtime dean, to train new pastors, so that by the early 1560s even Strasbourg's most distant parishes had their own pastors, who were educated in the city, examined by the Compagnie des Pasteurs, and closely supervised through the annual visitations. The system was so successful that in 1559 the Elector Palatine briefly acquired Marbach's services to install it in his territories, although Strasbourg itself did not formally mandate these practices, along with the Formula of Concord, until 1598.

The controversy between Marbach and Johannes Sturm both underlined the importance of Marbach's work and marked the nadir of his career. It began in December 1569 when Sturm threatened to resign his position as "lifetime" rector of the academy on the grounds that the pastors and the students and professors in the theology faculty claimed to be self-governing—that is, exempt from the authority of the nontheologians on the academy's faculty. Marbach replied that it was "unheard of" for theologians to be subject to the discipline of what he characterized as basically an arts faculty. In so doing he appealed both to the authority of his office as "superintendent" and to the precedent of older universities.

Marbach lost this battle. The civil authorities declared that they and they alone were the "superintendents" of the city's church and that Marbach merely presided over the meetings of the pastors and represented them before the government. As a result, Marbach was stripped of his deanship, and Sturm acquired the authority to approve theses for disputations in the theology faculty itself. Marbach did not live to see it, but in 1581 a debate on much the same issues—between his eventual successor, Johann Pappus, and Sturm—reversed the initial outcome. Pappus did not receive the title "superintendent," but he did get all of Marbach's authority and responsibilities and at last saw the adoption of the new church order of 1598, which survived until the French Revolution. Marbach's career thus reveals the middle stages of the process by which the Lutheran Reformation became not just a coherent body of doctrine but also an established church that by and large conducted its own business according to agreed-upon procedures.

BIBLIOGRAPHY

Abray, Lorna Jane. *The People's Reformation: Magistrates, Clergy, and Commons in Strasbourg, 1500–1598.* Ithaca, N.Y., 1985. Reliable summary but lacks theological sophistication.

Adam, Johann. *Evangelische Kirchengeschichte der Stadt Strassburg bis zur Französischen Revolution.* Strasbourg, 1922. Good overview written from a Reformed perspective but somewhat thin on sources.

Horning, Wilhelm. *Dr. Johann Marbach.* Strasbourg, 1990. Good on basic chronology but written by an obvious partisan.

Kittelson, James M. "Marbach vs. Zanchi: The Resolution of Controversy in Late Reformation Strasbourg." *Sixteenth-Century Journal* 8.3 (1977), 31–44. These writings treat the actual functioning of the church in Strasbourg.

———. "Successes and Failures in the German Reformation: The Report from Strasbourg," *Archive for Reformation History* 73 (1982), 153–175.

Röhrich, Timotheus-Wilhelm. *Geschichte der Reformation im Elsass und besonders in Strassburg.* 3 vols. Strasbourg, 1830–1832. Has the advantage of being written before the shelling of the Strasbourg archives but the disadvantage of a strong Reformed bias against Marbach.

Verzeichnis der im deutschen Sprachbereich erschienenen Drucke des XVI. Jahrhunderts. Stuttgart, 1983–. See vol. 13, nos. 901–912.

JAMES M. KITTELSON

MARBURG, COLLOQUY OF. When their protest at the second imperial Diet of Speyer did not achieve the recognition for which they had hoped, several of the protesting imperial estates united in a temporary alliance on the day of the recess (*Reichsabschied*), 22 April 1529. This action was taken less against the Turks, who had reached Vienna and were thus threatening the empire, than against Emperor Charles V, who had achieved momentary supremacy through his peace agreements with the pope and with the king of France, thus triggering fears of a military strike that would finally allow him to administer the Edict of Worms. It cannot be determined who initiated this alliance. The driving force in bringing it to fruition was Landgrave Philipp of Hesse, who was seeking to build a united front of all Protestant powers within the empire, which was in turn supposed to become the center of a large anti-Habsburg coalition that would encompass all of Europe. However, this endeavor was obstructed by the fundamental theological differences that separated the Wittenberg reformers from their co-religionists in south Germany and Switzerland. These antagonisms became instrumental in the Schwabach Articles, in which Martin Luther once more summarized his theological teachings, but which did not meet with the approval of the Swiss Zwinglians. In order to overcome these theological differences, which were obstructing his political plans, and in order to reach a consensus among the reformers, Landgrave Philipp, as early as 22 April, invited the important representatives of the reformers to a colloquy. He wanted to prevent the failure (for theological reasons) of his proposed alliance, and he especially wanted to assure the participation of the Swiss, who were militarily important. As the site for the meeting he set his own castle in the town of Marburg, his residence, which had shortly before been raised to the status of university town.

There is insufficient information on the course of the colloquy to trace events in detail. The notes recorded from memory vary greatly in details—even with respect to the number of participants. Among those certainly present from Wittenberg were Martin Luther himself, Philipp Melanchthon, Justus Jonas, Caspar Cruciger, Oswald Myconius, and Justus Menius; from Nuremberg came Andreas Osiander and Veit Dietrich, from Augsburg Stephan Agricola, from Württemberg Johannes Brenz. The Swiss reformers were represented by Huldrych Zwingli and Johannes Oecolampadius. From the Upper Rhine, Jakob Sturm, Martin Bucer, Caspar Hedio, and Heinrich Bullinger participated. The chief protagonists were Luther and Zwingli. The former had initially rejected the colloquy—as had his sovereign, the elector of Saxony—because he feared that this disputation might lead to a watering down of the Protestant teachings and a profanation of the word of God; moreover, he was not interested in the projected political alliance. Because of these deep reservations Luther had only consented at the last minute. Zwingli, on the other hand, who was especially courted by the landgrave as an important force in his political plans, placed far higher expectations on the meeting and was confident of a positive outcome.

The talks began on 1 October in the presence of Landgrave Philipp and his cousin, Duke Ulrich of Württemberg, with an address by the landgrave's chancellor, Johann Feige. In a friendly manner, Feige asked all participants for unity. In order to avoid a clash of the two main participants right at the beginning of the meeting, the landgrave first had Luther talk with Oecolampadius and Zwingli with Melanchthon. The talks dealt with all relevant topics. There was a closing of the gap in some areas, prejudice and misunderstandings were removed in others, and in some few cases agreements were in fact reached.

The decisive meetings took place on 2 October. Central was the disputation between Luther and Zwingli as well as Oecolampadius on the question of the Lord's Supper, the heart of the intra-Protestant theological quarrels since 1525. It was primarily about the words of institution: *Hoc est corpus meum.* Luther, always fond of theatrical gestures, had written them in chalk on the table at the beginning of the talks. There were fierce debates about the question of their interpretation in a literal or a metaphoric sense: how is Christ present in the form of bread and wine? Luther, wholly in line with his understanding of scripture, strongly affirmed the bodily transformation of bread and wine, that is, the real presence, while Zwingli rejected it; he granted a spiritual presence of Christ. This question was discussed intensely, and the two parties became increasingly hostile; agreement could not be reached. Zwingli also rejected the compromise formula proposed by Luther according to which the consecrated body and blood of Christ were present "substantive et essentialiter, non autem quantitative vel qualitative vel localiter."

Since the talks deadlocked and the two fronts hardened, discussions had to be continued on 3 October. Now the Strasbourg theologians took a more active part and proposed a compromise that Luther rejected. He was acting in accord, maybe even in verbal agreement, with Melanchthon, who feared that an obvious rapprochement of Wittenberg with the south Germans might lead to the failure of the desired agreement with the emperor. Despite widespread progress in specifics, there was no breakthrough in the central question.

The landgrave, who would have been satisfied with a loose compromise, did everything to achieve his goal of agreement among the Protestants. He tried to propel the negotiations forward through individual talks and personally invited several participants to meals. Political reasons above all motivated him. With this in mind, Luther asked for the results of the colloquy to be put down in writing. On 4 October he presented the fifteen Marburg Articles, which, on the one hand, summarized the points on which agreement had been reached or seemed feasible and, on the other hand, recorded the remaining disagreement. The first fourteen points were concerned with matters of general faith in which the common ground was certain—the Trinity, baptism of infants, and the position toward governmental authority. Point fifteen was reserved for the cardinal question of the disagreement over the Lord's Supper. Here, too, there were rapprochements, such as the insistence on an abolition of the Mass and for Communion under both kinds. On the key question of the real presence views continued to differ. While a consensus had been reached, dissent remained. In this manner, no one lost or was coerced into anything, but the crucial questions remained unresolved. Luther's fifteen Marburg Articles, which constituted a clear modification of the Schwabach Articles, were approved and signed by all present; there are two copies, one in Marburg and one in Zurich. The parties agreed to overcome the remaining differences in Christian love and to continue the conversation. The last article concluded with the assurance that they would abide with one another "in true understanding."

Views on the significance of the fifteen articles that resulted from the Colloquy of Marburg differed widely. Each party felt victorious. So the result of the colloquy was overestimated; the common ground that had been reached could not hide the fact that the talks had basically failed. There were various reasons for this failure. In addition to the mutual personal dislike of the two major reformers, which was apparent in Marburg, there were fundamental differences on political and ideological questions. Eventually it became clear that the two camps of reformers could not be reconciled to one another: the humanist rationality of Zwingli, who saw the teachings of scripture as rationally comprehensible, was ranged against the combative dogmatism of Luther, who constantly referred to the words of the Bible, was not interested in the political consequences of his decision (even though it reflected not only Melanchthon's but also Saxony's stance), and readily accepted the breach which he had perceived right from the start. He succinctly summarized his general sense: "If your spirit and our spirit are not in harmony, it is obvious that we do not have the same spirit." Efforts to conclude the colloquy with a common celebration of the Lord's Supper failed.

The Colloquy of Marburg was the first significant attempt at bringing together the different Protestant camps that had evolved in German-speaking areas. Its failure became the point of departure for the division of the movement of reform; in Marburg the opposing positions were clarified and became more obvious. The resolution of theological differences, which had been formulated as a goal, did not occur, and the desired political alliance did not materialize. So the Marburg Articles have in fact become a document of the division within Protestantism. But the colloquy linked the German Protestants more closely; the basis here, however, was not the Marburg Articles but the Schwabach Articles, which were soon revised. A few years later, the Wittenberg Concord (1534) and the Württemberg Concord (1536) found a common denominator, which, however, excluded the Swiss reformers. The Colloquy of Marburg was supposed to be a crucial milestone on the reformers' way to determining their church and to establishing an alliance for the self-assertion. But it became in fact an important step toward the formation of different Protestant traditions.

[*See also* Bucer, Martin; Hedio, Caspar; Luther, Martin; Oecolampadius, Johannes; Philipp of Hesse; *and* Zwingli, Huldrych.]

BIBLIOGRAPHY

Bezzenberger, Günter. *Was zu Marpurgh geschah: Eine Einführung in die Geschichte des Marburger Religionsgesprächs im Jahr 1529*. Kassel, 1979.

Bizer, Ernst. *Studien zur Geschichte des Abendmahlsstreits im 16. Jahrhunderts*. 2d ed. Darmstadt, 1962.

Köhler, Walther. *Das Marburger Religionsgespräch, 1529: Versuch einer Rekonstruktion*. Leipzig, 1929.

———. *Das Religionsgespräch zu Marburg, 1529*. Tübingen, 1929.

May, Gerhard, ed. *Das Marburger Religionsgespräch, 1529*. Gütersloh, 1970.

Schirrmacher, Friedrich Wilhelm, ed. *Briefe und Acten zu der Geschichte des Religionsgespräches zu Marburg, 1529*. Gotha, 1876.

Schubert, Hans von. *Die Anfänge der evangelischen Bekenntnisbildung von 1529/30*. Leipzig, 1928.

ALOIS SCHMID

MARBURG CONFESSION. The Marburg Colloquy of 1–4 October 1529 was convened by Landgrave Philipp of Hesse in order to settle the controversy over the Lord's Supper that had begun to divide the reformers. The discussions of 1–3 October, mainly between Luther and Melanchthon on one side, Zwingli and Oecolampadius on the other, helped the protagonist to get a better understanding of their opponents' views, but no agreement could be reached over the issue of Christ's corporeal presence in Communion. The landgrave was undaunted. Doctrinal agreement was a precondition to the realization of the strategy he had pursued ever since the second Diet of Speyer earlier in 1529: political alliance of all evangelical princes and imperial cities, including the southwestern German cities tending to Zwinglianism, and even the Swiss centers of the Reformation, Zurich and Basel. Accordingly Philipp urged the parties to make further attempts to reach agreement. The Lutherans offered at least three formulas that contained a mild doctrine of the presence of Christ in the sacrament, but the Swiss and Strasbourg theologians rejected them. The Lutherans in turn refused the proposal to affirm Communion without an agreement on the Eucharist. When these negotiations of 3–4 October had failed, the landgrave asked Luther to record the articles on which the parties had reached agreement as well as those on which they remained divided. The text Luther produced is called the Marburg Confession (also known as the Marburg Articles).

As a model for his work Luther used the seventeen Schwabach Articles, a confession drawn up in 1529 by the Wittenberg theologians, mainly Melanchthon and Luther, for Elector John of Saxony. These had been meant to serve as a theological basis of the Protestant alliance as pursued by Philipp of Hesse, but had had as their objective the exclusion of Zwinglianism. Luther now changed the order of the seventeen articles and reduced their number to fifteen; the text was shorter, less polemical, and more popular than that of the Schwabach Articles. Although it was written on the following day, the Marburg Confession was dated 3 October. It obviously was to be regarded as a summary of the discussions of 2 and 3 October. Articles 1–4 deal with the doctrines common to the universal church: Creation, the Trinity, Incarnation and Virgin Birth, the person of Christ, his death and resurrection, and Original Sin. In articles 5–11 the distinctive evangelical doctrines are summarized: salvation by faith in Christ alone; faith as a gift of God, given by the Holy Spirit into our hearts "as it pleases him when we hear the Gospel"; faith as righteousness before God; the work of the Holy Spirit through the preaching of the gospel; baptism; good works produced "by the efficacy of the Holy Spirit"; and "confession or the seeking of counsel from one's minister or neighbor." Articles 12–14, on magistracy, human traditions, and infant baptism, are directed against the Anabaptists. The final article deals with the controversial issue of the Lord's Supper. First the points of agreement are stated: Both bread and wine are to be used in the Lord's Supper; "the Mass is not a work by which one obtains grace for another, dead or living"; "the Sacrament of the Altar is a sacrament of the true body and blood of Jesus Christ"; "the spiritual partaking" of it "is especially necessary for every Christian"; "the use of the sacrament, like the Word, was given and ordained by Almighty God in order to move weak consciences to faith, by the Holy Spirit." At last comes the disagreement: "Although we could not agree at present as to whether the true body and blood of Christ are bodily present in bread and wine, nevertheless each party should show Christian love to the other, so far as conscience permits; and both parties should fervently pray Almighty God that he may confirm to us, by his Spirit, the right understanding."

Luther's first draft, which has been lost, was read to Zwingli and Oecolampadius for approval. Apparently they suggested several revisions—greater emphasis was laid on the direct action of the Holy Spirit in man, and certain terms were replaced by others that were more familiar to them. Three copies of the confession were then made. These were signed by Luther, Justus Jonas, and Melanchthon of Wittenberg; by Andreas Osiander, Stephan Agricola, Johannes Brenz, south German Lutherans; by Oecolampadius and Zwingli of Switzerland; and by Martin Bucer and Caspar Hedio of Strasbourg. Later that day three additions—concerning monastic vows, the Mass, and celibacy—were made on a separate sheet. Two of the signed copies have been preserved, one at Kassel and one at Zurich. The confession was immediately printed and was widely circulated.

Thus a document had been produced that affirmed doctrinal unity in fourteen articles and in five of six points of the fifteenth. The suspicions each party had harbored concerning the other's orthodoxy were removed, and the disagreement was reduced to the single—and perhaps resolvable—issue of the bodily presence of Christ in the sacrament. From the beginning, however, there was controversy—and modern scholars have carried on the debate—regarding whether the Marburg Confession really was a document of unity, a "concord." Despite the fact that he had revised the text according to the wishes of Zwingli and Oecolampadius, Luther and his followers claimed victory on the grounds that Zwinglians had denied the real presence of Christ only for political reasons. Zwingli, Bucer and Oecolampadius, meanwhile, attempted to show that the confession was fully in agreement with the doctrine they had always taught. On 24 October 1529, after his return to Zurich, Zwingli explained the Marburg Confession from the pulpit: he emphasized that his notion that salvation came only through the Holy Spirit and faith, the sacraments being only signs and not instruments of grace, was present in the text. Luther certainly would not have accepted Zwingli's argument, but every theological formula provides room for interpretation. In this light the Marburg Confession may be seen as a document of concord, though not of doctrinal uniformity.

Still hoping to achieve his political goals, Landgrave Philipp called on Elector John of Saxony and Margrave George of Brandenburg-Ansbach to accept the confession as a theological basis for the proposed Protestant alliance. The two rulers, however, insisted on assent to the Schwabach Articles. These in turn were unacceptable to the cities of Strasbourg and Ulm, which were sympathetic to Zwinglianism. Hence the alliance did not materialize.

The Marburg Confession is a classic document of the reformers' struggle for unity. It represents an important stage in the process leading to the Augsburg Confession.

BIBLIOGRAPHY

Primary Sources

D. Martin Luthers Werke: Revisionsnachtrag. Weimar, 1970. Critical edition of the original German text of the Schwabach Articles and the Marburg Confession. Important supplements in the *Revisionsnachtrag.*

Huldreich Zwinglis Sämtliche Werke. Corpus Reformatorum, vol. 93, pt. 2. Zurich, 1991. Critical edition of the Latin text of Zwingli's annotations to the Marburg Confession.

Reu, Johann Michael. *The Augsburg Confession: A Collection of Sources with an Historical Introduction.* 2 vols. Chicago, 1930. English translations of the Schwabach Articles and the Marburg Confession.

Sasse, Hermann. *This Is My Body: Luther's Contention for the Real Presence in the Sacrament of the Altar.* Minneapolis, 1959. Reconstruction and good, though one-sided, discussion of the Marburg Colloquy and the Marburg Confession. Presented from a Lutheran viewpoint. Reliable English translation of the confession.

Secondary Sources

Bornkamm, Heinrich. *Luther in Mid-Career, 1521–1530.* Philadelphia, 1983. Contains a balanced chapter on the Marburg Colloquy and the Marburg Confession. Also available in original German: *Martin Luther in der Mitte seines Lebens.* Göttingen, 1979.

Köhler, Walther. *Zwingli und Luther: Ihr Streit über das Abendmahl nach seinen politischen und religiösen Beziehungen.* 2 vols. Leipzig and Gütersloh, 1924–1953. The fundamental study of the controversy over the Lord's Supper. The Marburg Colloquy and the Marburg Confession are dealt with in vol. 2.

Potter, George Richard. *Zwingli.* Cambridge and New York, 1976. The Marburg Colloquy and the Marburg Confession are seen within the frame work of Zwingli's biography.

GERHARD MAY

MARCELLUS II (born Marcello Cervini; 1501–1555), pope in 1555. Born into a noble family from the north-central Italian town of Montepulciano, Marcellus rose to ecclesiastical prominence in part from the patronage of Paul III (1534–1549). He served as episcopal administrator of Nicastro in southern Italy (1539–1540) and of two dioceses in north-central Italy, Reggio nell'Emilia (1540–1544) and Gubbio (1544–1555). Tutor and later secretary to the papal grandson Alessandro Farnese, he participated in legations to Francis I of France and to Holy Roman Emperor Charles V in 1539 and 1540. He received appointment to the cardinalate in 1539 and served as one of the three legates to the Council of Trent in its early sessions, along wth Giovanni del Monte (later Pope Julius) and Reginald Pole.

Marcellus made a number of significant contributions to the reform of the traditional church. As legate he directed the group of theologians responsible for drafting the Tridentine decree on justification in 1547. His pastoral administration in Reggio nell'Emilia and in Gubbio resulted in effective clerical reform, and as with others before him (Gian Matteo Giberti, for example), such efforts fed into the program of episcopal renewal developed in the later sessions at Trent. He promoted learning in his own household as cardinal, reorgainzed the Vatican library (which he began to oversee in 1548), and sponsored a variety of publication projects, for which he became known as the virtual founder of the Vatican press. He actively participated in Inquistorial proceedings, both in the dioceses he oversaw and in the directorship of the Roman tribunal. In his few days as pope he worked quickly to effect the curial reform put off by his predecessors and rejected all nepotistic considerations in his inital appointments. He died, apparently of a stroke, on 1 May 1555.

BIBLIOGRAPHY

Alberigo, Giuseppe. *I vescovi italiani al Concilio di Trento (1545–1547).* Florence, 1959.

Hallman, Barbara McClung. *Italian Cardinals, Reform and the Church as Property, 1492–1563.* Berkeley, 1985.

Hudon, William V. *Marcello Cervini and Ecclesiastical Government in Tridentine Italy.* DeKalb, Ill., 1992. Study of Cervini's career as legate, episcopal administrator, and pope.

Jedin, Hubert. *A History of the Council of Trent.* 3 vols. Saint Louis, 1957–1963. Originally published as *Geschichte des Konzils von Trient,* 5 vols., Freiburg, 1950–1975.

Morison, Stanley. "Marcello Cervini, Pope Marcellus: Bibliography's Patron Saint." *Italia medioevale e umanistica* 5 (1962), 301–318.

Moroni, Gaetano. "Marcellus II." In *Dizionario di erudizione storico ecclesiastica,* vol. 42, pp. 238–246. Venice, 1840–1879. Old-fashioned but still useful biographical sketch.

Pastor, Ludwig. *The History of the Popes from the Close of the Middle Ages.* 40 vols., 3d ed. Saint Louis, 1938–53. Volume 14 covers Marcellus. Originally published as *Geschichte der Päpste seit dem Ausgang des Mittelalters* in Freiburg, 1866 to 1938.

WILLIAM V. HUDON

MARGARET OF NAVARRE. *See* Marguerite d'Angoulême.

MARGARET OF PARMA (1522–1586), duchess of Parma and governess-general of the Netherlands. The illegitimate daughter of Emperor Charles V and Johanna van der Gheynst, Margaret was born at the end of July 1522 in Pamele near Oudenaarde (county of Flanders) and was married to Alexander de Medici in 1536. After her husband was murdered in 1537, she took over the administration of Florence temporarily. In 1538 she married Ottavio Farnese, duke of Parma.

When in 1559 King Philip II was seeking a successor to Emmanuel Philibert of Savoy as governor-general of the Netherlands, Margaret was recommended by Antoine Perrenot de Granvelle, who then became the most influential member of her council of state in Brussels. As a fervent defender of royal centralization, Granvelle engendered a great deal of resistance from the nobles on the council of state. By 1563, for Farnese dynastic reasons as well as because of the opposition of the nobles, Margaret considered it no longer opportune to maintain Granvelle in his position, and his departure in 1564 signified an important victory for the nobles, led by William of Orange, Lamoral of Egmont, fourth count of Egmont, and Philip of Montmorency, count of Hornes.

On the marriage of Margaret's son Alexander (November 1565), a number of Protestant nobles formed a "league" opposed to Philip II's placards against heresy and to the Inquisition. With like-minded Catholic nobles they formed a confederation consisting largely of the lesser nobility and on 5 April 1566 presented to the governess-general a request for the suspension of the placards and the convening of the States-General. Under the pressure of circumstances, Margaret modified the application of the placards, but this "moderation" was rejected by radical Protestants and ultra-Catholics alike.

In the meantime massively attended open-air Reformed services often got out of hand, and the iconoclastic fury that broke out in August 1566 left a trail of destruction through the Netherlands. On 23 August Margaret allowed Protestant preaching to continue in places where it had begun, but she balked at further concessions contained in local settlements, such as the religious peace in Antwerp of 2 September 1566. When such Protestant-dominated cities as Tournai and Valenciennes rose in rebellion, she did not hesitate to suppress them with the help of the army. She then rejected the idea of convening the States-General, withdrew the permission to preach, quartered a garrison in Antwerp, and corresponded with the king about building a citadel there. She also launched judicial inquiries in order to identify and punish those responsible for the violence in each locality in 1566 (the Wonderyear).

Yet when Philip II sent Fernando Álvarez de Toledo, duke of Alba, with a powerful army to the Netherlands in 1567, Margaret was not pleased. She pointed out that she had the situation again under control, that a greater military presence would have unfavorable consequences for the country, and that news of the arrival of the duke of Alba had led many to emigrate. When it became clear that the duke of Alba had been given wide powers, Margaret asked the king to relieve her from her task as governess. Philip II then appointed the duke of Alba himself to the post of governor-general. In light of the duke of Alba's rules, contemporaries generally judged the governorship of Margaret of Parma mildly, but, in fact, she prepared the way for repression under her successor.

When the states of the Netherlands turned away from John of Austria in 1577 and offered the governorship to Archduke Matthias, Granvelle advised the king to send Margaret of Parma to the Netherlands to thwart Matthias. But it was not until after the reconciliation of the Walloon provinces (1579) that the king appointed Margaret of Parma governess-general. Her son Alexander, who had succeeded John of Austria as governor-general in 1578, would retain only command of the troops. This arrangement pleased neither of them. Although Margaret came to the Netherlands, she did not occupy her new function. Finally, on 25 July 1583, she received permission from Philip II to leave again. She died in Ortona in Italy on 1 January 1586.

BIBLIOGRAPHY

Primary Sources

Gachard, L.-P., ed. *Correspondance de Philippe II sur les affaires des Pays-Bas.* 5 vols. Brussels. 1848–1879.

———. *Correspondance de Marguerite de Parme avec Philippe II.* 3 vols. Brussels, 1867–1881.

Reiffenberg, Baron de, ed. *Correspondance de Marguerite d'Autriche duchesse de Parme avec Philippe II.* Brussels, 1842.

Thiessen, J. S., and H. A. Enno Van Gelder, eds. *Correspondance française de Marguerite d'Autriche, duchesse de Parme, avec Philippe II.* 3 vols. Utrecht, 1925–1942.

Secondary Sources

Essen, Léon. van der. *Alexandre Farnèse prince de Parme, gouverneur général des Pays-Bas, 1545–1592.* 5 vols. Brussels, 1933–1937. A magisterial biography of Alexander Farnese.

Ionghe, J. de. *Madama: Margaretha van Oostenrijk, hertogin van Parma en Piacenza, 1522–1586.* 3d ed. Amsterdam, 1981. A biography of Margaret.

Janssens, Gustaaf. *"Brabant in het Verweer": Loyale oppositie tegen Spanje's bewind in de Nederlanden van Alva tot Farnese 1567–1578.* Standen en Landen—Anciens Pays et Assemblées d' Etats, 89. Kortrijk, Belgium, 1989. On the loyal opposition in the Netherlands.

———. "Pacification générale ou réconciliation particulière? Problèmes de guerre et de paix aux Pays-Bas au début du gouvernement d'Alexandre Farnèse, *1578–1579.*" *Bulletin de l'Institut historique belge de Rome* 63 (1993), 251–278.

Maltby, William S. *Alba: A Biography of Fernando Alvarez de Toledo, Third Duke of Alba, 1507–1582.* Berkeley, 1983.

Parker, Geoffrey. *The Dutch Revolt.* London and New York, 1985.

Repetto Alvarez, A. "Acerca de un posible segundo gobierno de Margarita de Parma y el cardenal Granvela en los Estados de Flandes." *Hispania* 32 (1972), 379–475.

Gustaaf Janssens

MARGUERITE D'ANGOULÊME (1492–1549), daughter of Louise of Savoie, and Charles d'Angoulême, sister of King Francis I, also known as Marguerite of Navarre because of her marriage to Henry of Albret, king of Navarre (1527), after the death of her first husband, Charles of Alençon. Religious instruction by Robert Hurault, future abbot of Saint Martin at Autun, and François de Rochefort, abbot of Saint Mesmin near Orléans, acquainted the young Marguerite with biblical texts and encouraged an enduring interest in scripture. During her marriage to the duke of Alençon (1509–1525), she supported French evangelicals engaged in reforming the diocese of Meaux to the north of Paris—Bishop Guillaume Briçonnet, whose correspondence with her (1521–1524) shows that he was an influential spiritual adviser; Jacques Lefèvre d'Étaples; Michel d'Arande; and Gérard Roussel. Given the conservativism of the Sorbonne, her support was badly needed. While Marguerite was in Spain negotiating for the deliverance of Francis I, captured by Charles V in 1525, efforts were made to extirpate "heresy." Lefèvre d'Étaples, Roussel, and others fled to Strasbourg. Perhaps influenced by his sister, Francis issued orders from Madrid that prosecution should cease. Upon his return to France, Lefèvre was named tutor of the royal children, and Roussel became Marguerite's almoner. Louis de Berquin, translator of Luther and Erasmus, also benefited from Marguerite's protection, and she is credited with saving him from death as a heretic on two occasions.

Berquin's Lutheran sympathies would not have offended Marguerite. Marguerite's *Pater noster* paraphrases a Lutheran text. In 1524 Antoine Papillon gave her a translation of Luther's *De votis monasticis,* proving that she retained her interest in him after his condemnation by the pope (1520). W. G. Moore maintains that Marguerite also encouraged the printing of Lutheran translations and aided their distribution in France. Her religious poetry is influenced by Luther's concept of Christian liberty as well as by principles of scriptural authority and *sola fides.*

Lutheran influence was not exclusive. Wolfgang Capito, who received Lefèvre d'Étaples during his stay in Strasbourg, indicates that the queen passed through a series of stages in her quest for spiritual truth. Scholars disagree on the nature and date of these stages, but they recognize that Marguerite drew on Fabrism, Lutheranism, Neoplatonism, Calvinism, and spiritual libertinism to create her own faith experience. This personal synthesis makes it difficult to fit her into any denomination, and the old theory of a Protestant Marguerite has few adherents among modern scholars.

Marguerite's reformist sympathies alienated conservative Catholics in her own time. Sponsorship of Roussel's Lenten sermons in Paris in 1533 combined with a second edition of her poem *The Mirror of the Sinful Soul* led to the Sorbonne's condemnation of *The Mirror.* The condemnation was withdrawn upon the insistence of Francis I. After the *Affaire des placards,* the posting of placards condemning the Mass in Paris and throughout France by militant reformers, Marguerite withdrew to Navarre and to her court at Nerac, where she created her own evangelical community. Lefèvre d'Étaples remained with her there until his death in 1536. Marguerite also welcomed others, including Calvin (1534) and the poet Clément Marot. She continued to correspond with colleagues in Strasbourg, to receive letters in behalf of the Reformed, and to remain in touch with foreign ambassadors.

Still, the activist Marguerite one encounters early in the reign of Francis I, when conditions favored the evangelicals, differs markedly from the sober Marguerite of later years. The older Marguerite had witnessed the bitter religious persecution that followed the *Affaire des placards* and experienced opposition to reform in her own territories. Royal commissioners sent to investigate the orthodoxy of faith in Navarre (1537) dared to criticize her, prompting an urgent and successful appeal to her brother. Politically and spiritually, however, Francis had been setting his own course for some time, and Marguerite increasingly sought solace in quiet contemplation.

After the king's death (1547) her ability to influence religious policy in France declined. Never able to defy her brother or break with Rome, Marguerite remained true to her personal mysticism and, at least officially, to Catholicism. She encouraged the spread of new ideas and was a role model of some significance for other women of the Reformation, certainly for her daughter Jeanne of Navarre and perhaps even for Elizabeth I, who, as a young girl, had translated Marguerite's controversial *Mirror* for Catherine Parr.

BIBLIOGRAPHY

Atance, Félix R. "Marguerite de Navarre et ses activités en faveur des novateurs." *Neophilologus* 60 (1976), 505–524. Provides almost a year by year summary of the queen's activities.

Clive, H. P. *Marguerite de Navarre: An Annotated Bibliography.* London, 1983.

Cottrell, Robert. *The Grammar of Silence: A Reading of Marguerite de Navarre's Poetry.* Washington, D.C., 1986. Blends a perceptive discussion of her mysticism and religious thought with techniques of modern literary criticism.

d'Angoulême, Marguerite. *The Heptameron.* Translated by Paul A. Chilton. New York, 1984. This collection of prose tales inspired by the *Decameron* displays a strong evangelical influence in the cornice dialogues and prologue.

———. *The Prisons of Marguerite de Navarre.* Translated by Hilda Dale. New York and Reading, England, 1989. Composed late in life, this work affords the most complete expression of Marguerite's mysticism.

PAULA SOMMERS

MARIANA, Juan de (1536–1624), Spanish political theorist and historian. Born at Talavera de la Reina on 2 April 1536, Mariana became a Jesuit in 1554 and, after studying at Alcalá, taught theology at the society's colleges in Rome, Sicily, and Paris. In 1574 he moved permanently to Toledo, where he composed all his major works.

Though his *Historiae de rebus Hispaniae*, first published in 1592, went through several editions in both Latin and Spanish, his reputation rests largely on *De rege et regis institutione*, a treatise written at the request of Philip II and published in 1599 after the monarch's death. In it Mariana attacks royal absolutism and argues for a constitutional monarchy based on the consent of the governed. Though most of his views were rooted in medieval precedent, Mariana's qualified defense of tyrannicide aroused widespread anti-Jesuit sentiment after the assassination of Henry IV of France in 1610 and was eventually condemned by the general of his order. Another treatise, *De monetae mutatione*, led to his imprisonment for a year in a Franciscan monastery (1610). One of the *Tractatus VII theologici et historici*, published at Cologne in 1609, it attacked the debasement of Spanish coinage and accused royal officials of fraud.

In this same period Mariana composed a history of the Jesuits. Published posthumously at Bordeaux in 1625, it revealed the internal workings of the society and attacked its policies. For more than two centuries it remained a standard source for anti-Jesuit polemicists. Though he was justly famed as an anti-Machiavellian political theorist, Mariana's hostility to the Jesuits, as well as his role in attracting anti-Jesuit sentiment after the assassination of Henry IV, helped to undermine the society's credibility and that of the Counter-Reformation as a whole.

BIBLIOGRAPHY

Astrain, Antonio. *Historia de la compañia de Jesús*. 7 vols. Madrid, 1902–25. See especially vols. 3 and 4.

Laures, John. *The Political Economy of Juan de Mariana*. New York, 1928.

Lewy, Guenter. *Constitutionalism and Statecraft during the Golden Age of Spain: A Study of the Political Philosophy of Juan de Mariana, S.J.* Travaux d'Humanisme et Renaissance 36. Geneva, 1960.

WILLIAM S. MALTBY

MARIAN EXILES. The suppression of the duke of Northumberland's attempted coup d'état and the accession of Queen Mary I in the summer of 1553 resulted in the restoration of Roman Catholicism in England. As early as January of the next year substantial numbers of English exiles were seeking refuge on the Continent, an exodus that would total in John Foxe's estimation upwards of eight hundred men, women, and children. It is now generally accepted that the migration was in effect two separate movements, one essentially religious in motivation, the other political. The exiles seeking freedom to practice Reformed beliefs set out for Germany and Switzerland, where they established expatriate churches; the political refugees, who generally did not leave England until somewhat later, after the failure of the rebellions of 1554, continued their political opposition and agitation from France and Venice. For this latter group, religion was very much a secondary concern: hostility to the Spanish marriage and their loss of office were more compelling reasons for continued activity against the queen.

The religious émigrés established substantial English communities in Germany and Switzerland during the years of the Marian diaspora: in particular at Emden, Wesel, Zurich, Strasbourg, Frankfurt, Basel, Geneva, and Aarau, although these last three were founded by divisions in or migrations from the original five. The suggestion by Christian Garrett in *The Marian Exiles* that these groups represented a careful plan of migration, that "the Protestant exodus of 1554 [was] an experiment. . . in religious colonization: the first to be undertaken by Tudor Englishmen, and the training school for all their later undertakings," by which she means the Puritan parliamentary opposition, has been largely revised. There was some degree of organization in the exodus and some attempts at coordination and intercommunication, but the essential motive was to ensure immediate survival and religious freedom rather than to prepare for future victory.

Despite the rigors of poverty and exile and the shared apprehension of persecution from the queen's government, the English in Germany and Switzerland were anything but a united and organized community. Their internal quarrels over matters of doctrine were divisive and destructive. The large Frankfurt congregation split acrimoniously between the faction of laymen and clerics wishing their expatriate church to follow *The Second Book of Common Prayer* of Edward VI (1552) as they had done in England and the more radical exiles who had no wish to maintain "an English face" on their religion, desiring rather a complete adoption of Calvinist worship. The conclusion to this debate was the separation of the Calvinists from the Frankfurt congregation and, under leadership of John Knox, their removal to Geneva to found another confessional community, although not before injecting a serious measure of dissension into the entire community of religious émigrés. Because Frankfurt enjoyed the fewest senior divines or even powerful laymen from the Edwardian regime, there was no effective brake on the formal and liturgical innovations among the group. Attempting to forge a singular form of worship for all the expatriate churches free from any residual aspects of English tradition, the Frankfurt congregation sent letters to the other exiles suggesting a revision of religious practice. The failure of this radical attempt to establish a single exile church resulted in the continuation of largely autonomous congregations on the Continent, each with its own confessional character but limited by the requirement of essential conformity with the regimen of the host city.

Thus, the religious and social character of the congregations of Marian exiles in Germany and Switzerland varied.

Besides the obvious religious disputes that divided the community at Frankfurt, other groups restructured themselves for different reasons. The community at Wesel, for example, had to face the hostility of the local inhabitants, who feared that this group of exiles, composed largely of artisans, particularly weavers, might compete for employment. It was only after the intervention of Melanchthon that the congregation was permitted to settle. Nevertheless, by August of 1557 the small Wesel community under its minister, the former Frankfurt pastor Thomas Lever, had moved to Aarau, further reduced by the departures of two of its natural leaders: the dowager duchess of Suffolk, together with her household and husband (Richard Bertie), had left for Poland, and John Bodley had gone to Geneva. Consequently, the congregation was the most humble in terms of social complexion, reduced largely to artisans, a few clerics (including Miles Coverdale), and John, Lord Audley.

Closely linked to the French exile church whose building of Saint André it was to share, the Strasbourg congregation was one of the most attractive not only because of the still-powerful memory of Martin Bucer and the presence of Peter Martyr Vermigli before his migration to Zurich, but also because of the geographical location of the city, which provided relatively easy communication both within the Continent and with the persecuted church in England. Moreover, this group was among the richer, with many of the most influential émigrés in residence there, and served as well as a magnet for aristocratic exiles from Italy who abandoned the peninsula in 1556. Sir Thomas Wrothe, Sir Anthony Cooke, John Ponet (the deprived bishop of Winchester), Sir Richard Morrison, Sir John Cheke, and Edmund Grindal (future archbishop of Canterbury), as well as a number of wealthy merchants and some students, gathered there. The nature of this community suggests that Strasbourg was the financial and coordinating center of the exodus (Garrett, p. 49). Certainly the concentration of many extremely wealthy men, especially the courtiers Morrison and Cooke and merchants such as Richard Chambers, might have produced cash when necessary. Strasbourg and Frankfurt were the two communities that received a considerable gift of money from the duke of Württemberg.

Zurich was made a center of authority in both theology and church government by the migration of Peter Martyr from Strasbourg to escape the strict Lutheran environment required by the city government. Followed by other prominent exiles from Strasbourg such as John Jewel and Edwin Sandys, Martyr was looked to for doctrinal determinations and pastoral advice.

Consequently, Zurich and the English community at Basel both enjoyed significant numbers of students in their exile churches. Some were apparently brought there by senior scholars and divines such as Robert Horne; others, including Sir Francis Walsingham and his three cousins, the sons of Sir Anthony Denny, left studies at Padua to enter the University of Basel. Many members of these communities lived in former monastic buildings as dormitories and used adjacent spaces for church services. Neither Basel nor Zurich, then, had to provide churches for the exiles, since their living quarters, like the Karakloster in Zurich, included appropriate meeting places. However, as at Frankfurt, the community at Basel was severely divided in matters of religion. In theory it, too, was to follow the last Edwardian prayer book, but many more radical Protestants desired further reformation of church practice. No split in this congregation seems to have occurred, however, despite the complaints of its leaders.

The community at Emden in East Friesland, composed in part of Jan Łaski's London congregation, was in place by the spring of 1554. This group has traditionally been identified with the powerful press campaign against Mary. The geographical location of this port and the presence of the press of Egidius van de Evrve, formerly in Łaski's congregation in London, support this contention. A number of Protestant treatises in translation and polemical tracts did issue from Emden, but other centers, including Basel and Geneva, also saw publicist activity. The effect of the Continental exile propaganda barrage was remarkable. Altogether, ninety-eight texts have been identified with the Marian exiles, and these continued to circulate in England, despite the definition of possession as a capital offense by the queen's government.

Of those tracts, three in particular have entered the literature of resistance theory: Ponet's *Short Treatise of Politike Power*(1556), Christopher Goodman's *How Superior Powers Ought to Be Obeyed* (1558), and John Knox's *First Blast of the Trumpet* (1558). It is not an accident that such material should have been produced by the experience of the Marian exodus. Separated from the controls of both ecclesiastical authorities and the Crown, in profound opposition to the policies and religion of the queen, and full of learned confessional convictions, the articulate members of the Marian diaspora saw themselves as sustaining a true and godly polity in the face of injustice and "popery." It is incorrect, however, to claim that the exiles were a party, an organized faction that would then lead the parliamentary opposition to Elizabeth after 1559. Certainly a sense of unity and conviction animated the leadership of the opposition under Elizabeth; certainly some parliamentary leaders had been in exile, including Sir Anthony Cooke and Sir Francis Knollys. However, the most active and successful Elizabethan coterie with shared experience of exile under Mary was formed largely of people who had been émigrés for political rather than religious motives and who had spent much of their time abroad in Venice, rather than in the exile congregations of Switzerland and Germany.

The Marian exiles did, however, help determine the character of the Elizabethan church through the experience abroad of many of its leaders and through the definition of its martyrology. John Foxe's *Acts and Monuments* was begun at Strasbourg and the first edition completed at Basel just as Elizabeth assumed her sister's crown.

[*See also* Mary Tudor.]

BIBLIOGRAPHY

Primary Sources

Foxe, John. *The Acts and Monuments of John Foxe.* Edited by J. Pratt, 8 vols. London, 1870. This edition is a revision with index of Townshend and Cattley's 1837–1841 text of the martyrology.

Whittingham, William. *A Brief Discourse of the Troubles at Frankfurt, 1554–1558.* Edited by E. Arber. London, 1908. First-hand account by one of the radical leaders of the events that divided the Frankfurt community of English expatriates.

Secondary Sources

Bartlett, Kenneth R. "The English Exile Community in Italy and the Political Opposition to Queen Mary I." *Albion* 13 (1981), 223–241. Article investigates the activities of the political exiles abroad under Mary.

———. "The Role of the Marian Exiles." In *The House of Commons, 1558–1603*, edited by P. J. Hasler. London, 1981. Vol. 1, app. 11, pp. 102–110. Study of the role played by the returned Marian exiles in Elizabeth's Parliament, correcting some of the contentions of Garrett and Sir John Neale.

Brett, John. *Narrative of the Pursuit of the English under Mary.* Edited by I. S. Leadham. Transcripts of the Royal Historical Society, vol. 11. London, 1897. Brett's narrative is a report on his mission to recall the most prominent exiles to England by royal command.

Collinson, Patrick. *Archbishop Grindal, 1519–1583: The Struggle for a Reformed Church.* London, 1979. Although a biography of Grindal, contains a useful chapter on the Marian exile communities in which the future archbishop was involved, including Strasbourg.

Garrett, Christina H. *The Marian Exiles: A Study in the Origins of Elizabethan Puritanism.* Cambridge, 1966. Although Garrett's argument that the exiles formed the core of Elizabethan Puritanism is now questioned, the work contains biographies of individual exiles which remain useful.

Knappen, M. M. *Tudor Puritanism: A Chapter in the History of Idealism.* Reprint, Chicago, 1966. Contains substantial and useful chapters on the Frankfurt and Genevan communities of exiles.

KENNETH R. BARTLETT

MARIOLOGY. [*This entry comprises two articles on Marian devotion in the sixteenth century. The first considers popular devotion to Mary, the impact of the Reformation, and the ways in which Mariology survived in Protestant areas, as well as changes in Roman Catholic Mariology; the second surveys the effects of the Protestant Reformation and the Counter-Reformation on learned devotion to Mary. For more general discussions, see* Devotional Practices; Popular Religion; *and* Saints, *articles on* Cult of Saints *and* Sainthood.]

Popular Piety

Toward the end of the Middle Ages, popular Marian piety was widespread throughout the Western church. At the dawn of the Reformation the main expressions of popular Marian piety were pilgrimages, veneration of pictures and relics, Marian antiphons, bells of the Angelus, early forms of the rosary, popular devotions, pious associations, and Christmas pageants. These and other forms of devotion were intended to keep alive the Christian faith—in particular, the veneration of the Blessed Mother of Jesus—and to relate these elements to all areas of life.

Necessary Renewal. The Lutheran Reformation did not attack the fundamental elements of popular Marian piety but rather criticized the forms of devotions practiced in the late Middle Ages that contained strong belief in miracles. The many Marian legends and miracle anthologies testify to this belief in the miraculous. Widely distributed was the *Dialogus miraculorum*, written by Caesarius of Heisterbach (c.1180–1240); the second part of this opus, which contains 746 narratives, begins with fifty-nine Marian miracles. Book 3 of his *Libri miraculorum*, which was actually written by a later editor, reports another eighty-three miracles. Equally influential was the *Legenda aurea* by Jacobus de Voragine (1228/30–1298). After explaining the etymology and the legends surrounding each Marian feast, he reports two or three related miracles. This kind of literature, widespread throughout Western Christianity, reached its peak between about 1100 and 1500. Though these writings reflect the passion for miracles connected with Marian devotions at that time, their importance cannot be limited to that aspect alone.

In the opinion of many reformers, medieval devotions to Mary suffered from distorted perceptions and practices, such as object-centered piety; magical concepts; a distorted view of indulgences; lack of a clear distinction between the holy picture and the person who is depicted, as well as between the adoration of God and the veneration of Mary and the saints; and overindulgence in alcohol and carousing during pilgrimages. In order to preserve authentic praise of God and Mary, Martin Luther criticized these deficiencies. The seventy-fifth of his theses calls it madness to believe, as Johann Tetzel apparently did, that papal indulgences could absolve a person who had violated Mary. He reacted similarly to stories circulating about the relics of the milk of Mary and called the rosary an abuse. Because of problems like these, Luther voiced his objections to pilgrimages to Rome, as well as to local shrines (Eichen, Grimmental, Birnbaum), not because pilgrimages as such were evil but because they led to evil. Luther took a moderate position on iconoclasm, asking the iconoclasts to let him keep a crucifix and picture of Mary, not to adore or use to effect miracles, but to serve him as reminders of faith.

Changed View. From the inception of the Reformation, Luther aimed beyond a merely external correction of popular devotions. His understanding of faith and grace demanded a considerably revisionist orientation to the veneration of Mary and the saints. In his opinion problems arose from the perception of Christ as a stern judge and of Mary as a caring mother. He used the *Salve Regina* to prove his point. According to Luther, Marian praises are to be sung only to celebrate God's infinite grace: the full depth of this grace is demonstrated in Mary's human poverty. His acceptance of the concepts of *Deus solus* and *sola gratia* made an expressed veneration of Mary, such as the *Salve Regina*, unacceptable to him. To give honor to God alone and to the one mediator Christ Jesus (*1 Tim.* 2:5), any praise of Mary must always keep in view the total powerlessness of the mother of Jesus. In 1531 Luther felt the tension of this theological dilemma: "It is true, she is to be praised and never enough, because she is too high and magnificent" (WA 34/2,400,1). As a consequence of his conviction that God alone confers grace and in the absence of any biblical foundation for the practice, Luther opposed from the beginning of the 1520s any direct call for Mary's intervention and the inclusion of her name in the absolution formula. Finally, he classified any prayer addressed to Mary as idolatry. Until 1530 Luther accepted Mary's (and the saints') general intervention for the church, but he denounced any specific intervention.

Luther's newly formed theological concept of Marian praises was that the *Ave Maria* was not a prayer but a reflection on the grace bestowed on the mother of Jesus. Luther's hymns portray a similar perspective. The theme of his chorale "She Is Dear to Me the Fair Maid" is not in honor of Mary but rather a paraphrase of *Revelation* 12:1–6 and refers directly to the church and only indirectly to Mary. Other hymns addressed to Mary were restructured and readdressed by Luther to Christ. In this context he mentions the motif of the Virgin Mother in the mystery of Christmas as particularly moving. Luther's reformation kept the Marian feast days of Purification, Annunciation, and Visitation. For the people's sake Luther wanted to continue, for the time being, the celebration of the feasts of Mary's birth and assumption. At least until 1528 he preached on the feast of Mary's conception. Liturgy and popular devotions relating to this feast, as well as the theological discussion at the Council of Basel (after 1437 it ceased to be a canonical council) had furthered its popularity. Gabriel Biel (c.1410–1495) refers to the decision at Basel to establish as doctrine Mary's immaculate conception, as does Johann of Paltz (1445–1511), Luther's teacher at Erfurt in 1505/06. Having been theologically introduced to the feast, Luther continued to celebrate the memory of Mary's purification before her conception, which was granted to her as the mother of God; even so, this did not, for him, preclude her remaining a needy, weak creature.

Despite Luther's liturgical reforms, various traditional devotional practices to Mary were still present in Protestant regions during the second half of the sixteenth century—for example, traditional religious plays, processions and pilgrimages, and bells of the *Ave*. In disregard of verdicts and church orders, people reportedly continued to venerate holy and miraculous pictures in Franconia, upper and central Baden, the Palatinate region, and the rural district near Ulm. Around 1600 more than one hundred processions took place annually in Protestant Berlin. Until 1831 it was the practice at Saint Mary's church at Greifswald to carry a wooden statue of Our Lady while the collection was being taken up. All of this shows the traditional strength of popular piety; ordinances issued by the authorities were often met by rejection and contradiction. The connection with tradition was represented in Lutheran regions by many medieval altars honoring Mary, as well as paintings and carvings of Our Lady, especially in northern Germany and Franconia (Nuremberg). During the post-Reformation period many new depictions of Mary appeared in biblical scenes in Bibles, individual paintings, and stained glass windows and on altars, pulpits, epitaphs, wall memorials, and choir loft panels. These artifacts render valuable testimony to the history of both art and Marian devotion.

Within the Calvinist tradition, popular devotion to Mary changed much more radically from the beginning, for example, in some German regions, especially Württemberg, southern France, Switzerland, and the Netherlands. Here the uncompromising attitude toward depictions of Mary and toward Marian devotions of any kind was in contrast to the opinion of John Calvin himself, who was personally convinced of Mary's special dignity and her importance as an example for Christian life. But, like Luther, Calvin opposed the direct invocation of Mary in both public and private prayer. In support of this, he referred to Can. 23 of the third. Synod of Carthage (397); gathered in the presence of Augustine, it prohibited all public prayer to the saints. Calvin expanded this prohibition to all private piety. From this time the rejection of every Marian prayer became a characteristic feature of the Reformed tradition.

Catholic Reform. Various steps were taken in Catholic areas to effect the renewal of traditional Marian veneration. The Council of Trent (1545–1563) declared that it was good and helpful to ask the saints for their intercession and asserted that their relics were worthy of veneration. As for depictions of the saints, the council stressed that a distinction should be made between the holy person and the representation and that people should be instructed on the distinction; the veneration should be directed to the person represented.

The Jesuit and Capuchin orders led Catholic renewal among the clergy and laity. The Jesuits offered their remarkable skills in the areas of education and pastoral care, while the Capuchins made their contribution through their close involvement with the people. Both orders were guided by a deep veneration of Mary. Colleges and universities became centers of intense theological reflections on the mother of Jesus. Pilgrimages were used as occasions for instructing many people in the official doctrine regarding Mary and the proper practice of Marian devotion.

More than at any earlier time, the epoch of the Catholic Reformation brought a surge of Marian pilgrimages. Every level of church and society was involved: clergy and laity, servants and citizens, and even the great and minor rulers. Elector Maximilian I of Bavaria (r. 1623–1651), the embodiment of a Catholic elector, quite often went on pilgrimages to the many devotional centers in his land, particularly to Altötting. In fact, he commenced his rule with a pilgrimage there. He also went outside Bavaria to Einsiedeln and Loreto. In those years Loreto had a powerful influence, which showed itself in the numerous chapels of Loreto in the Italian-speaking area of Switzerland, in southern Germany and Austria, and in the Hradschin in Prague. Of particular significance in the Marian piety of Maximilian is the "Blutweihebrief" of Altötting, in which the elector and his son wrote their dedication to Mary in their own blood. Just as the Bavarian dukes and electors made pilgrimages to Altötting, so too did the Habsburg rulers to "Magna Mater Austriae" in Mariazell and the Polish kings to Jasna Góra in Czestochowa. Relevant causes for pilgrimages included marriage arrangements, childlessness, personal illness, epidemics, political needs, and wars. Similar causes spurred the faithful, either individually or in groups, to go on pilgrimages to the numerous sites within their own regions. They were moved to implore God and Mary for the many needs of their lives. Still other reasons for pilgrimages were thanksgiving and repentance; votive offerings and thanksgiving plaques attest to this. In the time of the Reformation and afterward, pilgrimages to Marian sites were also made by Catholics in order to atone for the abuse that she received at non-Catholic hands. Finally, the link between religious dissent and political protest must be mentioned; it was often only by honoring Mary that oppressed groups could articulate their dissent.

Prayer forms, which at this period had impregnated themselves deep into the hearts of the Catholic faithful, were the Hail Mary (in its present form), the rosary, the Angelus, and the litany of Loreto. These were prayers that had originated in the liturgy but in their common use had gone beyond it. As prayers of the people they were intended to sanctify the days and lives of the faithful through the remembrance of the central event of salvation. The extent to which Marian piety was central to the lives of the Catholic faithful is also confirmed by the visual arts. The Baroque period, which began in these years, was, in all its shades—from its highest expressions to popular art—in part an eloquent expression of the high regard of the people for Mary and a refutation of Protestant ideas.

Since the second half of the sixteenth century, Marian veneration has been a source of controversy among denominations and has continued to be perceived as the focal point of Catholicism. Under these circumstances Marian veneration among Protestants remained a part of popular religion only, and by the end of the sixteenth century fewer and fewer authentic traces of even popular devotion can be found in Protestant areas.

[*See also* Devotional Practices; Popular Religion; *and* Saints, *article on* Cult of Saints.]

BIBLIOGRAPHY

Beissel, Stephen. *Geschichte der Verehrung Marias im 16. und 17. Jahrhundert.* Freiburg, 1910.

Cole, William. "Was Luther a Devotee of Mary?" *Marian Studies* 21 (1970), 94–202.

Courth, Franz. "Mariens Unbefleckte Empfängnis im Zeugnis der frühen reformatorischen Theologie." In *Im Gewande des Heils*, edited by G. Rovira, pp. 85–100. Essen, 1980.

———. "Das Marienlob bei Martin Luther." In *Münchener Theologische Zeitschrift* 34 (1983), 279–292.

———. "Die Gestalt Mariens in der frühen reformatorischen Theologie." In *De cultu mariano saeculo XIV. Acta Congressus Mariologici-Mariana Internationalis 1979*, vol. 3, pp. 132–160. Rome, 1985.

———. "Mariologie und Geschichte: Zum Marienbild der reformatorischen Theologie und Frömmigkeit des 17. und 18. Jahrhunderts." In *Veritati Catholicae: Festschrift für Leo Scheffczyk*, edited by A. Ziegenaus, F. Courth, and Ph. Schäfer, pp. 407–439. Aschaffenburg, 1985.

Delius, Walter. *Geschichte der Marienverehrung.* Munich, 1963.

Gorski, Horst. *Die Niedrigkeit seiner Magd: Darstellung und theologische Analyse de Marientheologie Luthers als Beitrag zum gegenwärtigen lutherisch/römisch-katholischen Gespräch.* Europäische Hochschulschriften, vol. 23, no. 311. Frankfurt a.M. and New York, 1987.

Gritsch, Eric W. "The Views of Luther and Lutheranism on the Veneration of Mary." In *The One Mediator, the Saints, and Mary*, edited by H. G. Anderson, J. F. Stafford, and J. A. Burgess, pp. 235–248, 379–384. Lutherans and Catholics in Dialog 8. Augsburg and Minneapolis, 1992.

Guth, Klaus. "Geschichtlicher Abriß der marianischen Wallfahrtsbewegungen im deutschsprachigen Raum." In *Handbuch der Marienkunde*, edited by W. Beinert and H. Petri, pp. 721–848. Regensburg, 1984.

Lemmer, Manfred. "Mirakel." In *Marienlexikon*, edited by R. Bäumer and L. Scheffczyk, vol. 4, pp. 460–464. St. Ottilien, Germany, 1992.

Poser und Groß-Naedlitz, Hasso von. "Protestantische Kunst." In *Marienlexikon*, edited by R. Bäumer and L. Scheffczyk, vol. 5, pp. 329–336. St. Ottilien, Germany, 1993.

Roth, Elisabeth. "Wallfahrten zu evangelischen Landkirchen in Franken." *Jahrbuch für Volkskunde* n.s. 2 (1979), 135–160.

Zeeden, Ernst W. *Katholische Überlieferungen in den lutherischen Kirchenordnungen des 16. Jahrhunderts.* Münster, 1959.

FRANZ COURTH

Theology

At the earliest stage in the history of the Christian church, there was not yet any formal "veneration" of Mary. In the theological thinking of the ancient church, however, the Mother of the Lord appears rather early. Ignatius of Antioch (d. around 110) carries out the systematic linking of the two early Christian traditions that circumscribed God's becoming human: at the very moment when Mary was overshadowed by the Holy Spirit, the preexistent one descended into her womb to take on human nature as his own from her. From there Ignatius but especially Irenaeus (d. around 200/

203) saw Mary, in sharp contrast to Gnosticism, as the guarantor of the true humanity of Jesus Christ. Justin (d. around 165) disputed the influence of pagan mythology and interpreted the mystery of the virginal conception of the Son of God in terms of creation theology. Justin and Irenaeus furthermore depict Mary as the new Eve who makes amends for the sin committed by the first Eve; she is the new progenitrix of mankind, and thus they attribute to her a place in salvation history.

From this starting point the entire subsequent development of Mariology can be understood. A widespread view in the early church that Mary's virginity served to exclude the sexual aspect should be deemed to be erroneous, obscuring the mystery of God's becoming human; it is more a matter of a requirement for the possibility of God's immediate indwelling in the world (H. Gese). At any rate this view was supported by the affirmation of Mary's perpetual virginity (*aeiparthenos, semper virgo*) by the Fifth Ecumenical Council of Constantinople in 553. The Council of Ephesus in 431 (a minor council convened by Cyril of Alexandria then considered to be an ecumenical council) had defined Mary as *theotokos* ("bearer of God"), but the primary significance of this council was its clarification of the christological problem. Nonetheless, the sources from that time show how intensely Mary was already felt to be an autonomous presence in the church. Thus, it only followed that in the fifth and sixth centuries the belief in Mary's assumption into heavenly glory—admittedly on the basis of questionable apocryphal texts—won over the hearts of Christians. In 1950 Pope Pius XII finally defined Mary's assumption as a dogma of the Catholic church.

The Eastern church did not go beyond the Marian dogmas that had been established up to the sixth century. Likewise, the Middle Ages in the West produced no new Marian dogmas. The question of Mary's immaculate conception, however, affirmed by the Franciscans but denied by the Dominicans, was the subject of lively and sometimes bitter debate, ending in 1854 with Pope Pius IX's definition of the Immaculate Conception as dogma.

In the late Middle Ages it is difficult to distinguish sharply between the development of Mariology and popular Marian devotion. The sermons of Gabriel Biel intimate how much Mary's active role in the incarnation and the passion of her Son, as well as her assumption into heaven, managed to dominate theological thought (H. Oberman).

The Protestant reformers (and the corresponding Protestant confessions) did not challenge the Marian dogmas that had been defined up to that time but made use of traditional notions, particularly those going back to the early church. Martin Luther sees Mary as a descendant of David. Through her the true humanity of Jesus Christ is ensured. Moreover, she is the new Eve. As for Mary's assumption, no thought should be given to it; it suffices to know that she, along with all the saints, lives in Christ. Luther shares the uncertainty about Mary's immaculate conception; his comments on the subject are contradictory (H. Düfel), but he considers the debate over the matter to be pointless. In contrast, he emphatically affirms the virginal conception, although the Hebrew *alma* in *Isaiah* 7:14 merely designates a young woman that has not yet married. That Luther brings his teaching on justification to bear on Mariology is shown by his exposition on the Magnificat in 1520/21: God has looked upon the nothingness of his handmaid because he is a God who makes something out of nothing. Luther's Mariology is, strictly speaking, theology. Luther acknowledges an affectionate attachment to the Lord's handmaiden, but this attachment is grounded in God's salvific action. Therefore, Mary should not be called Queen of Heaven nor can she be an advocate (cf. Irenaeus: *advocata*); at most she is an intercessor. Thus, the Ave Maria is neither a prayer nor an invocation. At issue is not Mary but always Christ. One should not rely on the Mother of God and her merits. Mary is a model of faith, in that she believes, for example, that the promise in *Genesis* 3:15 is fulfilled in her.

Huldrych Zwingli agrees with Luther on all essential points. In a lively argumentation (directed against Helsidius) he defends Mary's perpetual virginity (*semper virgo*). Joseph is given to her only as a shield and protection. What is most instructive is the admittedly apologetic sermon on the ever-pure maiden Mary. Although Mary was the descendant of David, she was still poor: God looked upon her lowliness. Christ in his innocence willed to assume human nature from her and to be born of her: that is her greatest glory. She is therefore most honored when the great deeds of Christ are recognized. Mary teaches us to believe and to resign ourselves to the will of God; we can also imitate her in her purity and innocence, as well as in her steadfastness in suffering. If we wish to recite the Ave Maria, we should realize that this is not a prayer but a greeting and a word of praise. We should not use it without doing the will of God ourselves. Nonetheless, Zwingli calls Mary the "giver of our salvation" and thus grants her a special status in her communion with Christ.

According to John Calvin, God saw nothing in Mary besides her poverty, and he chose her purely by grace. It was not even her humility but rather her smallness (*petitesse*) that God willed to take into account. She has no value for her person in and of herself, but her whole act of praise consists in the fact that she submitted herself in faith to the angel's word.

[*See also* Saints, *article on* Sainthood.]

BIBLIOGRAPHY

Bäumer, Remigius, and Leo Scheffezyk, eds. *Marienlexikon*, vols. 1–5. St. Ottilien, 1988–1993.

Düfel, Hans. *Luthers Stellung zur Marienverehrung*. Göttingen, 1968.

Gese, Hartmut. "Natus ex virgine." In *Vom Sinai zu Zion*, pp. 130–146. Munich, 1974.

Oberman, Heiko. *Spätscholastik und Reformation.* Vol. 1. Zurich, 1965.

Räisänen, Heikki, Heiner Grote, and Reinhard Frieling. "Maria/Marienfrömmigkeit." In *Theologische Realenzyklopädie*, vol. 22, pp. 115–161.

Söll, Georg. "Mariologie." In *Handbuch der Dogmengeschichte*, vol. 3. Freiburg, 1978.

Tappolet, Walter, ed. *Das Marienlob der Reformatoren: Martin Luther, Johannis Calvin, Huldrych Zwingli, Heinrich Bullinger.* Tübingen, 1962.

ULRICH WICKERT

Translated from German by Robert E. Shillenn

MARNIX VAN SAINT ALDEGONDE, Philip

(1540–1598), Low Countries humanist, Calvinist reformer, and leader in the Revolt of the Netherlands. He was among the first of the nobles of the Low Countries to convert to Calvinism. After receiving a humanist education, he enrolled in Calvin's academy at Geneva in 1560. Two years later he renounced his prebend and returned to the Low Countries, where he would play out his role in the Reformation.

Throughout his adult life Marnix was active in Calvinist affairs. His most significant work came in the form of publications that generally served to promote Calvinism among the Netherlandish speaking populace. His most famous work, *Den Byencorf der Heilige Roomsche Kercke* (The Beehive of the Holy Roman Church; 1569), is a biting satire that mocked the clergy, sacraments, and history of Catholicism. Written in response to a pamphlet by the Catholic polemicist Gentian Hervet, the *Byencorf* clearly marked the differences between what Marnix regarded as the human invention of Catholicism and the true church of the Reformed, which was founded on the word of God. He later published an expanded translation of the *Byencorf* under the title *Tableau des differends des religions* (1590). He also translated the *Psalms* (1583) into Dutch, and produced a volume of hymns, *Het Boeck der heylige Schriftuerlicke Loftsangen* (1591).

His position on religious toleration has generated the most scholarly debate about him. He was an energetic opponent of the Anabaptists and the spiritualists because he felt they placed themselves above the authority of scripture by advocating an inner spiritual life. With the exception of the Schwenckfeldians, he repeatedly opposed the toleration of these people. Among his attacks on them was *Ondersoeckinge ende grondelijcke wederlegginge de geesterijvische leere* (Examination and Refutation of the Teaching of the Spiritualists; 1595), which argued that they should be subject to punishment by the state. Yet, while he also found Catholicism to be incorrect, he was willing to tolerate the existence of Catholics in the Low Countries. The difference was that Marnix regarded both Calvinism and Catholicism as churches that disciplined and instructed conscience, even if the Catholics were wrong; by contrast, the spiritualists and Anabaptists had no such external discipline among their members. Marnix believed that when a church failed to discipline its members, it was then—and only then—the duty of the state to provide the necessary discipline. The same idea also explains his participation in the Revolt of the Netherlands.

The most interesting aspect of Marnix's involvement in the revolt was his justification for the rebellion against Philip II of Spain. While insisting on external religious discipline, he also argued that the governancy of conscience belonged not to the sphere of the state, but solely to the realm of the church. It was the job of the church, not the state, to educate and discipline the conscience of the faithful. Only when a church failed to provide this discipline should the state intervene. To Marnix, Calvinism met this standard. Because Philip attempted to use state authority to prevent the exercise of the Reformed conscience, Marnix felt rebellion against Philip was justified. He was called to political rebellion because of the efforts of Philip II and his government to suppress the exercise of Marnix's conscience, not because his Calvinist conscience called him to rebellion.

The Wonder Year of 1566 found Marnix involved in the resistance to the religious policies of Philip II. His first significant political writing was *Vraye narration et apologie des choses passées au Pays-Bas* . . . (1567), which defended not only the *Gueux* ("beggars"), but also the iconoclasts. In neither case was sedition involved, for the *Gueux* defended Netherlandic privileges and the iconoclasts defended true religion. During the 1570s Marnix was active as a propagandist for William of Orange and probably wrote the words to "Wilhelmus van Nassouwen," which later became the Dutch national anthem. He frequently represented William in negotiations; most significant of these was his involvement in the Pacification of Ghent (1576). Marnix was a consistent defender of the pacification because its religious settlement, which was later carried into the Union of Utrecht, embodied his position on toleration. In the 1580s his political career ended in discredit. After serving as a representative of the States-General in their negotiations with François de Valois, duke of Anjou, Marnix shared in the blame when French soldiers rioted at Antwerp in 1583. The following year his friend William of Orange was assassinated, and in 1585 Marnix surrendered Antwerp to the Spanish. He retired to Walcheren and later died at Leiden, where he had earlier helped to found the university.

BIBLIOGRAPHY

Primary Sources

Marnix van Saint Aldegonde, Philip. *Philips van Marnix van St. Aldegonde: Godsdienstige en kerkelijke geschriften.* 3 vols. Edited by J. J. van Toorenenbergen. The Hague, 1871–1878. Contains most of Marnix's religious writings but is only available at a few major university libraries.

———. *Oeuvres de Philippe de Marnix de Sainte Aldgonde.* Edited by Albert Lacroix. Six volumes bound as three. Reprint, Geneva, 1971. Contains the *Tableau* as well as most of Marnix's significant political writings.

———. *Den Byencorf der H. Roomsche Kercke.* Edited by W. A. Ornóe and S. L. Strengholt. Zutphen, 1975. The modern edition of *Byencorf,* though it has been condensed in places.

———. *De onuitgegeven briefwisseling van Marnix van Sint-Aldegonde.* Edited by Aloïs Gerlo. Brussels, 1985. A collection of Marnix's correspondence which had not been previously published.

———. *Marnixi Epistulae: De briefwisseling van Marnix van Sint-Aldegonde.* Vol. 1, *1558–1576.* Edited by Gerlo Alois and Rudolf De Smet. Vol. 2, *1577–1578.* Brussels, 1990 and 1992. The first two volumes of a complete critical collection of Marnix's letters.

Secondary Sources

Beemon, F. E. "Poisoned Honey or Pure Manna: The Eucharist and the Word in the *Beehive* of Marnix of Saint Aldegonde." *Church History* 61 (1992), 382–393. Examines the metaphor of the beehive as a means of communicating Calvinist doctrine to a popular audience.

———. "Calvinist Conscience and Rebellion: Marnix of Saint Aldegonde's Justification for the Dutch Revolt." *Fides et Historia* 24 (1992), 91–99. Examines Marnix's formulation of his ideology of rebellion.

Bergsma, Wiebe. "Marnix and the Schwenkfeldians: Some General Remarks." *Mennonite Quarterly Review* 62 (1988), 236–248. Recounts Marnix's correspondence with the Frisian Aggaeus van Albada.

Graaff, B. J. W. de. *Dichter-soldaat: Uit het leven van Filips Marnix.* 2 vols. Utrecht, 1971. A nonscholarly Calvinist hagiography.

Kramer, C. *Emmery de Lyere et Marnix de Sainte Aldegonde: Un admirateur de Sebastian Franck et de Montaigne aux prises avec le champion des calvinistes néerlandais.* The Hague, 1971. Addresses the issue of religious toleration in an exchange between de Lyere and Marnix with Marnix as the heavy.

Schelven, A. A. van. *Marnix van Sint Aldegonde.* Utrecht, 1939. The best biography of Marnix.

Verhoef, C. E. H. J. *Philips van Marnix, Heer van Sint Aldegonde.* Weesp, Netherlands, 1985. This most recent biography is little more than pamphlet length, though it does a good job of summarizing the traditional disputes over Marnix.

F. E. BEEMON

MAROT, Clément (c.1496–1544), French poet and creator of metrical psalms. Son of the French court poet Jean Marot, Clément studied law in Paris before entering the service of Marguerite d'Angoulême (c.1518). The evangelical tendencies encountered in Marguerite's entourage led to his imprisonment for religious heterodoxy in 1526. He succeeded his father as court poet to Francis I in the same year. After the Affaire des Placards (1534) he fled to Ferrara and the fragile protection of Duchess Renée of France, but abjured and returned to France in 1536. In 1542 he was again in exile in Geneva; but he moved to Savoy, then Italy, a year later. He died in Turin. Marot's religious position has been hotly debated, but he was clearly in favor of a reformation of the Church on evangelical lines, and as clearly he was at home neither in Paris nor in Geneva.

Marot's poetic output was prolific, varied, and on the whole lighthearted, graceful, and witty; his style is simple and lucid. In 1533 he began a series of versifications in French of *Psalms;* he dedicated a collection of thirty metrical psalms to the king of France in 1539. In the same year, however, Calvin adopted some of these psalms (each provided with a melody) as the hymnbook of his Strasbourg congregation, and subsequently of the Geneva church (1542). They thus became viewed as heretical by the Paris theologians, who banned them in 1544. By the time of his death Marot had created fifty metrical psalms; the series was completed by Théodore de Bèze in 1562. Marot's psalms are remarkable for their fidelity to the original, their solemn musicality, their simplicity, and their metrical variety (contrast the metrical psalms in English); they constituted the most significant poetic and musical challenge to the esthetics of Ronsard and the Pléiade, and became the rallying point of the French Reformed church, for which they were—and still are—the major expression of corporate participation in worship.

BIBLIOGRAPHY

Primary Source

Marot, Clément. *Oeuvres poétiques.* Edited by Gérard Defaux. 2 vols. Paris, 1990–1993.

Secondary Sources

Screech, Michael A. *Marot évangélique.* Geneva, 1967. A polemical refutation of Claus Mayer's *La religion de Marot* (Geneva, 1960), but the most judicious statement of Marot's religious position.

Smith, Pauline M. *Clément Marot: Poet of the Renaissance.* London, 1970. The only recent study of Marot in English.

FRANCIS M. HIGMAN

MARPECK, Pilgram (c.1495–1556), civil magistrate turned social reformer and Anabaptist leader. Marpeck's life and thought shed light on the theology and practice of the Roman Catholic church and of various reform movements of the sixteenth century from the perspective of an interested lay German burgher who was acquainted with the social, economic, and political interests of his fellow burghers, the nobility, and the commoners. He influenced the present-day Mennonite tradition, which, since the rediscovery of most of his writings in the twentieth century, has embraced his theology as representative of Anabaptism. That interest is due, in part, to his position being less sectarian than that of other Anabaptists (e.g., Swiss Brethren and Hutterites), his continued professional activities, and his sensitivity to social justice issues.

Marpeck was born to a politically prominent family in the

Tirolean mining town of Rattenberg on the Inn. Having moved to the Tirol from Bavaria, Marpeck's father, Heinrich, served as district magistrate, burgomaster, and city councilman. Following the death of his first wife, Sophia, with whom he had one daughter, Margareth, Pilgram Marpeck married Anna and adopted three foster children. Professionally, he worked for the city hospital, organized the city's crossbow competition, and acted as purchasing agent for the mining guild's infirmary before assuming the office of mining magistrate in 1525. Politically, Marpeck served on the outer and inner city councils and as burgomaster (1522), represented Rattenberg's craftsmen in a territorial dispute, negotiated the release of a reform-minded Augustinian prior (Stephan Castenbaur, later Stephan Agricola), and oversaw the hiring of a priest (Wilhelm Kern) to serve in the city parish church. As mining magistrate, in 1527 Marpeck was ordered to extradite miners who were sympathetic, as was he, to the Anabaptist preachers Leonhard Schiemer and Hans Schlaffer. Following initial consent, Marpeck resigned his office a few days after Schiemer's execution, forfeited his substantial estate, and traveled to the Bohemian mining town of Krumau, where he was likely baptized and commissioned as an Anabaptist elder.

In 1528 Marpeck entered Strasbourg's gardener-wagoner guild and bought citizenship. He also became a leader of a group of social radicals involved in a communal collection for the care of the city's poor and refugees of religious persecution elsewhere. He held meetings of Anabaptists in his home and was arrested in October 1528 along with Fridolin Meyger, a notary in the episcopal chancery, Jakob Kautz, a spiritualizing Anabaptist, and Wilhelm Reublin, the Swiss Anabaptist leader. Released by 1530, Marpeck was hired as the city's wood and mining administrator in the Kinzig Valley.

Marpeck published two tracts in 1531 in Strasbourg that helped delineate the distinctions among the city's Anabaptist groups—the Spiritualists, the Melchiorites, the Swiss Brethren, and Marpeck's group. *Clave verantwurtung ettlicher Artickel. . .* (A Clear Response. . .) and *Ain klar / vast nützlicher unterricht. . .* (A Clear and Useful Instruction. . .) were directed primarily against the spiritualizing positions of Johannes Bünderlin and Christian Entfelder, as well as the apocalyptic visions and monophysite Christology of Melchior Hoffman. Marpeck also composed a "Confession of Faith" (1531) that distinguished his positions on baptism, the covenants, and the relationship of church and state from those of the magisterial reformer Martin Bucer. A debate between the two was held in council chambers and ended with Marpeck's expulsion from Strasbourg early in 1532. During this period, he may also have written the *Aufdeckung der Babylonian hürn. . .* (Exposure of the Babylonian Whore. . .), a text that criticizes the use of the power of the civil authority in matters of Christian faith.

During the years 1532–1544, Marpeck lived in Switzerland and traveled periodically to the Tirol, Moravia, south Germany, and Alsace. He established congregations and had contact with other Anabaptist groups, such as the Hutterites and Swiss Brethren. In an attempt to unify various groups of Anabaptists, Marpeck translated and edited Bernhard Rothmann's Low German *Bekenntnisse van beyden Sacramenten. . .* (Confession Concerning Both Sacraments) and published it as the *Vermahnung* (Warning; c.1542). This is also the period of Marpeck's christological controversy with the Silesian nobleman Kaspar von Schwenckfeld.

From about 1544 to his death in 1556, Marpeck lived in Augsburg, where he supervised lumbering in the city's forest and contributed to the renovation and extension of the city's water works as city engineer. Although he was warned three times to desist from Anabaptist activities, Marpeck persisted in the leadership of a group that often met in his home on municipal property. He maintained correspondence with Anabaptist groups in Switzerland, Alsace, south Germany, and Moravia. Of particular concern to him was the poor quality of leadership and the too strict exercise of the ban among the congregations in the Swiss village of Appenzell.

Marpeck's activities and theology have much in common with those of other lay theologians of the sixteenth century. First, he drew eclectically from such diverse sources as Luther and Zwingli, medieval mystical traditions (*Theologia Deutsch*), spiritualizing reformers (Schwenckfeld and Sebastian Franck), apocalyptic restitutionists (Bernhard Rothmann), local reform-minded pastors (Castenbaur and Kern), and itinerant Anabaptist preachers (Schiemer and Schlaffer). Second, he combined an emphasis on the Bible, a medieval anthropology, a notion of a sacred community, and a sense of vocation to redeem the world.

Marpeck expressed the last concern as a commitment "to be diligent in all things unto the fulfillment of all justice, not only internally before God, but also externally before humanity." This justice had as its foundation and source the historical reordering of the human person of Christ in the Incarnation and the extension of that order by the outpouring of the Holy Spirit in the Crucifixion. The Holy Spirit in turn gathers those who willingly receive it into a new, sacred community, Christ's "unglorified body," which mediates that Spirit to still others and awaits union with Christ's "glorified body" in heaven. The reception of the Spirit is sealed by baptism, the "covenant of good conscience"; justifies the believer; progressively reorders the believer's internal life; and leads to a commitment to participation in the reordering of the external life—both personal and social.

With respect to the establishment of God's just order, Marpeck was neither chiliastic nor revolutionary. He conceived of a reordered community of reordered persons that reordered the larger human community by patiently offering the Holy Spirit. Because of the unconstraining nature of Christ's Spirit, Marpeck argued against the use of the state's sword in matters of faith (e.g., his debate with Bucer) and rejected a coercive legalism within the church (e.g., his objection to these tendencies among the Hutterites and Swiss Brethren). He advocated not a monastic withdrawal from society, but a critical participation. He supported the swearing of the civil oath, obedience as far as possible to civil authority, and the payment of taxes. But he criticized and worked to alleviate economic injustice (e.g., he criticized the goals of the Fuggers, the Augsburg banking family, in financing the Schmalkald War, and he participated in Strasbourg's poor relief) and refused to use deadly force.

Marpeck affirms the "once-for-allness" of Christ's work—not in the sense that Christ and his work remain external, limited in space and time to Palestine fifteen hundred years earlier, but in the sense that the Incarnation initiated the ongoing existence and work of the salvific community, or body of Christ. One is saved by Christ alone, who has been embodied in the lives of Christians through successive generations since the Resurrection. As for salvation by grace alone, Marpeck insists that grace is not experienced from and in oneself, but only in relation to others in the new community. Receptivity to that grace is prepared by the recognition of one's vulnerability and need that issues from the experience of suffering. Marpeck's position concerning a reliable authority for doctrine and practice might be closer to certain late medieval Catholic views than Protestant ones. He implies that scripture alone, without the authenticating testimony of tradition, is insufficient. However, the kind of tradition that authenticates the scriptural witness is not the cumulative theological reflection passed on in learned texts interpreted by a clerical magisterium, but the reordered and reordering wisdom and life of the believing community as it has been passed on to the viator (wayfarer).

BIBLIOGRAPHY

Primary Sources

Klassen, William, and Walter Klaassen, eds. *The Writings of Pilgram Marpeck.* Scottdale, Pa., 1978. Translation of most of Marpeck's writings.

Marpeck, Pilgram. *Verantwurtung über Casparn Schwenckfelds Judicium* (1542). Vienna and Leipzig, 1929.

———. *Vermanung.* In *Gedenkschrift zum 400-Jährigen Jubiläum der Mennoniten....* Ludwigshafen, 1925.

Secondary Sources

Bergsten, Torsten. "Pilgram Marbeck und seine Auseinandersetzung mit Caspar Schwenckfeld." *Kyrkohistorik Arsskrift* (1957–1958), 39–100, 53–87. Best analysis of Marpeck's controversy with Schwenckfeld.

Blough, Neal. *Christologie Anabaptiste: Pilgram Marpeck et l'humanité de Christ.* Geneva, 1984. Excellent analysis of Marpeck's Christology, debt to Luther, and controversy with Schwenckfeld.

Boyd, Stephen. *Pilgram Marpeck: His Life and Social Theology.* Durham, N.C., and Mainz, 1992. The most comprehensive biographical treatment based on new archival material placed in Marpeck's social and political context with attention to social ethical issues, such as church and state. With extensive bibliography.

Fast, Heinold. "Pilgram Marbeck und das oberdeutsche Täufertum: Ein neuer Handschriftenfund." *Archiv für Reformationsgeschichte* 47 (1956), 212–242. Description of *Das Kunstbuch,* the devotional book containing most of Marpeck's extant letters. A critical edition is in preparation.

Klaassen, Walter. "Investigation into the Authorship and the Historical Background of the Anabaptist Tract 'Aufdeckung der babylonischen Hürn....' " *Mennonite Quarterly Review* 61 (1987), 251–261. Description of this important tract and argument for its inclusion among Marpeck's writings.

Klassen, William. *Covenant and Community.* Grand Rapids, Mich., 1968. Helpful treatment of Marpeck's hermeneutics and other theological issues.

Wray, Frank. "The 'Vermanung' of 1542 and Rothmann's 'Bekentnisse.'" *Archiv für Reformationsgeschichte* 47 (1956), 243–251. Identification of and argument that the *Warning* is Marpeck's translation and interpolation of Rothmann's *Confession.*

STEPHEN B. BOYD

MARPRELATE TRACTS. Consisting of six books and one broadside, the Marprelate Tracts appeared pseudonymously in 1588–1589. Brilliantly satirical, they attacked both the hierarchy and the distinctive tenets of the Church of England as well as espousing presbyterian principles. The tracts were part of the increasingly bitter pamphlet disputes within the established church between conformists and presbyterians. Enmity toward the bishops intensified as a result of Archbishop John Whitgift's campaign to enforce uniformity through the imposition of ecclesiastical articles and reliance on the High Commission, with its controversial oath *ex officio* requiring people to incriminate themselves. The immediate inspiration for the Marprelate Tracts was threefold: the publication of a treatise by John Bridges, dean of Salisbury, entitled *A Defence of the Government Established in the Church of Englande* (1587), which refuted a presbyterian book, *A Briefe and Plaine Declaration* (1584), probably by William Fulke; a Star Chamber decree of 23 June 1586 prohibiting the publication of unlicensed books; and the experiences of Job Throkmorton, Robert Waldegrave, and John Penry at the hands of the state.

Throkmorton, who in 1572 had defended John Field and Thomas Wilcox's *An Admonition to Parliament,* sat for Warwick in the Parliaments of 1586 and 1587. As an M.P. he spoke in favor of executing Mary Stuart, imposing presbyterian polity on the Church of England, and siding with the Netherlands against Spain; the last speech forced him to go into hiding. The authorities destroyed Waldegrave's press after he printed Throkmorton's *The State of the Church of Englande* (1588). Shortly after writing *A Treatise Containing the Aequity of an Humble Supplication* (1587), Penry was summoned before the High Commission and imprisoned. These men thus opposed what they saw as a policy of persecution inspired by the prelates, and all three were involved with the Marprelate Tracts.

More than twenty persons have been tentatively identified as "Martin Marprelate," including the Puritans John Udall,

John Field, and Dudley Fenner and the Separatist Henry Barrow. The strongest cases have been made for Throkmorton, almost certainly the author, and Penry, who coordinated the project. The printing was done on two secret, mobile presses, one controlled by Penry and the other by John Hodgskin.

The initial Marprelate tract, the *Epistle,* which appeared in October 1588, refuted Bridges's *Defence.* The *Epistle* contained a sweeping indictment of the episcopal hierarchy, whose members were depicted as petty antichrists and popes as well as enemies of the gospel, and a defense of prominent presbyterians. The *Epitome,* published a month later, continued the themes of the *Epistle* and attacked Bishop John Aylmer for failing to uphold the reformist tenets espoused in his *Harborowe for Faithfull and Trewe Subiectes* (1559). In *Certaine Mineralls, and Metaphisicall School Points* (January 1589) Marprelate accused the bishops of working for the devil and accepting polygamy, and attacked such Anglican practices as pluralism, the use of the sign of the cross in baptism, and wearing the surplice. *Hay Any Worke for Cooper* (March 1589), which refuted Bishop Thomas Cooper's *An Admonition to the People of England* (1589), focused on three themes: presbyterian polity; a rejection of the view that adopting it was difficult or dangerous; and the faults of church officials.

The progression of tracts continued in July 1589 with *Theses Martinianae,* which upheld Reformed tenets on polity, castigated bishops as unscriptural, and denounced both the oath *ex officio* and the role of bishops in the Privy Council and the House of Lords. The same month Marprelate published *The Just Censure and ReProofe of Martin Junior,* mocking the failure of the authorities to identify him and calling for a conference to discuss conformist-Puritan differences. Authorities seized the next manuscript, *More Worke for Cooper,* in August 1589 while it was still in press. From the last Marprelate tract, the *Protestatyon,* we know that *More Worke for Cooper* depicted the godly character, loyalty, and purpose of a "Martinist" and satirized those who had attacked the tracts. The *Protestatyon* proclaimed boldly that "Marprelate" would continue his campaign until the church was reformed.

In fact, no further tracts appeared. A grand jury indicted Throkmorton in October 1590, but his case was subsequently deferred and later suspended. Penry and Waldegrave fled to Scotland, where the latter found employment as a printer for James VI. Penry eventually returned to England, where he was executed as a Separatist in May 1593. During the search for the Marprelate press the government uncovered a network of presbyterian classes, prosecuted its leaders in Star Chamber and the High Commission, and effectively destroyed presbyterian organization. Ironically, many presbyterian leaders had disowned the tracts from the outset, but the government seized the opportunity to discredit all presbyterians.

BIBLIOGRAPHY

Anselment, Raymond A. "Rhetoric and the Dramatic Satire of Martin Marprelate." *Studies in English Literature 1500–1900* 10 (1970), 103–119. Helpful introduction to the use of satire in the tracts.

Carlson, Leland H. *Martin Marprelate, Gentleman: Master Job Throkmorton Laid Open in His Colors.* San Marino, Calif., 1981. Persuasively argues the case for Throkmorton's authorship of the tracts.

Collinson, Patrick. *The Elizabethan Puritan Movement.* Reprint, Oxford, 1990. Provides indispensable background for the tracts.

Marprelate, Martin. *The Marprelate Tracts, 1588–1589.* Leeds, 1967. Facsimile edition.

McGinn, Donald J. *John Penry and the Marprelate Controversy.* New Brunswick, N.J., 1966. Argues that Penry wrote the tracts.

Pierce, William. *An Historical Introduction to the Marprelate Tracts: A Chapter in the Evolution of Religious and Civil Liberty in England.* London, 1908. Suggests that the tracts came from the pen of a member of Parliament, though not necessarily Throkmorton.

RICHARD L. GREAVES

MARRANOS. *See* New Christians; Spain.

MARRIAGE is the institution through which men and women are united in a relationship of social and legal dependence for the purpose of founding and maintaining a family. Though the Reformation did not alter this fundamental definition, the reform of marriage was certainly one of its most visible institutional initiatives. By rejecting the received Catholic notions of marriage as a sacrament and of clerical celibacy as a spiritually superior way of life, sixteenth-century reformers created a new understanding of the religious content and purpose of marriage, an understanding argued through their publications and exemplified by their lives.

Catholic doctrine regarding the sacramental character of marriage and the spiritual merits of celibacy rested primarily on the teachings of Paul. His epistle to the Ephesians, in which he discusses the relationship between husband and wife and the mysterious union of Christ and his church, is a classic text for Catholic sacramental theology and especially for the Catholic definition of marriage. The Vulgate translation of the crucial Greek *mysterion* as *sacramentum* (*Ephesians* 5:32)—Protestants never tired of calling it a fundamental linguistic error—justified the understanding of marriage as a divine institution transmitting grace and the control of marriage through an extensive corpus of ecclesiastical regulations. The traditional glorification of celibacy and its elevation over the estate of marriage stemmed from Paul, too (for example, *1 Corinthians* 7:32–34). Elaborated over centuries, the relative merits of the two in the teachings of the Catholic church have been more frequently caricatured than analyzed. One of the best remembered examples is Jerome's opinion of the virtue of marriage as limited to the creation of new generations of virgins. Though theologians and moralists gave pride of place to the celibate life, this did not result in a complete denigration of marriage as such. For example, Albrecht von Eyb, a fifteenth-century Bamberg canon, wrote *Ehebüchlein* (Little Book of Marriage; 1472), a charming pamphlet in praise of marriage. Without lessening the value they placed on virginity, penitential preachers of the fourteenth and fifteenth centuries also praised the married estate in terms that Protestants would echo a century later. Distinctions of this sort could not, however, drown a growing chorus of cries for reform that focused on issues of the sacramental theology of the Catholic church and the sexual discipline of its clergy. By the fifteenth century this was strengthened by voices arguing the case for marriage on the basis of notions from classical antiquity. These notions, which saw marriage as the highest expression of love and the primordial pattern for the social order, had such literary manifestations as Leon Battista Alberti's *Della famiglia* (Concerning the Family; c.1435), Francesco Barbaro's *De re uxoria* (Concerning the Nature of Wives; reprint 1514), and Desiderius Erasmus's *Encomium matrimonii* (In Praise of Matrimony; 1497), as well as the thought of such figures as Coluccio Salutati and Lorenzo Valla.

In *De captivitate Babylonica ecclesiae praeludium* (The Babylonian Captivity of the Church; 1520) Martin Luther addressed the sacramental theology of the Catholic church and dismissed it as a spiritual prison rather than a source of grace: sacraments were restrictive rather than liberating. In the course of his argument, he contended that marriage could not be included among the sacraments of the Christian faith. Marriage, he pointed out, had existed since the very beginning of time and was common to Christians and heathens alike. Moreover, while upholding the sanctity of marriage, scripture offered no justification for defining it as a sacrament. Though it was a symbol and metaphor for the mystery of the relationship between Christ and his church, marriage was not the relationship itself and did not contain words of divine promise nor words of dominical institution. Thus, it failed to conform to Luther's definition of a sacrament. Marriage did not transmit the grace of God as a means of obtaining salvation.

Its spiritual value rested elsewhere, an idea mentioned only indirectly in 1520 but developed in detail later by Luther, his associates, and other reformers. Critical of the Catholic regulation of marriage, Luther reserved particular scorn for the notion that ordination—and, therefore, celibacy—was superior to marriage. Not only did this lift human legislation above divine institution, but it endangered the spiritual well-being of those members of the clergy who felt driven to marry or commit fornication in violation of their vows.

Luther eventually linked the dangers of celibacy and the purpose of marriage. The first reformer to do so openly was Andreas Bodenstein von Karlstadt. In his *De coelibatu monachatu et viduitate* (Concerning Celibacy, Monkery, and Widowhood; 1521) he rejected celibacy and vindicated marriage as a more worthy state because it was consistent with human nature, preserved souls from sin, and increased the body of the faithful. Later the same year Luther set forth his own very similar case against celibacy in the treatise *De votis monasticis* (On Monastic Vows; 1521). There he declared that the Bible offered no support for the supremacy of the celibate life and that vows of celibacy violated the Christian's faith in baptism, the individual's freedom of conscience, and the created nature of human beings.

These and all other arguments in favor of clerical marriage took as their basic premise the degeneracy of human nature and the necessity of human sexuality. In this context the reason for extolling marriage was essentially negative; it served as a means of attacking the Catholic practice of clerical celibacy. Yet the assumption that God created marriage as a refuge from the sins of lust and fornication could also serve as the basis for a positive assessment of the married state, as Luther demonstrated in his treatise *Vom ehelichen Leben* (On the Married Life; 1522). In it he emphasized the spiritual advantages of marriage rather than the spiritual dangers of celibacy.

Marriage existed in order to satisfy righteously the irresistible, natural, and necessary urge to procreate. God created humans with such a disposition that they simply must have children as a matter of nature rather than choice. Exempted from this natural ordinance were only those who had been castrated, those who were impotent, and those who practiced chastity. All others must marry. Were there no such institution for the pious, moral, and legal begetting of offspring, humans would still respond to this primordial urge through fornication, adultery, or "secret sins." Marriage worked for the salvation of souls, therefore, by allowing human beings to act according to their created nature without sin.

Sexuality was the reason for marriage, and marriage was the ideal state for nearly all human beings. By contrast, chastity was a rare and special gift of God—a spiritually rich and exalted state—but one that could not be hazarded without a special calling. Few people capable of marrying and having children could abstain and work for the kingdom of God.

Impotency was similarly problematic. Because of their created nature, the spouses of impotent persons had to be given an outlet for their sexuality. Luther proposed radical solutions, such as a secret contract to beget children with a close relative of the impotent person or, in cases where this was not acceptable, abandonment, flight, and remarriage in some distant land. The natural imperative of procreation superseded the social ordinance of fidelity.

Likewise, this order abrogated human ordinances that regulated marriage. Luther rejected nearly the entire Catholic canon of marital impedimenta. Consanguinity and affinity had to be limited to the second degree as prescribed in *Leviticus*, but they remained valid because they were biblically justified. Coercion, too, continued to be a grounds for annulling marriage because it violated the spiritual freedom of all Christians. All other rules and statutes that barred certain persons from wedding legally—a considerable list, including spiritual relationship, legal kinship, mixed religion, criminal condemnation, public decorum, solemn vows, personal error, personal unfreedom, holy orders, episcopal prohibition, restricted seasons, local custom, and physical defect—were swept aside by the necessity of marriage.

Ironically, that necessity necessitated divorce as well. If human beings were driven to marry by their sexual nature, then they had to be permitted to separate and remarry when their union no longer provided the intended spiritual refuge. Impotency was an obvious and easy case in point. More problematic were adultery and abandonment. Though justified by Jesus' own teaching (*Matthew* 19:3–9), adultery as a grounds for divorce troubled Luther. In his opinion it served as an expedient at best for those persons who could not tolerate infidelity. Yet it did not please him because it encouraged unchristian behavior. Under ideal circumstances the faithful should forgive such lapses, but, if not, the guilty should be executed and the innocent allowed to remarry. Abandonment, too, could serve as a pretext for dishonest dealings when spouses parted by mutual consent—that is, a sort of private repudiation and divorce. Legitimate cases, however, deprived the abandoned spouse of both material support and licit sexuality. Here again divorce and remarriage served as a remedy for marital dysfunction and a means of preserving souls from sin. In all cases human nature dictated the universality, the purpose, and, ultimately, the dissolubility of marriage.

The extended treatment of Luther's views on marriage, as articulated in 1522, is justified by the fact that most magisterial reformers adopted very similar positions. Huldrych Zwingli raised the topic of marriage in his most systematic theological statement, *De Vera et Falsa Religione* (Concerning True and False Religion; 1525), and John Calvin followed the same line of reasoning with no substantial deviations in the first edition of his great summa, *Institutio Christianae religionis* (Institutes of the Christian Religion; 1536). All interpreted marriage as a holy estate but not a sacrament; all valued it as a hospital for the soul, unable to resist its own predeliction to sin; and all rejected clerical celibacy as contrary to God's will and human nature.

Radical reformers, however, developed an altogether different notion, the so-called covenantal marriage. Though in agreement with the magisterial Reformation's rejection of both the sacramental character of marriage and the spiritual superiority of celibacy, the radical Reformation clung to a more religious sense of marriage, one that tied it directly to an emphasis on redemption through a conscious commitment to Christ. The point of marriage had little or nothing to do with procreative drives or weakened and sinful wills. Rather, it was a covenantal relationship between a man and a woman as freely consenting and fully responsible members of the conventicle of the faithful. This identification of both husband and wife as members of a congregation of believers was critical because it elevated the character of marriage from that of a remedy for human sinfulness to a direct expression and result of redemption and salvation. Even as it seemed closely associated to Protestant lines of argumentation regarding the sacraments and celibacy, covenantal marriage repudiated the Protestant notion of marriage as an institution predicated on human nature, insisting in terms reminiscent of the Catholic church on its spiritual character, subject to church ordinance. Thus, on the question of marriage, the radical Reformation occupied a position somewhere between those of Protestantism and Catholicism.

Among mid-century Anabaptists this view of marriage converged with another, increasingly important tenet, the use of the ban to assure the reality of a church "without spot or wrinkles." This ban was understood by some rigoristic Anabaptists as the categorical shunning of the person; it even included the breaking of all ties ("bed and board") with a spouse. Thus, among the rigoristic Anabaptists the believer's covenant with Christ was more important than the earthly covenant with one's spouse. Neither Catholicism nor Protestantism allowed for such priority.

Competing definitions of marriage held by competing churches and sects confronted the people of sixteenth-century Europe with a series of hitherto seldom encountered experiences and problems. Mixed and clerical marriages were among the most common. Mixed marriages were a novelty of the sixteenth century. Though condemned by religious leaders, such unions were not prohibited by secular authorities provided they did not create a public disturbance. Estate records suggest that families of mixed religion were not uncommon, if not exactly commonplace, especially in biconfessional communities.

More striking still were clerical marriages. Scholars have emphasized the immediate impact of the call for clerical marriage in terms of the number of religious who abandoned the cloister and celibacy to join the forces for religious change in the sixteenth century. Certainly Luther and all his associates at Wittenberg had married and established households by the end of 1525.

Whether this was the case generally cannot be determined, but clerical marriage remains undoubtedly one of the most visible and controversial innovations of the Reformation. Despite evidence that the practice of concubinage had become increasingly commonplace among the clergy and that the laity were more and more willing to accept these illicit relationships in the late Middle Ages, the open legal marriage of priests was a tangible sign of a new religious order, one even the illiterate and uninformed could not fail to notice and understand. It violated an ancient ecclesiastical custom, however, and probably sowed as much anxiety and confusion among the laity as it did among the clergy themselves. Whatever sexual irregularities celibacy might have caused, it was a sign of the mystical power and sacerdotal authority of the clergy. In many cultures, including that of pre-Christian Europe, celibacy indicated a unique relationship with the supernatural; once married, a priest appeared only as a neighbor with no more ability to intercede before God than the village blacksmith. The mixed feelings of laypeople were nowhere more evident than in England; Henry VIII initiated a thoroughgoing reform of the church but steadfastly enforced celibacy among its priests. Even the second and third generations of reformers continued to attack celibacy and defend clerical marriage long after the consolidation of the Reformation, a reliable indication that centuries-old practices were not so easily discarded.

Apart from justifying clerical marriage, Protestant diatribes against celibacy may also have narrowed socially acceptable roles for and fueled latent hostilities toward unmarried persons in society at large. Luther, Zwingli, and Calvin made perfectly clear that sexual incontinence plagued the laity, as well as the clergy, and women more than men. Those who failed or refused to marry would fall into immorality. It is impossible to prove statistically that Protestantism altered marital behavior by, for example, increasing rates of marriage or lowering ages at marriage. A connection may have existed, however, between changing attitudes toward celibacy and various established sixteenth-century phenomena, such as the increasing loss of public visibility among women that followed their expulsion from guilds and cloisters, the resulting subjugation of these women to the authority of their fathers and husbands, and the virulent persecution of women for witchcraft that claimed the elderly and unmarried as its most frequent victims. Marriage became not only the preferred estate for adult Christians but also a safe haven in a society that viewed the marginal and deviant with increasing unease.

Against the dangers of celibacy Protestants set the advantages of marriage. These were implicit in treatises on its theological nature and explicit in a growing body of sermons and guidebooks that addressed the mutual rights and responsibilities of husband and wife. All reformers recognized the ethical implications of the symbolism of Christ and the church. Clearly marriage was intended to quench sexual desires without sin, but it also provided mutual support in a relationship marked by patriarchy, amity, and communality. Spouses should especially love and tolerate one another. Husbands were bound to love, protect, and sustain their wives; wives should demonstrate their faith and love through obedience to their husbands. As Zwingli put it, marriage was a union of fortunes and a common fate.

None of these espousals were particularly new in the sixteenth century or unique to Protestantism. Catholic moralists had long lauded companionate marriage as a social and spiritual good; and little separated their arguments from those of their Protestant adversaries. The common ground occasionally became clear when, for example, a conservative Lutheran pastor, such as Cyriakus Spangenberg, applied the metaphor of an abbot and monk to the relationship of a husband and wife in his *Ehespiegel* (Mirror of Marriage; 1565). What was new among sixteenth-century reformers was a more urgent sense of responsibility not only for marriage but also for the quality of marital relations.

The conviction that marriage was central not only to the salvation of the spouses but also to the spiritual well-being of entire communities probably arose from the coincidence of two separate but complementary developments: the rise of the absolute state, with its universal authority to police its subjects, and the Protestant understanding of marriage as a nonsacramental, religious institution, with its broad disciplinary implications. The former resulted in a growing body of legislation as early as the fifteenth century designed to eliminate legal immunities within a state's jurisdiction and to expand its oversight of marriage. The latter seemed to justify an even further assumption of marital regulation by secular authorities.

The Catholic church had always conceded a certain civil competence in disputes pertaining to the ceremony, morality, and property of marriage (the so-called *res mixti fori*) but steadfastly reserved matters affecting the existence of conjugal bonds (the *substantia vinculi*) to its own courts. The growing power and self-confidence of secular governments led them to attempt to narrow the considerable political and legal authority of the Catholic church within their jurisdictions, especially in those matters that seemed to touch civil affairs most directly. Marriage, especially as an institution involving sometimes considerable transfers of property, qualified as one of these areas of contention.

Indeed, most Protestants demanded that a Christian magistracy assume the authority to regulate marriage by reforming rituals, legislating ordinances, and establishing tribunals to adjudicate disputes related to marriage. Governments usually obliged with omnibus reform programs or specialized marital statutes that were among their first acts of religious reform. The Reformation signaled a break with episcopal authority and provided the opportunity for cities and states to assume its powers summarily. As a result, marriage became both fully public and fully policed, simultaneously a means of social control and the object of social control.

The control of marriage began with the ceremony itself. From the twelfth century the Catholic church had upheld the importance of consent on the parts of the spouses in establishing a valid marriage. A free, honest, and immediate will to marry constituted an indissoluble bond regardless of consummation or consecration. Yet this principle seemed to permit an array of abuses, the most widely condemned of which were clandestine marriages between minors without the agreement of their parents and deceptive marriages that involved a swindle of one or both spouses. Not until 1563 did the Catholic church take steps against secrecy and swindle in the Tridentine decree *Tametsi*, which required the presence of witnesses and a ceremony in church as part of a valid marriage. Protestants rejected the sufficiency of consent, however, and insisted on publicity as well. Ordinances in most reformed states specified that marriage had to be an open contract involving the consent of parents, the presence of witnesses, and the participation of the community. This was one of the enduring legacies bequeathed to marriage by the Reformation. More immediately and broadly, however, the requirement of publicity created opportunities for magisterial oversight and control; marriages that failed to conform to Protestant strictures could be prevented, as well as prohibited.

Beyond rituals, reformed marital ordinances laid out the contours of acceptable married life. Just as a religious understanding of marriage dictated that it be characterized by monogamy, amity, communality, and patriarchy, the requirements of social order led magistrates to legislate more vigorous sanctions against fornication, adultery, abuse, and abandonment. Unique sexual privilege, uninterrupted cohabitation, and material support were the necessary signs of domestic tranquillity and stability, and these goals were to be achieved through a stringent social control of marriage.

Enforcing this legislation were specialized marriage courts and omnicompetent consistories, central institutions in the control of marriage and morality after the Reformation. Marriage courts were civil institutions that superseded episcopal courts and extended the *ius commune* of the government to marriage. Marriage courts heard complaints and suits most frequently on two general issues: the validity of marital contracts and the legality of marital behavior. They reviewed more suits to enforce agreements to marry than any other kind of litigation. Apart from the new list of admissible grounds, however, these suits differed little from those resolved for centuries by the tribunals of diocesan officials. If a plaintiff, usually a woman in such cases, could establish through witness testimony that a man had promised to marry her—and especially if she could prove his intention by the receipt of some tangible indication or pledge of his earnest—the courts acted swiftly to compel him to fulfill his commitment. Through enforcement of an ideal of marriage behavior (based on monogamy, amity, and cohabitation), adultery, abuse, and abandonment became grievances for which injured spouses might seek legal redress. This was true in medieval Catholic jurisdictions, too, but the determination of magistrates, inspired by Protestant teachings, had hardened, as had the range of sanctions.

Paramount among these was the possibility of divorce and remarriage, which served as the ultimate remedy for dysfunctional relationships, dissolving the bonds between husband and wife and permitting at least the innocent partner—and occasionally both spouses—to enter new marriages. Adultery and impotency were universally admitted grounds for divorce because they prevented marriage from serving its divinely intended purpose as a refuge from the sins of the flesh. Abuse, abandonment, and other problems, however, might lead to divorce at the discretion of these courts.

Divorce might have changed the nature of marriage in the sixteenth century but for the fact that it was closely regulated by the magistrates. Determined to uphold the sanctity of marriage and prevent frivolous procedures, suits of this sort were closely scrutinized and discouraged at every turn. As a result, divorce never became a common solution to marital problems, and it did not alter marriage during the Reformation.

It may, however, have had some effect on the material aspects of marriage. Protestants were well aware that marriages formed communities of fortune, creating new units of production and consumption in an age when household and workshop were usually identical. Thus, marriages established the economic preconditions for a family's material well-being through the exchange of property.

An agreement to marry usually specified the exact amount and type of property that each spouse would bring to their union. The fathers of brides offered dowries; husbands customarily supplied an equal amount of wealth. The sums offered varied according to social strata. Artisanal families might offer no cash but the fixed capital needed by the young couple to participate in a handicraft; elite families traded vast fortunes or even entire states, thus allying wedded bliss with political calculation. Only the poorest, most marginal members of sixteenth-century society, those for whom the spontaneous and fluid arrangements of common-law marriage and private repudiation were the rule, ignored the dictates of dowries. So important was this transfer of property between generations and households that its lack constituted a serious, sometimes insurmountable barrier to matrimony. Young women without dowries were as good as condemned to spinsterhood. For this reason a favorite form of early modern charity supplied modest dowries to poor girls as a means of helping them marry and achieve the material security that only matrimony offered them. Likewise, fathers carefully stipulated and guaranteed the size of their daughters dowries in their testaments. So crucial a transaction simply could not hinge on something as inscrutable as mortality, nor could it be left to the vagaries of legal innovations, such as divorce.

In most reformed communities new property laws were drawn to protect the interests of the innocent and to nullify any advantage to a guilty spouse in the event of a divorce. The transfer of property effected at marriage was carefully reversed. *Mitgift* and dowry were returned to the donors. The authorities then divided any communal property into shares and distributed it to the interested parties. Guilty spouses, however, lost all control of their share. It passed in propriety to the offender's children or nearest kin, and only one-third of it was reserved to provide the offender a pension. If no communal property existed, the guilty became wards of the state, living on charity for the rest of their lives.

Divorce clearly threatened familial interests in the communal property: the state arbitrarily redistributed this wealth, and spouses and their kin had no enforceable claims to it. In at least one instance marriage contracts changed as a result of the introduction of substantial divorce—that is, the dissolution of a conjugal union with the right to remarry—by a Protestant regime. Families in the city of Strasbourg gradually abandoned a tradition of universal communality of goods in favor of the stipulation of all property as the private possession of one spouse or the other. In this way the marrying couple and their families tried to ensure an equitable redistribution of property in the event that divorce disrupted the material community of a marriage.

Material community and the economic potential and security it provided was a purpose and cause of marriage as compelling and real in early modern Europe as emotional or physical attraction. Young men delayed marriage until they had reached a stage in life at which they could independently support a family. Women, too, did not marry until they were able to contribute to a domestic economy with their labor and ensure its longevity through the bearing of children. Modern scholars have long recognized the tangible evidence of these calculations in the so-called European pattern of marriage. Throughout Europe a surprisingly large number of people either never married or married so late as to constitute an effective limit on fertility. This pattern seems to have been deliberate, a strategy to promote the accumulation and preservation of wealth in families over generations. Marriage, therefore, was a crucial variable in the material calculations on which all families in the sixteenth century depended for survival.

Luther admitted that property concerns were very important and often created problems for couples. Yet he did not believe that such mundane matters should interfere with an institution of such spiritual consequence. What determined marriageability, in his opinion, was the onset of fecundity. At that point young people should have faith and marry regardless of material concerns; God would provide an honest means of support. The behavior of marrying couples and their families suggests that this proposal did not fit the realities of the age. Men and women continued to marry as they always had—that is, for a variety of emotional and economic reasons. That marriage changed suddenly and radically in the sixteenth century is a dubious proposition at best. Beginning with the Reformation, however, marriage became an institution celebrated in church but controlled by the state.

[*See also* Celibacy and Virginity; Courts, *article on* Marriage Courts; Divorce; Family; Polygamy; Social Disipline; Weddings; *and* Women.]

BIBLIOGRAPHY

Goody, Jack. *The Development of the Family and Marriage in Europe.* Cambridge, 1983. Anthropological study of changing cultural and social aspects of marriage.

Goody, Jack, and S. J. Tambiah. *Bridewealth and Dowry.* New York, 1973. Useful study of the history of European marriage practices taken from an anthropological perspective.

Gottlieb, Beatrice. "The Meaning of Clandestine Marriage." In *Family and Sexuality in French History*, edited by Robert Wheaton and Tamara K. Hareven, pp. 49–83. Philadelphia, 1980. Pioneering study of secret marriage as a social and legal phenomenon in the late medieval and early modern periods.

Hajnal, J. "European Marriage Patterns in Perspective." In *Population in History*, edited by D. V. Glass and D. E. C. Eversley, pp. 100–143. London, 1965. Classic statement on the European marriage pattern and its social and economic consequences.

Howell, Martha. *Women, Production and Patriarchy in Late Medieval Cities.* Chicago, 1986. Close study of women in the labor forces of several late medieval cities; useful for insights on connection between marriage and women's work.

Hughes, Diane Owens. "From Brideprice to Dowry in Mediterranean Europe." *Journal of Family History* 3 (1978), 262–296. Establishes connection between marriage practices and gender discrimination in the medieval and early modern worlds.

Joyce, George H. *Christian Marriage: An Historical and Doctrinal Study.* London, 1948. Useful study of the history of marriage in Catholic doctrine.

Levine, David. *Family Formation in an Age of Nascent Capitalism.* New York, 1977. Demographic study of early modern marriage and family using the techniques of family reconstitution on English parishes.

Mitterauer, Michael, and Reinhard Sieder. *The European Family: Patriarchy to Partnership from the Middle Ages to the Present.* Chicago, 1983. Very useful overview of current scholarship on marriage and family.

Ozment, Steven. *When Fathers Ruled: Family Life in Reformation Europe.* Cambridge, Mass., 1983. Study of marriage and family as objects of reform; weakened by reliance on prescriptive literature.

Roper, Lyndal. "Going to Church and Street: Weddings in Reformation Augsburg." *Past and Present* 106 (1985), 62–101. Insightful essay on marriage ceremonies and their meaning in a reforming city.

Safley, Thomas Max. *Let No Man Put Asunder: The Control of Marriage in the German Southwest; A Comparative Study, 1550–1600.* Kirksville, Mo., 1984. Concise study of impact of Protestant and Reformed legislation on the institutions of marriage and family.

Shorter, Edward. *The Making of the Modern Family.* New York, 1975. Classic statement on emergence of modern family that places too much emphasis on affection and sexuality and is weakened by gender biases.

Stone, Lawrence. *The Family, Sex and Marriage in England, 1500–1800.* New York, 1977. Monumental study of marriage and family in early modern England that sets the terms of the debate over the history of the modern family.

Watt, Jeffrey R. *The Making of Modern Marriage: Matrimonial Control and the Rise of Sentiment in Neuchâtel.* Ithaca, N.Y., 1992. Study of marriage courts and litigation in Neuchâtel offers conclusions on long-term effects of Reformation marriage courts on marriage and family.

Wrigley, E. A., ed. *An Introduction to English Historical Demography.* London, 1966. Essential overview of demographic history of early modern England with essential findings on marriage and family life.

THOMAS MAX SAFLEY

MARRIAGE, DEFENSES OF. Nearly all Protestant reformers advocated both clerical and lay marriage, and nearly all themselves were married, though Huldrych Zwingli and Thomas Cranmer did so secretly. Some wrote actual treatises in defense of marriage, such as *On Married Life*, by Martin Luther and *On Matrimony, Widowhood, and Virginity* by Johannes Brenz. But for the most part they expressed their views in other contexts. The most significant was the wedding sermon, a Protestant innovation that in the course of the sixteenth century grew into a prominent homiletic genre. Collections of these sermons—especially by second-generation reformers, such as Johann Freder (Ireneus), Caspar Huberinus, Johannes Mathesius, and Johannes and Cyriakus Spangenberg—were numerous and were often published. Because many weddings were now performed in the presence of a congregation, the wedding sermon served as the principal means of persuading Protestants of the rectitude, indeed the necessity, of marrying.

Other than in sermons, the reformers' views on marriage can often be found in their commentaries on the first chapter of *Genesis* and on other pertinent Bible passages, in works on the legal aspects of marriage, and even in dramas such as Paul Rebhun's *Hochzeit zu Kana* and *Susanna*. Luther's much publicized relationship with Katharina von Bora constituted its own defense of marriage, as (it seems from his correspondence after being widowed) did John Calvin's less displayed union with Idelette de Bure.

The preacher-reformers' specific arguments in defense of marriage were, naturally, not identical. In general, however, they advocated marriage for several major reasons: (1) God had ordained marriage in the Garden of Eden when he created Eve and presented her to Adam. Anyone who took a vow of celibacy rejected God's wishes. (2) For the propagation of the human race, God had implanted an irresistible sexual desire equally in men and women. Refraining from marriage thus led to fornication and disorder. The connubial bond provided a "remedy for sin." (3) Women as the "weaker vessel" required the care and the discipline that the married condition was supposed to provide. (4) Only the Christian married couple could carry out the crucial work of raising pious, obedient children, the godly society's new generation. (5) Wives and husbands were lovingly to serve, comfort, and console one another. They were helpmates and companions. The sexes, however, were to be confined to their appropriate and complementary roles—the husband as breadwinner and lord in the household, the wife as obedient homemaker and rearer of children. (6) The trials (the "cross") of married life, whether personal illness or the loss of a child, were God's means of testing people's faith. (7) The worst slanders of women that could be found in certain classical, medieval, and contemporary authors were rejected, including those collected by the mystic reformer Sebastian Franck. Women, too, were worthy creatures, equal inheritors of God's grace.

The reformer-preachers differed in the emphasis they placed on such traditional opinions as women's greater predilection to sin and men's duty to hold their wives within bounds (by beating them if necessary). They also disagreed about the circumstances under which divorce might be granted. Freder and Cyriakus Spangenberg were more positive and liberal, while Rebhun and Mathesius were more negative and conservative. Anabaptist leaders upheld the dominance of men over women far more than has occasionally been asserted. Even in the aberrant Anabaptist community in Münster in 1534–1535, patriarchy held firm. The reforming generations of clergy agreed that the family needed renovation along with religion and that the proper Christian marriage, replicated throughout society, would secure the fundament of a godly order on earth.

[*See also* Celibacy and Virginity; Family; Marriage; *and* Women.]

BIBLIOGRAPHY

Baldwin, Claude-Marie. "Marriage in Calvin's Sermons." In *Calviniana: Ideas and Influence of John Calvin*, edited by Robert V. Schnucker, pp. 121–129. Kirksville, Mo., 1988.

Douglass, Jane Dempsey. *Women, Freedom, and Calvin*. Phildadelphia, 1985. Asserts that despite Calvin's conventional utterances on women, he leaves women's public participation in church leadership in the category *adiaphora*, those things that individual congregations may decide for themselves or that may change with circumstances.

Dugan, Eileen T. "The Funeral Sermon as a Key to Familial Values in Early Modern Nördlingen." *Sixteenth Century Journal* 20 (Winter 1989), 631–644.

Hendrix, Scott. "Christianizing Domestic Relations: Women and Marriage in Johann Freder's *Dialogus dem Ehestand zu ehren*." *Sixteenth Century Journal* 23 (Summer 1992), 251–266. Presents Freder's generous views on women.

Karant-Nunn, Susan C. "*Kinder, Küche, Kirche*: Social Ideology in Sermons of Johannes Mathesius." In *Germania Illustrata: Essays on Early Modern Germany*, edited by Andrew C. Fix and Susan C. Karant-Nunn, pp. 121–140. Sixteenth Century Essays & Studies, vol. 18. Kirksville, Mo., 1992. Summarizes this pastor's far less generous views on women.

Miller, Thomas Fischer. "Mirror for Marriages: Lutheran Views of Marriage and the Family, 1520–1600." Ph.D. diss., University of Virginia, 1981. Available through University Microfilms, Ann Arbor.

Ozment, Steven E. *When Fathers Ruled: Family Life in Reformation Europe*. Cambridge, Mass., 1983. Criticized by many social historians, reaffirms the traditional view that the Reformation improved women's position in men's esteem and in society.

Roper, Lyndal. *The Holy Household: Religion, Morals and Order in Reformation Augsburg*. Oxford, 1989. Argues that authorities did think it necessary to reform women and the family.

Wiesner-Hanks, Merry. "Luther and Women: The Death of Two Marys." In *Disciplines of Faith: Religion, Patriarchy, and Politics*, edited by Jim Obelkevich, Lyndal Roper, and Raphael Samuel, pp. 295–308. London and New York, 1987.

SUSAN C. KARANT-NUNN

MARRIAGE COURTS. *See* Courts, *article on* Marriage Courts.

MARTIN, Gregory (1542?–1582), English Roman Catholic clergyman, translator of the Latin Vulgate into English (Douai-Rheims), and author of *Roma Sancta* (1581) and polemical works. Born in Sussex, Martin was appointed in 1557 as one of the first scholars at the new Saint John's College, Oxford. He earned his B.A. (1561) and M.A. (1564–65) there and taught Greek (1564–68) but resigned his fellowship to work as a tutor for the duke of Norfolk's sons, one of whom became the martyr Philip Howard. After the duke's imprisonment, Martin departed England (1569/70) for the newly established Douai College, where in 1573 he received his baccalaureate in theology and in 1575 his licentiate.

In 1573 he was ordained a priest at Brussels. From 1575 to 1576 he taught at Douai, and then in Rome (1576–1578) at the English Hospice (later the Venerable English College); he returned briefly to Douai before moving to Rheims, where he taught Greek and Hebrew. While preparing Catholic priests for the mission to England, Martin translated the Vulgate (New Testament printed at Rheims in 1582; Old Testament at Douai in 1609–1610) with help from William Allen, Richard Bristow, and John Reynolds. Because of his associations with the Jesuits it is believed he contemplated joining them. Among his friends was Edmund Campion, with whom he studied and taught at Oxford; the two also studied together at Douai and later corresponded. Martin died at Rheims on 28 October 1582. Besides biblical translations, Martin wrote polemical works: *A Treatise of Schism Shewing that Al Catholikes Ought in Any Wise to Abstaine Altogether from Heretical Conventicles*(1578) and *A Discoverie of the Manifold Corruptions of the Holy Scriptures by the Heretikes of Our Daies*(1582). Martin's unpublished *Roma Sancta* (1581) presents Rome as unrivaled for its "holiness" at a time when Catholics in England were experiencing increasing pressure to conform to the Church of England.

BIBLIOGRAPHY

Cooper, Thompson. "Gregory Martin." In *Dictionary of National Biography*, vol. 12, pp. 1162–1164. Oxford, 1967–1968. Provides additional biographical details on Martin's life and works.

Martin, Gregory. *Roma Sancta* (1581). Edited by George Bruner Parks. Rome, 1969. Parks's "The Life and Works of Gregory Martin" (pp. 11–32) provides a succinct and sympathetic portrait of Martin. Gives a full list and chronology of Martin's writings. Highly recommended.

Pertile, Lino. "Montaigne, Gregory Martin and Rome." *Bibliothèque d'Humanisme et Renaissance* 50.3 (1988), 637–659. Gives a good critique of Martin's idealistic view of Rome.

FREDERICK J. MCGINNESS

MARTINUZZI, George Utješenović (1482–1551), ecclesiastical and political figure in Transylvania. Born in Kamičic, Croatia, in 1482, Martinuzzi was the son of a Croatian father and a Venetian mother. Throughout his life "Friar George," as he was popularly and not always respectfully known, preferred to use the name of his Venetian mother, Martinuzzi, rather than that of his Slavic father. He had a brief military career before entering the Pauline order and the service of János Zápolya of Hungary. Zápolya was then waging an ongoing campaign against Ferdinand I for the Hungarian throne. He was named bishop of Nagyvárad (Grosswardein, Oradea Mare) by Zápolya, and in this capacity he negotiated the Treaty of Oradea (1538), by which Zápolya recognized the right of the Habsburgs to succeed him in Transylvania in exchange for the Habsburgs' recognition of his claim to be king and ruler of Transylvania. Shortly before his death, however, Zápolya married Isabella Báthory, who bore him a son, János Zsigmond.

In 1540 Martinuzzi promised the dying Zápolya, who repudiated the treaty with Ferdinand, to defend the claims of his infant son as governor of Transylvania. After the Turks captured Buda in 1541, however, Martinuzzi began negotiations with the Habsburgs concerning an alliance against the Turks and an eventual reunification of Hungary. Ten years later a treaty was accepted, and Martinuzzi was named archbishop of Esztergom and Hungarian primate, as well as a cardinal of the church. But he continued to maintain contacts with the Turks, Isabella Zápolya and her son, and the anti-Habsburg forces in Transylvania. Therefore, Martinuzzi was distrusted by Ferdinand and his military commanders, who probably arranged his assassination in Alvinc, Transylvania, on 17 December 1551.

BIBLIOGRAPHY

Horváth, Mihaly. *Utyeszenich Frater Gyorgy (Martinuzzi bibornok) élete.* Pest, 1872.

Juhász, Koloman. "Kardinal Georg Utjesenovich (gest. 1551) und das Bistum Tschanad." *Historisches Jahrbuch* 80 (1961), 252–264.

Utiešnović Ostrožinski, Matthias. *Lebensgeschichte des Cardinals Utiešenović genannt Martinusius.* Vienna, 1881.

DAVID P. DANIEL

MARTYR, Peter. *See* Vermigli, Peter Martyr.

MARXISM. An ideological outlook deriving from German philosopher Karl Marx (1818–1883) and fundamentally hostile to a religious understanding of historical movements, Marxism has nevertheless proved a creative and positive stimulus to Reformation studies. Marx's significance for Reformation historiography derives less from his specific statements than from the far-reaching impact of his methodological presuppositions, which questioned earlier assessments of the relationship between religion and social change. Committed to the Hegelian dialectic, which linked historical movements to the development of the human spirit, Marx replaced Hegel's idealistic focus with a material one based on close analysis of human society. Viewing all religion as a mythical human construct, he saw the Reformation as a failed revolution and a foil for the true revolution to come, but his judgments relied on colorful epigram rather than sustained historical analysis.

Marx's collaborator Friedrich Engels (1820–1895) established detailed Marxist historical analysis of the Reformation through his book on the 1525 German Peasants' War, written in the wake of the failed 1848 revolution. For Engels the 1525 revolt represented the beginning of the age of bourgeois revolutions and, given the church's central role in medieval civilization, the attack on the hated system necessarily took the form of theological heresy, cloaking class interests.

Contending groups involved in the Reformation conflict included conservative Catholics, intent on maintaining existing conditions; Lutheran bourgeois reformists (a propertied opposition, including lay princes desiring more independence); and revolutionaries led by Thomas Müntzer, who wanted radical change. After Martin Luther's short-lived revolutionary phase, he was forced to choose between competing interests and aligned himself with burghers and princes rather than the popular movement, while Müntzer abandoned theology for political agitation. In the end, however, Müntzer was a heroic failure, as the time was not ripe for revolutionary change.

Engels's study was original and stimulating, though it posed more questions than it answered. He used historical materialism as a guide rather than a straitjacket and freely recognized the role of noneconomic forces in historical causation. His later writings underlined the intimate connection between Catholicism and feudalism and developed the theme of a battle between feudalism and the bourgeoisie in three stages—the Reformation, the Great Rebellion (for which Calvin provided the "ideal costume"), and the final bourgeois triumph of the French Revolution.

Engels's associate Karl Kautsky (1854–1938) included the Peasants' War as one chapter in a broader study of communism in the Reformation era. An orthodox Marxist, he was nevertheless keenly interested in Christianity, especially its earliest phase, in which he detected a form of genuine communism eventually transformed by a clerical elite. Kautsky studied radical Hussite and Taborite movements closely while according Luther a secondary role. Müntzer, on the other hand, was seen as a central figure whose religious views were genuine rather than pretense. For Kautsky the failure of Christian communism was predictable, as the economic changes that would have supported it still lay ahead.

At the turn of the century British socialism provided an intellectual home for the elaboration of Marxist historical analysis of the Reformation. In three separate works published over the decade 1894–1903, Ernest Belfort Bax aimed to provide a general view of social conditions and popular movements of the Reformation era, setting Luther's achievement in its social context. Heavily dependent on Engels and sharing his awareness of complex patterns of causation, Bax identified the Reformation as the ideological aspect of Europe's economic and social transformation from a cooperative to an individualistic mode of activity. Bax condemned Luther's "betrayal" of the popular cause of the peasants without pausing to ask if he had ever supported it. On the other hand, Thomas More's *Utopia* was identified as a work of idealistic communism.

The first substantial and comprehensive English contribution after Bax was Roy Pascal's *The Social Basis of the German Reformation* (1933). For Pascal the Reformation was no chance occurrence or product of great personalities but part of more comprehensive political, economic, and intellectual changes. His materialist conception of history avoided crude economic determinism, yet class structure remained the presupposition of his historical understanding. Unlike earlier Marxists, Pascal accorded Luther a key role and acknowledged the centrality of his theological concerns, locating them firmly in their social context. Luther's historical role had been to define the moral and spiritual principles of the newly emerging individualistic society. The doctrine of justification was imbued with this spirit, while his social outlook highlighted the domination of the church by the state. Unconsciously Luther was the leader of a rising bourgeoisie striving for greater autonomy but still dependent on the continuance of social order.

Among Continental writers of the same period, there were few signs of a creative development or reinterpretation of the Marxist tradition. An exception was Ernst Bloch (1885–1977), who emphasized a strong connection between Müntzer and the chiliastic tradition. Müntzer's success with peasants was in Bloch's view largely the result of his capacity to inspire his followers with a vision of justice drawn from primitive Christian sources—an implicit recognition that economic factors were not necessarily the ultimate motive force in history.

From the time of Marx's early observations on the Reformation to the end of World War II, a generally cohesive tradition among Marxist writers did not preclude flexibility, adaptability, and an ability to modify views in light of discussion. Although critics maintained that they had forced the Reformation into an ideological straitjacket, their views proved a valuable corrective to the preoccupation of some scholars with narrow theological issues. Moreover, if the Marxists were at times highly dogmatic, they were no more so than many church historians of the period.

The connections between Marxist Reformation scholarship and Marxist political fortunes, hitherto tenuous and remote, acquired a new significance with the advent of communist regimes across eastern Europe in the aftermath of World War II, and especially with the incorporation of the Saxon-Thuringian heartland of the Reformation into the German Democratic Republic. As Engels had linked the failure of the German revolutionary tradition of 1525 with that of 1848, the new regime sought to link it with the triumph of 1949, and a swift historiographic revolution in which scholars joined with politicians and party leaders led to hard-line orthodoxy sanctioned by political power and patronage.

The first substantial expression of postwar Marxist orthodoxy came from Russian scholar M. M. Smirin (1895–1975), whose defense and restatement of Engels was translated into German in 1952. More orthodox than the later Engels, Smirin reaffirmed the image of Müntzer as the inspired and advanced leader of the oppressed masses whose religious message cloaked a fundamentally political program. Discussion focused increasingly on the concept of the "early bourgeois revolution," which Engels had introduced in later writings and which sat uneasily with the notion of Müntzer as a protocommunist. Vigorous debate on this issue in Soviet circles indicated that common commitment to Marxist principles did not preclude diverse views on particular issues.

In 1952 East German party leader Walter Ulbricht joined with historian Leo Stern to call for a revision of German history. For Stern this implied rejection of traditional German historicism in favor of a progressive polemical historiography focused on the German revolutionary tradition. In a 1967 address marking the 450th anniversary of the Reformation, Stern identified the religious controversy of the Reformation as the result rather than the cause of the development from feudalism to early capitalism.

In a similar vein his colleague Max Steinmetz (1912–1989) described Luther's thought as the theological expression of the economic struggle of the bourgeoisie and the masses against the feudal order embodied in the papal church. Advancing capitalism had rendered the feudal order—and hence Catholic ideology—anachronistic. Luther's struggle against that ideology, after an unsuccessful attempt to identify with it, was the intellectual expression of the economic and political struggle of the masses against the old church, and his theology represented the new ideology of the bourgeois church. Luther, therefore, was an unconscious agent of a secularizing dialectical process. The Reformation and the Peasants' War were parts of a single revolutionary process—occurring from 1517 to 1526 in three stages—that began with Luther's attack on the feudal order in the Ninety-five Theses, continued with Müntzer's people's reformation, and culminated in the Peasants' War, with the Münster experiment a kind of epilogue. The reductionist nature of this outlook was roundly criticized by Western historians, while a number of Marxist scholars began to question the assumed relationship between the Reformation and an "early bourgeois revolution," not the least because of difficulties in locating significant bourgeois participation in the alleged revolution. Marxist scholars responded to this problem in a number of ways, some by redefining the relationship and others by virtually ignoring it.

Reassessments of Luther emerged, generally distinguishing between the early revolutionary and the later reactionary, while Gerhard Zschäbitz broke with the notion of Luther's betrayal of the peasants, asserting that he had never supported their extremism and, far from being an opportunist, was merely defending his own Reformation. Müntzer was also reinterpreted as a deeply religious man uniting mystical and socialist revolutionary elements. Meanwhile, Josef Macek's study of the peasant leader Michael Gaismaer and Johannes Schildhauer's studies of the Hanseatic cities showed how Marxist scholars could produce impressive empirical studies free of obvious dogmatic bias and incorporating broad social analysis not unlike that carried out in the West.

Despite the efforts of leading scholars, there was little progress during the 1970s toward overcoming the ideological divide. By the 1980s, however, there were increasing signs that Marxist historiography was moving out of its isolation to become part of the broad area of social history, while Western historians were recognizing the role of ideological values in their own work. How that rapprochement between East and West would have developed will never be known since the abrupt collapse of eastern European regimes from 1989 removed leading Marxist historians from their academic posts. Their legacy to Reformation studies, however, is permanent and ongoing.

BIBLIOGRAPHY

Bak, Janos. "'The Peasant War in Germany' by Friedrich Engels: 125 Years After." In *The German Peasant War of 1525*, edited by Janos Bak. London, 1976. An extended discussion among seven historians, including East German Marxists, about the significance of Engels's work.

Bax, E. B. *German Society at the Close of the Middle Ages*. London, 1894.

———. *The Peasants' War in Germany, 1525–1526*. London, 1899.

———. *The Rise and Fall of the Anabaptists*. London, 1903.

Blickle, Peter. *The Revolution of 1525*. Baltimore, 1982. Interprets the Peasants' War as the revolution of the "common man" and addresses problems and issues posed by East German Marxist historians about the connection between Reformation doctrine and social discontent.

Brendler, Gerhard, and Max Steinmetz, eds. *Weltwirkung der Reformation*. Berlin, 1969. A commemorative volume incorporating a series of essays by East German Marxists.

Dickens, A. G., and John Tonkin. *The Reformation in Historical Thought*. Cambridge, Mass., 1985. See chap. 10 for a short but detailed analysis of Marxist interpretation of the Reformation from Marx himself to East Germany in the mid-1980s.

Friesen, Abraham. *Reformation and Utopia: The Marxist Interpretation of the Reformation and Its Antecedents*. Wiesbaden, 1974. A full-length study of Marxist interpretation in the context of late medieval reform movements.

Kautsky, Karl. *Communism in Central Europe in the Time of the Reformation* (1897). Reprint, New York, 1966. A broad study by a close associate of Engels, purporting to find versions of communism in Christian tradition, especially in the late medieval and Reformation period.

Krieger, Leonard, ed. *The German Revolutions*. Chicago, 1967. Includes *The Peasant War in Germany* and *Germany: Revolution and Counter-Revolution*, containing the fundamental writings of Engels. The former was based on earlier work of Wilhelm Zimmermann rather than original research and was the first detailed Marxist study of the early Reformation period.

Niebuhr, R, ed. *Karl Marx and Friedrich Engels on Religion.* New York, 1964. An excellent selection of extracts from the writings of Marx and Engels, illustrating both their general theories and specific statements on the Reformation. Useful for tracing the development of Engels's views over time.

Pascal, Roy. *The Social Basis of the German Reformation: Martin Luther and His Times.* London, 1933. Unusual among Marxist works for the prominence it gives to Luther and its recognition of the centrality of religion to him.

Scott, Tom. "The Peasant War: A Historiographical Review." *Historical Journal* 22 (1979), 693–720, 953–974. An impressively comprehensive bibliographical study including analytical and interpretive comments on Marxist historians among others.

Scribner, Robert W. "Is There a Social History of the Reformation?" *Social History* 2 (1977), 483–505. Discusses approaches to the social history of the Reformation, especially the interaction of East German Marxists with Western scholars.

Scribner, Robert W., and Gerhard Benecke, eds. *The German Peasant War: New Viewpoints.* London, 1979. A collection of translated articles reflecting the best of German scholarship from the previous decade, including Marxist contributions.

Smirin, M. M. *Die Volksreformation des Thomas Müntzer und der große Bauernkrieg.* 2d ed. Reprint, Frankfurt a.M., 1976. The first major Marxist work from postwar Eastern Europe; more orthodox than the later Engels.

JOHN TONKIN

MARY, QUEEN OF SCOTS. *See* Mary Stuart.

MARY I OF ENGLAND. *See* Mary Tudor.

MARY OF HUNGARY AND BOHEMIA (1505–1558), archduchess of Austria from birth, queen of Hungary (1521) and Bohemia (1522), regent of the Netherlands (1531–1555), and sister of Emperors Charles V and Ferdinand I. From childhood Mary played an important role in the plans of her grandfather, Emperor Maximilian I, who intended with her marriage to reinforce Habsburg claims. In 1515 she married the heir to the Hungarian and Bohemian thrones, Louis II (1506–1526); at the same ceremony Maximilian I acted as proxy in a wedding for one of his grandsons with Louis's sister Anna (1503–1547).

Mary took an active part in politics from an early age. From 1522 onwnard she and her court in Hugary and Bohemia represented the interests of her Habsburg brothers. In the interest of her own power, however, she supported the expropriation of the Fugger Thurzo mining company (in northern Hungary) in 1525.

When Louis II died in the Battle of Mohács (1526), the Hungarian estates elected and crowned as king the governor of Transylvania, János Zápolya. A minority of powerful magnates gathered around Mary and elected as king Archduke Ferdinand (Ferdinand I), who had already been elected king of Bohemia. In 1531 Mary succeeded her aunt, Archduchess Margaret (Margaret of Austria), as governess of the Netherlands for Charles V. Her governorship was characterized by financial burdens resulting from the European policy of Charles V and the effort to unify the provinces. Mary distinguished herself by her political and organizational efforts and even succeeded in raising money for the wars through her personal credit. But she did not succeed in preserving the Netherlands' neutrality nor, with her sister Eleanor, queen of France, in mediating peace (Cambrai, 1535).

Her life demonstrates how much the family's interest in power politics determined the actions of its members and how personal inclinations were articulated only within these limits. Her interests in hunting, music, and, above all, the intellectual trends of her time must have been triggered by her education in Mechelen and Innsbruck. In Hungary and Bohemia she was surrounded by people who shared criticism of the Roman Catholic church as expressed by the reformers. Before 1525 Mary—like many educated people who eventually remained within the Catholic church—showed an interest in Martin Luther's writings. Her actions during this period, which showed her sympathies for the Reformation, usually were also motivated by her political interests. For example, in order to regain political influence and royal domains in Bohemia Mary backed, in 1523, a group of Utraquists leaning toward Luther, as well as the Bohemian Brethren, against the former officials now collaborating with papal attempts to reach an agreement between the moderate Utraquists and the Roman Catholic church. Mary thereby prevented the political destruction of the Hussite movement. The papal emissaries, however, as early as 1524–1525 blamed the failure of their political plans on the Protestant inclinations of Mary and her German court. Her efforts to achieve a balance of religious power may also be judged as running parallel to imperial policy in those years.

Mary admitted to having read Luther's writings before 1525. She is also said to have written two Protestant hymns. Through her behavior and the attitudes of some members of her court, she provoked rumors of being a Protestant in Hungary. After the death of Louis II, Luther himself dedicated "Four Comforting Psalms to the Queen of Hungary" (Wittenberg, 1 November 1526). From the five questions she addressed to Luther in 1530 through her preacher John Henckel, we may conclude that Mary favored Protestantism. On the other hand, those questions also show that she subordinated her inclinations to the interests of the House of Habsburg. She made Henckel inquire of Luther whether it was sufficient to take Communion only under one kind in public but under both elements in secret if political conditions required it. Luther was not prepared to accept this separation of public appearance and private religious practice. Mary, because of the policy of her family, was not willing to profess in public to the new doctrine. In the question of faith she would take no action, she said in a letter to her brother Ferdinand in 1527, that would harm the reputation of the Habsburg family. Her personal sympathy for the Protestant doctrine did not show any effect on her religious policy during her governorship of the Netherlands, either. When she was appointed to this position, her brothers had particularly warned her not to show the slightest signs of doubt about the Catholic doctrine in these provinces.

Mary was an interested reader of Desiderius Erasmus. Through Jakob Piso (a teacher of Louis II), John Henckel (apart from short interruptions, her chaplain from 1525 to 1531), and Nicholas Olah (Mary's secretary from 1531 to 1542 and archbishop of Esztergom from 1553 to 1568), she had contact with Erasmus, who dedicated his *Vidua christiana* to her in 1530. In her function as governess she worked hard for Erasmus's return to the Netherlands, but the project failed at the last moment because Erasmus fell seriously ill.

BIBLIOGRAPHY

Boogert, Bob van den, and Jacqueline Kerkhoff, eds. "Maria van Hongarije, 1505–1558: Koningin tussen keizers en kunstenaars." Zwolle, 1993. Catalogue of the exhibitions in the Rijksmuseum Het Catharijneconvent in Utrecht and in the Noordbrabants Museum in 's-Hertogenbosch, 11 September to 28 November 1993, with articles on the involvement of Mary in the religious controversies, on the culture of her court, on her library, her collection of paintings and sculptures, the music at her court, etc.

Heiss, Gernot. "Politik und Ratgeber der Königin Maria von Ungarn in den Jahren 1521–1531." *Mitteilungen des Instituts für Österreichische Geschichtsforschunq* 82 (1974): 119–180. Discusses the policy of Mary and her court during her years in Hungary, Bohemia, and Austria.

———. "Mary of Austria." In *Contemporaries of Erasmus,* edited by Peter G. Bietenholz, pp. 399–401. Toronto and London, 1986.

Jongh, Jane de. *Mary of Hungary.* London, 1959. Good conventional biography.

Die Korrespondenz Ferdinands I. Vol. 1, *Familienkorrespondenz bis 1526.* Edited by Wilhelm Bauer. Vol. 2, *Familienkorrespondenz, 1527–1530.* Edited by Wilhelm Bauer and Robert Lacroix. Vol. 3, *Familienkorrespondenz, 1531–1532.* Edited by Herwig Wolfram and Christiane Thomas. Vienna 1912–1984. Political letters from and to Mary, mostly in French.

Schwob, Utte M. "Der Ofener Humanistenkreis der Königin Maria von Ungarn." *Südostdeutsches Archiv* 17/18 (1974/75), 50–73.

Spruyt, Bart Jan. "'En bruit d'estre bonne lutheriene:' Mary of Hungary and Religious Reform." *English Historical Review* 109 (April 1994), 275–307. An expanded English version of Spruyt's article, "Verdacht van Lutherse Sympathieen: Maria van Hongarije en de religieuze controversen van haar tijd."

Gernot Heiss

MARY STUART (1542–1587), Queen of Scotland. Scotland had long experience of minorities: no king since 1406 had succeeded as an adult. Nevertheless, the accession of Mary Stuart, Queen of Scots, in December 1542 at the age of one week did not usher in just another minority, if a particularly lengthy one. Her father, James V, was the first king to preside over a Scotland infiltrated by reforming ideas. Before his own minority ended, an Aberdeen schoolmaster had been summoned for Lutheran heresy as early as 1521, and parliamentary legislation against the bringing in of heretical literature started in 1525. And his personal rule had witnessed his strenuous efforts to maintain religious orthodoxy in partnership with the greatest churchman, David Beaton, cardinal of Saint Andrews. Jockeying for control during Mary's minority therefore involved confessional motivation as well as political ambition in both domestic and foreign affairs. This did not mean clear direction. The immediate aftermath of James's death was a lurch toward Protestantism and the England of the increasingly megalomaniac Henry VIII; that megalomania turned a possible marriage alliance between Mary and the future Edward VI into war, the "Rough Wooing" of 1544–1550, and drove the Scots back to their old allies, the French, for both help at home and a haven for their infant queen. In 1548 Mary was sent to France, where she was naturally brought up as a Catholic—emerging as *politique* rather than *dévot*—and brought up in a cocoon of luxury and adulation that seems to have significantly undermined any talent she might have had for political rule, despite the efforts of her uncle, Charles, cardinal of Lorraine, to educate her. The joint efforts of the French king Henry II and Mary's mother, Mary of Guise, regent in Scotland from 1554, ensured a French marriage; in April 1558 Mary married the Dauphin Francis, signing a secret treaty by which Scotland became an appanage of the French crown. The success of Mary of Guise in maintaining strong links with France and the existence of the Catholic Mary Tudor on the English throne left the emerging Protestant party in Scotland in limbo. Their only chance, at the time of the marriage, was that Mary would remain in France, thereby being less able to restrain the Protestants of her own kingdom, which is no doubt why some of them supported the marriage. But it was hardly a hopeful position.

The remarkable change in that position, and the Protestant success of 1560, could hardly have been foreseen in April 1558. In November Mary Tudor died, and Elizabeth's accession immediately transformed the international situation, offering a potential ally for the Scottish Protestants. The new threat, when France and Spain made peace in April 1559, leaving Henry II free to menace the heretics of his daughter-in-law's kingdom, lasted only until Henry's own death in July. In the summer of 1560, the death of Mary of Guise, French internal problems, and English intervention cleared the French out of Scotland and made the triumph of the Protestant party almost inevitable, a triumph sealed by the Reformation Parliament in August.

Nevertheless, if God at last seemed to have shown his favor to the Calvinist faithful of Scotland, there is no doubt that he gave them an extra bonus in the person of their queen. For Mary stayed in France, allowing the Protestants, whom she immediately denounced as rebels—her half brother Lord James Stuart, the earls of Argyll, Glencairn, and others—to consolidate their position at home. Even after the death of her husband, Francis II, in December 1560, she was determined to remain abroad, searching for a second husband from the royal houses of France and Spain, neither of which was in the least willing to oblige her. She was finally forced back to Scotland in August 1561, a year after the Reformation Parliament. She had made any chance of restoring Catholicism harder, although given the strength of Catholicism in Scotland, it was not yet too late. But she was no Mary Tudor. Scotland, let alone a Catholic Scotland, came low on the list of Mary Stuart's priorities. She wanted the English throne, which became the cornerstone of such policy as she had, even though Elizabeth was still a young woman, expected to marry and to produce an heir. That policy did not sit well with Catholic restoration at home.

Thus Jesuits visiting Scotland in 1562–1563 described the demoralization of the Catholics, despite their considerable presence in the northeast and southwest, and noted that they were still in the majority in Edinburgh itself, close to the Catholic queen, who insisted on her right to hear Mass in her private chapel in Holyrood but did nothing for them. The paradox of her position, indeed, had no bounds. She backed the persecution of priests for saying Mass. She actually financed the Reformed church, in the first attempt to endow it, when two-thirds of existing benefices remained with their holders, while the Crown took the other third and used it to maintain the church. That in itself was a measure of the potential for Catholic restoration. The structures of the old church were intact, its clergy drawing their revenues, the monks lingering in the monasteries; only during the next decade would the Reformed church begin to establish conformity in the dioceses and parishes of Scotland. Yet from the beginning, the initiative lay with the Protestants.

Lack of royal direction was equally apparent in government. Mary stirred up considerable hostility because of her household, staffed with foreigners—mainly French, although the most famous was an Italian musician, David Riccio—and filled with her Catholic friends. Her council, which, contrary to Scottish practice, she rarely attended, was dominated by Protestants. From 1561 until 1565, the makers of policy were her half brother, James, now earl of Moray, and her secretary, William Maitland of Lethington. Both were prepared to support her demands to be recognized as Elizabeth's heir in the interests of good relations with Protestant England; both upheld the Protestant faith in Scotland without hindrance from the queen.

In the summer of 1565, there was a dramatic change. Partly, perhaps, because of her continuing failure to find a husband in the early 1560s, partly because even the Marian worm eventually turned, Mary struck out on a new and independent policy. She married Lord Henry Darnley, apparently because his claim to the English throne—as the grandson of Margaret Tudor, from whom Mary's own claim came—would strengthen hers, although in fact hers was the better claim anyway. He was Catholic, or supposedly so; and the queen, who was by now being criticized by the pope for failure of zeal, began to pursue a Catholic line. She emphasized her friendship with France; she encouraged Catholics at court; she brought Catholics onto her council. Moray was thus provoked into unsuccessful rebellion. Defeating him was the only success that Mary had.

By early 1566 the witless and drunken Darnley was a pawn in the hands of the Protestant lords, drawn into the first great scandal of these years, the murder of Riccio, suspected—wrongly—of being a papal agent and the queen's lover, and more accurately, the sacrificial victim of Mary's ambivalent dealings with her household and government. Mary, then six months pregnant, survived what may have been a plot directed against her; but the halfhearted and ineffective Catholic policy was over. Only the birth of her son James in June 1566 gave her any claim to achievement. Darnley's irresponsible questioning of James's legitimacy and secret dealings with the Catholic powers led to the second great scandal, his murder in February 1567. The queen who had so significantly failed to rule failed to give a lead now. Instead, she rushed into the arms of the principal suspect of the murder—James, earl of Bothwell—married him by Protestant rites, and pushed the majority of her most powerful subjects into a coalition, the Confederate Lords, which defeated and imprisoned her in June and forced her to abdicate in July.

A year later escape and then a second defeat lengthened the list of her astonishing follies. She fled to England and spent the next eighteen years in boredom and conspiracy, entering with alacrity into any plot to kill Elizabeth, the queen who desperately tried to preserve her life in the teeth of repeated howls for blood from her councillors and parliaments and despite the danger to herself. It ended at Fotheringay in February 1587, when Elizabeth accepted reality, and, in agreeing to execute Mary, gave her the chance for a last act of unrivaled theater—as well as admitted courage.

She has been the stuff of romance ever since. Her son James, less romantically, and with singular lack of filial respect, wrote of her on her succession as "a double curse, both a Woman of sex and a newborn babe of age." The second was rectified by time; the first may be put into context by the sheer number of effective women rulers in mid-sixteenth-century Europe. Her problem lies elsewhere: in her unique refusal to take the awesome responsibility for the souls of her subjects now enjoined on the rulers of fragmented Christendom.

BIBLIOGRAPHY

Cowan, Ian B. *The Enigma of Mary Stuart.* London, 1971. An interesting collection of extracts from books on Mary, with connecting commentary, bringing out the violently contrasting views of her.

Donaldson, Gordon. *Mary Queen of Scots.* London, 1974. Brief, rather uncritical, but reasonably sober.

———. *All the Queen's Men.* London, 1983. A seminal work, with subtle analysis of the queen's supporters and opponents, their motives, and the way their ground could shift.

———. *The First Trial of Mary Queen of Scots.* Reprint, Westport, Conn., 1983. An interesting and useful account of the first attempt to resolve the problem of Mary after her flight to England.

Fleming, D. Hay. *Mary Queen of Scots.* London, 1897. An old work, but still of considerable value—not least in its footnotes, which are longer than the text and contain a great deal of information.

Fraser, Antonia. *Mary Queen of Scots.* London, 1969. The "standard" biography: full, carefully researched, and readable. But it still concentrates heavily on the personality and personal life of the queen rather than on her role as a ruler—a curious feature of Marian historiography, and one that markedly distinguishes the treatment of her as compared to other monarchs.

Lee, Maurice, Jr. *James Stewart, Earl of Moray.* Reprint, Westport, Conn., 1971. Excellent and balanced discussion of the leading Protestant and politician of the reign. A "must."

Lynch, Michael, ed. *Mary Stewart: Queen in Three Kingdoms.* London, 1988. A collection of essays, ranging over France, Scotland, and England, containing new material and interpretations, and offering both favorable and unfavorable analyses.

Phillips, J. E. *Images of a Queen: Mary Stuart in Sixteenth Century Literature.* Los Angeles, 1964. A fascinating account of the growth of the conflicting legends of Catholic martyr and Protestant whore and murderess, and the political reasons for them.

Wormald, Jenny. *Mary Queen of Scots: A Study in Failure.* London, 1988. An attempt to get away from the heavily personal approach and assess Mary as a ruler.

JENNY WORMALD

MARY TUDOR (also Mary I; 1516–1558), queen of England from 1553 to 1558. She was the only surviving child of Henry VIII by his first wife, Catherine of Aragon. Catherine, a cultivated and pious woman, ensured that her daughter received a sound, humanist education, learning Latin and a number of modern languages. Juan Luis Vives, Thomas Linacre, and Desiderius Erasmus all wrote books of instruction for her, and Mary at the end of her father's reign was able to undertake a translation of Erasmus's paraphrase of John's gospel. By the late 1520s, however, Henry's desire for a male heir and his love for Anne Boleyn brought his marriage to an effective end, although there was no formal divorce until 1533; Mary was, for a time, pushed to the periphery of the court. But the deaths of Catherine and Anne, the birth of Edward (later Edward VI), and the mollifying influence of Henry's sixth and last wife, Katherine Parr, restored Mary to her rightful position as a princess.

Mary's childhood was interspersed with marriage proposals. She had been betrothed briefly to the French Dauphin, and James V of Scotland, the duke of Milan, the brother of the king of Portugal, and even Mary's cousin, Holy Roman Emperor Charles V, were at various times mentioned as possible partners. But Mary remained single at her father's death; a small, frail, and rather plain woman, she was fond of her household and her old friends, with whom she played cards, listened to music, and danced.

Although her relations with her young brother were cordial, if distant, Mary found it impossible to accept the religious changes that took place after her father's death. Both she and Edward had a high sense of what was due to them, and both shared their father's temper. The dispute became so bitter that in 1550 Mary planned to flee to the Continent. In the end, constant pressure from Charles V and England's need for an ally against the French secured for Mary permission to continue hearing Mass within her own household; even so, a number of her servants were imprisoned for their failure to comply with the law.

Edward died on 6 July 1553, leaving the Crown by will to his Protestant cousin Lady Jane Grey in direct contravention of the 1544 Succession Act. But Mary was able to rally support in East Anglia and the Thames Valley, and she was proclaimed queen in London on 19 July. The motives of those supporting the princess were mixed, but a dislike of John Dudley, duke of Northumberland, whose protégé was Jane Grey, and a love of the old religion seem to have been the most significant factors.

Those hostile to Mary's accession declared that both her religion and her unmarried state would produce problems, and this turned out to be true. Although Mary made it known at once that she intended to restore Catholicism, the formal reconciliation of England to Rome did not take place until late 1554. Even so, under the direction of Cardinal Reginald Pole, appointed archbishop in succession to Thomas Cranmer, and many of the restored Henrician bishops, traditional liturgies and practices were soon in place. It is now generally recognized that the Restoration was actively welcomed in some areas and opposed in few, but Mary's willingness to pursue intransigent Protestants even to death has, nonetheless, sullied her reputation. Her attitude to heresy was that of most contemporary rulers, who believed that ridding the realm of a few "bad apples" would save the remainder. There is little evidence that, in general, Mary personally favored severity—indeed, she specifically ordered that punishment should be undertaken "without rashness." Mary always felt, however, that those "as by learning would seem to deceive the simple" were especially wicked, which may explain the decision to burn Cranmer even after he had recanted.

Mary was the first woman to be crowned as ruler of England, which gave rise to a number of anxieties. When she decided in the autumn of 1553 to marry a foreigner, Charles V's son, Philip, those anxieties prompted a rebellion led by a Kentish gentleman, Sir Thomas Wyatt. Both xenophobia and dislike of Mary's religious policy were prevalent among Wyatt's followers, some of whom planned to replace Mary with Anne Boleyn's daughter, Elizabeth. Although nothing could be found to implicate Elizabeth directly in the plot, Mary ordered that she should be imprisoned and thereafter regarded her with suspicion. Nonetheless, the marriage to Philip in July 1554 went off without incident, and for a time all went well. By the autumn Mary believed herself to be pregnant, and there was general rejoicing at the prospect of a settled succession. Mary's hopes were misplaced, however, and in the summer of 1555 the preparations for the birth were quietly discontinued.

Events abroad now claimed Philip's attention, in particular both the continuing conflict between his family and Henry II of France and the tension in Italy, heightened by the election to the papacy in 1555 of Cardinal Gian Pietro Carafa (thus becoming Paul IV), a great enemy of Habsburg interests in that area. Philip's visits to England were infrequent, and it became increasingly unlikely that Mary would bear a child. The outbreak of war between England and France, which led in January 1558 to the loss of England's last French possession, Calais, is often blamed on Philip's influence over his wife, but the truth is that conflict between the two countries was endemic: Mary's policy toward France was no different from that of her Protestant brother, her father, or her grandfather.

In 1551 Paul IV, summoned Pole to Rome, but Mary refused to allow him to go: the last years of a reign that had seen England restored to Roman obedience were thus marked by considerable tension between the English Crown and the papacy. Although obedient to the see of Rome in matters of dogma, she seems to have regarded the political aspirations of individual popes with the same pragmatic skepticism as many of her predecessors on the throne.

By the autumn of 1558 Mary's health, never robust, gave cause for concern. Finally, acknowledging Elizabeth as her successor, and comforted both by the sacrament and (poignantly for a woman whose maternal hopes had all been dashed) by dreams of "little children like angels," she died on 17 November.

Pole died on the same day as Mary, and the church was therefore without a leader when it came under assault at the beginning of Elizabeth I's reign: ultimately, the refusal of the Marian bishops to accept the royal supremacy forced Elizabeth into the arms of the Protestants. The dismantling of the Marian church and the publication in 1563 of John Foxe's *Acts and Monuments* (often known as *The Book of Martyrs*) caused a revulsion against Mary; Foxe's book was one of the great best-sellers of all time, and his judgment on Mary has endured. Foxe believed that Mary had been a failure, for, despite her efforts, Protestantism had won. He therefore emphasized what he described as the "arguments of God's great wrath and displeasure . . . the shortness of her time . . . [and] the unfortunate event of all her purposes, who never seemed to purpose anything that came luckily to pass." But Foxe was not only writing the history of English Protestantism, he was providing it with a martyrology, and he therefore stressed the cruel practices and terrible persecutions of her reign, the burning, imprisoning, murdering, famishing, racking, and tormenting of the pitiful bodies of Christ's blessed saints. That judgment—failure and cruelty—dominated all writing about Mary and the Catholic Restoration until well into the twentieth century. Research into other aspects of the reign, however, has revealed that her secular administration was sound, if unimaginative, and that, despite great economic crises, the period was one of surprising stability. Investigations of religion at the parish level have proved that Catholicism remained popular well into Elizabeth's reign, especially in the north and west. Mary herself has been revealed as a generous benefactor of both the church and, as befitted her enlightened upbringing, the universities, from which she believed would emerge a new generation of clergy, learned in the scriptures and well able, through catechizing, to teach their flocks.

BIBLIOGRAPHY

Dowling, Maria. *Humanism in the Age of Henry VIII.* London, 1986.

Foxe, John. *Acts and Monuments of the English Martyrs.* Edited by S. R. Cattley. 8 vols. London, 1837–1844.

Loades, David. *The Reign of Mary Tudor.* 2d ed. London, 1991.

———. *Mary Tudor: A Life.* Rev. ed. Oxford, 1992.

Prescott, H. F. M. *Mary Tudor.* London, 1952.

JENNIFER LOACH

MASS. *See* Eucharist; Liturgy, *article on* Roman Catholic Liturgy; Transubstantiation.

MASSACRE OF WASSY. *See* Wassy, Massacre of.

MATHESIUS, Johannes (Ger., Johann Matz; 1504–1565), Lutheran theologian, reformer of Jáchymov (Joachimsthal), and first biographer of Martin Luther. Born in Rochlitz, northwest of Chemnitz, Mathesius's home was marked by piety flavored with criticism of the church. His preparatory schooling begun locally and in nearby Mittweida, ended in Nuremberg where as an orphan he participated in the customary singing in return for food. After university studies at Ingolstadt, Mathesius tutored the children of a minor nobleman in Munich. His reading included Martin Luther's 1520 treatise *Von den guten Wercken* (On Good Works), which sparked much soul-searching. In 1529 Mathesius traveled to Wittenberg, heard Luther's Pentecost sermon on baptism, and decided to attend Luther's lectures.

In 1532 Mathesius taught briefly at Altenburg before moving to Jáchymov, located in northern Bohemia. As school rector he continued his private studies while overseeing a curriculum, typical of Reformation and humanist education, that included the study of catechetics and languages. He returned to Wittenberg in 1540 for further study and recorded some of Luther's *Tischreden* (Table Talk). He received his M.A. in 1540 and was ordained by Luther in 1542 before returning to Jáchymov. He married Sibylla Richert with whom he had seven children. Despite calls elsewhere, Mathesius remained in Jáchymov but preached widely in the area. His long, close oversight provided stability, and he defended his city before imperial officials in Prague during the Schmalkald War. His sense of responsibility for Jáchymov prompted him to decline requests to teach at Leipzig University or to be an observer at the Council of Trent, preferring to carry on preaching and writing after the war. Those hostilities, his wife's death, struggles within Lutheranism, and new religious persecutions all weighed on Mathesius in his last years.

Many of Mathesius's nearly fifteen hundred sermons on pericopes, catechism, and doctrine were published. His *Sarepta* explained biblical references to mining in a homily book for mining families in his Jáchymov congregation. Most famous are his sermons on Luther' s life, published as the first biography of the reformer in 1566 and reprinted into the early twentieth century under various titles.

BIBLIOGRAPHY

Primary Source

Mathesius, Johann. *Historien von des Ehrwirdigen in Gott seligen thewren Manns Gottes D. Martini Luthers*. Nuremberg, 1566. The collection of biographical sermons presents a positive view of Luther and Reformation theology.

Secondary Sources

Beyerle, Stefan. "Mathesius, Johannes." In *Biographisch-Bibliographisches Kirchenlexikon*, edited by Friedrich Wilhelm Bautz, vol. 5, nos. 1,000–1,011. Hamm, Germany, 1970–1994.

Beyreuther, Erich. "Die lutherische Kirche des 16. Jahrhunderts im Spiegelbild der Predigten von Johannes Mathesius, 1504–1565." In *Reformatio und Confessio: Festschrift für D. Wilhelm Mauer zum 65. Geburtstag am 7. Mai 1965*, edited by Friedrich Wilhelm Kantzenbach and Gerhard Müller, pp. 130–140. Berlin, 1965. Looks at Reformation theology, filtered through Mathesius's sermons, on the eve of the age of Lutheran orthodoxy.

Loesche, Georg. *Johannes Mathesius: Ein Lebens- und Sitten-Bild aus der Reformationszeit* (1895). 2 vols. Reprint, Nieuwkoop, 1971. Along with an extensive examination of Mathesius's life and work, the second volume includes an edition of his correspondence, his bibliography, and a short list of sources for more information on the reformer.

Volz, Hans. *Die Lutherpredigten des Johannes Mathesius: Kritische Untersuchungen zur Geschichtsschreibung im Zeitalter der Reformation.* Quellen und Forschungen zur Reformationsgeschichte, vol. 12. Reprint, New York, 1971. Detailed analysis of Mathesius's presentation of Luther. Includes an extensive table identifying the sources used in the sermons.

ROBERT ROSIN

MATTHIAS (1557–1619), king of Hungary and Bohemia, later Holy Roman Emperor. The third son of Emperor Maximilian II, Matthias was born in Vienna. Unlike his two elder brothers, Rudolf and Ernst, Matthias was raised at his father's court and not in Spain. He was therefore acquainted at first hand with the yeasty religious heterodoxy that marked that establishment; as late as 1573 his pious mother, the sister of Philip II, and her husband battled over whether Matthias and his younger brother, Archduke Maximilian, should be allowed to take their first Communion.

Precisely how all this controversy influenced him, if at all, is not clear. What did drive him was a burning need for self-justification and office, feelings intensified by his father's nonchalant provision for all but his eldest son, Emperor Rudolf, who succeeded Maximilian II in 1576. Matthias launched a hectic series of political adventures, getting himself elected governor general of the Netherlands in 1578 in a futile effort to save those provinces for the German empire and for his house. Returning ignominiously to Austria in 1581, he found himself relatively free to maneuver since, after 1583, Rudolf resided almost continuously in Prague. His efforts to unseat the increasingly reclusive emperor led Matthias to grant religious concessions to Protestants in the various Habsburg lands in return for their support. By 1608 Rudolf had yielded the Hungarian crown, the rule in Austria above and below the Enns and in Moravia to the younger archduke.

In 1611 Matthias became king of Bohemia and in 1612, Holy Roman Emperor. His energy, however, was at an end. He spent his remaining years trying to avoid the Protestant-Catholic warfare that had threatened central Europe since the formation of rival military leagues in 1607/1608. Matthias lived to see the outbreak of these hostilities in 1618. He died heirless in Vienna the following year, succeeded by his nephew, Ferdinand II.

BIBLIOGRAPHY

Hamann, Brigitte, ed. *Die Habsburger: Ein biographisches Lexikon*. 3d corr. ed. Munich, 1988.

Parker, Geoffrey. *The Thirty Years' War*. Reprint, London, 1987.

Schindling, Anton, and Walter Ziegler, eds. *Die Kaiser der Neuzeit, 1519–1918: Heiliges Römisches Reich, Österreich, Deutschland*. Munich, 1990.

PAULA SUTTER FICHTNER

MATTHIJS, Jan (d. 1534), Dutch Anabaptist leader. A resident of Harlem; Matthijs was a baker by trade. Not much is known about his background, education, or early life. Probably in the very early 1530s he was converted to Melchiorite Anabaptism in the Netherlands. Melchior Hoffman, convinced of the imminence of the end, had advised his followers not to perform believer's baptism, which had brought much persecution to the Anabaptists; the faithful should suffer quietly until the end came. In November 1533 Matthijs announced to the Dutch disciples of Hoffman that the time of tribulation was over and that believer's baptism should again be administered. Together with five followers Matthijs traveled through Holland announcing that the time of persecution was over, that no Anabaptist believer would henceforth be persecuted, and that God would shortly establish his thousand-year reign and destroy all tyrants.

Together with John of Leiden and other Anabaptists from the Netherlands, Matthijs found his way to Münster after the Anabaptists there, under the leadership of Bernhard Rothmann, had succeeded in obtaining political control of the city. Soon after his arrival in Münster Matthijs declared that the elect could defend themselves with the sword against their godless oppressors. After the elections to the city council of 23 February 1534, Matthijs effectively assumed leadership in the city, even though formally the city council continued to exist. Matthijs insisted that only those who had been truly baptized could remain in Münster. It was rumored that he personally executed a blacksmith who had publicly called him a deceiver.

For some two months Matthijs was the effective ruler of Münster, now besieged by the forces of Bishop Franz von Waldeck. It is not altogether clear if the changes undertaken in the city, under Matthijs's leadership, were the result of biblical understanding or a reaction to the economic and psychological necessities of the siege. The steeples of the several parish churches were flattened (which can be seen as iconoclasm or military necessity, since canons were promptly placed there), books were destroyed (with only the Bible spared), and communal living mandated. On a sortie against the besieging forces on Easter Sunday, 4 April 1534, Matthijs lost his life. Accordingly, he did not witness the debacle of the Münsterite New Jerusalem.

Matthijs was a charismatic personality who succeeded in leading the Münster Anabaptists—including Rothmann, their theologian—onto a path of chiliastic frenzy. He clearly saw himself as a crucial part of the last days. Unlike Hoffman, who had formed his tenets through biblical exegesis, Matthijs claimed direct revelation from God as support for his notions.

BIBLIOGRAPHY

Kirchhoff, K.-H. "Die Endzeiterwartung der Täufergemeinde zu Münster 1534/35." *Jahrbuch für Westfälische Kirchengeschichte* 78 (1985), 19–42. Excellent essay about Matthijs's role in Münster.

Rammstedt, Otthein. *Sekte und Soziale Bewegung: Soziologische Analyse der Täufer in Münster, 1534–1535*. Cologne, 1966. Places Matthijs in the context of the Münster Anabaptists.

Stayer, James M. "Christianity in One City: Anabaptist Münster, 1534–1535." In *Radical Tendencies in the Reformation: Divergent Perspectives*, edited by Hans J. Hillerbrand, pp. 117–134. Kirksville, Mo., 1988.

HANS J. HILLERBRAND

MAULBRONN, COLLOQUY OF. Held in 1564, this colloquy was attended by representatives of the Lutheran (Württemberg) and Reformed (Palatinate) confessions to discuss the Lord's Supper and Christology. It was Elector Frederick III's introduction of Calvinistic theology into the Palatinate in 1563 that aroused tensions with Lutheran neighbors, led by Duke Christoph of Württemberg. Negotiations between the Lutherans and Frederick reached a climax in a meeting between these two princes at Hilsbach in February 1564, when they agreed to a colloquy of their theologians on the most pressing issues dividing them—the real presence of Christ's body and blood in the Lord's Supper and related christological questions. Five theologians from each side assembled at the Württemberg abbey of Maulbronn on 10–15 April 1564 for ten inconclusive sessions of intense discussion. Jakob Andreae was the sole spokesman for the Württemberg side and was accompanied by Johannes Brenz, senior Württemberg theologian; Balthasar Bidembach, a court preacher; Dietrich Schnepf, Andreae's colleague at the University of Tübingen; and Valentin Wanner, abbot of Maulbronn. The Palatinate theologians included four Heidelberg professors—Peter Boquin, Kaspar Olevianus, Zacharias Ursinus, and Peter Dathenus—as well as the court preacher Michael Diller. Andreae not only served as the only Lutheran interlocutor but also directed the course of the discussions.

A brief exchange outlining differences on the Lord's Supper began the colloquy. The Palatine side insisted that Christ is received through faith, but they also argued that his body and blood are not received orally and not by unbelievers, positions held by the Württembergers. The topic then turned to Christology, beginning with the longtime disagreement between Calvinists and Lutherans on the nature of God's right hand, at which Christ is seated. The former defended a local interpretation of the term that the right hand of God is a place in heaven; the latter insisted that it designates the investiture of Christ with full divine power and majesty. The Reformed side criticized the Christology of Brenz and Andreae as "ubiquitistic," because it taught that the human nature of Christ is present everywhere by virtue of the communication of attributes. Andreae rejected the term as an invention of his foes, at the same time affirming that Christ's simple human nature does indeed share the divine nature's characteristic of omnipresence or ubiquity. In their debate the two sides only skirted an analysis of the presupposition that divided them, the Reformed belief that "the finite is not capable of bearing the infinite."

Hermeneutical issues arose at many points, particularly over whether the scriptures teach the communication of attributes between the two natures of Christ explicitly or implicitly. The debates revolved around syllogistic arguments, often poorly constructed, inviting ridicule from the opposite side.

Although the Hilsbach agreement had forbade the publication of protocols from the colloquy, Palatine boasts of victory provoked Brenz to have the Württemberg version printed; the Palatinate theologians replied with their own printed reports. The colloquy provided no advance in understanding between the two sides and left them hardened and in place for the coming "age of orthodoxy." The published reports decisively alienated the Philippist theologians of Wittenberg from their fellow Lutheran Württembergers. The colloquy demonstrated to Duke Christoph that the Palatinate was determined to reject the theology of the Augsburg Confession as he understood it and moved him to work for exclusion of this principality from the protection of the Peace of Augsburg at the Diet of Augsburg in 1566.

BIBLIOGRAPHY

Bizer, Ernst. *Studien zur Geschichte des Abendmahlsstreits im 16. Jahrhundert.* 3d ed. Darmstadt, 1972. See pp. 335–362 for a review of the flow of the debate at Maulbronn and an analysis of the rationalizing tendencies of both sides.

Hollerbach, Marion. *Das Religionsgespräch als Mittel der konfessionellen und politischen Auseinandersetzung im Deutschland des 16. Jahrhunderts.* Frankfurt a.M., 1982. See pp. 230–242 for a summary of the political developments and the form of the colloquy.

ROBERT KOLB

MAURICE OF NASSAU. *See* Nassau, Maurits van.

MAURICE OF SAXONY. *See* Moritz of Saxony.

MÄUßLI, Wolfgang. *See* Musculus, Wolfgang.

MAXIMILIAN I (1459–1519), king of Germany (1486–1519) and Holy Roman Emperor (1493–1519). An outstanding exception in a dynasty noted for gravity and steadfast application to detail, he was the son of the legendarily phlegmatic Emperor Frederick III and Eleanor of Portugal. The young archduke was early the despair of his tutors, who found him unable to keep his mind on anything for very long.

Maximilian's excessive energy, however, sustained him through a life marked by great responsibility and equally great disappointment. In 1477 he married Mary, the daughter and sole heir of Duke Charles of Burgundy, who died that same year. Louis XI of France immediately undertook to recover the Burgundian holdings for the French Crown, and Maximilian had no choice but to defend his wife's lands. After Mary died in 1482, Maximilian had only a shaky claim to these territories, encouraging Louis and his successor, Charles VIII, to challenge him further. Burgundy itself was lost to France in 1493 through the Treaty of Senlis. That same year Maximilian turned over the governorship of the remaining possessions to his son, Archduke Philip.

Elected German king (king of the Romans) in 1486, Maximilian became emperor in 1493 but was never crowned by the pope. As emperor, he was a key military figure in the Italian Wars, which were set off by Charles VIII's invasion of the peninsula in 1494. He was heavily involved in maintaining peace within Germany and had grandiose plans for a crusade against the expanding Ottoman empire. Few of these activities bore lasting fruit. The same was true of his efforts to reform the administration and defense of his Austrian lands, not to mention the empire itself. A diet meeting at Worms in 1495 sanctioned an imperial declaration of eternal peace and the establishment of the *Reichskammergericht*, a standing imperial court that would play a significant legal role during the Reformation. But the estates turned down a tax, the Common Penny, for support of a perpetual army, which Maximilian believed crucial to the success of his entire program. Thus thwarted, he flaunted the imperial constitution in subsequent years, a policy that only furthered disarray in the political and administrative life of the German lands.

He was considerably more successful in advancing the fortunes of his house. In 1496 Archduke Philip married Juana of Castile, thus opening the way for future Habsburg successions on the Iberian Peninsula. Maximilian also engineered the Vienna Accord of 1515, through which his grandson Ferdinand I, the second son of Philip and Juana, was betrothed to Anna, the daughter of King Václav of Hungary and Bohemia. The young archduke's sister, Mary, was promised to Anna's brother, Louis, the heir-apparent to these two east-central European crowns. With these arrangements in place, Maximilian dropped an idea with which he had toyed for some time—making a kingdom of the Habsburg Austrian patrimony. His gamble that Bohemia and Hungary would eventually bring the Habsburgs royal titles proved correct when King Louis died fleeing a battle against the Turks in 1526.

Though disdaining formal schooling, Maximilian was an enthusiastic patron of arts and letters and a practitioner of them as well. He participated in the writing of at least two autobiographical renderings of his youth and young manhood, *Weißkunig* and *Freydal.* He commissioned *Theuerdank*, an allegorical account of his journey to his Burgundian bride. He raised the cultivation of music, already underway at his father's court, to high levels, thereby furthering a practice to be followed by almost all his successors. The composer Ludwig Senfl and the organist and composer Paul Hochhaimer were special favorites. Maximilian brought outstanding scholars to Vienna as well. Perhaps most important among these was Conradus Celtis, whose work helped inspire interest in German antiquities and a sense of German identity among later generations.

A devout Catholic, Maximilian worked to remedy the moral defects of papal rule; he supported the Council of Pisa, which met in 1511–1512 to address the question. Seen in this light, his proposal to unite the papal and imperial office, made in 1511, was perhaps less frivolous than it sounds. Like so many of his schemes, however, it came to naught. When he died in Wels in 1519, his chief legacy to his heirs was a mountain of debt. He was buried in Wiener Neustadt; the body has never been moved to the grandiose tomb he commissioned in Innsbruck.

BIBLIOGRAPHY

Benecke, Gerhard. *Maximilian I, 1459–1519: An Analytical Biography.* London, 1982. Quirky, but useful for understanding Maximilian's environment.

Bonney, Richard. *The European Dynastic States, 1494–1660.* Oxford, 1991. Part 1 contains a good picture of Maximilian's diplomatic and military activities.

Brady, Thomas A., Jr. *Turning Swiss: Cities and Empire, 1450–1550.* Cambridge, 1985. Maximilian and his activities in the empire.

Wiesflecker, Hermann. *Kaiser Maximilian I: Das Reich, Österreich und Europa an der Wende zur Neuzeit.* 5 vols. Vienna, 1971–1986. The definitive work. It has been usefully abridged as *Maximilian I: Die Fundamente des habsburgischen Weltreiches,* Vienna, 1991.

PAULA SUTTER FICHTNER

MAXIMILIAN II (1527–1576), king of Bohemia and Hungary, later Holy Roman Emperor. The eldest son of Emperor Ferdinand I (r. 1558–1564), Maximilian was one of the most intellectually gifted and personally complex rulers of his day. Having received an excellent education, he was an adept linguist and a discerning patron of both arts and letters. His unusually probing mind ranged over a wide area of concerns, including religious questions, which began to preoccupy him around 1550. His interest in Lutheranism, which he pursued both in private and in correspondence with some of the leading Protestant princes and writers of his day, lent credence to the thought that he not only supported the general cause of the new confession but might actually convert to it. He allowed the Lutheran sympathizer Kaspar von Nidbruck access to the court library in Vienna where the latter gathered material for the *Magdeburg Centuries,* a historical apology for the Lutheran reform. Maximilian's court preacher, Sebastian Pfauser, supported the Protestant reform strongly, leading Emperor Ferdinand I to banish the clergyman from his son's court in 1560. When Ferdinand demanded that Maximilian swear allegiance to the church of Rome or lose his inheritance, the younger man gave in, taking an oath before his father and younger brothers in 1561. Nevertheless, his earlier behavior, coupled with his steadfast antipapalism, did much to ingratiate him with the German secular Protestant electors, who voted for him as king in 1563 and supported his elevation to the imperial office.

Maximilian's first years as emperor were taken up with a massive military campaign against the Turks in Hungary. The abject failure of this undertaking in 1566 humiliated him and apparently triggered the passive behavior that subsequently marked his reign. Maximilian shaped his religious policies around the Peace of Augsburg, the spirit of which he would recommend not only in the German lands but in religiously troubled areas such as France and the Netherlands. Though distressed by the political implications of sedition in any form, he consistently recommended that his brother-in-law, Philip II of Spain, follow a conciliatory policy in his rebellious Netherlands.

Within Austria and Bohemia, Maximilian was under constant pressure to widen freedom of worship for Protestants, especially Lutherans, who often linked such demands with financial inducements. In 1568 the estates of Lower Austria promised to assume his massive indebtedness in return for religious concessions. Maximilian took the opportunity to promote the reunification of the traditional faith and the new. But the results, the so-called Austrian Ecclesiastical Agenda of 1571, which granted the nobility and knights (though not the towns) of Lower Austria exercise of Lutheranism in their castles, only furthered Protestantism. The need for funds to mount a defense against the Turks coupled with his wishes to see his son Rudolf recognized as his successor in Bohemia forced Maximilian in 1575 to assent verbally to the Bohemian Confession. This act effectively granted religious freedom to a coalition of Utraquists, Lutherans, and the Bohemian Brethren. Religiously isolated within his family—his pious wife, Maria, was Philip II's sister—he refused the last rites of the church, leaving contemporaries and historians alike unsure of his true beliefs.

BIBLIOGRAPHY

Bibl, Viktor. *Maximilian II: Der rätselhafte Kaiser.* Dresden, 1929. Though this book has no scholarly apparatus, it is based on extensive and sound research.

Holtzmann, Robert. *Maximilian II. bis zu seiner Thronbesteigung 1527–1564.* Berlin, 1903. Excellent, though not widely available, study emphasizing the development of Maximilian's religious heterodoxy.

PAULA SUTTER FICHTNER

MEAUX. French bishopric, wool-cloth manufacturing center, and early stronghold of the Reformation, Meaux was the most important town of the Brie, a region to the east of Paris. Its population of notables, merchants, artisans, vine growers, and day laborers is estimated to have numbered around seven thousand in the sixteenth century. Parisian notables and merchants owned an increasing fraction of the land in the region. Paris was also the primary market for its grain, cloth, wine, and cheese. The clergy of the diocese tended to be nonresident Parisians.

The reformation at Meaux was initiated by its bishop, Guillaume Briçonnet. But its appeal lay in the growing religious fervor, rising literacy, and increasing hostility to ecclesiastical power on the part of the townspeople evident from the late fifteenth century. With the help of Jacques Lefèvre d'Étaples—as well as other reform-minded humanists, such as Gérard Roussel, Pierre Caroli, and Michel Mazurier—Briçonnet attempted to introduce an evangelically based reform of the diocese including reform of the hôtel-dieu, insistence on the residence of the clergy, and the introduction of a system insuring regular preaching based on the gospel (1518–1523). Reform at Meaux was assisted by the support of the royal court, especially the king's sister, Marguerite d'Angoulême. Royal patronage was the culmination of a growing commitment of the monarchy to ecclesiastical reform, as well as diplomatic maneuvering between the monarchy and the papacy in the wake of the German Reformation.

By December 1521 Briçonnet was calling upon the king to begin the reform of the whole French church on the basis of the gospel. In 1523 the New Testament translated by Lefèvre appeared under royal license. But the advance of Briçonnet's moderate reform was disrupted by the appearance of a more extreme form of evangelicism inspired by Martin Luther. In October 1523 Briçonnet issued a decree against Luther's teachings and denounced those among the preachers who had denied the existence of purgatory and questioned the efficacy of prayers to the Virgin and the saints. Briçonnet's disavowal of heretical opinions at this point coincided with the beginning of a rapprochement between the French monarchy and the papacy.

The withdrawal of official patronage led to the radicalization of the Meaux reform. Economic discontent and an intensified sense of political and social grievance led the people to heed the preaching of the wool comber Pierre Le Clerc and other religious radicals. Partly stemming from their desire to meet the threat of extremism and partly reflecting their own attraction to Luther, Huldrych Zwingli, and Johannes Oecolampadius, Lefèvre and Roussel cautiously began to take a more evangelical stance. The publication of *Les Epistres & evangiles pour les cinquante & deux sepmaines de l'an* (1525) represented an attempt by Lefèvre and his associates to promote an evangelical faith while avoiding as far as possible a direct challenge to Catholic orthodoxy.

But it was too late for such compromises. Iconoclastic outrages at the end of 1524 and the beginning of 1525 intensified the hostility of the Franciscans, the Faculty of Theology of Paris, and the Parlement of Paris. The captivity of the king following his defeat at Pavia (24 February 1525) removed the last hope of royal protection. Pierre Le Clerc and other radical preachers were put under arrest. In the summer of 1525 Briçonnet was forced into a trial against the Franciscans of Meaux that ended in his being fined for allowing heresy to spread in his diocese. In October warrants were issued for the arrest of Lefèvre, Roussel, and others involved in the Meaux experiment. Lefèvre and Roussel were obliged to flee to Strasbourg.

The reformation at Meaux continued for the next two decades as an underground movement among the people. In 1546, in the wake of war and renewed economic hardship, a church following the pattern laid down by John Calvin at Strasbourg was established in the *marché* of the town. Sixty-four members of the congregation were arrested by the *liéutenant du bailliage* on 8 September 1546. Fourteen of these, including the leaders, the merchant Étienne Mangin and the wool comber Pierre Le Clerc, were burned to death by order of the Parlement.

Persecution seemed only to increase the attraction of the new faith. By the outbreak of the religious wars, virtually the whole town had become Calvinist. Calvinism had also strongly implanted itself in the nearby bourgs and villages. In December 1560 a wave of icononclasm swept the town and region. The bishop was besieged in his palace. Eighteen months later new disturbances took place, including marches by bands of militants calling themselves *nus-pieds* led by a minister who went from village to village preaching the gospel. During the Saint Bartholomew's Day Massacre the homes of rich heretics were singled out for attack. Some six hundred Huguenots were killed. Despite this catastrophe there were still some eight to nine thousand Huguenots in the *bailliage* of Meaux at the conclusion of the religious wars.

[*See also* Briçonnet, Guillaume; Lefèvre d'Étaples, Jacques; Marguerite d'Angoulême; *and* Roussel, Gérard.]

BIBLIOGRAPHY

Briçonnet, Guillaume. *Correspondance de Guillaume Briçonnet et Marguerite d'Angoulême, 1521–1524.* 2 vols., edited by Christine Martineau, Michel Veissière, and Henry Heller. Geneva, 1975–1979. Briçonnet's letters to Marguerite embody the evangelical and mystical ideas behind the Fabrist reform, at least up to 1524.

Du Plessis, Toussaint. *Histoire de l'église de Meaux.* 2 vols. Paris, 1731. The most important collection of documents.

Heller, Henry. "The Briçonnet Case Reconsidered." *Journal of Medieval and Renaissance Studies* 2 (1972), 223–258. Study of the Meaux experiment from a political perspective.

———. "The Evangelicism of Lefèvre d'Étaples." *Studies in the Renaissance* 19 (1972), 43–77. Investigates the impact of German and Swiss Reformation ideas on Lefèvre's thought.

———. "Famine, Revolt and Heresy at Meaux, 1521–1525." *Archiv fur Reformationsgeschichte* 68 (1977), 133–157. Social and economic context of the Meaux experiment.

———. *The Conquest of Poverty: The Calvinist Revolt in Sixteenth-Century France.* Leiden, 1986. Includes a chapter on the social and economic background of the development of the Reformation at Meaux.

Lefèvre d'Étaples, Jacques. *Épistres et évanqiles pour les cinquante & deux sepmaines de l'an.* Introduction by M. A. Screech. Geneva, 1964. Facsimile of the edition of 1525. Introduction by Screech understates the radicalism of the text.

Lovy, René-Jacques. *Les origines de la réforme française: Meaux, 1518–1546.* 2d ed. Paris, 1983. History of the development of the Reformation from a Protestant point of view.

Mousseaux, Maurice. *La Brie protestante: Aux sources françaises de la réforme; textes et faits.* Paris, 1967. Essential documentation on the Reformation in the Brie.

Veissière, Michel. *L'éveque Guillaume Briçonnet, 1470–1534.* Provins, France, 1986. Excellent biography from a Catholic perspective.

HENRY HELLER

MEDICI, Giovan Angelo de'. *See* Pius IV.

MEDICI, Giovanni Damaso Romolo de'. *See* Leo X.

MEDICI, Giulio de'. *See* Clement VII.

MEDICI, HOUSE OF. A Florentine family of merchant bankers who became unofficial heads of the government of Florence, the House of Medici also developed close financial and dynastic ties with the papacy. The elevation of Giovanni de' Medici in 1489 as the youngest cardinal ever, his subsequent election as Pope Leo X in 1513, followed by the election of his cousin as Clement VII in 1523, mark the high tide of Medici relations with the church.

The Medici bank lay at the center of the family's ties with Rome. The volume of financial business the papacy generated necessitated the presence of bankers, designated *curiam sequentes* ("following the curia"). Giovanni di Bicci (1360–1429), founder of the Medici bank in 1397, became depositor general to the schismatic Pope John XXIII. The Medici bank continued as papal depository general throughout much of the fifteenth century. Under Giovanni's son Cosimo (1389–1464), the bank enjoyed its heyday, and the curial branch alone generated more than half the total profits of all Medici banking, commercial, and manufacturing enterprises.

Upon his death Cosimo was designated *pater patriae* ("father of his country"). He also distinguished himself as a learned man and cultivator of the arts and humanism, thereby establishing the reputation of his family for extensive cultural patronage. He actively supported monastic reform and was instrumental in bringing observant Dominican friars to the convent of San Marco, whose library he endowed and where he kept a private cell. At the end of the century San Marco was the ambiance from which Savonarola issued his strident calls for moral and church reform.

In 1469 Cosimo's grandson Lorenzo the Magnificent (1449–1492) became head of the family and first citizen of Florence. Rivalry with another Florentine banking family desirous of becoming depositor general precipitated the 1478 Pazzi Conspiracy, which had the support of Sixtus IV and his nephew Girolamo Riario. Assassins attacked Lorenzo and his brother during mass in the cathedral of Florence. Only Lorenzo survived. Subsequently Lorenzo tightened control of the Florentine government.

Lorenzo sought rapprochement with the papacy, and following the election of Innocent VIII in 1484 worked to reestablish the Medici bank in Rome and to launch his son Giovanni (1475–1521) in an ecclesiastical career. Lorenzo's reputation for statesmanship earned him the respect of Innocent, who sought his advice to such an extent that one ambassador noted that the pope slept with the eyes of Lorenzo. Lorenzo used the opportunity to establish a dynastic foothold within the curia. The marriage in 1487 of his daughter Maddalena to Franchescetto Cibo, Innocent's son, proved instrumental. The Medici bank once again became a player in Rome; Lorenzo acquired important benefices for Giovanni; and in 1489 the thirteen-year-old boy was named cardinal. Lorenzo's instructions to his young son on the occasion are emblematic of the cultural values associated with the Medici. Giovanni was to display moderation and to surround himself with a few antiques and beautiful books and a small, learned staff rather than a large and pompous retinue. Lorenzo supported observant reform within Florentine territory and in monasteries that Giovanni held as benefices. Plagued by gout and ill health, Lorenzo died in 1492 at age forty-three. In the last years of his life he wrote much religious poetry and was instrumental in bringing Savonarola to Florence.

In 1494 Lorenzo's heirs were exiled from Florence, and eighteen years passed before Cardinal Giovanni, aided by Julius II and a Spanish army, reestablished the Medici as *de facto* rulers. His 1513 election as Leo X ushered in what contemporaries referred to as a golden age of Renaissance culture in Rome. Both Leo X and his cousin Clement VII found the papacy embroiled in the Italian Wars, occasioned by invading French and Spanish armies, which by contrast must have made the events of the early Reformation in Germany seem insignificant. Clement spent eighteen months as a virtual Spanish hostage in a Roman fortress following the 1527 Sack of Rome. Attempts to reconcile with France resulted in the 1533 marriage of his niece Catherine (1519–1589) to the future Henry II of France. His nephew Ippolito (1511–1535) became the new family cardinal. When the last of Lorenzo the Magnificent's male issue died, a collateral line of the family took over Florence, now as grand dukes of Tuscany with Spanish backing. Duke Cosimo I's (1519–1574) granddaughter Marie (1573–1642) married Henry IV of France. Thus, over the course of 150 years, this Florentine family of merchant bankers had joined the ranks of princes of the church, of popes, and of the ruling houses of Europe.

BIBLIOGRAPHY

Ady, Cecilia M. *Lorenzo dei Medici and Renaissance Italy.* Reprint, London, 1970. Brief but sound overview of Lorenzo de' Medici's role in the politics and diplomacy of the Italian states.

Bizzocchi, Roberto. *Chiesa e potere nella Toscana del Quattrocento.* Bologna, 1987. The best recent study of the cooperation between church and lay authorities to control ecclesiastical institutions in Tuscany. The Medicis figure prominently.

Gutkin, Curt S. *Cosimo de' Medici, Pater Patriae, 1389–1464.* Oxford, 1938.

Hale, John R. *Florence and the Medici: The Pattern of Control.* Reprint, New York, 1983. Survey of three generations of Medici history in Florence with general bibliography.

Pastor, Ludwig. *History of the Popes.* Translated by Ralph Francis Kerr. Vols. 7–10. London, 1923. In the absence of any recent biographies of the Medici popes, Pastor remains a fundamental source.

Picotti, G. B. *La Giovinezza di Leone X.* Reprint, Rome, 1981. Study of Medici relations with the church in the late fifteenth century with an appendix of illustrative documents.

Roover, Raymond de. *The Rise and Decline of the Medici Bank, 1397–1494.* New York, 1966. Classic study of Medici business operations in various parts of Europe.

Rubinstein, Nicolai. *The Government of Florence under the Medici, 1434 to 1494.* Corr. ed. Oxford, 1968. The fundamental political analysis of how the Medici managed political control in Florence.

MELISSA MERIAM BULLARD

MEDICINE AND HEALING. Standard histories of medicine have often tended to slight the Reformation. Moving quickly from "the medicine of the Renaissance" to "the medicine of the seventeenth century," they highlight the anatomical discoveries of the Renaissance and illuminate the achievements of the "scientific revolution," while implicitly denying the existence of a singularly Reformation (or, for that matter, sixteenth-century) contribution to medicine and healing. Treatments of medicine and the Reformation often revolve around major figures, such as Paracelsus, Ambroise Paré, Girolamo Fracastoro, and Felix Platter. Less frequent attempts have been made toward establishing firm connections between medicine and society. But the Reformation was not incidental to the shaping of medicine and healing, nor can it be regarded merely as the working out of a humanism born in the Renaissance or the staging ground for the more salient "scientific" contributions of the next hundred years.

In three particular ways the Reformation was intimately linked to medicine. The reformers' attack on magic and superstition paved the way for the introduction of new systems of healing at the popular and academic levels. The Reformation's contributions to the restructuring of charity and charitable institutions, including hospitals, worked together with a revived civic culture to generate a set of charitable and communal prerogatives and initiatives that persisted through the eighteenth century. Finally, a new emphasis on literacy, on Bible reading, and on catechization, when joined to the technology of printing, generated a vast number of popular texts on health, thereby creating a popular health literature that combined the "great" and "little" traditions.

The environment of the sixteenth century assisted in these transformations as well. European contact with the Americas and the slow rise of a world economic system were reshaping Europe epidemiologically as well as economically. In the sixteenth century syphilis ravaged European bodies and psyches while fostering new anxieties about sexuality and affecting attitudes toward women as well. The "old" diseases of plague and dysentery did not vanish but remained major problems throughout the early modern period. The role of women as healers (and workers) was also altered by the teachings of religious reformers on the family.

The Assault on Magic and Superstition. The most important philosophical connection between the Reformation and medicine derived from the assault on the superstition and magic that reformers deemed characteristic of the medieval church. Magical healing was a central pillar of the medical system that served medieval and Renaissance people. Charms, amulets, prayers, and incantations, as well as astrological signs and portents, were completely embedded in, and indissoluble from, both the theory and practice of medicine. When the reformers attacked these "superstitious practices," they also subverted a style of healing that had endured for hundreds of years and that (at the very least) extended some psychological comfort to people confronted with illnesses and afflictions for which academic medicine offered no cures and few palliatives. "Wise men" and "cunning folk" divined and charmed, found lost goods and raised curses, as well as provided magical "cures." After the reformers called the orthodoxy of such healers into question, little remained to protect people from the maleficent magic of witches, which often expressed itself in an ability to strike people or animals with illness. While the Reformation's offensive against superstition never completely banished magical cures (which survived well into the nineteenth century), it did to some extent drive them underground by associating them with "popery" and even heresy. The Tridentine Catholic church likewise went far in denying the functional magic of Christianity and of the Christian clergy, confronting and disavowing to a large extent both the propriety and efficacy of magical and religious healing. In the late sixteenth and early seventeenth centuries, magical and religious healing were discredited because of their association with brutal sectarian strife. Religious enthusiasm and spiritual healing characterized many religious radicals. Thus, the growing numbers of those who recoiled from religious excess, and the violence it seemed to engender, rejected religious therapies as well.

Secularization. Historians have often regarded the secularization of charitable enterprises as one of the Reformation's most profound and lasting innovations. Luther (perhaps influenced by the Christian humanists and by early Catholic reformers) outlined the principles of "Christian" charity in his "An den Christlichen Adel deutscher Nation" (1520), linking poor relief to work. Ability to work, however, depended on a certain degree of health, and this precept, as well as the organizational and religious ones contained in Luther's program, had major repercussions on medical care. Many countries, most notably England, disbanded religious and nursing orders, closed hospitals once run by Catholic monks and nuns, and drove out their "inmates." According to this interpretation, the Reformation thus formed a watershed in the history of charity and of hospitals. But the assertion that the Reformation singlehandedly secularized charity has proved rather shaky, and the reform in poor relief and in hospitals is now generally seen as only one stage in a much slower transformation that spanned at least two centuries.

Hospitals in early modern Europe tended overwhelmingly to be urban institutions in whose management and financing city governments and lay organizations had assumed a major role already in the Middle Ages. Thus, modifications in hospital administration should be connected to that rekindling of civic life the Reformation fostered. Even in England, for example, where the communal tradition burned perhaps not as brightly as in many German city-states, the dissolution of monasteries and nursing orders and the abandonment of hospitals resulted in the worsening of conditions for the destitute and the ill, but only temporarily. Cities and private citizens quickly moved to take over, rebuild, and even construct new hospitals. In many reformed areas, little changed.

The Reformation, urban culture, and medicine were intertwined in other crucial ways as well. With the promulgation of Protestant church ordinances (*Kirchenordnungen*) came the introduction of statutes regulating medical practice, licensing practitioners, authorizing quarantine procedures, and activating urban "cleanup" programs, if on a small scale. Yet once again, important medieval precedents existed. Cities in the later Middle Ages had been the first to enact public health measures, but the new medical ordinances of the sixteenth century grew out of the revitalization of civic life that the Reformation stimulated and that the *Kirchenordnungen* embodied. Many *Kirchenordnungen* contained paragraphs on midwifery, apothecaries, physicians, and on the general practice of medicine, stipulating "Christian life-styles" as integral to professional competence. Johannes Bugenhagen's *Kirchenordnung* for Hamburg (1528), for example, discusses the appointment and duties of a city physician, a city barber surgeon, and a city midwife. These rules brought the regulation of medicine and health under the umbrella of the "good governance" (*Gute Zucht und Ordnung*) judged necessary to maintain a Christian community intact. Medical ordinances in other places similarly emphasized an embryonic social medicine. The most famous of these, and the one that served as model for others, was Joachim Struppius's *Nützliche Reformation Zu guter gesundtheit/ vnd Christlicher Ordnung* (1573). Under the rubric of "Christian order," Struppius called for the establishment of a *Collegium medicum* empowered to supervise the entire paraphernalia of health for the city of Frankfurt. In 1582 Protestant Augsburg was actually the first to set up a *Collegium medicum* on Struppius's model. Several other German cities, reformed and Catholic alike, including Ulm, Vienna, Nördlingen, and Nuremberg, soon followed.

Printing. While printing, of course, predates the Reformation, reformed teachings, particularly the emphasis on the use of the vernacular and Bible-reading, nurtured the proliferation of printed materials of all kinds. By the middle of the sixteenth century, a wide choice of vernacular medical texts was available. Paracelsus wrote in German, thus making his teachings accessible not only to an educated medical elite but also to a far broader segment of the population, appealing to them in terms they understood and with which they could associate. Paracelsus's message similarly harmonized with the views of the spiritual reformers. He dismissed and attacked Galenism both on medical grounds and as an artifact of a disintegrating and pagan, Mediterranean world.

At the same time popularly written, cheaply printed forms of medical literature cascaded off printing presses throughout Europe. What was once a trickle of popular medical works swelled into a flood by the middle of the sixteenth century. Innumerable books and pamphlets discussing "regimen"—that is, individual hygiene and health preservation—appeared in Latin and in the vernacular. Thomas Moulton's *Mirror or Glas of Health,* for example, went through at least seventeen editions between 1530 and 1580. A striking number of these works, such as Walther Hermann Ryff's famous and often pirated *Schwangerer Frawen Rosengarten* (1545), addressed the care of pregnant women, lactating mothers, and children. "Plague" tracts, such as John Caius's *A Boke or Conseill Agst. the Disease Commonly Called the Sweate, or Sweatyng Sicknesse* (1552), were specifically directed to the "common man" and discussed the prevention and means of treating several epidemic diseases, not merely bubonic plague. These were frequently reprinted and often distributed by governments when epidemics threatened. Calendars containing medical advice, astrological prognostications, and other useful information proliferated rapidly. Cheap and handy as such calendars were, many households possessed one or more. "Health catechisms" began to be popular and were clearly modeled after such religious classics as Luther's Small Catechism. Thus, in both form and content, the learned and popular medical literature of the sixteenth century converged with the theory and practice of the Reformation.

[*See also* Paracelsus *and* Social Welfare.]

BIBLIOGRAPHY

Ackerknecht, Erwin H. *A Short History of Medicine*. Rev. ed. New York, 1968. Somewhat old-fashioned but still useful introduction to the history of medicine.

Eccles, Audrey. *Obstetrics and Gynecology in Tudor and Stuart England*. London, 1982.

Maclean, Ian. *The Renaissance Notion of Woman: A Study in the Fortunes of Scholasticism and Medical Science in European Intellectual Life*. Cambridge, 1980.

Pagel, Walter. *Paracelsus: An Introduction to Philosophical Medicine in the Era of the Renaissance*. Basel and New York, 1958. Standard biography of Paracelsus, extremely learned and best overall analysis of the impact of his work.

The Plague Reconsidered: A New Look at Its Origins and Effects in Sixteenth- and Seventeenth-Century England. Matlock, England, 1977. Excellent discussion of major issues involved in outbreaks of plague; refutes several misconceptions about plague; especially good on epidemiology and mortality.

Thomas, Keith. *Religion and the Decline of Magic: Studies in Popular Beliefs in Sixteenth-Century England*. London, 1971. Classic study; offers a detailed and probing treatment of the reformed assault on superstition and magic as well as an excellent chapter on magical healing.

Wear, Andrew, Roger French, and I. M. Lonie, eds. *The Medical Renaissance of the Sixteenth Century*. Cambridge, 1985.

Webster, Charles, ed. *Health, Medicine and Mortality in the Sixteenth Century*. Cambridge, 1979. Several important articles on a wide range of medically related topics, including mortality, epidemics, diet, institutions, and medical practitioners.

MARY LINDEMANN

MEGANDER, Caspar (Ger., Grossmann; 1484–1545), Swiss clergyman, reformer of Bern, and humanist. Megander was a leading proponent of the Swiss reformer Huldrych Zwingli's theology following the latter's death in 1531. Born in Zurich, Megander studied in Basel before returning to his native city in 1518 as a priest in the hospital. His support of Zwingli and his preaching from 1519 facilitated the latter's establishment in the city. Megander acknowledged Zwingli to be the better theologian and preferred to play a supporting role. In 1522 he cosigned the petition to the bishop concerning celibacy of priests; in 1524 he followed Zwingli's example and married his housekeeper, he stood by Zwingli before the Zurich council in 1525 to demand the abolition of the Mass; and he participated in the disputation of 1525 with the Anabaptists and represented Zurich at the Bern Disputation in 1528. Megander was an energetic preacher and worked with Leo Jud to edit Zwingli's biblical commentaries and sermons.

Following the Bern Disputation in 1528, Megander was called to Bern to serve as the principal theologian in the newly reformed state. The years between 1528 and 1537 were marked by accomplishments, bitter quarrels, and loneliness. In Bern Megander worked to establish a Zwinglian Reformation through his preaching, the founding of a theological college, church visitations, and debates with the Anabaptists. In Bernese politics Megander worked as Zwingli's informant and agent. His advocacy of an alliance with Zurich led to his suspension from the pulpit in the wake of the Second Kappel War. Following his reinstatement, Megander fought every attempt by Wolfgang Capito and Martin Bucer to reconcile the Swiss with the German Lutherans. The particular point of contention was the Wittenberg Concord of 1536. Although Megander was the most capable churchman in the city, his obdurate character and refusal to compromise on any point isolated him from his colleagues and made him a political liability to the rulers of Bern.

Megander has received too little credit for his role in the reformation of the Pays du Vaud and Geneva after 1536. He headed the Bernese delegation at the Synod of Lausanne (1536), which established the Reformation in these French-speaking lands, and later wrote their church ordinances. In Lausanne Megander met the young John Calvin and wrote to Heinrich Bullinger in Zurich testifying to the doctrinal soundness of the Genevan reformers, thus strengthening Calvin's position in Geneva and contributing to the ties between the German- and French-speaking Reformed churches in Switzerland.

Megander fell victim to the split in Bern between the Lutherans and Zwinglians that he had created. He quarreled openly with Bucer and Capito over his Zwinglian catechism and was forced by the council to leave in 1537. Megander's departure alleviated the immediate crises, but his influence on the church in Bern was enduring, if not somewhat ambivalent. Through his learning and forcefulness he had ensured that the Bernese church remained Zwinglian, but his contentiousness provoked the magistrates to an unusually firm control of church affairs.

BIBLIOGRAPHY

Gordon, Bruce. "Switzerland." In *The Early Reformation in Europe*, edited by Andrew Pettegree, pp. 70–93. Cambridge, 1992. Sets the problems in Bern within the wider context of the Swiss Reformation.

Locher, Gottfried. *Die Zwinglische Reformation im Rahmen der europäischen Kirchengeschichte*. Göttingen, 1979. Reference work on the events and persons connected with the Zwinglian Reformation.

Verzeichnis der im deutschen Sprachbereich erschienenen Drucke des XVI. Jahrhunderts. Stuttgart, 1983–. Vol. 8, nos. 3484–3488.

BRUCE GORDON

MELANCHTHON, Philipp (also Melanthon; humanist name of Philip Schwartzerdt; 1497–1560), German humanist and reformer, educator, philologist, theologian, neo-Latin poet, and textbook author. Born on 16 February 1497 in Bretten, a city in the electoral Palatinate (present-day Kreis Karlsruhe, Germany), Melanchthon was the eldest son of George, a respected armorer, and Barbara, daughter of a prosperous merchant. In 1518—after comprehensive studies in Pforzheim (1508–1509), Heidelberg

(1509–1512), and Tübingen (1512–1518) and at the recommendation of Johannes Reuchlin—he received a call to a newly established teaching position in Greek at the University of Wittenberg in electoral Saxony.

There he came under the influence of Martin Luther and began to study theology. The proclamation of God's grace freely given became the enduring mainstay of his life. As this experience penetrated his intellectual world, it led him to develop the Reformation's message systematically. His theses for the baccalaureate in theology (9 September 1519) emphasized the authority of the scriptures and criticized the doctrine of transubstantiation. His most important work, the *Loci theologici*, through which he created not only the first dogmatic of the Lutheran Reformation but also a new genre in theological literature, arose out of the application of scriptural authority to his work on the biblical text itself.

Part of the curriculum for theologians still included lecturing on Peter Lombard's *Sentences*. Melanchthon wanted to circumvent this normative structure for dogmatics and to offer instead a scripturally based exposition of doctrine. For this purpose he employed an ancient method, recommended by Desiderius Erasmus, of noting the basic concepts—*topoi*, or *loci communes*—of a text in order to appropriate more fully its content. Whereas Erasmus continued to impose upon the text his own list of *loci communes*, Melanchthon required that the *loci* and their organization arise out of the text itself. Although unable consistently to apply this fruitful hermeneutic approach, he nevertheless took from *Romans* the central themes of sin, law, and grace as his organizational principles. To the original, purely soteriological *Loci theologici*, he added in the new edition of 1535 the *loci* of the doctrine of God and Christology from the gospel of John as a defense against the antitrinitarians. In 1543 he completely rewrote the book for a third time. Finally, dissatisfied with the translations of Georg Spalatin and Justus Jonas, he produced a German edition in 1555, which he dedicated to the wife of his friend Joachim Camerarius. During his lifetime translations appeared in Italian, French, Croatian, and Dutch.

For Melanchthon the rediscovery of the gospel—that is, the message concerning the believing sinner's acceptance by grace alone for the sake of Christ—is the central concern of the Reformation. It opposes all attempts to obtain this salvation through human efforts, even partial or preparatory ones. Only the gift of grace bestows certainty; every human component brings with it doubt and leads finally to despair. For this reason the gospel must be proclaimed in sharp contrast to the law. Those who do not follow this distinction and instead limit grace through elements of the law must be rejected. This meant scholastic theologians and, with them, their philosophical partner, Aristotle, who stood for the entire system of scholastic theology and philosophy that humanist thinkers had attacked before Luther and Melanchthon. In the struggle against Aristotle, humanist aversion to sophistic dialectics of the schools became allied with the Reformation's insistence upon faith's freedom from the law. Consequently, he substituted both simpler, humanist lectures for the scholastic ones and expounded theology by means of justification of the sinner by grace alone without human moral work. As a result, the law, and, too, the moral philosopher, Aristotle, could again be studied without prejudice.

The distinction between law and gospel offered the key. For Melanchthon it became the central formula for Luther's evangelical insight. Scholastic theologians, as well as some voices within the Reformation, did not differentiate between the demands of the law and the gift of the gospel and thereby, according to Melanchthon, endangered the certainty of salvation that clings in faith to the gift of grace alone. If, therefore, the "justification of the sinner" occurs only through the judgment of God and may be received only in faith, nevertheless there remains next to this "gospel" the "law," which itself demands further investigation and more precise definition by the theologian.

In this investigation Melanchthon discovered three uses, or functions (*usus, officium*), of the law. Its theological dimension is the completely unfulfillable demand to do good, which drives human beings to recognize their failure and prepares them for faith in the forgiveness offered by Christ for their sin and guilt. The law also contains a general human dimension (*usus civilis*), which orders the common life of all people, visible to everyone and binding on all, even Christians, who perform the good of themselves by virtue of their God-given renewal. For Christians, too, require the instruction and guidance of the law (*tertius usus legis*). According to Melanchthon, the gospel never abrogates civil law. In terms of content the "law," which is inscribed in the hearts of all people by the creator, may be found in the writings of the Old and New Testaments, although, to be sure, the time-bound ceremonies of the Jews do not belong to the generally binding moral laws. Moreover, natural law is also contained in the wisdom of all peoples, in fact most perfectly so in the works of the philosopher Aristotle. The early Reformation polemic against him was intended only to attack the mistaken application of his ethics to the concept of righteousness in theology. His writings on logic, rhetoric, and the natural sciences were in any case exempted from criticism.

Beginning in 1527 Melanchthon lectured on the ethical and political writings of Aristotle. Deciphering the Greek original posed considerable difficulties given the compactness of his style. Melanchthon, however, never managed a complete translation. What he published as commentaries in rapid succession from 1529 were brief, interpretative summaries of the content that amounted to introductions to the proper use of these philosophical texts by Christians. This study of the sources resulted in the particular, systematic delineation of a Christian philosophical ethic. It first appeared in 1538 under the title *Philosophiae moralis epitome* and, like all of Melanchthon's textbooks, underwent many revisions.

At that time Melanchthon had already been working for years on Aristotle's physics. Here he dispensed with the preparatory work of commentary and strove immediately to produce a systematic account reflecting the current state of knowledge—a difficult undertaking for which he sought out the aid of several experts, including the Tübingen professor of medicine and botany Leonhard Fuchs and the Wittenberg professor of medicine Jacob Milichius. Paul Eber, Melanchthon's student and later successor to Johannes Bugenhagen at the city church in Wittenberg, was the co-author. In 1540 his anthropology *De anima* appeared as this work's first section, receiving its final form in 1553. In 1549 the physics was completed. Together these books surveyed teaching about the human being and inanimate objects, including the stars. Melanchthon followed classical and contemporary authors up to the point where they seemed to him to require deviations from the Christian doctrine that the world is not eternal and the soul is immortal. According to Melanchthon's firm conviction, however, even purely philosophical observation refuted the atomism of Democritus: the world did not come into existence by accident but instead is a work whose design points to a rational creator.

Melanchthon was also given administrative duties, not only for his own territorial lords but also for other German and European princes and cities. In this task he always represented a moderating position. During Luther's absence from Wittenberg in 1521–1522 (when he was at Wartburg castle), Melanchthon tried to moderate the effects of the Wittenberg movement, while at the same time being counted among the driving forces behind the reform. Thus, the first evangelical celebration of the Lord's Supper took place among his circle of students. At the University of Wittenberg the scholastic curriculum had to be changed into a humanist and evangelical one. Scholastic lectures on logic and natural science were first expanded to include classical sources and then replaced by them. Alongside formal logic (dialectics), rhetoric was more strongly cultivated, so that beginning in 1523 declamations were interspersed with the regular disputations at the university. Melanchthon's rectorate from 1523 to 1524 was a milestone of this reform. In 1525 the teaching position in Greek was filled by one of his students, and Melanchthon himself obtained a special status that allowed him to serve in the theology faculty without having to give up his extensive responsibilities in philosophy.

As adviser for the reform of school, university, and church, he was often called upon to travel outside electoral Saxony—in 1525 and 1526 to Nuremberg, in 1536 to Tübingen, in 1539 to Leipzig, in 1547 to Jena, in 1557 to Heidelberg, and in 1543 with Martin Bucer to Bonn for an attempted reform of the archbishopric of Cologne, subsequently blocked by Emperor Charles V. His influence extended to Hesse, Anhalt, electoral Brandenburg, Mecklenburg, Pomerania, Prussia, Denmark, and Transylvania. During the Peasants' War he was called upon to arbitrate the dispute in his Palatine homeland, where he, in agreement with Luther, opted for reforms within the existing order. He was greatly involved in the construction of an evangelical territorial church in electoral Saxony, as shown by his work as a visitor in Thuringia from 1527 to 1529. In this connection he wrote the *Unterricht der Visitatoren* (Instruction for Visitors), a brief doctrinal handbook for pastors that also contained a short but influential order for schools.

In place of the outlawed Luther, Melanchthon became the most important theological spokesman of the Protestants at imperial diets and religious colloquies, beginning in Speyer in 1529. At the Diet of Augsburg in 1530 he brought into their final form both the Latin and German versions of the Augsburg Confession and wrote its defense, the Apology. His amicable cooperation with Luther rested upon a fundamental theological agreement that did not exclude differences on particular issues. In the controversy with Erasmus regarding the freedom of the will, Melanchthon held back. When, as visitor in 1527, he experienced firsthand the results of misunderstood and misleading evangelical sermons, he no longer doubted that what was certain for both him and Luther needed to be expressed much more clearly than before—namely, that the freedom of the Christian was not a freedom from the duties and laws of human society but rather an inner freedom before God, which liberated the Christian for service to the neighbor. This freedom obligated a person to act responsibly, although this did not suffice for true liberation. It was limited to relative good and foundered on the absolute. To this extent Melanchthon was of one mind with Luther. Nevertheless, he did not speak about a "bound will." With Erasmus he appealed to freedom as an obligation in the human sphere, to which Luther raised no objection. Melanchthon's carefully nuanced teaching on free will found its way into the Augsburg Confession and thus became normative for Lutheranism. Regarding the doctrine of justification, Melanchthon searched in vain for a compromise with the Roman Catholics at the religious colloquies in Augsburg (1530) and Regensburg (1541).

In Melanchthon's view the episcopal constitution of the church was also worth keeping since the emergency office of bishop exercised by territorial rulers was suspect in his eyes. In place of a church ruled by privy councilors, he hoped for the greater autonomy of an independently constituted church. Such a church could even have a single ruler at its head, albeit only according to human, not divine, right. At the signing of the Schmalkald Articles, which Luther had prepared for the prospective council of the church, Melanchthon affixed his name with the proviso that he would recognize a pope who did not hinder the gospel as the head of the church according to human, not divine, right. At the same time, he wrote in his *Tractatus de potestate papae* that the actual papacy belonged to the realm of the antichrist.

Melanchthon possessed the ability to live in a community with which, while not fully in agreement, he saw himself united in the fundamentals. The abuses he found among the Roman Catholics were unacceptable to him, particularly the exaggerated cult of the saints, the idolatrous adoration of the Host, and the coercion of the conscience in the sacrament of penance that nevertheless could not offer certainty of salvation.

In the Lord's Supper controversy with the Zwinglians, Melanchthon stood completely on Luther's side through the Colloquy of Marburg of 1529. At the Diet of Augsburg (1530) he began to support Bucer's efforts to mediate the dispute. After the diet the political authorities were able to convince the theologians of electoral Saxony that a defensive military alliance was acceptable. In 1531 negotiations for the formation of the Schmalkald League were successfully concluded. The imperial cities of south Germany also belonged to it. These cities provided much of the financing and were thus indispensable partners, but, like Strasbourg, Ulm, Constance, Lindau, and Memmingen, they were more inclined toward Zwingli's view and as a result had not subscribed to the Augsburg Confession. On the other side, Nuremberg remained aloof and loyal to the emperor. An alliance without a common confession was considered highly problematic, but it became imperative only to overcome major doctrinal differences, in this case those concerning the doctrine of the Lord's Supper. The driving force behind this rapprochement was Bucer, the reformer of Strasbourg, but Melanchthon built bridges to the initially skeptical Luther, and when a formal agreement was reached, it was he who wrote the text of the Wittenberg Concord. He also fundamentally reworked and expanded the Latin version of the Augsburg Confession, changing article 10 on the Lord's Supper in light of the Wittenberg Concord. Adherents to this *Confessio Augustana variata* of 1540 no longer had to confess what some objected to, that the "Body of Christ [was] in the bread." Instead, it sufficed to believe that "with" the bread the body of Christ was offered and that Christ was present, perhaps not in the elements but certainly in the celebration of the Lord's Supper. The belief that he was truly present also sufficed for Luther, who did not demand a more precise explanation. Later orthodox Lutherans, however, resented Melanchthon for these changes and pronounced him a "crypto-Calvinist." *The Book of Concord* (1580) and, following it, the current authoritative edition of the confessional documents reproduce not only for dogmatic reasons but also for historical ones the original edition of 1530. At the conclusion of the Peace of Augsburg in 1555, however, the *Augustana* in current circulation was the *Variata,* which was accepted without any difficulty. Elector Frederick III ("the Pious") of the Palatinate could cite it with a clear conscience, even after he had introduced the Heidelberg Catechism.

After the defeat of the Schmalkald League in 1547, Melanchthon volunteered his services to his new territorial prince, Moritz of Saxony, and thus prevented the dissolution of the University of Wittenberg. He succeeded both in preserving evangelical doctrine within electoral Saxony and in avoiding the imposition of the imperial edict on religion (the Augsburg Interim). Nevertheless, concessions regarding external matters that he held to be indifferent (adiaphora) earned him many attacks, even from former students. The resulting battles over doctrine weakened Lutheranism and impaired its ability to negotiate in the new political situation, as became clear at the Colloquy of Worms in 1557. The so-called adiaphoristic controversy thus deserves attention beyond its immediate context because it makes clear that logically coherent thought can founder on irrational emotions, that the formation of political consensus cannot be negotiated with theories alone, and that the effect of symbols on human feelings must also be taken into account. Melanchthon's lifework aimed at the formulation of clear, commonly accepted doctrine. This he never achieved. Instead, he was able to develop a sense for exact formulations and thus prepared the way for orthodoxy. The doctrinal disputes that embittered the last years of his life were the logical consequences of his quest for purity in doctrine because all who thought they had found this purity had to defend it vehemently.

Despite all these controversies Melanchthon achieved in the last decade of his life the height of his theological and intellectual influence. In 1551 he wrote the *Confessio Saxonica* for the Council of Trent; his embassy to Trent in 1552 ended abruptly in Nuremberg on account of the Revolt of the Princes. The 1552 church order of Mecklenburg, a model for other territories, included his theological textbook *Examen Ordinandorum,* which appeared separately in both Latin and German. Close cooperation with the University of Leipzig, where his friend Camerarius had worked since 1541, as well as with the government in Dresden regarding the formation of an educational system for electoral Saxony, led him again in the spring of 1560 to an examination of candidates held in Leipzig. On the trip he caught a cold from which he died in Wittenberg on 19 April. He was laid to rest next to Luther in the castle church.

Melanchthon's historical significance may chiefly be seen in his recognition of the problem of the relation between humanism and the Reformation (that is, the Greco-Roman and biblical heritage in the history of the West), his coming to terms with the problem, and his introduction of the results of his solution into the thought and organization of both ecclesiastical and educational reform in Germany. In so doing he avoided the twin dangers that either the fledgling reform movement would get sidetracked into an anti-intellectual spiritualism or, at the opposite extreme, philosophy would be imposed upon theology, knowledge upon faith, and reason upon revelation. Because Melanchthon allowed both poles to retain their own characteristics, he was able to bring about a fruitful joining of the two. He was certainly not the only one who did this, but he was one of the first, and his solution was ingeniously simple and enlightening, based as it was on the distinction between law and gospel. Together with Luther and several others, Melanchthon created a Christian and humanist educational system that was taken up and further developed by others, and it continued to be influential through the Enlightenment and nineteenth-century neohumanism into the twentieth century.

BIBLIOGRAPHY

Primary Sources

Bretschneider, Carl Gottlieb, and Heinrich Ernst Bindseil, eds. *Philippi Melanthonis Opera quae supersunt omnia.* 28 vols. Reprint, Frankfurt a.M., 1963. Corpus Reformatorum, vols. 1–28.

Scheible, Heinz, ed. *Melanchthons Briefwechsel: Kritische und kommentierte Gesamtausgabe.* Stuttgart, 1977–.

Stupperich, Robert, ed. *Melanchthons Werke in Auswahl.* 7 vols. Gütersloh, 1951–1975; partial 2d ed., 1978–1983.

Supplementa Melanchthoniana: Werke Philipp Melanchthons, die im Corpus Reformatorum vermißt werden. 5 vols. Reprint, Frankfurt a.M., 1968.

Secondary Sources

Bayer, Oswald. "Die Kirche braucht liberale Erudition: Das Theologieverständnis Melanchthons." *Kerygma und Dogma* 36 (1990), 218–244.

Fraenkel, Peter. *Testimonia Patrum: The Function of the Patristic Argument in the Theology of Philip Melanchthon.* Travaux d'Humanisme et Renaissance, vol. 46. Geneva, 1961.

Green, Lowell C. *Melanchthon in English: New Translations into English with a Registry of Previous Translations. A Memorial to William Hammer, 1909–1976.* Sixteenth Century Bibliography, vol. 22. Saint Louis, 1982.

Hammer, Wilhelm. *Die Melanchthonforschung im Wandel der Jahrhunderte: Ein beschreibendes Verzeichnis.* 3 vols. Quellen und Forschungen zur Reformationsgeschichte, vols. 35, 36, 49. Gütersloh, 1967–1981.

Hartfelder, Karl. *Philipp Melanchthon als Praeceptor Germaniae.* Reprint, Nieuwkoop, 1972.

Manschreck, Clyde L. *Melanchthon: The Quiet Reformer.* Reprint, Westport, Conn., 1975.

Meijering, E. P. *Melanchthon and Patristic Thought: The Doctrines of Christ and Grace, the Trinity and the Creation.* Studies in the History of Christian Thought, vol. 32. Leiden, 1983.

Rhein, Stefan, and Heinz Schieble, eds. *Melanchthonschriften der Stadt Bretten.* Sigmaringen, Germany, 1988–.

Rogness, Michael. *Philip Melanchthon: Reformer without Honor.* Minneapolis, 1969.

Scheible, Heinz. "Philipp Melanchthon." In *Gestalten der Kirchengeschichte,* edited by Martin Greschat, vol. 6, pp. 75–101. Stuttgart, 1981.

———. "Luther and Melanchthon." *Lutheran Quarterly* n.s. 4 (1990), 317–339.

———. "Melanchthon." In *Theologische Realenzyklopädie,* pp. 371–410. Berlin and New York, 1992.

Stupperich, Robert. "Melanchthon." In *Neue Deutsche Biographie,* vol. 16, pp. 741–745. Berlin, 1990.

Wengert, Timothy J. *Philip Melanchthon's Annotationes in Johannem in Relation to Its Predecessors and Contemporaries.* Travaux d'Humanisme et Renaissance, vol. 220. Geneva, 1987.

HEINZ SCHEIBLE

MELANTRICH OF AVENTIN, George

MELANTRICH OF AVENTIN, George (Czech, Jiřík Roždalovský; 1511?–1580), a publisher and printer in Prague (1547–1580). Having received a B.A. from Prague University (1535), Melantrich probably obtained some experience abroad without matriculating at foreign universities. He supposedly stayed in Wittenberg, Basel, and Nuremberg.

He began his public activities as the translator of the works of the German Lutheran humanist and theologian Urbanus Rhegius: *Dialog über Christi Gespräch mit zwey Jüngern auf dem Wege nach Emaus* (1545), from the German, and *Catechesis,* from the Latin, which was Melantrich's first publication in Prague, dated 6 July 1547, "on the day of Master Jan of Husinec, the faithful apostle of God in Bohemia." After his victory in the Schmalkald War, the Bohemian king Ferdinand I prohibited all public printing in Bohemia with the exception of his court printer, Bartoloměj Netolický. Melantrich found resort in his printing works and in 1549 they published together and with the royal privilege the entire Czech Bible. When the king again began to licence printing works by others than his court printer, Melantrich bought in 1553 Netolický's printing works and began to undertake his own business. During those years he gained wealth and social prominence, and thanks to his managerial gifts, well thought out publishing policy, and broad cultural outlook, he was able to publish large works of weighty content and high artistic quality; two of them successfully found their way into foreign book markets (Pietro Andrea Mattioli, the physician of the Hapsburgs who lived in Prague: *Epistolarum medicinalium libri quinque,* 1561, and, by the same author, *New Kreuterbuch,* 1563, both published in cooperation with the Venetian printer Vincento Valgrisio). Melantrich printed at least 225 publications, of which 111 were in Czech, 75 in Latin, 3 in German, and 1 in Italian; the rest were multilingual textbooks and a dictionary. He also printed the official minutes of governmental assemblies, humanist writings, political news, moral treatises, writings of legal, administrative, astronomic, economic, and medical content, calendars, and last but not least, religious works. He published works of at least 85 authors.

Melantrich's role in spreading the Reformation was indirect, but efficient. It resulted from his printing, above all from his five illustrated editions of the entire Vulgate Bible for the Bohemian Utraquist church. Included among the works he published by choice and his own initiative, each accompanied by his own introduction, were books by Urbanus Rhegius, Desiderius Erasmus, the Dominican court preacher Mathias Sittard, Girolamo Savonarola, the Saxon preacher Thomas Günther, and the martyr Embulus Methudius.

BIBLIOGRAPHY

Bohatcová, Mirjam. "Vydavatelský rámec Českých předbělohorských biblí" (The Publishing Context of Czech Bibles from the Time before the Battle of White Mountain). *Strahovská knihovna*5/6 (1970/1971), 255–277.

———. "Prager Drucke der Werke Pierandrea Mattiolis aus den Jahren 1558–1602." *Gutenberg-Jahrbuch*, pp. 167–185. N.p., 1985.

———. "První český nakladatelský dům" (The First Czech Publishing House). In *Česká kniha v proměnách staletí* (Bohemian Books throughout the Centuries), edited by Mirjam Bohatcová et al, pp. 214–227. Prague, 1990. With further information on older literature.

Horák, František. 'Signety starých českých tiskařů" (The Signets of Old Bohemian Printers). *Ročenka českých knihtiskařů* 24 (1941), 35–96.

———. *Česká kniha v minulosti a její výzdoba* (The Czech Book and its Decoration in the Past). Prague, 1948.

MIRJAM BOHATCOVÁ

MELCHIORITES. An Anabaptist sect crystallized around the personal authority and beliefs of Melchior Hoffman, in a narrow sense the Melchiorites did not last beyond 1540, when, under the influence of a religious compromise devised by Martin Bucer, they were reconciled with the established churches of Hesse and Strasbourg. But distinctive Melchiorite traits marked all Anabaptist groups in north Germany, the Baltic lands, the northern and southern Netherlands, and England—the Münster Anabaptists, the Batenburgers, the followers of David Joris, and the Mennonites were all Melchiorite offshoots.

In June 1529 the lay preacher Melchior Hoffman arrived in Strasbourg following his expulsion from the Scandinavian and Baltic lands, where he had worked energetically to spread the Reformation but had become an increasingly irritating thorn in the side of the Lutheran pastorate. He soon had similar difficulties with the Strasbourg preachers, but threw himself into lively interaction with the religious dissenters of the town, particularly Clemens Ziegler and Kaspar von Schwenckfeld. He entered a circle of lay "prophets" in Strasbourg; Lienhard and Ursula Jost, Barbara Rebstock, and Johannes Eisenburg were its most distinguished members. Even in his earlier activity in the Baltic lands Hoffman preached an apocalyptic message centered on 1533; now his apocalyptic focus was reinforced by persons like Rebstock who had been earlier touched by the apocalyptic Anabaptism of Hans Hut. This prophetic circle convinced Hoffman that he was the returned Elijah of *Revelation* 11, one of the witnesses of the apocalypse, and that Strasbourg was the spiritual Jerusalem from which 144,000 apostles would go out to convert the world.

Even more characteristic of Melchiorite ideas was the unique twist Hoffman gave to the christological discussions of the Strasbourg dissidents. He held that the body of Christ was "heavenly," that it had resided in but was not "of" the Virgin Mary, and that only through being free of sinful human nature could Christ be an effective redeemer. This Christology, which interpreters have often labeled "docetic," is the signature of northern, "Melchiorite" Anabaptism, shared by Bernhard Rothmann, David Joris, Georg Schnabel, Anabaptists executed in England, and Menno Simons, but foreign to Pilgram Marpeck, Melchior Rinck, the Hutterites, and the Swiss Brethren. Besides the characteristic apocalyptic and christological ideas, Hoffman and his Strasbourg followers affirmed the widespread Anabaptist view that God's grace was universally extended and that salvation depended on the response of human free will.

Hoffman also wrote a work on baptism, *Die Ordonnantie Godts* (The Ordinance of God; 1530), in which he endorsed believers' baptism. In 1530 he baptized extensively in Emden in East Frisia, but when in 1531 nine of the newly baptized Melchiorites, now active in Amsterdam, were executed by the Habsburg government of the Netherlands, Hoffman suspended baptism for two years. It was to be resumed, apparently, only as an accompaniment of the events of the end time. The Melchiorites opposed infant baptism, but theirs was a spiritualist orientation, attaching less value to the external rite. Hence they had only a weak commitment to believers' baptism, a definite factor in their eventual return to the established church. Melchiorite offshoot sects, such as the Batenburgers and the followers of Joris, likewise found reasons to abandon external adult baptism.

Melchiorite ideas spread from Strasbourg to the Netherlands and from the Netherlands to Münster. Preachers who came to Münster from Wassenberg in Jülich, Heinrich Roll and Hermann Staprade, won the reformer of Münster, Bernhard Rothmann, to a Melchiorite critique of infant baptism in the summer of 1533. Meanwhile in May 1533 Hoffman was imprisoned in Strasbourg, expecting that the end of the world would soon bring his release. In the uncertainties of late 1533 Jan Matthijs, the Haarlem baker, proclaimed that he, too, was an apocalyptic witness and that he had a divine commission to resume adult baptism. Matthijs and his followers gained control of the Melchiorite movement in Münster in January 1534; when they won political power there in an apparent miracle in the following month, the Melchiorite sect in the Netherlands fell under the control of the new prophet. The imprisoned Hoffman was himself impressed: "At Münster they have a prophet named Jan Matthijs who says he is one of the divine witnesses. Münster shall not be overcome." Only after the resistance of the Münster Anabaptists was finally broken in June 1535 did it become apparent to the disoriented remnants of Melchiorite Anabaptism that topics like the physical kingdom of God on earth (which Hoffman seemed to endorse in one of his last writings before being imprisoned) and polygamous marriage required a searching reexamination.

The representatives of various Münsterite-Melchiorite remnant groups who met at Bocholt in Westphalia in August 1536 tried but failed to halt the splintering process. The Bocholt meeting signaled the separate identity of four groups that were to some degree alienated from the Strasbourg Melchiorites such as Jost, Rebstock, and Eisenburg: a Münsterite remnant based in Oldenburg, the Batenburger terrorists, the followers of Obbe Philips (later replaced by Menno Simons), who had rejected prophetic militancy, and now the adherents of a new spiritualizing leader, David Joris of Delft. Nonetheless, Jan Matthijs of Middelberg, a prominent Dutch Anabaptist during the siege of Münster, whom Henry VIII was to burn at Smithfield in 1538, presented himself at Bocholt as an unreconstructed Melchiorite, still waiting for pious rulers and prophets to bring on Christ's earthly kingdom. Another group of Melchiorites affiliated with the Strasbourg "mother church" were the Hessians, led by Georg Schnabel.

Both Jan van Batenburg and Joris made trips to Strasbourg to convince the Melchiorite congregation there of their credentials as the anointed successor of the imprisoned Hoffman. Joris's visit of June 1538 is well documented. He and Barbara Rebstock exchanged prophetic imprecations, but the chief weight among the Melchiorites had passed from the prophets to two Latin-educated leaders, Johannes Eisenburg and a newcomer, Peter Tasch from the Cologne area. Eisenburg and Tasch insisted that Joris validate his calling on the basis of scripture, which he did not do to their satisfaction.

Later in 1538 Tasch took the occasion of a debate between Bucer and Melchiorite Anabaptists imprisoned in Hesse to initiate secret discussions aimed at a reconciliation of the Melchiorites with the established church. The Hessian Melchiorites produced a confession in December 1538 in which they withdrew their condemnation of infant baptism, without, however, recognizing it as scriptural. For his part, Bucer worked to introduce an order of discipline into the Hessian church, affirming the Anabaptist insistence on the need for an improvement of life among the adherents of the official Reformation. In the period 1538 to 1540, the Melchiorite movement, in the precise sense of the term, was dissolved. The Strasbourg prophet Lienhard Jost returned to the Reformed church; Eisenburg and Tasch, the educated Melchiorites who resisted David Joris, now toured the prisons advocating acceptance of the compromise confession of December 1538. The exiled John Calvin worked for the conversion of French-speaking Melchiorites in Strasbourg. An estimated two hundred Melchiorites rejoined the Hessian church. In Strasbourg some Melchiorite Anabaptists rejected the apostasy of the Melchiorite leaders and became Swiss Brethren. In April 1539 Tasch and Eisenburg visited Hoffman in prison and won from him a statement accepting infant baptism and calling on his followers to do so. While the authenticity of the retraction of a sick prisoner at the end of six years of dentention can naturally be questioned, the document has a good deal of plausibility. The recantation made no mention of Christology; but the well-informed contemporary, Nicholas Blesdijk, reports that Hoffman eventually disavowed his Christology, too, and circulated this retraction among his followers. The Melchiorite Christology was, however, continued among the Mennonites well beyond the sixteenth century.

BIBLIOGRAPHY

Brecht, Martin. "Die Theologie Bernhard Rothmanns." *Jahrbuch für Westfälische Kirchengeschichte* 78 (1985), 49–82. Emphasizes the assimilation of Melchiorite ideas in Münster in 1533, well before the first rebaptisms of January 1534.

Deppermann, Klaus. *Melchior Hoffman: Social Unrest and Apocalyptic Visions in the Age of Reformation.* Translated by Malcolm Wren. Edinburgh, 1987. English translation of *Melchior Hoffman: soziale Unruhen und apokalyptische Visionen im Zeitalter der Reformation*, Göttingen, 1979. This is the major recent work on Hoffman; it stresses his connection with the prophetic Strasbourg Melchiorite movement and that movement's decline following the fall of the Münster kingdom.

Krahn, Cornelius. *Dutch Anabaptism: Origin, Spread, Life and Thought, 1450–1600.* 2d ed. Scottdale, Pa., 1981. This appraisal, while written from a Mennonite perspective, contains two extensive chapters on Melchior Hoffman, the Melchiorites, and the Münsterites.

Packull, Werner O. "Melchior Hoffman—a Recanted Anabaptist in Schwäbisch Hall?" *Mennonite Quarterly Review* 57 (1983), 83–111. Although the speculation that Hoffman may have survived his imprisonment is doubtful, as Packull admits, the article corrects Deppermann on the character of the discussions between the Strasbourg pastors and Hoffman in 1539 and afterward.

———. "The Melchiorites and the Ziegenhain Order of Discipline, 1538–1539." In *Anabaptism Revisited: Essays on Anabaptist/Mennonite Studies in Honor of C.J. Dyck*, edited by Walter Klaassen, pp. 11–28. Scottdale, Pa., 1992. Contains a substantial treatment of the discussions between Martin Bucer and Peter Tasch and the subsequent dissolution of the Melchiorites.

Stayer, James M. *Anabaptists and the Sword.* 2d ed. Lawrence, Kans., 1976. One section is devoted to the various ideas held by Melchiorite sects on government and violence, with a more inclusive definition of "Melchiorite" than in this article.

———. "Was Dr. Kuehler's Conception of Early Dutch Anabaptism Historically Sound? The Historical Discussion of Anabaptist Münster 450 Years Later." *Mennonite Quarterly Review* 60 (1986), 261–288. A discussion of the recent historiography of Münster Anabaptism that stresses its Melchiorite background.

Waite, Gary K. *David Joris and Dutch Anabaptism, 1524–1543.* Waterloo, Ont., 1990. Stresses the interweaving of David Joris's career with the Melchiorite movement and its offshoots from 1532 to 1539, with a special chapter devoted to his encounter with the Strasbourg Melchiorites in 1538.

JAMES M. STAYER

MELIUS, Péter Somogyi (also Juhász; 1536–1572), pastor, theologian, and superintendent of the Reformed church in Hungary. He was born into a noble family in Horhi (in Somogyi county), southern Hungary, which was occupied by the Turks. Melius (the Greek version of his family name, Juhász) received his basic education in Hungary, studying from 1549 to 1552 in Tolna under two Lutheran teachers, Mátyás Tövisi and Imre Eszéki, and from

1552 to 1554 with István Szegedi Kis, who taught in the spirit of the Helvetic Reformed movement. On 25 October 1556 he matriculated at the University of Wittenberg, where he became the senior of the Liber Bursae Wittenbergae (Hungarian Coetus) and earned his master's degree.

His stay in Wittenberg was brief, however, for in 1558 he was called to Debrecen to succeed Márton Kálmáncsehi. He remained in Debrecen for the rest of his life, and during his pastorate he made the city the center of Reformed theology in Hungary; he was aided by Gallus Huszár, who in 1561 settled and set up a printing press in Debrecen. Melius was a productive if eclectic theologian and drew extensively from the works of Martin Bucer and Heinrich Bullinger, as well as John Calvin, Johannes Brenz and Philipp Melanchthon. In 1558 Melius, then only twenty-two years old, quickly emerged as a leader of the Reformed in Hungary when he prepared material that became the basis for the Confession of Maros Vásárhely (Neumarkt) on the Lord's Supper. The first Protestant confession prepared in the Hungarian language, it is in conformity with, but not totally dependent upon, the views of Huldrych Zwingli. According to the confession, believers, through the physical reception of the elements and the mediation of the Holy Spirit, receive the benefits of the Sacrament, while unbelievers do not receive the body of Christ.

The issuance of this confession, however, initiated years of struggle among the Hungarian Protestants which resulted in the production of a considerable number of polemical works and confessions. In 1561 Matthias Hebler, the Saxon Lutheran superintendent in Sibiu (Hermanstadt, Nagyvárad), Transylvania, appealed to the German universities to condemn the views of Melius, to which Melius responded with his *Refutatio* defending his own views and those of the Reformed. Although he translated a catechism of Calvin and developed his own catechism on the basis of Calvin's writings (1562), he was much influenced by Bullinger. On the request of János Fejérthóy, Bullinger sent an open letter to the Hungarian Reformed, which was published in 1559 by Huszár in Magyaróvár (Altenburg) and Caspar Heltai in Cluj (Klausenburg). When the bishop of Eger sought to force the predominantly Reformed inhabitants of his residence to return to Catholicism, Melius and Gregor Szegedi prepared for them the Confessio Catholica, also known as the Confessio Debrecinensis, the longest Reformed confession to be printed during the sixteenth century. In it doctrinal, moral, legal, and even medical and scientific questions are discussed. As senior of the Reformed, Melius attended the Synod of Tarczal-Torda (1562), which adopted a confession of Théodore de Bèze and thus Reformed formulations concerning questions on the Lord's Supper and predestination. Melius, however, had to contend with the growing influence of antitrinitarianism among the Magyar Reformed. Francis Dávid, whom Melius had earlier converted from Lutheranism to the Reformed faith, had been influenced by Giorgio Biandrata, who had been spreading antitrinitarian views throughout eastern Hungary and Siebenbürgen. In February 1567 Melius called a synod to meet in Debrecen. It brought together seventeen seniors from along both sides of the Tisza River, and they accepted the Confessio Catholica in Latin and Hungarian versions that had been prepared by Melius and were directed against the antitrinitarians. The synod also adopted the Second Helvetic Confession and can be said to be the constitutive synod of the Magyar Reformed church. Two years later Melius sought to distance the Reformed even more from the antitrinitarians and prepared a tract that became the basis of the Confessio Csengerina adopted by the synod at Csenger in July 1570. Thus, the Reformed in Hungary had decided to follow the ecclesiastical practices of Zurich, remove altars and pictures from the churches, utilize Hungarian in the liturgy, celebrate Communion only on festival days, and abolish the use of ceremonial ecclesiastical vestments, the ringing of bells, and funeral services held in the church. It retained, however, the use of spiritual songs alongside the Psalter. Melius died in Debrecen on 15 December 1572 and was survived by his wife and two daughters.

BIBLIOGRAPHY

Primary Sources

Melius (Juhász), Peter. *Kristus közbe iarasarol valo predicacioc, mellyeket Melius Peter a döbrötzöni lelki pasztor irt.* Debrecen, 1561.

———. *Catekismus: Az egesz keresztieni tudomannac fondamentoma es sommaia a szent irasbol ezue szedettetet es meg emendattatot . . . Calvinus Ianus irassa szerint az Somogi Melius Petertol.* Debrecen, 1562.

———. *Confessio catholica de praecipuis fidei articulis exhibita, sacratissimo et catholico Romanorum imperatori Ferdinando et filio sue i. maiestatis d. regi Maximiliano, ab universo exercitu equitum et peditum s.r.m. a nobilibus item et incolis totius vallis Agrinae, in nomine Sanctae Trinitatis ad foedus Dei custodien. iuramento fidei copulatorum et decertantium pro vera fide et religione, in Christo ex Scripturis Sacris fundata.* Debrecen, 1562.

———. *Confessio ecclesiae Debreciensis de praecipuis articulis et quaestionibus quibusdam, necessariis ad consulendum turbatis conscientiis, exhibita ut sit testimonium doctrinae et fidei contra calumniatores sanae doctrinae.* Debrecen, 1562.

———. *Apologia et abstersio Ecclesiae Debreciensis a calumniis quibus temere apud Academias et principes accusatur.* Debrecen, 1564.

———. *Refutatio confessionis de coena Domini Matthiae Hebler, Dionysii Alesii et his coniunctoru(m), una cum iudiciiquatuor academiaru(m), quae Saxonibus Transylvanicis diplomatis papalis instar missa sunt anno D. 1561.* Debrecen, 1567.

———. *Articuli ex verbo Dei . . . politiam ecclesiasticam et formandam vitam Christianam in omnibus ordinibus necessariam.* Debrecen, 1567.

———. *Brevis confessio pastorum ad synodum Debrecii celebratam 24, 25, et 26 Februa. anno D. 1567 convocatorum.* Debrecen, 1567.

———. *Az egész Szent Irásból való igaz tudomány.* Debrecen, 1570.

———. *Principia quaedam in theologia et philosophia immota.* Debrecen, 1570.

Secondary Sources

Bucsay, Mihály. "Leitgedanken der Theologie Bullingers bei Petrus Melius: Ein Beitrag zur Austrahlung des Zürcher Reformators nach Ungarn." In *Heinrich Bullinger, 1504–1575: Gesammelte Aufsätze zum*

400. *Todestag,* edited by Ulrich Gäbler and Erland Herkenrath, vol. 2, pp. 197–214. Zurich, 1975.
Kathona, Géza. "Méliusz Péter és életmúve." *Studia et Acta Ecclesiastica* 2 (1967), 105–192.
Révész, Imre. "Méliusz és Kálvin." In *Kálvin élete és a Kálvinizmus,* pp. 295–340. Debrecen, 1936.
Szinnyei, Joszef. *Magyar irók: Élete es munkai.* Vol. 8. Budapest, 1902. Bibliography of Melius's writings.

DAVID P. DANIEL

MELVILLE, Andrew (1545–1622), Scottish Presbyterian leader and educational reformer, and the youngest son of an Angus laird. Educated at Montrose grammar school, where he gained a knowledge of Greek, and St. Andrews University, which he entered on the eve of the Reformation, Melville pursued further studies abroad: at Paris, where he heard Petrus Ramus lecture; Poitiers, for law; Geneva, for divinity under Théodore de Bèze; and Lausanne, to hear Ramus again. In 1574 he returned home after a decade's absence to become principal of Glasgow University. There he introduced far-reaching reforms in the structure and content of teaching. The outmoded system of "regenting," whereby a teacher conducted his class through the entire curriculum, was discarded in favor of specialist teaching, and a humanist curriculum on Ramist lines replaced the dominance of the philosophies in arts. In divinity, instruction was offered in Hebrew and Aramaic.

By 1580 Melville left for St. Andrews University to head St. Mary's College, reconstituted as a divinity school. Although he is largely remembered as an early protagonist of Presbyterianism—the man who was later to call King James VI "God's silly vassal"—there are grounds for believing that in his own day his academic reforms were far more innovative than any changes he advocated for the church. The Reformed church, after all, claimed to adhere to the tradition of the "best reformed churches" on the Continent in theology and polity. Melville's intention was not to contradict Reformation principles but, in reinforcing them, to remedy some defects in ecclesiastical administration. Unlike the church, which had experienced a thoroughgoing Reformation in 1560, the three universities, as seminaries for the ministry, seemed at best to be half reformed until Melville gave a lead by integrating them more closely in the work of the Reformed church. At the same time, using the General Assembly as his platform, he helped guide the church away from its fleeting experiment with episcopacy in 1572 and toward a more committed Presbyterian structure, as depicted in the second *Book of Discipline* of 1578, which he helped draft.

In the end only the ingenuity of James VI and his relentless determination to outwit the Presbyterians prevented Melville's complete ascendancy. Forbidden by the king from attending Assembly and presbytery meetings, deprived of his rector's office in St. Andrews, and imprisoned in the Tower of London (1607–1611), Melville was forbidden to return home and died in exile in France, though many of the ideals he espoused received tangible expression in the Presbyterian revolution of the 1640s.

BIBLIOGRAPHY

Durkan, John, and James Kirk. *University of Glasgow, 1451–1577.* Glasgow, 1977.
Kirk, James. *Patterns of Reform: Continuity and Change in the Reformation Kirk.* Edinburgh, 1989.
McCrie, Thomas. *Life of Andrew Melville* (1819). Edinburgh, 1956.

JAMES KIRK

MENIUS, Justus (also Joducus Menig; 1499–1558), Lutheran pastor and theologian whose many years of labor in the western part of Saxony earned him the title "Reformer of Thuringia." After a humanist education at Erfurt, he studied under Philipp Melanchthon and Martin Luther at Wittenberg. From 1523 until the year before his death, his work centered on Thuringia, most notably as a teacher and pastor in Erfurt (1525–1528) and as church superintendent in Eisenach (1529–1547) and Gotha (1546–1556). In 1557 he went to the Saint Thomas church in Leipzig, where he died in August of the following year.

Menius's concerns were pastoral. He participated in the first (1528–1529) and subsequent church visitations in the Ernestine Saxon lands of Thuringia and, after its acceptance of Lutheranism in 1539, in Albertine Saxon territories both within and beyond Thuringia. This work prompted him to publish an abbreviated form of Luther's Small Catechism for use in the parishes (1532). Pastoral concern for moral renewal led him to address the place of good works in the life of the Christian and also to write a book on the proper character of a Christian household (*Oeconomia Christiana*; 1529, with many reprints). To his persuasive preaching is attributed the espousal of the Reformation in Mühlhausen (1542–1544).

Menius was a translator of Luther and Melanchthon's Latin works, most notably of Luther's 1535 *Galatians* commentary (1539). He wrote a commentary on *I Samuel* (1532). His attendance at some of the major Reformation events—the Marburg and Hagenau/Worms colloquies (1529 and 1540–1541, respectively) and conferences resulting in the Wittenberg Concord (1536) and the Schmalkald Articles (1537)—as well as laudatory prefaces by Luther and Melanchthon in some of his books, attest to his stature. He is remembered primarily, however, for his controversial writings. While in Erfurt he attacked the city's Roman Catholic party in two tracts of 1527. Anabaptist preaching in Thuringia, prompted Menius to become a most knowledgeable and prolific opponent, writing four books against Anabaptism between 1530 and 1551. Having argued in his *I Samuel* commentary that there are boundaries to lawful rule and, therefore, the possibility of legitimate political disobedience and resistance, he contributed to the Lutheran cause in the Schmalkald War its most thorough argument for the right of resistance to political authority (*Von der Notwehr Unterricht*; 1547). All of Menius's controversial works bear intemperate language; in this case Melanchthon quietly exorcised his text while it was at the printer so that it appeared in two quite varied forms, violent and moderate. He attacked the Augsburg Interim (1548), Emperor Charles V's program for restoring religious unity to Germany, in opinions that he wrote to the young princes ruling Ernestine Saxony on behalf of their imprisoned father; these opinions he then reworked into a confession (1549) that appeared under the names of the young princes.

His final controversies were with fellow Lutherans and correspond to the deep divisions in Lutheranism after the Schmalkald War. He supported an adiaphoron—exorcism in baptism—in an argument in 1550. He wrote against Andreas Osiander's doctrine of justification in 1552, after which Duke John Frederick of Ernestine Saxony sent him to Prussia in an unsuccessful attempt to win its court away from those teachings. Shortly thereafter Nikolaus von Amsdorf drew Menius into the struggle the Gnesio-Lutherans were fighting against Melanchthon, Georg Major, and the other Wittenberg and Leipzig theologians (the Philippists). Amsdorf demanded Menius's condemnation of Major's proposition "good works are necessary to salvation," which he refused to do, reflecting his long-standing concern that his parishioners fashion upright lives, as well as his most recent book against Anabaptists, which included an accusation of moral laxity among them. A flurry of treatises ensued from both sides (1555–1558). Despite Menius's long service to the princes of Ernestine Saxony, Amsdorf succeeded in forcing him from their lands, and Melanchthon secured for him the call to Leipzig for what turned out to be his final service to the Lutheran movement.

BIBLIOGRAPHY

Horst, Alvin H. "The Theology of Justus Menius." Th.D. diss., Concordia Seminary, 1973. Adequate examination of Menius's theological works.

Kolb, Robert. *Nikolaus von Amsdorf, 1483–1565: Popular Polemics in the Preservation of Luther's Legacy*. Nieuwkoop, 1978. Chapter 3 contains a masterful analysis of Menius's last battle.

Oyer, John S. *Lutheran Reformers against Anabaptists: Luther, Melanchthon and Menius and the Anabaptists of Central Germany*. The Hague, 1964. Gives full descriptions of Menius's tracts against the Anabaptists.

Peterson, Luther D. "Justus Menius, Philipp Melanchthon, and the 1547 Treatise, *Von der Notwehr Unterricht*." *Archiv für Reformationsgeschichte* 81 (1990), 138–157. Explains the complicated authorship and the political theory of the treatise.

Schmidt, Gustav L. *Justus Menius: Der Reformator Thüringens* (1867). 2 vols. Reprint, Nieuwkoop, 1968. The standard biography, long-winded and hagiographical; despite its length, it does not examine some of the important tracts and events.

Verzeichnis der im deutschen Sprachbereich erschienenen Drucke des XVI. Jahrhunderts. Struttgart, 1983–. Vol. 13, nos. 4536–4604.

LUTHER D. PETERSON

MENNONITES. This term is presently used to designate most of the churches descending from sixteenth-century Anabaptism. Since the rise of Anabaptism predates Menno Simon's joining the movement by some ten years, not all groups have adopted the term. Communal Anabaptists, or Hutterites, are named after their most important leader, Jacob Hutter (1500?–1536). The Amish are named after their most important leader, Jacob Ammann (c.1644–c.1730). Since 1796 the Dutch followers of Menno have called themselves Doopsgezinde; Swiss Anabaptists still prefer the term Taufgesinnte. Under the influence of Ludwig Keller (1849–1915) and his writings, German Mennonites in the late 1800s toyed with the idea of calling themselves altevangelische Taufgesinnte. Since the term Menist was first used in an edict of 1545 at Emden by Countess Anna of East Friesland in an attempt to distinguish the peaceful followers of Menno from those of David Joris and Jan van Batenburg, it seems proper to begin with Menno. But since Menno joined a movement already underway, it is more accurate to begin with the origin of the movement in the Netherlands.

It is generally agreed that Anabaptism came to the northern regions of the Holy Roman Empire through the activity of Melchior Hoffman (1495?–1543). He burst on the scene in 1523 as a Lutheran lay missionary in Livonia. Quickly moving his appeal for reform from the ruling circles to the masses, Hoffman became suspect and was forced in June 1525 to return to Wittenberg for a certificate of orthodoxy from Martin Luther. With this in hand he returned to Livonia, only to be expelled from Tartu (Dorpat) and then Reval (Tallinn), eventually being forced to seek sanctuary in Stockholm, where he published his commentary on *Daniel* in 1527. By this time his sermons, too, had begun to concentrate on apocalyptic themes. For a time he was in Lübeck, where he briefly came into the good graces of Frederick I, king of Denmark, and was appointed deacon at the Nikolai Church in Kiel. Here he acquired a printing press that he used increasingly to attack Luther's surrogates. He returned to Wittenberg in 1527, but this time there was no certificate of orthodoxy waiting for him. He now also began to attack Luther's doctrine of the real presence. Little wonder that his ideas were condemned at the Flensburg Disputation of 1529, forcing Hoffman to flee.

Like a number of other dissidents from Luther's views on the Eucharist, Hoffman journeyed south to Strasbourg, but even here his radical ideas were rejected, and so Hoffman turned his back on the magisterial Reformation. He came under the influence of spiritualist Anabaptists led by Hans

Denck and the "Strasbourg Prophets." Under their influence he came to extol the "inner word," free will, and a grace that illuminates all men. He also came to differentiate between a first and second justification. The first consisting of the cancellation of original sin through the redemptive death of Christ; the second coming through the Holy Spirit by means of which one could achieve perfection. In dialogue with Kaspar von Schwenckfeld (1489–1561), he developed a doctrine concerning the "heavenly flesh of Christ," according to which Christ passed through Mary like water through a sieve. The most important change, however, was the development of his apocalyptic thinking. He argued that Christ's return was imminent but had to be prepared by an act of cleansing in the world. These apocalyptic views might have derived from the latter part of Martin Cellarius's *De Operibus Dei* as reflected in Wolfgang Capito's commentary on *Hosea*. Hoffman came to regard himself a new Elijah and began to predict the return of Christ in Strasbourg for 1533.

In the meantime, Hoffman returned to Emden, East Friesland, where in 1530 he baptized some three hundred persons. There can be little doubt that the soil in northern Germany and the Netherlands had been prepared by the Sacramentarians and the Brothers of the Common Life, for the spread of the movement was phenomenal. But with the spread of the movement there also came persecution, which forced Hoffman to leave Emden and return to Strasbourg. In his place he left Jan Volkertszoon (also known as Trijpmaker). In Strasbourg Hoffmann maintained a low profile, returning to the Netherlands in 1531, when he is said to have baptized another fifty or so persons. But when Volkertszoon and ten others were executed at The Hague on 5 December 1531, Hoffman ordered a suspension of baptizing—perhaps under the influence of Sebastian Franck and Schwenckfeld, who had advocated a suspension of the apostolic ceremonies until a new command was received from God through a new prophet. The suspension was to last two years, though preaching and admonition were to continue. The decree was issued by Hoffman from Strasbourg, to which he had once more returned. When the authorities were made aware of his presence in the city, he was expelled. Once more he traveled north, perhaps to Hesse and from there to Leeuwarden, where Obbe Philips, one of his followers, was staying. But in the spring of 1533 he returned yet again to Strasbourg, this time to await Christ's return and the terrible slaughter of the godless that would precede it. The city council interpreted the prediction as a threat of revolution and had Hoffman incarcerated. There he died some ten years later a forgotten man.

Meanwhile, the former Lutheran Bernhard Rothmann had begun another Anabaptist movement in the Westphalian city of Münster. Educated at the universities of Cologne and Wittenberg, Rothmann by the early 1530s was moving through Zwinglianism to advanced radicalism. He knew Philipp Melanchthon well and was also acquainted with Luther. Around May 1531 he, too, came to Strasbourg where he met Martin Bucer and Capito and may also have come to know Cellarius and Schwenckfeld. By this time he was already familiar with Franck and Hoffman. It has recently been suggested that it may have been from Cellarius and Capito—at precisely that time under Cellarius's influence—that Rothmann received, at the very least, a predisposition to apocalyptic speculation. Cellarius, seen as the fount of this speculation, first published his views in the concluding sections of his *De Operibus Dei*. In any case, Rothmann probably returned to Münster within the year and immediately began to reform the city, a reform that was given a radical turn with the arrival of Heinrich Roll, one of the so-called *Wassenburger Predikanten*, in August 1533. Strongly influenced by Franck and Hoffman himself, Roll confirmed Rothmann in his new direction.

A major milepost on this new road was the August 1533 colloquy that took place in Münster between Rothmann, his followers, and some Lutheran and Catholic clerics. In this debate—for which Rothmann had prepared by writing his *Bekenntnisse van beyden Sacramenten, Doepe vnde Nachtmaele der predicanten tho Münster* (Confession Concerning the Two Sacraments)—Rothmann categorically rejected infant baptism and any kind of sacramental power in the Eucharist. He challenged both his Lutheran and Catholic opponents at the colloquy, therefore, to justify their practices on the basis of *sola scriptura*. Unable to do so, the Lutherans as well as the Catholics were forced to fall back on tradition.

Karl-Heinz Kirchhoff has demonstrated that Rothmann now began to build a peaceful Anabaptist congregation in Münster. He did not differentiate, however, between the Old and New Testaments—a Hoffman legacy—as clearly as did the Swiss Brethren. Together with Hoffman he asserted a parallelism between the two, with the Old Testament consisting of pictures or types of what was in the New Testament; the need to follow pictures or types, however, had come to an end with the reality of Christ's appearance. Circumcision, for example, he held to be a fleshly or tangible sign of God's covenant with Abraham; now, however, it had to be seen as a type of the spiritual and true covenant Christ wished to establish with his followers.

The arrival in Münster on 13 January 1534 of John of Leiden and Gerard Boekbinder, two disciples of Jan Matthijs, began to change things. These were followed on 24 February 1534 by the prophet himself, who had arrogated Hoffman's mantel to himself after Christ had failed to appear in Strasbourg in 1533. Matthijs now proclaimed that Münster instead would be the New Jerusalem; at the same time, he lifted Hoffman's ban on baptism with the baptism of Rothmann and his followers into the movement. With these newcomers came also a renewal of Hoffman's apocalyptic message—now, however, not of the restitution of the apostolic church but of the inauguration of the kingdom of God on earth. This shift from the apostolic church to the kingdom of God led to a renewed emphasis on the Old Testament, with Rothmann rejecting the argument that the latter was irrelevant to the Christian in his restitution of 1534. Arguing that Christ and his apostles had known no scriptures but the Old Testament, he now asserted a greater continuity between the two than he had been willing to concede earlier. There was only one gospel, and its prophecy of the kingdom of God on earth had not yet been fulfilled.

This shift also brought with it a change in attitude toward the use of the sword by the Christian, a change introduced by Matthijs himself. Arguing that the "time of harvest" was at hand, Matthijs helped complete the transition from a defenseless and suffering church to one that was entitled to defend itself until the inauguration of the kingdom of God that mandated the offensive use of the sword against the godless. Having gained control of the city through the support of the guilds in early 1534, John of Leiden began the transformation to the New Jerusalem after the death of Matthijs in early summer 1534. By August the former had proclaimed himself a new King David. Rothmann became his royal orator, and Berndt Knipperdolling, a former mayor of the city, became his chief minister. The institution of a community of goods followed, with polygamy just a little later.

For about a year, from summer 1534 to 24 June 1535, the city was under siege by the combined forces of Hesse and Franz von Waldeck, Catholic bishop of Münster. Gradually food ran out, and rumors of cannibalism surfaced. Inhabitants began to seek to escape, only to be cut down by the besieging forces. In early June some escapees informed the enemy of how to gain entrance to the city. On 24 June entry was accomplished. A great slaughter followed, but John of Leiden, Knipperdolling, and some others were taken alive. Rothmann, however, was never found—dead or alive. He was rumored to have been seen in Lübeck; others stated he lived out his days as a tutor to the children of a Dutch nobleman. The other leaders were interrogated, tortured, and finally executed. The bodies of John of Leiden, Knipperdolling, and one other person were placed in three separate cages and hoisted to the top of the spire of the Saint Lambert church. There they remained until the nineteenth century as a warning to all who would rise in revolt against the authority of church and state. It was at this point that Menno began to cast his lot with the movement. Was he a follower of the Münsterites, or a fellow traveler who sought to separate himself from them after they had been overwhelmed with disaster? Was he ever under their influence? Menno's relationship to the Münster revolution is critical for an overall assessment of the movement.

Menno Simons (c.1496–1561) was born in the small Frisian village of Pingjum in the vicinity of Witmarsum. Little is known of his early life, and it is assumed that he entered the priesthood at Utrecht at age twenty-eight, relatively late, probably having received his education in a monastic school. He knew Latin and some Greek and appears to have received a fairly good education for his time. He also possessed some acquaintance with the writings of the church fathers. In 1524, at age twenty-eight, Pingjum became his first parish. He speaks of playing cards to while away his time and of leading a relatively frivolous life in his first year as a priest. How did this young priest develop in the years between his first appointment and the events that transpired at Münster ten years later?

His theological development, Menno tells us, began one year after he became a priest—that is, in 1525. Perhaps through the reading of Reformation pamphlets, he began to doubt the doctrine of transubstantiation. Having heard of the importance of the Bible in matters Christian from these same pamphlets, Menno began "to examine the New Testament diligently" on the Eucharist. It was not long before he arrived at the conclusion that the church had deceived him on the subject. Torn between the authority of the Bible and the authority of the church, Menno turned to the writings of Luther, Huldrych Zwingli, and other reformers. Although the reformers did not agree on the interpretation of the issue, they did convince him that the authority of the Bible was to be considered greater than that of the church.

In 1531 the execution of Sicke Snyder in Leeuwarden for rebaptism forced Menno back to the Bible again, this time in quest of justification for infant baptism. He consulted Luther and then Bucer and Heinrich Bullinger, and they all appeared to have different reasons for retaining the practice, none of which Menno could find confirmed in the Bible. By the time he was transferred to Witmarsum in 1532, Menno tells us that he had "acquired considerable knowledge of the scriptures" and was considered by some an evangelical preacher. Approximately one year later rebaptism was introduced into his vicinity; probably in 1534 Münsterite emissaries appeared.

By the time Menno first encountered the Münsterites, he had been grappling with Reformation issues and studying the Bible for some nine years. What is significant about this period of study is that Menno had to find his own way through the teachings of the Catholic church, the reformers, the Münsterites, and the Bible to formulate his own theology. Would such a man have been seduced by the crude teachings of Matthijs and John of Leiden? It is important in assessing Menno's relationship to the Münsterites to recall that the original Melchiorites were not revolutionaries, and scholarship has confirmed Rothmann's assertion that the original Anabaptist movement in Münster was nonviolent. Furthermore, another group of Melchiorites centered around Obbe and Dirk Philips also rejected the revolutionary doctrines of the Münsterites. If one adds to this the fact that Pilgram Marpeck, the south German Anabaptist leader, could incorporate Rothmann's *Bekenntnisse van beyden Sa-*

cramenten nearly verbatim in his own *Vermanung; auch gantz klarer gründtlicher vnd unwider sprechlicher bericht zu warer Christlicher puntsvereynigung* (Admonition and Clear, Fundamental and Incontestable Account; 1542), then it may be asserted with some confidence that early Dutch and north German Anabaptism was not revolutionary. Even Philipp of Hesse wrote the Münsterite leaders on 16 February 1535 saying they had earlier "taught that the Christian was to suffer rather than resist evil, to turn the other cheek, and to obey evil as well as pious rulers. At the beginning," he continued, "you asserted one was not to war nor to defend himself, but to suffer."

Menno tells us that he, too, opposed the emissaries of revolution: he recognized them as zealous but erring in doctrine. In January 1535 these revolutionaries sought to capture Amsterdam; in March, with Menno's brother Pieter among them, they took over the Old Cloister in Bolsward, only to be defeated and massacred by the authorities. This marked a turning point in Menno's life. He seems to have read all the Münsterite literature he could acquire, especially Rothmann's writings, and seems to have gained an awareness of the transition from nonviolence to revolutionary chiliasm in Rothmann's writings. Perhaps immediately after his brother's execution, Menno penned his first tract, *Een gantz duidelijck ende klaer bewijs . . . Tegens de grouwelijcke ende grootste blasphemie van Jan van Leyden* (Against the Blasphemy of John of Leiden). Not published until 1627, it is a frontal attack on John of Leiden. Probably written before the collapse of the Münster kingdom (the tract speaks of John of Leiden in the present tense, as still alive), it attacks the "false prophets" for subverting the movement, but in it Menno also associates himself with "all the true brethren of the covenant scattered abroad." He accuses the "false prophets" of having "deserted the pure doctrine of Christ" and calls the misled and "erring sheep" back to their more orthodox beginnings. Yet Menno does not denounce every tenet of the Münsterite faith: he is always specific, referring to the "doctrine and practice . . . in regard to king, sword, rebellion, retaliation, vengeance, polygamy and the visible kingdom of Christ on earth." Never does he mention the Melchiorite doctrine of the heavenly flesh of Christ, a doctrine he adhered to. Clearly influenced by Melchiorite thought himself, Menno wished to restore the movement.

Menno wrote the tract in anger, and, in the process, Christ's words in *Matthew* 7 about the splinter in his brother's eye and the beam in his own came back to haunt him. Hypocrite that he was, he knew what was right and how the "erring sheep" could be helped, yet, for his ease and comfort, he had remained in the Catholic church. He had attacked the "splinter" in John of Leiden's eye in his *Blasphemie*; now he came to see the "beam" in his own. His inaction despite knowing the truth damned him every bit as much as John of Leiden's folly. This recognition, Menno tells us, compelled him to submit his life, as well as his mind, to the cause of Christ and the "erring sheep." He now began to teach the new doctrines openly and within nine months had left the Catholic church.

Early in 1526 Menno left for Groningen, where Obbe and Dirk Philips, who had also opposed the Münsterites, pressed him to join their movement. From them he probably received baptism and ordination. For a time he withdrew for study in order to associate with "the pious" and begin to cleanse the movement. Perhaps Menno's *Blasphemie* could not be published before the collapse of Münster; more likely he now refused to have it published after recognizing his own "hypocrisy." In any case, "The Spiritual Resurrection" (1536) and "The New Birth" (1537) seem to reflect his own conversion experience and demonstrate how central to the life of the Christian Menno saw the "new birth." His "Meditations on the 25 Psalm" (1538) was followed in 1539 by his most important book, *Ein Fundament vnd klare Anwisinge, van de heylsame vnd Godtsellyghe Leere Jesu Christi . . .* (The Foundation of Christian Teaching). Known as the Fundamentboek, it became the book around which Menno reorganized the movement. As a motto he chose *1 Corinthians* 3:11: "For no man can lay any foundation other than the one already laid, which is Jesus Christ." This remained his motto in all his other writings, indicating the Christ-centeredness of his theology. It was a theology that stressed discipleship within the context of the church, and it could be argued that Christ and the church are the two poles of his theological thought. Christ's work of salvation must be made effective in the church; the latter is to consist of regenerate souls willing to bear the cross of Christ.

Through his writings and itinerant preaching, Menno sought to regroup and rebuild the scattered members of the covenant into peaceful congregations. The revolutionaries had to be reformed; if that was not possible, they had to be removed by the ban. In 1542 a price was placed on his head, forcing Menno to move first to Frisia and then up the Baltic coast at least as far as Lübeck, perhaps even to Gdańsk. By 1545 his followers were being called "Mennists" for the first time. He spent time in Cologne until it became too dangerous for him and he eventually settled in Oldesloe, near Lübeck, under the protection of the count of Ahlefeld. Here he was allowed his own printing press and was able to publish his writings in relative peace. Though Menno appears never to have heard of the Swiss Brethren and never mentions such names as Felix Mantz or Conrad Grebel, his theology was, in the end, strikingly similar to that of the Swiss Brethren, or Swiss Anabaptists. He did differ with them on the Incarnation and on the use of the ban, but the essential features were strikingly similar.

From the collapse of Münster and his association with the movement onwards Menno was forced to work on two fronts—to cleanse the movement from within and to defend it against attacks from without. The attacks from without were severe, for virtually everyone now associated the movement with revolution and excesses such as polygamy. Internally, Menno had to move almost immediately against the remaining Münsterite sympathizers in the person of Jan Battenburg and his followers; he was forced to take issue with and reject David Joris, a spiritualist, and his followers. In 1547 Adam Pastor, ordained by Menno and Dirk Philips in 1542, had to be excommunicated for denying the preexistent divinity of Christ. As early as 1540 Obbe Philips—overcome by doubts about his own "calling," which had come through the Münsterites—left the movement. Externally, Menno debated Jan Łaski in 1544 and Martin Micron in 1554.

As early as 1542, in his *Vermanung* (Admonition), Marpeck had appropriated Rothmann's *Bekenntrisse* (Confession) virtually verbatim, thereby tacitly acknowledging similarities between the early Melchiorite movement in the north and the Swiss Brethren in the south. Yet there were contentious issues that divided the two movements as they made contact with one another. One of these—the "question of the origin of Christ's flesh"—was discussed at a conference held 24 August 1555 in Strasbourg. The conference decided that it was more important to observe Christ's commands than to speculate about the mystery of how Christ had become flesh. In 1557 a second conference took place in Strasbourg; this time the issues were the doctrine of original sin and the severe application of the ban, the latter having become a problem in the Low Countries. The first, an internal Swiss and South German problem, was resolved amicably, but the second, which was directed at the Dutch, remained divisive. Menno, who had sought to win the High Germans to his views in the spring of 1557, was rejected, though the conference expressed the hope that an outright rupture between the two groups would not occur. This was not to be, however, for Menno and his partner, Leenaert Bouwens, rejected the proffered hand, and in 1559 the Dutch elders pronounced a ban on the High Germans.

Menno, who died in 1561, regretted having agreed with Bouwens in favor of a severe application of the ban in their congregations. Already in 1555–1556 the "Waterlanders" separated from Menno, Bouwens and Dirk Philips over precisely this issue. They took their name from the lakes and river region north of Amsterdam in which they lived. By 1568 they began to hold their own church conferences and call themselves Doopsgezinde. Another division from Menno's group took place in 1567 when Flemish Anabaptists who had fled persecution in Belgium and settled among the Frisians separated. Cultural and other differences exacerbated attempts to resolve the disputes, and even Dirk Philips' intervention could not heal the rupture. These internal divisions had a ripple effect and spread over northern Europe, creating conservative and more moderate groups. Even among the Flemish themselves a division occurred between conservatives and moderates in 1594, with the conservative group calling itself "Old Flemish." Only four years later a similar split divided the Frisians.

Not everyone accepted these increasing divisions, however. Some members left the churches; others sought ways of healing the ruptures. The more moderate groups—in spite of the opposition of the "Old Flemish" and "Old Frisians"—insisted upon reunion. In 1591 the so-called Young Frisians and the High Germans united on the basis of the "Concept of Cologne," an agreement reached before the attempt at merger. Soon a number of Waterlanders, under the leadership of Hans de Ries, joined the union. But an invitation to the Old Flemish and Old Frisians in 1603 was once again rejected. Nevertheless, the attempts at reuniting the various groups of Dutch Anabaptists did have some success in the early years of the seventeenth century. Yet in the next few centuries the High German Mennonites came increasingly under strong pietist influences, while Dutch and north German Mennonites came under the influence of rationalism. This resulted, in the nineteenth century, in three regional Mennonite centers: the Verband of Mennonite churches in the south; the Vereinigung, representing most Mennonite churches in northern Germany and Prussia; and the Doopsgezinde of the Netherlands. In the north the more conservative groups had tended to migrate eastward and beginning in 1803 settled in the Crimean Peninsula of Russia. In North America and the rest of the world, the descendants of these Dutch, German, and Swiss Anabaptists are all called Mennonites today, with the exception of the Hutterites, the Amish, the Holdemann people, and a few other groups.

[*See also* Grebel, Conrad.]

BIBLIOGRAPHY

Brunk, Gerald R., ed. *Menno Simons: A Reappraisal.* Harrisonburg, Va., 1992.

Clasen, Claus-Peter. *Anabaptism: A Social History.* Ithaca, N.Y., 1972.

Deppermann, Claus. *Melchior Hoffman.* Edinburgh, 1987.

Doornkaat Koolman, J. ten, *Dirk Philips, vriend en medewerker van Menno Simons, 1504–1568.* 2d ed. Scottdale, Pa., 1981.

Dyck, C. J. *An Introduction to Mennonite History.* 3d ed. Scottdale, Pa., 1993.

Estep, William R. *The Anabaptist Story.* Reprint, Grand Rapids, Mich., 1989.

Goertz, Hans-Jürgen. *Die Täufer.* Munich, 1980.

Horsch, John. *Menno Simons: His Life, Labors, and Teachings.* Scottdale, Pa., 1916.

Keller, Ludwig. *Geschichte der Wiedertäufer und ihres Reiches zu Münster.* Münster, 1880.

Krahn, Cornelius. *Dutch Anabaptism.* 2d ed. Scottdale, Pa., 1981.

Kuehler, W. J. *Geschiedenis der Nederlandsche Doopsgezinde in de zestiende eeuw.* Reprint, Haarlem, 1961.

Meihuizen, H. W. *Menno Simons: Ijveraar voor hut herstel van de Nieuwtestamentlische gemeente, 1496–1561.* Haarlem, 1961.

Stupperich, Robert, ed. *Die Schriften Bernhard Rothmanns.* Münster, 1970.

Vos, Karel. *Menno Simons, 1496–1561: Zijn leven en werken en zijne reformatorische denkbeelden.* Leiden, 1914.

Williams, George H. *The Radical Reformation.* 3d. ed. Kirksville, Mo., 1992.

Zijpp, H. van der. *Geschiedenis der Doopsgezinden in Nederland.* Reprint, Delft, 1980.

Abraham Friesen

MENNO SIMONS (c.1496–1561), priest of Witmarsum, Friesland, who became a leader of the nonviolent wing of Dutch Anabaptists (hence Mennonites). Ordained in Utrecht about 1524, Menno became a vicar in Pingjum, Friesland. Presumably influenced by the sacramentarian ideas of early Dutch reformers and by his reading of the New Testament around 1526, he came to harbor doubts about the doctrine of transubstantiation. Between that year and 1531 he regarded himself as an "evangelical" preacher, although he remained within the traditional church. In 1531 he was promoted to a pastorate in Witmarsum. When the Dutch adherents of Melchior Hoffman (the covenanters, or Melchiorites) began administering baptism to adults in 1530/31, Menno too could find no biblical support for infant baptism. Although he did not yet join the covenanters, it appears from his earliest-known writing, *Van de Geestelijke Verrijenisse* (The Spiritual Resurrection; 1534), that his thought was turning in an increasingly Melchiorite direction.

In April 1535 several hundred Anabaptists, inspired by messengers sent out from the Anabaptist city of Münster, captured the Oldeklooster monastery near Bolsward, Friesland. After a short siege, most were killed or captured, and among those slain was Pieter Simons, presumably Menno's brother. Menno could not escape feeling responsible for the debacle, and he composed a tract against the Münsterite leadership entitled *Een gantsch duydelyck ende klaer bewys . . . tegens . . . de blasphemie van Jan van Leyden* (The Blasphemy of Jan van Leyden). Although his pacifism was limited—he acknowledged that self-defense might be necessary and allowed that a Christian ruler might suppress false teachers—he opposed the Münsterite use of the sword to establish the kingdom of God on earth. Because of the defeat of Münster two months later, Menno did not publish the tract. (It did not appear until 1627.) Around January 1536 he left his ecclesiastical office to lead the remnant of Anabaptists away from further violence. Probably at this time he was baptized, and about a year later he was ordained an elder by the Melchiorite leader Obbe Philips. From this point on, Simons was a hunted individual, living at times in Groningen, Holland, the archbishopric of Cologne, and for the last thirteen years of his life in Schleswig-Holstein. On 31 January 1561 he finally succumbed to the illness that had long afflicted him.

As seen in his magnum opus, *Dat Fundament des Christelycken leers* (The Fundament; 1539), Menno was deeply influenced by both traditional Catholic spirituality and the pacifistic piety of Erasmus. Menno promoted salvation as a process of discipleship resulting in the "new man in Christ." His spirituality at this point was reminiscent of Catholic penitential theology, emphasizing penance and obedience. Evidence of true repentance must precede divine grace. Baptism, the sign of membership in the church, must therefore be preceded by inner spiritual renewal and could be administered only to believing adults. Menno departed from traditional Catholic forms of spirituality by his revision and reduction of the sacraments, as well as by his strong anticlericalism and biblicism. Moreover, as a result of the failure of the broader Anabaptist attempt to reform the church, he organized many of the peaceful Anabaptists into voluntaristic church fellowships, following the apostolic model of the New Testament. In these fellowships believers could support each other on the difficult path of discipleship and sanctification.

Other aspects of Menno's ecclesiology developed as a result of his conflicts with other Anabaptist leaders. For example, although he consistently opposed revolutionary violence, in the 1539 edition of *Dat Fundament* he had called the Münsterites "dear brothers." Such magnanimous language reflected the fact that both the militant and the nonviolent Dutch Anabaptists traced a common heritage to Melchior Hoffman. Reformed and Catholic critics alike, however, increasingly accused Menno and his followers of being secret Münsterites, justifying their persecution. To defend his movement Menno therefore denied any connection with militant Anabaptism. His reference to Münsterites as "dear brothers" was therefore removed from later editions of *Dat Fundament.* But he maintained Hoffman's doctrine of the "heavenly flesh of Christ," in spite of the severe criticism it received from Reformed theologians.

Menno also opposed the Anabaptist leader David Joris on several issues, especially Joris's exalted sense of mission and divine calling, his allowing his followers to conform outwardly to approved religion to avoid persecution, and his denigration of external ceremonies, such as water baptism. Largely in response to Joris's spiritualistic approach Menno developed his later emphasis on church discipline and order. In the course of the 1540s and 1550s it became increasingly important, especially for Menno's key associates, Dirk Philips and Lenaert Bouwens, to define more precisely the ethical standards required for continued membership in that church. Those who fell into error or forbidden behavior could be placed under the ban and separated from the fellowship. Although Menno hoped to moderate the more rigorous application of this practice sought by Philips and Bouwens, their view carried the day among most Anabaptists who described themselves as Mennonites. Others, such as the more open-minded Waterlanders, called themselves *Doopsgezinde* ("baptist-oriented"), to distinguish themselves from their stricter brothers and sisters. Regardless of such internal disagreements, Menno's reputation as the preserver of peaceful Dutch Anabaptism remains.

BIBLIOGRAPHY

Augustijn, C. "Erasmus and Menno." *Mennonite Quarterly Review* 60 (1986), 497–508. Convincingly shows that the central features of Menno's theology can be traced back to Erasmus.

Bergsma, W., and S. Voolstra, eds. *Uyt Babel ghevolden, in Jerusalem ghetogen: Menno Simon's verlichting, bekering en beroeping.* Amsterdam, 1986. The best discussion of Menno's conversion to Anabaptism; includes an edition of Menno's own account of his departure from the priesthood.

Bornhäuser, Christoph. *Leben und Lehre Menno Simons: Ein Kampf um das Fundament des Glaubens (etwa 1496–1561).* Neukirchen, 1972. An important discussion of Menno's thought.

Brunk, Gerald R., ed. *Menno Simons: A Reappraisal.* Harrisonburg, Va., 1992. Contains several excellent studies of Menno's thought that summarize well the latest research on the subject. Especially noteworthy are M. Blok, "Discipleship in Menno Simons' *Dat Fundament*: An Exercise in Anabaptist Theology," pp. 105–130; H. Isaak, "Menno's Vision of the Anticipation of the Kingdom of God in His Early Writings," pp. 57–82; and S. Voolstra, "Themes in the Early Theology of Menno Simons," pp. 37–56.

George, Timothy. *Theology of the Reformers.* Nashville, 1988. Contains a useful overview in English on Menno's life and thought.

Grislis, Egil. "The Doctrine of Incarnation according to Menno Simons." *Journal of Mennonite Studies* 8 (1990), 16–33. Concludes that Menno's Christology had precursors in the late-medieval devotional and mystical traditions of the Low Countries.

Horst, Irvin B. "Menno Simons: The New Man in Community." In *Profiles of Radical Reformers*, edited by Hans-Jürgen Goertz, pp. 203–213. Scottdale, Pa., and Kitchener, Ont., 1982. A useful English introduction to Menno's life and thought.

Klaassen, Walter. "Menno Simons Research, 1937–1986." *Mennonite Quarterly Review* 60 (1986), 483–496.

———. "Menno Simons Research 1837–1937, 1986–1990." In *Menno Simons: A Reappraisal*, edited by Gerald R. Brunk, pp. 181–197. The two bibliographical essays by Klaassen provide the essential starting point for Menno research.

Krahn, Cornelius. *Menno Simons, 1496–1561: Ein Beitrag zur Geschichte und Theologie der Taufgesinnten.* North Newton, Kans. 1982. A reissue of the classic 1936 biography of Menno.

Meihuizen, H. W. *Menno Simons: IJveraar voor het Herstel van de Nieuwtestamentische Gemeente.* Haarlem, Netherlands, 1961. Although in Dutch, this is the most recent full-length biography of Menno. There is still no recent, comparable study in English.

Visser, Piet., ed. *Selectieve Bibliografie van Publicaties met Betrekking tot de Geschiedenis van het Doperdom in de Nederlanden Verschenen tussen 1975 en 1990.* Amsterdam, 1991. Includes the most thorough listing of recent Menno research.

Voolstra, Samme. "True Penitence: The Core of Menno Simons' Theology." *Mennonite Quarterly Review* 62 (1988), 387–400. An important examination of Menno's thought in the context of late-medieval penitential theology.

Waite, Gary K., ed. and trans. *Anabaptist Writings of David Joris.* Classics of the Radical Reformation, vol. 7. Waterloo, Ont., 1994.

Wenger, J. C., ed. *The Complete Writings of Menno Simons.* Scottdale, Pa., 1956. Remains the standard and generally reliable translation of Menno's writings into English.

Zijlstra, S. "Menno Simons and David Joris." *Mennonite Quarterly Review* 62 (1988), 249–256. Examines well the differences and similarities between Menno and Joris.

GARY K. WAITE

MERICI, Angela. *See* Ursulines.

MERULA, Angelus (Dutch, Engel Willemszoon de Merle; 1482–1557), Dutch priest and scholar who was condemned to death as an obstinate heretic. Merula came of a leading family in Den Briel (Voorne, South Holland) and studied theology at Paris. Ordained in 1511, he returned to Den Briel, where he held several nonparochial offices before his appointment in 1532 as parish priest of Heenvliet, a village in Oostvoorne. The benefice was a gift of the Van Cruiningen family, whose members inclined to evangelical doctrines; Merula's predecessor also held heterodox opinions. Almost at once Merula too fell under suspicion, but despite grave charges, he survived, presumably protected by his patron. The authorities conducted another investigation around 1540, again without result. Indeed such was Merula's standing as a theologian that only illness prevented him from being sent to the Council of Trent in 1551. The succession of a less sympathetic patron weakened Merula's position, and he had to reinstate certain aspects of the Mass that he had omitted. In 1552 the provincial court of Holland instituted fresh proceedings; depositions were taken and Merula's books and papers searched. In 1553 he was taken into custody in The Hague and examined by the Inquisition. In the autumn of 1554, at the point of condemnation for heresy, this "old and broken priest" retracted his opinions; his penance was to be lifelong imprisonment. His removal from the county of Holland to Louvain in Brabant was widely regarded as contrary to privileges and provoked an outcry in the provincial states. At Louvain he resumed his defiance of the Inquisitors. As a relapsed heretic, he was condemned to be burned at Mons in Hainault on 26 July 1557 but died on his way to the place of execution.

In many respects Merula concurred with the theology of the Protestant Reformation. He recognized no authority apart from that of the scriptures, and he staunchly professed the doctrine of justification by faith alone together with predestination. Though his evangelical theology was clearly indebted to the "young" Luther, he repudiated his eucharistic teaching. God was invisible and should be worshiped "in spirit and in truth." In his unpublished treatises and in his sermons, Merula openly opposed the veneration of images and pilgrimages and discouraged his parishioners from bringing votive offerings. Though the church for Merula was primarily spiritual, the assembly of the faithful, he did not reject ceremonies and sacraments and continued to celebrate the Mass. But he sought biblical warranty for the liturgical rites, and where he found none, he modified the service; for example, he omitted the *Salve regina.* He also set a high value on preaching.

Luther was by no means the only influence on Merula. His theology was drawn from a variety of sources, patristic as well as biblical, humanist as well as Protestant. Apart from his considerable debt to Luther, Merula's understanding of the Eucharist was influenced by Augustine and possibly Zwingli; he agreed with Erasmus regarding the need for interior piety rather than outward observance and regarding the lifelong importance of baptismal vows. Melanchthon and Lefèvre d'Étaples also informed his theology.

Though Merula enjoyed a reputation as a scholar, the impact of his teaching was probably quite restricted, for none of his writings were published. His trial, however, became a *cause célèbre*, and an account appeared soon after in the Dutch Calvinist martyrology of Adriaan Corneliszoon van Haemstede. In the seventeenth century, however, the Remonstrant historian, Brandt tried to appropriate Merula for his cause. Subsequently he was admired as a representative of the so-called "national Reformed" movement, a supposedly indigenous element in the Dutch Reformation, though this interpretation no longer commands widespread support.

BIBLIOGRAPHY

Brandt, Geeraerdt. *The History of the Reformation and Other Ecclesiastical Transactions in and about the Low Countries* (1720). Reprint, London, 1990. Fullest account in English, based on original sources; see especially vol. 1, pp. 111–119.

Bussy, A. de. "De eerste informatie naar Merula's ketterij, 1533." *Nederlandsch archief voor kerkgeschiedenis* n.s. 16 (1921), 129–143. Depositions concerning the first investigation into Merula's doctrines.

Flinterman, R. A. "Merula, Angelus." In *Biografisch Lexikon voor de geschiedenis van het nederlandse protestantisme*, vol. 2, pp. 327–327. Kampen, 1983. Brief, up-to-date biography which supplements Moll's account; with full bibliography.

Hoog, I. M. J., ed. *De verantwoording van Angelus Merula volgens het handschrift berustende in het archief der Oud-Bisschoppelijke Clerezy te Utrecht.* Leiden, 1897. Documents relating to the trial of Merula.

Moll, Willem. *Angelus Merula de hervormer en martelaar des geloofs 1530–1557*. Amsterdam, 1851. The standard biography, but now dated.

Weernekers, Jan. *De theologie van Angelus Merula met name onderzocht op invloeden vanuit de reformatie.* Amsterdam, 1983. An examination of Merula's theology, with a summary in German.

ALASTAIR C. DUKE

MEUSEL, Wolfgang. *See* Musculus, Wolfgang.

MICHELANGELO BUONARROTI (1475–1564),

Italian sculptor, painter, architect, and poet. The most celebrated artist in sixteenth-century Europe, Michelangelo had an incalculable impact on the history of religious art. His masterpieces of sculpture and painting, among them the *Pietà* (in Saint Peter's basilica, 1499), *David* (1501–1504), the Genesis cycle on the ceiling of the Sistine chapel (1508–1512), *Moses* (for the tomb of Julius II, c.1515), and the *Last Judgment* (on the altar wall of the Sistine chapel, 1536–1541)—have left an indelible impression on the Western imagination and have influenced the way many Christians visualize the divine. His architecture is equally significant and includes the Medici chapel (1520–1534) and Laurentian Library (1524–1559) in Florence, as well as the Campidoglio (1537–1564) and Saint Peter's basilica (1547–1564) in Rome.

Michelangelo was Florentine but spent much of his adult life in Rome, settling there permanently in 1534. He served a succession of popes, from Julius II to Pius IV, and from 1505 was almost continuously occupied with major papal commissions. He undertook his most important assignment for the Roman Church at the age of seventy-two, when he became architect of Saint Peter's. The basilica had been begun four decades earlier, but progress had been slow in the intervening time. Michelangelo introduced a new design, a simplified and improved version of the Greek cross plan proposed by Donato Bramante in 1506, and directed the project for the next seventeen years; by the time of his death the building was complete but for the cupola, corner chapels, and facade. This was the most ambitious artistic undertaking of the Renaissance and, given the enormous symbolic significance of Saint Peter's as the mother church of the Catholic faith, one that was intimately linked to the politics and propaganda of the Counter-Reformation.

Michelangelo's long career spanned a tumultuous period in the history of Italy and of the church, and his art seems to reflect his own responses to the changing climate in which he lived. One sees this most clearly when comparing his frescoes on the vault of the Sistine chapel, commissioned by the worldly Julius II at the height of the high Renaissance, with his *Last Judgment* on the altar wall of the same chapel, commissioned a quarter of a century later by the reformer Paul III. In both works Michelangelo relied on the idealized male nude as the primary vehicle for his artistic expression, but the gracefulness, assurance, and optimism of the earlier work gives way in his later work to a bleak vision of humanity cowering before its god and of souls torn between salvation and damnation. The *Last Judgment* gave rise to a heated controversy. The conspicuous nudity of the figures and especially of Christ and his saints offended Counter-Reformation sensibilities, and soon after 1563, when the Council of Trent denounced what it termed "lasciviousness" in the representation of sacred subjects, the offending subjects were painted over with drapery.

Michelangelo was himself profoundly devout. In his old age, under the influence of his close friend Vittoria Colonna, his thoughts turned increasingly to religion, and his late works reveal a vision at once sublime and tormented. He died at the age of eighty-nine and was buried in San Croce, Florence.

BIBLIOGRAPHY

Ackerman, James S. *The Architecture of Michelangelo.* Rev. ed. Reprint, Harmondsworth, 1986.

De Maio, Romeo. *Michelangelo e la Controriforma.* 3d ed. Florence, 1990. Focuses on the controversy surrounding the *Last Judgment.*

Tolnay, Charles. *Michelangelo.* 5 vols. 2d ed. Princeton, 1969–1971. The best general monograph on Michelangelo's life and work.

LOUISE RICE

MICRON, Maarten (1523–1559), Dutch Reformed minister and theologian. One of the foremost theologians and polemicists of the early Dutch Calvinist congregations, Micron played a seminal role both in the organization of the first Reformed churches in exile and in the formulation of church doctrine. Born in Ghent, Micron seems to have converted to the Reformation before his departure from the Netherlands in 1546. He studied first in Strasbourg and then in Basel before turning to the practice of medicine. His first published writing was a medical textbook, *In libros de placitis Hippocratis et Platonis argumenta* (1549).

The turning point in his career came with a visit to Zurich in 1548, where Micron became an intimate of the English exile John Hooper and a strong supporter of the doctrine of the Zurich church and its *Antistes*, Heinrich Bullinger. When Hooper returned to England in 1549, Micron accompanied him and soon became involved in the complicated negotiations leading to the foundation of the London exile church. The foundation charter of 1550 named Micron as one of the first ministers in the Dutch congregation. Micron soon emerged as an important collaborator, with the superintendent Jan Łaski, in the establishment of the church's institutions and discipline. Although Łaski is generally credited with the creation of the church's organizational structures, it was probably Micron who guided the church toward a doctrinal position close to that of Zurich, particularly in the crucial matter of eucharistic doctrine. Micron was certainly responsible for two of the most influential writings of the London congregation: the *Christlicke Ordinancien* (1554), a shortened Dutch version of Łaski's Latin church order, and the shorter catechism (1552). Both these writings contained the *Korte Ondersoeckinghe des Gheloofs*, a brief summary of doctrine that in frequent reprints became one of the most popular catechismal works of the early Dutch Calvinist congregations.

On the accession of Mary Tudor in 1553, Micron was one of the church leaders who accompanied Łaski on the search for a new refuge abroad. This ill-starred voyage through Denmark and northern Germany brought Micron once more into prominence as a principal defender of the church's doctrine and provided materials for the major polemical writings that occupied Micron up to his premature death at Norden (East Friesland) in 1559. These years saw the publication both of tracts against the Lutheran theologian Joachim Westphal, the most tenacious opponent of the Reformed in the second sacramentarian controversy (*Apologeticum scriptum*, 1557), and two confutations of the Anabaptist prophet Menno Simons. These works, the *Waerachtigh verhael* of 1556 and the *Apologie* of 1558, were the product of an acrimonious dispute with Menno at Wismar in January 1554 and ranged widely over the controversial points at issue between the Reformed and radical groups. Through these early Emden editions and later reprints, these works proved to have an enduring influence in the Dutch Reformed church. In this respect Micron must be seen as one of the key figures in the process by which the early Dutch Reformed congregations gradually articulated a separate identity from the then numerous sectarian groups.

BIBLIOGRAPHY

Dankbaar, W. F., ed. *Marten Micron, De christlicke ordinancien der Nederlandscher Ghemeinten te Londen* (1554). The Hague, 1956.

———. *Een waerachtigh verhaal der t'zamensprekinghen tusschen Menno Simons ende Martinus Mikron, van der Menschwerdinghe Jesu Christi.* Documenta Anabaptistica Neerlandica 3. Leiden, 1981.

Gerretsen, J. H. *Micronius: zijn leven, zijn geschriften, zijn geestesrichting.* Nijmegen, 1895.

Pettegree, Andrew. *Foreign Protestant Communities in Sixteenth-Century London.* Oxford, 1986. See chapter 3.

———. "The Struggle for an Orthodox Church: Calvinists and Anabaptists in East Friesland, 1554–1578. *Bulletin of the John Rylands Library* 70.3 (1988), 45–59. For the controversies with the Anabaptists.

Verzeichnis der im deutschen Sprachbereich erschienenen Drucke des XVI. Jahrhunderts. Stuttgart, 1983–. Vol. 13, nos. 5168–5179.

ANDREW PETTEGREE

MIJLE, Adriaan (also Adriaan Arendszoon van der Mijle; 1538–1590), moderate Calvinist and politician in Holland and supporter of William of Orange. He was a member of one of the most important families in his native town of Dordrecht in the county of Holland. In 1563, soon after his successful legal studies in Louvain, he was appointed to the Council of Holland (*Hof van Holland*). When the repressive Fernando Álvarez de Toledo, duke of Alba, arrived in the Netherlands in 1568, Mijle went to Italy under the pretext of weak health. In reality it was because he shared the new Calvinist ideas.

In 1573, after a short term on the court of the Elector Palatine Frederick III in Heidelberg, he decided on the elector's advice to return to Holland to help Stadtholder William of Orange and the States of Holland in their revolt against the sovereign, Philip II of Spain. He at once became a member of the government council, which assisted the Prince of Orange. William consulted him many times in subsequent years, and the States of Holland commissioned him for important matters such as peace negotiations in the 1570s, contacts with England and France, and preparations for choosing a new sovereign.

In 1583 he took office as president of the Council of Holland. After the death of William in the following year, he supported William's son Maurits van Nassau as the new stadtholder. His friend Johan van Oldenbarnevelt, the advocate of the states after 1586, took the same view. Because of his position, Mijle's attitude toward Robert Dudley, earl of Leicester, had to be tactful—Leicester was the English governor in the Netherlands during the period 1585–1587, and Mijle seemed to be among his supporters. Mijle, however, truly belonged to the anti-Leicesterians, who finally triumphed. In 1588, after the departure of Leicester, Mijle also became a member of the Council of State (*Raad van State*) of the rebellious States General, though on the condition that he should not be obliged to negotiate peace with the Spanish. He died in 1590, leaving behind his wife, Magdalena van Egmond van Nijenburg, and his two children, Cornelis and Cornelia.

In matters of religion Mijle argued for peace and tolerance. He belonged to the Erastian moderates who were opposed to the orthodox Calvinists in their ideas about strict adherence to the Belgic Confession and the autonomous position of the church vis-à-vis the state. His diplomatic qualities, however, made him a suitable person for mediations in ecclesiastical conflicts—for example, in 1582 in the case of Gouda pastor Hermannus Herbertszoon, a popular preacher of spiritualist leanings. Characteristic also was his political behavior during the Leicester period. When deputies from the synod of south Holland complained about the fact that the States of Holland did not confirm the church order promulgated by ecclesiastical authorities in 1586, Mijle replied that confirmation by the states was not necessary because Leicester had already done so. In this way he avoided an escalation of conflict for the time being. In sum, he blended political and religious interests for the sake of his own convictions and those of many others.

BIBLIOGRAPHY

Balen Jansz, M. *Beschrijvinge der stad Dordrecht . . . verscheyde hopre Konst-platen.* Dordrecht, 1677.

Bartelds, J. C. E. "Adriaan van der Mijle." In *Nieuw Nederlandsch Biografisch Woordenboek*, edited by P. C. Molhuysen, P. J. Blok, and F. J. Kossmann, vol. 8, cols. 1190–1192. Leiden, 1930.

Belonje, J. "Het ambacht van de Mijle met zijn leenkamer." *Hollandse studiën* 3 (1972), 159–169.

Schotel, G. D. J. *Het geslacht van der Mijle.* Dordrecht, 1858.

Tex, Jan den. *Oldenbarnevelt.* 2 vols. Haarlem, 1960–1962. Published in English translation, Cambridge, 1973.

Vecht, H. A. W. van der. *Cornelis van der Mijle, 1579–1642.* Sappemeer, 1907.

JOOP W. KOOPMANS

MILAN. For the state of Milan, which then encompassed the better part of Lombardy, the early sixteenth century was a time of political turmoil and religious disarray. While the area suffered severely from the devastations caused by the long-drawn conflict between France and the Habsburgs for the control of Italy, religious conditions reached an all-time low. Even though the basic loyalty of most of the populace to the established church was never seriously in question, there was widespread dissatisfaction with its personnel. Clerical absenteeism (epitomized by the fact that neither Milan nor Pavia had a resident bishop during the first half of the century); a poorly trained and often semiliterate parish clergy frequently guilty of negligence and even immorality; the notorious worldliness then rampant in several monasteries and convents; the heavy-handed meddling of secular authorities and of the local aristocracy in church affairs; the maladministration of ecclesiastical endowments—all these things combined to generate resentment among the laity and to create a climate of opinion in which ideas and programs of reform were bound to have considerable appeal.

In such a context one would expect the infiltration of Protestant ideas, the more so as Milan had long entertained close commercial contacts with German lands, and merchants from that country were frequent visitors in Milan, Pavia, and Cremona. Not surprisingly, from the early 1520s to the 1560s the existence of heretical groups and the diffusion of Lutheran and, later, Calvinist books and tracts smuggled in by merchants became a source of concern for the local authorities, especially when unorthodox ideas were broadcast from the pulpit by popular preachers like the Augustinians Giuliano da Milano in Cremona and Agostino Mainardi in Pavia before audiences that were all too eager to listen to a message of reform. It was, however, political authorities (the last Sforza duke, Francis II; the Milan senate; and, after the annexation of the state to the Habsburg monarchy in 1535, the Spanish governors) rather than church authorities who first took action to repress heresy that they regarded as a threat to the public peace; and it was the government rather than a negligent church leadership that tried, in the first half of the century, to curb clerical abuses and misconduct in response to popular complaints.

The diffusion of Protestant ideas was paralleled, from the 1530s, by the formation of small groups of devout laypeople and clerics whose goal was to improve religious standards within the framework of the Catholic church and in full loyalty to it. Their efforts, it is true, had been preceded in the fifteenth century by the so-called observant movement, that is to say the emergence within some of the older monastic orders (Benedictines and Augustinians) as well as within the orders of friars (Franciscans and Dominicans) of religious houses intent on restoring the founder's rule in all its pristine purity. As a result, by the close of the fifteenth century one could find in a single city, such as Milan, monasteries of the same order that were notorious for their moral laxity next to observant communities with a reputation for piety and asceticism.

While the observant movement can rightly be viewed as a forerunner of Catholic reform, its impact on religious standards at large was inevitably limited as the movement itself remained confined within monastic walls. Of far greater importance were the new orders of clerks regular, which, by dropping some of the strict requirements of monastic life such as the daily choral recitation of the Divine Office and a secluded life, proved better suited to meet the religious needs of the masses. One such new order was that of the Clerks Regular of Saint Paul (better known as Barnabites after the name of their main church) founded in 1530 in Milan by a physician, Antonio Maria Zaccaria, a lawyer, Bartolommeo Ferrari, and a nobleman, Giacomo Morigia. As laymen the three had been members of the Oratory of the Eternal Wisdom, a small, informal group of priests and laypeople that had formed in Milan in the early years of the century under the inspiration of Arcangela Panigarola, an Augustinian nun and mystic. The group was dedicated to raising religious standards among both clergy and laity and stressed personal commitment as a prerequisite to institutional reform. In the same spirit, the Barnabites emphasized intense devotion, blameless moral conduct, and preaching; in this way they hoped to serve as models for the clergy at large. Only later in the century did they make education their primary mission and begin to open schools. To the same milieu belonged Countess Ludovica Torelli della Guastalla, the founder in 1535 of a religious community for women (the Angelic nuns) and, in 1557, of a boarding school for girls from impoverished noble families (Collegio della Guastalla) that represented a sharp break with tradition in that it was run entirely by laywomen.

In the state of Milan the work of the Barnabites was soon to be complemented and indeed overshadowed by that of the new religious orders founded elsewhere in Italy and abroad, such as the Capuchins, the Theatines, the Somaschi, and the Jesuits. The Barnabites, however, continued to play a significant role, notably during the tenure of Carlo Borromeo, who, as archbishop of Milan (1560–1584), recruited from among them some of his closest associates.

The Catholic reform movement in Lombardy can also count among its distinctive achievements the creation in 1536 of a confraternity involving primarily lay participation whose influence was far-reaching and extended well beyond the borders of the state. This was the "Company of Reformation in Charity," later renamed "Company of Christian Doctrine." Its purpose was, in the words of its founder, Castellino da Castello, "to teach boys and girls how to read, write, and lead Christian lives, free of charge and for the love of God." Besides teaching literacy, it engaged in religious instruction and developed a network of schools of Christian doctrine that, by the end of the century, enrolled nearly forty thousand pupils.

Until midcentury, most manifestations of religious renewal (and to those already mentioned one should add the many lay confraternities, whether devotional or charitable, that sprang up in that period) came into being with little encouragement or guidance from the church hierarchy. As such, they all shared a spontaneous but at the same time fragmented and uncoordinated character. From about 1550, however, things began to change as a reflection of the new spirit generated at the top by the Council of Trent (under way since 1545). In 1550 Milan received its first resident archbishop in fifty years, Giovanni Angelo Arcimboldi. His work was primarily administrative and aimed at restoring a measure of discipline among the clergy as well as at suppressing heterodox ideas; it lacked the scope and the pastoral vision of the program soon to be pursued by his successor, Carlo Borromeo, under whose leadership Catholic reform in the state of Milan achieved its full dimension and its most enduring results.

Borromeo's commanding personality, the veneration he elicited from the masses long before he was canonized in 1610, and the vast resonance of his achievements throughout Catholic Europe should not, however, obscure the important work of a number of lesser, yet distinguished reforming prelates of his generation. Among them were Niccolò Ormaneto, who was closely associated with Borromeo as his vicar in the 1560s and later served as bishop of Padua; Carlo Bascape, a Barnabite and Borromeo's secretary, who rose to become bishop of Novara; and especially Ippolito de' Rossi, bishop of Pavia from 1564 to 1591. Like Borromeo the scion of a powerful noble family, de' Rossi rose to high church office thanks to his family connections, but he too chose from the start to take residence in his diocese, thus breaking with a long tradition of absenteeism, and adopted for himself and his household a lifestyle that bore little resemblance to that of most Renaissance prelates. In Pavia he founded one of the earliest seminaries and organized periodic conferences aimed at updating and improving the theological preparation of the clergy.

With men like Borromeo and de' Rossi the program of Catholic renewal formulated at Trent can be said to have become firmly established in the state of Milan. It remained for later generations and for prelates like Federico Borromeo, Carlo's younger cousin who held the Milan see from 1595 to 1631, to carry on and consolidate their legacy.

[*See also* Borromeo, Carlo; Italy; Monasticism; Ormaneto, Niccolò; *and* Religious Orders.]

BIBLIOGRAPHY

Bendiscioli, Mario. "Politica, amministrazione e religione nell'età dei Borromei." In *Storia di Milano*, vol. 10, pp. 3–351. Milan, 1957. Indispensable for the late sixteenth and early seventeenth centuries.

Bernorio, Virginio L. *La Chiesa di Pavia nel secolo XVI e l'azione pastorale del Cardinal Ippolito de' Rossi,1560–1591*. Pavia, 1972. A study of a nearly forgotten yet important churchman whose approach to religious renewal differed from Borromeo's.

Cattaneo, Enrico. "Istituzioni ecclesiastiche milanesi." In *Storia di Milano*, vol. 9, pp. 509–721. Milan, 1961. Comprehensive coverage of institutions and devotional practices in the Milan church in the early sixteenth century.

Chabod, Federico. *Lo Stato e la vita religiosa a Milano nell'epoca di Carlo V*. Turin, 1971. This is a reprint of a book originally published in

1938. Despite its age, it is still the classic work on the first half of the century and is especially useful on the spread of Lutheran ideas and the government's intervention in religious affairs.

Cochrane, Eric. *Italy, 1530–1630.* Edited by Julius Kirshner. London and New York, 1988. Chapter 7 provides an excellent, concise overview of religious trends with numerous references to Milan.

Headley, John M., and John B. Tomaro, eds. *San Carlo Borromeo: Catholic Reform and Ecclesiastical Politics in the Second Half of the Sixteenth Century.* Washington, D.C., 1988.

Majo, Angelo. *Storia della Chiesa Ambrosiana.* Vol. 2: *Dall'età comunale a San Carlo Borromeo.* Milan, 1982. Especially useful on the personality of individual archbishops.

Maselli, Domenico. *Saggi di storia ereticale lombarda al tempo di San Carlo.* Naples, 1979. Documents the presence of Protestant groups in the second half of the sixteenth century.

Prosdocimi, Luigi. *Il diritto ecclesiastico dello Stato di Milano dall'inizio della signoria viscontea al periodo tridentine, secc. XIII-XVI.* Milan, 1941. Still the chief authority on church-state relations in Milan.

DOMENICO SELLA

MILLENARIANISM. This term is often applied to any religious outlook that foresees a radical transformation of earthly life and the advent of a golden age. It refers most properly, however, to the belief of some Christians that the Savior will return to establish a kingdom of righteousness on earth. Christian millenarianism is based above all on *Revelation* 20, which speaks of a thousand-year period (Lat., *mille anni*) when Satan will be bound and Christ will reign among his people. More or less synonymous terms include *millennialism* and *chiliasm* (from Greek *chilias*, a thousand); the latter is frequently reserved for the most literal biblical readings. The concern here is with any apocalyptic eschatology that looks to Christ's rule, either personal or spiritual, before the end of time.

Such beliefs were common among the earliest Christians, who were influenced by Jewish hopes for the establishment of a messianic kingdom. Several prominent church fathers taught of a golden age to follow the return of Christ. From the time of Augustine (d. 430), leading clerics and thinkers worked to discourage such expectations. Nevertheless, in Europe the high and late Middle Ages saw a general resurgence of apocalyptic thought, including prophecies of a new spiritual age. Of central importance were the conceptions of the Cistercian abbot Joachim of Fiore (d. 1202). Joachim introduced a dynamic trinitarian vision of history and foresaw a new age of the Holy Spirit; these ideas influenced countless later writers who shared hopes of an earthly spiritual fulfillment.

Late twentieth-century scholarship downplays the traditional tendency to associate this hope with outbursts of social discontent and revolutionary dissent in Western history, and emphasizes instead the role of millenarian and other apocalyptic notions in the everyday outlook of premodern Europeans. Belief in the imminent establishment of a godly kingdom was not simply a reaction to oppression or upheaval; it was a common way of making sense of the world. While millenarianism was often an expression of frustration or dissent, it could and did also support established authorities by giving them positive roles in the divine drama. Thus despite official theological discouragement, millenarian schemes were widely adopted in the pre-Reformation centuries. They served a variety of interests, both lay and clerical, learned and popular, ranging from radical reformism to imperial propaganda.

During the Reformation era, most ecclesiastical leaders and theologians still formally rejected explicit belief in the coming earthly triumph of the saints. Like the defenders of the Roman Church, the leading figures of early Protestantism all denounced the idea that a new historical dispensation would or could be established. In general, they understood the thousand-year bondage of Satan as a period in the past when the church had been relatively free of corrupt teachings and practices. The Augsburg Confession (1530) denounced "certain Jewish opinions which are even now making their appearance and which teach that, before the resurrection of the dead, saints and godly men will possess a worldly kingdom and annihilate all the godless" (article 17). The Helvetic Confession of 1566 used similar language.

This conception of millenarian heresy was shaped partly by the dangers the magisterial reformers had come to associate with Anabaptist separatism and popular rebellion. Among various "radical" groups and thinkers millenarian visions did play a role, but it is difficult to generalize about the precise nature and significance of such ideas. Anabaptists, spiritualists, and independent prophets expressed a swirling variety of end-time notions. By no means were all such figures millenarians; many waited in simple expectation of the end of the world. Numerous prominent radicals, however, including Thomas Müntzer, Hans Hut, and Melchior Hoffman, preached that the elect would establish some form of godly rule on earth. These thinkers and many of their followers were influenced not only by biblical prophecies but by Joachimite notions of a final age of spiritual purity as well. They also breathed new life into Old Testament ideas about the triumph of God's chosen people; this element helped evoke the charge of "Judaizing."

Among many "radical" figures, this final earthly triumph was understood as a time of restitution preceding the actual return of Christ and the Last Judgment itself. Yet definite theological or metaphysical conceptions were on the whole less important than the overriding conviction that the last times were bringing a final pouring out of the spirit. This outpouring meant that the elect would carry out the purification of the church; believers shared responsibility in the process of the final cleansing. For some, this preparatory cleansing meant merely separation from all existing godless structures. For a few, including the leaders of the Anabaptist rising at Münster in 1534–1535, it demanded a more active campaign to restore purity before the end. It was the idea of radical cleansing, far more than millenarianism per se, that led to the intense persecution of Anabaptists and other extreme dissenters.

It is often difficult to distinguish clearly between millenarian and other apocalyptic conceptions of the end time in the Reformation era. The notions of the coming end and of the coming kingdom were so plastic that in some cases it is not easy to know whether a particular thinker meant to picture an earthly triumph. Moreover, millenarianism continued to take highly varied forms and appeared across a broad spectrum of theological, social, and political views. To be sure, those who felt most urgently called to play a role in the execution of God's plan often believed that this plan would have some sort of temporal fulfillment. Yet some "radicals" such as Hans Denck were evidently not millenarians; one can also find established figures such as the Lutheran preacher Philipp Nicolai (d. 1608) who hoped for a final victory of the true church before the end. The fundamental issue in sixteenth-century thinking about the last times thus cut across the category of millenarianism; it had to do with human activity or passivity in the execution of God's will.

In spite of the strictures of the early magisterial reformers, the general eschatological assumptions of early Protestantism did much to prepare the way for new forms of future-directed hope that gave a sense of unity and purpose to emerging religious, social, and political groups. The Reformation emphases on the promise of coming redemption and the fulfillment of biblical prophecy—especially evident in Luther—encouraged intensified efforts to understand all of history in terms of a transcendent scheme. Virtually all Protestants believed that the papacy stood revealed as the Antichrist, and the question of whether that satanic power might fall before the end of history was widely debated. The proliferation of speculation on such subjects inevitably encouraged some thinkers to move in the direction of millenarianism.

Calvinism would provide the field in which Protestant millenarianism saw its most significant flowering. Already in the second half of the sixteenth century, Calvin's own extreme reserve toward the historical interpretation of prophecy was waning among many of his heirs. By the early decades of the next century, in the writings of figures such as Johann Heinrich Alsted and John Amos Comenius, Calvinist millenarianism had already lost much of its genuinely apocalyptic aspect and shaded off into historical meliorism, a vision of continuing earthly progress. This tendency was present in German Pietism as well. But a sense of the prophetic immediacy of a godly kingdom was still on the rise in England, first among thinkers such as Thomas Brightman, John Napier, and Joseph Mede, then in a flood of prophetic scenarios during the era of the Civil War and interregnum (c.1642–1660). Most famous in this latter period were the "Fifth Monarchy Men," who adopted an old millenarian interpretation of the book of Daniel. Such thinking became less popularly visible but by no means died out in later decades. The form of millenarianism known as "dispensationalism," which had its roots in seventeenth-century England but did not flower until the nineteenth century, is influential among certain groups in the United States and elsewhere to this day. Dispensationalist teachings, a key source of modern biblical fundamentalism, include the ideas of a secret "rapture" of believers and the personal reign of Christ for a thousand years.

The atmosphere in much of Catholic Europe, especially Italy and Spain, was less favorable to the general circulation of millenarian views. Yet here too shifting conditions brought new adaptations of medieval hopes for a final earthly flowering of love and truth. Prophecies of a great angelic pope who would usher in such an age continued to appear. Joachimite notions of a new historical dawn influenced not only visionaries like Guillaume Postel and Tommaso Campanella but also more than a few conservative churchmen. Many Jesuits saw their order as the movement of spiritual men that Joachim himself had foreseen as heralding the new era. Still bolder were the assumptions of the many Franciscans who saw their New World enterprise in openly millenarian terms. Some scholars have found a darker and more exclusively emotional form of millenarianism underlying the Catholic violence of the French Wars of Religion; here a growing sense of eschatological panic in the face of heresy may have fueled the sort of purificatory zeal that characterized the Saint Bartholomew's Day Massacre (1572).

Among both Catholics and Protestants, then, beliefs in the imminent earthly realization of Christ's kingdom helped to legitimize and support a variety of interests. That both English Puritans and Spanish Franciscans viewed the New World with millenarian assumptions points both to the flexibility and to the centrality of such hopes in the history of the early modern West. Yet the very flexibility of the category suggests its limitations for understanding the actual social meaning of a given thinker's outlook.

[*See also* Anabaptists; Antichrist; *and* Apocalypticism.]

BIBLIOGRAPHY

Ball, Bryan W. *A Great Expectation: Eschatological Thought in English Protestantism to 1660*. Leiden, 1975.

Cohn, Norman. *The Pursuit of the Millennium: Revolutionary Millenarians and Mystical Anarchists in the Middle Ages*. Rev. ed. London, 1984.

List, Günther. *Chiliastische Utopie und Radikale Reformation: Die Erneuerung der Idee vom tausendjährigen Reich im 16. Jahrhundert*. Munich, 1973.

McGinn, Bernard. *Visions of the End: Apocalyptic Traditions in the Middle Ages*. New York, 1979.

Phelan, John Leddy. *The Millennial Kingdom of the Franciscans in the New World: A Study of the Writings of Geronimo de Mendieta, 1525–1604*. Berkeley, 1970.

Reeves, Marjorie. *Joachim of Fiore and the Prophetic Future.* London, 1976.

Tuveson, Ernest Lee. *Millennium and Utopia: A Study in the Background of the Idea of Progress.* Reprint, Gloucester, Mass., 1972.

Williams, George H. *The Radical Reformation.* 3d ed. Kirksville, Mo., 1992.

Zakai, Avihu. *Exile and Kingdom: History and Apocalypse in the Puritan Migration to America.* Cambridge and New York, 1992.

ROBIN B. BARNES

MILTITZ, Karl von (1490–1529), papal diplomat. The descendant of an ancient noble family in Saxony, Miltitz studied law at the University of Cologne from 1508. He moved to Bologna in 1510 and to Rome in 1514; there he became a papal privy chamberlain and *notarius sacri palatii.* Besides many other prebends he obtained two in the chapters of the cathedrals of Mainz and Meißen and was provost in Koblenz.

Having been active in Rome as an agent of Saxon princes, he immediately became involved in the events of the beginning of the Reformation. In 1518 he was commissioned to deliver the *Golden Rose* (Rose of Virtue), a letter of indulgence, and a privilege of confession to Elector Frederick of Saxony. Together with Cardinal Cajetan, Miltitz sought to explore Luther's attitude, an effort that resulted in the so-called *Miltitziade.* First, he delayed in handing over the *Rose* to Frederick, and at Altenburg in early 1519 he negotiated a moratorium with Luther, as condoned by Cajetan. Luther was to appear before a learned German bishop who would act as arbiter in the matter. Further activities along these lines came to naught owing to the controversies that followed the Leipzig Disputation of June-July 1519.

After the election of Charles V as emperor the papal court was no longer interested in close relations with the Saxon elector. Nevertheless Miltitz made further attempts to intervene and persuaded Luther during a meeting at Lichtenburg to publish the *Open Letter to Leo X* and the conciliatory tract *On the Freedom of the Christian.* After the failure of his diplomatic initiatives Miltitz became an adversary of Luther in accordance with Girolamo Aleandro and Hieronymus Emser. After 1521 he played no important role in diplomacy. Miltitz spent the last years of his life in Mainz. He died by drowning in the river Main.

BIBLIOGRAPHY

Bautz, Friedrich Wilhelm, ed. *Biographisch-bibliographisches Kirchenlexikon.* Hamm, Germany, 1970. See vol. 5, nos. 1538–1539.

Borth, Wilhelm. *Die Luthersache (Causa Lutheri), 1517–1524: Die Anfänge der Reformation als Frage von Politik und Recht.* Lübeck,1970.

Kalkoff, Paul. *Die Miltitziade.* Leipzig, 1911.

Leder, Hans-Günter. *Ausgleich mit dem Papst? Luthers Haltung in den Verhandlungen mit Miltitz 1520.* Stuttgart, 1969.

Neue Deutsche Biographie. See vol. 17, p. 532.

KARLHEINZ BLASCHKE

MINERS' REVOLT. At the end of the fifteenth century, miners in several of the mining centers of Upper Hungary (Slovakia), where the Thurzo-Fugger mining company was active, openly expressed their discontent. During the years 1516–1519 a struggle developed between the municipal council of Banská Bystrica and the social-religious Brotherhood of the Body of Christ over the administration of the fraternity's funds while, after 1522, the discontent of the mine and foundry workers was increased when they were paid in devalued currency. The tense situation was made worse by the decay of royal authority, the avariciousness of the nobility, the declining economy, and the spread of Reformation ideas.

Banská Bystrica, which was the administrative center of the Thurzo-Fugger Company in Hungary and the home of a large number of mine and metal workers, became the focus of the revolt when, in June 1525, about 500 armed miners from nearby settlements sought redress of their grievances. The royal authorities tried to forcefully crush the miners' movement. At the same time, Nicholas of Sabinov, Pastor of the city, accused Conrad Cordatus and John Kreysling of fomenting rebellion. They were advocates of Lutheran reforms and had been invited to preach in the city by members of the municipal council. The Association of Miners wrote to the archbishop of Esztergom to seek their release from prison.

In February 1526, armed miners attacked Banská Bystrica and imprisoned Bernard Beheim, the head of the Mining Chamber. But they failed to take the city castle and withdrew a fortnight later. A court, headed by the so-called royal commissioners, Stephen Verböczy and Gaspar Raskay, sentenced, in absentia, the leaders of the uprising to death and ordered the confiscation of their property. In August the city was attacked again and plundered by the miners.

The municipal authorities and patricians from the other nearby mining towns joined with the nobility to send troops to put down the insurrection, but the miners avoided an open fight and retreated from the city. Some of the leaders were arrested in the surrounding mountains, others in Moravia, and eventually were executed.

The royal court and the papal nuncio agreed with Nicholas of Sabinov, despite little real evidence, that the uprising of the miners had been instigated by the spread of "the Lutheran heresy." However, the revolt was a sign of the social, economic, and political tensions and conflicts that helped Reformation ideas spread throughout the *Montana*, or mining region, of Upper Hungary during the late 1520s and early 1530s.

BIBLIOGRAPHY

Heckenast, Gustáv. "A besztercebányai banyászfelkelés 1525–1526." *Századok* 86 (1952), 364–396. Primary focus on social and economic causes of the revolt.

Ratkoš, Peter. "Banícke povstanie 1525–1536 a reformačná ideológia na Slovensku." *Československý časopis historický* 2 (1954), 400–415. Evaluates the impact of Reformation ideology upon the revolt of the miners.

———. *Dokumenty k banickemu povstaniu na Slovensku 1525–1526.* Bratislava, 1957. A collection of documents that served as a basis for the following study.

———. *Povstanie baníkov na Slovensku roku, 1525–1526.* Bratislava, 1963. A comprehensive study of the revolt of the miners.

JOZEF VOZÁR

MIRACLE PLAYS. *See* Drama.

MIRACLES.

During the later Middle Ages, miracles were a fundamental component of the Christian religion. Two dominant perceptions governed the notion concerning these supernatural events: first, that miracles were performed by God through the intercession of the saints; second, that the saints' aid was attained through an exchange. Seeking help in hopeless circumstances, the faithful approached the saints at local shrines with prayers and vows of pilgrimages and votive gifts. In return, they received intercession for their devotion. Invoking the saint seemed to create a contractual obligation, and if the request was granted, the votant was required to complete the terms of his or her vow. Miracles consequently provided concrete proof of a particular saint's effectiveness, even as they satisfied an often intense desire to see the hand of God at work in the world. In contrast to the post-Enlightenment conception, what were perceived as miracles in the Middle Ages were not only extraordinary violations of the laws of nature but also unusual and unexpected resolutions to vexing problems. For example, in the absence of effective medication, illnesses were frequently perceived as life threatening; their successful cure through recourse to the saints might consequently be interpreted as cases of miraculous intervention.

In this regard, European shrines were in large part centers of "faith healing," revered because the saints cured and resolved dilemmas there in ways more effective than by other institutions. In this religious system, shrines were the predominant venue in which most miracles were recorded, although by the later Middle Ages most intercessions occurred not within the saints' sanctuaries but at the place in which the faithful prayed for relief. With their requests granted, the faithful journeyed to a saint's shrine and testified to the aid they had received. The clergy publicized these intercessions through oral pronouncement, artistic depiction, and, by the late fifteenth century, small, printed miracle books. The claim of miracles consequently buttressed the esteem of a shrine among the laity and enhanced the site's claim to indulgences, the "official" churchly seal of approval and another important spiritual currency in the late medieval world.

During the decades immediately preceding the Reformation, reports of miracles were increasing in many regions of Europe. Yet even as they mounted, they were becoming more controversial. Humanist hagiographers labored to make the saints less a focus for the laity's supernatural beliefs and more models for their pious emulation. Ecclesiastical officials, too, attacked the disruptions that new wonder-working sites produced. Fearing the enormous enthusiasm that spontaneous pilgrimages sometimes caused, they often condemned unsanctioned devotions as idolatries and even demonically produced inventions.

The Protestant reformers attempted to transform this preexisting dissatisfaction into a campaign that would rid the countryside of shrines and expunge the appetite for miracles. For Luther, the wonders reported at local shrines were alternately frauds, delusions, and even satanically produced acts, while the leaders of the emerging Reformed tradition were even more vitriolic in their attacks. Preaching, pamphlets, and illustrated broadsides popularized the Protestant critique among the people, sparking resentment, sporadic outbreaks of iconoclasm, and anticlerical violence. In Germany a declining belief in the efficacy of the saints is evident in the roughly five decades following 1520, even in regions remote from the center of religious controversy. In the duchy of Bavaria, where the miracles of the saints are amply documented from the fifteenth century until modern times, the miracle reporting of the laity declined most precipitously between 1520 and 1570.

In this period Lutheran pastors and theologians like Ludwig Rabus at Ulm labored to reform traditional belief in the saints. During the 1550s Rabus published a multivolume martyrology that stressed the importance of faith rather than supernatural intervention as the primary component of sainthood. His work extolled the confessing saints of the early church as the supreme model for Protestant piety. Yet even as efforts like these continued, more traditional perceptions were often being accommodated within the new Protestant confessions. From the earliest years of the Reformation, Luther had been portrayed in pictorial images in ways similar to the medieval saints. Stories of his prophecies continued to circulate within Lutheran circles long after the Reformation had become institutionalized. Following his death, accounts of images of Luther that wept or were preserved from fire and attack continued to inspire pilgrimages and invocations from Lutherans until the eighteenth century.

Beneath this "Luther cult," a lush undergrowth of stories about miracles worked in nature continued to satisfy the desires of Lutherans, as well as those of Catholics and Calvinists, for cases of divine intervention. In Protestant regions in particular, where saints' cults and miracles were being increasingly condemned as forms of diabolic magic, reports of prodigies multiplied most prolifically in the decades after 1550. The continuing appetite for miracles was now satisfied by a vigorous popular press that circulated tales about strange births, astral phenomena, and meteorological events through the medium of the illustrated broadside. These accounts were often interpreted in traditional Augustinian fashion as signs of God's mercy intended to warn the faithful and call them to repentance. But they were sometimes given an apocalyptic cast and promoted as portents of the imminent conclusion of world history.

As the end of the sixteenth century approached, a new cadre of counter-reforming clergy working in Germany, France, and the various Catholic regions of Europe began to renew the Roman church's claims to miracles. Theologically, the final sessions of the Council of Trent in 1563 had reaffirmed the invocation and veneration of the saints as "good and useful," in part because of the saints' power to work miracles. In the ensuing decades Catholic hagiographers began compiling voluminous testimonies to the miracles worked by the historical saints of the church. In this regard, the Cologne Carthusian Laurentius Surius's *Proofs of the Historical Saints,* published between 1571 and 1575, was typical. Collecting source material from monastic libraries throughout Europe and from other published works, Surius's almost seven hundred saints' lives included more than eight thousand miracle accounts. Like other late sixteenth-century Catholic martyrologies, his work was addressed primarily to an elite clerical audience. Yet it was also edited and sold in cheaper, digested versions. Even in its most modest forms, a work like this one did not exercise direct influence on the religion of the people. Its impact was more indirect in that the lives and miracles it retold frequently became the source material for Counter-Reformation preachers and artists.

The works of Catholic hagiographers attempted a rehabilitation of the Roman church's claims to supernatural authority through the evidence of a venerable tradition of miracles. Yet at least two additional features concerning miracles were discernible in the Counter-Reformation offensive against the Protestant religions. First, miracles were explicitly promoted as tangible proofs apostolicity of the Roman church. Second, the ability to intercede and to effect miracles was more systematically made a preserve of the clergy than it had been in the Middle Ages. At Rome, the new saints canonized during the course of the Counter-Reformation were, with only rare exceptions, members of the clergy. Moreover, in the regions in which the new counter-reforming orders were active, priests often claimed the power to work contemporary miracles through Catholic rite. This claim was especially advertised to the laity through public exorcisms. At Laon in France in 1566, perhaps the first of these dramas was worked on the young Nicole Obry, touching off a string of similar events in France, Germany, England, and Austria. Designed to prove the miraculous power of Catholic rite and priesthood, these exorcisms sparked bitter attacks from Protestant theologians and polemicists, even as they inspired Lutheran and Calvinist imitators. Because of the character of Roman exorcistic rite—its reliance on the cross, saintly images, the Eucharist, prayers, and incantations—Protestant polemicists and theologians increasingly denounced Catholic exorcisms and miracles generally as forms of magic and even witchcraft.

The Counter-Reformation clergy did not rely only on historical miracles and contemporary exorcisms as propaganda for the church's renewal. By the late sixteenth century, they were also working for a revival of the humbler conventions of thaumaturgic miracle recording that had played an integral role in late medieval saintly devotion. Through the scribal recording of miracles and their subsequent publicizing through oral, artistic, and printed media, the Catholic clergy aimed to demonstrate the continuing miraculous potency of the Roman church. Many of the dominant perceptions regarding these miracles remained those common to the Middle Ages, often revealing little long-term Reformation impact. Both the laity who reported these testimonies and the priestly scribes who recorded them still interpreted miracles as products of contractual exchanges between the saints and the faithful. Yet the lessons that the Catholic clergy drew from these accounts now took on both interior and confessional dimensions. The retelling of a miracle story in Catholic devotional literature and sermons was frequently coupled with the admonition that knowledge of these events should lead to a change in life and diligent observance of parochial duties.

By any measure, the renewal of thaumaturgic and intercessory miracles accomplished at early modern Catholic shrines was enormous, outstripping even the rising devotion of the fourteenth and fifteenth centuries. Despite the continuing attacks of Protestants, the numbers of miracles recorded at many Catholic shrines from the late sixteenth through the eighteenth century sometimes rose to the tens of thousands. This revival reveals the continuing importance that accounts of saintly intercession and divine intervention played in early modern Europe. It must also be accounted as one of the sources of the popularity of the Counter-Reformation program in those regions in which it exercised force.

[*See also* Magic; Prodigies and Portents; *and* Witchcraft.]

BIBLIOGRAPHY

Burke, Peter. "How to Be a Counter-Reformation Saint." In *Religion and Society in Early Modern Europe, 1500–1800*, edited by Kaspar von Greyerz, pp. 45–55. London, 1984.

Eire, Carlos. *War Against the Idols: The Reformation of Worship from Erasmus to Calvin.* Cambridge, 1986. The most thorough and approachable work in its field. Treats the attitudes of the major Protestant Reformers toward late medieval worship, with special emphasis on the invocation of the saints.

Kolb, Robert. *For All the Saints: Changing Perceptions of Martyrdom and Sainthood in the Lutheran Reformation.* Macon, Ga., 1987. Monographic examination of Lutheran works on the saints, focusing in particular on the multivolume martyrology of Ludwig Rabus of Ulm.

Scribner, R. W. *For the Sake of Simple Folk: Popular Propaganda for the*

German Reformation. Cambridge, 1981. Pioneering study of Lutheran visual propaganda.

———. *Popular Culture and Popular Movements in Reformation Germany.* London, 1987. Collection of Scribner's articles. Especially important for their examination of the role of ritual in late medieval religion. Two essays, "Incombustible Luther" and "Luther Myth," also demonstrate the residual appeal of miracles among early modern Lutherans.

Sigal, Pierre-André. *L'homme et le miracle dans la France médiévale, 11e–12e siècle.* Paris, 1985. The best work concerning the conventions of medieval miracle reporting and the contractual exchanges that governed relations between the saints and the faithful.

Soergel, Philip M. *Wondrous in His Saints: Propaganda for the Catholic Reformation in Bavaria.* Berkeley, 1993. Monographic examination of the Bavarian Counter-Reformers' use of shrines and miracles as one component of their campaign to revive the Roman church.

Walker, D. P. *Unclean Spirits: Possession and Exorcism in France and England during the Late Sixteenth and Early Seventeenth Centuries.* Philadelphia, 1981. Short yet brilliant study of the role that exorcism played in Catholic and Protestant propaganda.

Weinstein, Donald, and Rudolph Bell. *Saints and Society: The Two Worlds of Western Christendom, 1000–1700.* Chicago, 1982. Pathbreaking statistical study of the changing nature of sanctity over seven centuries.

PHILIP M. SOERGEL

MIRANDA, Bartolomé de. *See* Carranza, Bartolomé.

MISSALS were Latin liturgical books prescribing the order of ritual for the Catholic Mass. In the early Middle Ages the words and gestures to be performed by priests, servers, and choirs in the Mass were established by several liturgical books (e.g., sacramentary, antiphonary, lectionary, and legendary); such books were designed for use by the different persons performing the ritual and thus did not describe the Mass as a ritual whole. The missal developed from and eventually superseded these older liturgical books. Manuscript missals first appeared during the twelfth or thirteenth century. Although church authorities did not require clergy to use missals until 1570, they came increasingly into use during the late Middle Ages for a variety of reasons: a growing complexity in the Eucharistic ritual, a corresponding emphasis among theologians on precise performance of the ritual, and periodic and local reforms of the clergy that resulted in increasing literacy among priests.

Because they were designed for clerical use, missals were invariably written in Latin and presented texts the priest was to read, along with rubrics prescribing his gestures. Most missals were divided into two parts. The Ordinary of the Mass (*ordo missae*) included the invariable prayers, blessings, and readings that constituted every Mass. The Proper of the Season (*proprium de tempore*) and Proper of the Saints (*proprium sanctorum*) contained prayers and readings that varied according to liturgical season or saint's feast. Additional rites, such as funerals, weddings, and baptisms, were sometimes appended.

Although the missal prescribed the ritual of the Mass in precise detail, the exact content of missals varied considerably before the mid-sixteenth century. Standardization of both rite and text developed only with the spread of printing after 1450, and papal reforms of the missal after 1570. The rite commonly identified as Roman was adopted in many parts of western Europe by the late thirteenth century, but individual cities, regions, religious orders, monasteries, and even churches sometimes retained their own local custom or use (as in the Use of Paris or Cistercian Use). The printing press facilitated standardization of texts, typically because bishops or other church authorities subsidized and supervised the printing of large editions of missals.

Lively sixteenth-century debates over liturgy and papal authority made reform of the missal a compelling issue for the Counter-Reformation popes. Commissions appointed by popes Pius IV and Pius V recommended a uniform missal of the Roman rite; Pius V's bull *Qui primum tempore* (14 July 1570) declared the *Missale Romanum ex decreto sacrosancti Concilii Tridentini restitutum, Pii V. Pont. Max. iussu editum* the church's authoritative missal. Only churches able to demonstrate two centuries of continuous use were permitted to retain a local rite. The new text reproduced substantially the *Missale Romanum* commonly used in late medieval Rome—with humanist Latin replacing some of its medieval "barbarisms." Popes Clement VIII (1604) and Urban VIII (1634) added minor changes to the 1570 missal, but there was no new edition of the Roman missal until 1920. Assisted by the printing press, the Counter-Reformation popes managed to establish the Roman missal as the authoritative liturgical text of the Catholic church.

[*See also* Hymnals *and* Hymns.]

BIBLIOGRAPHY

Jungmann, Joseph A. *The Mass of the Roman Rite: Its Origins and Development.* Translated by Francis A. Brunner. 2 vols. Reprint, Dublin and Westminster, Md., 1986. For Tridentine reform of the Roman Mass and missal, see vol. 1, pp. 127–141.

Kingdon, Robert M. "Patronage, Piety, and Printing in Sixteenth-Century Europe." In *A Festschrift for Frederick B. Artz*, edited by David H. Pinkney and Theodore Ropp, pp. 19–36. Durham, N.C., 1964. Important article on the publishing history of sixteenth-century liturgical books which includes a case study of the production, sale, and distribution of the Roman breviary by Antwerp printer Christoffel Plantijn. Information about Plantijn's production of the Roman missal of 1570.

Leroquais, V. *Les sacramentaires et les missels manuscrits des bibliothèques publiques de France.* 4 vols. Paris, 1924. Important catalogue of hundreds of missals from all over Europe, the vast majority medieval but a few post-1500. Includes excerpts from liturgical texts.

Mayer, A. L. "Renaissance, Humanismus und Liturgie." *Jahrbuch für Liturgiewissenschaft* 14 (1934), 123–171. Discusses sixteenth-century reform of the Roman missal.

VIRGINIA REINBURG

MISSIONS. During the sixteenth century, missionary work among non-Christian peoples was undertaken mostly by Catholics. The reason for this was not theological but practical: the driving forces behind early European expansion were Portugal and Castile, and these two powers not only remained strictly Catholic but also considered that their gaining overseas territories was a compensation for the losses the church had suffered in Europe through the Reformation. In addition, the Reformation had, through its abolition of the religious orders, deprived itself of the only ecclesiastical organization with the necessary infrastructure and motivation for missionary work.

The missions began as a collaboration between the two Iberian crowns and the orders. In theory, at least, the papacy also played an important role, but in practice, well into the seventeenth century, when the *Congregatio de Propaganda Fide* was founded in 1622, its role was only minor. Indeed, in the eyes of Iberian politicians the papacy was actually a hindrance, for the missions were originally founded under royal patronage, a system of royal control of church and missions. This patronage gave the monarchs sweeping powers over the church, but in return obliged them to maintain and finance the church and the missions. Over the years 1418 to 1493, papal bulls were issued that, while granting the Iberian powers numerous rights over the church (rights that they probably would have taken anyway), also charged them with the duty of spreading the faith and developing the church in the new territories. In Portugal these rights, which were originally the prerogative of the Order of Christ, were later conferred upon the king. In 1493 the pope granted the Spanish rulers the exclusive mandate for missionary work in the West Indies, and the Portuguese that for the East Indies; in 1501 he granted them the church tithes, on the condition that they then assume the sole responsibility for building and endowing churches; and in 1508 he made the Spanish king the "Universal Patron of America," which in practical terms meant the right of appointment to all church benefices. Both crowns guarded their church prerogatives jealously, even (or rather particularly) from papal interference.

All explorations of discovery were accompanied by missionary activities, beginning with even the earliest Portuguese expeditions to circumnavigate the African continent. The initially promising missionary contacts with the kingdom of the Congo turned out to be rather disappointing; interest shifted toward India, and the slave trade got the upper hand in Africa. In India missionary successes were at first confined to the limited Portuguese area of influence, although the bishopric of Goa, founded in 1534, became an archbishopric in 1558, with suffragan bishops in Cochin and Malacca. The inclusion in 1579 of Macao and in 1588 of Funay in Japan was the result of the activities of the missionary Order of Jesus. The Jesuits, particularly through the efforts of Francis Xavier (1506–1552), deliberately expanded their operations first over, and then beyond, the Portuguese area of influence, and in 1549–1551 created the conditions for the rapid flowering of their mission in Japan. The religious and political pluralism in this country and the Jesuits' skillful adaptation to the Japanese mentality through Alessandro Valignano (1539–1606) were the essential preconditions for this success. But the Jesuits' position was called into question following Japanese reunification in 1573, after which it was dependent on the missionaries' ability to cooperate with the Portuguese traders coming to Japan with Chinese goods. The appearance of other Europeans made the Portuguese and the Jesuits dispensable as well as suspect in Japan. After a period of persecution, Christianity was banned, and in 1639 the country was closed to foreigners.

The Jesuits, however, drew on their successful adaptation to Japanese conventions when they moved into China and India. In 1583 Matteo Ricci (1552–1610) was able to establish himself in China in the guise of a quasi-Confucian scholar from the West. Others followed this example, and in southern India, beginning in 1607, Roberto de Nobili attempted to overcome the usual identification of Christianity with Europe by blending Hindu elements with his message. Missionaries had, up until this point, always taken for granted the doctrine that the unbaptized would, without exception, automatically suffer eternal damnation (*Mk.* 16:16), but the idea began to take root that salvation was also possible for some "noble heathens," such as the followers of Confucius. Despite the Jesuits' considerable philological and philosophical achievements in this field, their approach was thwarted by the efforts of their political opponents, combined with a rejection of Jesuit adaptations by Augustinian theologians.

In Ibero-America, however, the missionary effort was, in terms of size and continuity, more successful than at any other period in the history of Christianity. By the year 1600 in Spanish America there were thirty bishoprics in the four church provinces of Santo Domingo, Mexico, Lima, and Bogotá. By the end of the sixteenth century a total of 5,428 missionaries had been sent to America at the Crown's expense, of whom 2,782 were Franciscans, 1,579 Dominicans, and 351 Jesuits (whose great moment was to come in the seventeenth century). At first the missionary ideal served to legitimize the *Conquista* and the exploitation of the Indians by means of the so-called *Encomienda*; in theory this system meant that in return for their labour the *Encomendero* was charged with attending to the spiritual needs of the Indians who were "entrusted" to him.

It is unique in the history of colonialism that from an early stage missionaries protested against this practice. From 1511 Dominicans fought for the rights of the Indians and for a peaceful evangelization. The most important protagonist was Bartolomé de Las Casas (1484–1566), who experimented with peaceful missions and produced initiatives at Court as well as numerous writings. An abridged version of his larger works, the *Brevissima relación de la destrucción de las Indias* (1542, printed 1552), was used by Spain's enemies for propaganda purposes, and has, up to the present day, shaped throughout the Protestant world the erroneous perception of Spanish genocide of the Indians. The Dominicans' efforts did not, however, go without some degree of success: Indian slavery was abolished, and the power of the *Encomienda* was weakened, at least in law, although it was admittedly never completely possible to enforce this in distant America. The early Franciscan missionaries in Mexico were much influenced by the eschatological ideals of the *spirituali* movement and dreamt of founding a Christian utopia among the Indians, whose poverty and simplicity closely resembled the Franciscan ideal; in this model state other Spaniards would essentially have been superfluous. In Tlatelolco a college was established for the purpose of educating the future elite of a Christian, but Indian, Mexico. The confrontation with the Indian religion led Bernardino de Sahagún (c.1500–1590) to amass a great body of material about the culture of the Aztecs; his *Historia general de las cosas de la Nueva España* has become one of the most important sources of our knowledge about the pre-Spanish history of Mexico.

But these same Franciscans also destroyed pagan writings and icons by the thousand. Almost universally missionaries regarded the religion of the Indians with complete abhorrence (the later Las Casas was a rare exception). From 1575 the Spanish Inquisition in America was no longer responsible for the Indians, but this was only because they were thought to be too weak in faith. In Guadalupe in the year 1531 the Virgin Mary appeared before an Indian, a sign perhaps that Spanish and Indian religious elements were indeed coming together, but on the whole, pagan rites continued to be widely practiced, cloaked in the mantle of Christianity. Strenuous efforts were made, particularly in Peru, to eliminate such customs.

In addition, from the 1560s onward the Crown tightened its control over the church. As a result, the missions found themselves having to maintain a more "pragmatic" line in their dealings with the Indians. The Jesuit José de Acosta (1540–1600) epitomized this approach in his work *De procuranda Indorum salute* (1588). The missions now concentrated their efforts in grouping the Indians together in special settlements (*misiones* or *reducciones*), where they received instruction on the principles of Christianity and were also taught the basics of agriculture and introduced to other elements of Spanish civilization. Because of their notoriously bad influence, all Spaniards, apart from missionaries and officials, were strictly prohibited from entering these Indian settlements. The wrongly so-called Jesuit state of Paraguay, founded in the seventeenth century, was nothing but a particularly thorough realization of these principles. It had by now become clear that the spread of Christianity, and of Spanish civilization, would take time; it even became possible to deny Indians the right to partake in the Eucharist. Philip II overruled this restriction, a move that Acosta supported on the grounds that the Eucharist was also intended for the weak. The ordination to the priesthood, however, was now out of the question for Indians.

Similarly, in other parts of the world, a kind of "pigmentocracy" was established, with exceptions made for East Asians, who were officially deemed to be whites. In Brazil, which in the sixteenth century had only the lone bishopric of Bahia, and in the Philippines, which as a subcolony of Mexico belonged to Spanish America, the situation was the same. The attempt was made to apply the lessons learnt in the Americas to the Philippines; by the massive deployment of missionaries it was hoped that the brutalities of the *Conquista* phase could be avoided.

Missionary activity of a different sort may be associated with the Anabaptists of the Reformation. Persuaded, as they were, that established Christendom, both Catholic and Protestant, was profoundly perverted and did not show the true way to salvation, the Anabaptists set out in a vigorous proselytizing activity throughout central Europe. Since they almost without exception failed in commanding governmental support for their understanding of the Christian faith and were indeed suppressed in most places, the propagation of their tenets could occur only through the proclamation of their Anabaptist message, not in non-European contexts but in their own regions. Accordingly, the spread of Anabaptism and the establishment of a network of Anabaptist congregations throughout central Europe was the result of such missionary activity. It was undertaken by theologically untrained missionaries.

From a modern perspective, the Christian missionaries of the sixteenth century presented the natives with a double hurdle. On the one hand, the newly discovered peoples were for the most part not only "pagans," and as such denied eternal salvation, but also, in the tradition of antiquity, "barbarians," and therefore denied the temporal salvation of the long tradition of European culture. On the other hand, because they were considered to be "white," and because they lived in advanced and literate civilizations, exceptions were made for the peoples of the Far East, who were judged to have a natural access to eternal salvation, a possibility no missionary was prepared to consider in the case of American Indian "barbarians."

[*See also* America; Discoveries in the New World; Jesuits; *and* Xavier, Francis.]

BIBLIOGRAPHY

Boxer, C. R. *The Christian Century in Japan, 1549–1650.* Reprint, Berkeley, 1974. Not so much a study of missions, but of the cultural and political encounter.

———. *The Church Militant and the Iberian Expansion, 1440–1770.* Baltimore, 1978. Brilliant chapters by an outstanding secular historian.

Enrique, D., ed. *Historia general de la iglesia en América latina.* Salamanca, 1981–. A multivolume series, regionally arranged.

Friede, Juan, and Benjamin Keen, eds. *Bartolomé de las Casas in History: Toward an Understanding of the Man and His Work.* De Kalb, Ill., 1971. Important collection of essays; basic information on Las Casas.

Henkel, Willi, ed. *Bibliographia missionaria.* Rome, 1937–. Annual bibliography.

Latourette, Kenneth S. *A History of the Expansion of Christianity.* 7 vols. Reprint, Exeter, 1971. The Protestant classic of mission history.

Lopetegui, Leon, Félix Zubillaga, and Antonio de Engana. *Historia del la Iglesia en la América española: Desde el descubrimiento hasta comienzos del siglo XIX.* 2 vols. Madrid, 1965–1966.

Minamiki, George. *The Chinese Rites Controversy: From Its Beginning to Modern Times.* Chicago, 1985.

Moran, Joseph. *The Father Visitor: Alessandro Valignano and the Early Jesuits in Japan.* London, 1992. The creator of new missionary strategies in the East.

Neill, Stephan Charles. *A History of Christianity in India: The Beginnings to A.D. 1707.* Cambridge, 1984. From a British missionary in India.

Phelan, John L. *The Millennial Kingdom of the Franciscans in the New World.* 2d rev. ed. Berkeley, 1970. A study of Franciscans in Mexico, especially of Gerónimo de Mendieta.

Ricard, Robert. *The Spiritual Conquest of Mexico: An Essay on the Apostolate and the Evangelizing Methods of the Mendicant Orders in New Spain, 1523–1572.* Reprint, Berkley, 1982. Originally published in French: *La conquête spirituelle du Mexique: Essai sur l'apostolat et les méthodes des ordres mendiants en Nouvelle Espagne de 1523 à 1572,* Paris, 1933. The classic on early missions in Mexico; in certain parts outdated, but still worth reading.

Rule, Paul A. *K'ung-tzu or Confucius? The Jesuit Interpretation of Confucius.* Sydney, London, and Boston, 1986.

Santos Hernández, Angel. *Las misiones bajo el Patronato portugués.* Madrid, 1977. On Portuguese missions and the royal *padroado.*

Schäufele, W. *Das missionarische Bewußtsein und Wirken der Täufer.* Neukirchen-Vluyn, 1966.

Schurhammer, Georg. *Francis Xavier: His Life, His Times.* 4 vols. Rome, 1973–1981. Originally published in German: *Franz Xaver: Sein Leben und seine Zeit,* 2 vols. in 4 pts, Freiburg, 1955–1973. Not only a very thorough biography, but a history of the times.

Shiels, W. *King and Church: The Rise and Fall of the Patronato Real.* Chicago, 1961.

Streit, Robert, et al., eds. *Bibliotheca Missionum.* 2d ed. Freiburg, 1960. Very thorough comprehensive bibliography.

Thompson, Donald Eugene. *Maya Paganism and Christianity: A History of the Fusion of Two Religions.* New Orleans, 1954.

WOLFGANG REINHARD

MITMÁNEK, Václav (c.1510–c.1553), Czech theologian, politician, and organizer of Bohemian non-Catholics. Originally a member (1530–1537) of the Unity of Brethren, or Bohemian Brethren, Mitmánek studied in Wittenberg, Basel, and Paris and then later in Italy, where he was ordained and received the degree of doctor of theology (Venice, 1540). Inspired by the reform ideas of Martin Luther, he left the Unity of Brethren (1537)—at that time a very conservative religious community—which turned the brethren clergy against him. Mitmánek understood the weaknesses of a spontaneous Lutheranization of a majority of the Czech population (Hussites—i.e., Utraquists or Lutheranized neo-Utraquists), and in 1539–1543 he tried to reorganize all non-Catholics in Bohemia into a Czech national church based on a Lutheran model. Supported by Czech Utraquist noblemen and patricians, he became a preacher in the most important Hussite church in Bohemia (the Church of Our Lady in the Old Town of Prague) in 1540, and in 1541 he was elected a member of the lower consistory, a central office of the Bohemian Utraquist clergy.

Mitmánek's political efforts to consolidate the neo-Utraquists and the brethren within the framework of a new church were opposed both by the autonomous Unity of Brethren and by King Ferdinand I of Habsburg. Ferdinand forbade the election of a neo-Utraquist bishop and the organization of a unified non-Catholic consistory and church administration in Bohemia. Ferdinand banished Mitmánek from the kingdom in 1543 and, after Mitmánek secretly returned home, sent him to prison in 1544. After his release in June 1544, Mitmánek lived in exile in Saxony, Poland, and elsewhere. The last record concerning Mitmánek is his letter dated "in Russia" 1 February 1553.

Mitmánek was not an original theological thinker but rather a receptive pupil of Luther and a courageous and confessional politician. He searched for a compromise of the Czech Hussite and Unity of Brethren traditions with Lutheran innovations. His aim was a church supported by the Protestant nobility and burghers but independent of the Catholic king. In the first half of the sixteenth century, support for this policy was too weak, but Mitmánek's goals were partly realized at the beginning of the seventeenth century.

BIBLIOGRAPHY

Janáček, Josef. *České dějiny. Doba předbělohorská I/1* (History of Bohemia, 1526–1547). 2d ed. Prague, 1971. Critical analysis of Mitmánek's confessional policies 1539–1543. See especially pp. 197–206.

Krofta, Kamil. "Václav Mitmánek a Bratří" (Václav Mitmánek and the Czech Brethren). *Časopis Musea Království českého* 91 (1917), 2–20, 143–156. A slightly one-sided apology of Mitmánek's relation to the Bohemian Brethren, minimizing the ideological differences between both parties.

Krofta, Kamil, ed. *Doktor Václav Mitmánek panu tatikovi milému* (Letters Written by Václav Mitmánek to His Father). Prague, 1931. Edition of Mitmánek's private correspondence from 1533–1553, with a synthetic biographical outline.

JAROSLAV PÁNEK

MODED, Hermannus (Heb., Modetus; Dutch, Herman Strijcker; 1520?–1603), Dutch Calvinist minister. Born in Zwolle, in the province of Overijssel, Moded studied and then briefly taught at the University of Cologne. In 1556 he became vicar at the Saint Michielskerk in Zwolle. He lost his living there after offering Communion in both kinds. In 1558 King Christian III of Denmark appointed him court preacher in Copenhagen, where he also taught at the academy. In 1560 he became minister to the Reformed church "under the cross" in Antwerp. With Antwerp as his base, Moded traveled to London, Emden, and Geneva; he also preached in various parts of the Netherlands. Seized by Catholic officials several times, he managed always to escape. Anecdotes circulated about his daring. After the iconoclastic riots of 1566, Moded could never shake the suspicion, probably unfounded, of having incited those in Antwerp. In 1567, with the arrival of Fernando Álvarez de Toledo, duke of Alba, Moded fled to England, where he served briefly as minister to the Dutch fugitives' church in Norwich. Between 1568 and 1571 he traveled extensively. In 1568 he served as secretary at the convent of Wezel, and in 1571 he attended the Synod of Emden. In 1572, when the Dutch Revolt began anew, Moded went to Zeeland, where he became minister in Zierikzee. He found it difficult to settle down, however, and was censured for his wanderlust. Moded was in Ghent in 1578–1579 but did not play a leading role in the revolution that brought a socially radical, Calvinist theocratic regime to power there.

In 1580 Moded was called to serve the young Calvinist congregation in Utrecht. Because of his age and experience he soon set the tone in Utrecht's consistory—a bold and combative one. He so alienated Utrecht's magistrates that they dismissed him in 1585. A new, pro-Calvinist stadtholder and magistracy restored Moded to his ministry in 1586. Moded then became chief religious adviser to the Calvinist, theocratic regime that controlled Utrecht between 1586 and 1588. He also wielded great influence with Robert Dudley, earl of Leicester, then governor-general of the Netherlands. He involved himself deeply in politics, even helping to execute a string of purges that eliminated all non-Calvinists from Utrecht's municipal and provincial governments. In 1587 he accompanied an unauthorized delegation that offered sovereignty over the Netherlands to Queen Elizabeth. In 1588 Moded conspired to overthrow the same Calvinist, pro-Leicestrian regime that he had helped to bring to power in 1586. Discovered, Moded fled Utrecht and was promptly dismissed from office. He spent the following years in Germany serving as a spy for the States of Holland. As of 1603 he had settled again in Zeeland, where he died. Three publications by Moded are known: an apology, an examination of the Lord's Supper, and a historical refutation of Anabaptism.

A firebrand, Moded earned the nickname "Immoded," given to him by Charlotte of Bourbon. Even other Calvinist ministers disapproved of his political involvements, which helped to give Calvinist ministers in the Netherlands a reputation for being seditious and power-hungry.

BIBLIOGRAPHY

Brutel de la Rivière, Guilliam Johannes. *Het leven van Hermannus Moded, een der eerste calvinistische predikers in ons vaderland.* Haarlem, Netherlands, 1879. Antiquated, but the only existing monograph on Moded. Includes his *Apologie.*

Kaplan, Benjamin J. *Calvinists and Libertines: Confession and Community in Utrecht, 1578–1620.* Oxford, forthcoming. Moded in Utrecht.

Molhuysen, P. C., and P. J. Blok, eds. *Nieuw Nederlandsch biografisch woordenboek.* 10 vols. Leiden, 1911–1937. Vol. 3, pp. 862–873, contains a detailed biography.

BENJAMIN J. KAPLAN

MOHÁCS, BATTLE OF. On 29 August 1526, the forces of the Ottoman sultan Süleyman I inflicted a major defeat on the Hungarian kingdom. On a plain west of the Danube River in southern Hungary a Turkish army led by the sultan himself decisively crushed the vastly outnumbered army of the Hungarian king. The unfortunate Louis II, the archbishops of Esztergom and Kalocsa, five bishops, twenty-eight magnates, five hundred nobles, and nearly sixteen thousand of the twenty thousand member Hungarian army fell. Over the course of the next fifteen months rival political factions in Hungary elected and crowned two different kings, János Zsigmond Zápolya and Ferdinand I. The competition for the throne eventually produced further opportunities for Turkish expansion. After Zápolya's death in 1540 Süleyman I moved quickly to capture the central third of Hungary, a region the Turks would control for the next century and a half.

Along with the enormous political and military consequences, the defeat at Mohács proved to be crucial for the subsequent religious development of Hungary. After Mohács conflict between the followers of Zápolya and those of Ferdinand I, the lack of effective leadership in the Catholic church, and the desperate military situation all combined to weaken the old church and to facilitate the spread of Protestantism. Neither King János nor Ferdinand I was able to retard the spread of Protestantism since both needed political and military allies in Hungary.

The defeat at Mohács hobbled the Catholic church not only because of the loss of leadership and the subsequent losses of ecclesiastical property, but also because Protestants readily associated the disaster with Roman corruption and wickedness. According to the Protestants the kingdom had fallen into defeat and disarray because it had followed the pope. Consequently Hungary could be revived only through a spiritual resurgence of true Christianity based on scripture that would wipe away popery. As long as the Roman church held sway, no recovery would be possible because God would continue to punish Hungary for its sins. For many Protestants the establishment of pure Christianity was not only more important than the problem of the Turks—it was a necessary precondition for the eventual expulsion of the Ottoman occupiers. Thus the disastrous military defeat at Mohács greatly weakened the Catholic church in Hungary and helped the spread of Protestantism.

[*See also* Hungary *and* Zápolya, János Zsigmond.]

BIBLIOGRAPHY

Bak, János M., and BélaKirály, eds. *From Hunyadi to Rákóczy: War and Society in Late Medieval and Early Modern Hungary.* New York, 1982.

A collection of recent articles on Hungarian history immediately before, during, and after the Battle of Mohács.

Hóman, Bálint, and Gyula Szekfü. *Magyar történet* (Hungarian History). 5 vols. Budapest, 1990. The events surrounding the historic battle are covered in vols. 3 and 4 of this classic synthesis of Hungarian history.

Kiss, Károly, and Tamás Katona, eds. *Mohács emlékezete* (In Memory of Mohács). Budapest, 1979. The collection contains eyewitness and contemporary accounts of Mohács from both western and Turkish sources.

Magyari, István. *Az országokban való sok romlásoknak okairól* (On the Many Causes of the Ruin of Nations). Budapest, 1979. The best summation by a Reformation-era Lutheran pastor of the Protestant argument that Catholicism had led Hungary to disaster.

Rúzsás, Lajos, and Ferenc Szakály, eds. *Mohács tanulmányok* (Mohács Studies). Budapest, 1986. Further articles on various aspects of the decisive battle and its aftermath.

PETER SCHIMERT

MOIBANUS, Ambrose (1494–1554), Lutheran pastor in Breslau and humanist author. Moibanus was the second Lutheran reformer in his native city of Breslau, but he made more changes than had the first reformer there, Johann Hess. Son of a shoemaker, Moibanus attended the Latin school in Neisse, and the universities of Kraków (1510–1514) and Vienna (1515–1517), earning a bachelor and master of arts, respectively. In Vienna he published three hymns by Pico della Mirandola, and a poem *(carmen)* of his own on the origin of religion and the mystery of the Trinity (1517).

In 1520 and 1521, Moibanus was in Wittenberg and made contact with Philipp Melanchthon. At the same time, he served as the head of the Breslau cathedral school and of the parish school of Saint Mary Magdalene, where he was the first to teach Greek and later Hebrew. He wrote a Latin grammar, *Paedia artis Grammatice* (1521; 2d ed., 1522), and edited letters by Erasmus for teaching purposes.

In 1523 again in Wittenberg, Moibanus studied theology. When the city council of Breslau acquired the patronage over Saint Elizabeth church, it offered Moibanus the position of chief pastor (18 May 1525) and paid for his promotion to doctor of theology in Wittenberg (26 June 1525). On 3 August 1525 Moibanus met the bishop of Breslau, Jacob von Salza, at Grottkau. The bishop welcomed him as a "doctor of Holy Scripture and acolyte," and handed him a letter of investiture as pastor of Saint Elizabeth. Although Moibanus never held any order higher than acolyte, he honored the bishops of Breslau as his ecclesiastical superiors throughout his life.

As pastor of Saint Elizabeth, Moibanus revised the canon of the Mass (by 1540), after he abolished the blessing of palms and other objects of worship (1525), for which Johannes Cochlaeus took him to task in *Defensio Ceremoniarum Ecclesiae adversus errores et calumnias Trium librorum D. Ambrosij Moibanusi* (1543). But Moibanus retained most of the artistic, musical, and ceremonial features of the medieval Latin Mass, which set the standard for all Lutheran parishes in Silesia. In 1526 he married Anna Boncke (d. 1569) of Schweidnitz, with whom he fathered twelve children.

Moibanus organized a municipal welfare service and was concerned about pastoral care for prisoners. He enabled the gifted poor to obtain a higher education and wanted to expand the Breslau high school system into a university by trying to establish a medical school. Moibanus also ordained Lutheran ministers for the Silesian countryside (1547–1551).

Moibanus issued a *Mandat Jesu Christi* (1537), prefaced by Luther, against the Schwenckfelders in Liegnitz, who had suspended the office of the ministry and the administration of the Lord's Supper. He published a German (1535) and three Latin editions (1537, 1544, and 1546) of a *Catechismus.* In an *Epistola de consecratione Palmarum et aliis ceremoniis Ecclesiasticis ad Episcopum Suffraganeum* (1541), Moibanus exhorted the Breslau *Weihbishof,* Johannes Thiel, to turn deserted cloisters into educational institutions for impecunious students, thereby preventing church property from falling into secular hands. He repeated this plea in an edition of Terence (1540) and in a poem published together with an *Epistola Gratulatoria* by Melanchthon on the occasion of the election of Balthasar von Promnitz as bishop of Breslau (1541). Moibanus wrote an *Epistola consolatoria ad Christianos fratres qui Turcarum tyrannide opprimuntur* (2d ed., 1544), and offered refuge to pastors who had been displaced by the Turkish conquests. Besides a German hymn and a German paraphrase of the Lord's Prayer, Moibanus composed many Latin epitaphs for Breslau patricians. In 1550 he corresponded with Calvin, and in 1552 he hosted and corresponded with Lelio Sozzini. Before his death he worked on an anthology from the works of Melanchthon and Seneca as well as the lives of Roman emperors.

BIBLIOGRAPHY

Bauch, G. *Geschichte des Breslauer Schulwesens in der Zeit der Reformation.* Breslau, 1911. Discusses Moibanus's contributions as a humanist school reformer.

Konrad, P. *Dr. Ambrosius Moibanus.* Halle, 1891. A biography of Ambrose Moibanus.

Sabisch, A. "Der Messkanon des Breslauer Pfarrers Dr. Ambrosius Moibanus." *Archiv für Schlesische Kirchengeschichte* 3 (1938), 98–126. Discusses Moibanus's liturgical reforms, as does Sander.

Sander, H.-A. "Die lateinischen Haupt- und Nebengottesdienste in 16. und 17. Jahrhundert." Diss., Uniwersytet Wrocławski, 1937.

MANFRED P. FLEISCHER

MOLINA, Luis de (1535–1600), Spanish Jesuit theologian and theorist of the interrelation of divine grace and human free choice. Born in Cuenca in Castile, Molina was received into the Society of Jesus at Alcalá in 1553. In Portugal, after studies at Coimbra, he taught theology at Évora from 1568 until 1583, when he was freed from teaching to prepare his lecture materials for publication. Molina began a commentary on part I of Thomas Aquinas's *Summa theologiae,* but his manuscript was so extensive on questions concerning divine foreknowledge, providence, and predestination, all in relation to free choice, that he lifted his treatment of these and brought out a separate work, the *Concordia liberi arbitrii cum gratiae donis, divina praescientia, providentia, predestinatione et reprobatione* (1588). His two-volume commentary on part 1 of the *Summa* treated natural knowledge of God, the Trinity, creation, and the angels (1592). But his main project after 1590 was *De iustitia et iure,* treating the major questions of personal and socioeconomic morality. He oversaw the publication of the first three volumes, while four others came out posthumously (1609). In 1600 he was called to teach moral theology in Madrid, but he died there shortly after arriving.

Molina was criticized, especially by a phalanx of Dominicans, for making the graced free decisions of the will a cause or precondition of divine predestination to eternal salvation. Molina distinguished in God various types of foreknowledge, by one of which, called *scientia media,* God knows the outcome of human choices in the hypothesis of the creation of a certain order of reality. God's decree predestining some persons to salvation is then logically subsequent to their foreseen meritorious actions. Against this view, the Thomists of Salamanca, headed by Domingo Bañez, denied such intermediate divine knowledge and held that predestination is prior to foreseen human meritorious actions. The dispute was argued but not resolved before a papal tribunal from 1597 to 1607, with both theories in the end being permitted. Molina's work generally exemplifies the shift of Catholic thought on grace and salvation away from the biblical personalism of the Decree on Justification issued by the Council of Trent (1547) to elaborate analysis, speculation, and technicality.

BIBLIOGRAPHY

Backer, Augustin de, and Carl Sommervogel, eds. *Bibliothèque de la Compagnie de Jésus.* 2d ed. Brussels, 1894. See vol. 5, cols. 1169–1179, for a list of Luis de Molina's works and related publications.

Costello, Frank B. *The Political Philosophy of Luis de Molina, S.J., 1535–1600.* Rome and Spokane, Wash., 1974.

Freddoso, Alfred J. *On Divine Foreknowledge.* Ithaca, N.Y., 1988. Translation of part 4 of *Concordia.*

Polgar, Lázló. *Bibliographie sur l'histoire de la Compagnie de Jésus, 1901–1980.* 3 vols. 6 pts. Rome, 1981–1990. Volume 1, pp. 473–475, lists studies on Molinism; vol. 3, part 2, pp. 544–549, lists studies on Molina's life, works, and thought. Annual continuation in *Archivum Historicum Societatis Iesu.*

Rabeneck, Johannes. "De vita et scriptis Ludovici Molina." *Archivum Historicum Societatis Iesu* 19 (1950), 75–145.

Smith, Gerard. *Freedom in Molina.* Chicago, 1966. Relates Molina's reactions to Reformation denials of free choice.

Stegmüller, Friedrich. *Geschichte des Molinismus.*Vol. 1, *Neue Molinasschriften.* Münster, 1935. Contains an 80-page biography and numerous edited shorter treatises and letters from manuscript. The planned history was not continued.

Jared Wicks

MONARCHY. *See* Magistracy.

MONASTERIES.

[*This entry comprises two articles on the fate of monasteries and convents during the sixteenth century, focusing on those confiscated, secularized, and forcibly closed and those that continued as Protestant institutions. The first considers monasteries and convents in England, Scotland, Wales, and Ireland; the second examines monasteries and convents on the Continent, including those in Roman Catholic areas that were reformed both before and after the Council of Trent. For related discussions, see* Monasticism, Nuns, *and* Religious Orders.]

The British Isles

The religious orders were an integral component of the pre-Reformation church in the British Isles. Their monasteries, nunneries, and friaries were among the most visible manifestations of the church's presence in society, and the religious themselves played a vital role in the social, economic, and political structures of their local communities. Thirteen hundred religious houses accommodating approximately fifteen thousand men and women of the various religious orders could be found scattered throughout the three kingdoms of England (including Wales), Ireland, and Scotland in the first decades of the sixteenth century. There were clear distinctions between the orders of monks, nuns, and canons regular, all of whom lived in stable communities governed by locally elected or appointed superiors, and the mendicant orders of friars, who were members of highly centralized international organizations and were moved from one house to another. Some orders were strictly contemplative, while others were more active. Houses for female religious were a minority, and in England there were a number of foundations where both men and women lived under the same roof. There were also a number of hospitals regulated by monastic rules, and the priories and commanderies of the hospitaler monk-knights of St. John of Jerusalem held extensive estates throughout the British Isles. The medieval religious foundations of all three kingdoms disappeared in the course of the sixteenth century, but in each case the process of dissolution was quite different.

England and Wales. At the beginning of the 1530s there were approximately 775 monasteries and friaries in England and Wales. These were scattered fairly evenly across the country, but Wales had a relatively small number (39), while there were large concentrations of houses in Yorkshire and Lincolnshire and around London. The largest and wealthiest were the ancient Benedictine foundations, such as Glastonbury, Westminster, St. Albans, and Bury St. Edmunds. All but two of the twenty wealthiest monastic houses in England were Benedictine foundations, and seven of the eight cathedral priories were also Benedictine (Canterbury, Winchester, Durham, Worcester, Ely, Norwich, and Rochester). Their conventual buildings were among the architectural wonders of the day and often contained the shrines of famous miracle-working saints. Their enormous landholdings across many counties generated income that was the basis of both economic and political power. The abbots, many of whom held seats in the House of Lords, lived the lives of powerful magnates. The monks, too, enjoyed a standard of living that was unequaled even among the aristocracy and had access to a university education within the monastic colleges at Oxford and Cambridge. Around half of the eighty-two Benedictine houses for monks provided such opportunities, while about a dozen of the sixty-odd Benedictine nunneries were moderately wealthy.

Unlike the wealthy Benedictine houses, the more numerous monasteries of Augustinian canons (160) and nuns (40) were small and poor. More than half of these houses had fewer than ten inmates and annual incomes of less than £200. Living conditions varied considerably at this lower end of the scale, but many monks and nuns must have had as precarious an existence as the rest of the peasantry. The Benedictines and the Augustinians were together the largest religious orders in England and Wales, but there were also many houses of Cistercians (74), Cluniac monks (16), and Premonstratensian canons (29). There were also nine houses of Carthusians, two of Bonhommes, and five of Trinitarians. The mendicant orders were well represented with nearly two hundred friaries. The great majority of these were impoverished foundations that were in an advanced state of decay by the 1530s. The observant reform movement had not made a significant impact upon the mendicant orders in England, with only six houses of Observant Franciscans in the whole country. England was unusual in having twenty-two monasteries in which both male and female religious lived under one roof, although they were strictly divided. The Brigittine abbey of Syon was the largest of these, as well as one of the wealthiest monasteries in the country. The other twenty-one mixed houses belonged to the native Gilbertine order. They were relatively small monasteries and were mostly located in Lincolnshire. England also had sixteen hospitals that appear to have been run along monastic lines.

The question of the spiritual, moral, and intellectual state of the monasteries prior to their dissolution has caused considerable debate during the twentieth century. Earlier writers made much use of the damning reports of the 1535 visitation commissioners, but most of this evidence has now been discredited. Although a large number of religious establishments, especially the smaller ones, were to a greater or lesser extent in need of reformation in the 1530s, there can be little basis for the inflated charges of "manifest sin, vicious, carnal and abominable living," which the act dissolving the lesser monasteries (1536) alleged to be prevalent in these houses. It is now generally agreed that the most observant houses were those of the Carthusians, the Observant Franciscans, and the Brigittine abbey of Syon. Many of the larger Benedictine foundations were likewise in a healthy spiritual condition despite their wealth, and the friaries in London, Oxford, and Cambridge continued to be centers of spiritual and intellectual exertion. For the majority of houses, however, slender financial resources and small communities combined to produce a rather lax approach to religious duties. Such generalizations cannot be made without some caution, for there are numerous examples of smaller nunneries in which the regular life was being faithfully observed in difficult financial circumstances.

The dissolution of the monasteries in England and Wales took place in five well-defined phases during the reign of Henry VIII (1509–1547). First the "lesser" monasteries were suppressed in 1536. Next, monasteries that were involved in the Pilgrimage of Grace were dissolved during 1537. The third stage began in late 1537, when a number of monasteries surrendered to the Crown of their own volition; then, in 1538, the mendicant orders were suppressed. Finally, the government under Thomas Cromwell decided to force the surrender of the remaining religious houses between late 1538 and early 1540. The last surrender was that of the hospitaler monk-knights in May 1540.

The dissolutions of the 1530s were not the first in English history. Henry V had dissolved all of the French alien priories in England and Wales as far back as 1414, while Cardinal Thomas Wolsey suppressed thirty smaller monasteries in the 1520s to provide endowments for his colleges at Oxford and Ipswich. The dissolutions under Henry VIII began in 1536 with the passing of an act of Parliament (27 Henry VIII, c. 28) authorizing the suppression of the lesser monasteries that had lands valued at under £200 per annum. The English monasteries had already been visited by royal commissioners in 1534 in order to procure the acquiescence of the monastic communities to Henry's break with Rome and to his statutory alteration of the royal succession. Then in 1535 visitators were dispatched to enforce better monastic observance and to inquire about the moral state of the individual religious. The reports of the visitation commissioners were collected together in a document known as the *Compendium compertorum,* which accused the religious of widespread corruption and immorality. Although these reports were full of exaggerations and rumors, Parliament was easily convinced that the smaller monasteries were in desperate need of serious and immediate reform.

Although reform was certainly one reason for the first dissolution act of 1536, it is clear that Cromwell was also motivated by a desire to confiscate for the Crown's benefit some of the vast wealth of the monasteries. The extent of this wealth had been revealed by the *Valor Ecclesiasticus*, a valuation of church property that was conducted simultaneously with the visitations of 1535 in order to assess the clergy for the new clerical tax of first fruits and tenths. The actual suppressions were carried out in the second half of 1536 by specially appointed royal commissioners. A new government department, the Court of Augmentations, was established by a separate act of Parliament (27 Henry VIII, c. 27) to receive and administer the estates of the dissolved monasteries. The superiors of the suppressed houses were provided with pensions, while the monks and nuns were given the choice of transferring to other houses of their own order or else of being dispensed of their vows and going out into the world. Only a handful of the thousand or so religious whose monasteries were dissolved decided to remain in the religious life, but nearly a third of the more than three hundred communities affected by the act were ultimately exempted from suppression and allowed to continue. This was particularly so in Yorkshire and Lincolnshire, where there were large numbers of small nunneries. It was also in these two counties that resistance by the laity to the dissolution was greatest. The 1536 dissolutions provided a focus for the complaints of those who participated in the Pilgrimage of Grace, a popular uprising that affected most of the north of England.

Despite the suppression in 1537 of those northern monasteries involved in the Pilgrimage of Grace, it would appear that the policy for a more general dissolution of the remaining monasteries did not develop until some time in 1538. In this year the wealthy monastic shrines were dismantled, and their accumulated treasures were confiscated by the Crown. At the same time, visitators were commissioned to suppress the two hundred friaries of the four mendicant orders. These activities not surprisingly generated an atmosphere of impending doom in the remaining religious houses. The monastic communities began to liquidate whatever assets they could spare. Long leases were granted in return for large entry fines (payments made by tenants when entering into new leases of lands), and superfluous movables were sold. Such action alerted Cromwell to the potential loss of profit to the Crown, and he therefore acted quickly to forestall the wholesale alienation of monastic property. Commissioners were authorized to receive the surrenders of the surviving monastic houses, and they were also urged to coerce those superiors and communities who proved hesitant. Several executions, most notably those of the abbots of Glastonbury, Reading, and Colchester, ensured compliance from uncooperative convents. There was little serious resistance, however, so that from late 1538 until early 1540 the remaining monasteries, the largest and wealthiest in the kingdom, surrendered to the Crown. These surrenders and suppressions were approved by Parliament in a second dissolution act of 1539 (31 Henry VIII, c. 13).

Life pensions were granted to virtually all the religious except those who had been friars. These pensions later proved to be an enormous drain on royal finances. The Crown disbursed a staggering £34,000 in pensions to ex-religious in 1540, and even by 1546 the annual outlay was still as high as £27,000. The fate of the dispossessed ex-religious has been the subject of considerable debate since Cardinal Francis Gasquet wrote his account of the dissolution (*Henry VIII and the English Monasteries*, London, 1888–1889). It is difficult to assess the ease or the success with which the ex-religious made the transition from regular to secular life because so little is known of what happened to the majority of them. Priests were able to gain preferment to livings, a number of abbots became bishops, and the chapters of the new cathedrals were largely made up of former monks. The nuns probably found it more difficult to adjust to their new lives, and many may have returned to live with their parents or else continued to live together in secular communities. Monks and nuns were prohibited from marrying until the time of Edward VI, when many took advantage of the relaxation in the English church's rules regarding clerical celibacy. Many were therefore punished during the reign of Mary Tudor for breaking their vows.

The monastic buildings met a variety of fates. The great monastic cathedrals remained in use, and the abbey churches of Westminster, Peterborough, Gloucester, Chester, and Bristol became new cathedrals. Some monastic churches were converted for use by parishes, and many large country houses were constructed on the remains of conventual buildings. In the majority of cases, however, the structure of the monastic buildings was systematically destroyed, or the lead was simply removed from their roofs so that the elements could accomplish what was often too expensive a task for the Crown. Other ex-monastic sites were used as quarries for building materials up until the early twentieth century. The monastic libraries were broken up. The most valuable volumes found their way into Henry VIII's royal library, others were saved by former monks, but the majority were sold for scrap. No satisfactory assessment has yet been made of the national impact of the dissolution upon charity, poor relief, hospitality, health care, and education, but it is generally believed that there was a considerable diminution in these social services after 1540, especially in urban areas. Some monastic land was later devoted to educational purposes, most notably the foundation endowments of Christ Church, Oxford, and Trinity College, Cambridge (1546), but it was not until the reign of Edward VI (1547–1553) that a number of grammar schools were founded on endowments that came partly from the ex-monastic estate.

The majority of the ex-monastic lands were either retained and administered by the Court of Augmentations or alienated by the Crown in order to reward royal servants and pay for the wars with France and Scotland in the 1540s.

A total of around sixteen hundred grants of ex-monastic land valued at £104,182 per annum had been made by the end of the reign. Ecclesiastical corporations received more than a quarter of these lands (28 percent), while the remainder went to members of the peerage (16 percent), officers of the royal household (14 percent) and of the government administration (14 percent), citizens of London (13 percent), and members of the county-based gentry and yeomanry (15 percent). Despite this enormous alienation program, the Crown continued to receive income in excess of £90,000 per annum from the ex-monastic estate in 1547. Alienation of ex-monastic lands continued during the reigns of Edward VI and Elizabeth I (1558–1603).

Attempts were made by Mary Tudor (r. 1553–1558) to restore monasticism in England by returning some of the surviving monks, nuns, and friars to their monasteries. The Brigittine nuns of Syon returned to their old convent at Richmond, and a group of Carthusian monks reopened the old charterhouse nearby at Sheen. The most impressive of the renewed foundations was at Westminster Abbey, where a composite Benedictine community was formed by surviving members of several of the ancient English Benedictine monasteries. Six communities had been reestablished by the end of 1557, but within a year they had been forced to disperse after the accession of Elizabeth I in 1558. The Brigittines moved first to the Low Countries and finally in 1594 to Lisbon, where they remained until their eventual return to England in 1861. The charterhouse of Sheen Anglorum settled in the Netherlands and continued as a community until its suppression by Joseph II of Austria in 1783. The current English Benedictine congregation claims succession from its medieval forebear through Dom Sigebert Buckley, the last of the monks of Marian Westminster.

Ireland. Irish monasticism in the early sixteenth century was dominated by the mendicant orders. The four orders of friars had nearly two hundred houses in Ireland, fifty-six of which had adopted the observant reform. There were only four Benedictine monasteries but more than thirty Cistercian foundations and about one hundred houses of canons regular. There were also thirty-seven nunneries. Irish monasticism was in a state of crisis in the early sixteenth century, and whatever vigor it managed to retain may be attributed to the observant friars. The monks and canons regular were among the wealthiest landowners in the kingdom and had become largely secularized well before the dissolution process began in the 1530s.

A dissolution bill was introduced into the Irish Parliament in 1536, the same year that the lesser monasteries were suppressed in England and Wales. This bill was not enacted until 1537, however, owing to considerable local resistance, and even then the act affected only thirteen of the smaller and more isolated monasteries on the borders of the lordship. The rest of the dissolution process in Ireland followed closely the timetable of the suppressions in England and Wales. The mendicant orders were dissolved in 1538, and a general program of suppression was initiated in 1539. By the middle of 1540 all the monasteries in the Pale and the earldoms of Ormond and Kildare had been dissolved. As in England, life pensions were granted to the dispossessed religious, but contrary to English practice, most of the monastic buildings were left standing.

The Henrician dissolution in Ireland was not as quickly or as thoroughly accomplished as that in England because a large part of the island remained outside the limits of English control. Only around one-tenth of the four hundred Irish religious houses had been dissolved by 1540, but, as the English extended their jurisdiction in the 1540s, more monasteries were suppressed. By 1547 the religious houses in the earldoms of Ulster and Desmond and in the lordships extending west from the Pale to Galway had come into the hands of the Crown. Despite this rapid advance of Crown control in the Gaelic areas, only about half the Irish monasteries fell during Henry VIII's reign. It was not until the end of Elizabeth's reign that the whole of Ireland was conquered, but even then many monasteries survived the Crown's attempts at suppression. It was also in this period and later, during the reigns of the Stuart kings, that approximately one hundred and fifty houses, mostly of observant friars, were refounded in Ireland. Forty-one of these refoundations continue to exist. Most of the Irish monastic land was redistributed soon after its acquisition by the Crown. Ex-monastic lands valued at nearly £2,000 per annum were granted by Henry VIII to the established Anglo-Irish administrators, nobility and gentry (53 percent); to new English settlers (38 percent); and to the lords deputy (8 percent), primarily as a means of stabilizing the newly acquired territories.

Scotland. The Scottish monasteries were few in number (102) and in a state of serious decline by the early sixteenth century. The thirty-eight friaries appear to have been in a satisfactory condition on the eve of the Scottish Reformation, but the several large and wealthy Benedictine, Cistercian, and Augustinian abbeys were subject to considerable interference by laymen who had been able to gain control of their financial resources. The practice of appointing these lay heads, known as "commendatory" abbots and priors, was virtually unknown in England and Ireland but was common on the Continent, especially in France. The imposition of lay monastic heads in Scotland was disastrous for the religious communities, both in terms of financial security and regular discipline. The smaller monasteries, including eleven nunneries, were mostly poor and isolated.

The dissolution of the Scottish monasteries and friaries did not begin until 1560. Some of the larger houses were dissolved immediately, but most of the communities were allowed to continue occupying their monasteries until death and defection reduced their numbers. As the monastic communities gradually disappeared, their estates were progressively incorporated into temporal lordships.

BIBLIOGRAPHY

Bettey, J. H. *The Suppression of the Monasteries in the West Country.* Gloucester, 1989. One of the better regional surveys of the dissolution and its aftermath.

Bradshaw, Brendan. *The Dissolution of the Religious Orders in Ireland under Henry VIII.* Cambridge, 1974. The only comprehensive account of the Henrician suppressions.

Cross, Claire, and Noreen Vickers. *Monks, Friars and Nuns in Sixteenth Century Yorkshire.* York, 1995. An impressive attempt to trace the afterlives of the ex-religious of Yorkshire.

Easson, D. E. *Medieval Religious Houses, Scotland.* 2d ed. Revised by Ian Borthwick Cowan. London and New York, 1976. Includes a comprehensive bibliography.

Ellis, Stephen G. *Tudor Ireland: Crown, Community and the Conflict of Cultures, 1470–1603.* London, 1985. A concise account of the whole process of dissolution during the Tudor age.

Gwynn, Aubrey, and R. Neville Hadcock. *Medieval Religious Houses in Ireland.* Dublin, 1970. A complete listing of the Irish monasteries with a full bibliography.

Harvey, Barbara. *Living and Dying in England, 1100–1540: The Monastic Experience.* Oxford, 1993. An overview of the lifestyle of monks at Westminster Abbey.

Hoskins, W. G. *The Age of Plunder: King Henry's England, 1500–1547.* London, 1976.

Knowles, David. *The Religious Orders in England.* Vol. 3, *The Tudor Age.* Reprint, Cambridge, 1979. The definitive treatment of the English monasteries in the sixteenth century.

Knowles, David, and R. Neville Hadcock. *Medieval Religious Houses, England and Wales.* 2d ed. London, 1994. A complete listing of monasteries with a full bibliography.

New, Anthony. *A Guide to the Abbeys of England and Wales.* London, 1985. Detailed descriptions of the surviving remains of monasteries.

Ordnance Survey. *Monastic Britain.* Southampton, 1978. Maps the location of monasteries in England, Wales, and Scotland, and includes a useful bibliography.

Richardson, Walter C. *History of the Court of Augmentations, 1536–1554.* Baton Rouge, La., 1961. Describes the administration of the monastic lands after the dissolution.

Savine, Aleksandr. *English Monasteries on the Eve of the Dissolution* (1909). Reprint, New York, 1979. Although outdated, this is still the best survey of the monastic estates at the beginning of the sixteenth century.

The Victoria History of the Counties of England. 1900–. Provides separate articles for each religious foundation.

Woodward, G. W. O. *The Dissolution of the Monasteries.* Reprint, London, 1972. A clear and concise account of the process of dissolution.

Youings, Joyce. *The Dissolution of the Monasteries.* London, 1971. Contains an excellent selection of primary documents.

PETER CUNICH

The Continent

The fate of monasteries and their occupants varied widely in continental Europe in the sixteenth century. In Protestant territories, most monasteries were dissolved or transformed into hospitals and schools. Their revenues were diverted to the political authorities, with a percentage reserved for charitable functions. In Catholic lands, monastic foundations also underwent a period of examination, resulting in reform and renewal, and in some cases a redirection of energies.

The men and women who formed these institutions also varied in their responses to the Reformation. Many of the earliest converts to the new message were monks and nuns. The ranks of the new Protestant clergy were filled from the monastery as well as from the secular clergy. The most notable example is Martin Luther himself, but his message inspired other monks to leave the cloister and to seek a new path to salvation and spiritual security. Convents were no less affected by the Lutheran message. Nuns heard the word through their chaplains and by means of letters and books smuggled into the convent. The future wives of Luther and William of Orange, Katharina von Bora and Charlotte de Bourbon, respectively, both entered the convent in their early teens and left it clandestinely to espouse the Protestant cause. Even the more radical wing of the Reformation drew from the religious orders. Michael Sattler started as a Benedictine monk near Freiburg. He left in the 1520s to join the Anabaptists and eventually became a major contributor to the Schleitheim Confession.

As the Reformation progressed, monastic foundations in Protestant territories found themselves under increasing pressure to dissolve and serve new purposes. While Luther never insisted on the abandonment of the cloister, requiring only the recognition that the monastic life carried with it no assurance of salvation or merit, secular authorities were more urgent in their demands. Philipp of Hesse's agents offered monks the opportunity to accept the new gospel or to accept settlement elsewhere. While 60 percent of the revenues from former monastic lands went toward charitable foundations of hospitals, schools, and universities, the remaining 40 percent was used for Philipp's court and administrative purposes.

Nuremberg's regular clergy were split by the religious conflict. At the council-sponsored 1525 debate, representatives of the Augustinian and Benedictine houses argued for Luther's interpretation, while preachers from the Dominican, Franciscan, and Carmelite houses defended the Catholic position. In the following months Nuremberg's monastic foundations were dissolved, and their possessions, including real estate, rents, and buildings, were turned over to the city. Most of the monks accepted annuities from the city or joined the Lutheran ministry. The last five Dominicans were pensioned off in 1543, while the Franciscans held out until 1562. The nuns proved more stubborn in their resistance. While forbidding any new professions, the city was forced to wait until the last of the sisters died before gaining complete control over the convent's property, a process that was to be lengthy: the last Dominican nun in Nuremberg died in 1596. The newly acquired properties were put to use variously as schools, libraries, homes for widows, and building sites for new housing. The monastic buildings of Nuremberg's Egidienkirche housed the new municipal secondary school (gymnasium) founded on Philipp Melanchthon's recommendation in 1526.

The new charitable foundations often maintained many of the characteristics of monastic life, even though the theological foundations had changed. For example, the hospital founded at Haina in Hesse required its patients to adopt a life of regular prayer, light work for those capable, and instruction from the Bible and Luther's teaching. In addition, Haina maintained the monastic tradition of hospitality and almsgiving. Pilgrims and travelers could find one night's food and lodging there, while widows, orphans, and other poor people could beg food. The monastic buildings were maintained and served the new functions admirably. Several of the former monks of Haina remained to help staff the hospital.

Not all monastic foundations were maintained in public service. The Augustinian cloister in Wittenberg, where Luther had been a monk, was given to him for housing his family and the myriad students and guests who stayed with him over the years.

In general, convents in Protestant territories seem to have been more successful at resisting dissolution or adapting to a new role than monasteries. Wiesner has studied several free imperial abbeys and convents in central Germany that were able either to maintain their Catholic identity or to accept the Reformation and transform themselves into Protestant institutions for women—in spite of the rejection of monasticism explicit in Protestant teaching. The high social status of the abbesses and many of the convents' residents helped them to resist political and sometimes military pressures. In addition, convents served an important social function as an honorable alternative to marriage for daughters from noble and wealthy families. Whereas former monks, canons, and priests could join the growing ranks of the Protestant clergy, the alternatives for women were less palatable. Some convents were forced to relocate in order to preserve their vows and their corporate way of life. After resisting the eloquence of Guillaume Farel, Pierre Viret, and Marie Dentière (a former nun), the Poor Clares of Geneva left the city in 1535 to resettle in a convent in Annecy in Catholic Savoy.

In Catholic lands, monasteries and convents also suffered various fates and responded in divergent ways to both the Reformation and the Counter-Reformation. While in Germany iconoclasm and reuse of monastic buildings was common, in France the Wars of Religion sometimes brought about the deliberate destruction of monastic property. While some structures were rebuilt or restored during the revival of monastic foundations in the seventeenth century, others never recovered. The abbey of Saint-Aignon d'Orléans, in central France, was destroyed by the English during the Hundred Years' War, rebuilt, and later destroyed by the Calvinists in the sixteenth century. It was never rebuilt again.

The Catholic revival of religious orders in the seventeenth century saw the rebuilding of old foundations, as well as the construction of new homes for new orders. The end of the religious wars brought a spate of new building in France in response to the need to replace old buildings damaged or destroyed in the wars, to house newly founded orders, and in response to royal patronage. French monastic architecture in the sixteenth century saw the introduction of the Italian classical style, which was also influencing royal architecture of the same period. New structures were designed by some of the foremost architects of the time. A large, classical, domed structure was designed for the Benedictine convent of Montmartre by Philibert de l'Orme in 1555, although never built. Under Anne of Austria's patronage, the Benedictine convent of Le-Val-de-Grâce was rebuilt both in thanks for the birth of the Dauphin (the future Louis XIV) and as a site for the entombment of royal hearts. The work was begun by François Mansart, carried on by Jacques Lemercier, and completed in 1665 by Le Muet. The Cistercian convent of Port-Royal was designed by Antoine Le Pautre between 1646 and 1648.

Royal privilege dominated church appointments in France in the sixteenth century, leading to some unusual situations. Odet de Coligny, a leading Huguenot, became the titular abbot of Fleury in 1662. Income from the abbey was still being paid in 1571, through an intermediary, to Odet's brother, Gaspard de Coligny, a Huguenot military leader.

The Spanish Hieronymite monastery of San Isidro del Campo, outside Seville, was a wealthy foundation with powerful patrons, but it also was a refuge for Protestants until discovered in the late 1550's. It served too as a distribution center for Castillian New Testaments hidden in the monastery. The prior, several members, and several nuns from the Jeronomite convent of Santa Paula, also near Seville, fled the Inquisition in the 1550s.

The Italian Benedictine Congregation of Santa Giustina of Padua tried to steer a middle course between the theologies of the reformers and the counter-reformers of Trent. Their reliance on the Greek patristic tradition, as developed by Don Luciano degli Ottoni, led to positions that were alternately condemned as Pelagian and Lutheran by Catholics at the Council of Trent and as heretical by John Calvin.

The Council of Trent called for the reform of religious orders under the strictest observance of their rule. The council limited religious professions to adults (over the age of 16) who had lived as a novice for at least a year. Appointments of abbots and abbesses were to be regulated and conferred only on worthy individuals with proven records of virtue and sanctity. The implementation of these reforms was sometimes slow, especially in countries like France that did not initially accept the council's decrees. Nonetheless, religious orders underwent a vigorous revival in the late sixteenth century and especially the early seventeenth century. Old orders were reformed, new orders founded, and the roles of women expanded, particularly in the education of young women and the care of the sick.

This revival resulted in a remarkable upsurge of interest and involvement. In addition to the establishment of the Jesuits, the Franciscans produced the Capuchins, who in France established 285 foundations between 1589 and 1643. Teresa of Ávila reformed the Carmelites in 1562. By 1648 there were over 240 convents in Spain, Italy, and France. The Ursulines, Visitation nuns, and Daughters of Charity were new foundations for women that grew to include hundreds of houses. Twelve out of forty-eight Franciscan monasteries in New Castille were founded between 1564 and 1575. Spain became the home for many relics from monasteries now faced with pillage or dissolution in Protestant lands. Two of the heads of the eleven thousand virgins martyred with Saint Ursula had been owned by the Carmelite convent of Saint Thomas near Groeninga in Flanders. They were given to one of Fernando Álvarez de Toledo's captains in gratitude for his protection of the convent from heretics, and were then transported to Spain, where they found permanent homes.

Women were particularly important to the revival. While strict enforcement of the cloister was a key feature of convent reform, new forms of religious service developed, allowing women an active role in the teaching of young girls and in tending the sick. This was particularly noticeable in cities, where contemporaries commented on the explosion of the female religious population. In Reims the cloistered population increased almost 500 percent between 1619 and 1658. Rapley has suggested that these new roles were attractive to women as an alternative to the more limited opportunities available in marriage, as well as fulfilling a sense of mission.

In both Catholic and Protestant lands, the monasteries and convents either continued to fulfill their functions and in so doing found renewed life, or they were replaced by new structures. Their educational and social roles in early modern life, especially as they applied to women, were too important to be erased by theological controversy alone.

BIBLIOGRAPHY

Christian, William A., Jr. *Local Religion in Sixteenth-Century Spain.* Princeton, 1981. There is a wealth of literature on individual monks, nuns, monasteries, and convents, but few general works in English on continental monasteries and convents during the Reformation. The fate of individual monasteries and convents is best researched through regional and local histories of which this is a good example.

Collett, Barry. "A Benedictine Scholar and Greek Patristic Thought in Pre-Tridentine Italy: A Monastic Commentary of 1538 on Chrysostom." *Journal of Ecclesiastical History* 36 (1985), 66–81.

Delumeau, Jean. *Catholicism between Luther and Voltaire.* Philadelphia, 1977.

Evans, Joan. *Monastic Architecture in France: From the Renaissance to the Revolution.* Cambridge, 1964.

Maué, Hermann. "Nuremberg's Cityscape and Architecture." In *Gothic and Renaissance Art in Nuremberg, 1300–1550*, pp. 27–50. New York, 1986.

Midelfort, H. C. Erik. "Protestant Monastery? A Reformation Hospital in Hesse." In *Reformation Principle and Practice: Essays in Honour of A. G. Dickens*, edited by P. N. Brooks, pp. 71–93. London, 1980.

Perry, Mary Elizabeth. *Crime and Society in Early Modern Seville.* Hanover, N.H., 1980.

Rapley, Elizabeth. *The Dévotes: Women and Church in Seventeenth-Century France.* Montreal, 1990.

Snyder, C. Arnold. "Revolution and the Swiss Brethren: The Case of Michael Sattler." *Church History* 50 (1981), 276–87.

Strauss, Gerald. *Nuremberg in the Sixteenth Century.* Bloomington, Ind., 1976.

Wiesner, Merry E. "Ideology Meets the Empire: Reformed Convents and the Reformation." In *Germania Illustrata: Essays on Early Modern Germany Presented to Gerald Strauss*, edited by Andrew C. Fix and Susan C. Karant-Nunn, pp. 181–95. Sixteenth Century Essays and Studies, vol. 18. Kirksville, Mo., 1992.

MARY JANE CHASE

MONASTICISM. Monasticism (derived from Greek *monos*, "unique") refers to a recognizable type of social structure which characterizes those whose lives are dedicated to God and have vowed to adhere to the ideals of stability, or more specifically, celibacy, poverty, and obedience to a spiritual superior. Friars, to be distinguished from monks, are members of one of the mendicant orders of the Roman Catholic Church; they are characterized by being bound to poverty even as an order and combine presence in the monastery with work outside.

Before the Reformation, the monastic life was a common and accepted part of Western Christendom. In almost every region and town monastic buildings were inhabited by robed and tonsured men and veiled women living the "religious life" within the cloister. Under vows and under the authority of an abbot or abbess, they lived holy lives separated from the world, yet praying to sustain and transform it. It was an innately heroic vocation, with its allure enhanced by the presence in the community of distinctly clad religious, distinguished by rituals, musical traditions, reputations for holiness, and the esprit de corps of each order. Religious houses, both male and female, also farmed land; produced manuscripts, books, wines, and medicines; conducted schools; and dispensed charity. Yet the call to holiness through solemn vows remained central to monasticism.

At the heart of monasticism was *stabilitas*—the belief that amid the turmoil of human existence a person might remain steadily locked into worship, contemplation, and service of the eternal God. The monastic vows were not ends in themselves but a personal means of achieving such stability, and the community life of the monastery sought to provide a suitable environment for it. The community was ideally a family of brothers or sisters separated from the world in common commitment, following their rule (generally that of Benedict) under a patriarchal abbot or matriarchal abbess. The central work of monasteries was the *opus dei* ("the work of God"), the celebration of liturgical worship, especially the daily Divine Office. This worship served also as the basis of personal devotions and discipline. The monastic life thus represented a search for holiness through stability, worship, and discipline.

A century before the Reformation, many wealthy monasteries had fallen under the control of nonresident abbots appointed by church or secular authorities. Consequently, Western monasticism had declined in piety, scholarship, and spiritual authority. For example, the Italian Benedictines were described as being "almost totally collapsed," although some contemplative orders, such as the Carthusians, continued to maintain strong monastic discipline and spiritual authority. After 1400 several lax monastic houses were reinvigorated by reforms, sometimes imposed by governments: for example, in the German city of Lüneberg, Duke Otto forcibly attempted to reform (and strip the assets) of the convent of Weinhausen in 1469. The most successful reforms came from within monasticism itself, when individual abbeys returned to a strict observance of their rule. As a protection from outside interference, monasteries sometimes united into a congregation under the centralized authority of a chapter-general. This congregational model of reform was first successfully used by the Congregation of Santa Giustina of Padua, which united almost all the more important Benedictine houses in Italy and several in southern France. Using the same model, the Congregation of Chezal-Benoît was reformed in France, and in northern and central Germany the Congregation of Bursfeld grew to ninety monasteries by 1520. Other congregational reforms occurred in Hungary (Pannonhalma), Poland, Dalmatia, and Catalonia.

During these reforms, monastic piety was increasingly based on biblical and patristic scholarship, emphasizing Christ's humanity and his sufferings on the cross for human redemption. These emphases influenced contemporary monastic devotional practices, art, and pastoral work, all of which were characterized by compassion toward the human condition. One must not exaggerate the extent of the revival: reforms were often resisted, and even reformed monasteries sometimes did little more than contribute to civic life and the status of families. Nevertheless the spiritual reinvigoration was sufficient to engender new levels of respect for monastic ideals of holiness, and toward the end of the fifteenth century the number of monastic professions increased. Paradoxically, the more a monastery became a house of prayer, the more the outside world intruded through gifts of laypeople wishing to be associated with monastic holiness. Increased monastic wealth during the late fifteenth century engaged many able monks and nuns in administration and politics, reviving the old monastic problem of otherworldly sanctity being mingled with worldly business such as buying and selling, and negotiating with tenants, other landowners, and governments. Consequently, monasteries were often distinguished as much by their worldly status as by their spirituality.

The spread of reform, the increase of numbers, the responses of the laity to monasticism, and lay piety itself all suggest vigorous religious sensibilities in Europe, which during the early sixteenth century were being stimulated by the *devotio moderna* and the invention of printed books. The quickening of religious devotion was characterized by a sense that laymen and laywomen in every calling could pursue holiness in their own way. This lay piety often included monastic-like devotions, such as reading the daily offices, methodical private devotions, and making private vows for particular intentions. The Italian Oratory of Divine Love (founded about 1500 under the inspiration of Catherine of Genoa) was a form of monasticism for laypeople who lived under its discipline but worked in the outside world. These developments were associated with considerable searching for new understanding and new practices of holiness within both the religious and the lay life. The value of monastic vows became less clear, especially as the level of lay education and the intensity of lay piety sometimes matched those found in monasteries.

The result was some uncertainty among the laity and monks and nuns themselves as to the objectives, practices, and value of the monastic life. An abbess told Richard Foxe, bishop of Winchester, that one of her nuns "wyste not what she was doing" when she took her vows. Such uncertainties were at this time exacerbated by the old monastic problems of political interference in monastic affairs and of quarrels within orders, between orders, and with secular clergy. But the problem of monasticism before the Reformation was not primarily laxity and corruption—a misinterpretation common to Protestants and Catholics—for pre-Reformation monasticism was unsettled by the much more profound problem that even in flourishing monasteries there were uncertainties about the purpose of monastic vows and the definition of holiness. Many orders tackled this problem by turning back to the rule, the Bible, and patristic writings in search of renewed theological understanding of the monastic life.

Immediately before the Reformation there was further criticism, mainly from humanist scholars, that the monastic life was prone to abuses, shallow piety, and institutional parochialism. At the crudest level, abuses included drunkenness, sexual misbehavior, maladministration, greed, and indifference toward devotional responsibilities. Monastic authorities themselves often had the sharpest eye for these failings, though witty scandalmongers such as François Rabelais and Ulrich von Hutten attracted a wider audience.

Some faults stemmed from unsuitability for the monastic life because young men—and more often young women—were persuaded or compelled by their families to embrace the religious life. The criticisms of shallow monastic piety were aimed at undue emphasis on outward shows of holiness, such as an almost snobbish monastic disdain of the world (*de contemptu mundi*). It was said that monastic vows and practices were too often merely outward trappings without true inward holiness.

The third set of allegations referred to the institutional parochialism of excessive loyalty to one's own monastic culture, praising it as an elite and holy corporation of celibates, giving more importance to its practices and institutional culture than to its spirituality. Obsessions with monastic culture sharpened the satire of critics. In *The Praise of Folly* (1511), Desiderius Erasmus mocked the "universally loathed" yet "gloriously self satisfied tribe" of monks and the "trivialities" of squabbles between the orders over "ceremonies and petty man-made traditions." The appetite of humanist critics was further aroused by most orders being strongholds of their scholastic opponents and by the ease with which printing presses enabled them to exercise their satire widely and profitably against monastic scholastics.

These were merely attacks upon the moral defects of otherwise venerable institutions, but two other criticisms, more fundamental, foreshadowed the Reformation theologians. One concerned the potential of monasticism to cultivate mere appearances of piety in order to impress those laypeople who expected tangible signs of holiness in monks and nuns. Jakob Wimpfeling accused monks of manipulating and deceiving the laity with unwarranted claims of holiness, and Erasmus argued that "those who dress up in the mask of religion . . . manage by dignified dress and the false semblance of holiness to acquire no little authority among the ignorant crowd" (*Antibarbarians*, 1520), thus deceiving others and themselves. The second fundamental criticism questioned the distinctive spiritual value of monasticism. In the *Enchiridion* (1503) Erasmus asserted that monasticism "may be useful or not useful" according to individual makeup and disposition. In *De Contemptu Mundi* (On Disdaining the World; 1521), he used a monastic theme to argue that "whoever is a true Christian is monk enough"; in other words, the monastic life may certainly be a way of true piety, but so also may the lay life. Thus, whatever its qualities, the monastic life was not necessarily the best way to salvation.

Some monks and nuns saw the situation as a challenge for monasticism to restore its spiritual excellence through even greater piety, austerity, and scholarship. In 1513, with a cartload of books, the Italian Tommaso Giustiniani withdrew from the world into the Camaldolese order, where he cultivated the ecstatic love of God. Others undertook even more rigorous austerity and contemplation. During the early years of the sixteenth century, continuing unease about the monastic vocation stimulated further efforts to intensify its piety and led Pope Leo X to impose reorganizations upon orders in 1516.

Some critics constructively encouraged zeal, scholarship, and piety within monasticism. In January 1517 Richard Foxe published a vigorous translation of the Benedictine rule for women, written in "oure moders tonge, commune, playne, round englisshe." Foxe emphasized the importance of leadership in the monastic life, especially the exercise of authority by women, asserting that the authority of an abbess is drawn from God, "whose royome and authority she hath and occupies." He assumed that abbesses and other senior nuns were women of considerable learning and ability, and that the chief responsibility of their monastic vocation was for them and their nuns to attain a burning love of God.

Only a few months later in 1517, Luther posted his Ninety-five Theses. In 1520 he attacked monastic abuses and the way monasteries and nunneries now went beyond their original function as schools, imposing vows on young men and women, thus making them "permanent prisoners" under abbots and abbesses who turned discipline into tyranny. In his *De captivitate babylonica ecclesiae* of 1520, Luther acknowledged that religious vows of celibacy, obedience, and poverty were "a recognized mode of life," but he argued passionately that these vows were not commanded by God, obscured the divine gifts of grace and faith, increased pride, and encouraged disdain for ordinary married Christians.

Luther thus denied any special spiritual value in monasticism, whose works, he said, "in God's sight are in no way whatever superior to the works of a farmer laboring in the field, or of a woman looking after her home." He feared that the example set by monks and nuns might lead "ordinary folk" into mere outward piety instead of encouraging them to live a spiritual life of "true godliness," through faith in the cross of Christ. He saw monasticism not as the religious life but as an illusion that perverted true religious life, and he urged those "in high places" to abolish "all vows and religious orders." In 1524 he abandoned his own vows and married a nun who like many others had left her convent.

Luther's attack on monasticism was ultimately theological. Justification by grace alone through faith disallowed the existence of any elite spiritual group that could attain degrees of holiness above that of ordinary Christians. On the contrary, the highest spiritual riches were to be found in the laity's secular vocation rather than in monasticism. Contemplation was not a work of merit for the cloisters but for all Christians as they contemplated grace, faith, and salvation. Protestantism therefore offered an alternative form of holiness, which was neither cloistered nor ascetic but a truly religious vocation outside monasticism, based on baptism and lives of ordinary work and marriage.

Luther's colleague Philipp Melanchthon, in his *Loci Communes* (1520–1521), extended Luther's criticism, holding that vows were a self-imposed slavery "at variance with faith and the freedom of the spirit." Like Luther, Melanchthon drew practical conclusions from his theological arguments: monastic celibacy encouraged rather than prevented concupiscent thoughts; monastic poverty encouraged begging rather than taking responsibility for others. The monastic goal of salvation by perfection through separation from the world was misguided, and any claim to achieve a state of perfection "from the appearance of external works" was superstitious godlessness.

From the mid-1520s the attack on monasticism and "monkery" became an entrenched element in Protestant culture, with the criticisms ranging from alleged abuses to theological error. The Swiss theologian Huldrych Zwingli mingled all elements in his vigorous criticisms. In 1523 he declared that "there is no body of people on earth richer than monks and none more avaricious . . . those fattened pigs in disguise," whose "three vows of obedience, chastity, and poverty are grounded solely in hypocrisy and idolatry" because they pursued a false god of salvation through outward works.

The Protestant laity mounted similar attacks on monasticism. At Nuremberg in 1524 Hans Sachs wrote a vigorous and self-confident pamphlet, *Ain Gesprech von den Scheynwercken der Gaystlichen und iren gelübdten* (A Conversation About the Illusory Works of the Cloistered and the Vows by Which They Blaspheme the Blood of Christ and Believe Themselves to Be Holy; Augsburg, 1524), asserting that celibacy deadens the senses and hardens the heart, and charity given to monastic houses is diverted from "the truly needy and sick." In 1527 Arndt von Aich published a similar Protestant *Handbook* at Cologne describing monasticism's doctrines and practices as mere human constructions and not of divine command. Protestant critics of monasticism saw true religious discipline not in sexual asceticism but in the discipline of Christian marriage, which had its own divine purpose and responsibilities. In the Swiss city of St. Gall, the burgomaster Joachim Vadian led a campaign to secularize the city's monasteries, though attempts to suppress the great abbey of St. Gall were unsuccessful.

Western monasticism was considerably eroded by the combined onslaught of criticism and Luther's alternative theology. In some areas, notably Scandinavia, monasticism fell into slow decline. In other Protestant lands, principally Germany, Switzerland, and England, religious houses were dissolved by secular governments, both for theological reasons and for the acquisition of their property. In places where politicians were pious, a portion of confiscated monastic wealth was put to social use.

Many monasteries surrendered relatively easily to government intervention, but those with a high standard of spirituality often resisted strongly. In England, despite a welter of theological ambiguity on the part of Henry VIII (who piously approved of celibacy and monasticism), all monastic houses were dissolved between 1535 and 1540, displacing about nine thousand monks and nuns. Some went willingly, but others clung to their monastic ideals and resisted. As a government tactic of terror, several Carthusians and others were executed for their resistance.

In the territory of the Protestant Duke Ernst of Brunswick, in Germany, all female convents opposed the Reformation. When Protestant preachers were imposed on them, the defiant nuns of one convent disrupted the sermons by burning old slippers and singing. Other nuns defended their vocation with theological arguments, citing the Bible on virginity and patristic writers and church tradition on consecrated convent life. More female religious houses survived in central Germany than did their male counterparts. They were able to resist attempts by Protestant rulers to suppress or convert them because of the independent economic and political power of their abbesses, and what a contemporary Lutheran described as "the resolution of the nuns." Some convents compromised eventually and accepted state-imposed Lutheran doctrines on the condition that they retain their independence and Catholic spiritual practices. In Germany a few convents actually became Protestant, each under a "Lutheran abbess," but belonging to no order and with their nuns not making formal vows. Both these kinds of convents survived because of the territorial, legal, and political power wielded by their abbesses, but doctrinal orthodoxy may have been less important than the desire by nuns to protect the existence of religious institutions for women.

In some parts of Protestant Europe the laity attempted to defend the monasteries from government attack. In 1537 Robert Aske, a leader of the unsuccessful English rebellion of 1536–1537 (the Pilgrimage of Grace), defended the monasteries for their schools, public works, and charity, describing the suppressed abbeys as "one of the beauties of this realm." Another lay partisan also praised English religious houses for their public virtues of hospitality, public works, and keeping down the price of corn. Their views on the value of monasteries were deeply felt, but ultimately what they praised could also be done by laypeople and was not a specific justification of monasticism. It was this factor, as well as the acquisition of monastic lands by both Protestant and Catholic families, that inhibited enthusiasm later for the restoration of monasticism when the Catholic Mary Tudor became queen in 1553.

Under Catholic governments monasticism was preserved, but both the church and secular authorities insisted on reforms and amalgamations that improved standards but inhibited growth. With fewer novices in Catholic areas and decline and dissolutions in Protestant areas, the Reformation crisis greatly reduced European monasticism; the Benedictines, for example, lost about eight hundred of their three thousand monasteries. In Protestant Europe a distinctive class of religious persons with their separate calling to holiness disappeared from the community. Monasticism had for centuries been a focal point of civic identity and prestige, with its churches, liturgy, and good works, and with monks and nuns drawn from local families, all of which abruptly vanished. Moreover, while the dissolution of convents may have released nuns from cloistered and controlled lives, it also removed an area in which women could exercise independent authority, and it seriously diminished the education of women.

Monasticism now became a flagship of Roman Catholic orthodoxy in a divided Europe. But the Protestant theological challenge drove monks and nuns into renewed questioning of their vocation. Biblical studies, already flourishing in some orders before the Reformation, intensified. New concepts and forms of monasticism emerged that broadened the focus from the cloister to society: the Theatines established seminaries for the training of secular priests living a communal monastic life under threefold monastic vows—similar to the patristic function of monasticism approved by Calvin. The Somaschi and Barnabites worked among the very poor in northern Italy, mingling an intensive study of Paul with open-air evangelism and practical charity. From these orders and the rejuvenated Benedictines emerged a new monastic intellectual elite, intensely scholarly, often of aristocratic background, but with new ideas about monasticism engaging in social service. The Ursulines, founded in Italy in 1535, also bridged the cloister and the world: during the early years of the order, the nuns took only simple vows and lived with their own families while they worked in education.

Monastic theologians took seriously the Protestant accusation that vows of chastity, poverty, and obedience were simply man-made good works masquerading as piety. The Benedictine monk Isidoro Chiari, whose order of Santa Giustina of Padua drew upon Greek patristic theology for its doctrines, maintained that the monastic life was more valid than the reformers realized. In an appeal (*Adhortatio*) to Protestants in 1536, Chiari asserted that he did not "vow this manner of life" to God believing it "to be the way to a just life and salvation or the justification of sins," for such motives would "deny . . . the Lamb of God . . . who washes all in his blood and justifies them." Vows did not sacrilegiously reject the grace of the cross: salvation lay only in that grace, not in human merit and "certainly not in my vows and works." Chiari argued that the monastic life was actually an outcome of the life of faith that Protestants themselves sought, a work of gratitude, simultaneously arising out of faith, deepening that faith, and reconstructing fallen and sinful human nature.

Chiari's argument indicates that Protestant and Catholic understandings of monasticism were complicated and had more in common than was suggested by polemic. Luther did not entirely abandon the monastic *opus dei*, but wove it into the music and hymn singing of Protestant worship. Neither was John Calvin, the reformer of Geneva, completely opposed to monastic ideals. During the 1540s, as he worked out the implications of his theology, he became increasingly opposed to monasticism, and in the 1559 edition of his *Institutes of the Christian Religion* he argued that patristic monasteries had been schools of discipline to train the clergy but had been distorted, becoming a fabricated kind of perfection, "a sacrilegious doctrine," which bullied young men and women to take upon themselves the "cursed halter" of the vow of chastity. Nevertheless, Calvin's biblical commentaries contain ideas, possibly drawn from Greek patristic sources, that resemble the monastic doctrine of sanctification. Through faith, said Calvin, the Christian is justified but also sanctified—the divine image is restored to a wholeness that includes social and personal relationships. Moreover, Calvin's doctrine of calling as a godly work, distinct from social status and pride, was similar to monastic teaching. Thus elements in Calvin resembled the views of Chiari and other contemporary monastic apologists.

In Rome itself, monasticism was reviewed for its abuses rather than its underlying theology. The *Consilium de Emendanda Ecclesia* of 1537 reported that monasteries were often lax and recommended much tighter discipline of both male and female religious houses. The Council of Trent (1545–1563) confirmed the traditional value given to the monastic life and formulated a Counter-Reformation strategy to restore religious houses "entirely to a discipline becoming the monastic life," promulgating detailed regulations intended to recover the "great splendor" of the monastic past. Individual houses were obliged to join together in congregations, which facilitated the supervision of discipline, education, the elections of abbots and abbesses, and the observance of the rule, all under the centralized oversight of the congregational authorities and subject to the "fatherly admonitions" of the bishops and the papacy. Female monasticism was to be improved by careful investigation to see whether any applicant had been "forced or enticed, and that she knows what she is doing." Nuns were to live within their convent, their monastic life enclosed and given to contemplation, mortification, and the choir work of the Divine Office, with regular confession and Communion.

After the Council of Trent, the redefined monastic sense of mission extended even further beyond the cloister. Pastoral work, especially among the poor, became a priority for male monastic orders of the Counter-Reformation. They concentrated on biblical and patristic scholarship, preaching, and publishing, and they undertook a re-Catholicizing program in areas influenced by Protestantism, for example in Styria at the end of the seventeenth century. Churches attached to abbeys were rebuilt, generally in the baroque style, and made available to the laity for pilgrimages, lay confraternities, and other devotions. This sense of mission to the outside world was extended into the Americas and Asia. The Spanish Benedictines of the congregation of Valladolid established monasteries in Mexico and Peru, and the Portuguese congregation founded several houses in Brazil.

Although changes in discipline and mission were considerable, there was less change in piety. Post-Reformation monastic piety concentrated on the Bible and sacramental devotions. It became intense, austere, and methodical (in some areas influenced by the Ignatian school), emphasizing the presence of God, the indwelling Holy Spirit, and steady personal transformation, yet trying to avoid Protestant theological objections that salvation was being earned by human merit. Post-Reformation monasticism expressed its sense of holiness through the stylized emotional splendor of baroque architecture and art, especially in Germany, cultivating an exuberant, almost theatrical, liturgy and sacramental piety. These styles were at some variance with post-Tridentine monastic asceticism, but they were favored by wealthy patrons who provided this setting for both monastic and lay spirituality.

The concept of monastic vows and the underlying notion of the path to holiness did not change at all. The old ideal of separation from the world remained, although the monastic goal of *stabilitas* was no longer entirely sought through a life spent in the cloister—except for nuns and the stricter male contemplative orders. The Reformation had been a crisis in understanding and vocabulary as much as a challenge to ecclesiastical authority, and this crisis had produced uncertainties about the concept of holiness at the heart of monasticism. These Reformation uncertainties strongly modified monasticism but did not change it fundamentally.

[*See also* Monasteries; Nuns; *and* Religious Orders.]

BIBLIOGRAPHY

Bossy, John. *Christianity in the West, 1400–1700.* Oxford, 1985. A scholarly survey which provides a wide context for monasticism during this period.

Butler, Edward Cuthbert. *Benedictine Monachism: Studies in Benedictine Life and Rule* (1924). 2d ed. Reprint, Cambridge and New York, 1962. A study based upon one rule, but with application to European monasticism in general.

Calvin, John. *Institutes of the Christian Religion.* Edited by John T. McNeill. Translated by Ford Lewis Battles. Reprint, London and Philadelphia, 1977. See book 4, chap. 13, pp. 7–21. For the flavor and force of contemporary polemic it is necessary to read Calvin himself. The translation is most readable.

Cameron, Euan. *The European Reformation.* Oxford, 1991. See especially 3:2, 4:4. A detailed, highly schematic work, valuable for reference to theological issues, events, and historiography.

Caraman, Philip George. *Saint Angela: The Life of Angela Merici, Foundress of the Ursulines, 1474–1540.* London, 1963. A hagiographical study, but the monastic ideals and struggles of the period strongly emerge from its scholarly details.

Collett, Barry. *Italian Benedictine Scholars and the Reformation.* Oxford, 1985. A full treatment of Chiari and of his congregation's unique response to the Reformation crisis, but post-Reformation monastic emphasis on the Holy Spirit is insufficiently described.

Haigh, Christopher, ed. *The English Reformation Revised.* Cambridge, 1987. A review of the historiographical debates together with several articles of recent revisionist research.

Jedin, Hubert. *Geschichte des Konzils von Trient.* 4 vols. Freiburg, 1949–1975. Vols. 1 and 2 translated by Dom Ernest Graf as *A History of the Council of Trent,* 2 vols., London, 1957–1961. An enormously detailed, although a little dated, study of the Council of Trent, including the preceding period. Much material on monasticism is embedded in the work.

Knowles, David. *The Religious Orders in England.* 3 vols. Reprint, Cambridge, 1971. See vol. 3. A very detailed analysis of English monasticism immediately before and during the Reformation.

———. *Christian Monasticism.* Reprint, New York, 1977. See chaps. 4–8, 10–12. A general historical survey of monastic ideals and practices.

Lekai, Louis. *The Cistercians: Ideals and Reality.* Kent, Ohio, 1977. A massive work with chapters on "Reforms and the Reformation" and the subsequent "Rise of the Congregation."

MacKenney, Richard. *Sixteenth Century Europe: Expansion and Conflict.* London, 1993. This work is divided between politics and religion, and provides a detailed context of the monastic milieu. It has a modern bibliography.

Schmitz, Philibert. *Histoire de l'ordre de Saint Benoît.* 7 vols. Gembloux, 1942–1956. An old-fashioned but enormously detailed compilation. Its strength lies in the details rather than the overall analysis of monastic life.

Taveneaux, René. "La vie intellectuelle dans la Congrégation Bénédictine de Saint-Vanne au XVIIe siècle." In *Sous la règle de Saint Benoît: Structures monastiques et sociétés en France du moyen age a l'époque moderne,* pp. 307–325. Geneva, 1982. A study of the intellectual achievements of one Benedictine congregation before, during, and after the Reformation, with several reflective analytic observations.

Wallace, Ronald, S. *Calvin's Doctrine of the Christian Life.* Reprint, Tyler, Tex., 1982. This work emphasizes the doctrine of transformation in Calvin.

Wiesner-Hanks, Merry E. "Ideology Meets the Empire: Reformed Convents and the Reformation." In *Germania Illustrata: Essays on Early Modern Germany Presented to Gerald Strauss,* edited by Andrew C. Fix and Susan Karaunt-Nunn, pp. 181–195. Sixteenth Century Essays and Studies, vol. 18. Kirksville, Mo., 1992. A brief but lively study of the interaction between religion, politics, and scholarship in German convents during the Reformation upheavals.

Zwingli, Huldrych. *Huldrych Zwingli: Writings.* Vol. 2, *In Search of True Religion: Reformation, Pastoral and Eucharistic Writings, 1523.* Edited and translated by H. Wayne Pipkin. Allison Park, Pa., 1984. See articles 26–30, pp. 202–225. An excellent translation of Zwingli's energetic search for "true religion" and his attack upon monasticism.

BARRY COLLETT

MONTAIGNE, Michel Eyquem de (1533–1592), French literary figure. Although it would be easy, if not facile, to picture him as a faithful Catholic, Montaigne's stance toward the Reformation remains an enigma, especially since tolerance was at the heart of his thinking. He lived in a part of France, the Perigord, where the Reformation had made significant inroads. In his own family, one of his brothers (Thomas) and also a sister (Jeanne) had become Calvinists. Furthermore, his mother, Antoinette de Louppes (Lopez), came from a *marranos* background. Thus Montaigne, living during turbulent times, like many of his contemporaries was guided by a sense of prudence, never devoid, however, of the most humane and tolerant convictions.

A case in point is that the Saint Bartholomew's Day Massacre is never mentioned explicitly in the *Essais.* Yet, Montaigne is implicitly far from condoning it since he devotes two essays to condemning cruelty and similar barbarous behavior ("De la cruauté" and "Couardise mère de la cruauté"). Furthermore, in his essay "De la liberté de conscience," he advocates moderation in defending one's faith and curses those "whose passion drives outside the bounds of reason, and makes them sometimes adopt unjust, violent, and even reckless courses." In fact, the hero in this essay turns out to be the Roman emperor Julian the Apostate, "a very great and rare man" who indeed may have renounced his Catholic faith but remained an exemplary figure of virtue and justice. No wonder then that the Vatican censors admonished Montaigne to mitigate his enthusiasm for this controversial personality.

In another ambivalent context, Montaigne's stance toward prayers is significant because he takes aim against both the church and the Reformation. He does so in the essay "De prières," where he states categorically that mere verbal recitation of texts is no substitute for turning a contrite heart toward God and away from vicious desires. Also in addressing both the church and the reformers, he stands against allowing interpretations and translations of the Bible because "in preaching and speaking, the interpretation is vague, free, mutable, and piecemeal; so it is not the same thing."

Be it within the church itself or with the advent of the Reformation, Montaigne remains staunchly against dogmatism and any religious environment that creates divisiveness within the national political scene. As for his being a Catholic, it is merely an accident of history and birth. In the proper social and political climate, reformers and Catholics should and can coexist. To make the point, Montaigne, in his *Journal de voyage en Italia*, indicates that on his way to Italy he stopped in Basel, where he sought out François Hotman, the Calvinist theologian. While in that city he also observed the diversity of reformers (followers of Zwingli, Calvin, Luther), and he called attention as well to the presence there of the Catholic bishop, who also looked after his own flock and even received from the civil authorities a huge yearly payment.

From his own experience as well as his moral and civic sense, Montaigne came to understand that the presence of the Reformation in France must be met with political accommodation and compromise. If this was not accomplished successfully earlier (see the end of "De la liberté de conscience"), Montaigne hoped that it would be done when the Reformed Henry of Navarre acceded to the throne (1589) and became Henry IV—a goal toward which Montaigne worked tenaciously and patiently and to which he contributed most diplomatically.

BIBLIOGRAPHY

Balmas, Enea. "'Montaigne et l'Inquisition." In *Le Parcours desEssais*, edited by Marcel Tetel, pp. 239–249. Paris, 1989. Shows how to varying degrees the *Essais* were censured by the Vatican, in the first Italian translation, and by the reformers.

Frame, Donald M., trans. *The Complete Works of Montaigne.* Stanford, Calif., 1958. The most readable English translation.

———. *Montaigne: A Biography.* Reprint, San Francisco, 1984. The standard biography, in English or in French.

Nakam, Géralde. *Montaigne et son temps: Les événements et les Essais.* Paris, 1982. The best study of the *Essais* set in the divided French religious climate.

Screech, M. A., trans. *The Complete Essays of Montaigne.* London and New York, 1991. The best and closest translation to Montaigne's text.

Smith, Malcolm. *Montaigne and the Roman Censors.* Geneva, 1981. The most thorough study of the attempted censorship by the church.

MARCEL TETEL

MONTBÉLIARD, COLLOQUY OF. This colloquy was held in the town and county of Montbéliard in the duchy of Württemberg in 1586 between Reformed leader Théodore de Bèze and Lutheran theologian Jakob Andreae. The primary issue was the doctrine of the Lord's Supper, but four other doctrines were added after the colloquy had begun: Christology, baptism, art and music in churches, and predestination. The immediate reason for the colloquy was the desire of French refugees to receive Communion according to their French Reformed liturgy and confession of faith. Although Francophone and Swiss Reformed from the time of its reformation in 1524, Montbéliard was a county within the strictly Lutheran duchy of Württemberg. The local population resisted efforts to conform Montbéliard to German Lutheranism, an attitude increased by the influx of refugees driven from France by the decrees of Henry III of France, especially the decree of July 1585 exiling all who refused to practice Catholicism.

A wider implication of the colloquy was Henry of Navarre's (Henry IV) request that German Lutheran princes support the Huguenots in the Wars of Religion. The sticking point was the doctrine of the Lord's Supper. The Lutherans would not do so unless the Huguenots accepted the real presence of Christ in the supper with its attendant doctrine of oral manducation of the body of Christ by all recipients. The people of Montbéliard and their French guests adhered to Calvin's doctrine of a true spiritual presence in which only the faithful, through the Holy Spirit, received Christ's body and blood by the "mouth of faith." The matter came to a head when Frederick, count of Montbéliard, invited to debate the issue Théodore de Bèze, Calvin's successor in Geneva, and Jakob Andreae, provost at the University of Tübingen and chief theologian in the court of Frederick's uncle and suzerain, Duke Ludwig of Württemberg.

A still wider concern behind the debate was the effort of Queen Elizabeth I of England to form a Protestant league. In addition to the problem of the German princes' allegiance to the Holy Roman Emperor were the theological difficulties between Lutherans and Reformed that prevented them from forming a league against the pope. Indeed, Andreae openly preferred Roman Catholic eucharistic doctrine to the Calvinist doctrine. The aid that Lutheran princes sent to Henry III of France was theologically as well as politically motivated.

The outcome of the colloquy spelled ultimate failure for the cause of the Reformed people of Montbéliard. Partial agreement was reached with regard to music and art in churches; no agreement was reached on the other topics. In fact, thirty years earlier, Pierre Toussain, pastor of the church of Montbéliard, had openly disagreed with Calvin and Bèze regarding predestination. Bèze's defense of double predestination was an unpopular position with the people and Count Frederick of Württemberg. Frederick denied the French petition to receive Communion without first accepting article 10 of the unaltered Augsburg Confession, which upheld oral manducation. There was to be no healing of differences between the German Lutherans and the Swiss and French Reformed and no theological ground of unity upon which to organize Protestants against the pope.

[*See also* Andreae, Jakob; Bèze, Théodore de; Eucharist; Frederick III of the Palatinate; Iconography; Predestination; Wars of Religion; *and* Württemberg.]

BIBLIOGRAPHY

Mabille, Florent. *Histoire succincte de la Réforme du Pays de Montbéliard.* Batchelor's thesis, University of Geneva, 1873.

Pfister, P. *Colloque de Montbéliard, 1586: Étude historique.* Geneva, 1873.

Raitt, Jill. "The Emperor and the Exiles: The Clash of Religion and Politics in the Sixteenth Century." In *Church History* 52 (June, 1983), 145–156.

———. "The Elector John Casimir, Queen Elizabeth, and the Protestant League." In *Controversy and Conciliation: The Reformation and the Palatinate, 1559–1583,* edited by Derk Visser, pp. 178–190. Allison Park, Pa., 1986.

———. *The Colloquy of Montbéliard: Religion and Politics in the Sixteenth Century.* New York, 1993.

Viénot, John. *Histoire de la réforme dans le Pays de Montbéliard depuis les origines jusqu'à la mort de P. Toussain, 1524–1573.* 2 vols. Paris, 1900. The second volume contains primary sources for vol. 1.

JILL RAITT

MONTE, Giovan Maria de' Ciocchi del. *See* Julius III.

MONTMORENCY, Anne de (1492–1567), French commander and statesman.

He was Francis I's boyhood companion and fought with him at Marignano (1515). In 1522 Francis made him a marshal. Montmorency was one of the many French captains captured with the king at Pavia in 1525. Upon the king's return, Francis rewarded him with the offices of grand master of the royal household and governor of Languedoc. Montmorency married late, in 1527. Thus his sons were too young to benefit from Francis I's favor; instead he promoted his nephews, the Châtillons.

From 1528 to 1541 Montmorency was the most powerful royal adviser and exercised a conservative influence, especially in regard to religion. His reward was the office of constable in 1538. Three years later he fell into disgrace until Francis died in 1547. The new king, Henry II, brought him back to power, and for the duration of Henry's reign, he was his closest adviser. However, he had to share influence with the Guises and Diane de Poitiers, Henry's mistress.

In 1549 Montmorency crushed the Gabelle Revolt in southwestern France and earned a reputation for harshness. Yet he also was a force for peace with the Habsburgs and cooperation with foreign Protestants, although he advocated severity toward French Protestants. Toward the end of Henry's reign, with his nephews showing Protestant leanings, he became less hostile to the reformers. In 1557 Montmorency was captured in the Battle of Saint-Quentin. Ransoming him was a factor in Henry's decision to agree to the Peace of Cateau-Cambrésis (1559). Celebrating the peace, Henry was mortally wounded while jousting. With the Guises dominating Francis II, Montmorency retired from the court and was a bystander for the first year of the religious strife that now erupted. The failure of the Colloquy of Poissy (1561) probably convinced him to join with the Guises against the Huguenots. In command of the Catholic-royal forces at the Battle of Dreux in 1562, he and the Protestant commander were both captured by their opponents, a unique event in history. Freed the next year, Montmorency returned to the field when the civil war resumed in 1567 and was killed in the Battle of Saint-Denis.

BIBLIOGRAPHY

Baumgartner, Frederic J. *Henry II, King of France.* Durham, N.C., 1988. Describes the duke's role in government during his period of greatest influence.

Bedos Rezak, Brigitte. *Anne de Montmorency: Seigneur de la Renaissance.* Paris, 1990. Largely deals with the duke's patronage of art and literature.

FREDERIC J. BAUMGARTNER

MONTMORENCY, HOUSE OF.

During the French Wars of Religion, this French aristocratic family held great influence at court and powerful connections in the provinces. With a lineage stretching back to the Middle Ages, impressive holdings in the Île-de-France, and control of the governorship of Languedoc, the family of Montmorency emerged as one of the most powerful noble families at the court of Francis I (r. 1515–1547), beginning with the appointment of Anne de Montmorency (1493–1567) as grand master and constable of France, the highest military offices a French noble could occupy. He retained these offices with all their prestige and influence under Henry II (r. 1547–1559), Francis II (r. 1559–1560), and Charles IX (r. 1560–1574). Although the constable remained a devout

Catholic throughout his life, he and his family opposed the Guise family at court under Henry II and Francis II. As the Guises became attached to a policy of persecution of Protestantism in the 1550s, some of the constable's sons and nephews were drawn to the Protestant movement and provided critical aristocratic support to the new religion as it came under royal attack. This was especially true during the short reign of Francis II, as the Guises dominated the young king and his court. (Francis II was married to Mary Stuart, daughter of Marie de Guise.) Thus, the significance of this family to the Protestant movement in France was in the form of noble patrons, supporters, leaders, and defenders of the Huguenots during the Wars of Religion.

Although the constable's eldest son, François de Montmorency, never converted to Protestantism, he served as a staunch opponent of the Guises at court. As a marshal of the army and governor of the Île-de-France, he continued in his father's footsteps as a moderating Catholic force who tried to rid the crown of Guise influence. The constable's second son, Henri de Montmorency, lord of Damville (1534–1614), played a direct role in supporting the Protestant cause during the religious wars. He was appointed as marshal, constable, and, in 1563, governor of Languedoc, a position he would hold for the next fifty years. As Languedoc, a province in the Midi, was already a region heavily populated with Huguenots by the time of his appointment as governor, Henri was in a critical position either to suppress the new religion (as many royal governors were doing elsewhere in the kingdom) or to support it. While his own personal religious beliefs were somewhat ambivalent (though officially he remained a Catholic), Henri chose the latter policy of supporting the Huguenot movement. When a Huguenot assembly met in Millau in 1574, he formed an alliance with them, offering his protection. When a Huguenot constitution was adopted at Nîmes in January 1575, Henri was officially recognized as a military commander and deputy to Henri I Condé. Advocating religious coexistence, Montmorency thus became an explicit component of the Protestant state within the state, as the Huguenots set up their own administrative, political, and military state in southern France, with Languedoc at its center. This placed him in opposition to the Crown during the fifth civil war (1575–1576), and he was a significant part of the Protestant alliance that exacted the Peace of Monsieur from the king in May 1576. Although Henri did leave the Huguenot alliance shortly thereafter and vowed to support the Crown, he was a moderating influence in Languedoc for the remainder of the religious wars and served as an opponent of the Guise-led Catholic League in the 1580s and 1590s.

Henri's younger brothers—Guillaume de Montmorency, lord of Thoré, and Charles de Montmorency, lord of Méru—also supported the Huguenot army as military commanders under Henri I Condé in the 1570s. But the most celebrated member of the Montmorency family to support and to lead the Protestant cause was a nephew of the constable, and thus the Montmorency brothers's first cousin, Gaspard II de Coligny (1519–72), lord of Châtillon and admiral of France. Coligny had actually converted to Calvinism at the outbreak of the civil wars in the early 1560s and had served as a military leader under the command of Louis I Condé. When the elder Condé was killed in battle in 1569, Coligny took over the Huguenot leadership and began to forge alliances abroad, particularly with William of Orange, who promised mutual support for the French Huguenots if Coligny would aid his attempt to wrest away the provinces of Holland and Zeeland from the control of an occupying Spanish army. At home in France, Coligny eventually was invited onto the royal council of Charles IX and continued his family's policy of opposing the Guises at court. All his activities were suddenly struck down by assassins in August 1572, when the murders of Coligny and several other Protestant nobles gathered in Paris sparked the Saint Bartholomew's Day Massacre. The assassination of Coligny and his fellow nobles touched off further religious violence that decimated the ranks of the Huguenot leadership and ended whatever hopes they had of further growth. Moreover, the Huguenots were robbed of one of their most able military leaders of the entire conflict.

Coligny's older brother, Odet, followed in his brother's footsteps and converted to Protestantism, even though he was a cardinal, bishop, and inquisitor in the French church. Coligny's younger brother, François, lord of Andelot, also converted to Protestantism and married a Calvinist wife. The entire Montmorency family, in fact, had forged strong marriage alliances with some of the most influential Calvinist families in France: the Lavals, La Marcks, La Trémoilles, and Bouillons, among others. This vast aristocratic network and that of several other noble families (such as the Bourbons) were critically important in sustaining Calvinist growth around midcentury, when the Crown began a policy of outright suppression of Protestantism under Henry II. Had French Calvinists been unable to draw upon the support and protection of families such as the Montmorencies—in the form of military support, payment of pastors, and general protection as nobles of the sword—the Protestant Reformation in France could easily have succumbed to the suppression of the Crown.

BIBLIOGRAPHY

Davies, Joan M. "Languedoc and Its *Gouverneur:* Henri de Montmorency-Damville, 1563–1589." Unpub. Ph.D. thesis, University of London, 1974. Although difficult to consult outside England, this unpublished thesis with that of Mark Greengrass are easily the best and most comprehensive studies of the career of Damville available. They have completely replaced the outdated and much older study by C. F. Palm.

De Crue de Stoutz, Francis. *Anne, duc de Montmorency, connétable et pair de France, sous les rois Henry II, François IX et Charles IX.* Paris, 1889. Although very outdated, this is the only large-scale study of the constable's career.

Greengrass, Mark. "War, Politics, and Religion in Languedoc during the Government of Henri de Montmorency-Damville, 1574–1610." Unpub. Ph.D. thesis, University of Oxford, 1979. Especially good on Damville's military alliance with the Huguenots.

Salmon, J. H. M. *Society in Crisis: France in the Sixteenth Century.* London and New York, 1975. Best survey of the religious wars in English, and one that demonstrates explicitly the role of the Montmorency family.

Shimizu, J. *Conflict of Loyalties: Politics and Religion in the Career of Gaspard de Coligny, Admiral of France, 1519–1572.* Geneva, 1970. Although marred by an attempt to distinguish political and religious motives, this is the most scholarly biography of Coligny in English.

Sutherland, N. M. *The Huguenot Struggle for Recognition.* New Haven and London, 1980. Perceptive study of the Huguenots attempts to survive suppression by the crown and Catholic church in France, outlining the role played by the Montmorencies.

MACK P. HOLT

MORAVIA. A full century before Luther's revolt launched massive changes in Europe, Moravia, in partnership with its larger neighbor, Bohemia, experienced its own religious reformation. Bordered by Austria, Bohemia, Silesia, and Hungary, the margravate of Moravia was dominated by its larger neighbors. Most of the population was Czech, but a significant German minority had established itself, especially in the royal cities and the towns that carried on Moravian commerce.

When the Reformation began, Moravia owed allegiance to the king of Hungary, Louis II, but when he died in the Battle of Mohács in 1526, Ferdinand I, archduke of Austria, moved quickly to assert his dynastic claim to become margrave of Moravia. Thus began a centuries-long Habsburg rule of Moravia. Often the local diet successfully asserted a measure of independence and resisted Ferdinand's efforts to establish greater religious and political control. Several commercial centers, however, were royal cities and thus stood directly under royal rule. During the Hussite Reformation most Czechs in Moravia had adopted some form of the movement. The landed gentry and most of the Czech population at large became Utraquist. A minority embraced a more radical form of dissent that eventually found expression in the Unity of Brethren (Bohemian Brethren). Most of the German urban population remained Catholic. During much of the fifteenth century, papal and imperial pressure—often expressed in crusade and interdict or by excommunication—established the view that Moravia was a home for heretics. At the same time, this relentless external opposition gave the Hussite movement a national identity defined in antipapal and anti-Austrian (or anti-German) terms. Fears about the independence of Moravia soon proved fully justified.

The Hussite movement, although it remained largely confined to the Czechs, so profoundly changed the religious configuration of Moravia that when the teachings of Martin Luther, Huldrych Zwingli, John Calvin, and other Reformation leaders came to this margravate, they were generally given a cordial reception as expressions of a kindred spirit. This did not mean, however, that the new views were adopted.

Luther's writings aroused considerable interest in Moravia. Luther's teachings early received a warm reception in Moravian towns with large German populations, and eventually most German-speaking parishes became Lutheran. In addition, a number of prominent Czechs, members of the Unity of Brethren, sensed a kindred spirit with Wittenberg. Soon after Luther's dramatic identification with Hussite views in 1520, Jan Roh (Horn), an adherent of the Unity of Brethren and a priest in Litomysl, together with other clergy of the Unity of Brethren, made the first of several journeys to Wittenberg. Contact between Luther and the Unity of Brethren continued; at the same time, Luther tried to form a common front with the neo-Utraquists, who were less inclined to seek rapprochement with Rome.

Champions of Luther's position, such as Paul Speratus (the later Lutheran bishop of Pomerania in Prussia), (1522–1523), explored possibilities of doctrinal ties; differences on the real presence, however, proved substantial. Similarly, Luther's emphasis on salvation by faith alone created some uneasiness. Another disagreement arose over the Unity of Brethren's insistence on clerical celibacy, a position they modified at the end of the century. Five visits by Roh to Wittenberg demonstrated the Unity of Brethren's strong desire for mutual acceptance. The two groups decided to remain separate but recognized each other, in Luther's words, as "true Christians." When the Unity of Brethren published a confession in 1535, Luther wrote a warm introduction.

By the mid-1520s some of Zwingli's writings began to appear in Moravia. A small group—supported by Jan Dubčanský, a Moravian noble, and a few Utraquist and Unity of Brethren priests—attempted in 1528 to establish a Zwinglian movement centered in the village of Habrovany. This effort failed to gain widespread support, despite a vigorous literary effort. A conference in 1535, attended by numerous Moravian nobles and religious leaders, failed to adopt the Zwinglian position. Differences in theology, especially in the doctrine of justification and the meaning of the sacraments, prevented closer ties. With the death of Dubčanský in 1543, this movement faded into the background.

In the second half of the sixteenth century, the Unity of Brethren became increasingly receptive to Calvinist theology. Indeed, some prominent leaders of the group urged formal union with Calvinist churches; others championed a close, fraternal, but separate relationship. The latter view prevailed. Thus, Moravian members of the Unity of Brethren recognized a spiritual affinity with Calvinism but maintained their ecclesiastical identity.

In 1526 the Anabaptist leader Balthasar Hubmaier arrived in Mikulov (Nikolsburg), which became the focal point of a significant Moravian experiment in religious and social reform. As forcible suppression of Anabaptism spread in many countries, adherents from numerous communities found toleration in Moravia. Here, local lords allowed the Anabaptists to settle and establish communal farms. Agricultural products, as well as the skilled labor of craftsmen, such as masons, carpenters, tailors, coppersmiths, hatters, and others proved decisive economic factors in persuading local authorities to allow religious nonconformity. Sometimes prominent nobles insisted on religious freedom and, at least in the case of Leonhart, lord of Liechtenstein, not only protected Anabaptist leaders like Hubmaier, but actually joined the movement in Mikulov.

As ever more Anabaptist refugees came to the area, several groups emerged. Ethnic diversity, different geographical origins, and theological disagreements all played a role in giving rise to new forms of Anabaptism. Disagreement with Hubmaier on the issue of pacifism caused one group to move to another location; during the journey to Slavkov (Austerlitz), the physical problems encountered led the group to begin sharing possessions. When the refugees found a new home, they continued the practice of voluntary communal living. Thus, Moravia gave birth to the Hutterite Brethren. Soon their number increased to perhaps twenty-five thousand, living in scores of communities. Most of the Anabaptist groups in Moravia were composed of those who had fled persecution elsewhere; only a small number of Czechs joined their ranks.

Toleration of the Anabaptists, however, was regularly opposed by Ferdinand. Despite his visit to the sessions of the Moravian diet in 1528, he could gain only modest support against the Anabaptists. In the royal cities, however, he insisted on execution of Anabaptists. Not infrequently, problems elsewhere forced Ferdinand to turn his attention to other matters. During much of the sixteenth century, with some notable exceptions, Anabaptists enjoyed relative freedom in Moravia. That changed dramatically with the beginning of the Thirty Years' War, early in the seventeenth century, as the Habsburg rulers determined to rid Moravia not only of Anabaptists but of all Protestants. This goal was largely achieved.

[*See also* Anabaptists *and* Bohemian Brethren.]

BIBLIOGRAPHY

Brock, Peter. *The Political and Social Doctrines of the Unity of Czech Brethren in the Fifteenth and Early Sixteenth Centuries.* The Hague, 1957. Examines the social implications of the beliefs of the Unity of Brethren.

Heymann, Frederick G. "The Impact of Martin Luther upon Bohemia." *Central European History* 1 (1968), 107–130. Shows how Luther gained a strong following in the larger Moravian cities and also exerted considerable influence on Utraquists.

Hrubý, Frantisek. *Die Wiedertäufer in Mähren.* Leipzig, 1935. Concludes that the number of Hutterites in Moravia may have approached twenty thousand.

Mecenseffy, Grete. *Geschichte des Protestantismus in Österreich.* Graz, 1956. A careful analysis of various Protestant movements in lands, including Moravia, under the Austrian Crown.

Odložilík, Otakar. "Der Widerhall der Lehre Zwinglis in Mähren." *Zwingliana,* 4.g (1925), 257–276. Demonstrates that, although some prominent Moravian leaders championed Zwingli's views for a short time, it was the Reformed position of Calvin that endured.

Říčan, Rudolf. *Das Reich Gottes in den böhmischen Ländern: Geschichte des tschechischen Protestantismus.* Stuttgart, 1957. A survey of Protestantism, including the spread of Lutheran, Reformed, and Anabaptist movements during the Reformation era.

Stayer, James M. *The German Peasants' War and Anabaptist Community of Goods.* Montreal, 1991. Includes numerous regional assessments of the numerical strength of Anabaptists in Moravia and reasons for their being tolerated for much of the sixteenth century.

Thomson, S. Harrison. "Luther and Bohemia." *Archive for Reformation History* 44 (1953), 160–181. Includes a discussion of the theological impact of Luther upon the Unity of Brethren and Utraquists in Moravia.

Williams, George H. *The Radical Reformation.* 3d ed. Kirksville, Mo., 1992. Examines the role of the Anabaptist movement in Moravia within the context of the larger radical reformation.

Zeman, Jarold K. *The Anabaptists and the Czech Brethren in Moravia, 1526–1628.* The Hague, 1967. A detailed analysis of the interaction of these two groups, with special emphasis on their many shared beliefs and practices.

———. "The Rise of Religious Liberty in the Czech Reformation." *Central European History* 6 (1973), 128–147. Shows how Moravia, prodded by Utraquists and members of the Unity of Brethren, became a pioneer in religious toleration.

Zieglschmid, A. J. F. *Die älteste Chronik der Hutterischen Brüder.* Philadelphia, 1974. Translated as *Chronicle of Hutterian Brethren, 1525–1665,* Rifton, N.Y., 1989. Recounts the origins and development of the Hutterites, their frequent persecution and forced wandering, their religious beliefs, social structures, and economic practices.

PETER J. KLASSEN

MORAVIAN BRETHREN. *See* Bohemian Brethren.

MORE, Thomas (Lat., Morus; 1477/78–1535), English lawyer, statesman, foremost early Tudor exponent of the active humanist life, Catholic controversialist, and martyr; knighted 1521, beatified 1886, canonized 1935. He was born in London, and was executed on Tower Hill, London. The second child and eldest son of John More (c.1451–1530), lawyer, later judge and Sir John, and Agnes, née Graunger (d. before 1507), he probably attended Saint Anthony's School in London, and was page in the household of John Morton, archbishop of Canterbury and lord chancellor, before being sent to the University of Oxford, (c.1492–1494). Returning to London, he began legal training and from 1499 practiced as a barrister. He lived some years in the London Charterhouse without taking vows. By January 1505 he had married Jane (or Joan) Colt (c.1488–1511), with whom he had three daughters and a son; at her death he married Alice Middleton (c.1471–1543), a widow.

Career. More may have been a member of the Parliament of 1504; he greeted the coronation of Henry VIII in 1509 with flattering Latin epigrams. The next year he was again an MP and was made freeman of the Mercers' Company, for whom he conducted negotiations. From 1510 to 1518 he was under-sheriff, an important City legal officer. In 1517 he helped to pacify and to enquire into the disturbances of Evil May Day. He served on his first Royal Commission in 1510. In 1515 More went to Flanders on the first of his six royal missions abroad. During this embassy he wrote the description of the utopian commonwealth that forms the second part of his best-known work. His most important later embassies were to the Field of the Cloth of Gold (1520) and to the "Ladies' Peace" of Cambrai (1529). Early in 1518 he joined the King's Council, becoming a sort of royal secretary. Made under-treasurer and knight in 1521, he was appointed speaker of the House of Commons in 1523, and in 1525 chancellor of the Duchy of Lancaster. The "Eltham Ordinances" of 1526 required More to be in constant attendance on the king.

Though More's reluctance to agree to the annulment of Henry VIII's marriage to Catherine of Aragon was already clear in 1527, when he was first consulted, he succeeded Thomas Wolsey as lord chancellor in October 1529, being only the second layman in that office. A month later, More opened the first session of the "Reformation Parliament," and further sessions in 1531 and early 1532. On 16 May 1532, the day following the Submission of the Clergy, More resigned. Thereafter, he lived as a private citizen, though continuing as religious and clandestine political controversialist. Implicated in the affair of the treasonable prophecies of Elizabeth Barton, the "Nun of Kent," in 1533–1534 but exonerated, he was examined concerning his views on the divorce and the supremacy before the King's Council on 6 March 1534. Having refused to swear the oath presented to him, the exact content of which is not known, he was committed to the Tower of London on 17 April. His imprisonment was regularized by an act of attainder of More and John Fisher, bishop of Rochester, on 3 November. Between 30 April and 14 June 1535, More was several times interrogated in the Tower. On 1 July he was tried and condemned in Westminster Hall under the High Treason Act of 1534, and executed on 6 July 1535, a fortnight after John Fisher (22 June).

Humanism. More was the friend and penitent of John Colet, dean of Saint Paul's, and a friend of Desiderius Erasmus from 1499. He probably learned Greek from William Grocyn and Thomas Linacre at the end of the fifteenth century and the beginning of the sixteenth and later translated, from Greek into Latin, epigrams with William Lilly and Lucian with Erasmus.

More had early written English poetry, but his European reputation—already secure by the end of the 1510s—was based on his humanist compositions. His learned contacts outside England included, among opponents, the Frenchman Germanus Brixius (Germain de Brie), and among friends and supporters in France Guillaume Budé and Jacques Lefèvre d'Étaples, in Spain Juan Luis Vives, and in the Netherlands Jerome Busleiden, Frans van Cranevelt, and Pieter Gillis, the dedicatee of *Utopia.* In 1509 Erasmus, staying in More's City house on his return from Italy, wrote and dedicated to More his *Praise of Folly (Encomium Moriae)*, with its Greek pun on More's name in the title. The More household became famous for learned piety and for care for female education. In the mid-1520s, when More had moved to Chelsea, Vives and the German mathematician and astronomer Nikolaus Kratzer were his guests. The Swiss painter Hans Holbein the Younger was welcomed there in 1526–1527 and drew and painted portraits of More and others of the household.

From 1514 to 1521 More supported Erasmus in the controversy over the *Folly* and Erasmus's Greek New Testament with translation *(Novum Instrumentum*, 1516; *Novum Testamentum*, 1519, etc.). His long Latin letters to Maarten van Dorp of Louvain, the University of Oxford, and an unnamed monk (John Batmanson) are eloquent statements of Erasmian evangelical humanism. They contain much strong criticism of scholastic dialectic and of reactionary views concerning the Latin Vulgate New Testament and its relation to the original Greek. Erasmus in turn made Europe better aware of More the man and the humanist, especially by promoting the publication of the Latin *Utopia* (Louvain, 1516; Paris, 1517; Basel, Froben, 1518 [twice, with Latin epigrams]; first English translation, 1551), and by describing him in a published letter to Ulrich von Hutten. About 1515–1518, More wrote Latin and English versions of a *History of Richard III*, which was a substantial contribution to the Tudor image of Richard as tyrant and monster.

Religious and Political Controversy. Though More publicly underplayed the early manifestations of Luther's revolt, he was already aware of the threat to a well-ordered English society presented by heresy and anticlericalism, as in the case of Richard Hunne (1514). The epitaph that he composed for himself in 1532 makes special mention of his severity toward thieves, murderers, and heretics. The writings in defense of Catholic orthodoxy, the unity of the church, and the ecclesiastical jurisdiction that occupied much of his later life opened on the European stage. More's first move from an Erasmian to a furiously anti-Lutheran position was prompted by his perception of the danger to Catholicism of Luther's attack on the sacraments. In 1521 he was—as he later wrote—"a placer and sorter out of the principal matters" contained in Henry VIII's *Assertio septem sacramentorum.* Soon after, in tandem with Fisher, More began himself to write against European heterodoxy. In 1521 Fisher preached at a burning of Lutheran books at Paul's Cross and in early 1523 published *Assertionis Lutheranae confutatio.* A little later in 1523 More followed with a *Responsio ad Lutherum,* in often scurrilous Latin, under two different pseudonyms. To Fisher's subsequent voluminous defenses, More also added, in late 1525 or early 1526 (published 1568), a long Latin letter in reply to the *Epistola ad Anglos* of Johannes Bugenhagen (1525), who was apparently under the impression that England was being won over to the Lutheran cause.

At about this time the English church, aided by the civil authority of More, was moving afresh against heresy. In 1524 the London booksellers were formally warned against trafficking in heretical works in English. In early 1526 More descended on the Hansa merchants in their compound at the Steelyard to examine and admonish them also. On 11 February 1526 Wolsey staged another ceremonial burning of books at Saint Paul's, and there were further formal prohibitions in 1530 and 1531. The works of William Tyndale (burned at the stake in 1536), strongly influenced by Luther and printed in Germany and the Low Countries, were being imported. Thomas Bilney (burned 1531), Thomas Arthur, Richard Bayfield (burned 1531), George Joye, Robert Barnes (burned 1540), and John Frith (burned 1533) in particular spread Lutheran doctrines. More took part in the examination of Bayfield, Frith, and others.

In early 1529 Simon Fish of Gray's Inn wrote his *Supplication for the Beggars.* Most of these works were printed in Antwerp. In Fish's tract the beggars of England are made to complain that alms that ought to go to support them in life are being diverted to the church for the release of souls from purgatory after death. Against Tyndale, Frith, Barnes, Joye, and Fish, More wrote at length during the years 1528 to 1533, becoming the chief spokesman in English on the Catholic side. This activity had been commissioned by Cuthbert Tunstall, his friend, fellow ambassador and bishop, on 7 March 1528. The first installment of almost a million words written in half-a-dozen years, for more than half of which More was lord chancellor, was published as the *Dialogue concerning Heresies* (for short) in June 1529 (second edition, May 1531). This was a refutation, less unpleasant in tone than some of his later controversial works, of Tyndale's Lutheran doctrines concerning justification by faith, the nature of the Eucharist, and the efficacy of religious observances such as devotion to the saints, veneration of images, and pilgrimage. It was also a rejection, spirit and letter, of Tyndale's English translation of the New Testament (1525–1526). In late 1529 two editions appeared of *The Supplication of Souls,* More's answer to Fish. Next came More's vast, unwieldy, harsh, and uncompromising *Confutation of Tyndale's Answer* (first part, spring 1532; second part, early 1533). In this work More dealt chiefly again with Tyndale's New Testament, his ideas of "feeling faith" and the real presence, the nature of the church and its authority, and the relative status of scripture and tradition, giving special attention to Barnes at the end of the second part and, according to his custom, denigrating the characters of his opponents. At the end of 1532 he contested the eucharistic doctrine of Frith, the chief English adherent of Johannes Oecolampadius, in his *Letter against Frith* (published early 1533).

With the exception of Fish, the authors of the tracts so far attacked by More had been English clerics. Toward the end of 1532 appeared an anonymous pamphlet from a new direction. A *Treatise concerning the Division between the Spiritualty and Temporalty* assaulted the clergy for their laxness, their greed for honor and money, and particularly their leniency in dealings with each other and their oppressiveness to laymen in the ecclesiastical courts. Such criticisms had been gathering force for half a century. Now they were being voiced by one of England's senior common lawyers, Christopher St. German (c.1460–1540/41). St. German's *Dialogue betwixt a Doctor of Divinity and a Student in the Laws of England* had sought to clarify the respective roles of the civil and ecclesiastical courts. In the *Treatise concerning the Division* and subsequent pamphlets recommending the bringing into line of the ecclesiastical with the civil courts by royal authority, St. German was writing with the approbation—at least—of Thomas Cromwell. More's first reply, *The Apology of Sir Thomas More, Knight,* published about Easter 1533, is part reiteration of previous arguments against Tyndale and Barnes in particular, part self-defense against charges of physical cruelty to and illegal imprisonment and interrogation of English heretics. Chiefly, however, it is justification of ecclesiastical court procedure and rebuttal of St. German's other complaints against the clergy. St. German replied and More retorted rapidly with *The Debellation of Salem and Bizance,* written in ten days and published about the end of October 1533. In both tracts More affects not to know his opponent's identity. This was necessary because he was meddling in politics after relinquishing the lord chancellorship in May 1532. At the end of 1533 he returned to matters of religion in *The Answer to the Poisoned Book Which a Nameless Heretic Hath Named "The Supper of the Lord,"* published at the beginning of 1534. This opponent is generally agreed to have been George Joye. It was More's final work in the genre. It is again a strong assertion of the Catholic doctrine of the Eucharist and the inviolable authority of the church and its tradition, as embodied in its own determinations, made under the direct inspiration of the Holy Ghost, and in the writings of the Fathers, "the old holy doctors," as More calls them.

Devotional Works. Imprisoned in the Tower, More reverted to the sacred and devotional writing that he had begun in the earlier years of the century with lectures on Augustine's *City of God* in the church of Saint Lawrence Jewry, his translation into English and adaptation of the *Life* of Giovanni Pico della Mirandola, written by Pico's nephew, Gianfrancesco, and Pico's maxims on the qualities of a lover and the weapons of spiritual battle. In the 1520s he wrote a brooding consideration of the "Four Last Things." The prayers and meditations More composed in the Tower, together with the annotations in the prayer book, a combined book of hours and psalter that was his constant companion there, and the incomplete meditation on the agony in the Garden, *De tristitia Christi* (which remained in manuscript until 1976), as well as *A Dialogue of Comfort against Tribulation* (first printed posthumously in 1553), are moving records of his spiritual certainties and uncertainties in his last months as he strove, in his own words, "to continually remember the immortality of the life to come." Throughout his life he had reinforced prayer and meditation with physical austerities such as abstinence and the wearing of a hair shirt; he was never an easy man, with himself as with opponents.

Reputation. Accounts of More's trial and death, rapidly diffused in Latin newsletters, shocked Europe; he was at once regarded as a martyr. Later biographies in English such as those written by his son-in-law William Roper, by Nicholas Harpsfield, and by one "Ro. Ba.," circulating in manuscript, reinforced this image among More's English coreligionists. Roper was first printed in 1626 at Saint Omer, the others not until the twentieth century. Authoritative for Catholic Europe, replacing Erasmus's letter to Hutten, was Thomas Stapleton's Latin biography, a prime document of the Counter-Reformation, printed in Stapleton's *Tres Thomae* (1588), which stressed the spiritual dimension. In England, except in the works of John Foxe, More's reputation as a man of holiness, kindness, uprightness, wit, and learning, as well as equitable paterfamilias and judge—a picture essentially based on Erasmus and Roper combined—long survived. It is still the estimate of R. W. Chambers in his frankly adulatory biography of 1935. Chambers also claimed for More an important position in the development of English prose. Nineteenth- and twentieth-century historians, from J. A. Froude to G. R. Elton, have laid emphasis on More's less attractive aspects as politician and controversialist, especially in his dealings with heterodoxy, discounting More's claim that it was the vice of heresy rather than the persons of heretics that he detested. Richard Marius's biography, the fullest and most satisfactory to date, seeks to counter Chambers.

BIBLIOGRAPHY

Primary Works

Miller, Clarence H. "Thomas More's Letters to Frans van Cranevelt, including Seven recently discovered Autographs." *Moreana* 31 (1994), 3–66.

More, Thomas. *English Works*. London, 1557. Collected by More's nephew William Rastell and published under Mary.

———. *Opera*. Basel, 1563; Louvain, 1565, 1566; and Frankfurt a.M., 1689.

———. *Correspondence*. Edited by Elizabeth F. Rogers. Princeton, 1947.

———. *Works*. 15 vols. New Haven and London, 1963–. Critical editions with substantial introductions and commentaries; lacking only vol. 1 (in press, 1994).

———. *Neue Briefe*. Edited by Hubertus Schulte Herbrüggen. Münster, 1966.

———. *Thomas More's Prayer-Book*. Edited by Richard S. Sylvester and Louis L. Martz. New Haven, 1969.

Secondary Sources

Chambers, R. W. *Thomas More* (1935). Reprint, London, 1982.

Gibson, R. W. and J. Max Patrick. *St. Thomas More: A Preliminary Bibliography of His Works and Moreana to the Year 1750*. New Haven and London, 1961.

Guy, J. A. *The Public Career of Sir Thomas More*. London and New Haven, 1980.

Kenny, Anthony. *Thomas More*. Oxford, 1983.

Marius, Richard. *Thomas More*. New York and London, 1984.

Morison, Stanley. *The Likeness of Thomas More*. Edited and supplemented by Nicolas Barker. London, 1963.

Smith, Constance. *An Updating of R. W. Gibson's St. Thomas More: A Preliminary Bibliography*. Saint Louis, 1981.

Sylvester, Richard S., and G. Marc'hadour, eds. *Essential Articles for the Study of Thomas More*. Hamden, Conn., 1977.

Trapp, J. B. *Erasmus, Colet and More: The Early Tudor Humanists and Their Books*. London, 1991.

Trapp, J. B., and Hubertus Schulte Herbrüggen. *"The King's Good Servant" : Sir Thomas More, 1477/78–1535*. Catalogue of the exhibition at the National Portrait Gallery. London, 1977.

J. B. TRAPP

MORÉLY, Jean (1524?–1594?), French Protestant theologian and advocate of the rights of the people in the church. Morély, sieur of Villiers, belonged to an affluent Parisian family that owned land in various sites around the capital. His father was a physician to King Francis I. After studying law and possibly theology, he converted to Protestantism in about 1545 and went to Zurich to continue his studies. In 1549 he accompanied two young Swiss nobles as a preceptor to Wittenberg, where he met Melanchthon. He then moved to Paris and from there to Lausanne in the middle of 1550. His friendship with Pierre Viret and with Calvin, who became his first son's godfather, dates from that time. He acquired the status of an inhabitant of Geneva in February 1554. He stayed in Geneva, with interruptions, until 1563. In following years he became involved in various political and diplomatic activities in France and, on one occasion, in England, on behalf of the French Protestant party. In 1556 he published a Latin translation of Machiavelli's *De arte della guerra*, a copy of which he presented to the council of Geneva. His relationship with the Genevan authorities soured in April 1560 after he made some incautious public statements about the ministers' involvement in the Conspiracy of Amboise, a failed attempt by a group of radical Huguenots to seize power in France.

A second and more serious conflict broke out after the publication of his *Traicté de la discipline et police chrestienne* in Lyon two years later. The Reformed churches were criticized for not observing Christ's church order, contenting themselves with half measures on the pretext that the times were not ripe for a full reformation of the church. In an unpublished book written while he was in England about thirteen years later, *De Ecclesiae ordine atque disciplina libri octo*, Morély completed his description of what he thought was the church's best government.

He never denied the right of pastors and elders to run the church but insisted that the assembly of the faithful had to exercise "supreme power" in the church. According to him it was the congregation that should finally decide about doctrinal and disciplinary matters. It also should have the power to elect and depose pastors, elders, and deacons. Delegates were to be sent to regional and national synods, but the "particular church" was to make the final decision. Referring to Aristotle's *Politics*, Morély advocated a model of mixed government, with Christ as king, the consistory as the aristocracy, and the assembly of the faithful as a "republic and democracy" (*Traicté*, p. 183). Only the male adults, having publicly confessed their faith, were to take part in the decision-making process. Morély argued that if the right church order, ordained by Christ, were followed, all disputes would be settled; with the help of the Holy Spirit the church would reach consensus.

Morély's proposals were first discussed at the Synod of Orléans in April 1562. The *Traicté* was said to contain "wicked doctrine" tending to the "confusion and dissipation of the church." In September 1563 Morély was excommunicated by the consistory of Geneva, and the council ordered his book to be burned publicly. He then tried to reconcile himself with the Reformed church by admitting his guilt but failed to convince the Genevan ministers of his sincerity.

Meanwhile he gained increasing numbers of disciples in France, particularly among the nobility. During the summer of 1566 he was chosen by Jeanne d'Albret, queen of Navarre, as the tutor of her son, who was to reign as Henry IV. Soon afterward, however, some compromising letters, in which he mocked the ministers in general and Théodore de Bèze in particular, were discovered and publicized. Though he was an excellent preceptor, the queen of Navarre was forced to dismiss him. Until 1572 nothing was heard from him, but his partisans, led by the French philosopher Petrus Ramus, continued to question the power given to the consistories and synods to the detriment of the congregation. Morély's condemnation was renewed and strengthened at two national synods, La Rochelle (September 1571) and Nîmes (May 1572).

After the Saint Bartholomew's Day Massacre in August 1572, Morély fled to England. On Lord Walsingham's recommendation, he became the guest of Herbert Davies, president of the council of Wales, in his Swansea castle. He met Richard Davies, the bishop of Saint David's, and wrote *De Ecclesiae ordine* for him in the hope of converting the Church of England to his ideas. By June 1578 he was back in France, but in 1585 the Edict of Nemours prompted him to flee once again to England. He died by 1594 at the latest.

BIBLIOGRAPHY

Primary Sources

Morély, Jean. *Traicté de la discipline et police chrestienne* (1562). New ed. Geneva, 1968.

———. *De Ecclesiae ordine atque disciplina libri octo ad Ecclesiae Anglicanae archiepiscopos atque episcopos authore Joanne Morelio Parisiensi.* Paris, Bibliothèque Nationale: Ms lat. 4361, 1574–1581. Only three books were found. The remaining five were probably never written.

———. *De Ecclesia ab Antichristo per ejus excidium liberanda, eaque ex Dei promissis beatissime reparanda Tractatus.* London, 1589.

———. *Le vray Agnus Dei pour descharmer le peuple Francois. Ecrit pour le Roy treschrestien Henri III. Roy de France de Pologne, sur le poinct de son Massacre.* London, 1589.

Secondary Sources

Denis, Philippe. "Penser la démocratie au XVIe siècle: Morély, Aristote et la réforme de la Réforme." *Bulletin de la Société de l'Histoire du Protestantisme Français* 137 (1991), 369–386.

———. "Viret et Morély: Les raisons d'un silence." *Bibliothèque d'Humanisme et Renaissance* 54 (1992), 395–409.

Denis, Philippe, and Jean Rott. *Jean Morély (ca 1524-ca 1594) et l'utopie d'une démocratie dans l'Église.* Geneva, 1993. This book is the latest biography of Morély and includes an extensive discussion of his theology. It takes newly-discovered documents into account, particularly Morély's *De Ecclesiae ordine.*

Kingdon, Robert M. *Geneva and the Consolidation of the French Protestant Movement, 1564–1572: A Contribution to the History of Congregationalism, Presbyterianism, and Calvinist Resistance Theory.* Geneva, 1967. The greater part of chapter 3, pp. 37–137, is devoted to the Morély dispute in France between 1562 and 1572.

Rott, Jean. "Jean Morély, disciple dissident de Calvin et précepteur malchanceux d'Henri de Navarre." In *Bulletin philologique et historique (jusqu'à 1610) du Comité des travaux historiques. Année 1969.* Paris, 1972. Also in Jean Rott, *Investigationes historicae,* vol 2, pp. 63–81, Strasbourg, 1986.

PHILIPPE DENIS

MORISCOS. *See* New Christians; Spain.

MORISON, Richard (also Morrison and Moryson; c.1510–1556), English humanist, politician, and reformer. Educated at Eton, Oxford (where he obtained his B.A. in 1528 at Thomas Cardinal Wolsey's new humanist college, later renamed Christ Church), and perhaps Paris, Morison first gained prominence on the fringes of Reginald Pole's establishment in Padua. While there Morison studied law and languages. His fortune was made when he won Thomas Cromwell's favor, probably in early 1536. Morison made the most of his first assignment as secretary to the committee that read Pole's *Pro ecclesiasticae unitatis defensione*, shortly after his return to England; he summarized the work adroitly, minimizing the damage Pole had done without entirely whitewashing the savagery of his attack on Henry VIII. This rhetorical skill typifies Morison's chief attraction to Cromwell. Shortly thereafter Morison tried his hand at theological controversy, drafting a reply to Johannes Cochlaeus's attack on royal supremacy. Morison's *Apomaxis calumniarum* was not published until 1538, having been delayed by more urgent business in the form of two polemical works against the Pilgrimage of Grace, *A Lamentation in Which Is Showed What Ruin and Destruction Cometh of Seditious Rebellion* and *A Remedy for Sedition* (both 1536). These tracts developed a highly Italianate, hierarchical view of the kingdom that may have owed something to Morison's familarity with Machiavelli's writings.

A staunch Protestant, Morison quickly gained a place in royal service, but Henry did not take to his new servant, and after Cromwell's fall in 1540 Morison went into the political wilderness. He executed at least one diplomatic assignment late in Henry's reign before becoming ambassador to Charles V under Edward. In 1554 he was forced into exile in Strasbourg, where he died. The trajectory of Morison's career tracks the ascent of a new class of state servants, as his works map some of the intersections between Italian humanism, English political vocabulary, and the more advanced varieties of Protestantism.

BIBLIOGRAPHY

Berkowitz, David Sandler, ed. *Humanist Scholarship and Public Order: Two Tracts against the Pilgrimage of Grace by Sir Richard Morison.* Washington, D.C., 1984. Introduction offers the most extensive (sometimes highly debatable) analysis of Morison's writing and career through 1536.

Elton, G. R. *Reform and Renewal: Thomas Cromwell and the Common Weal.* Cambridge, 1973. Sets Morison's early reform efforts in the context of the "Tudor Revolution."

Mueller, Janel M. *The Native Tongue and the Word: Developments in English Prose Style, 1380–1580.* Chicago, 1984. Final section of chapter five is by far the best treatment of Morison's style.

Slavin, A. J. "Profitable Studies: Humanists and Government in Early Tudor England." *Viator* 1 (1970), 307–325.

Zeeveld, W. Gordon. *Foundations of Tudor Policy.* Reprint, Westport, Conn., 1981. Basic work on Pole's circle; especially important for the question of Morison's Machiavellism.

THOMAS F. MAYER

MORITZ OF SAXONY (1521–1553), duke of Albertine Saxony, prince elector of Saxony after 1547. The first prince elector from the Albertine line of the house of the Wettins that emerged from the Leipzig division of 1485, Moritz of Saxony exerted a decisive influence on politics in the Holy Roman Empire of the German Nation around the middle of the century. Born in Freiberg as the first son of Henry, who introduced the Reformation in 1539, and of Catherine, a princess of Mecklenburg, Moritz soon became involved in the disputes of the various religious parties. During his education at the courts at Halle (1533–1534, Cardinal Albrecht), Dresden (1534–1537, Duke George), and Torgau(1537–1539, Elector John Frederick), he saw first hand the fluctuating and contradictory positions of imperial and religious politics. He was deeply influenced by Philipp of Hesse, whose daughter Agnes he married in 1541, and by his contact with his councilors after he assumed the government in 1541. The years 1546 and 1548/49 signaled radical changes in Moritz's policies.

During the first period of Albertine policy under Moritz between 1541 and 1546 (the beginning of the Schmalkald War), the duchy of Saxony became an evangelical territory. Efforts to create an overall ecclesiastical order did not succeed. There were too many differences in the positions of the key figures involved in the church reform. Johannes Pfeffinger, Anton Lauterbach, and Caspar Zeuner, the superintendents alongside Daniel Greiser who were influenced by Wittenberg and Luther, were countered by the views of George of Anhalt and of the court councilors. Among the achievements in domestic policy was the creation of an educational system based on the Reformation, including the establishment of prince's schools in Meissen and Schulpforta in 1543, the reform of the University of Leipzig, and the expansion of the city schools. The resources for this ecclesiastical and educational reform came from the sale of ecclesiastical property. With the appointment of his brother August as administrator of the bishopric of Merseburg in the spring of 1544 and the appointment of George of Anhalt as coadjutor of ecclesiastical affairs in Merseburg, Moritz, by dividing ecclesiastical and temporal power, attempted to promote the territorial integration of Merseburg and further the cause of the Reformation. In 1545 consistories were established in Merseburg and Meissen; they relied on the traditional structures of the bishoprics of Meissen and Merseburg that had become dysfunctional.

Even though both electoral and ducal Saxony had accepted the Reformation, tensions continued. Moritz's pro-Habsburg policy came to the fore when the duke fought against the Turks in Hungary in 1542 and joined forces with Charles V against France. In the second Braunschweig War of 1545 Moritz came to the aid of his father-in-law against Duke Henry the Younger. At that time attempts were made to achieve a rapprochement with Hesse and Ernestine Saxony. The proposed alliance was unacceptable to the leaders of the Schmalkald League, while Moritz shied away from taking a clear position in favor of the Protestants.

With the Regensburg Treaty of 19 June 1546 Moritz definitively broke with the Schmalkald League. He pledged himself to neutrality. Thus began a second phase in Albertine policy that lasted until 1548. Moritz acted as an ally and partner of the emperor. Only with difficulty could the young prince hold his ground against the prevailing public opinion, which was pro-Ernestine and anti-imperial. Many saw him as the "Judas of Meissen" who had betrayed his lord (John Frederick). The promise of the electoral title in mid-October 1546 finally led to his involvement in the Schmalkald War. Only with the emperor's support was Moritz able to prevail against his cousin. After his defeat at Mühlberg on 19 May 1547, John Frederick, now a prisoner, was forced to sign the Wittenberg Surrender, which meant the loss of the electoral title and of parts of electoral Saxony. In Thuringia a remnant Ernestine territory continued to exist, and its rulers dreamt for decades of a restoration. This marked for Moritz the beginning of his political ascent, which was hampered by the religious question and the unexpected imprisonment of Philipp of Hesse.

On 24 February 1548 the new Prince elector was solemnly sworn in by Charles V in Augsburg. At the same time the emperor took advantage of this increase in his power to push through a religious settlement (the Interim). Moritz opposed this settlement with great skepticism since it conceded to the Protestants only a married clergy and Communion under bread and wine. Influenced by the Wittenberg theologians, Moritz refused to give his assent. The growing alienation between Charles V and Moritz had not yet become explicit. The dispute over the Interim in Albertine Saxony marked the third and decisive period in Moritz's political career. He had reached the pinnacle of his power.

In 1548 the Diet of Leipzig considered the draft of a religious settlement. It did not agree with the emperor's Interim and was sharply rejected by Matthias Flacius Illyricus's circle of allies. It remained a topic of negotiations with Charles V and Ferdinand. Magdeburg became the focal point of resistance against it, and Moritz began to command the siege of the city at the end of 1550. He successfully discussed the enforcement of the Interim with King Ferdinand and at the same time negotiated an alliance with France. The disagreements between Charles V and his brother over succession in the empire advanced Albertine policies. Moritz succeeded in uniting the opposition to "imperial servitude" and in recommending himself to France as the important German ally. The agreement between France and the princes opposed to the emperor materialized and was signed by Henry II at Chambord on 1 January 1552.

In return for his considerable financial aid, which had made the princes' war against Charles V possible, Henry II obtained the imperial vice-regency over Cambrai, Metz, Toul, and Verdun. The warring princes moved swiftly and effectively south in March 1552. Charles V was forced to retreat. Against the opposition of France and Margrave Albrecht Alcibiades, who at first had been allied with Moritz, an agreement was reached in Passau in August 1552; the emperor gave his consent to it only after he had been defeated by France. The religious parties renounced the use of force against one another. The Interim became invalid. Philipp of Hesse and John Frederick of Saxony regained their freedom. The power of the emperor had been broken and the princes had prevailed. Moritz succeeded in discrediting the charge of betrayal. His success in the princes' war set the stage for the Peace of Augsburg of 1555. The attempts by Charles V to revise the Treaty of Passau were in vain. In his disappointment he increasingly yielded the initiative in the empire to his brother. Moritz's death on 11 July 1553 sealed the fundamental changes in religious policy that had been negotiated at Passau. No political decisions could be made in the empire without Saxony.

Until the conversion of August the Strong in 1697, Albertine Saxony dominated in German Protestantism. Moritz ruled for twelve years. Without regard to his capabilities Moritz pursued his offensive policies. He achieved success because he divorced his political decisions from religion. During the Interim this led Lutheran theology into a great crisis. Moritz contributed decisively to Charles V's withdrawal from politics. No other German prince of the Reformation era succeeded in moving from being the object of the emperor's power politics to becoming a successful opponent of the emperor. Thus he prepared the way for the empire's movement into the early modern period as a biconfessional state where the princes had a decisive voice.

BIBLIOGRAPHY

Primary Source

Moritz of Saxony. *Politische Korrespondenz des Herzogs und Kurfürsten Moritz von Sachsen.* 4 vols. to date. Edited by Erich Brandenburg, Johannes Herrmann, and Günther Wartenberg. Berlin, 1982–. Vols. 1 and 2 (which were originally published in 1900 and 1904, respectively) cover the period 1541–1546; vols. 3 and 4, 1547–1551. Vols. 5 and 6 are in preparation.

Secondary Sources

Blaschke, Karlheinz. *Moritz von Sachsen: Ein Reformationsfürst der zweiten Generation.* Göttingen, 1983.

Wartenberg, Günther. "Moritz von Sachsen, 1521–1553." In *Theologische Realenzykopädie*, vol. 23, pp. 302–311. Berlin and New York, 1994. Includes extensive bibliography.

GÜNTHER WARTENBERG

Translated from German by Robert E. Shillenn

MÖRLIN, Joachim (1514–1571), German Lutheran controversial theologian involved in ecclesiastical politics. Born in Wittenberg on 8 April 1514, Mörlin was the son of a professor of metaphysics at the University of Wittenberg who accepted the position of minister near Coburg soon after the birth of his son. Consequently, Mörlin grew up in financially modest circumstances, which barely allowed university studies. From 1532 he studied in Wittenberg, earning the degree of master of arts in 1536 and specializing in theology. He was promoted to the doctorate in theology in 1540 at the express request of Martin Luther. In 1540 Luther recommended him to Arnstadt as superintendent, but there he had a falling out with the sovereign, Count Günther of Schwarzburg, and despite Luther's protest, he was dismissed. In 1544 he was called to Göttingen as superintendent, but the adoption of the Interim in 1548 brought an end to his activities. This was followed by two years of precarious existence, after which Duke Albert of Prussia offered him a new position. He was appointed preacher at the cathedral in Königsberg, which included the position of inspector over the churches.

Mörlin considered himself a student of Luther and Philipp Melanchthon, which prompted his participation in the various religious controversies. He intervened in the dispute between Andreas Osiander and Melanchthon, as well as others, over the doctrine of justification, the Mass, and confession, and he sought to mediate between the antagonists, a tactic that Osiander roundly rejected. The dispute was carried out both verbally and in writing and by 1552 had become increasingly tense. The sentiment of the Protestant churches was for the most part against Osiander, who died in the middle of the dispute. Duke Albert had sympathized with Osiander's views and had observed Mörlin's activities with uneasiness and displeasure, especially since Mörlin saw himself superior to Osiander but was clearly not his intellectual equal.

When Duke Albert introduced the mediating Württemberg position, Mörlin opposed it from the pulpit and soon after (1553) was dismissed. Offers of employment came from Braunschweig, Lübeck, and Count Wilhelm of Henneberg. Mörlin decided on the superintendency in Braunschweig, but not without taking his assistant Martin Chemnitz with him. Here he presided over the Lutheran church and defended it against external influences. In order to prevent the inroads of Calvinism, he required all ministers to sign a *Corpus doctrinae* (the Lutheran Confession of Braunschweig; 1563). In 1556 he was called to mediate in Bremen the dispute between Johann Timann and Albert Hardenberg (an opponent of the Lutheran concept of ubiquity) over the Lutheran doctrine of the Sacrament. In the Heidelberg dispute over Communion he sided with the Lutheran Tilemann Hesshus against the Calvinist position of Thomas Lüber. He tried unsuccessfully to settle the controversy between Melanchthon and Matthias Flacius Illyricus. In the 1557 Colloquy of Worms he sided with the followers of Flacius, cooperated on the revision of the Weimar Confutation, advocated the convocation of a Lutheran synod, and participated in the 1561 convention of Lüneburg.

His *Erklärung aus Gottes Wort* was adopted in Braunschweig as a confession. Mörlin had a distinct view of church and ministerial office and of ecclesiastical and secular authority. Completely in line with the meaning of the Lutheran doctrine of two kingdoms, he emphasized the boundaries between church and state.

In 1567 he was called back to Königsberg at the insistence of the estates to order ecclesiastical affairs there; Braunschweig allowed him only a leave of absence. He drafted the *Repetitio corporis doctrinae christianae* for the Prussian church. This confession was submitted to the synod and was published after endorsement by the estates. After Braunschweig had discharged him honorably, Mörlin became the bishop of Samland in Prussia in 1568. His significance lies less in his own theological efforts than in the consolidation of the Lutheran confession and the Lutheran church. In Braunschweig and Lower Saxony he laid the foundation for the Formula of Concord (1577).

BIBLIOGRAPHY

Primary Source

Koch, F. "Briefwechsel Joachim Mörlins mit Herzog Albrecht." *Altpreußische Monatsschrift* 39 (1902), 517–596. Letters written during Mörlin's first stay in Prussia.

Secondary Sources

Roth, E. "Ein braunschweigischer Theologe des 16. Jahrhunderts: Joachim Mörlin und seine Rechtfertigungslehre." *Jahrbuch der Gesellschaft für niedersächsische Kirchengeschichte* 59 (1952) 59–81. A treatment of Mörlin's works and influence in Braunschweig, based on primary sources.

Stupperich, Martin. *Osiander in Preußen*. Arbeiten zur Kirchengeschichte 44. Berlin, 1973. See pp. 120–220 for the best summary of the results of new research on the relationship between Osiander and Mörlin during the Osiander dispute in Königsberg.

SIGRID LOOß

Translated from German by Susan M. Sisler

MORONE, Giovanni (1509–1580), Italian cardinal and diplomat. He was the son of Girolamo Morone, the grand chancellor of the duke of Milan, Francesco II Sforza, who was ruined by the failure of the anti-imperial conspiracy that had been planned following the battle of Pavia. The not yet twenty-year-old Giovanni had to seek in an ecclesiastical career the means for dealing with the crisis of his family, which had been forced to go into debt to pay for the father's ransom. He interrupted his law studies in Padua and went to Rome to ask for the aid of Clement VII. In 1529 he was appointed bishop of Modena, but he was able to take possession of the diocese only in 1533, after reaching a difficult compromise with the Duke Ercole II of Este.

He had an early opportunity to show his exceptional talent as a diplomat during the period he spent in Germany between 1536 and 1542 as apostolic nuncio to the Habsburg court, where he was charged with the task of setting the stage for the upcoming convening of the council. Here, in direct contact with the great religious crisis of the Germanic world and through his participation in the colloquies of Worms, Hagenau, and Regensburg, he developed the conciliatory and reformist orientations that were to characterize his pastoral and political activity. At the 1542 Diet of Speyer Morone played a decisive role in obtaining the diplomatic agreement concerning the site of the council. Thereafter Morone was finally able to return to Italy to face the serious problems caused by the spread of heretical dissent in his own diocese of Modena.

He was made a cardinal in June 1542, when he was just thirty-three years old, and shortly thereafter he was designated a papal legate during the first unsuccessful convocation of the council. At this time Morone underwent a profound religious turn, influenced by his meeting with the English cardinal Reginald Pole and by his reading of the works of Juan de Valdés and the *Beneficio di Cristo*. This led him to move away from the conciliatory theological attitude characteristic of Cardinal Gasparo Contarini, which he had espoused up to then. Inquisitors would later interpret this turn as an actual "seduction" into the Lutheran heresy. This turn, which led Morone to assume a leading role among the so-called spirituals, soon also began to manifest itself on the pastoral plane, both in Modena and in Bologna (where he was papal legate between 1544 and 1548), namely by the puzzling stances he took in favor of heterodox preachers and dissident groups, by the suspect doctrinal positions he expressed on more than one occasion, and by his ever closer ties with men and circles that were capable of combining openness to northern heresies with their own positions at the top echelons of the institutional church.

All this did not prevent Morone from retaining in those years a very influential role in the Curia Romana, which was reinforced by the personal favor of Ferdinand I and Charles V, or from becoming involved in the curial commissions in charge of reforms and organizing the council. In 1550 he resigned from the diocese of Modena, which he governed once again between 1564 and 1571, while between 1552 and 1560 he was bishop of Novara. But in 1555 Gian Pietro Carafa (Paul IV)—the undisputed leader of the intransigent party, which in the last conclaves had managed to prevent the election of both Pole and Morone by airing serious allegations of heresy—ascended the papal throne. Immediately inquisitorial proceedings were opened against Morone; at first they were secret, but then they were made official and became public upon his arrest at the end of May 1557. Only the death of the pontiff in August 1559 made it possible for Morone to leave the prison of Castel Sant'Angelo and thus avoid an almost certain condemnation. He was admitted to the conclave and then was solemnly acquitted by Pius IV in March of the following year; he then again assumed leading positions within the Curia Romana. He was even appointed to chair the final and decisive session of the Council of Trent in 1563, and he managed to bring it to a successful conclusion with extraordinary diplomatic skill.

Toward the end of 1565 the election of Pius V, who in the past had headed the curial commission charged with investigating him, marked a new and definitive decline in Morone's fortunes in the Curia. The new pope, however, was not able to arrest him because of Morone's personal prestige, the protection of the emperor, and the obvious need to avoid disavowing the previously granted pardon and to safeguard the credibility of the council. Even so, the proceedings against Morone were secretly reopened in 1570.

In the following years Morone contniued to play an important political role as a great diplomat: in 1570/71 during the negotiations for the conclusion of the Catholic League; in 1575 in a difficult mission to Genoa, where he was able to find a lasting solution to the political conflicts of the republic; and in the following year when he was sent as a papal legate to the Diet of Regensburg. Morone died in 1580 while dean of the Sacred College. He was the last of a generation of intellectuals who had lived at the crossroads of the Reformation and the Counter-Reformation and participated in the profound and conflicting tensions that formed the backdrop to the Tridentine era. These tensions were reflected in succeeding Counter-Reformation historiography, in which Morone's legacy oscillated between the figure of a crypto-Lutheran heretic investigated by Paul IV and that of the savior of the council under the guidance of Carlo Borromeo.

BIBLIOGRAPHY

Bernabei, Nicola. *Vita del cardinal Morone.* Modena, 1885. Outdated and unreliable biography.

Constant, Gustave. *La légation du Cardinal Morone près de l'empereur et le concile de Trente, avril-décembre 1563.* Paris, 1922. Edition of documents.

Dittrich, Franz, ed. *Nuntiaturberichte aus Deutschland.* Vol. 17, pt. 1, *1533–1559.* Reprint, Gotha, 1981.

———. *Nuntiaturberichte Giovanni Morones vom deutschen Königshofe, 1539–1540.* Paderborn, 1892. Basic documentation on Morone's political and diplomatic role.

Firpo, Massimo. *Inquisizione romana e Controriforma: Studi sul cardinal Giovanni e il uso processo d'eresia.* Bologna, 1992. Collection of essays particularly dealing with Morone's religious experience in the years 1540–1560.

Firpo, Massimo, and Marcatto Dario. *Il processo inquisitoriale del cardinal Giovanni Morone.* 6 vols. Rome, 1981–1995. See vol. 5. Critical edition of the extensive documentation on the proceedings.

Jedin, Hubert. *History of the Council of Trent.* 3 vols. London and New York, 1957–1963. On Morone's role in the preparation and direction of the council.

Lutz, Heinrich. "Kardinal Morone: Reform, Konzil und europäische Staatenwelt." In *Il Concilio di Trento e la riforma tridentina,* pp. 363–381. Rome, 1965.

"Morone, Giovanni." In *Theologische Realenzyklopädie,* vol. 23, pp. 318–324. Berlin and New York, 1977–.

Peyronel Rambaldi, Susanna. *Speranze e crisi nel Cinquecento modenese: Tensioni religiose e vita cittadina ai tempi di Giovanni Morone.* Milan, 1979. Deals with Morone's pastoral activity in the diocese of Modena.

Sclopis, Federico. *Le cardinal Jean Morone.* Paris, 1869. Chiefly about his diplomatic missions.

Schweinzer, Sylvia. "Das Ringen um Konzil und Kirchenreform: Die Mission des Nuntius Giovanni Morone auf dem Speyer Reichstag

1542." In *Reichstage und Kirche*, edited by E. Meuthen, pp. 137–189. Göttingen, 1991.

Massimo Firpo
Translated from Italian by Robert E. Shillenn

MORRISON, Richard. *See* Morison, Richard.

MÜHLHAUSEN. *See* Müntzer, Thomas.

MÜNSTER. Located in northwest Germany, Münster was the capital city of the territory and diocese of the same name. Under the leadership of Bernhard Rothmann, a Protestant congregation was formed in Münster in August 1532 and included six parishes. The resistance to change shown by the Catholic cathedral chapter and the bishop, Count Franz of Waldeck, ended through the mediation of Landgrave Philipp of Hesse; the resulting Treaty of Dülmen (14 February 1533) allowed the city council, which gained a Protestant majority in March 1533, to adopt a new church order drafted by Rothmann. The order did not subscribe to Luther's teaching on the sacrament of the altar and infant baptism—a stance that was later reinforced when Rothmann welcomed into town several preachers (including Hinrick Roll) who had been expelled from the Netherlands and Jülich. Jan Bockelson, better known as John of Leiden, whose mother came from Darup (twenty-five kilometers to the west of Münster), stayed in Münster for several weeks in the summer of 1533. The city council and the leaders of the guilds, assisted by Hessian clergy, attempted unsuccessfully to halt the spread of Anabaptist tendencies. In Strasbourg, meanwhile, Melchior Hoffman had prophesied that the world would end at year's end; by early November, Protestants in Münster were deeply divided, for some of them had turned to Melchiorite Anabaptism.

In the meantime, Jan Matthijs had assumed the leadership of the Melchiorites in Amsterdam and had begun to administer adult baptism there. On 5 January 1534 two of his emissaries came to Münster and baptized Rothmann and others; when John of Leiden arrived a week later, some fourteen hundred persons were reportedly baptized. Following the precedent of the apostolic congregation in Jerusalem, the "Congregation of Christ" lived in expectation of the Last Judgment, whose date had been postponed (probably by Matthijs) to Easter.

In a first letter about these developments, the bishop of Münster informed Landgrave Philipp in late January that "the damned sect and teachings of rebaptism" had spread to Münster, that infant baptism had been abolished, that the community of goods was being practiced, and that all governmental authority had been rejected. The bishop recommended that known preachers be arrested as revolutionaries; the city council responded by upholding freedom of worship. Matthijs consequently identified Münster as the site of the future New Jerusalem where all the baptized should gather in order to survive God's judgment. Amid ecstatic calls for penance, this announcement was made on 8 February. Threatening confrontations with Lutherans and Catholics followed, prompting the heretofore-peaceful Anabaptists to begin arming themselves in self-defense. Unusual phenomena appeared in the sky on 9–11 February that were interpreted as the signs of the Last Judgment as prophesied in the Gospels. The city council, fearing imminent civil conflict as well as military intervention by the bishop, renewed its toleration mandate. Word spread that Münster was God's elect city and that all true believers were to gather there. The several hundred who responded to this call—from the vicinity of Münster, the Lower Rhine, Holland, Frisia—were lodged in the vacated monasteries.

The bishop of Münster prepared a siege. He mobilized the knights, hired mercenaries, and on 23 February established his headquarters in Telgte, some 15 kilometers outside town. That same day a new city council was elected in Münster—twenty-four men who had the confidence of both the baptized and the unbaptized citizens, including Knipperdolling and Kibbenbrock as mayors. The next day Matthijs arrived in Münster and assumed the leadership of the Anabaptist congregation. In response to the siege, the Anabaptists expelled all citizens who refused rebaptism; some two thousand men and women left town.

When the Second Coming did not occur on Easter (5 April), Matthijs engaged in an attack outside the city walls and was killed. John of Leiden, his successor, established a council of twelve elders to organize the distribution of goods, the trades, and defense. Owing to the large number of unmarried women in the city, polygyny was introduced, despite strong resistance from the congregation. In September 1534, John of Leiden was crowned king on the throne of David. The organization of the Anabaptist kingdom was regulated by royal court order; of 148 royal officials identified by name, sixty-six came from Münster. Rothmann wrote in his *Restitution* (October 1534) that the Münster kingdom was to prepare the kingdom of Christ on earth, that the age of the perversion of the gospel had ended in 1533, and that the time of the restitution of the church of Christ had begun. Just as David had given his kingdom to his son Solomon, the new David, chosen by God in these final days, would hand over the kingdom begun in Münster to his successor, Solomon-Christ (*Bericht von der Rache*, December 1534).

Unable to carry out the siege on his own, the bishop of Münster initially received military and financial support from Landgrave Philipp of Hesse and, after lengthy negotiations, from the neighboring rulers along the Rhine, from the Habsburgs in Brussels, and eventually from the empire. Finally, on 25 June 1535, the city was taken. John of Leiden,

Knipperdolling, and Bernd Krechting were executed in the Münster marketplace on 22 January 1536.

The Münster variant of Anabaptism endured for a time in small clandestine groupings. Heinrich Krechting, formerly the king's chancellor, had escaped; new prophecies told of a reconquest of Münster and the coronation of a new king by the end of 1538. Within two years, however, Münsterite Anabaptism, severely persecuted, had disappeared.

The rise of the Anabaptist kingdom in Münster was once interpreted as a revolution of the poor, as a communist, socialist, or fascist revolution. Within the past fifty years, however, the period has become the focus of a new and more informed discussion, one that takes into account both theological matters and aspects of urban history. It has been noted that the bipolar constitution of Münster, whereby city council and guild leaders were elected annually, enabled the oppositional movement of 1532–1533 to place its representatives in important positions and thereby to implement its communal and confessional goals. Thus, in a Catholic city a Protestant congregation emerged, and later an Anabaptist congregation that declared Münster to be the New Jerusalem. Hoffman's prophecy regarding the Last Judgment was recast by Rothmann, who held that the restitution of the true church of Christ had begun; the rule of the "new David" would be followed by the eternal (or, as some believed, the thousand-year) rule of Christ. In February 1534, in the face of the territorial ruler's move against the city, civic resistance and eschatological hope became merged in the minds of citizens irrespective of social stratum.

The opposition of the ecclesiastical and secular authorities came in response to the Anabaptists' stance against existing governmental structures and denial that subjects were to be held accountable for civic obedience and orthodox religious belief. Claiming to follow only Christ, Anabaptists refused the oath, military service, and the exercise of governmental offices, and so became a threat to the public order. Imperial laws of 1526–1529 prohibited the unauthorized establishment of Anabaptist congregations and the administration of rebaptism on the grounds that these were insurrectionary, just as Protestant preaching had once been suppressed. Thus persecuted, the initially pacifist Anabaptists found justification for taking up arms in self-defense.

Warned repeatedly by the bishop of Münster that Anabaptists meant to destroy all rulers and conquer the world, the great Catholic powers finally united with evangelical rulers and cities to stamp out the Münster congregation. All rights and privileges were rescinded. An occupation force remained until 1541, and citizens had to wait until 1553 to regain the right to elect the city council. Together with the Anabaptist congregations, the nascent Lutheran movement was destroyed in and around Münster; the Counter-Reformation in Germany had scored its first success.

[*See also* Anabaptists; John of Leiden; Matthijs, Jan; Mennonites; *and* Philipp of Hesse.]

BIBLIOGRAPHY

Cornelius, Carl Adolf, ed. *Berichte der Augenzeugen über das Münsterische Wiedertäuferreich.* Geschichtsquellen des Bistums Münster, vol. 2. Münster, 1853. Includes sources, reports, chronicles, and correspondence from the years 1534–35 and the confessions of the Anabaptist leaders John of Leiden, Berndt Knipperdolling, and Bernd Krechting.

Detmer, Heinrich, ed. *Hermanni a Kerssenbroch Anabaptistici furoris Monasterium inclitam Westphaliae metropolim evertentis historica narratio.* Geschichtsquellen des Bistums Münster, vols.5–6. Band, Münster, 1899–1900. The Latin chronicle of Hermann of Kerssenbrock, headmaster in Münster, who died in 1585. The edition identifies the sources and cites relevant literature.

Hillerbrand, Hans J., ed. *Anabaptist Bibliography, 1520–1630.* Saint Louis, 1991.

Kirchhoff, Karl-Heinz. "Was There a Peaceful Anabaptist Congregation in Münster in 1534?" *Mennonite Quarterly Review* (1970), 357–370. Correction of Hermann of Kerssenbrock's account of the origins of the Congregation of Christ.

———. *Die Täufer in Münster 1534/35: Untersuchungen zum Umfang und zur Sozialstruktur der Bewegung.* Münster, 1973. Names, home ownership, property, and trade and profession are used to demonstrate (in contradiction of the thesis of a proletarian revolution) the involvement of a large number of burghers.

———. "Das Phänomen des Täuferreiches zu Münster 1534/35." In *Der Raum Westfalen* 6/1, edited by Franz Petri, pp. 277–422. Münster, 1989. Report on four centuries of research on Anabaptism with notes on the eschatological elements in Münster.

Littell, Franklin Hamlin. *The Anabaptist View of the Church.* Boston, 1958.

Stayer, James M. *Anabaptists and the Sword.* Lawrence, Kans., 1972.

Stupperich, Robert. *Die Schriften der münsterischen Täufer und ihrer Gegner.* pts. 1–3. Münster, 1970–. The writings and letters of B. Rothmann (1. Teil) and a selection of the writings of Catholic (2. Teil) and Protestant (3. Teil) polemists.

KARL-HEINZ KIRCHHOFF
Translated from German by Hans J. Hillerbrand

MÜNSTER, Sebastian (1480–1553), sixteenth-century German Hebraist, theologian, and exegete. He was born in Ingelheim and died in Basel. Münster studied Hebrew with Konrad Pellikan at the Franciscan monastery at Roufach. After converting to Protestantism in 1524, Münster taught Hebrew at the University of Heidelberg until 1528. He then moved to the University of Basel and held the position of professor of Hebrew and theology until his death twenty-five years later.

The scope of his interest in Hebraica was immense, and by the end of the sixteenth century over 100,000 volumes of his more than sixty publications were in circulation. With the exception of Jewish Cabbalistic studies, which he disliked, he contributed significantly to virtually every aspect of Hebraica. After publishing several good dictionaries of his own creation, in 1525 he published the excellent *Sefer Ha-Dikduk: Grammatica Hebraicae Absolutissima,* which incorporated the work of the leading Jewish grammarian of the day, Elijah Levita, with whom he started a lifelong collaboration. This publication was reprinted seven times. The next several years witnessed Münster's publication of Levita's many other grammatical writings, and in 1547 he published many of them in his *Opus grammaticum consummatum ex variis Elianis libris concinnatum.* He was also a devoted student of Aramaic, the language of the apostles. In 1523 he added a brief Aramaic addendum to a large Hebrew dictionary and published the excellent *Chaldaica Grammatica* in 1527. For scholars less familiar with Hebrew but knowing Greek or Latin, he produced *Shilush L'Shonot, Dictionarium Trilinguae* (1530), which was reprinted in 1543 and 1562.

Münster also made significant contributions to scriptural studies, and the inclusion of Jewish scholarship became a hallmark of his publication. He published accurate Old Testament texts along with Rabbi David Kimchi's commentary for *Joel* and *Malachi* (1530), *Amos* (1531), and *Isaiah* (1535). In 1525 Münster published his *Dictionarium Hebraicum ex rabbinorum commentoriis collectum,* and ten years later he produced an adaptation of Kimchi's classic grammatical dictionary in his *Dictionarium Hebraicum Sefer Hashorashim im Nigzarim.* The work proved popular and was reprinted three times. Most important was Münster's *Hebraica Biblia* (1534–35), the first new translation of the Hebrew Old Testament into Latin, together with his own annotations, which were filled with information drawn from medieval rabbinic sources.

His publications in the area of Jewish rabbinic thought were more controversial and provoked repeated charges of Judaization. In addition to several editions of Josephus, he also published selections from Abraham Ibn Ezra, Maimonides, Rabbi Solomon, and Moses ben Jacob of Coucy. Münster also published several missionary works directed at the Jewish community, including *Vikuach* (1539), a debate between a Jew and a Christian. The *Torat ha-Maschiach* (1537) was a Hebrew translation of the gospel of Matthew, the first translation into Hebrew of any part of the New Testament. Eventually, accusations of Judaization by Luther and others depressed Münster, and he devoted the last years of his life to the study of geography.

BIBLIOGRAPHY

Burmeister, Karl Heinz. *Eine Bibliographie mit 22 Abhandlungen.* Weisbaden, 1964. Most complete listing of Münster's writings.

———. *Sebastian Münster: Versuch eines biographischen Gesamtbildes.* 2d ed. Basel and Stuttgart, 1969. Best available study of Münster.

Hantzsch, Victor. *Sebastian Münster: Leben, Werk, Wissenschaftliche Bedeutung.* Nieuwkoop, 1965. Until the publication of Burmeister's works, this was the standard work on the subject. Still valuable, it provides a somewhat traditional, Protestant confessional view of Münster.

Friedman, Jerome. *The Most Ancient Testimony: Sixteenth-Century Christian Hebraica in the Age of Renaissance Nostalgia.* Athens, Ohio, 1983. Most recent analysis of Münster's Hebraica, and the most complete assessment of his reliance upon Jewish teachers. The only work which describes and analyzes Münster's missionary writings and their place within the overall corpus of his writings.

Perles, Joseph. *Beiträge zur Geschichte der Hebräischen und Aramäischen Studien.* Munich, 1884. This classic study discusses Münster's importance from the vantage point of the development of medieval semitic studies.

Verzeichnis der im deutschen Sprachbereich erschienenen Drucke des XVI. Jahrhunderts. Stuttgart, 1983–. See vol. 14, nos. 6645–6728.

JEROME FRIEDMAN

MÜNTZER, Thomas (also Münzer; d. 1525), German theologian, preacher, and leader of the Peasants' War. He was born in Stolberg, a town in the Harz region of central Germany. His birth year (before 1491) is unknown. Müntzer gave as his place of origin Quedlinburg, situated north of the Harz, when he enrolled at the University of Leipzig for the winter semester of 1506/07. He matriculated at the University of Frankfurt an der Oder during the winter semester of 1512/13. The curriculum he pursued is not known in detail. Müntzer concluded his studies in the philosophy faculty with a master's degree and attained the lowest advanced degree in theology (*baccalaureus biblicus*). He was ordained a priest in the diocese of Halberstadt sometime before May 1514. At Braunschweig (Brunswick) on 6 May 1514 he was installed as a chantry priest; the endowment for this prebend yielded a small income, which he continued to receive until February 1522. There is evidence that in 1515–1516 Müntzer was a confessor at a convent of canonesses at Frose, near Aschersleben, east of the Harz. There he also tutored privately the sons of some citizens of Braunschweig. His circle of friends at Braunschweig included goldsmiths and merchants engaged in long-distance trade.

According to several sources, Müntzer was at Wittenberg between the winter semester of 1517/18 and the spring of 1519. During this period he continued his humanist and theological studies, but to what extent and under what influences have been debated. Fragments of the notes that Müntzer took on a lecture on Jerome by the humanist Johannes Rhagius Aesticampianus have survived. He had contact with Andreas Bodenstein von Karlstadt and Martin Luther. Once he preached at Wittenberg, and from there he undertook a journey to Franconia. At the start of 1519 he stayed at Leipzig and afterward at Orlamünde an der Saale, where he read the sermons of the mystic Johannes Tauler. Tauler's mysticism had a great influence on Müntzer's thought. At Easter 1519 Müntzer attacked the church hierarchy in three sermons at Jüterbog (east of Wittenberg). In the winter of 1519/20 he withdrew from the controversy and acted as the confessor at a convent of Cistercian nuns at Beuditz, near Weissenfels (Thuringia). Self-critical, he now waited for God to call him through Jesus Christ.

In May 1520 Müntzer came to the church of Saint Catherine at Zwickau (in Saxony) in order to substitute as a preacher for the humanist Johannes Sylvius Egranus. After Müntzer's appointment to the Zwickau church of Saint

Mary in October 1520, he became involved in a conflict with Egranus, whom Müntzer now regarded as the incarnation of a dead, literalistic learning. Against this, Müntzer expressed his commitment to an interior, living voice of God. Müntzer now saw himself as called directly by God to a mission of worldwide significance. After being dismissed from Zwickau in April 1521, he undertook two missionary trips to Bohemia and Prague. There is evidence that he stayed at the Czech city of Žatec (Saaz) on his first journey to northern Bohemia. On 20 June 1521 Müntzer entered Prague, the goal of his second journey. Initially he was able to preach in several churches, but soon the authorities prohibited him from preaching. During his stay at Prague he made marginal notations in a volume containing works by Cyprian and Tertullian. This reading influenced his *Prager Protestation*, (Prague Protest, also known as the Prague Manifesto) of November 1521. In the *Prager Protestation* he cited the *Historia ecclesiastica* (Church History) of the church father Eusebius of Caesarea (d. 339), according to whom, soon after the age of the apostles, the church became a whore. After the *Prager Protestation*, the restitution of the apostolic church became the goal of Müntzer's mission, the essential feature of which would be the visible working of the Holy Spirit. In addition to rejecting the Roman Catholic church, which Müntzer and Luther shared, already at this time Müntzer had developed positions that deviated from those of Luther, especially Müntzer's emphasis on living revelations that supplemented those in holy scripture and his consciousness of participating as a servant of God in an imminent Last Judgment.

Müntzer had to leave Prague without success. In the spring of 1522 he appeared at Wittenberg or the surrounding area. For the next year only a few of the places where he stayed are known: during Passion Week 1522 he preached at Stolberg, his hometown, and at Nordhausen he was unable to gain a foothold (July and September 1522). His activities as a confessor and preacher at a convent of Cistercian nuns at Glaucha, near Halle (Christmas 1522 until March 1523), again ended with his expulsion.

From March 1523 until August 1524 Müntzer was a minister at the church of Saint John at Allstedt, a small Thuringian town in electoral Saxony. The city council installed him without obtaining the approval of the territorial prince, Frederick III, who held patronage rights to the benefice. The *Prager Protestation* had predicted an eschatological battle with the Turks in 1522; after this battle failed to occur, Müntzer's expectations again assumed a longer time frame. Surprisingly, soon after 29 July 1523, he married Ottilie von Gersen, a nun who had fled her convent. She bore a son on Easter 1524 (27 March).

As soon as Müntzer arrived at Allstedt on Easter 1523, he began reforming the liturgy. He saw this as part of his educational work among the people, and he strengthened the role of the community as a liturgical participant. His aim was to lead the elect to an inner purification before the Last Judgment took place. In the course of the year 1523 he composed the works of his German liturgy: *Deutsches Kirchenamt* (German Church Office) and *Deutsch-evangelische Messe* (German Evangelical Mass), both of which were published in 1524. Beforehand, the *Ordnung und Berechnung des deutschen Amts zu Allstedt*, (Order and Justification of the German Service at Allstedt; Eilenburg, 1524) appeared as an explanation of the order of the German Mass as it was practiced at Allstedt. While retaining much of the old ritual, Müntzer reoriented the traditional liturgical texts toward his theological position by freely translating the texts and composing his own songs. In the liturgical works—as well as in a letter to his followers at Stolberg, *Ein ernster Sendbrief an seine lieben Brüder zu Stolberg, unfüglichen Aufruhr zu meiden*, (An Earnest, Open Letter to His Dear Brothers at Stolberg, to Avoid Inappropriate Rebellion; Eilenburg, July 1523)—Müntzer's initial efforts to reach a compromise with Luther failed. In the *Sendbrief* he made an effort to counter the reputation as a rebel he had gained among the Wittenbergers since his stay at Zwickau. Luther, however, remained mistrustful of "prophet Thomas." At the turn of the year 1523/24 Müntzer then shifted to a literary conflict with Wittenberg theology. In his *Protestation oder Entbietung. . . von dem rechten Christenglauben und der Taufe* (Protest or Offering. . . about True Christian Faith and Baptism), as well as the work *Von dem gedichteten Glauben* (On Contrived Faith; both printed at Eilenburg, 1524), he contrasted Luther's faith, which rested solely on the grace of God, with his own notion of a faith that was tested in persecution. "Contrived faith" is a faith without works and suffering. With this assertion Müntzer effectively attacked a weak point in Luther's message, namely the deficient impact of the new teaching on actual life.

Tension with secular rulers first began to develop in the summer of 1523. The neighboring Count Ernst of Mansfeld forbade his subjects from visiting Müntzer's liturgical services. In his sermons Müntzer rebuked the count and on 23 September 1525 warned him by letter. This continually escalating conflict remained with Müntzer to the end of his period at Allstedt. In addition, Duke George of Saxony took measures against Müntzer's followers. Müntzer, in turn, attempted to mobilize his own territorial lords, Elector Frederick III and Duke John of Saxony, against those who were persecuting his followers. The rulers of electoral Saxony kept Müntzer at a distance. This changed after 24 March 1524, when citizens of Allstedt burned down the nearby chapel at Mallerbach. On 13 July 1524 Müntzer preached a sermon before Duke John of Saxony and his son, John Frederick, at the castle at Allstedt. This *Fürstenpredigt* (Sermon to the Princes) on *Daniel* 2 was published at Allstedt under the title *Auslegung des andern Unterschieds Danielis des Propheten* (An Exposition of the Second Chapter of Daniel the Prophet). Here, Müntzer offered himself to the princes as a new Daniel—that is, as a counselor who would have the tasks of expounding the meaning of apocalyptic history and of interpreting visionary dreams. The way in which the prophet Daniel could recognize and interpret dreams as the voice of God belonged to the "knowledge of God" (*Kunst Gottes*), and he believed that certain dreams could be the living word of God. At Allstedt Müntzer had an old and a young man with him whose dreams he interpreted in order to gain guidelines for action. The visionary experiences behind Müntzer's decisions cannot be known today, which makes many of them appear surprising and puzzling. In the *Fürstenpredigt* Müntzer called on the Saxon princes to take action against lords who suppressed the gospel. The princes, however, ignored Müntzer's appeal.

Confronted by escalating threats to his followers in the territories surrounding Allstedt, Müntzer established a league, or covenant (*Bund*), with about five hundred members, including the Allstedt council. Duke John reacted by summoning Müntzer to a hearing on 1 August at Weimar at which Müntzer was forbidden to preach or publish. The Allstedt print shop, which did Müntzer's publishing, was closed. Müntzer had agreed to remain for the time being at Allstedt, but in anticipation of an expulsion order he felt was imminent, he fled from Allstedt over the city wall during the night of 7–8 August. Luther's *Brief an die Fürsten von Sachsen von dem aufrührerischen Geist* (Letter to the Princes of Saxony Concerning the Rebellious Spirit) played a role in these events. Luther urged the princes to expel Müntzer for insurrection. Müntzer responded to this letter, which resembled the indictment of a public prosecutor, with his *Hochverursachte Schutzrede und Antwort wider das sanftlebende Fleisch zu Wittenberg* (Highly Provoked Defense and Reply to the Soft-living Flesh at Wittenberg), a work that presented the defendant's response to the charges and his own counter-accusations against Luther, which Müntzer laid before the tribunal of Christ. At the same time, Müntzer set forth his final reckoning with Luther's theology of the "big Jacks" (*grossen Hansen*) in his *Ausgedrückte Entblössung des falschen Glaubens der ungetreuen Welt* (Printed Exposure of the False Faith of the Unfaithful World). Müntzer was able to get both writings published later in the fall of 1524 at Nuremberg. After the princes not only refused to participate in an alliance but also, in fact, turned against Müntzer, he was convinced that political power must be transferred from the feudal authorities to the common people in order to carry out God's will. With this, Müntzer beame revolutionary in a political sense.

From 15 August 1524 Müntzer was at Mülhausen in Thuringia, a free imperial city with about 7,500 inhabitants. Already in September, together with the preacher Heinrich Pfeiffer, he supported unrest, with the goal of altering the city's constitution and electing a new council. Müntzer and Pfeiffer, however, were expelled from Mülhausen. A journey through southern Germany took Müntzer first to Nuremberg, where he wanted to see to the publication of his *Ausgedrückte Entblössung* and *Hochverursachte Schutzrede.* A surviving document from this Nuremberg period is a correspondence with Christoph Fürer, a member of the patriciate, concerning problems with Luther's theology. Müntzer then traveled via Basel to Griesen in the Klettgau region. From here he preached for several months to the peasants in the Hegau and Klettgau regions.

On 22 February Müntzer was again at Mülhausen, where he became pastor at the church of Saint Mary. The Eternal League of God, a covenanted organization he promoted at Mülhausen, supported his actions during this period. On 16 March 1525 the old city council was deposed, and on the next day an "Eternal Council" elected. In the rebellion of the Thuringian peasants and towns, known as the Peasants' War, Müntzer increasingly assumed a leadership role. Between 26 April and 6 May 1525 he took part in a campaign of the Mülhausen band in the Eichsfeld region. On 10 May he set off with his Mülhausen contingent to support a peasant band assembled at Frankenhausen. Müntzer saw the Peasants' War as an apocalyptic event in which God would place political power in the hands of the faithful and reestablish the apostolic church. Based on the model of Gideon (*Judges* 6–8), Müntzer identified with the role of charismatic army commander. On 15 May princely troops annihilated the unified band of the Thuringian insurgents outside Frankenhausen; Müntzer was taken captive, and on 27 May he was decapitated outside the walls of Mülhausen.

Initially Müntzer had no further significant public impact. His liturgical works continued to be used anonymously. Enlarged versions of his *Deutsch-evangelische Messe* continued to be printed at Erfurt into the 1550s. Elements of Müntzer's theology continued to survive among dissidents (e.g., Hans Hut and Hans Denck) and crypto-dissidents during the sixteenth and seventeenth centuries. The text of his *Ausgedrückte Entblössung* was printed in 1526 under the pseudonym Christian Hitz of Salzburg with the title *Ein gründlicher Unterschied von dem rechtgeschaffenen Glauben wider die Heuchler und angenommene Weise der falschen Christenheit* (A Basic Distinction of Truly Generated Faith, Against the Hypocrites and the Presumptuous Manner of False Christendom). Through the writings of Johannes Bünderlin, Müntzer's hermeneutics influenced Weigelianism. The radical Pietist Gottfried Arnold—who evaluated Müntzer positively, in part by excluding the revolutionary dimension of his character—republished Müntzer's *Von dem gedichteten Glauben* in his *Unparteiische Kirchen- und Ketzerhistorie* (Impartial History of the Church and Heresy; 1699–1700).

Mediated by the liberal historian Wilhelm Zimmermann (*Allgemeine Geschichte der Bauernkrieges*, vol. 3, 1843) and by Friedrich Engels (*Der deutsche Bauernkrieg*, 1850), the German workers' movement and the German Democratic Republic (1949–1990) came to view Müntzer as a figure who symbolized social revolution, a protagonist of the revolutionary classes in the so-called early bourgeois revolution (*frühbürgerliche Revolution*). The celebration of Müntzer's five hundredth birthday in 1989 was the high point and end of the socialist veneration of a mythical and symbolic Müntzer with whom the historical Müntzer had little in common. On the one hand, the ideologically motivated appropriation of Müntzer promoted international historiographic interest in him; on the other hand, it impaired the critical level of this historiography. The question of Müntzer's identity as a revolutionary must be explained anew in the context of new research, begun in the late twentieth century, exploring his biography, his theology, and his long-neglected visionary-charismatic sense of self-identity. Research free of the distortions imposed by the dichotomy between Marxist and so-called bourgeois interpretations of Müntzer will no doubt continue through the end of the twentieth century.

BIBLIOGRAPHY

Primary Sources

Baylor, Michael G., ed. and trans. *The Radical Reformation.* Cambridge, 1991. Offers several pieces from Müntzer's writings and correspondence in an English translation which is more exact in part than the translation of Matheson.

Matheson, Peter, ed. and trans. *The Collected Works of Thomas Müntzer.* Edinburgh, 1988. A complete edition in English translation; the numerous errors in translation and commentary are partly the result of using the Franz edition of 1968. Included for the first time are Müntzer's marginal notes to Cyprian and Tertullian.

Müntzer, Thomas. *Schriften und Briefe: Kritische Gesamtausgabe.* Edited by Günther Franz. Gütersloh, 1968. The only complete German edition; contains many errors.

Secondary Sources

Bräuer, Siegfried, and Helmar Junghans, eds. *Der Theologe Thomas Müntzer: Untersuchungen zu seiner Entwicklung und Lehre.* Berlin, 1989. This volume, to which several authors contributed, puts Müntzer's theology at the center of the research and shows how contested are the details of its origins and structure.

Bubenheimer, Ulrich. *Thomas Müntzer: Herkunft und Bildung.* Leiden, 1989. A biographical reconstruction of Müntzer's life up to 1519 that depicts elements of his humanistic education. The small number of sources leads to many hypotheses that need further confirmation. The second part of the work offers editions of both old and new sources.

Elliger, Walter. *Thomas Müntzer: Leben und Werk.* Göttingen, 1975. Remains the most comprehensive Müntzer biography. The strength of the work is its detailed theological analysis of Müntzer's writings, whereas the biography in the strict sense is not satisfying.

Friesen, Abraham. *Thomas Müntzer, a Destroyer of the Godless: The Making of a Sixteenth-Century Religious Revolutionary.* Berkeley, 1990. The biographical parts have been superseded by more recent research. Friesen's original contribution consists of three speculative chapters on Müntzer's relations to Tauler, Eusebius, and Augustine that present a challenge for further research.

Goertz, Hans-Juergen. *Thomas Müntzer: Mystic-Apocalyptic Revolutionary.* Edinburgh, 1993.

Gritsch, Eric W. *Reformer without a Church: The Life and Thought of Thomas Muentzer, 1488[?]-1525.* Philadelphia, 1967. The first English-language biography; remains worth reading.

———. *Thomas Müntzer: A Tragedy of Errors.* Minneapolis, 1989. The focal point is an ecumenical interpretation of the conflict between Luther and Müntzer. The biographical parts are inferior to Gritsch's 1967 work.

Junghans, Reinhard. *Thomas-Müntzer-Rezeption während des "Dritten Reiches": Eine Fallstudie zur populär(wissenschaftlich)en und wissenschaftlichen Geschichtsschreibung.* Frankfurt a.M., 1990. The author depicts comprehensively the German interpretation of Müntzer between 1933 and 1945. A corresponding retrospective examination of the interpretation of Müntzer in the German Democratic Republic is now called for.

Martinson, Steven D. *Between Luther and Müntzer: The Peasant Revolution in German Drama and Thought.* Heidelberg, 1988. This history of Müntzer and the Peasants' War in dramas is concerned with "Luther," "Müntzer," and "Peasants' War" as ideological symbols in German intellectual history over the last two centuries.

Scholz, Günter, ed. *Thomas Müntzer vor 1491–1525: Prediger, Prophet, Bauernkriegsführer.* Böblingen, 1990. Contributions by Ulrich Bubenheimer and Dieter Fauth offer some new dates for Müntzer's life and impact. The accessible volume contains a selection of sources, maps, illustrations, and a detailed chronology of Müntzer's life.

Scott, Tom. *Thomas Müntzer: Theology and Revolution in the German Reformation.* New York, 1989. The best English-language biography of Müntzer, offering new information especially about Müntzer's role at Allstedt, at Mühlhausen, and during the Peasants' War.

Vogler, Günter. *Thomas Müntzer.* Berlin, 1989. Among the newer biographies, this one contains the most accurate dates.

Warnke, Ingo. *Wörterbuch zu Thomas Müntzers deutschen Schriften und Briefen.* Tübingen, 1993.

ULRICH BUBENHEIMER
Translated from German by Michael G. Baylor

MURNER, Thomas (1475–1537), Franciscan preacher and satirist, foremost critic of Luther during the early 1520s. Born in Alsace (Oberehnheim), Murner studied at various universities, taught in Franciscan schools, and lectured at the University of Freiburg im Breisgau, where he also earned the doctor of theology degree (1506). Murner is noted for his wide-ranging intellectual interests, critical insights, literary talent, and unwavering defense of traditional Catholicism.

His literary activities (satire, polemic) fall into three stages: 1499–1509, Latin tracts against astrology and witchcraft and the critique of Jakob Wimpfeling's *Epitome Rerum Germanicum*, the first history of Germany; 1510–1520, German satirical works in the "fool" tradition inaugurated by the satirist Sebastian Brant's *Narrenschiff* (Ship of Fools); 1520–1530, polemical writings against Luther. The satirical works reflect both the moral concern and the colloquial tone of Murner's sermons while revealing considerable literary talent and a sense of the artistic impact of linking word and image; some of the woodcuts used to illustrate his works are believed to be his own. His literary roles as exorcist of fools (*Narrenbeschwörung*, 1512), guildmaster of rogues and rascals (*Schelmenzunft*, 1512), and critic of love-possessed women and men (*Mühle von Schwindelsheim*, 1515, and

Gauchmatt, 1519/20) were inspired by Brant, but Murner is more provincial and realistic in his approach to human folly and more severe in his condemnation of it.

In response to three major tracts of Luther (1520), Murner urged caution in the emphasis on scripture to the neglect of beliefs and rituals confirmed by tradition and criticized the priesthood of all believers as a fallacious concept that envisioned too great a role for the laity. Murner's pamphlets criticizing Luther's teachings and defending the Pope took issue with Luther the man and with his perception of the role of the papacy. Polemic and satire are effectively combined in "Von dem Großen Lutherischen Narren" (1522), which was confiscated by the Strasbourg censors before its social impact could be felt; modern assessments confirm its literary value and Murner's rank as a leading satirist of the German Reformation period.

BIBLIOGRAPHY

Primary Sources

Murner, Thomas. *Der schelmen Zunft*. Halle, 1912.

———. *Die gottesheilige Messe von Gott allein erstiftet*. Halle, 1928.

———. *An den grossmächtigsten und durchlauchtigsten Adel deutscher Nation*. Halle, 1968.

Secondary Sources

Grimm, G. E., and F. R. Max, eds. *Deutsche Dichter: Leben und Werk deutschesprachiger Autoren*. Vol. 2, *Reformation, Renaissance, Barock*. Stuttgart, 1988. Short evaluations of lives and works of selected sixteenth-century writers based on most recent research.

Kawerau, Waldemar. *Thomas Murner und die Kirche des Mittelalters*. Schriften des Vereins für Reformationsgeschichte, vol. 8, no. 30. Halle, 1890. Biographical study relating Murner's satires to his relationship to the church.

———. *Thomas Murner and die Deutsche Reformation*. Schriften des Vereins für Reformationsgeschichte, vol. 8, no. 32. Halle, 1891.

Könneker, Barbara. *Wesen und Wandlung der Narrenidee im Zeitalter des Humanismus*. Wiesbaden, 1966. Analysis of the "fool" tradition as related to humanism and the Reformation; general study of satire.

Liebenau, Theodor. *Der Franziskaner Dr. Thomas Murner*. Freiburg, 1913. The standard biography of Murner, though modern assessments have changed certain views.

Schultz, F., ed. *Thomas Murners Deutsche Schriften*. 9 vols. Strasbourg, 1918–1931. Standard edition of Murner's collected works.

RICHARD ERNEST WALKER

MUSCULUS, Andreas (1514–1581), German Lutheran professor at Frankurt an der Oder and codrafter of the Formula of Concord. Born in Schneeberg, Saxony, of a prominent middle-class family, Musculus studied at Leipzig (1531–1534) and Wittenberg (1538–1541) before becoming a parish pastor in Frankfurt an der Oder (in Brandenburg), where his brother-in-law, Johann Agricola, directed ecclesiastical affairs. He became a professor of theology at the local university (1542) and worked to bring the Reformation to the surrounding countryside.

His career was filled with controversy as he defended his understanding of Luther's teaching. His gentle opposition to the Augsburg Interim, in part authored by Agricola, gave way to sharp polemic against Andreas Osiander, Francis Stancarus, and Friedrich Staphylus. In 1558 he began a long, bitter dispute with his Philippist colleague Abdias Praetorius over the necessity of good works. Though accused of antinomianism, he did not espouse Agricola's position. He taught that the law does not motivate good works in believers but rather that they do God's will "from a free and merry spirit." His sharp condemnation of sin in the lives of church members, particularly in his use of the *Teufelbuch* genre (e.g., his attack on unseemly dress in the *Hosenteufel* [Trousers Devil], *Eheteufel* [Marriage Devil], and *Fluchteufel* [Curse Devil]), reveals his strong emphasis on the accusing force of the law.

Musculus conducted a running battle with local officials in defense of the independence of clergy and church, but he served his princes faithfully and was named general superintendent of the Brandenburg church after 1566. With Georg Coelestin, court preacher in Berlin, he prepared a new ecclesiastical constitution for Brandenburg in 1572. In 1576–1577, with his Frankfurt colleague Christoph Körner, Musculus represented Brandenburg on the committee that framed the Formula of Concord, setting his views alongside contrary views in its sixth article, "On the Third Use of the Law." His literary activities marshaled biblical and patristic material and took form in catechetical, devotional, and doctrinal-polemical treatises.

BIBLIOGRAPHY

Ebel, Jobst. "Die Herkunft des Konzeptes der Konkordienformel." *Zeitschrift für Kirchengeschichte* 91 (1980), 237–282. Summary of Musculus's involvement in the composition of the Formula of Concord.

Koch, Ernst. "Andreas Musculus und die Konfessionalisierung in Luthertum." In *Die lutherische Konfessionalisierung in Deutschland*, edited by Hans-Christoph Rublack, pp. 250–273. Gütersloh, 1992.

———. "'Das Geheimnis unserer Erlösung': Die Christologie des Andreas Musculus als Beitrag zur Formulierung verbindlicher christlicher Lehre im späten 16. Jahrhundert." In *Veritas et Communicatio, Festschrift Zum 60. Geburtstag von Ulrich Kühn*, edited by Heiko Franke et al., pp. 143–156. Göttingen, 1992.

Spiecker, Christian Wilhelm. *Lebensgeschichte des Andreas Musculus*. Reprint, Nieuwkoop, 1964. A thorough nineteenth-century critical overview.

Verzeichnis der im deutschen Sprachbereich erschienenen Drucke des XVI. Jahrhunderts. Stuttgart, 1983–. See vol. 14, nos. 7117–7266.

ROBERT KOLB

MUSCULUS, Wolfgang (also Müsli[n], Mäußli, Meusel, Dusanus; 1497–1563), Reformed theologian. Born at Dieuze, near Salzburg, Musculus attended Latin schools in Rappoltsweiler, Colmar, and Schlettstadt but never studied at a university. At the the age of fifteen, he entered the Benedictine monastery at Lixheim, where he remained as singer, organist, and preacher until 1527. During his early years in the monastery he studied the classics. Turning to theology at the age of twenty, he became acquainted with Luther's writings in 1518 and soon became an adherent of the new theology. Though widely known as "the Lutheran monk," he was not forced to leave the monastery until 1527, at which time he married. In 1528 Musculus became Martin Bucer's secretary at Strasbourg, and the next year, an assistant to Matthias Zell. While at Strasbourg, he also studied Greek and Hebrew and was introduced to Reformed theology.

From 1531 to 1548 Musculus was pastor at the Church of the Holy Cross in Augsburg. Though he was a Zwinglian when he arrived in Augsburg, he also was concerned about Protestant unity. He was thus a participant in the drafting of and a signatory to the Wittenberg Concord of 1536. However, he soon returned to his earlier position on the Eucharist when it became apparent that Bullinger and the Zwinglians would not accept the concord. When Musculus arrived in Augsburg, there was still a significant Catholic minority that controlled eight churches in the city, including the cathedral. Musculus urged the city magistrates to effect total reform, and he himself held the first evangelical service in the cathedral in July 1537. Musculus also participated in the discussions between the Catholic and Lutheran theologians at Hagenau, Worms, and Regensburg in 1540–1541 and engaged in a literary dispute with Johannes Cochlaeus in 1545. In 1544 he was instrumental in introducing the Reformation at Donauwörth. He left Augsburg in 1548, when the city accepted the terms of the Interim.

Musculus, along with his wife and eight children, fled to Constance; later, after brief periods in Basel and St. Gall, they found temporary refuge in Zurich. Then in February 1549 he was invited to replace Simon Sulzer as professor of theology at Bern. He remained at Bern until his death on 30 August 1563. His ministry was the beginning of a family dynasty of pastors in Bern, with the last of the family, Daniel Müslin, dying in 1821.

While at Bern, Musculus was involved in the negotiations with Calvin concerning the conflict in the Vaud over church discipline. Musculus's understanding of the relationship between the church and the civil government was quite similar to Bullinger's. The two men corresponded regularly from 1544 to 1563, and it is likely that Musculus's theory of the state church was influenced by Bullinger; more than a hundred letters from Musculus and a few from Bullinger are extant. Musculus in turn exerted influence on Thomas Lüber (Erastus) and the English in the matter of church discipline and the relationship between church and state. His influence can also be traced to Poland and Hungary.

Musculus's writings fall into three main groups: translations, biblical commentaries, and theological works. The most important of his writings was his *Loci communes sacrae theologiae* of 1560 (published in English translation as *Commonplaces of the Christian Religion* in 1563), which evidences his basically Zwinglian theology.

BIBLIOGRAPHY

Bäumlin, Richard. "Naturrecht und obrigkeitliches Kirchenregiment bei Wolfgang Musculus." In *Für Kirche und Recht: Festschrift für Johannes Heckel zum 70. Geburtstag,* edited by Siegfried Grundmann, pp. 120–143. Cologne, 1959. Argues that Musculus's teaching on natural law is the key to understanding his theory of the state church as expressed in his *Loci communes.*

Dellsperger, Rudolf. "Wolfgang Musculus, 1497–1563, Prädicant bei Hl Kreuz von 1531 bis 1548." In *Die Augsburger Kirchenordnung von 1537 und ihr Umfeld,* edited by Reinhard Schwarz, pp. 91–100. Schriftenreihe des Vereins für Reformationsgeschichte 196. Gütersloh, 1988. Deals with Musculus's time in Augsburg and his influence on the reform there during the 1530s.

Grote, Ludwig. *Wolfgang Musculus, ein biographischer Versuch.* Hamburg, 1855. Standard biography.

Ives, Robert B. *The Theology of Wolfgang Musculus.* Ph.D. diss., University of Manchester, 1965. Short biography followed by a study of the theology of Musculus.

Schwab, Paul Josiah. *The Attitude of Wolfgang Musculus toward Religious Tolerance.* Yale Studies in Religion 6. Scottdale, Pa., 1933. Argues that Musculus was relatively more tolerant than most of his contemporaries in his attitude toward those who differed with his religious views.

Streuber, Wilhelm Theodor. "Wolfgang Musculus oder Müslin: Ein Lebensbild aus der Reformationszeit." In *Berner Taschenbuch auf das Jahr 1860,* edited by Ludwig Lauterburg, Jahrgang 9, pp. 1–79. Bern, 1860. Short biography.

Verzeichnis der im deutschen Sprachbereich erschienenen Drucke des XVI. Jahrhunderts. Stuttgart, 1983–. See vol. 14, nos. 7270–7316.

J. WAYNE BAKER

MUSIC.

MUSIC. Of all the arts, none was of greater concern to the leading reformers than music. In the early phases of the Reformation, widespread iconoclasm erupted in often violent forms as a predictable and immediate rejection of medieval piety and practice, but music, because of its long-standing active role in worship, remained a subject of ongoing criticism, support, and reform.

The Reformers on Music. Not since the patristic period was music subjected to the intense scrutiny given it by the reformers. For nearly a millennium musical developments, together with the visual arts, had followed the expansion and elaboration of Western theology, liturgy, and piety. Well before the Reformation, it is true, critics began to deplore the secular elements in liturgical music and the abuses of both clergy and church musicians. But soon Girolamo Savonarola would attack the arts as worldly vanity; humanist educators would complain of the burdensome requirements of the liturgy at the expense of study; and Desiderius Erasmus would attack the needless complexity of polyphony, the musical distortions of the liturgy, the loss of time for preaching, the unintelligibility of sung texts, and the theatrical pomp of raucous voices, loud instruments, organs, drums, and secular styles—all designed for popular appeal (Miller, 1966).

These critics, however, exercised essentially practical, aesthetic, or moral judgments; not even an outspoken humanist like Erasmus seriously questioned the legitimacy of music in worship. But the principal reformers, who held the scriptures to be the sole authority for faith and practice, saw worship and music as fundamentally theological problems. Although Martin Luther, Huldrych Zwingli, and John Calvin proceeded from this common assumption, they arrived at radically different conclusions.

Martin Luther. Luther's devotion to music, especially sacred music, appears to have been boundless. Though he agreed with Augustine's dictum "Who sings well prays twice," unlike him Luther did not fear its sensuous appeal but desired to use it in whatever way it might serve the gospel. For this reason he was determined to provide the laity with their own sacred songs for active participation in the liturgy. He knew and loved the musical treasures of the past and of his contemporaries and urged his followers to preserve and cultivate them for the good of the church.

In his writings Luther repeatedly paid tribute to music, praising its unique nature, power, and practical value. Although his ardent affection for music from boyhood on may have predisposed him to argue in its defense, his biblical studies and his personal musical experiences, especially when linked to the sacred texts, led him to conclude that music was an extraordinary divine gift, second only to the word of God; and if so, it was inherently good and intended for the worship of its creator. Perhaps his most systematic and extended statement is the preface to *Symphoniae jucundae* (1538), an anthology of short Latin motets. In it he acknowledges the powerful psychological and moral force of music so well understood by the ancients, but adds, "the gift of language combined with the gift of song was only given to man . . . that he should praise God with both word and music, namely, by proclaiming [the Word of God] through music and by providing sweet melodies with words" (*Luther's Works*, American ed., vol. 53, Philadelphia, 1965, p. 323f; cited henceforth as *LW*).

He thus allied music with preaching, for struck by Paul's insistence that faith depended on *hearing* the gospel (*Rom.* 10:17), he envisioned music and the word bound together as servant and master, a more powerful "living voice of the Gospel." Although Luther did not ignore potential abuses of sacred and secular music, he firmly believed that the testimony of scripture (*Ps.*, *Eph.* 5:19, *Col.* 3:16), reason, and the benefits of music outweighed every objection. "We want the beautiful art of music to be rightly used to serve her dear Creator and his Christians. He is thereby praised and honored and we are made better and stronger in faith when his holy Word is impressed on our hearts by sweet music" (preface to *Christliche Geseng Lateinische Deudsch, zum Begrebnis*, 1542, *LW* 53:328).

Huldrych Zwingli. An Erasmian humanist with university degrees and a highly accomplished amateur musician, Zwingli became the people's priest at the Grossmünster in Zurich in 1519 and soon declared his sympathies with the Reformation. Instituting few changes at first, he called in 1523 for radical alteration in the worship life of the community. Among these changes was to be the elimination of all music from the services at the Grossmünster, finally achieved in Zurich in the spring of 1525. A radically simplified vernacular liturgy was introduced, the organs were removed or silenced, and no music was heard in public worship.

Zwingli, whose musical training and experience far exceeded Luther's, was perhaps even more aware than Luther of the affective power of music for evil as well as good, for he recognized that its effects were spontaneous and uncontrolled by the intellect and judgment. By virtue of its creatureliness, music was undeniably a gift, but Zwingli could find no reason to link it with the work of the Holy Spirit or any theological warrant whatsoever. Music, therefore, had no divinely ordained role in worship. Moreover, for Zwingli music was a hindrance, a detriment to true worship, as he defined it. His opposition was not simply a reaction against the medieval cultus. He sought to restore the practice of the primitive church by relying exclusively on the New Testament, from which he concluded that ideal worship was individual, internal, silent prayer. He saw the gathered assemblies of the Pauline letters as occasions of corporate instruction and memorial; their prayers, psalms, and hymns were to be silent or spoken. He insisted that *Ephesians* 5:19 and *Colossians* 3:16 meant that the melodies were to be from or "in your hearts" and not sung aloud. Zwingli did not, in fact, condemn music. He loved it but saw no place for it in church.

John Calvin. As with Zwingli, most comments on Calvin's relation to music have considered it almost totally negative, emphasizing his restrictions on music in worship and his legalistic attitude toward its place in social life. More recent scholarship has recognized the magnitude of his achievement in initiating and fostering a unique form of metrical psalmody and overseeing the development of the enormously influential Genevan Psalter as the sole hymnody—and, in fact, the only music—of Reformed public worship for generations.

Calvin's theological, legal, and Christian humanist background introduced him to biblical, classical, and patristic views on music, but unlike Luther and Zwingli he showed no apparent interest in it before his conversion. Like Erasmus and Zwingli, however, he was critical of the medieval church and desired a reconstruction of worship faithful to the New Testament. His primary sources for reconciling his eventual understanding of music with scripture were the same Pauline passages used by Zwingli, along with the witness of church history and the testimony of the Fathers, especially Augustine. Just how close he came to Zwingli's purism is unclear, but by the time he had made his earliest reference to music in the first edition of the *Christianae religionis Institutio* (Institutes of the Christian Religion; 1536) he had gone to Basel and heard the congregational chorales introduced there by Johannes Oecolampadius a decade earlier. In it Calvin did not condemn music, but in writing of private prayer he asserted that only when words or song were deeply felt and came "from the heart" were they acceptable to God. Moreover, in his instructions for the Lord's Supper, he permitted psalms before Communion and called for "sung praises to God" afterward.

Calvin eventually became a fervent supporter of congregational psalm singing after experiencing it firsthand in Strasbourg with the sympathetic guidance of Martin Bucer. He was so convinced of its value that there Calvin devoted his energies to preparing a small book of French psalms for his congregation of refugees in the city. Printed in 1539, it was the first step in what was to become the Genevan Psalter of 1562.

True to the Reformation, Calvin took scripture as his primary authority, drawing support from church history and the Fathers, specifically Augustine. The Pauline texts indicated the character, if not the form, of ideal worship and the role of music in it, justifying heartfelt singing to build up the church. He found further support for that "gift of God" in Augustine's *Confessiones* (book X, 33), which testified to music's powerful effect on the emotions but which also warned against attending to its melodic beauty at the expense of the sacred texts. For that reason and acknowledging his own experience of the emotional force of psalms in worship, Calvin insisted on a sacred style clearly distinct from that of social music making or entertainment, a style serious, majestic, and fit for its task. Moreover, since the heart needed to be joined to the intelligence and the understanding (*1 Cor.* 14:5), the songs had to be sung by the congregation only in their own language, preferably from memory (also recommended by Luther), as one voice in unison, and unaccompanied.

There was, however, another reason for concern with musical style. Music was given as one of the principal sources of human refreshment and pleasure, but it was all too easily misused, added to which was Plato's reminder that it had the extraordinary power to arouse the passions and affect moral behavior. If this were in fact true, as patristic authors claimed, then music needed regulation. Instrumental music belonged to the Old Covenant, and wordless music was a form of "tongues"; hence, only music with words was permissible, but the words had to convey salutary meaning. To explain his reasons Calvin resorted to the funnel metaphor: music connected with evil words served to pour their harmful contents into the depths of the heart (Augustine had referred to sacred truths poured out in his heart on hearing singing in church [*Conf.* IX, 6]). The solution, therefore, was to require only good, holy texts, and what better choice than the *Psalms*, the songs given by the Holy Spirit (albeit in the metrical versions of Clément Marot and Théodore de Bèze)? And for these songs a style had been fashioned, Calvin maintained, uniquely sacred and suited to its lofty purpose in gravity, majesty, moderation, and modesty.

Sacred Music in the Century of the Reformation. Luther, Zwingli, and Calvin represent the main currents in the approaches to the music of the Reformation, and their influence persisted as their followers held, more or less, to the principles they had established. Circumstances and conditions, especially political and social factors, led to variations, but each instance can be traced to one of these three positions. Roman Catholic practice, on the other hand, responded with few essential changes until the reforms following the Council of Trent. The sharpest distinctions in practice and style occurred in the liturgical and musical action of the congregation.

This article focuses rather on sacred music in general, and here Luther's attitude had momentous historical significance. He insisted that liturgy, music, and even language were indifferent—that is, they were adiaphora—insofar as they accorded with the gospel and love for the neighbor. In theory this gave the widest latitude to decisions affecting worship, music, and the use of Latin or the vernacular, and it helps explain how the several confessions, despite their differences, could in some instances freely share in a community of musical styles.

Vocal music. On the eve of the Reformation, Latin plainsong (the so-called Gregorian chant) was the most universally used music in the Western church. In cathedrals, collegiate churches, parish churches (both large and small), royal and princely chapels, and monasteries and convents it was sung by choirs and individuals in the Mass and the daily hours. Its styles ranged from simple recitation formulas (e.g., psalm tones) to lengthy, richly elaborate and evocative melodies. Although polyphonic (many voiced) art music had attained an impressive level of beauty and refinement by this time, Latin chant continued to dominate Catholic worship in most churches and institutions. Sacred polyphony, however, which had its earlier flowering in the major intellectual centers, gradually spread to the private worship of the ruling courts of Europe, to the papal chapel, to the lesser courts, to the cathedrals and churches of thriving towns, and to their pious confraternities and foundations. By the end of the sixteenth century, aided by the expansion of music printing, it was cultivated wherever resources were available. Nevertheless, in most places chant was the normal day-to-day music, with polyphony reserved primarily for high feasts and other special occasions.

The leading type of composition in high Renaissance polyphony was the mass, a cycle of movements set to the unchanging texts of the five main sections of the sung *Ordinarium missae*: the *Kyrie*, the *Gloria in excelsis*, the *Credo*, the *Sanctus* (with the *Benedictus*), and the *Agnus Dei*. It reached its first peak in the masses of Johannes Okeghem, Jacob Ob-recht, and Josquin Desprez, for whom Luther expressed the greatest admiration. These movements make up only part of the sung liturgy, but as general acclamations (true in a sense even of the *Credo*) all of them, with seasonal exceptions, are included in every celebration of the Eucharist.

A second principal source of Catholic liturgical music was the Divine Office or canonical hours (eight services sung daily), to which the clergy and religious institutions were obligated. All of them included the chanting of the *Psalms,* but the most important for music were Matins (or Nocturns), Lauds, Vespers, and Compline, each of which contained portions often selected for polyphonic elaboration—namely, office hymns, canticles (i.e., Biblical songs), responsories (related to the readings), and antiphons, which usually framed psalms and canticles. Of unusual historical interest is the *Te Deum,* the ancient unmetered hymn of praise sung to conclude Matins of Sundays and feasts; from the late Middle Ages on it has resounded with organ, bells, and trumpets at major celebrations of church and state. Vespers, however, acquired the greatest musical significance, in part because the laity frequently attended and because its psalms and especially its canticle, the Magnificat (Mary's song at the Annunciation; *Luke* 1:46–55), attracted generations of composers. Although each of the eight hours contained a metrical Latin hymn, such hymns, in contrast to Protestant usage, were not admitted to the Mass.

From its origins in the thirteenth century the term *motet* has had a checkered history, but modern writers have tended to use it to designate polyphonic compositions of the sixteenth century in two different but not mutually exclusive ways. One usage assigns it to specific types of polyphonic structure associated primarily with a sacred text in Latin. By this definition a four-voice introit or antiphon would be called a motet. On the other hand, because by midcentury printed collections began to use *motetus* and *cantio sacra* interchangeably, a more historically accurate usage applies the term to a polyphonic piece in Latin that is usually sacred but not technically liturgical because it is not strictly part of the Mass or the Divine Office.

Luther's insistence on freedom in externals allowed the conservative branch of the Reformation to retain much of the liturgico-musical tradition of medieval worship. His *Formula missae* (1523) approved all of the Latin choral Mass Ordinary and Proper except the Tract, Offertory, and most Sequences. Although Luther urged that German songs be sung by the congregation at certain points, the service could be sung entirely in Latin chant. Similarly, nothing in the content of the polyphonic mass prevented its use, while a Proper with objectionable text could be replaced or altered. With Luther's sanction, many churches continued to use Latin chant and polyphony to a greater or lesser degree. In this way masses, often by leading Catholic composers, contributed to the growing body of Lutheran sacred music. Whereas the same was true of only certain parts of the Office, the approval of Latin also encouraged the use and development of the motet, which was increasingly in the forefront of musical developments.

Luther's pastoral concerns, however, focused also on the need for a liturgy in the vernacular for the common people. With his *Deudsche Messe* (1526) he introduced and established the German hymn as an essential element in the liturgy. Except for a simple *Kyrie* chant in Greek, the whole service was in German, and metrical hymns and songs replaced most of the choral parts of the Latin Ordinary and some of the Proper. Although Luther surely intended the whole congregation eventually to participate as much as possible, the liturgical use of vernacular hymns (chorales) motivated polyphonic settings for choir or voices and instruments. Some were very simple; more complex were those modeled on the secular art songs of Heinrich Isaac, Thomas Stoltzer, and especially Ludwig Senfl. Still others incorporated the structural sophistication of Catholic motets based on chant melodies. The chorale settings of Johann Walter exemplify all these, and he was followed by such composers as Balthasar Resinarius, Sixt Dietrich, Johannes Eccard, and Hans Leo Hassler. Emerging later in the century was a new German motet based not on chorales but freely composed to appealing biblical and devotional texts. This new type of Lutheran choral music was best represented by Joachim a Burck, Leonhard Lechner, Gallus Dressler, Melchior Franck, Michael Praetorius, and eventually Johann Hermann Schein and Heinrich Schütz.

The choral music of the English Reformation, like the Lutheran, was in part indebted to the traditional forms of the Mass and the Divine Office but with distinctively English features. First came the exclusive use of the vernacular in public worship (exceptions were limited to private services). Then, based for the next hundred years on *The Book of Common Prayer* (1552), which superseded the conservative first Edwardian book of 1549, the deviations from tradition were substantial. Although the prayer book made no provision for congregational singing, the choral sections in the Mass, now called Holy Communion, were reduced to the *Credo* and the *Gloria,* with the latter transferred to the end. The *Kyrie* became a reworded single petition following each of the Ten Commandments, choral settings of which have been preserved. A modified *Sanctus* without the *Benedictus* was included, but it was rarely sung polyphonically if at all. Morning Prayer and Evening Prayer (Evensong), abbreviated conflations of Matins-Lauds-Prime and Vespers-Compline, were token remnants of the Divine Office, but they assumed considerable musical importance, for the extended, rich texts of the canticles and their alternative psalms called for musical elaboration. In both services psalms were appointed to be sung daily in a manner that evolved into Anglican chant.

From the time of Queen Elizabeth I, composers increasingly developed expansive and impressive liturgical settings called services. Distinct from the service and not acknowledged in the prayer book until the Restoration, the anthem made its way into the choral liturgy as a result of the queen's intentionally ambiguous injunction in 1559, which stated that before or after Morning Prayer and Evensong "there may be sung a Hymn, or such like song . . . in the best sort of melody and music that may be conveniently devised," provided that it be intelligible. Like the motet, to which it is analogous and with which it shares a common origin in the votive antiphon, the anthem became the vehicle for more personal sacred musical expression. Crystallizing in the late sixteenth century were two general types of anthems: the "full" anthem, a polyphonic work for choir; and the "verse" anthem, with "verses" for one or more solo voices accompanied by organ or instruments, each followed by a choral reply or a refrain. The service music and anthems of Thomas Tallis, John Sheppard, Richard Farrant, Christopher Tye, Robert White, William Byrd, Thomas Morley, Orlando Gibbons, and Thomas Tomkins, to name the best known, together with the Latin works of some of them, are among the reasons this period has been called the golden age of English church music.

It is well to remember, however, that this was the music of the cathedrals, collegiate churches, institutions with choral endowments, and, above all, the Chapel Royal. These offered few opportunities, if any, for active participation in worship for the people in attendance. That was gradually provided by the metrical psalms, inspired by the examples of Strasbourg, Geneva, and the "Stranger" churches and made available in the English Psalter. With texts and tunes easy for ordinary parishioners to learn, they became the unofficial liturgical music of the laity for generations.

Instrumental music and the liturgy. The Western church has employed some form of instrumental music in its rites since the late Middle Ages, but before 1500 only the organ has solid documentary evidence for its widespread and accepted use. In these instances it participated actively in the liturgy but did not normally accompany singing. After the Reformation as before in Catholic and some of the Protestant areas, the organ alternated with the voices in certain chanted or polyphonic movements of the Ordinary, the Proper, and the Divine Office. Its simple or involved treatment of the prescribed chant melody in effect replaced that section with textless music. In the late sixteenth century two new genres for instrumental ensemble emerged in Italy: the imitative *ricercar* and the *canzone.* Although non-liturgical in origin, both types eventually made their way into the church and also, in some cases, replaced the singing.

Where the Reformed tradition was influential, drastic reduction or total elimination of organ music occurred. The former was largely true for much of England, except apparently in the Chapel Royal; the latter, of course, was typical in regions of strict Reformed observance. In those Lutheran territories where conservative church orders retained the Latin liturgy, traditional instrumental practices to some extent survived, employing the older types of music and later in the century the newer Italian ones as well. The specifically Lutheran additions to the instrumental repertory were those pieces elaborating on chorale-based vocal works or otherwise incorporating the chorale tune.

Devotional music. The sixteenth century witnessed an abundance of sacred music intended not for church use but for personal and family devotion, for education, and for pious music making and recreation. The most striking phenomenon was the widespread interest in the Psalms. Inspired by them Luther created the metrical psalm chorale and completed several by 1523. These and others spread with astonishing speed, were widely imitated, and were disseminated by presses in Strasbourg, Augsburg, and Nuremberg. In France the fateful beginnings of the Genevan metrical psalm occurred about a decade later. Marot, caught up in the sympathy for reform emerging in Paris, even at court, produced his first skillfully poetic psalm versifications, apparently at the urging of the devout, evangelically minded Renée of France, whom he visited briefly in Ferrara in 1535. Not long after his return home his psalms were enthusiastically received. Somehow a dozen or so came into Calvin's possession in Strasbourg before publication; someone in court circles must have recognized their significance and sent them on. These and other versions of metrical psalms appeared in the Low Countries, Germany, England, France, and Switzerland, and although for Calvin only monophonic, unaccompanied psalms were permissible in church, simple harmonizations sprang up based on these several versions. Calvin's call for the psalms to replace secular music may have had an effect, for the demand for musical arrangements of psalms resulted in an outpouring of publications of personal psalters, books of harmonized settings, and collections of polyphonic psalms ranging from the simplest textures to the most sophisticated and challenging motets. These psalm settings number in the thousands.

As important as the psalms were in the religious life of the several confessions, much other devotional poetry and music was created, published, and sung. Among Catholics the lay confraternities supported music in their communities, both in church and in their separate devotions. In Italy they sang vernacular *laudi spirituali,* which in the sixteenth century were simple part-songs that later served the Catholic reform, as exemplified in the work of Filippo Neri in Rome. Similar organizations in northern cities such as Antwerp actively sponsored devotional polyphony, as well as music for the liturgy. French chansons and Italian madrigals, the most sophisticated types of Renaissance secular polyphony, were rivaled by *chansons spirituelles, madrigali spirituali,* and *odes spirituelles,* the French types composed by both Catholics and Huguenots, as were the *noëls.* In Germany and France the Jesuits used music for religious devotion and moral education, notably in their school dramas. Lutherans contributed devotional songs and polyphonic settings in great numbers; some of the finest were by Lechner, Hassler, and Melchior Franck. There is also the neglected genre of polyphonic table graces, which appeared throughout sixteenth-century Europe in Latin and the vernacular in both Catholic and Protestant traditions. Not to be overlooked are the late works of Byrd, composed for his recusant friends, himself, and other faithful Catholics; these include three Latin masses and two books of *Gradualia* (1605, 1607), ostensibly for the Catholic liturgy but, ironically, works of religious devotion for those forced to worship in secret.

Music in Worship. Despite local variations, Catholic musical practices were relatively constant from the late Middle Ages until the Council of Trent (1545–1563). In its few sessions devoted to music the council delegates questioned the liturgical propriety of polyphony. Its influential advocates prevailed, however, and the decrees passed were general, moderate, and brief. Music in the liturgy had to arouse the devotion of the faithful; anything redolent of the secular, such as profane tunes and styles, was to be scrupulously avoided, and the style of music and its performance had to render the text and its meaning clear and intelligible. The council, however, assigned the working out of the specific details to the provincial councils, synods, and the Commission of Cardinals, led by Vitellozzi Vitellozzi and Carlo Borromeo. Their investigations included auditioning works of Jacobus de Kerle, Vincenzo Ruffo, and Giovanni Pierluigi da Palestrina.

In the sixteenth century the Ordinary of the Mass continued to be performed in the traditional ways, most often with each of the verses or subsections of the five movements taken alternately (*alternatim*) by chant and organ, chant and polyphony, or, more rarely, organ and polyphony. Opposition to the organ in the *Credo*, however, was so strong that after Trent it was severely limited or prohibited entirely. As polyphony in the Mass gained wider and wider appeal, especially for high feasts, the newer complete Ordinaries contained fewer subdivisions suitable for organ *alternatim*. In the more common chanted Mass, of course, organ settings in the Ordinary were the practical equivalent of the polyphonic choir. Not infrequently the organ replaced the Gradual and the Offertory and played at the Elevation. The motet reportedly also assumed some of these same functions, most often at the Offertory and the Elevation, but also in place of the *Deo gratias* at the end of the Mass.

On occasion late in the century instrumental pieces were similarly employed. The use of instruments (usually trombones and *cornetti*) to reinforce choral polyphony increased without official sanction, but it also provided the very useful function of stabilizing the pitch of the choir, which the organ similarly began to do more than before. Understandably, decrees allowing the organ alone had little effect because discretion was left to individual bishops, a fact contributing to relatively wide variations in musical practices by 1600. The same applies to both the Divine Office and the Mass. Depending on the solemnity of the feast and local circumstances, various types of polyphony enriched Matins, Lauds, Vespers, and Compline, with and without *alternatim* and with and without the organ and instruments. The increasingly rich panoply of liturgical music in many parts of the services was evidently designed to appeal to worshipers and was undeniably successful in furthering the Catholic reform.

The most conspicuous feature of Lutheran worship in the sixteenth century is the variety in detail from one place to another. Although one cannot speak of *the* Lutheran church at this time, evangelical Protestants in sympathy with the Augsburg Confession shared broad areas of agreement and exhibited certain differences. Their liturgies embodied more or less Luther's idea of freedom within an orderly tradition, congregational participation, and the use of the vernacular hymn. Some—influenced, for example, by Zwingli, Strasbourg, Württemberg, or Calvin—fashioned simple orders of worship in which prayer and preaching were central. The song of the congregation, though valued highly, was almost the sole means of musical expression in church. Missing in these, however, was the strong Lutheran preference for as much musical enrichment as available resources and good judgment allowed, a tradition with far-reaching consequences for the future of Protestant church music. From the most conservative to the most eclectic Lutheran practice, the essential minimum was, of course, the inclusion of the congregational hymn. Beyond that, one can in general deduce three models of liturgical musical structure: the historic Latin form, with artistic choral music and chant; a vernacular text throughout, emphasizing the congregational song; and a broad spectrum of compromise between the two.

The conservative Lutheran Mass adhering strictly to Luther's *Formula missae* was undoubtedly rare in its pure form, limited with few exceptions to the major feasts of the year and largely in educated communities. In its close external resemblance to the Roman rite, it is a useful model with which to begin. The details of its liturgical order and musical performance were almost identical to the Catholic practices described above. Theoretically usable were the complete polyphonic Latin Ordinary and the polyphonic Introit, the Alleluia, the major festival Sequences, a rare Gradual, and the *Communio*, although the latter was usually dropped or sung during the distribution along with the *Agnus Dei*, chorales, or responsories. When any of these items was chanted, it also, like the Latin chants normally used on ordinary Sundays, alternated with the organ, as in the Catholic Mass. In very conservative centers such as Nuremberg (which had an atypical solution), congregational hymns appear not to have found a place in the festival liturgy other than during the distribution. This rigidity, however, was usually relaxed in certain ways to allow the people to sing. On the other hand, in some localities almost everything was sung in the vernacular using chorale substitutes like those in Luther's German Mass, although this liturgy itself was not necessarily adopted. Where practicable the organ or a choir probably alternated with the congregation stanza by stanza.

Between these two extremes local and territorial church orders present a great many variations and compromises. A few samples of addition, substitution, and *alternatim* will illustrate some of the procedures. The simplest *alternatim* was the exchange of hymn stanzas by the congregation and choir (or organ), a method analogous to antiphonal psalmody. But the choir might elaborate on this design by varying each choral stanza—for example, one sung in unison, another in simple harmony, a third as a polyphonic chorale setting, and another as a complex chorale-motet—and comparable possibilities were also available to the organist. Furthermore, the organ sometimes functioned as a third participant, not only intoning but also supplying one or two alternate stanzas or even free interludes during the hymn (a cause for complaint when too long). The most common substitution in the Lutheran Mass was Luther's *Wir glauben all* for the Latin *Credo*. Similarly, the classic example of addition alternated the versicles of *Victimae paschali laudes* (the Easter Sequence) with stanzas of *Christ lag in Todesbanden.*

Tradition and innovation coalesced in other ways affecting liturgico-musical practice. Lutherans in many areas retained much of the Mass Ordinary but modified its use in language, music, and function. Besides the frequent replacement of the *Credo*, the *Agnus Dei* and later the *Sanctus* were often delayed until the distribution. This left the *Kyrie* and *Gloria* as the only movements of the polyphonic Ordinary, hence the term *Missa brevis* for a composed "Lutheran mass."

Lutherans not only drew from the rich Catholic liturgical tradition but also recognized the value of its musical heritage. Even the chorale was not an original creation of the reformers. For their Latin chant the churches used their old manuscript choir books because most of the music was suitable for the Proper of their revised calendar. Some recent Catholic polyphony was also usable, but most of it was in manuscripts available only to a few, and little was yet in print. Around 1535, however, it became clear that Lutherans needed publications of Latin polyphony arranged more specifically for their use. Tentative beginnings were made in Nuremberg in 1537 with the publication of eight Magnificats of Senfl (a nominal Catholic) and a collection of Latin motets. They were followed the next year by the first of twelve liturgical prints of music for Mass and Vespers, skillfully prepared by Georg Rhau and published in Wittenberg from 1538 to 1545 for urban parishes, schools, and municipal *Kantoreien* (volunteer choirs where local schools lacked adequate resources). Most of the composers in these collections were Catholics or recent Lutheran converts. (In some cases texts were modified for Protestant use.) It soon became apparent that confessional boundaries did not apply to most Latin liturgical music. Lutheran princely courts and imperial free cities adopted changes in Catholic practice. For example, conservative Lutherans shared the Catholic preference for motets as liturgical substitutes and devotional music, and they employed them even more extensively at Mass and Vespers, especially the many motets that were both liturgical and biblical. With respect to instrumental music, Catholics and Lutherans later in the century increasingly used organ music to replace certain of the Propers, but the Lutherans tended to play motets, whereas Catholics preferred the newer instrumental compositions for organ or ensemble, of prime historical significance and adopted by Lutherans mainly in the next century.

Beginning in the 1550s a wave of motets on biblical passages by Lutheran composers entered the market. A dominant feature of both the Latin and German types was the preference for sayings from the Gospels, resulting in the so-called Gospel motet. This has given rise to the belief that it was used as a substitute for the corresponding portion of the liturgical lection. Circumstantial evidence hints that it may have been done, but although the hypothesis accords with the many Gospel cycles composed into the next century, nothing has been uncovered to demonstrate that the practice was widespread. On the other hand, sources report that in some churches where the Gospel lesson was postponed and read from the pulpit before the sermon, a motet on a Gospel text was sung in its place. More to the point is the evidence that these motets were legitimately performed in place of the Responsory at Vespers, as substitutes for the *Deo gratias* and the Sequence, and as responses to the Gospel readings.

The Reformation of worship and music in England proceeded along two nearly parallel courses; one was guided by tradition and the needs of the monarchy, while the other was driven by aggressive clergy inspired by Zwingli, Calvin, and like-minded reformers on the Continent. Before his death Henry VIII helped maintain the great English choral tradition by founding no fewer than a dozen new cathedrals from wealthy secularized monastic houses. In the brief reign of Edward VI, however, Puritan determination significantly reduced choral and organ music in parishes and some cathedrals, and although Mary Tudor moved to reverse the trend, it was not permanently halted. With the return of the exiles at Elizabeth I's accession, opponents renewed their condemnation of the cathedral services as vain and extravagant remnants of "popery," idolatrous and intolerable for excluding congregational participation. The queen, on the other hand, worked shrewdly for a compromise to allow both sides their due.

The break with Rome had placed all the cathedrals under the Crown. Then, with the growing sentiment for reform embodied somewhat in the prayer book of 1549 and more so in that of 1552, there was reason to hope for a renewal of worship. Though the texts and the language did change, the medieval notion of the Divine Office and the Mass as the

Opus Dei apparently did not. Drastically reduced, it nevertheless survived as the ongoing, perpetual service of prayer, praise, and memorial, which was said and sung daily in the cathedrals and some of the other endowed institutions (Lehmberg, pp. 9–12). The services assumed no gathered congregation, they had no pedagogical intent, nor did their purpose include the edification of the church preached by the apostle Paul. Instead, honor to God was their avowed obligation. Their music and ceremonial may well have evoked awe, devotion, and religious feeling among those in attendance, but critics complained that the complex music often rendered the words unintelligible, while the chanting was too often indifferent and mechanical, a gross offense to the Almighty. In Morning Prayer and Evensong the musical settings of the canticles and psalms enriched with beauty an otherwise detached experience for the listener, who had to worship in silence. In spite of the attacks on the cathedral services, others were later to affirm that at its best the music intoning the elevated language of the prayer book added to the affective power of those words, a witness to the faithfulness of the church to its Lord.

Circumstances in the parish churches were far different from those in the cathedrals. As a result of secularization, fewer and fewer churches were left with a choir or organist, especially with the loss of chantry endowments on the accession of Edward VI. Although legally bound to the prayer book liturgy, these parishes had no ready means of worshiping with music, an outcome acceptable to those Puritans of Zwinglian persuasion but hardly true of most laity.

The desire of the people to sing metrical psalms in church, however, was so astonishingly great that not only were they sung after the prayer services, but people attending sermons in cathedrals sang them both before and after the sermon, a familiar practice on the Continent. This apparent license opened the way to the liturgical use of these psalms in the churches. Without choir or organ the liturgies of *The Book of Common Prayer* had been entirely spoken or read responsively, but as corresponding metrical versions of psalms and canticles became increasingly available by 1559 in the psalters of John Day, congregations apparently started to sing them in place of some prescribed texts. By 1562 Day's *Whole Booke of Psalmes* contained most of them. The evidence points to considerable local variation. For example, in addition to the sermon psalms, the congregation could have sung the psalms appointed for the day in meter and read the canticles responsively from *The Book of Common Prayer.* On the other hand, the appointed psalms could have been read, whereas the people could have sung the metrical versions of appropriate sections of the liturgy. Remarkably, the so-called Elizabethan Settlement produced this extraordinary coexistence of Reformed worship patterns in the churches with Anglo-Catholic liturgico-musical practices in the cathedrals and the Chapel Royal, both under the rubrics of one official liturgical order.

In the Reformed churches of Switzerland, France, and the Low Countries, music was far from unimportant, but it was totally subservient to a firm conviction about the nature and purpose of worship and life under the majesty of God. The use of music in the German Reformed churches, however, was less uniform. Except for a few territories like the Palatinate, the crucial issues were theological ones related to the Lord's Supper, among which music was hardly an urgent problem. Besides, in many areas the confessional allegiance shifted several times with changes in government and political circumstances. Some nominally Calvinist churches allowed harmonized or simple polyphonic psalms to be sung by choirs in church, especially Ambrosius Lobwasser's version with the Claude Goudimel settings. Presumably used in Reformed churches, some hymnals were published with freely composed songs and Lutheran chorales, as well as with metrical psalms. Organs were kept in good repair and used, though rarely within the service. Besides the German love of music, there was a practical motive: the illegal status of Calvinism in the Peace of Augsburg (1555) advised against publicizing its identifying features, just as leading Nuremberg patricians hoped their conservative liturgy and music would allay suspicions of crypto-Calvinism.

Secular Use of Sacred Music. The extraordinary popularity of music at all levels of Renaissance society meant, of course, that people valued it for more than worship and personal devotion. But the close interrelationship of the sacred and the secular—inherited from the Middle Ages—which acknowledged the intimate coexistence of the temporal and the spiritual, also meant that in the sixteenth century secular occasions often made use of sacred music, or at least its styles and forms. Conclaves of the church, coronations of kings, and royal weddings certainly relied on sacred rites, but their liturgical function was on the whole secondary. Celebrations of military victories, treaties of peace, births of a royal heir, and other good fortune required music, especially, as mentioned above, a festive *Te Deum,* with at least a choir and the organ. Of all other types, motets most often served these and other ceremonial events, as their impressive effect was particularly suited to such functions, regardless of whether the texts were sacred or secular.

Closely related was the use of music for political motives. Although Queen Elizabeth permitted frankly Protestant worship in English cathedrals and parish churches, she ordered the services in the Chapel Royal to be conducted with ceremonial and music almost indistinguishable from Roman use. According to recorded testimony, their effect, enhanced at times by Latin polyphony, served to minimize England's distance from the Catholic faith of visiting emissaries from the Continent. The wary patricians of Nuremberg appear to have followed a similar strategy in their conservative liturgy and music, a measure that perhaps smoothed relations with the emperor and the Catholic states.

Music in Education and Social Life. Although the importance of music in Renaissance social life and education can now be taken for granted, it is also true, as the popularity of psalms has shown, that the Reformation achieved a somewhat favorable balance, if not an increase, in the relation between sacred expression and the secular. In the schools the students not only participated regularly in worship, in many instances providing musical leadership, but also studied sacred polyphony to learn notation and develop their performing skills. School regulations generally prohibited "frivolous" music, insisting on examples of sacred polyphony, such as motets and hymns. To make such music accessible to younger students, printers issued collections of two- and three-part excerpts from well-known works of the past. Some composers prepared sets of motets, chorale settings, and catechism pieces, all arranged for youthful voices. Even the poor students (*Kurrenden*) who sang for bread at the homes of the citizenry were required to sing only sacred music. How much this emphasis on the sacred influenced morality is still being debated, but few question its impact on music history.

Evidence of this trend in social life, however, should not necessarily be generalized. The following examples, though drawn from the upper social strata, are illustrated and of intrinsic interest. A telling symptom is the music used in the home. Although much has been lost, some pertinent artifacts survive—for example, stone table tops on which are engraved the vocal parts of table prayers, motets, and chorales, so arranged that persons seated around them could conveniently perform them. At least one beautifully embroidered tablecloth was known to have a setting of *Ein' feste Burg* by Martin Agricola (Sohr; Sore) sewn on it in this arrangement. A number of the surviving music manuscripts contain sacred pieces copied for home use. The practice continued because the printing of music partbooks was still cumbersome and costly. There is, however, evidence that occasionally a motet, for example, was printed on an inexpensive broadsheet, which could then be cut into separate parts for each performer. It is also symptomatic of the appeal of this music that people at home enjoyed performing sacred polyphony with instruments as well as with voices and that dozens of printed lute and keyboard collections contain textless arrangements of motets, chorales, and mass sections for personal use. On a broader social plane, in spite of Reformed prohibition against organ music in the service, popular desire for it was so great that lengthy performances were held before or after church, especially in Reformed Holland and Germany, leading eventually to the return of the organ in worship in some of these churches.

Music, Communication, and Influence. Hundreds of songs were composed to express partisan conviction, provide moral support, attack opposition, and persuade public opinion. Most of them were printed on broadsheets or in small pamphlets and were to be sung in the streets and wherever people gathered. The prints usually suggested one or more familiar tunes for each song. The poetry, however, was clearly not for church. Poems by followers of Luther, for example, mercilessly satirized the pope and Catholic clergy, doctrine, and practice on every conceivably vulnerable point. Luther himself, although he did not hesitate to use the saltiest language in his writings, generally refrained from it in his songs and hymns.

The Schmalkald War provoked bitter songs deploring the violence of the imperial soldiers, especially the Spanish troops, whose brutality was compared with the Turks in "A Saxon Maiden's Lament." The Augsburg and Leipzig Interims apparently did not evoke as many songs as might have been expected, probably because there was ample reason to fear reprisal. Those preserved were usually printed without identification, circulated in manuscript, or printed in Magdeburg, where Matthias Flacius Illyricus and his followers openly and vehemently resisted. Andreas Osiander also expressed his well-known opposition in a lively song; it was modeled on a vigorous tune and is traceable to a printer in Bern in 1552, when the danger was almost over. Possibly the most famous broadsheet of the Augsburg Interim period is the satiric woodcut (often reprinted, as in Blume, p. 81) lampooning its clerical proponents, who appear to be singing the actual notes of a four-voice motet beginning *Beatus vir qui non abiit* (*Ps.* 1:1), seemingly ignorant of the German continuation that condemns the Interim as of the devil. The same motet, apparently composed by cantor Martin Agricola of Magdeburg, is contained on another broadsheet, printed for singing around a table.

After 1555 polemical songs took up conflicts between Protestants and the Jesuits, between Lutherans and Calvinists, and between Gnesio-Lutherans and Philippists (or crypto-Calvinists). The real presence in the Lord's Supper was the most contentious issue, along with exorcism, baptism, and, after 1577, the Formula of Concord. Catholic response, however, turned from initial hostility to a somewhat conciliatory attitude toward Lutheran songs, and by the late sixteenth century, led by the Jesuits, Catholics looked increasingly to their own traditions, believing polemical songs to be counterproductive.

The motet served political expression in Italy as elsewhere, and a remarkable group of motets tied to historical events is preserved in a manuscript set of partbooks in the Biblioteca Vallicelliana, once the library of Filippo Neri's oratorium in Rome (Lowinsky). Although only a few of its ninety pieces contain specific references to actual events, well over a dozen additional motets contain enough other clues to connect them to the courageous stand of the short-lived Florentine republic, a struggle in which the spirit of Savonarola was still alive. Within a few years the Reformation itself became a personal issue at the court of Ferrara, where Duke Ercole II had to contend with the overt Protestant sympathies of Duchess Renée of France, who had sheltered Marot and Calvin in 1535. His determination to oppose heresy may well have prompted his court composer, Maistre Jhan, to compose a polyphonic setting of the *Te Deum*, to which he also fitted a somewhat earlier textual parody beginning *Te Lutherum damnamus*, printed later in Venice in 1549. Ferrara and Mantua both had reason to use music to political and religious ends (Nugent).

There are other concrete examples of musical connections with historical personages. Some are polemical, while others are laudatory or neutral. Luther's first song, *Ein neues Lied wir heben an*, a narrative ballad reporting the martyrdom of two young Augustinians at Brussels in 1523, established the martyr ballad typology of the Reformation. The reformers received their share of sung praise and criticism, as did clergy and political leaders, especially those of electoral and ducal Saxony. Luther, of course, stood out as the object of both kinds, but the following is of a different category from these. A source from about 1529 and dedicated to a duke of Saxony (presumably Elector John the Constant) contains a parody of the Easter Sequence *Victimae paschali laudes*, fitted to the chant in praise of Luther. It opens with "Invicti Martini laudes intonant Christiani." In rebuttal, a Catholic parody to the same chant (preserved in Basel) attacks him with "Pessimas Lutheri fraudes fugiant Christiani" (Nugent, pp. 234f).

The Late Phase. In France the Huguenots' intermittent successes and tragic failures, eventuating in the relatively tolerant Edict of Nantes (1598), brought about no significant changes in their music for worship other than the increasing availability of Genevan psalms published in Lyon and Paris. The popularity of polyphonic psalm settings, however, grew even among Catholic composers, as did the popularity of new versions and translations. The Jesuits were also active in France, initiating tighter restrictions on liturgical music in their provincial colleges. With the enthusiastic reception of Orlando di Lasso's sacred works, French composers seemed temporarily reluctant to produce music for the liturgy, but toward the end of the century men like Jacques Mauduit and Eustache du Caurroy exhibited signs anticipating the later French sacred style. In Dutch Reformed areas church music was again limited almost exclusively to psalms, but Jan Pieterszoon Sweelinck must be mentioned not only for his masterly polyphonic Genevan psalms but also for his brilliant Latin motets and highly influential organ works, all from the early seventeenth century. His career (and that of others like him) as a Protestant organist of the Old Church in Amsterdam can be explained by an extraordinary circumstance. Although the Synod of Dordrecht (1574) decreed the abolition of organ playing in church, several town councils refused to give up the organ recitals played before and after the services. Faced with this defiance, the synods only gradually surrendered and by 1638 agreed to accept organ playing as "a neutral thing" left to the discretion of the congregation. In England the accession of James I saw a continuation of the division between music of the cathedrals (and some colleges) and parish churches, except that the separation became progressively wider as the Anglican taste for more formal ceremonial succeeded in adding far more elaborate and colorful music to the cathedral services than earlier. The impressive full anthems and attractive verse anthems with soloists and instruments not only overshadowed the liturgical service music but also prompted the cathedrals to reduce the number of metrical psalms for the people, thereby contributing to the Puritan disaffection that led to revolution. As noted, Calvinists in the empire were, with a few exceptions, somewhat more liberal in their use of music than was the Genevan model. Their attitude toward organ playing was rather like that of the Dutch, which in a way had been anticipated in Basel beginning as early as 1561.

Italy. By the time the Counter-Reformation was under way, Italians had begun to assume musical leadership in Europe and would hold it for at least the next two centuries. That dominance was eventually stronger in secular music, but at this time, having assimilated northern contrapuntal skills, Italy took the lead in sacred music as well. The impetus for the latter undoubtedly came from the vitality of Catholic reform and the new opportunities it offered to musicians and other creative artists. Two trends emerged. One was conservative and centered in Rome; the other, somewhat later and more progressive, emanated from Venice. The new seriousness of Catholic piety combined asceticism and a restrained mysticism, to which smooth, at times sonorous, harmonious polyphony was ideally suited. Not surprisingly, however, the style owed some of its spiritual intensity to Spain in the person of Cristóbal de Morales, whose ten years in Rome from 1535 to 1545 left their mark on Giovanni Pierluigi da Palestrina, the perfecter and chief proponent of Roman polyphony. A remarkable achievement, the style came as close as any to reconciling the Tridentine insistence on textual intelligibility with the more elusive mission suggested in one of the canons (but not stated in the final decree) that music in worship should somehow prefigure the celestial harmonies enjoyed by the blessed. None of Palestrina's followers quite equaled him, but there was one, the Spaniard Tomás Luis de Victoria (1548–1611), who in his two decades in Rome not only mastered the style but gave it a Spanish devotional ardor and luminosity.

In music Venice represents a quite different aspect of the Counter-Reformation, if one is even willing to accept the validity of a connection. Its political independence and worldly mentality, its religious rites intimately bound to civic ceremony, its distance from Roman hegemony (symbolized by its Byzantine-inspired basilica), and its exotic setting all call up the image of a thoroughly secular culture of energy, willfulness, and colorful splendor. The sacred music reflective of this culture took shape in the last decades of the century in the works of Andrea and Giovanni Gabrieli. In grand motets of two, three, and four choirs, with solo voices, organs, and instruments and in kaleidoscopic patterns of brilliant sonorities, energetic rhythms, and intense feeling, this music anticipates the baroque and the sensuousness of Jesuit productions in the next period. By overwhelming the senses with sound and pageantry, it seems calculated to evoke a vision of the Church Triumphant.

Evangelical Germany. The new generation in Germany was less willing to learn the old repertory of hymns to which the liturgy was still almost exclusively confined. Faced with hostility from outside the evangelical community and political and confessional conflicts from within, not to mention the host of everyday hardships, people reportedly found the current mode of worship inadequate to their needs. About this time and for similar and other plausible reasons, choral music assumed an even more dominant role in the principal church services. Just as in Catholic churches, the attractiveness of polyphonic music gained in popularity among the upper classes, but for Lutherans it was at the expense of congregational singing and in favor of passive contemplation, if not simply aesthetic enjoyment. For example, Friedrich Lindner, a Lutheran cantor in Nuremberg, expressed the educated music lover's view in a foreword to an anthology of masses he edited in 1590. It was his task, he noted, to provide music in church "which may be sung devoutly in the celebration of the Holy Name and of divine worship and which may be heard with a pious feeling of delight because of their pleasant harmony." Most of this fine choral music was composed by Catholics, beginning in the 1560s with Orlando di Lasso and later some younger northerners in the imperial chapels, several Italians, Victoria, and a great many others. Very little of it contained anything theologically objectionable, even without textual emendation, but almost all of it set Latin texts and did little to revive the congregation.

At the same time, however, there was growing concern to reverse the deteriorating participation of the congregation, for the problem existed in churches even where German music was the norm. One of the first known strategies of any lasting importance was an unpromising collection of fifty chorales in simple harmony with the tune in the topmost voice. It was printed in Nuremberg in 1586 by Lucas Osiander, a theologian associated with the Württemberg court in Stuttgart. In his foreword Osiander agrees that there are fine songs in Latin, the finest of the ages, but points out that not everyone understands Latin. There are fine German chorales, but they are set in artistic counterpoint, and thus a layman cannot sing along; he must merely listen. Osiander's hope was that his simple arrangements for the choir would gradually teach the chorales to the people until eventually "the whole Christian congregation can sing along." This so-called *cantional lied* was not Osiander's invention; a comparable style had appeared much earlier in humanist odes, some Reformed psalm settings, and several other types. Nor was it to be, as might be assumed, merely a choral accompaniment to congregational singing, for although the people were to sing with the choir, media *alternatim* was still the fundamental practice. The real significance of his experiment was rather that it proposed to restore the congregation once again to its rightful place as an active and equal participant in the liturgy with the polyphonic choir (*figurata musica*) and the organ.

Starting shortly before 1600 a series of chorale collections by well-known composers began to be published, and these were frankly modeled on Osiander's book in style and its standard Lutheran repertory. Well into the seventeenth century these and similar collections had a remarkably receptive market in evangelical lands. In his preface each composer usually acknowledged the lack of artistry in the style, and although admitting that he had made the settings at the urging of the governing authorities, he was pleased to say that they were musically effective in church while of genuine benefit to the people.

Consequences and Implications. After 1555 matters of faith and practice in the fragmented Christian communities rested more than ever with secular authority and political circumstance, but, despite the variety of liturgico-musical forms, a musical heritage common to Lutherans and Catholics lasted amicably for perhaps a generation. The progress of the Counter-Reformation and intra-Lutheran disputes put this stylistic community at risk. Lutherans called for more sacred music on German biblical and devotional texts. French Calvinists proudly maintained their unique tradition of monophonic psalmody, shared, though less stringently, by their Dutch and German counterparts. Anglicans and Puritans went their separate ways in uneasy toleration, with each musically distinct from the other and from styles on the Continent. In part the fruit of Luther's legacy, these manifold differences accentuated confessional separation.

For this reason (along with pragmatic and aesthetic one), some Lutherans retained Latin chant and polyphony as they came to value the stylistic community in church music as a way of living in continuity with a venerable tradition. They not only sang Latin chant (occasionally in German translation) and the polyphony of older Catholic composers but also were receptive to the exciting new sacred music produced in Italy, so much so that they sent their own talented young musicians to study there. Travelers, merchants, and students brought Italian vocal and instrumental music home, and before long German printers published their own Italian anthologies to distribute at the great book fairs. German composers imitated Italian motets and also incorporated features of the madrigal and simpler forms such as the *villanella* into their sacred works. Princely courts and large urban communities, enamored of the brilliant and colorful polychoral works from Venice and elsewhere, ordered their performance for high festivals, celebrations, and weddings. When the humanist experiments in Florence and Rome produced the dramatic forerunners of opera and oratorio, Lutherans in their conservatism hesitated at first but eventually made their own adaptations of them as a natural rhetorical means of exegesis and of bringing the word to life, as demonstrated later by Heinrich Schütz and Johann Sebastian Bach. They also looked to the north and west. Attracted by the reputation of the Reformed town organ recitals, many aspiring organists went to Amsterdam to study with Sweelinck, the "maker of German organists," and helped establish a north German organ tradition, much as the Venetian-trained organists, such as Hassler, had done in the south. Lutheran sacred organ music included free compositions (e.g., Italian toccatas, *ricercari*, *canzoni*, and chant-based pieces) as well as various types based on chorale tunes. These newer developments, especially in Italy, exposed Lutherans to music the expressive force of which intensified to an astonishing degree. This escalation of emotional temperature was perhaps unknown before in the West and was a symptom of a new, unsettling, and at times exhilarating view of the world.

The processes of change included two related developments, both signs of modernity, involving music in general and church music in particular. These were the shift from a participatory to a more individualistic or professional approach to music making and the growth of a more thoroughly secular attitude toward music at the expense of the concept of a sacred style. By the early sixteenth century music was as much for the enjoyment of performers as for the pleasure of an audience. Greater leisure and a more broadly educated middle class increased the demand for music, which composers and publishers, aided by improved print technology, satisfied with music designed for the widest market. By the end of the sixteenth century, however, new styles both of composition and performance required far more soloistic virtuosity than before. Amateurs became listeners rather than performers, creating new audiences, who in turn demanded more brilliant performances. Before and even after the advent of public opera houses and public concerts in the seventeenth century, few but the wealthy had the means to hear such performances, with one important exception—in church when performances took place at Vespers, at Mass, or at special devotional services sponsored by local confraternities. Predictably, the taste for soloistic, individualistic performances affected music in the churches.

Western Catholic and Lutheran traditions, on the one hand, and the Reformed tradition, on the other, each helped advance the secularization of church music in the wake of the Reformation. Of the three traditions, Lutheran church music was the most open to secular influences since it was theoretically the most free of stylistic dogma. Although it is true that the several church orders set liturgical guidelines, they were relatively flexible and set not by church but by secular authorities. Conversely, even though it was theoretically subject to hierarchical regulation, Catholic church music was not immune to secularization, for liberties in musical style and practice were taken where clerical oversight was lax, if not, in fact, sympathetic. The Reformed tradition, however, proved the most paradoxical. Its churches, committed more or less to Calvin's teachings, accepted the concept of a uniquely sacred style to which all its church music was to conform. It is therefore ironic that Calvinism contributed so much to the shift in balance toward the secularization of all music. Calvin did successfully achieve a unique "sacred style." Though its significance was misunderstood by most of his critics, the end result was in a way positive for music. In restricting church music entirely to metrical unison psalms, Calvin in effect defined as secular all art music, which, though "a gift of God," was to be used only for human enjoyment, refreshment, and, it was hoped, moral betterment. England offers a prime example. Denied musical satisfaction in church, especially during the Commonwealth, the middle class turned to musical entertainments, embryonic opera, and, soon after the Restoration (which brought prospects for profit), the first public concerts. There and elsewhere, the concert hall was later to replace the church as the temple of music.

The Catholic tradition of sacred music took two divergent directions after 1600: chant plus a canonized "old style" of polyphony (*stile antico,* derived from Palestrina) and a succession of "modern" styles adapted readily from secular music. Composers and choirmasters were expected to employ the sacred style in church, but they were free to follow current innovations in secular music, such as soloistic madrigals, and apply them to devotional works. With the creation of the early musical antecedents of opera in Florence and Rome at the end of the sixteenth century, this "second style" of sacred music (not quite "church" music yet) gradually adopted some of its dramatic features as well. Before long, though contingent on local ecclesiastical policy, it was admitted into the liturgy, most commonly in the music for Vespers.

The Lutheran musical tradition, on the other hand, did not canonize a sacred musical style. Lutherans did, of course, limit its theoretical freedom—for example, in restricting the number of hymns approved for use. Undoubtedly some decisions were also based on aesthetic preferences, but the fundamental criteria were theological, functional, and flexible; music was judged appropriate if it faithfully served the Christian community, a point not lost on Catholic proponents of vernacular song. The chorale, it is true, maintained a central position in the tradition, but by no means an exclusive one. Again, musical style was not an issue, for its melodic origins were as diverse as Gregorian chant, French chansons, German art songs, and Genevan psalms. With regular use these tunes and their associated texts became symbols of the faith, the identity, and the memories of a branch of the church universal. The principle of freedom also led, though less directly than Calvinism, to a broadening of secular musical culture. Carried on in church, at court, in the schools, and in social gatherings, the tradition promoted musical activity in communities large and small, where the leading musicians were the rectors, cantors, teachers, and organists. Amateurs and appreciative audiences prepared the groundwork for composers to contribute to the wider community of Western music. The significance and consequences of this musical tradition are easily subject to differing judgments; freedom led to conflict and decline, as well as to advance. In its openness, breadth, and inclusiveness, however, the tradition can be said to be truly catholic, and as a Reformation movement it has proved since Vatican II to have been Luther's major legacy to ecumenicity.

[*See also* Devotional Practices; Hymnals; *and* Hymns.]

BIBLIOGRAPHY

Abraham, Gerald, ed. *The New Oxford History of Music.* Vol. 4, *The Age of Humanism, 1540–1630.* Reprint, Oxford, 1994. A generous survey, only moderately technical, of Renaissance, Reformation, and early Baroque music with topical chapters written by acknowledged specialists. Representative bibliographies of scholarly editions and studies.

Blume, Friedrich, et al. *Protestant Church Music: A History.* New York, 1974. The one major comprehensive and authoritative book in English on Protestant music from the Reformation to the twentieth century; a translation of *Geschichte der evangelischen Kirchenmusik,* Kassel, 1964, with new chapters on Scandinavia, the United States, and England; extensive classified bibliography.

Brown, Howard Mayer. *Music in the Renaissance.* Englewood Cliffs, N.J., 1976. Excellent general introduction, from c.1420 to 1600, with a brief chapter on the Reformation.

Butler, Bartlett R. "Liturgical Music in Sixteenth-Century Nürnberg; A Socio-Musical Study." 2 vols. Ph.D. diss., University of Illinois at Urbana-Champaign, 1970. Documents the background, basis, and repertory of the conservative liturgico-musical tradition of this Lutheran city.

Caldwell, John. *The Oxford History of English Music.* Vol. 1, *From the Beginnings to c.1715.* Oxford, 1991. Incorporates recent scholarship, including music of the English Reformation.

Fellerer, Karl Gustav. "Church Music and the Council of Trent." *Musical Quarterly* 39 (1953), 576–594. A good general introduction in English, with many excerpts from primary sources before and after the council.

Fellerer, Karl Gustav, ed. *Geschichte der katholischen Kirchenmusik.* Vol. 1, *Von den Anfängen bis zum Tridentinum*; Vol. 2, *Vom Tridentinum bis zur Gegenwart.* Kassel, 1972–1976. A thorough survey with bibliographies, important for sections on medieval sacred vernacular songs and their use, the impact of the Reformation, and Counter-Reformation developments after Trent.

Fenlon, Iain, ed. *The Renaissance: From the 1470's to the End of the Sixteenth Century; Man & Music.* Englewood Cliffs, N.J., 1989. Beginning with the editor's fine introduction, "Music and Society," major musical centers are treated by individual scholars, including Robin Leaver on Reformation Wittenberg and Leipzig.

Garside, Charles. *Zwingli and the Arts.* New Haven and London, 1966. Notable for a rare and successful attempt to give the biographical and theological bases for Zwingli's attitude toward music.

Lehmberg, Stanford. *The Reformation of Cathedrals: Cathedrals in English Society, 1485–1603.* Princeton, 1988. Thorough historical study. See especially chaps. 1, 5, and 8 for liturgy and music.

Le Huray, Peter. *Music and the Reformation in England, 1549–1660.* 2d rev. ed. London, 1978. The standard survey, with good bibliography and many examples; terminology somewhat technical.

Lowinsky, Edward. "A Newly Discovered Sixteenth-Century Motet Manuscript at the Biblioteca Vallicelliana in Rome." *Journal of the American Musicological Society* 3 (1950), 173–232. A classic example of interdisciplinary scholarship that uncovers relationships between musical works and their historical context.

Mattfeld, Victor H. *Georg Rhaw's Publications for Vespers.* Brooklyn, 1966. A thorough exposition of the theological, liturgical, and musical bases for Rhau's printed anthologies of Latin polyphony for Lutheran use.

Miller, Clement A. "Erasmus on Music." *The Musical Quarterly* 52 (1966), 332–349. Useful for its compilation and analysis of many pertinent quotations.

Müller, Karl Ferdinand, and Walter Blankenburg, eds. *Die Musik des evangelischen Gottesdienstes.* Vol. 4, *Leiturgia: Handbuch des evangelischen Gottesdienstes.* Kassel, 1961. Comprehensive and well-documented essays by several authors on various aspects of liturgical music, including congregational song, chant, choral polyphony, and performance practices of vocal and instrumental music. Indispensable for serious study.

Nettl, Paul. *Luther and Music.* Philadelphia, 1948. Semipopular but informative work of a reputable music historian; lacks documentation except for basic bibliography.

Nugent, George. "Anti-Protestant Music for Sixteenth-Century Ferrara." *Journal of the American Musicological Society* 43 (1990), 228–291. An impressive historical essay centering on the musical consequences of the conflict between Ercole II d'Este of Ferrara and his duchess, Renée of France, resulting from her openly Protestant sympathies.

Reese, Gustave. *Music in the Renaissance.* Rev. ed. New York, 1959. Still the basic work in English; encyclopedic, emphasizing both cultural-historical and technical aspects. Comprehensive bibliographies for its time.

Sadie, Stanley, ed. *The New Grove Dictionary of Music and Musicians.* 20 vols. London, 1980. Authoritative, compact articles on Calvin, Luther (and Lutheran music), Zwingli, chorale, psalms (metrical), and most pertinent topics. Remarkably comprehensive, with basic scholarly bibliographies.

Schalk, Carl. *Luther on Music: Paradigms of Praise.* Saint Louis, 1988. Assembles Luther's words on music, indicating its crucial importance to him and the Lutheran tradition.

Schalk, Carl, ed. *Key Words in Church Music: Definition Essays on Concepts, Practices, and Movements of Thought in Church Music.* Saint Louis, 1978. Useful mini-encyclopedia of generally accurate historical and practical information. Strong Lutheran emphases but with fair treatment of the principal traditions. Selected readings for further study.

Temperley, Nicholas. *The Music of the English Parish Church.* 2 vols. Cambridge, 1979. A masterly study of a neglected topic, its first three chapters cover the Reformation to the early seventeenth century, including the metrical psalm. Exhaustive bibliography of primary and secondary sources.

Wienandt, Elwyn A. *Choral Music of the Church.* New York, 1965. Surveys sacred choral music from the Middle Ages to the twentieth century with emphasis on form and style, and with reference to historical context, especially for the periods of the Renaissance and the Reformation.

BARTLETT R. BUTLER

MÜSLI, Wolfgang. *See* Musculus, Wolfgang.

MUTIANUS RUFUS, Conrad (also Mutian; 1471–1526), German humanist. Born in Homburg, Mutianus was raised in prosperous circumstances, for his father was a patrician, a popular city councilor, and mayor. He enjoyed financial independence during his Italian travels and for years as a canon at Gotha in Saxony, though he spent lavishly on books and friends and ended his life in true apostolic poverty. He owed much to his education with the Brethren of the Common Life at Deventer, but under the spell of Neoplatonism he held that there is a divine revelation in all religions and that Christ is the universal spirit inspiring all. As discussion leader and informal mentor of groups of youths at Gotha, Mutianus influenced numerous young humanists. In his *Table Talks* Luther dismissed him as a skeptic.

In 1486 Mutianus entered the University of Erfurt, which, along with the University of Heidelberg, was an early center for humanist and classical studies. He received his B.A. degree in 1488 and his M.A. degree in 1492. Mutianus wished to be thought of as a philosopher (*vates*), not merely as a humanist poet (*poeta*), or a philologist, rhetorican, or *literatus* in the purely humanist sense of the word poet. He reacted vigorously against the sacramental-sacerdotal system as it had developed in the late Middle Ages and against scholastic philosophy. His correspondence reveals his animus for current beliefs and practices, but he was incapable of offering a viable alternative—that is, a constructive theology or evangelical revival. He was closer to the negativist criticism of Sebastian Brant, Crotus Rubeanus, and Ulrich von Hutten than to the Reformation theologians who were more concerned with matters of substance and doctrine. Mutianus's philosophy can best be characterized as a kind of religious universalism. The significance of Christ to Mutianus lay in the spiritual qualities that he essentially represented, as opposed to the historical Jesus, the one who taught, was crucified, was buried, and rose again. Man, an intermediate being in the universe, can be drawn toward God, truth, and goodness but is bound by the sensual. Mutianus's interpretation of Paulinism was essentially moralistic, not fideistic or soteriological, fostering a kind of piety well suited to the *Beata Tranquillitas*, the name he gave to his library, for he was a learned man, though a diffident author.

BIBLIOGRAPHY

Gillert, Karl. *Der Briefwechsel des Conradus Mutianusus, Geschichtsquellen der Provinz Sachsen und angrenzender Gebiete.* Vol. 17. Halle, 1890. Since Mutianus published virtually nothing, his importance lies in his very extensive correspondence, edited carefully in this volume of his correspondence and in the collection of Krause.

Krause, Carl. *Der Briefwechsel des Mutianusus Rufus.* Kassel, 1885.

Spitz, Lewis W. "Mutianus: Intellectual Canon." In *The Religious Renaissance of the German Humanists*, pp. 130–154, 320–325. Cambridge, 1963.

LEWIS W. SPITZ

MYCONIUS, Friedrich (Ger., Mecum; 1490–1546), German humanist, Lutheran theologian, and associate of Martin Luther and Philipp Melanchthon. Born in Lichtenfels, north of Bamberg, Myconius attended Latin school in Annaberg, where in 1510 he met Johann Tetzel, who was offering indulgences. Myconius's spiritual troubles prompted his entrance into the Franciscan order, first in Annaberg and then in Leipzig and Weimar, where he was ordained a priest in 1516. Though deeply impressed by such theologians as Peter Lombard, Alexander of Hales, and Gabriel Biel, Myconius was also attracted to Luther because of his struggle against indulgences. Myconius became an early supporter of Luther and actually met him when Luther passed through Weimar for his 1518 meeting with Cardinal Cajetan in Augsburg. Authorities sought to restrict Myconius's preaching and writing, but he managed to break loose, becoming a preacher at a Zwickau hospital in 1524 and in the village of Buchholz. That same year Saxon Elector John ("the Steadfast") relayed a call from Gotha for Myconius to reform the parish and city schools. Correspondence from Luther and Melanchthon offered considerable encouragement as he met apathy and resistance from local clerics and some city officials.

His preaching and personal pastoral example brought success in Gotha and attracted attention elsewhere. He accompanied John Frederick (who succeeded his father, John, as elector of Saxony) as preacher on several official trips, and he worked with Melanchthon on the 1527 and 1533 church visitations in Thuringia. He also participated in several major theological discussions: the 1529 colloquy at Marburg, the 1536 colloquy at Wittenberg, the 1537 assembly at Schmalkald, the 1539 negotiations at Frankfurt and Nuremberg, and the 1540 gathering at Hagenau. In December 1536 Luther finished the Schmalkald Articles, anticipating a general council called by Rome for the next year (and then postponed until the Council of Trent). Although the Schmalkald League hesitated to adopt officially the articles at its February 1537 meeting, Myconius added his name to the original eight signatories from December.

In 1538 Myconius joined a delegation sent to England to discuss the Augsburg Confession with theological advisers of Henry VIII, returning a half year later after little progress. He met more success as part of the effort to introduce evangelical theology in ducal Saxony after the 1539 death of Duke George (who had been an ardent foe of the Reformation), working in his old base of Annaberg and then Leipzig, where he preached the first evangelical sermon in Saint Nicholas. His pastoral style again helped overcome opposition during his nine-month effort in the territory. Although he was asked by the citizenry to stay, Myconius's poor health prompted his return to his Gotha congregation in 1540. When bronchial problems prevented preaching, Myconius busied himself with administrative tasks and with collecting information documenting the course of the Reformation.

That material became part of his *Historia reformationis* covering the years 1517 to 1542.

His early spiritual problems paralleled Luther's, and his encounter with the evangelical message through Luther's early writings made Myconius a staunch advocate of Wittenberg's theology and a firm friend of Luther and Melanchthon. A capable theologian but not a prolific writer, Myconius proved most valuable because of his preaching, pastoral style, and ability to prescribe and execute administrative reforms.

BIBLIOGRAPHY

Primary Sources

Menius, Justus. *Ein tröstliche Predigt vber der Leich vnd Begrebnis des Erwirdigen Herrn Friderichen Mecums, Pfarrherrn vnd Superattendenten zu Gotha.* Wittenberg, 1546. The funeral sermon for Myconius delivered by his good friend Justus Menius, in whose behalf Myconius had signed the Schmalkald Articles.

Myconius, Friedrich. *Historia reformationis vom Jahr Christi 1517 bis 1542.* Edited with a preface by Ernst Salomon Cyprian. Leipzig, 1715. The first published edition of Myconius's historical observations. Also available as *Geschichte der Reformation,* edited by Otto Clemen, Voigtländers Quellenbücher, vol. 68, Leipzig, 1914.

———. *Der Briefwechsel der Friedrich Mykonius, 1524–1546.* Tübingen, 1960.

Secondary Sources

Delius, Hans-Ulrich. "Friedrich Myconius: Das Leben und Werk eines Thüringischen Reformators." Diss., Westfälische Wilhelms-Universität Münster, 1958.

Koch, Ernst. "Aktenstücke zur Visitation in Thüringen 1528/29 als Ergänzungen zum Briefwechsel Melanchthons und Friedrich Myconius." In *Herbergen der Christenheit 1987/88: Jahrbuch für deutsche Kirchengeschichte,* edited by Karlheinz Blaschke, pp. 53–58. Beiträge zur deutschen Kirchengeschichte, vol. 26. Berlin, 1988. Edited collection of Myconius's letters commenting on his first Saxon church visitation.

Ledderhose, Karl Friedrich. *Friedrich Mykonius, Pfarrherr und Superintendent von Gotha: Ein Leben aus der Reformationszeit.* Hamburg, 1854. Done with devotion but without footnotes, this popular biography looks at Myconius in detail, often through extensive quotation of his own letters.

Ulbrich, Heinrich. *Friedrich Myconius, 1490–1546: Ein Lebensbild und neue Funde zum Briefwechsel des Reformators.* Schriften zur Kirchen- und Rechtsgeschichte, vol. 20. Tübingen, 1962. While devoted especially to Myconius's correspondence, the book begins with a useful biographical chapter.

ROBERT ROSIN

MYCONIUS, Oswald (Ger., Oswald Geisshüsler; 1488–1552), Swiss reformer who worked in Zurich with Huldrych Zwingli and in Lucerne and Basel. Born in Lucerne, Myconius attended university at Basel, where he became acquainted with the work of Desiderius Erasmus and learned of the young Zwingli. He taught at the canon's school in Zurich in 1516 and early on showed a critical stripe, writing a 1518 tract arguing for obedience to Rome only as long as the pope did not run counter to the Christian faith. Myconius took part in calling Zwingli to Zurich and then took a call himself to Lucerne. Correspondence with Zwingli helped forge a friendship and carried him through considerable resistance at home. That opposition eventually prompted him to leave in 1522 to teach briefly at Einsiedeln before accepting a call to Zurich's Fraumünster school. He lectured on the New Testament while working behind the scenes on Zwingli's reforms.

After Zurich's defeat and Zwingli's death at Kappel in 1531, Myconius no longer wanted to stay in Zurich and moved to Saint Albans in Basel. He added to his parish duties in 1532 by accepting a university appointment as successor to Johannes Oecolampadius. Although Myconius agreed to that arrangement on a temporary basis and wanted someone else to assume the university post, he continued that dual role until his death. He complicated matters for himself by bringing to the university faculty the former Wittenberg professor Andreas Bodenstein von Karlstadt, who precipitated a row by charging that Myconius wanted clerics to dominate civil authorities; Bodenstein led a group to make the university dominant over the parishes. Myconius weathered the storm.

Although Myconius greatly admired Zwingli, he differed with him on the Lord's Supper, seeing it as a mystical or spiritual meal with Christ present in more than historical memory. He incorporated that view into the 1536 First Helvetic Confession. Myconius came close to Martin Bucer's mediating position, arguing that Zwingli and Luther were talking past each other and held more common ground than they realized.

BIBLIOGRAPHY

Brändly, Willy. *Geschichte des Protestantismus in Stadt und Land Luzern.* Luzern, Geschichte und Kultur: Eine Monographienreihe, II; Staats- und Kirchengeschichte, vol. 4. Lucerne, 1956. Includes information on Myconius's early career.

———. "Oswald Myconius in Basel." *Zwingliana* 11 (1959–1963), 183–192. Examines Myconius's later career as pastor and professor.

Hagenbach, Karl Rudolf. *Johann Oekolampad und Oswald Myconius, die Reformatoren Basels: Leben und ausgewälte Schriften.* Elberfeld, 1859. Includes the more significant writings of Myconius except for his Zwingli biography. Also available on microfiche from Inter Documentation Company, in the collection *Reformed Protestantism,* section 1, *The Swiss Urban Reformation,* Zug, 1982.

Kirchhofer, Melchior. *Oswald Mykonius: Antistes der Baslerischen Kirche.* Basel, 1813.

Neander, August F., ed. *Vitae Quatuor Reformatorum: Lutheri a Melanchthone, Melanchthonis a Camerario, Zwinglii a Myconio, Calvini a Theodore Beza.* Berlin, 1841. Contains Myconius's biography of Zwingli, which is also available in English as "The Original Life of Zwingli," in *Ulrich Zwingli: Early Writings,* edited by Samuel Macauley Jackson, pp. 1–24, reprint, Durham, N.C., 1987.

ROBERT ROSIN

MYSTICISM. If the Reformation of the sixteenth century can be described as the final act of a crisis of reform beginning in the thirteenth century, it is no less true that the varieties of mysticism found in that era need to be viewed against their medieval background to be properly understood. Late medieval debates about the nature of mysticism and its relation to reform provide the context for the ways in which the reformers—Catholic, Protestant, and radical—adopted, transformed, or rejected the mystical elements in Christian traditions.

The term *mysticism* did not exist in the sixteenth century. The adjective *mystical* had long been used to describe the inner reality of many aspects of the Christian life, as in the "mystical sense" of scripture, "mystical contemplation," and "mystical theology," which was understood as a particular kind of knowledge of God. It was not until the early seventeenth century that substantive uses first occur, notably the French *la mystique* (best translated as "mystics," in analogy with "mathematics"). As Michel de Certeau has shown, the identification of mystics as a self-conscious and distinct discipline marked a major shift in the history of Western mysticism. This change was already brewing in the sixteenth century, which therefore should be seen as a time of transition. In order to grasp the importance of this shift, a brief glance at the development of Christian mysticism is needed.

Under the influence of the monastic movement, the mystical element in Christianity—meaning that dimension of Christian belief and practice that concerns the preparation for, the consciousness of, and the consequences of direct contact with God in this life—emerged in explicit fashion. In Western Christianity, mysticism remained closely bound to monasticism until the thirteenth century, when reforms in religious life, especially the Beguines and the Mendicants, marked an important change. Older forms of mysticism, based on withdrawal from the world and programs of ascesis and contemplative prayer, did not die out, but they were challenged by new lifestyles encouraging types of mysticism that were democratic, in the sense of being open to all (and therefore also communicated in the vernacular), as well as "secular" in not demanding flight from the world. Women played a large role in the creation of these new forms and in the shifts in mystical practices and teaching they entailed. The most notable of the changes in mystical practice was an emphasis on ecstatic experience; the most important of the new teachings was a conception of union of identity, or indistinction, with God, as contrasted with traditional teaching concerning the loving union of wills (*unitas spiritus* of *1 Cor.* 6:17). The union of indistinction is found in Meister Eckhart and some of the Beguines. It was thought, at least by some, to encourage a "freedom of spirit" (*libertas spiritus* of *2 Cor.* 3:17), which resulted in antinomianism and denial of the mediation of the institutional church and its sacramental system. Another possible implication of this emphasis on inner identity with God was the marginalization of the Bible. Few, if any, late medieval mystics went this far, but a change in the role of the Bible in the mystical tradition is evident in the late Middle Ages and was to continue into the sixteenth century. Monastic mysticism had been based upon meditation on the biblical text (*lectio divina*) and was expressed largely through biblical commentary. In the later Middle Ages and sixteenth century, the text of the mystics' experience took on an ever larger role.

The errors of the "free spirit" mystical heresy were condemned in 1311, and in 1329 Pope John XXII rejected Eckhart's teaching. These condemnations set the stage for debates over mysticism in which both inquisitors and mystical writers took part. The issues at stake remained powerful in the sixteenth century. Along with the theoretical question of what kind of union with God was possible in this life, there were many practical issues concerning the relation of the mystical element in Christianity to the total life of the believer. Did mystical practices imply an elitist, superior form of Christian life? Did mystical union lead to antinomian behavior? Did mystics put so much stress on the interior presence of God that they no longer had need of the Bible, the institutional Church, and perhaps even the redemptive mediation of Jesus Christ? Each of the three major currents of sixteenth-century reform had to work out its answers to these questions. Their responses form a set of variations on common themes, but the range of adaptations among Catholic reformers, proponents of the classical Reformation, and radical reformers differed greatly.

A discussion of sixteenth-century mysticism can begin with the Catholic reformers. Geographically, Catholic mysticism of the sixteenth century centers on Spain. French mysticism will not be discussed because, though the circles that marked its inception were active from the last decade of the sixteenth century (Benet Canfield's *Reigle de perfection* [The Rule of Perfection], the earliest major work, was written around 1590), French mysticism is properly a seventeenth-century phenomenon. Mystical texts of a late medieval character continued to be produced into the sixteenth century. An anonymous female mystic of the Netherlands wrote *Die evangelische Peerle* (The Evangelical Pearl; 1535) and *Vanden Tempel onser Sielen* (Temple of Our Souls; 1543), the last direct witnesses to properly Eckhartian mysticism. The Benedictine François Louis de Blois's *Institutio Spiritualis* (Book of Spiritual Instruction; 1551), which fused a notion of mystical union taken from John Tauler with many traditional sources, was a textbook that could be used by people in all walks of life. (Blois was a pioneer in the use of the technical term *unio mystica.*)

An important characteristic of the newer elements in Catholic mysticism of the sixteenth century was their relation to the movements for reform in religious life, first evident in Italy and soon also in Spain. Although it is legitimate to speak of a Counter-Reformation spirituality that sought to defend Roman Catholicism against Protestantism, at least by the time of Pope Paul III (1534–1549), sixteenth-century Catholic mysticism was primarily rooted in internal religious reforms seeking a return to strict asceticism, a deeper internal life, and often new types of apostolic commitment.

The concern for reform, both personal and institutional, puts sixteenth-century Catholic mysticism in continuity with the democratizing trend in late medieval mysticism, which tried to create new religious models that would make the ideal of perfection accessible in all walks of life. An example can be found in Catherine of Genoa (1447–1510), a married contemplative who devoted her life to care of the sick. Catherine wrote nothing, but her teachings were put together and eventually published (1551) by her followers. Catherine's brief texts illustrate a powerful and, in some ways, novel form of mysticism. The stress on the centrality of purgation in the path to perfection links her with Juan Álvarez (John of the Cross), and her concern for absolutely pure love mirrors a traditional mystical theme that was to become a burning issue in the seventeenth century. She might be most significant, however, as a lay mystic immersed in apostolic activity during the decades prior to the crisis that destroyed medieval Christianity. Catherine exercised considerable influence on a group of Italian ecstatics who wrote at the end of the sixteenth century. These include the Dominican Catherine dei Ricci (1522–1590), the Carmelite Mary Magdalene dei Pazzi (1566–1607), and Isabella Bellinzaga (1551–1624), whose *Breve Compendio intorno alla Perfezione Cristiana* (Summary of Christian Perfection; c.1584) was widely read.

To be sure, not all mystics couched their doctrine in terms accessible to the laity and intended for general consumption. Some, even the great Juan Álvarez, obviously thought that heights of the mystical path were reached by only the "smallest number" (*Noche Oscura* 1.14.1), and those, presumably, were cloistered contemplatives. Francisco de Osuna, in his *Tercer Abecedario* (Third Spiritual Alphabet; 1527), was more typical when he insisted, "No kind of prayer is to be denied married people if they are inclined to it and desire to practice it" (treatise 8, chapter 1).

The reform circles of early sixteenth-century Spain, located both in religious orders and in lay circles, were the context for the greatest sixteenth-century flowering of mysticism. The sources for this movement toward austerity and interiority were many—Erasmian humanism, Italian reformism, and the *devotio moderna*—and a good deal of late medieval mysticism filtered through the works of the Franciscan Hendrik Herp (d. 1477) and the translations and editions produced by the Carthusians of Cologne. Spain's position as a newly unified (and culturally fragile) nation, a sudden global power through the discovery of America, and a self-appointed guarantor of orthodoxy helps to explain important aspects of the development of Spanish mysticism, which was in many ways a plant that flourished in the midst of (and perhaps partly because of) severe opposition. The suspicion of mysticism evident since the late thirteenth century was revived in Spain in the 1520s with the Inquisition's attacks on the *Alumbrados*, or Illuminated, who were accused of much the same errors as were the medieval "free spirits" (and often of a "Lutheranism" that had nothing to do with Luther). The condemnation of forty-eight propositions concerning mystical abandonment to God (*dejamiento*) in 1525 played a role in Spanish mysticism similar to that of the 1311 condemnation in the late Middle Ages. A climate of fear was created that both restricted and challenged the mystics. The flow of mystical literature was also hampered, especially by the Index of 1559. Many of the great mystics (Ignatius Loyola, Teresa of Ávila, Juan Álvarez) were investigated by the Inquisition; others, such as Luis de Léon, suffered in its prisons.

The attack on the *Alumbrados* forms the background to two of the early masters of Spanish mysticism, both reformed Franciscans. Francisco de Osuna (1492–1541?) wrote six lengthy works called *Abecedario Espiritual* (Spiritual Alphabets). The third of these considered "recollection" (*recogimiento*), which was his term for the process of interior prayer culminating in truly mystical states. Quoting a wide variety of standard authorities (especially Augustine, Pope Gregory I the Great, Bernard of Clairvaux, and Jean Gerson), he endeavored to provide a map of prayer that was accessible to all and guaranteed by tradition. Though scarcely as penetrating as Juan Álvarez, Francisco's work influenced Teresa of Ávila and other mystics. In places (e.g., the analysis of the four kinds of rapturous recollection in treatise 21, chapter 7) his work remains a significant mystical text. Francisco's emphasis on *recogimiento* rather than *dejamiento* was designed to counter the dangerous tendencies of the time. It saved him from the Inquisition in his day, even though his book later came under suspicion.

Contemporary with Francisco was Bernardino de Laredo (1482- 1540?), whose *Subida del Monte Sión* (also known to Teresa) first appeared in 1535. The three parts of Bernardino's work—dealing, respectively, with the necessity of self-knowledge, the imitation of Christ, and finally contemplative prayer—provide a good picture of the standard spiritual handbook of the time. Bernardino laid great stress on the absolute priority of divine activity in the path toward the "sleep of the faculties" in which mystical contemplation is found. Other Franciscan writers also contributed to Spain's golden age of mystical literature. Peter of Alcántara (1499–1562), a friend of Teresa's and supporter of her movement, wrote a *Tratado de la Oración y Meditación* (Treatise on Prayer and Meditation). Diego de Estella's *Meditaciones devotisimas del Amor de Dias* (Very Devout Meditations on the Love of God; 1576) was used by Blaise Pascal and Francis of Sales, and Juan de los Angeles's *Triumphos del Amor de Diòs* (Triumphs of the Love of God; 1589) and *Lucha espiritual y amerosa entre Dios y el Alma*

(Spiritual Conflict of Love between God and the Soul; 1600) make use of Richard of Saint Victor's notion of violent charity.

Perhaps the greatest Spanish mystic of the first half of the sixteenth century was Ignatius Loyola (1491?-1556), whose career was so bound up with the Counter-Reformation that it challenges the claim that Catholic mysticism was largely connected with Catholic reform. Ignatius's mysticism, or better, the mystical side of his complex personality, is undeniable, not only on the basis of the famous experience at Manresa in 1522, a classic account of what Augustine described as an intellectual vision, but especially through the fragmentary spiritual diary he kept between 1544–1545, which is one of the purest examples of direct reporting of mystical experiences in Christian history. Ignatius's profoundly trinitarian mysticism centering on the reception of the Eucharist cannot be separated from his apostolic activity. The ancient Christian ideal of the interpenetration of the highest contemplation with the most active apostolicity, put forth by authorities like Gregory I the Great and Thomas Aquinas, never found a more perfect representative than the founder of the Jesuits (though it was Jerome Nadal, his successor, who actually invented the phrase commonly ascribed to Ignatius—"simul in contemplatione activus," or "active at the same time as being in contemplation"). Ignatius's break with the traditions of medieval monasticism and his insistence that his followers "seek God our Lord in all things" (*Constitutions* 288) are in line with the democratized and secularized tradition of mysticism of the later Middle Ages, though they also served the new situation of militant Catholicism. As H. Outram Evennett noted, however, "The mystic and the active man merged naturally in St. Ignatius himself. They were not encouraged to do so in the society." Though there certainly were Jesuit mystics, especially in the seventeenth century, a tension between action and contemplation developed in the Society of Jesus, as is evident in the campaigns against contemplative prayer of later generals, such as Everard Mercurian and Claudio Acquaviva.

Spanish mysticism of the second half of the sixteenth century was a remarkably varied phenomenon, though the brilliance of the two Carmelite giants, Teresa of Ávila (1515–1582) and Juan Álvarez (1542–1591), has often blotted out the contributions of their contemporaries. Any number of authors would deserve more extended review. Although Luis de Granada (1504–1588) wrote little that was directly mystical, his connection with Teresa and aspects of his *Libro de la Oración y Meditación* (Book of Prayer and Meditation; 1554) show that not all Dominicans agreed with Melchior Cano's rigid opposition to mysticism. The second generation of Carmelite mystics (e.g., Jerome Gracian and Thomas of Jesus), who tried to coordinate the views of the two authorities of the order and to make them available to a wider audience, also deserve their due. One figure who cannot be neglected is the Augustinian Luis de León (c.1527/28–1591), a mystic who produced the first edition of Teresa's works and who would have been an ornament to any era. Like Juan Álvarez, Luis was both a poet and a theologian. His major work, the deeply biblical *De los Nombres de Cristo* (Names of Christ; 1583), is an adaptation of the Dionysian mystical tradition that fuses a Neoplatonic dialectic view of God with the "affective Dionysianism" that became popular in the later Middle Ages and a Renaissance humanist concern for the harmony of humanity and nature. Love reigns supreme in Luis's mysticism: "The soul is like a vessel with huge sails filled by winds of love, sailing a sea of honey, burning with secret fire" (*De los Nombres de Cristo* 2).

Both Teresa and Juan were important as key representatives of Catholic mysticism. (Juan was declared a doctor of the church in 1926 and Teresa in 1970.) Though they were closely allied in the Carmelite reform movement, in reading Teresa and Juan it is the differences in their personalities that is most striking. Both present the reader with paradoxes, though of different sorts. With Teresa the interpreter is confronted with a seeming artlessness in recording extraordinary mystical experiences (especially in her two most important works, the *Vida*, written in 1562–1565, and the *Moradas*, in 1577), which seems in conflict with the shrewdness and energy of a woman who usually got her way against overwhelming odds. With Juan Álvarez, the paradox rests in the contrast between the intensity of the poems that represent the experiential text and the complex and often dry exposition of the four lengthy works that comment upon them (the *Subida del Monte Carmelo* and the *Noche Oscura*, really one work; the *Cantico Espritual* and the *Llama de Amor viva*). In both Teresa and Juan the ambiguity of sixteenth-century mysticism's relation to the biblical text becomes clear. Teresa's book *is* her experience, as is suggested by the famous passage in the *Vida*, chapter 26, where Christ promises to give her a "living book." She does not disregard the Bible, but her access to it as a woman was, of necessity, indirect. Juan Álvarez was a trained exegete who used all the procedures of spiritual interpretation, but he based his exposition on his own poems, which were new renditions of the *Song of Songs*, updated by the Holy Spirit, because, as Max Huot de Longchamp puts it, "the mystic *insofar as he is a mystic* encounters Scripture on the same level as its inspiration, that is, on the level where the Holy Spirit reveals a divine reality in a human one." Despite the attention that both Juan and Teresa give to the investigation of interior states, it would be a mistake to see them as merely constructing a phenomenology of mysticism. As Rowan Williams reminds us, for both Teresa and Juan "'mystical states'. . . have authority only within a frame of reference which is believed in on quite other grounds, and are therefore properly to be tested according to their consistency with this."

The broad agreement of these two Carmelites on key elements in the debates within mysticism was important for subsequently establishing them as leading Catholic authorities. First, both laid emphasis on the priority of the divine initiative in the path to perfection and therefore insisted that, in the higher stages of purgation and prayer, the soul was completely passive to the divine, "theopathic" action. Second, despite Teresa's concern with analyzing her ecstatic states, she agreed with Juan (who frankly distrusted such experiences) that the fundamental thing was conformity to the divine will. Third, although they used metaphors and symbols that at times suggest the possibility of total identity with God, both Carmelites adhered to the traditional view of mystical union that insisted the soul never gains more than oneness of spirit, a loving union of wills. For both mystics, then, the theme of loving knowledge of God is crucial, and the similarity in their teaching on the spiritual betrothal and marriage as the culmination of the mystical life (see *Moradas* 7 and *Cantico Espiritual* 13–35) gave new form to the ancient traditions of erotic mysticism.

There are, however, significant differences between Teresa and Juan. Teresa was fundamentally positive in her approach to God and completely Christocentric. Though she recognized the need for purgation, she added little to traditional teaching. Juan, on the other hand, was perhaps the most austerely apophatic mystic in the Christian tradition, one whose emphasis on the necessity for the passive purgation of both sense and spirit was a significant new development. For Juan, nothing (*nada*) is everything. The journey to God is called night, not only because the soul must deprive itself of all things but also because the path upon which it must walk is the darkness of faith and because the goal is "God, who, equally, is dark night to the soul in this life" (*Subida del Monte Carmelo* 1.2.1).

In turning to the role of the mystical element in the classic Reformation figures, one is immediately confronted with the question of Martin Luther's relation to mysticism. Older views saw only his opposition to mysticism, but both Catholic and Protestant scholars have become willing to admit the importance of mysticism to Luther. Still, one would be hard put to call Luther a mystic in the same way that Teresa was. It is more accurate to say that Luther adopted and transformed aspects of late medieval mysticism in the service of his *theologia crucis*.

Luther's opposition to speculative mysticism is as well known as his praise for John Tauler and for the *Theologia Deutsch*, a fourteenth-century mystical text he edited and published. What Luther found in these works was an experiential Christocentric mysticism, which he used to help present the union with Christ that all believers gain through baptism. "To believe in Christ is to put him on, to become one with him" (WA 2:535, 524). This union with Christ in faith is a mystery: "The Christ of whom faith takes hold is sitting in this darkness as God sat in the midst of the darkness on Sinai and in the temple" (WA 40.1:229, 215ff.). Luther's "faith-mysticism" produces no vision of God; we hear but do not see. In a sense, Luther rewrote the traditional mysticism of the *via negativa* in terms of his notion of the *via contrarii*, in which God becomes one with man in *Anfechtung*, or temptation, and in the suffering of the Crucifixion. Luther can describe the "happy exchange" by which the human hands over sin in return for Christ's righteousness in terms of the mystical marriage, but this embrace, which is also a rapture or ecstasy, never becomes our possession. If the formula *simul justus et peccator* aptly summarizes Luther's view of redemption, then, as Heiko Oberman puts it, "The very same reality. . . can be expressed in the language of mystical spirituality, and that means for Luther in the language of the personal experience of faith, by the formula, 'simul gemitus et raptus.' " It is fascinating in this connection to reflect on how Luther and Juan, so different, share a common emphasis on the centrality of the dark way of faith in the Christian life. Furthermore, Luther's stress on a mystical union established in baptism, on the priesthood of all believers, and on the vocation (*Berufung*) that each believer receives in the world can all be seen as a continuation of that tendency in medieval mysticism that sought to open the goal of perfection to believers in every walk of life.

One would be even less likely to think of John Calvin as a mystic than Luther, but the importance of the believer's union with Christ given by the Holy Spirit led Calvin to use the term *unio mystica* to characterize this central mystery (e.g., *Institutiones Christianae Religionis* 3.11.10) and, at times, to speak of a spiritual marriage between Christ and the believer (*Institutiones Christianes Religionis* 2.8.18). For Calvin, as for Luther, this union remains an experience of faith, and it is not developed in terms of contemplative prayer or even (unlike Luther) in the language of rapture or ecstasy. Calvin's stress on the doctrine of sanctification, however, led him to speak of two communions with Christ: the first was total in relation to justification; the second was partial and growing as the believer responds to God's action (*Institutiones Christiane Relgionis* 3.6.2). Thus, the teachings of both Luther and Calvin indicate that a mystical element played a role in classic Reformation theology. It was, therefore, no deformation of Reformation faith when Johann Arndt in 1606 issued his *Vier Bücher vom wahren Christentum* (True Christianity), in which the mystical aspects of Luther were brought together through the new emphasis Arndt gave to the role of loving contemplation in the journey of faith. More difficult to classify is Jacob Böhme (1575–1624). Böhme was a mystic; he also thought of himself as a follower of Luther, whatever his theosophical tendencies. Even so, Böhme's mysticism belongs properly to the seventeenth century.

The movements generally referred to as the radical Reformation display complex relations with the mystical element in Christianity. Not all the radicals should be thought of as mystics, but a significant number, especially among those often spoken of as the spiritualists, had ties to late medieval mysticism and constitute a definite chapter in the history of Christian mysticism. It was the radical reformers, far more than the shadowy Spanish *Alumbrados*, who were the real heirs of the tendency toward uncompromising insistence on interior religion found in some strands of late-medieval mysticism. On the theoretical side, these links centered on the immediate experience of God within as the essence of religion. This was evident in their adoption of a mystical anthropology emphasizing the presence of a divine spark within the soul (*Seelengrund* or *synteresis*), something that was anathema to Luther. Closely connected with this was the use of various themes from German mysticism, such as *Gottesgeburt*, or birth of the word in the soul, and the notion of *Gelassenheit*, the letting go of all creation so that God can work in the soul. The key text in the dissemination of these mystical themes to the radicals was the *Theologia Deutsch*, though Tauler and even at times Eckhart were also known. These themes center on the union of indistinction, but the radical Reformation mystics were more ethical than metaphysical in orientation and do not provide discussions of the nature of union with God that compare with those of their medieval predecessors or Spanish contemporaries.

On the practical side, the spiritualists did what the Free Spirits and *Alumbrados* had been accused of doing—that is, they took the priority of inner religion so seriously that they called into question the need for external religion at all. There were, of course, many variations in their attitudes toward the role of the visible church, the sacraments, and the Bible. Many distinguished between an inferior visible church and the true invisible church of the elite. Most saw the sacraments (especially the all-important sacrament of the Lord's Supper, so much debated in the sixteenth century) as a mere external sign of an interior communion and, therefore, one that could be dispensed with if need be. As far as the Bible was concerned, they were opposed to the "heretics of the letter," insisting, as Valentin Weigel put it, that "truth runs into no one by a pipe." The letter of the Bible meant nothing for salvation unless it had already been experienced within. The spiritualists were probably no more antinomian than their medieval predecessors (despite some unguarded formulas), but they were seen as no less dangerous both by Catholics and Protestants.

Some of these radicals managed to exist within the framework of their respective communions. Valentin Weigel (1533–1588) lived as a Lutheran pastor, but the posthumous publication of his works revealed him as a classic example of a spiritualist reformer. Most of the other figures encountered persecution that drove them outside the established communions. Hans Denck (c.1500–1527) was one of the earliest representatives; the confession he made before the Nuremberg authorities in 1525 was the *Magna Carta* of the movement in Protestant circles. The most important figures were Kaspar von Schwenckfeld (1489–1561) and Sebastian Franck (1499–1542), both Lutherans who ran afoul of Luther for understandable reasons. Franck's 1535 defense is a succinct and effective presentation of this particular sixteenth-century adaption of mysticism. Among the others affected by this tradition were Calvin's opponent Sébastien Castellion (1515–1563) and Hendrik Niclaes (d. about 1580), the founder of the Family of Love.

Sixteenth-century mysticism was more varied and complex than has ordinarily been allowed. Each of the three major channels of reform, however, sought to utilize mystical elements for its own purposes. In Roman Catholicism, mysticism was a plant nurtured by internal reform and was often suspect in the defensive atmosphere that grew after 1520. This did not prevent an extraordinary flowering of mysticism in Spain, paradoxically the most repressive country of all. Classical Protestant reformers, such as Luther (and to a lesser extent Calvin), made use of mystical themes but within the framework of a theology that dissolved and recombined the inherited mystical elements. Finally, the radical spiritual reformers absorbed important aspects of late medieval mysticism but within an ethical and individualistic framework that was distinctly postmedieval.

[*See also* John of the Cross; Ignatius Loyola; Saints, *article on* Sainthood; Sanctification; *and* Teresa of Ávila.]

BIBLIOGRAPHY

Certeau, Michel de. *The Mystic Fable.* Vol. 1: *The Sixteenth and Seventeenth Centuries.* Chicago and London, 1992. Difficult, idiosyncratic, brilliant; deals more with seventeenth century.

Cognet, Louis. *Post-Reformation Spirituality.* The Twentieth Century Encyclopedia of Catholicism, vol. 41. New York, 1959. A brief and lucid overview, with good treatments of Teresa of Ávila and Juan Álvarez.

Dicken, E. W. Trueman. *The Crucible of Love: A Study of the Mysticism of St. Teresa of Jesus and St. John of the Cross.* New York, 1963. Still a classic study, though it tends to homogenize its subjects.

Dupré, Louis, and Don Saliers, eds. *Christian Spirituality III: Post-Reformation and Modern.* World Spirituality, vol. 18. New York, 1989. Contains useful essays on Jesuit spirituality by John O'Malley and Spanish mysticism by Kieran Kavanaugh.

Evennett, H. Outram. *The Spirit of the Counter-Reformation.* Edited with a postscript by John Bossy. Cambridge, 1968. A succinct and beautifully written evaluation.

Haas, Alois M. "Luther und die Mystik." *Deutsche Vierteljahrsschrift für Literaturwissenschaft und Geistesgeschichte* 60 (1986), 177–207. Argues for the importance of mysticism in Luther.

Iserloh, Erwin. "Luther's Christ-Mysticism." In *Catholic Scholars Dialogue with Luther*, edited by Jared Wicks, pp. 37–58. Chicago, 1970. Classic paper on Luther as mystic.

Jones, Rufus M. *Spiritual Reformers in the Sixteenth and Seventeenth Centuries.* London, 1928. Somewhat dated but still helpful account by the great Quaker scholar of mysticism.

Longchamp, Max Huot de. "Les mystiques catholiques et la Bible." In *Le temps des Réformes et la Bible*, edited by Guy Bedouelle and Bernard Roussel, pp. 586–612. Bible de tous les temps, vol. 6. Paris, 1989. One of the few discussions of the role of the Bible in Catholic mysticism of the sixteenth century.

Maritain, Jacques. *Distinguish to Unite, or The Degrees of Knowledge.* 4th ed. New York, 1959. Chapters 6–9 contain a famous discussion of mystical knowing based on Juan Álvarez.

McGinn, Bernard. "Love, Knowledge, and *Unio mystica* in the Western Christian Tradition." In *Mystical Union and Monotheistic Faith: An Ecumenical Dialogue,* edited by Moshe Idel and Bernard McGinn, pp. 59–86. New York, 1989. Discusses the development of basic models of mystical union in Christianity through the sixteenth century.

Oberman, Heiko A. "*Simul Gemitus et Raptus*: Luther and Mysticism." In *The Reformation in Medieval Perspective,* edited with an introduction by Steven E. Ozment, pp. 217–251. Chicago, 1971. A seminal study.

Ozment, Steven E. *Mysticism and Dissent: Religious Ideology and Social Protest in the Sixteenth Century.* New Haven and London, 1973. Considers the relation between the radical reformers and medieval mysticism.

Peers, E. Allison. *Studies in the Spanish Mystics.* 2d ed., 2 vols. London and New York, 1951. Still the most complete English account of the full range of Spanish mysticism by its most celebrated English student.

Raitt, Jill, Bernard McGinn, and John Meyendorff, eds. *Christian Spirituality II. High Middle Ages and Reformation.* World Spirituality, vol. 17. New York, 1987. Important essays, not only on late medieval mysticism by Alois M. Haas, but especially on Luther by Marc Lienhard, Calvin by William J. Bouwsma, and the radical Reformation by Timothy George.

Senn, Frank C., ed. *Protestant Spiritual Traditions.* New York and Mahwah, N.J., 1986. Useful essays on Lutheran spirituality (Frank C. Senn), Reformed spirituality (Howard G. Hageman), and especially Anabaptist spirituality (Peter C. Erb).

Wicks, Jared. "Luther, Martin." In *Dictionnaire de spiritualité,* vol. 9, pp. 1206–1243. Paris, 1976. A summary of Luther's spirituality by a Catholic scholar.

Williams, Rowan. *Teresa of Avila.* London, 1991. A brief but penetrating account of Teresa as mystic.

BERNARD MCGINN

N

NADERE REFORMATIE. Dutch for "further Reformation," this term was used by the Calvinist preacher Jean Taffin, a close associate of William of Orange (1533–1584). In the Netherlands the *nadere reformatie* received its impetus to a large extent from refugees returning from the Palatinate, including pastors and professors educated there, and from the presence in the Netherlands of such English pietistic scholars and divines as William Ames (Amesius). The great debate over a new "code of discipline," which disrupted the Palatinate from 1568 to 1570 (reflected in Zacharius Ursinus's commentary on the Heidelberg Catechism), set the political framework for the *nadere reformatie*'s program. The strict disciplinists in Heidelberg had wanted to subject worldly magistrates to ecclesiastical censure, but Dutch magistrates favored an Erastian religious settlement. They resisted even such demands by the synods as the enforcing of traditional sumptuary laws and allowing the church a share in control over marriage law. Repeated complaints from the synods about desecration of the sabbath, noisy guard processions during church service, processions around cemeteries, and excessive drinking during the meals of guilds and civic guard corporations indicate that city fathers did not enforce the laws promoting and maintaining public order.

Although its ideals may be traced back to the late sixteenth century, the *nadere reformatie* within the Reformed church of the Netherlands is primarily a seventeenth-century movement that sought a "deepening and broadening" of the theological Reformation through a further reforming of the moral life of the community (*gemeente*). The movement was enhanced by the Reformed insistence on doctrinal and moral discipline as a major task of the church, organized in consistories.

Scholarship in the Netherlands describes the *nadere reformatie* as a turning "against the general poor conditions prevailing in the Reformed Church. . . to achieve a radical and complete sanctification of all facets of life." This was to be achieved through an "interiorisation of the fruits of God's Word," the results of which would be "a pious lifestyle and a theocratic concept of all social [and political] relationships." These relationships take the form of three types of worship—in the family, the parish (*gemeente*), and the church (the community of saints) as a whole, which ideally should coincide with the state. The objectives could best be achieved on the basis of the Reformed "Belgic" Confession and the Heidelberg Catechism, the official teaching handbook from the establishment of the Dutch Reformed church.

Family worship (*huisdevotie*, or "small church worship") and private devotion were the hallmarks of the movement. They included prayer, meditation, examination of one's conscience, the reading of Bible and devotional tracts, and the singing of hymns and spiritual songs. Lay and clerical writers provided many works to assist in these activities. Magistrates, as well as many pastors, were suspicious of this "privatization" of religion.

Representative pietistic works are Willem Teellinck's *Sleutel der Devotie* (Key to Devotion; 1624) and Petrus Wittewrongel's *Oeconomia Christiana* (The Christian Householder; 1661), as well as many translations of Puritan writings. In the end the *nadere reformatie* laid the groundwork for eighteenth-century Pictism.

The Reformed church was the established church but remained in most places only a minority church. After the Synod of Dordrecht (1618) no regular national synods were held, and thus the Reformed church had no effective means of pressing its objectives in the political arena. The particularism of Dutch constitutional arrangements—in effect, a pyramidal structure of confederations of local, regional, and provincial jurisdictions—made the establishment of one national church with a uniform code of doctrinal and moral discipline impractical if not impossible. Perhaps the most significant check on the *nadere reformatie* was the experience of the early years of the armed struggle against Spain (1568–1609), which was understood by many as a struggle for liberty of conscience against tyranny. This tyranny they remembered as having been supported by the Spanish Inquisition. It was symbolized by the Council of Troubles (organized by Fernando Álvarez de Toldeo, duke of Alba, and nicknamed the Council of Blood), which equated such deviant behavior as adherence to ideas of ecclesiastical and religious reform with political subversion. In the 1580s a delegate from the States of Holland, speaking to a consistorial examination of a wayward pastor, put the matter in a nutshell: "Gentlemen, I have read the history of the inquisition, but never saw I so lively a picture of it as here." Ecclesiastical discipline as practiced by the consistories was seen by some as reintroducing papal monarchy in another guise.

Because of these limitations the *nadere reformatie* focused on improving the private and family piety of the members of the Reformed church. In some cases local consistories developed catalogs of sins that are much more detailed (twenty six in one case) than the categories used by modern researchers in their studies of the application of church discipline. Here, too, there were built-in limitations, since censured members sometimes joined a Mennonite or Lutheran congregation or even "lapsed" and went back to the Roman Catholic church. Consistory records also show that for some sinners admonition in their home, in consistory, or in church before the parishioners—each of these successive steps was repeated up to three times—was not effective. The ultimate sanction—exclusion from the Lord's Supper—was meted out only to a few, some of whom remained obdurate.

There were also different shades of opinion on discipline within the church. Many parishioners apparently abstained voluntarily from the Lord's Supper so as to avoid confessing their sins in consistory the week before the Sunday celebration. Other churchgoers were known as *liefhebbers*, or those who liked to attend but who did not become communicating members, partly because they did not want to subject themselves to the discipline required of members who participated in the Lord's Supper. At the other end of the spectrum were not only proponents of the *nadere reformatie*, but also the followers of Jean de Labadie (1610–1674), who left the Reformed church because of what they saw as its shortcomings in achieving the Christian ideal.

BIBLIOGRAPHY

Duke, Alistair C. "Building Heaven in Hell's Despite." In *Britain and the Netherlands*, edited by Alistair C. Duke and C. A. Tamse, pp. 45–75. The Hague, 1981. A useful presentation of the problems facing the reform-minded.

Graafland, C. "De Nadere Reformatie en haar culturele context." In *Met het woord in de tijd*, edited by L. Westland, pp. 117–138. The Hague, 1985. Provides the best definition of the movement and its objectives.

Groenendijk, L. F. "Opdat de mensche Gods volmaeckt zy" (That God's People May Be Perfect). *Pedagogische Verhandelingen* 9 (1986), 16–54. An insightful discussion of seventeenth-century pietistic literature of the *nadere reformatie*; bibliography in notes.

Lieburg, Fred A. van. "From Pure Church to Pious Culture: The Further Reformation in the Seventeenth-Century Dutch Republic." In *Later Calvinism: International Perspectives*, edited by Fred W. Graham, pp. 409–430. Kirksville, Mo., 1994. Useful analysis in English of recent attempts by Dutch scholars to define the role of the movement. Concentrates on the years after the Synod of Dordrecht (1618).

Spiertz, M. G. "Die Ausübung der Zucht in der IJsselstadt Deventer, 1592–1619." *Rheinische Vierteljahrsblätter* 29 (1985), 139–172. Uses modern research categories of "sin" for the study of moral discipline. Compares a Dutch case with practices in France and the Palatinate.

Visser, Derk. "Establishing the Reformed Church: Church and State in the Low Countries (1572–1620)." In *Later Calvinism: International Perspectives*, edited by Fred W. Graham, pp. 389–497. Kirksville, Mo., 1994. Describes the years after the establishment of the Reformed church including the first provincial synods after the Council of Dordrecht, which demonstrated the need for further reform.

DERK VISSER

NANTES, EDICT OF. In full the "Edict of the King and Declaration on the Preceding Edicts of Pacification," this document was signed by King Henry IV of France at Nantes on 13 April 1598. It provided a temporary measure of religious freedom for French Protestants. What is commonly termed the Edict of Nantes actually comprises four texts: the warrant of 3 April 1598, whereby the king granted an annual subsidy to the Reformed ministers; the edict proper, consisting of ninety-two articles and declared to be "perpetual and irrevocable"; the fifty-six "secret" articles complementary to the edict; and the warrant of 30 April, comprising twenty-three articles (the "second secret articles") securing a defensive military organization for the Protestants. The edict of ninety-two articles was the only one of these texts to be registered by the parlements. Having ordered a general amnesty with respect to past disputes (articles 1–2), the king declared his intention to restore civil and religious peace with two main aims in view: first, to reestablish the Catholic, apostolic, and Roman church (articles 3–5), to reinstate worship wherever it had been interrupted, and to cause the churches, houses, and goods formerly belonging to the clergy to be restored; and second, to allow the exercise of the "so-called Reformed Religion" under a strict ruling (articles 6–16; secret articles 1–3).

Although the principle of freedom of conscience was confirmed in accordance with the preceding edicts of pacification (1563, 1570, 1576, and 1577), the exercise of Reformed worship was allowed only on the fiefs of lords having high justice, that is to say, the authority over capital crimes (as well as on the estates of other lords, on the condition that their domiciles were not situated in a town or village where high justice was administered by a Catholic lord); in the places and towns where worship had been authorized by the Edict of 1577 or where it had been publicly and continuously held from 1596 to the month of August 1597; and in two places or towns in each "bailiwick, seneschalsy, or government." Conversely, Reformed worship was forbidden in all places of residence of the royal court, in places within five leagues of the city of Paris, and in the other towns mentioned in the conventions stipulated by the dukes of Guise and of Mayenne. The Protestants were assigned special cemeteries (articles 28–29). As for marriages, the edict defined the legitimate degrees of consanguinity for Protestant couples and ensured that their children should be protected (article 23, secret articles 40–41). The Protestants were entitled to have schools and to found universities (secret article 37). The edict allowed (secret article 34) Protestants to maintain their ecclesiastical organization (religious assemblies, consistories, colloquies, and provincial and national synods) in all the places where their form of worship was allowed.

The Protestants had access to all offices and public functions (article 27; secret article 10). The warrant of 3 April guaranteed the ministers an annual subsidy of 45,000 écus. Concerning the administration of justice, the edict reestablished (articles 30–57) the "Chambres de l'Édit" (in Paris, Rouen, and Rennes) and the "Chambres mi-parties," in which the functions of president and counsel were equally divided between Protestants and Catholics. The edict ordered the dissolution of political assemblies (article 82), while provisionally maintaining (second secret article 22) the assemblies in progress (in Châtellerault, subsequently Saumur) until the verification of the edict by the Parlement of Paris. The Protestants held in pledge hostage cities (warrant of 30 April), which "were to remain in their care under the authority and obedience" of the king for the duration of eight years. The localities given in pledge (slightly over 150) comprised towns and castles occupied by the Protestants from August 1597 by their own garrisons; the free royal cities occupied by the Protestants from 30 April 1598; and localities in the Dauphiné. The king granted the Protestants the sum of 180,000 écus for the maintenance of their garrisons.

Principal Causes and Actors. The Edict of Nantes marked an important truce after thirty-six years of religious and civil wars. It was the only means whereby Henry IV could prevent the renewal of hostilities and ensure durable peace. Its promulgation was necessary because the kingdom had become ungovernable owing to constant divisions and strife. The king could not exercise his sovereignty without bringing his subjects back under his obedience. In these circumstances, reasons of state yielded convenient solutions to problems that had intrinsically to do with civil liberty and religious conscience.

The Edict of Nantes was the result of protracted negotiations between the royal commissioners (e.g., Gaspard de Schomberg, Emery de Vic, Soffrey de Calignon, Pierre Forget, and Jacques-Auguste de Thou) and the representatives of the Protestant political assemblies (notably Jean de Cazes, Jean Courtaumer, Pierre Vulson, and Philippe Duplessis-Mornay). Henry IV had to proceed carefully with his adversaries, who included some of his former co-religionists (Henri of La Tour-d'Auvergne, duke of Bouillon, and Henri, duke of La Trémouille), as well as the leaders of the Catholic League (Charles of Lorraine, duke of Mayenne, Philippe-Emmanuel of Lorraine, duke of Mercoeur, and Jean-Louis of Nogaret, duke of Épernon, among others). At the same time, foreign interventions were not to be disregarded: while the Protestants could muster political support among the Protestant powers (England and the United Provinces), the league could avail itself of the aid of the Catholic states (Spain and the Holy See). After his victorious siege of Amiens (25 September 1597), which he recaptured from the Spaniards without the help of the insubordinate Protestant commanders, the king seized the opportunity to impose religious concord within the kingdom via the edict and to conclude to his advantage the peace with foreign powers (at Vervins on 2 May 1598).

These historical circumstances explain why the Edict of Nantes was more a royal ordinance than a treaty involving reciprocal, contractual agreements. Yet the texts of Nantes remain a compromise between contradictory exigencies. Indeed, the edict was far from representing the unanimous will of the preponderant forces. Both parties requested modifications of the "final text": the Protestants because they were not satisfied with the rights obtained, and the members of the parlements and the clergy because they were worried by the violations of the fundamental laws of the kingdom (on account of religious tolerance). Torn between the restrictions required by the latter and the extensions claimed by the former, Henry IV had to struggle for another year in order to obtain the registration and enactment of the edict by the Parlement of Paris (25 February 1599).

Relevance for the Reformation in France. Although it was in line with the preceding edicts of pacification, which had often been infringed as soon as they had been promulgated, the Edict of Nantes distinguished itself by its longevity—eighty-seven years. The Wars of Religion were episodically rekindled (1621–1622, 1625–1626, and 1627–1629), but the edict was nevertheless confirmed by repeated declarations of Louis XIII and Louis XIV in 1610, 1615, 1643, and 1652. Though its "rigorous" application from the 1660s onward had gradually reduced its benefits for the Reformed, its revocation was not proclaimed until 1685. These eighty-seven years were thus characterized by comparative internal peace, which allowed considerable development in the economic, social, and religious sectors of the kingdom.

In the history of French Protestantism, the edict was, in effect, the first recognition, not so much of religious tolerance (which was only limited and temporary), but of the right of Protestantism to exist without being considered legally as a heresy. Moreover, the civil rights of the Protestants were, for the first time in France, proclaimed to be equal to the rights of those of the king's subjects who shared his creed. Thus, the Edict of Nantes has, for the Reformation as well as for modern France, an importance that can hardly be overemphasized.

Historical Question. The tendency since the eighteenth century to celebrate the Edict of Nantes as a precursory landmark of the Enlightenment—and, consequently, to perceive its revocation as dictated by anachronistic obscurantism—has caused the perspective of historians to shift and to misrepresent both the circumstances that determined its adoption and the real meaning of its content. In this respect a historical question is raised by the duration of the edict, which in its preamble is defined as "perpetual and irrevocable."

This feature has been variously commented on by historians, Protestant as well as Catholic, and triggered a lengthy debate on its internal interpretation and on the legitimacy of its revocation. As historians focused their attention on the problems with religious tolerance, they were led to highlight the "tolerance" element of what indeed became commonly known as the Edict of Tolerance. In so doing, however, they neglected the main aspect of the legislators' intent, which was to secure the preconditions of a provisional regime of tolerance so as to obtain in the long run, not the coexistence of two religions, but religious and civil "concord"—that is, the confessional reunification of all the subjects under the religion of the king and his predecessors. Therefore, in order to place the Edict of Nantes in its proper historical perspective, one has to take as a starting point its interpretation by the lawyers of the time, who were Henry IV's closest collaborators: they defined the legislative texts of the edict as the "Law of Concord" or "Law of Union and Pacification."

[*See also* Calvinism; Henry IV of France; Huguenots; La Rochelle, Synod of; *and* Wars of Religion.]

BIBLIOGRAPHY

Primary Sources

Anquez, L. *Histoire des assemblées politiques des réformés de France, 1573–1622.* Reprint, Geneva, 1970. The first version of the four texts appears on pp. 456–502.

Benoist, E. *Histoire de l'Édit de Nantes et de sa révocation.* 5 vols. Delft, Netherlands, 1693–1695. The edict appears in vol. 1, pp. 62–94. See also vol. 1, pp. 526–562, for a partial English translation.

Fontanon, A., ed. "Edict du Roy et Declaration sur les precedens Edicts de Pacification: Publié à Paris, 1599." In *Les edicts et ordonnances des rois de France,* vol. 4, pp. 361ff. Paris, 1611. The "official" version of the edict.

Golden, Richard M., ed. *The Huguenot Connection: The Edict of Nantes; Its Revocation, and Early French Migration to South Carolina.* Dordrecht, Netherlands, 1988. A recent English translation of the edict appears on pp. 86–134.

Haag, Émile, and Eugène Haag. *La France protestante, ou vies des protestants français.* Reprint, Geneva, 1966. See vol. 10, pp. 225–257.

Isambert, F., et al., eds. *Recueil général des anciennes lois françaises. . . .* Reprint, Ridgewood, N.J., 1964–1966. See vol. 15, pp. 170–210.

Mousnier, R. *L'assassinat d'Henri IV, 14 mai 1610.* Reprint, Paris, 1992. See pp. 294–334. Also available in English, *The Assassination of Henry IV,* translated by Joan Spencer, New York, 1973.

Secondary Sources

Beloy, Pierre de. *Conference des edicts de pacification.* Paris, 1600. The best legal, canonical, theological, and historical comment; the author (c.1540–1613) was a Catholic royalist who, after being persecuted and imprisoned by the Ligueurs, was appointed by Henry IV as advocate general of the king in the Parlement of Tolouse.

Faurey, J. *Henri IV et l'Édit de Nantes.* Bordeaux, 1903.

Pagès, G. "Les paix de religion et l'Édit de Nantes." *Revue d'histoire moderne* 11 (1936), 394–413.

Sutherland, N. M. "The Crown, the Huguenots, and the Edict of Nantes." In *The Huguenot Connection: The Edict of Nantes, Its Revocation, and Early French Migration to South Carolina,* edited by Richard M. Golden, pp. 28–48. Dordrecht, Netherlands, 1988.

Turchetti, Mario. "Une question mal posée: La qualification de 'perpétuel et irrévocable' dans l'édit de Nantes." *Bulletin de la Société de l'Histoire du Protestantisme Français* 139 (1993), 41–78.

MARIO TURCHETTI

NAOGEORGUS, Thomas.

See Kirchmeyer, Thomas.

NAPLES.

Between the years 1504 and 1713, a series of viceroys governed the city and kingdom of Naples in the name of the kings of Spain. Backed by the well-disciplined and battle-hardened Spanish infantry, they found themselves in a stronger position than most of the kings of Naples who had preceded them. Most historians today agree that the viceroys conscientiously strove to provide good government according to the standards of the age. They kept the peace, inaugurated numerous building projects, provided adequate supplies of food, and sought diligently to solve the real problems that they faced. Most notably, they brought the independent Neapolitan barons, who for centuries had resisted royal control while pursuing their own ambitions, under effective central supervision. They certainly faced resistance to their rule: they put down serious rebellions in 1547, 1585, and 1647. For the most part, however, they presided over a stable and prosperous realm.

Although the viceroys recognized forums in which Neapolitans could express their desires and grievances, their policies naturally reflected the interests of the Spanish empire. During an age of considerable religious experimentation and theological turmoil, they sought to ensure that Neapolitan thought and culture conformed to the Spanish understanding of Christian orthodoxy. To this end, they exercised careful supervision over cultural institutions in Naples. They closely watched the University of Naples, for example, controlling its budget, faculty, students, and curriculum. By the middle of the sixteenth century, the university provided solid instruction in practical disciplines like law and medicine, but it was not a site of independent thought: students and faculty rarely posed political or religious challenges, but rather respected the conservative and orthodox ideals of the Spanish regime. The viceroys also kept a sharp eye on the humanist academy of Naples, which since 1447 had provided a forum for men of letters and learning. In 1542, however, the academy's organizer fell under suspicion of heresy, and Pedro de Toledo (viceroy from 1532 to 1553) took the opportunity to close its doors. The viceroys even attempted twice (in 1510 and 1547) to introduce the Spanish Inquisition into the viceroyalty of Naples. On both occasions Neapolitans mounted intense and concerted popular resistance, based on the fear that the Inquisition would become a political tool, so that the viceroys abandoned their project. Nevertheless, the viceroys were generally quite effective in promoting Roman Catholic orthodoxy and discouraging alternatives.

Under these circumstances, it is not surprising that the Roman church flourished in Naples and that Neapolitans made important contributions to its tradition. The Neapolitan nobility—particularly the Carafa, Acquaviva, and Caracciolo families—provided a series of cardinals for the Roman church. One of them, Gian Pietro Carafa, even became Pope Paul IV (1555–1559). Other Neapolitans who made especially important contributions to the cause of the Roman church included Tommaso de Vio, better known as Cardinal Cajetan (1469–1534), general of the Dominican order and early interrogator of Martin Luther; Girolamo Seripando (1493–1563), general of the Augustinian order and a leading figure at the Council of Trent; Guglielmo Sirleto (1514–1585), who defended the Vulgate against the criticism of humanist New Testament scholars; and Cesare Baronio (1538–1607), who prepared the *Annales ecclesiastici* (Ecclesiastical Annals), an exhaustive orthodox interpretation of the Roman Catholic church, as a response to the Lutheran view presented in the *Magdeburg Centuries* (*Ecclesiastica historia secundum centurias*).

By no means, however, did all Neapolitans cast their lots with the Roman church. Indeed, the Neapolitan realm generated a small collection of unorthodox thinkers of various types, including several of the genuine free spirits of the sixteenth century. Bernardino Telesio (1509–1588) outlined an empirical philosophy of the natural world that rejected the authority of Aristotle. Tommaso Campenella (1568–1639) was another empiricist and philosopher of nature. His best-known work, *Civitas solis* (City of the Sun), sketched a utopian realm blessed by rational government and religion. His openness to new ideas brought suspicion upon him, however, and the Spanish government of Naples imprisoned him for some twenty-seven years as a conspirator against the regime. Most notorious of all the Neapolitan thinkers was Giordano Bruno (1548–1600), whose speculations about the infinity of the universe earned him a trial and conviction for heresy, followed by a fiery death at the stake. Although each of these men found a following in other lands, none of them attracted many disciples within the Neapolitan realm, much less a school of like-minded thinkers.

The city of Naples attracted a fair number of religious dissidents, but only in one case did a circle of reformers become established there over a long term. During the late 1530s, Bernardino Ochino of Siena (1487–1564) preached throughout the Italian peninsula. In Naples his sermons had such powerful effect that the city's laboring classes openly discussed points of Pauline theology in the streets. Meanwhile, between 1535 and 1541, the Spanish reformer Juan de Valdés (1500/10–1541) lived in Naples and hosted weekly prayers and discussions at his luxurious villa. A native of Toledo, Valdés had fled Spain because his *Dialogo de doctrina cristiana* (Dialogue on Christian Doctrine) had raised the suspicions of the Inquisition. He went first to Rome, where he served as a papal secretary, then to Naples, where he found a post in the viceregal administration. In his published works he taught a simple, ethical piety, so that as a reformer he resembled Erasmus more than Luther. He did not inaugurate a genuine reforming movement, but his pious influence touched many of the cultural and religious leaders of his age, including Bernardino Ochino, Peter Martyr Vermigli, Pier Paolo Vergerio, and Vittoria Colonna.

Under the watchful eyes of the Spanish viceroys, however, it was impossible for a vigorous reforming movement to emerge in the Neapolitan realm, which remained well within the fold of the Roman Catholic church. Only in the late seventeenth and eighteenth century did a genuine cultural revival take place in Naples. The inspiration came not from humanism or the Reformation, but rather either entered from abroad, in the form of the Cartesian rationalism that helped Pietro Giannone to develop his anticlerical vision of history, or else arose *sui generis,* in the form of the remarkable reflections that helped Giambattista Vico to construct his new science of society.

[*See also* Italy *and* Paul IV.]

BIBLIOGRAPHY

Bacco, Enrico. *Naples: An Early Guide.* Edited and translated by Eileen Gardiner. New York, 1991. Presents a description of the city of Naples at mid-seventeenth century.

Bentley, Jerry H. *Politics and Culture in Renaissance Naples.* Princeton, 1987. Analyzes the cultural history of Naples in its political context.

Calabria, Antonio, and John A. Marino, eds. *Good Government in Spanish Naples.* New York, 1990. Translations of six important articles on the political, social, economic, and cultural history of Spanish Naples.

Cantimori, Delio. *Italian Heretics of the Sixteenth Century.* 3d ed. Translated by Hilary A. Smith. Cambridge, Mass., 1979. Thoughtful survey of Italian reformers, including Neapolitans and others who lived in Naples.

Cochrane, Eric. "Southern Italy in the Age of the Spanish Viceroys: Some Recent Titles." *Journal of Modern History* 58 (1986), 194–217. Review of recent scholarship dealing with political, social, economic, and cultural themes.

Croce, Benedetto. *History of the Kingdom of Naples.* Translated by F. Frenaye. Chicago, 1970. Classic interpretation by one of the great historians of the twentieth century.

JERRY H. BENTLEY

NAS, Johannes (1534–1590), Catholic convert, Franciscan preacher, and polemicist of the Counter-Reformation period. Nas rose through the ranks of his order to become auxiliary bishop of Brixen (1580). He was an effective and relentless defender of Catholicism whose satirical writings, especially the six-volume *Centuria* (1565–1569), addressed doctrinal errors of Luther and his supporters and attempted to capitalize on dissension among the reformers after Luther's death.

Nas was widely respected as a popular preacher, a leader of the Catholic polemical offensive against the reformers, and one who devoted much time to the preparation of published sermons (Corpus Christi cycle, 1572) that could serve as manuals for inexperienced preachers or as inspirational texts for laypersons. His polemical tracts and sermons reveal a broad, eclectic reading taste, scholarly concern for detail, a strong sense of history and tradition, and a philological interest in words and ideas. His interest in languages (Hebrew, Greek, Latin) and in the process of translation was reflected in his critique of Luther's Bible translation (*Centuria*, vol. 3) and in the numerous puns and manipulations of words and phrases that characterize his polemic.

In addition to his polemical writings against Johannes Aurifaber, Johannes Brenz, Johann Friedrich Cölestin, Andreas Osiander, Cyriakus Spangenberg, Michael Stifel, and others, Nas maintained an active involvement in the affairs of the Franciscan order in Bavaria (guardian, 1569), subsequently overseeing the province of Strasbourg, Austria, and Bohemia (commissioner, 1562). As successor to Peter Canisius as court preacher to Archduke Ferdinand (1572), Nas was a central force in the effort to revitalize the Catholic faith in southeast Germany and the Tirol and saw his role as a fulfillment of the concepts and principles that had emerged from the Council of Trent (1547).

BIBLIOGRAPHY

Goedeke, Karl. *Grundriss zur Geschichte der deutschen Dichtung* (1896). Reprint, Nendeln, 1979. Earliest objective assessment of Nas's literary importance and complete listing of works known at the time are presented in vol. 2, pp. 486–491.

Newald, Richard. *Geschichte der deutschen Literatur vom Humanismus bis zum Tod Goethes.* In *Annalen der deutschen Literatur*, edited by Heinz Otto Burger, 2d rev. ed., pp. 330–335. Stuttgart, 1971. Comprehensive assessment of Nas's literary contributions and place in context of German literature of sixteenth century.

Schöpf, J. B. *Johannes Nas, Franziskaner und Weihbischof von Brixen.* X. Programm des K. K. Gymnasiums zu Bozen. Bozen, 1860. Comprehensive biography of Nas with brief analyses of his works and his relationships to contemporaries. Complete list of published works.

Walker, Richard Ernest. *The Corpus Christi Sermons of Johannes Nas, 1534–1590.* Göppingen, 1988. Only modern collection of Nas's sermons; comprehensive commentary on people, events, controversial concepts, and texts alluded to or cited in the sermons.

RICHARD ERNEST WALKER

NASSAU, Maurits van (Eng., Maurice; 1567–1625), prince of Orange, Dutch general, and politician. Born on 13 November at Dillenburg castle in Germany, he was the son of William of Orange and his second wife, Ann of Saxony. From 1572 onward—after his father returned to the Netherlands to lead the revolt and while his mother was imprisoned for infidelity—he was brought up at Dillenburg by his Lutheran (later rigidly Calvinist) uncle John VI of Nassau. In 1577 he was sent for by his father in the Netherlands. There in 1583 he matriculated at Leiden University, where his lasting interest in mathematics was awakened.

Maurits broke off his studies when his father was murdered in 1584. The following year he was, as his father's successor, created stadtholder of Holland and Zeeland, as well as captain- and admiral-general over the army and the navy of both these provinces. In 1590 he was also invested with these dignities in the provinces of Utrecht, Gelderland, and Overijssel.

In the 1580s, Maurits—in cooperation with his cousin William Louis, the stadtholder of Friesland and Groningen—reformed the army of the United Provinces; between 1590 and 1604 this army conquered forty-three towns and fifty-five strongholds in order to fortify the borders of the Dutch Republic. As a greatly respected commander in chief, Maurits often clashed with the *de facto* political leader of the republic, Johan van Oldenbarnevelt, grand pensionary of Holland. Above all, they disagreed about the desirability of a peace or truce with Brussels and Madrid. When a twelve-year truce was concluded in 1609, it was over Maurits's opposition.

As Maurits had feared, conflicts within the republic broke out once the war was suspended. In particular, the debate over predestination between the followers of Franciscus Gomarus and Jacobus Arminius now took on political overtones. From 1609 Gomarus and the Contra-Remonstrants had behind-the-scenes support from Maurits, while Arminius's supporters, the Remonstrants, were in close contact with Oldenbarnevelt.

By 1617 religious and political conflicts had become so intermingled that a moderate solution was no longer possible. Maurits now sided openly with the Contra-Remonstrants and forced a solution. Choosing the right moment and using the Dutch army as a weapon, he replaced many town regents with compliant ones and arrested Oldenbarnevelt and his closest collaborators. During a political trial the pensionary was sentenced to death. The religious problems were solved by the national Synod of Dordrecht (1618–1619), which condemned the views of the Remonstrants.

When the war with Brussels and Madrid resumed in 1621, Maurits stood alone at the center of power but did not prove an inspiring leader. A now docile States-General acquiesced in his preference for a defensive strategy, but successes were few. He died on 23 April 1625, just before the city of Breda, his first capture (1590), was conquered by Spanish troops. Having never married, he left only illegitimate descendants.

In the absence of a modern biography, most of Maurits's religious ideas must be inferred from his actions. When in 1590 he conquered by surprise the Roman Catholic city of Breda in the duchy of Brabant, he granted local Calvinists a privileged position, but since there were far too few capable Calvinists to fill all posts in the magistracy, Maurits also appointed moderate Protestants and some Roman Catholics, even hard-liners. He also conceded the parish priest, a moderate man, a certain liberty of speech and action. His aim seems to have been to avoid trouble in the city.

During the Twelve-Year Truce, he attended services until 1617 in the court chapel in The Hague, his residence, where Johannes Wtenbogaert, the well-known Remonstrant leader, was the minister. Maurits thought it possible to keep both Remonstrants and Contra-Remonstrants within one church if both were allowed to have their own services, but it was the Contra-Remonstrants who rejected this solution. Why then did he join their ranks? Perhaps his Calvinist upbringing at Dillenburg played a part as well as the influence of his nephew, William Louis, and the idea that the Remonstrants were far too tolerant toward the Roman Catholics, who were considered to be supporters of their co-religionists in the southern Netherlands and Spain. In both cases Maurits was primarily concerned with political and military considerations. Nowhere can any interest in dogmatics or a real piety be discovered. His public statements seem to express a civic religion rather than a deep personal conviction.

BIBLIOGRAPHY

Deursen, A. Th. van. *Honni soit qui mal y pense? De Republiek tussen de mogendheden, 1610–1612.* Amsterdam, 1965.

———. "Maurits." In *Vaderlands Verleden in Veelvoud,* edited by G. A. M. Beekelaar, et al., vol. 1, pp. 133–159. The Hague, 1980.

———. *Bavianen en slijkgeuzen: Kerk en kerkvolk ten tijde van Maurits en Oldenbarnevelt.* Reprint, Franeker, Netherlands, 1991.

Hallema, A. *Prins Maurits. 1567–1625: Veertig jaar strijder voor 's lands vrijheid.* Assen, 1949.

Kemp, C. M. van der. *Maurits van Nassau, prins van Oranje.* 4 vols. Rotterdam, 1843.

Scherft, P. *Het sterfhuis van Willem van Oranje.* Leiden, 1966.

S. GROENVELD

NASSAU, Willem van. *See* William of Orange.

NAUMBURG, DECLARATION OF. Negotiated and signed by German Lutheran princes who met at Naumburg (Thuringia) from 20 January to 8 February 1561, the Declaration of Naumburg was a product of the theological conflicts that agitated German Lutheranism during the second half of the sixteenth century. At Naumburg the princes were attempting to build consensus in their territories through resubscription to the Augsburg Confession. The princes were concerned about the continuing disagreements over theology, as well as Roman Catholic accusations that the Lutherans had abandoned the Augsburg Confession and were therefore no longer entitled to protection under the Peace of Augsburg (1555).

The main issue was the relative status of the two versions of the confession, the *invariata* and the 1540 *variata* (which contained changes from the *editio princeps,* particularly in the article on the Lord's Supper). The Naumburg declaration affirmed the Apology to the Augsburg Confession (1531) and both versions of the confession itself. The preface, however, approved the *variata* in a manner that gave it priority over the *invariata.* The Gnesio-Lutheran princes, led by John Frederick of Saxony, objected to this preface and refused to sign. Eventually, on the advice of their respective theologians, almost all of the original twenty-six princes who signed the Declaration of Naumburg withdrew their signatures.

The Declaration of Naumburg itself failed to establish a distinctively Lutheran basis for confessional unity among German Lutherans. Still, the Naumburg meeting helped German Lutheranism to affirm the 1530–1531 edition of the Augsburg Confession (the *invariata*) as its primary confessional symbol and eventually to accept the Formula of Concord. This is also evident in the emphasis at Naumburg on confessional unity, the prominent role played by the princes, and the expressed need for a "new" confessional writing (which ultimately led to the formula).

[*See also* Augsburg Confession.]

BIBLIOGRAPHY

Bente, F. *Historical Introductions to the Book of Concord.* Reprint, Saint Louis, 1965. Interprets the Declaration of Naumburg in the context of the emerging Lutheran confessional consensus; see especially pp. 241–242.

Richard, James W. *The Confessional History of the Lutheran Church.* Philadelphia, 1909. Pays close attention to primary sources and includes translations of materials unavailable elsewhere; see especially pp. 290–307.

Schmauk, Theodore E., and C. Theodore Benze. *The Confessional Principle and the Confessions of the Lutheran Church.* Reprint, Saint Louis, 1981. Draws on some of the best nineteenth-century confessional scholarship.

Tappert, Theodore, ed. *The Book of Concord.* Philadelphia, 1959. See espcially pp. 3–16. The 1580 preface makes explicit reference to the princes' meeting at Naumburg.(See Tappert's extended and generally accurate footnote on p. 5.)

WILLIAM R. RUSSELL

NAVARRE, HOUSE OF. While there never was a "House of Navarre," the ambitions that swirled around the little kingdom at the western end of the Pyrenees provide a focus for the coalescence of several great families that had an important influence upon the French civil and religious wars of the sixteenth century. Navarre was a product of the Moorish conquest of Spain and the subsequent Christian *Reconquista;* Basque magnates achieved independence in the ninth-century breakup of the Carolingian empire and announced a royal title. The greater part of the principality comprised Haute Navarre on the southern flank of the mountains, with Basse Navarre a fragment on the northern side. In addition to local products and a transit trade between the Bay of Biscay and the Mediterranean, the principality was important for the only pass through the western Pyrenees (Roncevaux); but perhaps most of all it was desired for its royal crown—disputed among Basques, the kings of Aragon in Spain, and the French royal line.

One of the most important families to emerge from these tumultuous politics was the House of Foix, dating from the early eleventh century. The counts of Foix figured prominently in the Crusades, in the Albigensian Wars, and then in the Hundred Years' War, adding one title after another to their holdings, including the duchy of Béarn. In 1483 a daughter and heiress of the house, Catherine, received the royal title of Navarre by inheritance, and by marriage she joined this illustrious legacy to another important family of southwestern France, traced from tenth-century origins in Gascony, the Albrets, who had collected lordships through marriage and conquest. The alliance of Foix and Albret, reinforcing the royal title of Navarre, might have signaled the emergence of an important new dynasty; but Navarre was a tiny kingdom caught between powerful and expansionist neighbors.

From the mid-1490s the crowns of France and Spain usually were at war with one another, and Navarre was an early victim. In 1512 Ferdinand of Aragon occupied Haute Navarre, and in 1515 he declared it annexed to the Crown of Castile. Catherine of Foix and Jean d'Albret were forced to withdraw into Basse Navarre (and the associated Béarnaise, Albret, and Foix territories); but they continued to claim the royal title and styled their son Henry II king of Navarre. Ferdinand seems never to have sought recognition *de jure*, perhaps perceiving the potential value of the Navarese title as a bargaining chip—which his successors exploited adroitly.

All three of the principal figures died soon after this coup—Ferdinand and Jean in 1516 and Catherine in 1517. Henry II of Navarre was probably greatly encouraged in 1527 when he was allowed to marry the widowed sister of King Francis I of France, Marguerite d'Angoulême, but he was to be disillusioned. With a royal title he was appropriate for a princess of France, and perhaps the king had some notion of strengthening the French presence in the Pyrenees; but Francis I never showed a serious interest in taking up the quarrel over Haute Navarre. In 1528 Marguerite gave birth to a girl, Jeanne, who was to be a highly significant figure of the mid-sixteenth century. Marguerite also established a reputation as a literary figure and a patroness of humanist scholars. Francis I, himself devoted to arts and letters, had sustained a rather indulgent patronage; but in the mid-1530s, when the disputes became embittered and appeared to challenge all authority, he became much more conservative and initiated some persecutions. Marguerite then provided refuge in the southwest for many controversial literary and religious critics. (Given the communications of the period, once away from Paris a person could effectively disappear.) In 1548, a year before her death, Marguerite saw one more success for her family when Jeanne d'Albret married Antoine de Bourbon-Vendôme.

While the royal Valois descended from the first son of Louis IX of France (mid-thirteenth century), the Bourbons descended from his sixth son, but they remained the closest cousins of the royal family. (The lines of the other four sons of Louis IX had become extinct in the male line.) Antoine came from a younger branch of the Bourbon family, La Marche-Vendôme, and he might not have been able to aspire to marriage with the heiress expectant of the royal title of Navarre but for a political scandal of the 1520s. By then the lands and titles of the senior branches of the House of Bourbon had become consolidated in the person of Charles de Bourbon-Montpensier, constable of France. However, after enjoying great favor early in the reign of Francis I, he later incurred the enmity of the king and of the queen mother, who tried to strip him of much of his land and wealth in the mid-1520s. Embittered, Bourbon left France to serve Charles V, Holy Roman Emperor, and died in 1527 leading imperial troops against French forces in Italy. For his treason his properties were confiscated, but the Crown did not wish to alienate the whole influential Bourbon clan; so after the royal family had taken what it wanted, the rest was distributed to Bourbons who had not been compromised by the constable. A major beneficiary was Antoine's father, Charles, duke of Vendôme. Thus, when his father died in 1537 Antoine was not only the scion of the House of La Marche-Vendôme but was much richer than his predecessors. This was the man whom Jeanne d'Albret married in 1548, producing a son in 1553 called Henri de Béarn. In 1555, when Henry II of Navarre died, Jeanne persuaded the Navarese that she and her husband should be proclaimed joint sovereigns, so Antoine became not only consort but king of Navarre. Like his father-in-law, he threw himself into the quarrel over Haute Navarre, engaging in an endless confusion of secret diplomacy and intrigue, though ultimately he achieved nothing. Either Henry II or Antoine might well have been charged with treason by the French Crown had the extent to which they compromised themselves with the king of Spain ever been established clearly. Antoine died during the civil wars in 1562, and the affairs of the family then devolved upon Jeanne until her death a decade later.

The queen of Navarre continued her mother's role as patroness of religious reformers, receiving and protecting many of them, though it put a terrible strain upon her marriage. During the late 1550s Antoine flirted with the reform movement, but around 1560 he returned to the traditional fold. (His chief motivation appears to have been a perception that the king of Spain would consider his pretensions to Haute Navarre more favorably if he were a Roman Catholic.) By contrast, Jeanne showed more and more commitment to the reform movement, and at Christmas of 1560 she received Communion in Calvinist rites. The next two years were very difficult, but after her husband's death she could move more freely—establishing regular communication with the Calvinist center in Geneva, appointing reform ministers to preaching and teaching posts, suppressing the practice of Roman Catholicism, and confiscating ecclesiastical property to endow ministries, schools, and even a Reformed seminary. By the time of Jeanne's death in 1572, there probably was no place outside her domains, except Geneva, that had so developed a Church of the *religion prétendue réformée.* Jeanne's last major action was the negotiation with the French queen mother of a marriage between Henri de Béarn and Catherine's daughter, Marguerite de Valois. The queen mother very much wanted this as a counterbalance to the power of the Guises despite the problems posed by religious differences, but the negotiations took the last of Jeanne's strength. She died, probably of tuberculosis, on 9 June 1572; she was forty-four.

The death of Jeanne d'Albret left the burden of the family of Fois-Navarre-Albret-Bourbon to her nineteen-year-old son. He was King of Navarre, sovereign lord in the duchy of Béarn and the count of Soule, duke and peer in Albret, duke of Vendôme and of Beaumont, and count of Foix, Bigorre, Armagnac, Rodez, Pèrigord, and Marle; in addition he held three viscounties and a host of lesser lordships, many of them dependent upon his greater titles. He also had grander prospects.

While no one could have predicted a crisis so early as 1572, the possibility was recognized. Henry II of France had four sons who lived into maturity, so the line appeared secure. But Francis II, who succeeded in 1559, reigned only months before dying childless; and his brother, Charles IX, died without legitimate heirs in 1574. The Crown then passed to the next brother, Henry III, who reigned until his murder in 1589; but he also produced no heirs. The prospect of a crisis therefore loomed when the fourth of the Valois princes, d'Alençon, died childless in 1584. Under the principles of the Salic Law (restricting the French succession to the male line) Henri of Navarre, *chef du parti* of the French Calvinists, suddenly was heir apparent to the throne of France.

With the murder of Henry III in 1589 Henry IV became king of France, but it took five years to defeat those who wished to wrest his crown from him. On the battlefield he defeated French ultra-Catholics and their Spanish reinforcements; and careful diplomacy brought essential foreign support. But the king did not have the strength to take ultra-Catholic Paris, and the Catholic nobles who supported him were becoming very restive by the mid-1590s. (Henry IV had issued several equivocal statements that he would undertake Roman Catholic instruction "when circumstances permitted," and Catholic noblemen who had interpreted this as a promise of conversion became disenchanted when the king time and again procrastinated.) Forced by these accumulating pressures, in 1593 Henry made a profession of faith in the Roman Catholic church, but contrary to often-repeated legend, it was not done cynically and did not come easily. (There is *no* documentary evidence for the phrase "Paris is worth a mass.") The king agonized for months, even years, over what he perceived as a growing necessity if he were to give his kingdom peace. He had great experience of the importance of religious declaration and of the obligation that it laid upon a prince. He had been baptized in a Roman Catholic sacrament; in 1560 his mother began taking him to Calvinist services; in 1562, with his mother exiled to her own domains, his father held him at the French court and forced him to go to Mass. After his father's death his mother was able to take him from the French court and back to Calvinist practices; then, in 1572 his marriage was followed by the Saint Bartholomew's Day Massacre of Calvinists, and after much resistance he was forced back to Mass. Following his second escape from court, in 1576, he returned to Calvinism.

In 1593 Henry IV was still his mother's son, with her piety deeply ingrained; for two decades he had been a practicing Calvinist, with many of his closest and most trusted associates deeply involved in the promotion of the reform. He knew both sides of the religious quarrels as well as anyone, and it is entirely possible that the reflection of his closest counselor, the duke of Sully, that the king sacrificed an important part of his conscience to the good of his people is considerably less naive than historians have assumed.

Before he was murdered in 1610, Henry IV issued the Edict of Nantes, giving freedom of conscience and a limited freedom of practice to his Calvinist subjects; and he made peace with Spain. Hence, his reputation as a pacifier is well grounded. In the reign of his son, Louis XIII, any separate influence of the Navarese title ended in 1621, when the family lands were annexed to the Crown of France.

[*See also* Antoine of Navarre; Bourbon, House of; Catherine de Médicis; Henry IV of France; Jeanne of Navarre; Marguerite d'Angoulême; *and* Philip II of Spain.]

BIBLIOGRAPHY

Buisseret, David. *Henry IV.* Reprint, London, 1989. A significant modern biography, as is Roelker's, of a major figure of the Navarese royal family of the sixteenth century.

Eurich, S. Amanda. *The Economics of Power: The Private Finances of the House of Foix-Navarre-Albret during the Religious Wars.* Kirksville, Mo., 1993. A different approach that adds important new dimensions to the whole subject.

Kingdon, Robert M. *Geneva and the Coming of the Wars of Religion in France, 1555–1563.* Geneva, 1956.

———. *Geneva and the Consolidation of the French Protestant Movement, 1564–1572.* Geneva, 1967. Kingdon's two volumes are useful for the growth of the reform in its early years.

Michaud, Joseph F. *Biographie Universelle* (1845–1865). 45 vols. Reprint, Graz, 1966. Unrivaled with respect to the many lesser figures of the family.

Roelker, Nancy L. *Queen of Navarre: Jeanne d'Albret, 1528–1572*. Cambridge, Mass., 1968.

Romier, Lucien. *Le Royaume de Catherine de Médicis* (1922). 2 vols. Reprint, Geneva, 1978. Remains justifiably a classic.

Rothrock, George A. *The Huguenots: A Biography of a Minority*. Chicago, 1979. A broad introduction to the religious quarrels.

Salmon, John H. M. *Society in Crisis: France in the Sixteenth Century*. Reprint, London, 1980. Essential for anything relating to the conflicts in sixteenth-century France.

Thompson, James W. *The Wars of Religion in France, 1559–1576*. 2d ed. New York, 1957. Remains very useful.

GEORGE ROTHROCK AND RONALD S. LOVE

NAVARRUS. *See* Azpilcueta, Martín de.

NEGRI, Paola Antonia (also Virginia; 1508–1555), Italian nun, mystic, and spiritual leader. For almost ten years, Negri dominated the spiritual life of the infant congregations of the clerks regular of Saint Paul (Barnabites, founded 1533) and their sister order, the Angelics. Her charismatic leadership of a mixed group, her combination of the active and contemplative lives, and her mystical illuminism all mark her as one of the many female *beate* (living saints) whose cults dotted the landscape of early sixteenth-century Catholicism. As this age of experiment drew to a close at midcentury, Negri was toppled by the newly censorious Roman authorities and sank into disgrace, vilified by her former followers as a manipulative, arrogant fraud.

Born in Castellanza in the state of Milan, Negri was one of the first professed nuns of the Angelics of Saint Paul (chartered 1535 in Milan), an unenclosed order founded under the spiritual direction of Antonio Maria Zaccaria and inspired by the Dominican Battista Carioni of Crema (c.1460–1534). She was appointed the mistress of novices of the convent in 1537. By 1544 chapter acts of the Barnabites show her, hailed as their "Divine Mother," supervising the priests' meetings on both spiritual and practical matters, managing group confessions, and meting out penances. Under her direction, the two orders combined meditation and study with social service in hospitals and homes for repentant prostitutes across northern Italy.

But the straitening ambience of the late 1540s soon brought official disapproval of these experimental religious forms. The state of Venice ejected the congregations from its territories (1551), objecting to the mixing of men and women, Negri's title of "Divine," and her sacral power within the group. The Roman Inquisition ordered an investigation, resulting in life imprisonment for Negri, the separation of the male and female groups, and enclosure of the nuns (1552). Carioni's writings, cleared twice before of heresy, were condemned as semi-Pelagian and placed on the Index of Prohibited Books of 1559.

The Barnabites and Angelics emerged from this crucible reforged into more conventional religious and institutional forms, and ever since have struggled to distance themselves from their early unorthodoxy, scapegoating Negri in the process. Nonetheless, loyal followers published her *Lettere spirituali della devota religiosa Angelica Paola Antonia de' Negri milanese. Vita della medesima racccolta da Giovan Battista Fontana de' Conti* (Spiritual Letters), on which our understanding of her spirituality is based (Milan, 1564; Rome, 1576; French editions, 1611, 1613).

The *Lettere spirituali*, written mostly between 1542 and 1551 to her disciples, are instructions to the elite band who sought "perfect perfection" through inner contemplation, group discipline, and imitation of Christ's sufferings. Faith is to be felt, not reasoned, to be found not only in "study" of scripture but in personal "experience" and "mental quiet." The road to perfection is a "continuous battle" against the passions; here, the Pauline epistles are cited extensively. For Negri, as for Carioni, the "open way to truth" was a difficult path to be trod only by the spiritually gifted, in community, who must nonetheless reach ever outward to their fellow Christians. She never criticized the church directly; the letters were doctrinally innocuous, and though the Inquisition reviewed them in 1576, it could find nothing to condemn.

Thus, Negri's persecution was "only in part thanks to doctrinal motives and suspicion of her 'illuminism'"; it must also be linked to the stifling, after 1550, of the many women who combined charismatic spirituality with earthly power and a high profile in society (see Gabriella Zarri). Negri's fall was also the harbinger of a more generalized drift toward reclusion of all religious women. The Angelics were the first to suffer this trend, which reached its fullest expression in the decrees of the Council of Trent on women religious (session 25, December 1563).

Some suspicion lingers about the authenticity of the *Lettere spirituali*. The Barnabite Gian Pietro Besozzi, formerly Negri's supporter, claimed in 1576 to have written the letters himself, and some have taken this claim seriously. While it is possible, even likely, that Negri had some help in the composition of the letters, a comparison with Besozzi's own writings reveals such differences in style, content, and tone that attribution to him would appear untenable.

BIBLIOGRAPHY

Baernstein, P. Renée. "The Counter-reformation Cloister: The Angelics of San Paolo in Milan, 1535–1635." Ph.D. diss., Harvard University, 1993. See chapter 2, "Foundation to Cloister, 1530–1552." The only work in English.

Cagni, Giuseppe. "Negri o Besozzi? Come nacque la 'vexata quaestio' della paternità delle *Lettere spirituali* dell'Angelica Paola Antonia Negri." *Barnabiti Studi Rivista dei Chierici Regolari di S. Paolo (Barnabati)* 6 (1989), 177–217. Exhaustive discussion of the disputed authorship of the letters, concluding that Negri and Besozzi collaborated to produce them.

Erba, Andrea. "Negri, Paule-Antoinette." In *Dictionnaire de Spiritualité*, vol. 11, pp. 87–89. Paris, 1982. Most accessible treatment of Negri's spirituality.

Firpo, Massimo. "Paola Antonia Negri da 'Divina Madre Maestra' a 'Spirito diabolico.'" *Barnabiti Studi. Rivista dei Chierici Regolari di S. Paolo (Barnabiti)* 7 (1990), 7–65. Best biography; deftly sets Negri in the context of Barnabite history.

Negri, Paola Antonia. *Lettere spirituali della devota religiosa Angelica Paola Antonia de' Negri milanese. Vita della medesima raccolta da Giovan Battista Fontana de' Conti.* Rome, 1576. First published, in a truncated edition, in Milan in 1564. The Roman edition includes a hagiography of Negri; it is more widely available than the Milanese, though still very rare. Originals of all 133 spiritual letters, including many never published, are in Archivio Generalizio dei Barnabiti, Rome. A modern critical edition of the letters is under discussion.

Petrocchi, Massimo. "Dottrine e orientamenti spirituali della scuola lombarda del Cinquecento." In *Storia della spiritualità*, vol. 2, pp. 61–109. Rome, 1978. Attributes the *Lettere spirituali* to Negri.

Premoli, Orazio M. *Storia dei Barnabiti nel Cinquecento.* Rome, 1913. Openly hostile to Negri, but still the most thorough treatment of early Barnabite history.

Prosperi, Adriano. "Dalle 'Divine Madri' ai 'padri spirituali.'" In *Women and Men in Spiritual Culture 16th–17th Centuries: A Meeting of South and North*, edited by Elisja Schulte van Kessel, pp. 71–90. The Hague, 1986.

Zarri, Gabriella. "Le Sante Vive: Per una tipologia della santità femminile nel primo Cinquecento." *Annali dell'Istituto storico Italo-germanico in Trento* 6 (1980), 371–445. The most important recent work on the subject. Situates Negri in the context of the many contemporary female mystics.

P. Renée Baernstein

NERI, Filippo (also Philip; 1515–1595), Roman Catholic church leader and saint. Known as the "Apostle of Rome" and still loved by the Roman population, this eccentric ecclesiastic came from Florence. His parents, Francisco and Lucrezia (da Mosciano), people of meager means, brought up their three children in the shadow of San Marco, the Dominican friary and church in which the spirit of the fiery reformer Girolamo Savonarola still lingered. Savonarola was burned at the stake in 1498. Filippo was born in 1515. His two siblings were Caterina and Elizabetta. All three received religious instruction from the friars.

When Neri was only eighteen, he was sent to San Germano to take over a business inherited from a childless cousin of his father. He was given a genealogical table to show his noble descent, but young Neri cared little for wealth or nobility. He tore up the genealogy, abandoned the business, and proceeded to Rome in search of something better.

The Rome of Paul III, to which Neri came, had forgotten the sack of 1527 and had returned to the gaiety of the days of Pope Leo X. The young man, who still carried the ghost of Savonarola in him, was deeply offended by this. Rome, he thought, was the Babylon of *Revelation.* Instantly he found his vocation to be the reform of Rome. He fasted, meditated, and prayed to prepare himself for it. He gathered young people, and anyone else who would listen to him, including the poor and sick, and took them to the basilicas and to the recently discovered catacombs. He organized his followers into a confraternity to tend the sick and the pilgrims, which actually was the beginning of the hospital of Santa Trinita dei Pelegrini. It was indeed a one-man crusade, led by a layman who had little formal education and no standing in the church. To remedy his lack of knowledge about the church, he enrolled himself in the newly founded Sapienza, the future University of Rome, for courses in philosophy and theology. Owing to the insistence of Persiano Rosa, his confessor and spiritual guide in Rome, he agreed to be ordained a priest in 1551.

Now with education and ordination, Neri gained access to the higher society of Rome. His circle of friends and followers included the highly educated humanists, wealthy nobility, and influential churchmen. With them he developed a daily gathering to discuss the scripture, religious life, church history, and church reform. Unorthodox religious services in combination with prayers and hymns in the vernacular and occasional religious concerts made these meetings popular but also suspect in the eyes of the Counter-Reformation church. Pius V wanted to stop these gatherings in 1567, but Neri by now had influential friends in the hierarchy, such as Carlo Borromeo, who were themselves deeply involved in the Oratory, the name by which these gatherings came to he known. The informal daily meetings led to the formation of a small permanent group who stayed with Neri at San Giovanni dei Fiorentini as a community. Gregory XIII elevated this group to the status of a religious congregation in 1575.

Neri's circle continued to widen and came to include reform-oriented churchmen and laymen from throughout Italy and Europe. Some of the great leaders of the Catholic Reformation—Carlo and Federico Borromeo, Jacopo Sadoleto, Gian Matteo Giberti, and Francis de Sales, to name a few—frequented the Oratory. Branches of the Oratory were also founded in many parts of Europe. The formal members of the Oratorian congregation themselves became great contributors to the cause of the Catholic Reformation. The most illustrious son of the congregation was Cesare Baronio, the author of the *Annales Ecclesiastici*, the massive history of the church that effectively refuted the central argument of the *Centuriae Magdeburgenses* (Magdeburg Centuries), the Lutheran work that attempted to demonstrate that the hierarchical order and papal supremacy in the church were aberrations.

Neri was indeed a central figure in the Catholic Reformation. He himself was a simple priest, and he refused to accept ecclesiastical dignity, but he shaped church policies and programs through the illustrious churchmen whose minds and hearts he influenced at the Oratory. His own personal touch to church reform was to add a sense of joy and even gaiety to religious devotions. Only Neri could have made religious pilgrimages to the basilicas into picnics and religious services into musical concerts without any irreverence, and here lies his genius. Neri died 26 May 1595. He was canonized by Gregory XV on 12 May 1622.

BIBLIOGRAPHY

Bacci, P. G. *Vita di S. Filippo Neri*. Rome, 1745.

Capecelatro, Alfonzo. *The Life of Saint Philip Neri, Apostle of Rome.* Translated by Alder Pope. London, 1926.

Jouhandeau, Marcel. *St. Philip Neri*. Translated by George Lamb. London, 1960.

Libero, Giuseppe de. *Vita di S. Filippo Neri*. Rome, 1960.

Ponnelle, Louis, and Louis Bordet. *St. Philip Neri and the Roman Society of His Times, 1515–1595*. London, 1932.

Trevor, Muriol. *Apostle of Rome: A Life of Philip Neri, 1515–1595*. London, 1966.

CYRIAC K. PULLAPILLY

NETHERLANDS. The course of the Reformation in the Low Countries is best understood in terms of the long dialectic of conflict between the yearning for evangelical religion in a region with strong traditions of lay piety, and a Habsburg government determined to repress heresy in its hereditary lands. Anecdotal evidence suggests that both hatred of clerical privilege and initial enthusiasm for Luther's ideas were as great here as in many parts of Germany. The persecution launched by Charles V deprived the inchoate Lutheran movement of the clerics and humanists who were its natural leaders, but in so doing it inadvertently gave further impetus to Anabaptism, which was much less dependent on members of an easily identifiable educated elite. Reformed churches, implanted in the southern provinces from the 1540s, were deeply colored both by the experience of living "under the cross" (that is, under a regime of persecution) and by competition with tightly disciplined Anabaptist communities. These struggles made of Calvinists in the Low Countries a kind of spiritual elite that was well suited for a leadership role, after 1572, in the northern provinces' protracted war for independence from Spain. But if the new Dutch republic sanctioned the public practice of "the Reformed evangelical religion" and no other, the historical memory of persecution also gave rise here to a strong attachment to freedom of conscience, a sentiment too diffuse to be captured by any organized church, but still strong enough to check the more ambitious plans of the Dutch Reformed church for achieving a godly commonwealth.

The Low Countries and Germany were connected by multiple channels of commerce and cultural exchange: overland from the great hub of Antwerp (in Brabant), by sea from Brugge (Flanders) and Amsterdam (Holland). Thus Wittenberg theology could travel west as readily as Flemish cloth or Brabantine retables traveled east. The religious culture of the Low Countries may have lacked some of the institutional features that abetted the spread of the Reformation in Germany (notably the endowed preacherships, whose incumbents often espoused the new theology). But some of the most important forms of late medieval lay piety (Brethren of the Common Life, Beguines) were either native to this region or richly represented here. Among a productive and relatively well-educated populace there was considerable demand for religious art and vernacular religious literature, and the privileges of gentlemen clerics (such as the canons of the Low Countries' seventy collegiate churches) were no less obtrusive than elsewhere. Not surprisingly, then, small groups for the study of scripture—and of Luther's writings—formed around parish chaplains, mendicant friars, and humanist schoolmasters in one city after another during the early 1520s.

Yet Charles V would have been derelict in his duty to the Catholic faith to allow the heresy that was spreading across Germany to infect his Burgundian lands. In 1521 he issued the first in a long series of placards banning, under pain of death, the possession of Luther's books and attendance at conventicles. Europe's earliest Protestant martyrs were two Augustinian friars from Antwerp, Hendrik Vos and Jan van den Esschen; they were burned in Brussels in 1523. Since the crime of heresy was nothing less than *lèse majesté divine* ("treason against God"), Charles expected his government in Brussels (Brabant) to behave as it would in cases of treason, that is, to brook no interference from local magistrates. But town governments saw new heresy laws as infringing on their privileges, and even Habsburg officials—members of the provincial courts, which Charles counted on to chivy town courts into compliance—were loath to follow the rigor of the placards. Foot dragging was most noticeable in northern provinces over which the central government had less control, such as Holland and (even more) Friesland. At the opposite end of the scale, the most aggressive campaigner against heresy was Pieter Titelmans, underinquisitor for Flanders, Lille, Douai, Orchies, and Tournai between 1545 and 1566; empowered to conduct ecclesiastical trials and remand unrepentant heretics to the secular courts for punishment, Titelmans dealt with an average of a hundred cases a year for much of his career. Some thirteen hundred men and women were put to death for their beliefs under Charles V and his son, Philip II, between 1523 and 1566. Persecution of this kind—as Andrew Pettegree has noted, its "sustained intensity" has no parallel elsewhere in Europe—cannot have been without effects on the religious history of the Low Countries, even if the effects were hardly those intended by Charles and Philip.

At all levels, officials responsible for implementation of the placards assumed that the danger to orthodox religion and to the social order came from the appeal of Luther's doctrines to persons distinguished by wealth or education. Repeatedly interrogated by civil and religious authorities, dissidents marked by their social position were sometimes confronted with a choice between martyrdom and recantation; more often they took refuge in exile, and many had notable careers in the Protestant churches of places like Bremen and Basel or in refugee churches that sprang up in London and elsewhere beginning in the 1540s. The authorities had at first no inkling of heterodox teachings other than Luther's, nor were they worried about the lower social orders, unruly to be sure but not deemed capable of causing real trouble unless their betters showed them how. But the hunt for Luther's books and for the men who could understand and expound them, insofar as it succeeded in its own terms, merely forced into new and unexpected channels a yearning for evangelical religion that could not be extinguished by fires and placards.

If the literature of this nascent Protestantism has "disappointingly few" references to justification by faith, Alastair Duke has found a passionate attachment to vernacular scripture (25 Netherlandish editions of the New Testament between 1522 and 1530). The *Epistola Christiana Admodum* of Cornelis Hoen (d. 1524), an advocate before the provincial court of Holland, was hardly inspired by Luther in its rejection of the real presence of Christ in the Eucharist; indeed, this text helped provoke a major Reformation debate when Zwingli published it in 1525. Such views could soon command the passionate loyalty of ordinary folk, like Wendelmoet Claesdochter, a housewife from the little town of Monnikendam (Holland), whose courage in the face of death (1527) inspired one of the earliest Netherlandish Protestant martyrdom accounts. This "sacramentarian" phase of the Netherlands Reformation is still poorly understood, but it seems to have prepared the ground for Anabaptism in the Low Countries after about 1530.

During Melchior Hoffman's sojourn (1530) in nearby Emden (East Friesland), his disciples brought the message to Amsterdam and thence to other parts of the region. Netherlandish Melchiorites followed their leader by embracing suffering as a preparation for the eschatological triumph of the saints, at times even turning themselves in to town officials; they also obeyed his injunction to suspend adult baptism for a time. But if Anabaptist communities, made up in the main of artisans and laboring folk, could not be readily detected by the authorities, the relative scarcity among them of a Latin-educated elite also left them vulnerable to the appeals of self-styled prophets.

Beginning in 1533, John Matthijs in Haarlem resumed adult baptism and preached of how the saints could hasten the final day by smiting the wicked. The episcopal city of Münster, not far away, offered Matthijs and his disciple, John of Leiden, a proving ground for their ideas. In the early months of 1534 blood-curdling "prophecies" emanating from Münster warned that God's wrath would strike all who did not seek refuge in the kingdom of the saints. Of those who now took ship for Münster, especially from Holland, some three thousand were detailed by the authorities at Genemuiden (Overijssel), but many others got through. While Münster itself lay under siege by Catholic and Lutheran princes (1534/35), local Münsterites sacked a Frisian cloister and stormed the Amsterdam town hall; they were also accused of plotting to seize Leiden (Holland).

In the wake of these events town magistrates exceeded the fondest wishes of the Habsburg government in their zeal to bring heretics to justice. But though Münsterite ideas lived on for a time after the fall of Münster among the church-robbing Batenburger sect, Menno Simons and David Joris were able in their different ways to rebuild Low Countries Anabaptism on peaceful foundations; their doctrines, not those of Münster, accounted for a growth of Anabaptist communities in the south, especially in Flanders. Meanwhile, as town governments took cognizance of nonviolent beliefs among Anabaptists, they reverted to their normal disinterest in applying the full rigor of the placards.

From the 1540s, Reformed communities are found not only in the French-speaking towns to which preachers from Geneva and France had ready access (Lille, Tournai, Valenciennes), but also in Netherlandish-speaking Ghent, Brugge, and Antwerp. The same artisan and laboring milieu that was the main recruiting ground for Anabaptist congregations was also fertile soil for Reformed preaching, notably in the small cities of West Flanders, such as Hondschoote, where new (lighter-weight) cloth industries had attracted large numbers of low-wage workers who lacked the protection afforded by guild regulations. (By contrast, the new faith had as yet little appeal for cloth workers in centers of the traditional industry, such as Ghent.) Unlike Anabaptism, Reformed preaching also attracted significant numbers of merchant families and men of learning—hence Johan Decavele's characterization of the earliest nucleus of Reformed faith in Ghent as "salon Protestantism." These fledgling congregations had to distinguish themselves from other movements claiming the mantle of evangelical religion, not only the growing Anabaptist congregations but also "libertine" spiritualists—followers of Loys Pruystinck or, later, Hendrik Niclaes and his Family of Love—who found it proper to conform outwardly to Catholic worship even while rejecting its premises. Geneva's well-defined doctrine and firm discipline thus provided a needed organizational backbone. But Reformed Christians in the southern Low Countries looked for leadership not so much to Geneva as to the refugee churches—such as those in London, Sandwich, Emden, and Wesel—whose ranks were swelled with each new wave of persecution. Of special importance was the London church, led by Jan Łaski and Maarten Micron (a Ghent refugee), until Mary Tudor's accession (1553) forced the congregation to find a new home in Emden. London and Sandwich reclaimed their importance when Elizabeth came to the English throne, and preachers returning from England were in good part responsible for the rapid growth of Reformed congregations after 1559, especially in Flanders.

The early expansion of Calvinism in the Low Countries

(c.1545–1566) was largely confined to the southern provinces. With the important exception of Antwerp, the centers of real growth in this period fell within the jurisdiction of Pieter Titelmans, the most zealous and most hated of Low Countries' inquisitors. Hence the Reformed movement in its initial stages was deeply colored by the brute fact of persecution. For one thing, living "under the cross" made internal bickering a dangerous luxury; London or Emden usually sought to resolve disputes by reconciling the parties rather than rendering a definitive judgment.

In these circumstances a certain theological eclecticism within the broad Reformed tradition was to be expected. Both the doctrine of the nascent church (the Belgic Confession) and its discipline (the earliest consistories date from the 1550s) were fully congruent with Calvin's teaching. Yet Netherlandish-language presses in Emden turned out only four editions of works by Calvin before 1572, but twelve of works by Heinrich Bullinger, including four of his *Hausbuch.* Only after the Reformed church was declared to be the official church of a new Dutch state would it matter that Calvin and Bullinger had not shared the same vision of a Christian polity. Further, it is likely, if not established, that the necessary secretiveness of a persecuted minority gave birth to an organizational feature that is distinctive to later Dutch Calvinism: the carefully maintained distinction between full members of the church, admitted to communion only after careful scrutiny, and the *liefhebbers* ("sympathizers") and *toehoorders* ("listeners"), who attended services but did not communicate. Finally, watching one's co-religionist subjected to a painful death for their beliefs tested the limits of Calvin's insistence on obedience to the lawful magistrate, just as it did for French Huguenots at about the same time. The London church, on an appeal from Antwerp, ruled against breaking one's co-religionists out of prison by force (1561), but this did not prevent the rash of prison breaks that began when Titelmans attempted to remove a prisoner from the industrial town of Belle, near Hondschoote. By 1562 (thus somewhat later than in France) there was public preaching guarded by armed men, again in Flanders; there was also a furious dispute over the appropriateness of resorting to violence, pitting Hermannus Moded, Antwerp's zealous preacher, against Pieter Delenus, minister of the London church and a faithful disciple of Calvin on this point.

Meanwhile, enforcement of the placards was beginning to meet with opposition all over the Low Countries, often in circumstances that suggest a nonconfessional withdrawal of allegiance from laws that required people to be put to death for their beliefs. For example, as the first of five condemned Anabaptists was being hanged in Rotterdam (1558), a torch applied to the foot of the still-living victim, then a woman's slipper flying into the staked-off "ring" of execution, sparked a riot that rescued the condemned persons and drove the magistrates to seek refuge in the town hall tower. In the 1560s, the call for moderation of the placards gained strength when Philip II's plans for new bishoprics (1561) touched off fears of a wider persecution (each new bishop would have an inquisitorial court), and gained legitimacy when it was taken up by William of Orange and other great nobles on the Council of State—the men who forced Antoine Perrenot de Granvelle's withdrawal (1564). This broad resistance to the placards provided, as it were, a protective coloring for incidents involving the use of violence by Calvinists; it was not always possible to tell whether people resorted to force out of zeal for true religion or out of an ingrained sense of due process instilled by persecution. Similarly, in the later Dutch republic, it would not be possible to settle the debate as to whether the long war against Spain was being fought *religionis ergo* (for the sake of religion), or *libertatis ergo* (for the sake of liberty).

By the summer of 1566 Margaret of Parma's government seemed to be losing its grip; some four hundred nobles had adhered to the compromise calling for suspension of the placards, illegal sermons in the countryside attracted tens of thousands in some places, and prominent citizens were stepping forward to fill positions in the consistories of cities such as Antwerp. Beginning at Steenvoorde (West Flanders) on 10 August, iconoclastic riots spread across much of the Low Countries, sometimes organized by preachers (especially those recently returned from England) or by local consistories, and sometimes expressing the spontaneous rage of local folk against the wood and stone emblems of Catholic devotion. The ruling oligarchies of most towns stood by helplessly, evidently fearing to test their authority by calling out burgher militias to defend the images. But though Margaret was forced to grant the Calvinists limited rights in the exercise of their religion, local elites, appalled by the implications of iconoclastic violence, rallied to the government. Meanwhile, Philip II refused to countenance any relaxation of the placards, and sent Fernando Álvarez de Toledo, duke of Alba, with an army of ten thousand to enforce his will; by the time the duke of Alba arrived, most of those who had participated in the Wonderyear of 1566/67 were already en route abroad to join one of the refugee churches.

The years of exile (1567–1572) were contentious, yet formative for the future Dutch church. Once gathered in Emden or London, refugees from various parts of the Netherlands found themselves in less than total agreement. Preachers from Flanders and Brabant and from the Walloon (French-speaking) provinces insisted on uniformity of doctrine, sometimes to the dismay of colleagues from Holland and Friesland, where Reformed congregations were newer and less organized and where persecution had been notably less severe. On issues relating to the revolt northerners readily followed the leadership of William of Orange, who had previously been stadtholder of Holland, but many southern ministers distrusted the then still Lutheran William because of past and present efforts to fashion a religiously disparate coalition of opposition. The crucial Synod of Emden (1571) was in some ways a victory for the southerners. Orthodox doctrine was defined in terms of the French and Belgic confessions of faith, as supplemented by the catechisms of Geneva and Heidelberg. Election of ministers and elders was to follow the practice of the Emden church, and the French church supplied a model for the organization of local churches into classes and provinces.

With the capture of Brill (Holland) by anti-Spanish rebels in 1572, the Dutch Reformed church began its career as the established church of the rebel northern provinces. In the turbulent early years of the republic the church's great strength was the organizational fit between Calvin's federative church structure and the civic culture that produced and sustained the complex federal structure of Dutch government. Calvin himself had not made discipline one of the marks of the true church, but the Belgic Confession did so, in keeping with the thinking of the refugee churches. In the northern Netherlands after 1572, a continuing influx of refugees from the south joined with members of local elites to form consistories that maintained a vigilant scrutiny of would-be communicants and kept a sharp eye on church members. (In some towns "watchers" reported to the elders on the behavior of their neighbors.) At the same time, they were slow and cautious in proceeding to the ultimate sanction of excommunication, as was prescribed by the Synod of Emden. The system of Reformed poor relief that in many places remained distinct from municipal charitable institutions was built up by deacons answerable to the consistory, not (as some have argued) as a way of recruiting indigent converts but so the Christian community could take care of its own.

Beyond the parish level, the classis, meeting quarterly or even monthly, was a preeminently clerical institution. (Regulations required elders to attend, but they usually did not.) The classis served as a platform for leaders of the new clergy, such as Hendrik van den Corput of Dordrecht (d. 1601), a refugee from Brabant, and Arend Corneliszoon of Delft (d. 1605), scion of a native patrician family. The classis was also an informal school of theology for ministers who lacked university training, a disciplinary body for wayward preachers, and an unfailing source of moral support for colleagues embroiled in conflict with dissenters or with their town governments. Finally, provincial synods (with circumscriptions not always identical to those of the civil provinces) served both as a forum for settling intractable local disputes and as a higher ecclesiastical authority that could claim to stand on equal terms with the provincial states to which towns sometimes referred their quarrels with the church. The Dutch church was thus, in Van Deursen's term, "a federation of classes," one that functioned no less effectively than its civil counterpart.

What made this church different from sister churches in Geneva or Scotland was that citizenship in the Netherlands did not entail membership in the official church. Anabaptist churches continued growing into the first half of the seventeenth century, despite numerous schisms, and competition with the moral purity of *Doopsgezind* communities is thought by scholars to have strengthened Reformed church leaders in their determination not to admit unworthy persons to full membership—in effect, stressing quality over quantity. Meanwhile, priests of the Holland Mission, operating from "stations" that were not quite parishes, rebuilt the religious loyalties of the Catholic flock; despite quarrelling between secular clergy and the religious orders, especially the Jesuits, Catholics in many places long outnumbered the Reformed. Reformed dominees never advocated that Catholics be punished by death, but the laws of the republic forbade Catholic worship even in private, and dominees did demand of the authorities stricter enforcement of the law, albeit with increasingly disappointing results.

Finally, the gravest intellectual threat to Calvinist orthodoxy came not from Anabaptists, among whom there were few theologians, nor from Catholics, forbidden to publish religious tracts, but from those few radical thinkers who, drawing on the heritage of the spiritual reformers, negated the doctrine of original sin and with it that deep sense of human sinfulness that was in this era fundamental to the spirituality of all three major churches (Cornelius Jansenius, eponym of the Jansenist movement among Catholics, was a Hollander by birth). For those who envisaged a perfectible human nature, the strictures of Calvinist discipline were nothing but the shackles of a new clerical tyranny. In this sense Dirk Volkertszoon Coornhert of Haarlem (1522–1590)—polymath, poet, pamphleteer, member of the Family of Love, and champion of religious liberty—was danger incarnate. Corneliszoon, with a Delft colleague, twice accepted Coornhert's challenge to a public debate, but both times the debate was suspended by commissioners from the States-General of Holland, evidently in the belief that open debate on fundamental theological issues served no useful civic purpose. The same civic authority that made the Reformed church an official church and reserved for its use the former revenues of the Catholic church nonetheless treated Reformed orthodoxy as but one of several religious viewpoints, all of which had to obey ground rules set by the government.

Thus the church's most important problem in these early years was that of achieving a *modus vivendi* with civic authorities. In most places during the 1580s and in some places as late as 1600, full members of the Reformed church were no more than 10 percent of the population. Yet no government of the period, least of all one in rebellion against its sovereign, could fail to place itself under divine protection; since Habsburg rule meant Catholic persecution and since Calvinists had a leading role in rebel armies, there could also be no question about the church to which the spiritual well-being of the body politic was to be entrusted. Hence the states of the several provinces, followed by the 1579 Union of Utrecht, banned the public practice of all but the "evangelical Reformed religion." At the same time, civil penalties for religious dissent were kept to a minimum. (Catholics in their *schuilkerken* ["hidden churches"] might now and then be harassed by the local sheriff, and office holding was limited in theory, if not always in practice, to members of the Reformed church.) Thus a church that regarded itself as a holy community living among the devil's flock was expected somehow to tend to the religious needs of the entire commonwealth, and to do so without infringing on the divinely sanctioned prerogatives of the *mogende heren* ("mighty lords") who ruled in the town halls and the provincial states.

In some ways, Netherlands dominees willingly embraced their assigned role as leaders of a "public church." For example, the baptism of all infants presented in the church, even those whose parents refused to return proper answers to the minister's prescribed questions, was justified on the grounds that God's covenant extended even unto the thousandth generation. The problem was that the church's idea of a commonwealth in which God's laws would not be flouted did not correspond to the political elite's notion of a nation under God. For many dominees, a godly commonwealth was one that averted God's wrath by denying succor to the foreign enemies of God (e.g., by not allowing Dutch merchants to trade with Spain) and by enforcing the laws against papists at home. For many of the *mogende heren*, especially among the patrician elite of the highly urbanized province of Holland, a Christian body politic was one in which preachers kept out of politics (permits for trading with the enemy were an important source of revenue) and bent their energies toward unifying the commonwealth rather than accentuating its divisions into warring doctrinal camps.

Over time church and state worked out an accommodation, based on the exclusion of extreme views that threatened the vital interests of one side or the other. The theocratic alternative, anathema to the state, was discredited during the years following the Pacification of Ghent (1576), when much of the south joined in the revolt against Spain; contrary to the express orders of William of Orange, radical preachers, especially in Ghent, insisted on the suppression of Catholicism and thus abetted a Catholic and pro-Spanish reaction in the south that culminated in the recapture of Antwerp (1585). The Erastian option, anathema to the church, was discredited bit by bit as orthodox dominees backed by their classes secured the dismissal of preachers who, with the support of the magistrates, espoused the latitudinarian vision of a civic church open to all Christians of good faith, rather than a church dominated by the "tyranny" of Calvinist discipline. For example, Caspar Coolhaes in Leiden appealed to the example of Zurich in support of his practice of admitting to the Lord's Supper all who asked to receive. Coolhaes would not be the only preacher who attempted to marshall Zurich theology (with its Erastian implications) against Calvinism, but the fact that he, along with his chief critic, was forced to resign his pulpit (1582) foreshadowed the outcome of similar struggles in other towns. As the two extreme positions fell away, what remained was a cordial disagreement (or a stressful entente) between church and state, in which each favored the other with its distinctive stamp of legitimacy, while refusing to cede ground on contentious issues. For example, the states did not recognize church orders drafted by synods, just as Holland synods refused to accept the ordinance drafted in the States-General of Holland (1591).

This equilibrium was disturbed but not overturned by the great Arminian controversy, ending with the triumph of the orthodox, or Contra-Remonstrant, party at the national Synod of Dordrecht (1618–1619). In hopes of achieving a better educated clergy, church and civic authorities had cooperated in providing scholarships for theological study at the universities of Leiden and Franeker (Friesland). But once girt by the mantle of a doctorate, a man who proved to have dissident views could not easily be dislodged from his post, especially not at Leiden, which was controlled by a town magistracy that was still not sympathetic to the claims of the church. Thus as Arminius found a following among students at Leiden, his opponents blocked the appointment of Leiden graduates holding suspect views, which led to the Remonstrance of 1610. Both the Remonstrants' appeal for intervention by the state in the affairs of the church and their hesitations about the Belgic Confession's formulation of the doctrine of predestination may be compared with the views of earlier dissidents, such as Coolhaes. But this later conflict had national repercussions, as local churches divided into factions, even if the still common characterization of these divisions—Arminian patricians versus loyally Calvinist commoners—is overly simplistic. (The support of Amsterdam's mercantile elite was crucial to the Contra-Remonstrant victory, while commoners in Rotterdam and elsewhere were found among the stoutest Remonstrants.)

The settlement at Dordrecht, made possible by Maurits van Nassau's coup d'état against the States of Holland and its leader, Johan van Oldenbarnevelt, was in some respects definitive; the question of predestination was placed for some time beyond dispute, and Remonstrant pastors and their congregants were excluded from the church. But some other things changed little or not at all. The church order adopted by the synod was accepted only where the provincial states chose to do so. More importantly, the division of civil society into separate confessions was anchored even more firmly in the visible fabric of Dutch life, as Protestant dissenters (even Remonstrants) and Portuguese Jews were soon allowed to build houses of public worship, while Catholics in their *schuilkerken* intoned the Latin liturgy without fear of disruption. Fittingly, a land whose erstwhile rulers had sacrificed so many victims to the medieval ideal of religious unity became, in the seventeenth century, a model for the modern ideal of religious pluralism.

BIBLIOGRAPHY

Augustijn, Cornelis. "Anabaptism in the Netherlands: Another Look." *Mennonite Quarterly Review* 62 (1988), 197–210.

Backhouse, Marcel. "The Official Start of Armed Resistance in the Low Countries: Boeschepe, 12 July 1562." *Archiv für Reformationsgeschichte* 71 (1980), 198–226.

Bangs, Carl. *Arminius: A Study in the Dutch Reformation.* 2d ed. Grand Rapids, Mich., 1985.

Bergsma, Wiebe. *Aggaeus van Albada, c.1525–1587: Schwenckfeldiaan, Staatsman en Stryder voor Verdraagzaamheid.* Meppel, Netherlands, 1983.

———. *De Wereld volgens Abel Eppens.* Groningen, 1988.

———. "Calvinismus in Friesland um 1600 am Beispiel der Stadt Sneek." *Archiv für Reformationsgeschichte* 80 (1989), 252–285.

Bonger, H. *Leven en Werken van Dirk Volkertszoon Coornhert.* Amsterdam, 1978.

Boom, Hendrik ten. *De Reformatie in Rotterdam, 1530–1585.* Hollands Historische Reeks, vol. 7. The Hague, 1987.

Briels, J. G. C. A. *Zuid-Nederlandse Immigratie in Amsterdam en Haarlem, ca. 1572–1630.* Utrecht, 1976.

Briels, J. G. C. A., ed. *Bronnen voor de Religeuze Geschiedenis van Belgie.* Bibliothèque de la Revue d'histoire écclésiastique. Brussels, 1968.

Crew, Phyllis Mack. *Calvinist Preaching and Iconoclasm in the Netherlands, 1544–1569.* Cambridge and New York, 1978.

Decavele, Johan. *De Dagraad van de Reformatie in Vlaanderen. 1520–1565.* Verhandelingen van de Koninklijke Akademie van Wetenschappen. Letteren en Schoone Kunsten van België, Klasse der Letteren, vol. 28. Brussels, 1975.

Decavele, Johan, ed. *Het Eind van een Rebelse Droom: Opstellen over het Calvinistisch Bewind te Gent.* Ghent, Belgium, 1984.

Deppermann, Klaus. *Melchior Hoffman.* Edinburgh, 1987.

Deursen, A. Th. van. *Bavianen en Slijkgeuzen: Kerk en Kerkvolk ten Tijde van Maurits en Oldenbarnevelt.* Assen, Netherlands, 1974.

———. *Plain Lives in the Golden Age: Popular Culture, Religion, and Society in Seventeenth Century Holland.* Translated by Maarten Ultee. Cambridge and New York, 1991.

Duke, A. C. "The Ambivalent Face of Calvinism in the Netherlands, 1561–1618." In *International Calvinism,* edited by Menna Prestwich, pp. 109–133. Oxford, 1985.

———. *Reformation and Revolt in the Low Countries.* London, 1990.

DuPlessis, Robert S. *Lille in the Dutch Revolt: Urban Stability in an Era of Revolution, 1500–1582.* Cambridge and New York, 1991.

Elliot, John Paul. "Protestantization in the Northern Netherlands, a Case Study: The Classis Dordrecht, 1572–1640," Ph.D. diss., Columbia University, 1990.

Estié, Paul. *Het Vluchtige Bestaan van de Eerste Nederlandse Lutherse Gemeente: Antwerp, 1566–1567.* Amsterdam, 1986.

———. *Het Plaatselilk Bestuur van de Nederlandse Lutherse Gemeente: Ontstaan en Ontwikkeling in de Jaren 1566 to 1686.* Amsterdam, 1987.

Evenhuis, R. B. *Ook Dat Was Amsterdam.* 5 vols. Amsterdam, 1965–1978.

Fatio, Olivier. *Nihil Pulchrius Ordine: Contribution à l'Etude de l'Établissement de la Discipline Écclésiastique aux Pays Bas, ou Lambert Daneau aux Pays Bas, 1581–1583.* Leiden, 1971.

Gelder, H. A. Enno van. "Nederland Geprotestantiseerd?" *Tijdschrift voor Geschiedenis* 81 (1968), 326–334, 445–464.

———. *Getemperde Vrijheid.* Groningen, 1972.

Geyl, Pieter. "De Protestantiseering van Noord-Nederland." In *Verzamelde Opstellen,* vol. 1, pp. 205–218. Utrecht, 1978.

Ginkel, Albertus van. *De Ouderling.* Amsterdam, 1975.

Groenhuis, G. *De Predikanten: De Sociale Positie van de Gereformeerde Predikanten in de Republiek der Vereenigde Nederlanden voor +/– 1700.* Groningen, Netherlands, 1977.

Groenveld, S., J. P. Jacobszoon, and S. L. Verheus, eds. *Wederdopers, Menisten, Doopsgezinden in Nederland, 1530–1980.* Zutphen, Netherlands, 1981.

Güldner, Gerhard. *Das Toleranz-Problem in den Niederlanden im Ausgang des 16en Jahrhunderts.* Historische Studien, no. 403. Lübeck, Germany, 1968.

Hamilton, Alastair. *The Family of Love.* Cambridge, 1981.

Hibben, C. C. *Gouda in Revolt.* Utrecht, 1983.

Horst, Irvin B., ed. *The Dutch Dissenters,* Leiden, 1986.

Jelsma, A. J. *Adriaan van Haemstede en zijn martelaarsboek.* The Hague, 1970.

Jones, R. L. "Reformed Church and Civil Authorities in the United Provinces in the Late Sixteenth and Early Seventeenth Centuries." *Journal of the Society of Archivists* 4 (1970–1973), 109–123.

Kamphuis, J. *Kerkelijke Besluitvaardigheid: Over de Bevestiging van het Gereformeerd Kerkverband in de Jaren 1574 tot 1581/2. . . .* Groningen, Netherlands, 1970.

Kaplan, Benjamin J. "Calvinists and Libertines: The Reformation in Utrecht, 1578–1618." Ph.D. diss., Harvard University, 1989.

Kok, J. A. de. *Nederland op de Breuklijn Rome-Reformatie: Numerieke Aspekten van Protestantiseering en Katholieke Herleving in de Noordelijke Nederlanden, 1580–1880.* Assen, 1964.

Krahn, Cornelius. *Dutch Anabaptism: Origin, Spread, Life and Thought.* 2d ed. Scottdale, Pa., 1981.

Lamet, Sterling A. "The *Vroedschap* of Leiden, 1550–1600: The Impact of Tradition and Change on the Governing Elite of a Dutch City." *Sixteenth Century Journal* 12.2 (1981), 15–42.

Marnef, Guido. *Het Calvinistisch Bewind te Mechelen, 1580–1585.* Standen en Landen, vol. 87. Kortrijk-Heule, Belgium, 1987.

Mellink, A. F. *Amsterdam en de wederdopers in de zestiende eeuw.* Nijmegen, Netherlands, 1978.

———. *De wederdopers in de noordelijke Nederlanden, 1531–1544.* Reprint, Leeuwarden, Netherlands, 1981.

Moreau, Gérard. "La Correlation entre le milieu social et le choix de religion à Tournai." In *Bronnen voor de Religeuze Geschiedenis van België,* edited by J. G. A. C. Briels, pp. 286–301. Brussels, 1968.

Nauta, D. "De Reformatie in Nederland in de Historiografie." In *Geschiedschrijving in Nederland,* edited by P. A. M. Geurts and A. E. M. Jansen, vol. 2, pp. 206–228. The Hague, 1981.

Nierop, Henk F. K. van. *Beeldenstorm en burgelijk verzet in Amsterdam, 1566–1567.* Nijmegen, 1978.

Nijenhuis, Willem. "De publieke kerk veelkleurig en verdeeld, bevoorrecht en onvriij." In *Algemene Geschiedenis der Nederlanden,* vol. 6, pp. 325–343. Haarlem, Netherlands, 1979.

———. "Variants within Dutch Calvinism in the Sixteenth Century." *Acta Historiae Neerlandicae* 12 (1979), 48–64.

Parker, Charles H. "The Reformation of Community: The Reformed Diaconate and Municipal Poor Relief in Holland, 1572–1617." Ph.D. diss., University of Minnesota, 1993.

Pettegree, Andrew. *Foreign Protestant Communities in Sixteenth-Century London.* Oxford, 1986.

———. *Emden and the Dutch Revolt.* Oxford, 1992.

Riemersma, Jelle C. *Religious Factors in Early Dutch Capitalism, 1550–1650.* The Hague, 1967.

Roey, J. van. "De Correlatie tussen het Sociale-Beroepsmilieu en de Godsdienstkeuze te Antwerpen op het Einde van de XVIe Eeuw." In *Bronnen voor de Religeuze Geschiedenis van België,* edited by J. G. C. A. Briels, pp 239–258. Brussels, 1968.

Rogier, L. J. *Geschiedenis van het Katholicisme in Noord-Nederland in de 16e en 17e Eeuw.* 3 vols. Amsterdam, 1947.

Roodenburg, Herman Willem. *Onder Censuur: De Kerkeliike Tucht in de Gereformeerde Gemeente van Amsterdam, 1578–1700.* Hilversum, Netherlands, 1990.

Schilling, Heinz. *Civic Calvinism in Northwestern Germany and the Netherlands.* Kirksville, Mo., 1991.

———. *Religion, Political Culture, and the Emergence of Early Modern Society.* Studies in Medieval and Reformation Thought, vol. 50. Leiden and New York, 1992.

Spaans, Joke. *Haarlem na de Reformatie: Stedelijk Cultuur en Kerkeliik Leven, 1577–1620.* Hollands Historische Reeks, vol. 11. The Hague, 1989.

Spiertz, M. G. *Gids voor de Studie van Reformatie en Katholieke Herleving in Nederland, 1520–1650.* The Hague, 1982.

———. "Die Ausübung der Zucht in der Ijsselstadt Deventer in den Jahren 1592–1619 im Vergleich mit den Untersuchungen in Languedoc und Kurpfalz." *Rheinische Viertelsjahrsblätter* 49 (1985), 139–172.

Steen, Charlie. *A Chronicle of Conflict: Tournai, 1559–1567.* Utrecht, 1985.

Tracy, J. D. "Heresy Law and Centralization under Mary of Hungary: Conflict between the Council of Holland and the Central Government over the Enforcement of Charles V's Placards." *Archiv für Reformationsgeschichte* 73 (1982), 284–307.

———. "The Calvinist Church of the Dutch Republic, 1572–1618/9." In *Reformation Europe: A Guide to Research,* edited by William Maltby, vol. 2., pp. 253–279. St. Louis, 1992.

Tukker, C. A. *De Classis Dordrecht van 1573 tot 1609.* Leiden, 1965.

Uytven, Raymond van. "Invloeden van het Sociale en Professionele Mileu op de Godsdienstkeuze: Leuven en Edingen." In *Bronnen voor de Religeuze Geschiedenis van België,* edited by J. G. C. A. Briels. Brussels, 1968.

Wee, Herman van der. "La Réforme Protestante dans l'Optique de la Conjuncture Économique et Sociale des Pays-Bas Méridionaux." In *Bronnen voor de Religeuze Geschiedenis van België,* edited by J. G. C. A. Briels. Brussels, 1968.

Woltjer, J. J. *Friesland in Hervormingstijd.* Leiden, 1962.

———. "De Vredemakers." *Tijdschrift voor Geschiedenis* 89 (1976), 299–321.

Zilverberg, S. B. J. *Dissidenten in de Gouden Eeuw: Geloof en Geweten in de Republiek.* Weesp, Netherlands, 1985.

JAMES D. TRACY

NETTESHEIM, Agrippa von. *See* Agrippa, Heinrich Cornelius.

NEW CHRISTIANS, or *Conversos,* were those in medieval Spain who had converted to Christianity from Judaism; the term also applied to their descendants. In rare cases the word was used for those converting from Islam. New Christians were so-called to distinguish them from Old, or non-Semitic, Christians and were in popular parlance vilified as *marranos,* or pigs. They had a significant effect on public life from 1391, when anti-Jewish riots in the major Spanish towns forced most Jews to convert to Christianity. Continuing anti-Jewish pressure—fed in part by the preaching of Vicente Ferrer and by a Christian-Jewish debate held before the pope at Tortosa in 1413—augmented the number of conversions, principally at the highest social levels. New Christians were no longer Jews and therefore had the right of access to public office; by the late fifteenth century they were an influential force in many towns, largely in the south of Spain, where the Jewish presence had been strongest, and could be found in the episcopate and in the royal councils. Many, however, were suspected of still following Jewish religious practices, which helped to bring about the establishment of the Spanish Inquisition in 1478 and the expulsion of the Jews in 1492. From 1480, when it commenced operations, to the 1520s, the Inquisition in Spain executed thousands of New Christians accused of secret Judaizing.

By the early sixteenth century Judaizers were becoming a rarity, and New Christians were more readily absorbed into Spanish life; virtually all were practicing Christians, and they cannot be identified as a separate cultural group. Some Jewish historians, such as Haim Beinart, maintain that all New Christians, or *anusim* in Hebrew, aspired to be Jews, but the evidence for this argument is weak. Geographically, New Christians coincided with the old areas of Jewish settlement: they were numerous in southern Spain and on the island of Majorca (where they were known as *chuetas*) but virtually nonexistent in Catalonia and the Basque provinces. Anti-Semitism was restricted largely to the Castilian lands. The most serious obstacle faced by New Christians was the existence of "pure blood" (*limpieza de sangre*) statutes, which originated in the late fifteenth century and excluded those of Jewish origin from access to some private institutions, such as universities and religious orders. The statutes did not have validity in public law and frequently were disregarded, even where, as in the chapter of Toledo cathedral in 1547, controversy led to the adoption of a *limpieza* rule. In part because many families of the ruling elite had New Christian ancestors, which brought disrepute on them, during the late sixteenth century a powerful movement, headed by the Inquisition itself and including prominent Jesuits, attempted to reform or abolish the statutes.

During the sixteenth century New Christians, whose number was never large, were active in economic, spiritual, and intellectual life. New Christian traders in Seville, such as Antón Bernal and Gaspar Jorge, played a role in the developing trade with the New World, and families, such as the Maluenda, were active in the trade between Burgos and northern Europe; their importance to such trade, however, was relatively small and restricted to the ports of Castile. Many relied for commercial contacts on Jewish and New Christian traders living abroad in Italy, the Netherlands, and France.

By contrast, they played a more significant role in intellectual life. In the early sixteenth century important groups of Castilian mystics known as *alumbrados* were composed largely of New Christians, and New Christian influences have been detected as a basic component of Castilian spirituality in the century. Some scholars, such as Américo Castro, have explained this as a conscious rejection of orthodoxy; others, such as Marcel Bataillon, have seen it as a consequence of their spiritual restlessness within the official framework. The fact is that some of the major figures of Castilian spiritual life during the century were of New Christian origin: John of Ávila, Teresa of Ávila, Diego Láinez, and many others.

The list of New Christians who contributed to the intellectual life of Spain is lengthy, ranging from Erasmian humanists, such as Juan de Vergara, and Juan Luis Vives, to poet Luis de León and writer Mateo Alemán; but they had no common cultural tradition, and there is little support for the emphasis once placed by Castro and his followers on the allegedly unique role played by New Christians in peninsular thought. Intellectuals frequently suffered discrimination because of their Jewish origin, and some fell foul of the Inquisition. A significant example was Vives, who spent all his career in the Netherlands and whose family background probably dissuaded him from returning to Spain: his father was burnt alive by the Inquisition in 1524 as a Judaizer. The most celebrated case was the arrest by the Inquisition in 1572 of Luis de León and two other New Christian professors at Salamanca University. New Christians were also suspected of helping to introduce Protestant heresy. The Seville preacher Constantino Ponce de la Fuente, who in 1558 died in the cells of the Inquisition, was a New Christian, but his writings show no evidence of the Protestant ideas attributed to him by the Holy Office. By contrast, some New Christians in exile, such as Marco Pérez, became active supporters of Calvinist teaching.

In general, New Christians can be found in most of the intellectual currents of the period, but, apart from the special case of the *alumbrados*,they played no distinctive role in any of them. It is difficult to identify any specifically New Christian features in their culture, although in professional terms some, such as Francisco López Villalobos (d. 1549) and Andrés Laguna (d. 1560), distinguished themselves in medicine.

[*See also* Alumbrados; Inquisition; *and* Vives, Juan Luis.]

BIBLIOGRAPHY

Bataillon, Marcel. *Erasmo y España*. Corr. ed. Mexico City, 1966. Classic survey of sixteenth-century literature and the place of New Christians in it.

Beinart, Haim. *Conversos on Trial: The Inquisition in Ciudad Real*. Jerusalem, 1981. Argues that New Christians saw themselves as Jews.

Braunstein, Baruch. *The Chuetas of Majorca: Conversos and the Inquisition of Majorca*. New York, 1973. History of one New Christian community.

Castro, Américo. *The Structure of Spanish History*. Princeton, 1954. Influential study, based on the Middle Ages, that argues that Jews and New Christians played a fundamental role in Hispanic culture.

Kamen, Henry. *Inquisition and Society in Spain in the Sixteenth and Seventeenth Centuries*. London and Bloomington, Ind., 1985. Brief and updated introduction to the subject.

Netanyahu, Benzion. *The Marranos of Spain from the Late Fourteenth to the Early Sixteenth Century, According to Contemporary Hebrew Sources*. 2d ed. New York, 1973. Argues that New Christians were not really Jews, but over-estimates their numbers.

Ortiz, Antonio Domínguez. *Los Judeoconversos en España y América*. Reprint, Madrid, 1988. Useful short survey, but unsystematic and now out-dated.

Sicroff, A. *Les controverses des statuts de 'pureté de sang' en Espagne du 15e au 17e siècle*. Paris, 1960. Good survey of the *limpieza* debates but superseded in its orientation.

HENRY KAMEN

NICLAES, Hendrik (1502–1580), German spiritualistic prophet and religious visionary who founded the Family of Love in the 1540s. Born in Westphalia, the son of a rich Catholic merchant, he had early religious questions culminating at age nine in a vision in which he experienced unity with God. He came under Lutheran influence in his early twenties, and although he rejected persecution of Lutherans on the basis of toleration, he never adopted Luther's solifidianism or sanctioned his revolt against the Catholic church. Nevertheless he was arrested in Münster in 1529 on suspicion of Lutheranism but released soon afterward for lack of evidence.

Under the influence of sources such as the *Theologica Germanica*, Niclaes believed that although Christ had died on the cross to redeem fallen humankind, only a few people had benefited from this enlightenment. Soon there came a second fall in which humanity once again turned away from God, the teachings of Christ were distorted, the Holy Spirit was ignored, and scripture became a dead letter. Niclaes believed that the last age of time had come and that God had sent him as another "new man" to enlighten the world and lead humankind once again to unity with God. His call would be the last one, Niclaes believed, and all who failed to answer it would be damned. He criticized the established churches for their formalism and neglect of the Spirit, and he opposed the Protestant reformers, who had only replaced one set of false ceremonies with another. He considered himself a Catholic and he continued outwardly to follow Catholic practices until the majority of believers would come to accept his idea that ceremonies and sacraments were of no real importance in religious life.

In 1531 Niclaes settled in Amsterdam, where he lived as a wealthy merchant. He was arrested on suspicion of Anabaptist sympathies and interrogated before the Court of Holland in The Hague, but released. In 1540 he had a revelation that led him to found the Family of Love: he was instructed to take three elders, write down the truth, go to a land of piety, and proclaim the kingdom of love. He then moved to Emden, where he lived for twenty years under an assumed name, wrote his first works, and organized his followers into a religious community. He traveled widely and often, spreading his religious beliefs while forming commercial ties and collecting followers such as the spiritualist Hendrik Jansen van Barrefelt and the humanist printer Christoffel Plantijn. In 1560 persecution forced him to leave

Emden, and after short stays with Plantijn in Antwerp and with his follower Augustine van Hasselt in Kampen, he settled in Rotterdam in 1565.

In 1567, in the midst of the religious crackdown by Fernando Álvarez de Toledo, duke of Alba, Niclaes had a vision telling him to take twenty-four elders and go to a land of peace where he could better organize his sect and revise his writings. He then moved to Cologne, where he organized the Family of Love into a priestly hierarchy with himself as highest bishop. This development led Barrefelt, Plantijn, and other of his followers to split from him. Niclaes spent the remaining years of his life in Cologne publishing new editions of his works. He died in 1580.

BIBLIOGRAPHY

Primary Sources

Fontaine Verwey, H. de la. "De geschriften van Hendrik Niclaes." *Het Boek* 27 (1940–42), 161–222. A guide to Niclaes's other works.

Niclaes, Hendrik. *Spiegel der gerechtigheid.* Antwerp, 1555–1560. Niclaes's first major doctrinal work. Argues that ceremonies and sacraments could be observed as remembrances and testimonies to God's truth but otherwise were of no importance in religious life.

———. *Ordo Sacerdotis.* Written shortly after 1570 in Cologne, but never printed. A modern edition of it can be found in: Hamilton, Alastair, *Cronica, Ordo Sacerdotis, Acta HN: Three Texts of the Family of Love,* Leiden, 1988. The *Ordo* describes the priestly hierarchy for the Family of Love that Niclaes developed at the end of his life. The other two works in this volume are by followers of Niclaes and describe his life and the history of the Family of Love.

Secondary Sources

Hamilton, Alastair. *The Family of Love.* Cambridge, 1981.

Lanceé, J. A. L. "Hendrik Niclaes." In *Biografisch Lexicon voor de Geschiedenis van het Nederlandse Protestantisme,* vol. 2, pp. 341–343. Kampen, 1983.

ANDREW C. FIX

NICODEMISM. John Calvin used the term Nicodemism to describe an attitude of compromise and a pattern of dissembling behavior on the part of Protestant evangelicals living in Roman Catholic territories. The name is suggested by the biblical character of Nicodemus, who came to visit Jesus by night, under the cover of darkness, thus suggesting a piety of simulation based on the fear of persecution (*Jn.* 3:1–3).

According to Théodore de Bèze Nicodemism was a special problem among Reformed believers in France, who were the objects of increased persecution from the 1540s onward:

> At this time also there were some persons in France, who, having fallen away at first from fear of persecution, had afterwards begun to be satisfied with their conduct as to deny that there was any sin in giving bodily attendance on popish rites, provided their minds were devoted to true religion. This most pernicious error, which had been condemned of old by the Fathers, Calvin refuted with the greatest clearness . . . the consequence was that from that time, the name of Nicodemite was applied to those who pretended a sanction for their misconduct in the example of that holy man Nicodemus.

The phenomenon of Nicodemism was a matter of persistent concern for Calvin throughout his career as a reformer. The following six treatises are among his most important anti-Nicodemite works: *De fugiendis impiorium illicitis sacris* (1536); *Petit traicté monstrant que doit faire un homme fidèle entre les papistes* (1543); *Excuse à messieurs les Nicodémites* (1544); *De vitantdis superstitionidus* (1545); *Quatre sermons* (1552); *Réponse à un certain holandois* (1562). Calvin never divulged the names of individual Nicodemites. He did distinguish several types and various motivations for dissimulation among them: those who retained benefices in the Roman church while still pretending to preach the gospel; those who sought to win ladies of nobility to the Reformed faith but who were insincere in their own profession; some philosophically inclined Christians overly influenced by Neoplatonic ideas; those Reformed believers among the artisans and common folk who where reluctant to take a public stand for fear of persecution.

Some French evangelicals accused Calvin of being too severe in his strictures against the Nicodemites. Calvin, however, saw only two alternatives for Protestant believers faced with unrelenting persecution: exile (the path he himself had taken) or faithfulness unto death (martyrdom). Calvin's counsel was motivated by his overriding fear of idolatry and his refusal to separate inward piety from public worship. By admonishing believers under duress to avow publicly their faith or else flee, Calvin encouraged the influx of religious refugees into Protestant strongholds such as Geneva. His exhortations to courage also lent support to the planting and establishing of Protestant congregations throughout France during the 1550s and 1560s. His refusal to counsel compromise contributed to the emerging sense of identity among French Protestants and strengthened their resolve to persevere in the tense environment preceding the Wars of Religion.

While Calvin's concern with Nicodemism focused primarily on France, the problem of religious simulation among Protestant minorities was evident in other situations of confessional strife as well. For example, German Lutherans were forbidden to worship according to Reformation standards following the Augsburg and Leipzig Interims of 1548, as were the English Protestants during the reign of the Catholic queen Mary Tudor. Both Wolfgang Musculus and Peter Martyr Vermigli wrote treatises attacking religious dissembling and compromise. Calvin's own writings against the Nicodemites were translated into German, English, and Italian.

The term "Nicodemite" was used as an epithet to describe various temporizing figures including Desiderius Erasmus. Some scholars have traced the origins of Nicodemism to the French evangelical movement led by Jacques Lefèvre d'Étaples, while others have located the headwaters of the movement in the writings of Otto Brunfels, a spiritualist reformer of Strasbourg. Brunfels's *Pandectae veteris et novis testamenti* (1527) has been interpreted by some as the first Nicodemite treatise. It is unlikely, however, that Nicodemism was a unified, coherent movement stemming from any single individual or writing. Some persons who may have been regarded as Nicodemites, such as Calvin's friend Nicholas Du Chemin, later returned to a public avowal of the Roman church, while others, such as Dirk Coornhert, embraced radical spiritualizing tendencies. As a general term Nicodemism covered a wide range of religious dissemblers who for various theological and prudential reasons preferred to camouflage their true convictions in time of persecution and distress.

BIBLIOGRAPHY

Eire, Carlos M. N. "Calvin and Nicodemism: A Reappraisal." *Sixteenth Century Journal* 10 (1979), 45–69.

———. "Prelude to Sedition?: Calvin's Attack on Nicodemism and Religious Compromise." *Archiv für Reformationsgeschichte* 76 (1985), 120–145.

Ginzburg, Carlo. *Il Nicodemismo.* Turin, 1970.

Matheson, P. C. "Martyrdom or Mission?: A Protestant Debate." *Archiv für Reformationsgeschichte* 80 (1989), 154–172.

Oberman, Heiko A. "The Impact of the Reformation: Problems and Perspectives." In *Politics and Society in Reformation Europe,* edited by E. I. Kouri and Tom Scott, pp. 3–31. New York, 1987.

Williams, George H. *The Radical Reformation.* 3d ed. Kirksville, Mo., 1992.

TIMOTHY GEORGE

NICOLAI, Philipp (1556–1608), German Lutheran theologian, pastor, and hymnist. Born in Mengeringhausen in Waldeck in northern Germany, the son of a Lutheran pastor, Nicolai is known primarily as the poet-composer of two hymns: "How Brightly Shines the Morning Star" and "Wake, Awake, for Night is Flying." As a student his obvious gifts were nurtured by teachers such as composer Joachim a Burck and hymnist Ludwig Helmbold, but he chose theology, completing formal study at Wittenberg in 1579. Returning to Waldeck to study privately and to preach, he was ordained in 1583 and assumed his first pastorate in Herdecke near Dortmund. Although Catholic hostility led him to resign in 1586, he then ministered secretly to Lutherans in Cologne.

Nicolai turned to polemics after he became Waldeck court preacher and tutor to Count Wilhelm Ernst in 1588. In defending the Formula of Concord (1577) and "ubiquity" (a complex rationale for the real presence), he attacked the Sacramentarians so vehemently that in 1590 the landgrave forbade the University of Marburg to grant him his earned doctorate (awarded by Wittenberg in 1594). Although called to Unna (Westphalia) in 1596 to uphold Lutheran teachings against Calvinist immigrants, Nicolai the pastor emerged in 1597–1598 when the plague took more than thirteen hundred of his parishioners. To comfort his flock he wrote his most influential devotional work, *Freudenspiegel des ewigen Lebens* (Mirror of the Joys of Eternal Life; Frankfurt a.M., 1599). His last and most important pastorate was Saint Catherine's in Hamburg (1601–1608), where he wrote more than half his published works.

Nicolai's publications, collected and edited after his death, fill six folio volumes. Although many are intensely polemical attacks on Reformed, Catholic, and other opponents of orthodoxy, most are essentially theological. Moreover, in *Freudenspiegel* and *Theoria vitae aeternae* (1606) he anticipated the warm, subjective piety of Johann Arndt's *Vom wahren Christentum* (On True Christianity, books 1–4, 1606; books 5–6, 1610). Like Arndt, he was a pioneer in Lutheran devotional literature, and his works inspired a relationship between it and Lutheran hymnody both old and new. Even more than Arndt, Nicolai recalled the biblically based elements of Luther's mystical thought and piety. Affirming that a "spiritual union" of the faithful with Christ was analogous to the "personal union" of his two natures and that divine omnipresence entailed a nonspatial, nonlocalized conception of heaven, Nicolai portrayed eternal life as actual for the Christian in the here and now.

The poetry of Nicolai's two great hymns embodies in miniature the essence of his piety, and although the melodies resemble earlier tunes, their coherence, intensity, and fidelity to the words are clearly his own. Nicolai heard the gospel word as the music of God, unmatchable in beauty and yet calling for symbolic expression in the music of voices and instruments. The cultivation of this piety and hymnody in orthodoxy led to those developments in Lutheran church music that culminated in Johann Sebastian Bach, who based two of his finest cantatas on Nicolai's hymns and whose orthodox faith and personal devotional life can best be understood within this heritage.

BIBLIOGRAPHY

Blankenburg, Walter. "Philipp Nicolai." In *The New Grove Dictionary of Music and Musicians,* edited by Stanley Sadie, vol. 13, pp. 214–215. London, 1980. Abridged from *Die Musik in Geschichte und Gegenwart,* edited by Friedrich Blume, vol. 9, cols. 1453–1455, Kassel, 1961. Both are brief, but original is preferable for musical details and somewhat fuller bibliography.

Buszin, Walter E. "Philip Nicolai." In *The Encyclopedia of the Lutheran Church,* edited by Julius Bodensieck, vol. 3, pp. 1751–1752. Minneapolis, 1965. Concise and useful sketch with additional bibliography and theological comment.

Elert, Werner. *The Structure of Lutheranism.* Translated by Walter A. Hansen. Saint Louis, 1962. On Nicolai, Luther, and the *unio mystica* see vol. 1, pp. 160–176. Translation based on the first volume of *Morphologie des Luthertums,* 2 vols., rev. ed., Munich, 1952–1953. Lucid exposition combining historical method and systematic theology; masterful analyses of texts from Luther and the dogmaticians to the early 18th century.

Lindström, Martin. *Philipp Nicolais Verständnis des Christentums.* Gütersloh, 1939. Translated from the Swedish, a critique of Nicolai's theology in relation to Lutheran orthodoxy and in general a rather negative assessment; short title list of works.

Nicolai, Philipp. *Freudenspiegel des ewigen Lebens.* (1599). Edited by Reinhard Mumm. Reprint, Soest, 1963. Classic text, including the chorales, with a brief foreword by the editor.

Piepkorn, Arthur Carl. "Philipp Nicolai, 1556–1608: Theologian, Mystic, Hymn Writer, Polemicist, and Missiologist; A Biobibliographical Survey." *Concordia Theological Monthly* 39 (1968), 432–461. Best summary in English to date of Nicolai's life and thought; includes a basic bibliography as well as translations of the lengthy titles of his published works.

Verzeichnis der im deutschen Sprachbereich erschienenen Drucke des XVI. Jahrhunderts. Stuttgart, 1983–. See vol. 14, nos. 1478–1495.

Zeller, Winfried. "Zum Verständnis Philipp Nicolais." *Jahrbuch der Hessischen Kirchengeschichtlichen Vereinigung* 9 (1958), 83–90. Sympathetic revaluation of Nicolai's work and its significance by a specialist in the devotional literature of the sixteenth and seventeenth centuries; unfortunately, not easily accessible.

———. "Protestantische Frömmigkeit im 17. Jahrhundert." In *Theologie und Frömmigkeit: Gesammelte Aufsätze,* vol. 1, pp. 85–116. Marburg, 1971. Illuminates the background and character of the devotional literature of orthodoxy and incipient Pietism.

BARTLETT R. BUTLER

NIELSSEN, Laurits. *See* Norvegus, Laurentius.

NIKLASHAUSEN, Pfeifer von. *See* Böheim, Hans.

NIKOLSBURG. A city and principality near Brünn (Brno) in the margraviate of Moravia, Nikolsburg (Mikulov) belonged from the mid-thirteenth century to the Lower Austrian branch of the Liechtenstein family. In the 1530s Nikolsburg became the center of Moravian Anabaptism, and throughout the sixteenth century it was a haven of religious toleration for a wide variety of dissenting and persecuted religious groups.

In 1524 Hans Spittelmaier and Oswald Glaidt established a Protestant congregation in Nikolsburg under the protection of Leonhard of Liechtenstein. Following the arrival of Balthasar Hubmaier in July 1526 and the subsequent baptism of Leonhard, the reform movement took on a distinctly Anabaptist character. Over the next decade Anabaptists from south Germany, Austria, and Switzerland—perhaps as many as twenty thousand in total—streamed to the city seeking refuge from persecution.

As the foremost leader of the Anabaptist group, Hubmaier published numerous tracts in Nikolsburg before his execution at the hands of Austrian authorities in May 1528, many of them dedicated to local lords and magistrates in the hopes of winning their support for Anabaptism. Hubmaier's cordial relations with state authorities aroused opposition within the Anabaptist group, especially among those led by Hans Hut, who argued against pedobaptism and the use of the sword, both of which seemed to be implied in Hubmaier's church-state alliance. Hubmaier and Hut engaged in at least two debates. An account of their final disputation, published in 1529 as the so-called *Nikolsburger Artikel,* aroused widespread interest in Anabaptist thought and evoked several refutations from Protestant and Catholic opponents. Some historians have speculated that the *Nikolsburger Artikel* were actually published by opponents in an effort to discredit the Anabaptists in the region.

The debate between Hubmaier and Hut reflected a broader division among the Nikolsburg Anabaptists. Those sympathetic to Hubmaier were known as the *Schwertler* ("sword-bearers") because they countenanced the use of the sword; their opponents, the *Stäbler* ("staff-bearers"), held that Christians could not in good conscience bear arms. In the spring of 1528 the *Stäbler* group was forced to leave Nikolsburg and eventually settled in Austerlitz. En route, however, they pooled all of their belongings, establishing thereby the principle of "community of goods," which became a distinctive feature of the group. By the 1550s descendants of the *Stäbler,* known as the Hutterian Brethren, returned from Austerlitz to the Nikolsburg area, where sympathetic lords permitted them to establish communities in acknowledgment of their economic contributions as farmers, craftsmen, and physicians.

Throughout the last half of the sixteenth century, Lutherans, Anabaptists, Hutterian Brethren, and a variety of other religious minorities continued to survive in the region in and around Nikolsburg. After 1575, however, when Emperor Maximilian II ceded the region to Baron Adam von Dietrichstein, their existence was threatened by a new round of persecution. In 1579 Dietrichstein invited the Jesuits into his territory to convert Lutherans and sectarians, thereby initiating a long polemical campaign against the Anabaptists. In the 1620s, following a wave of peasant unrest, Cardinal Franz von Dietrichstein began to make systematic efforts to eradicate Hutterian communities. A mandate of expulsion was issued in Brünn in September 1622, and by the end of the decade some twenty-four Hutterian Brethren communities were destroyed, bringing an end to the Anabaptist presence in Nikolsburg.

[*See also* Anabaptists *and* Moravia.]

BIBLIOGRAPHY

Bergsten, Torsten. *Balthasar Hubmaier: Anabaptist Theologian and Martyr.* Translated and revised by W. R. Estep, Jr. Valley Forge, Pa., 1978. Pp. 314–333 offer a basic overview of the Anabaptist reformation in Nikolsburg. Originally published as *Balthasar Hubmaier:*

Seine Stellung zur Reformation und Täufertum, 1521–1528, Kassel, 1961.

The Chronicle of the Hutterian Brethren. Vol. 1. Rifton, N.Y., 1987. Has numerous references to Nikolsburg and the story of the Hutterian Brethren in the region.

Williams, George. *The Radical Reformation.* 3d ed. Kirksville, Mo., 1992. Pp. 314–354 outline the broader context of the radical Reformation in Bohemia and Moravia.

Zeman, Jarold K. *The Anabaptists and the Czech Brethren in Moravia, 1526–1628.* The Hague, 1969. Provides the best systematic history and overview of the Anabaptist, Hutterian Brethren, and Utraquist movements in Moravia.

JOHN D. ROTH

NÎMES, SYNOD OF. The eighth national synod of the French Reformed churches was held in 1572. This synod was called principally to deal with proposals for ecclesiastical reform raised by Jean Morély. Morély's program, as advanced in his *Traicté de la discipline et police Chrestienne* (Treatise on Christian Discipline; 1562), placed the responsibility for discipline on the congregation as a whole rather than on the pastors and elders; further, it insisted on more direct congregational involvement in the nomination and selection of all church officers. Although Morély provided for a form of consistory in local churches, its functions were to be far more administrative than disciplinary. He also called for colloquies, provincial synods, and, reluctantly, national synods, though in all cases with greatly reduced authority.

Morély's ideas were promptly condemned by the third national synod (Orléans, 1562) under the moderatorship of Antoine de la Roche Chandieu; this condemnation was repeated by the fifth national synod (Paris, 1565). Chandieu prepared a response to Morély entitled *La confirmation de la discipline ecclésiastique* (1566), a book that became the semiofficial defense of the French Reformed churches' polity. The controversy continued when Morély was appointed tutor to Henry of Navarre, the future Henry IV. Morély was eventually dismissed, more because of the outbreak of yet another round in the Wars of Religion than to his ecclesiastical views.

The quarrel revived again because of a number of decisions passed by the seventh national synod held at La Rochelle in 1571, but by this time Morély had won a champion for his cause in the person of Petrus Ramus, a logician, educator, and intellectual well respected in the international Protestant community. Ramus sent a report to Heinrich Bullinger highlighting three particular actions of the synod that were sure to raise the ire of Zurich: the synod's insistence that churches retain the right of excommunication, its condemnation of those who argued that the church was subordinate to the state, and its use of the term *substance* with respect to Christ's presence in the Lord's Supper. The alarmed Bullinger fired off a letter to Théodore de Bèze—the moderator of the Synod of La Rochelle—complaining about these decisions; Bèze replied by denouncing Morély's character and insisting that all the actions were taken to respond to threats from within the French Reformed community and were not intended as an attack on Zurich.

Meanwhile, the indefatigable Ramus convinced the provincial synod of the Île-de-France (Lumigny-en-Brie, 1572) to adopt some of Morély's ideas by increasing lay participation in the local church. This compromise, which took only a small step toward Morély's position, seems to have satisfied Ramus, although Bèze and other Reformed leaders were adamantly opposed to it. This provincial synod set the stage for the final confrontation over Morély's ideas at the Synod of Nîmes in 1572.

The Synod of Nîmes was watched closely not only by the churches of Geneva and France but also by those of Zurich and Bern; as a result, the synod had to act carefully to avoid a confrontation with the Zwinglian churches. Nonetheless, the synod condemned point by point every proposal of the reform party. The provincial synod of the Île-de-France was ordered to destroy all records of the Synod of Lumigny and was forbidden to introduce ecclesiastical innovations independently. The national synod also ordered the provincial synod of the Île-de-France to summon Morély, Ramus, and the other instigators of the reform program to the Colloquy of Beauvoisin and there either repent or be treated as schismatics. This was to be the last act of the story; the Saint Bartholomew's Day Massacre later that year claimed Ramus as a victim and essentially rendered further discussion irrelevant.

At the same time as it condemned the Morélian reform program, however, the synod backed away from some of its earlier eucharistic statements. While retaining the use of the term *substance* within France, the synod added that foreign churches were free to reject it. They also softened the wording of the statement on the nature of Christ's presence in the Supper to make it more compatible with Zurich's position.

The Synod of Nîmes also introduced a chapter on colloquies to the *Discipline ecclésiastique*, the church order of the French Reformed churches. The previous national synod (La Rochelle, 1571) had produced an edition of the *Discipline* that included chapters on each level of ecclesiastical government except the colloquy; with the addition of this chapter, the Synod of Nîmes completed the reorganization of the *Discipline*.

[*See also* Bèze, Théodore de; Chandieu, Antoine de la Roche; Henry IV of France; Morély, Jean; Ramus, Petrus; *and* Synods.]

BIBLIOGRAPHY

Primary Sources

Aymon, Jean. *Tous les synodes nationaux des Eglises Réformées de France.* 2 vols. The Hague, 1710. On microfiche: Inter Documentation Company, Reformed Protestantism: Sources of the sixteenth and seventeenth centuries on microfiche 2b (France), KPRS 109. The only French edition of the Acts of the National Synods, including Nîmes; generally inferior to the English translation by Quick.

Morély, Jean. *Traicté de la discipline et police Chrestienne* (1562). Reprint, Geneva, 1968. The work which started the debates culminating in the Synod of Nîmes.

Quick, John. *Synodicon in Gallia Reformata: or, The Acts, Decisions, Decrees, and Canons of Those Famous National Councils of the Reformed Churches in France.* 2 vols. London, 1692. On microfilm: UMI, Early English Books 1641–1700 selected from Donald Wing's Short Title Catalogue, reel 473 (Wing Q209). The best published text of the Acts of the National Synods, including Nîmes.

Sunshine, Glenn S. "French Protestantism on the Eve of St. Bartholomew: The Ecclesiastical Discipline of the French Reformed Churches, 1571–1572." *French History* 4 (1990), 340–377. Includes an annotated text of the *Discipline* of 1571/72 and an introductory essay setting this text into the context of the ecclesiastical development of the French Reformed churches.

Secondary Source

Kingdon, Robert M. *Geneva and the Consolidation of French Protestantism, 1564–1572: A Contribution to the History of Congregationalism, Presbyterianism, and Calvinist Resistance Theory.* Madison, Wis., 1967. The best available discussion of the ecclesiastical debates sparked by Morély, including an account of the Synod of Nîmes.

GLENN S. SUNSHINE

NOBILITY. The role of the nobility in introducing, defending, and combating the Reformation has not been studied as extensively as have the roles of other social groups, such as the urban bourgeoisie or the peasantry. This may be because the Reformation in Germany was essentially an urban movement, and the direction of research in central and western Europe has been shaped by the critical importance of the bourgeoisie to the Reformation within the Holy Roman Empire.

Two important historiographic points need to be made concerning the nobility's relationship with the religious reform movement that swept across Europe in the sixteenth century. First, there is general agreement that in most of Europe noble support was important, even crucial, to the success of the new religions. Nobles often provided protection and status to the nascent Protestant churches, and, once converted, they would also increase the size of a congregation by bringing in their retainers, clients, and relatives. John Calvin, Théodore de Bèze, and other magisterials clearly recognized and appreciated the importance of the nobility to the success of the reform movement. Second, there were regional variations in the level and extent of noble commitment to the new religions owing to local political, economic, and social factors. A general consensus among researchers is that the German nobles were less enthusiastic supporters of the Reformation from its inception than were nobles in France, the Netherlands, and Poland. In the latter three areas the Reformation was seen as a religious and ideological movement that could be used to defend local and class privileges against centralizing monarchs.

These regional differences in the attitude of the nobility become apparent upon examination of individual countries. Within the Holy Roman Empire there were many levels of nobility, ranging from free imperial knights, who controlled small holdings, to dukes and counts, who controlled vast areas. According to Volker Press, a leading historian of the German nobility's reaction to the Reformation, there was a general pattern among the imperial knights: they exhibited a period of initial enthusiasm for the Reformation, then a longer period of indecision lasting until the 1550s, followed by a late period of support for the Reformation during the second half of the sixteenth century. A number of historians have supported this conclusion, arguing that the nobility as a whole tended to be cautious and unwilling to commit themselves wholeheartedly to the reform movement until the latter part of the sixteenth century.

Historians have emphasized that the following factors must be taken into account when trying to understand the reasons for the German nobility's hesitation in supporting the Reformation: their traditional ties to feudal lords, sovereign princes, and the emperor, ties that often affected a nobleman's decision about religious affiliations; their dependence on patronage; and their involvement in the highest levels of the pre-Reformation church in Germany, which has been described as an *Adelskirche*, or nobles' church. All of these things meant that from the outset the nobility would not opt for the Reformation in large numbers, except for a few groups, such as the imperial knights of the Rhineland and Franconia and the nobles in the Habsburg lands in Austria and Styria.

The Peace of Augsburg (1555)—based on the principle that the religion of the ruler should be the religion of all, as long as it was either Catholicism or Lutheranism—altered the confessional situation within the empire for the nobility, since lesser nobles were not exempt from the terms of the settlement. This meant that in theory the knights were bound to follow the religion of their prince, for the structure of the imperial and territorial constitutions was such that they often worked against the German nobility's freedom to follow an independent course in their religious affiliation. After 1555 an increasing number of knights and nobles did join Protestant churches, often because their princes had done so.

The nobility's role in actively promoting the new religious movements in France, Poland, and the Netherlands was stronger than in Germany. While there are some striking parallels between the French and German situations, in general the French nobility were far more active in advancing the Reformation, especially after the mid-sixteenth century. Lutheranism made little headway among the French nobility, whereas the missionary church of John Calvin had a more lasting impact. He made a special effort to convert the French nobility because he recognized how important they could be to his new church, and he was dramatically successful. Conversions among the nobility increased rapidly beginning in the 1550s, and according to some estimates close to 50 percent of the French nobility were Calvinist (termed Huguenot) by the late 1560s.

Calvin was successful for several reasons: he aimed his well-organized missionary efforts directly at the nobility; his theological doctrines, which rejected the efficacy of works and emphasized predestination, appear to have found a ready audience among both the rural and urban literate elites; and his activities coincided with a period of political crisis in France. After the death of Henry II in 1559, the monarchy fell to a series of three weak and ineffective kings. The leading French noble houses fought among themselves for control of these kings, who remained steadfastly Catholic under the watchful eye of the queen mother, Catherine de Médicis. Religious and political rivalries became intertwined, and for some nobles conversion to Calvinism was a way of demonstrating opposition to the monarchy and of extending their own economic and political authority. The large and powerful group of French nobles who did convert, protected and defended the Reformed movement from Catholic counterattacks throughout the second half of the sixteenth century, with their efforts culminating in the Edict of Nantes (1598), which extended toleration to Huguenots.

In eastern Europe it was the nobility of Poland who were the most successful in pushing for religious reform. Lutheranism did not win many followers among the Polish nobility, although they often disobeyed royal edicts of the 1530s and 1540s aimed at suppressing Protestantism and allowed Lutherans and other Protestants to live on their estates. As in France, Calvinism was much more successful among the elites, and many Polish nobles were converted from the 1550s on. Even those nobles who were outwardly Catholic pushed for church reform. For example, the nobility took the initiative at a diet in 1556 and adopted a nine-point reform program for the Polish church. Among the items they wanted to enact were permission for priests to marry and the rejection of the legal authority of bishops in civil suits.

The Polish nobility also worked for religious toleration. In 1573 they forced Henry of Anjou (Henry III of France from 1574 to 1589) to declare his assent to an agreement of mutual religious toleration by both Catholics and Protestants. This policy was abandoned, however, by later Polish kings, largely because of the efforts of the Jesuits. In fact, as a result of the Counter-Reformation, the Reformed church was effectively destroyed as an organization in Poland by the 1630s.

The history of the Reformation in England was unique, as it was Henry VIII's divorce and his break with the papacy, not theological factors, that led to religious change. This state Reformation won its most willing adherents among those with influence: aristocrats who wanted to gain favor with the king, country gentlemen who were willing to enforce religious change as a way of increasing their own power, and those who had acquired land following the dissolution of the monasteries. Research has indicated that a large and influential segment of the aristocracy and gentry were won over to Protestant opinions, and that their support was primarily responsible for the success of both the Henrician reform and the Elizabethan Settlement.

The reaction of the Scottish nobility to Calvinism was mixed, which is somewhat surprising since John Knox, following Calvin's lead, placed a great deal of emphasis on the conversion of the nobility. But here, as elsewhere, political factors played a major role in the decisions of many nobles. Attempts at winning over the nobility to the Reformed religion met with limited success, which was extremely frustrating to Knox, who repeatedly told them to accept their important role in God's plan for the renewal of his church on earth. But the Scottish nobility hesitated, partly because of their influential position within the Catholic church and partly because their power in the local communities came to be challenged by the national Reformed church, termed the Kirk. The result was that many nobles stood aloof from the Reformed movement, and it was the bourgeoisie, artisans, professionals, and others who embraced Calvinism with more fervor.

Calvinism had greater success among the Dutch nobility, as large numbers converted to the Reformed church. This pattern, however, has to be seen as part of the larger political and socioeconomic struggles taking place in the Low Countries during the 1550s and 1560s, which were rooted in the growing hostility to Spanish rule. Political opposition to what were seen by many in the Netherlands as Spanish abuses came to be joined by religious opposition to the Catholic church and its Inquisition, with religious toleration becoming the slogan of the revolutionaries. Calvinism won many followers among the Dutch nobility not only because of Calvin's missionary efforts in their direction and the appeal of Reformed theology but also because of socioeconomic and political tensions.

This last point leads to an important conclusion about the nobility and the Reformation. Because of the extensive economic and political power of the European nobility in the sixteenth century, their reasons for accepting or rejecting Protestantism cannot be reduced solely to theological factors. In every country there were local political, social, and economic conditions that helped to shape nobles' decisions. If the religious choices of the nobility are to be understood, they have to be seen as part of a broader set of decisions each individual made about the economic, political, and religious future of his or her family.

[*See also* Peasants.]

BIBLIOGRAPHY

Brady, Thomas A. "Social History." In *Reformation Europe: A Guide to Research*, edited by Steven E. Ozment, pp. 161–181. Saint Louis, 1982. Includes a discussion of noble responses to the Reformation across Europe, especially in the Holy Roman Empire.

Delumeau, Jean. *Naissance et Affirmation de la Réforme.* Reprint, Paris, 1991. Emphasizes the importance of the large number of noble conversions to the success of the Huguenot churches in France.

Fritze, R. H. "'A Rare Example of Godlyness Amongst Gentlemen': The Role of the Kingsmill and Gifford Families in Promoting the Reformation in Hampshire." In *Protestantism and the National Church in Sixteenth-Century England*, edited by Peter Lake and Maria Dowling, pp. 144–161. London, 1987. Argues that the conversion of the gentry to Protestantism was crucial to the success of the Elizabethan Settlement.

Haigh, Christopher. *The English Reformation Revised.* London, 1987. Concludes that the Reformation in England made proportionally more progress among the literate social elites (gentry, merchants) than among the lower orders.

Kirk, James. *Patterns of Reform: Continuity and Change in the Reformation Kirk.* Edinburgh, 1988. Argues that the Protestant cause in Scotland by the 1550s was a strong national movement in all classes of society from *lairds* to artisans.

McNeill, John T. *The History and Character of Calvinism* (1954). Reprint, London and New York, 1973. An older but solid survey of the spread of Calvinism through Europe, including Germany, Poland, Bohemia, and Hungary.

Press, Volker. "Adel, Reich and Reformation." In *The Urban Classes, the Nobility and the Reformation*, edited by Wolfgang J. Mommsen, Peter Alter, and Robert W. Scribner, pp. 330–383. Stuttgart, 1979. Excellent survey of the reactions of the German nobility to the Reformation. Contains a summary in English.

Roelker, Nancy Lyman. "Family, Faith and *Fortuna:* The Châtillon Brothers in the French Reformation." In *Leaders of the Reformation*, edited by Richard L. DeMolen, pp. 247–277. London, 1984. A case study that demonstrates the importance of noble support for the success of the Reformation in France.

Scribner, Robert W. "Religion, Society and Culture: Reorientating the Reformation." *History Workshop* 14 (1982), 2–22. Argues that the towns rather than the nobility were the locus of the German Reformation.

Smit, J. W. "The Netherlands Revolution." In *Preconditions of Revolution in Early Modern Europe*, edited by Robert Forster and Jack Greene, pp. 19–54. Baltimore, 1970. Argues that the nobility in the Netherlands did convert to Calvinism in large numbers, but that this has to be seen in the context of the larger political and socioeconomic struggles that were taking place there during the 1550s and 1560s.

Wormald, Jenny. "'Princes' and the Regions in the Scottish Reformation." In *Church, Politics and Society: Scotland, 1408–1929*, edited by Norman Macdougall, pp. 65–84. Edinburgh, 1983. Concludes that the influence of the Scottish nobility in pushing the Reformation forward in their own regions was more limited than previous research had indicated.

ROBERT J. KALAS

NOMINALISM. The term *nominalism* covers philosophical theories purporting to account for "universals" (common nouns such as "human being," "horse," "stone") as mere names, since genuine reality is judged to consist solely of individuals. There have been three major philosophical efforts to account for universals. The first was that of Plato, whose extreme "realism" stipulated a world of eternal, universal Forms or Ideas, imitated and participated in by things in our experience; those things, known by sense, he termed "shadows of images." The Platonizing Augustine made divine Ideas of Plato's Forms; Christian Platonists have largely followed him in this. Plato's theory was opposed by the mature Aristotle, who proposed a "moderate realism" according to which the individual beings of experience are constituted by forms-in-matter. Those forms can be abstracted from sense data by the human intellect, which "makes all things" and which then "becomes all things" by adapting itself to the form of the "other as other." Finally, we can know the individual as individual by returning to the sense impressions by which the real individual was first grasped and from which impressions the process of understanding began, but now equipped to predicate the abstracted universal of the individual as its subject. Third, and many centuries later, various forms of "nominalism" were contrived in reaction to all realisms, for even the most moderate were thought by the nominalists to be excessive. The many forms of nominalism may be said to share family resemblances.

Proto-Nominalism. There is evidence of primitive forms of nominalism dating back to the late eleventh and early twelfth centuries, but documentation is meager and stems exclusively from those who opposed it. An obscure early nominalist, Raimbertus of Lille, was opposed by Herman, a future bishop of Cambrai, and also by Anselm of Bec. Raimbertus was said to have taught dialectic "as vocal" (*in voce*), and so to have departed from the realist tradition (*in re*), "of Boethius and of the ancients." In two letters and in a major treatise Anselm complained about another nominalist, Roscelin, having spoken of universals as nothing more than "vocal blasts" (*flatus vocis*). Anselm permitted himself the pun that thinkers who applied this to trinitarian theology "ought to be blasted away" (*exsufflandi*). Peter Abelard, too, bore witness against the same Roscelin. Having studied dialectic under him, Peter moved to another teacher, William of Champeaux, who taught "realistically" (*in re*). Abelard liked the explanations of his new teacher, William, no better than those of Roscelin. He refuted two successive positions of William. First, William held for an essence in common; then, under pressure from his difficult student, William proposed a community of "indifference" that Abelard refuted as well. Abelard's personal position seems to have been akin to William's second explanation: Abelard held that a universal term expresses a "status" rather than an essence or indifference. Such a term is a "word with meaning" (*sermo*). A universal term does duty for a corresponding concept in the divine Intellect representing the things of nature, but in a human intellect only such things as we can produce—swords, for instance, and houses. It is not unfair to list Abelard's solution among the nominalisms. As for the more extreme form ascribed to Roscelin, John of Salisbury later in the twelfth century reported that his nominalism had died with its author. Still, the terms "nominalists" (*nominales*) and "realists" (*reales*) were coined before the century was out. Both were used by Godfrey of Saint-Victor in his *Fountain of Philosophy*, a seriocomic presentation of academic Paris in the 1170s.

The great masters of the thirteenth century, Albert the Great, Bonaventure, and Thomas Aquinas, all held forms of moderate realism on universals. In their personal ways they held with Albert that there is a universal "before the thing" (*ante rem*), in the divine Mind; "in the thing" (*in re*), as its form; and "after the thing" (*post rem*), in the human mind, understanding the class to which an individual thing might belong. Between those moderate realists, whose position would become known as "the ancient way" (*via antiqua*) and the "modern way" (*via moderna*) of the nominalists, stands "the Subtle Doctor," John Duns Scotus (c.1265–1308).

It was characteristic of the thought of Scotus that he distinguished in things a number of "formalities," intelligible structures that differ from each other in a way that is "less than real" but "more than logical." An individual being was thus metaphysically analyzed into a broad class and then into increasingly limited formalities: for example, "animal," "rational," "Greek," "philosopher," and finally the "thisness" (*haecceitas*) in no sense shared by any other being and expressed in the nonuniversal name "Socrates." With this formalism went a characteristically Scotistic emphasis on the divine Will as against the traditional emphasis on the divine Intellect.

Classical Nominalism. Scholastic tradition, with Scotus as its most immediate transmitter, supplied William of Ockham (c.1285–c.1349) with a number of positions that would come to be identified with him but that were in fact no less characteristic of Scotus. Chief among them was the principle of parsimony according to which "entities are not to be multiplied without necessity"—a commonplace since Aristotle—which, although it had been used frequently by Scotus, is widely called "Ockham's razor." So too theological tradition, mediated by Scotus, provided Ockham with the distinction between "intuitive" and "abstractive" knowledge. By intuitive knowledge we know through sensation existing individual things, and this type of knowing normally carries existential weight: what is thus known is as a rule real. By abstractive knowledge we know the classes into which our thought and language associate things seen to resemble each other. These classes that engage abstractive knowledge cannot be real; hence, abstractive knowledge carries no existential implication. Ockham, who reacted sharply against the multiple formalities of Scotus, the "Subtle Doctor," has been called with some justice the "More Than Subtle Doctor." An instance of this is to be found in what appears to be his last theological work, given final shape while he was at Avignon waiting for a decision on the case against him for heresy: it shows traces of the articles urged against him (Wey, p. 28). In *Quodlibet* 6.6 (Wey, pp. 604–607) Ockham wrote that intuitive knowledge of a star could persist after the annihilation of the star by divine intervention: there was no patent contradiction to shackle divine power. In 5.5 (Wey, pp. 495–500) he had held that God could indeed "cause a 'creditive' act" in such circumstances and that such an act would "be abstractive, not intuitive" (Wey, p. 498). Natural reason cannot prove that God is One (1.1; Wey, pp. 1–11), nor that God is First Efficient Cause of all else (2.1; Wey, pp. 107–111); articles of faith cannot be demonstrated (2.3; Wey, pp. 117–123).

During Ockham's lifetime Adam Wodeham (d. 1350) and Robert Holkot (d. 1349) supported the *via moderna*. John of Mirecourt suffered a condemnation of his work in that vein (1347), as did Nicholas of Autrecourt in the same year.

As was usual with Ockham, he used his indubitable logical expertise to set out a theory of abstractive human knowing based on logic. Universals thus fall into a triple division in accord with "supposition theory," a threefold way in which a universal term can usefully, and with truth, "stand for" (*supponere pro*) a thing or things in a world of real individuals without the baggage of an impossible "universal reality." Ockham's terminology can be misleading for modern readers. First, "personal supposition" is not restricted to persons, but to any and all individual things which the term at stake can name. "Simple supposition" refers to the paradoxical situation in which a universal concept in a human intellect is, in itself, an individual mental episode. Finally, "material supposition" has nothing to do with matter, but refers to usages in which a term might "stand for" itself: " 'Horse' is a noun."

It would be difficult to overemphasize another distinction, older than Scotus (it can be found in Thomas Aquinas, *Summa theologiae*, 1.25.3–4), between the "absolute" and the "ordered" power of God. The first was seen by Ockham to be limited by the law of noncontradiction only; the second he held to be limited by divine decisions that have constituted various "orderings" of created things. Although by his absolute power God might reverse moral prescriptions—that he be hated might, in theory, become a precept and thus a virtuous act—the order he has freely established removes this from the realm of serious possibility. Thus Ockham could be sure of a divine response to the sacraments, to virtuous and to nonvirtuous living by humans, and, with the exception of miracles, to the normal order of the world of experience.

Nor did the *via moderna* end with the deaths of the first generation. John Buridan (who disappeared from the records in 1366) counted himself a discerning Ockhamist. Albert of Saxony (d. 1390) was the first rector of the University of Vienna; with Henry Totting of Oyta (d. 1397) and Henry

Hainbuch of Langenstein (d. 1397) Albert brought the *via moderna* into German-speaking circles. The two Henrys, incidentally, have been shown to represent an effort to meet Jewish resistance to trinitarian theology; because it did not seem possible to avoid paralogisms in using Aristotelian logic, they appealed to a "Platonic logic," a particularity not otherwise observable in nominalists (Shank). An important point is that causes for Ockham are individuals, observed to precede others; effects are individuals observed to follow others (*Quodlibet* 4.1; Wey, pp. 293–300). Abraham was the "cause" of Isaac and so, indirectly but truly, the "cause" of Jacob, his grandson (3.4; Wey, p. 215). Our empiric observation of such sequences guarantees that effects have causes and vice versa; on this basis, Ockham has been dubbed "a medieval Hume." In fact, his influence on future philosophers of the first rank is undeniable, especially on British empiricists. John Locke (1632–1704) began book 2, chapter I.2 of his *Essay* with the Ockhamist assertion "All our knowledge [is] about external sensible objects, or about the internal operations of our minds"; George Berkeley (1685–1753), no empiricist, in his *Treatise Concerning the Principles of Human Knowledge*, introduction paragraph 12, spoke of "an idea which considered in itself is particular, becomes general by being made to represent or stand for all other particular ideas of the same sort." David Hume (1711–1776) opened section IV, part I, of his *Enquiry Concerning Human Understanding* with the Ockhamist pronouncement "All the objects of human reason or inquiry may naturally be divided into two kinds, to wit, relations of ideas, and matters of fact." Ockham's anticipation of Hume's "customary causality" has been noted.

Nominalism and the Reformation. The influence of nominalism upon the Reformation ought not to be ignored, but neither should it be exaggerated. Nominalism was neither a primary cause nor an occasion of the Reformation. The young Luther was taught by at least one nominalist professor, Johann Nathin, who had been a student of Gabriel Biel at Tübingen; and Biel was an explicit admirer of Ockham, as his *Collectio vel epitome* (Collection or Abridgement) of Ockham's theology bears witness. But the University of Erfurt, where Luther met Nathin, welcomed Scholastics of all persuasions—Scotists, Thomists, and Albertists—to say nothing of humanists. What Luther came to dislike about Scholasticism (which for a moment he seems to have favored [McSorley, p. 218]) was the use of philosophy in theology, particularly that of Aristotle. He could not have been unaware of a range of academic options. Furthermore, at a time when Rome still hoped that he might be persuaded to remain in communion with the pope, two Thomists were sent to interview him: first Sylvester Mazzolini and then Cajetan (one of the classical commentators on Aquinas). Luther's objection to Scholasticism was not precisely its nominalist incarnation but rather what he perceived to be a Pelagian or semi-Pelagian insistence that to "do what is within one's power" was a quasi-automatic "cause" of grace and the scholastics' rationalizing of this by distinguishing between merit "out of justice" (*de condigno*), and merit "out of fairness" (*de congruo*). To the extent that nominalist theologians held such views, Luther was moved to oppose them. It may be noted in this connection that twentieth-century Roman Catholic theologians in dialogue with their Lutheran counterparts have held that Luther was theologically correct in this opposition. One of them has lamented that a year after Luther's death the Council of Trent defined the issue in favor of Augustine, the Second Council of Orange (A.D. 529), prenominalist scholastics, and Martin Luther (McSorley, p. 272).

BIBLIOGRAPHY

Boehner, Philotheus. *Ockham: Philosophical Writings; A Selection Edited and Translated.* Reprint, New York, 1962. In Latin with English translations.

Brecht, Martin. *Martin Luther: His Road to Reformation, 1483–1521.* Translated by James L. Schaaf. Philadelphia, 1985. Originally published in German: *Martin Luther: Sein Weg zur Reformation, 1483–1521*, Stuttgart, 1981.

Farthing, John L. *Thomas Aquinas and Gabriel Biel: Interpretations of St. Thomas Aquinas in German Nominalism on the Eve of the Reformation.* Durham, N.C., and London, 1988.

McSorley, Harry J. *Luther: Right or Wrong? An Ecumenical-Theological Study of Luther's Major Work, "The Bondage of the Will."* New York, 1969.

Shank, Michael H. *"Unless You Believe, You Shall Not Understand": Logic, University, and Society in Late Medieval Vienna.* Princeton, 1988.

Wey, Joseph C. *Venerabilis Inceptoris Guillelmi De Ockham Quodlibeta Septem.* Saint Bonaventure, N.Y., 1980.

EDWARD A. SYNAN

NONCONFORMITY With respect to Tudor England, the term *nonconformity* is customarily used to refer to the practice of those who refused to wear the clerical garb prescribed in *The Book of Common Prayer* but who nevertheless remained in the Church of England. Most of these people were Puritans, but doubts about the mandatory surplices and square caps troubled some, such as the young John Whitgift, who opted to wear the required clothing rather than risk losing the opportunity for a productive career in the church. The problem first surfaced when John Hooper (d. 1555) temporarily refused to use the traditional vestments after he was nominated to the bishopric of Gloucester.

The issue was rejoined in the mid-1560s in the Vestiarian Controversy. Two former Marian exiles, Thomas Sampson and Lawrence Humphrey, condemned the required vestments because of their association with Catholicism, especially the "idolatrous" doctrine of transubstantiation. Because of such associations, the bishops had made no attempt to enforce uniformity after the 1559 Elizabethan Settlement.

Subsequently troubled by the disorder in the church caused by those who refused to conform, Queen Elizabeth in 1565 ordered Matthew Parker, archbishop of Canterbury, to enforce uniformity. Parker offered the "precisianists," as the Nonconformists were called, a compromise, the terms of which required them to wear the surplice but not the alb, chasuble, and cope in parish churches, though the eucharistic garments were still mandatory in cathedrals and collegiate churches. In 1566 Parker and Edmund Grindal, bishop of London, who accepted the cope and surplice only reluctantly, demanded that 130 London clergy subscribe to articles embodying Parker's terms; 37 refused and were suspended, prompting public demonstrations. Humphrey and Sampson urged Heinrich Bullinger of Zurich to support their position on vestments, but Bullinger sided with the queen. He and Théodore de Bèze did, however, advise the Nonconformists to take their case to Parliament, which they did, unsuccessfully, in 1566/67.

The debate continued both in print and in Parliament. The Puritan case appeared in such publications as *A Brief Discourse Against the Outward Apparel and Ministering Garments of the Popish Church* (1566), probably by Robert Crowley and others, and *The Fortress of Fathers* (1566), probably by John Bartlett; the latter work incorporated selections from the writings of such Continental reformers as Bullinger, Martin Bucer, Peter Martyr Vermigli, and Philipp Melanchthon. Walter Strickland, member of Parliament for Scarborough, proposed the removal of the detested vestments in the 1571 Parliament, but his attempt failed when Sir Francis Knollys, a privy councillor, argued that such matters were part of the royal prerogative. The following year the controversy over vestments was dwarfed by the demand of radical Puritans for the virtual abolition of the episcopalian hierarchy.

The debate over conformity, especially ecclesiastical vestments, was the crucible out of which the Puritans emerged. The dispute was significant for two reasons. First, it raised the crucial issue of authority and ultimately led to challenges against both the royal prerogative in religion and episcopal polity in the church. Second, the symbolism involved in the traditional vestments and such practices as the sign of the cross in baptism and use of the marriage ring signified to advanced Protestants that the Reformation in England had stopped well short of its goals, thus mandating renewed efforts to purge the church.

[*See also* Baptists; Congregationalism; Puritans; *and* Separatists.]

BIBLIOGRAPHY

Collinson, Patrick. *The Elizabethan Puritan Movement.* Reprint, Oxford, 1990. Standard account of the emergence of the Puritans.

Primus, John H. *The Vestments Controversy.* Kampen, 1960. Fullest treatment of the Vestiarian dispute.

Solt, Leo F. *Church and State in Early Modern England, 1509–1640.* New York, 1990. Chapter 3 includes a useful overview of the Puritan challenge.

Trinterud, Leonard J., ed. *Elizabethan Puritanism.* New York, 1971. Contains a useful summary of the Vestiarian controversy and selections from key primary sources.

RICHARD L. GREAVES

NORFOLK, Duke of. *See* Howard, Thomas.

NORTHUMBERLAND, Duke of. *See* Dudley, John.

NORVEGUS, Laurentius (Nor., Laurits Nielssen; 1538–1622), Norwegian Jesuit. Norvegus played a leading role in the Counter-Reformation in northern Europe for over fifty years. Born in Tønsberg in southeastern Norway, he was given the name Laurits Nielssen at baptism. Usually known by his Latinized name, he is also known as Klosterlasse ("Laurits of the Cloisters"), which many Scandinavians use in a pejorative fashion. The background of his parents is unknown, though his father was presumably a middle-class merchant. His early education was at Tønsberg, followed by a stint at the Oslo cathedral school.

At the age of twenty, while studying at the metropolitan school in Copenhagen, Norvegus came in contact with some undercover Jesuits posing as merchants. (This contact has led some to postulate the existence of a secret Jesuit college in Copenhagen, but no documents in the Vatican Library substantiate this theory.) In August 1559 Norvegus enrolled at the Jesuit college in Louvain. While agonizing over his decision to convert to Roman Catholicism, he underwent the spiritual exercises laid out by Ignatius Loyola and became convinced of his course in life. In 1564 he became a Jesuit novice and the following year was ordained a Roman Catholic priest. One of his teachers at Louvain, who was to remain a lifelong friend, was the well-known Roberto Bellarmino. Within a short time, Norvegus gained a reputation for being a zealous and effective evangelist for the Jesuits. His sixty-year-old father came to visit him at Louvain in 1568 and returned to Norway a devout Roman Catholic. Norvegus himself returned to Norway two years later to head up a special Jesuit mission. Little came of this venture, though contact was maintained with a close circle of supporters in Tønsberg through the next decade. Many had been raised in the tenets of the old church and were naturally predisposed to Roman Catholicism. Since there had never been a grass-roots movement toward Lutheranism in Norway, laypersons often tended to regard Lutheranism as the new faith imposed by a foreign Danish sovereign. Because of the shortage of Lutheran clergy, the parish from which

Norvegus came had long been served by a Roman Catholic priest, whose Lutheran sympathies were questionable.

In 1562 John, duke of Finland, who was also a brother of Erik XIV, king of Sweden, married the Polish princess Catherine Jagiellon, the sister of King Sigismund II of Poland. Although imprisoned for a short time by his brother, John succeeded in overthrowing him in 1568 and proclaiming himself John III, king of Sweden and Finland. His Roman Catholic wife was now able to bring to Sweden her Jesuit spiritual advisers. In a letter to one of her Roman Catholic supporters, the queen dedicated herself to the conversion of her husband to Roman Catholicism.

In 1572 Pope Pius V died, as did Sigismund II of Poland. John III's son by Catherine succeeded to the Polish throne since he had been raised a Catholic by his mother. The new pope, Gregory XIII, was much more aggressive in direct negotiations with heretical Protestant rulers than his predecessor had been. When John III indicated his openness to be received into the Church of Rome, the principle of *cuius regio eius religio* (whoever the King, his religion) became very attractive from a Roman Catholic perspective. Returning Sweden-Finland to Roman allegiance loomed as an increasing possibility. Such an opportunity could not be missed and the Roman Curia swung into high gear.

From John III's perspective, Poland was worth a mass, though the prize went to his son, who was already a Catholic. In addition, his Polish consort had a huge fortune in Bona Sforza that Philip II of Spain had frozen. Conversion would undoubtedly free this immense wealth for use by a Catholic Vasa house. It was obvious that Philip did not want this wealth to fall into the hands of a Protestant monarch who could build a huge fleet to aid the Dutch Protestants, with whom Philip was engaged in conflict.

In 1571 the Lutheran archbishop of Uppsala, Laurentius Petri, published his long-awaited church order. The queen's Roman Catholic chaplain, Johan Herbst, immediately attacked it, instigating a pamphlet war. The Vatican, afraid that Herbst's brash tactics would alienate John III, replaced Herbst in 1574 with a Polish Jesuit, Stanislas Warszewicki. He had resided in Protestant Germany for several years and knew Lutheranism well. He quickly made a positive impression on John III with his learning and friendly demeanor. Though Warszewicki's stay lasted only a few weeks, he found the Swedish king amazingly open to much of Roman Catholic doctrine and practice. How to persuade the king to embrace Rome became a burning question. What was needed was a tried and true Scandinavian Jesuit to head up a mission to Sweden.

Norvegus, who spoke Swedish fluently and who had just returned to Louvain from Norway, was a logical choice. In the fall of 1575, Pope Gregory XIII appointed Norvegus to lead a secret Jesuit mission to Sweden (*Missio Suetica*) and to serve as the queen's chaplain. Norvegus was thirty-seven years of age when he assumed the role of a secret agent of the Counter-Reformation. His task was to build a cadre of Roman Catholic clergy that would be ready to assume strategic positions throughout the Swedish church and state as soon as the king publicly declared his new religious affiliation. It was a delicate operation since everything had to be done in secret. The Saint Bartholomew's Day Massacre was still vividly engrained in the minds of European Protestants. It was rumored that Jesuits had landed in Stockholm sometime in April 1576. Indeed they had, in the person of Norvegus and his cluster of trustworthy friends whom he had brought with him. At first John III was somewhat suspicious of Norvegus, who was a subject of his archenemy, the Danish king. But Norvegus quickly made friends of the German merchants and Swedish clergy in Stockholm. They viewed him as a distinguished theologian who sought to raise the theological level of the clergy in Sweden.

Two years before the arrival of Norvegus, John III had promulgated his liturgical reforms in his Red Book (*Liturgia Suecanae Ecclesiae*). The king was known to be a liturgical dilettante who preferred a high church style of worship. The theological college in Stockholm (Collegium Regium Stockholmense), which was opened in 1576 to sixty students, was thought to be a Lutheran high church theological college sponsored by the king in opposition to the low church theological faculty at the University of Uppsala. In reality it was the heart and soul of the secret Jesuit mission to Sweden. An inner-core Roman Catholic seminary was formed within the theological college to prepare students for their studies in Rome. But otherwise it appeared to the Swedish people as a Lutheran institution endowed by the king. Little did most people know that the king had become a Roman Catholic under the tutelage of Norvegus.

Now the question became how to get the king to declare his new religious allegiance publicly. Before he would do that, John III insisted that the pope allow clerical marriage in Sweden, vernacular worship, and Communion in both kinds. Operating out of a Tridentine mind-set, Pope Gregory XIII refused. Norvegus counseled caution but the pope dispatched the secretary of the Jesuit order, Antonio Possevino, to Sweden to force the king's hand by publicly announcing that the king had become a Roman Catholic. The move boomeranged. Instead of the desired result, John III denied he had ever converted to Roman Catholicism and quickly exposed the secret Jesuit mission. Norvegus and the Jesuits were expelled from Sweden in 1580. Three years later Catherine Jagiellon died and her Jesuit chaplains were forced to leave as well. After the failure of *Missio Suetica,* Norvegus fled to Poland, where he and Possevino wrote the Vatican seeking to account for their failure from their respective viewpoints. For all his courage and learning, Norvegus could act naively at times as well as independently, which behavior disconcerted his superiors. All the participants in the Swedish mission eventually assembled in Rome for a debriefing on what went wrong. Norvegus encouraged Rome not to give up on Sweden or for that matter on the whole of Scandinavia. To that end he drew up a *Confessio Suetica* for later use.

During the years that followed, Norvegus was assigned to various schools (Vienna, Olmutz, and Prague) in the Austrian province of the Jesuits. In 1604 he published his *Confessio Christiana de via Domini*, which was translated into Danish the next year. In question-and-answer catechetical style, he sought to outline the basic doctrinal differences between the Roman Catholic and the Lutheran churches. At the same time (1604) a law was promulgated in Copenhagen making it illegal for Danish and Norwegian students to study abroad at Jesuit institutions. Norvegus therefore went to Denmark in 1606 on an ill-fated mission but was summarily ordered out of the country by the Danish king, Christian IV.

The remaining years of Norvegus's long life were spent teaching, writing, and no doubt dreaming of what might have been. In 1622, the same year that the Congregation for the Propagation of the Faith was founded, Norvegus passed away in Vilna, Poland. To the end of his life, Norvegus never abandoned the hope of seeing Scandinavia return to the fold of Rome. So frightened were Scandinavian Lutherans of the real and imagined activities of Jesuits like Norvegus that laws were passed forbidding their abode in Scandinavia that were not rescinded until the 1950s.

BIBLIOGRAPHY

Brandrud, Andreas. *Klosterlasse: Et Bidrag til den jesuitiske Propagandas Historie i Norden.* Christiania [Oslo], 1895.

Garstein, Oskar. *Rome and the Counter-Reformation in Scandinavia.* 3 vols. Oslo and Leiden, 1963–1992.

Helk, Vello. *Laurentius Nicolai Norvegus S.J.* Copenhagen, 1966.

Norvego, Laurentio N. *Exemplum literarum, quas studiosi ex Daniæ et Norvegiæ Regnis extra Patriam . . . degentes ad Professores Acadimicæ Hafniensis.* Rostock, Germany, 1603.

———. *Confessio Christiana de via Domini.* Kraków, 1604.

———. *Examen confessionis fidei synodi Upsalensis in regno Sueciae anno Domini 1593.* Edited by Oluf Kolsrud. Oslo, 1965.

TRYGVE R. SKARSTEN

NORWAY. In the sixteenth century Norway was entering a rather prosperous phase of development. Its population grew and the principal industries, agriculture and fishing, expanded. In the beginning of the century the population was 200,000, and of these about 10,000 lived in towns. With a population of about 6,000, Bergen was the most prosperous, a center of trade and commerce. Trondheim had about 2,000 inhabitants, Oslo about 1,000.

In 1536, when Norway formally became a province of Denmark, Bergen lost much of its former importance to Oslo, which became the center of administration, economy, and defense, principally because of its better communications with Copenhagen. Immigration of skilled occupational groups such as miners and merchants as well as government employees from Denmark contributed to the increase of the population. The merchants and artisans emigrated from Denmark and Germany, the miners from Germany. Finnish farmers moved from the western parts of Sweden to Norway, and Norway began to export timber to the Netherlands, thereby improving its finances.

Historical Background and Church Politics. Christian II (r. 1513–1523) wanted to limit the financial power of the church by incorporating it in the state. The church was an important factor in trade and fishing, and for a long time it had been exempted from taxation. It had its own administration of justice with the fines payable to the bishop.

These plans of reform were advanced by the king at the same time Luther published *An den christlichen Adel* in 1520. These ideas soon arrived in Copenhagen. In the same year Christian wrote to Saxony asking for clergy "who do sing well, preach well, and have good knowledge of the New Testament." Martin Reinhart came to Copenhagen. In the spring of 1521 Andreas Bodenstein von Karlstadt visited Copenhagen but soon left the city. Abroad Christian was generally regarded as Lutheran and it was assumed that Luther would take refuge at his court. But Christian's legislation indicated that his goal was a reformed Catholic national church that would avoid breaking with Rome. He wanted to incorporate the church in society by restricting its economic and legal power without affecting its doctrine or liturgy. His attempts at reform ended in the spring of 1523 when the nobility and the church leaders revolted against the king's policy, which they found too compliant to the farmers and the burghers. Christian then left for Germany.

In 1523 Christian's uncle, Frederick, duke of Schleswig-Holstein, supported by the nobility and the higher clergy, was proclaimed king of Denmark (r. 1523–33). In a restrictive coronation charter he had to support the Catholic church and fight against Lutheranism. The power of the nobility was thus strengthened and the authority of the king reduced. Farmers and burghers were deprived of their privileges.

In a privy council meeting in Bergen in 1524 loyalty to Christian was revoked and Frederick was formally elected king of Norway. He confirmed a coronation charter drawn up by the councilors. The difference was not so remarkable since Christian's ecclesiastical reforms had not been valid in Norway. But Frederick had to commit himself to defend the interests of the Catholic church and its clergy and to prevent heretics, Lutherans as well as others, from preaching and teaching.

Theological Background. As early as 1526 the Scandinavian countries were politically connected with Prussia, a leading Protestant territory, where church policy was characterized by the rule of the prince over the church, the reduction of church property, and evangelical preaching, which became a source of inspiration for other commonwealths. In spite of his coronation charter Frederick I issued a letter of protection for the Lutheran preachers in 1526, in which he placed them under royal patronage. In 1529 he issued letters of protection for Herman Frese and Jens Viborg in Bergen, who were to "preach and teach the word of God to the poor and simple people" in the Church of the Holy Cross (Korskirken), where an evangelical service was introduced. In the same year the city council of Lübeck complained that "some new preachers" were allowed to stay in Norway, especially in Bergen. Lutheranism was supported by Vincens Lunge, a councilor in Bergen, who was protected by the king against the archbishop of Trondheim. With Frederick I's death in 1533 protection of Lutheranism came to an end. The succession to the throne was decided by an intense civil war between 1533 and 1536.

In 1523 Olav Engelbrektssøn had become archbishop of Norway and thereby head of the Norwegian church as well as leader of the Norwegian Council. When Christian II, who had turned to Catholicism again, returned to Norway in November 1531 to regain his realm, the clergy and peasantry supported him. For this adventure they had to pay a high price after Christian's attempt had failed and he was imprisoned in Denmark in 1532.

In August 1533 the archbishop summoned the Norwegian Crown Council to a meeting at Bud in Romsdal to discuss Lutheranism and decide who would be elected as new king. Their firm condition was that they should find a "Christian" (i.e., Catholic) king. During the civil war the archbishop had supported the claims of the imprisoned Christian II. To attain this goal he made himself an enemy of the Crown Council and even murdered some of the councilors.

Norway Becomes Part of Denmark. In 1536, the year before the Reformation was formally introduced through the Church Ordinance of 1537, Norway as a consequence of its rebellious role in the civil war ceased to be an independent kingdom. At the Diet of Copenhagen in 1536 the new king, Christian III, inserted a provision in his coronation charter that implied that Norway should be connected to Denmark in the future like the other Danish provinces (Jutland, Fyn, Sealand, and Scania) "and hereafter should not be nor be called a kingdom of its own." This was never fully accomplished, and Norway continued to be called a kingdom and kept many of its institutions. It remained, however, a satellite state until 1814. In this way the future of the Norwegian church was also decided: rules concerning the Danish church also applied to the Norwegian church, even though Norway succeeded in obtaining some special regulations.

The Reformation in Norway. No great reformer brought the evangelical message to Norway. The only exception to this general rule was Bergen, which had good connections with Germany and the Hanseatic towns and where an important middle class existed. Lutheran clergymen had been preaching there already during the reign of Frederick I. In 1526 a little-known friar named Antonius propagated Lutheran doctrines in the city. There also is some indirect evidence indicating that the new doctrine was known in the country. Thus King Frederick I donated the monastery of Nonneseter in Bergen to Vincent Lunge in 1528, who kept it as a secular fief.

On the whole, the Reformation came late to Norway, where it was formally introduced by a royal decree in the absence of a reformer. Even though the events introducing the Reformation in Norway were not dramatic, they nevertheless marked a radical change. The church lost its independent position in state and society. The change did not, however, arise from protests against the moral and religious degradation in the Catholic church, as had been the case in Denmark. Because of the isolated geographical location of Norway as well as the poverty of the country, such ecclesiastical evils had not been so obvious as in other countries.

In April 1537 Archbishop Olav accepted the political and theological consequences of his defeat and left Trondheim. The powerful head of the Catholic church in Norway and leader of the Norwegian State Council left the country. The same year all bishops were dismissed and ecclesiastical property was confiscated by the Crown. The first step toward the introduction of Lutheranism was then made.

The Reformation was formally introduced by the letter of Christian III on 16 June 1537 to Eske Bille, the tenant-in-chief of Bergen. The king instructed that the Reformation should be introduced cautiously. No priest should be removed from office and the church should retain most of its property. At a later time, when a new bishop was nominated, the organization and the doctrines of the church should be reformed. The task of the tenant-in-chief should now be confined to administering church property.

At this point no clergy had any experience of Lutheran theology or ethics. The king could not find anyone to whom he could entrust the task of carrying out the Norwegian Reformation. This was the reason why he ordered the tenant-in-chief Eske Bille to administer the diocese of Bergen, thereby avoiding social unrest until the king had presented a plan of how to accomplish reform. The Catholic clergy kept their former status not only in Bergen but also in the entire country.

Neither Luther nor any of the leaders of the evangelical movement in Germany seems to have had any direct contacts with Norway. Neither was any Norwegian document on the Reformation published. The burghers did not form an important social group that supported the evangelical message as they did in other countries.

The king's main purpose was to keep peace and order, and nothing was said either about doctrinal questions or about ecclesiastical abuse. The independence of the bishops, the deans, and the clergy was limited by the church ordinance of 1537/39 which was valid also in Norway. All had to swear an oath of allegiance to the king. The ordinance included a paragraph devoted especially to Norway. The king promised, when visiting Norway, to issue special stipulations because of "the provisions in this Ordinance that could not be valid in that country, in which in many cases another Church Ordinance ought to be issued."

On 26 August 1537 Bugenhagen consecrated Geble Pedersøn as the first Lutheran bishop (superintendent) in Norway. Bergen was for a long time the only diocesan town to have a bishop. Its first incumbent had been appointed by the former Catholic chapter in Bergen as "electus." Pedersøn was a humanist scholar who was zealously interested in education and in organizing a new school system.

In 1539 Oslo and Hamar were united into a single diocese. At the command of the king Pedersøn traveled throughout the new diocese to inform the people about the evangelical doctrine and the church ordinance, which was sanctioned on behalf of Norway by a meeting in Oslo in June 1539, attended by the clergy as well as laymen. The clergy of the new diocese applied to the king to send them a man of learning to teach them "the right understanding of the holy scripture." Christian III sent the former Catholic bishop, Hans Rev, to his old diocese after he had turned evangelical. In Oslo Rev founded a Latin school in order to train new evangelical clergy.

It was a long time before all four dioceses (Bergen, Oslo, Stavanger, and Trondheim) got their evangelical superintendents/bishops. In 1541 Jon Guttormsen arrived at Stavanger, where he founded a school and reconstructed churches in disrepair. Not until 1546 was Thorbjørn Olafsson Bratt nominated bishop (superintendent) in Trondheim. The king had previously sent him to study in Wittenberg for over two years. He was the first Lutheran bishop in Norway who had studied evangelical theology. Like the other superintendents, he founded a chapter school and rebuilt churches.

All the evangelical bishops of the first generation were Norwegian except Hans Rev, who was Danish. In the next generation all were Danes save Jens Nilssøn in Oslo (1530–1600), who had a Norwegian mother, though his father was Danish.

Theology. It was many years before the doctrinal disputes among the Lutherans on the Continent reached Norway. The Reformed doctrine was not yet felt as a menace to the Lutheran church and was still allowed. Bishop Jens Nilssøn sent his son to study at Saint Andrews in Scotland and used the Wittenberg catechism (1571), which may be labeled Philippist, for his teaching.

Norwegian students unhesitatingly attended Philippist and Calvinist universities in Germany and many of them were influenced by Niels Hemmingsen in Denmark. David Cythræus in Rostock had close contacts with Norwegian church leaders who accepted his irenic theology. Works by Calvin are often found in estate inventories of Norwegian clergymen.

Resistance against Catholicism was vivid. In 1572 Jens Skielderup, bishop in Bergen, published *A Christian Instruction from the Holy Writ about the Considerations a Christian Should Take on Idolatry in the Churches*, the only religious booklet written in Norway during the Reformation period.

Laurentius Norvegus (1538–1622) grew up in Norway, but during studies in Louvain in 1569 he had contact with the Jesuits. Between 1576 and 1580 he propagated the Counter-Reformation in Sweden and also tried to propagate it in Denmark. In 1604 a royal patent prohibited persons who had studied in Jesuit schools from holding office either in the church or in schools. In 1613, Catholics were prohibited from staying in the kingdom. At last, in 1624, monks, Jesuits, *presbyteros saeculares*, and other members of the Catholic clergy were forbidden on pain of death to reside in Denmark and Norway.

The Consolidation of the Reformation. Bishop Jens Skielderup (1557–1582) as well as his successor, Anders Foss (1583–1607), summoned the clergy of the diocese of Bergen to synods on the pattern of Denmark. In Stavanger and Trondheim too synods were held to justify Reformation practice. Bishop Jens Nilssøn (1580–1600) of Oslo did not convene any synods but traveled his diocese visiting the parishes. The efforts of these bishops had the same objective: carrying out the Reformation among the clergy as well as the parishioners. Schools were established to teach Lutheranism and special sermons on the catechism, addressed to the youth, were decreed to be given in the churches.

The tenant-in-chief in Trondheim, Christian Friis, drew the king's attention to the financial conditions in some parishes, which were too small to support an evangelical pastor with a family. The king, inspired by the German rules of visitations, appointed a royal commission, made up of the tenant-in-chief, the bishop, and three clergy to suggest improvements, and in 1589 they submitted their report, "Den Trondheimske Reformats." The commission gave an account of its observations and reported on the kind of improvements it undertook. Remarkably, secular and ecclesiastical authorities cooperated in consolidating parishes and closing churches to improve the economic conditions of the parishes.

The importance of education had been emphasized already by Luther and the German reformers. In Norway too this ideal was to be implemented. The diocesan synod at Stavanger in 1573 decided that only those older than twelve who knew the catechism should be permitted to take Communion. Typical sermons of this period are found in Bishop Jørgen Erikssøn's *Jonæ prophetis skiøne historia, udi 24 predicken begrepen* (The Wonderful Story of the Prophet Jonah, Told in 24 Sermons), printed in Copenhagen in 1622. The piety of Bishop Erikssøn seems to have been more influenced by Melanchthon than by Luther.

The Norwegian Church Ordinance of 1607. Not until the reign of King Christian IV (1588–1648) was the Reformation in Norway accomplished. Norway received its own church ordinance, which had been promised for a long time.

It was written by the bishop of Oslo, Anders Bendsøn Dall (1601–1607), together with his colleagues in Bergen (Anders Foss), in Trondheim (Isak Grønbech), and in Stavanger (Jørgen Erickssøn). The king had commissioned the four bishops only to prepare a draft, which was handed him in 1604. The king then had the Danish Chancellery and the professors of Copenhagen University revise it. Their main interest was to protect the unity of the kingdom, and therefore they excluded rules that were too specifically Norwegian. In 1607 Christian IV approved the Norwegian church ordinance in its revised form. At a solemn meeting in the cathedral of Stavanger the king in the presence of the bishops of the country presented the church ordinance as a gift to the Norwegian church. Although the new ordinance endeavoured to follow closely the one of 1537, one may recognize traces of an early stage of absolutism. As regards church discipline the responsibility was moved from the local to the diocesan level, from the clergy to the bishop and the consistory, which was introduced as a new ecclesiastical institution. The consistory received the decisive responsibility for excommunication after consultation with dean, chapter, and bishop.

Liturgy and Divine Service. The divine service in Norway was mostly prescribed by the Danish liturgical books, but the development came one generation later. The earliest evidence of Norwegian liturgical practice can be found in the statutes of the first synods of western Norway (1569–1589) and in a letter from the bishop of Oslo in 1580. Almost every Catholic priest remained in his parish after the Reformation. The Latin church ordinance of 1537 (the Danish translation came in 1539) laid down only the general outline for the liturgical reorganization. Peder Palladius's *Service-Book* (Book of Common Prayer) of 1556, the hymnal of Hans Thomissøn of 1569, and Niels Jesperssøns gradual of 1573 gave more detailed information about the liturgical order. The statutes of the synod in Bergen (1584) gave the impression that the clergy had their own version of the church ordinance. The bishop of Bergen, however, complained in his synodal sermon in 1589 that not every clergy followed the directions given. Somewhat earlier, in a letter of 1580, the bishop of Oslo intimated the same. The synod of 1584 identified the cathedral of Bergen as the normative church of the diocese as regards liturgical practice in spite of the prescriptions in a royal letter of 1568 that identified the Church of Our Lady in Copenhagen as the norm. Such an adjustment was typical for the Reformation in Norway. As late as in the draft of the church ordinance of 1604 the bishops reminded the clergy that not only bread but also wine should be distributed at Communion.

After the Reformation, reredos (*katekismetavler*) representing one or more parts of the catechism were often placed over the altar instead of Catholic altar pieces. The superintendent of Bergen, Jens Skielderup, was the first to introduce the idea of painting sentences from the Bible on Norwegian reredos. It was decreed in the statutes of the Bergen synod in 1589 that altar pieces should be set up without pictures, containing only "the wonderful sentences from the holy Bible," these "wonderful sentences" being parts of the catechism. Seventy-eight such reredos are preserved in Norway. After the Reformation the pulpit received a more conspicuous place in the churches and pews were installed because of the importance and length of the sermon.

New marriage laws with betrothal, bans in church for three Sundays in succession, and finally church weddings were introduced in Norway in 1589, seven years after Denmark. The 1556 service book by Peder Palladius was replaced in 1580. The Bible of Christian III appeared in 1550, and three years later sixty-five copies were distributed to those churches in the diocese of Oslo that had paid for it. In 1556 there were ninety-six Bibles in Norway. In 1589 the Bible of Frederick II appeared and in 1607 the cheap Bible edition of Bishop Hans Poulsen Resen.

By the beginning of the seventeenth century ecclesiastical books were in common use in Norway, and in 1604 Norway had its own law and in 1607 its own church ordinance. The Reformation was finally realized in Norway.

BIBLIOGRAPHY

Aarflot, Andreas, and Carl Fredrik Wisløff. *Norsk kirkehistorie.* Oslo 1966. See vol. 1.

Bang, A. C. *Den norske kirkes historie i Reformations-aarhundredet, 1536–1600.* Kristiania, 1895.

Brohed, Ingmar, ed. *Reformationens konsolidering i de nordiska länderna, 1540–1610.* Oslo, 1990.

Christopherson, Kenneth Eugene. "Norwegian Historiography of Norway's Reformation." Ph.D. diss., University of Michigan, 1985.

Garstein, Oscar. *Rome and the Counter-Reformation in Scandinavia.* 4 vols. Oslo, 1963–1992.

Grell, Ole Peter. *The Scandinavian Reformation: From Evangelical Movement to Institutionalisation of Reform.* New York, 1995.

Quam, John Elliott. "Jørgen Erikssøn: A Study in the Norwegian Reformation, 1571- 1604." Ph.D. diss., University of Michigan, 1982.

INGUN MONTGOMERY

NUNS. Monastic profession offered women an alternative to marriage and motherhood, an opportunity to broaden their intellectual and administrative talents in a community of socially compatible peers, whether in a wealthy rural convent for noble women or in a small-town house sheltering a handful of women supported by handiwork. The endemic warfare and plague of the fourteenth century reduced their numbers and resources, but in the late fifteenth century convents again had more applicants than their resources could support. Loosely cloistered nuns retained ties to family, friends, and neighbors. They helped troubled relatives and patrons in emergencies with spiritual alms accumulated by prayer and self-mortification and with corporal alms for the sick and needy from private funds or earned income. Nuns undertook the education of women and children and gave hospitality and nursing to the poor, the old, and the orphaned.

Hagiography enshrined women who defied family, friends, and sometimes the church itself in order to fulfill a religious vocation. It was, however, virtually impossible to gain a place in a convent without financial support. Young women and widows had to supply their own dowries, though undowered women were incorporated as *conversae*, sisters devoted to housework or external errands, who were ineligible to participate in governance or choir. Thus, fathers had the final power to assign their daughters to marriage or to the convent. Popular fiction fantasized the complaints and peccadilloes of frustrated girls forced into the celibate life by hard-hearted and closefisted parents. Most young women obeyed their fathers, and their relative chances of happiness in a convent or in an arranged marriage were about even. In sixteenth-century England royal commissioners who investigated convents—with the dual motive of persuading the nuns to leave their communities and discrediting those who refused—found few dissolute nuns and few who would agree to break their vows.

Both clergymen and laymen distrusted women who lived outside their moral and physical control, viewing unmarried women as anomalies in the social order. Nuns were never incorporated into the ecclesiastical hierarchy. They were excluded from the educational, preaching, and evangelizing efforts of the international orders. Their communities, which tended to be smaller, poorer, and more restricted in scope, were placed under episcopal jurisdiction and were dependent on local patrons. Clerical fears were reflected in sermons of revolting prurience, and most monastic orders refused female members or made their strict enclosure a condition of spiritual supervision. In 1295 the papal bull *Periculoso* decreed claustration for all women religious regardless of their original vocation, though it was rarely enforced in the chaotic fourteenth century.

In the fifteenth century many nuns accustomed to a relatively open life resisted male reformers who forcibly imposed strict cloistering, voluntary poverty, a common treasury, and a common table. Such women as Colette of Corbie and Birgitta of Sweden and many abbesses of great royal monasteries, however, successfully implanted the same reforms in hundreds of convents. By the sixteenth century German and Scandinavian nuns fiercely opposed a new generation of Protestant reformers who sought to force them out of their cloisters and into marriage. Many convents had to be left to die out when it proved impossible to dislodge the nuns; Martin Luther noted that convents served a social purpose in sheltering unmarried women, though he denied that their religious services had any usefulness and defined their vocations as "selfish." German Catholic women were supplanted by Protestant women who maintained the conventual life through the eighteenth century. At least one English community, the Brigittines of Syon, escaped to the Continent, while individual nuns took refuge on their families' estates or in foreign convents. By Elizabethan times Catholic families began to endow English communities in France or the Spanish Netherlands, which continued to offer English women the alternative of celibacy. The nuns themselves clearly believed in the worth of their vocations and defended them with courage and persistence.

Spiritually ambitious women of the sixteenth century saw the cloister as the logical apex of their careers. Even before the Council of Trent and before Pius V (*Circa Pastoralis*, 1566) reiterated that cloister defined all nuns, Teresa of Ávila inspired women of every order to seek a "hidden apostolate" where their prayers might give strength and purpose to a clergy distracted by worldly concerns. As their public presence shrank, nuns increased their austerities, prayers, and sometimes self-torture in order to multiply the spiritual alms they contributed to the Counter-Reformation and the overseas missions.

As late medieval reformers gradually persuaded nuns to retreat deeper into the cloister and to dedicate themselves to prayer and contemplation, their charitable activities were taken over by married women who devoted themselves to pious practices while living in the world. With their husbands or with women of similar sympathies, Frances of Rome, Catherine of Genoa, and others established various enterprises, such as hospitals and soup kitchens, for poor relief. But when widowhood intervened to make a deeper religious life possible, such women generally retired to a cloister and abandoned their active lives. Other women did not, however, for many women of the early sixteenth century were inspired to undertake an active apostolate emulating the missionary work of the Jesuits. Angela Merici's Company of Saint Ursula embraced the apostolic ideal of becoming one with the poor they served. Upper-class ladies acted as supervisors and patrons for lower-class women who, living at home or with employers, devoted themselves to the care of the sick and needy, as well as to the religious education of poor girls. Their ideal was to help the poor help themselves and join as equals in the care of others. In the early sixteenth century, the Ursulines spread from Italy into France, where they were principally devoted to the education of girls from every class. Mary Ward's institute spread from an educational mission in the Spanish Netherlands to active charitable and missionary work in Protestant England.

These charitable activities by nuns were often directed specifically to women, for many scholars have noted that poverty was increasingly feminized in the sixteenth century. Social restraints and guild regulations hampered poor women's ability to support themselves and their children and many lost their husbands to war or overseas migration. The feminization of poverty accelerated in Protestant countries with the transfer of monastic property to male institutions. Docile and virtuous women might be classed as "embarrassed poor," gentry whose incomes failed to support their social status. Nunneries for noble women became strong candidates for charity when inflation and overpopulation threatened their standard of living, but this dependency only enhanced the feeling of many reformers that nuns were socially useless.

Unmarried Catholic women with a vocation to religion were systematically submitted to their bishops. In convents this led to mixing together many types of enclosed women, such as prostitutes, prisoners, refugees from home, and penitents, as well as genuine nuns. Convents were frequently forced to take criminal or disturbed women into their cloisters in exchange for financial support.

Increasingly, however, the public tended to confuse women who ministered to the poor and sick with their charges. Fear of contagion from disease and even from poverty engendered deep suspicion of beguines and beatas, women who voluntarily crossed the deepening gulf between the classes. Highly successful in the early sixteenth century, most of the active women's enterprises were dissolved in the wake of the Council of Trent. Wealthy women who organized charities became preoccupied with protecting embarrassed gentlefolk from contact with the vulgar poor. They often funded soup kitchens or hospitals but sent their servants to do the dirty work. They demanded that girls of good family be separated from lower-class girls, even in the schools where nuns continued to serve poor day pupils. Gradually the Ursulines were cloistered and found it increasingly difficult to educate poor girls as wealthy boarders absorbed their attention, though they added the education of girls to their monastic vows. Similarly, the few nuns who made their way to the missions of the New World found themselves diverted into caring for white women rather than the Indians whom they had come to serve. Mary Ward's institute and similar groups of would-be "Jesuitesses" were condemned and dissolved by the resurgent papal hierarchy. The seventeenth-century Daughters of Charity, who took only temporary "simple" vows, succeeded in reviving the active apostolate for women, but the Roman Catholic church steadfastly refused to classify such women as nuns.

[*See also* Anticlericalism; Celibacy and Virginity; Monasteries; Monasticism; Religious Orders; Roman Catholicism; *and* Trent, Council of.]

BIBLIOGRAPHY

Bilinkoff, Jodi. *The Avila of Saint Teresa: Religious Reform in a Sixteenth Century City.* Ithaca, N.Y., 1990.

Châtellier, Louis. *Reformation and the Formation of a New Society.* Cambridge, 1989.

Cohen, Sherrill. "Asylums for Women in Counter-Reformation Italy." In *Women in Reformation and Counter-Reformation Europe: Private and Public Worlds,* edited by Sherrin Marshall, pp. 166–188. Bloomington, Ind., 1989.

Daichman, Graciela S. *Wayward Nuns in Medieval Literature.* Syracuse, N.Y., 1986.

Janssen, Johannes. *History of the German People at the Close of the Middle Ages.* New York, 1966.

Ledochowska, Teresa. *Angela Merici and the Company of St. Ursula According to the Historical Documents.* Translated by Mary Teresa Neylan. Rome, 1969.

Leibowitz, Ruth P. "Virgins in the Service of Christ: The Dispute over an Active Apostolate for Women during the Counter-Reformation." In *Women of Spirit,* edited by R. R. Ruether and E. McLaughlin, pp. 131–152. New York, 1979.

Oliva, Marilyn. *The Convent and the Community in the Diocese of Norwich, 1350-1540.* Ph.D. diss., Fordham University, 1991.

Power, Eileen. *Medieval English Nunneries, 1275–1535.* Cambridge, 1922.

Rapley, Elizabeth. *The Dévotes: Women and the Church in Seventeenth Century France.* Montreal, 1990.

Rohrbach, Peter-Thomas. *Journey to Carith: The Story of the Carmelite Order.* Garden City, N.Y., 1966.

Trexler, Richard C. "Charity and the Defense of Urban Elites in the Italian Communes." In *The Rich, the Well-born and the Powerful,* edited by Fred Jaher. Urbana, Ill., 1974.

Wiesner, Merry E. "Nuns, Wives and Mothers: Women and the Reformation in Germany." In *Women in Reformation and Counter-Reformation Europe: Private and Public Worlds,* edited by Sherrin D. Marshall. Bloomington, Ind., 1989.

Wilson, Katharina, ed. *Women Writers of the Renaissance and Reformation.* Athens, Ga., 1987.

JO ANN MCNAMARA

NUREMBERG.

Under much pressure from preachers and the community, Nuremberg was one of the first cities actually to reform the church by civil decree. The eminent economic status of the city (with probably more than 40,000 inhabitants) was based upon its advanced production of trade goods and its expansive foreign trade and money transactions. It was governed by a stable patrician class, was a cultural center shaped by humanism, and reigned over a territory that included six cities, seven trade centers, and more than seventy villages.

The piety that was characteristic in Nuremberg during the late Middle Ages and that was also the subject of artistic expression culminated in the townspeople's interest in securing their salvation through good works (e.g., indulgences, donations, and pilgrimages). As late as 1 October 1517 Pope Leo X granted any Nuremberg citizen who donated a sum equivalent to a day's cost of living a complete absolution. This, along with other expressions of piety, was an indication of an intact religious-ecclesiastical life. Yet when Johannes von Staupitz, who repeatedly spent time in Nuremberg, attacked the practice of indulgences in his Advent sermons of 1516, and when he drew attention to God's mercy, his views were well received in the town, which had long sought to wrest ecclesiastical authority from the bishop of Bamberg.

Beginnings of the Reformation. Stimulated by Staupitz, a circle of respected townspeople—among whom were some council members, as well as the council's consultant, Christoph Scheurl; the council's clerk, Lazarus Spengler; and the painter Albrecht Dürer—held conversations about religious topics at the Augustinian monastery. When Wenceslaus Linck came from Wittenberg to Nuremberg in the spring of 1517, he became a central figure in this circle that was opening itself up to thoughts of reform. The interest in Martin Luther is also documented by letters from Scheurl and by the translation of the Ninety-five Theses into German by Kaspar Nützel. On 5 and 23 October 1518 Luther stayed in Nuremberg during a journey to Augsburg. The first public lay testimony in Luther's defense was Spengler's *Schutzrede und christliche Antwort eines ehrbaren Liebhabers göttlicher Wahrheit der Heiligen Schrift* ... (Supportive Speech and Christian Answer of an Honorable Admirer of the Divine Truth of Holy Scripture . . . ; 1519), in which he presented Luther's teachings as liberating to one's conscience and as based upon Christ and scripture. When, in the same year, the Ingolstadt theologian Johann Eck was ridiculed in the satirical pamphlet *Eccius dedolatus*, whose author was believed to be the humanist Willibald Pirckheimer, Eck also included the names of Spengler and Pirckheimer in the bull of 15 July 1520 threatening Luther with an ecclesiastical ban. The council was thus challenged for the first time and supported the efforts of both to lift the ban, although not successful until August 1521.

The appointment of a reform-minded clergy set the city's course of support for the reform movement. In 1520 Hektor Pömer and in 1522 Georg Pesler, who both had studied in Wittenberg, were appointed as provosts. In 1521/22 Andreas Osiander, Dominikus Schleupner, and Thomas Venatorius were appointed as preachers, and Wolfgang Volprecht was made prior. For the time being, however, religious services and the ecclesiastical order were left unchanged, but disruptions of sermons, mock processions, and violations of the obligation to fast—mostly perpetrated by craftsmen and journeymen—testified to a spreading anticlericalism. The council criticized some of those acts, but its tone was generally moderate so that the Protestant message was able to reach a broad spectrum of the population.

When the Edict of Worms of May 1521 was presented to the council, the way in which the council enforced its regulations was sometimes lenient, sometimes restrictive, depending on circumstances. Since Nuremberg was made the seat of the imperial regiment and the imperial court and since between 1522 and 1524 three imperial diets were held here, the council and the reformers acted during those years in full view of the estates of the empire who were temporarily present. Consequently, concerns about foreign policy influenced the actions of the council, which strove for a harmony between obedience toward the gospel and obedience toward the emperor. But at the beginning of 1523, when the papal nuncio demanded the arrest of the new preachers, the council protected them. It could not ignore the anticlerical sentiment and the growing unrest in the city, and it did not shy away from a conflict if a curtailment of its rights and disturbance of the peace in the city were threatened.

Although there was growing pressure from the community for a renewal of the ecclesiastical structure, the city government did not yet give in to that pressure. The council issued an order regulating the giving of alms in 1522 but still did not allow Communion in both kinds; thus, only Volprecht practiced it on Easter 1523. Some ceremonies disrespected for their external "pomp," however, were removed. Thereupon, on 1 June 1524, the provosts in their own right introduced a restructuring of the religious service. Although they provided the council and the bishop of Bamberg with a justification for their actions, they produced a continuing conflict. In retrospect, the council sanctioned the innovations, aware of the impending state of unrest in the city.

Intensification of the Conflict and Colloquy on Religion. Through the pressure exercised by the reform movement, two facts became manifest—an interest in definitive decisions by the council and a stronger social orientation. From 1523 Diepold Peringer, the "peasant of Wöhrd" (a former monk), propagated Lutheran thought in a populist way. In 1523/24 the painter Hans Greiffenberger defended in seven pamphlets the layman's right to relate directly to the Bible and demanded the pure preaching of the gospel. In 1523 Hans Sachs effectively summarized the typical charges levied against the clergy and their greed for money in the allegorical animal table *Die Wittembergisch Nachtigalle* (The Wittenberg Nightingale). In 1524 he propagated in four prose dialogues the idea that the clergy should work and accept civil duties, and he leveled a polemic against those who called themselves "Lutheran" but whose lifestyle was not exemplary of that designation.

The confluence of the religious and a social movement are documented, particularly after May 1524, by peasants' meetings in the rural areas belonging to the town and by the refusal to pay the tithe to the clergy and their institutions. The council asked the townspeople to abstain from those activities, and it sought to isolate the city from them. Nevertheless, there followed opposition to the taxation of foodstuff and support for the establishment of guilds (which had not existed since 1348). The council responded with comprehensive military precautions and sometimes severe punishment of participants in the city as well as in its rural surroundings.

When Thomas Müntzer and Andreas Bodenstein von Karlstadt were expelled from the electorate of Saxony, Müntzer, Heinrich Pfeiffer, and Martin Reinhard made an effort in the fall of 1524 to establish contacts in Nuremberg. This was thwarted, and the spread of other views that differed from Lutheran doctrine was halted. This development is exemplified by the trial of the painters Hans Sebald Beham, Barthel Beham, and Georg Pencz, as well as of the schoolmaster Hans Denck (who ended up being expelled from the city in January 1525), but also in the course of action against the spreading influence of Huldrych Zwingli in the city. In general, the council acted according to the principle that salvation was not a matter of personal judgment but subject to the authority of the city council, which was therefore interested in "unanimous preaching."

In order to eliminate "discordant preaching," the council convened a colloquy on religion from 3 to 14 March 1525, which enjoyed great attendance by the townspeople. Catholic believers and reformers were called upon to prove the scriptural conformity of their doctrines. In the end the council judged the Catholic preachers as disproved. On 17 March they were barred from preaching and from taking confession. The council also accounted for its decision in favor of the Lutheran doctrine by arguing that it wanted to avoid civil unrest. As a matter of fact, during the time of the Peasants' War the situation once again became dangerously acute, but the council was successful in keeping the commune uninvolved in those events by military measures and by a number of concessions (small tithe, low taxation, etc.).

The reform movement had achieved the following: the acceptance of Protestant preachers in the town and its rural areas, the abolition of the "papal" Mass and the restructuring of religious services, the abolition of processions and ceremonies dedicated to saints, the establishment of a "common chest" (civic welfare fund), the subsumption of clergy under civil law, the dissolution of most monasteries, and the establishment of a school for higher education. The results of these measures were the communal administration of churches, the detachment from the bishop of Bamberg as ecclesiastical authority, and the release of believers from spiritual and material burdens. Secular and ecclesiastical authority now lay in the hands of the council.

Defense of Reforms. After the decisions in principle, the issue became above all the inward and outward defense of the reforms already achieved, a process in which lawyers and theologians actively supported the council, especially Spengler and Osiander. Acting against the temporarily strong influence of Zwingli, the activities of the Anabaptists, and the orthodox resistance in the remaining monasteries, the council strove to preserve the civil peace by means of "unanimous preaching."

The bishop of Bamberg sought to reestablish his rights with the aid of the Swabian League. In spite of its objection, a commission of theologians and councilmen, in compliance with the margravate of Brandenburg-Ansbach, visited the rural parishes in September and October 1528 and the city parishes in May 1529. The ecclesiastical order, which had been prepared in 1529 by a commission of theologians under the supervision of Osiander, was put into force in the city on 1 January 1533 and in the rural areas on 9 February. The bishop of Bamberg and Eck did enter their protest against it, but during the following period it became a model for a number of ecclesiastical orders in other towns and territories.

During the imperial Diets of Speyer in 1526 and 1529, Nuremberg was resolutely on the side of the Protestant estates of the empire, but it refrained from forming alliances in order not to lose the emperor's favor. As a result, the city came under the suspicion of turning its back on the new faith. At the imperial diet at Augsburg in 1530, Nuremberg approved in spite of the Augsburg Confession, but it did not join the Schmalkald League, founded shortly thereafter. In light of the risk of being without protection, only a limited cooperation with its members ensued (an alliance between Augsburg and Ulm was founded in 1533), and in 1535 Nuremberg joined the imperial alliance. During the Schmalkald War of 1546–1547, the city sought to stay out of the conflict, but upon the defeat of the Schmalkaldians it was forced to accept the Interim. When the imperial Diet of Augsburg negotiated and endorsed the Peace of Augsburg of 1555, Lutheranism was firmly established in the imperial city of Nuremberg.

[*See also* Linck, Wenceslaus; Pirckheimer, Willibald and Caritas; Scheurl, Christoph; *and* Staupitz, Johann von.]

BIBLIOGRAPHY

Engelhardt, Adolf. "Die Reformation in Nürnberg." *Mitteilungen des Vereins für Geschichte der Stadt Nürnberg* 33 (1936), 1–258; 34 (1937), 1–402.

Grimm, Harold J. *Lazarus Spengler: A Lay Leader of the Reformation.* Columbus, Ohio, 1978.

Pfeiffer, Gerhard, ed. *Quellen zur Nürnberger Reformationsgeschichte: Von der Duldung liturgischer Änderungen bis zur Ausübung des Kirchenregiments durch den Rat, Juni 1524-Juni 1525.* Nuremberg 1968.

———. *Nürnberg: Geschichte einer europäischen Stadt.* Munich, 1971.

Schmidt, Georg. "Die Haltung des Städtekorpus zur Reformation und die Nürnberger Bündnispolitik." *Archiv für Reformationsgeschichte* 75 (1984), 194–232.

Schmidt, Heinrich Richard. *Reichsstädte, Reich und Reformation: Korporative Religionspolitik, 1521–1529/30.* Stuttgart, 1985.

Seebaß, Gottfried. *Das reformatorische Werk des Andreas Osiander.* Nuremberg, 1967.

———. "Stadt und Kirche in Nürnberg im Zeitalter der Reformation." In *Stadt und Kirche im 16. Jahrhundert*, edited by Bernd Moeller, pp. 66–86. Schriften des Vereins für Reformationsgeschichte, vol. 190. Gütersloh, 1978.

Strauss, Gerald. *Nuremberg in the Sixteenth Century.* Rev. ed. Bloomington, Ind., 1976.

Vogler, Günter. *Nürnberg 1524/25.* Studien zur Geschichte der reformatorischen und sozialen Bewegung in der Reichsstadt. Berlin, 1982.

———. "Imperial City Nuremberg, 1524/25: The Reform Movement in Transition." In *The German People and the Reformation*, edited by R. Po-Chia Hsia, pp. 33–49. Ithaca, N.Y., 1988.

GÜNTER VOGLER

Translated from German by Wolfgang Katenz

NUREMBERG, PEACE OF. Negotiated by the adherents of the Augsburg Confession and Charles V, the agreements of the Peace of Nuremberg provided a temporary truce between the two factions. At the Diet of Augsburg in 1530, an attempt was made to settle the relations between Protestants and Catholics on the basis of renunciation of violence until the convening of a council. Initial efforts toward an agreement failed, owing to the emperor's intransigent views on politics in religion. But since the support of the Protestant estates in the war against the Turks was indispensable, the electors Albrecht of Mainz and Ludwig V of the Palatinate, who were interested in a settlement, made an effort toward negotiation. The major obstacle turned out to be the Protestants' demand to dismiss all religious suits before the imperial cameral court.

Following exploratory talks between electors Albrecht and John of Saxony at the turn of 1531/32, Charles V decided to deal with the issue of religion at the Diet of Regensburg. But since there was fear of disruptions by the Catholic estates of the empire, the negotiations were held separately from the imperial diet, the first occurring from 1 April to 7 May 1532 in the Franconian city of Schweinfurt. Seven princes were represented (including those of Saxony and Hesse) and fourteen cities (including Nuremberg, Strasbourg, Ulm, Lübeck, and Magdeburg). Charles V was willing to grant only a limited "suspension," but his main objective was the dissolution of the Schmalkald League. Issues of contention were the *jus reformationis* (the right of a territorial ruler or a city council to "reform" the church in their territory), the disposition of ecclesiastical property, the jurisdiction of the bishops, the recognition of the Augsburg Confession and of its apology, the treaty's inclusion of those estates that would at a future date subscribe to the Augsburg Confession, and the appointment of a national council in Germany. A solution to this deadlocked situation was found by suspending several controversial issues, while the Protestants concentrated on their demand to be included in the general public peace (from which they had been excluded in 1530). Thus, the aim was no longer a theological concord but a political settlement.

Following a break the negotiations were continued on 8 June in Nuremberg with the emperor's approval and the support of the Curia Romana. On 23 July the electors of Mainz and the Palatinate, as the main negotiators, signed the treaty that had been negotiated with the Protestants; on 3 August an imperial mandate made the agreement public. For the sake of the preservation of peace in the empire, the followers of the Augsburg Confession were guaranteed the status quo until the next council or the next imperial diet. Until then neither of the parties was to exercise or support force against the other. The emperor agreed to support the convening of a council. A declaration that was not issued publicly but made available to the leaders of the negotiating parties provided that lawsuits involving religious matters—inasmuch as they concerned Protestants covered by the treaty—would be suspended.

The expectations were only partially fulfilled. It became possible for the estates to act in concert against the Turks. The recess of the Diet of Augsburg was no longer valid, and the Augsburg Confession was temporarily recognized. But the agreements did not become part of the recess of the Diet of Regensburg, and hence they were not binding for the estates. Since the emperor had left the signing of the treaty to the leaders of the negotiating parties, he could declare the treaty valid or annul or alter it. It was not until 24 November 1535 that Charles V ordered the suspension of religious suits. It remained controversial what, according to the agreements, would be considered a "religious issue." From the standpoint of constitutional law a provisional situation had been created. Also, the stipulations contradicted earlier imperial decrees. But the reform movement was able to consolidate itself under the auspices of the "religious peace." The provisional situation became permanent, and the efforts toward a conciliation opened a path that led—via the Peace of Frankfurt in 1539, the recesses of the imperial diets of 1541 and 1544, and the Treaty of Passau in 1552—to the Peace of Augsburg in 1555.

[*See also* Charles V *and* Schmalkald League.]

BIBLIOGRAPHY

Aulinger, Rosemarie. "Die Verhandlungen zum Nürnberger Anstand 1531/32 in der Vorgeschichte des Augsburger Religionsfriedens." In *Aus der Arbeit an den Reichstagen unter Kaiser Karl V. Schriftenreihe der Historischen Kommission bei der Bayerischen Akademie der Wissenschaften*, vol. 26, edited by Heinrich Lutz and Alfred Kohler, pp. 194–227. Göttingen, 1986.

"Der Reichstag in Regensburg und die Verhandlungen über einen Friedstand mit den Protestanten in Schweinfurt und Nürnberg 1532." In *Deutsche Reichstagakten, jüngere Reihe*, vol. 10, pt. 1, edited by Rosemarie Aulinger, pp. 129–146. Göttingen, 1992.

Engelhardt, Adolf. "Der Nürnberger Religionsfriede von 1532." *Mitteilungen des Vereins für Geschichte der Stadt Nürnberg* 31 (1933), 17–123.

Wolgast, Eike. "Die Wittenberger Theologie und die Politik der evangelischen Stände." *Quellen und Forschungen zur Reformationsgeschichte* 47 (1977), 203–224.

GÜNTER VOGLER

Translated from German by Wolfgang Katenz

O

OATHS. *See* Vows and Oaths.

OBSERVANTISM. Lasting from the mid-fourteenth century until the Council of Trent (1545–1563), observantism was a reform movement within almost all of the monastic and mendicant male and many female religious orders of Latin Christendom. It called for a return to the spirit of each order's founder and a strict observance of the primitive rule.

During the fourteenth century religious orders experienced a notable decline in their discipline. Wars and civil unrest, periodic plagues, the Great Western Schism, and papal and royal interferences in both the government and finances of orders all contributed to the disruption of regular life. The disciplines of common life were further undermined by legitimate dispensations for the sake of the apostolate and by human nature's resistance to asceticism.

Observants tried to eliminate all communal and personal dispensations from the rule and to restore the equality and austerity of common life. Cloister was enforced, simple clothing replaced soft and costly robes, meals were to be taken in the refectory, and dietary rules were to be observed. Private rooms and suites were to be abandoned for the dormitory and cell. No longer were religious to have outside sources of revenue for their personal needs or hold external offices that brought them exemptions from the order's rule. Instead of idleness and secular pursuits, religious were to devote themselves to prayer, study, manual labor, and pastoral ministries. At chapter meetings these reforms were legislated, and encyclical letters from superiors urged compliance. Visitors were sent to ensure observance. Those found at fault were admonished, penalized with fasts or restrictions of movement, removed from office, sent into exile, or even imprisoned.

Support for reform was widespread. Although the councils of Konstanz and Basel, the popes, and numerous ecclesiastical and civil officials gave their support to reform efforts, the principal protagonists came from within the orders themselves and were often encouraged by superiors.

The chief instrument of observant reform was the congregation, a particular historico-juridical organizational structure. Monastic congregations were often based on a shared customary. Those congregations that preserved the autonomy of individual monasteries were frequently unable to prevent a relaxation of discipline and thus failed, while those succeeded that had supra-abbatial officials who could intervene to promote and maintain discipline. Mendicant congregations functioned differently by providing parallel autonomous governmental structures within the order. Often these congregations were begun by the general of the order, who removed from the jurisdiction of local provincials and subjected to his direct authority, usually exercised through a vicar, those houses in which the observance had been installed. Eventually this autonomy was confirmed by conciliar or papal decrees that granted the observants the right to elect their own officials and protected them from interference by the conventuals, the nonreformed members of their order. The plan was to win over to the observant cause more and more houses until the observants became the majority. Those conventual houses that resisted reform would be denied new recruits, and when the observant congregation had absorbed most of the houses in a region, it would cease to exist as a congregation and become the reformed province. Although this scheme worked in various places for the Dominicans and Augustinians with the vigorous support of their reforming generals, it failed for the Franciscans, who split into two separate orders. Reform did not sweep the whole of most orders until the implementation of the decrees on religious enacted by the 25th session (1563) of the Council of Trent.

[*See also* Monasteries; Monasticism; *and* Religious Orders.]

BIBLIOGRAPHY

Elm, Kaspar. "Verfall und Erneuerung des Ordenswesens im Spätmittelalter: Forschungen und Forschungsaufgaben." In *Untersuchungen zu Kloster und Stift,* edited by the Max-Planck-Institut für Geschichte, pp. 188–238. Göttingen, 1980. Survey of current scholarship on the observant reform movement in various religious orders.

Elm, Kaspar, ed. *Reformbemühungen und Observanzbestrebungen im spätmittelalterlichen Ordenswesen.* Berliner Historische Studien, 14, Ordensstudien, 6. Berlin, 1989. Collection of thirty articles in various languages on the whole range of observant movements among monks, canons, knights, friars, and nuns; and on the role of popes, councils, prelates, and laity in promoting this reform. The first article, by Elm, provides a useful overview of the observant movement.

Fois, Mario. "L''osservanza' come espressione della 'ecclesia semper renovanda.'" In *Problemi di storia della chiesa nei secoli 15/17,* edited by Il Consiglio di Presidenza dell' Associazione italiana dei Professori di Storia della Chiesa, pp. 13–107. Naples, 1979. Reprinted in an abridged form with an ample systematic bibliography as "Osservanza, congregazioni di osservanza" in *Dizionario degli istituti di perfezione,* edited by Guerrino Pelliccia and Giancarlo Rocca, cols. 1036–1057, Rome, 1980. Excellent survey of the observant movement in the various monastic and mendicant orders.

Gutiérrez, David. *History of the Order of St. Augustine.* Vol. 1, pt. 2, *The Augustinians in the Middle Ages, 1357–1517.* Translated by Thomas Martin. Villanova, Pa., 1983. Vol. 2, *The Augustinians from the Protestant Reformation to the Peace of Westphalia, 1518–1648.* Translated by John J. Kelly. Villanova, Pa., 1979.

Moorman, John. *A History of the Franciscan Order from Its Origins to the Year 1517.* Oxford, 1968.

NELSON H. MINNICH

OCHINO, Bernardino (1487–1564), Italian theologian and reformer. Bernardino di Domenico Tommasini was born in Siena in the district of Oca, hence the nickname Ochino. Beginning in 1503–1504 he was an observant Franciscan and he rapidly advanced within the order until he was elected vicar general in 1533. During those years he took part in the discussions within the Franciscan movement for and against the creation of the Capuchin branch; he initially sided with the general of the order, Paolo Pisotti, against the separation proposed by Matteo Serafini da Bascio and Ludovico da Fossombrone. Then when the new order was born thanks to the protection it received from Clement VII and Paul III through the offices of Caterina Cybo and Vittoria Colonna, he requested and obtained permission to join it and even took part in drawing up the first constitutions (1536). In June 1538, when his fame as a popular preacher was already at its height, he was elected general of the order.

It is difficult to date the beginning of Ochino's heterodoxy: it surfaced as early as 1530 according to Franciscan historians, in 1534 according to what he himself wrote in the *Responsio ad Mutium Brixiensem* (1543). What is certain is that in 1536 there surfaced the first denunciation of his heterodoxy, made by Theatine zealots who detected it in the course of one of his sermons at Naples. What is certain is that in Naples, along with Peter Martyr Vermigli, he collaborated in spreading the teachings of Juan de Valdés from the pulpit.

A great popular preacher in the classic Franciscan tradition, Ochino moved from city to city, stirring up people in the public squares, threatening divine punishments, promoting reconciliations between factions, but especially spreading the new Protestant word "behind a mask" (i.e., covertly, without indiscretions). He preached in Italy from Advent of 1536 in Perugia to Lent of 1542 in Venice, passing though all the more important cities of the Italian peninsula. His fame was such and his authority was so great that whenever he was called into question, Paul III intervened personally, taking upon himself responsibility for the choice of sending Ochino.

In 1539 new accusations concerning his orthodoxy forced him to go to Venice for a public defense, but the following year he again aroused suspicions and protests in Naples because of his way of preaching against "the church laws on fasting and the authority of the pope." Again in Venice during Lent 1542 he admonished the authorities of the republic not to prosecute the Augustinian hermit Giulio della Rovere, who had been in jail on charges of Protestantism since the previous year. From all his constant preaching activity there remain only a few texts collected by followers and admirers without his knowledge (the *Prediche nove* and the *Prediche lucchesi*) and in addition the *Dialogi sette,* in which the theology of justification by faith alone is grafted onto the as yet unrepudiated Franciscan mysticism that speaks of "confidence in God" that leads to the "annihilation" of human will.

Even before the reorganization of the Roman Inquisition (21 July 1542) he received a summons from Rome (15 July) that led him to suspect the possibility of his arrest. He therefore headed from Venice to Bologna for a conversation with Cardinal Gasparo Contarini, who was dying. Hence he continued on to Florence and met up with Vermigli, and from there they fled together to Geneva. He reached Geneva in September 1542, and although he almost immediately (in October) published a volume of *Prediche* (sermons in Italian), all reflecting rigid Calvinist orthodoxy, his relations with the Genevan leadership were not cordial. Calvin, owing to the suspicion he felt toward Italians, was rather cautious and decided to receive him and entrust him with a pastoral post only after a rigorous doctrinal examination. During this period Ochino wrote the *Epistola alla Balìa di Sienna* to justify his flight; the *Immagine di Antichristo,* a small satirical work, destined to an extended career both cultural and editorial; and the *Esposizioni* of the letters of Paul to the Romans and to the Galatians, in which his obvious Calvinist orthodoxy does not conceal the earlier Franciscan mystical vein and the surfacing of doctrinal problems (such as the right of armed resistance, the morality of the patriarchs, etc.), which would subsequently undergo rather different development.

After leaving Geneva (where he had married a woman from Lucca), not as yet because of differences with Calvin, he went first to Basel and strengthened his ties of friendship with Celio Secondo Curione and Sébastien Castellion, and from there to Strasbourg, where he again saw his companion in flight, Vermigli, and where, despite Martin Bucer's help, he did not find a stable situation. Then he went on to Augsburg, where he arrived completely impoverished in the autumn of 1545. After obtaining from the municipality the church of Saint Anne, he again took up preaching to the Italian community, becoming the idol of the rich and cosmopolitan urban social strata. While there he cultivated his ties with Kaspar von Schwenckfeld and Francis Stancarus. He even remained in the city while it was besieged by imperial troops during the Schmalkald War. Upon capitulation, an odious clause provided for handing over Ochino to the imperial authorities, but the residents of Augsburg aided him in his escape from the city. After brief stays in Basel and Strasbourg, Ochino decided to accept the invitation of the archbishop of Canterbury and, along with Vermigli, landed in England in 1548. His stay there was relatively calm and prosperous. Freed of compelling pastoral obligations, he was able to devote himself to the composition of *Tragoedie or Dialogue of the uniuste primacie of the Bishop of Rome.* Despite the favor he enjoyed in groups close to the court of Edward VI, he was still denounced by the head of the Italian church of London, Michelangelo Florio, for doctrinal deviations. But events precipitated Mary Tudor's elevation to the throne. Thus even before anti-Anglican and anti-Protestant persecutions broke out he left England and returned to Switzerland.

He arrived in Geneva on the day of the execution of the antitrinitarian Michael Servetus and became involved in debates on Servetus within the Italian community. He just barely had the time to publish there the *Apologhi* before he once again set out on a journey without a destination that took him to Chiavenna, then back to Basel, and from there to Zurich. Only after he accepted the doctrinal discipline of the synod and after he swore allegiance to the civil magistrate, was he able to exercise the charge of pastor of the Italian community. This was the period of Ochino's greatest literary activity: he published *Dialogo del Purgatorio, Syncerae et verae doctrinae de Coena Domini defensio,* and *Laberinti del libero o ver servo arbitrio,* all volumes that stirred up bewilderment and controversies among the Swiss churches and the Zurich authorities even when, as in the case of *De Coena Domini defensio,* he was upholding Zwinglian teaching. Ochino was admonished to stop publishing without previous authorization of the Zurich authorities. Thus, as he had already done with the *Laberinti,* with the help of Pietro Perna, Castellion, and Curione, it was again in Basel that he published his new volume, *Dialogi XXX* in 1563. The contents of the work, involving a condemnation of the use of force against heretics, condemnation of the right to armed resistance, *fundamentalia fidei,* and discussions on polygamy, provoked harsh reactions: the council of the city, even before hearing Ochino's arguments in his defense, unanimously decided to banish him. The protests of the Sienese exile were to no avail and neither were Ochino's requests to delay the execution of the sentence. In December 1563, with four small children, he was forced to leave the city. He spent the winter in Nuremberg, and from there—after having denied rumors of his possible return to Catholicism—he arrived in Poland, where Francis Lismanino had already imported his various manuscript works and where Stancarus was stirring up anti-Calvinist debates on the Trinity.

Ochino's stay there was brief. Although he had been warmly received in court circles, he was included in Parczow's decree that in order to put a brake on the tensions caused by constant doctrinal disputes, expelled all non-Catholic foreigners. Ochino refused the naturalization offered to him by the noble Ivan Karminski and once more set out on his way to his final exile. After losing three of his four small children to the plague, he arrived in Moravia in the city of Schlackau (Austerlitz) and was received into the household of the Venetian Anabaptist Niccolò Paruta, where he died in 1564.

BIBLIOGRAPHY

Primary Sources

Ochino, Bernardino. *Apologie des Bernardino Ochino.* Leipzig, 1907.

———. *Dialogue de M. Bernardin Ochin, senois, touchant le Purgatoire* (1559). Paris, 1878.

———. *Seven Dialogues.* Ottawa, 1988.

———. *Tragedy of the Unjust Usurped Primacy of the Bishop of Rome* (1549). London, 1960.

Secondary Sources

Bainton, Roland H. *Bernardino Ochino: Esule e riformatore sinese del Cinquecento.* Florence, 1940.

Benrath, Karl. *Bernardino Ochino von Siena* (1892). 2d ed. Reprint, Nieuwkoop, 1962.

Campi, Emidio. "Conciliazone de dispareri: Bernardino Ochino e la seconda disputa sacramentale." In *Reformiertes Erbe,* edited by Heiko Oberman, pp. 77–92. Zurich, 1993.

Cantimori, Delio. "Bernardino Ochino uomo del Rinascimento e riformatore." *Annali della Scuola normale superiore di Pisa* 30 (1929), 1–40.

———. *Eretici italiana del Cinquecento.* 3d ed. Edited by Adriano Prosperi. Turin, 1992. (An earlier edition is available in English translation: *Italian Heretics of the Sixteenth Century.* Cambridge, Mass., 1979).

Marchetti, Valerio. *Gruppi eretici sinesi del Cinquecento.* Florence, 1975.

Rozzo, V., ed. *I "Dialogi sette" e altri scritti del tempo della fuga.* Turin, 1985.

PAOLO SIMONCELLI

Translated from Italian by Robert E. Shillenn

OCKHAMISM refers to speculative positions of the English Franciscan thinker William of Ockham (c.1285–c.1349). Ockham first appears around 1309–1319 as an Oxford theology student lecturing on the *Sentences* of Peter Lombard (c.1100–1160) and then as a lector in philosophy at the London convent of his order. He was known as "the Venerable Inceptor," literally a "formed bachelor" of theology, ready to "incept," that is, to deliver an inaugural lecture in the presence of the Oxford masters of theology, and so to achieve status as one of their number. This ceremony did not take place; Ockham remained an "inceptor" because in 1324 the chancellor of Oxford, John Luttrell, delated him to the papal court at Avignon on suspicion of heresy. While a commission was examining his theology, Ockham aligned himself with the Franciscan "Spirituals" who opposed Pope John XXII in the name of apostolic poverty. Before the resolution of his own case, Ockham slipped away from Avignon with Michael Cesena, minister general of the Franciscans, and two others, to take refuge with Louis IV of Bavaria. Excommunicated owing to his flight, Ockham seems to have attempted a reconciliation with Pope Clement VI; he disappears from history without having achieved it, most probably as a victim of the Black Death.

Philosophy. Ockham proposed a logicized physics and metaphysics with such fidelity to the traditional principle that "entities are not to be multiplied without necessity" that this is often called "Ockham's razor." The world is composed exclusively of individuals; nothing "universal" is, or can be, real. Despite a pledge of allegiance to Aristotle in philosophy (*Summa logicae*, p. 182), Ockham admitted only "primary substance" and "quality" as real; the other nine accidents are but human perspectives on individuals and their qualities. "Intuitive" knowledge bears on existing individuals known in sensation; "abstractive" knowledge bears on universal names and concepts without existential import. Universal names "stand for" either concepts, or individuals, or themselves; this is a "supposition theory" of universals. Causality is the usual sequence between single events, but God can effect directly what he normally does through secondary agents. The existential security of even intuitive knowledge may be invalidated by a miracle. Thus Ockham belongs among the British empiricists, in the line extending from Robert Grosseteste (c.1175–1253) and Roger Bacon (c.1220–1292) to John Locke (1632–1704) and David Hume (1711–1776). That God is, or is One, cannot be demonstrated by philosophical argument.

Theology. Ethics as discourse on the moral good Ockham relegated to theology. Actions are "good" because God freely decreed them to be so; he was free to will their contraries. God has been revealed to be a Trinity of persons, and here Ockham made an exception to his habitual denial of the "formal distinction" emphasized by John Duns Scotus (c.1265–1308); the three divine persons are "formally distinct" from each other. Not every critic of Ockham failed to note this inconsistency. Strongly influenced by Scotus, Ockham made a basic distinction between "absolute" and "ordered" divine power. God is untrammeled except by the principle of noncontradiction and by his freely chosen "order." The efficacy of sacraments, effective repentance for sin, moral precepts, merit, and grace constitute such an order, freely willed by God, who could have chosen otherwise. Merit and grace Ockham accounted for by God's "acceptance"; to do "what lies within one's power" entails that grace will not be denied. Succeeding generations, Luther and Reformed theologians in particular, would see a semi-Pelagianism in the position that one can merit the first grace of justification. Regarding the Eucharist, Ockham denied the consensus that the perduring "appearances" of bread and wine inhere in the quantity of each element; having denied the category of quantity, Ockham held that the appearances inhere in nothing.

Ecclesiology. In 1302, during his quarrel with Philip IV of France over the papal office, Boniface VIII issued the contentious letter on the church *Unam sanctam*, an unforeseen result of which was new theological tracts on the nature of the church and the civil power. Ockham's last period of defending Louis of Bavaria resulted in treatises that deal exclusively with the respective roles of king and pope; the "Conciliarists" of the future would mine selectively this antipapal collection: a council, but not a king, he wrote, can depose an unworthy pope. Their sustained attack on this Ockhamist basis could not but contribute to the growing disequilibrium of western Christendom as the Reformation approached.

BIBLIOGRAPHY

Primary Sources

William of Ockham. *Epistola ad fratres minores.* Edited by Charles Kenneth Brampton. Oxford, 1929.

———. *The "De sacramento altaris" of William of Ockham.* Edited and translated by Thomas Bruce Birch. Burlington, Iowa, 1930.

———. *The "De imperatorum et pontificum potestate" of William of Ockham.* Edited by Charles Kenneth Brampton. Oxford, 1927.

———. *Guillelmi de Ockham: Opera politica.* Edited by J.G. Sikes et al. Manchester, 1940.

———. *Summa logicae.* Edited by Philotheus Boehner. Saint Bonaventure, N.Y., 1951.

———. *Ockham: Philosophical Writings.* Edited and translated by Philotheus Boehner. New York, 1962. A selection in Latin with English translations.

———. *Guillelmi De Ockham: Opera philosophica et theologica.* Saint Bonaventure, N.Y., 1967–.

———. *Ockham's Theory of Terms.* Edited by M. J. Loux. Notre Dame, Ind., 1974. Part 1 of *Summa logicae.*

———. *Ockham's Theory of Propositions.* Translated by A. J. Freddoso and H. Schuurman. Notre Dame, Ind., 1980.

Secondary Sources

Hoffmann, F. *Die erste Kritik des Ockhamismus durch den Oxforder Kanzler Johannes Lutterell.* Breslau, 1941.

———. *Die Schriften des Oxforder Kanzlers Johannes Lutterell.* Leipzig, 1959.

Koch, J. "Neue Aktenstücke zu dem gegen Wilhelm Ockham in Avignon geführten Prozess." *Recherches de théologie ancienne et médiévale* 7 (1935), 353–380; 8 (1936), 79–93 and 168–197.

Moody, Ernest A. *The Logic of William of Ockham.* New York, 1935.

Tierney, Brian. *Ockham, the Conciliar Theory, and the Canonists.* Philadelphia, 1971.

Edward A. Synan

ODENSE, DIETS OF.

Faced with the imminent return of the ousted Danish king, Christian II (r. 1513–1523), Frederick I (r. 1523–1533) called the Diet of Odense in 1526 to prepare for the defense of Denmark. New taxes were to be levied, and church bells were to be confiscated and made into cannon. Bishops in the future were not to seek confirmation from the pope in Rome but from the Danish archbishop in Lund (today part of Sweden). Confirmation money for episcopal appointments, usually sent to Rome, was to go into the royal treasury for the defense of the realm. In effect, a national Catholic church was set up with a much weakened hierarchy. Ties to the pope were broken, but Catholic doctrine and liturgy were to remain unchanged.

Unrest continued to increase as the evangelical preachers spread their Lutheran doctrine throughout the country. With the apparent threat from Christian II lessened, Frederick I called another diet to meet the next year in Odense to deal with problems in the church. The bishops immediately brought forth their grievances, chief of which were the "letters of protection" that the king had been granting to the evangelical preachers and the whole matter of clerical marriage. The latter the king would not forbid nor promote. The preachers would have to be answerable to God if they married. Nor would he withdraw his letters of protection as long as the preachers proclaimed the gospel and taught from the scriptures. Those who wished to follow the preachers could do so by setting up their own congregations. In the meantime, the disputed matters could continue to be proclaimed until they were declared heretical by some future ecumenical council.

The two Odense diets have been seen as a turning point in the history of the Reformation in Denmark. An older generation of historians have also heralded them for establishing religious freedom in Denmark, but contemporary historians have been more modest in their claims.

BIBLIOGRAPHY

Grell, Ole. "Herredagen 1527." *Kirkehistoriske Samlinger* (1978), 69–88.

Paludan-Müller, Caspar. *Herredagene i Odense 1526 og 1527*. Copenhagen, 1857.

Scharling, Suno W. "Frederik I:s Kirkepolitik." *Kirkehistoriske Samlinger* (1974), 40–88.

Sjøberg, E. "Odense-Privilegiet af1527." *Historisk Tidsskrift* (Copenhagen) 12.2 (1966–1967), 337–360.

TRYGVE R. SKARSTEN

OECOLAMPADIUS, Johannes (Ger., Huszgen; 1482–1531), Swiss reformer. Born Johannes Huszgen in Weinsberg in the Palatinate, he was the son of a prosperous family. He studied law at Bologna and theology in the attenuated schools of the *via antiqua* at Heidelberg, Tübingen, and Basel. Jakob Wimpfeling met him at Heidelberg and became a friend and mentor. It was under the influence of humanism that Johannes Huszgen became Johannes Oecolampadius ("shining light" or "lantern").

Thanks to Wimpfeling, Oecolampadius was named by Elector Philipp of the Palatinate as the tutor to his sons. He interrupted his studies and moved to Mainz, where the young princes were gathered. After leaving Mainz in 1510, his parents endowed a living for him as a preacher at Weinsberg, which was under the rule of Duke Ulrich of Württemberg. Oecolampadius was ordained and began to preach. His biographer, Wolfgang Capito, interprets this development as motivated by Oecolampadius's desire to work for the reform of the church.

Urged by Wimpfeling and others, Oecolampadius began his remarkable writing career in 1512 by publishing a treatise on the Seven Last Words of Christ, a work that allows a glance at his theological development. There are clear humanist elements, but Oecolampadius also reached back to the tradition of the mystic, contemplative experience of Christ that Augustine first delineated.

After less than three years of preaching, he took leave of Weinsberg in order to continue his theological studies. He came to know Philipp Melanchthon and his great uncle, Johannes Reuchlin, who, according to Capito, encouraged Oecolampadius to study Greek and Hebrew. From 1514 Oecolampadius was identified as a member of Reuchlin's humanist circle. When he left Tübingen to return to Heidelberg, his studies were again interrupted by the request that he lecture at the university on Greek. He was glad to comply and wrote a Greek grammar for the lectures and also intensified his study of Hebrew with the Jewish convert Matthew Adrianus. At this time he began his friendship with Wolfgang Capito, who in 1515 became professor of theology at the University of Basel and preacher at Basel's minster. At almost the same time Oecolampadius was called by Johann Froben to come to Basel. Oecolampadius helped Desiderius Erasmus finish the notes and commentary that the humanist added to the text of his edition of the Greek New Testament (*Annotationes*) and also wrote the epilogue to the work. As this work was drawing to an end, Oecolampadius matriculated in the theological faculty of the University of Basel and began the prescribed course for the doctoral degree. By the autumn of 1516 he returned to Weinsberg as a licentiate in theology. At this time he had the services of an assistant, Johannes Brenz the future reformer of Schwäbisch-Hall and Württemberg.

In addition to literary pursuits, Oecolampadius fulfilled his obligation as preacher and confessor at Weinsberg. His experience as confessor was destined to influence his attitude toward the development of a Reformed doctrine of excommunication. Indeed, while still at Weinsberg he began to translate and publish works on the subject of excommunication in the early church.

Returning to Basel in 1518, Oecolampadius published his Greek grammar with Andreas Cratander, who later became his general editor and publisher. The work was of great significance and went through many editions; among its users were the future archbishop of Canterbury and martyr, Thomas Cranmer, and the south German reformer Erhard Schnepf. The humanist Willibald Pirckheimer recommended Oecolampadius to the vacant post of preacher and confessor (*Domprediger*) at the Augsburg cathedral. Oecolampadius met the requirement for the position, a doctorate in theology, late in 1518. At Augsburg he continued to write, hear confessions, and support church reform. He resisted Reuchlin's effort to have him appointed professor of Hebrew at Wittenberg on the grounds that he had been invited to Basel as *poenitentiarius* ("confessor"). Much to the surprise of his friends, he entered the Birgitten monastery at Altenmünster near Augsburg in 1520. The reason for his decision was his intellectual turmoil caused by the radicalization of the younger members of the humanist movement and the early impact of Luther's writings. Oecolampadius sought a quiet retreat to read the church fathers and Luther.

Oecolampadius's friend, Bernhard Adelmann, asked him for his opinion of Luther. The answer came quickly: "Martin is closer to the evangelical truth than any of his opponents." The publication of Oecolampadius's manuscript, *Judicium de Luthero,* which Adelmann sent to Capito, and Capito passed on to others, among them Johannes Sylvius Egranus, who published it, made his judgment of the Roman documents against Luther clear.

The situation at Basel was extremely complicated. Thanks to its printers, the city had become the center for the publication of Luther's writings in western Europe. The town council had seen the commercial value of these publications but had not realized how they might affect Basel. By 1522 the call for a reform according to the Lutheran model was heard from some pulpits. The Lenten fast was violated. The following year there was open discussion of Huldrych Zwingli's reform at Zurich, which caused even greater division in the city.

The Reformation in Basel might well have failed because of widespread disunity had it not been for Oecolampadius's diplomacy, firm leadership, and friendship with Zwingli, who became a source of endless good advice when Oecolampadius first wrote to him in December 1522. His friendship with Zwingli did not mean that he broke with Luther, for the two continued to correspond with one another. His relationship with Melanchthon was closer, and Melanchthon offered him asylum at Wittenberg in case the situation at Basel became too difficult. The clearest break was between Oecolampadius and Erasmus.

When he first returned to the city, he kept himself free of controversy and busied himself with his editorial labors. By 1523 he was lecturing on *Isaiah* at the university. A year later a series of lectures on the letter to the Romans was published. For over a year he had also been preaching at Saint Martin's church.

At no time was he merely a disciple of Zwingli. For instance, he made his own way from affirming the real presence of Christ in the elements of Communion to a spiritual interpretation, which by late 1524 found him in agreement with Zwingli and also Andreas Bodenstein von Karlstadt. He was skeptical of what could be achieved by disputations, though he understood why Zwingli favored them.

The reason for his doubt was his own experience of academic debates at the university and what he had seen at Basel. There, after the city council issued an order to the clergy in the summer of 1523 (*Predigtmandat*) to preach only the gospel and to avoid attacking others, several disputations had brought only further disagreement. Guillaume Farel's offer to debate while he visited Basel briefly was supported by Oecolampadius, but no one appeared to represent the other side. The situation at Basel made it impossible to have a disputation to introduce the Reformation. The council wished to remain neutral and leave the question of religious persuasion to individuals and groups. This policy naturally led it to the censorship law of December 1524, which was intended to keep the peace.

The next step in introducing the Reformation at Basel was taken during the Peasants' War in 1525. Oecolampadius had continued to think and write about the nature of the Lord's Supper, and he began to publish his opinions in the summer of 1525 (*Genuina expositio*). For the first time he made his "symbolic" view of the Lord's Supper clear and argued that the bread and wine signified the body and blood of Christ, which were eaten spiritually. His public expression of these views caused the final break with his old friend Pirckheimer. In less than a year Bucer was advising Zwingli and Oecolampadius on how to answer Luther's long preface to the German edition of the *Syngramma,* which flatly rejected their conception of the Lord's Supper. Above all Bucer asked them to remember their former "love" for Luther. The radicalism that faced the council on all sides caused it to be more conservative and eventually to abandon plans for a disputation concerning the Lord's Supper. For a short time the council's authority was also weakened and Oecolampadius took advantage of this weakness: on All Souls Sunday he and his friends began to replace the Mass with the Lord's Supper. Following Zwingli's example, Oecolampadius paved the way for this development by preaching two sermons on the subject of the Lord's Supper. A lengthy discussion with the council followed, but he was allowed to continue celebrating the Lord's Supper.

At the same time the council began to secularize the monasteries and endowments of the church, leaving the endowments for parish churches, care of the poor, and schools in tact. This development made it clear in which direction the city was moving. Nevertheless, the councilors continued to hedge. They greeted the new Bishop of Basel on 23 September 1527, the same day they released the clergy from saying Mass and the people from attending the service.

The traditionalist interest was still quite strong in Basel and since 1525 Johann Fabri, the counselor to King Ferdinand, and Johann Eck, the theologian, had been hard at work to strengthen the supporters of the old church. The council's decision meant that their help had come too late. With the exception of Oecolampadius and his colleagues at Saint Martin's church, the Augustinians, and the canons of

Saint Leonhard, all priests who no longer said the mass were forced by the council to give up their livings.

A month later the council issued a mandate that no one should be coerced for reasons of faith. In February 1528 the Council again proclaimed that matters of faith were the work of God; the citizens should not hate one another on account of differing religious views. The council clearly hoped to maintain some kind of religious toleration.

Oecolampadius had distinguished himself at the Baden Disputation (May 1526) by defending the Zwinglian view of the Lord's Supper against Eck and by arguing with Eck over purgatory. When Eck quoted Luther against him, Oecolampadius answered that he had never been a Lutheran. The majority of the Swiss present at Baden disliked Zwingli and it required boldness to speak on behalf of Zwingli's theology. The differences between Oecolampadius and Fabri over intercessory prayers to the saints continued long after Baden. Baden brought no final decision regarding the reform movement in the Swiss Confederacy.

In 1528 the great success of the Bern Disputation opened the way for Oecolampadius to achieve his goal. He attended the disputation with his friends Capito and Bucer. The outcome certainly tipped the balance in favor of the reform party at Basel. The council accepted Zwinglianism as the faith of Basel; Oecolampadius had won a great victory.

Among his various activities in the period between 1528 and his death in November 1531 several stand out. He took part in the Colloquy of Marburg in 1529, where he loyally defended Zwingli's view of the Lord's Supper. Oecolampadius had engaged in a printed exchange with Balthasar Hubmaier, and by January 1530 the first executions of Anabaptists began. He viewed the spiritualist Kaspar von Schwenckfeld as an ally against the Lutherans. After the council's decision, he spent much time developing a Reformation order for the new state church, a task he had begun in his *Agenda* of 1526.

The new state church was introduced by popular attacks upon the images in the churches and by a series of oaths that recognized the obligation of the Council to provide the people with the right religion (11 February 1529). Two days later representatives of the *Christliche Burgrecht* ("Christian alliance") and the council swore that the Bible should be at the center of Basel's religion. The guilds then swore obedience to the council in the presence of Basel's allies. In effect the control of religion had been put in the hands of the council.

On 1 April 1529 the Reformation order became law for the cantonal church. Dissatisfaction arose almost immediately over Oecolampadius's plan to place control of excommunication in the hands of the church. In the spring of 1530 the newly established synod considered the question. Oecolampadius wrote a treatise on the subject (*Oratio de reducenda excommunicatione*) and was invited to speak before the council. He proposed that each congregation elect lay elders who with the pastor would form a presbytery. Oecolampadius asserted that the church needed a court of its own and sought to limit the council's authority over the church. Finally the council agreed to the idea of twelve censors to be chosen by the council to punish bad behavior.

Oecolampadius looked to his friends, especially Zwingli, who appeared to agree with him, for support. He hoped to win over all the members of the *Christliche Burgrecht* for his conception of church discipline. When the allies met at Aarau in September 1530, however, they rejected the proposal and later decided that each member should make its own decision. The Zurich council had prevented Zwingli from attending. When in the following year Oecolampadius turned to Bullinger, his idea was flatly rejected.

This disappointment did not prevent Oecolampadius from continuing to publish his works. His Dialogue on the Lord's Supper was a defensive act, but he still sought ways to find agreement with Luther. There was also time to help reform the university. Oecolampadius died in his prime just a month after Zwingli died at Kappel.

BIBLIOGRAPHY

Hammer, Karl. "Der Reformator Oekolampad, 1482–1531." In *Reformiertes Erbe*, edited by Heiko Oberman, vol. 1, pp. 157–170. Zurich, 1992.

Muralt, Leonhard von. "Renaissance und Reformation." In *Handbuch der schweizer Geschichte*, vol. 1. Zurich, 1972.

Poythress, Diane M. "Johannes Oecolampadius' Exposition of Isaiah, Chapters 36–37." Ph.D. diss., Westminster Theological Seminary, 1992.

Rupp, E. Gordon. *Patterns of Reformation.* London, 1969.

Staehelin, Ernst. *Briefe und Akten zum Leben Ökolampads: Zum vierhundertjährigen Jubiläum der Basler Reformation.* 2 vols. Leipzig, 1927.

———. *Das theologische Lebenswerk Johannes Oekolampads* (1939). Reprint, New York and London, 1971.

———. *Ökolampad-Bibliographie.* 2d ed. Nieuwkoop, 1963.

Wackernagel, Rudolf. *Geschichte der Stadt Basel.* 3 vols. Basel, 1924.

ROBERT C. WALTON

OECONOMUS. *See* Hofmeister, Sebastian.

OLÁH, Nicholaus (1493–1568), archbishop of Esztergom, royal official, and humanist. The scion of a Romanian nobleman, Oláh was born in Sibiu and, after studies (1505–1510) at the chapter school in Oradea (Nagyvárad, Grosswardein) and a stay at the court of Ladislav II, was ordained a priest in 1518. He subsequently obtained a number of benefices and, in 1526, entered the service of Louis and Mary of Hungary. After the Battle of Mohács (1526) he supported the Habsburg candidacy for the Hungarian throne; he served as a counselor of the widowed queen both in Hungary and in the Netherlands, where he maintained contacts with the local humanist community. He was named bishop of Zagreb (1543), bishop of Eger (1548), and, finally, archbishop of Esztergom (1553). He also served as the chancellor of Hungary (after 1543) and royal governor (after 1562).

Holding the highest ecclesiastical and political offices in Hungary, Oláh sought to strengthen the authority of the Habsburgs in middle Europe and to revitalize the Catholic church. He supported Ferdinand in his struggles with János Zápolya and against the Bohemian estates (1547), as well as attempting, in vain, to halt the spread of the Protestant Reformation in Hungary by improving Catholic education and ecclesiastical discipline. He petitioned the pope and the Council of Trent on behalf of the Hungarian clergy, asking that they be allowed to marry and to distribute both bread and wine during Mass. He began to compile a list of all clergy under his jurisdiction (1559) and sent visitors to investigate parish conditions. He published liturgical materials (*Brevarium*, 1558; *Pontificale ordo et ritus*, 1560), conducted regular synods (1560–1564), established a seminary for parish priests (1566), reorganized the school in Trnava as an academy (1558), sought to establish schools for each parish, invited the Jesuits to Trnava in 1561, and actively opposed Protestantism in the diets of Hungary. Oláh also fostered the spread of Catholic humanism in Hungary, maintained contacts with Erasmus and other humanists throughout Europe, and wrote numerous works on a wide range of topics.

BIBLIOGRAPHY

Békefi, Remig. "Oláh Miklós nagyszombati iskolájának szervéte." *Századok* 31 (1897), 881–902.

Bucko, Vojtech. *Reformne hunutie v arcibiskupstve ostrihomskom do r. 1564*. Bratislava, 1939.

———. *Mikuláš Oláh a jeho doba, 1493–1568*. Bratislava, 1940.

Schleicher, P. *Oláh Miklós és Erasmus*. Budapest, 1941.

Szemes, J. *Oláh Miklós*. Esztergom, Hungary, 1936.

DAVID P. DANIEL

OLDENBARNEVELT, Johan van (1547–1619), Dutch statesman. Born on 14 September 1547 in Amersfoort in the province of Utrecht, Oldenbarnevelt was the eldest son of Gerrit Reyerszoon van Oldenbarnevelt and Deliana van Weede, both, it seems, of the lower gentry. Having worked at a lawyer's office in The Hague (1564–1566), he matriculated in the faculty of law at Louvain (1566–1567), Bourges (1567), Cologne (1567–1568), Heidelberg (1568–1569), and perhaps Padua (1569–1570).

As a lawyer in The Hague, he sided with William of Orange when, in 1572, the Revolt of the Netherlands intensified, serving as a revenue agent and occasionally as a soldier. In 1575 the States of Holland appointed him as their advocate before the Court of Holland. At the end of 1576 he was named pensionary (legal official) to the city of Rotterdam. Meanwhile, in 1575, he married Marie of Utrecht, a wealthy woman probably of illegitimate birth.

As pensionary, Oldenbarnevelt often served as one of Rotterdam's deputies to the States of Holland and was frequently deputed by the States to important meetings outside the province. After 1582, as one of Holland's delegates to the States-General, he supported free trade with the southern Netherlands and conferred frequently with William of Orange. Oldenbarnevelt showed himself a true pupil of William following the prince's assassination in 1584.

In 1585 Oldenbarnevelt was a member of the embassy that went to England to offer sovereignty of the rebel provinces to Elizabeth I. The queen declined but instead agreed to send six thousand troops under the command of her confidant, Robert Dudley, earl of Leicester, who was to act as her representative in the government of the revolting provinces. Oldenbarnevelt, however, intended to prevent Dudley from gaining too strong a position. Before Dudley's arrival, Oldenbarnevelt arranged the appointment of William's son Maurits van Nassau as the stadtholder of Holland and Zeeland. In February 1586 he himself was named grand pensionary of the States of Holland. In this capacity Oldenbarnevelt became the unofficial president of the States of Holland. At meetings of the States-General—held from 1593 daily in a room near where the States of Holland convened—he in effect guided a polity consisting of seven rebel provinces, among which Holland was the wealthiest, most populous, and most influential.

Taking up residence in Utrecht in 1586, Dudley issued edicts forbidding Holland's lucrative trade with the enemy in the southern Netherlands and Spain. He also cultivated good relations with strict Calvinists in Utrecht, although in Holland more moderate Calvinists held sway. His one-sided policy caused many clashes, but Dudley was unable to bend to his will either Oldenbarnevelt or his pupil, Maurits van Nassau. A year after Dudley's departure in 1587, the search for a sovereign prince was abandoned; the United Provinces became the Dutch Republic.

Oldenbarnevelt's greatest political success came in 1609, when the Dutch Republic concluded the Twelve-Year Truce with Brussels and Madrid. In his view the truce would ease the burden of war finance, promote trade, and allow the republic to flourish. Maurits, however, saw things differently, and their disagreements were fought out during the truce.

Oldenbarnevelt did not often speak of his religious beliefs. During his stay at Heidelberg, it is certain that he set aside the Catholicism of his youth for a moderate Calvinism. He laid stress on personal reading of the Bible, rejected mediation by the clergy, but felt troubled about predestination: he was willing to believe that God preordained all faithful Christians to salvation but not that God predestined others to damnation. When theologians assured him that his beliefs sufficed for a layman, he was confirmed as a member of the Heidelberg community.

The ideas of Thomas Lüber were hotly debated at Heidelberg in these years, and Oldenbarnevelt was to be a lifelong Erastian. He preferred an open, popular church, wherein not only Calvinists but also moderate Lutherans, Mennonites, and even Roman Catholics could find a place. Those who nevertheless wanted to remain outside were to be granted toleration on condition they professed their religion in private. Oldenbarnevelt thus felt little sympathy for the strict Calvinists in the republic, although Johannes Wtenbogaert did persuade him to become a member of the congregation in The Hague in 1592.

When the debate between Remonstrants and Contra-Remonstrants intensified during the Twelve-Year Truce, Oldenbarnevelt stuck to his Erastian views. The Contra-Remonstrants favored a resolution of the issues at the national level, but Oldenbarnevelt, knowing that the Arminians were strong only in Holland, insisted on each province taking its own measures, as provided in the Union of Utrecht.

In Holland, then, Oldenbarnevelt took steps he considered necessary. After the Arminians had asked the States for protection, he first organized a colloquy between Arminians and Gomarists (1612). When this failed he ordered that both parties should be tolerant toward each other (1614). The anticlerical Oldenbarnevelt believed that unrest was promoted only by a small group of extremist ministers and that ordinary lay people would obey the civil authorities. In fact, ordinary Gomarist believers began separating themselves from churches dominated by their adversaries and forming their own congregations.

In the summer of 1617 Maurits broke the deadlock by siding with the Gomarists; using his control of the army as a threat, he forced the provinces to agree to the convening of a national synod at Dordrecht (1618–1619), which would pass resolutions confirming the Gomarist, orthodox interpretation of the dogma of predestination. Meanwhile, in August 1618, Oldenbarnevelt was arrested on the basis of a rather vague resolution of the States-General. This body founded a court of justice of its own, where Oldenbarnevelt was charged with high treason. This charge turned out to be unprovable, but the old pensionary was nevertheless condemned, sentenced to death, and then executed on 13 May 1619 in The Hague. Although the verdict did no justice to Oldenbarnevelt's great service to the republic, it was the outcome of a political deadlock to which his staunch character and the Erastian assumptions of his own policy had in no small measure contributed.

BIBLIOGRAPHY

Conring, Enno. *Kirche und Staat nach der Lehre der niederländischen Calvinisten, in der ersten Hälfte des 17. Jahrhunderts.* Neukirchen-Vluyn, Germany, 1965.

Deursen, A. Th. van. *Bavianen en slijkgeuzen: Kerk en kerkvolk ten tijde van Maurits en Oldenbarnevelt.* Reprint, Franeker, Netherlands, 1991.

Gerlach, H. *Het proces tegen Oldenbarnevelt en de "Maximen in den Staet."* Haarlem, Netherlands, 1965.

Jones, R. L. "Reformed Church and Civil Authorities in the United Provinces in the Late Sixteenth and Early Seventeenth Centuries, As Reflected in Dutch State and Municipal Archives." *Journal of the Society of Archivists* 4 (1970–1973), 109–123.

Tex, Jan den. *Oldenbarnevelt.* 2 vols. Cambridge, 1973.

S. GROENVELD

OLDENDORP, Johannes (1480/90–1567), German jurist and reformer. He was born in Hamburg, but his date of birth is unknown. A nephew of the Hamburg canon Albert Krantz, Oldendorp studied from 1504 to 1516 in Rostock, Cologne, and Bologna. He began his academic teaching career in Greifswald in 1517. Although he left for Frankfurt an der Oder in 1520, he returned the following year to Greifswald, where he was twice elected rector of the university. From 1526 to 1534 he served as syndic, or legal counsel, to the Rostock city council and here took an active part in the introduction of the Reformation. From 1534 to 1536, Oldendorp was a legal adviser to Wollenwever and syndic to the city of Lübeck. Consequently, he became deeply involved in Lübeck's war against Denmark, the so-called *Grafenfehde.* After he left Lübeck in 1536, his whereabouts are unknown until he appeared in Cologne in 1538 and offered his services as a private lecturer, eventually succeeding in being named professor. He became embroiled in the controversies surrounding the Archbishop of Cologne, Hermann von Wied, whose attempts at reform in Cologne were thwarted by the intervention of the emperor. He was forced to leave in 1543 and followed a call to Marburg, where, until his death in 1567, he successfully served as professor, reformer of the university, and counselor to Landgrave Philipp of Hesse.

Oldendorp's treatise *Wat byllick vnn recht ys,* published in Rostock in 1529, establishes him as the founder of Protestant natural law. His *Ratmannenspiegel* (1530) also published in Low German, constitutes an influential contribution to police regulations. His most important works appeared in Cologne: *Formula investigandae actionis* (1538, German edition 1567); *Eisagoge iuris naturalis* and *Actionum iuris civilis loci communes* (1539); *Variorum lectione libri* and *Enchiridion exceptionum forensium* (1540); *De iure et aequitate forensis disputatio;* and *Collatio iuris civilis et canonici* (1541). His collected works appeared in 1559 as *Opera Omnia.* The numerous editions of the *Enchiridion oder Handbüchlein von Chamergerichts Terminen vnd Processen,* a translation of one of Oldendorp's Latin treatises, indicate the practical utility of his work in the sixteenth century. Furthermore, his theory of natural law, developed primarily in the *Eisagoge* of 1539, was not only adopted by the Protestant orthodox tradition and handed on in a multitude of commentaries but also became a focus of the academic discussion during the heyday of secular natural law in the seventeenth and eighteenth centuries.

BIBLIOGRAPHY

Primary Sources

Oldendorp, Johannes. *Wat byllick vnn recht ys.* Rostock, 1528.
———. *Van radtslagende, wo men gude Politie . . . erholden möghe (Ratmannenspiegel; 1530).* Reprint, Frankfurt.
———. *Formula investigandaeactionis.* 1538; German ed., 1567.
———. *Actionum iuris civilis loci communes.* 1539.
———. *Eisagoge iuris naturalis.* 1539.
———. *Enchiridion exceptionum forensium.* 1540.
———. *Variorum lectione libri.* 1540.
———. *Collatio iuris civilis et canonici.* 1541.
———. *De iure et aequitate forensis disputatio.* 1541.
———. *Enchiridion oder Handbüchlein von Chamergerichts Terminen vnd Processen.* N.d.
———. *Opera Omnia* (1559). Reprint, Aalen, 1966.

Secondary Sources

Bautz, Friedrich Wilhelm, ed. *Biographisch-bibliographisches Kirchenlexikon.* Hamm, Germany, 1970–. See vol. 6, nos. 1178–1180.
Berman, Harold J. "Conscience and Law: The Lutheran Reformation and the Western Legal Tradition." *Journal of Law and Religion* 5 (1987), 177–202.
Pettke, Sabine. "Johannes Oldendorp." In *Theologische Realenzyklopädie,* vol. 25. Berlin and New York, 1977–.
Verzeichnis der im deutschen Sprachbereich erschienenen Drucke des XVI. Jahrhunderts. Stuttgart, 1983–. See vol. 16, nos. 538–621.
Wolf, Erik. *Große Rechtsdenker der deutschen Geistesgeschichte.* Tübingen, 1963. See pp. 138–176.

SABINE PETTKE

OLEVIANUS, Kaspar (1536–1587), German theologian and Calvinist reformer. After studying law at Paris, Orléans, and Bourges, he devoted himself to theology and studied under the masters of the Reformation—John Calvin, Peter Martyr Vermigli, Théodore de Bèze, and Heinrich Bullinger. In 1559 he returned to the city of his birth, Trier, to preach Reformed doctrine. He then went to Heidelberg toward the end of 1560, the period when Calvinism was replacing Lutheranism in the city's churches and academy. He obtained a doctorate in theology and distinguished himself as a professor of dogmatic theology at Sapientia College. There he was also active as a preacher and reorganized the city's churches on the model of the church of Geneva.

In particular, he attempted to establish Calvinist ecclesiastical discipline, which gave the right of excommunication to the consistory. In doing so he encountered the opposition of Thomas Lüber (Erastus), who, following the Zurich model, conferred this same right on the magistracy. Just as Lüber followed the directives of Bullinger, Olevianus followed Bèze, whose confession of faith he translated. Using Calvin's catechism as a model, he wrote the Heidelberg Catechism, which was translated by Ursinus Zacharias and published in 1563 (*Ordnung der evangelischen Kirchen in Frankreich . . . und christlichen Catechismus* [Order of the Evangelical Churches in France . . . and Christian Catechism]). Olevianus pursued the controversy over ecclesiastical discipline (giving ministers the power to monitor morals) against Lüber with such fervor that in 1569 Bèze had to intervene to urge him toward moderation.

Upon the death of Elector Frederick III in 1576, the return of Lutheranism forced Olevianus to leave the Palatinate. He then carried on his pedagogical and pastoral activity at Berleburg (in the service of Count Ludwig of Wittgenstein) and from 1583 in Herborn (at the request of Count Johann of Nassau-Dillenburg). In that city he distinguished himself by his works on dogmatic theology (including the publication of his major work, *De substantia foederis gratuiti inter Deum et electos* [On the Substance of the Free Covenant between God and the Elect]). Thus, he achieved the same status as his colleague Johannes Piscator (Johannes Fischer), the famous exegete. In 1586 he published a scholarly edition of Calvin's chief work (*Epitome institutionis religionis christianae Calvini*). On 13 July he was appointed moderator of the general synod at Herborn, to which he imparted a strongly Calvinist direction.

BIBLIOGRAPHY

Primary Sources

Olevianus, Kaspar. *Vester Grund, das ist, Die Artickel des alten, waren, ungezweiffelten Christlichen Glaubens.* Heidelberg, 1567.
———. *Exposition of the Symbole of the Apostles, or rather of the Articles of Faith* (1576). Translated by J. Field. London, 1581.
———. *De substantia foederis gratuiti inter Deum et electos.* Geneva, 1585.

Secondary Sources

Bautz, Friedrich Wilhelm, ed. *Biographisch-bibliographisches Kirchenlexikon.* Hamm, Germany, 1970–. See vol. 6, nos. 1197–1200.
Beeke, Joel R. "Faith and Assurance in the Heidelberg Catechism and Its Primary Composers." *Calvin Theological Journal* 27 (1992), 39–67.
Bierma, L. D. "Lutheran-Reformed Polemics in the Late Reformation: Olevian's Proposal." In *Controversy and Conciliation: The Reformation and the Palatinate, 1559–1583,* edited by Derk Visser, pp. 51–71. Allison Park, Pa., 1986.
———. "Covenant or covenants in the theology of Olevianus?" *Calvin Theological Journal* 22 (1987), 228–250.
Steenkamp, J. J. "Ursinus, die opsteller van die Heidelbergse Kategismus, Olevianus en die Heidelbergse teologie." *Hervormde Teologiese Studien* 45 (1989), 611–625.
Sudhoff, Karl. *C. Olevianus und Z. Ursinus.* Elberfeld, 1857.
Verzeichnis der im deutschen Sprachbereich erschienenen Drucke des XVI. Jahrhunderts. Stuttgart, 1983–. See vol. 16, nos. 696–709.

MARIO TURCHETTI
Translated from French by Robert E. Shillenn

OLIVÉTAN, Pierre Robert (also Louis Olivier; Lat., Olivetanus; c.1506–1538), French Protestant reformer and translator of the Bible into French. Born in Noyon, in northern France, and a relative of John Calvin, Pierre Robert was nicknamed Olivetanus ("midnight oil") as an allusion to his study habits. He studied at Orléans around 1528 and may have been one of those who introduced Calvin to Reformation beliefs. He was obliged to leave France because of his convictions and settled in Strasbourg (1529–1531), where he studied Greek and Hebrew. He refused to become a pastor on account of his "poor elocution" and elected to teach. A tutor in Neuchâtel, Switzerland, in 1531, he moved to Geneva in May 1532.

Expelled from Geneva in October of that year together with Guillaume Farel, he accompanied Antoine Saulnier to Piedmont, where he composed his *Instruction des enfans,* an exposition of the Lord's Prayer, Apostles' Creed, and the Ten Commandments entirely made up of scriptural quotations (published 1533). After a second stay in Geneva, which ended again with his expulsion for various disorders, he returned to the Piedmont Alps and worked on his translation of the Bible into French. (The dedicatory epistle is dated "from the Alps, 12 February 1535.") His "translation" is, in fact, a revision of Jacques Lefèvre d'Étaples's 1530 Bible in the light of several Greek, Hebrew, and Latin editions and commentaries, most notably by Desiderius Erasmus, Robert I Estienne, and Sante Pagnini. Although the changes to Lefèvre's New Testament are not extensive, his reworking of the Old Testament is more thorough. His Bible, published at Neuchâtel in 1535, remained the basis, with frequent modifications up to 1588, from which all subsequent French Protestant Bibles were derived until Ostervald's new translation in 1744.

Nothing further is known about Olivétan, except that he appears to have died in 1538 at Rome. Typically, reeditions of parts of his Bible published in 1536 and 1537 were signed "Belisem de Belimakom" (Hebrew for no-name, no-place).

BIBLIOGRAPHY

Barthélémy, Dominique, Henri Meylan, and Bernard Roussel. *Olivétan, celui qui fit passer la Bible d'hébreu en français.* Biel, Switzerland, 1986. Brief but unique study of the shadowy figure of Olivétan. There are no studies in English of the reformer.

Berthoud, Gabrielle. "L'édition originale de l'*Instruction des enfans* par Olivétan." *Musée neuchâtelois* (1937), 1–10. Information on the only other work by Olivétan apart from his Bible translation.

Delarue, Henri. "Olivétan et Pierre de Wingle à Genève." *Bibliothèque d'Humanisme et Renaissance* 8 (1946), 105–118. Establishes Olivétan's movements in 1533 and thereabouts.

FRANCIS HIGMAN

OMENS. *See* Prodigies and Portents.

OPORINUS, Johannes

OPORINUS, Johannes (Ger., Hans Herbst; 1507–1568), Basel scholar-printer and humanist. Master of his own shop from 1542 to 1564, he was the most active printer in Basel during the period and one of the most important publishers in Europe. Basel's relative tolerance and its position on the border between France and the Holy Roman Empire and on the principal route north from Italy made it a gathering place for refugees from Catholic and Protestant persecution. Once in Basel, these scholars were drawn to Oporinus's establishment. Oporinus had been trained in classics as a boy and had resigned a position as professor of Latin and Greek at the University of Basel to enter printing full time.

Although he had one great commercial success, Andreas Vesalius's *De Humani Corporis Fabrica* (1543), the first accurate work on human anatomy, Oporinus's printing program was guided primarily by his scholarly tastes and sentiments toward religious tolerance. Besides a large number of Greek and Latin classics, Oporinus published a long list of contemporary works, including the first printed Latin edition of the Qu'ran (1543), the *De Hereticis* of Sébastien Castellion (1554), and the Latin first edition of John Foxe's *Book of Martyrs* (1559). Both Castellion and Foxe, exiles from Savoy and England, respectively, worked as editors for Oporinus, who published and marketed their works.

Works like the Qu'ran and the *De Hereticis* brought Oporinus into conflict with the municipal censors. The Qu'ran was released for publication only after Luther himself requested it in order to aid Christians in fighting its heresies. The *De Hereticis* (an impassioned plea against the execution of heretics occasioned by Geneva's burning of Michael Servetus) was banned from sale in Basel, though enough copies escaped to inspire movements for religious tolerance everywhere in Europe.

Oporinus was celebrated for his courage in publishing works reflecting his horror and revulsion at religious persecution. His support of Castellion, Foxe, and other like-minded authors helped their ideas promote the development of religious freedom.

BIBLIOGRAPHY

Bietenholz, Peter G. *Basle and France in the Sixteenth Century: The Basle Humanists and Printers in their Contacts with Francophone Culture.* Geneva, 1971. Valuable discussion of the milieu of Johannes Oporinus and his colleagues that devotes an informative chapter to Sébastien Castellion.

Fisch, Max H. "The Printer of Vesalius Fabrica." [Medical Library Association] *Bulletin* 31 (1943), 240–258. Brief account in English of Oporinus's life and career.

Mozley, J. F. *John Foxe and his Book.* London, 1940. Includes account of Foxe's activities in Basel and an appreciation of the Latin edition of the *Book of Martyrs.*

Steinmann, Martin. *Johannes Oporinus: Ein Basler Buchdrucker um die Mitte des 16 Jahrhunderts.* Basel, 1967. The full account of Oporinus's life and career. Lists 807 letters to or from Oporinus in print and manuscript; the work also contains an extensive bibliography (principally German works) on printing in Basel and on Oporinus's associates.

HARRY CLARK

OPUS TRIPARTITUM

OPUS TRIPARTITUM. A manual of Hungarian customary law, the *Opus Tripartitum* was composed in 1514 by the lawyer István Werbőczi and first published at Vienna in 1517. The *Tripartitum*, so called for its division into three main sections, never received the sanction of the king and therefore remained an unofficial compilation; but its authority in judicial matters was generally acknowledged over the next three centuries, during which it passed through some fifty further editions.

Werbőczi (1458–1541) was a petty noble who rose to positions of great influence in the Hungarian state. His *Tripartitum* enshrines the ideals of a typical contemporary member of his class: first, it asserts the privileges of the noble estate against the claims of the Crown; second, it proclaims the equal rights of every member of that estate against the pretensions of the magnates; and third, it perpetuates the harsh legislation just enacted against the serfs, whose fierce rebellion against their lords was harshly repressed in the very year 1514. The long-lasting influence of the *Tripartitum* mirrored, and itself contributed to, the remarkable conservatism of Hungary's feudal constitution and society in the early modern period.

The appearance of the *Tripartitum*—in the same year as Luther's Ninety-five Theses—had an indirect significance for the subsequent spread of the Reformation in Hungary, which coincided also with the collapse of the country's medieval monarchy at the Battle of Mohács (1526). In the absence of any strong central authority, Werbőczi's codification of noble liberties enhanced the scope for religious dissidence, even though he himself railed against Protestant heresy. In due course the estates came to press for freedom of worship to be statutorily added to their existing freedoms, a demand realized at the Peace of Vienna in 1606.

[*See also* Hungary *and* Mohács, Battle of.]

BIBLIOGRAPHY

Csekey, István. *Werbőczi és a magyar alkotmányjog*. Kolozsvár, 1941. Includes a bibliography of the *Tripartitum*.

Fraknói, Vilmos. *Werbőczi István életrajza*. Budapest, 1899. Still the standard life.

Márkus, Dezsö, ed. *Corpus Iuris Hungarici: Magyar törvénytár*. Vol. 1. Budapest, 1899. Latin text of the *Tripartitum*, with Hungarian translation.

R. J. W. Evans

ORATORY OF DIVINE LOVE is a term that applies to a large number of locally organized institutions whose inspiration came from the devotional life and charitable work of Caterina Fieschi Adorna (or Saint Catherine of Genoa, 1447–1510), and whose best example lies in the sixteenth-century history of the Roman Oratory of Divine Love. These institutions were the source of a significant pre-Tridentine, pre-Lutheran reform movement that exemplifies the close connection between lay and clerical interest in Catholic religious revival and reform in the Reformation era. As a result, historians interested in defining a "Catholic Reformation" that was something other than a mere reaction to the challenge expressed by Luther consider them of crucial significance.

Ettore Vernazza (c.1470–1524), a wealthy notary and businessman who became a colleague of Caterina in her work for the sick, founded the original Oratory of Divine Love in Genoa in 1497, along with three other Genoese citizens, Giovanni Battista Salvago, Nicolò Grimaldi, and Benedetto Lomellino. Linked to earlier Italian confraternities and to the religious revival promoted by preachers like Bernardino of Siena (1380–1444) in the later Middle Ages, the oratory had a dual focus: the inward renewal of its members through religious exercises, common prayer, and frequent reception of the sacraments; and charitable work for the sick and poor in Genoa. Its rule received approval during the pontificate of Leo X on 24 March 1514, with a restricted (and secret) membership that guaranteed the lay character of the organization—thirty-six laymen and four priests. The rule required a fixed program of prayers that included recitation of the Divine Office in common, as well as a weekly fast, monthly confession, and reception of Communion at least four times a year. A father prior ruled the body, along with two counselors and three assistants to the counselors, for a six-month period. Vernazza must have considered humility a key virtue to be promoted among the members, as priors going out of office were to take the "lowest place" in the choir. The energetic charitable work of this first oratory is best seen in the hospital for incurables founded in Genoa by Vernazza in 1499, another first of its kind in Italy. Such charitable activities by members of the oratory, evidence of the link between it and the spirituality of late-medieval Italian confraternities, came to be seen incorrectly, by some historians, as nothing other than an anti-Lutheran expression of the value of works.

The oratory stood at the center of a large number of charitable institutions distributed on a national scale, as similar ones were founded in Milan, Florence, Verona, Lucca, Vicenza, Brescia, Faenza, Padua, Rome, and Naples. In addition, new confraternities sprang up and others were revived that reflected the outward-looking values and intentions of the oratory, without following its specific model. Examples of these are found in the Roman Confraternità della Carità, established in 1519, the confraternity of San Girolamo della Carità in Vicenza, and the confraternity of Saints Filippo and Paolo in Milan, all of which sought to address one or another particular social problem afflicting their respective cities. Such problems ranged from incurable diseases, like syphilis, to prostitution, and from the need for rudimentary education to the insurance of the spiritual welfare of condemned prisoners on their way to the scaffold.

Vernazza apparently helped to organize the Roman branch of the oratory, which met at the church of Saints Silvestro and Dorothea, in Trastevere, sometime between

1514 and 1517. It disbanded after the Sack of Rome (1527) but was of lasting significance because of the later prominence of many of its members and because it served, in part, as the inspiration behind the foundation of the Theatine order. Members like Gian Matteo Giberti (bishop of Verona, 1525–1543), Luigi Lippomano (1500–1559), and Gasparo Contarini (1483–1542) undertook work in diocesan administration for the improvement of lay and clerical devotional life that fed into the revision and clarification of the specific duties and responsibilities of bishops that eventually emerged as law from the Council of Trent. Two other members, Gaetano da Thiene (c.1480–1547) and Gian Pietro Carafa (1476–1559, later Pope Paul IV, 1555–1559), founded the Theatine order. The Theatine rule clearly reflects the directions and motivations of the oratory, and the order was created at least in part because of the recognition that an institution like the oratory, without a strict organization and stable, permanent membership, could have only a limited impact on the church at large.

BIBLIOGRAPHY

Black, Christopher F. *Italian Confraternities in the Sixteenth Century.* Cambridge, 1989. Includes limited information on the oratory but essential background on other confraternities of the period.

Catherine of Genoa. *Purgation and Purgatory, the Spiritual Dialogue.* Translated by Serge Hughes. New York, 1979. Presents translations of two texts by the married lay woman whose work inspired the foundation and early work of the oratory. Includes a helpful introduction.

Jorgensen, Kenneth J. "The Oratories of Divine Love and the Theatines: Confraternal Piety and the Making of a Religious Community." Ph.D. diss., Columbia University, 1989. Approximately 150 pages are devoted to the background, origin, and development of the oratory.

Olin, John C., ed. *The Catholic Reformation, Savonarola to Ignatius Loyola: Reform in the Church, 1495–1540.* New York, 1992. Chapter 2 presents limited background material and an edition of the rule of the original Genoese branch.

Paschini, Pio. *Tre ricerche sulla storia della chiesa nel Cinquecento.* Rome, 1945.

Pastor, Ludwig. *The History of the Popes from the Close of the Middle Ages.* 40 vols., 3d ed. Saint Louis, 1938–1953. Volume 10 includes ten useful pages on the oratories. Originally published as *Geschichte der Päpste seit dem Ausgang des Mittelalters*, 21 vols., Freiburg, 1866–1938.

Pullan, Brian S. *Rich and Poor in Renaissance Venice: The Social Institutions of a Catholic State, to 1620.* Oxford, 1971. Limited information on the origins and rule of the Genoese branch.

Rusconi, Roberto. "Confraternite, compagnie, devozioni." In *Storia d'Italia, Annali n. 9.* Turin, 1986. A forty page monograph on late medieval and early modern confraternities, surveying all recent literature.

Solfaroli Camillocci, Daniela. "Le confraternite del Divino Amore: Interpretazioni storiografice e proposte attuali di ricerca." *Rivista di storia e letteratura religiosa* 27 (1991), 315–332. A useful, but not entirely complete, overview of late nineteenth- and twentieth-century analysis of the oratory and its importance for the Catholic Reformation.

WILLIAM V. HUDON

ORDINATION. In ancient Rome *ordination* was the technical term for the appointment of civil servants, but from the eleventh century on it principally referred to the act of admission into the status of priest. Later, under the influence of the school of Saint Victor, ordination gained significance as the sacrament that conferred authority to celebrate the Eucharist. Its basic meaning of "vocation to particular service in the church" was retained in the churches of the Reformation.

During the Reformation two distinctions were important and left their mark on the church at the beginning of the sixteenth century; these were the division of *ordo* and *jurisdictio* following the Gregorian reform (*Dictatus papae* 1075) and the debates on canon law during the high and late Middle Ages. Canon lawyers drew a distinction between *hierarchia ordinis* (consisting of deacons, priests, and bishops) and *hierarchia jurisdictionis*, with the pope at its head (*papa est nomen jurisdictionis*). This led in some places to the custom of archdeacons and cardinal deacons exercising church leadership. The English Catholic reformer Reginald Pole (1500–1558), cardinal from 1536, was not ordained as a priest until 1555, following his appointment as archbishop of Canterbury. From the twelfth century on there was also a new approach to the understanding of the priestly office. According to theologians, its function was principally focused on the body of Christ present in the sacrament of the Eucharist and less on the representation of Christ in the church. The tendency to see the significance of the office in worship and in the eucharistic sacrifice was strengthened by an influential current in late medieval theology. This theology, which followed Jerome and Peter Lombard, sought equality of priests and bishops on the grounds that the significance of the sacrament of ordination was the offering of the sacrifice of the Mass and the forgiveness of sins, which a minister can exercise once he is ordained. The Council of Florence had fixed as an obligatory dogma in *Decretum pro Armenis* (1439) that the substance of the sacrament of ordination was the *traditio instrumentorum* (in the case of the presbyterate, the chalice and paten, and in the case of the diaconate, the gospel book). The form of the sacrament of priestly ordination was seen in the sentence "accipe potestatem offerendi sacrificium in Ecclesia pro vivis et mortuis, in nomine Patris et Filii et Spiritus Sancti" (accept the power of offering the sacrifice in the church for the living and the dead in the name of the Father and the Son and the Holy Spirit). *Potestas ordinis* meant the general authority of the ordained to administer the sacraments, especially the authority to celebrate the Eucharist. Pope Pius XII was to reintroduce in the apostolic constitution "Sacramentum Ordinis" (1947) the early (and Eastern Orthodox) practice, with the laying on of hands understood as substance and the ordination prayer as form. In a liturgical sense the limitation of ordination to the sacrifice of the Mass is thus done away with. *Potestas jurisdictionis* means the authority of the minister to teach, enact, and interpret the law and to make legal decisions.

Martin Luther does not present a unified or distinct theology of ministry on the theme of ordination. A turning point in his theology of ministry came in 1525, the year of the Peasants' War. After 1525 Luther distanced himself increasingly from the radical left wing of the Reformation. Fundamental to his understanding of ordination was baptism. Baptism is the true ordination to the priesthood. Any differentiation between the clergy and the laity on the grounds of ordination is unbiblical. Ordination as a sacrament and, linked with it, the *character indelebilis* of the priest is an invention of the church without foundation in scripture. All the baptized belong to the universal priesthood and are priests. In his treatise *De instituendis ministris Ecclesiae* of 1523, Luther claims for the universal priesthood all the authority that the Roman church restricted to the ordained office: proclamation of the word, authority to baptize and consecrate the elements, power to retain and absolve sins and to offer a sacrifice on behalf of others, and prayer and the making of judgments on questions of faith. Found at an early stage and increasingly gaining importance after 1525 is the argument that functions belonging to all cannot be assumed by one person; a person's authority must be given by the entire congregation. For the sake of order this authority must be exercised with the general consensus of all. Only in an emergency may an individual claim this authority without express consent. The fundamental function of the universal and the particular ministry is the preaching of the word, *ministerium verbi,* or, better, *ministerium Evangelii.* A minister who no longer performs this service loses his office (which is a functional understanding of the ordained office). After 1525 Luther emphasized an objective calling through an external sign from God or through a commission by the authorities. A proper calling is, however, no guarantee of authentic teaching. The particular ministry always remains under the authority of the word, that is the gospel. The first Lutheran ordination took place in Wittenberg in 1535.

Philipp Melanchthon's position can be found in the Lutheran *Bekenntnisschriften* ("confessional documents"). Melanchthon held that in an emergency the congregation has the right to baptize and forgive sins and to elect the minister, but, in general, a calling or election to public ministry according to proper order is necessary. The true church maintains the right to call and ordain ministers. Ordination with laying on of hands is confirmation of the prior election. A hierarchically structured ministry is as alien to Melanchthon as it is to Luther. The pastor is to a certain extent the bishop of the locality. In order to distance himself from the Roman understanding of the sacrificial priesthood, Melanchthon describes the ministry as the preaching office and the minister's role as the preaching of the word, or gospel, and the administration of the sacraments. The Augsburg Confession requires the installation of servants of the word according to the gospel by the bishop. It threatens bishops with serious consequences (schisms) if they do not fulfill their duty according to *Acts of the Apostles* 5:29 and *1 Peter* 5:2f. In such cases the congregation obviously has the right to appoint its minister. According to the Lutheran understanding, the actual act of installation is a matter of human law. The vagueness of the confessional statement (Augsburg Confession, article 14: *rite vocatus*; the spiritual emphasis on *vocatus,* not *ordinatus,* is significant) reveals a large range of interpretations and formulations concerning ordination. Not until later developments in Lutheranism, after initial uncertainty, was ordination recognized as a single, unrepeatable call to office valid for the church at large (distinguished from the relative and repeatable induction, or installation, into office in a particular congregation). The participation of the congregation decreased as the secular ruler increasingly assumed the function of church leadership.

Huldrych Zwingli's view is found most clearly in his treatise *Von dem Predigtamt* (Of the Preaching Office). Teaching and preaching in a parish require a divine calling. This may arise in two ways: either it follows an inner call and is then, if from God, always accompanied by miracles, or it may occur through election by the congregation. At the core there is only one particular ministry, namely the office of preaching, and this needs to be distinguished from the universal priesthood, which means the equality of all before God. In practice Zwingli's church order was above all established in Zurich. There the church was a local church under the leadership of the secular authority, the city council, assisted by Zwingli, the religious prophet. The marriage court (a forerunner of the consistory in Geneva) consisted of members of the city council and the clergy. The city council led the church and had the power to install ministers.

John Calvin had a strong interest in questions of church order. The *Institutio religionis Christianae* (Institutes of the Christian Religion; 1559) offers a summary of his views. Like Melanchthon and Zwingli, he endeavored to find the basis of the office of minister in the New Testament (*Eph.* 4:11–14). More strongly than Melanchthon, Calvin emphasized that the office must be exercised by men who thereby receive responsibility and authority. Together with other reformers he opposed the hierarchical structure of ministry in the Roman church. He recognized, however, different incumbents for different types of ministry. In the New Testament and in the practice of the early church, he identified four ministries necessary for the church at all times since they were instituted by Christ; these are shepherds (*pastores*), teachers (*doctores*), elders (*seniores*), and deacons (*diaconi*). For the installation of officeholders a calling by election is necessary. Calvin understands this election as confirmation of a decision (vocation) previously made. When someone is installed in office, he does not thereby hold sovereign authority over the congregation. The officeholder has power or authority only insofar as he fulfills the responsibility with which he has been entrusted. The congregation has to monitor whether this happens. Calvin's position thus lies between the classical Lutheran and the Roman Catholic understandings. Calvin does not value Luther's typical argument of the universal priesthood very highly in his elaboration of order; he uses it only in a controversial way against the Roman Catholic understanding of order.

In the Church of England the ordinal—or the *Form and Manner of Making, Ordaining and Consecrating of Bishops, Priests, and Deacons* (1550, as a supplement to *The Book of Common Prayer*)—presupposes in its preface the existence of a threefold order in the church from the time of the apostles that must be maintained. Ordination takes place through the laying on of hands and the prayer of the bishop. Not until the ordinal of 1661 was ordination seen as the specific function of the bishop. The custom of anointing with oil was no longer performed. The deacon had responsibilities derived from the Roman Catholic tradition. The term *priest* is used, without hesitation, for the second order, although it was no longer in use by Protestant churches in continental Europe. The responsibilities of the priest are teaching, administration of the sacraments, and church discipline. The ordinal places particular value on the personal faith and the way of life of the priest. The tasks of the bishop include proclaiming the word, being a guardian of the faith, leading an exemplary life, promoting peace in his diocese, and almsgiving. A distinctive feature of the Church of England in the sixteenth century and thereafter was the oath of allegiance to the monarch, which was required of every minister. The Thirty-nine Articles do not list ordination as a sacrament.

The Roman Catholic understanding of ordination in the sixteenth century was formulated at the Council of Trent (1545–1563). The council formulated its position in opposition to the reformers (the ministry as proclamation of the word) but avoided any resolution of internal Catholic disagreements (relations between the pope and the episcopacy, the source of the jurisdiction of bishops, and the sacramentality of consecration of bishops). The council made the following pronouncements: ordination is a sacrament that can be granted only once, although in various grades. Named are seven grades (doorkeeper, reader, exorcist, acolyte, subdeacon, deacon, and sacerdotium, the latter as an all-inclusive term for the presbyterate and episcopate). The hierarchy is divided into three parts—bishop, priest, and *ministri*. Only after the council was there further clarification that only ordination to the diaconate and priesthood and consecration of bishops had sacramental character. The bishop is the administrator of ordination. Individual cases exist in which ordination was administered by nonbishops (normally priests). These were known at the time the sixteenth-century Spanish theologian Gabriel Vazquez (1549–1604) mentioned such privileges for Benedictine abbots and Franciscan missionaries in India, although without citing any evidence, but these were not systematically considered at the Council of Trent. The sacerdotal image of the priest is predominant. The priest (and thereby ordination) is defined by the celebration of the Eucharist and the forgiveness of sins. The issues concerning the authority of the bishop in relation to the pope—for instance, regarding the question of choosing, presenting, and ordaining candidates right up to the episcopate—were much discussed, but no decision was reached.

[*See also* Diaconate *and* Vocation.]

BIBLIOGRAPHY

Calvin, John. *Institutes of the Christian Religion.* Translated by Ford Battles Lewis. 2 vols. Philadelphia, 1960.

Luther, Martin. *De instituendis ministris Ecclesiae ad Clarissimum Senatum Pragensem Bohemiae.* Wittenberg, 1523.

Zwingli, Ulrich. "Von dem Predigtamt." In *Corpus Reformatorum*, vol. 91, pp. 382–433. Berlin, 1905.

Noll, Mark A., ed. *Confessions and Catechisms of the Reformation.* Leicester, 1991. Contains an English translation of the canons and decrees of the Council of Trent.

WOLFGANG KLAUSNITZER

Translated from German by Christoph Schuler and Lars Simpson

ORLAMUNDE. *See* Bodenstein von Karlstadt, Andreas.

ORMANETO, Niccolò (1515/17–1577), Italian promoter of Catholic reform and diplomat. Born in Verona and trained in law (Padua University), he became an archpriest (of Bovolone) and served the model reforming bishop of Verona, Gian Matteo Giberti. He also traveled for and with Cardinal Reginald Pole, especially during his 1554 visit to England, helping draw up Pole's reform plans (*Reformatio Angliae*). Ormaneto's experience of reform under Giberti and Pole specifically led Carlo Borromeo, cardinal archbishop of Milan, to appoint him as his vicar general (1564–1566). Thus Ormaneto launched Milan's diocesan reform ahead of Borromeo's own residency; he called the first diocesan synod (August 1564), started the first Milan seminary, prepared the first Provincial Council (October 1565), and inaugurated a rigorous confrontational campaign to ensure clerical residency and the proper enclosure of nuns. Surviving correspondence shows that Ormaneto was as much a teacher of Borromeo as his disciple and prepared the way for Borromeo's more famous legislation, homilies, and dictatorial reforms.

Though wishing to resume his parish duties, Ormaneto was summoned by Pius V to reform the Roman diocese itself (1566–1570); there he rigorously and contentiously sought to improve the standards of parish priests and confessors, to prune the papal court, and to reform, banish, or enclose prostitutes. Created bishop of Padua (1570), he found that his reformatory rigidity soon led to serious conflict with local patricians and Venetian republican authorities, notably over disciplining mediocre priests and depriving nuns of family contacts. Against his wishes he was sent as nuncio to Spain (1572–1577), where notably he encouraged Teresa of Ávila and her reform of the Carmelite order. Ormaneto played a crucial role in transmitting reform procedures from the Giberti-Pole circle to the post-Tridentine generation of Borromeo and Cardinal Gabriele Paleotti, but his rigidity and lack of sensitive pastoral care generated unhelpful confrontation.

BIBLIOGRAPHY

Marcora, Carlo. "Nicolò Ormaneto, vicario di S. Carlo, giugno 1564-giugno 1566." *Memorie storiche della diocesi di Milano* 8 (1961), 209–590. Invaluable for printing extensive correspondence between Ormaneto and Borromeo, and other documents preserved in the Biblioteca Ambrosiana, Milan.

Monticone, Alberto. "L'applicazione del Concilio di Trento a Roma: I 'Riformatori' e l'Oratorio, 1566–1572." *Rivista di storia della Chiesa in Italia* 8 (1954), 23–48. Crucial for evidence on his Roman reforming campaign.

Pastor, Ludwig von. *History of the Popes from the Close of the Middle Ages*. London, 1898–1953. The most readily available material for English-language readers. Original edition: *Geschichte der Päpste seit dem Ausgang des Mittelalters*, Freiburg, 1886–1933.

Preto, Paolo. "Un aspetto della riforma cattolica nel Veneto: L'episcopato padovano di Niccolò Ormaneto." *Studi Veneziani*, o.s. 11 (1969), 325–363. For evidence of his troubles as a reforming bishop.

Robinson, Cuthbert. *Nicolò Ormaneto: A Papal Envoy in the Sixteenth Century*. London, 1920. A brief guide to much of his career; worthy, using some old sources, but needs updating as the only modern biographical study.

CHRISTOPHER F. BLACK

ORTHODOX CHURCH. *See* Eastern Orthodoxy.

ORTHODOXY.

In the context of the Reformation, orthodoxy does not enjoy a good press. It is seen as a theological position via which the creative and generous insights of the reformers became fixed in an arid scholastic system. The lively faith that marked the beginnings is seen as turning into dry legalism, while the theology of revelation degenerated into rationalistic ontology. This is a grave error in perspective that not only fails to take account of the movement of history but also creates a mythical picture of the beginnings of the Reformation. It is true that the period during which orthodoxy arose witnessed a proliferation of theological summas that are beyond the grasp of most twentieth-century readers; there was a return to metaphysics and an overall institutionalization of the Reformation. But, were not these manifestations the expression of a necessary establishment in time and space of the churches that arose from the preaching of the reformers?

The generation of pastors and theologians to whom responsibility fell for these young churches, both Lutheran (in Germany and Scandinavia) and Calvinist-Zwinglian (in Switzerland, the Netherlands, France, Hungary, and Scotland), in the mid-sixteenth century had to address a series of problems. It was necessary to provide for or consolidate the organization of the churches in all the states that had decided to adopt the Reformation. To this end, not only ecclesiastical regulations were needed but also creedal texts that would make it possible to define, teach, and live the new faith; hence the proliferation of confessions of faith, catechisms, and liturgical books. Provision had to be made for the formation of competent ecclesiastical personnel; therefore academies were created that were to become the birthplace of the great theological summas of Protestant scholasticism. There was also the need to defend the Reformation theologically, spiritually, and sometimes even physically against the Roman Catholic counteroffensive. Thus an interdenominational debate of increasing subtlety emerged that made use of the finer points of formal logic, which imparted to theology an ever more polemical and rationalizing tone. Finally, it was necessary to give answers to new ethical, political, and cosmological questions that the reformers had only touched upon. To this end it was necessary to call on the resources of secular philosophy, generally Aristotelian, enlightened by the word of God.

This brief summary helps one to grasp the process of orthodoxy and to understand the crucial role played in it by academy professors, servants and interpreters of the Protestant heritage, who also often exercised leadership positions within their respective churches, such as Johann Gerhard in Jena, Abraham Calov in Wittenberg, and François Turrettini in Geneva. They were responsible for defining the faith and for forming a clergy who in turn imbued the faithful with the new belief. Thus one can say that the history of Protestant orthodoxy is tied to that of its academies.

The age of orthodoxy runs from the mid-sixteenth century to the end of the seventeenth century. Starting from the second half of the seventeenth century a shift in thought began that was to have major repercussions on theology, devotion, and worldview and would sound the death knell of orthodoxy. This crisis was to relegate theology to a place below the other sciences, which, in complete independence from the Bible, Ptolemy, and Aristotle, were discovering the laws of nature and of thought, spurred on by Galileo and Newton by way of Descartes and Gassendi.

The beginnings of Lutheran orthodoxy can be traced back to the Formula of Concord, which came from the pen of Jakob Andreae (1528–1590), chancellor of the University of Tübingen. As the culmination of a long process of conciliation within Lutheranism, the Formula of Concord, adopted in 1577, was presented as a commentary on the Augsburg Confession, defining pure doctrine in conformity to the word of God on points that had been in dispute for forty years. For example, against Philipp Melanchthon and Georg Major, it rejected the power of free will in the process of conversion and regeneration. In agreement with Matthias Flacius Illyricus, it held that in times of persecution no concession should be made in the area of adiaphora (moral and religious principles of indifference). Against the Calvinists, it affirmed the *manducatio indignorum et impiorum* ("the eating by the unworthy and impious" of the Lord's Supper) and the ubiquity of the body of Christ at the Lord's Supper. It opposed the twofold predestination that tended to drive the faithful to despair while comforting the impenitent in their disordered living. The Formula of Concord presented itself as a text for fighting against Calvinism and the followers of Melanchthon, and, by unifying Lutheranism, it formally recognized the division of Protestantism into two opposing blocks. It took its place in the *Book of Concord*, alongside the three ecumenical creeds, the Augsburg Confession and its Apology, the Schmalkald Articles and Melanchthon's treatise *De potestate et primatu papae*, and the large and small catechisms of Luther. The canon of Lutheranism was thus definitively established.

From that time on the *Book of Concord* was signed by all new Lutheran pastors and served as a doctrinal framework and a guide for reflections in Lutheran high orthodoxy, which had developed in the schools of theology. The most steeped in history was that of Wittenberg, the *cathedra Lutheri* ("chair of Luther"); the most illustrious were Jena, Tübingen, Strasbourg, Leipzig, Giessen, Rostock, and Königsberg. There were no conspicuous differences of thought or serious conflicts among these institutions. The monumental theological summas they produced testify to the effort made by orthodoxy to encompass all the questions posed by revelation, from creation to redemption. With astonishing biblical and patristic scholarship, thanks to their genuine mastery of the Aristotelian *organon*, the orthodox theologians strove to present in a clear and methodical manner all that humans could hope to know about God and his work. The certitude of their statements reflected their boundless confidence in the possibility of coming to an absolute knowledge of truth. This confidence parallels that expressed by the return of theologians like Jacob Martini (1570–1649) to Aristotelian metaphysics. This return to ontology and fundamental natural theology rested on the certitude that there exists a perfect congruity between the means of knowledge (*intellectus*) and things perceived (*res*).

The magnitude and precision of this theology are illustrated in the work of the three principal masters of Lutheran high orthodoxy. Johann Gerhard (1582–1637), professor at Jena and superintendent of the duchy of Coburg, was the author of *Loci theologici* (1610–1621), which filled nine volumes. For his part, Abraham Calov (1612–1685), professor at Rostock, Königsberg, Danzig, and beginning in 1600 at Wittenberg, where he was likewise superintendent, wrote a twelve-volume summa of "fundamentalist" Lutheranism, the *Systema locorum theologicorum* (1655–1677). His father-in-law (and yet his junior!), Johann Andreas Quenstedt (1617–1688), who was also a nephew of Gerhard (here the dynastic character of Protestant orthodox theology is apparent), professor at Wittenberg, in 1685 published his *Theologica didactico-polemica sive Systema theologicorum.* Though less voluminous than the previously mentioned works, it was no less valued and served as a compendium for Lutheran orthodoxy.

Without going into an analysis of these great summas, it should still be pointed out that one of the main concerns of their authors, in common with Reformed Protestants, was sacred scripture. For a confession that made the *sola scriptura* principle the basis of its faith and preaching, it was necessary to ask in what manner God reveals himself in and through the scriptures and thereby to reinforce the affirmation of the divine authority of scripture. Since scripture was the norm for salvation and the arbiter of religious disputes, its attributes were emphasized: its sufficiency for salvation (to the exclusion of tradition as held by the Catholics and the private revelations of the spiritualists), its intelligibility in passages necessary for salvation (*facultas se ipsam interpretandi*, "ability to interpret itself"), and its efficacy. This vision of scripture rested on the doctrine of literal inspiration. Moving away from Luther's position, which gave greater importance to some biblical books than others, the orthodox theologians considered the prophets and apostles to be "the hand and the pen" of the Holy Spirit. This led Quenstedt to conclude that the vowel points of the Hebrew text had a revealed character and to hold particularly for the formal infallibility of the Bible.

While Lutherans, with their *Book of Concord*, had established a final and definitive doctrinal corpus, Reformed Protestants did not provide themselves with creedal books of definitive and universal value. While many Reformed confessions of faith were marked by the Calvinist imprint, their very multiplicity referred readers to scripture. This fundamental difference with respect to Lutheranism heralded an openness and even a doctrinal multiplicity that led to the first schism (in the strict sense) in the history of Protestantism, the Arminian schism in the Netherlands.

But in order for there to have been a schism, there had to be an orthodoxy, and the origins of this orthodoxy have been rightly traced back to Théodore de Bèze (1519–1605), a colleague and later the successor of Calvin as the head of the church and the academy of Geneva. Bèze distinguished himself by his teaching, often based on the reference work of Reformed Protestantism, Calvin's *Institutio religionis Christianae* (Institutes of the Christian Religion; 1559–1560), by his work as a biblical editor and annotator, by his tireless anti-ubiquitarian and anti-Roman polemical activity, by his shaping of the doctrine of twofold predestination in his famous "Tabula praedestinationis" (a part of his significantly titled *Summa totius christianismi*), and by his role as a consultant for almost half a century to the Reformed churches of Europe. In his greatness Bèze embodied the essence of Calvinism. Alongside him, men such as Lambert Daneau (1530?–1595) adapted Calvinist doctrine to the requirements of academic transmission, utilizing the resources of dialectics and rhetoric to structure theology while making careful use of some elements of metaphysics to deal with the *loci theologici* that the reformers had merely touched upon, such as the essence of God. Imbued with classical and patristic culture, tinged with a veneer of medieval Scholasticism, their still awkward attempts foreshadowed the deeper and more balanced syntheses of the Reformed theologians of the seventeenth century, such as the theologian and philosopher Bartholomaeus Keckermann (*Systema S. S. theologiae*, 1611) and the Basel theologians Amandus Polanus of Polansdorf (*Syntagma theologiae christianae*, 1624) and Johannes Wolleb (*Christiane theologiae compendium*, 1620).

The mention of these three names underlines the fact that from the last quarter of the sixteenth century, Geneva ceased to be the only center of Reformed orthodoxy. Other academies were created or developed: in Switzerland, Basel boasted Amandus Polanus, Johannes Wolleb, Theodor Zwinger, Lukas Gernler, Johann-Rudolf Wettsteins (father and son, both had the same name), Johannes Buxtorfs I and II (father and son), and Peter and Samuel Werenfels; in Germany, Bremen and Heidelberg had Girolamo Zanchi, Urainus, Kaspar Olevianus, Herborn, as well as Pezel, J. Piscator, and Alsted. But most particularly the schools of theology in the Netherlands became the privileged land of Reformed orthodoxy. The creation of the school in Leiden in 1575 was followed by the opening of schools in Franeker (1586), Groningen (1616), and Utrecht (1634). In Leiden the Arminian affair broke out and subsequently shook the Reformed churches and schools of theology throughout Europe during the seventeenth century, leading to the definition of the orthodox doctrine of predestination at the Synod of Dordrecht.

Charged with refuting the latitudinarian opinions of the Dutch moralist Dirk Volkertszoon Coornhert, Jacobus Arminius (1559–1609) disappointed the expectations of the orthodox party by calling into question twofold predestination. Like Melanchthon, Arminius held that Christ died for all and that the grace offered to all is accepted by virtue of a decision by the will of each person. After being appointed professor at Leiden, Arminius clashed with his colleague Franciscus Gomarus (1563–1641), who defended supralapsarianism, according to which God determined (predestined) some to salvation and others to damnation even before (*supra*) deciding to create the universe and to allow the Fall. According to Gomarus, the theories of Arminius were Pelagian.

The controversy continued beyond Arminius's death and was complicated by political interests. In a remonstrance dating from 1610, the Arminians (who were also called Remonstrants) rejected several points that had seemed key to orthodox Calvinists since Bèze. The Arminians refused to consider grace to be irresistible; they based predestination on the foreknowledge of God rather than basing it exclusively on God's will expressed in his deliberate decree. They reiterated that Christ did not die only for the elect, but for all, although they acknowledged that salvation was granted only to believers.

The Synod of Dordrecht (1618–1619), which gathered representatives of all the Calvinist churches (except that of France, which was prevented from attending by Louis XIII), was a sort of Reformed council. The synod moved away from supralapsarianism in favor of the more moderate position of infralapsarianism, according to which God issued his decree of predestination after (*infra*) his decree of creation and that of the Fall. Nonetheless the synod condemned the Arminians, who were forced underground. It also ruled that God chooses the elect not on account of the faith he foresees in them, but on account of his own predilection alone; it further affirmed that grace is irresistible and cannot be lost; and it reaffirmed the primacy of the initiative and glory of God, a central dimension of the theology of Calvin and Bèze. Once they were accepted by the Reformed churches, the decisions of Dordrecht determined the teaching and the debates within Calvinist orthodoxy. These decisions marked the great summas of Dutch theologians such as Gijsbert Voet (1589–1676), professor at Utrecht and an adversary of Descartes, and Samuel Desmarets (1599–1673), Gomarus's successor at Groningen.

The main debate over the decisions of Dordrecht took place in France at the academy of Saumur. Founded in 1599–1600, the academy of Saumur accepted into its ranks a series of professors who attempted to bring the teaching of Dordrecht more in line with biblical statements. Moïse Amyraut (1596–1664) in particular formulated the theory of hypothetical universalism in order to tone down the particularism of orthodox predestination, which reserved salvation to the elect alone. According to him, God wills to save all—on the condition that they believe. Despite these universalist intentions, Amyraut did not escape particularism, since he made faith, the condition for salvation, dependanat on the predilection of God. Nonetheless his theses stirred up lively debates. Pierre Du Moulin (1568–1658), professor at the academy of Sedan, and his brother-in-law André Rivet (1572–1651), professor at Leiden from 1632, defended Calvinist orthodoxy. Saumur became a synonym for "novelties" and attacks on orthodoxy. Amyraut had colleagues that included the Hebrew scholar Louis Cappel (1585–1658), who rejected the divine inspiration of the vowel points of the Old Testament, and Josué de la Place (1596–1656), who disputed the immediate and mechanical imputation of Adam's sin to his descendants. To halt the advance of these novelties, professors Johann Heinrich Heidegger (1633–1698) of Zurich, François Turrettini (1629–1687) of Geneva, and Lukas Gernler (1625–1675) of Basel drew up in 1675 the last creedal formula of Calvinist orthodoxy, the *Formula consensus ecclesiarum helveticarum reformatarum* (*Consensus helveticus*). This text defended the literal inspiration and the absolute integrity of the Hebrew text, including the vowel points. It reaffirmed the teaching of Dordrecht (limiting salvation to the elect alone) and the immediate imputation of Adam's sin to all his posterity.

One of its authors, Turrettini, published in 1679 the three volumes of his *Institutio theologiae elencticae*, a work of Calvinist orthodoxy monumental for its structure and clarity. Shortly after this work appeared, the age of Reformed orthodoxy came to a close, after having begun upon the publication of the last edition of Calvin's *Institutes.* In Geneva, under the influence of Jean-Alphonse Turrettini, the son of François Turrettini, who adapted the heritage of the reformers to the Enlightenment, the requirement of signing the *Consensus helveticus* was abandoned in 1706 and in 1725 the requirement of signing the canons of Dordrecht was likewise rescinded. Thereafter nothing more was required beyond faithfulness to the Bible and Calvin's catechism.

In the year the *Consensus helveticus* was drawn up, the *Pia desideria* (1675) of Philipp Jacob Spener was published. This work, which was really the charter of Pietism, by comparison made the *Consensus helveticus* appear to be a last desperate fight and orthodoxy to be an outdated movement. By both his statements and his criticisms, Spener points out the weaknesses of orthodoxy, both Lutheran and Calvinist, as it was showing signs of exhaustion. Orthodoxy had become too exclusively polemical, even rationalizing, and ended up erecting a screen between the Bible and the faithful, leading students to lose sight of the fact that theology is not an end in itself, but a means to salvation, and causing pastors to forget that they must preach a faith that is lived and visible by its fruits. Finally, Spener brings out the fact that orthodoxy, despite its links with political power, had been unable to push through the moral reforms that society needed. Only individual conversion could henceforth lead to real moral change, and, for this purpose, it is not necessary for the church to be connected to civil jurisdiction.

The demand for faith that was lived and the criticism of theology that was too far removed from the life of the faithful should not make one forget the importance of the age of orthodoxy for Protestant piety. This was the age that saw the development of the practice of family worship, in which Bible reading, singing of psalms and chorales, prayers, and a providential explanation for events set the rhythm of daily family life. It was during this time that monumental works of Protestant devotion were published, such as *Vier Bücher vom wahren Christentum* (1605–1609) by Johann Arndt (1555–1621) and *Consolations de l'âme fidèle contre les frayeurs de la mort* (1651) by Charles Drelincourt (1595–1669). This was also the time when in the context of sufferings and sadness, Paul Gerhardt, a champion of orthodoxy, composed remarkable hymns of hope and joy. The providentialist mind-set, which saw the hand of God in every event, did not have the effect only of leading the faithful to a growing trust in the word of God. On the contrary, many resorted to ancestral practices verging on magic, paying attention to comets, believing in sorcerers and evil spirits, and taking part in traditional feasts intended, in the most pagan manner, to ward off the perils of nature and humankind with each passing season. The age that produced expressions of faith as sumptuous as the musical works of the likes of Heinrich Schütz or, later, Johann Sebastian Bach, contemporaries of the last glow of Lutheran orthodoxy, is also the age that considered it necessary to burn sorcerers and witches at the stake to safeguard its faith.

BIBLIOGRAPHY

Barth, Hans-Martin. *Atheismus und Orthodoxie: Analyse und Modelle christlicher Apologetik im 17. Jahrhundert.* Göttingen, 1971.

Baur, Jörg. *Die Vernunft zwischen Ontologie und Evangelium.* Gütersloh, 1962.

Bizer, Ernst. *Frühorthodoxie und Rationalismus.* Zurich, 1963.

Fatio, Olivier. "L'orthodoxie protestante." In *L'aventure de la réforme: Le monde de Jean Calvin,* edited by Pierre Chaunu, rev. ed. Paris, 1992.

Geiger, Max. *Die Basler Kirche und Theologie im Zeitalter der Hochorthodoxie.* Zollikon, Switzerland, 1952.

Greschat, Martin. *Zwischen Tradition und neuem Anfang: Valentin Ernst Löscher und der Ausgang der lutherischen Orthodoxie.* Witten, 1971.

Hornig, Gottfried. "Von der Frühorthodoxie bis zur Aufklärungstheologie des 18. Jahrhunderts." In *Handbuch der Dogmen- und Theologiegeschichte,* edited by Carl Andresen, vol. 3. Göttingen, 1984.

Laplanche, François. *L'écriture, le sacré et l'histoire.* Amsterdam, 1986.

Muller, Richard A. "'Vera Philosophia cum sacra theologia nusquam pugnat': Keckermann on Philosophy, Theology and the Problem of Double Truth." *Sixteenth Century Journal* 15 (1984), 341–365.

———. *Christ and the Decree: Christology and Predestination in Reformed Theology from Calvin to Perkins.* Grand Rapids, Mich., 1986. See pp. 1–13 for an excellent discussion of historiography.

———. "Scholasticism Protestant and Catholic: Francis Turretin on the Object and Principles of Theology." *Church History* 55 (1986), 193–205.

Ratschow, Carl-Heinz. *Lutherische Dogmatik zwischen Reformation und Aufklärung.* Gütersloh, 1966.

Sparn, W. *Wiederkehr der Metaphysik: Die ontologische Frage in der lutherischen Theologie des frühen 17. Jahrhunderts.* Stuttgart, 1976.

Weber, H. E. *Reformation, Orthodoxie und Rationalismus.* Reprint, Gütersloh, 1967.

OLIVIER FATIO

Translated from French by Robert E. Shillenn

OSIANDER, Andreas (1496?–1552), German reformer and Luthern theologian. As a reformer of the imperial city of Nuremberg and later because of the conflict over the doctrine of justification named after him, Osiander won a lasting and significant place in the theological and ecclesistical history of Protestantism. The publication of the chief work of Nicolaus Copernicus with an anonymous preface written by him caused Osiander's name also to go down in the history of science.

He was most likely born in the year 1496 in Gunzenhausen on the Altmühl River in Franconia. He began his studies at the University of Ingolstadt in 1515 and quickly opened himself up to the influence of humanism. His concerns over the text of the Bible are reflected in his attempt at a revision of the Vulgate (1522) and his *Harmonia Evangelica* (Harmony of the Gospels; 1537). Through the works of Johannes Reuchlin, Osiander found his way to the Cabbalistic tradition; he learned Hebrew and Aramaic, and later, in a work published anonymously, he came out against the accusation of ritual murder leveled against Jews. In 1520 he was ordained a priest, teaching Hebrew in the Nuremberg Augustinian monastery and in 1522 became a preacher at the parish church of Saint Lorenz.

When, after several unsuccessful attempts, the evangelical preachers of the city introduced a reformed order of worship, Osiander drafted the written defense for the two provosts. In March of the following year he was the spokesman for the evangelical side at the religious discussion that resulted in the official enactment of the Reformation by the council.

In the following years Osiander's opinion was constantly sought regarding the manifold problems associated with the Reformation. The detailed minutes of the consultations with him as well as his written opinions are extant and and have been edited from the Nuremberg manuscipts.

Osiander came out with equal harshness against Catholic, Zwinglian, and spiritualist tendencies in the city and later expressed skepticism about Martin Bucer's endeavors to attain a united evangelical church community. Over the editing of the Brandenburg-Nuremberg church order (1533) that had essentially come from him along with its catechetical sermons, which many cities and territories adopted, serious tensions arose with his colleagues and the council clerk Lazarus Spengler. Despite this, Osiander frequently represented the city and its theologians—for example, at the Marburg religious discussions in 1529, the Augsburg Imperial Diet in 1530, the Schmalkald conference in 1537, and the religious discussions in Hagenau and Worms in 1540–1541. Because of the rigid ecclesiastical regime of the council, which was unwilling to tolerate any independent ecclesiastical discipline, any independent ordinations, or any reformed marriage laws as Osiander understood them, disputes constantly arose. Even relations with the Wittenberg theologians did not remain free of tension, as when Osiander, between 1533 and 1536, spoke out vehemently against "general absolution" and in favor of private confession and absolution. Perhaps because people at that time already feared this obstinate and self-righteous man, endeavors in the 1530s to bring him to Tübingen as a professor and to Augsburg as city superintendent never got beyond the early stages of consideration. Nevertheless, Palatinate Count Ottheinrich entrusted him with the reformation of his principality, Palatinate-Neuburg, for which Osiander drafted a new church order in 1543, based on the Margravial-Brandenburg church order of 1540 and the Brandenburg-Nuremberg church order of 1533.

When, after earlier consultations undertaken without summoning its theologians, the Nuremberg council decided in 1548 to introduce a new order of worship that was congenial to the Interim, Osiander left the imperial city and went to Königsberg in East Prussia. Here, on the basis of his long-standing connections with Duke Albert, he became not only pastor of the old city but also—in violation of the statutes—professor at the university. Since this post required him to set forth his theology in a more coherent fashion, the peculiarities of his views were immediately evident to disciples of Luther and Philipp Melanchthon. In a problematic absolutizing of the traditional assertion that there is nothing accidental in God, Osiander, who took recourse to Cabbalistic traditions, came to the thesis that, even without the Fall, the son of God would have had to become man. Moreover, in a one-sided reflection of some of Luther's occasional remarks, he paralleled the ancient church's Christology of the two natures in Christ with the Reformation's basic concept that man becomes justified not by works but by faith. Because he equated Christ's human nature with works and his divine nature with faith, he understood the justification of man before God as an inpouring or infusion of Christ's divine nature.

The Osiander controversy originated not only on the basis of these ideas, but also against the background of disputes with his colleagues at the university. It continued even after Osiander's death on 17 October 1552. In his Christology his opponents denounced a tendency toward Nestorianism, in which Christ's humanity is insufficiently valued, while discerning a tendency toward Catholicism in his doctrine on justification since it brought the inpouring of divine nature into the context of a *gratia infusa.* As problematic as Osiander's position was on particular points, he did recognize that a merely forensic understanding of justification did not do justice to Luther's theology. Furthermore, he noted that the connection of Christology with the doctrine of justification by way of Anselm's doctrine of satisfaction left much to be desired. Nonetheless, apart from the Württemberg theologians, who were influenced by Johannes Brenz and seeking a path of mediation, Osiander's theology, which Duke Albert of Prussia ordered examined in the Protestant territories of the empire, met with unanimous rejection; this was confirmed in the Formula of Concord.

BIBLIOGRAPHY

Primary Sources

Osiander d. Ä, Andreas. *Gesamtausgabe.* Volumes 1–6, edited by Gerhard Müller, volumes 7–10, commissioned by the Heidelberg Academy of Sciences, edited by Gottfried Seebaß. Gütersloh, 1975–1995.

Seebaß, Gottfried, ed. *Bibliographia Osiandrica: Bibliographie der gedruckten Schriften Andreas Osianders d. Ä, 1496–1552.* Nieuwkoop, 1971.

Secondary Sources

Fligg, Jörg Rainer. "Herzog Albrecht von Preußen und der Osiandrismus, 1522–1568." Ph.D. diss. Bonn, 1972.

Hirsch, Emanuel. *Die Theologie des Andreas Osiander und ihre geschichtlichen Voraussetzungen.* Göttingen, 1919.

Seebaß, Gottfried. *Das reformatorische Werk des Andreas Osiander.* Einzelarbeiten aus der Kirchengeschichte Bayerns, vol. 44. Nuremberg, 1967.

Stupperich, Martin. *Osiander in Preußen, 1549–1552.* Arbeiten zur Kirchengeschichte 44. Berlin and New York, 1973.

GOTTFRIED SEEBAß

Translated from German by Robert E. Shillenn

OSIANDER, Lucas II (1571–1638), orthodox Lutheran theologian and polemicist at the University of Tübingen. The son of the Württemberg court preacher Lucas Osiander the Elder, he studied at Tübingen, served as deacon in Göppingen (1591), pastor at Schwieberdingen (1597), superintendent at Leonberg (1601) and Schorndorf (1606), and abbot at Bebenhausen (1612) and Maulbronn (1616). After earning his doctorate, he was named full professor of theology at Tübingen (1619) and university chancellor and provost (1620), posts he held until the end of his life. Like other members of the renowned Osiander family, Lucas was endowed with a keen mind and made a reputation as an orthodox Lutheran dogmatist. He was one of the most vehement polemicists of his age and did not hesitate to take a firm stand on some of the thorniest theological issues. He wrote a number of tracts and treatises, among them four lengthy *Enchiridia controversiarum,* against Anabaptists, Schwenckfeldians, Jesuits, and Calvinists (notably the Heidelberg theologian Abraham Scultetus).

Osiander became best known through the krypsis-kenosis controversy, which arose in the early seventeenth century between the universities of Giessen and Tübingen over the question whether Christ, in the state of humiliation, abstained from the use of divine attributes (kenosis) or whether he used them secretly (krypsis). The controversy was important since it involved the development of orthodox Lutheran Christology after the Formula of Concord. The Giessen Lutherans (Balthasar Mentzer, Justus Feuerborn) defended the kenotic view; Osiander and his colleagues at Tübingen (Melchior Nicolai, Theodor Thumm) opposed it.

Another well-known confrontation resulted from Osiander's sweeping denunciation of Johann Arndt's *Wahres Christentum* in 1623. Osiander found Arndt's title offensive, charged that his work preached mysticism (*Taulerdom*), and called it a "book of hell" because, he claimed, it contained papist, Schwenckfeldian, and Calvinist heresies. Osiander's criticism of individual passages, while defensible from the perspective of orthodox Lutheranism, did not justify his condemnation of the entire work and was not endorsed by other members of the Tübingen faculty; Arndt's book remained very popular in southern Germany.

BIBLIOGRAPHY

Brecht, Martin, ed. *Theologie und Theologen der Universität Tübingen.* Tübingen, 1977. Detailed analyses of Osiander's theological controversies.

Farren, John A. *The Lutheran Krypsis-Kenosis Controversy: The Presence of Christ, 1619–1627.* Washington, D.C., 1974. Theological analysis by Dominican scholar.

Verzeichnis der im deutschen Sprachbereich erschienenen Drucke des XVI. Jahrhunderts. Stuttgart, 1983–. See vol. 15, nos. 1159–1282.

Wangemann and Bossert. "Lukas II Osiander." In *Realencyclopädie für protestantische Theologie und Kirche,* 3d ed., 24 vols., edited by Albert Hauck, vol. 14, pp. 512ff. Leipzig, 1896–1913. Focuses on Osiander as polemicist.

BODO NISCHAN

OSUNA, Francisco de (1492–1541?), Spanish Franciscan theologian and devotional author. He was born around 1492 in Osuna (Sevilla province), where his family was in the service of the ducal family. He participated in the campaign in Tripoli (1510) and, after a pilgrimage to Santiago de Campostela, became a member of the Castillian province of the Franciscan order. He studied theology at the University of Alcalá de Henares. After his ordination to the priesthood, he moved to the hermitage of La Salceda, where he wrote his first devotional writings. An extensive journey through Europe in the service of his order and to advance the publication of his writings followed in the 1530s.

Osuna was especially active in teaching Christians to nourish a personal relationship with God through mental prayer. Of the two forms of mental prayer in use at the time, Osuna defended *recogimiento,* or recollection, as opposed to *dejamiento,* or abandonment. *Dejamiento* was the preferred practice of the *Alumbrados* ("enlightened ones"), whom the Inquisition prosecuted for denying the efficacy of virtuous deeds, vocal prayer, and the sacraments and for their insistence that true prayer rendered them powerless to do anything except surrender to divine grace.

Osuna's major work, *Tercer Abecedario espiritual* (The Third Spiritual Alphabet; 1527), is evidence that he did not share the quietism of the *Alumbrados.* Orthodox in its mysticism, the *Abecedario* is a description and explanation of the soul's inward journey in terms of recollection. Recollection is Osuna's name for prayer, including vocal prayer, mental prayer, and the passive prayer identified with the higher stages of the mystical way. Rather than denoting any one mode of prayer, recollection is the process wherein the soul becomes increasingly aware of God's presence and eventually is infused with the wisdom that surpasses rational understanding.

Osuna wrote five other major treatises, two of them also in alphabetical form. Through his teachings and writings he not only helped his contemporaries to reform their religious lives in the direction of greater simplicity and interiority but also influenced a number of later mystics, most notably Teresa of Ávila.

BIBLIOGRAPHY

Primary Source

Osuna, Francisco de. *Tercer Abecedario espiritual* (1527). Madrid, 1972. English translation by Mary E. Giles, New York, 1981.

Secondary Sources

Calvert, Laura. *Francisco de Osuna and the Spirit of the Letter.* Chapel Hill, N.C., 1973. A meticulous study, especially of imagery.

Prien, Hans-Jürgen. *Francisco de Osuna: Mystik und Rechtfertigung; Ein Beitrag zur Erforschung der spanischen Theologie und Frömmigkeit.* Hamburg, 1967.

Ros, Fidèle. *Un maître de sainte Thérèse: Le Père Francisco d'Osuna, Sa vie, son oeuvre, sa doctrine spirituelle.* Paris, 1936.

MARY E. GILES

OTTOMAN EMPIRE. In sixteenth-century Europe the Ottoman empire comprised the entire Balkan Peninsula south of the Danube and that part of the Hungarian kingdom that stretched from the Danube to Buda. These vast territories were conquered by the Turks between the fourteenth and the first half of the sixteenth century. A variety of ethnic groups inhabited the Ottoman empire in Europe: mostly southern Slavs in the central and western peninsula, Greeks in the southern part and Constantinople, Albanians on the western and southwestern borders, Magyars in Hungary, and Ottoman Turks scattered throughout the empire but primarily in Constantinople, Adrianople, and adjacent lands.

With the exception of the Hungarian part of the empire, where the inhabitants were either Catholic or Protestant, the dominant Christian faith of the peoples of the Balkan Peninsula was Eastern Orthodoxy. Catholics were found in small numbers among Bulgarians and Albanians; however, a significant number of Bosnians and Albanians had converted to Islam in previous centuries and, of course, the Turks were Muslim.

Although the Ottoman empire included part of historical Hungary in the first half of the sixteenth century, that part, because of the special regimen that it enjoyed, was not regarded as an integral part of the so-called core empire, which comprised the territories south of the Danube. Nor, for that matter, were the vassal states of Moldavia, Wallachia, and Transylvania—inhabited primarily by Romanians—or the city-state of Dubrovnik integral parts of the Ottoman empire. Therefore, in any consideration of Ottoman policies relevant to religious or political aspects of the Protestant Reformation, one must appraise and understand such policies in terms of governmental structures and policies determined by the Turkish sultans as rulers of the core empire.

Because of their conquests in east-central Europe and military successes in the Mediterranean, as well as their Muslim faith, the Turks were generally regarded as mortal enemies of Christendom, as the "scourge of God," and as a force that had to be removed from the European continent. Whereas appeals for crusades against the "infidel" emanating from the papacy and the Holy Roman Emperor were falling on deaf ears by the sixteenth century, the Turks remained a constant catalyst for rallying Christendom to causes and ideologies unrelated to the grossly exaggerated "Turkish threat." In reality, the threat to Western Christendom was minimal after the conquest of Turkish Hungary, and the presumed need for liberating Christians under the "Turkish yoke" from cruelty and repression was not evident. Indeed, the Turkish sultans were more tolerant of religious diversity than any European ruler. The Christians in the core empire—overwhelmingly Orthodox—were organized in a "millet," which, in accordance with Islamic tradition and practice, was the community of non-Muslim people that formed a legal-administrative unit; in this instance it was under the jurisdiction of the Orthodox patriarch of Constantinople. The same level of toleration was extended to the Jewish and Armenian millets.

The initial link between Protestantism and the Turkish empire was related to the perceived "Turkish threat" and focused on the medieval concept of heresy. Since Islam was patently heretical to all Christians and since the papacy was patently heretical to Luther and other theologians of the Reformation, the equating of the heretical papacy and Catholic church with heretical Islam became *de rigueur* for most Protestant reformers, if for no other reason than to assert the theological purity of Protestantism. Notwithstanding Luther's uncompromising, albeit erroneous, view of the Turks and of the Turkish menace, it was perhaps the greatest irony that Lutheranism in Germany and Protestantism in general in eastern and central Europe were the ultimate beneficiaries of the religious toleration and foreign policies of the Ottoman empire.

Within the confines of the core empire Protestantism was not an issue because it had not penetrated the Orthodox millet and because in general the imperial authorities were not wont to differentiate among Christian denominations. It was of critical significance, however, in Turkish Hungary and in vassal Transylvania, where the survival and consolidation of Protestantism was to a considerable extent a function of the Ottoman presence in Hungary and of the special position enjoyed by Transylvania in the Ottoman order in east-central Europe. Whereas the Turks had no conscious policy toward Calvinists, Lutherans, and Unitarians other than that of tolerating religious diversity, the Turks were clearly cognizant of the policies of their Transylvanian vassals, which policies benefited the Porte (i.e., the Ottoman empire) through a common opposition to the Catholic Habsburg Holy Roman Empire.

Specifically, the repressive anti-Protestant enactments of the Hungarian diet prior to the destruction of the old Hungarian kingdom by the Turks at the Battle of Mohács in 1526 that, in the case of Lutherans, provided for their being "rooted out of the country and, whenever they be found, seized without restriction not only by the clergy but also by laymen, and be burned," were indicative of the prospective fate of Protestantism. Under Turkish rule, however, Protestantism spread rapidly, most notably among intellectuals and the aristocracy. By the mid-sixteenth century the Hungarian school system was predominately Protestant and the defection of the nobility to Calvinism was such that by the 1570s "only three of the great families of Hungary" were reputedly "still Catholic."

The acceleration of the adoption of Calvinism, however, was partly accountable to the massive migration of the aristocracy to Transylvania, where Protestantism flourished perhaps to a greater degree than anywhere else in sixteenth-century Europe. Recapitulating only the most significant legal enactments and activities of Protestant leaders, one should note that Transylvania was at the forefront of religious tolerance from as early as the middle of the century. The Diet of Torda granted the Lutherans freedom of worship in 1550, in 1557 the same diet recognized the Lutheran church as an "accepted religion," in 1564 it extended the same status to the Calvinist church, and in 1568 it legislated universal freedom of worship. This unusual tolerance allowed unhindered preaching by such distinguished Protestant theologians as Johannes Honterus, who spread Lutheranism among the Saxons, and Francis Dávid and Giorgio Biandrata, who founded the most famous Unitarian church in Europe at Klausenburg in 1556.

Crucial for the survival and expansion of Protestantism in Hungary and Transylvania, Ottoman policies also played a decisive role in the consolidation, expansion, and legitimation of Lutheranism in Germany. The contribution of the Turks was indirect and intimately related to their being the principal opponents of the Habsburg quest for hegemony in Europe in the first half of the sixteenth century. Habsburg expansionism eastward, focusing on the succession to the Hungarian crown by Ferdinand, was resisted by the Turks, who rejected all Habsburg claims to Hungary. The protracted confrontations between Habsburgs and Turks in and over Hungary following the Battle of Mohács expanded to naval warfare in the Mediterranean and in North Africa as the Turks became allies of Francis I after 1535; this situation helped the Protestant cause in Germany.

The Protestants readily linked the problems presented to the Habsburgs by direct and indirect Ottoman aggression with their own struggle for survival, consolidation, and expansion in Germany. Most significantly, they utilized the Habsburg dependence on German assistance for the protection of the empire and the attainment of Hungarian aims to further their own cause. Almost all major concessions wrested from the Habsburgs from 1526 were connected with Ottoman activities in eastern and western Europe, and the all-important Lutheran campaign for legal recognition in Germany exploited the insoluble Habsburg-Ottoman conflict over Hungary. The Recess of Speyer of 1526, the Peace of Nuremberg of 1532, the Compact of Cadan, the Frankfurt Anstand, the Declaration of Regensburg, the Recess of Speyer of 1542, the Treaty of Passau, and the Peace of Augsburg of 1555—all milestones in the Protestant struggle for recognition and the course of the German Reformation—were deeply influenced by the ebb and flow of Ottoman aggression.

The relationship between Protestantism and the Ottoman empire was most significant in the heroic age of confrontation and consolidation that ended with the legal recognition of Protestantism in countries and areas affected directly or indirectly by Turkish political actions. The very survival and expansion of Protestantism in its various confessions in Germany, Hungary, and Transylvania was to a considerable extent a function of two interrelated aspects of Ottoman-Islamic imperialism: military action and religious toleration.

[*See also* Hungary; Mohács, Battle of; *and* Transylvania.]

BIBLIOGRAPHY

Coles, Peter. *The Ottoman Impact on Europe.* New York, 1968.

Fisher-Galati, Stephen. *Ottoman Imperialism and German Protestantism, 1521–1555.* Reprint, New York, 1972.

———. "Judeo-Christian Aspects of Pax Ottomanica." In *Tolerance and Movements of Religious Dissent in Eastern Europe,* edited by Béla K. Király, pp. 185–197. Boulder, 1975.

———. "The Protestant Reformation and Islam." In *The Mutual Effects of the Islamic and Judeo-Christian Worlds: The East European Patterns,* edited by Abraham Ascher, Tibor Halasi-Kun, and Béla K. Király, pp. 53–64. Brooklyn, 1979.

Inalcik, Halil. *The Ottoman Empire: The Classical Age, 1300–1600.* Reprint, New Rochelle, N.Y., 1989.

Király, Béla K. "The Sublime Porte, Vienna, Transylvania and the Dissemination of Protestant Reformation in Royal Hungary." In *Tolerance and Movements of Religious Dissent in Eastern Europe,* edited by Béla K. Király, pp. 199–221. Boulder, 1975.

Setton, Kenneth M. "Lutheranism and the Turkish Peril." *Balkan Studies* 3 (1962), 113–168.

STEPHEN FISCHER-GALATI

OXFORD, UNIVERSITY OF. The response of the University of Oxford to the Reformation was shaped by at least four factors: the memory of the theologian John Wycliffe and his condemnation, its geographical location, the influence of local recusancy, and the strength of the university's theological tradition and of its loyalty to it. The controversy surrounding Wycliffe (d. 1384) had brought Oxford into unprecedented conflict with its historic patrons and protectors, the royal government and the English bishops. Moreover, it had precipitated the first and only papal intervention in the teaching of the Oxford faculty of theology (by Gregory XI in 1377), a consequence of Wycliffe's ideas having been taken into the national arena by rival factions within the court. In the following century, therefore, Wycliffe's legacy to the university was chiefly the memory of affront to its independence and of the supervision maintained over its masters in the next generation by the successive archbishops of Canterbury, William Courtenay (1381–1396) and Thomas Arundel (1396–1397, 1399–1413). While Wycliffe retained a following for a generation or so among certain theologians in the faculty, the evidence suggests that by the middle of the fifteenth century his views had been absorbed rather uneventfully into the generous fabric of Oxford's theological tradition. This in the late Middle Ages was eclectic if predominantly Scotist, characterized not so much by speculation as by pastoral concern and apologetic works against the influence of Wycliffe, along with a growing scholarly taste for exegetical and patristic texts.

Oxford received its first identifiable Protestant adherents from Cambridge, where proximity to the Continent had insured early contact with reforming thought. Ironically, these were men recruited by Thomas Wolsey to staff his new foundation, Cardinal College (1526), one of whose aims was the extirpation of heresy. Vigorous action by Wolsey and the authorities banished a group of some twenty-two dissidents from the university by 1528, and while Luther's works undoubtedly continued to be read, attracting some discreet adherents, clearly his opinions did not elicit a wide, sympathetic interest. Oxford was also conspicuously reluctant to support Henry VIII's cause in the royal divorce. The efforts of the government visitors in 1535 to enforce the new religious settlement and the dissolution of the religious houses in the following years brought about signal changes, but Oxford remained conservative.

Under Edward VI (r. 1547–1553) the government intervened directly to purge the traditionalists and introduce Protestant theology. The former was to be the work of another royal visitation, this time in 1549. It at least exposed the scale of the problem. The latter was achieved by appointing a committed Protestant, Richard Cox, as both dean of Christ Church and chancellor of the university and a distinguished Continental theologian, Peter Martyr Vermigli, as regius professor. Their impact, if brief, was immense. The introduction of Protestant thought nevertheless proved an uphill struggle, and after the accession of Mary Tudor the tables were turned. There is no evidence that the university as a whole regretted the passing of the previous reign, which had exposed it to government intervention and deprivations on a hitherto unimagined scale. Moreover, under Mary the fortunes of Oxford improved dramatically with a revival of numbers; new endowments from the Crown, which tripled the university's revenue; the appointment of two Spanish theologians, Juan de Villa Garcia and his successor, Peter de Soto; and the endowment of two new colleges, Trinity and Saint John's, by Catholic laymen. In 1554–1556 the trials and executions for heresy of bishops Thomas Cranmer, Hugh Latimer, and Nicholas Ridley—all Cambridge men—made it clear that the university was no place for confessing Protestants.

With the advent of Elizabeth I (r. 1558–1603) the roles again reversed. Marian exiles returned (though few to Oxford itself), and the Catholics went abroad. The grip of the government on the university, a principal consequence of the Reformation in both places, was ensured by the earl of Leicester (Robert Dudley) as chancellor (1564–1588), who was the first to appoint his vice-chancellors. A new visitation (1559) initiated the process of removing Catholic heads and fellows, although only a few colleges, such as Magdalen and Christ Church, were converted with comparative ease. In 1569 a special commission was sent to Oxford to search out Catholic books. All those matriculating or taking degrees were required to subscribe to the Articles of Religion, and catechesis was carefully prescribed.

Now at last a Protestant university slowly emerged, its Protestantism bearing an inflection characteristic of the place. In considerable part it was shaped in response to issues raised by learned Catholic graduates now writing from exile or prison, such as William Allen, Edmund Campion, John de Feckenham, Nicholas Harpsfield, Gregory Martin, Robert Parsons, Nicholas Sanders, and Thomas Stapleton. Moreover, Oxford was preoccupied to a degree unknown in Cambridge with the challenge of a continuing Catholic presence in the university, supported in the academic halls and by local recusant families living at the very boundaries of the university. One result was that Oxford theologians took but a small part in the controversies of the 1560s about the nature of the Elizabethan church, devoting their energies instead to combating the Roman positions. As the reign progressed the general tenor of Oxford theology was firmly Calvinistic; the leading names include John Jewel, Laurence Humphrey, John Rainolds, and Richard Hooker. Yet even late in the century evidence from the schools more typically shows concern about defining Protestant doctrine against that of Rome than about exploring debate between the reformed traditions. In the end Oxford Puritanism was chiefly of the conforming variety, with its controversies less violent than those at Cambridge and its more extreme proponents either departing or moderating their views. Moreover, as the writings even of such a firm Protestant as Rainolds show, Oxford masters of the time maintained an eclecticism and a deference to the unbroken tradition of commentary which is likewise reflected in Hooker's *Laws of the Ecclesiastical Polity,* the chief monument of the English church to emerge from Elizabethan Oxford. If it is said that the sixteenth century belonged to Cambridge in religion, then the claims of comprehensiveness that would be voiced in the seventeenth century were being formed in Oxford.

[*See also* Cambridge, University of.]

BIBLIOGRAPHY

Catto, Jeremy I. "Theology after Wycliffism." In *Late Medieval Oxford,* edited by J. I. Catto, pp. 263–280. The History of the University of Oxford, vol. 2. Oxford, 1992. Especially valuable for the manuscript sources cited, Catto's two chapters are the most recent and comprehensive study of late medieval theology in Oxford.

———. "Wyclif and Wycliffism at Oxford 1356–1430." In *Late Medieval Oxford,* edited by J. I. Catto, pp. 175–261. The History of the University of Oxford, vol. 2. Oxford, 1992.

Cross, Claire. "Oxford and the Tudor State, 1509–1558." In *The Collegiate University,* edited by James McConica, pp. 117–49. The History of the University of Oxford, vol. 3. Oxford, 1986. Describes the increasing dominance of the government in university affairs with the advent of the Reformation.

Curtis, Mark H. *Oxford and Cambridge in Transition, 1558–1642.* 2d ed. Oxford, 1965. Established study that places religious developments in the context of wider intellectual changes, notably the advent of humanism in the universities.

Loach, Jennifer. "Reformation Controversies." In *The Collegiate University,* edited by James McConica, pp. 363–396. The History of the University of Oxford, vol. 3. Oxford, 1986. Focuses on the debate within the university over the Tudor period.

Loades, David. *The Oxford Martyrs.* London, 1970. Detailed account of the background and trials of Thomas Cranmer, Hugh Latimer, and Nicholas Ridley.

Williams, Penny. "State, Church, and University, 1558–1603." In *The Collegiate University,* edited by James McConica, pp. 397–440. The History of the University of Oxford, vol. 3. Oxford, 1986. Discussion complementary to that of Cross with more emphasis on the presence of Puritanism in Elizabethan Oxford than is found in Loach.

James McConica

P

PACIFICATION OF GHENT.

As stated in the document itself, the Pacification of Ghent of 1576 was a "peace, alliance, and union" between the northern and southern provinces of the Netherlands, a "treaty . . . between the prelates, nobles, towns and members of Brabant, Flanders, Artois, Hainault, Valenciennes, Lille, Douai, Orchies, Namur, Tournay, Utrecht and Mechlin, representing the States of those countries, and the prince of Orange, the States of Holland, Zeeland, and their associates." Luxembourg remained aloof.

In the sixteenth century, the Netherlands was Habsburg territory. The provinces enjoyed some self-determination under Emperor Charles V, who had been born in Ghent. Charles attempted to suppress Anabaptism and Lutheranism; his son Philip II of Spain, who succeeded him in 1556, took sterner measures to establish absolutism, levy new taxes, and suppress the Calvinism then infiltrating from France. A rebellion rose. William of Orange took leadership of it in 1568, and Sea Beggars took Holland and Zeeland in 1572; finally, full-scale civil war broke out. William, who embraced Calvinism in 1573, strove to unify the religiously divided Netherlands.

Opposition to Spain coalesced with the outbreak of the Spanish Fury at Antwerp on 4 November 1576 when uncontrolled troops killed thousands. The pacification was signed on 8 November; it called for expelling the Spanish, suspending antiheresy edicts, ending the Inquisition, and guaranteeing freedom of movement. It forbade attacks on Roman Catholicism outside Holland and Zeeland, and implicitly allowed the Reformed religion there.

The pacification's wording was open to interpretation. It did not determine what would be the structure of government in the absence of the Spaniards, nor did it solve religious divisions. Calvinists continued to proselytize and expand political control, while anti-Catholic action was punished. A new royal governor was allowed to assume duties after accepting the pacification and ordering Spanish troops out (February 1577), but he resumed hostilities on 6 January 1579. Artois, Hainault, and the city of Douai formed the Union of Arras (precursor to modern Belgium) and capitulated to the Spanish on favorable terms. On 29 January 1579 the seven northern provinces of the Netherlands signed the Union of Utrecht; in 1581 they declared independence from Spain.

BIBLIOGRAPHY

Griffiths, Gordon. *Representative Government in Western Europe in the Sixteenth Century: Commentary and Documents for the Study of Comparative Constitutional History.* Oxford, 1968. Summary of the situation in the Low Countries in the sixteenth century and bibliographical sources (pp. 298–328); text of the Pacification of Ghent in Dutch with Van Meteren's translation into French (pp. 433–47).

Koenigsberger, H. G. *Estates and Revolutionaries: Essays in Early Modern History.* Ithaca, N.Y., 1971. See especially "The Organization of Revolutionary Parties in France and the Netherlands during the Sixteenth Century," pp. 224–252, for an analysis of the role of Calvinist congregations as a highly organized minority in the Revolt of the Netherlands.

Kossman, E. H., and A. F. Mellink, eds. *Texts concerning the Revolt of the Netherlands.* London, 1974. Summary of the situation in the Netherlands from 1555 to 1586 and description of the documents, pp. 1–51; English text of the Pacification of Ghent, pp. 126–132.

Opstand en pacificatie in de Lage Landen: Bijdrage tot de studie van de pacificatie van Gent. Ghent, 1976.

Rowen, Herbert. "The Dutch Revolt: What Kind of Revolution?" *Renaissance Quarterly* 43.3 (Autumn 1990), 570–590. A summary of the Revolt of the Netherlands in the sixteenth century, its historiography, and a bibliography; critical of Koenigsberger's view of the role of Calvinism in the revolt; views the Pacification of Ghent as the high point of William of Orange's achievement.

JEANNINE E. OLSON

PACIFISM.

A term used anachronistically when applied to the rejection of the sword of war and justice in the sixteenth century, pacifism has always existed in some form in the Christian church. The early church was pacifist. Christians began to appear in the Roman army toward the end of the second century and became common after Constantine. After its articulation by Ambrose and especially Augustine in the fourth and fifth centuries, the idea of a justifiable war developed into the cultural consensus of the medieval church, and the notion of crusade, or aggressive war in pursuit of a holy cause, became an additional defense of war. Only with the major Reformation confessions, however, did either justifiable war or justifiable revolution attain official or creedal status. The pacifist tradition, at least nonparticipation in war, was maintained in the Middle Ages by the sectarians and through the idea, not always adhered to, that monastics and clergy, both secular and religious, ought not participate in warfare. Christian humanists and Anabaptists expressed pacifist views in the sixteenth century.

Desiderius Erasmus (1467?–1536), the most renowned humanist scholar, based his virtually absolutist pacifism on both theological and philosophical grounds. For example, in defense of a gospel of love and nonviolence, the two parts of *Dulce bellum inexpertis*, which first appeared in the 1515 edition of the *Adages*, argued that war is contrary both to human nature and natural law and to the example and teaching of Christ. Erasmus advocated pacifism as relevant advice for rulers, which eventually proved to be a forlorn humanist program to produce peace among the great princes—Henry VIII, Charles V, and Francis I. Pacifism constituted a theme throughout Erasmus's career and influenced a variety of pacifist and antiwar currents among an international circle of humanists. *Utopia*, by Thomas More (1477/78–1535), whose publication Erasmus arranged a year after *Bellum*'s appearance, echoed most points of Erasmus's social reform and his attitude toward war. François Rabelais (1483?–1553) pointed out the trivial causes of war and opposed aggressive wars and spreading the gospel by force, while Michel Eyquem de Montaigne noted the stupidity of committing a cause to the capricious outcome of a battle. Josse van Clichtove (1472/73–1543) and Juan Luis Vives (1492?–1540) centered on the impropriety of war among Christians. John Colet (1467–1519) and Heinrich Cornelius Agrippa (1486–1535) called for strict application of justifiable war criteria, in effect ruling out most wars. Spiritualist Paracelsus (1493–1541) appealed to both the biblical injunction against killing and a profound respect for human life, while Sebastian Franck (1499–1542) invoked the suffering church and Christ's command that the sword be done away with. Oswald Myconius (1488–1552) wrote an Erasmus-influenced pacifist manuscript, never published, which was one of the pacifist sources for Conrad Grebel (c.1498–1526). While Erasmus's influence cannot be demonstrated definitively, Grebel and Menno Simons (c.1496–1561) among Anabaptists knew Erasmus's writings and reflected his pacifism.

The discussion of pacifism is closely linked to the evolving historiography of Anabaptism. The historiography of the early twentieth century described early Anabaptism as a violent, revolutionary movement beginning with Thomas Müntzer (d. 1525) and reaching its logical apogee with the failed uprising at Münster in 1534–1535. Only following Münster, it was thought, did Menno Simons turn the movement to the pacifist position for which the Mennonites, the Anabaptist bearers of Menno's name, became known. In the 1940s Mennonite church historian Harold S. Bender (1897–1962) inaugurated a new era in North American Anabaptist studies. Following up directions indicated earlier by C. A. Cornelius and other Europeans, Bender distinguished Anabaptists from revolutionaries. He placed Anabaptist origins in the rejection of Huldrych Zwingli's reformation by the circle of Grebel and argued that an absolute rejection of the sword by Christians on a biblical and christological basis constituted a central component of Anabaptism. Swordbearers were by definition not Anabaptists. Clarence Bauman indicated a few exceptions to the absolutist position. Hans J. Hillerbrand described them more fully as a "minority within the minority." James M. Stayer depicted Anabaptism as a pluralistic movement with several points of origin and a spectrum of views on the sword.

At one end of the spectrum is the absolutist, apolitical pacifism of the circle of Zurich Anabaptist Conrad Grebel. Although the early Swiss Anabaptist movement displayed a range of ideas on the sword, the absolutist view of men like Grebel became the normative position of the Swiss Brethren after Michael Sattler (c.1490–1527) reformulated it in the Schleitheim Articles (February 1527) with a strong sense of separation from the world. Based on appeals to the teachings and example of Jesus, Grebel rejected use of the sword under any circumstances, whether for defense or justice, by Christians. The Schleitheim Articles allowed that the sword of the magistrate served the God-ordained purpose of punishing the wicked and protecting the good but called it "outside the perfection of Christ" and forbade Christians to wield it or to hold political office.

Balthasar Hubmaier (1480/85–1528) came to Anabaptism via the Swiss Brethren but had a position on the sword and government similar to that of the magisterial reformers. First at Waldshut and then at Nikolsburg (Mikulov), Hubmaier introduced Anabaptist reforms through local governmental action. His writings argued that Christians could serve as soldiers and defended the idea of a Christian magistrate who exercised the sword of defense and of justice. Under the influence of the Schleitheim Articles and apocalyptic preaching by Hans Hut (c.1490–1527), *Stäbler* ("staff bearers," in contrast to *Schwertler*, "sword bearers") refugees to Moravia objected to Hubmaier's view of the sword and magisterial approach to reform in Nikolsburg. From the resulting schism developed the several pacifist communitarian Moravian Anabaptist groups, the best known of which was the Hutterites, named for Jacob Hutter (1500?–1536). They adopted a position on the sword similar to the Schleitheim Articles. Clemens Adler wrote the first Moravian Anabaptist treatise on nonresistance in 1529. In the early 1540s *Rechenschaft* by Peter Riedemann (1506–1556) institutionalized separatist nonresistance within the Hutterite code of behavior.

The south German Anabaptist movement, with one of its roots in medieval mysticism, produced several sorts of pacifism. Revising Müntzer's revolutionary outlook in the aftermath of the Peasants' War, Hut developed an interim, sheathed-sword pacifism. He believed that Christ would return at Pentecost in 1528, when the judgment of the ungodly would begin and Christ would call the godly to seize the sword and destroy the wicked. Meanwhile, in the short interim until the judgment, Hut called for his followers to leave the sword sheathed. The inner, mystical suffering they would endure until then would purify them for the coming of Christ and their mission of judgment.

Another version of south German Anabaptism went beyond Hut's interim pacifism to a complete rejection of the sword for Christians. The foundation was less directly lodged in an appeal to the Bible and the example of Jesus, as for Grebel or Sattler, and rooted more in the inner, mystical experience of *Gelassenheit*, or yieldedness. This yieldedness, nourished by the indwelling word of God, purified the individual and enabled the Christian to follow the example of Jesus. Representatives of this position included Hans Denck (c.1500–1527), who had baptized Hut, and Hut's followers Leonhard Schiemer (d. 1528) and Hans Schlaffer (d. 1528).

Melchior Hoffman (1495?–1543) had another version of apocalyptic pacifism. He held a view of the sword of justice and punishment much closer to Luther than to the Schleitheim Articles, but advocated pacifism for individual believers. Hoffman expected the return of Christ about 1533, with Strasbourg as the leader of the free imperial cities that would protect the gospel and the true believers. While Hoffman considered his Anabaptist followers pacifists who should not bear the sword themselves, they could assist the imperial forces through prayer and in building the defenses of cities such as Strasbourg. The actual extermination of the godless would be carried out by the Turks, who would be destroyed in turn once their task was accomplished. Hoffman left the initiative to God in eliminating the godless and establishing the kingdom.

At the opposite end of the spectrum from the absolutist Swiss Brethren were the revolutionary Münsterites, whose position developed out of Hoffman's. They shifted the origin of the revolution from heaven to earth in the belief that the time had come for the righteous to unsheathe the sword and to slay the wicked in preparation for the coming kingdom of God.

From within the Melchiorite movement the brothers Obbe Philips (c.1500–1568) and Dirk Philips (1504–1568), as well as Menno Simons, who joined the Melchiorite Anabaptist movement in 1537, objected to the revolutionary direction of the movement while maintaining Hoffman's rejection of the sword for Christians and his idea of a Christian magistrate. Menno's pacifism, but not his espousal of a Christian magistrate, resembled that of the Swiss Brethren. Late in his life Menno added opposition to capital punishment to his description of the Christian magistrate. From the south German Anabaptist movement, Pilgram Marpeck (c.1495–1556), who held office as city engineer in Strasbourg and Augsburg, had views similar to Menno on the sword and the possibility of a Christian magistrate.

Following the death of Menno Simons, his followers came to espouse apolitical separatism like that of the Swiss Brethren and the Hutterites, but the Dutch Mennonites, who attained toleration and acculturation more quickly than the Swiss, also reached the first compromises with military service. In response to the Revolt of the Netherlands against Spain, Mennonites collected money in 1572 as a gift to Prince William of Orange in anticipation of his friendship toward the church if he came to govern the Netherlands. In 1575 William's representative issued a decree exempting Mennonites from military duty in exchange for either noncombatant duties, such as digging ditches and erecting earthworks, or payment of fines. Such arrangements continued to the end of the century.

The Minor church of the antitrinitarian Polish Brethren, separated in 1565 from the Reformed church of the Calvinists, had a strong pacifist component, based on the teaching of Christ and opposition to participation in government. Piotr Giezek of Goniadz (Lat., Gonesius; 1532–1572), who accepted the ideas of adult baptism and nonresistance from Hutterites in Moravia, precipitated the separation. Some influence of Erasmian pacifism also extended to the Polish Brethren. In 1574 Grzegorz Pawel (Lat., Gregorius Paulus; 1525–1591) wrote the first surviving tract on the pacifist views of the antitrinitarians in response to the minority position in defense of war, penned by Jacobus Palaeologus. A second pacifist response, appealing to the imitation of Christ and the way of the cross, came from Marcin Czechowic (1532–1613). Szymon Budny (1530–1593) was another prowar voice. Although Italian immigrant Fausto Sozzini (1539–1604), who molded the diverse antitrinitarians into a compact denomination, did not silence the debate among the antitrinitarians, he articulated a principled pacifist stance coupled with a more moderate attitude toward participation in the state. Sozzini's later qualifications of pacifism opened the way to full and uninhibited participation in the military by the Polish antitrinitarians.

BIBLIOGRAPHY

Adams, Robert P. *The Better Part of Valor: More, Erasmus, Colet, and Vives on Humanism, War, and Peace, 1496–1535*. Seattle, 1962.

Bainton, Roland H. *Christian Attitudes toward War and Peace: A Historical Survey and Critical Re-evaluation.* Nashville, 1960.

Bauman, Clarence. *Gewaltlosigkeit im Täufertum.* Studies in the History of Christian Thought, vol. 3. Leiden, 1968.

Bender, Harold S. "The Zwickau Prophets, Thomas Müntzer, and the Anabaptists." *Mennonite Quarterly Review* 27 (1953), 3–16.

———. "The Pacifism of the Sixteenth Century Anabaptists." *Church History* 24 (1955), 119–131.

Boyd, Stephen B. "Anabaptism and Social Radicalism in Strasbourg, 1528–1532: Pilgram Marpeck on Christian Social Responsibility." *Mennonite Quarterly Review* 63 (1989), 58–76.

Brock, Peter. *Pacifism in Europe to 1914.* Princeton, 1972.

———. *Freedom from Violence: Sectarian Nonresistance from the Middle Ages to the Great War.* Toronto, 1991.

Goldammer, Kurt. "Friedensidee und Toleranzgedanke bei Paracelsus und den Spiritualisten, I: Paracelsus." *Archiv fur Reformationsgeschichte* 46 (1955), 20–46.

Hillerbrand, Hans J. "The Anabaptist View of the State." *Mennonite Quarterly Review* 32 (1958), 83–110.
———. *Die politische Ethik des Oberdeutschen Täufertums.* Leiden, 1962.
———. "The Lonely Individualist: Sebastian Franck." In *A Fellowship of Discontent,* pp. 31–46. New York, 1967.
Olin, John C. "The Pacifism of Erasmus." In *Six Essays on Erasmus, and a Translation of Erasmus' Letter to Carondelet, 1523,* pp. 17–31. New York, 1979.
Schrag, Dale. "Erasmian and Grebelian Pacifism: Consistency or Contradiction?" *Mennonite Quarterly Review* 62 (1988), 431–454.
Stayer, James M. *Anabaptists and the Sword.* 2d ed. Lawrence, Kans., 1976.
———. *The German Peasants' War and Anabaptist Community of Goods.* McGill-Queen's Studies in the History of Religion, vol. 6. Montreal and Kingston, Ont., 1991
Yoder, John H. "'Anabaptists and the Sword' Revisited: Systematic Historiography and Undogmatic Nonresistants." *Zeitschrift für Kirchengeschichte* 85 (1974), 126–139.

J. DENNY WEAVER

PACK AFFAIR. Involving Philipp of Hesse and the ducal Saxon counselor, Otto von Pack, the affair nearly brought a preventive strike by the evangelical territories against their Catholic neighbors. It remains one of the more intriguing events of the German Reformation. In early 1528 Pack apprised Philipp that he had seen an antievangelical treaty and produced a forged copy. Ferdinand of Habsburg, Duke George of Saxony, the dukes of Bavaria, the elector of Brandenburg, and the archbishops of Mainz, Würzburg, and Salzburg had supposedly agreed to use force against the evangelicals.

Philipp convinced the Saxons to conclude the Weimar Alliance (9 March 1528), which called for a preventive strike against the bishops in June of that year. Philipp also concluded an agreement with King Frederick I of Denmark to protect his northern flank. Fortunately, the Catholic powers convinced the Saxon officials, who were already skeptical, that there was no antievangelical alliance. Nevertheless, the Hessian and Saxon armies had already been mobilized and effectively used their powerful position to compel Mainz to renounce its ecclesiastical jurisdiction in their territories.

The general consensus today, based on documentary evidence, is that Pack was the author of the forged treaty, although reputable nineteenth-century scholars claimed otherwise. Philipp believed the forgery, because he was always suspicious of potential enemies. Moreover, during 1527 tensions with the Habsburgs had increased.

Disagreement today centers on the question of Philipp's response to Pack's lies. Some historians believe Philipp used the forgery to undertake a preventive strike he had already planned. This belief is based on the questionable dating of a single letter, however.

The Pack Affair was significant in that Mainz renounced ecclesiastical jurisdiction and the evangelicals showed their resolve. Equally significant, the Saxons came to distrust the landgrave permanently, judging him reckless, hotheaded, and overly aggressive.

[*See also* Holy Roman Empire *and* Philipp of Hesse.]

BIBLIOGRAPHY

Dülfer, Kurt. *Die Packschen Händel: Darstellung und Quellen.* Marburg, Germany, 1952. Best modern treatment of the affair.
Fabian, Ekkehart. *Die Entstehung des Schmalkaldischen Bundes und Seiner Verfassung, 1524–1529 and 1531–1535: Gregor Brück, Philipp von Hessen und Jakob Sturm.* 2d ed. Tübingen, 1962. Fabian argues that the affair should be called the Landgrave's Bishops' War. He argues that although Philipp may not have been an author of the forgery, he bears some responsibility for the outcome.
Hauswirth, René. *Landgraf Philipp von Hessen und Zwingli, 1526–1531.* Schriften zur Kirchen- und Rechtsgeschichte, vol. 35. Tübingen, 1968. Like Fabian, Hauswirth claims Philipp had some responsibility for the outcome, an argument that is in keeping with his general thesis that represents Philipp as the leader in the Zurich relationship.
Hillerbrand, Hans J. *Landgrave Philipp of Hesse, 1504–1567: Religion and Politics in the Reformation.* Reformation Essays and Studies, vol. 1. Saint Louis, Mo., 1967. Excellent introduction to the studies of Philipp; introduces the reader to the appropriate literature.
Meinhardus, Otto. *Der katzenelbogische Erbfolgestreit.* 2 vols. Wiesbaden, 1899. Excellent source to begin a search for older arguments that claimed Philipp was an author of the forgery and that it was all an example of "realpolitik."

WILLIAM J. WRIGHT

PAGNINI, Sante (1470–1536), Italian Dominican friar. Born in Lucca, Pagnini studied and worked first in various religious houses of his order at Fiesole, Florence, where he became the pupil of the converted Jew Clement Abraham, as well as at Lucca. With the patronage of Leo X (d. 1521), then the encouragement of Clement VII, he left to teach at Avignon after 1523, and then went on to Lyon, where he met compatriots and printers who were to help him publish part of his writings.

Numerous writings of Pagnini, which remained in manuscript form, should be considered as lost, particularly some annotations on the Bible and sermons. One fragment (*Ps.* 1–29) of a Psalter in four languages is extant in manuscript form. The focus of Pagnini's activity must be considered his Latin translation of the Bible, published in Lyon, accompanied by various ancillary pieces and letters: *Interpretatio nominum hebraicorum: Habes in hoc libro prudens lector utriusque instrumenti novam translationem . . .* (1527–1528). The Latin version of the Old Testament reflects a very careful study of the Hebrew text, while that of the New Testament is not merely borrowed from Erasmus. The publication of grammars and dictionaries supplemented this version, which was the great work to which Pagnini devoted himself: *Enchiridion expositionis vocabulorum Haruch, Thargum, Midrascim . . . Midbar Rabba* (Rome, 1523), *Isagogae ad linguam graecam capessendam septem continentes libros* (Avignon, 1525), *Hebraicae insitutiones* (1526), and *Thesaurus Linguae Sanctae* (Lyon, 1529). The publication in 1536 of *Isagogae ad sacras Litteras . . . ad mysticos Sacrae Scripturae sensus* (Lyon) shows that Pagnini's scholarly work did not lead him to break with traditional hermeneutics.

The influence of Pagnini's books was extensive. Those of his generation who translated the Bible into the vernacular languages, such as Antonio Brucioli and Pierre Robert Olivétan, and teachers such as Vatable, judging from notes taken in his courses, refer to the *Thesaurus* as well as to his translation of the Bible. Agostino Steuco, Sebastian Münster (who criticized it), Leo Jud and his Zurich colleagues, as well as numerous exegetes of the time including Martin Bucer used his translation.

Some of his works underwent numerous editions, sometimes reworked or expanded, which further widened Pagnini's sphere of influence. Michael Servetus contributed to a new edition of Pagnini's Bible in Lyon in 1542. The Dominican friar's version is used in volume 6 of the *Biblia Sana polyglot* published in Antwerp in 1572. The Estiennes reprinted his Hebrew grammar, while the *Thesaurus* was published in several abridged editions (e.g., 1548, 1616); in 1575 Hebrew scholars of the Reformed church (Jean Mercier, Antoine Chevallier, and Bonaventure C. Bertram) contributed to expanding and improving the accuracy of the references of a new complete edition of the *Thesaurus*.

Pagnini's legacy was thus picked up under various denominational auspices and was integrated into the work of Hebrew scholars for decades to come. His influence can be detected even beyond the circle of biblical scholars: Rabelais may well have taken some words from the *Thesaurus*. François Secret, in his studies of Christian Cabbala, observes that Pontus de Tyard (1522–1605) kept a Pagnini Bible in his library and that Ignazio Landriani (1579–1642), an Olivétan monk, was a critical and enlightened reader of it.

Along with Johannes Reuchlin, Konrad Pellikan, Sebastian Münster, and the publisher Daniel Bomberg, Pagnini made one of the most significant contributions to opening up Jewish lexicographical, grammatical, exegetical, and biblical traditions to Christians of the sixteenth century. Could it be, as some think, that he wrote a treatise *Adversus Judaeos*? In looking over the whole of his writings, one sees that through him Christians at the beginning of the sixteenth century recovered the memory of what they owed to the Jews. But his scholarship no more succeeded in turning the tide of anti-Judaism common to both Catholics and Protestants than did that of the other Hebrew scholars of the time who were his colleagues and competitors.

BIBLIOGRAPHY

Bedouelle, Guy, and Bernard Roussel, ed. *Bible de tous les temps*. Vol. 5, *Le temps des Réformes et la Bible*. Paris, 1989.

Centi, Timoteo M. "L'attività letteraria di Santi Pagnini (1470–1536) nel campo dell scienze bibliche." *Archivum Fratrum Praedicatorum* 15 (1945), p. 5–51.

Moris Guerra, A. "Santi Pagnini traducteur de la Bible." In *Théorie et pratique de l'exégèse: Actes du 3e colloque international sur l'histoire de l'exégèse biblique au XVIe siècle*, edited by Irena Backus and Francis Higman, pp. 191–198. Geneva, 1990.

Pagnino, G. *Vita di Santi Pagnini*. Rome, 1653.

BERNARD ROUSSEL

Translated from French by Robert E. Shillenn

PALATINATE.

This German territory on the upper Rhine was centered on Heidelberg, whose ruler, the elector palatine, was one of the seven electors of the Holy Roman Emperor. The Palatinate (*Kurpfalz*) took its name from its ruler's title, count palatine (*comes palatinus*), which had originated in the early Middle Ages. The counts palatine did not establish a territorial basis along the upper Rhine until the twelfth century. The Wittelsbach dynasty acquired the Palatinate in 1214, and the Treaty of Pavia (1329) gave the count palatine control of the upper Palatinate. The Golden Bull (1356) assured the count palatine's privilege of voting in imperial elections, making him the elector palatine. As imperial vicar (*Reichsvikar*), the elector palatine represented the emperor in the case of a vacancy of office. Since the Wittelsbachs often practiced partible inheritance, many cadet branches also bore the title count palatine, while only the ruler of the *Kurpfalz* was known as the elector palatine.

In the sixteenth century the Palatinate encompassed two territories: the lower, or Rhine, Palatinate (*Unterpfalz*) along the Rhine and Neckar, which contained the cities of Alzey, Kaiserslautern, Neustadt, and Germersheim; and the upper Palatinate (*Oberpfalz*), a northern Bavarian territory with its administrative center in Amberg. The lands of the lower palatinate were scattered alongside the domains of the bishoprics of Speyer and Worms. The elector palatine was the most powerful ruler in the vicinity and used his lordship over the Rhine and Neckar and rights over safe conducts on the regional highways to extend his hegemony. The lower Palatinate had no formal assembly of estates, largely because most of the local nobility were free imperial knights, though they traditionally served at court. Alternatively, the upper Palatinate was an enclosed territory and possessed territorial estates. The elector's heir apparent normally served as stadtholder (*Statthalter*) of the upper Palatinate. The chief administrative institution of the Palatinate was the high council (*Oberrat*), which usually met daily and made decisions based on the preference of the majority, though the will of the elector was ultimately decisive. The *Hofgericht* was the supreme court of the Palatinate, and the elector's subjects, under the terms of the Golden Bull, could not be cited to external courts. The *Hofgericht* also heard cases of individuals and entities who were not the elector's subjects (e.g., from neighboring imperial cities) and thus enhanced the elector's regional influence.

Ludwig V to Ottheinrich. The late fifteenth century had been a time of both territorial aggrandizement and cultural flowering, with the Heidelberg court serving as base for such humanists as Conradus Celtis. The defeat of the Palatinate, however, in the Bavarian Succession War (*Landshuter Krieg*, 1503/04) not only curbed Palatine expansion but also determined the passive role that the Palatinate would play in imperial politics for the next half century.

As the Reformation began, the Palatinate was ruled jointly by Elector Ludwig V (r. 1508–1544) and his brother Fredrick II, who served as stadtholder in the upper Palatinate. Ludwig moved cautiously, using his vote for Charles V in the 1519 election to consolidate the Palatinate's position in the empire and to have its extraterritorial privileges confirmed. Palatine regional influence increased, and by 1529 Ludwig's brothers served as bishops of Speyer and Worms. Initially Ludwig did not take definitive action for or against the Reformation but sought a middle ground while remaining close to the Habsburgs. Although Martin Luther won a number of followers at the Heidelberg Disputation (1518), the reformer had little direct impact on the Palatine territory or the university. The 1520s were lean years for the University of Heidelberg, as salaries were too meager to retain prominent faculty, and enrollment plummeted. The only action Ludwig V undertook on behalf of the Lutheran movement was abstaining from the vote to place Luther under the imperial ban at the Diet of Worms (1521).

Involvement in the Knight's Revolt (1523) and the Peasants' War (1525) diminished Ludwig's openness to Protestantism. Ludwig's forces helped suppress the revolt led by his former councillor Franz von Sickingen, which threatened the regional power balance. The peasant bands that rose on Palatine territory west of the Rhine were disbanded through Ludwig's personal mediation. The peasants' program was the Twelve Articles, and the revolt had an imported rather than indigenous character and thrived in the agriculturally rich but densely populated Rhine plain. Palatine forces also took part in suppressing the revolt in the bishoprics of Speyer and Würzburg. Although these experiences brought Ludwig closer to the old church, he continued to play a political game of confessional neutrality to the end of his reign.

The reformation of the Palatinate began in earnest during the reign of Fredrick II (r. 1544–1556), when the Lord's Supper was celebrated in evangelical form, priests were allowed to marry, and a new church order was proclaimed (1546). While professing his loyalty to Charles V, Fredrick attempted to remain neutral in the Schmalkald War (1546), although he sent a contingent with Duke Ulrich of Württemberg honoring a mutual defense agreement. The imperial victory forced Fredrick to humbly submit to the emperor. Fredrick accepted the Interim (1548) and did not reintroduce Protestant usages after the defeat of the emperor in 1553.

Although the confessionally flexible Fredrick II had favored Protestantism, it fell to his nephew Elector Ottheinrich (r. 1556–1559) to establish Protestantism in the Palatinate. Ottheinrich had in 1543 introduced Lutheranism into his own territory, Pfalz-Neuburg, but was forced into exile by his estates for financial malfeasance. An outstanding German Renaissance prince, Ottheinrich was a great builder and patron whose book collection enhanced the Bibliotheca Palatina. Ottheinrich issued a new church order (1556) and established a church council headed by a general superintendent. The Strasbourg Lutheran Johannes Marbach undertook the first church visitation of the Palatinate. The mandated removal of images (1557) degenerated into popular iconclasm. Failing to lure Marbach permanently from Strasbourg, Ottheinrich appointed Tilemann Hesshus as church general superintendent upon the recommendation of Philipp Melanchthon. Though Ottheinrich's reform was definitely Lutheran, confessional diversity reigned in Heidelberg, and Reformed Protestants—such as the theologian Pierre Boquin, the physician Thomas Lüber (Erastus), and the jurist and future councillor Christoph Ehem—were appointed to the university. These recruits, paired with the financial strengthening of the university through the transfer of monastic income by both Fredrick II and Ottheinrich, facilitated the university's later prominence. Although his reign was brief, Ottheinrich placed the Palatinate in the Protestant camp and recruited the individuals who would direct future church developments.

The Second Reformation. With Ottheinrich's death the electoral line of the Wittelsbach dynasty died out, and Frederick III ("the Pious"; r. 1559–1576) of the house of Pfalz-Simmern became elector. Impressed by the performance of Boquin and Lüber at the Heidelberg Disputation (1560), Frederick moved toward a Reformed interpretation of the Eucharist. The Heidelberg Catechism and church order of 1563 confirmed the Reformed confession's ascendency. Foreign religious refugees, especially Netherlanders, began to stream into the Palatinate. Palatine policy reflected a new openness toward Western European Protestantism, and Frederick's son Johann Casimir led Palatine forces on behalf of Protestants in France and in the Netherlands. Frederick avoided falling under the imperial ban at the Diet of Augsburg (1566) by claiming faithfulness to the Variata version of the Augsburg Confession. With the Reformed confession now tacitly accepted in the empire, the Calvinist preacher and church council member Kaspar Olevianus began to agitate for the adoption of a Geneva-style consistory to monitor church discipline. An antidisciplinist party arose around the Zwinglian Lüber, who favored leaving moral oversight and the power of excommunication in state hands. As the elector was preparing to announce the new edict, which established a consistory though retained some aspects of the state-church system, two of Lüber's sympathizers, Adam Neuser and Johannes Sylvanus, were discovered to be antitrinitarians (1570). Sylvanus was executed in 1572, while Neuser died a Muslim in Istanbul. With the likely ascension of his Lutheran son Ludwig, Frederick sought to make provision for the continuance of the Reformed confession by carving out a principality for Johann Casimir, his like-minded son, from the Palatine domains. When Frederick died in 1576, the people braced themselves for yet another confessional change.

Ludwig VI (r. 1576–1583) reestablished Lutheranism in the Palatinate and expelled the Reformed theologians and clergy. Ludwig's requirement that the university faculty sign the Formula of Concord in 1580 caused another exodus. Meanwhile, Johann Casimir's territory, *Pfalz-Lautern,* maintained the Palatine Reformed tradition. When Ludwig VI died in 1583, Johann Casimir (regent from 1583 to 1592) returned to Heidelberg as regent for Fredrick IV. After excluding his Lutheran coregents, Johann Casimir reestablished the Reformed confession in the Palatinate. The Palatinate remained Reformed after another regency crisis following the death of Elector Fredrick IV (r. 1583–1610). The Reformed faith alienated the Palatinate from the local, mostly Lutheran imperial knights. In the later years of the sixteenth century, the Palatine subjects, especially the educated, increasingly identified with the Reformed confession and supported the Palatinate's role as a militant leader of Reformed Protestantism.

The history of the Reformation in the Palatinate turned tragic during the reign of Elector Fredrick V (r. 1610–1623). Under the influence of Christian von Anhalt, the Palatinate played an aggressive political role in the empire, becoming the leader of the Protestant Union. After the Bohemian estates revolted against Emperor Ferdinand II (1618), Fredrick unwisely accepted the Bohemian crown. His brief reign in Prague won him the appellation "Winter King" and initiated the catastrophe that become the Thirty Years' War. Bavarian forces conquered the Palatinate, and Duke Maximilian of Bavaria demanded the Palatine electoral dignity from the emperor as compensation for his assistance. As a result of the Peace of Westphalia (1648), Fredrick V's descendants received their principality back (without the upper Palatinate) and an eighth vote in the electoral college to compensate for Bavaria's confiscation of the Palatine electoral dignity. In 1803 the *Kurpfalz* was incorporated into several neighboring territories, and today *Pfalz* generally denotes only the western side of the Rhine.

BIBLIOGRAPHY

Burchill, Christopher J. "The Heidelberg Antitrinitarians." In *Bibliotheca Dissidentium XI,* edited by André Séguenny. Baden-Baden, 1989.

Clasen, Claus-Peter. *The Palatinate in European History, 1559–1618.* Oxford, 1963. A suggestive study, but now superseded by the work of Volker Press.

Cohn, Henry J. "Territorial Princes in Germany's Second Reformation, 1559–1622." In *International Calvinism, 1541–1715,* edited by Menna Prestwich, pp. 135–166. Oxford, 1985.

———. *The Government of the Rhine Palatinate in the Fifteenth Century.* Reprint, Oxford, 1991. Best starting point in English regarding the administration of the Palatinate.

Parker, Geoffrey, ed. *The Thirty Years War.* Reprint, London, 1988. Good coverage of the intrigues leading to the war.

Press, Volker. *Calvinismus und Territorialstaat: Regierung und Zentralbehörden der Kurpfalz, 1559–1619.* Stuttgart, 1970. The classic work on the Palatinate in the sixteenth century.

———. "Die 'Zweite Reformation' in der Kurpfalz." In *Die reformierte Konfessionalisierung in Deutschland: Das Problem der "Zweiten Reformation,"* edited by Heinz Schilling, pp. 104–129. Schriften des Vereins für Reformationsgeschichte 195. Gütersloh, 1986. Concise overview of the entire century.

Schaab, Meinrad. *Geschichte der Kurpfalz.* 2 vols. Stuttgart, 1988–1992. Up-to-date treatment of the Palatinate. Especially strong on the exterritorial extension of Palatine power; valuable maps.

Sehling, Emil, ed. *Die evangelischen Kirchenordnungen des XVI. Jahrhunderts.* Vol. 14, *Kurpfalz.* Leipzig, 1983. Contains both source material and useful introductions.

Visser, Derk. *Zacharias Ursinus: The Reluctant Reformer.* New York, 1983.

Wolgast, Eike. *Die Universität Heidelberg, 1386–1986.* Berlin and New York, 1986.

CHARLES D. GUNNOE, JR.

PALEOTTI, Gabriele (1522–1597), cardinal and bishop of Bologna. In late-twentieth-century historical research Paleotti has been gaining in importance as an example of a pastoral approach that diverged from that of the Council of Trent, representing a more human and open approach as compared with the Counter-Reformation disciplinary rigor of his contemporary and friend Carlo Borromeo, archbishop of Milan. That he descended from a family steeped in the vital humanist tradition of Bologna, combined with his law education in the school of Alciato led him to an academic career and to teach law in Bologna. His most original work from this first phase in his career was *De notis spuriisque filiis* (1550), a forthright defense of the rights of illegitimate offspring.

The turning point in his life came when as auditor of the Rota he was sent to the Council of Trent during its final phase (1562–1563) to work alongside the presiding cardinals, particularly Giovanni Morone, in drawing up the conciliar reform decrees. In this context his contribution was decisive in reaching agreements that made it possible to bring the final sessions of the council to a positive conclusion. His diaries also represent one of the most important sources for understanding the work of the council. Named a cardinal by Pius IV in 1565 and then bishop of Bologna in 1566, he devoted himself to implementing the decrees of Trent by maintaining continuous residence, conducting pastoral visitations throughout his diocese, and holding annual synods—the fruit of these experiences being preserved mainly in the volumes *Episcopale Bonoiensis civitatis et diocesis* (1582) and *Archiepiscopale Bononiense* (1594). The principles underlying this activity aimed at restoring the pastoral function of the bishop, fostering the tradition of the local church, and promoting preaching with particular attention to the world of culture and academia as well as raising the level of the rural masses.

Paleotti gave significant attention to the problem of the representational arts, which he saw as an instrument to translate the scriptures and the tradition of the church into a language that all could understand (*Discorso intorno alle imagini sacre e profane*, 1582), and he also championed the devotional art of the Po Valley, which was based on a piety grounded in the everyday, in contrast to the Counter-Reformation triumphalism of the Roman baroque.

These positions led him into frequent conflicts with the Curia Romana over the "obstacles" to the work of reform in his diocese that came from the temporal government itself and papal centralization in the administration of the universal church. For this reason he devoted his last years to drafting proposals for reforming the Curia Romana, and in particular the college of cardinals, in order to restore its functions as a true senate of the universal Church (*De sacri Consistorii consultationibus*, 1592).

BIBLIOGRAPHY

Prodi, Paolo. *Il cardinale Gabriele Paleotti, 1522–1597*. 2 vols. Rome, 1959–1967.

PAOLO PRODI
Translated from Italian by Robert E. Shillenn

PALESTRINA, Giovanni Pierluigi da (1525/26–1594), Italian composer whose work was widely admired and respected during his lifetime. Shortly after his death Palestrina was already becoming the legendary figure he was to remain throughout the next three centuries, celebrated as the "savior of church music" and as the model for all who wished to compose in the strict contrapuntal style, or *stile antico*. It is one of the great ironies of music history that these attributes are based on inaccuracy and wishful thinking and that Palestrina's superb achievement as a composer is in reality not dependent on either of them.

Palestrina's early musical training was in Rome. He returned to his hometown for a time but in 1551 was appointed by Julius III as maestro of the Cappella Giulia at Saint Peter's basilica. From here he moved to the Sistine Chapel but, being married, was discharged by Paul IV, who wished to enforce the Sistine Chapel's rule of celibacy. After serving at San Giovanni Laterano and Santa Maria Maggiore, he returned to the Cappella Giulia in 1571 and remained there for the rest of his life.

A book of masses (1554) was Palestrina's first important publication. He went on to publish collections of masses, motets, and other sacred music, as well as secular and spiritual madrigals. His music was successful, frequently reprinted in Rome and Venice, and his reputation spread. He spent some years in the service of Cardinal Ippolito II d'Este, was an artistic adviser to Duke Guglielmo Gonzaga of Mantua, and was proposed for the position of imperial choirmaster in Vienna.

At his death a good deal of Palestrina's music was as yet unpublished. His total output includes 104 masses, nearly 400 motets, volumes of Offertories and other liturgical music, and a surprising number of madrigals. In all this music, beauty of melodic line is combined with polyphonic expertise and use of a full but brightly clear harmonic palette. His style can indeed serve as a model, but in fact rather little of his music was knowing during the centuries he served as patron saint of the *stile antico*. Instead, musicians used rules codified by theorists who allowed seepage of elements of later music, and compositions by seventeenth- and even eighteenth-century epigones were hailed as *alla Palestrina*, often on shaky stylistic grounds.

Palestrina's relation to the Counter-Reformation was important. He was known to most of the prelates concerned with reform of ecclesiastcal music and was commissioned by Gregory XIII to begin, along with Annbale Zoilo, a thorough revision of plainchant (although he never finished this work, the *Editio Medicea* of 1614 might provide a clue for what he would have done). But his reputation as "savior" of religious polyphony is based on fanciful accounts of the effect his *Missa Papae Marcelli* had on reform-minded cardinals anxious that the sacred text be clearly audible. Palestrina remained a polyphonist who never wrote the simple "reform" music that Vincenzo Ruffo and others did. Nonetheless, his settings of the Mass Ordinary are perhaps the most sumptuous musical monuments of the Counter-Reformation period, and a real achievement transcending legend.

BIBLIOGRAPHY

Jeppesen, Knud. *The Style of Palestrina and the Dissonance*. London, 1927.

Lockwood, Lewis. *The Counter-Reformation and the Masses of Vincenzo Ruffo*. Vienna, 1970.

———. "Palestrina, G. P. da." In *The New Grove Dictionary of Music and Musicans*, edited by Stanley Sadie, vol. 14, pp. 118–137. London, 1980.

Lockwood, Lewis, ed. *Pope Marcellus Mass*. New York, 1975.

JAMES HAAR

PALLADIO, Andrea (born Andrea di Pietro della Gondola; 1508–1580), Italian architect and author of architectural treatises. Trained in Padua and Vicenza, Palladio was an architectural classicist who inventively combined a knowledge of Vitruvius and of actual Roman antiquities in his innovative designs for villas, palaces, and churches. He also produced illustrations for the humanist Daniele Barbaro's annotated edition of Vitruvius (1556) and wrote several works of his own, most importantly the *Quattro Libri di Architettura* (published 1570).

While all evidence of Palladio's own religious beliefs points toward his orthodoxy, his adoptive home city of Vicenza was an important center for the dissemination of Reformation ideas, and a number of his patrons and friends among the aristocracy of that city were associated with Protestant movements. Among those accused of, or espousing, heterodox views (some more fervently than others) were his mentor, Giangiorgio Trissino; Francesco, Odoardo, and Marco Thiene; and Francesco and Mario Repeta, as well as the Venetian Daniele Barbaro, most of whom commissioned palaces or suburban villas from the architect. On the basis of his contacts with such men, certain art historians have attempted to seek out reform ideas in Palladio's architecture and writings. For instance, the highly visible placement of the altar in his Venetian churches of San Giorgio Maggiore and Il Redentore (no longer separated from the laity by a monks' choir) has been associated with Protestant ideas, and the general use of formal elements proper to religious architecture (e.g., domes, temple fronts) in his villa designs has been linked by Tafuri to the Anabaptist doctrine of bringing the sacred down to a worldly or personal realm. The connections of the architect to such ideas, however, remain largely conjectural; one may safely say that at the very least Palladio benefited from working for a clientele that valued freedom of thought and experimentation—architectural as well as spiritual.

BIBLIOGRAPHY

Boucher, Bruce. *Andreas Palladio.* New York, 1993.

Burns, Howard, Lynda Fairbairn, and Bruce Boucher. *Andrea Palladio, 1508–1580: The Portico and the Farmyard.* London, 1975. Exhibition catalog, with useful short sections on Palladio's Vicentine patrons and associates.

Isermeyr, Christian Adolf. "Le chiese del Palladio in rapporto al culto." *Bollettino del Centro internazionale di studi di architettura Andrea Palladio* 10 (1968), 42–58. Examines Palladio's writings on and designs for church architecture in relation to Reformation and Counter-Reformation ideas.

Puppi, Lionello. *Andrea Palladio.* Translated by Pearl Sanders. Reprint, London, 1989. Introductory section deals with Palladio's relation to the intellectual climate of Vicenza, summing up much of the Italian literature on the topic through the late 1960s.

Tafuri, Manfredo. "Committenza e tipologia nelle ville Palladiane." *Bollettino del Centro internazionale di studi di architettura Andrea Palladio* 11 (1969), 120–136. The article cautiously proposes a reading of Palladio's villa architecture in light of the reform ideas shared by his patrons.

ANDREA BOLLAND

PALLADIUS, Niels (c.1510–1560), Danish Lutheran bishop. Born into a middle-class family in Ribe (southern Denmark), Palladius was a younger brother of Bishop Peder Palladius. With support from King Christian III and Danish noble circles, he began studies at Wittenberg University in 1534, received a master's degree in 1540, and was called in 1544 to the office of lecturer at the Maribo convent in southeastern Denmark. At the same time, he was to work there as an assistant to the bishop of Fyn's diocese. In 1550, after another stay in Wittenberg, he was called to be a parish priest at Our Lady's Church in Copenhagen, and as early as 1551 he was chosen to be bishop of the Lund diocese.

Like his brother, Palladius was prolific as an author of theological and educational books, and he left about twenty Latin, Danish, and Icelandic writings. Many of them, however, were reworkings of writings of the German reformers. He was particularly interested in practical-theological subjects, and his *Regulæ quædam utiles ac necessariæ concionatoribus obsevandæ* (1556) is the first pastoral-theological handbook in the Danish reformed church. In *Oratio de vera et catholica ecclesia* (1556), he strongly recommends the holding of yearly parish synods as part of the reeducation of the Catholic priesthood to Lutheranism, and with the translation of *Summaria offuer vor christelig lerdom* (A Summary of the Christian Doctrine), he introduced Veit Dietrich's collects into Danish religious services, and they have remained until our time.

Methodologically and theologically he was above all a pupil of Philipp Melanchthon. This is true of his ideas on church and administration, and it is seen also in his *Tractatus brevis de articula prædestinationis* (1554). But he seems nevertheless to diverge from Melanchthon in his concept of the Eucharist and in his opinion of images, because in *Commonefactio de vera invocatione Dei et de vitandis idolis* (1557) he rejects all forms of religious imagery.

In his writings to laymen, he dealt with social moral questions, as, for example, drunkenness and matters concerning personal religious life. He wrote about marriage and made the first Danish contribution to the literature on *ars moriendi.* He also translated Andreas Musculus's writings on marriage and the Last Judgment.

BIBLIOGRAPHY

Lausten, Martin Schwarz. *Biskop Niels Palladius: Et bidrag til den danske kirkes historie, 1550–1560.* Kirkehistoriske II, no. 27. Copenhagen, 1968.

MARTIN SCHWARZ LAUSTEN
Translated from Danish by Walter D. Morris

PALLADIUS, Peder (1503–1560), first Lutheran bishop of Zealand (Sjælland), Denmark, theological professor, and royal adviser. He was born in Ribe to the family of a shoemaker, from which occupation he took the name Palladius. Not much is known of his early childhood except that he went to school in Ribe, Assen, and Roskilde. By 1530 he was the rector of the Latin school in Odense. Biblical humanism was widespread in the schools of Denmark largely through the work of Paul Helie and his students. It is not certain when Palladius became the rector at Odense or when he resigned his position. But on 3 September 1531 Palladius matriculated at the University of Wittenberg to begin studying for his doctor's degree. Did he arrive in Wittenberg as a disciple of Luther or was he converted to the evangelical faith after he attended some lectures? Either is possible. A rector at Odense would certainly have become acquainted with Lutheran doctrine through the decrees issued by the Diet of Odense in 1527. In a letter to the Icelandic bishop Jon Arason, Palladius states that the pericope text about Mount Tabor in *Luke* 9:35 powerfully affected him in his journey to Lutheranism. The year this occurred, however, is not clear. It is clear that the clarion cry of biblical humanism, *ad fontes* ("back to the sources"), and Luther's call for faith and life based on the "word alone" joined to form a strong resonance in the heart of Palladius. Like so many other Scandinavian students who studied at Wittenberg and who had previously been influenced by biblical humanism, Palladius was strongly drawn to Philipp Melanchthon. Later theological works of Palladius are permeated with Philippist theology.

In 1537, after he had completed his final doctoral exams at Wittenberg, Palladius was summoned by Christian III to assume the highest office in the Danish church, superintendent (bishop) of Zealand together with its accompanying responsibilities as theology professor at the University of Copenhagen. In the new ecclesiastical structure of the Danish church, Lund no longer served as an archbishopric, and the bishopric of Zealand was moved from Roskilde to the more populous Copenhagen. In 1537 Palladius journeyed back to Denmark in the company of Johannes Bugenhagen, parish pastor and university lecturer in Wittenberg. The latter had been called by the Danish king to draw up a church ordinance for the church of Denmark-Norway. From 1537 to 1539 Bugenhagen resided in Copenhagen and proceeded to restructure the Danish church. Seven new evangelical superintendents (one for Norway) were installed (not ordained) into their dioceses by Bugenhagen. One of the seven was Palladius. This act was designed as a deliberate break with the historic episcopate since Bugenhagen had only the ordination of a presbyter. In addition, Bugenhagen conducted the coronation ceremony and drew up a new evangelical charter for the reopening of the University of Copenhagen.

For the next twenty-three years, Palladius entered into his various duties with vigor, making him the leading churchman of his time. In addition to serving as one of the three theological professors at the university and the superintendent of Zealand, he also served as the king's spiritual and theological adviser and the overseer of ecclesiastical affairs in Norway, Iceland, and the Faeroes. Palladius realized that the spiritual loyalty of the people could not be won by royal decree alone. He therefore saw his task as educating the people into an evangelical commitment. Palladius was thoroughly committed to education as the way to consolidate the evangelical political victory of 1536, which declared that everyone in Denmark-Norway was to become Lutheran.

One of the stipulations of the 1537 church ordinance was that the superintendents faithfully visit the parishes in their diocese. This Palladius studiously did; it took him six years on the first round to visit the 390 parishes under his jurisdiction. As a result of his experience and in order to assist his fellow superintendents in their parish visitations, Palladius drew up a manual for conducting such visitations. The manuscript was obviously never intended to be published and is thus all the more valuable because of its intimate details regarding contemporary life and foibles. In 1866 it was discovered in the Danish Royal Library and published some years later for the first time. Palladius began his visitations in the fall of 1537. His *Visitatsbog* covered the whole gamut of concerns from the state of a congregation's altar furnishings, to the doctrinal position of the local priest/pastor, to his spiritual life and piety, to the ethical/moral life of the laity in the parish. Palladius would preach to the laity every day for a week or two and give lectures in Latin to the local clergy and monastics. Through these pastors' conferences and synod meetings, Catholic priests and monks were reschooled for evangelical ministry. Palladius became a role model for what an evangelical bishop should be and do. Inspection of the local schools and care for the poor and homeless were included in the visitations as well. Through his *Alterbog* (1556), evangelical worship in the vernacular was standardized; the *Alterbog* remained the official liturgical manual until 1685. Through devotional writings and theological publications such as *De poenitentia et de iustificatione* (1558), Palladius exerted a tremendous influence on the next generation of parish clergy in Denmark and Norway as they sought to emulate the example of their teacher and bishop. Where there was no grass-roots movement toward the evangelical persuasion, Palladius counseled a pastoral approach emphasizing the need for education rather than hasty action. But when the Polish nobleman Jan Łaski and his followers arrived in Denmark (1553) fleeing the wrath of Mary Tudor in England, where they had first sought a haven, Palladius was less tolerant and counseled the king not to allow them to land in Denmark unless they became Lutherans. They refused to give up their Calvinist views, and so they were forced to seek asylum elsewhere.

BIBLIOGRAPHY

Andersen, Niels K. "Peder Palladius i Wittenberg." *Dansk Teologisk Tidsskrift* 8 (1945), 1–30.

Ertner, Jørgen. *Peder Palladius' lutherske teologi.* Copenhagen, 1988.

Heiberg, A. C. L. *Peder Palladius: Sjællands første evangeliske biskop.* Copenhagen, 1840.

Jacobsen, Lis. *Peder Palladius' visitatsbog.* Copenhagen, 1925.

Lausten, Martin Schwarz. *Biskop Peder Palladius og kirken, 1537–1560.* Copenhagen, 1987.

———. *Christian d. 3 og kirken, 1537–1559.* Copenhagen, 1987.

TRYGVE R. SKARSTEN

PALMIER, Jean-François du. *See* Salvart, Jean-François.

PAMPHLETS. A novel sixteenth-century medium of communication, pamphlets, or *Flugschriften*, were extensively used by the advocates of reform. Pamphlets did not address themselves to a specific group or class within society but sought to make their messages widely available to a wide public, possibly even through the oral propagation of their content. The message in the pamphlets was intended to affect the views, convictions, and values of the readers. The pamphlets did not primarily seek to communicate knowledge, provide entertainment, or edify the reader; pamphlets were intended to influence opinion.

In contrast to the book format, which was generally several hundred pages in length, pamphlets were lightweight in several respects: appearance, cost, distribution, the complete absence of formal norms for their production, and, importantly, the character of the commodity. The external appearance of the pamphlets was generally characterized by the use of handy, fairly readable fonts. The quarto format was used as a rule; the octavo format was the exception. Even though a large number of pamphlets were fairly long (occasionally as much as one hundred pages), the overwhelming majority were modest in size. More than half the known pamphlets are only eight pages, while the average is roughly twice that length. Only about one-fourth of the pamphlets are longer than sixteen pages.

The use of woodcuts as ornamentation on the title page, found on 75 percent of pamphlets, was meant to enhance the sales of the pamphlet. Most often the woodcuts are purely ornamental (though occasionally figurative) and serve simply to frame the title proper. Some 20 percent of the pamphlets have title-page illustrations with landscapes, portraits, coats of arms, and other motifs that more or less explicitly refer to the content of the pamphlet. The woodcuts were frequently created by eminent artists, such as Lucas Cranach the Elder.

There were various literary forms employed by the authors: sermons, missives, epistles, and tracts are found alongside poems, songs, prayers, letters, reports, and archival publications. In addition, there are genuine and fictitious documents, lectures, and mandates. Some pamphlets offer name lists, often without commentary—for example, of participants of imperial diets or punished revolutionaries—while others provide compilations of theological errors, sometimes along with tedious responses.

The use of the dialogue, reintroduced by Ulrich von Hutten, is important to mention. Some seventy pamphlets are known to have used the dialogue format. The dialectic structure, with its ability to personify points of view and convictions, made it possible to confront intellectually the conflicting views and goals of the competing parties. Moreover, dialogues made it possible to bestow positive or negative qualities on the conversationalists, and thereby to evoke loyalties or at least to influence the reader (or listener). Several stereotypes held by the partisans of the Reformation—such as the mature, Bible-conversant layman; the pious peasant; and the unlearned, arrogant, irresponsible, and immoral Catholic priest—were formed and propagated by the dialogue. Several dialogues possess an extraordinary aesthetic quality, which explains the extensive preoccupation with Reformation dialogues by literary scholars.

The topics of the pamphlets are as diverse as the literary forms employed by their authors. Essentially, every topic of possible interest in the early sixteenth century found expression. This meant, primarily, questions about the Christian faith, the order of the church, and the role of its servants in society, but it also meant the Turkish threat, the uprising of the "common man," the legitimacy of that uprising, and the appropriateness of the punishment meted out after the "common man" had gone down in defeat. Other topics were imminent wars, battles, treaties, and peace accords; aspects of economic life; the burdens imposed by the church on the faithful; the role of the great trading companies and monopolies; interest and usury; ominous miraculous signs and prophecies, including their causes and meaning; and the virtues and liabilities of foreign peoples and cultures.

Generalizations about this diversity of themes and topics are difficult to formulate. Theological themes clearly dominate. Moreover, biblical quotations were the authority cited by the authors of the pamphlets to give credence to their argumentation, quite apart from the religious or political orientation of the author. Despite the brevity of most of the pamphlets, the argumentation is anything but crude or simplistic. In most instances the authors are singularly differentiating and circumspect in their judgments.

This takes us to the question of the age, social status, education, and religious and political orientation of the authors. Although the authors liked to portray themselves as "poor, unlearned, God-fearing laymen," most were educated, and many were clerics. One thinks immediately of Martin Luther, whose writings in pamphlet form probably constitute about 20 percent of the total number of pamphlets published in Germany. The number of lay authors is not large; a dozen or so, including several women, are generally mentioned. This small group of lay authors includes artisans, nobles, and patricians.

There were also a number of anonymous pamphlets. One might presume that fear of punishment for the author or printer precipitated anonymity. However, in most instances the content of the anonymous pamphlet is not at all radical. It seems that the use of anonymity was an intriguing and convenient way for an educated author to claim to be an uneducated and simple layman.

Most of the established printers in Augsburg, Wittenberg, Nuremberg, Strasbourg, Basel, and Leipzig published pamphlets, and many smaller printing shops seem to have thrived economically on the printing of pamphlets. Since the format (and thus the weight) of the typical pamphlet was modest, most pamphlets were sold by peripatetic booksellers, who used fairs, markets, and other convenient occasions to sell their wares. This, in turn, meant a particularly fast and wide distribution. Still, despite the rapid sale of pamphlets, only a few copies could be disbursed within a geographic locale. Copies of the original edition were used for unauthorized reprints, often by clandestine print shops. This might happen several times and have a snowball effect. For example, the famous Twelve Articles of the peasants were published in 1525 in no less than twenty-four editions by at least eighteen printers in fifteen cities (from Wrocław to Strasbourg and from Magdeburg to Zurich).

No firm statements can be made about the cost of a typical pamphlet. What is known is from sporadic notations by owners, making it difficult to generalize. An average price of two pence per *Druckbogen* ("printed sheet") may be assumed. This would entail a price of sixteen pence for a typical pamphlet of sixteen pages. This amount was roughly equivalent to one-third the daily wage of an artisan apprentice or the price of one of the following: a chicken, two pounds of beef, a pound of wax, or a pitchfork. Although low, the price was not at all modest at a time when the lower classes of society in particular had virtually no cash; on the other hand, the price of the typical pamphlet can hardly be called prohibitive.

No comparative studies of the ideological orientation of the individual printers in the early sixteenth century are available. Such studies would be enormously helpful, however, as they would cast light on the question of whether the business interests of a trade influenced the intellectual, political, and social changes in early modern German society. Such studies would also provide information on whether the dominant motivation of the printers was ideology or economics. A detailed answer to these questions could also solve the intriguing question of why Catholic voices are so blatantly underrepresented in the pamphlet literature. Was it an erroneous understanding of the effectiveness of this new medium, was it incompetence, or was it the unwillingness of the old church to use this new vehicle of communication? At any rate, the absence of Catholic pamphleteers had fateful consequences for the viability of the conservative position.

The protagonists of the Catholic church found irritating and unfamiliar (and thus difficult to affirm) the concept of open and equal discourse with a critical and self-confident laity. When, as in Johann Dietenberger's *Dialogue Between a Priest and a Peasant,* the priest concedes the thoughtfulness of the peasant's interpretation of scripture, that point is not carried through in the remainder of the pamphlet. The bulk of the *Dialogue* consists of the priest's tedious sermonic exhortation to the illiterate peasant. No matter how seriously some Catholic authors, such as Thomas Murner, tried to adjust to new circumstances, the essential emancipation implied in the reformers' notion of the priesthood of all believers meant a significant advantage for the Protestant polemicists.

It is also important to ask who were the intended and who were the actual readers of the pamphlets. As most of the pamphlet authors (including the anonymous ones) were well educated, it is not surprising that many publications were directed toward partisans and antagonists from the same social background as the author. An additional group of intended readers was the holders of power, both political and economic, such as mayors and council members of cities, the nobility and lords, the pope and emperor, and their advisers. Then there was the "common man." A large number of pamphlets explicitly addressed themselves on the title page to the "common man," the "simple people," or the "unlearned pious laymen"—that is, the mythical figure of the peasant, who was unable to read or write.

Attempts were made to overcome the problems of reaching uneducated readers. One strategy, for example, was the replacement of Latin with the German language. After the outbreak of the indulgences controversy, a veritable flood of German-language publications dramatically reversed the ratio of Latin to German-language publications—from seventy-two Latin and twenty-eight German publications in 1519 to twenty-six Latin and seventy-four German in 1521. By 1522 the percentage of Latin publications had dwindled to 9.5 percent—a decline from 72 percent in just three years.

Undoubtedly the pamphlet authors deliberately addressed themselves not only to readers but also to nonreading listeners, to whom the content of pamphlets was communicated orally. Even more important, the authors were clearly conscious of the necessity to adjust their argumentation and style to the intellectual and literary level of their intended readers. They were able to do so because most of them were clerics and experienced preachers.

It is important to note that the general literacy rate in early sixteenth-century central Europe was no more than 10 to 15 percent, although in the cities it was significantly higher (probably 30 percent of the male population in the cities were literate). But 90 percent of the population was rural, making the 10 to 15 percent range more significant. The significance of the pamphlets becomes even more impressive when one recalls that between 1521 and 1525 a veritable pamphlet boom took place. During the five years between Luther's appearance at Worms and the end of the Peasants' War, ten pamphlets for each literate person must have been in circulation.

Pamphlets were singularly capable of effecting a quick transfer of information without any alteration in the information transmitted. The use of illustrations enhanced the communication. The necessity of literate readers to appropriate the content of the pamphlets, however, restricted their impact. The authors' goal of reaching all of society presupposed, then, that communication occurred in stages, with the readers of the pamphlets transmitting their content in a second stage through sermons, talks, discussions, and public readings. In each instance communication occurred through social interaction. In that context a high potential for changing (or, for that matter, confirming) positions and opinions existed. The primary significance of the pamphlets must not be seen, therefore, as changing convictions among the people; undoubtedly sermons were far more effective in that regard. Pamphlets were effective in efficiently and quickly raising the level of familiarity with the issues at hand. The pamphlets also served the role of turning vague, general sentiment—for which one may use the labels insecurity, dissatisfaction, or desire for reform—into a fairly precise set of ideas. By that the pamphlets became targets of public opinion with which one agreed or disagreed. Most important, the pamphlets helped create a well-informed and like-minded group of followers for the leading reformers. The remarkable flood of pamphlets, so characteristic of the German scene between 1520 and 1525, finally began to subside after 1525, thus signifying a new phase in the course of the German Reformation.

Much of what has been described above—drawn exclusively from the German scene—is applicable to other European countries, notably France and England. In particular, the use of the vernacular, the appeal to the laity, and the use of a fairly brief format are general characteristics of the French and English pamphlet literature. Unfortunately the level of scholarship in those countries has not equaled the scholarly preoccupation with the German pamphlet.

[*See also* Literacy *and* Printing.]

BIBLIOGRAPHY

Cole, Richard. "The Pamphlet and Social Forces in the Reformation." *Lutheran Quarterly* 17 (1965), 135–195.

Hirsch, Rudolf. *Printing, Selling and Reading, 1450–1550*. Wiesbaden, 1974.

Houston, R. A. *Literacy in Early Modern Europe: Culture and Education, 1500–1800*. London and New York, 1989.

Köhler, Hans-Joachim. *Bibliographie der Flugschriften des 16. Jahrhunderts*. Pt. 1, *Das frühe 16. Jahrhundert, 1501–1530*. Tübingen, 1991.

———. "Die Flugschriften: Versuch der Präzisierung eines geläufigen Begriffs." In *Festgabe E. W. Zeeden*, pp. 36–61. Münster, 1976.

———. "Die Flugschriften der frühen Neuzeit: Ein Überblick." In *Die Erforschung der Buch- und Bibliotheksgeschichte in Deutschland*, edited by Werner Arnold, Wolfgang Dittrich, and Bernhard Zeller, pp. 307–345. Wiesbaden, 1987.

Laube, Adolf. *Flugschriften der frühen Reformationsbewegung, 1518–1524*. 2 vols. Berlin, 1983.

Moeller, Bernd. "Flugschriften der Reformationszeit." *Theologische Realenzyklopädie*, vol. 11, pp. 240–246. Berlin, 1983.

Moore, Will Grayburn. *La Réforme allemande et la litterature française: recherches sur la notorieté de Luther en France*. Strasbourg, 1930.

Scheible, Heinz. "Reform, Reformation, Revolution. Grundsätze zur Beurteilung der Flugschriften." *Archiv für Reformationsgeschichte* 65 (1974), 108–134.

Tompert, Hella. "Die Flugschriften als Medium religiöser Publizistik. Aspekte der gegenwärtigen Forschung." In *Kontinuität und Umbruch: Theologie und Frömmigkeit in Flugschriften und Kleinliteratur an der Wende vom 15. zum 16. Jahrhundert*, edited by Josef Nolte, Hella Tompert, and Christof Windhorst, pp. 211–221. Stuttgart, 1978.

Watt, Tessa. *Cheap Print and Popular Piety, 1550–1640*. Cambridge, 1991.

HANS JOACHIM KÖHLER AND HANS J. HILLERBRAND

PAPACY.

PAPACY. Religious historiography has maintained that in the sixteenth century an utterly worldly (and from time to time actually pagan) Renaissance papacy came to be replaced by a reformed papacy exclusively oriented toward the saving of souls. This viewpoint has further held that during the new secularism of the baroque period the reformed papacy then "relapsed." Of course, such general trends cannot be denied—the differences between an Alexander VI, a Pius V, and an Urban VIII are patently obvious. Research in the late twentieth century, however, emphasized the essential continuity of ideology, institutions, economic foundation, and rules of social behavior that channeled this development and kept it within limits.

The popes from the High Renaissance to the end of the Age of the Reformation are as follows.

- 1471–1484, Sixtus IV (Francesco della Rovere)
- 1484–1492, Innocent VIII (Giovanni Battista Cibo)
- 1492–1503, Alexander VI (Rodrigo de Borja)
- 1503, Pius III (Francesco Todeschini Piccolomini)
- 1503–1513, Julius II (Giuliano della Rovere)
- 1513–1521, Leo X (Giovanni de' Medici)
- 1522–1523, Adrian VI (Adriaan Florensz)
- 1523–1534, Clement VII (Giulio de' Medici)
- 1534–1549, Paul III (Alessandro Farnese)
- 1550–1555, Julius III (Giovanni Maria Ciocchi del Monte)
- 1555, Marcellus II (Marcello Cervini)
- 1555–1559, Paul IV (Gian Pietro Carafa)
- 1559–1565, Pius IV (Giovanni Angelo de' Medici)
- 1566–1572, Pius V (Michele Ghislieri)
- 1572–1585, Gregory XIII (Ugo Buoncompagni)
- 1585–1590, Sixtus V (Felice Peretti)
- 1590, Urban VII (Giovanni Battista Castagna)
- 1590–1591, Gregory XIV (Niccolò Sfondrato)
- 1591, Innocent IX (Gian Antonio Facchinetti)
- 1592–1605, Clement VIII (Ippolito Aldobrandini)
- 1605, Leo XI (Alessandro de' Medici)
- 1605–1621, Paul V (Camillo Borghese)
- 1621–1623, Gregory XV (Alessandro Ludovisi)
- 1623–1644, Urban VIII (Maffeo Barberini)

The papacy moved hesitantly toward reform only as a result of the increasing pressure of the Protestant Reformation, gradually coming to realize that reform lay in its own interest. Despite the shock of the Sack of Rome in 1527, which was regarded as a historical turning point by many of his contemporaries, Clement VII remained firmly resistant to change and thereby unintentionally fostered the Protestant movement in Germany. Paul III, on the other hand, recognized the new needs of the papacy and acted accordingly by appointing religiously orientated cardinals, such as Gasparo Contarini and Gian Pietro Carafa (later Paul IV), by initiating certain reforms and establishing effective means of control (recognition of the Jesuits in 1540 and the setting up of the Roman Central Inquisition in 1542), and, most importantly of all, through the summoning of the Council of Trent. Once Paul IV's brutal measures had weakened the opposition to innovation and the once-so-feared council had been tamed, the "reform popes" Pius IV, Pius V, Gregory XIII, and Sixtus V were able to push its reform program through and in this way increase still further the long-term significance of the papacy. The pope confirmed the council's decrees in 1564, only to assume total control over how these conclusions were to be interpreted by founding the Congregation of the Council. Despite the pope's newly defined spiritual priorities, papal activities nevertheless remained within the boundaries of the old system; the Roman reform was a typically conservative reform.

The twin notions of papal infallibility and of papal supremacy over ecclesiastical and temporal matters were reflected not only in the writings of members of the Curia Romana and in the papal program of artistic commissions but also in the pronouncements and behavior of the pope himself. When the Jesuit Roberto Bellarmino attempted to restrict the pope's authority over the world to an indirect one, Sixtus V promptly placed his work on the Index of Prohibited Books. The pope was naturally fearful of the council's possible claim to represent the highest doctrinal authority if it could not, like the Fifth Lateran Council (1512–1517), be kept under close Roman control. Appeals to the council were repeatedly forbidden by the pope, but it remained an instrument of antipapal polemics used not only by Martin Luther. Clement VII's hostility toward the council was, therefore, based on more than simple fear of losing office on the grounds of his illegitimacy. It can be counted among the considerable achievements of certain papal diplomats, in particular Giovanni Morone's, that although the Council of Trent pushed through its doctrinal definitions and structural reforms, it held back from deciding on the question of papal primacy and the reform of the Curia.

This was not to say there was no support for reform in pre-Tridentine Rome; on the contrary, reform belonged to the standard repertoire of all official pronouncements. There was certainly no shortage of concrete plans for reform, even under Alexander VI, or clear resolutions, such as those adopted in 1514 during the Fifth Lateran Council. Neither the pope nor the church, however, took them very seriously. Only fear of the Reformation brought about an eventual change of heart in Rome and forced the painful transition from words to deeds, enabling the resolutions of the Council of Trent to be implemented. Introduced in 1564 was a Tridentine confession of faith, which priests and other people in strategic positions were required to take on oath. In the same year an Index of Prohibited Books was drawn up, followed by a catechism in 1566, a breviary in 1568, a missal in 1570, a new edition of the Vulgate in 1592, and a ritual in 1614, which together formed a uniform and binding code of rules for the whole church. Founded in Rome were various central training colleges for priests, including the Collegium Romanum in 1551, the Collegium Germanicum in 1552, the Seminarum Romanum in 1565, amd the Collegium Anglicum in 1579. In order to help strengthen Rome's overall control, informative processes for the selection of candidates for bishoprics were introduced, bishops were required to submit regular reports, and a dense network of papal nuncios was established, backed up wherever possible by apostolic visitors. The aim of the Roman reform program had always been to centralize authority under the leadership of the pope, but now the emphasis shifted from humanist moralizing to pastoral spirituality.

Contrary to the traditional view, the continuity of the theocratic program meant that even from a political perspective the "reform papacy" was indeed an extension, if not an accentuation, of the "Renaissance papacy," and this concerned not just the expansion of the Papal States between Alexander VI and Sixtus V. Under the double monarchy of the popes, the church went through a kind of state-building process whereby it was both archetype and rival to the emergent modern European states. At this point the lines of confrontation did not yet lie between "church" and "state" but between spiritual and temporal princes, who, despite their different legal positions, believed themselves to be equally responsible for both areas. For this reason the pope ruled over the church in an absolute sense only in the Papal States, and he found himself more and more in the role of a prince among princes. Likewise, it was the more spiritually orientated popes, such as Pius V, who took the fight against the enemy of Christianity, the Ottoman empire, most seriously (for example, in 1571 at the Battle of Lepanto), whereas Innocent VIII and Alexander VI were generally prepared to engage in lucrative dealings with the sultan.

As princes among princes, the popes in the fifteenth century were part of the Italian pentarchy and, following the 1494 Italian campaign of the French king Charles VIII, therefore found themselves drawn into the permanent conflict between the European powers—that is, between the Valois and the Habsburgs. The popes were unable to hold their own in this power struggle, unlike in the Italian theater, and were in danger of becoming dependent first upon the Habsburg empire of Charles V and later upon the Spanish empire of Philip II, which along with Milan and Naples controlled key political and financial positions in Italy. In light of this, the pro-French tendencies shown by many popes could be regarded as a political necessity, but France was weakened by the Wars of Religion, placing Rome in a serious predicament. This situation manifested itself in the papal elections, which were subjected to open pressure from 1521 onward, and to massive pressure from 1549 by the great powers, particularly from Spain. Nevertheless, even those popes that Philip II himself championed were able to assert their relative independence from this guardian of Catholicism: Henry IV of France, for example, had no difficulty receiving papal absolution in 1595 once the credibility of his latest denominational switch had been verified. In conclaves a balance developed between four power blocs—the French, the Spanish, and the nepotal factions of the two preceding popes—which allowed for a certain degree of coalition building among the cardinals.

Similar forces within the church, the Curia, and the Papal States led to the establishment of a centralized papal absolutism, which formed a remarkable parallel to events in the European states. Whereas in the latter the assemblies of the states were neutralized, the papacy deprived of power not only the council but also the college of cardinals. Out of a corporation claiming a dyarchic partnership with the ruler, there developed a compliant and unassertive nobility of service and officialdom, still able to enforce electoral agreements but never able to have them respected by the new elect. The assembly of cardinals—the *Consistorium*, originally the political "senate" of the church—slipped into empty ritual, while the cardinals carried out day-to-day administration in committees known as congregations, a system that Sixtus V made permanent in 1588. As was the case in the great monarchies, secretaries of state became the popes' right-hand men. For a period of almost two hundred years, control of the apparatus of government was entrusted to a close relation of the pope, the cardinal-nephew, a practice that also had its parallels in the ruling "favorites" of western Europe.

Notwithstanding these administrative changes, the traditionalists among the church officials knew how to stand up for themselves and had some success blocking more drastic reforms. The very thing that made these officials such a particular thorn in the side of reformers right up to Martin Luther—the fact that they were a part of a cleverly thought-out finance and credit system—also made them largely immune from attack. These officials had lawfully purchased their positions, and from where was any pope to get the money he needed to compensate them for their loss of vested rights? Because these venal offices, which should be viewed as a sort of life annuity, formed one of the pillars of papal credit (along with the more modern state annuity, the "Monti," introduced in 1527), any sudden attempt to abolish them would have meant not only the loss of the pope's line of credit but also the loss of the papacy's freedom to maneuver. The only way the pope could finance extraordinary expenditure, whether it was for wars, councils, construction projects, or donations to his family, was through credit. Even the authoritarian Pius V had great difficulty separating the apostolic penitentiary, which was the tribunal responsible for cases of conscience, from its contentious affiliation with the collecting of fees; his eventual and neat solution was not the outright abolition of this transaction but simply its relocation to the chancery, thereby assuring the accustomed beneficiaries of their continued income. The great reformer Pope Sixtus V, in order to finance his expensive projects, had extended to extremes the system of venal offices.

Officially, of course, it was not ecclesiastical appointments or benefices that were sold but rather administrative posts. It had become customary, however, for the previous offices and benefices of a newly appointed cardinal to revert automatically to the pope, and this practice opened up interesting perspectives for both parties. At least three popes were able to expedite their rise to the papacy through this mechanism. Well before the Reformation the revenues that the pope needed to pay the interest on his credit and to cover ordinary running expenses no longer came largely from contributions of the Universal Church (as in the Middle Ages) but from taxes levied on the papal states. It is often forgotten, however, that considerable sums, particularly from benefices in Naples, Milan, and Spain, continued to flow to cardinals and other members of the Curia in Rome. Although the Council of Trent specifically forbade the accumulation of bishoprics, it did not do so in the case of abbeys given *in commendam*, or pensions. On this point the papacy found itself obliged to disregard the will of a clear majority of the council in order to ensure the survival of the Roman social system. It is certainly true that, unlike earlier periods, under the reform papacy large sums were expended on the fight against the Turks and heretics, but similar amounts poured into the pockets of the papal nephews and other senior church dignitaries.

Beginning at the very latest when Sixtus IV created a permanent two-thirds to four-fifths majority in the college through his appointment of thirty-four Italian cardinals, the papacy and the Curia became the private domain of the central and northern Italian urban upper classes. Alexander VI fitted this mold, though Adrian VI was considered antipathetic. The Roman identity of the papacy came to be regarded as the natural order of things. An important indication of the stabilization of the papacy is the fact that, from the election of Julius III in 1550 onward, the popes were almost exclusively a product of the system. They tended to be either career prelates from the church administration (Julius III, Pius IV, Gregory XIII, Clement VIII, Paul V, Gregory XV, and Urban VIII) or members of religious orders (Pius V and Sixtus V, who had been successful inquisitors). Although career prelates needed to come from a family with a solid financial background, it was possible to achieve social advancement through a mendicant religious order.

Whatever the individual case, society in Europe at the time revolved around patronage, and the key factor to advancement was the patron-client relationship; this was reflected in the choice of names that the popes took for themselves and in the cardinals' coats of arms. In 1557 Paul IV and his inquisitor, Michele Ghislieri, imprisoned Cardinal Morone in the Castle of Saint Angelo for suspected heresy, but when Morone's close relation and compatriot Giovanni Angelo de' Medici became Pope Pius IV, the cardinal was rehabilitated and subsequently rose to become the pope's most trusted adviser. On the other hand, the members of Paul IV's nepotal clique, who had already been removed from office by their uncle, were now brought to trial. Ghislieri, once he had become Pope Pius V, was generally more restrained in such matters but nevertheless arranged for the rehabilitation of his patron Paul IV's family—this despite having adopted the name of his predecessor, Pius IV, whose nephew Carlo Borromeo had been instrumental in his reaching the papacy.

It was in contexts such as these that papal nepotism played its role; an extreme case was the personal union between Florence and Rome under Leo X and Clement VII. During the age of the rise of the modern state, however, in contrast to the Middle Ages, the traditional system of noble family rule no longer functioned so unequivocally in favor of the papacy. On the contrary, it had a disintegrating effect on the Papal States—for example, in 1547, when Paul III gave the duchy of Parma and Piacenza to his Farnese family. The usual practice, whereby each nepotal family was advanced to the ranks of the high nobility, was certainly a spoils system, but one that was recognized as socially acceptable so long as certain generously measured boundaries were not overstepped and so long as the subsequent nepotal family was not, in turn, deprived of similarly golden opportunities. Nonetheless, as patron of the pope's clientage and as the head of the secretariat of state, the cardinal-nephew performed an important function in the papal government apparatus. With time these responsibilities came to be more closely defined. It was not so much that the nepotal system itself was modified but that the customary behavior of the papal nephews altered; there are more than mere differences of character between Borromeo and Cesare Borgia.

Under the competitive pressure of Protestantism on the one hand and thanks to the reformers within the church (whose influence was out of proportion to their numbers) on the other, public expectations of the moral and religious conduct of church leaders were raised. In stark contrast to established opinion, Sixtus IV, Alexander VI, Julius II, or Leo X cannot be denied a fundamentally religious approach to office nor sincere piety. Conspicuous zeal in carrying out pious works, active engagement in pastoral needs, and sexual abstinence (at least after ordination) were now expected of the priesthood. Under Paul IV and Pius V attempts to raise ethical standards in Rome went hand in hand with religious renewal. It is also significant that these two popes abandoned Rome's traditionally liberal policy toward the Jews. This development should be seen in terms of an interdenominational and pan-European process, which, as an inevitable part of the relentless growth of state power, reflected the increasing number of restrictions and regulations in society as a whole.

Even the physical face of Rome was transformed, not only because the formerly independent municipal authorities had now fallen completely under the control of the papacy but also as a direct consequence of the popes' patronage of the arts and, most particularly of all, as a result of their ambitious building program. The inscriptions on many of the buildings in Rome give testimony to the fact that they were erected by the popes as monuments dedicated to the glory of themselves and the prestige of their families; rulers of the period were inordinately fond of such enterprises, and the popes were no exception. From the Renaissance onward the church-building program continued to have absolute priority among the various schemes, and the enormous project to rebuild Saint Peter's basilica in Rome was the centerpiece of this activity. At the same time, huge sums continued to be expended on the construction of palaces and fortresses, roads and bridges, and fountains and obelisks. In a process culminating under Pope Sixtus V, the popes and the Roman patriciate dedicated themselves to their ambitious building program and their lavish patronage of the arts with a clear objective in mind—namely, to turn Rome into the worthy capital of Christendom and to make the authority of the papacy clear for all to see. Millions of the faithful were to see this message for themselves; an estimated 1.2 million pilgrims made the journey to Rome in 1600.

[*See also* Catholic Reformation; Italy; Papal States; *and* Roman Catholicism.]

BIBLIOGRAPHY

Archivum Historiae Pontificiae. Rome, 1963–. Contains studies and an extensive bibliography on the history of the papacy.

Bauer, Clemens. "Die Epochen der Papstfinanz: Ein Versuch." *Historische Zeitschrift* 138 (1927), 457–503. Also available in: Bauer, Clemens, *Gesammelte Aufsätze zur Wirtschafts- und Sozialgeschichte,* Freiburg, 1965; see pp. 112–147. Research has made some progress in the meantime, but Bauer's magisterial essay is still the only synthesis available.

Becker, Hans-Jürgen. *Die Appellation vom Papst an ein Konzil: Historische Entwicklung und kanonistische Diskussion im späten Mittelalter und in der frühen Neuzeit.* Cologne, 1988. The essential book on a crucial aspect of papal power.

Delumeau, Jean. *Vie économique et sociale de Rome dans la seconde moitié du XVIe siècle.* 2 vols. Paris, 1957–1959. A thorough study of the economic and social history of Rome in the age of the Counter-Reformation that now requires some correction but is still valid in many respects.

Firpo, Massimo. "Der Kardinal." In *L'uomo del Rinascimento,* edited by Eugenio Garin, pp. 79–142. Frankfurt a.M., 1990. Also available in English: *Renaissance Characters*. Translated by Lydia Cochrane. Chicago, 1991. An excellent introduction to the lives and personalities of Renaissance cardinals.

Firpo, Massimo, and Dario Marcatto, eds. *Il processo inquisitoriale del cardinal Giovanni Morone*. 5 vols. Rome, 1981–1989. Documents one of the most important figures of the Curia; elucidates the social world of the Curia and the procedures of the Inquisition.

Frommel, Christoph L. "The Planning of Rome during the Renaissance." *Journal of Interdisciplinary History* 17 (1986), 39–65. Good outline from Nicholas V to Paul III.

Hallman, Barbara McClung. *Italian Cardinals, Reform, and the Church as Property*. Berkeley and London, 1985. An instructive study of the economic and social role of the top group of the Curia during high Renaissance times.

Jedin, Hubert, ed. *History of the Church*. Vols. 4 and 5. New York, 1980. Original German edition: *Handbuch der Kirchengeschichte*. Vols. 3.2 and 4, Freiburg, 1967–1968. Contains chapters by Karl August Fink, Erwin Iserloh, and Jedin himself on the history of the papacy which are still the most recent and up-to-date summary.

Magnuson, Torgil. *Rome in the Age of Bernini*. Vol. 2, *From the Election of Sixtus V to the Death of Urban VIII*. Stockholm, 1982. Rome from the point of view of art history and urban studies.

Müller, Gerhard. *Die römische Kurie und die Reformation 1523–1534*. Gütersloh, 1969. A thorough study of the policy of Clement VII based on the reports of his nuncios. These have been edited by Müller in the *Nuntiaturberichte aus Deutschland*, supplementary vols. 1–2, Tübingen, 1963–1965.

Partner, Peter. "Papal Financial Policy in the Renaissance and Counterreformation." *Past and Present* 88 (1980), 17–62.

Pastor, Ludwig. *The History of the Popes from the Close of the Middle Ages*. 40 vols. London, 1891–1954. Original German edition: *Geschichte der Päpste seit dem Ausgang des Mittelalters*. 16 vols. in 22 pts. 12th ed. Freiburg, 1955–1956. Papalistic but essential because of its tremendous richness of information.

Prodi, Paolo. *The Papal Prince: One Body and Two Souls; The Papal Monarchy in Early Modern Europe*. Cambridge, 1987. Original Italian edition: *Il sovrano pontefice: Un corpo e due anime; La monarchia papale nella prima eta moderna*, Bologna, 1982. Important reinterpretation of the dual monarchy of the popes in the light of recent research on early modern state building.

Reinhard, Wolfgang. "Papal Power and Family Strategy in the Sixteenth and Seventeenth Centuries." In *Princes, Patronage, and the Nobility: The Court at the Beginning of the Modern Age*, edited by Ronald G. Asch and Adolf M. Birke, pp. 329–356. Oxford, 1991. Summary of recent research (mostly by the author and published in German) on the social history of the papacy and the Curia.

Stumpo, Enrico. *Il capitale finanziario a Roma fra cinque e seicento: Contributo alla storia della fiscalite pontificia in eta moderna, 1570–1660*. Milan, 1985. Important contribution to the history of papal finance.

Trisco, Robert. "Reforming the Roman Curia: Emperor Ferdinand I and the Council of Trent." In *Reform and Authority in the Medieval and Renaissance Church*, edited by George F. Lytle, pp. 143–337. Washington, D.C., 1981. Papal policy between council and political pressure.

WOLFGANG REINHARD

PAPAL DIPLOMATIC CORPS. The history of the Papal Diplomatic Corps, which during the sixteenth century acquired the form it was to keep until the end of the ancien régime, is the history of the politics of the Counter-Reformation and of the popes' attempts to implement their ecclesiastical reforms. Papal diplomacy developed, parallel to that of other rulers, as part of the process of ecclesiastical "state building." What lent its development particular momentum, though, were interests particular to Rome. During the Middle Ages the popes pursued many of their ecclesiastical reforms and church policies by sending out cardinals who, delegated with broad powers, were then able to intervene in all aspects of church life on their behalf. Later on, although such *Legati a latere* continued to be entrusted with special missions, most of their powers were transferred to permanent nuncios, usually known as *Nuncius cum potestate legati de latere*, with the exception of the representative at the French court, who remained nuncius without that distinction. They were also supposed to be clerics (as a rule with the rank of bishop), but this was initially by no means always the case, for the origins of the nuncios can be traced to two other older institutions as well: *Collectores* and diplomatic agents.

Collectores, originally representatives of the apostolic chamber, were, as their name suggests, responsible for collecting duties where they were due. In contrast to the legates, they could be appointed to their districts for long tenures. In Naples, Portugal, and Spain, insofar as the office continued to exist, their responsibilities were transferred to the nunciature. By the beginning of the sixteenth century, however, the popes had established permanent diplomatic agents of junior rank (often laymen) in the capitals of most of the important powers. Venice was probably the first place where a permanent nuncio was sent, followed by the Holy Roman Empire in 1513. The first stage of this development was completed during the pontificate of Paul III. In response to the religious turmoil of the period, from then on almost exclusively Italian bishops were appointed as papal diplomats, to be directed by the cardinal-nephew, later by the secretary of state; *Nuntius* became the regular title. In 1545 there were permanent nuncios in Venice, Spain, France, and at the imperial court; by 1572 Florence, Naples, Turin, Portugal, and Poland had all been added to the list. Gregory XIII dispatched special "reform nuncios" to the lower Rhine, Austria, and Switzerland to enforce the Tridentine decrees. This led to the establishment of permanent nunciatures in Cologne, Graz, and Lucerne; Brussels was added in 1592. Even the traditionally more "political" nuncios took on new reform duties, not least the scrutiny of candidates for bishoprics by so-called "informative processes."

The nunciatures, with their auditors, abbreviators, and secretaries, adapted to the structure of the curial bureaucracy; the Spanish one even had its own court of law, the *Rota*. Roman prelates came to see the office of nuncio as a normal step in their careers. Having successfully completed a term of office, the occupants of important nunciatures were practically assured of a cardinalate upon their return to Rome. The rulers by whom they had been accredited did their best to ensure this eventuality, for having a friend in the college of cardinals meant more than just a question of prestige. The pope, meanwhile, was interested in rewarding his followers for faithful service; personal loyalty still counted for more than the integrity of office. It therefore comes as no surprise to learn that of the approximately three hundred nuncios between the years 1560 and 1650, only three were non-Italians. The correspondence between the nuncios and the Vatican in Rome is regarded as one of Europe's most important historical sources, and, following the opening of the Vatican archives, is being steadily published by the nations concerned.

BIBLIOGRAPHY

Biaudet, Henri. *Les nonciatures apostoliques permanentes jusqu'en 1648.* Helsinki, 1910. Contains more-or-less complete lists of all papal nuncios.

Blet, Pierre. *Histoire de la représentation diplomatique du Saint Siège des origines à l'aube du XIXe siècle.* Vatican City, 1982. Synthesis by one of the leading experts, who was a professor at the Gregorian University and editor of some of the French volumes.

Bues, Almut. "'Acta Nuntiaturae Polonae': Zur Erschließung einer Quellengattung für die osteuropäische Geschichte." *Zeitschrift für Ostforschung* 41 (1992), 386–398. Report on the new Polish series, which is not included in other reports; extensive bibliographic information.

De Witte, Charles Martial, ed. *La correspondance des premiers nonces permanents au Portugal, 1532–1553.* 2 vols. Lisbon, 1980–1986. New edition covering another territory that is not included in the usual overviews.

Jaitner, Klaus, ed. *Die Hauptinstruktionen Clemens VIII. für Nuntien und Legaten an den europäischen Fürstenhöfen, 1592–1605.* 2 vols. Tübingen, 1984. An outstanding and pioneering achievement.

Müller, Gerhard. *Causa Reformationis: Beiträge zur Reformationsgeschichte und zur Theologie Martin Luthers.* Gütersloh, 1989. A collection of essays, many of them dealing with the role of papal nuncios in early Reformation Germany.

Rainer, Johann. "Nuntiaturberichte: Forschungsstand und Forschungsprobleme." *Innsbrucker Historische Studien* 9 (1986), 69–90. General overview by the editor of the correspondence of the nuncios at Graz, including a complete bibliography of editions up to publication date.

WOLFGANG REINHARD

PAPAL STATES. The traditional justification for the existence of the Papal States was that they guaranteed the independence of the papacy; this did not mean, however, that in the sixteenth century they were regarded merely as an appendage to, or instrument of, the church. On the contrary, they were an integral part of the concept of a papal double monarchy, in which the separation between the church and the state was blurred. Over the years they became the setting for the final bid to realize the enduring dream of an all-encompassing papal theocracy, which in political terms meant an absolutism of unparalleled radicalism. Experts are still divided about whether this calculated attempt at state building could have been successful. The structural advantages enjoyed by church organizations and the unique situation lent by having a single government over both spiritual and temporal spheres would seem to indicate that it might well have been. The weakness of the popes during the fifteenth century, however, speaks against such a view.

Following the 1357 *Liber Constitutionum Sanctae Matris Ecclesiae* of Cardinal Egidius Albornoz, the state comprised six separate parts: Rome and its environs (Agro romano); Campagna and Marittima, both of which extended south to the border with Naples; the so-called Patrimonium of Saint Peter, located from the north of Rome to the border with Tuscany, which included Sabina and extended as far as Umbria in the northeast; Umbria, which once belonged to the ancient duchy of Spoleto but, following the recapture of Perugia, became increasingly identified with this city and its area of influence; the Mark of Ancona on the Adriatic coast, later known simply as "the Marches"; and finally, to the north, the Romagna with Ravenna, and Bologna. In addition to these can be counted the two exclaves Benevento and Pontecorvo in Naples, as well as Avignon and the Comtat Venaissin in southern France. The Venetian expansion along the Adriatic coastline, along with the rise of the duchy of Milan (and the subsequent territorial confrontations), rendered the situation in the northern Italian peninsula extremely complicated. As lords of Ferrara the house of Este were papal vassals of the Pope, whereas they held Modena as fief of the empire.

Many parts of the Papal States were fiefs or vicariates and as such beyond the jurisdiction of the papacy's provincial governors or treasurers. Examples of such local ruling families were the Colonna and the Gaetani in Campagna and Marittima, the Orsini in the Patrimonium, and the Montefeltre of Urbino between Umbria and the Marches. Autonomous towns, which (apart from Orvieto and Viterbo) were found only in the northern and eastern parts of the state, were regarded as under the direct authority of the Holy See and its officials. In fact, these towns were largely self-governing, although their relations with the papal administration could vary considerably. The only city to lose its municipal independence almost completely was Rome, where the Curia Romana showed a tendency to swallow up the urban administration. The true ruler of the city was the papal vice-chamberlain, or *Governatore.* Other towns in central and northern Italy came under the control of local *signori,* who had their position legitimized by being raised to the status of *vicarii* of the pope. In the fifteenth century one finds examples of these, such as the Manfredi in Faenza, the Ordelaffi in Forli, the Malatesta in Rimini and in other places, the Sforza in Pesaro, and the Varano in Camerino, to mention just a few. In Bologna the Bentivoglio were advanced to the rank of *signori,* and the Baglioni in Perugia seem to have come close to achieving a similar elevation.

During the fifteenth and sixteenth centuries the two great

themes around which the history of the Papal States revolved were the (often strained) relations with these small principalities and the stabilization of the political situation in the eastern and northern regions. The popes, therefore, ensured that their nephews occupied senior positions in the military and in the state administration. In addition to this, the popes appointed their nephews as lords of newly won territories, a strategy that over the short term promised better control than the alternative of communal autonomy. This policy, however, was also liable to have a destabilizing effect when, for instance, following the death of its patron, a nepotal dynasty tried to assert its position. The last and most crass instance was the foundation of the duchy of Parma and Piacenza, land that the pope took over from Milan in 1512, and that in the year 1545 was conferred upon Pope Paul III's son Pier Luigi Farnese. These arrangements, relying upon feudal forces of social mobility, could be said to be indicative of the Renaissance popes' lack of proper planning in the art of state building.

The high point of this nepotal policy was reached under Alexander VI when, at the time of the French invasion of Italy, the Orsini had some of their land to the north of Rome requisitioned, and subsequently the Colonna, the Gaetani, and the Savelli were dispossessed outright, all so that two new nepotal principalities might be created out of their properties. While this was happening, the pope's son Cesare Borgia, the "duke of Romagna," systematically destroyed all the seigniories in the Northeast, with the single exception of the Bentivoglio seigniory in Bologna, and was on the verge of reaching beyond the Papal States and attacking Siena. Following the fall of the House of Borgia, the Venetian Republic seized Romagna for itself. Masterfully taking advantage of "international" politics, Julius II then forced Venice to return all its recent conquests and placed them, along with the greater part of Cesare Borgia's former dominions, under the direct authority of Rome. The Roman barons were reinstated, and a number of the signori were allowed to return, in particular the Montefeltro of Urbino.

Julius II is generally acknowledged to be the founder of the modern Papal States, at least to the extent that the borders he established remained steady and that over all these territories direct papal rule was henceforth recognized as the principal authority. In addition to this, he did not rely upon the services of nephews. Under his successors still most of the highest offices of state continued to be filled by nephews until the seventeenth century, and there was no shortage of attempts by nephews to establish new principalities; however, while the Farnese enjoyed great success during the sixteenth century, this was not repeated by the Barberini in the seventeenth. Following the comprehensive halt (1567) to the practice of granting fiefs, it became impossible to transform the fiefs of Ferrara (1598) and Urbino (1625), which had fallen by escheat to Rome, into nepotal principalities. Most nepotal families had to be content with an elevation to the ranks of Roman barons by the means of their title-laden landed properties. The nature of those offices that the nephews continued to occupy tended to be bureaucratic or social rather than political, at least insofar as the offices had not been reduced to straightforward sinecures. This development, however, took time. Julius II had not yet been able to reform the administrative apparatus. The pope's direct sovereignty over the state was necessarily based upon individual arrangements with the local oligarchies, who enjoyed a greater degree of independence than under their former signori. This helped secure their loyalty while at the same time keeping the administrative costs low. One gets the distinct impression that neither party was entirely satisfied with this division of power and that during the sixteenth century, when Rome demanded readjustments, this was based not so much on the interests of deliberate absolutist centralization but rather a consequence of short-term fiscal bottlenecks, which would entirely correspond to developments in other "absolute" monarchies.

Up until the seventeenth century the proportion of Rome's income that came directly from the church was in fact much higher than has hitherto been supposed, particularly if one takes into account the transfer of funds from benefices in other lands, which had only an indirect effect upon papal finances. The fixed costs, however, in particular the interest payments due on the state annuities of the venal offices (*uffizi*), and the *Monti* introduced in 1527 were borne by the Papal States and were mostly paid from farmed-out taxes and duties. Occasionally, in order to raise taxes, force had to be used. The economic resources were, after all, fairly primitive. In 1656 the first census to cover the forty-four thousand square kilometers of the state (not counting the exclaves) revealed a population of about 1.7 million; only those of Venice and Naples were larger. The population density was lower in the south and greater in the north of Italy. The border between these two regions ran precisely through the middle of the Papal States, which meant that the area with the dominant (if principally agrarian) economy and the higher population lay beyond the Apennines. Apart from the ubiquitous textile manufacture and the already heavily taxed salt industry, the only other economic factor to play a significant role was the alum deposits discovered at Tolfa in the Patrimonium in 1461.

Rome and the surrounding countryside, on the other hand, found itself trapped in an economic *circulus vitiosus*. Rome, whose population during the sixteenth century had risen from about fifty thousand to more than one hundred thousand, was in an economic sense barely productive, but its huge demand for luxury items and foodstuffs had to be satisfied, and this provided ample opportunities for speculators. Because the production of meat and milk products entailed lower costs and brought in higher profits, the great landowners moved out of cereal cultivation and into livestock. The *Campagna romana* began to go to ruin. The popes issued halfhearted prohibitions, but they themselves had an interest in this development, as the tax on livestock was one of their most important sources of income. The consequence of this pauperization was a notorious scourge of bandits on the one hand and a growing state interference with baronial autonomy on the other.

The revision of feudal property titles pushed through by Gregory XIII has been interpreted as an antifeudal absolutist move and as a purely fiscal measure. It was, however, only during the pontificates of Sixtus V and Clement VIII that contemporary writers themselves first referred to the "absolutism" of the Papal States. What they were alluding to was the removal of the last vestiges of power from the college of cardinals, the definitive reorganization of the central administration into congregations and secretariats, and the recognition that the reins of power were now firmly in the hand of a clerical career bureaucracy. The relationship between the center and the state had hardly altered at all. In Ferrara, Bologna, Ravenna, Macerata, Perugia, Viterbo, and Frosinone (or Ferentino), a cardinal sat as legate, represented by a vice-legate or a *Governatore.* The office of treasurer was franchised out. This system was not, however, universally applied. Especially in the Marches a number of urban and rural districts (Fermo, Camerino, Fano, Iesi [Jesi], Ancona, Ascoli, Loreto, Fabriano, San Severino, Matelica, and Montalto) had their own governors and were directly answerable to Rome. At the same time and in contradiction to the very notion of absolutism, the local and feudal authorities continued to exert their influence, so that one really ought to speak of a dyarchy between papal officials and local oligarchies. On this point the Papal States do not, in fact, differ from other absolutist regimes.

Admittedly, in one particular regard the clerical-absolutist governmental apparatus was extraordinarily successful: in its use of the Inquisition to suppress the Reformation. In Rome and Viterbo some members of the "evangelical" circle, which had formed around the teachings of Paul and the doctrine of justification, actually overstepped the dividing line to Protestantism. Indeed, in Rome during the mid-sixteenth century, secret evangelical parishes are thought to have flourished. Bologna became a third focal point, not least as a result of the influence of the neighboring evangelical strongholds Modena and Ferrara. By the end of the century the Protestant movements in all these places had been completely eradicated by the Inquisition. The surviving protagonists left Italy for other countries. The Protestants were plainly unable to count upon the support of either the oligarchies or the people.

[*See also* Italy *and* Papacy.]

BIBLIOGRAPHY

Black, Christopher F. "Perugia and Papal Absolutism in the Sixteenth Century." *English Historical Review* 96 (1981), 509–539. Examplary study of the dyarchy of papal officials and the local oligarchy.

Caravale, Mario, and Alberto Caracciolo. *Lo Stato pontificio da Martino V a Pio IX.* Turin, 1978. Latest synthesis.

Carocci, Giampiero. *Lo stato della chiesa nella seconda metà del secolo XVI.* Milan, 1961. A pioneering study that includes much important information.

Coing, Helmut, ed. *Handbuch der Quellen und Literatur der neueren europäischen Privatrechtsgeschichte.* Munich, 1973–1976. See vol. 1, pp. 712–717, and vol. 2.2, pp. 135–146. Studies law and legislation; extensive bibliography.

Delumeau, Jean. *Vie économique et sociale de Rome dans la seconde moitié du XVIe siècle.* 2 vols. Paris, 1957–1959. Requires some correction, but still a rich source of information on the Papal States.

———. *L'alun de Rome, XVe-XIX siècle.* Paris, 1962. On the alum mine of Tolfa, the only important industrial enterprise of the Papal States.

Monaco, Michele. *Lo stato della chiesa.* Lecce, 1975. A synthesis by an expert of sixteenth-century financial history.

Partner, Peter. *The Lands of St. Peter: The Papal State in the Middle Ages and the Early Renaissance.* Berkeley, 1972. Good synthesis of the prehistory of the Reformation period.

———. "The Papal State, 1417–1600." In *Conquest and Coalescence: The Shaping of the State in Early Modern Europe,* edited by Mark Greengrass, pp. 25–47. London, 1991. The best short summary available in English.

Polverini Fosi, Irene. *La società violenta: Il banditismo dello Stato Pontificio nella seconda metà del Cinquecento.* Rome, 1985. Latest study on the bandits of the Papal States, based on the processes of the court of the *Governatore di Roma.*

Prodi, Paolo. *The Papal Prince: One Body and Two Souls; The Papal Monarchy in Early Modern Europe.* Cambridge, 1987. Original Italian edition: *Il sovrano pontefice: Un corpo e due anime; La monarchia papale nella prima età moderna,* Bologna, 1982. Important reinterpretation of the dual monarchy of the popes in the light of recent research on early modern state building.

Scotoni, Lando. *I territori autonomi dello Stato Ecclesiastico nel Cinquecento: Cartografia e aspetti amministrativi, economici e sociali.* Galatina, 1982. Thorough study of an essential part of the political geography.

Volpi, Roberto. *La regioni introvabili: Centralizzazione e regionalizzazione dello Stato Pontificio.* Bologna, 1983. Studies the role of the regions and their development in the Papal States.

Zenobi, Bandino Giacomo. *Ceti e potere nella Marca pontificia.* Bologna, 1976. Another exemplary study of the dyarchy of officials and oligarchies.

WOLFGANG REINHARD

PAPPUS, Johann (also Johannes; 1549–1610), German professor, president of the Compagnie des Pasteurs (Company of Pastors) in Strasbourg, church organizer, and controversialist. Born the son of a furrier in Lindau and educated there and at Tübingen, Pappus came to Strasbourg in 1564 as a teacher of Hebrew at the academy and a decade later became a professor in the theology faculty. In 1581 he succeeded his fellow Lindauer, Johann Marbach, as president of the Compagnie des Pasteurs and therefore became the city's highest ecclesiastical official. He is best known for his controversy with Johannes Sturm, the rector of the academy, and for codifying the city's new church order of 1598, by which Strasbourg at last officially subscribed to the Formula of Concord. For many scholars his career thus marks the city's entry into the ranks of Lutheran Orthodoxy.

The controversy with Sturm followed an earlier one that Pappus's predecessor lost. This bitter struggle began in late 1580, when Pappus announced and defended a series of theses regarding the *condemnamus* of the formula. In this, its last section, the subscribing "theologians of the Augsburg Confession" condemned the teachings of their non-Roman opponents and in particular those of the Reformed persuasion. The Lord's Supper was the central issue.

Pappus, however, knew well Sturm's close relations with the Reformed and those in certain areas of the Palatinate. Hence, he chose not to defend the doctrines of the formula as such but raised in his theses the question of whether one could condemn a person's teachings without at the same time condemning the person. Sturm, who was fundamentally a humanist educator for whom such distinctions were fraudulent, was outraged. The ensuing debate centered on the question of whether any well-educated person or only a trained and certified theologian could dependably judge matters of doctrine. At base it was the same issue that had fueled the controversy with Pappus's predecessor six years and more earlier. On this occasion Sturm made the mistake of offending the (now Lutheran) elector palatine, Ludwig I, and he was dismissed.

Pappus became president of the Compagnie des Pasteurs in December 1581, but another sixteen years elapsed before Strasbourg's ruling authorities authorized him and the company to draft the church order of 1598. By virtue of its official adoption, the city not only endorsed how its church was already in fact functioning but also the Formula of Concord itself, and Strasbourg, once allied confessionally with the Swiss, became formally Lutheran.

Pappus was, however, more than a controversialist and a churchman. He was also an intellectual with decidedly humanistic tastes in his own right. The extant catalog of his personal library, with more than six thousand volumes, reveals that more than 40 percent of it consisted of works in rhetoric, grammar, history, the ancient languages, and the sources of classical antiquity—that is, precisely the writings that were most precious to the humanists of his day. During the last years of his life, Pappus began increasingly to devote himself to the study of church history and in particular to that of the ancient church. On the other hand, he employed these studies to defend the correctness of Lutheran teaching according to the ancient traditions. Hence, his career is not only a study in the development of Lutheranism as such but also the roles that humanism played in it.

BIBLIOGRAPHY

Horning, Wilhelm. *Dr. Johann Pappus von Lindau, 1549–1610*. Strassburg, 1891. A basic chronology but highly partisan and to be used with care.

Kittelson, James M. "Humanism in the Theological Faculties of Lutheran Universities during the Late Reformation." In *The Harvest of Humanism in Central Europe: Essays in Honor of Lewis W. Spitz*, edited by Manfred P. Fleischer, pp. 139–157. Saint Louis, 1992. An overview of the career of Johann Pappus and an examination of his personal library.

Verzeichnis der im deutschen Sprachbereich erschienenen Drucke des XVI. Jahrhunderts. Stuttgart, 1983–. See vol. 15, nos. 319–344.

James M. Kittelson

PARACELSUS (also Philippus Aureolus Theophrastus Bombastus von Hohenheim; 1493–1541), German alchemist and physician. Paracelsus was born on 17(?) December in Einsiedeln, in the canton of Schwyz. His father, the physician Wilhelm von Hohenheim, came from a family of the Swabian petty nobility from around Stuttgart in southwest Germany, his mother from a family with service ties to the monastery in Einsiedeln. The young Hohenheim went to school in Villach (Kärnten) where his father worked as the town physician and as a teacher in the local mining school. In 1509/10 he left Villach for Vienna. In 1512 he was in Italy, where he matriculated at Ferrara and passed examinations in the two arts of healing (*Leib-und Wundarznei*). Here he seems to have first come into contact with the Florentine Neoplatonism of Marsilio Ficino and Giovanni Pico della Mirandola; from this period came his first studies of the "French disease," syphilis.

In the following years Paracelsus traveled throughout Europe collecting information on folk medicine and coming into contact with the radical reform movements. During this time he visited the centers of traditional Galenic medicine at Paris, Montpellier, and Salerno. He spent 1524 at Salzburg as a physician and published his first medical writings; his support for the rebellious peasants forced him to flee the city. Two years later he applied for citizenship at Strasbourg as a physician (*Wundartzt*). From there he followed a call to Basel as city physician after he had successfully treated the city's most famous publisher, Johannes Froben (1527). A faculty appointment to the university established him as a member of the learned community. He lectured in Latin as well as in German on medical and philosophical topics. During this time he developed and published his theory on stone-forming illnesses (*tartarische Krankheiten*).

But the acrimony between Paracelsus and the medical establishment increased over his unorthodox healing methods, his use of German in the lecture hall, as well as his irreverent comments about school medicine. The climax was reached when—at the summer solstice of 1527—he burned some traditional medical treatises in a public gesture of contempt for his physician colleagues at the university. This act earned him serious public censure and considerable professional hostility (a pamphlet called him "Cacophrastos") and forced him to flee to Colmar. Here he undertook his first experiments using mercury in an attempt to cure syphilis. A year later (1529) in Nuremberg his polemics against the use of Guajar wood to treat syphilis brought him into conflict with the Fugger family, who held the monopoly in the

Guajar trade. It is around this time that he began to sign his works "Paracelsus."

In 1530 he worked on the *Opus Paragranum*, the first comprehensive exposition of his theories on medicine, science, and natural philosophy (magic). During the same year, at Regensburg, he wrote the *Opus Paramirum*, which developed his *Entientheorie*, the theory that each disease has its own being (*ens*). He based his theories on the idea that all human life consists of three basic components: sulphur, mercury, and salt. These components were produced by the four elements: fire, air, earth, and water. He also began work on the "invisible illnesses," diseases of the mind such as visions, melancholy, and delusions.

In 1536 he completed his most successful work, the *Große Wundarznei*. Printed in Ulm and Augsburg, it is dedicated to Ferdinand I of Austria. Shortly thereafter he published his *Prognostication auf XXIIII jahr zukünfftig* at Munich, and he began the major exposition of his esoteric philosophy and cosmology, the *Astronomia magna oder die ganze Philosophia sagax der großen und der kleinen Welt*. He returned to Villach and then went to Saint Veit, where he wrote a chronicle of Kärnten; a polemical tract, *Vom Irrgang der Aerzte*; and the *Defensiones*, an apologia of his life and work. In 1540 he received a call to Salzburg from Archbishop Ernst von Wittelsbach. On 24 September 1541 he died at Salzburg, where he is buried at the cemetery for the poor, Saint Sebastian.

Paracelsus wrote most of works in German, liberally mixing in Latin terms and phrases. Seeking language that could adequately express his philosophical, theological, and medical speculations, he invented many new words and categories that already during his lifetime earned him the honorific "Luther of Medicine." The historian Daniel Specklin has called 1517 a stellar year because it witnessed the creative genius of three great men, Paracelsus, Luther, and Dürer.

Despite his sympathies for the radical reformers, Paracelsus never left the Catholic faith. He did, however, reject what he called the *Mauerkirche*, the walled church, in favor of a more direct, evangelical relationship to God. He felt that the church had fallen from its erstwhile state of purity and that the true church could be found only in the writings and actions of those who were wrongly called heretics, many of them radical reformers. His commentaries on biblical and patristic texts express an acerbic criticism of the church and an intense engagement with the poor. While he did not abandon many of the misogynist tenets of his time, he stated repeatedly that woman was created of one flesh—was of the same nature—as man and thus his equal. Although never married, he praised marriage as a divinely ordained state, and he rejected adult virginity and celibacy as contrary to nature and to the human task to live in familial harmony.

Paracelsus believed his world to be near its end; his prognostications of the last days circulated widely. He recommended study of the Bible, especially the book of *Revelation*; he also fervently defended the study of the physical world, the "book of nature." He believed that God revealed himself to humanity in the pages of these two books.

According to Paracelsus, humanity was placed into the midst of a cosmos formed of the elements, the stars, and heaven. Natural philosophy, *scientia magica*, dealt with all aspects of this cosmos. Alchemy taught humanity how to control and manipulate the forces hidden in the elements. Basic to Paracelsus's epistemology was the ancient notion that the microcosm, the human being, was constituted in direct analogy to the macrocosm, the universe. The heavenly, the celestial, and the elemental worlds found their reflection in a person's body and soul. The human mission on earth was to strive for an ever deeper understanding of the universal powers, good and evil, spiritual and elemental. Created last, the human being unites in the self all aspects of the universe, which means that a person who is one of the wise, the adept, the magi can manipulate the forces of the universe.

A fervent defender of the efficacy of natural, white, licit magic, Paracelsus distanced himself vigorously from all suspicion that he practiced black, satanic magic. Although he rejected judicial astrology, his prognostications were very popular, printed repeatedly, and circulated widely. He believed that the instability of the time announced the nearing of the Last Judgment, at which time God's promise was to be fulfilled and full knowledge of the universe granted to humanity.

Paracelsus's restless wanderings and his tireless search for knowledge find expression in the positive valuation of experience and of curiosity. Only those who saw, heard, and read for themselves could attain true understanding. Paracelsus had only scathing criticism for the scholar who stayed in the study and ignored the world of experience, of nature.

BIBLIOGRAPHY

Primary Sources

Goldammer, Kurt, ed. *Sämtliche Werke. 2. Abt.: Theologische und religionsphilosophische Schriften.* 14 vols. Wiesbaden, Germany, 1955–1965.

Peuckert, Will-Erich, ed. *Theophrastus Paracelsus Werke.* 5 vols. Reprint, Basel, 1982. Since the Sudhoff/Goldammer editions are generally not easily accessible, the Peuckert edition provides a serviceable entry into the materials.

Sudhoff, Karl, ed. *Sämtliche Werke. 1. Abt.: Medizinische, naturwissenschaftliche und philosophische Schriften.* 14 Vols. Berlin, 1922–1933. 2d edition with index volume published in Einsiedeln, Switzerland, 1960.

———. *Bibliographia Paracelsica.* Besprechung der unter Hohenheims Namen 1527–1893 erschienenen Druckschriften. Graz, 1963. Sudhoff was and remains the foremost Paracelsus specialist whose edition of Hohenheim's works has canonical status among Paracelsus researchers.

Secondary Sources

Debus, Allen. *Science, Medicine, and Society in the Renaissance.* New York, 1972.

———. *The Chemical Philosophy: Paracelsian Science and Medicine in the Sixteenth and Seventeenth Centuries.* New York, 1977. Debus studies Paracelsus in the European context and presents him as an important intellectual influence in early modern science and philosophy.

Dopsch, Heinz, Kurt Goldammer, and Peter F. Kramm, eds. *Paracelsus, 1493–1541: "Keines andern Knecht. . . ."* Salzburg, 1993. A collection of informative articles on all aspects of Paracelsus's career and work on the occasion of the 500th anniversary of his birth.

Goldammer, Kurt. *Der göttliche Magier und die Magierin Natur: Religion, Naturmagie und die Anfänge der Naturwissenschaft vom Spätmittelaltert bis zur Renaissance.* Suttgart, 1991. Good introduction and overview over the development of natural magic and Paracelsus's contributions to the field by one of the foremost scholars on Paracelsus.

Kaiser, Ernst. *Paracelsus in Selbstzeugnissen und Bilddokumenten.* Reinbek, Germany, 1969. This is a serviceable introduction to Paracelsus.

Merkel, Ingrid, and Allen G. Debus, eds. *Hermeticism and the Renaissance: Intellectual History and the Occult in Early Modern Europe.* London, 1988.

Metzke, Erwin. *Coincidentia Oppositorum.* Witten, 1961. A collection of essays on the concepts of time, experience, and nature in Paracelsus.

Pagel, Walter. *Paracelsus: An Introduction to the Philosophical Medicine in the Era of the Renaissance.* Basel, 1958.

———. *Das medizinische Weltbild des Paracelsus: Seine Zusammenhänge mit Neoplatonismus und Gnosis.* Wiesbaden, Germany, 1962. Pagel's studies, numerous and extremely learned, are still required reading for students and scholars.

Peuckert, Will-Erich. *Pansophie: Ein Versuch zur Geschichte der Schwarzen und Weißen Magie.* 2d ed. Berlin, 1956–1967. Peuckert's studies show an astonishing knowledge of sources, and they make fascinating and instructive reading; because annotations are sparse and many of the sources cited are impossible to locate, rather frustrating reading as well.

Telle, Joachim. *Pererga Paracelsica: Paracelsus in Vergangenheit und Gegenwart.* Stuttgart, 1991.

Vickers, Brian, ed. *Occult and Scientific Mentalities in the Renaissance.* Cambridge, 1984. A collection of essays on the close relationship between science and the occult and Paracelsus's role in this development.

Webster, Charles. *From Paracelsus to Newton: Magic and the Making of Modern Science.* Cambridge, 1982. A straightforward, knowledgeable account of the close association of magic and science and of magic's seminal influence on early modern scientific thought.

Weimann, Karl H. *Paracelsus Bibliographie, 1932–1960.* Wiesbaden, 1963. Continues where Sudhoff left off.

GERHILD SCHOLZ WILLIAMS

PARIS. With a population estimated to have risen during the sixteenth century from fewer than 200,000 to more than 300,000 persons, the administrative capital of the French monarchy was the largest city in northern Europe and one of the most volatile. Its importance for the Reformation lies in both opposition to religious change on the part of its theologians and magistrates and popular resistance on the part of its fiercely Catholic population.

At the University of Paris, the learned doctors of the Sorbonne condemned 104 of Luther's propositions as heretical in April 1521. Five months later, the high court of the Parlement of Paris ordered all bookstores and individuals possessing subversive books to surrender them immediately. Despite these condemnations, Luther's teachings found a ready audience prepared by the evangelical reformers of the Circle of Meaux. The first Parisian converts were Augustinian monks and university faculty and students. King Francis I's position was a complex one. Sympathetic to humanism and open to Erasmian reform, he was hostile to heresy and opposed to division in the church. He encouraged Parlement and the Sorbonne in their opposition to Lutheranism, but he tried to restrain their broader attacks on Christian humanists. The king soon had to return to his wars in Italy, however, and Parlement and the Sorbonne were able to step up their persecution of religious dissidents. The first executions by burning in Paris occurred in 1525.

In 1528 the desecration of a statue of the Virgin Mary on a Parisian street corner aroused public ire against the new religion. The solemn procession of reparation, in which the king himself took part, was the first of many demonstrations of Parisian solidarity against the heretics. But Protestant teachings continued to spread secretly within the university, the clergy, and the mercantile bourgeoisie. In 1533 the university's new rector, Nicolas Cop, gave a controversial sermon, perhaps written with the aid of his friend Calvin, that provoked the intervention of the Sorbonne and Parlement and resulted in the flight of both men and the arrest of others. When an evangelical priest, Gérard Roussel, was chosen to preach at Notre-Dame in 1534, the public was outraged and invaded the cathedral. In October of the same year, placards posted against the Mass in Paris and other locations, including on the door to the king's bedchamber, aroused Francis I's ire and resulted in an abrupt increase in the prosecution of dissidents. Strict restraints were put on the book trade, and houses were invaded to seek out banned books. Throughout his lifetime, however, Francis I continued to try to defend those he viewed as humanist reformers against the extremists of Parlement and the Sorbonne. His son, Henry II, was less moderate when he came to the throne in 1547. Establishing a special chamber in Parlement, the *Chambre ardente*, especially for the prosecution of accused heretics, Henry II instituted policies that greatly increased the number of arrests and executions for heresy.

During the 1540s Calvinist ideas began to penetrate the clandestine Protestant community. Informal meetings for the reading of scripture, prayer, and discussion soon failed to satisfy the converts, who also wanted access to the sacraments. In September 1555 a Calvinist group chose one of its members, La Rivière, to act as minister and set up a consistory on the Genevan model. In 1556 Calvin sent several experienced ministers from Geneva to assist the nascent church, which acquired a second regular minister in 1557 in the person of Antoine de la Roche Chandieu. In September of that year, Calvinists leaving a secret meeting in the rue Saint-Jacques were discovered and set upon by locals. The authorities imprisoned about 130 persons who had not dared to leave. Most secured their freedom by recanting, but seven were executed before the end of October. By May 1558 church members had recovered their courage, and they gathered publicly to sing psalms on the Pré-aux-Clercs. Important nobles like Antoine, the king of Navarre, joined in. Angered by rumors of Protestant plots, Henry II forbade further assemblies and issued new laws against heresy. Despite the danger, Chandieu organized the first national synod of Reformed churches in Paris in May 1559. The synod adopted a common confession of faith and discipline. With some revision, these remain the theological and institutional foundations of the French Reformed church.

Henry's sudden death in July 1559 led to a period of increased persecution, as the young king, Francis II, was dominated by his wife's uncles, members of the arch-Catholic house of Guise. Parlementaire Anne du Bourg, whose arrest was one of the last orders given by Henry II, was but the most famous victim whose death by burning was cheered by Parisian crowds. At the same time, incidents of popular violence against suspected Calvinists multiplied. Even before Francis II's own premature death in December 1560, however, a new period of toleration began. As regent for her son Charles IX, Catherine de Médicis relaxed repressive measures and encouraged leaders of the two faiths to seek compromise. Protestants took advantage of the situation to preach more publicly. To the great distress of Paris's priests, magistrates, and populace, Protestant numbers swelled. The situation grew tense; in December 1561 fighting broke out between Catholics worshiping at Saint-Médard and a nearby Protestant assembly. When a new edict of toleration was issued in January, the city protested mightily.

Fresh from his attack on the Protestants of Wassy, Francis, duke of Guise, was greeted as a hero when he entered Paris on March 16. Violent clashes in the city prevented compromise as the first of the Wars of Religion began. The Parisians armed and formed a militia whose radical tendencies escalated the cycle of violence it was intended to inhibit. Confessed Protestants were expelled from Paris in May, but many who claimed to be orthodox Catholics were subsequently driven out by secret denunciations and harassment. Parisian delegations protested attempts by Catherine de Médicis to negotiate peace, and the settlement reached in March 1563 was so bitterly opposed that Parlement feared to register it. For six months the militia resisted laying down its arms, and few Protestants dared to return.

The pattern was similar in each of the subsequent Wars of Religion, especially the second, which began in September 1567 with the Huguenots encircling Paris after their abortive attempt to seize the king at Meaux. Rumors of a Huguenot attack set off a wave of panic, and Protestants who remained in the city feared for their lives. Peace was made in March 1568, but neither side disarmed. Few Protestants returned to Paris until after the Peace of Saint-Germain in August 1570. This settlement was no more palatable than earlier ones to the Parisian populace, whose bitterness found echo in angry sermons and violent acts, including a long contest over a monument known as the Cross of Gastines, whose removal was ordered by the king in compliance with the peace but resisted by the city.

It is in this context that the Saint Bartholomew's Day Massacre, 24 August 1572, must be viewed. Less a concerted plot on the part of the king and his advisers than a reaction of fear against a rumored Protestant coup, the intended execution of Huguenot leaders became, through the participation of the Parisian masses, the bloody slaughter of more than two thousand persons. Surviving Protestants recanted their faith, fled the country, or went underground.

Reaction against the massacre encouraged the growth of a new faction of moderate Catholics known as *politiques*. Catholic extremists also hardened their opinions and began openly to oppose the Valois monarchy, which was seen to be bankrupting the country with fruitless wars and frivolous pleasures. Parisians especially hated Henry III, king after his brother's death in 1574. Henry III managed to co-opt and defuse a Catholic league formed in 1576 but was unable to perform the same feat when a new league arose late in 1584. In May 1588, on the Day of Barricades, the league seized control of Paris, and Henry III fled to Blois. Ordering the assassination of the Catholic league's leader, Henry, duke of Guise, Henry III forfeited any hope of regaining the allegiance of his rebellious capital. He designated the Protestant Henry of Navarre (Henry IV) his legitimate successor before dying of an assassin's wounds in August 1589.

The new king, Henry IV, had a hard fight to retake Paris, which he weakened from without by a long siege, while factional divisions within slowly broke the hold of the league. Henry IV's conversion to Catholicism in 1593 further weakened resistance in the capital, which he entered without opposition in March 1594. Pardoning all but the most ardent leaguers, Henry IV set about restoring order and repairing the damages of war. The Edict of Nantes (1598), reaffirming earlier edicts forbidding Protestant worship in Paris, confirmed the capital's status as a Catholic city and forced its small Protestant community to troop out to the countryside, to Charenton, to hold services.

[*See also* Calvin, John; Catholic League; Chandieu, Antoine de la Roche; Cop, Nicholas; France; Francis I of France; Gallic Confession; Henry II of France; Henry III of France; Henry IV of France; Lorraine-Guise, House of; Parlement; Saint Bartholomew's Day Massacre; *and* Valois, House of.]

BIBLIOGRAPHY

Babelon, Jean-Pierre. *Paris au XVIe siècle*. Paris, 1986. A good synthesis of older and recent research.

Crouzet, Denis. *Les guerriers de Dieu: La violence au temps des troubles de religion*. 2 vols. Paris, 1990. Massive and not exclusively on Paris, but important on popular violence and the religious content of the league.

Descimon, Robert. *Qui étaient les Seize? Mythes et réalités de la Ligue parisienne, 1584–1594*. Paris, 1983. The best recent study of the social background of the league.

Diefendorf, Barbara. "Prologue to a Massacre: Popular Unrest in Paris, 1557–1572." *American Historical Review* 90 (1985), 1067–1091. Narrative account of events leading up to Saint Bartholomew's Day Massacre.

———. "The Catholic League: Social Crisis or Apocalypse Now?" *French Historical Studies* 15 (1987), 332–344. Review essay on recent studies of the league.

———. *Beneath the Cross: Catholics and Huguenots in Sixteenth-Century Paris*. New York and Oxford, 1991. Social, political, and religious history; focusing on the period prior to Saint Bartholomew's Day.

Farge, James K. *Orthodoxy and Reform in Early Reformation France: The Faculty of Theology of Paris, 1500–1543*. Leiden, 1985. Useful background on the positions taken by theologians of the University of Paris.

Imbart de la Tour, Pierre. *Les origines de la Réforme*. 4 vols. Reprint, Geneva, 1978. Still the essential work on the origins of the French Reformation.

Kingdon, Robert M. *Geneva and the Coming of the Wars of Religion in France, 1555–1563*. Geneva, 1956. One of the few works in English on the spread of Calvinism in France.

Knecht, R. J. *Francis I*. Cambridge and London, 1982. Reconciles some apparent contradictions in the religious policies of François I.

Richet, Denis. "Aspects socio-culturels des conflits religieux à Paris dans la seconde moitié du XVIe siècle." *Annales, économies, sociétés, civilisations* 32 (1977): 764–89. Reprinted in Denis Richet, *De la Réforme à la Révolution: Etudes sur la France moderne*, pp. 15–52, Paris, 1991. A seminal article on the social roots of religious change in Paris.

Salmon, J. H. M. "The Paris Sixteen, 1584–94: The Social Analysis of a Revolutionary Movement." *Journal of Modern History* 44 (1972), 540–576. The best work in English on the Paris League; superseded but seldom contradicted by Descimon.

———. *Society in Crisis: France in the Sixteenth Century*. New York, 1975. Still the best general work on the French religious conflicts.

BARBARA B. DIEFENDORF

PARIS, UNIVERSITY OF. *See* Faculty of Theology of Paris.

PARIS FACULTY OF THEOLOGY. *See* Faculty of Theology of Paris.

PARKER, Matthew (1504–1575), English reformer and first archbishop of Canterbury to Elizabeth I (r. 1559–1575). Parker has always existed in the shadow of his great predecessor, Thomas Cranmer, yet he was second only to Cranmer in defining the nature of the Church of England in the sixteenth century. He was not a distinguished theologian or liturgical specialist: his initial fame derived from his preaching skills. As Archbishop he contributed to the church an outstanding capacity for organization and a passion for education. Above all he sought to make the fledgling Elizabethan Settlement acceptable by linking the Church of England to its ancient roots, and by an emphasis on good order and harmony.

Parker was born in Norwich in 1504, the son of a prosperous weaver. He received his university education at Corpus Christi College, Cambridge, an institution to which he remained loyal throughout his life. His fine manuscript collection, reflecting his ecclesiastical preoccupations and his passion for Anglo-Saxon antiquities, was left to the college at his death. His identification with Protestant ideas must have emanated from Cambridge, which in the 1520s was the major English center for the reception of Lutheranism. In the 1530s Parker developed a reputation as a preacher, which eventually brought him to the attention of Anne Boleyn. Anne appointed him one of her chaplains in 1535 and promoted him to a profitable East Anglian benefice. He remained at Corpus Christi and in 1544 was made master there. He moved steadily through academic offices, becoming vice-chancellor twice, in 1545 and 1548. He married in 1547 (two years before clerical marriage was sanctioned by Parliament). Under Mary he lost all his promotions but succeeded in living obscurely with his family, perhaps protected by William Cecil. Two of his rare writings belong to this period: a metrical translation of the Psalter, and a defense of priests' marriage.

Parker was Elizabeth's first choice as archbishop, both because he had avoided exile under Mary, and hence the danger of identification with a specific form of Continental Protestantism, and because of his loyalty to her mother. Although he had not held high administrative office in the church, he was known as an efficient organizer within the university. He was initially most reluctant to accept the queen's appointment but was persuaded by William Cecil: his years as archbishop were often unhappy, and he recalled the pleasures of academic obscurity with longing. Nevertheless, he committed himself wholeheartedly to the reconstruction of English Protestantism. His own priorities were the provision of a well-trained and resident body of parochial clergy and the proper ordering of the ecclesiastical hierarchy. He had no apparent reservations about the episcopal order; indeed, he saw the hierarchy as a crucial defense against the democratic proclivities of Protestantism. "God keep us," he wrote in 1559, "from. . . the people to be orderers of things." It was difficult to provide adequate clergy in the parishes after the upheavals of the mid-century. Parker tried a variety of devices including systematic surveys of the state of the clergy, regular visitations, and the provision of readers who would serve when qualified men were not available. In his own diocese he increased the number of resident clergy by at least twenty-five percent. He continued to give close attention to the universities as the future nurseries of the clergy. He oversaw the passage of the Thirty-nine Articles through convocation in 1563 and the publication of the Bishops' Bible in 1568: the former showed that he was willing to accept the theology of Switzerland, the latter that he already saw Geneva and its Bible as a threat to orthodoxy.

Much of Parker's archiepiscopate was devoted to defending the new church from external threat. Lay interest in the church and its property was one danger. Parker tried to counter this with appeals to Cecil and with strong emphasis on the needs of the church for the payment of a learned ministry and the provision of hospitality. There was the obvious challenge from Catholicism to be countered by cleansing the universities and the organization of propaganda. Then there was the growing problem of Protestant nonconformity. Parker was firmly committed to the order imposed by the Elizabethan Settlement, and he spent much of his last years embattled against Puritanism. The *Advertisements* of 1566 were his first major attempt to impose uniformity of worship and apparel on the clergy. These were followed in 1571 by the Articles of Religion, which regulated preaching. In his last years Parker's determined efforts to attack new presbyterian ideas of church government were undermined by the most insidious threat to full uniformity, Queen Elizabeth herself. The archbishop was rarely given freedom to act or full power to enforce discipline: Elizabeth willed the ends, but wished to avoid the political odium of the means. The Thirty-nine Articles did not receive parliamentary ratification until 1571, the *Advertisements* were issued solely on the bishops authority, and Parker was never certain that the queen would endorse his views publicly. It was this uncertainty that made his last years so exhausting. His last letters suggest that only his attempts to improve the ministry, and his antiquarian pursuits, still satisfied him. Nevertheless, his legacy extended beyond his manuscripts and views on a preaching ministry: his vision of an ordered, hierarchical church, assimilating Protestant theology and a reformed Catholic structure, did much to determine the future direction of Anglicanism.

BIBLIOGRAPHY

Brook, V. J. K. *A Life of Archbishop Parker.* Reprint, Oxford, 1965. The only full modern biography, valuable on the archbishop, though the interpretation of Elizabethan ecclesiastical politics is dated.

Collinson, Patrick. *The Elizabethan Puritan Movement.* Reprint, Oxford, 1990. For Parker's struggles with nonconformity.

Haugaard, William P. *Elizabeth and the English Reformation.* London, 1968. Good analysis of the problems of the episcopate in the 1560s.

Hudson, Winthrop S. *The Cambridge Connection and the Elizabethan Settlement of 1559.* Durham, N.C., 1980. For the establishment of Elizabeth's church.

FELICITY HEAL

PARLEMENT. The sovereign court of France, the Parlements registered and published royal decrees and oversaw the maintenance of public order in their territories in addition to their judicial role. In the sixteenth century there were eight Parlements, although in theory they formed one body. The most important was the Parlement of Paris, which, in addition to its other functions, could act as a court of peers. Its jurisdiction covered most of northern France and extended south through Auvergne. The provincial courts were, in order of creation, the Parlements of Toulouse, Bordeaux, Grenoble, Dijon, Rouen, Aix-en-Provence, and (after 1554) Rennes. Each court was sovereign in its own right; its decisions could not be appealed, and it had an independent power to register royal decrees. This sovereignty allowed the courts to become effective defenders of provincial liberties, since they had the right to remonstrate with the king when they believed his edicts ran counter to earlier laws or the public interest, and the process of registration allowed them to alter or propose amendments to royal decrees. The king could override a court's remonstrances by sending *lettres de jussion* ordering registration of an edict or by appearing in person to order obedience to his will in a ceremony known as a *lit de justice.*

Heresy cases did not initially come under the purview of the Parlements. As a religious crime, heresy fell under the jurisdiction of ecclesiastical courts, which released convicted heretics to the secular arm for punishment. The Parlements dealt with ancillary issues such as censorship and sedition but not with doctrinal questions. With the spread of the Reformation, however, church authorities proved to be poorly equipped to pursue suspected heretics, and special commissions, which coupled magistrates with theologians, were sometimes set up. Appeal to Parlement was allowed, which permitted the courts to become more directly involved in heresy proceedings. In 1540 the Edict of Fontainebleau, defining false doctrine as sedition, turned over to lay courts all heresy cases except those involving clerics. Prisoners were to be tried immediately by the criminal chambers of the appropriate Parlement. The clergy protested their loss of authority, and later edicts attempted to restore doctrinal questions to ecclesiastical jurisdiction. The Parlements fought meanwhile to maintain their claim to judge religious dissidents through a broad interpretation of heresy's effects.

On his accession in 1547, Henry II set up a special chamber in the Parlement of Paris to try heresy cases. Known for its zeal as the "burning chamber," the *Chambre ardente* was discontinued in 1550 and its functions returned to Parlement's regular criminal chambers. In 1551 cases of simple heresy were returned to the clerical courts by the Edict of Châteaubriand. The same edict, however, broadened the Parlements' mandate where the effects of heresy were concerned, and so increased rather than decreased their role in religious persecution.

The situation began to turn in the other direction with the Edict of Romorantin (May 1560), which narrowed the Parlements' role. The edict of July 1561, while prohibiting Protestant assemblies, forgave past religious offenses and forbade inquiry into matters of conscience. The edict of January 1562 went further in the direction of freedom of conscience and even allowed Protestants certain limited rights of assembly. The refusal of the Parlement of Paris to register this edict until March, after receiving two *lettres de jussion*, was one of the issues that pushed Protestants into open war. The settlements negotiated after each of the Wars of Religion generally reaffirmed the measures of toleration advanced in the edict of January 1562. During each war, the courts prosecuted violations of sedition laws, but execution for religious crimes became increasingly rare.

The Parlements are often considered to have been solidly Catholic and opposed to all religious toleration. Recent research has shown that this was not the case. A number of courts excluded certain counselors from office as Protestants during the Wars of Religion, and even Catholic magistrates disagreed among themselves over how strictly the laws against heresy should be enforced. In the Parlement of Paris, these disagreements first came to a head at the *mercuriale*, or special disciplinary session, held in the presence of King Henry II on 10 June 1559. The arrest of five counselors who spoke out in favor of leniency in the judging of heresy cases (and the subsequent execution for heresy of one of these men, Anne du Bourg) stunned the court. The hard-liners became more vocal and active, and the moderates appeared to be in retreat, but differences of opinion persisted within the court. In many respects, the divisions that were later to separate *politiques*, who looked for a compromise solution to the religious conflicts, from ultra-Catholics, who made religious unity their first priority, had their roots in these disagreements.

[*See also* Chambre Ardente *and* Châteubriand, Edict of.]

BIBLIOGRAPHY

Diefendorf, Barbara B. *Beneath the Cross: Catholics and Huguenots in Sixteenth-Century Paris*. New York and Oxford, 1991. See especially chapter 10 on the Parlement of Paris and popular opinion during the religious wars.

Hanley, Sarah. *The Lit de Justice of the Kings of France: Constitutional Ideology in Legend, Ritual and Discourse*. Princeton, 1983. On the relationship between the king and the Parlement of Paris in the sixteenth century; should be read in company with Holt, "The King in Parlement."

Holt, Mack P. "The King in Parlement: The Problem of the *Lit de Justice* in Sixteenth-Century France." *Historical Journal* 31 (1988), 507–523. Demonstrates the important effect religious issues had on relations between the Crown and the parlements.

Knecht, R. J. *Francis I*. Cambridge and London, 1982. A good, brief account of the Parlement's increasing role in heresy cases under Francis I.

Mentzer, Raymond A., Jr. *Heresy Proceedings in Languedoc, 1500–1560*. Transactions of the American Philosophical Society, vol. 74, pt. 5. Philadelphia, 1984. One of the few studies of provincial tribunals; essential on the Parlement of Toulouse.

Sutherland, Nicola M. *The Huguenot Struggle for Recognition*. New Haven and London, 1980. Particularly valuable for the appendix of religious edicts.

Taber, Linda L. "Religious Dissent within the Parlement of Paris in the Mid-Sixteenth Century: A Reassessment." *French Historical Studies* 16 (1990), 684–699. Useful article that may be supplanted by Taber's book-in-progress on the same subject.

Zeller, Gaston. *Les institutions de la France au XVIe siècle*. 2d ed. Paris, 1987. Old but still useful for chapter 3, "Le Parlement, les parlements."

BARBARA B. DIEFENDORF

PARLIAMENT. In England Parliament played an active role in implementing and enforcing the Reformation. Few historians would now agree with Sir Maurice Powicke's confident assertion that "the one definite thing which can be said about the Reformation in England is that it was an act of State" (*The Reformation in England*, Oxford, 1941, p. 1), for the various forces behind religious change are better understood today than they were when Powicke wrote. Nevertheless, it remains true that statutes passed by Parliament effected the break with Rome and continued to define the basic character of the Church of England.

By the beginning of the sixteenth century, Parliament was well established as an integral part of the English constitution. It was composed of two branches—the House of Lords and the House of Commons. The Lords were summoned to Parliament because of their personal status, either as hereditary peers (the lords temporal) or as religious leaders (the archbishops, bishops, and heads of the larger monasteries, collectively called the lords spiritual). Before the Reformation the two groups were evenly balanced, with about fifty lords in each category, but nearly thirty abbots and priors disappeared after the dissolution of the monasteries in the 1530s, leaving the lords spiritual in a minority. The members of the Commons were elected. Each county in England returned two knights of the shire, while cities and towns that enjoyed representation named two burgesses. (Because of its size London had four burgesses, and the Welsh counties and boroughs, which gained representation in Parliament after 1536, sent single members.) A uniform franchise applied in the counties or shires—a forty-shilling freehold conferred the right to vote—but arrangements in the boroughs varied, and the franchise was generally restricted to the wealthier inhabitants. The size of the Commons rose from about three hundred members at the beginning of the sixteenth century to nearly twice that number at its end, mainly as a result of the enfranchisement of additional boroughs. It was rare for elections to be contested during the Tudor period; generally closed discussions took place before the election and a single candidate was presented for each position. The monarch enjoyed the power of summoning Parliament whenever it was thought desirable (usually when taxation was required) and could terminate sessions at will. Legislation required the affirmative vote of both houses and the assent of the sovereign, who had an absolute veto power and exercised it on several occasions. At the beginning of the Tudor period, the Lords were probably of greater importance than the Commons, but the role of the lower house grew significantly during the sixteenth century, and the Commons solidified a leading position during the reign of Elizabeth I. The Lords, however, retained more influence than the writings of Sir John Neale suggest.

The Henrician Reformation. Parliament's involvement in religious affairs began in 1529 with the summoning of what was to become known as the Reformation Parliament. During the summer of that year, a papal legatine court had met in London to consider Henry VIII's divorce from Catherine of Aragon. When the pope adjourned the court and revoked the case to Rome, Henry VIII dismissed his chief minister, Cardinal Thomas Wolsey. The king was probably unsure of his future course—certainly he had not yet determined to repudiate papal jurisdiction in England—and hoped that parliamentary discussion might assist his cause. The first session was primarily given over to complaints about Wolsey and about the greed of churchmen generally. In 1531 all the clergy of the realm were charged with violating the medieval statute of praemunire by supporting papal authority; they bought their pardon by paying more than £100,000 and acknowledging that the king was the supreme head of the church in England "as far as the word of God allows." In 1532 an act in conditional restraint of annates gave the king power to cut off financial payments to the papacy; the Supplication against the Ordinaries contained further charges against the church, and the Submission of the Clergy abandoned the principle of the independence of the church by acknowledging the king's right to assent to canons or veto them.

Henry's marital problems were not confronted directly until 1533. By then he had found a new chief minister of great ability, Thomas Cromwell, and he had replaced a conservative archbishop of Canterbury, William Warham, with a more flexible reformer, Thomas Cranmer. The Act in Restraint of Appeals gave the archbishop of Canterbury, not the pope, power to render a binding decision about the king's marriage, but its final version went much further and extinguished all papal jurisdiction in England. The famous preamble, drafted by Cromwell, declared that the realm of England was a self-contained "empire" not subject to any external authority, either secular or religious, and that Henry VIII was an emperor with greater powers than those held by mere kings. Following the passage of the act, Cranmer declared that Henry's marriage to Catherine had never been valid and ratified his marriage to Anne Boleyn.

In 1534 Parliament passed a variety of additional bills cutting all ties with the papacy and establishing the Church of England as a national institution, the king being its supreme head and the archbishop of Canterbury its religious leader. Payments previously sent to Rome (annates, or first fruits and tenths) were transferred to the monarch, who was also given binding power to designate bishops in England and Wales. The power of granting dispensations was transferred to the archbishop of Canterbury. The dissolution of the monasteries was begun under an act of 1536, which called for the closing of houses receiving an income under £200 a year; the suppression of larger religious houses was confirmed by a second statute passed in 1539. Two new financial bureaus were established, the Court of First Fruits and Tenths to handle collection of payments from the clergy and the Court of Augmentations to oversee the dissolution of the monasteries and administer their estates.

The Reformation Parliament was dissolved in 1536. Its activities were not limited to religious change; social and economic reforms of considerable significance were also enacted under Thomas Cromwell's leadership. Several parliaments met later in Henry's reign. These continued to deal with Henry VIII's marital problems and with succession to the throne. They also reflected growing tensions in religion, as conservatives led by Stephen Gardiner, bishop of Winchester, and Thomas Howard, duke of Norfolk, opposed reforms espoused by Cromwell and Cranmer. Among the conservative measures passed by Parliament were the Act of Six Articles (1539), which reaffirmed belief in transubstantiation and clerical celibacy (although Cranmer himself had married), and the Act for the Advancement of True Religion (1543), which limited the right of lay people to read English translations of the Bible.

Edward VI and Mary. Protestant reform reached its high point in England during the brief reign of the boy king Edward VI (r. 1547–1553). A parliamentary act confirmed the dissolution of the chantries, whose endowments were taken over by the government in 1547 on the grounds that prayers for the dead were superstitious and unavailing. The first *Book of Common Prayer* was brought into use by the 1549 Act of Uniformity, and Cranmer's more radical revision of 1552 was also confirmed by statute.

Although Mary Tudor (r. 1553–1558) believed that Parliament should not have been involved in the establishment of religion, she was forced to use Parliament as the constitutional instrument for the restoration of papal jurisdiction. Her first Act of Repeal (1553) undid the work of Edward's parliaments, thus restoring the Latin Mass in place of the vernacular prayer book, and her second act (1554) repealed Henry VIII's legislation as well, reestablishing the church as it had been before 1529. It was at a joint session of the two houses of Parliament that Cardinal Reginald Pole, Mary's archbishop of Canterbury, absolved the realm of the sins of heresy and schism and received England back into the papal fold.

The Elizabethan Settlement. When Mary died without heirs in 1558, the throne passed to her half sister Elizabeth, Henry VIII's daughter by Anne Boleyn. Unlike Mary (Catherine of Aragon's daughter) Elizabeth had been brought up as a Protestant, and it was inevitable that Mary's religious program would be reversed. The Elizabethan Settlement was enacted by the Parliament of 1559. It contained two major pieces of legislation—the Act of Supremacy, which gave the queen the title "Supreme Governor of the Church" rather than "Supreme Head," and the Act of Uniformity, which again mandated the use of *The Book of Common Prayer.* The prayer book of 1559 was based on the 1552 version but incorporated a few significant changes in the direction of ambiguity and moderation. Sir John Neale's dramatic account of the split between conservatives in the Lords and reformers led by Marian Exiles in the Commons was based on inadequate evidence and has now been discredited by Norman Jones and Sir Geoffrey Elton. Nevertheless, it remains true that the Elizabethan Settlement was a moderate compromise intended to make it possible for people of divergent personal views to find a home in the established church. The Thirty-Nine Articles of Religion, based on the Forty-Two Articles written by Cranmer shortly before the death of Edward VI, were ratified by Parliament in 1563, completing the settlement by giving it a staunchly Protestant theological basis.

Elizabeth never conceded that there were major flaws in the settlement of 1559, imperfect though it might have been, and she never countenanced further religious change through statute. Puritan reformers introduced bills calling for additional reforms in most of her parliaments. Designed to eliminate remaining bits of "popery and superstition," these would have reduced the powers of bishops and provided for further revision of the prayer book. The queen found various ways of preventing such measures from becoming law, and although she held the veto power, she was not forced to use it. Neale's account of the Elizabethan parliaments focuses attention on the Puritans and identifies a "choir" of Puritan leaders who were active in the Commons, but Elton and other later writers demolish the notion of an organized "choir" and suggest that pressure for reform was more sporadic and less well coordinated. During Elizabeth's last years the reformers finally realized that there would be no change in the state church during the queen's lifetime. Some Separatists left the church, and a few even left England in pursuit of religious freedom.

The Elizabethan parliaments were more active in fields other than religion. Frequent tax bills provided funding for military activities, including the defeat of the Spanish Armada, as well as wars in the Netherlands and Ireland. Economic and social measures were especially important. The Statute of Apprentices or Artificers (1563) confirmed the seven-year period of apprenticeship for craftsmen and attempted to regulate working conditions and wages. The Poor Law of 1601 codified existing legislation dealing with poverty and vagrancy, placing the responsibility for poor relief on the parish rather than the central government. When the queen's early parliaments urged her to marry, she countered the requests with eloquent but meaningless answers. The threat to Elizabeth's security posed by Mary Stuart was discussed in several sessions; Parliament advocated her execution some years before the queen acquiesced. The problem of succession to the throne also concerned Parliament, but Elizabeth was never willing to designate a successor despite Parliament's insistence that she do so. Elizabeth delivered her famous "Golden Speech" at the end of her last parliament in 1601, and members are said to have wept as they pressed forward to kiss her hand.

The parliamentary privileges of free speech and freedom from arrest during sessions were first requested formally by Sir Thomas More, speaker of the Commons in 1523, although they may have been traditional earlier. The monarch granted these privileges at the beginning of each session, but the right of free speech was often thought to extend only to appropriate topics, not including religion unless that subject was opened to debate by royal consent. Elizabeth sent several members of the Commons to the Tower for criticizing her religious policies (among them the notable Puritan brothers Peter and Paul Wentworth), and the Stuart sovereigns frequently reprimanded Parliament for trespassing on the royal prerogative by discussing religion, foreign policy, or the private life of the king and his favorites. Several documents dating from the early seventeenth century—the Apology of Commons (1604), the Petition of 1610, and the Great Protestation (1621)—reflect the Commons' growing insistence on the right to debate all issues of national concern. Our knowledge of parliamentary activity is fuller after 1547, when the Commons Journal becomes available. The Lords Journal exists, with gaps, from 1509. Individual members began keeping private diaries during Elizabeth's reign; since the official journals are brief and formal, these add greatly to our understanding of parliamentary debate. It has been suggested that rhetoric grew increasingly elaborate at the beginning of the seventeenth century, partly because members began following the rhetorical traditions of ancient Greek and Roman oratory and partly because of the interest in historical precedent demonstrated by a number of highly learned lawyers in the Commons. The early Stuart kings complained on several occasions that Parliament spent too much time talking, and not enough dealing expeditiously with proposed legislation.

The Early Stuarts and the Civil War. Parliament was not actively involved in religious matters under the early Stuarts. The Puritans did present James I with the notable Millenary Petition in 1603, calling for a wide variety of reforms, but the king's response was to have their issues discussed in a special gathering, the Hampton Court Conference (1604), rather than in Parliament. The increasingly Arminian complexion of the church under Archbishop William Laud (consecrated in 1633) would almost certainly have been attacked by Parliament but for the fact that Charles I summoned no sessions between 1629 and 1640 (the period of his "personal rule"). Accumulated religious grievances, both in England and in Scotland, and the insensitivity of the king and archbishop to the religious views of subjects can be counted among the underlying causes of the English Civil War.

Charles I's religious policies for Scotland, in particular his attempt to force a service book on the unwilling Scottish church, led to the outbreak of warfare between the Scottish Covenanters and the king. After his failure to defeat the Scots in the First Bishops' War (1639), Charles was forced to summon Parliament in the hope of obtaining funds for his army. The Short Parliament (1640) broke down without any agreement between the king and the Commons, but the problem persisted and Charles convened the Long Parliament later in the year. The demands of the Scots following the Second Bishops' War were so insistent that the king had to accept various reforms in order to obtain money. Charles's attempt to arrest five members of the Commons thought to be the leaders of opposition to his policies failed in January 1642 and led to further estrangement between the two sides. Both the king and Parliament raised armies, and the English Civil War began in August. After serious military defeats the king surrendered in 1646. He was condemned to death by a court convened on the order of Parliament and was executed 30 January 1649. By this time the royalists had left Parliament, and the House of Commons had been subject to Pride's Purge, in which moderates were prevented from taking their seats, leaving only religious and political radicals in the Commons. This remnant was nicknamed the Rump.

Parliament and the Interregnum. Both the monarchy and the House of Lords were abolished in 1649, when England was turned into a Commonwealth and Free State governed by the House of Commons. The religious policy of the Commonwealth mandated both a Presbyterian state church and toleration for the Independents. Such a settlement had become inevitable after the conclusion of the Solemn League and Covenant between England and Scotland (1643); the establishment of Presbyterianism in England, as in Scotland, was the price the English had to pay for a military alliance with the Scots in the civil war. The Anglican church was dismantled, and the properties of the bishops and cathedral chapters were confiscated. Parliament was reshaped in various ways during the Interregnum (1649–1660). The Parliament of Saints, also called the Nominated Parliament or Barebones' Parliament, met in 1653. Its members were nominated by Independent congregations and actually selected by army officers. When this system of government failed, England experienced the novelty of a written constitution, drafted by army leaders and called the Instrument of Government, which recognized Oliver Cromwell's paramount position as commander of the army by making him lord protector of England, Scotland, and Ireland. The composition of Parliament was reformed by the Instrument of Government. Later a second house, comparable to the former House of Lords, was instituted by a second written constitution, the Humble Petition and Advice (1657). But the government remained unstable, and the Protectorate came to an end following the death of Cromwell in 1658 and the resignation of his son and successor the following year.

The Restoration, 1660. The traditional structure of Parliament was restored along with the monarchy in 1660, when Charles II was crowned king. Parliament ordered the restoration of the Church of England as well. Lands confiscated from bishops and cathedrals were returned to their original owners. Although Charles himself favored a broad state church with toleration for those who wished to remain outside it, a narrow Anglican establishment was instituted by Parliament. The so-called Clarendon Code, somewhat inappropriately named for the king's chief minister Edward Hyde, earl of Clarendon, ratified the 1662 *Book of Common Prayer*, which was similar in substance to the 1559 book. More than two thousand Nonconformist clergy were deprived under the 1662 Act of Uniformity. The Clarendon Code also included the Conventicle Act and the Five-Mile Act, both of which established penalties for unauthorized Nonconformist worship. Parliament forced Charles to abandon his plan to grant toleration to Roman Catholics through a Declaration of Indulgence and, following the trumped-up Popish Plot of 1678, it passed the Papists' Disabling Act, under which Catholics continued to be excluded from Parliament until the nineteenth century.

An important development of Charles II's reign was the growth of rival political parties. Although competing factions can be identified as early as the 1530s, fully developed parties that contested parliamentary elections on the basis of differing policies did not exist until the 1670s. The Tories grew out of the court party, which supported the pro-French and pro-Catholic position of Charles II, while the "country" party developed into the Whigs, a staunchly Protestant group that included Nonconformist sympathizers, who opposed Charles's actions. The chief policy of the Whigs was exclusion: they sought to prevent a Roman Catholic like Charles's brother James, duke of York, from succeeding to the throne. Exclusion bills were introduced in several parliaments, but Charles was able to block their passage, and James became king in 1685.

The Glorious Revolution. Although James II promised that he would not tamper with the existing religious settlement, he soon began to introduce pro-Catholic measures, including a new Declaration of Indulgence. Opposition came to a head in 1688, when James's second wife, Mary of Modena, gave birth to a son, James Francis Edward (later to be known as the Old Pretender). Prior to this time James's heirs had been his daughters Mary and Anne, whose mother, Clarendon's daughter Anne Hyde, had brought them up as Protestants. When a son who would be raised a Catholic supplanted them as heir apparent, leaders of both parties joined in the Glorious Revolution. James was forced to flee to France, and Parliament conferred the crown on Mary and her husband, William of Orange, as joint rulers. A few conservative Anglican clergy felt unable to swear the oath of loyalty to the new rulers required by Parliament since they thought it contravened the divinely ordained principle of hereditary succession. For a generation these nonjurors formed a small unofficial branch of the Anglican church; their differences from the established body lay more in the area of political theory than in theology or liturgy.

Although the Glorious Revolution enjoyed bipartisan support, it was in some sense a victory for the Whigs, and the Whig party dominated politics during most of the early eighteenth century. The parliamentary settlement enacted following the revolution justified the exclusion of Roman Catholics from the throne and from Parliament. Indeed, some new restrictions were placed on Catholics. Protestant Nonconformists benefited from the Toleration Act of 1689, which granted religious freedom to those Nonconformists who professed belief in the Trinity.

Parliament played a major role in determining religious policy in England during the period following the Reformation. The state church was established by statute, and penalties on those who remained outside it were mandated by parliamentary acts. Parliament itself grew in power during these years. Once Parliament legislated about religion, as it did under Henry VIII, it could not be kept out of ecclesiastical matters. Its involvement in religious issues provides one of the key strands in the development of Parliament's role in sixteenth- and seventeenth-century English politics.

[*See also* Acts of Supremacy; Acts of Uniformity; *and* Elizabethan Settlement.]

BIBLIOGRAPHY

Elton, G. R. *The Parliament of England, 1559–1581*. Cambridge, 1986. A revision of Neale; demolishes the concept of a Puritan choir.

Graves, Michael A. R. *The Tudor Parliaments: Crown, Lords and Commons, 1485–1603*. London, 1985. A brief general account, particularly useful for the period before 1529.

Jones, J. R. *The First Whigs*. Reprint, Westport, Conn., 1985. Perhaps the best account of Parliament and politics in the later seventeenth century.

Jones, Norman L. *Faith by Statute: Parliament and the Settlement of Religion, 1559*. London, 1982. Revises Neale's interpretation of the Elizabethan Settlement.

Lehmberg, Stanford E. *The Reformation Parliament, 1529–1536*. Cambridge, 1970.

———. *The Later Parliaments of Henry VIII, 1536-1547*. Cambridge, 1977. These volumes provide a narrative of Parliament's activity, summarize legislation, and discuss the membership of the two houses.

Loach, Jennifer. *Parliament and the Crown in the Reign of Mary Tudor*. Oxford, 1986.

Neale, J. E. *Elizabeth I and Her Parliaments, 1559–1581*. London, 1953.

———. *Elizabeth I and Her Parliaments, 1584–1601*. London, 1957. Neale's classic narrative is marred by his excessive concentration on issues which divided the queen and the Commons.

———. *The Elizabethan House of Commons*. Rev. ed. London, 1976. Focuses on membership, elections, and procedure.

Notestein, Wallace. *The House of Commons, 1604–1610*. New Haven, 1971. Although based on a lifetime of scholarship, this study was already old-fashioned at the time of its publication.

Russell, Conrad. *Parliaments and English Politics, 1621–1629*. Corr. ed. Oxford, 1982.

———. *The Causes of the English Civil War*. Oxford, 1990.

———. *The Fall of the British Monarchies, 1637–1642*. Oxford, 1991. Rather surprisingly, these studies by the acknowledged master of Stuart parliamentary history play down the importance of Parliament in English politics.

STANFORD E. LEHMBERG

PARMA, DUKE OF. *See* Farnese, Alessandro (1542–1592).

PARR, Katherine (1513/14–1548), first Protestant queen of England, and sixth wife (and widow) of Henry VIII. Parr is triply significant as a founding figure of the English Reformation: (1) in the educational and nurturing roles she played as cherished stepmother of two eventual monarchs, Edward VI and Elizabeth I, and guardian of Lady Jane Grey; (2) in her patronage of such early Protestant luminaries as Hugh Latimer, Miles Coverdale, John Cheke, Roger Ascham, Anthony Cooke, Nicholas Udall, and John Parkhurst; and (3) in her authorship of two pioneering vernacular works of Reformation piety, *Prayers or Meditations* and *The Lamentation of a Sinner.*

Thanks to prudent provision by her widowed mother, Katherine became a childhood intimate of Princess Mary Tudor (b. 1516). Katherine's mother, Lady Maud Parr, was one of Catherine of Aragon's principal ladies-in-waiting, and apparently also the administrator of the royal nursery, where she could arrange for her three children's education together with Princess Mary's (Katherine was 2 years older than Princess Mary). Under Juan Luis Vives's state-of-the-art tutelage, the girls received a grounding in Latin and the core texts of Christian humanism. Meagerly dowered, Katherine at thirty was left wealthy, widowed, and childless after two marriages to great landed lords of the north, both Catholic and both many years her senior. Marriage to the first, Edward, Lord Borough of Gainsborough, lasted from 1526 to 1529; and to the second, John Neville, Lord Latimer, from 1533 to 1543. Within weeks of resuming court life, the disinclined Katherine found herself the latest nuptial choice of King Henry VIII, whom she married in a public ceremony in July 1543 at which Stephen Gardiner and Thomas Cranmer officiated. Quickly making stellar virtue of dire necessity, Katherine won not only Henry's political trust (he formally named her regent of the realm during his military campaign in France in July–October 1544) but also his personal compliance (through her efforts he reconciled with his daughters, Mary and Elizabeth, rejoining them with the young Edward in the immediate family circle).

Given the impeccable Catholic affiliations of her past, Katherine's embrace of Protestantism proves the crucial (though nowhere directly documented) development of this same period; apparently she was converted by Cranmer, with whom as principal councillor she, as regent, consulted daily throughout the summer of 1544. With time Henry would confront evidence of his queen's Protestantism, but from this earlier date its repercussions are clearly discernible. Edward was nearly five and Elizabeth twelve when Katherine became their stepmother; with the power of the regency she stepped forward as the guarantor of their education under Protestant humanists by securing Cheke's and Ascham's (and subsequently Cooke's) appointment as their tutors. Loving letters addressing Katherine as "mother" and crediting her with inspiring their studies survive in Edward's and Elizabeth's youthful handwriting.

By 1545–1546 Katherine had gained a controversial reputation for reading and discussing scripture in her chambers; in this connection Hugh Latimer and Nicholas Ridley attended on the queen and her circle of ladies. The conservative court faction led by Gardiner nearly succeeded in alienating Henry's affections from Katherine on imputations of the capital offense of heresy. By a timely act of submission to the king's superior wisdom, she was able to save her credit and her life, although not that of her friend, Ann Askew, who went to the stake in July 1546. Undeterred but ever circumspect, Katherine moved to provide more widely for vernacular scriptural instruction by sponsoring a translation of Erasmus's Latin *Paraphrases in Novum Testamentum* (Paraphrases upon the New Testament; 1519) and recruiting Princess Mary's help with the project. On its eventual publication in 1548–1549, early in Edward's reign, the English *Paraphrases* bore four dedications to Queen Katherine from Nicholas Udall, general editor (with Coverdale) of these two large volumes that were to share with the English Bible the honor of being prescribed by royal injunction for public access in the parish churches of the realm.

Most significantly, in the risky era of Henry's declining years, Katherine braved authorship to put her Protestantism on record under her own name, dedicating to her jealous, irascible spouse her *Prayers or Meditations* in December 1545. Subtly recasting and reordering excerpts from the *Imitation of Christ* in Richard Whytford's translation, this work excises the original's monastic framework and makes its Christic affectivity directly accessible to pious laity of both genders. In her second work, however, Katherine's devotion gradated too daringly into social complaint and authoritative assertion to make publication a possibility before November 1547, nine months after Henry's death. By turns evocative of Erasmus, Cranmer, and Latimer, *The Lamentation of a Sinner* begins in Lutheran-Pauline self-accounting (including notable declarations on justification by faith and the crucifixion of Christ as the central truth of God's word) but subsequently opens into a survey of the estates of the realm, whom Katherine exhorts to a new sense of vocation and zeal for God's kingdom by taking scripture to their hearts as she has done. Here her first-person reflections on wifehood, household duties, and social comportment strikingly anticipate later Puritan treatments of gender roles and marriage (for example, William Gouge's *Of Domestical Duties*, 1622). Likewise prescient of later Puritan bibliocracy (such as Milton's *Paradise Regained*, bk. 4, ll. 286–364) is Katherine's letter to the fellows of Cambridge University in February 1546. They had implored her to intercede with Henry and prevent his confiscation of their properties; in return for her success with the king she urges them to set the gospel first in their learning and make Cambridge much more famous for divine philosophy than Athens ever was for natural and moral philosophy.

In May 1547 Katherine, a royal widow for four months, married for the fourth time in her first love match—with Thomas Seymour, younger brother of the lord protector, Edward Seymour, duke of Somerset, both uncles of the now boy-king. Soon Katherine, no less than Edward VI, became a pawn in the struggle that locked the power-hungry Seymour brothers in an elimination contest. The new regime sharply curtailed certain of her former prerogatives, suspending (on divergent grounds) Katherine's close intimacy with both Edward and Elizabeth. Her romantic passion for Thomas Seymour bore fatal fruit, moreover, in her one and only pregnancy: the daughter, Mary, whom Katherine bore in late August 1548 before dying six days later of puerperal fever. The former queen's Protestant funeral, comprised of scripture readings, psalm-singing, and a sermon by Coverdale, was the first such for royalty in England. As for the infant Mary—an ongoing subject of speculation by her mother's biographers—she was orphaned by her father's execution for high treason in March 1549 and, according to John Parkhurst's Latin epitaph on her in his *Ludicra sive epigrammata juvenilia* (1573), followed her parents in death before she had learned to speak.

BIBLIOGRAPHY

Martienssen, Anthony. *Queen Katherine Parr.* London and New York, 1973. Builds on the compilation of documentary sources (especially Parr's letters) and on summaries of the accounts by Reformation chroniclers. Regrettably, no full-length annotated biography of Katherine Parr exists.

Mueller, Janel. "A Tudor Queen Finds Voice: Katherine Parr's *Lamentation of a Sinner.*" In *The Historical Renaissance*, edited by Heather Dubrow and Richard Strier, pp. 15–47. Chicago and London, 1988.

———. "Devotion as Difference: Intertextuality in Queen Katherine Parr's *Prayers or Meditations.*" *Huntington Library Quarterly* 53 (1990), 171–197.

Strickland, Agnes. "Katharine Parr, Sixth Queen of Henry VIII." In *Lives of the Queens of England* (1861), vol. 2, pp. 390–473. Reprint, Bath, 1972.

JANEL MUELLER

PARSONS, Robert (also Persons; 1546–1610), English Jesuit missionary, controversialist, and superior. Elected a fellow of Balliol College, Oxford, in 1568, Parsons resigned his position in 1574 for religious reasons. He entered the Jesuits the following year. Ordained in Rome in 1578, he was named superior of the small group of Jesuits who initiated the society's mission to England in 1580. Shortly after the capture of his fellow Jesuit Edmund Campion in 1581, Parsons returned to the Continent to write and to confer with William Allen, the president of the English college in Douai.

Throughout the 1580s Parsons and Allen were involved in negotiations concerning a possible invasion of England or Scotland to aid James VI of Scotland and the captive Mary Stuart. After the execution of Mary in 1587 and James's reconciliation with Queen Elizabeth I, Allen and Parsons abandoned the Stuarts and supported Princess Isabella of Spain as Elizabeth's successor. After the defeat of the Spanish Armada in 1588, Parsons worked in Spain on the establishment of more seminaries and colleges for the preservation of English Catholicism. These included Valladolid and Seville in Spain and Saint Omers in Flanders. At the same time, he used his influence with King Philip II of Spain to prevent royal interference in an intra-Jesuit battle between a Spanish faction and Claudio Acquaviva, the Jesuit superior-general.

Because of disturbances at the English college in Rome, he was named rector there in 1597. The problems, however, were aggravated the following year with the introduction of two novel structures: an archpriest to govern the secular clergy in England and a prefect (Parsons) to coordinate the activities of English Jesuits in the Continental seminaries and on the mission. Both resulted in conflict. Nevertheless, he remained rector and prefect until his death in 1610.

The majority of Parsons's thirty books treat the political and controversial issues of the period. His most important, *The First Book of Christian Resolution* (subsequently called *The Christian Directory*), was later purified and published for Anglican use.

BIBLIOGRAPHY

Primary Source

Allison, A. F., and D. M. Rogers. *The Contemporary Printed Literature of the English Counter-Reformation between 1558–1640*. Vol. 1, *Languages Other Than English*; vol. 2, *English*. London, 1989, 1994. Contains full bibliographical details regarding the works of Parsons, many of which were written under an alias.

Secondary Sources

Clancy, Thomas H. *Papist Pamphleteers: The Allen-Persons Party and the Political Thought of the Counter-Reformation in England, 1572–1615*. Chicago, 1964.

Holmes, Peter. *Resistance and Compromise: The Political Thought of the Elizabethan Catholics*. Cambridge, 1982. Holmes rejects the traditional division of English recusants into factions and insists that all their political writings follow the same pattern. Unfortunately this pattern often seems to be rather an imposition by the author than a conclusion from the evidence.

McCoog, Thomas M. *Monumenta Angliae*. Rome, 1992. See vol. 2, pp. 432–433, for a full bibliography on Parsons.

Reynolds, E. E. *Campion and Parsons*. London, 1980. Despite the title, this says little about Parsons after the death of Campion.

THOMAS M. MCCOOG, S.J.

PATRISTICS.

The writings of the early church became available in the course of the fifteenth century. Italian humanists such as Leonardo Bruni and Guarino of Verona were interested in Greek and Latin patristic writings primarily as educational material and found that the works of, for example, Basil of Caesarea and Jerome provided excellent moral as well as stylistic models for their pupils. Moreover, theological activity around the church councils, particularly the Council of Florence (1438–1445), meant an increase of interest in the writings of the Greek church, which were made available to the West in Latin translation. Although the translations were by and large tendentious and of poor literary quality, some works of Eusebius of Caesarea, the Cappadocian fathers, Cyril of Alexandria, and so on, were available only in that form until well into the sixteenth century. Among the most important "conciliar" translators or patrons of translators were George of Trebizond (1396–1486), Ambrogio Traversari (c.1386–1439), the General of the Camaldolese order favorable to a union with the Greek church; and Cardinal John Bessarion (1403–1472). In addition, certain monastic communities became centers of patristic learning, partly because of their desire to reform and partly because of general interest in classical culture that extended to pagan and Christian writings. Notable communities included the Benedictine Congregation of Santa Giustina of Padua and, to a certain degree, the Augustinian friars in Germany, some of whose congregations became centers of an Augustine renaissance.

Interest in the early church continued and indeed increased with the Reformation, when it became necessary to evaluate the relationship between patristic testimony and that of the scripture. Thus, although the main medieval collections of patristic testimonies—Thomas Aquinas's *Catena aurea*, the *Decree of Gratian*, and the glossed Bible—continued to be used and used extensively, the reformers and their opponents could also draw on and add to the stock of early Christian writings that had become available in their own time. Both the Protestants and the Roman church produced their share of eminent theologians who were also patristic scholars, such as Philipp Melanchthon, Johann Fabri, and in the later generation Théodore de Bèze, Matthias Flacius Illyricus, and Roberto Bellarmino.

The Reformers' View of the Early Church. Martin Luther's attitude is difficult to sum up in a few words. He uses patristic material extensively in his *Biblical Commentaries*, often taking it from medieval collections such as the glossed Bible. In his 1523 *Order of Service* he expresses strong approval of additions to the service made by what he calls "the first Fathers," claiming among other things that it was Athanasius and Cyprian who added the psalms to be sung before the *Benedictus.* The reformer knew patristic writings well enough to be able to assess in the *Von den Konziliis und Kirchen* (1539) the value of their authority as against that of scripture and to note that, unlike scripture, each Father and each council treated only a few subjects, never "the entire doctrine of the Christian faith." In the *Von den Konziliis* Luther enumerates the main Fathers and their principal contributions to Christian doctrine in a way that suggests familiarity with the early Christian writings that had become available in his own time.

Luther's colleague, Melanchthon, a patristic scholar himself, went more deeply into questions of patristic authority, although his basic view is not radically different from Luther's. Melanchthon too insists that the Fathers and councils treated only some aspects of Christian doctrine and are not to be quoted indiscriminately even on such aspects of it as they did treat. Melanchthon's patrology, *De ecclesia et de authoritate verbi Dei* (translated into French in 1543 and 1550), is a brief and careful assessment of the "strong and weak points" of the church councils and Fathers. While Melanchthon's exact criteria for sifting patristic evidence have not yet been established, it is plain that he sets out to criticize all early Christian doctrine that bears a resemblance to the Roman abuses criticized by Luther (e.g., Cyprian's pronouncements on grace are to be treated with circumspection) and to commend all patristic teaching that bears out the early creeds, particularly as regards doctrines such as the Trinity or infant baptism for which there is no clear biblical support. The reliability of each early Christian author is commensurate with his proximity to apostolic times. Melanchthon's *De ecclesia* was a precursor of the patrologies of Martin Chemnitz (published in 1591) and Johann Gerhard (published posthumously in 1653).

This view of patristic authority meant that the early creeds assumed a new importance. The Nicene Creed and the Apostles' Creed (the latter especially for the Swiss and Genevan Reformed churches) became the documents that linked scripture to the early church. The Apostles' Creed lent itself particularly well to that interpretation, given that the medieval tradition attributing each of the twelve articles to one of the apostles (based on Pseudo-Augustine's *Sermon* no. 240) was not shaken by Erasmus's attempts to redate the creed as a fourth-century document in his *Ratio* of 1520.

In the context of the Swiss and Strasbourg Reformation one witnesses for the first time a wholesale attempt to appropriate and in some ways neutralize the writings of the early church, prior to evaluating their merits and demerits in a more nuanced manner. The Swiss reformers were familiar with contemporary patristic scholarship. Zwingli had a large personal library containing a number of editions of the Fathers (notably Origen, Jerome, and Augustine) that he annotated. Johannes Oecolampadius was responsible for a considerable number of editions and (Latin) translations of the Fathers, several dating from before his conversion. Particularly well known at the time was his 1520 Latin translation of (Pseudo-) John of Damascus's treatise on prayers for the dead, a translation characterized by its Lutheran slant.

Yet the Swiss reformers' method of appropriating the early church did not have to do with any a priori favorable attitude to the early church but with the theological pressure placed on them by their Roman adversaries, especially Johann Eck and Johannes Fabri. In the Baden Disputation of 1526 Oecolampadius could not argue from scripture without exposing himself to the charge of spiritualism or subjectivity. He thus had recourse to early Christian writings and found himself citing the same patristic sources (e.g., the newly discovered *Adversus haereses* by Irenaeus) as did Eck to prove the opposite viewpoint, finally yielding to Eck's superior debating skills. At the Bern Disputation of 1528 the reformers redefined the doctrine of the true church and identified the latter with the minority of the faithful, distinct from the official (Roman) church. (This doctrine was first developed in the conciliar period by William of Ockham and others and then elaborated by Luther.) Thus the reformers could place the Fathers among the faithful minority stretching from scripture, through the Apostles' Creed, and all the way to the reformers themselves.

This tacit appropriation of the early church is particularly evident in Martin Bucer's *Gospel Commentaries* (1527–1528), in which the Fathers, although hardly mentioned by name, are seen to serve as the direct source of his exegesis. In his *Romans Commentary* (1536), Bucer cites the Fathers overtly, and his view of their exegesis is much more critical. So far as ecclesiological and liturgical matters are concerned, Bucer's compilation of extracts from the Fathers, begun in the late 1530s, makes it plain that the Strasbourg reformers saw the early church as a direct model and that medieval collections of patristic excerpts, and especially the *Decree of Gratian,* were as important to them as more recent editions.

The same can be said of the Genevan reformer John Calvin. There is no doubt that he initially acquired his knowledge of the Fathers from medieval collections such as the *Decree of Gratian* and supplemented it subsequently by a reading of Erasmian and other editions. Although seeing his doctrines as being in line with the pure doctrines of the early church, Calvin is both critical and cavalier in his use of patristic writings and occasionally "adjusts" them to suit his own teaching. The tendency to use early Christian writers as precursors to the Reformation or to the doctrines of the Roman church without paying much attention to their historical contexts became a widespread phenomenon in the later sixteenth century.

Erasmus and the Humanists. Erasmus's contribution to the diffusion of patristic writings was quantitatively and qualitatively of great importance. Between 1516 and 1536 he edited or partially edited works of Jerome, Cyprian, Arnobius the Younger, Hilary of Poitiers, John Chrysostom, Irenaeus, Ambrose, (Pseudo-)Athanasius, Augustine, Lactantius, Basil of Caesarea, and Origen. Some have seen Erasmus's interest in the early church as an attempt to recapture the "golden age" of theology, while others have viewed it as part of a program to reform the church, a program announced by the 1516 edition of the New Testament. It is also likely that Erasmus used the Fathers as moral and linguistic models and also as examples of fluidity of doctrine, thus making the point that it was not advisable to lay down hard-and-fast distinctions between orthodoxy and heresy in his own time.

Much more critical in his approach than most of his contemporaries, Erasmus was the first to address himself seriously to the problem of misattribution of early Christian writings. Using largely stylistic criteria, he was sometimes led astray (e.g., in questioning Basil of Caesarea's authorship of *De Spiritu sancto*). At other times he persisted in misattributing certain works (e.g., Arnobius the Younger's *Psalms Commentary* to Arnobius the Elder) in the face of stylistic and external evidence. In his *Treatise of the Corruption of Scripture, Councels and Fathers* (1611) Thomas James (c.1573–1624), one of the first Protestant scholars to concern himself with textual accuracy over and above his polemical interests, while praising Erasmus's achievements, criticized him for never citing variant readings and for not giving any precise description or location of manuscripts he had used. Criticized frequently by the Roman church, Erasmus's patristic editions found favor with the reformers.

Erasmus's combination of interest in both doctrine and text of early Christian writings was not shared by Christian humanists such as Beatus Rhenanus. Editor of Eusebius Rufinus's *Ecclesiastical History*, Cassiodorus's *Historia tripartita* (1523), and the *Works* of Tertullian (1521), Rhenanus, while taking the early church as model for the church of his own time, rarely assesses the subtleties of its doctrine.

Reformation and Counter-Reformation Patristic Scholarship. Outside Christian humanist circles patristic scholarship rapidly polarized into "Protestant" and "Catholic," each side claiming its descent from the apostolic church and identifying the adversary with ancient heretics. Both sides considered splinter groups such as the antitrinitarians a revival of Arianism. Patristic materials were therefore published to serve more as polemical weapons than as works of reference or history. Among the leading Protestant patristic scholars of the period are the Bern reformer Wolfgang Musculus, the Schwenckfeldian Johannes Lange, the physician Janus Cornarus, and, in Calvinist circles, the Estiennes, Théodore de Bèze, and Simon Goulart. In Protestant and Roman Catholic circles alike, much of the work of propagating the early Christian writings was accomplished by learned printers or printers' correctors. Among the Protestants, the best examples are the Estiennes in Geneva and Johann Froben's corrector Sigismund Gelenius (c.1498–1554), who edited the 1547 Latin translation of Chrysostom.

While Robert I Estienne's Greek editions, such as that of Justin Martyr of 1551, do not show any overt confessional prejudice, Musculus's 1540 Latin translation of Basil's *Ascetica magna* was produced with the express aim of showing that the Capadocian was a direct precursor of the Reformation, and that his rule had been written for nonmonastic Christian communities. Similarly Lange's *Justin Martyr* (1565) contained marginal glosses on the Eucharist that were distinctly Schwenckfeldian in tone. Equally marked by polemical interests is Théodore de Bèze's 1570 Greek-Latin edition of *Dialogi quinque de sancta Trinitate* (wrongly attributed by him to Athanasius) and other patristic pieces. Bèze states he is using the works to show the antitrinitarians that their doctrines are a revival of Arianism and to prove to the (Polish) Roman church that the trinitarian teaching of the reformers is in line with that of Athanasius and therefore could not have given rise to antitrinitarianism.

Other noteworthy examples of Protestant patristic scholarship include the *Historia ecclesiae Christi*, familiarly known as the *Magdeburg Centuries*. Covering the period from New Testament times to the thirteenth century, the work (in 13 volumes) was published in Basel (1559–1574) after having been written, partly in Magdeburg, by various authors on the idea of Matthias Flacius Illyricus. Based on a wealth of patristic material, it presents the events of each century in sixteen commonplaces: doctrine, heresies, and so on. Lutheranism is depicted as a return to the apostolic church, free from all error. Cesare Baronio's *Annales ecclesiastici* (1588–1607) constituted the Roman response to it.

Patristic writings did, to some extent, penetrate to the wider mass of the faithful in Reformation territories. A large number of extracts from the Fathers, or *florilegia* (mostly based on Hermannus Bodius's *Unio dissidentium* of 1527), on topics such as justification by faith appeared between 1530 and 1565. They were no doubt intended for preachers and are to be sharply distinguished from *florilegia* that some reformers compiled for themselves, such as that of Martin Bucer. In Lutheran circles the expurgated editions of medieval *Vitae patrum*, published in the 1530s and 1540s, were expressly destined for the "ministers of the word." The church ordinances of Braunschweig, Soest, and Bremen drawn up in the 1530s order that parish libraries contain the works of Augustine, Ambrose, and Jerome.

In Calvinist circles some attempts were made to translate early Christian writings into the vernacular, for example, Marie Dentière's French translation of Cyprian on female apparel issued in 1561 as support for the Geneva ordinances on clothing, or the (more ambitious) 1578 French translation of Theodoret of Cyrrhus by Simon Goulart.

Roman Catholic patristic scholarship was characterized by its energetic efforts to uncover and publish early Christian writings, particularly during and after the Council of Trent. The manuscript collection of Cardinal Guglielmo Sirleto was unmatched in Protestant circles. Among other distinguished Roman Catholic patristic scholars are Pietro Francesco Zini; translator of several Greek fathers into Latin, Antonello Arcimboldi; the Jesuit Antonio Possevino; and the "reformists" around Cardinal Gasparo Contarini, who saw the early church as a viable model for moderate reforms. Patristic studies also flourished in France, thanks to the efforts of men like Jacques de Billy, Joachim Perion (both Benedictines), Gentien Hervet, and Margarin de la Bigne, the somewhat careless compiler of the first (controversial) *Bibliotheca patrum sanctorum* (1575–1579), a precursor to the *Patrology* of J.-P. Migne. Printers also played a part, the most interesting example here being the Parisian widow Charlotte Guillard, who worked out a program of publication of the major Greek and Latin fathers to combat (the Protestant) heresy. Produced by Guillard's corrector, Louis Miré, the Carthusian Gottfried Tilmann, and others, the Guillard publications showed great confessional prejudice. Only toward the end of the century did scholars such as Thomas James on the Protestant side and the French Jesuit Fronto Ducaeus, one of the most eminent patristic scholars of the late sixteenth century, show an interest in textual criticism, without, however, abandoning their polemical stance.

In Reformed circles the first years of the seventeenth century mark the appearance of patristic manuals by Abraham Scultetus (*Medullae Patrum Syntagma* in four parts, 1598–1613), André Rivet (*Criticus sacer*, 1612), and Jean Daillé (*Traicté de l'employ des saincts pères*, 1631, translated into Latin in 1656). All of these set out to clarify the status of the Fathers in relation to the immutable authority of the scripture but also provide information on available editions, situate the Fathers in their historical context, and take account of Roman Catholic scholarship, while often disputing its conclusions.

Alongside scripture, the writings of the early church (especially Augustine, Ambrose, Jerome, and Origen) played a crucial role in determining the doctrines of both the Reformation and the Counter-Reformation. While it would be incorrect to consider the late Middle Ages as a "patristic desert," the religious controversies of the sixteenth century acted as a spur to the publication of new material (whatever its quality) and in the long run to the development of accurate methods of textual criticism.

BIBLIOGRAPHY

Backus, Irena. *Lectures humanistes de Basile de Césarée: Traductions latines, 1439–1618*. Collection des Etudes Augustiniennes. Série "Antiquité" 125. Paris, 1990. This volume examines the confessional slant of the different editions and translations. It also includes a table of *incipits*.

———. "Some Fifteenth- and Sixteenth-Century Translations of Basil of Caesarea and Justin Martyr." In *Studia Patristic*, edited by Elizabeth A. Livingstone, papers of the 1983 Oxford Patristic Conference, vol. 18, no. 4, pp. 305–321. Kalamazoo and Louvain, 1990.

———. "Calvin's Judgment of Eusebius of Caesarea: An Analysis." *Sixteenth Century Journal* 22.3 (1991), 419–437.

———. *The Disputations of Baden, 1526 and Berne, 1528: Neutralizing the Early Church*. Studies in Reformed Theology and History, vol. 1, no. 1. Princeton, N.J., 1993.

———. *La Patristique et les guerres de religion en France: Etude de l'activité littéraire de Jacques de Billy, 1535–1581, O.S.B. d'après le MS. Sens 167 et les sources imprimées*. Collection des Etudes Augustiniennes. Serie "Moyen-Age-Temps Modernes," vol. 28. Paris, 1993. Examines Billy's scholarship in its context and discusses also his vernacular patristic anthologies intended for the general public of his period.

Backus, Irena, and Benoît Gain. "Le cardinal Guglielmo Sirleto, 1514–1585: Sa bibliothèque et ses traductions de saint Basile." *Mélanges de l'Ecole française de Rome* 98.2 (1986), 889–995. An exhaustive listing of Sirleto's patristic materials.

Béné, Charles. *Erasme et saint Augustin ou influence de saint Augustin sur l'humanisme d'Erasme*. Travaux d'Humanisme et Renaissance, 103. Geneva, 1969.

Bury, E., and B. Meunier, eds. *Les Pères de l'Eglise au XVII siècle Actes du colloque de Lyon, 2–5 octubre, 1991*. Paris, 1993. Several articles deal with sixteenth- and early seveteenth-century patristics.

Fraenkel, Pierre. *Testimonia Patrum: The Function of the Patristic Argument in the Theology of Philip Melanchthon*. Travaux d'Humanisme et Renaissance, 46. Geneva, 1961. A pioneering study.

Kristeller, Paul O., and F. Edward Cranz, eds. *Catalogus Translationum et Commentariorum : Mediaeval and Renaissance Latin Translations and Commentaries; Annotated Lists and Guides*. Washington, D.C., 1960. Particularly useful for biographical details of translators and editors, but volumes published so far include very few church fathers.

Meijering, E. P. *Calvin wider die Neugierde: Ein Beitrag zum Vergleich zwischen reformatorischem und patristischem Denken*. Bibliotheca humanistica et reformatoria, 29. Nieuwkoop, Netherlands, 1980. Sees Calvin's lack of interest in speculation on the nature of God's commandments as analogous to that of Irenaeus, Tertullian, and Augustine.

Monfasani, John. *Collectanea Trapezuntiana*. Binghamton, N.Y., 1984. A descriptive catalog of manuscripts and editions of all of George of Trebizond's works, including his patristic translations.

Old, Hughes Oliphant. *The Patristic Roots of Reformed Worship*. Zürcher Beiträge zur Reformationsgeschichte, 5. Zurich, 1975. Although somewhat dated, still reliable on transmission of patristic elements into Reformed worship.

Petitmengin, Pierre. "Deux 'Bibliothèques' de la Contre-Réforme: La *Panoplie* du Père Torres et la *Bibliotheca sanctorum patrum*." In *The Uses of Greek and Latin: Historical Essays*, edited by A. C. Dionisotti, A. Grafton, and J. Kraye, pp. 127–153. Warburg Institute Surveys and Texts, 16. London, 1988.

Rice, Eugene F. *Saint Jerome in the Renaissance*. Baltimore and London, 1985. Includes chapters on art, popular culture, etc.

Schär, Max. *Das Nachleben des Origenes im Zeitalter des Humanismus*. Basler Beiträge zur Geschichtswissenschaft, 140. Basel, 1979. Very thorough.

Scheible, Heinz. *Die Entstehung der Magdeburger Zenturien*. Schriften des Vereins für Reformationsgeschichte, vol. 72, no. 183. Gütersloh, 1966. The most comprehensive study available to date, but lacks detailed analysis of patristic sources.

Schindler, Alfred. *Zwingli und die Kirchenväter*. Zurich, 1984.

Schucan, Luzi. *Das Nachleben von Basilius Magnus "Ad adolescentes": Ein Beitrag zur Geschichte des christlichen Humanismus*. Travaux d'Humanisme et Renaissance, 133. Geneva, 1973. Useful for bringing out the links between classical and patristic scholarship.

Staehelin, Ernst. "Die Väterübersetzungen Oekolampads." *Schweizerische Theologische Zeitschrift* 33 (1916), 57–91. A complete list although no evaluation of Oecolampadius as translator.

Stinger, Charles L. *Humanism and the Church Fathers: Ambrogio Traversari, 1386–1439, and Christian Antiquity in the Italian Renaissance.* Albany, N.Y., 1977.

IRENA BACKUS

PATRONATO REAL is the juridical institution that from the Middle Ages regulated the relations between the church and the monarchy in the kingdoms of Spain and Portugal and their respective overseas possessions. The term *patronato real* (*patronato* in Spanish, *padroado* in Portuguese) normally refers to the particular juridical institution that was essentially a series of rights and duties that, by virtue of explicit concessions by the Holy See, pertained to the Iberian sovereigns beginning in the fifteenth century.

Although, on a strictly juridical level, the institution of the *patronato real* was more broadly applied in Spain and in its possessions, its origins go back to the first papal concessions made in favor of the Portuguese sovereigns after the latter had embarked upon a dynamic policy of expansion. Beginning in the mid-fifteenth century, Popes Nicholas V and Calistus III had sanctioned the rights acquired by the Portuguese Crown over its African conquests and had recognized its right to erect and confer ecclesiastical benefices in its overseas territories. In 1506 Pope Julius III granted King Manuel I the right of patronage (*patronato*) over the dioceses of Portugal. An analogous right over the overseas territories was explicitly recognized in 1514. That same year Pope Leo X granted the sovereign and his successors the right of nominating the candidates for all the churches and the ecclesiastical benefices in the territories already conquered and those that would be conquered thereafter. The pope created a new diocese in Funchal, on the island of Madeira, granting the Crown the right to nominate the bishop, who was given spiritual jurisdiction over all Portuguese territories of Africa, the East Indies, and Brazil.

Subsequent papal concessions led to the creation of new dioceses in the oversees territories. By the end of the sixteenth century, the kings of Portugal exercised the rights of *patronato real* not only over the dioceses of the mother country but also over all its possessions, from Brazil—where the first diocese (Bahia) was erected in 1551—to Africa and the Far East. There the diocese of Goa assumed major importance. It was established in 1534 and elevated to a metropolitan and primatial see by Paul IV in 1558. The ecclesiastical province of Goa subsequently continued to expand with the inclusion of the suffragan diocese of Macao in 1576, with spiritual jurisdiction over all of China, and that of Funai in 1588, with jurisdiction over the islands of Japan.

In the meantime, particularly on the basis of a series of provisions by Paul III in 1534, rights and obligations began to be spelled out. The Crown had the right to submit to the Holy See the names of candidates to be appointed archbishops and bishops, as well as to other offices. It also had the right to expropriate a portion of the ecclesiastical revenues and to prevent missionaries from going to Portuguese missionary territories without obtaining prior royal authorization. In return, the sovereigns assumed, in the oversees territories, the obligation of building churches and other sacred buildings, of providing for the needs of worship, and of guaranteeing the support of the clergy.

Analogous rights and obligations had also been acquired by Spain. In the Middle Ages, the kings of Castile and León had unsuccessfully attempted to obtain from the Holy See the right to nominate the bishops of the two kingdoms. It was only in 1486 that the Catholic monarchs, Ferdinand of Aragon and Isabella of Castile, obtained from Innocent VIII the right of *patronato real* for Granada, the Canary Islands, and Puerto Real (Cádiz), in view of their conquest of the kingdom of Grenada, which was still in the hands of the Muslims. For their part, the sovereigns agreed to build and endow the churches of the territories they had not yet recovered. From that time on, because of the moral authority derived from the merits they had acquired in the reconquest of the peninsula from the infidels, the sovereigns insisted on obtaining an extension of the papal concession to all of Spain. This was to be achieved by Charles V in 1523; the king of Spain and his successors were granted patronage by Pope Adrian VI over all the consistorial bishoprics and benefices (i.e., all those assigned by the pope in consistory).

By that time the Crown had also obtained patronage over the West Indies, the so-called *patronato real de Indias.* In 1504 Julius II had granted King Ferdinand only the right of nomination for the three dioceses of Yaguata, Magua, and Baynúa. Then, between 1508 and 1511, the king was granted patronage over all the bishoprics and benefices of the Indies, as well as the right to expropriate a part of the ecclesiastical revenues. Finally, in 1518 Charles, who was not yet emperor, obtained a privilege that went beyond the institution of the *patronato real,* inasmuch as Leo X granted him, albeit only for the diocese of Yucatán, the right to modify its boundaries.

As to the *patronato real* over the Indies, Philip II gave it a broad interpretation through a special commission in 1574. This commission drafted a document known as the "Magna Carta" of the *patronato real.* This document assigns broad powers to the Spanish sovereigns, including oversight of ecclesiastical life and punishing and exonerating clergy who did not fulfill their obligations. On this basis the royal jurists worked out a theory, which the Spanish kings never made their own, whereby the sovereign could intervene in the internal affairs of the church of the Indies by virtue of the claim to be the vicar of the Supreme Pontiff (the so-called theory of the *Regio Vicariato Indiano*).

Apart from this radicalization of the position of royal

power, however, one should note that although the institution of the *patronato real* removed the churches of both Spain and Portugal, as well as those of their territories in the East and in the West, from the direct control of the Holy See, it did make it possible for the Iberian monarchs to carry out a vast and intense work of evangelization that the papacy, at least until the first half of the seventeenth century, would not have had the means to promote.

BIBLIOGRAPHY

Cárdenas, Eduardo. "Das königlische Patronat und Vikariat in der überseeischen Besitzungen Spaniens." In *Conquista und Evangelisation 500 Jahre Orden in Lateinamerika*, edited by Michael Sievernich, Arnulf Camps, Andreas Müller, and Walter Senner, pp. 147–166. Mainz, 1992.

Egaña, Antonio de. *La teoría del Regio Vicariato español en Indias*. Analecta Gregoriana 95. Rome, 1958.

Hermann, Christian. *L'Église d'Espagne sous le patronage royal, 1476–1834: Essai d'ecclésiologie politique*. Bibliothèque de la Casa de Velásquez 3. Madrid, 1988.

Jordão, Levy Maria, ed. *Bullarium Patronatus Portugalliae Regum in ecclesiis Africae, Asiae atque Oceaniae: Bullas, brevia, epistolas, decreta, actaque Sanctae Sedis ab Alexandro III ad hoc usque tempus amplectens*. 4 vols. Olisipone, 1868–1872. See esp. vol. 1. The most complete collection of pontifical documents relating to the Portuguese patronage of the Far East.

Leturia, Pedro. *Relaciones entre la Santa Sede e Hispano-América*. 3 vols. Rome and Caracas, 1959–1960. See vol. 1.

Metzler, Josef, ed. *America Pontificia primi saeculi evangelizationis, 1493–1592:, Documenta Pontificia ex registris et minutis praesertim in Archivo Secreto Vaticano existentibus*. 2 vols. Collectanea Archivi Vaticani 27.1–2, Pontificio Comitato di Scienze Storiche, 3.1–2. Vatican City, 1991. The most recent and complete collection of papal documents relating to Spanish and Portuguese America.

Rêgo, António da Silva. *Le patronage portugais de l'Orient: Aperçu historique*. Lisbon, 1957. French translation from the Portuguese.

———. *O padroado português no Oriente e a sua historiografia, 1838–1950*. Lisbon, 1978. See esp. pp. 15–18.

Shiels, William Eugene. *King and Church: The Rise and Fall of the Patronato Real*. Chicago, 1961. A useful summary work; however, the user should be mindful of the corrections made by Quintin Aldea in "A propósito del Patronato Real," *Miscelánea Comillas* 37 (1962), 485–491.

Suberbiola Martínez, Jesús. *Real Patronato de Granda: El arzobispo Talavera, la Iglesia y el estado moderno, 1486–1516; Estudios y documentos*. Granada, 1985. A thorough study of the juridical foundations for the right of *patronato real* in the Kingdom of Grenada and its exercise during the initial phase.

AGOSTINO BORROMEO

Translated from Italian by Robert E. Shillenn

PAUL III (born Alessandro Farnese; 1468–1549), pope from 1534 to 1549. The son of Pier Luigi Farnese and Giovannella Gaetani, he received a humanist education, further developed through study at the University of Pisa and at the famous court of Lorenzo the Magnificent (1449–1492) in Florence. He served in a variety of ecclesiastical offices, initially under the patronage of Rodrigo Borgia (Pope Alexander VI, 1492–1503), who was intimate with Farnese's sister, Giulia. As cardinal (appointed 1493) but prior to his priestly ordination (1519), he kept a mistress and fathered four children, three of whom (Pier Luigi, Paolo, and Ranuccio) were legitimized during the papal reigns of Julius II and Leo X.

Many consider Paul III the first pope committed to efficacious reform of the Catholic church in the sixteenth century. The reasons for this include his election announcement of his intention to hold a general council, as well as his consistent promotion of qualified candidates to the rank of cardinal. Among these were Gasparo Contarini, Gian Pietro Carafa (Paul IV), Reginald Pole, Jacopo Sadoleto, and Gregorio Cortese. He commissioned from them and others the reform document *Consilium de emendanda ecclesia* (1537), presided over the approbation of the Society of Jesus, and encouraged other new religious orders, such as the Theatines, Barnabites, Somaschi, and Ursulines. He revived the Roman Inquisition in 1542, and after long, frustrating delays and despite fear of conciliarist tendencies among prelates, he convened the Council of Trent (1545–1563). He also demonstrated commitment to initiatives associated with later Catholic reform in his work as bishop in the north-central Italian diocese of Parma, where as early as 1516 he personally undertook a visitation. Still, he unabashedly promoted the interests of his family through the papal office, naming two teenage grandsons cardinal (Alessandro Farnese and Guido Ascanio Sforza) and bestowing the rank of duke of Parma and Piacenza upon his son Pier Luigi (1503–1547) in 1545 against considerable opposition. This fact—combined with his notorious indecisiveness, especially over issues faced at the early sessions of the Council of Trent—reduce his stature to one who began, but lacked consistency in applying the reform so many desired.

No comprehensive assessment can omit his patronage of art, of learning, and of the city of Rome itself. Here, too, Paul stood as a man of contradictions, as he spent enormous sums supporting everything from carnivals and astrologers to the restoration of the Roman university and the work of artists such as Raphael and Michelangelo. In 1548 he placed the Vatican library under the directorship of the humanist Marcello Cervini (Pope Marcellus II, 1555) and enhanced its holdings at considerable expense. He reconvened the painting school of Raphael, whose members had scattered after the Sack of Rome (1527). He enlisted the participation of Michelangelo in extensive building projects throughout the papal state, in addition to that artist's more celebrated work in the Sistine Chapel and in formulating the design for the rebuilding of Saint Peter's basilica. Paul also undertook urban planning that anticipated the later work of Sixtus V (r. 1585–1590). He left no doubt that the years of austerity following the sack were over.

Paul faced consistent frustration of his political aims, especially in formulating policies that would simultaneously satisfy the archrivals Charles V (Holy Roman Emperor, 1519–1556) and Francis I (king of France, 1515–1547) while maintaining his own neutrality. This problem was exacerbated by Paul's need to secure a truce in their conflict in order to convene a council, by his concern to organize adequate defense of Italy against the naval power of the Ottoman Empire, and by his commitment to the enrichment of his family through nepotism. No better example of his nepotism exists than the sequence of events that led to the assassination of the pope's son Pier Luigi in 1547. As duke of Parma and Piacenza, Pier Luigi held a territory that had been created for him by his father out of papal holdings. Ferrante Gonzaga, the governor of Milan, arranged the assassination, which simultaneously rid him of an undesirable neighbor and held out hope that Charles V might strengthen his position in Italy. The event confirmed Paul in his conviction that the emperor represented the greatest threat to his political plans. Paul entered his final illness and died in 1549 in the context of renewed conflict over the disposition of the same territories—this time involving his grandson Ottavio (1520–1586), who was the beneficiary of the last act of this inveterate nepotist, which occurred virtually at the hour of his death.

BIBLIOGRAPHY

Battifol, Pierre. *La Vaticane de Paul III à Paul V, dáprès des documents nouveaux.* Paris, 1890. Study of the development of the Vatican library.

Brizzi, Gian Paolo, et al. *Università, principe, Gesuiti: La politica farnesiana dell'istruzione a Parma e Piacenza, 1545–1622.* Rome, 1980.

Capasso, Carlo. *Paolo III. 1534–1549.* 2 vols. Messina, 1924. Comprehensive and thorough analysis of the pontificate.

Dorez, Léon. *La Cour du Pape Paul III.* 2 vols. Paris, 1932. Extensive study of the finances and artistic patronage of Paul III.

Edwards, W. H. *Paul der Dritte. oder die geistliche Gegenreformation.* Leipzig, 1933. Analysis of his work as a reformer.

Fragnito, Gigiola. "Evangelismo e intransigenti nei difficili equilibri del pontificato farnesiano." *Rivista di storia e letteratura religiosa* 25 (1989), 20–47.

Hallman, Barbara McClung. *Italian Cardinals, Reform and the Church as Property, 1492–1563.* Berkeley, 1985.

Jedin, Hubert. *A History of the Council of Trent.* 3 vols. Saint Louis, 1957–1963. Originally published as *Geschichte des Konzils von Trient.* 5 vols. Freiburg, 1950–1975.

Pastor, Ludwig. *The History of the Popes From the Close of the Middle Ages.* 40 vols., 3d ed. Saint Louis, 1938–1953. Volumes 11 and 12 still constitute the best extended study of Paul III, and the only one in English. Originally published by Pastor as *Geschichte der Päpste seit dem Ausgang des Mittelalters* in Freiburg from 1866 to 1938.

Prodi, Paolo. *The Papal Prince. One Body and Two Souls: The Papal Monarchy in Modern Europe.* Translated by Susan Haskins. Cambridge, 1987.

Stinger, Charles L. *The Renaissance in Rome.* Bloomington, Ind., 1985.

WILLIAM V. HUDON

PAUL IV (born Gian Pietro Carafa; 1476–1559), pope from 1555 to 1559. A member of one of the most important noble families of the Neapolitan region, Paul IV received a thoroughly humanistic education and enjoyed the admiration of even Desiderius Erasmus for his abilities. He displayed the beginnings of his fervent religiosity by attempting to enter the Dominican monastery of San Domenico Maggiore in Naples at age fourteen, but he was returned to his family. At twenty-six he began his ecclesiastical career under the patronage of his uncle, Cardinal Oliviero Carafa, and was named bishop of Chieti in 1504. He served as papal legate to Spain and to England under Pope Leo X (r. 1513–1521).

Prior to his election as pope, he made two principal contributions to the church's reform. In 1524 he founded, along with Gaetano da Thiene and two other members of the Roman Oratory of Divine Love, the Theatine order of regular clerics. He wrote a primitive "rule" for the order, whose members became famous for the care of souls and practical works of charity. His second principal contribution began in 1542, when he assumed directorship of the revived Roman Inquisition. He served as head of that institution until his election to the papacy, gradually steering the tribunal toward more vigorous, repressive, and even violent activity than was apparently intended by Paul III, the pope who had revived the institution. Paul IV's fanatical but groundless prosecution of Cardinal Giovanni Morone and that intended against Cardinal Reginald Pole are two cases in point.

Although "excluded" from pontifical election by Charles V, he gained the office in 1555 because of the strong support of Cardinal Alessandro Farnese (great-grandson of Paul III), and acknowledged that support by choosing the name Paul V. His temperament, correctly described as "hot blooded" and "volcanic," led to unpredictable, perhaps irrational behavior during his pontificate. Personally frugal and austere, he nevertheless maintained a generous table as pope. Although committed to rigorous clerical reform, he remained blind to the shortcomings of family members, such as his nephew Carlo Carafa, whom he appointed to numerous ecclesiastical benefices and to the position of papal secretary of state. Carlo held this position from 1555 until he was discredited in 1559. Paul's hatred of Spain and of the Habsburg family knew no bounds and provoked a disastrous war (1556–1557) in which this fanatic for orthodoxy even employed German Protestant mercenaries. He lacked experience and practicality in political affairs, and this contributed to his impetuosity.

Paul gained a well-deserved reputation for draconian severity in ecclesiastical reform and in other matters pertaining to his administration of Rome. Clerics who refused to follow the strictures he imposed (especially regular clergy living outside their monasteries without permission) served time in the galleys, were scourged, or, in the case of secular clerics, suffered the loss of property. He attempted to force alterations in the constitutions of the new Society of Jesus, apparently because he believed their lack of prayer in choir indicated laxity. Opposed categorically to the continuation of the suspended Council of Trent, he insisted that a vigorous Roman Inquisition was the key to success in ecclesiastical reform. So convinced was he that after appointing his handpicked protégé, Antonio Ghislieri (later Pius V), as grand inquisitor-for-life, he continued to attend its weekly meetings. He even had one of its meetings held in his own room as he lay bedridden with his final illness.

Paul IV stood alone among his contemporaries and quite out of the mainstream in much of this work. His attempt to deprive Morone and Pole (and any other cardinal in the future who might hold similar beliefs) of their vote in the conclave on the basis of a mere indictment before the Inquisition was rebuffed by the college of cardinals. He published a lengthy Index of Prohibited Books which was significantly modified by his successor. He also imposed severe restrictions upon the Jewish population of Rome, including a crushing taxation and rigid segregation, in contradiction of the policy of his predecessors. Because of such measures and the reputation they generated, popular rejoicing greeted Paul's death in August 1559, when he succumbed in the midst of a three-day fast. Before he actually died a mob began to attack the palace of the Inquisition, destroying the building and many of its records. The statue of himself that Paul had erected on the Capitoline was also attacked by a mob, which threw the head into the Tiber.

BIBLIOGRAPHY

Aubert, Alberto. "Alle origini della controriforma: studi e problemi su Paolo IV." *Rivista di storia e letteratura religiosa* 22 (1986), 303–355.

Caracciolo, Antonio. *De vita Pauli qauarti pontificis maximi collectanea historica.* Cologne, 1612. Most reliable of early works on the life of Paul IV, virtually all of which are marred by attempts to rehabilitate him.

Firpo, Massimo, and Dario Marcatto. *Il processo inquistoriale del Cardinale Giovanni Morone.* 5 vols. Rome, 1981–89. This magisterial edition of the documents from the trial of Morone includes information on all related persons, including Paul IV. Of particular importance is the critical analysis of secondary biographical sources on Paul in vol. 1, pp. 91–172.

Monti, Gennaro Maria. *Ricerche su papa Paolo IV Carafa.* Benevento, Italy, 1923.

Paschini, Pio. S. *Gaetano Thiene, Gian Pietro Carafa e le origini del chierici regolari teatini.* Rome, 1926. Important study on Paul's co-founding of the Theatine order.

Pastor, Ludwig. *The History of the Popes From the Close of the Middle Ages.* 40 vols., 3d ed. Saint Louis, 1938–1953. Vol. 14 still constitutes the best extended study of Paul IV, and the only one in English. Originally published as *Geschichte der Päpste seit dem Ausgang des Mittelalters,* 21 vols., Freiburg im Breisgau, 1866–1938.

Santosuosso, Antonio. "An Account of the Election of Paul IV to the Pontificate." *Renaissance Quarterly* 31 (1978), 486–498.

Simoncelli, Paolo. "Inquisizione romana e riforma in Italia." *Rivista storica italiana* 100 (1988), 1–125. A controversial article that calls into question the very existence of "Catholic reform" through analysis of inquisitorial records.

Stow, Kenneth R. *Taxation, Community and State: The Jews and the Fiscal Foundations of the Early Modern Papal State.* Stuttgart, 1982. Examines the shift in papal policy toward the Jews by Pope Paul IV and his followers.

WILLIAM V. HUDON

PÁZMÁNY, Péter (1570–1637), archbishop of Esztergom (1616–1637) and cardinal, leader of the Counter-Reformation in Hungary. Although Pázmány came from a Calvinist noble family, he became the leading Catholic prelate in early seventeenth-century Hungary. Orphaned while still a minor, he was educated by the Jesuits at Kolozsvár (Cluj), Kraków (where he formally joined the society in 1588), Vienna, and Rome. After his consecration Pázmány taught in the Jesuit school at Graz from 1597 to 1600 and again from 1603 to 1607. His intellect and influential Hungarian patrons, as well as his desire to serve the Roman church in his native land, directed Pázmány away from an academic career. From 1601 to 1603 and again from 1607 to 1616 he served as a Jesuit missionary in western Hungary and developed close contacts and friendships with influential Catholic laymen and ecclesiastics. His distant relative Ferenc Forgách, the archbishop of Esztergom and primate of Hungary, acted as Pázmány's chief patron. By the time Forgách died in 1615 Pázmány was widely recognized as the most able Catholic cleric in Hungary. The following year he succeeded Forgách as the archbishop of Esztergom.

Pázmány's contributions to the revival of Catholicism in Hungary were unparalleled in their scope and effectiveness. In the sphere of religious debate he reversed the Protestant tide that had dominated vernacular publication and religious argument during the sixteenth century. As a defender of Catholicism he moved from strident attacks on various Protestant teachings to a position of supreme self-confidence from which he sought to dictate the terms of the debate. Having gained the intellectual initiative, Pázmány forced his Protestant rivals to discuss the issues that were most congenial to Roman Catholicism. His later works reveal an able and assured writer who emphasized the truth of Catholic teaching on scripture, ecclesiology, and the role of tradition. Pázmány restored the intellectual respectability and attractiveness of the old church.

As a Jesuit and later as archbishop Pázmány helped to convert a number of Protestant aristocrats to Roman Catholicism. By the mid-seventeenth century the Catholics in Hungary had succeeded in returning thirty-nine Protestant magnates to the Roman fold. Pázmány played a direct role in at least twelve conversions of Protestant aristocrats to Catholicism. In converting Protestants Pázmány made use of his knowledge of religious dogma, his personal contacts among the aristocracy, his political connections at the Habsburg court, as well as fully deploying the power of the Roman church as an institution of patronage.

Pázmány also helped to revive Catholicism by implementing the decisions of the Council of Trent. As primate he presided over several church synods and reinvigorated Catholic education for both clergy and laymen. Using his considerable ecclesiastical income and Jesuit teachers, he established a seminary for training Hungarian clergy in Vienna, a school for the education of youths in Pozsony (Bratislava), and a university in Hungary at Nagyszombat (Trnava). Pázmány left his imprint on the Roman church in his homeland through his numerous writings, his pastoral work, and as the founder of educational institutions.

BIBLIOGRAPHY

Primary Sources

Pázmány, Péter. *Opera omnia . . . series latina.* Edited by Stephanus Bognar, Adalbertus Breznay, and Desiderus Bita. 6 vols. Budapest, 1894–1904. Includes Pázmány's Latin-language publications and university lectures.

———. *Összes munkái* (Collected Works). Edited by the Department of Theology of the Budapest Royal Hungarian University. 7 vols. Budapest, 1894–1905. Contains Pázmány's Hungarian-language religious polemics and sermons.

———. *Petri Cardinalis Pázmány epistolae collectae.* Edited by Ferenc Hanuy. 2 vols. Budapest, 1910–1912.

Secondary Sources

Bitskey, István. *Humanista erudíció és barokk világkép* (Humanist Erudition and Baroque Worldview). Budapest, 1979. A recent analysis of Pázmány's sermons that greatly contributes to an understanding of his sources and themes.

Frankl [Fraknói], Vilmos. *Pázmány Péter és kora* (Péter Pázmány and his Time). 3 vols. Pest, 1868–1872. The standard biography on Pázmány.

Lukács, László, and Ferenc Szabó, eds. *Pázmány Péter emlékezete* (In Memory of Péter Pázmány). Rome, 1987. A representative sample of recent scholarship on Pázmány.

Öry, Miklós. *Pázmány Péter tanulmányi évei* (Péter Pázmány's Years of Education). Eisenstadt, Austria, 1970. The best work on Pázmány's youth.

Sik, Sándor. *Pázmány, az ember és az író* (Pázmány, the Man and the Writer). Budapest, 1939. The most extensive analysis of Pázmány as a writer.

PETER SCHIMERT

PEACE OF ______. *See under latter part of name.*

PEASANTS. "Reformation and peasant" forms a German theme. Nowhere in Europe did the peasants participate to such a great extent in the Reformation as in Germany, particularly in upper Germany (south Germany, and parts of Austria and Switzerland). This is evidenced by the Peasants' War of 1525, the greatest mass uprising in Europe before the French Revolution. In England the peasants rose up against the introduction of a new faith. In Scandinavia the Reformation was introduced from above, without noticeable reaction on the part of the population, and in France, Calvinism won out among the rural population essentially through the efforts of the nobility, who led peasants under their control to the Reformed confession. No thoroughly accepted thesis has yet been developed to explain why Germany was the exception; nevertheless, plausible reasons for the reception of the Reformation in rural society can be advanced.

Concept. The concept of peasant has a broad and a narrow significance. In the broad sense, peasants are the producers of plant (farming) and animal (breeding) foods and raw materials in the framework of an independent, economically self-sufficient unit (farm), which they cultivate and direct by their own labor. In this sense, peasants are a historically universal phenomenon. In European history, however, peasants are not only defined by their activities but also to a great extent by their social position in a society organized into estates. European society was conceptualized as divided into three parts—priests (*oratores*), warriors (*bellatores*), and peasants (*laboratores*)—in the high Middle Ages, and peasants received their defined social "place." This division was marked in theory by the complementary character of the three estates, and in practice by the fact that peasants fed the priestly and warrior classes with their work. This order was understood as God-willed, and it was not basically overcome until the French Revolution brought about a thorough transformation, first in France and finally everywhere in Europe with the removal of the privileges of the ruling classes and the corresponding liberation of the peasants. Then peasants became on the one hand farmers and on the other hand citizens of the state.

Between 1300 and 1800 peasants were also defined as being subject to noble and church domination (manor, seigneurie, *Grundherrschaft*). A large part of their net income was delivered to their lords in the form of duties and taxes, while a special priestly class cared for their salvation. The system of estates explains why there were always areas of conflict between peasants and lords (authorities) and peasants and ministers of salvation (priests). In times of great upheaval, to which the Reformation undoubtedly belongs, these conflicts could only intensify.

Peasants at the Beginning of the Reformation. The position of peasants in Germany was differentiated greatly according to economic burden, personal legal position, market involvement, degree of community organization, and political rights. The south German, east and north Swiss, and Habsburg areas (from the Tirol into Alsace) show a certain similarity, and it was not by accident that these were also the areas in which the peasants entered the Reformation camp with flags flying. The following is essentially a discussion of these areas.

In the fourteenth and fifteenth centuries, the role of agriculture was changed dramatically by the explosive growth of the cities and their populations. Up to then productivity had not increased over the years, providing enough grain only for maintenance taxes. But then, with a greater input of work, productivity increased providing noticeable surplus in some areas for peasants to see in the markets. Historians figure that in some regions one-third of the farms were in a position to produce for the market (Sabean). This also had its effect on the agrarian organization. In the fifteenth and the early sixteenth century a broad improvement of the types of rental for the peasant farms occurred. The traditional loan was replaced by the lifelong inherited fief, with the result that taxes could not be increased even with a change of ownership, and the closest relatives were the actual inheritors of the farm. The older form of the use of land, labor, and their products, which belonged theoretically to the landed ruler after production costs had been deducted, was changed so that the lord got certain established contributions, while the peasants could keep the rest of their profits. This change was pushed through by the peasants against the interests of the lords through uprisings and legal proceedings.

The result for the peasants was a stronger bond to their lords to ensure the steady production of agricultural goods. Freedom of movement was made more difficult, partially because of the expansion and the intensification of serfdom, particularly in the southwestern part of the empire. Serfs could not freely choose their lords. They were limited in their marriage choices to their master's serfs (*ungenossame Ehe*) and had to leave a part of their property at their death to their master. Toward the end of the Middle Ages, there was a tendency to level the great legal differences between peasants, making servitude or serfdom the legal status of all peasants in the whole territory. With or without the legal title of serfdom, the authorities also tended to hinder geographic mobility.

Thereby the pressure of the authorities on the peasants was increased. The territorial formation of states in the empire began in the late Middle Ages. It found expression mainly in territorial legislation and in the related expansion of government and courts (Strauss). With their own university-educated lawyers, and with the idea of the "good police," proper administration, the princes took over more and more political functions, which found legal expression in territorial laws. In this sense the time around 1500 was an important one in German legal and constitutional history. What has long been described as "the reception of Roman law" was, in practice, primarily the establishment of state legislation and the elimination or bypassing of courts that judged according to customary, usually unwritten law, in which the peasant men had taken part as jurors. Writing replaced oral tradition. The law displaced right, to put it succintly; the law set up norms for judgment that limited the accommodations that could be made for individual cases and also limited the subjective ethical perception of the judges.

In counterpoint to the establishment of governing authorities on the territorial level, cities and villages, as new forms of settlement and social structures, grew explosively in the late Middle Ages. The number of cities grew from fifty in the year 1200 to four thousand in 1500; tens of thousands of villages probably came into existence from settlements and from the enlargement of hamlets. In the cities and villages, business and social intercourse were organized more and more along the lines of self-rule, with mayors and councilors in both the cities (*Bürgermeister* and *Rat*) and the villages (*Ammann* and *Vierer*).

Next to the family, the village became the primary social and political sphere for the peasants. The regulation of agriculture and the security of village life (safety of the streets, measures for fire protection, guarding of public establishments such as smithies, taverns, bakeries, and bath houses) were accomplished essentially by means of representative, often elected, organs of villagers and tenants. Often they succeeded in being accepted into diets (the Tirol, Salzburg, northern Austria, Württemberg) or in forming their own corporations on a territorial level (*Landschaft*), and this strengthened their political influence through participation in the approval of taxes and cooperation in the territorial statutes. There was therefore among the peasants a clearly recognizable striving for political participation. This may partially explain why peasants took such an active part in the Reformation movement.

The "Peasant Reformation." As a mass movement, the Reformation was long considered to be exclusively a city phenomenon. A. G. Dickens's description of the Reformation as an "urban event" became a watchword. Since the early 1980s, scholars have also spoken of a "peasant Reformation" (Conrad). From the demands, programs, and actions of the peasants, their perception of the Reformation can be reconstructed. It was expressed theologically in the demand for the preaching of the "pure gospel," election of preachers by the congregation, and, in cases of conflict between the old and new faith, theological decisions by the congregation. In church organization it was expressed in the demand for the residency of the preacher, for an inexpensive church, and for the elimination, or at least a limitation, of the authority of clerical courts.

Both the theological and the organizational demands, which were naturally connected, can be traced to the theology of the Reformation. The "pure" gospel, as the peasants understood it, was the slogan for a gospel "without human tradition," "without human additions," "without human doctrine." This corresponds precisely to the language of the Reformation. But the peasants also added something to this understanding of the gospel: the conviction that the gospel contained the basic instructions for a just social and political order. The scriptures became the source of the peasants' ideas of natural rights, for example, in the demand for the abolition of serfdom.

From such considerations they finally developed at the end of 1524 (Klettgau, Allgäu) and the beginning of 1525 (Upper Swabia) the concept of "divine law." "Divine law" eventually became a key concept of the Peasants' War of 1525. Positive law was exchanged for a divine natural law that was to some extent codified in the scriptures. This was to be the measure for legitimate rule. The obvious criterion was the Christian nature of government, and this meant, as the situation demanded, the acceptance of the Reformation. Where the authorities refused this, they became suspect. The development of divine law as a category is one of the essential accomplishments of the peasants in the Reformation. It was probably related to a sharpening of the interpretation of the gospel by the Christian humanists in the south German cities, especially by Huldrych Zwingli, who as early as 1523 in his *Schlussreden* had taken the position that the secular order had to be improved on the basis of the gospel and the "divine law."

The hope of the peasants to be able to use the gospel as law was rooted in the severe discrediting that justice, law, and the administration of justice experienced in the late Middle Ages. Law had previously been "created" and "found" by jurors who obligated themselves by oath to make judgments according to their best knowledge and conscience. More and more it became the practice, however, for the authorities to establish norms of civil and criminal laws with uniformly normalized punishments and fines and to force the peasant judges, who were not legally trained, to apply them. This no longer allowed for justice to be modified according to individual situations and was therefore considered to be a loss of fairness and justice. Seen in this connection, the "divine law" had for the peasants a liberating function.

Next to the gospel, the election of the minister by the congregation was an important point for the peasants. It became a non-negotiable demand in the whole south German area, and it spread from Thuringia to Zurich and from Alsace to Salzburg. In the context of the theological argumentation of the Reformation, the election of ministers was meant to assure the proclamation of the pure gospel, which was also seen by the peasants as necessary for salvation.

In the matter of the election of ministers, the peasants agreed with the position of the Reformation theologians. Of the Twelve Articles that the peasants finally presented in 1525, Martin Luther considered only the first, which demanded the election of ministers, to be justified. Together with Zwingli in Zurich and Martin Bucer in Strasbourg, Luther had allowed the congregation of the faithful the right to name its pastor and to determine religious belief.

Fuhrmann has pointed out that the demand for the election of the minister has roots in the late Middle Ages. During the hundred years before the Reformation, rural communities often founded benefices to improve the circumstances of the priest. The charters outlined the duties related to the benefice and in this way assured the communities a considerable voice in the granting of the benefices.

It was inherent in the logic of the demand for the election of the minister that the community also decide on which faith to accept. If the clergy in office stated that he was preaching the pure gospel, but the community wanted another minister, the community claimed the right to decide who had the best theological arguments. Along with the well-known disputations in the cities (the first in Zurich, 1523) there were also parallels in rural areas (for example, Ilanz in Grisons).

If the election of the minister had become general custom, which obviously was not possible after the failure of the Peasants' War, the entire church would have gone through a process of communalization. It was necessary and logical that the peasants, along with the election of ministers, also demand the control of the means for his support, that is, the tithe. The commmunity was to determine its use. The tithe, together with any benefice, was meant to provide the minister with a satisfactory living.

The peasants' conception of the Reformation focused on the one hand on the pure gospel and the divine law that developed from it, and on the other on the election of pastors by the "political community." Their further notions can be understood as growing out of these basic concepts. They regarded the sermon as necessary for salvation, which may explain why the peasants demanded the residency of the minister and no longer wanted to tolerate absences caused either by accumulation of benefices or by incorporation of the parish into an ecclesiastical institution. To have a minister in the village for the daily religious services, baptism of the newborn, and support for the dying had been a strong motive for the creation of benefices by villages as early as the fifteenth century. If a minister was properly given benefices and tithes, there was no reason to demand fees for duties such as baptisms, burials, and marriages. The church could become "inexpensive."

Where the church hierarchy was no longer respected, there was no longer any reason to accept the jurisdiction of the episcopal courts. The complaints of the peasants about the abuses of church courts were no different at the time of the Reformation from those of the late Middle Ages. But now the fact that church taxes, as well as interest and revenue payments, demanded by church courts could be enforced by means of ban and interdiction (temporarily excluding people from the means of salvation) was even less tolerable since the reformers had emphatically attacked these abuses.

The "peasant Reformation" deserves a broader interpretive basis to the extent that it shares many of its manifestations with the "urban Reformation." "Pure gospel," "election of the clergy," "confessional choice," "inexpensive church," and "removal of church courts" were also central demands of the towns people. The similarities have been tentatively expressed in the concept "communal Reformation." The main difference between the peasant and urban Reformation was that the peasants developed the concept of "divine law" into a criterion for all law and the legitimacy of rule, and with this radical move developed theoretically a new political order that constituted the revolutionary nucleus of the Peasants' War of 1525.

The Reformation movement became undoubtedly an all-inclusive, social, intellectual, and cultural event because the large burgher and peasant groups accepted the theology and ethics of the Reformation to the extent that they had access to them and understood them. There is no thesis about whether or how Protestant teachings might be explained by late medieval social developments so fascinating and worthy of discussion as Max Weber's notion of the connection between Protestantism and modernism (expressed metaphorically in capitalism). Fertile ground for such a thesis may lie in something like the concept of the "communal Reformation." At any rate, the communal focus of all Protestant denominations has a predecessor in the growth of communal organizations for the handling of everyday social problems, whether they were in city, village, or rural communities.

Results of the "Peasant Reformation." Some scholars have seen the peasants as illiterate and unable to understand the concerns of the Reformation, particularly Luther's doctrine of grace (Schilling). This reproach is in error, because with the millions of pamphlets the ability to read had undoubtedly increased more than has commonly been assumed, and because the Lutheran understanding of grace is undoubtedly less complicated than the Catholic one; in addition, south Germany was strongly under the influence of Zwingli. Today no one denies that one can speak of a "peasant Reformation." What is controversial, however, is the significance of the defeat of the peasants in the Peasants' War of 1525, which meant that the concept of reform they espoused had no chance of success. The fundamental debate that the peasants wished to instigate on natural law in the form of "divine law" did not take place, and Lutheranism was not built on community churches but on national churches. The decision, which was still unresolved in the late Middle Ages, on whether the empire would take a communal or a territorial path was decided in favor of the territories. Otto Gierke argued as early as the mid-nineteenth century that the year 1525 represented a deep break in German history with consequences in all areas including religion.

[*See also* Capitalism; Common Man; Nobility; *and* Peasants' War.]

BIBLIOGRAPHY

Blickle, Peter. *Gemeindereformation: Die Menschen des 16. Jahrhunderts auf dem Weg zum Heil.* Munich, 1985. Also available in English: *Communal Reformation: The Quest for Salvation in Sixteenth-Century Germany,* translated by Thomas Dunlap, Atlantic Highlands, N. J., and London, 1992.

———. *Studien zur geschichtlichen Bedeutung des deutschen Bauernstandes.* Stuttgart, 1989.

Conrad, Franziska. *Reformation in der bäuerlichen Gesellschaft: Zur Rezeption reformatorischer Theologie im Elsaß.* Stuttgart, 1984.

Franz, Günther. *Der deutsche Bauernkrieg.* Munich, 1933.

Fuhrmann, Rosi. "Dorfgemeinde und Pfründstiftung vor der Reformation." *Zeitschrift für Historische Forschung* supplement 9 (1989), 77–112.

Patze, Hans, ed. *Die Grundherrschaft im späten Mittelalter.* 2 vols. Sigmaringen, 1983.

Sabean, David W. *Landbesitz und Gesellschaft am Vorabend des Bauernkriegs.* Stuttgart, 1972.

Schilling, Heinz. "Die deutsche Gemeindereformation." *Zeitschrift für Historische Forschung* 14 (1987), 325–332.

Strauss, Gerald. *Law, Resistance, and the State: The Opposition to Roman Law in Reformation Germany.* Princeton, 1986.

PETER BLICKLE

Translated from German by Walter D. Morris

PEASANTS' WAR. One of the greatest popular risings of modern European history, the German Peasants' War of 1524–1526 is traditionally said to have commenced on 24 June 1524 with the rebellion of the peasants of the county of Lupfen and Stühlingen; it actually began in the nearby Black Forest on 30 May 1524, when subjects of the abbey of Saint Blasien refused to render feudal dues and services to their overlord. It was not at first an armed uprising, but more of a public demonstration or strike, yet it quickly involved peasants of various lordships in the Klettgau and Hegau regions along the Swiss border. Its chief characteristic was efficient organization of local assemblies into a large regional band of rebels prepared to negotiate with the lords about joint grievances.

Skillful peasant leaders, such as Hans Müller of Bulgenbach, also sought alliances with towns such as Waldshut and Zurich. Their involvement led to the introduction into the rebellion of radical religious ideas linking acceptance of the gospel to redress of secular grievances and social justice. By the beginning of 1525 the peasants had begun to appeal to the word of God as justification for their disobedience. Between December 1524 and February 1525 the rebellion spread along the northern shores of Lake Constance, into Swabia and the Algäu. This was followed by the formation of supraregional bands and alliances, culminating in the creation on 7 March 1525 of the Christian Union of Upper Swabia, a revolutionary organization of the inhabitants of all the allied regions, equipped with political and military structures and pledging allegiance to the word of God. It produced as its manifesto the Twelve Articles of Memmingen, the most significant document of the rebellion, which was disseminated throughout Germany as both a symbol of, and a spur to, rebellion.

From the Black Forest and Upper Swabia, the revolt spread out in waves over April and May 1525: into Franconia, Alsace, and the Rhine Palatinate, the Tirol and the archbishopric of Salzburg, and northward to the Thuringian Forest and Saxony. As it did so, its character and achievements became more diverse. The Franconian revolt was militarily the most successful, sweeping aside the feeble opposition of the nobility and seizing the city (but crucially not the garrison) of the episcopal seat of Würzburg. Indeed, on the western fringes of this region, the Odenwald-Neckar Valley band achieved the most significant symbolic victory of the war when the archbishopric of Mainz capitulated to the rebels' demands on 7 May. The Franconian rebellion also produced the most ambitious plans for a "reformation" of politics and society in the Holy Roman Empire, Friedrich Weigandt's "Draft of an Imperial Reformation" of 18 May, which was to have been presented to a "peasant parliament" in Heilbronn later that month.

The Thuringian revolt was characterized by the powerful revolutionary vision of Thomas Müntzer; by numerous urban revolts, which, however, too often failed to combine with rural discontent; and by the reluctance of the peasantry to entertain any wider political vision beyond a general adherence to the Twelve Articles and the settlement of local grievances. It was easily put down in mid-May. The revolt in Alsace, which broke out in mid-April 1525, produced the most efficient military organization in southwest Germany but lacked a wider political vision and was easily defeated after only five weeks. Bands on both sides of the Rhine in the Palatinate and the bishopric of Speyer were indecisive and easily fobbed off in late May by empty promises to call a diet to consider rebel grievances, allowing the Elector Palatine time to help repress the Franconia revolt before putting down his own rebels on 26 June.

The last wave of revolt occurred in the Alpine lands, in the Archbishopric of Salzburg, the Tirol, Styria, Carinthia, and Upper Austria from the second week of May and was notable for virulent anticlericalism and the participation of miners. Archduke Ferdinand stifled rebellion in his territories by calling a territorial diet in which rural estates were represented and promising a new territorial constitution. This was first published in the spring of 1526 and effectively defused revolt in the Austrian lands. The Salzburg rebels seized Salzburg and besieged the archbishop in his castle but were bought off with promises of a diet to redress grievances. When this diet was indefinitely adjourned without any firm results, a second revolt broke out in March 1526, which attracted some elements from the Austrian revolt (excluding the miners), but was repressed in July 1526. The revolt in the Alpine lands was notable for the only peasant military victory, at Schladming on 3 July, and for the political vision of its leader, Michael Gaismaier, whose draft territorial constitution for the Tirol offered a model for an egalitarian republic inspired by radical Christian social principles.

The causes of the rebellion have always been controversial, but no doubt it was provoked by frustration with growing burdens that threatened peasant means of subsistence. Lists of grievances provide the best evidence for the causes of discontent, and they encompass legal, political, and intensely local issues alongside the purely economic. It is impossible, however, to separate causes into simplistic categories, since many legal complaints had economic or political elements, while political changes, such as the growth of bureaucratic government in fledgling territorial states, often had wide-ranging economic and legal consequences. Long-term structural changes undeniably played a part. Economic recovery from the late medieval agrarian depression benefited those best placed to take advantage of it, whether feudal lords or substantial peasant farmers. Structural conflicts between the interests of town and country, especially over access to markets, played an important role and may have hindered the formation of crucial alliances between urban and rural rebels. The effects of population growth and inheritance customs contributed by producing peasant impoverishment. The strategies evolved by lords, towns, and even the peasants themselves to deal with structural and conjunctural changes meant that political and legal measures were inseparable from economic and social change.

Nonetheless, some crucial features stand out. Demands for increased rents, services, dues, fees, taxes, and tithes, whether they originated from feudal lords, rulers, or the church, had a decisive impact on a rural economy close to subsistence, provoking numerous social conflicts, often within peasant ranks themselves, as everyone struggled to maximize income. Serfdom and the tithe were the most prominently cited grievances. The former involved a complex cluster of political, legal, and economic issues; the latter invoked both economic and religious discontents, especially an ever-present anticlericalism.

At least one feature of rebel demands stands out clearly. The peasants seem to have internalized an idealized view of the feudal contract, by which they supplied dues and services in return for their lords' protection. Many felt that this contract had become so one-sided that they were justified in abrogating it, as expressed in many calls for the lords to explain what they did for their tenants in return for services rendered. It was a short step from this essentially conservative position to the conclusion that the contract was inherently one-sided and unjust. There was certainly no lack of social hatred expressed during the rebellion, and in places this could appear close to a primitive class consciousness. An alternative to a hierarchical view of feudal society was presented by strong communal ideas, which undoubtedly played a leading ideological role and provided a common antifeudal platform on which urban and rural discontent could unite.

In addition, longstanding urban conflicts blazed up anew during the rebellion, especially opposition to rule by self-interested oligarchies, demands for greater political participation in municipal government, and fundamental civic rights such as free assembly, freedom from arbitrary arrest, communal control over government expenditure, and better accountability to the civic commune. But the specific nature of these grievances meant that any alliance between town and country was only temporary. The economic and political interests of urban and rural dwellers were often so fundamentally opposed that unity between them was only possible around the broadest slogans. The promotion of religious reform and the desire to advance the word of God was certainly one such slogan, found alongside the demand to elect one's own pastors and to take local control of religious affairs. But the rebellion was so often used in towns to force through radical religious change against the wishes of the ecclesiastical hierarchy and holders of patronage rights that it smacked of opportunism and manipulation by ruling elites. Mainstream reformers moved quickly to distance themselves from the idea of reformation as a coup d'état. The failure to build lasting and solid communities of interest between town and country undoubtedly played a major part in the failure of the rebellion.

No one would doubt the importance of evangelical ideas in inspiring many leaders and participants of the rebellion. Religious reformers who spoke of the need for social justice and advocated reform of politics and society based on evangelical principles certainly provided a strong ideological foundation for dissidence and even revolt. Some of Luther's more populist ideas, such as the liberty of the Christian and the right of the believing community to elect its own pastors, had a powerful impact, as did humanist-Zwinglian ideas of reshaping daily life according to evangelical principles. The mainstream reformers backpedaled furiously to deny the political implications of their own positions even as the first signs of a coming rebellion were apparent in 1523 and 1524, but it was too late to turn back the clock. Too many preachers and propagandists were inspired by the idea of a demand for social justice founded on the renewed religious fervor released by the early evangelical movements. The role of preachers, radical or otherwise, in injecting an evangelical inspiration into peasant discontent was crucial for the ideological thrust of the rebellion. Once the Twelve Articles, the most successful peasant manifesto, had enunciated the idea that the word of God in the Bible should serve as a guide for adjudging the justice of many social practices, a powerful link had been forged that made the peasant rebellion a potential revolution. Equally, it encouraged both rulers and major reformers of all tendencies to repudiate any link between religious reform and social discontent, and in the wake of defeat any preachers attempting to raise broad social issues in religious terms were stigmatized as seditious. Meanwhile, the reformers evolved an interpretation of the rebellion, even before it was fully defeated, that ascribed it to false preaching that had distorted the "pure" message of the gospel through "fleshly" reading, and especially a misunderstanding of the notion of Christian liberty. Reformers of all persuasions began to preach obedience and passivity to the unprivileged classes of both town and country.

In its military aspects, the Peasants' War was a curiosity. The rebels dominated the initial theaters of revolt because of the failure of the forces of law and order. The feudal nobility was too unreliable as a policing force, while the Swabian League was too cumbersome in structures and procedures to respond rapidly to such an unprecedented wave of rebellion. The authorities were also short of troops to deploy in an army of repression, since the most experienced mercenaries were engaged in Italy and became available only after the imperial victory at Pavia on 24 February 1525. Peasant forces operated unchecked for several months before the army of the Swabian League took the field under Georg Truchsess von Waldburg on 29 March, and the first full-scale military encounter took place at Leipheim on 3–4 April, a defeat for the outnumbered and poorly equipped peasants. The Baltringen Band submitted meekly shortly thereafter, when other bands failed to come to its aid. Truchsess von Waldlburg negotiated an armistice on 17 April in the Treaty of Weingarten by which the rebels in the well-organized and formidable Lake Constance Band agreed to disband pending a hearing of grievances. This was a decisive point in the military progress of the rebellion. The league army was never seriously tested in battle and was free to concentrate on repressing several other smaller and less experienced rebel bands.

Peasant armies did not lack experience or organization: the presence of former mercenaries, many of peasant origins, ensured a considerable military potential. They lacked cavalry, artillery, and firearms in significant quantities, however, so that they were outgunned almost everywhere they engaged the lords' forces. Some military failures are attributable to lack of political will on the part of the leaders, some of whom had placed themselves at the head of peasant bands for reasons of expediency. The rebels did produce some formidable leaders from their own ranks, but not in sufficient numbers to make a military difference, while the campaigns were too brief to allow such leaders to gain experience or wider reputation. Military success was never purely a matter of open battle but as much of securing strategic places dominating major roads, passes, and river crossings. The highly successful campaigns in Franconia and Thuringia reflected that awareness, destroying or rendering ineffectual castles, abbeys, and convents, and constituted a significant weakening of the coercive power of feudal lords. But failure to seize the garrison in Würzburg or to capitalize on the surrender of Freiburg im Breisgau on 24 May 1525 deprived the rebels of potential strongholds that might have served as a focus for resistance. In the long run the rebels never achieved that crucial domino effect that enabled one success to build on another until the initiative rested in their hands; instead it was the lords who profited from this process.

There can be no doubt about the wider significance of the Peasants' War. In the short term, it served as a terrible warning to the authorities and did lead to minor amelioration of the lot of the peasantry. Certainly, any major concessions were quickly rescinded in the wake of victory, but fear of renewed rebellion weighed heavily on the minds of rulers for the next generation and may have served to prevent the deterioration in peasant status that was to characterize the peasantries of eastern Europe in the following two centuries. Harsh penalties were initially imposed on the defeated rebels, although most lords were aware that to impoverish the payers of rent or tithe was self-defeating. The peasants were certainly not cowed in defeat, and their recalcitrance did not cease after 1526. Many defeated rebels found a place in the emerging Anabaptist movement, providing continuity with some of the social and religious ideals of the revolt. No further outbreak of rebellion on the same scale occurred before the nineteenth century, but peasant resistance remained, as it had always been, part of the local politics of Germany.

[*See also* Müntzer, Thomas; Twelve Articles; *and* Zwickau Prophets.]

BIBLIOGRAPHY

Blickle, Peter. *Die Revolution von 1525*. 3d. ed. Munich, 1993. Most recent interpretation of the Peasants' War. An earlier edition is available in English translation: *The Revolution of 1525: The German Peasants' War from a New Perspective*, translated by Thomas A. Brady and H. C. Erik Midelfort, Baltimore and London, 1977.

Buszello, Horst, Peter Blickle, and Rudolf Endres, eds. *Der deutsche Bauernkrieg*. Paderborn, 1984. An overview.

Franz, Gunther. *Der deutsche Bauernkrieg* (1933). 11th ed. Reprint, Darmstadt, 1984. Long the standard account.

Scott, Tom, and Robert W Scribner, eds. *The German Peasants' War: A History in Documents*. Atlantic Highlands, N. J., 1991. Comprehensive collection of documents; offers a succinct history and some fresh interpretations.

Stayer, James M. *The German Peasants' War and Anabaptist Community of Goods*. Montreal, 1991. Emphasizes continuity with the Anabaptist movement.

Winterhager, Friedrich. *Bauernkriegsforschung*. Darmstadt, 1981. Historiographic overview.

ROBERT W. SCRIBNER

PEDERSEN, Christian (c.1480–1554) Danish author, printer, and publisher. Born in Helsingør, he took his baccalaureate degree in Greifswald and during his period of study at the University of Paris (1508–1515) received a master of arts. After a short stay in Louvain, he traveled home to Lund, where he was a canon at the cathedral and an altar priest. In 1522 he became chancellor for Archbishop Johan Weze in Lund, and in 1526 he joined the exiled King Christian II in the Netherlands, where he converted to Lutheranism. After Christian II's imprisonment, Pedersen settled in Malmö (1531), where he continued his work as an author and printer, a profession he had practiced since his years in Paris. Now he placed himself in the service of the Reformation, but during the civil war (Counts' War) he sold his materials to the Copenhagen printer Hans Vingaard, though he continued as a translator and author until his death.

In his extensive literary production, there is a characteristic movement from humanism and reformed Catholicism to Lutheranism. His most significant literary accomplishment was his publication of *Gesta Danorum* (Paris, 1514) by Saxo Grammaticus (c.1150–after 1216), Denmark's greatest medieval historian. This work, which patriotically reproduces old legends and historical reports on Danes up to the author's own time, brought praise from Desiderius Erasmus of Rotterdam and made Pedersen internationally famous. Typical for this period as well were his pedagogical writings for students and his Danish books intended to educate the lay people. In *Vor Frue Tider* (Breviary of the Blessed Mother; 1514) he translated the breviary so that lay people could understand the religious texts. In *Bogen om Messen* (The Book of the Mass; 1514) he discusses the benefits one receives from attending Mass, and he presents an allegorical interpretation of the Mass. Among the authors he built upon were the Dominicans Johannes Herolt (d. 1468) and Vincentius Ferrerius (d.1419). His *Postille* (Book of Sermons; 1515) about the epistolary and Gospel texts, which emphasize the moralizing aspect, were his most popular works, and typically he defended his use of Danish by saying that all people should know the scriptures in their mother tongue, for no language is holier than another. Each sermon ended with a fantastic or grotesque miracle or example that pointed more to late Catholic piousness than toward reformed Catholicism. The book of sermons, which was also based on foreign sources, was in this sense an attempt at harmonizing.

In his Lutheran period his main work was his Danish translation of the New Testament (1529). His source was the Vulgate, but typically enough he turned also to Erasmus and Martin Luther as sources. He replaced Luther's prefaces with his own, however, and in this one can read his new evangelical understanding of the redeeming word of God, his rejection of the significance of good deeds, and his polemics against the Catholic clergy, who wanted to prevent the common people from having access to the scriptures. Here Pedersen went against his own sermons and warned the people against their Catholic fables.

Consistent with this, he then published writings of Peter Laurentsen and other Malmö reformers. During the early period of the reformed church, he completed a translation into Danish of the whole Bible, which was reviewed by a commission under the leadership of Peder Palladius and appeared in 1550 as *Christian III's Danske Bibel,* the first complete Bible in Danish. Pedersen's Danish, which was fluent and often conversational, became orthographically normalizing for the early standard Danish language.

His humanistic background continued to play a role, a fact seen in the general educational materials, medical writings, and chronicles and popular romances he then published. When the latter were criticized for their "Catholic" content, he defended himself with a humanist sense of history and an appeal for tolerance.

BIBLIOGRAPHY

Boserup, Ivan, ed. *Saxostudier* (Studies on Saxo). Opuscula Graecolatina, vol. 2. Copenhagen, 1975.

Brandt, C. J. *Om Lunde-kanniken Christiern Pedersen og hans skrifter* (On the Lunde Canon of Christiern Pedersen and His Writings). Copenhagen, 1882.

Hallingskov, Lisbet. "Til belysning af Christiern Pedersens bog om messen" (Elucidation of Christiern Pedersen's Book on the Mass). In *Kirkehistoriske Samlinger,* 7th ser., no 4, pp. 426–473. Copenhagen, 1960–1962.

Hens, H. A. "Pedersen Christiern." In *Dansk Biografisk Leksikon,* edited by Svend Cedergreen Bech, vol. 11, pp. 202–205. Copenhagen, 1982.

Lausten, Martin Schwarz. *Reformationen in Danmark* (The Reformation in Denmark). 2d ed. Copenhagen, 1992.

Pedersen, Christiern. *Christiern Pedersens Danske Skrifter* (Christiern Pedersen's Danish Writings). Edited by C. J. Brandt and R. Th. Fenger. 5 vols. Copenhagen, 1850–1856.

Verzeichnis der im deutschen Sprachbereich erschienenen Drucke des XVI. Jahrhunderts. Stuttgart, 1983–. See vol. 15, nos. 1106–1108.

MARTIN SCHWARZ LAUSTEN

Translated from Danish by Walter D. Morris

PELAGIANISM. The term *Pelagianism* stems from the ancient controversy between Augustine and Pelagius regarding the relationship between human beings and God in justification, sanctification, and salvation. The meaning of the term has varied throughout the centuries. As Heiko A. Oberman has noted, if one applied the standards of the Council of Trent, no medieval theologian would have been a true Pelagian. Even Pelagius never taught that one could be justified by one's own works "without divine grace."

The heart of the controversy between Augustine and Pelagius stemmed from their different understandings of grace, human nature, and freedom. Identifying freedom with choice, Pelagius believed that human beings were created with free will. Sin was not an inevitable condition but a series of immoral acts for which people were responsible because they chose and acted freely. Divine grace was defined in terms of creation and revelation. Pelagius thought it was an act of grace that God created the human being with a mind and a free will. The goodness of human nature was itself a manifestation of grace. Beyond the grace of creation, God also revealed his will in the law and in the example of Christ. Because of these assumptions about grace and human nature, Pelagian theology revolved around obedience and justice. The deity was not an unjust god who gave commands that could not be fulfilled. Humanity owed God complete obedience because the very existence of a command implied the ability to obey. Moreover, God was just and created all people in an equal condition; salvation or damnation depended not on predestination but on one's freely willed moral choices.

Augustine also believed that people were created in an equal condition for which they were responsible. But that condition was that of Original Sin, the main effect of which was the bondage of the will. Sinners experienced an activity or facility of the will, but on the deepest level of their being their wills were enslaved to sin. Human beings were born with disordered loves: they loved God with the lower love of use while they loved creation and the self with the ultimate love of enjoyment. Only divine grace could gradually heal and reorder the soul. True freedom transcended moral choice; freedom was an unchangeability of a soul rooted in the proper love of God and the inability to sin. This freedom, attained fully only in the heavenly city, was granted to the elect. These assumptions led Augustine's theology to revolve around the promise of divine mercy. Out of the "mass of perdition," God predestined some to salvation. Predestination was an act of mercy since, according to justice, all should be condemned to hell.

Pelagianism was repeatedly condemned in the fifth century. The condemnation most frequently cited in the Middle Ages was that by the Council of Ephesus in 431. The heresy was condemned again at the Council of Orange in 529. This council affirmed that the freedom of the will was so corrupted by sin that sinners could not, by their natural powers, believe in or love God. Even the desire for faith was the result of grace. Divine grace was necessary for salvation and tied primarily to baptism. The council thus affirmed the existence of Original Sin. However, double predestination was anathematized and the irresistibility of grace was omitted. The Council of Orange was the victory of a moderate Augustinianism over Pelagianism.

The Reformation has been interpreted as a continuation of late medieval attacks on the resurgence of semi-Pelagianism. The late Middle Ages was an era of complex theological debate. The late fourteenth and fifteenth century witnessed a "renewed search for the authentic interpretation of Augustine" (Oberman, *Forerunners of the Reformation,* 1981, p. 126). During this search, however, elements of the Pelagian controversy resurfaced. The teaching by some late medieval nominalists about God's absolute power and the divine *acceptatio* of contracted merits preserved Augustine's emphasis on the sovereignty of God. Nonetheless, for some theologians, the principle that "God does not withhold his grace from those who do their very best" came to exemplify the Pelagian view of works and free will. Debates about the ability to perform merits of congruity and condignity deepened the fear that Christianity was falling into Pelagianism. Theologians such as Thomas Bradwardine (d. 1349) and Johannes von Staupitz (d. 1524) thus wrote against what they considered the resurgence of Pelagianism in their time. In doing so, they insisted on the depth of human sin, the sinner's dependency on divine grace to do good and meritorious works, and the insufficiency of human action before God. They attempted to revive both the Augustinian emphasis on divine sovereignty and the Augustinian view of human sinfulness.

In view of the anti-Pelagian debates of late medieval thinkers as well as earlier theologians who maintained strong Augustinian doctrines of justification, it may seem strange that in his *Disputatio contra Scholasticam theologiam* (1517), Martin Luther charged all medieval theology with Pelagianism. Was his attack properly aimed only at some late medieval nominalists? In the preface to the second *Wider die Antinomer* (1538), Luther differentiated between earlier and later theologians and insisted that the Ockhamists simply had become "even worse Pelagians." The theology of the Reformation was born largely out of such an assault on medieval "Pelagianism."

The anti-Pelagian attack of reformers such as Luther, Huldrych Zwingli, and John Calvin was rooted in a twofold argument: the defense of a correct doctrine of human nature and the denial that justification was a process. In their insistence on the proper understanding of human nature, these reformers emphasized the radical effects of the Fall on both the mind and the will. The noetic effect of sin wreaked havoc on the mind so that human beings could no longer perceive the nature of God, the relationship between God and the self, or the true depth of sin. Human deception led to idolatry, false religious zeal, and a mistaken drive to earn salvation through merits. Moreover, the Fall caused the bondage of the will so that without election and grace, people would be incapable of loving God, having faith, or truly serving the neighbor. Any denial of the radical depravity of sin called forth accusations of Pelagianism. Luther accused Desiderius Erasmus of reviving the Pelagian heresy because of his attribution of freedom to the fallen human will. Even among these three reformers we see such a debate; in 1525 Zwingli had denounced the "papist" fables about "hereditary sin," and he at times distinguished Original Sin from guilt. Nonetheless, he emphasized the noetic effect of sin, the bondage of the natural, fallen will, the inability to earn merits, and that the sin of Adam clung to human nature and was "truly a sickness." The ambiguities in Zwingli's statements regarding the nature of Original Sin explained Luther's constant accusations that he had denied the orthodox Augustinian doctrine of Original Sin.

If sixteenth-century reformers had stressed only human depravity and the necessity for grace, they would not have deviated from the Augustinian tradition within the Catholic church. The theological rupture was caused by their anti-Pelagian attack on the medieval doctrine of justification. In medieval theology, the Christian was a viator who received the grace of the justice of Christ in baptism and penance. Cooperating with this grace, the Christian was gradually transformed into holiness by supplementing the justice of Christ with his or her own inherent righteousness. The merits earned by Christians prepared them for the Last Judgment, where they were judged by the justice of God. Medieval theologians assumed that justification was a process whereby Christ's justice was completed by the meritorious actions of the Christian, who must still proceed onward to face the justice of God.

The charge that this view of justification was Pelagian was aimed precisely at this notion of a process that was completed by the cooperation and works of the Christian. The doctrine of justification by faith alone insisted that Christ's atoning work was completely sufficient for the justification of the sinner. No works, even those inspired by grace, were required for salvation. By arguing that the believer was justified by faith, Luther, Zwingli, and Calvin reunified the justice of Christ and the justice of God. Their doctrines of justification, therefore, denied that justification was a process. Works of love followed justification but did not contribute to it. Therefore the Christian was completely justified at the beginning of sanctification.

In their various arguments against the medieval view of justification, these Reformation theologians made several anti-Pelagian points. They lowered the view of human nature so that humans had no possibility of contributing to salvation in or out of a state of grace. They also expounded a doctrine of justification that corresponded to this lowered anthropology; that is, they denied that the Christian needed to earn merits that completed the work of Christ. Finally, they defined Christian freedom as the freedom from having to earn salvation or to confront the final and terrifying justice of God.

Such central Reformation insights did not mean that these reformers simply reiterated or recovered Augustine. Their definition of freedom was not the state of unchangeability yearned for by Augustine; in Reformation theology the believer was sinful, just, and free at the same time. More importantly, their complete denial of meritorious actions was not the Augustinian teaching. For Augustine it was the theological virtue of love, rather than faith, that justified the Christian. For Augustine the spiritual renewal of the Christian, through faith that worked through love, was necessary for justification; justification was not an imputation of an alien (Christ's) righteousness but "being made righteous" through grace. The reformers were, in some ways, more anti-Pelagian than Augustine himself.

But the charge of Pelagianism was not limited to the arguments between Luther, Zwingli, and Calvin and their Catholic opponents. The emergence of religious radicalism incited even more charges against this ancient heresy. The accusation of Pelagianism was often aimed indiscriminately against the "radicals" but was most often leveled against the "evangelical Anabaptists." Their belief in believer's baptism, the voluntary church, and free will made them immediately suspect. Their criticisms against the doctrines of Original Sin and predestination only strengthened the belief that they had fallen into Pelagianism.

Nonetheless, it was primarily their separatism and their emphasis on holiness of the life of sanctification that roused the ire of those preaching justification by faith. Zwingli's polemics were usually aimed against the practice of adult baptism, but in his treatise *In catabaptistarum strophas elenchus*, he attacked the deceptive appearance of sanctity and the seeming devotion to good works among the Anabaptists. In his arguments against their alleged rejection of citizenship and the magistery, Zwingli insisted that neither the monks nor the Anabaptists attained the state of perfection that could do without civil authority. He went on to deny that the separated, gathered church of the Anabaptists had any claim to salvation or election.

Luther and Calvin more frequently criticized the dangers of the Anabaptists' supposed claim to holiness. Calvin repeatedly attacked the Anabaptists for being the new Novationists and the new Donatists, that is, those who would cause schism because they maintained that the church must be pure and perfect. Luther was more explicit about the dangers of such a demand for holiness. According to him, the Anabaptists were the "new monks" or the "false apostles" and "new jurists" who taught another form of salvation by works. According to Luther, the Anabaptists repeated the ancient error of turning Christ into Moses and relying on the works of the law for redemption. In particular, Luther argued that the Anabaptists' emphasis on suffering was just another way of relying on one's own works for righteousness.

Nonetheless, we must note that the charge of Pelagianism grew out of a theological problem common to all the Protestant reformers: the task of explaining the relationship of justification by faith alone and the resulting ethical life of the believer. Despite their many differences, the Anabaptists, spiritualists, and rationalists all shared a common disappointment in the failure of the Reformation to effect any real moral improvement in society or the church. The radicals insisted on making ethical results the ultimate test of doctrine. Luther, Zwingli, and Calvin considered these attempts to make ethics the norm of doctrine to be yet another resurgence of the Donatist-Pelagian heresies.

The final Tridentine decree on justification stands as another important stage in the sixteenth-century debates about Pelagianism. Trent rejected the attempts at reconciliation forged by the ecumenical movement of the early 1540s and made complete the doctrinal incompatibility of Protestant and Catholic views of justification. The fifth and sixth sessions of the Council of Trent roundly condemned the Pelagian views of human nature and the role of human works. Several of the canons appended to the sixth chapter on justification reaffirmed the essential elements of the Council of Orange so that once again Pelagianism was publicly condemned. Nonetheless, Trent also affirmed that justification was a process whereby the Christian was not reputed as just but was indeed made just by the remission of sins, the voluntary reception of grace, and the sanctification and renewal of the inward person. By cooperating with the grace of justification, the Christian increases and grows into holiness, a process completed in purgatory. The debate about Pelagianism that had resurfaced as a major issue with the emergence of late medieval "nominalist" theology did not result in a decision for or against Pelagius but in differing views about what constituted Pelagianism in Christian theology.

[*See also* Patristics.]

BIBLIOGRAPHY

Brown, Peter. *Augustine of Hippo.* Reprint, New York, 1986. Discusses ancient Pelagian heresy.

Edwards, Mark U. *Luther and the False Brethren.* Stanford, Calif., 1975.

Grane, Leif. *Contra Gabrielem.* Copenhagen, 1962.

———. *Modus loquendi theologicus: Luthers Kampf um die Erneuerung der Theologie, 1515–1518.* Leiden, 1975.

Hillerbrand, Hans J. *A Fellowship of Discontent.* New York, 1967.

Jedin, Hubert. *A History of the Council of Trent.* Translated by Ernest Graf. 2 vols. Saint Louis, 1949.

McGrath, Alister E. *Iustitia Dei: Beginnings to 1500.* Cambridge, 1986. See pp. 30–36 for a discussion comparing Augustine to the sixteenth-century reformers.

Oberman, Heiko A. *The Harvest of Medieval Theology.* Reprint, Durham, N.C., 1983. Discusses late medieval nominalism and Luther's relationship to this movement and the medieval tradition.

———. *Luther: Man between God and the Devil.* Translated by Eileen Walliser-Schwarzbart. New Haven, 1989.

———. "Duns Scotus, Nominalism, and the Council of Trent." In *Dawn of the Reformation,* pp. 204–233. Reprint, Grand Rapids, Mich., 1992.

———. "'Iustitia Christi' and 'Iustitia Dei': Luther and the Scholastic Doctrines of Justification." In *Dawn of the Reformation,* pp. 104–125. Reprint, Grand Rapids, Mich., 1992. Includes an analysis of the debate by modern historians about Luther's attack against Scholasticism.

Ozment, Stephen. *Mysticism and Dissent: Religious Ideology and Religious Dissent in the Sixteenth Century.* New Haven, 1973.

Pelikan, Jaroslav. *The Christian Tradition: A History of the Development of Doctrine.* Vol. 1, *The Emergence of the Catholic Tradition, 100–600.* Chicago, 1971.

———. *The Christian Tradition: A History of the Development of Doctrine.* Vol. 4, *Reformation of Church and Dogma, 1300–1700.* Chicago, 1984. See pp. 138–155 regarding the attack by Protestant reformers on medieval Pelagianism.

Plinval, G. de. *Essai sur le style et la langue de Pélage.* Fribourg, 1947.

Reese, B. R. *The Letters of Pelagius and His Followers.* Suffolk, England, 1991.

Rupp, E. Gordon. *Patterns of Reformation.* Philadelphia, 1969.
Steinmetz, David C. *Reformers in the Wings.* Philadelphia, 1971.
———. *Luther in Context.* Bloomington, Ind., 1986. See pp. 59–71.
Trinkaus, Charles, and Heiko A. Oberman, eds. *The Pursuit of Holiness in Late Medieval and Renaissance Religion.* Leiden, 1974.
Vignaux, Paul. *Justification et prédestination au XIVe siècle: Duns Scot, Pierre d'Auriole, Guillaume d'Occam, Grégoire de Rimini* (1934). Reprint, Paris, 1981.
Williams, George H. *The Radical Reformation.* Kirksville, Mo., 1992.

SUSAN E. SCHREINER

PELARGUS, Ambrosius

PELARGUS, Ambrosius (1493–1561), German Dominican opponent of the Reformation active in Basel and at the Council of Trent. Born in Nidda in Hesse, Pelargus entered the Dominican order as a young man and remained a lifelong champion of the old church. By the mid-1520s he was preaching in Basel, where he became a vigorous advocate of the Catholic Mass against Swiss reformer Johannes Oecolampadius. In 1527 the undecided city council accepted Pelargus's arguments for retaining both the Mass and Reformed services until a general council of the church pronounced on the matter.

This stratagem provoked the reformers to exert increasing pressure on the town fathers to forbid the Mass as "papal idolatry." In 1529 Oecolampadius urged the confiscation of a tract in which Pelargus pointed out inconsistencies in the reformer's stance on church authority—invoking it against Anabaptists while rejecting it for his own party in the religious struggle. These subtle polemics proved no match, however, for the fiery rhetoric of the reformers, and Pelargus fled the city on the eve of a popular uprising and wave of iconoclasm that brought an end to Catholic worship in Basel.

From his refuge in Freiburg, Pelargus continued his attacks against Protestant religion, particularly its more radical manifestations in social turbulence, image breaking, and Anabaptism. He disagreed sharply with the view of Johannes Brenz that recalcitrant Anabaptists simply be exiled if they were not actively promoting public disorder. Pelargus insisted on the death penalty for heretics.

In Freiburg the strict Dominican developed an unlikely friendship with the ageing and chastened Desiderius Erasmus. Their correspondence, including Pelargus's commentary on the *Apologia* Erasmus prepared for the Sorbonne in 1531, was published in 1539.

From 1533 until his death in 1561, Pelargus held a professorship at the University of Trier, where he also served as procurator to the archbishop. In 1540 he was a major speaker at the religious colloquy in Worms, and at the Council of Trent he contributed to deliberations on the Eucharist, confession, the Mass, and extreme unction. In 1561 Pelargus was instrumental in the admission of the Jesuits to the philosophy and theology faculties of the University of Trier.

BIBLIOGRAPHY

Paulus, Nikolaus. *Die deutschen Dominikaner im Kampf gegen Luther.* Freiburg, 1903. See pp. 190–212 for an extensively annotated essay covering the life and major writings of Pelargus.
Schottenloher, Karl, ed. *Bibliography zur deutschen Geschichte im Zeitalter der Glaubensspaltung.* Stuttgart, 1957.
Walz, A. *Lexicon für Theologie und Kirche.* Vol. 8. Freiburg, 1965. See p. 252 for more recent bibliographical data.

KARIN BRINKMANN BROWN

PELLIKAN, Konrad

PELLIKAN, Konrad (Lat., Conradus Pellicanus; also Kürschner; 1478–1556), Protestant theologian and Hebrew scholar. Born in Rufach in Upper Alsace, he was brought up in Heidelberg by his uncle Jodokus Gallus, who belonged to the humanist circle of Bishop Johann von Dalberg. In 1493 he was placed as a novice in the Franciscan monastery of his native town. From 1495 he studied Latin, Greek, and theology at the monastery of Tübingen. He was taught Hebrew by Johannes Reuchlin, and in 1501 Pellikan was the first Christian to publish a Hebrew grammar.

As a lector in the monastery in Basel, he belonged to the reform circle of Bishop Christoph von Utenheim and worked with the printer Johannes Amerbach. From 1516 he was closely associated with Desiderius Erasmus, who had a profound influence on his theological thinking. Pellikan contributed decisively to the Reformation in Basel by publishing Martin Luther's writings. In 1523 the council of Basel appointed him professor of theology at the university together with Johannes Oecolampadius. In 1526 he was nominated by Huldrych Zwingli in Zurich, where he accepted the Old Testament chair, which he occupied until his death.

Pellikan was a typical representative of the middle way and did not take part in confessional polemics. To his contemporaries Pellikan was above all a Hebrew scholar. He translated many Jewish commentaries, mostly into Latin, but he did not publish any of them. His influence as a Bible commentator was more important. He wrote the only complete Latin Bible commentary of the Reformation. From his German commentaries only that on the book of Ruth was printed. In its account of the early years, his autobiography gives insightful information about the Franciscan order in the Upper Rhine area, which was caught between late Scholasticism and humanism. At the same time, it is an interesting source for the history of education at the time of Zwingli in Zurich.

BIBLIOGRAPHY

Primary Sources

Conradi Pellicani de modo legendi et intelligendi Hebraeum. Strasbourg, 1501.
Commentaria bibliorum. 7 vols. Zurich, 1532–1539.
Riggenbach, Bernhard, ed. *Das Chronikon des Konrad Pellikan.* Basel, 1877. Pellikan's autobiography, written in Latin.

Secondary Sources

Degler-Spengler, Brigitte. "Barfüsserkloster Basel." In *Helvetia Sacra,* pt. 5, vol. 1, pp 133–135. Bern, 1978. Contains biographical and bibliographical information on Pellikan as a Franciscan.

Zürcher, Christoph. *Konrad Pellikans Wirken in Zürich, 1526–1556.* Zurich, 1975. Studies Pellikan's years in Zurich. Contains an extensive bibliography.

CHRISTOPH ZÜRCHER

PENANCE. The Latin word for penance—*penitentia* (as well as its Romance language cognates and the German *Busse*)—has three overlapping meanings in medieval religious thought and practice. The first, usually translated as "repentance" and identified with contrition, implies sorrow for sin and the intention to amend. In a second distinct but not unrelated meaning, penance (or penances) refers to the penitential activities (primarily prayer, fasting, and almsgiving, in that order of importance) voluntarily undertaken on one's own or at the direction of an ecclesiastical authority, usually a confessor, as satisfaction for the temporal punishments owed for sin and as proof of the sincerity of repentance. Finally, the word in medieval and Roman Catholic usage refers principally to the sacrament of penance itself. This sacramental penance includes the first two meanings—repentance and penitential activities—and adds the individual, private confession of sins to a priest and the absolution of the penitent by the priest. In medieval religious discourse the sacrament of penance is habitually assigned three parts: contrition, confession, and satisfaction. In medieval religious reality the sacrament of penance has a fourth part, which by the end of the Middle Ages had become the most important: the absolution of a priest, whose ordination gives him the "key of power" that forgives sin. By the thirteenth century absolution was pronounced in the indicative, "I absolve you" (*ego te absolvo*), which is consistent with the proposition of late medieval sacramental theology that the sacraments of the new law are efficacious *ex opere operato* (that is, they work automatically when a baptized adult penitent meets the basic criteria for "valid" reception). In short, contrition, confession of sin, performance of penances, and submission to the priestly keys are parts of "doing penance" in one sacrament.

Late Medieval Theologies of Penance. The teaching of three theologians and their schools defined the range of medieval explanations of how the penitent's sorrow and the priest's absolution obtain divine forgiveness (and some confidence in the reality of that forgiveness). In the twelfth century Peter Lombard asserted that confession is necessary but that forgiveness occurs outside the confessional as soon as a penitent becomes "contrite." Peter Lombard's nominalist successors, such as William of Ockham and Gabriel Biel, continued to assert the necessity of confession to a priest even as they called for a contrition motivated by love and ascribed a lesser power to priestly absolution. The belief that God requires penitents to do only what they are capable of (*facere quod in se est*) mitigated the strictness of the demands on the penitent.

Duns Scotus and his late medieval followers identified two ways to forgiveness. A spiritual elite might achieve a sorrow for sin sufficient in itself for forgiveness. Ordinary Christians have the sacrament of penance, which he redefined as "that absolution of a priest having jurisdiction." Scotus further strengthened the power of the confessor by asserting that the penitent need only be "a very little attrite" (*parum attritus,* sometimes mistaken as an endorsement of a sorrow based solely on fear) and that only the "obstacle" of a mortal sin while confessing can impede the efficacy of absolution. Scotus himself realized that these concessions to human weakness reduced the penitent's insecurity about his worthiness to be forgiven. Johann von Palz, on the eve of the Reformation, concluded that sacramental power is so great that even with minimal preparation one "could scarcely be damned."

In Thomas Aquinas's middle way the priest's absolution is the "instrumental" cause of forgiveness (a difficult concept), which preserves a decisive role for the penitent's contrition and the work of confession but which, like Scotism, strengthens the power of the priest. Both systems provide a logical basis for indicative absolution, but nominalists, as well as Scotists and Thomists, found ways to enhance the psychological advantages of confession by emphasizing the power of absolution to add something that the penitent does not bring to the encounter. Some speak of the power of the keys to raise an inadequate to a sufficient sorrow during confession. Even among historians who differ about confession's actual psychological consequences and its role in the Reformation, there is wide agreement that speculations by medieval theologians addressed the psychological problems that Luther made central.

Roman Catholic Economy of Sin and Forgiveness. Baptism, the first plank of salvation, removes the guilt of Original Sin but not its effect of making all humans prone to sin. When the grace from baptism is lost by "actual" mortal sin, the sacrament of penance ("the second plank after the shipwreck" of the Fall of man) is available to restore grace as many times as relapses into sin make it necessary.

Imagine a female penitent. With the commission of any mortal sin she incurs guilt (*culpa*), which makes her liable to eternal damnation, and a penalty (*poena*), a debt precisely commensurate with the gravity of her sin. Her contrition and confession, in combination with the priest's absolution, remove her guilt. If she dies, she will not go to hell, but a penalty demanding satisfaction remains. The penances prescribed by the priest (usually prayers) have a special efficacy because his keys put her penitential activity into contact with the suffering of Christ (the ultimate source of all forgiveness, whether of *culpa* or *poena*). When she dies she must suffer in purgatory for any unexpiated punishment. Medieval religious culture encouraged fear of purgatory, and a papal bull of 1343 officially formulated the doctrine on indulgences (Heinrich Denzinger, *The Sources of Catholic Dogma*, Saint Louis, 1957, nos. 550–552). The massive increase in the late Middle Ages of masses for the dead and the accumulation of indulgences (with financial advantage to the clergy) is compelling evidence of the centrality of this element in pre-Reformation penance. The temporal values of indulgences (*tantum valent quam sonant*—"their value is as stated") ought undoubtedly to be understood as equivalences to an identical period of penance in the ancient church, but the notion was widespread (see, for example, Desiderius Erasmus's *Enchiridion Militis Christiani*) that they represented a simple reduction in the number of days or years one was destined to suffer in purgatory.

Luther's Revolutionary Theology of Penance. Philipp Melanchthon once summarized Martin Luther's achievement in a succinct judgment: "He taught the correct manner of penance and the correct use of the sacraments." In focusing on penance, Melanchthon identified a practice and theological idea that encompassed every major contested issue in the theology of forgiveness: justification, grace and works, contrition, confession, satisfaction, absolution, indulgences, purgatory, and hell and heaven. After Luther all Protestant doctrines of penance centered on salvation by faith, which entailed the rejection of basic features of the Catholic medieval tradition of penance.

The basic outlines were fixed by 1520. In spite of Luther's determination to retain confession and absolution, the sacraments were reduced to two—baptism and the Lord's Supper—both of which have a visible sign and the effective promise of the forgiveness of sins to all who believe. Righteousness, no longer equated with works, is imputed and passive. Human merit—whether "condign" (actually worthy in the eyes of God) or "congruent" (not actually worthy but acceptable because it is as good as the sinner can offer)—has no place in Luther's theology. To those who believe that the suffering and death of Christ forgave their sins, forgiveness has been promised and is already given. Baptism and the Lord's Supper remain the continual sacramental sources that turn penance into forgiveness.

Luther realized the antinomian tendencies of this doctrine even before the Antinomian controversy or the Peasants' War. He insists, on the contrary, that a penitent Christian does works, but they are a result, not a cause, of his justification. Even rigorous penance can be appropriate if, as in the ancient church, it is considered not as satisfaction for sin but as a sign of sincerity. Christian liberty requires the subjugation of the outer man "for the purpose of keeping the body under control" (*Three Treatises*, pp. 294, 308). The focus of his theology, however, is the forgiveness of *culpa*, not the remission of *poena*, through salvation by faith.

Penance in the Reformed Tradition. The Swiss and south German reformers accepted Luther's reformulation of penance and justification but stressed even more than Luther the connection between repentance and the penitent, regenerate life. The long section devoted to penance in John Calvin's *Institutes* (book III, chapters 3–10) begins by affirming that "with good reason, the sum of the gospel is held to consist in repentance and forgiveness of sins." By treating penance before justification, Calvin anticipates Roman Catholic charges that justification by faith would encourage moral laxity. Calvin's penance incorporates change of life, mortification of the flesh, and vivification of the spirit. He distinguishes legitimate "mortification of the flesh" from practices he considers extravagant or misguided, and he quotes approvingly Saint Bernard's warning that "sorrow for sins is necessary if it be not unremitting." Nevertheless, he insists on the lifelong practice of sobriety and the taming of the flesh. Calamities and the need to avert divine vengeance may even call for public penance in the form of fasting, which is primarily a public confession of guilt. Yet he always stresses internal over external acts. This teaching connects directly with the characteristic Reformed doctrine on regeneration (the continual and often slow restoration of the almost obliterated image of God) and sanctification (a purification, always short of perfection) of the life of the regenerate. Even vivification is not pure joy but rather "the desire arising from rebirth" to live a holy and devout life. At the same time, Calvin excoriates scholastic theology's doctrine of penance, especially the scholastic habit of meticulously identifying its various human and divine parts. Like Luther, he tried to eliminate false notions of human effort—that repentance is a human preparation for forgiveness and that forgiveness is the reward of penance—even though he affirmed his own vision of holy asceticism. As the title to book III, chapter 7, puts it: "The Sum of the Christian Life: The Denial of Ourselves."

The Council of Trent rejected the Protestant critique in its entirety and made traditional scholastic definitions a rule of faith. Penance, the fathers of Trent assert, is a virtue, a sacrament, and a work of satisfaction. Auricular confession to a priest is divinely ordained and necessary to salvation. The council makes no apology for its insistence that penance be performed according to certain laws and standards, but it could not settle the scholastic debates about attrition, contrition, and the power of the keys. Most emphatically the fathers condemn the "vain confidence of the heretics," the heart of evangelical and Reformed repentance and justification. Sinners are to conceive of themselves as actively contributing—by the work of their sincere contrition, conscientiously complete confession, and dutiful performance of penances—to the forgiveness of guilt and the remission of punishment owing to sin. When priests say "I absolve you," they do more than declare that God has already forgiven a contrite sinner and more than confirm the promise contained in a gospel of fiduciary faith and imputed righteousness. Somehow priestly absolution works, and its effects are real. Thus, the Council of Trent reaffirmed the medieval scholastic doctrine against which the reformers protested and fixed a Catholic theological discourse about sin, penance, and forgiveness that remained remarkably stable for almost exactly four hundred years.

[*See also* Confession *and* Indulgences.]

BIBLIOGRAPHY

Calvin, John. *Institutes of the Christian Religion.* 2 vols. Edited by John T. McNeill, translated and indexed by Ford Lewis Battles. Library of Christian Classics, 20 and 21. Philadelphia, 1960. Intended as a definitive summary of theology; two user-friendly volumes that offer the editors' impressive erudition, in explanatory notes and extensive indexes, to the intense or merely browsing reader. See especially book 3, chapters 5–7, on penance (vol. 1, pp. 592–725).

Cameron, Euan. *The European Reformation.* Oxford, 1991. Basic survey of the religious and political issues, with a careful presentation of the place of penance in the conflicting explanations of the motivations behind the Reformation. See especially pp. 9–19, 79–93, 111–135, 156–185, 305–313, 406–422.

Luther, Martin. *Three Treatises.* 2d rev. ed. Philadelphia, 1970. Nothing can substitute for the passion, concreteness, love of paradox, and persuasive power of Luther's own prose—even in translation. See especially the passages on baptism and penance in *The Babylonian Captivity of the Church,* pp. 178–218, and *The Freedom of a Christian* in its entirety, pp. 277–316.

McGrath, Alister E. *Iustitia Dei: A History of the Christian Doctrine of Justification.* 2 vols. Cambridge, Mass., 1986. A scholarly survey of the whole history of forgiveness of sins, grace, and free will, and the creation of "orthodox" definitions of those doctrines.

Oberman, Heiko. *The Harvest of Medieval Theology.* 3d ed. Durham, N.C., 1983. A learned and incisive examination of the relationship between late medieval theology and the Reformation—especially the theology of grace, works, and penance.

Poschmann, Bernhard. *Penance and the Anointing of the Sick.* Translated and revised by Francis Courtney. New York, 1964. A general survey of the history of the sacrament of penance and extreme unction from antiquity to the Counter-Reformation by the twentieth century's foremost authority on the subject.

Schroeder, H. J., trans. *Canons and Decrees of the Council of Trent.* Reprint, Rockford, Ill., 1978. Straightforward language—in chapters that expound doctrine, and canons that condemn heretical error—designed to establish clear boundaries for orthodoxy. Especially relevant are the sixth session on justification and the fourteenth session on the sacrament of penance, pp. 29–46, 88–105.

Steinmetz, David. *Luther in Context.* Bloomington, Ind., 1986. Scholarly and accessible: individual studies explain the inspirations—both negative and positive—of Luther's reformation of theology.

THOMAS TENTLER

PERETTI, Felice. *See* Sixtus V.

PÉREZ DE PINEDA, Juan (Lat., Pierius; c.1500–1568), converted Spanish priest, Reformed minister in Switzerland and France, and author and translator.

Juan Pérez was born on an unknown date in Montilla (Andalusia). Nothing is known of his early life, education, and ordination, although he did obtain a doctorate. After diplomatic service in Italy, he was—as director of the college of the Niños de la Doctrina in Seville—one of a small group teaching reformist doctrine. Around 1549, after the Inquisition began enquiries into Juan Gil, he fled to Paris and shared a house with Juan Morillo, who not long before had been in Trent as a Catholic theologian. At the house they received reform-minded Spaniards and taught Protestant doctrine.

Pérez next traveled to Geneva some time before 1556, when he was sent to Frankfurt with Calvin as one of a commission to mediate between Valérand Poullain and his congregation. Pérez stayed on for two years in Frankfurt and was a signatory of the Frankfurt Recess.

In Geneva he had already produced a number of books in Spanish to be used for spreading evangelical ideas in his homeland. This continued after his return. In addition to original works, these include versions of Calvin's catechism, the New Testament, and *Psalms* (claimed by some as revisions of versions by Francisco de Enzinas) and adaptations of the works of others. The discovery of smuggled copies of these in Seville triggered the savage persecutions of Protestants in Spain and their eventual total suppression.

For some years Pérez was pastor of a small Spanish congregation in Geneva, but after freedom of worship was granted to French Protestants, he became a minister in France in 1562 and was one of those deputed to meet Louis I Condé in Orléans in March 1563 to discuss whether the January Edict allowed Protestants to bear arms. Against all advice, Condé signed the Pacification of Amboise, restricting Protestant liberties and curbing the right to call foreign ministers.

Pérez was invited to become minister of the French Protestants in London. Instead he went in late 1564 to serve René of France as domestic chaplain, along with Antonio del Corro. There he worked on revisions of his various publications, particularly the translation of the New Testament. This prevented his accepting a call to minister to French-speaking Protestants in Antwerp. In 1568 he went to supervise the printing of these works in Paris, where Corro, on his way to Antwerp, arrived just in time to be at Pérez's deathbed. The books were seized and burned.

Pérez was an unswerving first-generation Calvinist, publicist of Reformed biblical teaching, and a respected pastor. Parts of his translation of the New Testament were incorporated into the Spanish Bible of 1569.

BIBLIOGRAPHY

Boehmer, Eduard. *Bibliotheca Wiffeniana: Spanish Reformers of Two Centuries.* London, 1883. See vol. 2, pp. 55–100.

Kinder, A. G. "Juan Pérez de Pineda (Pierius): A Spanish Calvinist Minister of the Gospel in Sixteenth-Century Geneva." *Bulletin of Hispanic Studies* 53 (1976), 283–300.

A. GORDON KINDER

PERIODICAL LITERATURE. Reformation studies have benefited from an extensive array of serial publications, many of which specialize in the field. The richness represented by these periodicals demonstrates both that Reformation studies are a major field of scholarship and that this scholarship is quite often interdisciplinary in nature. The geographic emphasis traditionally has been Germany.

The most important journal in the field has been the *Archiv für Reformationgeschichte.* First published in 1903, it has continuously appeared ever since (with the exception of several years during and after World War II). The *Archiv* is published under the auspices of the German Verein für Reformationsgeschichte and has enjoyed a number of distinguished German Reformation scholars as editors—for example, Walther Friedensburg and Gerhard Ritter. In 1951, when Germany was still suffering from the ravages of World War II, the American Society for Reformation Research offered, in a gesture of financial support by North American Reformation scholars, to participate jointly in the publication of the *Archiv.* The English version of the title of the journal was added at the time (*Archive for Reformation History*), and the Verein and the American society have been the copublishers ever since. A European and a North American managing editor jointly edit the *Archiv.* In the main, the *Archiv* has struck a balance between German- and English-language contributions. Traditionally it has focused on the German Reformation and theological topics, reflecting the orientation of Reformation scholarship during most of the twentieth century. Although the *Archiv* interprets *Reformation* in a very broad sense, it does remain focused on the Reformation—that is, religious change, not the sixteenth century in its entirety. An important augmentation of the *Archiv* (since 1972) is the annual *Literature Survey* (*Literaturbericht*), which lists, in annotated form, literature on a whole range of aspects of the sixteenth century.

The *Sixteenth Century Journal,* published by the Sixteenth Century Studies Conference since 1972, excels the *Archiv für Reformationsgeschichte* in its comprehensiveness of scope. Its title is programmatic in that the journal focuses on the entire sweep of the sixteenth century. This has meant that theological themes have not held the same kind of prominence in its essays as has been the case in the *Archiv.* The journal is truly interdisciplinary in nature.

In addition to these two comprehensive journals, several other major journals focus on particular aspects of the sixteenth century. Of these, *Zwingliana* is the oldest. As its name conveys, it emphasizes Zwingli and the Zwinglian Reformation in Switzerland. Published by the Zwingli Verein in Zurich, it first appeared in 1897/1903 and has been published ever since. *Zwingliana* is indispensable for the student of Zurich and Swiss reform.

The *Mennonite Quarterly Review* was founded by the Anabaptist scholar Harold S. Bender in 1927 and is published by the Mennonite Historical Society of Goshen, Indiana. During the three decades of Bender's editorship, it was, despite its stated focus on the entire Anabaptist-Mennonite heritage, a publication concentrating on sixteenth-century Anabaptism. Most of the writings of Anabaptist revisionism associated with Bender and Robert Friedmann were published in the *Mennonite Quarterly Review.* In recent years the focus of the review has returned to contemporary aspects of the Mennonite tradition.

Two periodical publications are devoted to Martin Luther and his influence on the sixteenth century and beyond. They are the *Luther-Jahrbuch,* published in Leipzig beginning in 1919, and *Luther: Mitteilungen der Luthergesellschaft,* also published since 1919. Of these, the *Luther-Jahrbuch* is more scholarly in its tone and articles; the latter publication has excelled in essays on the continuing significance of Luther's life and thought. The *Luther-Jahrbuch* is published annually as a single volume and includes a valuable Luther bibliography. With more than a thousand entries each year, the quantity of annual publications signifies the importance of contemporary Luther research.

Mention must be made of several regional periodicals, all, of course, with a broader chronological scope than the Reformation but notable for the importance they place on sixteenth-century topics. These include *Jahrbuch der hessischen kirchengeschichtlichen Vereinigung; Blätter für pfälzische Kirchengeschichte; Jahrbuch für Geschichte des Protestantismus in Österreich,* and *Jahrbuch für Westfälische Kirchengeschichte.* In addition to these German serials, also of note are the French publications *Revue d'histoire de l'eglise de France* and *Bulletin de la Societe de l'Histoire du Protestantisme Français,* as well as the Swiss *Zeitschrift für schweizerische Kirchengeschichte* and the Italian *Rivista di storia della chiesa in Italia.*

Also important are the two serial publications *Quellen und Forschungen zur Reformationsgeschichte* and *Schriften des Vereins für Reformationsgeschichte,* the former published since 1921 in continuation of the series Studien zur Kultur und Geschichte der Reformation. As the title *Quellen und Forschungen* (Sources and Studies) indicates, two types of publications are here combined. The first are Reformation sources (*Quellen*), of which fifty-seven volumes have been published, notably the collection of Anabaptist sources (the Täuferakten, at present sixteen volumes) and the writings of several reformers, such as Andreas Osiander. The second (*Forschungen*) is a monograph series that has included some of the most important contributions to Reformation scholarship in the twentieth century. The related series, *Schriften des Vereins für Reformationsgeschichte,* has published no less than 196 shorter monographs since 1883.

The *Reformationsgeschichtliche Studien und Texte* was conceived as a Catholic counterpart to the publication efforts of the Verein. The underlying notion was that for Catholics, too, the sixteenth century was a period of immense importance. The series is published by the Gesellschaft zur Herausgabe des Corpus Catholicorum. The Texte, begun in 1906, consists of 132 volumes (plus two supplementary volumes), while the *Corpus Catholicorum* itself, editions of the writings of sixteenth-century Catholic theologians, has published 43 volumes since 1919. A further series under the same sponsorship is entitled *Katholisches Leben und Kirchenreform im Zeitalter der Glaubensspaltung,* begun in 1927. It is a Catholic parallel to the *Schriften des Vereins für Reformationsgeschichte* and has published 49 volumes.

In Holland the *Doopsgezinde Bijdragen* cover Anabaptist-Mennonite history, primarily Dutch, while for Poland the *Odrozenie i reformacja w Polsce* must be mentioned. Important for Jesuit studies is the *Archivum historicum Societatis Iesu.*

Other important journals include the *Conrad Grebel Review,* with its Anabaptist orientation; *Recusant History,* with its emphasis on late sixteenth-century English Catholicism; and *Moreana,* with its concentration on Thomas More. Moreover, there are a number of general journals of broad historical and church historical character that include scholarship on the Reformation, such as *Historisches Jahrbuch der Görresgesellschaft; Zeitschrift für Kirchengeschichte; Church History; Journal of Ecclesiastical History; Journal of Medieval and Renaissance Studies; Revue d'histoire ecclesiastique;* and *Nederlands archief voor kerkgeschiedenis.* The advent of online bibliographies has produced Clio and Religion Abstracts. The latter is particularly useful, as it also includes reviews.

In sum, periodicals have played an important role in Reformation scholarship. Two general conclusions may be offered. One is that journals have provided an avenue for essays and contributions of a regional nature. A great deal of the groundwork relevant for Reformation studies pertains to its regional manifestations, and journals have supplied that need. Second, journals have been the vehicles for major theses and hypotheses regarding the Reformation.

HANS J. HILLERBRAND

PERSECUTION. The suppression, legal or otherwise, of religious dissent or deviation relates to societal intolerance and absence of religious freedom. It is a consequence of the inability (or unwillingness) to accept the "other." The point of departure for persecution in the sixteenth century is the medieval European notion of the unity of society. It was the basic assumption that society was one and was characterized by Christian principles. Theologians divided society functionally into church (*sacerdotium*) and state (*imperium*), with the church laying claim to its superiority over the state. In this view, the state's function was confined to maintaining external security and domestic law and order while the church functioned to offer eternal bliss. Christianity, that is, the Roman Catholic church led by the Roman pontiff, was the prescribed religion of all European states and commonwealths. This preeminence was not only buttressed by a number of dogmas that enjoined adherence to the proper Christian tenets—for example, infant baptism—but also, in the course of the Middle Ages, by suppression and penalties for theological dissent. In the early medieval period the persecution of dissent was fairly lax, but the emergence of organized groupings of heretical dissenters in the high Middle Ages prompted the formation of the Inquisition, which eventually had three manifestations (papal, Roman, and Spanish) and became the touchstone for the maintenance of orthodoxy.

By the early sixteenth century religious deviation was subsumed under three charges, each of which entailed persecution by church and state: blasphemy, heresy, and insurrection. Blasphemy was any act that entailed offending, such as using epithets against God, swearing false oaths (while invoking God), or deliberately destroying or damaging crucifixes or sacred images. The church dealt with blasphemy initially, but secular courts increasingly assumed jurisdiction. The penalties for blasphemy were fines, expulsion, pilgrimages, whippings, and, most severely, execution. Tellingly, cutting off the culprit's tongue was a frequent penalty.

Heresy, in turn, was dissent from church dogma. Initially, heresy was an ecclesiastical offense (*delictum mere ecclesiasticum*), but as early as 1139 the Second Lateran Council invoked the support of secular authorities for the persecution of heresy. From then on, the secular persecution of heresy as well as secular trials and penalties (after the church had rendered the theological verdict) became the norm. In the thirteenth century the legislation of Emperor Frederick II stipulated as punishment for heresy death by burning, carried out by secular authorities.

The charge of insurrection was widely used in the sixteenth century as a rationale for suppression and persecution of religious dissent, particularly against the Anabaptists. The charge had an intriguing relationship to that of heresy. Heresy was seen, for example by Emperor Frederick II, as an offense against the divine majesty, while insurrection was seen as a *crimen laesae majestatis,* a crime against secular majesty.

In the sixteenth century persecution of dissent in the form of blasphemy, heresy, or insurrection was mostly an intra-Christian phenomenon. By the same token, persecution also meant the Christian suppression of non-Christians, such as, in late fifteenth-century Spain, of Jews. The treatment of the native peoples in regions occupied by European explorers in the course of the sixteenth century also comes under the label of persecution. Finally, the European witch craze, which began late in the fifteenth century with the publication of the famous *Witchhammer,* exposed its victims, mainly women, to severe persecution. Much like the prominent intra-Christian religious persecution, it lasted with intriguing oscillations well into the seventeenth century.

The philosophical basis for persecution in the sixteenth century was a generally held concept of truth that allowed only for a single truth, and no diversity or pluralism. Accordingly, since one's own tenets constituted truth, any deviation was error—blasphemy, heresy, or both. Juridically, the justifications for persecution were legal statutes already on the books when the Reformation controversy erupted.

The point of departure was always a legal act that one might call a "uniformity" statute. A legal bill of particulars—generally old, but sometimes new—stipulated the parameters of theological uniformity. These statutes (for example, Henry VI's Six Articles Act) also provided relevant punishment and penalties.

The extent to which the penalties provided for heterodox thinking were actually applied depended on the disposition of the political authorities. The Six Articles Act is a good case in point; its stipulation that any denial of the doctrine of transubstantiation entailed the death penalty (a pronouncement that surely would put the fear of God into English Protestants) was never applied. Religious dissent in the Reformation was thus both a theological and a secular matter. As far as the Catholic church was concerned, Protestants were heretics and were not to be tolerated. Luther's excommunication and the Edict of Worms set the stage as to how Luther and his followers were to be treated: the condemnation of one as a heretic by the church was to be followed by punishment according to secular law. An ecclesiastical and a secular verdict joined to deal with religious dissent. The Bamberg *Halsgerichtsordnung* ("penal code") of 1507, in force in the Holy Roman Empire until 1527, stipulated that someone found to be a heretic by an ecclesiastical tribunal was to be turned over to the secular authorities for execution by burning. If the Edict of Worms did not set the stage for the persecution of Luther and his followers, it was only because any number of territorial rulers and cities, notably Luther's Elector Frederick, were unwilling to carry out existing legal mandates. While some territories, Bavaria, for example, proceeded to administer the edict, most of the territorial rulers did not. The papal bull of excommunication should have entailed the persecution (and punishment) of Lutheran partisans, but for complex reasons it did not.

The religious and political stalemate between Catholics and reformers that quickly characterized the German scene explains why Catholics undertook little actual persecution of "Martinians." Persecution would have disturbed the precarious equilibrium in the empire, where, after all, the Protestant rulers were an important political force. The Protestants in their territories, in turn, could not really persecute Catholics for much the same reason, especially since, as in Augsburg in 1530, the Lutherans made a point of insisting that there were no real differences between them and the Catholic church. Accordingly, the persecution of mainstream Protestants was rare in Germany. It occurred in non-German lands, such as France and Spain, where different political realities prevailed.

A different situation obtained with respect to the Anabaptists. They lacked political stature and were promptly subjected to vehement persecution by Catholics and Protestants alike. Both reiterated the traditional medieval notion that dissent was connected with insurrections. In particular, King Ferdinand expanded the notion that the Anabaptists—that is, all fringe or radical reformers—were a threat to the public order. Accordingly, the Anabaptists were declared to be revolutionaries and punished with execution by the sword. Ferdinand's mandate against the Anabaptists of 1528, which followed this line of reasoning, was made imperial law at the Diet of Speyer in 1529. This gave the political authorities the sole jurisdiction for the persecution of Anabaptists. All persecution, legal proceedings, and trials against Anabaptists in the sixteenth century were conducted by secular authorities.

Luther's 1525 treatise against Thomas Müntzer made the fateful connection between theological heresy and civic disobedience that was to characterize the legal case against the Anabaptists and other radicals throughout the sixteenth century. In 1528 Johannes Brenz addressed the issue of the role of governmental authority—*Ob ein weltliche öberkeit mit Götlichem vnd billichem Rechten, mög die Widderteuffer durch fewer, odder schwerd, vom leben zum tode richten lassen* (If Government May by Divine or Civic Law Condemn the Anabaptists to Death by Fire or Sword), a theme which Luther reiterated in his 1536 tract *Das weltliche Oberkeit den Widerteuffern mit leiblicher straffe zu wehren schuldig sey* (That It Is the Responsibility of Government to Suppress the Anabaptists with Physical Punishment).

As early as 1520 Emperor Charles V had issued for his hereditary lands a mandate against Luther and his followers; two years later he appointed a Brabant councilor as general inquisitor, thereby removing the jurisdiction for the suppression and persecution of the Lutheran heresy from the church. Charles wanted this move, which implied that the Lutheran heresy had also infected the church, to strengthen his centralizing objectives.

In the early years of the Reformation, Luther had vigorously protested against the use of force in religious matters, placing himself against the consensus of his time. Indeed, his use of a quotation in one of his writings ("to burn heretics is contrary to the Holy Spirit") was included among the 41 propositions condemned in the bull *Exsurge Domine*, which formed the basis for his eventual excommunication. But Luther was soon overwhelmed by the medieval legacy of the uniform society, and he became concerned about how heretical dissent disrupted law and order in society and jeopardized the spread of the gospel. Still, Luther distinguished between the mere holding of religious beliefs on the one hand and the public exercise of such belief on the other. People were free to believe but were not free to advocate publicly their beliefs. Of course, the first part of this position was gratuitous in that belief as an intellectual exercise could hardly be subject to governmental (or ecclesiastical) surveillance. Since public advocacy meant speaking, writing, publishing, or preaching, any public expression of one's belief was precluded.

The radical fringe of the Reformation was on the receiving end of most of the religious persecution in the sixteenth century. In Germany, as elsewhere, numerous mandates were issued against the Anabaptists, which buttressed the case (and thus the persecution) against them. From the first mandate issued in Zurich in 1525 to the mandates promulgated at the end of the century, the common motif was that, in addition to being heretical, the Anabaptists were political revolutionaries. The political authorities associated revolutionary tendencies with theological radicalism. The authorities were undoubtedly convinced of this, since they had no reason to advance a rationale in addition to that of heresy. Accordingly, the legal proceedings against Anabaptists in the sixteenth century were uniformly conducted by secular tribunal officials, though theologians were present as theological advisers. The punishment for Anabaptists was severe—confiscation of property, expulsion, death. The estimate of the number of executed Anabaptists is around five thousand during the century. Only toward the end of the century did persecution of Anabaptists cease.

The number of victims of sixteenth-century persecution elsewhere is equally difficult to ascertain. Some three hundred persons fell victim to the Marian persecution in England, an astoundingly low number given the notoriety of Mary Tudor's policy. In other countries the numbers appear to have been more modest. But these figures only tell about those who were executed, not about those who were jailed, expelled, or deprived of their property.

England, which deserves primacy of place for the most frequent ecclesiastical changes during the century, saw persecutions of widely different sorts flourish throughout the century. A parliamentary statute provided the legal rationale for persecution and suppression since the disavowal of the authority of Rome had rendered the existing old statutes invalid. Under Henry VIII, the Treason Act and the Act of Succession, two statutes that seemingly dealt with matters of state, had not-so-subtle theological ramifications. Nonetheless, actual persecution under Henry was sporadic, and the celebrated trials and executions of John Fisher and Thomas More had rather more symbolic than typical significance. When the Six Articles Act, with its decidedly Catholic orientation, was promulgated in 1540, its harsh penalties were scarcely applied. Mary Tudor, who succeeded in 1553, was of a different temper: she was resolved to return England to the fold of the Roman church and she determinedly persecuted the "gospellers." Under Elizabeth I, both ardent Puritans and committed Catholics were on the receiving end of what was, in general, a fairly broad-minded ecclesiastical policy.

Elizabeth's policy of religious uniformity along the lines of a fairly moderate religious settlement shows once more the close proximity of ecclesiastical and political considerations. Elizabeth was convinced of the political expediency of the settlement, and both the ardent Puritans and the Catholics were a threat to the political stability of the realm, the latter not the least for the obvious political implications of their alleged ties with Spain. Catholics were the greater threat and frequently found themselves the objects of latent persecution.

The Catholic perspective had clarity with respect to how to deal with dissent: blasphemy and heresy were unthinkable. The challenge of the Protestant heresy caused Pope Paul III to establish in his bull *Licet ab initio* (1542), an inquisitorial commission of six cardinals with the charge to deal with heresy, morality, Jews, and the ecclesiastical order. This mandate broadened the most extensive existing inquisitorial machinery, the Spanish Inquisition, whose preoccupation in the late fifteenth century had been with Jews and Muslims.

A modest tradition dissented from this societal consensus and called for religious freedom. Sebastian Franck's *Chronica* set the tone. The major sixteenth-century work was Sébastien Castellion's *De haereticis: an sint persequendi* (Concerning Heretics: If They Are to Be Persecuted), published under the pseudonym Martin Bellius. It skillfully used quotations from Jerome, Augustine, Erasmus, Luther, and a host of other Protestant reformers (including Calvin) against the persecution of "heretics." Of similar fervor was Camillo Renato's *Carmen* against Calvin's role in Michael Servetus's execution, an impassioned appeal for broad-minded toleration. Later in the century, Jacobus Acontius's *Strategemata Satanae* made the case for religious toleration even more forcefully. Among these voices, Castellion had sounded the fundamental tone: it is impossible to be a judge of doctrine, when so many divergent factions all claim to be sole possessor of the truth. These advocates of toleration clearly embraced a different concept of truth. They rejected the notion of an easily accessible and absolute single truth as much as the notion that government had a function in maintaining religious uniformity.

Despite these voices of toleration, mainline sixteenth-century sentiment held that society had to be uniform in its religious orientation. Pluralism was unthinkable, and the tools of government had to be employed to prevent it. In an era of rising importance—not to mention self-confidence—of political rulers in Europe, this insistence on uniformity was what the rulers, too, preferred.

[*See also* Anabaptists; Antisemitism; Books of Martyrs; Marian Exiles; Nicodemism; Recusancy; Refugees; Spiritualism; *and* Toleration.]

BIBLIOGRAPHY

Brändi, Willy. "Täuferprozesse in Luzern im XVI. Jahrhundert." *Zwingliana* 8 (1944), 65–78.

Ginzburg, Carlo. "Cheese and Worms: The Cosmos of a Sixteenth-Century Miller." In *Religion and the People, 800–1700*, edited by Jim Obelkevich, pp. 87–167. Chapel Hill, N.C., 1979.

Haliczer, Stephen, ed. *Inquisition and Society in Early Modern Europe.* Totowa, N.J., 1987.

Kamen, Henry. "Toleration and Dissent in Sixteenth-Century Spain: The Alternative Tradition." *Sixteenth Century Journal* 19 (1988), 3–23.

Kaplan, Yosef, ed. *Jews and Conversos: Studies in Society and the Inquisition.* Proceedings of the Eighth World Congress of Jewish Studies, 16–21 August 1981. Jerusalem, 1985.

Kelly, Henry Ansgar. "Inquisition and the Prosecution of Heresy: Misconceptions and Abuses." *Church History* 58 (1989), 439–451.

Köhler, Walther. *Reformation und Ketzerprozess.* Tübingen, 1901.

Menchi, Silvana Seidel, Hans R. Guggisberg, and Bernd Moeller, eds. *Ketzerverfolgung im 16. und frühen 17. Jahrhundert.* Proceedings of an international conference, Wolfenbüttel, Germany, 1–5 October 1989. Wiesbaden, 1992.

Monter, E. William, and John Tedeschi. "Toward a Statistical Profile of the Italian Inquisition, Sixteenth to Eighteenth Centuries." In *The Inquisition in Early Modern Europe: Studies on Sources and Methods*, edited by Gustav Henningsen, John A. Tedeschi, and Charles Amiel, pp. 130–157. De Kalb, Ill., 1986.

Nalle, Sara T. "Inquisitors, Priests, and the People during the Catholic Reformation in Spain." *Sixteenth Century Journal* 18.4 (1987), 557–587.

Perry, Mary Elizabeth, and Anne J. Cruz, eds. *Cultural Encounters: The Impact of the Inquisition in Spain and the New World.* Proceedings of an international conference, Los Angeles, 1988. Reprint, Berkeley, 1991.

Schraepler, Horst W. *Die rechtliche Behandlung der Täufer in der deutschen Schweiz, Südwestdeutschland und Hessen, 1525–1618.* Tübingen, 1957.

Tedeschi, John. "The Roman Inquisition and Witchcraft: An Early Seventeenth Century 'Instruction' on Correct Trial Procedure." *Revue de l'Histoire des Religions* 200 (1983), 163–188.

———. "The Organization and Procedures of the Roman Inquisition: A Sketch." In *The Spanish Inquisition and the Inquisitorial Mind*, edited by Angel Alcala, pp. 187–215. Boulder, Colo, 1987.

———. "Inquisitorial Law and the Witch." In *Early Modern European Witchcraft: Centres and Peripheries*, edited by Bengt Ankarloo and Gustav Henningsen, pp. 83–118. Reprint, Oxford, 1993.

Wappler, Paul. *Inquisition und Ketzerprozesse in Zwickau zur Reformationszeit dargestellt im Zusammenhang mit der Entwicklung der Ansichten Luthers und Melanchthons über Glaubens- und Gewissensfreiheit.* Leipzig, 1908.

HANS J. HILLERBRAND

PERSONS, Robert. *See* Parsons, Robert.

PETER MARTYR. *See* Vermigli, Peter Martyr.

PETER OF ALCÁNTARA

PETER OF ALCÁNTARA (1499–1562), Spanish Franciscan reformer and mystic and Roman Catholic saint. Born Pedro Garavita, he studied at the University of Salamanca (1511–1515) before joining the Friars Minor. Ordained a priest in 1524, elected provincial of San Gabriel in 1538, and appointed commissary general of the Spanish Conventual Franciscans in 1559, Peter of Alcántara devoted himself to a life of intense asceticism and prayer and to the improvement of his order. Though he did not initiate it, he became the leader of the Discalced reform among Spanish Franciscans, and saw to its diffusion in Europe, the New World, and the East Indies. His followers became known as Alcantarines.

Peter had a profound impact on Teresa of Ávila and her reform of the Carmelites, for it was he who finally convinced Teresa and her confessors of the divine origin of her mystical experiences, which he recognized as similar to his own. He also induced the bishop of Ávila to allow the establishment of Teresa's first Discalced convent of Saint Joseph in 1562. According to Teresa, Peter of Alcántara was a man with a "beautiful intellect," worn so frail by his austerities that he looked "as if made from tree roots" (*Autobiography*, 27.18). Clad in sackcloth and sandals, often sleeping no more than two hours a night in a sitting position, Peter encouraged an unflinching embrace of total poverty and a commitment to mental prayer and *recogimiento* ("inwardness") among his followers. Though this spirituality would emerge triumphant in Tridentine Catholicism, it was mistrusted and disdained by many academic theologians in Peter's own day, having been dubbed "theology for carpenters' wives" by the inquisitor general, Fernando de Valdés. Peter's *Tratado de la oración y meditación* (1556), which owes much to John of Ávila, has gone through more than 175 editions and translations. He was beatified in 1622 and canonized in 1669.

BIBLIOGRAPHY

Barrado Manzano, A. *San Pedro de Alcántara, 1499–1562: Estudio documentado y crítico de su vida.* Madrid, 1965.

Bilinkoff, Jodi. *The Ávila of Saint Teresa: Religious Reform in a Sixteenth-Century City.* Ithaca, N.Y., 1989. Analyzes Peter of Alcántara's place among Spanish clerical reformers of the sixteenth century.

Fernández y Fernández, J. *El perfil bíblico de San Pedro de Alcántara.* Badajoz, 1950.

Jiménez Duque, Baldomero, ed. *Un hombre de ayer y de hoy: San Pedro de Alcántara.* Madrid, 1976. A collection of essays.

Ledrus, M. "Grenade et Alcantara: Deux manuels d'oraison mentale." *Revue d'ascétique et de mystique* 38 (1962), 447–460.

Peers, E. Allison. *Studies of the Spanish Mystics.* Reprint, London and New York, 1951. See especially vol. 2, pp. 97–120.

CARLOS M. N. EIRE

PETRI, Olaus and Laurentius

PETRI, Olaus and Laurentius (Swed., Olof and Lars Petersson; 1493–1552 and 1499–1573, respectively),

Swedish Lutheran reformer and first Lutheran archbishop of the Church of Sweden, respectively. The Petri brothers worked closely together to further the Reformation in Sweden. They were born in Örebro, the sons of a blacksmith. Olaus is often called the "Martin Luther of Sweden." After studying at the University of Uppsala for a time, Olaus continued his studies at Leipzig and then moved on to Wittenberg, where he studied for two years while Luther was lecturing on the letters to the Galatians and the Hebrews (1516–1518). Here he heard Luther's maturing views on the nature of law and gospel and on justification by grace through faith. He heard Luther's critique of indulgences as well as the claims John Tetzel was making for his indulgence letters. He was present in Wittenberg when Luther wrote the Ninety-five Theses. With other Wittenberg students he discussed the "theology of the cross" as their professor, Luther, elaborated on it during the spring of 1518, before and after the gathering of Augustinians in Heidelberg. As Philipp Melanchthon arrived in Wittenberg to take up his new professorial duties, Olaus Petri left for his native Sweden the last week of August 1518. Olaus brought with him a conservative understanding of the Reformation based on the early reforming ideals of Luther. Still to come was Luther's debate with Johann Eck at Leipzig, Luther's attack on the sacramental system of Rome found in the *De captivitate Babyloniaca* (Babylonian Captivity of the Church), and Luther's famous "Here I Stand" declaration at the Diet of Worms in 1521.

Olaus settled down at Strengnäs, where he was ordained a deacon and soon was appointed secretary to Bishop Matts (Mattias Gregorii). Here he met Laurentius Andreae, an archdeacon involved in the ongoing ecclesiastical details of running the Strengnäs diocese. Olaus, a zealous evangelical, won over Andreae to the new doctrines emanating from Wittenberg. Soon complaints were being heard from the neighboring diocese of Linköping, where Hans Brask was bishop, about the heretical Lutheran preaching in Strengnäs.

On 8 November 1520 the infamous Stockholm Bloodbath occurred. At least eighty nobles and two bishops were executed (one of them Olaus Petri's bishop from Strengnäs). This act galvanized Sweden into revolution under the leadership of Gustavus Vasa. After three years Sweden won its political independence and extricated itself from the Kalmar Union and Danish domination. In 1523 Vasa was acclaimed king at Strengnäs. While there Vasa made the acquaintance of Olaus Petri, whom he heard expounding the evangelical notions he had learned in Wittenberg. Laurentius Andreae, the king's new chancellor, was apparently responsible for the introduction. Within a year's time, Olaus was summoned to Stockholm as the town clerk and given the prestigious pulpit of Saint Nicholas. Thus in 1524 Lutherans occupied two important sounding boards for evangelical reform in the nation's capital. Bishop Brask continued to object to the spread of Lutheran doctrine, while the king continued to promise that he would never allow heresy to be preached in his realm but only sound doctrine based on the word of God. In 1525 Olaus Petri scandalized the inhabitants of Stockholm by taking a wife (Kristine) on 11 February 1525, a few months before Luther's marriage. The king defended Olaus's action and came increasingly to be seen as Olaus's protector. It has been contended that the Swedish Mass was first used at Olaus's weddding, but evidence indicates that it was not until 1529 that it came to be used, being eventually published in 1531. The Swedish Mass was accompanied by a strong defense of vernacular worship in a pamphlet entitled *Orsack hwar före messan böör wara på thet tungmål som then menighe man forstandælighit är* (Why the Mass Ought to be Held in Swedish).

The ten years following Olaus Petri's marriage proved to be his most productive literary years. During this time he published sixteen books in Swedish. Previously only eight books existed in the vernacular. Early in 1526 the first evangelical book in Swedish appeared entitled *En nyttig undervisning* (A Useful Instruction) modeled after Luther's *Betbüchlein* of 1522. In late summer of 1526, Olaus published his Swedish translation of the New Testament with a foreword expounding his Lutheran view of the authority of scripture as over against tradition. In 1527 and 1528 he published a series of polemical works aimed against Paul Helie of Denmark and made clear that he sided with Luther in the controversy over free will.

At this point (1527) Olaus was joined by his younger brother, Laurentius, who had just returned from his studies in Wittenberg. Together with Laurentius Andreae, the three formed a powerful evangelical voice in Sweden. Gustavus Vasa proceeded to appoint Olaus to be his secretary in 1527 and called the four estates together for a national assembly to be held at Västerås. The Diet of Västerås (1527) proclaimed that God's word should be preached purely and plainly throughout the kingdom. This vague statement allowed for the continuance of Lutheran preaching. The Västerås Recess of 1527 also stipulated that the surplus property and wealth of the church belonged to the state. Any properties given to the church before 1454 were to be returned to their rightful heirs. There was no formal break with the papacy, but the handwriting on the wall was clear for everyone to see, including Bishop Brask, who hastily left Sweden after the diet adjourned, never to return to his native land. Vasa, who had threatened to resign as king, was given a vote of confidence by all the estates and persuaded to continue ruling the country.

Olaus continued his literary activity and in 1528 published *Een liten boock om sacramenten* (A Little Book about the Sacraments), a translation of the Brandenburg *Ratslag* of 1525 expounding the Lutheran position regarding the seven sacraments of the Roman Catholic church. The same year Olaus published a tract on marriage, a book of sermons, and various other writings. In 1529 he published *Een handbock påå Swensko* (Swedish Manual), a liturgical handbook that enabled the clergy to conduct the rites in an evangelical manner. Two years later he published a mass in Swedish, which enabled worship to be conducted in the vernacular. He also was appointed chancellor by the king in 1531, but Olaus quickly revealed he had no aptitude for political matters and went back to preaching.

His brother, Laurentius, was appointed in 1531 as the first Lutheran archbishop of Uppsala. This was a most fortuitous appointment, as Laurentius was blessed with good health and continued to occupy the office of archbishop for the next forty-two years. He had a patient temperament and the gift of common sense so he was able to bide his time until he eventually saw his church ordinance ratified in 1571, two years before his death. It was not until 1593 that any formal subscription to the Lutheran confessions was made since both the Petri brothers based their reforming work on the *sola scriptura* principle of the early Luther. When Laurentius was ordained archbishop of Uppsala in 1531, the historic episcopate was preserved since the Roman Catholic bishop of Västerås, Petrus Magni, was the consecrator.

During the 1540s, Vasa sought to centralize his government still further by reigning in the semiautonomy of the evangelical church that was emerging in Sweden. His ideal was a structure similar to that outlined in the 1539 church ordinance of Denmark-Norway. George Norman, a German nobleman and tutor for the king's son, was appointed superintendent of the church. The role of the Swedish bishops was correspondingly downgraded. Both Olaus Petri and Laurentius Andreae were accused of treason and sentenced to death because they had not revealed a possible coup d'état that had been told to each of them in pastoral confidence. Saner heads prevailed, however, and the executions were not carried out, though the exact legal status of the church remained in question.

In 1552 Olaus died, followed by the death of Andreae two weeks later. This ended the first phase of the Reformation in Sweden and left Laurentius Petri as the leader of the gradual ecclesiastical transformation that was evolving. When Vasa died in 1560, Laurentius was confronted with Erik XIV (r. 1560–1568), an avowed Calvinist. The archbishop had hoped to introduce a Lutheran church ordinance in 1561 but was forced to wait until the reign of the next king, John III (r. 1568–1592). The new king was anxious to regularize the ecclesiastical transformation that had transpired in sixteenth-century Sweden and was not a Calvinist. Later events were to reveal his propensity for a high church Lutheran liturgy and even Roman Catholicism as he came under the influence of his Polish wife's Jesuit chaplains. In the meantime, Laurentius Petri marked the crowning achievement of his long career as archbishop of Uppsala with the legal adoption of his church ordinance in 1571, which placed the Church of Sweden on a solid evangelical foundation.

BIBLIOGRAPHY

Ahlberg, Bo. *Laurentius Petris nattvards uppfattning.* Lund, 1964.

Bergendoff, Conrad. *Olavus Petri and the Ecclesiastical Transformation in Sweden.* Philadelphia, 1965.

Ingebrand, Sven. *Olavus Petris reformatoriska åskådning.* Uppsala, 1946.

Petri, Olavus. *Samlade skrifter af Olavus Perti.* Edited by Bengt Hesselman. Uppsala, 1914–1917.

Yelverton, Eric E. *The Manual of Olavus Petri, 1529.* London, 1953.

———. *An Archbishop of the Reformation: Laurentius Petri Nericius Archbishop of Uppsala, 1531–73.* London, 1958.

TRYGVE R. SKARSTEN

PETSCHIUS, Petrus. *See* Láni, Eliáš.

PEUCER, Caspar (1525–1602), German humanist, physician, and supporter of Philippist theology in Lutheranism. Born in Bautzen, east of Dresden, Peucer attended the Latin school in Goldberg, Silesia, led by Valentin Trotzendorf, the famous educator trained by Philipp Melanchthon. In 1540 Peucer matriculated at the university in Wittenberg and on Trotzendorf's recommendation was taken into Melanchthon's home. He attended Melanchthon's lectures; studied with the humanist mathematicians Erasmus Reinhold, Jakob Milich, and Joachim Rhäticus; and pursued arithmetic privately with Johann Stifel, pastor at nearby Holzdorf. After obtaining an M.A. in 1545, Peucer stayed to teach, beginning in the arts faculty in 1548. He became professor of mathematics in 1554 and professor of medicine in 1560.

In 1550 Peucer married Magdelena Melanchthon and continued living in Melanchthon's house, serving his father-in-law as household manager, traveling companion, and personal physician. After Melanchthon's death, Peucer edited some of the reformer's letters and writings and completed Melanchthon's work on the *Chronicon carionis*, picking up the unfinished project after Charlemagne and carrying through to the 1519 Leipzig Disputation.

As university rector in 1560, Peucer attracted the attention of the Saxon elector August and in 1563 moved to Dresden as court physician. He quickly gained August's confidence, evidenced when August asked Peucer to be sponsor for the baptism of the infant prince Adolf. The close relationship gave Peucer an opportunity to lobby on behalf of Wittenberg, where he remained on the medical faculty. He also promoted Lutheran theology as interpreted by the Philippists, a movement that both echoed and pressed beyond some of Melanchthon's views, including free will in conversion, the necessity of good works, and a Christology that entailed a more spiritualized presence of Christ in the Lord's Supper. Peucer assembled and worked for Saxony's adoption of the *Corpus doctrinae*, also called the *Corpus philippicum* because the collected documents included much from Melanchthon, notably his revised *Loci communes* (with its controversial position on the human will) and the Variata of the Augsburg Confession (with its weaker view of the real presence). Conservative Gnesio-Lutheran critics called this crypto-Calvinism. Peucer, however, enjoyed August's confidence and continued to influence university faculty appointments and publish carefully couched arguments for his position.

Everything changed in 1574 with the publication of *Exegesis perspicua*, which clearly advocated a Calvinist view of the Lord's Supper. August understood the Philippist position and moved to clean house, as he was upset by Philippist theology and also angered by what he took to be deception. Peucer was linked to the treatise, arrested, and imprisoned until 1586, when the widowed August remarried, and Prince Joachim Ernest of Anhalt, his new father-in-law, secured Peucer's release. He served the princes of Anhalt as physician and adviser during his last years, remaining committed to Melanchthon's theology.

BIBLIOGRAPHY

Calinich, Robert. *Kampf und Untergang des Melanchthonismus in Kursachsen in den Jahren 1570 bis 1574*. Leipzig, 1866. Recounts Peucer's involvement in the crypto-Calvinist problem.

Friedensburg, Walter. *Geschichte der Universität Wittenberg*. Halle, 1917. Includes material on Peucer's academic activities.

Kolb, Robert. *Caspar Peucer's Library: Portrait of a Wittenberg Professor of the Mid-Sixteenth Century*. Sixteenth Century Bibliography, vol. 5. Saint Louis, 1976. A catalog of what Peucer owned and may have read; contains a short biography.

Verzeichnis der im deutschen Sprachbereich erschienenen Drucke des XVI. Jahrhunderts. Stuttgart, 1983–. Vol. 15, nos. 1950–2039.

ROBERT ROSIN

PEUTINGER, Conrad (1465–1547), German humanist and antiquarian. Born into an old Augsburg family, Peutinger was appointed in 1492 to serve as city secretary and later became a syndic of the city. One of the first of the German humanists to publish Roman inscriptions, he was inspired perhaps by his close connections as privy counselor with Emperor Maximilian I, the idol of the German humanists. While studying law in Italy, he developed a passion for classical learning and collected coins, art works, statues, and classical manuscripts. His name has always been associated with a most valuable historical document, the *Tabula peutingeriana*, which was a map of the military roads of the western Roman Empire with only the westernmost panel missing. Conradus Celtis discovered it and gave it to Peutinger to publish.

Peutinger also published an edition of the *Historia Gothorum* of Jordanes, a sixth-century Goth and a notary, who converted to Christianity, probably became a monk, and wrote this history of the Goths condensed from a work by Cassiodorus and extended to A.D. 551. Along with Julius Caesar, Aemianus Marcellinus, and Tacitus, Jordanes provided one of the few sources of information about the early Germans. Peutinger also edited Paul the Deacon's *Historia Langobardorum* (History of the Lombards), who invaded, inhabited, and beautified Lombardy in northern Italy. Peutinger also demonstrated the value of numismatics for broader classical and historical learning.

The prosperous cities of southern Germany served as central foci of humanist and artistic activity. Augsburg, home of the Welsers, Fuggers, Paumgartners, and other wealthy families, rivaled Nuremberg as a center of northern Renaissance culture. Peutinger acted as an agent for the Welsers and achieved prominent status in the city. His efforts to write an imperial history failed, for he was not up to the task.

Similarly, in his religious stance he was a mediator and seemed to lack strong convictions of his own. Sent to Rome to represent Augsburg during the pontificate of Innocent VIII, he wrote of the shocking venality in the capital of Christendom. His criticism of the Roman church, however, was concerned largely with moral abuses. His advocacy of reform measures remained on the level one might fairly characterize as Erasmian. He was an ardent student of the patristic writers as well. A Reuchlinist, he played host to Martin Luther when he came to Augsburg in 1518. He corresponded with the Swabian-Swiss reformer Johannes Oecolampadius in Basel. In the end he held back from the Lutheran Reformation and urged all to await the calling of a general ecumenical council to resolve the problems of church reform.

BIBLIOGRAPHY

Primary Source

Peutinger, Conrad. *Briefwechsel*. Edited by Erich König. Munich, 1923.

Secondary Sources

Borchardt, Frank L. *German Antiquity in Renaissance Myth*. Baltimore, 1971.

König, Erich. *Peutingerstudien*. Freiburg, 1914.

Lutz, Heinrich. *Conrad Peutinger: Beiträge zu einer politischen Biographie*. Augsburg, 1958.

LEWIS W. SPITZ

PFLUG, Julius (1499–1564), German bishop and theologian. Son of the chancellor of the duke of Saxony, Pflug was very young when he became caught up in the turmoil generated by the Lutheran Reformation. After studying law in Bologna and Rome, he was deeply influenced by humanism and admired Desiderius Erasmus and Philipp Melanchthon. Quickly he won the confidence of George, duke of Saxony, who had remained faithful to the Roman church. This allowed him to come into contact with the theological circles of the two denominations that dominated the political and religious scene in Germany from 1530 to 1560. George took him along to the Diet of Augsburg in 1530 and subsequently entrusted him with various missions.

Although eloquent and cultured, Pflug had little theological training. His ambition led him to take up an ecclesiastical and diplomatic career. He quickly accumulated several benefices as a canon in the chapters of Meissen (where he became dean in 1537), Zeitz, Merseburg, and Magdeburg before being elected prince-bishop of Naumburg-Zeitz (1541), a post he was unable to occupy until after the victory of Charles V over the forces of the Schmalkald League (1547).

Moritz and August, the successors of George, were both Lutherans and appreciated Pflug's moderation. As a humanist and out of a desire to retain his benefices, he played a leading role in the various talks between 1540 and 1559 that attempted to reconcile Catholics and Lutherans and restore religious unity. He favored making significant concessions to the Lutherans, particularly the marriage of priests and offering the Communion chalice to the laity. After 1540 he became an instrument of the imperial policy of conciliation with the Lutherans and shared Charles V's vision of Catholicism as the state religion. In 1540 he took part in the colloquies held in Hagenau and Worms and then in the Colloquy of Regensburg, where in 1541 he brilliantly manifested his talents as a diplomat and conciliating theologian on several occasions.

In 1547 he was finally able to settle into his post as bishop of Naumburg. He took active part in the negotiations at the Diet of Augsburg. He again worked on the Pflug-Helding memorandum that had been drafted during the Diet of Regensburg in 1546 and that, after a few modifications, became the basic text of the Augsburg Interim.

In the years that followed, he devoted himself to the work of the Council of Trent, which he saw as the only means of restoring unity. Thus, he endeavored in vain to rally the Protestants to the council. In the 1550s he continued to favor conciliation with the Lutherans but without sacrificing any dogmas, all the while professing sincere loyalty to the apostolic see.

This notoriety, along with the respect that the Lutherans had for him as a person, led to his being asked to preside over the Colloquy of Worms in 1557. Two years later Emperor Ferdinand I personally invited him to attend the Diet of Augsburg. This diet could do nothing more than acknowledge the failure of the talks. Pflug, however, took advantage of the presence of the entire German episcopate to propose a program of reforms, *Formula reformationis,* which consisted of a renewal of letters and a purification of religion.

His ideas are contained in speeches, homilies, and a voluminous correspondence. Two major themes stand out, the first of which concerns moral decline. In Pflug's view the religious schism had brought about a slackening of moral standards, and the name of Christ had become no more than a pretense to cover up shameful vices. Second, he emphasized the need to preach penance, charity, and good works, and this included criticism of the catechesis of Lutheran preachers.

As for Lutheran doctrines, he accepted them in part but was also at pains to delineate points on which he diverged. He recognized the scriptures as the word of God, the priority of divine initiative and grace in any movement toward salvation, and the centrality of Christ as redeemer and of the Crucifixion. But, at the same time, he distanced himself by refusing to reject the doctrine of merit or to deny devotion to the saints or purgatory. He deplored the degradation of marriage, which in his eyes became a secular matter, and also the transfer of some of the church's prerogatives to civil authority. He saw the emphasis on earthly vocation *(Beruf)* as tantamount to giving greater importance to the here and now at the expense of the hereafter.

Pflug remains a major figure of the German episcopate in the middle of the sixteenth century. By his example and his work, he laid the groundwork for the restoration of Catholicism in Germany—the reform of the chapter of Naumburg, the foundation of a seminary for the education of the clergy, and the publication of treatises with an apologetic content. After fighting for the restoration of unity up until 1599, he rightly believed that only local efforts made by bishops were capable of rebuilding Catholicism in the German empire.

BIBLIOGRAPHY

Lau, F. "Pflug, Julius." In *Die Religion in Geschichte und Gegenwart,* edited by K. Galling, vol. 5, p. 319. 3d ed. Tübingen, 1961.

Muller, Otfried. "Schriften von und gegen Julius Pflug bis zu seiner Reise nach Triente 1551–1552: Ein Bericht aus der Stiftsbibliothek Zeitz." In *Reformata Reformanda: Festgabe für H. Jedin,* edited by E. Iserloh, vol. 2, pp. 29–69. Münster, 1965.

Pflug, Julius. *Correspondance.* Collected and edited with an introduction and notes by J. V. Pollet. 6 vols. Leiden, 1969–1982.

Pollet, J. V. *Julius Pflug, 1499–1564, et la crise religieuse dans l'Allemagne du XVIe siècle.* Leiden, 1990.

BERNARD VOGLER

Translated from French by Robert E. Shillenn

PHILIP II OF SPAIN (1527–1598), king who opposed the Reformation and believed himself the bulwark of the Counter-Reformation. Historians have often taken sides for or against him, depending upon their religion or nationality, and impartial accounts of his reign are difficult to find before the twentieth century. A member of the house of Habsburg, he was born in Valladolid 21 May 1527, son of Emperor Charles V and Isabel of Portugal. A list of inherited titles reveals the extent of his dominions: king of Castile and the Indies, Aragon, Navarre, Naples, Sicily, and Sardinia; duke of Milan, Brabant, and Luxembourg; count of Flanders, Holland, Zeeland, and the Franche-comté; lord in Africa and Asia. In 1565 Spaniards sailing from Mexico began to colonize the Philippines, which were named after him.

Education and Family Life. Philip's education was supervised by Charles V and reflected Charles's Christian humanist and chivalric education, experience of statecraft, and hostility toward Protestantism. Philip's mother and Castilian tutors inculcated in Philip the reserved demeanor that contemporaries often perceived as cold arrogance; and Charles, who was absent for much of Philip's boyhood, failed to temper Philip's character with his own ability to be affable.

Philip proved an affectionate son, brother, and father. He maintained close bonds with his two sisters, Maria (1529–1603; married Emperor Maximilian II) and Juana (1535–1573; married Prince John of Portugal). Each, after being widowed, retired to Madrid.

After his mother died in 1539, Philip began to act as regent of Spain during Charles's absences. In 1543 he married Maria Manuela of Portugal, who died in 1545 after giving birth to the unfortunate Don Carlos. Philip's second marriage, to Mary Tudor, queen of England (r. 1553–1558), in 1554 was political and left no issue. His third, to Elizabeth of Valois in 1559, seems to have been his happiest; she died in 1568, leaving him two daughters, Isabel Clara Eugenia (1566–1633; married Archduke Albert of Austria) and Catalina Micaëla (1567–1597; married Duke Charles Emmanuel of Savoy). In 1570 Philip married Ana of Austria, whose only child to live long was to become Philip III (1578–1621). After her death in 1580, Philip did not remarry.

The death of Don Carlos in 1568 stimulated speculation of heresy, treason, and love for his stepmother, Elizabeth. The prince suffered from mental instability and Philip reluctantly put him under confinement, where his hunger strikes, malaria, and dysentery combined to kill him. In this case and others Philip felt deep grief and withdrew into melancholy, yet a stubborn sense of obligation always brought him back to what he believed to be his duties.

Science and Learning. If one can set aside the religious intolerance that characterizes his age, Philip II provides the prototype of an enlightened despot. He collected books on all subjects, including a Qur'an. In the tradition of Queen Isabella I, who supported publication of the Complutensian Polyglot Bible, Philip backed Antwerp printer Christoffel Plantijn in publishing an extended version, the Biblia Polyglotta (1568–1572). Throughout his life he read avidly when time allowed, favoring works of religion, history, and science.

He patronized music and the fine arts, and his monastery-palace of El Escorial, with its chapel, library, and mausoleum, reflects Renaissance Christian humanist ideals. He promoted mathematics and science and was an avid collector of flora and fauna for his botanical gardens and zoo at Aranjuez.

Several renowned scholars he subsidized were not entirely orthodox in religion. Benito Arias Montano, librarian of the Escorial, was a secret Familist; and Justus Lipsius, editor of Tacitus, Philip's favorite ancient historian, embraced Lutheranism and later Calvinism before being reconciled with Rome.

Government and Church. Philip believed his chief obligations to his subjects were to provide justice, to maintain the Roman Catholic religion, and to defend them from enemies, domestic and foreign. He notoriously detested war but for most of his reign waged it in defense of his obligations. Escalating war costs drove him three times to renegotiate his debts (1557, 1575, 1597). He persuaded the *cortes* of Castile to raise taxes to levels that in time impaired Spain's economy, while the fair imposition he sought was compromised by local authorities and foreign creditors.

He supervised the appointment of judges and the administration of justice, and he promoted the codification of laws, particularly for Spain's overseas empire. To collect more information about his subjects, he launched ambitious census projects in Spain and its empire, carried out only in part. Resident in Spain for most of his reign, he governed his other realms in Europe and overseas through an elaborate system of councils at court, viceroys, and local institutions.

Many of the people and much of the funding for Philip's governments came from the church. Churchmen served in state administration and justice. Through arrangements with Rome, Philip collected two important subsidies annually from every diocese in Spain and revenue from sales of indulgences, in which Rome insisted there be no abuses, for the crusade against Turks and heretics.

Relations between Philip and Rome were often strained. Although he promoted a third session (1562–1563) of the Council of Trent, he favored episcopal power over papal and proved reluctant to publish Trent's final decrees, which he believed unduly favored the papacy. In 1570 for reasons of state he delayed the publication of Pius V's bull that excommunicated Queen Elizabeth I of England, and in 1593 he refused to accept Rome's absolution and recognition of Henry IV of France.

Long-standing concordats with Rome permitted Philip to nominate candidates for bishoprics and other benefices, a power he took seriously. Like Charles he showed special favor to the Hieronymite order and respect for the Augustinians, Dominicans, and Franciscans, whose overseas missionary activities he encouraged. He supported the Jesuits while their generals were Spaniards; after the death of Francis Borgia, his relations with them cooled, as Italians succeeded to the generalship and their ultramontanism became more evident.

Of Spain's religious institutions, the Inquisition was most notorious and enjoyed Philip's full support. He perceived a world around him troubled by heresy, Judaizing, and Islam, all related in causing the damnation of souls and promoting the triumph of the Antichrist. In his "Adoration of the Name of Jesus," El Greco catches this vision, depicting Philip on his knees with his back to the gaping mouth of hell and his eyes fixed on the holy name.

When Philip succeeded Charles in Brussels in 1555–1556, he was disturbed by heretical ideas he found circulating in England, Germany, and the Netherlands. He arranged to strengthen church institutions in the Netherlands by increasing the number of bishops from four to eighteen and by appointing two inquisitors to each diocese. These actions stirred powerful opposition.

On his return to Spain in 1559 he was shocked to find that the Inquisition had discovered Protestant cells in Valladolid and Seville. In his first major public appearance, Philip attended an auto-da-fe in Valladolid. Subsequently he attended autos-da-fe during his travels in Spain and to Lisbon (1581), after his annexation of Portugal, to show his support for the maintenance of purity of faith. Against interference from Rome, he backed the Inquisition's right to prosecute Archbishop Bartolomé de Carranza of Toledo, once his court preacher. Fearing that Spanish students who studied abroad might become contaminated with heretical ideas, he forbade them to study outside the Iberian peninsula, save in Rome and Bologna.

Foreign Relations and War. Defense of religion and the dynastic rights of the house of Habsburg, in both Madrid and Vienna, underlay Philip's foreign policies and wars. Until 1578 Philip's Mediterranean possessions were involved in a monumental struggle with the Turkish Ottoman empire, highlighted in 1565 by the relief of Malta and in 1571 by the victory at the Battle of Lepanto. In 1568–1570 a Morisco uprising in Granada was subdued, but control of Tunis was lost to the Turks, with whom Philip achieved a truce in 1578. He aided Morocco in keeping its independence of them, but King Sebastian of Portugal invaded Morocco in 1578, against Philip's wishes, and fell in battle. Claiming dynastic right, Philip annexed Portugal and its overseas empire in 1580.

For western Europe Philip accepted the order established by the Treaty of Cateau-Cambrésis (1559) but saw it undermined by the clash of Calvinism and the Counter-Reformation. The Revolt of the Netherlands that erupted in 1568, following years of rising tensions, came to consume his attention, along with the preservation of Catholic government in neighboring France.

In the Netherlands' northern provinces Calvinist rebels, led by William of Orange, established the Dutch Republic, while army mutinies resulting from Philip's financial straits and Mediterranean wars frustrated his governors, Margaret of Parma, Fernando Álvarez de Toledo (the duke of Alba), Luis de Requeséns y Zúñiga, and John of Austria. After 1578 Alessandro Farnese, duke of Parma, who succeeded John, consolidated Philip's rule and the sway of Catholicism over the southern provinces, the germ of modern Belgium. English intervention, crucial to the rebel republic, led to a war (1585–1604) marked by the defeat in 1588 of his Spanish Armada, intended to overthrow Elizabeth I and to restore Catholicism in England.

He repeatedly intervened in the French Wars of Religion to support the Catholic side, and his opposition to Henry IV brought war in 1595, which papal mediation ended with the Peace of Vervins in 1598. In a final attempt to end the Netherlands revolt, Philip granted the provinces independence under his daughter Isabel and Albert VII of Austria in the vain hope that they might negotiate peace and win the rebel provinces back to Rome. Philip died at the Escorial on 13 September 1598.

BIBLIOGRAPHY

Braudel, Fernand. *The Mediterranean and the Mediterranean World in the Age of Philip II.* 2 vols. Translated by Siân Reynolds. London and New York, 1972. Though a magisterial study of societies, economies, and events, it reveals little about personalities and less about religion. A 1992 reprint by HarperCollins is abridged.

Fernández Armesto, Felipe. *The Spanish Armada.* Oxford, 1988. Good on ordinary lives and religious sentiments.

Goodman, David C. *Power and Penury: Government, Technology and Science in Philip II's Spain.* Cambridge, 1988. A detailed survey that includes the occult.

Marañón, Gregorio. *Antonio Pérez.* 2 vols., 8th ed. Madrid, 1969. Offers a fascinating portrait of the king and court. An abridged translation into English (London, 1954) is available.

Martin, Colin, and Geoffrey Parker. *The Spanish Armada.* Reprint, New York, 1992. The best treatment of planning and the campaign.

Mattingly, Garrett. *The Armada.* Reprint, Norwalk, Conn., 1989. A classic, remains the best for mood and diplomacy, with a moving portrait of Philip.

Merriman, Roger B. *The Rise of the Spanish Empire in the Old World and in the New.* Vol. 4, *Philip the Prudent.* Reprint, New York, 1962. The first modern and most thorough study in English of the man and his reign; it surveys well the vast and controversial historiography.

Parker, Geoffrey. *Philip II.* Reprint, London, 1988. Offers a fine intimate portrait of the king based on newly located archival material but confines references to notes.

Pierson, Peter. *Philip II of Spain.* London, 1975. Broad treatment of the reign; it updates Merriman's survey of the literature.

PETER O'M. PIERSON

PHILIPPISTS. The death of Martin Luther in 1546 marked the beginning of more than a quarter century of strife among his followers in the Saxon homeland of his Reformation, a strife also felt in other parts of Germany and elsewhere in central and northern Europe where the Lutheran (or evangelical) faith had spread. This strife exposed to public view the fact that within the evangelical movement, even at its center at Wittenberg University and among those who had led it from its earliest days—Luther and colleagues such as Philipp Melanchthon (1497–1560) and Nikolaus von Amsdorf (1483–1565)—some variety of religious thought had emerged over the years that could erupt into controversies once the reformer's powerful presence was gone. The Augsburg Interim, the religious settlement that Emperor Charles V imposed on Protestant cities and territories of Germany upon defeating the Lutheran Schmalkald

League in April 1547, provided the context for the controversies, for its intent was to restore Roman Catholic theology and practice.

Quickly two rival camps emerged in the conflict, Gnesio-Lutherans and Philippists. The former were set upon complete opposition to Charles V, certain that they were upholding not only Luther's defiant stance but also his theology, and the latter, while also claiming Luther's mantle, rallied around Melanchthon and reflected his willingness to compromise and his more humanist/rationalist theological program. Controversy between the two raged until the mid-1570s, when the will to settle the issues in conflict coalesced, driven primarily by Jakob Andreae (1528–1590) and Elector August of Albertine Saxony (r. 1553–1586). Andreae had been party to neither side, and August, after years of supporting the Philippists in his universities, Wittenberg and Leipzig, now suddenly arrested some and deported others. The result was the Formula of Concord (1577), which had gained the support of most of evangelical Germany by the time it was issued as the *Book of Concord* on the fiftieth anniversary of the Augsburg Confession, 25 June 1580, and remains normative in Lutheran churches today.

The positions of the Formula of Concord on the issues dividing the two camps were for the most part those of the Gnesio-Lutherans, although upon closer examination one observes perspectives in it fought for by Philippists also. Philippism as a movement had been damaged by the conflict, so that those Germans who continued to hold Philippist views generally found this possible only in those places where the authorities went over to the Reformed church, such as Bremen, and territories in the northwest, the Palatinate, Anhalt, and, later, Brandenburg; still, Philippism remained stronger in Saxony after Elector August's crackdown than has been recognized by historians. It should be noted that current scholarship on "confessionalization" argues that for the winning of souls and for purposes of ecclesiastical and political centralization, all three Christian churches present in Germany at the time, Roman Catholic, Reformed, and Lutheran, had to arrive at settled, easily perceived religious stances, clearly delineated from each other. The Lutheran church opted for the Gnesio-Lutherans. The much-maligned loser in its struggle with the Gnesio-Lutherans, the Philippists and their religious perspectives have since then received relatively little study of a balanced and scholarly sort.

Most of the adherents to both parties in the struggle had been students of Melanchthon as well as Luther. From Melanchthon they had gained a solid grounding in the humanist educational program and Aristotelian logic, so that in spite of their battles they shared his linguistic interests and especially his theological method and terminology. They agreed enough on the doctrine of salvation (soteriology) that in the midst of their battles in the early 1550s they joined forces to protect the idea of imputed righteousness that they had learned together in Wittenberg from the maverick ideas of Andreas Osiander (1496–1552). The Philippists espoused ideas that had begun to mark Melanchthon's distinctive perspectives within Wittenberg theology as early as the late 1520s, in particular in theological anthropology, where he sought means to stress ethical responsibility, and in the doctrines of the Lord's Supper and the person of Christ, prompted by growing discomfort over expressions—for example, from Luther—of actual physical consumption of Christ's body and blood by communicants. The Philippists' allegiance went even further. They agreed with Melanchthon that after the recent military defeat the Protestant religious cause might only be saved through negotiation and concessions to the victorious emperor. More than their opponents, they tended to seek religious authority for their beliefs in the doctrinal and liturgical practices of the early church and the church fathers. Again like Melanchthon, they were reluctant participants in controversies, preferring amnesty for past differences and negotiation for simple consensus statements of faith. Some scholars have found them more willing than their opponents to accept external political direction in their churches. During the war, however, they took up and developed arguments that had percolated quietly over the previous fifteen years on the issue of resistance to political authority. They unleashed a number of pamphlets in which they not only justified resistance by lower to higher political authority, but also by subjects—those anyway who held the divinely consecrated place of heads of households—against wrongful authority, a very radical stance. So the truth of the scholars' observation is simply to be explained by the fact that the Philippists saw themselves in different political circumstances in later years, circumstances in which they thought they had political leaders with whom they could work without significant hindrance to their preaching office. There was a firm bond of friendship in this party, which comprised an intellectual elite that included not only theologians but some physicians, philologists, and court jurists also. The label "Philippist" was coined by the Gnesio-Lutherans, one of the last of the epithets that they hurled in derision at their opponents.

Wittenberg became the Philippist center because Melanchthon agreed to return there at the end of the war out of a sense of loyalty to Luther and of its importance to the continuing fortune of the Reformation. At the time he was the religious leader of the Lutherans. He was joined by the remaining members of the theology faculty, Johannes Bugenhagen (1485–1558), Caspar Cruciger (1504–1548), and Georg Major (1502–1574), and by Paul Eber (1511–1569) and Johann Forster (1496–1558). But the university was restored under threatening circumstances. Charles V was at the height of his power. Thus the Augsburg Interim, issued on 20 June 1548, was not to be ignored. While Melanchthon and almost all German Protestants denounced it, the emperor's troops quickly fell to enforcing it and evicting recalcitrant pastors in those parts of the country they controlled, mainly in the south and west. Nor did the Saxon situation seem any rosier. Whereas Wittenberg had been in the Ernestine part of Saxony, its current ruler, John Frederick (r. 1532–1554), was in the emperor's jail, and Charles had awarded the city and title of elector to his ally in the war, Moritz of Saxony. Before joining with Charles he had extracted a vow from him that his lands could remain Protestant, and he had promised Melanchthon in their negotiations for his return that Wittenberg would be unchanged. But he also had installed Roman Catholics as bishops of the two dioceses of his lands and now feared Charles's response if he did not introduce a religious settlement similar to the Interim. He pressured Melanchthon and his Wittenberg colleagues along with Johann Pfeffinger (1493–1570) and Joachim Camerarius (1500–1574) of the university at Leipzig and former evangelical bishop Prince Georg III of Anhalt (1507–1553) to negotiate with the two bishops and his own counselors, whom he had inherited from his staunchly Catholic uncle, in order to come up with a suitable settlement. Compromise was necessary. The theologians employed Melanchthon's idea of adiaphora ("indifferent things"): as long as essential doctrines were proclaimed correctly, many of the external practices were adiaphora and could be used or not, depending on such things as whether they contributed to solemnity, unity, or propriety. Other external forms, however, were not at all indifferent but in fact contradicted doctrine, such as processions, invocation of saints, private masses and masses for the dead, consecration with oil and some exorcisms, all of which were prescribed in the Augsburg Interim; the theologians resorted to subtle means to evade these. In line with this idea, there could be no compromise on doctrines deemed essential.

The resulting Leipzig Interim (24 December 1548) gave nuance to some Augsburg commands: enjoining obedience to bishops who function "according to God's command"; celebration of the seven sacraments, but not using the word "sacrament" for those five that Protestants had eliminated; and use of the traditional Mass without mentioning specifically the canon or masses for the dead. This latitude was sufficient that Melanchthon could agree to them reluctantly as adiaphora, as he did also for other provisions regulating practice, for example those ordering clergy to wear the traditional surplice and churches to celebrate a list of saints' festivals, even that of Corpus Christi. In addition to practices, the Augsburg Interim and therefore also the Leipzig focused much attention on soteriology, for Lutherans the most essential doctrine. Melanchthon and Cruciger wrote the draft document for this part, and expressed alongside a Lutheran insistence that Christ was the sole source of justification the view that the individual has the responsibility of aligning his or her will to God's call. They spoke also of the necessity of good works for salvation. Melanchthon earlier had used such language in searching for an anthropology by which he could urge humans to responsibility, that is, for a place for sanctification in evangelical theology; he apparently hoped that drawing upon these ideas here would satisfy the bishops short of Catholic expressions of infused grace, whereby the believer's love or works as well as faith count in his or her justification before God, as stated in the Augsburg Interim. But the bishops did demand insertion of the term "inherent righteousness," thereby aligning the two interims and rendering the Leipzig a theological muddle that would be acceptable to virtually no one.

The Adiaphora Controversy. In the following years a series of controversies erupted among the Lutherans, all but the last of them stemming from the interims. In 1549 Matthias Flacius Illyricus (1520–1575) and Nikolaus Gallus (1516–1570) joined Nikolaus von Amsdorf in Magdeburg, far from the emperor's troops, to publicize and attack the interims and anyone who had anything to do with them, especially Melanchthon and the other Wittenberg and Albertine theologians. Thus began the opposing party, whom the Philippists derided as "Flacians" and, later, Gnesio- ("true") Lutherans. Soon the triumvirate was joined by pastors in other northern cities, especially Braunschweig, Hamburg, Lübeck, and Lüneburg, and together they unleashed a flood of books against the "Interimists" and "Adiaphorists." They charged that many of the Leipzig Interim's practices were harmful to true doctrine, not indifferent. Furthermore, even those that might otherwise have been considered adiaphora, if they were reintroduced in this time of crisis, would confuse and harm many lay people; such a time called for firm confession of faith, not compromise (*nihil est adiaphora in casu confessionis et scandali*).

The Wittenberg theologians were not much more satisfied with the situation than were their opponents, for the prescribed practices were ones they had eliminated over the years. Their mournful defense was that in this circumstance it was better to suffer "tolerable" hardship, meaning one whereby something of Lutheranism would be able to continue, than to risk all in defiance or abandon parishioners by fleeing; otherwise their writings bemoaned the treachery of their erstwhile friends in Magdeburg.

The Majorist Controversy. A second controversy erupted in 1551, when Amsdorf accused Georg Major of having stated that "good works are necessary to salvation," a proposition that the Gnesio-Lutherans rejected as a return to Catholic soteriology that placed human effort ("good works") alongside God's grace as the means of salvation, and which appeared in the interims. Whether or not this is what Major had said—in reply he both denied and implied that he had—the accusation brought to the forefront soteriological doubts about Melanchthon since the second edition of his *Loci communes* (1535) as well as about the Wittenberg and Albertine theologians on account of the Leipzig Interim. While Melanchthon never wavered from a Pauline/Lutheran "justification by grace through faith" (*sola fide*), in the light of the moral laxity among believers that continued on in the new evangelical age, he sought to present a soteriology that considered the anthropological dimension and that could urge human responsibility. Apparently it was not enough, he seemed to be saying, to present the justification event from God's perspective of moving the sinner like a block of wood to the side of the ledger marked "righteous," where he or she would simply remain until death; nor in turning to ethics was it enough to say that this saved individual would freely respond to God's mercy in love of his or her neighbor. So on the latter, ethical, issue Melanchthon wrote that change of life, though freely occurring, must happen: "Good works are necessary to eternal life, since they must necessarily follow after the reconciliation." When the Leipzig Interim introduced the Catholic notion of inherent righteousness and said virtues such as love "must be in us and are necessary to salvation," its opponents were aroused to defend the Lutheran *sola fide* from any Catholic-like soteriological expressions, no matter their source.

Printed sermons of 1549 and 1550, before Amsdorf's attack, indicated that Major had taken up Melanchthon's concern about moral laxity. To emphasize its seriousness, he drew this ethical issue into soteriological discourse, treated always from an anthropological perspective. He continually asserted that justification of the sinner occurred *sola fide*, but in his schema, as in Melanchthon's, this was succeeded by regeneration and sanctification (a topic other Lutherans seemed reticent to discuss), in which the Holy Spirit enabled a new godly life. For this believers had to hold God's law before themselves, and obedience defined the human's relation to God. Fruits of the Spirit (that is, works) were "sure testimony" for the believer of his or her salvation, and returning to sin meant loss of the Spirit and of salvation—from this perspective Major's audience heard nothing about a divine grace that would persevere even when they faltered. Those works were always explained as doing what the Decalogue commanded, rejecting those of "human invention" (pilgrimages, for example).

Flacius, Gallus, and others joined Amsdorf's attack on the "Majorists," and Major replied in four tracts over the following two years, most notably in his long-winded *Sermon on the Conversion of Saint Paul.* He gave enormous space to distinguishing his teaching from Catholic soteriology, rejecting the idea of inherent righteousness and affirming his commitment to solifidianism. But he refused to back down on his call for moral regeneration, saying that it was "necessary" for those saved by faith to "leave adultery, prostitution, and other sins," and espousing the by-now-famous proposition. For him the key word in it was "salvation," by which he referred solely to the stage after justification, that is, regeneration and sanctification; to make this clear he amended it: "Good works are necessary to the justified for salvation." His opponents replied that evangelicals normally used "salvation" interchangeably with "justification," and so no matter what he intended, the laity would understand from it the Catholic view that works were a precondition of grace. They in fact had the better of him: for example, they said his use of "necessary" introduced coercion into an event of free grace and free response in love, to which he answered that this coercion was of the gospel, wherein the believer put himself freely under Christ's yoke; they asked how one converted at his or her deathbed could have confidence in salvation, since that person would have no works, which he answered by distinguishing "inner works" of faith and trust from "external works"—that person would have the inner works, which were the ones more dear to God.

Still the dispute did not end. A few years later Justus Menius (1499–1558) espoused the statement "the new obedience is necessary to salvation," which provoked Amsdorf to utter "good works are harmful to salvation." As Amsdorf's proposition indicated, any light shed by the debate on the proper character of Lutheran soteriology had degenerated into mere heat. By now one was defined by party affiliation, and party antagonisms divided northern Germany. Since Ernestine Saxony with governmental support was taking leadership of the Gnesio-Lutheran party in the later 1550s, Menius had to flee from his position as a superintendent there. Major returned to the debate in 1567 and 1570 with pamphlets in which he angrily blamed Flacius for the intensity of the controversy, wearily protested that he had never meant what he was accused of, and wished that the controversy would end. In its resolution of the controversy, the Formula of Concord leaned in the main to the side of the Gnesio-Lutherans. Yet it rejected Amsdorf's statement as well as Major's, and it distinguished justification and regeneration, saying that love or good works would follow the latter by renewal through the Holy Spirit, and even that the works were "necessary" because they were done as a freely given obedience (articles 3 and 4).

The Crypto-Calvinist Controversy. In the last of the controversies, this one flourishing in the 1560s and early 1570s, the Gnesio-Lutherans accused a younger generation of Philippists of secretly harboring Calvinist ideas on the Lord's Supper and Christology. These issues had been the most prominent source of division among Protestants from the very beginning of the Reformation. In the "First Lord's Supper Controversy" of the 1520s, Luther and the Swiss reformer Huldrych Zwingli (1484–1531) split over the intent of Christ's words "This is my body," Luther insisting the words could only have meant Christ's real presence in the bread and wine and Zwingli that the "is" merely signified the heaven-dwelling human nature of Christ, trivializing—in Lutheran eyes—the sacrament into a remembrance ceremony. The Lutheran position was stated in simple form in Melanchthon's Augsburg Confession (the so-called Invariata of 1530): the "body and blood . . . are truly present . . . under the form of bread and wine and are there distributed." Lutherans drew the corollary, based on *1 Corinthians* 11:29, that unbelievers who eat these elements do so to their own condemnation *(manducatio impiorum).* As a christological understanding of real presence Lutherans often offered the idea of ubiquity—that Christ's risen body shared the attributes of his divine nature *(communicatio idiomatum)* and therefore, since the divine nature is present everywhere, was able to be physically present in the bread and wine. To the Swiss ubiquity was destructive of the human nature of Christ, whose sacramental presence was instead spiritual in nature and experienced only by believers. Nonbelievers derived nothing from partaking.

Melanchthon's position shifted toward a more spiritualized understanding of the Lord's Supper, influenced by his reading of church fathers in the early 1530s. He held to real presence, thus maintaining that the impious ate to their peril, but like the Swiss opposed ubiquity. His altered (or Variata) Augsburg Confession of 1540 displayed in a few words his effort to preserve an integrity to each of Christ's natures and an analogous difference between the bread and wine and Christ by the words "with the bread and wine the body and blood . . . are truly offered to those who eat." When in 1551 the Hamburg pastor Joachim Westphal (1510–1574) launched the "Second Lord's Supper Controversy" against Calvin's doctrine, which he simply and incorrectly lumped with that of Zwingli, Calvin publicly called on the Wittenberg theologians for support, believing that they agreed with him. They remained silent, and there may be a number of reasons why, but one crucial reason must have been their recognition, despite similarities in Christology, that their understanding of real presence remained a significant difference from Geneva. Westphal's cause became a Gnesio-Lutheran cause; that the Wittenbergers did not lend support to him only made these rivals more suspicious of them.

Evangelical Germany, however, was preoccupied with other controversies in these years. On the political stage, Elector Moritz's defection from and victory over the emperor ended implementation of the interims in 1552. August succeeded Moritz the next year; he continued state support of the Wittenberg and Leipzig theologians out of the belief that their theology was that of Luther as well as Melanchthon, and because of the connection between Gnesio-Lutheran attacks and the bitter rivalry of the Ernestine house. Then came the Peace of Augsburg (1555), which was important to the intra-evangelical conflict in two ways: it intensified princely control of churches throughout Germany, and gave legal status to those Protestants who adhered to the Augsburg Confession, or could hide their beliefs under it. The controversies themselves increasingly took on the appearance of a referendum on Melanchthon's place within the evangelical movement. The Gnesio-Lutherans sought no less than the personal humiliation of Melanchthon as the betrayer of Lutheranism. A sign of the times was the behavior of Gnesio-Lutherans at the Colloquy of Worms in 1557, which, to the delight of the Roman Catholic delegates, they torpedoed, refusing to participate unless Melanchthon and his fellow Albertine theologians acknowledged their errors. The Gnesio-Lutherans in Ernestine Saxony got Duke John Frederick (r. 1554–1567) to require all clergy of the state to subscribe to their anti-Philippist *Confutations Book* and to undermine accords worked out at princely conferences in Frankfurt (1558) and Naumburg (1561) because they regarded them as Melanchthonian. At the latter conference Elector Frederick III (r. 1559–1576) of the Palatinate succeeded in obtaining legal recognition in the empire for his Calvinist reforms, having argued that they conformed to the Variata of the Augsburg Confession; the decision was only to intensify Gnesio-Lutheran convictions about what Melanchthon's purposes had been in making the changes from the Invariata. A final effort to resolve the differences between the parties, held in Altenburg in 1568–1569, failed to find a solution even to its initial topic, justification and good works. If a Philippist treatise on the conference, *Final Report and Declaration* (1570), can be believed, the Ernestine theologians dwelt primarily on attacking Melanchthon.

Such was the context in which gradually Melanchthon's friends took on the aspect of a party, joined together to promote the Melanchthonian perspective within Wittenberg theology. In 1560 the Wittenberg theologians printed a volume of six of his works along with the three ancient creeds, the *Corpus doctrinae Philippicum* (or *Corpus doctrinae Misnicum*), which was, according to the title, a "Complete Summary of the Right, True Christian Doctrine of the Holy Evangelists" and which became obligatory for all Albertine clergy in 1566. They often published on the controversies of the day under the collective authorship of "the theologians of Wittenberg and Leipzig." A particularly revealing volume was a collection of Wittenberg orations by eight Philippists, explicating from their common Melanchthonian viewpoint the issues in conflict (*Concerning the Principal Controversies of This Time,* 1571). The Philippist stock claim, repeated in treatise upon treatise, was that the work of Melanchthon and Luther was a unified whole, so that, for example, printing only the former's works in their *Corpus doctrinae* should not be understood as depreciating the latter's; they even came to portray the two in the image of the Hebrew prophetic team of Elijah and Elisha.

Because of its connection to Calvinism, the dispute over the Lord's Supper more than the preceding controversies determined Philippism's fate. Calvinism's spectacular growth from the late 1550s heightened political and religious tensions in Germany as well as elsewhere. In 1559 Duke Christoph (r. 1550–1568) of Württemberg at Jakob Andreae's urging required his clergy to subscribe to the doctrine of ubiquity as a means to stem Calvinist influence. Melanchthon students Albert Hardenberg (1510–1574) in Bremen and Zacharius Ursinus (1534–1583) in Breslau (in today's Poland) were removed from office, after bitter controversies, for promoting Calvinist sacramental theology; Ursinus became a leading light of Palatinate Calvinism after his arrival in 1561. So it was a valid question whether there could be a legitimate evangelical understanding of the sacrament from a Melanchthonian perspective. Or, as Gnesio-Lutherans believed, was the Philippist position a self-delusion and a fatal step in one's descent to Calvinist falsehood, or even an instrument of some Calvinist conspiracy?

The Albertine Saxon story over these years provides materials for a range of answers to these questions, because among its clergy, theologians, and learned elite were men who sought sincerely to hew to a Melanchthonian evangelical line and some whose beliefs appear to have been close to those of Calvin, which they would have had to cloak, knowing Elector August's opposition to Calvinism. Thanks to Pfeffinger, the University of Leipzig held solely to Melanchthon's sacramental theology; he even locked a lecture hall to prevent Jena refugee Viktorin Strigel from teaching the Calvinist view. In Wittenberg Paul Eber led the moderates. With his death in 1569, Caspar Peucer (1525–1602), professor of medicine and Melanchthon's son-in-law, and the theologian Christoph Pezel (1539–1604) assumed center stage, abetted by Peucer's connections with August. With the support of electoral counselor Georg Cracow (1525–1575), they steered the university toward the Genevan position. In the same year they began a secret correspondence with Calvin's successor, Théodore de Bèze (1516–1605). Publication of Pezel's Latin edition of *Catechesis contexta* in 1571, which stated that Christ's body was transferred to heaven, signaled for many the ascendancy of crypto-Calvinism; not only did Gnesio-Lutherans criticize it, but so also did Nicholas Selnecker (1530–1592), then aligned with the moderate Philippists and later one of the authors of the Formula of Concord—he charged that it deviated on the Lord's Supper even from the *Corpus doctrinae Philippicum*. August's suspicions were raised when Johann Casimir (r. 1578–1592) of the Palatinate asked him what the differences were between this catechism and the Palatinate's (Calvinist) Heidelberg Catechism. Two clerical officials at court, theologian Johann Stössel (1524–1578) and court pastor Christian Schütz (1526–1594), delivered a deceitful refutation in order to allay August's concerns and for him to send to the Palatinate in protestation of their claim of concord. But the other Philippist view of the Lord's Supper was heard soon after the *Catechesis contexta*, in October 1571 at the Albertine court in Dresden at a gathering of the theologians of both universities along with other members of the church hierarchy. The result was the Dresden Consensus. At its core was the rejection of ubiquity, which over the previous decade had emerged as the central theme of Philippists on the Lord's Supper—this rejection also may explain the failure of Jakob Andreae's union mission in the electorate prior to 1574. The consensus argued that the notion of Christ's human body sharing in the divine nature was never known in the ancient churches, and that if the human body were with the divine, it would be "in all places, in stone and wood." Instead it advanced as the true understanding of the real presence a simple "sacramental union": Christ's word of institution promised his body and blood in the Lord's Supper; therefore they were truly "with" and "under" the bread and wine, and the unworthy partakes to his judgment. It claimed that this was Luther's teaching as well as Melanchthon's, and cited church fathers and the Council of Nicaea (325) in agreement. In fact sacramental union was always a characteristic Lutheran explanation of real presence, and in its simplicity and comprehensiveness was the foundational formula for the Wittenberg Concord (1536), which joined most south Germans to the Wittenberg theology. Although the Gnesio-Lutherans and most historians since have regarded the consensus as nothing other than a crypto-Calvinist veiling of their true beliefs from a now suspicious Elector August, it was consistent with and a comprehensive outline of the views of all Philippists then and also of the Albertine church over the next decade.

In April 1574 Elector August arrested Peucer, Cracow, Stössel, and Schütz for crypto-Calvinism; Peucer and Schütz remained in prison until the end of August's reign twelve years later; the others died in jail. August also expelled Pezel, who later led Bremen to the Reformed church. Political factors played a role in August's act: even greater Lutheran aversion to Calvinism and the desire to protect its legality in the wake of the Saint Bartholomew's Day Massacre in France (1572), and the end of the Ernestine rivalry—and banishment of its Gnesio-Lutherans—with his assumption of a regency government for the duchy in 1573. And then a Calvinist tract on the Lord's Supper, written anonymously by a Silesian physician, Joachim Cureus (1532–1573), and printed surreptitiously in Leipzig, appeared, leading August once again to suspect a Calvinist cabal among his theologians. The arrests and subsequent change in Albertine Saxon religious policy to support of Andreae's union drive, leading in 1577 to the Formula of Concord, historians have interpreted as a fatal blow to Philippism in Saxony. Such was not the case, however. Crypto-Calvinism disappeared for the remainder of August's reign, but even though some Wittenberg Philippists, who appear not to have been connected with Peucer's program, were dismissed (with pay), the new state policy, led by the theologians Paul Krell (1531–1579), Peter Glaser (1528–1583), and Caspar Eberhard (d. 1575), deviated little from the Eber line: the Wittenberg catechisms were replaced by Luther's and the *Corpus doctrinae Philippicum* and Dresden Consensus remained normative. At governmental command new editions of Melanchthon's and Luther's sacramental writings and the latter's Schmalkald Articles (1537) appeared. In the elector's correspondence, in books, and in the prefaces to these editions, Melanchthon's and Luther's essential unity was asserted constantly—the divergences that one would discover in a reading of those editions were attributed merely to differences in their personalities and in the circumstances under which they were writing. Repeated attacks on Albertine Saxon religious policy, particularly regarding the thesis of Melanchthon and Luther's unity, by probably the most prolific of the younger generation of Gnesio-Lutherans, Johann Wigand (1523–1587), were further evidence of its continuity before and after April 1574 and of a sustained Philippist presence.

Articles 7, "The Lord's Supper," and 8, "The Person of Christ," of the Formula of Concord indicated the effects of the crypto-Calvinist controversy in the explicitness with which they distinguished Lutheran from Zwinglian and Calvinist thought. The articles carried on a running commentary on and debate with those who professed adherence to the Augsburg Confession but taught "sacramentarian"—meaning here Swiss— doctrines, that is, the crypto-Calvinists. Thus the Philippists' christological objection to the *communicatio idiomatum,* since they shared this with the Swiss and their crypto-Calvinist colleagues, was condemned. In article 8 there is a detailed argument for this distinctively Lutheran doctrine. Ubiquity was affirmed, although not in name, a small concession to Philippist sensitivities, while their preferred means of explaining the physical presence of Christ with the bread and wine, the sacramental union, found copious expression. The Formula of Concord was not the last chapter in the saga of crypto-Calvinism, however, even within Albertine Saxony. August's son and successor, Christian I (r. 1586–1591), had been educated by Schütz and from 1584 became an enthusiastic supporter of the counselor Nikolaus Krell (1552/53–1601), who envisioned changes in Saxon religious policy along the lines of a frequently heard Calvinist notion—Luther's Reformation had gone halfway, and it was time to complete it. Upon assuming power Christian and Krell ended official sanction of the Formula of Concord, replaced a host of professors and church authorities (including Selnecker), and issued a new Bible that replaced Luther's introductions with Calvinist explanations. Most visible to the laity were a new hymnal with Reformed as well as Lutheran hymns and liturgical directions in sacramental theology that ended exorcism in baptism (a Calvinist criticism of Lutheran practice) and prescribed Calvinist rites and understanding of the Lord's Supper. Upon Christian's death these policies were overturned, and Krell was executed for his part in the adventure after a long trial and imprisonment.

Although Melanchthon's theological methodology remained a foundation of the evangelical church in the seventeenth century, Philippism's gift to the theological enterprise in the age of Lutheran orthodoxy was mainly these three issues, along with the Synergist Controversy, that theologians debated endlessly, ever finding the Philippists to have been in error. Philippism's legacy in Germany remained visible only in Reformed territories and in the irenic theology of the University of Helmstedt. For a more lasting positive legacy of the Philippists one must look to the evangelical movements in Hungary, Habsburg lands, and especially Scandinavia, where Melanchthon student Niels Hemmingsen (1513–1600) developed a rich humanist atmosphere and trained a generation of clergy with Philippist perspectives at the University of Copenhagen prior to his removal in 1579 on suspicions of crypto-Calvinism.

[*See also* Synergist Controversy.]

BIBLIOGRAPHY

Primary Sources

Christliche Bekentnis der Kirchen Gottes in des Churfürsten zu Sachsen Landen / Von dem heiligen Nachtmal des Herrn Christi / in der Christlichen versamlung zu Dreßden gestellet [.] Mit einhelligem Consens beider Vniuersiteten Leipzig vnd Witteberg / der dreien Geistlichen Consistorien vnd allen Superintendenten in diesem Landen. Wittenberg, 1571. Otherwise known as the Dresden Consensus. This and the Major and Pfeffinger volumes are in the Herzog August Bibliothek in Wolfenbüttel, Germany.

Major, Georg. *Ein Sermon von S. Pauli vnd aller Gottfurchtigen menschen bekerung zu Gott.* Leipzig, 1553. His major work.

Melanchthon, Philipp. *Loci Communes* (1543). Translated by J. A. O. Preus. Saint Louis, 1992. A competent translation of the third edition (or "age") of the *Loci,* which indicated the changes in Melanchthon's thinking between the first and second ages; the original texts are in vol. 21 of *Corpus reformatorum,* edited by Bretschneider and Bindseil.

Pfeffinger, Johann. *Grüntlicher vnd Warhafftiger Bericht der vorigen vnd jetzigen / für vnd nach dem Kriege ergangen Handlungen / von den Adiaphoris oder Mittledingen. Sampt eine Christlichen Kurtzen verantwortung.* Leipzig, 1550. His defense of adiaphora and the high liturgical practices of the Albertine Saxon churches.

Tappert, Theodore G., ed. *The Book of Concord: The Confessions of the Evangelical Lutheran Church.* Philadelphia, 1959. Includes Melanchthon's Augsburg Confession (Invariata) as well as the Formula of Concord; for scholarly work one should instead use *Die Bekenntnisschriften der evangelisch-lutherischen Kirche,* edited by Hans Lietzmann, H. Bornkamm, H. Volz, and E. Wolf.

Secondary Sources

Blaschke, Karlheinz. "Religion und Politik in Kursachsen, 1586–1591." In *Die reformierte Konfessionalisierung in Deutschland: Das Problem der "Zweiten Reformation,"* edited by Heinz Schilling, pp. 79–97. Gütersloh, 1986. Best recent study of the "Indian summer" of crypto-Calvinism in Saxony under Elector Christian I.

Calinich, Robert. *Kampf und Untergang des Melanchthonianismus in Kursachsen in den Jahren 1570 bis 1574 und die Schicksale seiner vornehmsten Häupter.* Leipzig, 1866. Detailed narrative of the events leading to the arrest of the crypto-Calvinists in 1574; unsympathetic to Philippism.

Junghans, Helmar. "Kryptocalvinisten." In *Theologische Realenzyklopädie,* vol. 20, pp. 123–129. Berlin and New York, 1990. Fine overview of crypto-Calvinism, though Junghans is not inclined to differentiate it from Philippism; good bibliography.

Koch, Ernst. "Der kursächsische Philippismus und seine Krise in den 1560er und 1570er Jahren." In *Die reformierte Konfessionalisierung in Deutschland: Das Problem der "Zweiten Reformation,"* edited by Heinz Schilling, pp. 60–77. Gütersloh, 1986. Koch's two articles are the most insightful studies of the Philippist movement from about 1560 onwards; his description of the events surrounding the 1571 letter of Johann Casimir varies from that set forth here.

———. "Auseinandersetzungen um die Autorität von Philipp Melanchthon und Martin Luther in Kursachsen im Vorfeld der Konkordienformel von 1577." *Lutherjahrbuch* 59 (1992), 128–159.

Kolb, Robert. "Georg Major as Controversialist: Polemics in the Late Reformation." *Church History* 45 (1976), 455–468. Good overview of the Majorist Controversy.

———. "Dynamics of Party Conflict in the Saxon Late Reformation: Gnesio-Lutherans vs. Philippists." *Journal of Modern History* 49.3 (1977), D[emand Publication Series] 1289-D1305. Identifies similarities and differences in the ways the two camps perceived the world around them.

———. *Nikolaus von Amsdorf, 1483–1565: Popular Polemics in the Preservation of Luther's Legacy*. Nieuwkoop, 1978. Focusing on Amsdorf after the Schmalkald War, this is an excellent introduction to the Adiaphora, Majorist, and Synergist Controversies; remarkably balanced.

Landerer, Albert, and Gustav Kawerau. "Philippisten." In *Realencyklopädie für protestantische Theologie und Kirche*, 3d ed., vol. 15, pp. 322–331. 1904. Most thorough brief description of the Philippists.

Peterson, Luther D. "The Philippist Theologians and the Interims of 1548: Soteriological, Ecclesiastical, and Liturgical Compromises and Controversies within German Lutheranism." Ph.D. diss., University of Wisconsin, 1974. The most thorough exploration of the Augsburg and Leipzig Interims and of the Adiaphora and Majorist Controversies.

———. "Melanchthon on Resisting the Emperor: The *Von der Notwehr Unterricht* of 1547." In *Regnum, Religio et Ratio: Essays Presented to Robert M. Kingdon*, edited by Jerome Friedman, pp. 133–144. Kirksville, Mo., 1987. Examination of the radical political ideas of Melanchthon and colleagues during the Schmalkald War.

Preger, Wilhelm. *Matthias Flacius Illyricus und seine Zeit.* 2 vols. Erlangen, 1859–1861. Important survey regarding Flacius's part in controversies.

Quere, Ralph W. "Melanchthonian Motifs in the Formula's Eucharistic Christology." In *Discord, Dialogue, and Concord: Studies in the Lutheran Reformation's Formula of Concord*, edited by Lewis W. Spitz and Wenzel Lohff, pp. 58–73. Philadelphia, 1977. Important though perhaps overstated claim of Melanchthonian influence on the Formula of Concord's treatment of the Lord's Supper and Christology.

Ritschl, Otto. *Dogmengeschichte des Protestantismus.* 4 vols. Leipzig, 1912–1927. The most thorough of a handful of late nineteenth- and early twentieth-century German studies of the period between Luther's death and the Formula of Concord; unsympathetic to Philippism.

Schilling, Heinz. "Confessionalization in the Empire: Religious and Societal Change in Germany between 1555 and 1620." In *Religion, Political Culture and the Emergence of Early Modern Society: Essays in German and Dutch History*, pp. 205–245. Leiden, 1992. Translation of an article that first appeared in *Historische Zeitschrift* 245 (1988), 1–46. This is a good introduction to the growing literature on "confessionalization"; see footnotes 4 and 8 for a brief bibliography.

LUTHER D. PETERSON

PHILIPP OF HESSE (also Philip; the "Magnanimous"; 1504–1567), landgrave, antagonist of the Habsburgs, architect of the Schmalkald League, and champion of the *via media* in confessional disputes. Although he was small of stature, contemporaries knew him as a man of decisive action and persistence. Luther commented: "When the landgrave burns, nothing can stop it." From his earliest days, too, he was known for his rational approach to matters. He listened to the advice of "graybeards" in his youth and continued to consider the advice of theologians and other advisers throughout his life. But he was also capable of making up his own mind and even of disagreeing with prominent theologians.

Philipp's early life was distinguished by traumatic experiences that undoubtedly sobered him but also left him suspicious of others. His father, Wilhelm II (1477–1509), was incapacitated by syphilis and died when Philipp was four. He was then separated from his mother by a noble regency. Anna of Mecklenburg (1485–1525) managed to gain control of the regency and rejoin her son in 1514, but the rebellious nobility continued to threaten Philipp's rule, even after his majority was declared (1518). Anna abandoned him again to undertake a second marriage in 1519.

From the mid-1520s, one may characterize the landgrave as the main German antagonist of the Habsburgs, as a lay counterpart to Luther, and as champion of the *via media* in confessional disputes. These roles were closely connected. The major political factor behind Philipp's antagonistic policy was the Katzenellenbogen dispute, which set Hesse at odds with the counts of Nassau and the Habsburgs.

In order to counter the Habsburg threat, Philipp promoted the idea of an evangelical (after 1529, Protestant) alliance. In 1524 the Torgau League allied electoral Saxony and Hesse. They were soon joined by some towns and smaller principalities. Philipp wished to include "all who adhere to the Gospel." Because of doctrinal and constitutional differences, however, he could not convince the Lutheran party, led by electoral Saxony and Nuremberg, to include the Upper Germans and Swiss. Hence through 1530 the landgrave fulfilled his need for a defensive arrangement with bilateral alliances. Philipp also developed a theory of resistance to imperial authority. This Hessian theory of resistance was the foundation for the later, better-known Magdeburg theory of resistance practiced by lesser magistrates.

Meanwhile, because the Saxons claimed alliances could be made only with co-religionists, Philip determined to hold a colloquy. He believed that the differences between the parties were not essential, but a matter of words. Hence Philipp sponsored the Colloquy of Marburg (1529) to end differences between Lutherans and Zwinglians. Although success eluded him at Marburg, Philipp continued to work for alliance at the Diet of Augsburg (1530), and he led the opposition to Charles V as he had at the previous diets. But the emperor's threats at Augsburg finally pushed the Saxon party to ally with the upper Germans. The resulting Schmalkald League (1531) provided security to the Protestants for years.

After Marburg, Philipp also continued to work for communion between the upper German towns and the Lutheran party, enlisting the aid of Martin Bucer of Strasbourg, with whom he became acquainted at Marburg. The demise of Zwingli (1531) lightened this task. Through Bucer, Philipp sponsored talks that led to the agreements at Württemberg (1534), Kassel (1534), and ultimately Wittenberg (1536), by which Luther accepted the upper Germans as co-religionists. Hence he ended the sacramentarian controversy. From 1527 until his death, Philipp remained the proponent of pan-Protestant union.

The Württemberg campaign of 1534 was Philipp's most significant stroke against the Habsburgs. Using superior siege artillery and diplomacy to isolate the enemy, Philipp easily restored the previously deposed Duke Ulrich (1487–1550) to his duchy (hence Philipp was nicknamed "the Magnanimous"). This act deprived the Habsburgs of the territory with which they had sought, since 1520, to bridge their Austrian and Burgundian lands. Moreover, it brought Protestantism to a large princely territory in the south. Gratuitously, the reform of Württemberg made progress in favor of Protestant union.

After Württemberg, Philipp sought an agreement with the moderate Roman Catholics and a rapprochement with the emperor. Having fulfilled his political ambitions regarding the Habsburgs, the landgrave became concerned with reducing irritations that might lead to war. He coordinated religious concerns with this policy, too. Philipp developed a deeper respect for the early church fathers as a basis for religious reform and agreement. Tradition came to mean the practices of the patristic church, not simply the scriptures. In this view, he followed Bucer and Melanchthon. Hence Philipp supported the emperor's famous Protestant-Catholic dialogues at Hagenau, Worms, and Regensburg (1540/41).

Philipp's bigamy (1541) undermined the league and helped provoke the disastrous Schmalkald War in 1547. The landgrave's resulting imprisonment by the emperor (1547–1552) has been seen as permanently neutralizing, indeed, breaking the previously active prince. More recent studies, however, downplay this idea. One need only note that he was behind the Peace of Augsburg (1555), which finally granted legal security to those who followed the Augsburg Confession. As an antagonist, furthermore, Philipp had enough energy to force a final, favorable revision of the Katzenellenbogen dispute in 1557. Philipp also continued to sponsor pan-Protestant talks. The threat of Counter-Reformation activities, led by Philip II of Spain, spurred him to overcome confessional differences that were intensifying in Germany and to aid the Huguenots in France.

Philipp was a heroic figure of great achievement: he was the lay defender of Protestantism and, under his rule, Hesse set examples of toleration, charity, and promotion of education. But he had weaknesses of heroic proportions too. One cannot gainsay the Wittenberg judgment of him as rash, hotheaded, and overly suspicious. The Pack Affair (1528), his support for the Zwinglian towns with their warlike inclinations, and his promotion of resistance all led to these conclusions. But Philipp proved to be a selective advocate of war. In the 1530s, rejecting Bucer's advice, he opposed war as a means of protecting church property. When Charles V gained the upper hand in the Schmalkald War, Philipp preferred to surrender to the emperor rather than fight a war that would probably lead only to much destruction of his land and people.

Philipp's sexually wayward life, which led to bigamy, represented his greatest weakness. Although he may have suffered from a sexual anomaly, this and other rationales offered have failed to explain fully, much less excuse, his waywardness or bigamy. The bigamy led ultimately to his division of Hesse as he attempted to satisfy his second wife and her children.

BIBLIOGRAPHY

Hancock, Alton O. "Philipp of Hesse's View of the Relationship of Prince and Church." *Church History* 35 (1966), 157–169.

Heinemeyer, Walter. "Landgraf Philipp der Grossmütige von Hessen—politische Führer der Reformation." In *Die Geschichte Hessens,* edited by Uwe Schultz, pp.72–81. Stuttgart, 1983. Latest assessment by a prominent Hessian historian who has written extensively on Philipp.

Hillerbrand, Hans J. *Landgrave Philipp of Hesse, 1504–1567: Religion and Politics in the Reformation.* Reformation Essays and Studies, vol. 1. Saint Louis, 1967. Best general introduction to the life and significance of Philipp in the English language.

Kleiner, John W. "The Attitudes of Martin Bucer and Landgrave Philipp toward the Jews of Hesse, 1538–1539." In *Faith and Freedom: A Tribute to Franklin H. Littell,* edited by Richard Libowitz, pp. 221–230. Oxford, 1987. Useful as an English introduction to the issues and literature regarding Philipp's policies of toleration.

Maurer, Wilhelm. "Theologie und Laienchristentum bei Philipp von Hessen." In *Kirche und Geschichte: Gesammelte Aufsätze,* edited by Ernst-Wilhelm Kohls and Gerhard Müller, pp. 292–318. Göttingen, 1970. The best treatment of Philipp's religious views and character, with attention given to his relationship to the magisterial reformers.

Press, Volker. "Landgraf Philipp der Grossmütige von Hessen, 1504–1567." In *Protestantische Profile,* edited by Klaus Scholder and Dieter Kleinmann, pp. 60–77. Königstein-Taunus, Germany, 1983. Excellent analysis of Philipp's accomplishments and character by a distinguished scholar of the Reformation.

Wright, William J. "The Homberg Synod and Philip of Hesse's Plan for a New Church-State Settlement." *Sixteenth Century Journal* 4 (1973), 23–46. Sets the early Hessian Reformation in the context of the general Lutheran movement.

———. "Philip of Hesse's Vision of Protestant Unity and the Marburg Colloquy." In *Pietas et Societas: New Trends in Reformation History,* edited by Kyle C. Sessions and Phillip N. Bebb, pp. 163–179. Sixteenth Century Essays and Studies, vol. 4. Kirksville, Mo., 1985. Shows that Philipp's vision of Protestant union and alliance was frustrated by differing constitutional views and national sentiments, not just religious differences.

WILLIAM J. WRIGHT

PHILIPS, Dirk (1504–1568), an early leader of Dutch Anabaptism. Born the son of a priest and the younger brother of Obbe Philips (c.1500–1568), he became a Franciscan monk, joining the observant Franciscan monastery at

Nieuw Galilea in Leeuwarden. Some have assumed that he received a university education; whatever the case, he knew Latin, Greek, and some Hebrew. Whether, like his brother Obbe, Philips joined the group of Sacramentarians in Leeuwarden that gradually came under the influence of Melchior Hoffman's doctrine is not known. Nevertheless, it was at Leeuwarden that Philips was rebaptized some time toward the end of 1533 by Pieter Houtzager, a disciple of Jan Matthijs, who also proclaimed the coming judgment and kingdom of God.

Early the next year Philips appears to have been ordained an elder by his own brother. During this period the group was bombarded with messages and messengers from Münster. But both Dirk and Obbe appear to have harbored serious doubts about the veracity of the message, especially after the persecution began, for, as Obbe put it in his confession, "all they told us would come upon the world, the tyrants and the godless on earth, that came upon us and upon them first of all, for we were the very first who were persecuted and put to death." They appear always to have opposed revolution, but their protests went unheeded until after the Münster disaster. That disillusioning experience allowed their voices to be heard. They thus became leaders of the peaceful Melchiorites after the fall of Münster and shortly thereafter won Menno Simons to their cause.

Philips ministered first in the Netherlands and then in East Friesland, Mecklenburg, and Holstein. Contrary to the earlier assumption that he lived in Gdańsk from 1550 on, his biographer (Doornkaat Koolman) argues that Philips probably resided instead in Het Falder, on the outskirts of Emden. Here he encountered many Flemish Anabaptist refugees. He clearly became one of the outstanding early leaders of Dutch Anabaptism, being singled out as such by the civil authorities as early as 1537. He participated prominently in various conferences of elders; was present at Goch in 1547, when Adam Pastor was banned for denying the divinity of Christ; and in 1554 was at Wismar where agreement was reached on a number of divisive issues. By virtually all accounts, however, Philips was a severe and at times obstinate man, and he entered into many disputes with Leenaert Bouwens, whom he suspended from office in 1565. Earlier, however, he had sided with him on the issue of the severe application of the ban (excommunication along with avoidance of the excommunicated). Together they had persuaded Menno Simons to accept their position, to the lasting detriment of the Dutch church. When the division between the Flemings and the Frisians took place in 1567, he took the side of the Flemings, perhaps because of his association with them. The latter thereupon immediately banned the Frisians, who had been joined by Bouwens. The Frisians, in turn, banned the Flemings, together with Philips. Undeterred, the latter completed his booklet on Christian marriage. He died a year later.

In opposition to Kuehler, Doornkaat Koolman asserts that Philips always played a secondary role to Menno, at least until 1554. This may well be confirmed by the fact that, beginning in 1545, Dutch and North German Anabaptists came to be called "Menists," whereas before Menno had joined the group they had been called "Obbenites" (after Philips's brother). For some time, however, the writings of Dirk and not those of Menno exerted the greater influence on the Dutch and north German Anabaptists. Toward the end of his life he had these collected and published in a single volume entitled *Enchiridion oft Hantboecxken van de Christelijcke Leere* (1564). Perhaps named after the famous "handbook" of Desiderius Erasmus, his more famous countryman, the volume of some 650 pages contained such tracts as, "Confession of Faith"; "Concerning the Incarnation"; "Concerning the True Knowledge of Jesus Christ"; "Apologia"; "The Call of the Preacher"; "Loving Admonition"; "Concerning the True Knowledge of God"; "Exposition of the Tabernacle of Moses"; "Concerning the New Birth"; "Spiritual Restoration"; "Three Thorough Admonitions"; and "The Church of God." Of these, perhaps the two most important are his tracts on the church and on spiritual restitution.

In the first Philips presents a delineation of the church organized on the apostolic model, which is based on a radical separation of the people of God from the children of the world. As in his tract on spiritual restitution—aimed directly at Bernhard Rothmann's tract of the same name—he rejects the visible kingdom of God on earth, remarking, "Out of this have come many errors, so that everyone has interpreted this restitution in a strange fashion in accordance with his own preconceptions in a physical manner, as many still do." That concept of the kingdom, Philips maintained, had been justified on the basis of an erroneous assumption about the relationship between the Old and New Testaments. Menno and Philips, on the other hand, were attempting to restore the New Testament model of the church—the apostolic church.

There is great uniformity of views between Menno and Philips, down to their agreement concerning the "heavenly flesh of Christ." Where Philips—with the help of Bouwens—exerted influence on Menno was in the matter of the severe application of the ban, which Menno regretted on his deathbed. When Dutch and north German Anabaptists began to take a more lenient approach to the ban in the seventeenth century, Philips's influence also waned. This is reflected in the editions of his works. Dutch editions appeared in 1564, 1578, 1579, 1600, and 1627. A French edition appeared in 1626, and the first German edition came out in 1715, followed by another in 1802.

BIBLIOGRAPHY

Primary Sources

Cramer, Samuel, and Fredrik Pipjer. *Bibliotheca reformatoria neerlandica.* Vol. 10. The Hague, 1914.

Philips, Dirk. *The Writings of Dirk Philips, 1504–1568.* Translated and edited by Cornelius J. Dyck, William E. Keeney, and Alvin J. Beachy. Scottdale, Pa., 1992.

Secondary Sources

Doornkaat Koolman, J. ten. *Dirk Philips, vriend en medewerker van Menno Simons, 1504–1568.* 2d ed. Scottdale, Pa., 1981.

Friesen, A. "Menno and Münster: The Man and the Movement." In *Menno Simons: A Reappraisal,* edited by Gerald R. Brunk pp. 131–162. Harrisonburg, Va., 1992.

Krahn, Cornelius. *Dutch Anabaptism.* 2d ed. Scottdale, Pa., 1982.

Kuehler, W. J. *Geschiedenis der Nederlandsche Doopsgezinde in de zestiende eeuw.* Reprint, Haarlem, 1961.

Vos, Karel. *Menno Simons, 1496–1561: Zijn leven en werken en zijn reformatorische denkbeelden.* Leiden, 1914.

Williams, George H. *The Radical Reformation.* 3d ed. Kirksville, Mo., 1992.

ABRAHAM FRIESEN

PHILIPS, Obbe (c.1500–1568), Dutch Anabaptist leader and theologian. Obbe Philips, elder brother of the Anabaptist leader and theologian Dirk Philips, was born the son of a priest in Leeuwarden. He made his living as a physician-surgeon. In the religious turbulence of the 1520s the two brothers had taken to reading Lutheran tracts and probably joined a Sacramentarian conventicle. Converted to Melchiorite Anabaptism by Melchior Hoffman, Obbe Philips witnessed the execution of the first Anabaptist martyr in the Netherlands. While Philips was away on an Anabaptist preaching mission, militant apocalyptic Anabaptists, followers of the other Leeuwarden convert of Melchior Hoffman, Jan Matthijs, announced that the end was near and undertook a rebellion. Philips was alleged to have been the ringleader—in all probability he was not—and fled to Amsterdam. There he encountered a militant form of Melchiorite Anabaptism at about the same time that the Anabaptists were beginning to rule in Münster increasingly with the same militant apocalyptic tendencies. Philips dissociated himself from this militancy, particularly when seven men and women in February 1535 ran naked through the streets of Amsterdam, proclaiming the "naked truth of God." When in the spring of 1535 a group of revolutionary Anabaptists sought to storm the Amsterdam city hall, Philips opposed them.

The debacle of Münsterite Anabaptism caused Philips deep soul-searching, doubting not only his own vocation as Anabaptist preacher—he had been ordained by the Matthijs faction which he had come to consider unbiblical—but also the legitimacy of those whom he, in turn, had ordained—his brother Dirk together with David Joris and Menno Simons. Eventually the gap between Obbe and the newly emerging "Mennonites," under the leadership of Menno Simons, became formidable, and by 1540 there occurred a parting of the ways. Nothing is known about Philips's life afterwards except that he died in 1568. Thus the intriguing question of his subsequent theological development—Did he return to Catholicism? Did he follow the spiritualist individualism of Sebastian Franck?—remains unanswered.

Obbe Philips has been described as a spiritualist Anabaptist, a northern Hans Denck, one who shared the basic Anabaptist tenets but abhorred the aapocalyptic militancy of Jan Matthijs and the Münster Anabaptists. Despite his eventual disappearance from the Anabaptists in the north, their early story is unthinkable without him. His only written work was his *Bekentnisse* (Confessions), published posthumously. All salient biographical facts about him are derived from this treatise.

BIBLIOGRAPHY

Primary Sources

Philips, Obbe. *Bekentnisse Obbe Philipsz.* (1584). *Bibliotheca Reformatoria Neerlandica* 7 (1910), 88–138.

———. *Confessions.* In *Spiritual and Anabaptist Writers.* Philadelphia, 1957.

Secondary Sources

Bautz, Friedrich Wilhelm, ed. *Biographisch-bibliographisches Kirchenlexikon.* Hamm, Germany, 1970–. See vol. 7, nos. 514–515.

Livestro, C. "Obbe Philips and the Anabaptist Vision." *Mennonite Quarterly Review* 41 (1967), 99–115.

Stroman, B. *Obbe Philipsz, Oudste der Doopers.* Hilversum, 1935.

Zijpp, Nanne van der. "Obbe Philips(z)." In *Mennonite Encyclopedia,* vol. 4, pp. 9–11. Scottdale, Pa., 1959.

HANS J. HILLERBRAND

PHILOSOPHY OF CHRIST. "Christian philosophy," or "philosophy of Christ" (*philosophia christiana* or *Christi*), was an expression most widely used and popularized by Desiderius Erasmus in the Reformation period. The phrase is especially visible in the introductory writings to his New Testament editions, most notably the *Paraclesis* (1516), and in the preface to his 1518 edition of the *Enchiridion* (the letter to Paul Volz), but it is also present in other writings, such as the *Adagia,* the *Paraphrases in Novum Testamentum,* and the annotations in the *Novum Testamentum.* Erasmus stressed that the Christian philosophy displayed in the Gospels and the letters of Paul has to do not with dialectic or intellectual comprehension but with true piety and transformed living according to the life and teachings of Jesus under the inspiration of the Holy Spirit. He set this philosophy over against scholastic disputation and monastic ceremonial religion. He thought it could be practiced as readily by laypersons as by trained theologians and monks.

In the past scholars have perceived in this expression a rationalistic, humanist moralism, particularly since in the *Paraclesis* Erasmus described the teaching of some of the ancient philosophers as in agreement with Christ's doctrine. In contrast with this interpretation, more recent scholarship has emphasized that the "philosophy of Christ" concerns the mystery of Christ known not to human reason but to faith, an understanding that has its roots in the Fathers. The patristic base of Erasmus's view was underlined already by Ernst R. Curtius in 1953. The term is found in Clement of Alexandria, Chrysostom, and, most importantly for the Western development, Augustine (*Against Julian* 4.14.72). The expression is employed in the Middle Ages in connection with the monastic life. In the Italian Renaissance, Petrarch anticipated Erasmus's usage with his phrase "philosopher of Christ." In the northern Renaissance, Rodolphus Agricola (Roelof Huysman) preceded Erasmus with the prominence he gave the term (*De formando studio*, 1484). Among Erasmus's contemporaries who used the expression were Jacques Lefèvre d'Étaples and Guillaume Budé.

Influenced by Erasmus, several of the Protestant Reformers utilized the expression "Christian philosophy" or its equivalents, "heavenly philosophy," "heavenly doctrine," and "sacred philosophy," such as Philipp Melanchthon, Heinrich Bullinger, and John Calvin. The term "Christian philosophy" is also found in the Roman Catechism of the Council of Trent.

[*See also* Christology.]

BIBLIOGRAPHY

Augustijn, Cornelis. *Erasmus: His Life, Works and Influence.* Translated by J. C. Grayson. Toronto, 1991. Chapter 7 gives an excellent description of the meaning of "philosophy of Christ" for Erasmus.

Erasmus, Desiderius. *Collected Works of Erasmus.* Vol. 66, edited by John W. O'Malley. *Spiritualia: Enchiridion, De Contemptu Mundi, De Vidua Christiana.* Toronto, 1988. The general introduction provides another fine summary of Erasmus's understanding of the expression.

Gilson, Etienne. *L'esprit de la philosophie médiévale.* 2d. rev. ed. Paris, 1944. The appendix contains an annotated bibliography of works from Augustine to the twentieth century which employ the expression "philosophy of Christ" or its equivalent or deal with the subject without using the term. The English translation lacks this appendix.

JOHN B. PAYNE

PICKEL, Conrad. *See* Celtis, Conradus.

PIERIUS. *See* Pérez de Pineda, Juan.

PIETY. The medieval world acknowledged readily that the essence of religion was piety, or "godliness." On the eve of the Reformation, one's "religion" referred as much to one's ritualistic behavior and spiritual demeanor as to beliefs and doctrinal position. It was the religious scholar and philosopher Wilfred Cantwell Smith who first emphasized (in *The Meaning and End of Religion*, New York, 1964) the peculiarly subjective and performative way in which the notion of religion was articulated in the literature of the Middle Ages. Rarely, he pointed out, did the noun-form *religio* appear in the manuscripts of Christian writers before 1500, and when it did surface, as in Augustine's treatise *De Vera Religione*, it referred not to an objective entity or institutional structure that might be thought of as a "church," but to a personal attitude of respect toward the holy. *De Vera Religione* should be interpreted, according to Smith, "not as 'On the True Religion,' (i.e., Christianity in contrast to other religions), but as 'On True Religiousness' or 'True Piety.' " Before the seventeenth and eighteenth centuries, and certainly before the spiritual battles of the sixteenth century, "the understanding of religions as alternative systems of belief embodied in mutually exclusive ideological communities" was not dominant.

This emphasis on personal piety in the medieval understanding of religion was conditioned by philosophical as well as political forces peculiar to early church history. The Reformation's wars and national conflicts relating to specific doctrinal issues contributed finally to engendering a sense of the sacred as a depersonalized system of metaphysical truths held by contraposed ideological communities. A new linguistic orientation eventually hypostatized subjective feelings into "things," and ultimately made the piety of Catholics different from the piety of Protestants, separating them both from Judaism, Islam, Hinduism, Confucianism, and various "heretical" sects. The modern conception of religion, in other words, evolving out of Reformation political struggles, involved a process of reification in which an attitude of mind became an objective entity and in which pious inclinations gradually came to be conceived of as institutionalized systems of belief.

It was with the medieval conception of *religio* as an attitude and posture of respect and honor toward the sacred that sixteenth-century writers wrote their devotional manuals for the instruction of the faithful. The Dutch humanist Desiderius Erasmus called his readers, in the little treatise *De contemptu mundi* (1521), to come "hither, to religion . . . to religion, where the unrestful roaring of the world does not rush in." In religion, or pious devotion, even the significant theological and institutional differences that divided Protestants from Catholics did not normally enter, for private devotional experiences appear to have been remarkably similar across Europe. The earliest Protestant communities in Germany, France, Switzerland, and England shared the same devotional readings as their Catholic counterparts—favoring Augustine's *De doctrina Christiana*, Thomas à Kempis's *De imitatione Christi*, the *Hortulus animae*, and prayer books featuring the Ten Commandments, the Lord's Prayer, and the Apostles' Creed. Even the Puritan laity, the individuals most radically opposed to traditional Catholic doctrine, adopted readings from a generally accepted collection of religious writers. Bernard of Clairvaux's *De diligendo Deo* and *De gradibus humilitatus et superbiae* mediated for Puritans the traditional Catholic program of spiritual exercise based on confession, self-abasement, and meditation on the joys of heaven. Luis de Granada's *Guia de pecadores* (1556) and *Libro de la oración y meditación* (1567) and Melchor Cano's *Tratado de la victoria de sí mismo* (1550) could be found in the private libraries of Calvinist as well as Lutheran families.

In England and the New World, the Protestant manuals of Thomas Becon, *The Pomander of Prayer* (1559) and *The Sicke Man's Salve* (1561), and of Lewis Bayly, *The Practice of Piety: Directing a Christian to Walk, That He May Please God* (1610), had a profound influence on the devotional experiences of Conformists and Nonconformists. What readers found attractive in these reformed treatises was systematic analysis of the traditional devotional disciplines of faith, prayer, and fasting, and an elaborate discussion about the proper ritual procedures to be taken in preparation for death. Reformed readers could also find in Protestant manuals such as Francis Quarles's *Emblems, Divine and Moral* and Richard Baxter's *The Saints Everlasting Rest* (1652) strategies for meditation and prayer that resembled in many respects Ignatius Loyola's *Exercitia spiritualia.*

These shared devotional readings reveal a fundamental commitment to the medieval conception that a pious life rests upon routine management of bodily activity and mental thought processes in order to conform to the image of Christ. Ideally, no distinction was drawn, in the Christian "state of godliness," between the inner life of the spirit and outward behavior. With respect to this ideal, many of the manuals of pious instruction were written to readers and listeners in their capacity as children (Philipp Melanchthon's *Enchiridion elementorum puerilium,* 1520), as husbands and wives (Richard Whitford's *A Werke for Housholders,* 1530), and as apprentices (Abraham Jackson's *The Pious Prentice, Or, the Prentices Piety,* 1640), asking that they strive to shape their personalities precisely to fit standards appropriate to their social positions. One of the most popular preachers of Protestant England, William Perkins, upheld a more generic code of piety that required of all believers, whatever their status in society, to seek purity of soul by attending to diet, which should be moderate; to laughter, which should be sparing; to conversation, which should be serious at all times; and to reading, which should avoid "idle discourses and histories, being nothing else but enticements and baits unto manifold sinners." Even the choice of clothes was in some manner tied to godliness. In the sternest Puritan conception, "clothing must be neat and suitable for one's occupation, neither too gay nor too somber but such as indicate sobriety of mind." This concern for outward appearance was to be extended to personal demeanor, which should be cheerful and discreet and always kindly toward neighbors. Similarly, Catholic lay piety recommended that kindness and charity toward others be exercised around the formula of the "seven acts of mercy," which involved feeding the hungry, giving drink to the thirsty, clothing the naked, lodging the homeless, visiting the sick, ransoming the captive, and burying the dead. Along with this religious praxis, Catholics were instructed to engage regularly in penitential acts such as fasting and pilgrimage to make their outward behavior conform to a spirit of ascetic concern for the afterlife.

The importance of external appearance for the expression of internal faith was thus shared by diverse spiritual groups of sixteenth-century Europe and demonstrates the continued vitality of ritual form in religious life. It was in fact to these outward observances that the term *religiones* referred in this period, and it was through these ritual ceremonies that ordinary people exercised their metaphysical prerogatives. According to Richard Trexler, it was largely "through ritual that a vocabulary of right action" was inculcated. The repetition of Latin words, the collective singing of biblical psalms, the genuflection of the body, the smell of warm incense, and the strategic ringing of bells all attuned human consciousness to the life of the spirit. "Under the rubric of routine ceremony," says Trexler, "lie legions of individual lives changed decisively by participation in ceremonies" ("Reverence and Profanity in the Study of Early Modern Religion," in *Religion and Society in Early Modern Europe, 1500–1800*, edited by Kaspar von Greyerz, London, 1984).

The tendency of Christian communities to conceive of the holy through a series of standardized acts as basic as prayer and churchgoing served an important psychological function. As Elaine Scarry has pointed out, to believe "is to perpetuate the imagined object across a succession of days, weeks and years; 'belief' is the capacity to sustain the imagined (or apprehended) object in one's own psyche, even when there is no sensorially available confirmation that that object has any existence independent of one's own interior mental activity" (*The Body in Pain,* New York, 1985). To the Catholic and Protestant churches of the sixteenth century, it was largely through formalized prayer and collective ritual that faith in an invisible God was sustained.

Within Catholic devotions specifically, the paramount means by which the invisible order of creation was perpetuated in the mind was through public and private exercises that made use of the visual. The Renaissance and Reformation years witnessed a burgeoning of religious art that represented through material objects the biblical and hagiographical tales of redemption. Every cathedral, parish church, and religious sanctuary possessed its painted image or statuary that was believed to contain supernatural powers. In addition to these fixed objects of meditation, Catholic culture carved out of the landscape special "holy" spots in which divine beings were thought to have made momentary appearances to human eyes. Pilgrimage shrines (Mary of the Cross in Castile, Our Lady of Rocamadour in central France) and sanctuaries containing relics of saintly personages (Santiago de Compostela, Canterbury, Cologne) drew pious Catholics away from the ordinary environment of their homes to extraordinary loci of sacred powers. It is undoubtedly true that much of Catholic religious reflection occurred in the presence of these tangible conduits of divine grace. "This visual externalization of faith," says Carlos Eire, "became the layman's theology" (*War against the Idols*, Cambridge, 1986).

Intensification of belief in Catholic communities was achieved as well by the forging of a special relationship to the temporal order that tied the natural seasons of the year to an annual christological life cycle. The biblical tale of Christ's birth, death, and redemption was incorporated into seasonal ceremonies consisting of Advent, Christmas, Epiphany, Lent, Easter, and Ascension, making these mystical events a common accompaniment to everyday life. To the christological calendar, which roughly accommodated the older pagan cycle of the solar and agricultural year, the church added across the centuries a series of holy days dedicated to saints. A host of local saints was also adopted into the Catholic calendar and distributed throughout the year to provide intercessionary avenues to heaven. Attention to their cults, it was believed, enhanced the material as well as spiritual status of devotees. Each day in the Catholic calendar, therefore, brought its personal exemplar of sanctity, and within each day the tolling of canonical hours brought its reminder of spiritual purpose. By tying belief to performative acts of homage such as these, to charity and penitence, to objects of art, to natural geography, and to the phenomenon of time, Catholic piety sought to grasp the transcendent by making it immanent. It was a devotional experience that blended the holy with the profane and conceived of the infinite within the finite.

Given the profound grasp of visual images and holidays upon the pious thoughts of Christians, one of the initial challenges in the establishment of the new Protestant churches was to elaborate distinctive types of liturgical and devotional etiquette. While doctrinal differences were articulated with relative ease and speed by Reformed theologians, establishing new sacred times, spaces, and objects was more difficult. The first steps in this direction were primarily negative, focused on abolishing the performance of masses, processions, and the use of holy water. The quintessential form of Protestant resistance to the religion of Rome was a passionate and vindictive iconoclasm that attempted to abolish the visual and temporal representations of a tradition that tied faith so closely to the imagination. Protestantism sought to generate an idea of God that could be held in place hour by hour, day by day, without mediatory signs and graven images to assist believers. It was a faith that took up the challenge of the original Hebraic conception of God as hidden and unrepresentable, one that put enormous pressure on the human capacity to apprehend through abstraction. To a degree unknown by Christian communities in the past, Protestantism relied on the power of the word, on the verbal purity of scripture, to sustain belief. Reformed theologians such as Martin Bucer and John Calvin condemned devotion to physical objects as idolatrous and dangerous to the "true" worship of a transcendental God. Their followers' ritualized acts of iconographic destruction, undertaken at strategic moments in the Catholic calendar, implicitly affirmed the importance of images and eventually brought about a heightened self-consciousness concerning their instrumental role in devotional life. Iconoclasm was the dialectical antithesis of a faith nurtured on visual objects in the imagination. By parodying the Mass, urinating on statues, and defiling the Host, participants were putting their sacred beliefs to the test, and by means of this anti-ritual they acquired a new form of religious conviction. Calvinists in particular challenged the metaphysical assumption that the divine was objectively present in material elements and affirmed the principle that "finitum non est capax infiniti" (the finite does not contain the infinite). The reformation of Christian piety therefore was itself a ritual process and a struggle for control over the "experiential" nature of faith.

It is not true, however, that the discarding of traditional visual receptacles of the sacred was ever thoroughly completed in the Protestant faith. Reading manuals widely used by the lay public exploited graphic as well as literary texts from the past. Protestant emblem books combined visual devotional aids with meditative verse and continued, in woodblock prints, the same symbolic tradition found in illuminated picture bibles, books of hours, and stained glass. Detailed drawings of the world of the spirit were also contained in the title pages of such prominent Puritan devotionals as John Downame's *The Christian Warfare Against the Devill World and Flesh* (1604), Johann Gerhard's *The Soules Watch or, a Day-Booke for the Devout Soule* (3d ed., 1621), and Lewis Bayly's *The Practice of Piety* (1610).

A more significant accommodation to traditional Catholic use of the visual imagination in prayer came in the Puritan exercise known as "composition of place." In this technique, biblical scenes of Christ were reenacted in the imagination during prayer. Francis de Sales articulated the technique to Catholic readers in his *Introduction à la vie dévote* (1608): "When you kneel before your spiritual father, imagine that you are on Mount Calvary, at the feet of Jesus Christ crucified, whose Precious Blood drops down on all sides to wash and cleanse you from your iniquities." In *The Plaine Mans Pathway to Heaven* (1601), Arthur Dent likewise enjoined Puritan readers to visualize the process of repentance through the image of the Crucifixion, advising the pious to "nail down all our sinnes and iniquities to the crosse of Christ, bury them in his death, bathe them in his bloud, hide them in his wounds, let them never rise up in judgement against us."

A more radically successful reconfiguration of pious etiquette was the development of a new series of public events for rescheduling people's lives around religion. In Strasbourg, where the Reformation was strongly supported by government magistrates, every day of the year offered the opportunity for collective religious instruction and devotion. Every morning at sunrise the pastors held early services with prayers and half-hour exhortations to piety. Three hours later, at eight or nine o'clock, the cathedral preacher gave a sermon on a biblical text, reading through the entire Old and New Testaments in the course of a year. Later in the afternoon, another worship service was available in the cathedral. To this daily schedule was added the celebration of the Lord's Supper on Sunday morning, which quickly became the focal point of the new evangelical calendar. For those who wished to partake in Communion, services were held on the preceding Saturday evening for public and private confessions of sins. Early on Sunday morning, small religious services were held in the parish churches for servants, followed by a later one offered for the community as a whole. This larger Sunday service began with organ recitals and hymn singing by the entire congregation and was succeeded by exhortations to humility, assurances of forgiveness, and general confession of sin. Additional singing ensued as the pastors moved to their pulpits to recite the Lord's Prayer with the congregation. Bible reading and preaching lasted another hour. At the end of the service came Communion, prayers for the well-being of parishioners, more singing, and, finally, a blessing to complete the liturgy.

This reconstruction of the Lord's Supper, meticulously designed to conform to biblical precedent and making extraordinary use of music and preaching for capturing the spiritual imagination, was eventually adopted by Puritan congregations in England and New England and became the devotional point of reference within Christianity in the West. The "sabbath" became the time to hear the word of God, to partake in the Eucharist, and to rest from secular work and play. The new calendar was different only in degree from the old, continuing to manage time by separating "sacred" from "secular" activities. For Reformed Protestantism, sabbath worship completely replaced the annual, irregular cycle of holy feast days with regular cycles of weekly memorials of the salvation drama. Catholics also readily accepted the heightened appearance of sabbath worship by integrating it into the old series of calendrical celebrations, all of which now regulated the flow of events in their lives. In England, the Anglican church compromised its members' relationships with sacred time by honoring all Sundays, the Mondays and Tuesdays of Easter week and Whitsun week, and some twenty-seven holidays with prayer and public worship.

The reform in ritual that took place in sixteenth-century Europe was nowhere more universally shared than in the experience of public and private devotion. Among all religious groups, the Reformation and Counter-Reformation movements resulted in a more intensified devotional experience based on meditational readings, silent reflection on sin, and prayer. The second half of the sixteenth century saw a great multiplication of manuals designed to facilitate private contemplation, including books of prayers, pious aphorisms, printed sermons, adaptations of the Psalms, moralized allegories, and manuals of religious etiquette, especially those concerned with the problem of how to die. If some Christian believers had found reliance on visual images a facile and problematic aspect of traditional piety, they all eventually embraced the power of words to shape the human imagination and transform the heart. The word of God—spoken, read, and sung—was believed to be the most powerful means by which the soul was infused with divine grace. When sixteenth-century Christians went to prayer, their minds were filled with stock phrases, whether from Luther's *Betbüchlein*, *The Book of Common Prayer*, or the French *Psalter*. Even the Puritans, who rejected the set phrases of published manuals in favor of extemporaneous language that flowed from the heart, relied, as their diaries and letters attest, on memorized sayings derived from scripture. This routine recital of prayer formulas was taught to adults as well as children, who were tested for their faith from time to time by ecclesiastical superiors in public performances. Prayer undoubtedly became the most highly ritualized aspect of lay piety during the sixteenth century.

It was in the arena of private devotion that the ritualization of prayer most profoundly influenced the religious consciousness of men and women during the period of the Reformation, intensifying the subjective nature of faith. There developed in this age of literary reproduction an elaborate structure to private prayer that was intended to enhance the individual's opportunities to venture directly into the presence of God. For this purpose, private devotion was arranged symbolically around the theme of the redemptive cycle of Christ's death and resurrection, and formulated as a spiritual pilgrimage through established stages that varied only slightly among denominations. One of the most popular prayer books in all of sixteenth-century Europe, written by the Spanish Dominican Luis de Granada, listed five parts to private devotion: preparation of the soul, reading, meditation, thanksgiving, and prayer, or "petition." These stages of pious devotion traced a continuous journey from sin to faith, rehearsing the cycle of pain and suffering, fear, repentance, and reconciliation that constituted the Christian drama of salvation.

Penitents generally began their devotions by examining their consciences for sin and reflecting upon the temptations that existed in their everyday lives. The psychological stages of conversion and progression in spiritual life were initiated with penitence and humility, or, in the stronger Puritan term, humiliation. This essentially subjective state was facilitated by corporal discipline such as fasting and, in more extreme cases, flagellation and the wearing of hair shirts. The position of the body during prayer was also of immense importance for the cultivation of humble sentiment. Among traditional Catholics, Peter the Chanter's *De penitentia* listed at least seven different prayer postures; four involved standing with hands arranged in various positions of strain, one involved kneeling, and two others involved lying prostrate on the ground. The inclination of the head, the glance of the eyes, and the movement of the lips were all carefully managed in private devotion in order to elicit proper emotional responses. Early Puritan meditative techniques were strikingly similar to these Catholic precedents of self-abasement. John Downame's recommendations in *A Guide to Godlynesse* listed various "Gestures of the Body" that the devout should adopt to "further the inward humility, reverence, and fervency of devotion." These included "standing, kneeling, uncovering the head, lifting up the eyes and hands, and in extraordinary and greater humiliation, prostrating ourselves upon the ground, casting down our eyes, as being ashamed to look towards heaven, and knocking of the breast, as bewailing the sinful corruption therein contained." It was also considered advantageous, in this first preparatory stage of devotion, to recite set verses such as the *Meditationes* of Augustine, the *Psalter* of David, or the new religious verse of such vernacular writers as Théodore de Bèze, Philippe Duplessis-Mornay, and Jean de Sponde. Such techniques again were designed not to give doctrinal instruction but to stimulate controlled individual reflection. Rhymed verse and poetic expression were employed to organize thoughts and stimulate meditation in an emotional as well as methodical way.

After this "humbling" of the soul there came a period of reading or lecturing designed to instruct the penitent in knowledge of self and God. In order to facilitate self-analysis, prayer manuals frequently offered detailed descriptions of "the seven deadly sins" or of behavior that might be offensive to God. Readers of Lewis Bayly's *The Practice of Piety* learned the nature and attributes of God, and they saw contrasted the miseries of the unregenerate life and the happiness that comes from regeneration. They were made aware of the many obstacles to genuine piety and were exhorted to lead godly lives in order to preserve the eternal welfare of their souls. Toward this end, they were given direction for proper conduct to ensure the attainment of heaven, and, in an emotional appeal to the traditional threats of hell and damnation, offered notable examples of God's judgment against sinners. The strategy of Luis de Granada's *Libro de la oración y meditación* was to provide readers with different scriptural passages for each of the seven days of the week, accompanied by lengthy discussions about the meaning of the texts.

Such explications were intended to stimulate the third, "introspective" stage of devotion, in which the laws of scripture were applied to readers' own lives. Meditation was considered to be the natural outcome of reading in that it fed off the substance of the written passages. The process of meditation in turn prepared the heart theologically for direct communion with Christ.

At the final devotional stages of "thanksgiving" and "prayer," penitents were expected to have gained confidence in the merciful nature of God and to release the affections in a grateful outpouring of love. It was here, in these culminating moments, that the devotional poetry of the period expressed its most poignant pleas for moral strength and forgiveness, its most submissive relinquishing to the will of providence, its most lavish praises of the power and majesty of the divine order, and its most delighted expectations of eternal life. The poetry of Christians at prayer serves to remind us that the desired goal of all the ritual formality of prayer was to enhance the believer's capacity for spontaneous expression of yearning and rejoicing in the presence of God. It was expected, moreover, that prayer of this kind would outlast the moment at hand and fortify the soul for a life of commitment to Christ. The enduring virtue of prayer, Luis de Granada suggested, "is the celestial ability and gift that inclines the will to desire with great spirit and longing all that pertains to the service of God."

Such an ideal purpose to prayer, whether or not it was consistently realized on a personal level, was what distinguished sixteenth-century spirituality from the spirituality of the Middle Ages. Following Martin Luther's call for a church in which all men and women became their own priests, devotional manuals of all languages were circulated in order to encourage individuals to experience in the privacy of their homes their own spiritual aspirations. Liturgy and literary form thus combined to vitalize personal devotion among the laity and enhance the subjective nature of faith.

[*See also* Devotional Practices; Liturgical Calendar; Popular Religion; and Time.]

BIBLIOGRAPHY

Abray, Lorna Jane. *The People's Reformation: Magistrates, Clergy, and Commons in Strasbourg, 1500–1598*. Ithaca, N.Y., 1985. Traces the nature of communal reforms from the early radical years.

Bataillon, Marcel. "De Savonarole à Louis de Grenade." *Revue de littérature comparé* 16 (1936), 23–39. Examines the devotional technique of the most popular Catholic preachers.

Cave, Terence C. *Devotional Poetry in France, c.1570–1613*. Cambridge, 1969. Examines the literary style as well as content of Catholic and Calvinist poets.

Chrisman, Miriam Usher. *Lay Culture, Learned Culture: Books and Social Change in Strasbourg, 1480–1599*. New Haven, 1982. Provides comprehensive literary and statistical analysis of devotional works read by the Lutheran public.

Christian, William A. *Apparitions in Late Medieval and Renaissance Spain*. Reprint, Princeton, 1989.

Cressy, David. *Bonfires and Bells*. London, 1989. Identifies the increasingly nationalistic character of the Tudor calendar.

Galpern, A. N. *The Religions of the People in Sixteenth-Century Champagne*. Cambridge, 1976. One of the first local studies to acknowledge the performative dimensions of religion.

Hambrick-Stowe, Charles E. *The Practice of Piety: Puritan Devotional Disciplines in Seventeenth-Century New England*. Chapel Hill, N.C., 1982. Ties Puritan devotion to earlier, especially Augustinian, piety.

Kaufman, Peter Iver. *Augustinian Piety and Catholic Reform.* Macon, Ga., 1982.

Martz, Louis L. *The Poetry of Meditation.* Rev. ed. New Haven, 1978. Testifies to a devotional revival in England by the popularity of religious poetry.

Moeller, Bernd. "Piety in Germany around 1500." In *The Reformation in Medieval Perspective,* edited by Steven E. Ozment, pp. 50–75. Chicago, 1971. Presents evidence for an "intensification of popular piety" on the eve of the Reformation.

Ozment, Steven E. *The Reformation in the Cities.* New Haven, 1975. Assesses arguments in secondary literature concerning the spiritual value and intensity of late medieval lay piety.

Pourrat, Pierre. *La spiritualité chrétienne.* Rev. ed. 4 vols. Paris, 1947–1951. Remains the most comprehensive guide to devotional trends.

Scribner, Robert W. "Ritual and Popular Religion in Catholic Germany at the Time of the Reformation." *Journal of Ecclesiastical History* 35 (1984), 47–77. Looks at the evangelical movement as a "ritual" process and struggle over control of liturgy.

Toussaert, Jacques. *Le sentiment religieux en Flandre à la fin du moyen âge.* Paris, 1963. Sees the cult of the saints as a symbolic network of human needs and social desires.

Trexler, Richard. *Public Life in Renaissance Florence.* Reprint, Ithaca, N.Y., 1991. Demonstrates the "sensual" and "performative" nature of Catholic piety.

White, Helen C. *The Tudor Books of Private Devotion.* Reprint, Westport, Conn., 1979. Her explication of Tudor readings acknowledges a shift in theme from the human implications of Christ's life on earth to the redemptive function.

MAUREEN FLYNN

PIGHIUS, Albertus (c.1490–1542), Dutch humanist and Catholic theologian. Born in Kampen in the province of Overijssel, he studied in Louvain, where he received a master of arts in 1509. From 1518 to 1522 he studied in Paris. In 1522 he followed his teacher, Pope Adrian VI, to Rome. Under Clement VII he became a papal privy councilor in 1525. In 1531 he returned to the Netherlands and worked in the following years for the retention of Catholic belief. He was an adviser of the nuncios, a participant in religious discussions, and the author of influential theological works. Against Luther's attacks on the papacy, he wrote a defense of the church hierarchy, stressed the significance of the papacy, and defended papal principles. In matters of belief, the pope was infallible: no pope in history, not even Honorius I, had been a heretic. In his theory of the council, Pighius also represented papal views. For the infallibility of the council, connection with the pope was necessary. Without the pope, councils had no validity. The decrees from the Council of Constance (1414–1418) on the superiority of the council had no binding force.

Pighius's *Apologia indicti concilii* was an answer to the rejection of the council by the Schmalkald League. He summarized the most important doctrinal differences between the old and new believers in his work *Controversiarum* and defended free will in *De libero hominis arbitrio.* (Calvin answered immediately with his *Defensio.*) Pighius presented suggestions for overcoming the division in belief in his *Ratio componendorum dissidiorum et sarcienda in religione concordia.* His last work, occasioned by the negotiations for church reunion at the Diet of Regensburg (1541), was against Martin Bucer, stressing that the Catholic church had not strayed from the truth of faith. The new church defended by Bucer did not have the apostolic succession, which for Pighius was the decisive mark of the true church. Pighius called the Reformation a revolution; to him it was understandable that Luther, one of the pseudoprophets Jesus had predicted, found so many adherents.

His views on justification, Original Sin, and papal infallibility had great influence. His doctrine of exculpability and Original Sin played a role in the discussions at the Council of Trent. His ideas on infallibility were affirmed by Roberto Bellarmino and numerous theologians and presented at the first Vatican Council (1870). Pighius belongs to the influential Catholic theologians of the 16th century. He died at Utrecht on 28/29 December 1542.

BIBLIOGRAPHY

Bäumer, Remigius. "Die Wiederentdeckung der Honoriusfrage im Abendland." *Römische Quartalschrift* 56 (1961), 200–214.

———. "Das Kirchenverständnis Albert Pigges." In *Volk Gottes,* edited by Remigius Bäumer and Heimo Dolch, pp. 306–322. Freiburg, 1967.

———. "Albert Pigge." In *Katholische Theologen der Reformationszeit I,* edited by Erwin Iserloh, pp. 98–106. Münster, 1984.

———. "Pighius (Pigge), Albertus." In *Marienlexikon,* edited by Remigius Bäumer and Leo Scheffczyk, vol. 5, p. 224. St. Ottilien, 1993.

———. "Pigge, Albertus." In *Theologische Realenzyklopädie,* vol. 24. Berlin and New York, 1994.

Feiner, J. *Die Erbsündenlehre Albertus Pigges.* Zurich, 1940.

Jedin, Hubert. *Studien über die Schriftstellertätigkeit Albert Pigges.* Münster, 1931.

Klaiber, W., ed. *Katholische Kontroverstheologen und Reformer des 16. Jahrhunderts.* Münster, 1978. See nos. 2510–2522.

Pfeifer, L. *Ursprung der katholischen Kirche und Zugehörigkeit zur Kirche nach Albert Pigge.* Würzburg, 1938.

Troxler, Walter. "Pighius, Albertus." In *Biographisch-Bibliographisches Kirchenlexikon,* edited by Friedrich Wilhelm Bautz, vol. 7, nos. 610–612. Hamm, Germany, 1994.

REMIGIUS BÄUMER
Translated from German by Walter D. Morris

PILGRIMAGE OF GRACE. Although used loosely to refer to a series of rebellions against Henry VIII in northern England in the autumn of 1536 and winter of 1536/37, the name Pilgrimage of Grace strictly refers only to the movement in Yorkshire between October and December 1536. The rebellion began with riots in the Lincolnshire market towns of Louth and Horncastle on 2 and 3 October, the capture of the neighboring gentry, and the razing of the countryside. By 7 October a force of several thousand had entered Lincoln, but by the end of the following week all had dispersed without conflict with the royal forces gathering to the south. By this time the rebellion had also spread northward into Yorkshire. The Yorkshire uprising may be seen as a more long-lived extension of the Lincolnshire movement, and it, in turn, spawned subsidiary uprisings in Lancashire, Westmorland, and Cumberland. York was entered by the pilgrims on 16 October, and Pontefract castle was surrendered to them by Lord Thomas Darcy on 21 October. A truce was negotiated with Thomas Howard, duke of Norfolk, at Doncaster on 27 October. As Norfolk was supported by an inferior number of troops of doubtful reliability, the pilgrims had a considerable military edge, but by accepting a truce and sending emissaries (Sir Ralph Ellerker and Robert Bowes) to the king, the pilgrims dissipated their advantage. On the return of Ellerker and Bowes, a congress was held at Pontefract to devise a program to be put to Norfolk at a second meeting at Doncaster, held on 6 December, after which the movement disbanded. There were further uprisings—in the East Riding of Yorkshire in January 1537 and in the Lake District in February—which were prompted respectively by fears that the Doncaster settlement would not be honored and by clumsy attempts to arrest the ring leaders of the earlier rebellion. In fact, none of the undertakings at Doncaster were honored, and by midsummer the more prominent "leaders" of the movement—Robert Aske, Thomas Darcy, and Sir Robert Constable—had been arrested, tried, and executed.

The Pilgrimage of Grace was certainly the greatest emergency that Henry VIII faced, but the motivation and character of the movement has been the subject of debate. That the rebellion was contained first within Lincolnshire and then within Yorkshire has encouraged some historians to regard the movement as essentially northern and therefore peripheral—the outburst of a particularly conservative and poor region. There was, however, little distinctively northern about the movement. It took place in the north of England, but the circumstances in which it began and the sympathy that it attracted suggest that it arose from general and not local factors.

There has also been a tendency to marginalize the movement by claiming that it arose out of a conspiracy led by a conservative court faction outmaneuvered in the factional politics of 1536. Conspiracy interpretations ignore the evidence of popular action; a close reading of the accounts of the first days of the uprising make it clear that the gentry were not in command. Such interpretations are also forced to explain key aspects of the movement by claiming that plans misfired or that central individuals lost their nerve. Finally, conspiracy theories lack firm proof (certainly none was discovered at the time). The evidence points to the movement having been a popular uprising that the gentry were compelled to lead and that they did so in the hope of taming the common people. This they successfully achieved in the Lincolnshire uprising; there are hints that a similar strategy was implemented in Yorkshire.

The primary cause of the outbreak of the Pilgrimage of Grace was rumors of the confiscation of church goods and the enforced closure of parish churches. There were no such plans, although the reports were plausible at a moment when the dissolution was in progress. There is some evidence that these reports were manufactured and circulated by the parochial clergy, who were irreconciled to both clerical taxation and reports that their ability was to be examined. Successive articles (drawn up by the gentry) tended to enlarge and muddy the pilgrims' aims to the point where the articles made at York on 3–4 December were a catchall of legal, economic, and ecclesiastical grievances. Although some of the pilgrims' articles express fiscal concerns, the primary aim of the pilgrims was (in their own words) "the maintenance of the faith of God, the right and liberty of his church militant and the destruction of heretics and their opinions and other public wealths in soul and body" (*Camden Miscellany* 31, London, 1992, p. 130).

[*See also* Aske, Robert.]

BIBLIOGRAPHY

Bush, M. L. " 'Up for the Commonweal': The Significance of Tax Grievances in the English Rebellions of 1536." *English Historical Review* 106 (1991), 299–318. Overstates claims.

Davies, C. S. L. "The Pilgrimage of Grace Reconsidered." *Past and Present* 41 (1968), 54–76.

———. "Popular Religion and the Pilgrimage of Grace." In *Order and Disorder in Early Modern England*, edited by Anthony Fletcher and John Stevenson, pp. 58–91. Cambridge, 1985.

Dodds, Madeleine Hope, and Ruth Dodds. *The Pilgrimage of Grace, 1536–1537, and the Exeter Conspiracy, 1538*. 2 vols. Cambridge, 1915. Detailed narrative not yet superseded; weak on analysis of motivation.

Elton, G. R. "Politics and the Pilgrimage of Grace." In *Studies in Tudor and Stuart Politics and Government*, edited by G. R. Elton, vol. 3, pp. 183–215. Cambridge, 1983. Influential, not fully persuasive.

Gunn, S. J. "Peers, Commons and Gentry in the Lincolnshire Revolt of 1536." *Past and Present* 123 (1989), 52–79. The necessary antidote to James.

Hoyle, R. W. *The Pilgrimage of Grace*. Oxford, 1995. The fullest modern account stressing the popular character of the rebellion known as the Pilgrimage of Grace.

James, Mervyn. "Obedience and Dissent in Henrician England: The Lincolnshire Rebellion, 1536." In *Society, Politics and Culture*, edited by Mervyn James, pp. 188–296. Cambridge, 1986. Denies the evidence of a rising of the commons.

R. W. Hoyle

PILGRIMAGES. One of the great religious institutions of pre-Reformation Europe, pilgrimage was closely tied to the medieval cults of the worship of saints and of relics. A pilgrimage officially was an act of penance or thanksgiving, or a journey to ensure spiritual salvation. Church authorities continually reminded pilgrims that the focus of their pilgrimage should always remain spiritual, uncorrupted by the material world through which they traveled. Ideally, pilgrims wore only the simplest clothes, rested at night within a monastery, and ate only the plain fare the monks provided. While on the journey the pilgrim's only aim and only thought should be of spiritual salvation; worldly affairs should not intrude upon his or her reflections. At its most spiritually idealistic, a literal pilgrimage mirrored a lifelong spiritual voyage toward grace and salvation.

Although the prime motivation for many pilgrims was spiritual, other motives also set pilgrims on their paths. For some, the desire to obtain relief from a distressing disease induced them to seek relief by begging the intercession of a saint. In extreme cases, when plague or another devastating disease ravaged a community, the whole community might embark on a pilgrimage. But many pilgrims were motivated by less worthy causes than consideration of their spiritual or physical well-being. A mixture of holiness or piety, boredom, restlessness, and curiosity sent hundreds of thousands of people across medieval Europe to the numerous holy sites available. Curiosity about the world beyond the home country, a desire to escape the routine of their lives, or, like Chaucer's worldly Canterbury pilgrims, the promise of good fellowship and an entertaining journey encouraged many men and women to begin a pilgrimage.

The major medieval pilgrimage sites were Jerusalem, Rome, and Saint James of Compostela in northwestern Spain; minor destinations included the hundreds, if not thousands, of local shrines scattered throughout Europe. Although most pilgrims longed to visit the Holy Land, cost and the sheer difficulty of the journey meant that most pilgrims contented themselves by journeying to Rome or Saint James. Those without the wealth or the time to visit one of the major sites made do with a journey to a local shrine. English pilgrims could visit the shrines at Canterbury, Glastonbury, Walsingham, and Saint Albans; French pilgrims flocked to the shrines at Chartres, Limoges, or Rocamadour; Italians visited the bones of Saint Mark at Venice or Saint Zita at Lucca; many Germans made a pilgrimage to a famous shrine in the small town of Wilsnak near Wittenberg. Pilgrimage was a big business, comparable to today's tourist industry, and churches, monasteries, and religious institutions of all types hoped to obtain the relic of some saint that would attract pilgrims. The competition for the possession of relics was so intense that the opportunity for forgeries was limitless; numerous clergy succumbed to temptation and begged, stole, or forged relics in order to attract pilgrims and their money.

Although sixteenth-century reformers attacked the practice of pilgrimage together with the cults of the saints and relics as one of the major abuses of the church, pilgrimage and pilgrims had attracted virulent criticism long before the Protestant Reformation. Some medieval critics believed that the journey itself, not the devotional goal, had become the primary object, and people embarked on a pilgrimage only in order to indulge their idle curiosity in this world, rather than embarking on a spiritual quest toward their salvation in the next world. More often, however, medieval churchmen and reformers alike accused pilgrims of immoral conduct. In the eighth century Saint Boniface urged the English church to prevent women from going on pilgrimages because so many of them became prostitutes along the way. After the eleventh century critics increasingly attacked pilgrimage as a practice that men and women corrupted with material or worldly desires; many believed the final result of pilgrimage was only laziness, vanity, idle living, and the moral corruption of its participants. Some of the most vehement critics of pilgrimage in the late fourteenth and early fifteenth century were the English Lollards, who particularly criticized the practice of pilgrimage for the moral corruption of its participants, although they also objected to pilgrims' veneration of images and argued that pilgrimage was spiritually redundant anyway because pilgrims began their journey cleansed by confession. Other European reformers, like the fifteenth-century Hussites, also attacked pilgrimage as an immoral and spiritually redundant practice.

The long tradition of medieval concern about and criticism of pilgrimage culminated in the sixteenth-century reformers' condemnation of the practice. The true Christian pilgrimage, argued Martin Luther, was not toward Rome or Compostela, but to the prophets, the *Psalms*, and the Gospels. Salvation lay in the Bible and in faith, not in the superstitious idolatry of the saints and relics or participation in any outward journey. One's neighbors might be more worthy of veneration than distant saints. Where in the scriptures did God indicate that he wanted his people to embark on pilgrimages? The reformers insisted that men and women could no longer seek divine help through intermediaries such as the saints. The individual had to rely on personal devotion and a personal relationship with God for salvation. Citing the patently fraudulent collections of relics about Europe as proof, other reformers argued that pilgrimage was a myth fabricated by corrupt clergy desperate to wrest as much wealth from the laity as possible.

Although the practice of pilgrimage was still strong in many European countries during the fifteenth century, the onset of the Reformation in the sixteenth century eventually spelled the end for pilgrimage in Protestant countries. This did not happen overnight, however, and while large-scale pilgrimages generally ceased within a few decades, it took church and civil authorities longer to stop the common people from wandering to local shrines. As a manifestation of popular religion (or superstition), it is probable that short pilgrimages to local holy sites within various Protestant countries continued for many generations. Many holy wells, originally sites of pagan worship that had acquired associations with saints during the medieval period, retained their popularity after the Reformation, except that now Protestants traveled to them to partake of the medicinal qualities of the waters. Shrines became spas; pilgrimages to the well of Saint Winifred at Holywell (among many other spas and wells) continued well into the seventeenth century.

Pilgrimage remained popular (and legitimate) in Catholic countries, as it does to the present day. Although the sixteenth-century Catholic church encouraged private worship and reaffirmed devotion to the saints, pilgrims and pilgrimages tended to be more regulated, especially after the Catholic Reformation of the late sixteenth and early seventeenth century. The Catholic church attempted to eliminate the worst abuses of pilgrimage; it carefully investigated any miraculous cures of saints and tried its best to discourage the revelry and immorality so often associated with medieval bands of pilgrims. Despite the efforts of the Catholic church, these reforms were only partly successful. For many Catholics, the meaning and purpose of pilgrimage remained very similar to their medieval precursors (although the medieval emphasis on undertaking a pilgrimage for the purpose of penance was gone). Pilgrims still sought the intervention of saints for spiritual consolation, health problems, or other personal reasons. Many continued to leave offerings at shrines, sometimes wax models of whatever part of the body had been cured. Groups of pilgrims not under the direction or supervision of clerics still enjoyed dancing, drinking, and other nocturnal activities during their nightly stopovers. Although most pilgrims traveled singly or in small groups, mass pilgrimages still occurred occasionally. These tended to be localized; a parish priest might mark a local festival by taking his parishioners on a short pilgrimage to a nearby shrine.

Many of the same destinations remained popular with Catholic pilgrims. The Holy Land itself remained one of the most desired destinations, even though increasingly only the most wealthy could afford the difficult journey to Jerusalem. The other popular medieval destination for pilgrims, Rome, continued to attract vast numbers after the Reformation, especially during jubilee years. In France many of the pre-Reformation holy sites retained their fascination for Catholic pilgrims, although during the sixteenth century French Protestants, the Huguenots, sometimes attacked and tried to destroy some pilgrimage sites. Chartres remained a popular destination for pilgrims from the seventh century through the era of the Reformation, and pilgrims also made their way to Mont-Saint-Michel, Saint-Martin of Tours, Sainte-Baume, and Rocamadour. Some new sites became popular—the church rapidly authorized the Shrine of Our Lady at Plancoët as a pilgrimage center in 1644, after locals claimed to have seen a vision of the Virgin Mary there. Even those Catholics trapped in Protestant countries still managed clandestine pilgrimages. In the late sixteenth century, local bishops in northern England (a stronghold of Catholicism in the Protestant nation) reported that many people still undertook pilgrimages to local holy sites as quietly and as unobtrusively as they could.

The Reformation clearly marked the end of the great age of pilgrimage; even in Catholic countries the number of pilgrims on the road after the Reformation was noticeably smaller. During the medieval period the majority of pilgrims had come from the northern European nations. After the Reformation their Reformed faith gave these people no justification to undertake the wonderful adventure of pilgrimage. Within Protestant countries the growing popularity of educational travel filled the void for educated men to some degree, but for women and many of the common people, one of the most popular avenues open to them to see the world was permanently closed.

[*See also* Devotional Practices; Popular Religion; *and* Saints, *article on* Cult of Saints.]

BIBLIOGRAPHY

Dickens, A. G. *The English Reformation.* 2d ed. London, 1989. Contains a section that discusses medieval religion and the impact of the Reformation; the material on pilgrimage is only minor, but useful.

Jusserand, J. J. *English Wayfaring Life in the Middle Ages.* 4th ed. London, 1950. Contains a chapter on English pilgrims and their practices and also discusses many of the criticisms of pilgrimage.

Lebrun, François. "The Two Reformations: Communal Devotion and Personal Piety." In *Passions of the Renaissance,* edited by Roger Chartier, pp. 89–93. A History of Private Life, vol. 3. Cambridge, Mass., 1989. Includes a synopsis of pilgrimage in France after the Reformation.

Sumption, Jonathan. *Pilgrimage: An Image of Medieval Religion.* London, 1975. The standard and most comprehensive work for medieval pilgrimage; includes a good bibliography for further reading.

Thomas, Keith. *Religion and the Decline of Magic.* Reprint, Harmondsworth, 1984. Covers the magic of the medieval church and the impact of the Reformation on medieval "magical" and "superstitious" practices, not only for pilgrimages, but also for the cult of relics, saints, and holy places.

Zacher, Christian K. *Curiosity and Pilgrimage.* Baltimore, 1976. Examines the close relationship in fourteenth-century thought between the vice of *curiositas* and the practice of pilgrimage.

SARA WARNEKE

PIO, Alberto (1475–1531), humanist prince of Carpi, diplomat, and writer. Born the eldest son of Lionello I, coruler of Carpi, and of Caterina Pico Pio, the sister of Giovanni Pico della Mirandola, noted humanist and philosopher, Alberto soon entered into a lifelong struggle to secure his rights over Carpi after his father's death in 1477. On the advice of his maternal uncle he was tutored by Aldo Manuzio in letters. His subsequent tutors included the Greek humanist Marcus Musurus and the philosophers Pietro Pomponazzi, Graziano da Brescia, and Juan Montesdoch. He became learned in classical letters, scripture, the church fathers, and scholastic philosophy and theology.

With support from his uncle Galeotto I Pico della Mirandola and from his stepfather Rodolfo Gonzaga di Mantua, Alberto secured title to half of Carpi in 1490 from Emperor

Maximilian I, who in 1509 and again in 1512 nullified the 1499 sale of the other half by Alberto's cousin to the d'Este of Ferrara and granted him full dominion over Carpi, which Alberto transformed into a small cultural center. Leaving the administration of Carpi to his brothers Leonello and Teodoro, Alberto took up a diplomatic career.

Pio became one of the most important diplomats of his generation, serving various rulers: Gian Francesco II Gonzaga di Mantua (1505–1507), Louis XII of France (1507–1511), Emperor Maximilian I (1511–1519), Francis I of France as his unofficial agent (1519–1521), Pope Adrian VI as governor of Reggio (1522), Francis I (1523–1527), and Pope Clement VII (1527–1531). This alternating service of rival rulers resulted in Charles V's decision to despoil him of Carpi (1523) and confer it formally on Alfonso I d'Este (1530). For fifteen years (1512–1527) the papal court was the base of Pio's operations, and he enjoyed there the personal friendship and confidence of Julius II, Leo X, and Clement VII. In 1518 he married Cecilia Orsini, the daughter of Leo X's first cousin, by whom he had two daughters and a son, Giulio, who soon died. A friend and patron of humanists and artists, Pio was an important figure in the Roman academy. On religious matters he espoused pious, learned, and conservative views.

Pio was opposed to heresy. In 1518 he ordered his officials in Carpi to turn over to the local inquisitor or to other deputies of the pope for punishment anyone holding errors about the Catholic faith. In 1522 he denounced Alfonso d'Este to Emperor Charles V for allowing an Augustinian friar to preach Lutheranism openly in Ferrara. Pio encouraged Juan Ginés de Sepúlveda to write his *De fato et libero arbitrio* (1526) against Luther, reading a draft of it and suggesting revisions to make it more effective. He himself found time, despite his numerous duties as ambassador, to write a refutation of Luther's teachings in such polished Ciceronian style as to be praised by Desiderius Erasmus. In this work, *Responsio accurata et paraenetica*, Pio accused Erasmus of having been the occasion for Luther's revolt by his destructive criticism of the church and by supporting Luther with words of praise, silence, or even an inept *Diatribe*. In large sections of this *Responsio*, Pio attacked Luther directly as an arrogant false prophet who contradicted what holy and learned men had taught for the past thirteen hundred years yet lacked any signs or miracles to confirm the truth of his own teachings. His twisting of scripture had produced a host of heresies, while his preaching of "Christian liberty" had led to the recent peasant revolts. By appeals to scripture, tradition, and logic, Pio defended the church's teachings on numerous topics. He ended with an appeal to Erasmus to write forcefully against Luther. This *Responsio*, written in Rome in 1526, was not published until 1529 in Paris, where Pio took up residence following the Sack of Rome.

When Erasmus denied in his *Responsio ad epistolam paraeneticam Alberti Pii*... (1529) that he had helped cause the Reformation or held views similar to Luther's, Pio spent the last two years of his life collecting quotations from Erasmus's writings demonstrating this similarity and providing refutations of Erasmus's and the Protestants' views on over twenty topics. Following his death in Paris on 8 January 1531 (for the previous fifteen or so years he suffered from debilitating bouts of gout), his friends published the partially revised manuscript Pio left behind as *Tres et viginti libri in locos lucubrationum variarum D. Erasmi Roterodami, quos censet ab eo recognoscendos et retractandos* (1531). Erasmus quickly penned a lengthy and bitter refutation, *Apologia adversus rhapsodias calumniosarum querimoniarum Alberti Pii*... (1531), and even a rejoinder to the table of contents of the *Tres et viginti libri* entitled *In elenchum Alberti Pii brevissima scholia* (1532). He also vented his venom by satirizing Pio's burial in the habit of a Franciscan in the colloquy *Exequiae Seraphicae* (1531). Pio's two works went through subsequent editions, both were translated into Spanish and the *Responsio* into French for presentation to Francis I, and his writings were recommended by Duke Albert of Bavaria in 1569 for inclusion in the monastic libraries of his territories.

BIBLIOGRAPHY

Avesani, Rino, et al., eds. *Società, politica e cultura a Carpi ai tempi di Alberto III Pio: Atti del convegno internazionale, Carpi, 19–21 maggio 1978*. 2 vols. Medioevo e Umanesimo, 46–47. Padua, 1981. A collection of twenty-two scholarly papers in various languages on Pio's position in the culture of his time and on the society and economy of Carpi.

Bernuzzi, Marco, and Thomas B. Deutscher. "Alberto Pio Prince of Carpi, 23 July 1475–7 January 1531." In *Contemporaries of Erasmus: A Biographical Register of the Renaissance and Reformation*, edited by Peter G. Bietenholz, vol. 3, pp. 86–88. Toronto, 1987. A brief overview of Pio's life that concentrates on his relations with Erasmus.

Gilmore, Myron P. "Erasmus and Alberto Pio, Prince of Carpi." In *Action and Conviction in Early Modern Europe: Essays in Memory of E. H. Harbison*, edited by Theodore K. Rabb and Jerold E. Seigel, pp. 299–318. Princeton, 1969. An overview of the debate between Erasmus and Pio.

———. "De modis disputandi: The Apologetic Works of Erasmus." In *Florilegium Historiale: Essays Presented to Wallace K. Ferguson*, edited by John Gordon Rowe and W. H. Stockdale, pp. 62–88. Toronto, 1971. A survey of Erasmus's style of disputing with his critics, especially Alberto Pio.

Guaitoli, Paolo. "Memorie sulla vita d'Alberto III Pio." In *Memorie storiche e documenti sulla città e sull' antico principato di Carpi*, vol. 1, pp. 133–313. Carpi, 1877. A chronological narrative of the major events in the life of Alberto Pio with particular reference to his relations with Carpi during the years 1495–1500 and 1507–1531.

Heesakkers, Chris L. "Argumentatio a persona in Erasmus' Second Apology against Alberto Pio." In *Erasmus of Rotterdam: The Man and the Scholar; Proceedings of the Symposium Held at the Erasmus University, Rotterdam, 9–11 November 1986*, edited by Jan Sperna Weiland and Willem Th. M. Frijhoff, pp. 79–87. Leiden, 1988. A study of the strategies used by Erasmus to undermine Pio's authority.

Minnich, Nelson H. "The Debate between Desiderius Erasmus of Rotterdam and Alberto Pio of Carpi on the Use of Sacred Images."

Annuarium Historiae Conciliorum 20 (1988), 379–413. A detailed examination of the validity of Erasmus's charges against Alberto Pio and of their differing views on the cult of images.

Rummel, Erika. *Erasmus and His Catholic Critics*. Vol. 2, *1523–1536*. Nieuwkoop, 1989. Pages 115–123 provide an overview of the controversy with particular attention to the styles of debating employed on each side.

Vasoli, Cesare. *Alberto III Pio da Carpi*. Carpi, 1978. An excellent study of Pio's life and thought.

NELSON H. MINNICH

PIO, Rodolfo (also Pio da Carpi; 1500–1564), Italian cardinal, bishop, and papal diplomat. Son of Lionello II da Carpi and Maria Martinengo, Pio studied under the humanist Aldo Manuzio, (1450–1515) and received degrees in philosophy and theology at Padua. He enjoyed a curial and diplomatic career that included administration of the dioceses of Faenza and Ostia, plus four legations to France. He became a cardinal in 1536, and a failed attempt to elect him pope in 1559 revealed both his proimperial politics and the French opposition to his candidacy. He served as legate in Ancona under Paul III (1534–1549) and reworked the fourteenth-century Aegidian constitution for the administration of the Papal States. A promoter of reform, he became a member of the Roman Inquisition in 1547 and encouraged the Jesuit apostolate to repentant prostitutes through patronage of their Compagnia della Grazia.

Pio embodied contradictions typical of the age. Despite diplomatic experience, his overly optimistic reports on the position of Francis I (1515–1547) contributed to the failure of negotiations for peace between him and Charles V (1519–1556) in 1537. A bishop committed to local reform, he published a new constitution for his diocese in 1533 but always administered through a vicar. He opposed Paul III's nepotism in Parma and Piacenza but ceded his own episcopal administration first to a brother (Teodor) and then to an assistant (Giambattista Sighicelli). His concept of reform apparently did not conflict with use and enjoyment of considerable wealth, as he maintained a large collection of books, manuscripts, statues, and bronzes in a sculpture garden he constructed on the Quirinal hill of Rome and in a palace in Campo Marzio. Influenced by the ideas and policies of Gian Pietro Carafa (Pope Paul IV, r. 1555–1559), he both doubted the orthodoxy of Cardinal Reginald Pole (1500–1559) and was an outspoken opponent of the censure of Carlo Carafa by Pius IV (r. 1559–1565).

BIBLIOGRAPHY

Baroni, Pier Giovanni. *La nunziature in Francia di Rodolfo Pio, 1535–1537*. Bologna, 1962. An edition of the documents from his second assignment as nuncio to France, this includes some biographical material, especially pp. xxiii-xxxvii.

Dorez, Léon. "Latino Latini et la Bibliothèque capitulaire de Viterbe." *Revue des bibliothèques* 2 (1892), 377–391; 5 (1895), 237–260. A study of the librarian to whom Pio left his considerable collection of manuscripts and books. Includes a list of the materials.

Eiche, Sabine. "Cardinal Giulio della Rovere and the Vigna Carpi." *Journal of the Society of Architectural Historians* 45 (1986), 115–133. A study of the history and layout of Pio's sculpture garden on the Quirinale, with reference to its social and political context.

Hoffmann, Christiane. *Kardinal Rodolfo Pio da Carpi und seine Reform der Aegidianischen Konstitutionen*. Berlin, 1989. This analysis of Pio's revision of a fourteenth-century administrative instrument for the Papal States includes thirty pages of biographical information.

Lanzoni, Francesco. *La controriforma nella città e diocesi di Faenza*. Faenza, 1925. Includes chapters on Pio and the reform constitutions he published for the diocese in 1533.

Mercati, Giovanni. *Codici latini Pico Grimani Pio e di altra biblioteca ignota del secolo XVI esistenti nell'Ottoboniana e i codici greci Pio di Modena*. Vatican City, 1938. Includes a chapter on the Latin books and manuscripts of Rodolfo and an inventory of his Greek manuscripts.

Pastor, Ludwig. *The History of the Popes from the Close of the Middle Ages*. 40 vols. 3d ed. Saint Louis, 1938–1953. Although the information on Pio is scattered throughout volumes 10 to 17, they provide virtually all the context one could hope for.

WILLIAM V. HUDON

PIRCKHEIMER, Willibald and Caritas (1470–1530 and 1466–1532, respectively), heirs to a Nuremberg patrician fortune, both remarkable for their learning, religious concern, and traits of character. Born on 5 December 1470, in Eichstätt, Willibald Pirckheimer was the son of a legal counselor to the learned bishop. His father later served the duke of Bavaria and the duke of Tirol and took young Willibald on his diplomatic missions to Italy, Switzerland, and the Netherlands. At eighteen Pirckheimer went to study in Italy and remained there for seven years, studying the law and the humanities—notably Greek philosophy (Platonism as opposed to Aristotelianism or Averroism)—at Padua before moving on to the university in Pavia. In 1495, however, he was summoned to Nuremberg to begin his adult life with his election to the city council, which he served until 1522. In 1499 he led the troops of the emperor and the Swabian League against the Swiss without distinction and with no decisive results, for the Swiss were determined to maintain their independence from imperial control. Despite the failure of the military enterprise, Emperor Charles V made Pirckheimer an imperial councillor.

Pirckheimer was a veritable polymath in the range of his intellectual interests—the occult, palmistry, astrology, and Greek and Latin classics. "Why should a man live," he asked, "if he cannot study?" Religiously, he heard in history the same "voice of God" that reverberated throughout the scriptures. He did scores of translations, prefaces, and classical editions not only of the wholesome Plutarch but also of the satirical Lucian, as well as of the Greek patristic writings. He was most likely the author of the *Eckius dedolatus*, "shaving the corner off" of Johann Eck, Martin Luther's

Dominican opponent. He also composed various reformist religious dramas. He was much taken with Plato and the Neoplatonists, but the context of his thought was always medieval Christian, and though he hosted Luther in his grand patrician house on the square in Nuremberg and encouraged his reform effort, he eventually returned to his Catholic and patrician roots.

For all his sense of duty and willingness to serve the state—a kind of civic humanism—Pirckheimer belonged to a patrician family renowned for its piety and devotion to the received religion. Georg, his uncle, was prior of a Carthusian monastery, and seven of Pirckheimer's sisters were nuns, four of whom became abbesses and one a prioress. Three of his five daughters took the veil with his blessing. The most renowned of his sisters was the saintly and learned Caritas. In Nuremberg the patrician council and the city secretary, Lazarus Spengler, introduced a whole catalog of reform measures, ending the Mass, introducing Communion in both kinds, and eliminating vigils and masses for the dead. The pastor Andreas Osiander and the clergy of Saint Lorenz and Saint Sebaldus churches adopted an order of service in the evangelical form. Caritas and the sisters were treated roughly by the Nuremberg mobs. Luther, however, was supportive—as he was with the Brethren of the Common Life, to whom he owed much—and declared that sisters and brothers should be allowed to live out their lives according to their vocations in peace and quiet. He admired the erudition of Caritas, just as Desiderius Erasmus had praised the daughters of Thomas More and the sisters of Pirckheimer.

Pirckheimer's relation to the Reformation was fraught with tension and unresolved questions. In the bull of excommunication against Luther, *Decet Romanum Pontificum* (2 January 1521), Pirckheimer and Spengler were named along with Ulrich von Hutten, which was perhaps a contrivance of Eck, the papal informant in Germany. Spengler became the tie between Wittenberg and Nuremberg, one of the first cities to decide for the evangelical Reformation. Pirckheimer's situation was more difficult than that of Spengler. In October 1518 Luther, on returning from his confrontation with Cardinal Cajetan in Augsburg, rested in Pirckheimer's splendid patrician house (destroyed by bombers in 1945). In his library Pirckheimer had 150 separate writings of Luther. He early assumed the role of conciliator between Luther and his papal opponents, as well as between Luther and various humanists, such as the vacillating Erasmus. Pirckheimer wrote many letters and largely unpublished tracts. Especially notable is his open letter to Pope Adrian VI on the causes of the Reformation movement in Germany and, following Lorenzo Campeggio and papal political maneuverings at the Diet of Nuremberg in 1524, his tract *De persequutoribus evangelicae veritatis, eorum consiliis et machinationibus* (On the Persecutors of Evangelical Truth, Their Counsels and Machinations; 1610).

After his resignation from the city council in 1522, Pirckheimer increasingly sought leisure for his classical studies, but he was thrown headlong into three major controversies—the defense of the convents, the sacramentarian controversy, and the debate over the second marriage of the clergy. As for Catholics and Lutherans, his final disposition, as befits a cranky and ill old man, was to wish a plague on both their houses, though, as he neared the grave, he inclined noticeably toward the comforts of the old church.

During his final years Pirckheimer was preoccupied with translating both pagan and Christian classics, such as the sermons of Gregory Naziansen, *Dr. Gregorii Nazianzeni orationes xxx* (Basel, 1530) which Erasmus edited. In the preface—which, as Pirckheimer had requested, was addressed to Duke George of Saxony, Luther's foe—Erasmus praised Pirckheimer, "whose last words breathed nothing but love of the fatherland and the most fervent love of the Christian religion." His bronze epitaph in Saint John's cemetery reads *Virtus interire nescit* ("Virtue Cannot Perish").

BIBLIOGRAPHY

Goodman, Anthony, and Angus MacKay. "Humanism in Germany." In *The Impact of Humanism on Western Europe*, pp. 202–219. London and New York, 1989. Provides an overview of humanism and the Reformation; see also Rabil.

Hagen, Rudolf. *Willibald Pirckheimer in seinem Verhälltnis zum Humanismus und zur Reformation.* Nuremberg, 1882. Maintains mistakenly that Pirckheimer remained loyal to the Reformation, but that he disliked confessionalism, an inadequate analysis of a superior and religiously complex personality.

Rabil, Albert, Jr. *Renaissance Humanisms: Foundations, Forms, and Legacy*. Vol. 3, *Humanism and the Disciplines*. Philadelphia, 1988. See pp. 381–411.

Reicke, Emil. *Willibald Pirckheimer: Leben, Familien und Persönlichkeit.* Jena, 1930. Brief popular biography.

Reicke, Emil, ed. *Willibald Pirckheimers Briefwechsel.* Munich, 1956.

Spitz, Lewis W. *The Religious Renaissance of the German Humanists.* Cambridge, Mass., 1963. See pp. 155–197 and 325–333.

LEWIS W. SPITZ

PIUS IV (Ital., Giovan Angelo de' Medici; 1499–1565), pope (1559–1565). The son of a Milanese notary of petty nobility and slender means, Angelo de' Medici studied at Pavia and obtained the doctorate in canon and civil law at the University of Bologna. Then he served the papacy in several governmental posts, rising to the episcopate and the cardinalate under his patron, Paul III. He was more noted for his administrative ability and political acumen than his religious spirit or advocacy of reform. In the lengthy conclave (sixteen weeks) following the death of Paul IV, he was the candidate of Duke Cosimo I of Florence (de' Medici), to whom he was not related. As pope, by sentencing to death two nephews of his predecessor (Cardinal Carlo Carafa and his lay brother, Giovanni, duke of Paliano), in contrast to his characteristic moderation, he dealt a lethal blow to the kind of nepotism responsible for founding principalities for papal families; nonetheless, he made some of his own nephews cardinals and others high officials in the Papal States. The most important was Carlo Borromeo, whom he set over the secretariat of state, but he reserved important policy decisions to himself. As his other new cardinals he chose some men for their scholarship and ecclesiastical prominence and some to please secular princes.

To forestall the convening of a national council in France, which might have separated that country from the Holy See and led to the triumph of Calvinism, Pius, after long negotiations with King Philip II, Emperor Ferdinand I, and the French court, convoked a general council; in spite of the opposition of France and the emperor, who demanded a new assembly, he decided to continue the Council of Trent, which had been suspended in 1552. He appointed legates to preside over the council, determined its agenda, followed its activities through the legates' reports, and gave them instructions through Borromeo. Meanwhile, anticipating any attempts of bishops and ambassadors at Trent to eliminate abuses in the church even at the highest level, he decreed reforms in several departments of the Curia Romana. To resolve a crisis in the council, he appointed a new president, Cardinal Giovanni Morone, who succeeded in bringing it to a close 4 December 1563. Disregarding the advice of curialists who wished him to proceed selectively and slowly, he promptly confirmed all the conciliar decrees (on doctrine and reform) and had them published, and he instituted a commission of cardinals (the Congregation of the Council) for the authentic interpretation and application of the reform decrees. By striving to enforce them and have them accepted and observed in Catholic lands, he made the papacy the leader of the reform movement in the Catholic church and gave a new impetus to the Counter-Reformation.

Pius also continued the work of the council in several ways. He issued a bull promulgating the Index of Prohibited Books initiated at Trent. Since the council had referred to him the Emperor's petition for the lay chalice (Communion under both kinds), he approved its use for some parts of the empire. He prescribed a Profession of Tridentine Faith (a brief summary of the dogmatic decrees) to be made by bishops, religious superiors, professors in universities, and those taking doctoral degrees.

Guided by Philip II, Pius showed limitless patience and forbearance toward Queen Elizabeth I, to whom he tried in vain twice to send an envoy. He looked to Mary Stuart to save Catholicism in her domain but could not help her materially.

In Rome Pius patronized architects and artists, especially Michelangelo, and undertook some grand projects for buildings, fortifications, and city planning. He had the best-preserved part of the Baths of Diocletian transformed into a magnificent church, Santa Maria degli Angeli, and there he has his tomb.

BIBLIOGRAPHY

Jedin, Hubert. *Geschichte des Konzils von Trient.* Vol. 4, *Dritte Tagungsperiode und Abschluss.* 2 vols. Freiburg, 1975. Clearly depicts Pius IV's role in the last period of the council.

Pastor, Ludwig. *The History of the Popes.* Vols. 15 and 16. Edited by Ralph Francis Kerr. London, 1928. A translation of the *Geschichte der Päpste im Zeitalter der katholischen Reformation und Restauration.* Vol. 7. Freiburg, 1920. Based on extensive archival research, this is the most thorough and detailed study of the pontificate, marked by attention to political and cultural affairs and a high papal ecclesiology.

Trisco, Robert. "Reforming the Roman Curia: Emperor Ferdinand I and the Council of Trent." In *Reform and Authority in the Medieval and Reformation Church,* edited by Guy F. Lytle, pp. 143–337. Washington, D.C., 1981. Pius IV is a principal figure in this struggle between emperor and council.

ROBERT TRISCO

PIUS V (Ital., Antonio Ghislieri; 1504–1572), pope from 1566 to 1572 and Roman Catholic saint. Famed for his austerity and repression of heresy that characterized the Catholic church under his administration, Pius V lived the life of a shepherd boy until he became a Dominican friar at age 14, choosing the name "Michele." He acquired prominence through the exercise of Inquistorial offices in the northern Italian towns of Pavia, Como, and Bergamo. Gian Pietro Carafa (1476–1559; Pope Paul IV, 1555–1559) impressed with his zeal and determination, found in him a kindred spirit. Carafa brought him to Rome (1551) and eventually appointed him cardinal (1557) and grand inquistor-for-life (1558). Ghislieri gained the papal office on the basis of support from Carlo Borromeo (1538–1584), whose uncle, Pius IV (r. 1559–1565), was his immediate predecessor. He thus chose the same papal name, although he was known to have disdained what he considered the "worldly" attitude of Pius IV. He maintained three major interests as pope: pursuit of disciplinary reform of the clergy, implementation of the decrees of the Council of Trent, and organization of a new crusade. In the first of these he mimicked the policy of Paul IV but undertook the work comprehensively, beginning with his own household, and without the lack of consistency and logic characteristic of his patron. To effect the reorganization decreed by Trent, he appointed rigorous diocesan visitors. War against the infidel was the one form of combat he supported, and he facilitated the stunning victory at Lepanto (Návpaktos).

Pius resembled Paul IV in his political ineptitude, which resulted in continual difficulties with European heads of state, but even exceeded his patron's reputation for hatred and intolerance of Jews. His status as a saint is a result of his reputation for a spiritual focus, for consistent efforts to raise the moral standing of the papacy, and for effective promotion of clerical renewal and missionary activity in various areas of the world.

BIBLIOGRAPHY

Brognoli, Vincenzo de. *Studi storici sul regno di S. Pio V.* 2 vols. Rome, 1883. Standard, still useful group of studies.

Catena, Girolamo. *Vita del gloriosissimo papa Pio quinto.* Rome, 1587.

Hallman, Barbara McClung. *Italian Cardinals, Reform and the Church as Property, 1492–1563.* Berkeley, 1985.

Hilliger, Benno. *Die Wahl Pius V zum Papste.* Leipzig, 1891. Standard history of the conclave that elected Pius.

Pastor, Ludwig. *The History of the Popes From the Close of the Middle Ages.* 40 vols., 3d ed. Saint Louis, 1938–1953. Volumes 17 and 18 still constitute the best extended study of Pius V, and the only one in English. The work was originally published as *Geschichte der Päpste seit dem Ausgang des Mittelalters,* 21 vols., Freiburg, 1866–1938.

Prodi, Paolo. *The Papal Prince. One Body and Two Souls: The Papal Monarchy in Early Modern Europe.* Translated by Susan Haskins. Cambridge, 1987.

Simoncelli, Paolo. "Inquisizione romana e riforma in Italia." *Rivista storica italiana* 100 (1988), 1–125. A controversial article that calls into question the very existence of "Catholic reform" through analysis of inquisitorial records.

Stow, Kenneth R. *Taxation, Community and State: The Jews and the Fiscal Foundations of the Early Modern Papal State.* Stuttgart, 1983. Examines the shift in papal policy towars the Jews by Pope Paul IV and his followers.

William V. Hudon

PLACARDS, AFFAIRE DES. In the early hours of 17 October 1534, a number of Protestants posted broadsheets or placards denouncing the Catholic doctrine of the Mass in Paris, Orléans, and several other cities. The placards carried the headline: "THE TRUE ARTICLES AGAINST THE HORRIBLE, GROSS, AND INSUPPORTABLE DOCTRINE OF THE POPISH MASS." The text had been written by Antoine Marcourt, a French refugee who had become pastor at Neuchâtel, Switzerland, where the placards had been printed and then smuggled into France.

The impact of this dramatic affront to Catholic doctrine and sensibilities was greatly increased by the posting of a placard on Francis I's chamber door at Amboise. The Parisian authorities quickly began a search for the perpetrators, and whereas in the past the king had stayed the hand of persecution, this time he encouraged it. By the end of November, six persons had been burnt for heresy, and dozens more had been clapped into prison. In January 1535 the "Sacramentarians," as those who denied the doctrine of Transubstantiation were called, struck again, spreading another of Marcourt's tracts around Paris. Francis responded with an edict against the publication of any new books and led a great prayer procession through Paris, which culminated in six more public burnings. The heresy trials continued to May, when the king's wrath cooled.

During the flare-up of persecution in France, a number of French Protestants fled the realm, among them John Calvin and Clément Marot. After a year of traveling, Calvin found himself in Geneva facing his destiny. The Affaire des Placards also forced Francis I to face the fact that not all those who called for church reform were the moderate humanists whom he had favored; some clearly had gone well beyond the bounds that he could tolerate and had descended into sedition. Persecution became the official policy of the French monarchy.

[*See also* Calvin, John, *and* Francis I of France.]

BIBLIOGRAPHY

Berthoud, G. *Antoine Marcourt.* Geneva, 1973. Fine biography providing evidence for Marcourt's authorship of the placards.

Kelly, Donald, R. *The Beginning of Ideology. Consciousness and Society in the French Reformation.* Cambridge, 1981. Places the Affaire des Placards in the development of a distinctive French Protestant world view.

Knecht, R. J. *Francis I.* Cambridge, 1981. Argues that the king's response to the affair was less severe than usually is maintained.

Frederic J. Baumgartner

PLAGUE. *See* Medicine and Healing.

PLANCIUS, Petrus (1552–1622), Dutch geographer, map maker, and Calvinist minister; vigorous opponent of Jacobus Arminius and the Remonstrants. After being educated in England and Germany, Plancius began his career in 1576 as a Calvinist preacher among the clandestine Reformed congregations (the "churches under the cross") in the southern provinces of the Low Countries. In 1585, after the conquest of Brussels by Alessandro Farnese, duke of Parma, and his Spanish troops, Plancius fled north to Amsterdam, where he served as a minister in the Reformed church for nearly forty years, even though he always hoped to return to the south. Plancius first achieved recognition for his work in astronomy and geography and as a maker of navigational instruments. Throughout his life he played an important role in Dutch exploration and trade and was involved first with the Dutch East India Company and later with the West India Company; he also strongly encouraged and promoted missionary work in the Dutch trading empire.

Theologically, Plancius was a strict Calvinist and a strong supporter of the doctrine of predestination. He was also a forceful advocate of a confessional church and believed that adherence to the confessional standards of the Dutch Reformed church—the Belgic, or Netherlands, Confession and the Heidelberg Catechism—should be used as a measure of Calvinist orthodoxy within the church; at the same time Plancius opposed the efforts of the States of Holland to promote theological tolerance in the church through their support of the Remonstrants. Plancius was also a champion of an independent church government and was deeply involved in the struggles to secure a uniform church order for the Dutch Reformed church.

Even before Plancius went to Amsterdam, he was recognized as a leader in the Reformed church of the Low Countries. In Amsterdam itself he led an attack against the Lutheran congregations there and became the head of the orthodox Calvinist party in the years of conflict with Arminius and the Remonstrants (1590–1620); because of Plancius's influence, Amsterdam was a center of Calvinist orthodoxy in the early seventeenth century. During Arminius's tenure in Amsterdam, Plancius frequently brought the issue of predestination to the pulpit and accused Arminius of deviation from Calvinist theology on the doctrines of grace, original sin, and predestination. He also unsuccessfully opposed Arminius's appointment to the theology faculty at the University of Leiden, and after Arminius's death he challenged the theological orthodoxy of Arminius's successor, Conradus Vorstius.

In 1611 Plancius participated in a conference at The Hague, organized by the States of Holland, at which he and other opponents of Arminius and the Remonstrants submitted their objections to the theology of the Remonstrance of 1610. Plancius then became a leader in the Contra-Remonstrant party, and he continued to oppose and preach against the Remonstrants until their theological opinions were declared unorthodox at the Synod of Dordrecht (1618/19). At this synod Plancius was appointed to work on an official translation of the Bible for use in the Reformed church of the Netherlands but was little involved in this project because of his death in 1622. Throughout his career Plancius distinguished himself as an opponent of Arminianism from the pulpit; unlike other leading Contra-Remonstrants he did not contribute to the theological debates of his time through writing and publication.

BIBLIOGRAPHY

Bangs, Carl. *Arminius: A Study in the Dutch Reformation.* 2d ed. Reprint, Grand Rapids, Mich., 1985. An excellent introduction to the theological controversy between Arminius and Gomarus, and Plancius's role in it.

Deursen, A. Th. van. *Bavianen en Slijkgeuzen: Kerk en Kerkvolk ten tijde van Maurits en Oldenbarnevelt.* Reprint, Franeker, 1991. Based on extensive archival research. The single best work on the development of Calvinism in the Netherlands and the significance of the Arminian controversy.

Keuning, J. *Petrus Plancius: Theoloog and Geograaf, 1552–1622.* Amsterdam, 1946. The standard biography of Plancius.

Nobbs, Douglas. *Theocracy and Toleration: A Study of Disputes in Dutch Calvinism from 1600 to 1650.* Cambridge, 1938. A detailed source of information but not readily available.

Tex, Jan den. *Oldenbarnevelt.* 2 vols. Translated by R. B. Powell. Cambridge, 1973. Excellent on the political context of the Arminian controversy.

MICHAEL A. HAKKENBERG

PLANTIJN, Christoffel (Eng., Christopher Plantin; 1520?–1589), French printer, bookbinder, and publisher. Born in Saint-Avertin, near Tours, Plantijn left Caen (where he married Jeanne Rivière) and Paris for Antwerp at the end of the 1540s. On 21 March 1550 the French bookbinder was registered as an Antwerp citizen, and in the same year he was admitted to the Guild of Saint Luke. Plantijn sought to make printing and publishing activities his main line of business, and in 1555 he got "the first fruit from the garden of [his] press," G. M. Bruto's *La Institutione di una fanciulla nata nobilmente.* The Plantijn printing press was incorporated in circumstances that have never been fully explained, and it is uncertain whether he obtained his initial working capital from the settlement of a legal claim or from businessmen imbued with the spirit of the Family of Love. In any case, Plantijn's dealings with the rich merchant Hendrik Niclaes, the founder of this spiritual movement, are characterised by a mixture of commercial and religious interest.

Plantijn's pious mysticism and indifference to sacraments, ceremonies, and dogma did not prevent him from conforming to the Roman Catholic church and displaying his loyalty to whomever was in power. Plantijn's bad experience with three of his journeymen, whose clandestine printing of the Calvinist *Briefve instruction pour prier* (1562) caused him to go into temporary exile in Paris (1562–1563), convinced him to dissociate himself from the troubles accompanying the Revolt of the Netherlands. Accordingly, after a successful partnership with the Calvinist Van Bomberghens (1563–1567), Plantijn and his partners settled their accounts without reviewing the partnership, although he did help them, albeit reluctantly, to set up an anti-Spanish press at Vianen. By strengthening his ties with influential Catholics such as Cardinal Granvelle, Plantijn tried to secure his safety. Attesting his Catholic orthodoxy in lengthy affirmations of faith, Plantijn was able to secure both the approval of Philip II and the financial backing for a new critical edition of the Bible. Supervision of the monumental *Biblia Polyglotta* (1568–1573) was entrusted to the king's chaplain, Benito Arias Montano, and the professional relationship between Arias and Plantijn grew into a close friendship. The two men joined with a circle of scholars and businessmen of various confessions in support of Hendrik Jansen van Barrevelt, an erstwhile follower of Hendrik Niclaes, who rejected his efforts to turn the Family of Love into a visible church. Plantijn also secured for himself many orders of Tridentine breviaries and missals in 1571. Moreover, as official prototypographus of the Spanish king (1570), he received government orders to print editions of the *Index of Prohibited Books* (1569–1570) and royal ordinances. The Spanish Fury (1576) put an end to the fruitful collaboration with Philip II and to Plantijn's peak years of expansion, during which he operated sixteen presses and employed about seventy men.

During the period of Calvinist rule Plantijn sought to gain favor with leading figures of the revolt in order to keep his press going, but he was never really involved in political action and managed to avoid publishing the most virulent anti-Spanish propaganda under his own name. In 1581 Plantijn was busy printing Barrevelt's works, but he remained, as always, outwardly loyal to Catholicism. Faced with the impending Spanish reconquest of Antwerp, Plantijn, on the insistence of Justus Lipsius, moved to the Dutch university town of Leiden (1583–1585), where he established a new *Officina* that could keep him solvent and take over the functions of the parent house if necessary. At Leiden Plantijn observed a large degree of neutrality in religion and politics, whereas in Antwerp his sons-in-law Jan I Moerentorf (Moretus) and Frans I van Ravelingen (Raphelengius) published at the same time anti-Spanish ordinances and Catholic liturgical books.

Plantijn returned to Antwerp when the city was recaptured by Spain, and his old contacts enabled him to resume a rate of publication that laid the foundations for the Counter-Reformation publishing business of Jan I Moerentorf. His other son-in-law, the Calvinist Frans I van Ravelingen, had at least nominal control over the Leiden branch, which specialized in academic works. During his career (1555–1589) Plantijn produced some 563 broadsheets and 1,887 books, including 391 humanist works, 312 theological treatises, 665 religious works of various kinds (not counting editions of scripture and the Fathers), and 196 liturgical books.

BIBLIOGRAPHY

De Nave, Francine, and Léon Voet. *Museum Plantin-Moretus Antwerpen.* Brussels, 1989.

Materné, Jan. "Ex Officina Plantiniana: Les impressions anversoises à caractère religeux destinées au marché du livre ibéro-américain." In *Flandre Amérique latine,* edited by Eddy Stols and Rudy Bleys, pp. 139–153. Antwerp, 1993.

Peira, Pedro, et al., eds. *Simposio Internacional sobre Cristobal Plantino.* 18–20 January 1990, Madrid. Madrid, 1991.

Voet, Léon. *The Golden Compasses: A History and Evaluation of the Printing and Publishing Activities of the Officina Plantiniana at Antwerp.* 2 vols. Amsterdam and New York, 1969–1972.

———. "Some Considerations on the Productions of the Plantin Press." In *Liber Amicorum Herman Liebaers,* edited by Frans Vanwijngaerden, et al., pp. 355–369. Brussels, 1984.

Voet, Léon, and Jenny Voet-Grisolle. *The Plantin Press, 1555–1589.* 6 vols. Amsterdam, 1980–1983. A bibliography of the works printed and published by Christoffel Plantijn at Antwerp and Leiden.

JAN MATERNÉ

PLAYS. *See* Drama.

POISSY, COLLOQUY OF. One of the last great expressions of sixteenth-century efforts to join religious reform with religious reconciliation, the Colloquy of Poissy of 1561 was something of a summit conference as well as a theological dialogue. It was set in the village of Poissy, just west of Paris, on the eve of the ruinous French Wars of Religion, to which it was a conceivable alternative. Moreover, while essentially a gathering of the Gallican church, this national council was played out against the background of the definitive sessions of a general council, the Council of Trent, and accordingly had implications for Christendom generally.

The unitive ideal, rooted in scripture (e.g., *Jn.* 17:21), survived the first generations of the Reformation and was never really disavowed. Desiderius Erasmus of Rotterdam was its foremost patron, and it counted a distinguished group, both Catholic and Protestant, committed to the inviolability of Christendom. In France, this moderating and ecumenical strain persisted through Jacques Lefèvre d'Étaples at the beginning of the century to Michel de Montaigne at the end, including in between the distinguished humanist chancellor, Michel de L'Hôpital, an ardent exponent of the colloquy. The queen mother and regent, Catherine de Médicis, championed the colloquy as an alternative to impending anarchy and war. Inevitably it pitted her against another Medici, Pius IV (no kin), determined upon his own ecumenical program via the Council of Trent. Although the first two periods of Trent (1545–1547 and 1551–1552) had come and gone, mutual animosities had prevented the general council from being fully ecumenical. The final period (1562–1563) would be decisive. The French court feared that a dogmatic Tridentine resolution would perpetuate the schism, while Rome feared that particular solutions such as Poissy could result in the alienation and schism of the Gallican church. Although both Luther and Calvin had called for a resolution of the religious crisis via a general council, this expedient would not be a council under Roman auspices; hence, a series of more national colloquies, such as Poissy.

The colloquy occurred within a larger context of an assembly of the Gallican church. It counted an eminent company, therefore, including the royal family and the princes of the blood, as well as six cardinals, more than forty bishops, plus a dozen theologians. The Reformed party, attending from Geneva, counted a dozen theologians, led by Théodore de Bèze, right hand and heir of Calvin to leadership of the international Reformed church. Bèze would be seconded by the learned theologian, Peter Martyr Vermigli, who enjoyed powerful support at court. The foremost Catholic spokesman was Charles of Guise, the cardinal of Lorraine. Diego Laínez, general of the Jesuits, also participated.

The setting was the refectory of an old convent, and the meetings ran intermittently for a month, beginning 9 September 1561. French was the medium of discourse in deference to the royal family. Bèze's opening speech was generally a model presentation of Calvinist faith. But the sacrament of unity eventuated as, ironically, "the apple of discord," as Thomas Cranmer, the English reformer, had termed it. When Bèze infelicitously declared that Christ's body was "as far removed from the bread and wine as is heaven from earth," the horrified prelates reacted with accusations of blasphemy. Lorraine interceded to secure the very continuance of the colloquy. The next week he himself responded for the Catholic side. His presentation was generally moderate in tone. Reviewing the much converted and critical rule of faith, he avoided scholastic language and attributed infallibility only to the word of God.

Generally, neither side was disposed to reconciliation, and a truncated colloquy continued, without the prelates. Bèze increasingly appealed to the Crown to take direct action and establish the Reformation in France. Lorraine, for his part, introduced the Augsburg Confession into the Calvinist-Catholic encounter, requiring Bèze's ascription to its eucharistic doctrine as a condition of continuance. This controversial act of the mercurial Lorraine has been called by one school of historians "the bomb" (Paul Geisendorf, *Théodore de Bèze*, Geneva, 1949): a ruse done in bad faith to advertise and exacerbate Calvinist-Lutheran divisions. But differences between Reformed and evangelical eucharistic doctrine had been painfully commonplace since the Colloquy of Marburg (1529). Lorraine's motives may have been mixed, like those of the colloquy itself, and as likely as not he introduced the Lutheran document in a desperate effort at mediation. It spared the Calvinists submitting to strictly Catholic terms. Nevertheless, Bèze declined the measure as inappropriate.

The colloquy eventuated in a still more private form at the royal court at Saint Germain-en-Laye. This has been called the *petit colloque.* There Claude d'Espence, Lorraine's theological adviser and one of the most genuinely ecumenical figures of the colloquy, attempted to mediate with various eucharistic formulas, but to no avail. Vermigli emerged to reinforce the orthodoxy of the Reformed. For his part, Laínez intervened in favor of the doctrine of Trent. A related colloquy on icons under the royal eye of Saint Germain between 27 January and 11 February 1562 was anticlimactic. Reunion failing, the queen mother opted for religious toleration in the edict of January 1562. But Frenchmen were apparently no more ready for toleration than they were for reconciliation. They had first to be schooled by war, some thirty years of which followed the Massacre of Wassy, 1 March 1562.

There was good will at Poissy, but most understood ecumenism in partisan terms. Few of the prelates could tolerate the Protestants, and the Reformed were more interested in gaining recognition and the opportunity to plead their case at court than in reconciliation. Calvinists were perhaps too close to the age of their martyrs and too confident in the victory of their cause to treat with the opposition. Both sides were more interested in conversions than in convergence.

The colloquy ended, ironically, a chapter in the Counter-Reformation. A few years earlier, the Catholic standard had passed from the relatively more ecumenical Charles V to his son Philip II, the inveterate foe of Poissy. The waning of the colloquy points up the rising convergence of Spanish power, Roman spiritual leadership, Tridentine doctrine, Jesuit élan, and confessional estrangement.

[*See also* Andreae, Jakob; Bèze, Théodore de; Catherine de Médicis; Charles IX of France; *and* Wars of Religion.]

BIBLIOGRAPHY

Evans, G. R. *Problems of Authority in the Reformation Debates.* Cambridge, 1992. Excellent for broad theological background.

Evennett, H. Outram. *The Cardinal of Lorraine and the Council of Trent.* Cambridge, 1940. Indispensable for the most controverted personage at Poissy and formative for the standard study of the colloquy, listed below.

Nugent, Donald. *Ecumenism in the Age of the Reformation: The Colloquy of Poissy.* Cambridge, Mass., 1974. The standard study. See for extended bibliography.

Rouse, Ruth, and Stephen Charles Neill, eds. *A History of the Ecumenical Movement, 1517–1948.* 4th ed. Geneva, 1993. Magisterial study of the movement up until its popular revival.

DONALD NUGENT

POLANCO, Juan Alonso de (1517?–1576), Jesuit administrator and historian. Polanco was born in Burgos, Spain, of a wealthy family. It has been frequently alleged, on dubious grounds, that his family was of Jewish ancestry. After humanistic and philosophical studies at the University of Paris, Polanco secured appointment as apostolic secretary in the papal curia, but when his friend Francisco Torres entered the Jesuits and had made the Spiritual Exercises, he too entered the Jesuits in 1541, despite bitter family opposition. After studying theology at Padua (1541–1546), he was ordained and appointed secretary of the Society of Jesus (i.e., a chief of staff for Ignatius Loyola); he retained that position under the next two Jesuit generals (1546–1573), Diego Laínez and Francisco Borgia. He was also assistant (supervisor) for the Spanish Jesuits from 1558 to 1573.

Much of Loyola's vast correspondence was actually drafted by Polanco, who was a skilled writer and Latinist. Polanco played a key role, second only to Loyola, in drawing up the Jesuit *Constitutions;* Loyola depended on him to do background research on monastic legislation, to propose alternative solutions to problems, and to polish the style, although it was Loyola who made final decisions about the *Constitutions.* Polanco was a skillful manager. Because of him, the records and correspondence of the early Jesuits are incomparably richer than those of earlier religious orders. Polanco used this material to write a life of Loyola and his *Chronicon* (Madrid, 1894–1898), a six-volume account of Jesuit activities, 1537–1556. His *Methodus ad eos adiuvandos qui moriuntur* (Rome, 1575) enjoyed several editions. Polanco was the logical choice as the fourth Jesuit general in 1573, but his alleged Jewish ancestry and Gregory XIII's desire that the new general not be another Spaniard probably worked against him; the electors chose a Belgian, Everard Mercurian.

BIBLIOGRAPHY

Dowling, Richard H. "Juan de Polanco, S.J., 1517–1576." *Woodstock Letters* 69 (1940), 1–20. Brief biography.

Englander, Clara. *Ignatius von Loyola und Johannes von Polanco: Der Ordensstifter und sein Sekretär.* Regensburg, 1956. Studies the interaction of Loyola and Polanco.

O'Malley, John W. *The First Jesuits.* Cambridge, Mass., 1993.

Ravier, André. *Ignatius of Loyola and the Founding of the Society of Jesus.* San Francisco, 1987. Polanco played a major role in this story.

Verzeichnis der im deutschen Sprachbereich erschienenen Drucke des XVI. Jahrhunderts. Stuttgart, 1983–. See vol. 16, nos. 3916–3919.

JOHN PATRICK DONNELLY

POLAND. By the beginning of the sixteenth century, the kingdom of Poland had been joined for over a century to the grand duchy of Lithuania in a personal, dynastic union under the rule of the Jagiellon family. Before that dynasty died out in 1572, the Union of Lublin in 1569 had transformed the relationship between the two countries into a constitutional, organic union, known officially as the Commonwealth of Both Nations (*Respublica Poloniae et Lithuaniae, Rzeczpospolita Obojga Narodów*). The combined realms occupied an area of about 1,140,000 square kilometers, making them the largest European polity. (Territorial losses and corresponding growth by Muscovite Russia reduced the commonwealth's rank to second by 1600.)

The historic Polish lands were centered in the basins of the Warta and Vistula rivers—that is, the regions of Great Poland (*Polonia maior, Wielkopolska*), Minor Poland (*Polonia minor, Małopolska*), Mazovia, and Kujavia. Expansion to the southeast in the fourteenth and fifteenth centuries had brought the regions of Halicz (Galicia) and Vladimir in Volhynia (Lodomeria) in Red Ruthenia and the territory of Podolia under Polish control. Farther to the south the feudal tributary of Moldavia had been taken from Poland by the Turks in the 1470s. In the north, as the result of successful fifteenth-century wars against the Teutonic Knights, Gdańsk Pomerania (the region around Gdańsk [Danzig]) and parts of western Prussia were incorporated into the kingdom and were known as Royal Prussia. The remaining lands of the Teutonic Knights were held by the grand master as a fief of the Polish Crown; they became known as Ducal Prussia after 1525. The capital of the kingdom was at Kraków, as it had been since the early Middle Ages.

The possessions of the grand duchy included the ethnically Lithuanian lands of Aukštota (the "upper country") and Samogitia (the "low country"), plus White Ruthenia (today Belarus) and Polesia in the upper basin of the Pripet River. Conquests during the fifteenth and sixteenth centuries had added Courland (Kurland) and Livonia in the north and the regions of Volhynia and Ukraine in the Dnieper River basin in the south to the Lithuanian state. The most important administrative centers in the grand duchy were at Vilno (Vilnius) and Kiev. At one point in the fifteenth century the combined territories of Poland-Lithuania stretched from the Baltic Sea to the Black Sea.

Population. The population of Poland-Lithuania was about 7.5 million in 1500, but it was unevenly distributed. In the kingdom of Poland, especially in Royal Prussia and the central regions of Great and Minor Poland, density may have approached fourteen to fifteen persons per square kilometer, but in Lithuania, where settlements were thinly scattered, the population was much sparser.

Compared with western Europe, especially Italy and the Low Countries, Poland-Lithuania was not strongly urbanized. Gdańsk had a population of about 30,000, but Kraków had only about 15,000 at the beginning of the century. Other cities did not exceed 10,000. Lwów, Toruń (Thorn), and Elbląg (Elbing) may have had 8,000, and Poznań (Posen) and Lublin about 6,000, but most urban settlements had a population of between 3,000 and 5,000. During the sixteenth century population growth in the two realms was robust; by 1650 the Polish-Lithuanian commonwealth probably had a population of eleven million, with an average density of eleven persons per square kilometer (again, unevenly distributed).

A Diverse Society. Within the borders of the Poland-Lithuania state, there was a society of diverse ethnic, linguistic, and religious groups. The ethnically Polish population was most heavily settled in the kingdom proper, though there had been much migration into the lands to the east and south conquered before the sixteenth century. In the grand duchy Lithuanians and Ruthenians predominated. But the commonwealth was a multinational state that also included Germans, Jews, Armenians, Walloons, Italians, Netherlanders, and Tatars, among others. Some had come to the towns as merchants and traders, others had been invited by medieval dukes seeking agricultural improvements on the land, and some had been incorporated into the Polish-Lithuanian state as it expanded.

Consequently, a babel of tongues could be found in the cities and the countryside. The aristocracy in Poland spoke Polish among themselves and at the various national and regional courts, and Polish was common in the countryside and among the lesser guilds of urban life. German predominated among the merchants, in some parts of the peasantry (especially western Poland), and in the towns of Prussia. In the grand duchy Lithuanian dominated the private life of the ruling elite, but Ruthenian (*ruski,* Old Byelorussian) was used for official life, though the nobility was fast becoming Polonized in the course of the sixteenth century. In commercial circles in the east, Armenian was common, while throughout the two countries Hebrew, Yiddish, and (among the Karaites) Tatar were used by the Jewish community. Latin, of course, remained the language of intellectual discourse, higher education, and the Catholic church.

The religious scene in Poland-Lithuania was equally diverse. Poland had been converted to Catholic Christianity in the early Middle Ages, and a single archbishopric for the whole Polish church was established at Gniezno (Gnesen) in 1000. A second Catholic archbishopric was created at Lwów in the fifteenth century, but Gniezno remained the seat of the Polish primate. Formerly pagan Lithuania had been christianized during the fifteenth century. The medieval expansion of Poland had brought it into contact with the Orthodox world of Ruthenia, so that within the state, even before the union with Lithuania, there were multiple Christian groups. The Armenian church had many members in Ruthenia, and Lwów was the seat of an Armenian archbishop. Near the end of the sixteenth century the Union of Brest (1596) brought an official—if not widely popular and effective—end to the schism between Catholicism and Eastern Orthodoxy with the establishment of the Uniate church, that is, an Orthodox church in communion with Rome and recognizing the pope as the head of the church. (The range of religious diversity was to increase with the Reformation.)

A significant element of the population in Poland-Lithuania was not Christian at all. The Jewish presence included both Karaites and Jews from the west. The former were derived from an eighth-century development among Jews in the Orient and had been brought to Lithuania in the fifteenth century. From the west Jews had been welcome in Poland since the early Middle Ages. Numerous ducal and royal privileges attracted large numbers of Jews, especially as antisemitism grew in the west. Following the expulsions from the Iberian Peninsula at the end of the fifteenth century, Jewish immigration to Poland increased. It is estimated that there were more than one hundred thousand Jews in Poland-Lithuania by the time of the Union of Lublin. Though constrained by legal limitations in many places, the foundations of later Jewish autonomy emerged under royal patronage in the sixteenth century. By 1550 the outlines of the *kahal* ("communal government") at the local level and the *vaad* ("council of the four lands") at the national level were well established. The Muslims in Poland-Lithuania were largely derived from Tatar settlements in the western areas of the grand duchy. They were loyal subjects, many were admitted to the ranks of the nobility, and, in the middle of the sixteenth century, there were more than one hundred mosques in Lithuania.

Government. Lithuania in the sixteenth century was a country ruled autocratically by its grand duke and by a small, powerful aristocracy. Jagiellonian Poland, on the other hand, was a polity that demanded power sharing and representation. The nobility there had emerged in the late medieval period as a status within society (the term *class* is misleading) eager to defend and extend their rights against what they perceived as potential royal absolutism. As a result, Poland was a hereditary monarchy ruled by a series of successively weaker kings. It was similar to many other European polities, where ruler (whether prince or king) and the estates of society (*Stände* in German) cooperated together in governance.

During the fifteenth century a series of rulers had granted to the nobility (the *szlachta*) the rights of due process (1422) and *habeas corpus* (1430), the right to be consulted in local diets (*conventiones particulares, sejmiki*) before troops or taxes were raised (1454), and the right to have a bicameral national parliament meet on a regular basis (1493). The lower house (the *Sejm*, or diet) was composed of noble deputies elected in the local diets; the upper house, or senate, consisted of the great magnates, high church officials, and appointed officers (councillors) of the Crown. Finally, in 1505 King Alexander (1461–1506; grand duke of Lithuania, 1492–1506; king of Poland, 1501–1506) promised in the decree *Nihil novi* that in the future "nothing new will be decided by us or our successors without the concurrence of the councillors and the deputies."

These and other privileges constitute the principle of consensual lawmaking rather than depending upon the whim of the ruler. These developments represent the foundations of what came to be known in the sixteenth and early seventeenth century as "the noble democracy," and in the late sixteenth century the *szlachta*, or those in society who possessed political rights, constituted nearly 10 percent of the Polish-Lithuanian population. At its best it ensured that arbitrary royal absolutism would not limit the republican freedoms of the *szlachta*. It was predicated upon the idea that unity and consent among all concerned were in the best interests of society.

Significant as these limitations, both real and potential, were upon the monarchy, rulers in Poland were not without power. Nowhere is this more clearly shown than in the events that led up to the Union of Lublin. Sigismund II Augustus (1520–1572; grand duke and king after 1548) had no heir. This raised the question of what would become of the Polish-Lithuanian union. The Polish *szlachta* was not united in its approach. The great magnates fought to establish government by oligarchy. The lesser *szlachta* fought to have the traditional laws protecting their status executed (and were consequently known as executionists); they wanted judicial, ecclesiastical, and economic reforms. In Lithuania the minor *szlachta* were politically immature and were dominated by the great magnates. But when confronted by the possibility of going it alone after Sigismund II Augustus's death, the Lithuanians found themselves and their freedoms threatened by the new Czar of Muscovy, Ivan IV ("the Terrible"), and the traditions of Russian autocracy. When the king proposed a transformation of the union from a personal to an organic one, the leading magnate faction resisted. The king showed his strength, however, by stripping three territories—Podlasia, Volhynia, and Ukraine—from Lithuania and incorporating them into the Kingdom of Poland. This forceful act was enough to bring all to agreement. The senate and diet of Lithuania met with those of Poland at Lublin on 1 July 1569 and swore a new act of union.

By the terms of the Union of Lublin, the parliaments of both countries were combined and were to meet as one assembly at Warsaw, a city in Mazovia conveniently located for both countries. (Within a generation Warsaw replaced Kraków as the capital.) The two states were to share one elected monarch. Lithuania kept its old law, treasury, and army; identical officers were established for the kingdom and the grand duchy. The Lithuanian nobility were granted the rights of the Polish *szlachta,* and within a generation they had become thoroughly Polonized. The monarchy and grand duchy had been transformed into a commonwealth with an elected monarch.

Renaissance Humanism in Poland. The strongest cultural current of the century was Renaissance humanism. Introduced into Poland during the course of the second half of the fifteenth century, it had in succeeding generations a great impact in art, literature, and all areas of learning and culture. Renaissance style was adopted and adapted in Poland in such important architectural monuments as the rebuilt Wawel Castle on Wawel Hill in Kraków and the planned city of Zamość, begun in 1580 by the royal chancellor Jan Zamoyski (1542–1605) in conformity with Renaissance principles. Neo-Latin prose and poetry by Polish writers ensured Poland a place in the mainstream of European culture. Johannes Dantiscus (Jan Dantyszek, 1485–1548), Andreas Cricius (Andrzej Krzycki, 1482–1537), and Clemens Ianicius (Klemens Janicjusz, 1516–1543) all produced works that were admired not only in Poland but throughout Europe. The Renaissance, by its emphasis on ancient history, culture, and language, also enhanced the development of a Polish national culture, which found particular expression in the creation of a vernacular literature of great power and beauty. Shaped by the religious and political literature of Biernat of Lublin (c.1465–c.1529), it was improved and enriched by Mikołaj Rej (1505–1569) and perfected by Jan Kochanowski (1530–1584).

Finally, the Renaissance, as well as the humanist, ideal that individuals and society could be reformed found its fullest expression in this period in the career and writings of Andreas Modrevius (Andrzej Frycz-Modrzewski, c.1503–1572), a royal secretary and author of *De republica emendanda libri quinque* (Five Books on the Reform of the Republic, published in 1554 in full and uncensored form in Basel). Modrzewski, who in some ways may be included in the complex and often self-contradictory executionist movement, called for strengthening the monarchy at the expense of the oligarchy of the noble magnates, for limitations upon the church, and for reform of the law so that it would protect all strata of society. The importance of humanism in Poland is reflected in the great influence that Desiderius Erasmus had there and in his famous comment that "Polonia mea est" ("Poland is devoted to me").

Church-State Relations. The Catholic church had prospered from royal patronage and protection, though the monarchy eventually came to exercise considerable influence over it. By the sixteenth century the church held 10 percent of the arable land in Great Poland, 15 percent in Minor Poland, and 25 percent in Mazovia. (By comparison, the Crown held 9, 7.5, and 5 percent, respectively, in these same lands.) Its bishops sat in the senate and wielded considerable political influence, and it had wide jurisdiction over laymen on church lands. Moreover, pluralities were common.

Although the Polish clergy were probably not by European standards particularly corrupt or immoral, the position of the church and its close ties to the monarchy roused complaints within society. The fifteenth century Hussite movement in neighboring Bohemia had found some echoes in Poland, but there had been only limited support for it among the nobility. By the sixteenth century, however, sentiment for a "national Catholicism" was growing, especially among the lesser *szlachta,* who resented the power of the church. Biernat of Lublin was one of the first to condemn the gap between scriptural precept and church practice.

The Reformation in Poland. Martin Luther's message came to Poland first in the German-speaking towns of the Baltic, and his Ninety-five Theses were taught in Gdańsk in the summer of 1518. Soon afterward King Sigismund I (1467–1548; r. 1506–1548) forbade the import of Luther's teachings into Poland. Nevertheless, Roman practice and jurisdiction were abolished by the Gdańsk city government in 1525. Catholicism was superficially restored soon thereafter when the king executed fifteen of the municipal leaders in what was to be, for Poland-Lithuania, an uncharacteristically violent and punitive response. In 1525 Albert of Hohenzollern, the Catholic grand master of the Knights of the Teutonic Order, converted to Lutheranism and secularized the order's territory, creating in the process the duchy of Prussia, for which he subsequently did homage to King Sigismund. Luther's ideas also made headway at the University of Kraków, where copies of his works were circulated and discussed. These examples of Lutheran inroads in Poland are, however, exceptions to the general pattern. The anti-German feeling of many Poles ensured that Lutheranism would have only marginal success outside the Germanized cities.

In Poland itself the Reformed tradition struck deeper roots. John Calvin's emphasis on the governing power of the lay elder appealed to the nobility in Poland, and the Gallic origins of the Reformed movement made it more acceptable to those hostile to German and imperial elements. In 1539 Calvin dedicated his commentary on the Mass to the heir to the Polish throne, Sigismund II Augustus, hoping to win his religious allegiance. The most famous Polish convert to the Protestant cause was Jan Łaski (John of Lasco; 1499–1560), nephew of the archbishop of Gniezno. He had been educated in Italy; was in contact with most of the leading reformers in Germany, Switzerland, and France; and was a close friend of Erasmus, whose library he eventually purchased and arranged to have transported to Poland. Appointed a bishop in Poland, he spent the years 1526–1539 involved in politics and diplomacy. He resigned his position in 1538, became a Protestant, and until his death was active in East Friesland, England, Germany, Denmark, and Poland as a reformer.

In the 1550s the powerful noble magnate Nicholas Oleśnicki converted a convent in Pinczów into a Calvinist academy, and in 1554 the first Calvinist synod in the Polish kingdom was held at Słomniki in Minor Poland. By this time the Protestant spectrum in Poland had been enriched by the arrival of the Bohemian Brethren, who had come to Poland in 1548 after being driven out of their native land by Emperor Ferdinand I. They gained adherents among the nobility. The diet held in 1555 was dominated by Protestant deputies, who demanded religious liberties from King Sigismund II Augustus that would have virtually created a national church. The religious sympathies of the new ruler were ambiguous. He was deeply religious and adhered to Rome as the state church (in which he had been brought up), though he was somewhat indifferent about religious forms and formal institutions. He was interested in theological issues, followed the Protestant movement sympathetically (he had many important Protestant nobles among his close advisers), and, when asked once by subjects which way they should lean on religious issues, replied, "I am not the king of your consciences."

In 1551 Lelio Sozzini (Laelius Socinus, 1525–1562) made a brief visit to Poland, and his antitrinitarian views soon found adherents. In subsequent years—especially after the 1578 visit and 1580 permanent residence in Poland of his nephew Fausto Sozzini (Faustus Socinus, 1539–1604)—the antitrinitarian movement, known as the Polish Brethren (or Minor church to distinguish them from the Calvinists, who were also known as the Major church), put down deep roots in the Polish-Lithuanian commonwealth. Their center was at Raków in Minor Poland, where they were protected by the great noble magnate Michał Sieniecki (1521–1582). As early as 1574 they had formulated a coherent unitarian catechism, pacifist in nature and socially communist, which was eventually refined in the more famous Racovian Catechism in 1605.

The threat of splits over doctrine forced Protestant groups to consider some kind of union following the Diet of Piotrków in 1562/63. In opposition to the antitrinitarians and the executionist party among the Catholics—who sought some kind of national church, perhaps on an Anglican model—the Calvinists, Lutherans, and Bohemian Brethren concluded the Consensus Sendomiriensis in 1570. This was designed to protect Protestants against Catholic repression and to promote understanding among the groups. By this time Protestants were nearly in the majority in the diet, and about one-sixth of the ecclesiastical parishes in the country were held by Protestants. This strength resulted in the legal establishment of religious toleration and equality in the commonwealth following the death of Sigismund II Augustus in 1572. Ironically, however, it also marked the high-water mark of the Reformation in Poland, for in succeeding decades the Catholic cause recovered.

Politics in the Commonwealth and the Catholic Recovery. The interregnum following 1572 saw the appointment of the archbishop of Gniezno, Jakub Uchański, as interrex at a gathering of the nobles called the Convocation Diet. His responsibilities included regulating the process leading to the election of a new king under the terms of the Union of Lublin. It was eventually decided, following the proposal of Jan Zamoyski, that the election would be held *viritim*—that is, with all nobles of whatever rank in the commonwealth eligible to participate in person at the site of the election, the field of Wola outside Warsaw. This effectively ensured the election of a Catholic since the majority of the *szlachta* had held firm to Rome. At the same time, a compact was reached by which absolute religious toleration without exception was granted to all *dissidentes de religione* (i.e., religious dissidents from the Catholic faith). This principle, which was approved even by the entire Polish episcopate (except one), was regarded by all as a guarantee against religious fanaticism. (The diet was held shortly after news of the Saint Bartholomew's Day Massacre in France reached Poland.) Henceforth, the principle of religious toleration was included in the terms of the *Pacta conventa* ("Acts of Agreement"), which every future Polish king was required to swear to uphold.

In the election diet held in April 1573, Henry of Valois (1550–1589), the younger brother of King Charles IX of France, was chosen. After he had sworn to uphold not only the *Pacta conventa* but also specific agreements known as the Henrician Articles, he came to Poland to rule. His reign lasted only 118 days, for when his brother died in 1574, he returned to France to become the ruler there (as Henry III). To replace him, the nobles elected Stephen Báthory, prince of Transylvania (1533–1586; r. 1576–1586), in December 1575. He proved to be an effective monarch, waging a successful war against Poland-Lithuania's Baltic neighbors, especially Czar Ivan IV, and reestablishing some measure of royal authority and respect for the Crown, particularly in judicial and financial matters. In religious matters Báthory upheld the letter of his oaths to respect toleration, but he was unequivocally pro-Catholic and favored the Jesuits. His successor, King Sigismund III Vasa (1566–1632; r. 1587–1632), was even more aggressive in his support of the Jesuits and of the Catholic Reformation and Counter-Reformation. His personal and family ambitions vis à vis Sweden led him into a foreign policy that was disastrous for Poland and that greatly weakened royal power in Poland.

The Catholic recovery in Poland can be said to have begun under the auspices of Archbishop Jan Łaski of Gniezno (1455–1531; uncle of the above-mentioned Jan Łaski) and of royal vice-chancellor and bishop of Kraków Piotr Tomicki (1464–1535), both of whom resisted Lutheranism and promoted reforms within the Polish church. But their efforts (and those of others) were essentially palliatives. A more principled and systematic "counter-reformation" took place under the leadership of Stanisław Hosius (1505–1579), after 1551 bishop of Warmia (Ermeland) and after 1559 cardinal, in which capacity he presided as one of the five presidents of the last assembly of the Council of Trent. In addition to a series of aggressive reform efforts in his see, one of the most Protestant areas of the kingdom, Hosius formulated for the provincial synod of Piotrków in 1551 a short Confessio, which was later expanded into a comprehensive, positive, and clear exposition of Catholic faith and morals, the Confessio fidei catholicae christiana. After his return to Poland from Trent in 1564, he lobbied the royal court successfully for the acceptance of the council's decrees in Poland. His work was complemented by the efforts of the Jesuits.

The Jesuits had first arrived in Poland in 1559, when Peter Canisius (1521–1597) had visited Kraków incognito. In 1565 Canisius sent King Sigismund II Augustus ten members of the order and arranged to have four colleges founded to educate the sons of the *szlachta* and to train native members of the order. By the end of the century there were more than 450 members of the Society of Jesus in the Polish province, and the most powerful preacher of the age, the Jesuit Piotr Skarga (1536–1612), was the court chaplain of King Sigismund III. Gradually the Protestant position in Poland-Lithuania was undermined. Although formally there was Protestant unity, in practice the divisions and conflicts among Lutherans, Calvinists, and Bohemian Brethren weakened their efforts. In addition, the association with the doctrinal and social radicalism of the Polish Brethren compromised the Protestants in the eyes of many leaders in society. King Sigismund III effectively repudiated his oath of toleration without resulting political or religious resistance, and as a culminating symbol of the Catholic recovery, the Polish Brethren were exiled to the west in 1660. By then the association of Poland-Lithuania with the Catholic church, which has endured in powerful ways down to the present, was well established.

BIBLIOGRAPHY

Dembkowski, Harry E. *The Union of Lublin: Polish Federalism in the Golden Age.* East European Monographs, no. 116. Boulder, Colo., 1982. A fine political history of the process leading to the union, including an excellent study of the "Executionist" movement, though weak on religious issues.

Fedorowicz, J. K., ed. and trans., with Maria Bogucka and Henryk Samsonowicz, co-eds. *A Republic of Nobles: Studies in Polish History to 1864.* Cambridge, 1982. Eight of the thirteen chapters bear directly upon sixteenth-century issues, including religion, and reflect current scholarship as of that date in Poland; contains good bibliographies to the Polish-language literature.

Fiszman, Samuel, ed. *The Polish Renaissance in Its European Context.* Bloomington, Ind., 1988. A brilliantly edited collection of essays resulting from an international conference in 1982 held to commemorate the coming anniversary of Jan Kochanowski's death; chapters treat all aspects of the period, including religion, not just Renaissance culture in a narrow sense.

Fox, Paul. *The Reformation in Poland: Some Social and Economic Aspects.* Baltimore, 1924. Argues that the underlying causes of the rise and development of the Reformation were social and economic in nature rather than religious or political. A standard work in English, though now somewhat superseded by more recent scholarship, especially in Poland.

Jobert, Ambroise. *De Luther à Mohila: La Pologne dans la crise de la chrétienté, 1517–1648.* Paris, 1974. Classic work, monumental in scope and coverage, of the subtle relationship between religious and political issues.

Kieniewicz, Stefan, ed. *History of Poland.* 2d ed. Warsaw, 1979. Two long chapters (7 and 8) by Janusz Tazbir (translated by Leon Szwajcer) provide a balanced treatment of political, religious, and socioeconomic developments in the sixteenth and early seventeenth centuries.

Kot, Stanisław. *Socinianism in Poland: The Social and Political Ideas of the Polish Antitrinitarians in the Sixteenth and Seventeenth Centuries.* Translated by Earl Morse Wilbur. Boston, 1957. Except for the more recent studies by George H. Williams, still the most valuable analysis of the antitrinitarians available in English.

Mączak, Antoni, Henryk Samsonowicz, and Peter Burke, eds. *East-Central Europe in Transition: From the Fourteenth to the Seventeenth Century.* Cambridge, 1985. Seven of the twelve essays (all by Polish scholars) treat Polish developments in a comparative context; none deal directly with religious matters.

Pollard, A. F. *The Jesuits in Poland* (1892). Reprint, New York, 1971. Despite its age, this slim volume is still a reliable narrative concerning the history of the Jesuits in Poland.

Raitt, Jill, ed. *Shapers of Religious Traditions in Germany, Switzerland and Poland, 1560–1600.* New Haven and London, 1981. Among the dozen essays in this volume, those by George H. Williams on Hosius and Skarga and Zbigniew Ogonowski on Fausto Sozzini provide a useful picture, with good bibliography and notes, of these individuals in their Polish context.

Reddaway, William F., et al., eds. *The Cambridge History of Poland.* 2 vols. Cambridge, 1941–1950. Chapters 13–21 in the first volume of this standard work provide a full and authoritative treatment of Polish history in the sixteenth century; now somewhat outdated (much in this volume was written before World War II), it is still reliable for its details. The chapters by Paul Fox on the Reformation and Józef Umiński on the Counter-Reformation are classics and should still be consulted.

Schramm, Gottfried. *Der polnische Adel und die Reformation, 1548–1607.* Wiesbaden, 1965. A careful and thoroughly reliable analysis of the involvement by the Polish nobility (the *szlachta*) in the Reformation; uses much archival material and was completely abreast of Polish scholarship at its publication.

Segel, Harold B. *Renaissance Culture in Poland: The Rise of Humanism, 1470–1543.* Ithaca, N.Y., and London, 1989. Primarily devoted to neo-Latin literature in Poland in this period, this fine study also treats humanism more broadly, including an interesting chapter on Copernicus as a humanist.

Stasiewski, Bernhard. *Reformation und Gegenreformation in Polen: Neue Forschungsergebnisse.* Münster, 1960. A careful assessment, from a Catholic perspective, of Marxist scholarship in postwar Poland; very good on recently edited archival materials.

Tazbir, Janusz. *A State without Stakes: Polish Religious Toleration in the Sixteenth and Seventeenth Centuries.* Translated by A. T. Jordan. New York and Warsaw, 1973. The classic study of Polish religious toleration by Poland's greatest student of the Reformation; translated from *Państwo bez stosów,* Warsaw, 1967. Tazbir's later collection of articles, *Dzieje polskiej tolerancji,* Warsaw, 1973, was published in a German translation as *Geschichte der polnischen Toleranz,* Warsaw, 1977. His most recent collection of articles, *Dzieje Reformacji w Polsce,* Warsaw, 1993, has not yet been translated.

Williams, George H. *The Radical Reformation.* 3d ed. Kirksville, Mo., 1992. The chapters on eastern Europe in general and Poland in particular are the best studies in any language of the antitrinitarian movement and other radical elements. Williams is also the editor, translator, and interpreter of thirty-five documents relating to the history and thought of unitarianism in the Polish-Lithuanian Commonwealth and in the diaspora, 1601–1685 (*The Polish Brethren,* 2 vols., Harvard Theological Studies 30, Missoula, Mont., 1980). Williams also has edited, translated, and interpreted Stanisław Lubieniecki (1623–1675), *History of the Polish Reformation and Nine Related Documents,* Minneapolis, 1995. Together this body of work makes available in English some of the most important resources for Polish religious, intellectual/cultural, and social history in the late sixteenth and early seventeenth century.

PAUL W. KNOLL

POLE, Reginald (1500–1558), antagonist of Henry VIII, leader of Italian reform, and archbishop of Canterbury under Mary Tudor. Pole is probably best known as a writer rather than a figure who had direct impact on the Reformation. His significance in the history of political thought rests both on his polemical defense of the church (*De unitate,* 1536; published 1539) and on his inauguration of a major stream of anti-Machiavellism ("Apologia ad Carolum Quintum," 1539). His interpretation of the Henrician Reformation has dominated not only Catholic historiography but almost all views of Henry and his chief minister Thomas Cromwell until the late twentieth century. Similarly, Pole had a major role in fostering the saintly image of Thomas More, as well as his own unblemished persona. He was also an important (if impecunious) cultural patron. Although perhaps most notorious for his political failures—from his first legation against Henry (1537) through the debate on justification at the Council of Trent (1546) and the abortive Marian Counter-Reformation—Pole nevertheless stood at the center stage of Europe for twenty years. In England, as the grandson of the duke of Clarence (brother of Edward IV), Pole always had major political standing.

Educated at Oxford and Padua (at Henry's expense) and following the usual path for one preparing for royal service, Pole first entered politics in 1529–1530 on a mission for Henry to the theological and canon law faculties of the University of Paris. Pole secured favorable opinions on Henry's divorce from both. This would quickly become the first episode in Pole's career to be rewritten as a moment not of service but of resistance. Perhaps by 1532 Pole had changed his mind about Henry and especially about the King's supreme headship over the English church; in any case, he left England then for what became a twenty-year exile.

The rest of Pole's career rested on his tortured relationship to his native country and on a religious conversion. By the time of *De unitate* or shortly thereafter, Pole had developed a heavily evangelical religion that stressed the centrality of faith and human impotence. Called to Rome by Paul III in 1536, Pole rejoined a nebulous group known variously as Italian evangelicals, or *spirituali,* who hoped for a reform of the institutional church and a rapprochement with the Protestants. From the time he joined the commission that produced the *Consilium de emendanda ecclesiae* (1537) until his departure from Rome in 1553, Pole stood very close to the pope, whether Paul III or his successor, Julius III. Paul III protected Pole in numerous ways and recommended him as his successor. Julius III—who succeeded Paul only after a long conclave in which Pole missed election by one vote—gave Pole a large role in the formulation of policy toward secular powers, especially the Holy Roman Empire. Here Pole's good relations with Charles V served him well at first.

Throughout his career in Rome, Pole continued both to lead the *spirituali* and to execute numerous diplomatic missions and legations (especially that of Viterbo, which he held from 1542 to 1546). Until his return to England under Mary, the two most significant episodes in Pole's career came in the aftermath of the Council of Regensburg (1541) and in the first session of the Council of Trent (1546). In the first case Pole refused to support the compromise on justification worked out by his ally Gasparo Contarini, perhaps because Pole held more extreme (possibly Calvinist) views, or as a matter of political calculation, or because of a lifelong habit of retreating in moments of crisis. Whatever his motives, Pole also withdrew from Trent when the same issue came up for debate, leaving the evangelical position without serious defense.

Pole is most famous as the architect of the Marian Counter-Reformation, which he undertook in 1554 after complicated negotiations between Charles, his son Philip, and the queen. As both archbishop of Canterbury and papal legate, Pole enjoyed more authority over the English church than any other prelate since Thomas Wolsey. Pole displayed a curious mixture of adroit maneuvering and stubborn obtuseness, which produced a checkered record of reform. While he could only with difficulty be persuaded to compromise on the score of church lands that had come into lay hands, for example, he could also lead a synod of the clergy that produced reform legislation (especially about the training of clergy) that had a major impact on Tridentine legislation and even more directly, through Pole's ally Niccolò Ormaneto, on Carlo Borromeo. As one of Mary's closest advisers, Pole could have dominated the government, but he chose to concentrate on religious matters and on efforts to make peace on the Continent. Despite the strong backing of the queen, these came to nothing at the conference of Ardres (1555).

In addition to this disappointment, the final years of Pole's life were blighted by the animosity of his erstwhile ally Paul IV (Gian Pietro Carafa). In 1556 Paul revoked Pole's legation and cited him to Rome to face charges of heresy, mainly on justification. With Mary's strong support, Pole resisted Paul's demands, but his position in England was badly crippled, and the difficulties of Mary's finances also hampered much further reforming activity. Nevertheless, Pole continued to try to roll back Protestantism, intervening above all in two famous cases—that of John Cheke (whom he persuaded to recant) and of Thomas Cranmer (with whom he ultimately failed, after early successes). Both cases testify to the power of Pole's personality and perhaps to the impact of his religiosity. It appears that Pole was otherwise not much in favor of the policy of repression that led to the burning of about 300 heretics during Mary's reign.

Throughout his life Pole wrote prolifically. In addition to the four books of *De unitate*, his most important works include two sets of dialogues on the papal office (those written in the conclave of Julius III were published posthumously in 1569 as *De summo pontifice*; the others remain in manuscript); *De concilio* (1562); a huge manuscript dialogue, "De reformatione ecclesiae"; and a large number of letters. The list of Pole's smaller works includes a "Discorso di pace" (1555), intended for Charles and Henry II of France.

BIBLIOGRAPHY

Donaldson, Peter S. *Machiavelli and Mystery of State*. Cambridge, 1989. See "Machiavelli and Antichrist: Prophetic Typology in Reginald Pole's *De unitate* and *Apologia ad Carolum quintum*," pp. 1–36. Develops a new approach to Pole's writings in terms of the personae they presented.

Dunn, Thomas F. "The Development of the Text of Pole's *De unitate ecclesiae*." *Papers of the Bibliographical Society of America* 70 (1976), 455–468. The only study of the text of any of Pole's writings. To be used with care.

Fenlon, Dermot. *Heresy and Obedience in Tridentine Italy: Cardinal Pole and the Counter Reformation*. Cambridge, 1972. Most important study of Pole's religion and politics.

Firpo, Massimo. *Tra alumbrados e "spirituali": Studi su Juan de Valdés e il Valdesianesimo nella crisi religiosa del '500 italiano*. Florence, 1990. One of Firpo's numerous works on the *spirituali*. Makes the first use of Pole's manuscript notes on *Psalms*.

Hallé, Marie [Martin Haile, pseud.]. *The Life of Reginald Pole*. London, 1911. Standard (if hagiographical) life in English.

Phillips, Thomas. *The History of the Life of Reginald Pole*. Oxford, 1764; 2d ed., without Phillips's name, London, 1767. First serious English biography, based mainly on the Latin adaptation of Ludovico Beccadelli's life of Pole (c.1561). It generated much controversy.

Schenk, Wilhelm. *Reginald Pole, Cardinal of England*. London, 1950. Interpretive essay.

Simoncelli, Paolo. *Il caso Reginald Pole. Eresia e santità nelle polemiche religiose del Cinquecento*. Rome, 1977. First important work on Pole historiography, and also an analysis of the politics of the *spirituali*. More controversial on the second head; see especially the work of Gigliola Fragnito.

Tellechea Idigoras, J. Ignacio. *Fray Bartolomé Carranza y el cardenal Pole: Un navarro en la restauracion católica de Inglaterra, 1554–1558*. Pamplona, 1977. Carranza was one of Pole's closest collaborators in England. Based on Tellechea's edition of Carranza's Inquisitorial trial.

Zeeveld, W. Gordon. *Foundations of Tudor Policy*. Reprint, Westport, Conn., 1981. Pioneering work on Pole's household.

Zimmermann, Athanasius. *Kardinal Pole, sein Leben und seine Schriften: Ein Beitrag zur Kirchengeschichte des 16. Jahrhunderts*. Regensburg, 1893. Perhaps the model for Hallé's work.

Thomas F. Mayer

POLISH BRETHREN. The first reports concerning antitrinitarianism reached Poland about 1530. A German, Andreas Fischer, an antitrinitarian from the Low Countries, "Belga Spiritus," and two Poles, Peter Gonesius of Goniadz and Lucas Delfin, were its first adherents. Gonesius supported the teachings of Michael Servetus as early as the synod held in Secemin (northern Minor Poland) in 1556. But these views were generally condemned.

The roots of the movement were threefold: Italian religious rationalism, represented primarily by the views of Servetus, a Spaniard, and Lelio Sozzini; the social ideas of German Anabaptism; and Calvinism, with its independent ecclesiastical organization. After discussions held from 1562 to 1565, the antitrinitarian Minor church separated from the Major church. Most of the Protestant preachers in Minor Poland joined the Minor church, but only a small number of the faithful and the gentry. Only one magnate, a Lithuanian, John Kiszka, a pupil of the Basel freethinkers, belonged to the first generation of the Polish Brethren (Bracia Polscy). The most prominent Arians among the nobility were a Cuiavian, John Niemojewski, and Jerome Filipowski and Stanislas Cikowski, from Minor Poland.

The Polish Brethren movement was initially like a loose association of religious freethinkers. The movement had three dominant dogmatic streams: tritheism, ditheism (Gonesius, Stanislas Farnowski), and Unitarianism (Gregory Paul Zagrobelny [Gregorius Pauli] of Brzeziny, Martin Czechowic), which also included a Judaized Unitarianism. Some of the Arians adhered to Anabaptism, others practiced infant baptism; some believed in the authority of the scriptures, and others were spiritualists. Many Arians of plebeian origin condemned feudal property, serfdom, feudal rent, wars, law courts, and even the authority of the state. The epitome of this view was the community founded in 1569 in Raków in central Minor Poland, which was intended to become a new Jerusalem.

This attempt soon failed. Arianism became a Unitarian and Anabaptist movement. Its social radicalism moderated, and it gravitated toward rationalism. This stemmed especially from the Italians Giorgio Biandrata and Fausto Sozzini and also the indigenous thinker Szymon Budny. Ditheism, which recognized only the Father and Jesus Christ as God, finally died out in the early seventeenth century.

In 1601 a synod in Raków demonstrated the initial success of Socinian Arianism, which was socially moderate but radical in its dogma. It accepted, for instance, the principle that rules and rites were not necessary for redemption and regarded Jesus Christ as a deified human being. The movement established schools and printing houses. About 1620 it achieved its greatest following, and although the Arians made up no more than 1 percent of the total population of the Polish-Lithuanian commonwealth, between 10 and 20 percent of the intellectuals were associated with them. Arians were particularly numerous in the regions of Sandecz, Lublin, and Volhynia. Apart from Poles, Arians could be found among Germans, Ukrainians, Belorussians, Slovaks, and Czechs. Besides undertaking missions abroad, most notably to Altdorf, close contacts were maintained with Unitarians in Transylvania, with the Remonstrants in the Netherlands, and briefly, with the Moscow Judaizers.

In 1638 persecutions of Arians began in the commonwealth. The most eminent men of this generation were Samuel Przypkowski, an Austrian, John Lewis of Wolzogen, and the grandson of Fausto Sozzini, Andrew Wiszowaty, the most distinguished Arian philosopher and the author of *Religio rationalis.* In 1655 a greater part of the Arians stood by the Swedish invaders for politico-religious reasons, and the diet of 1658 ordered their expulsion. Some of them stayed in the country, however, and while formally converting to Catholicism or Protestantism, they remained crypto-Arians. Others left for exile, especially for eastern Prussia, Transylvania, and the Netherlands, where they edited eleven volumes of *Bibliotheca Fratrum Polonorum* as a recapitulation of their teachings. One can assume that these expatriates had died out by the end of the eighteenth century. Nevertheless, during the Enlightenment, the Polish Arians were viewed, especially in England, as the co-originators of Deism and the idea of toleration.

[*See also* Antitrinitarianism *and* Poland.]

BIBLIOGRAPHY

Chmaj, Ludwik. *Bracia polscy.* Warsaw, 1957.

Kot, Stanisław. *Ideologia polityczna i społeczna Braci Polskich zwanych arianami.* Warsaw, 1932. Also available in English translation as *Socinianism in Poland,* Boston, 1957.

Odrodzenie i Reformacja w Polsce. Vol. 1. Warsaw, 1956.

Ogonowski, Zbigniew. *Arianie polscy.* Warsaw, 1952.

Sandius, Christophorus. *Bibliotheca antitrinitariorum* (1684). Facsimile ed. Warsaw, 1967.

Urban, Wacław. *Der Antitrinitarimus in den Böhmischen Ländern und in der Slowakei im 16. und 17. Jahrhundert.* Baden-Baden, 1986.

Wallace, Robert. *Antitrinitarian Biography.* Vols. 1 and 2. London, 1850.

Wilbur, Earl Morse. *A History of Unitarianism, Socinianism and its Antecedents.* Reprint, Boston, 1977.

Williams, George H. *The Radical Reformation.* 3d ed. Saint Louis, 1992.

WACŁAW URBAN

POLITI, Ambrogio Catarino

POLITI, Ambrogio Catarino (Ital., Lancellotto de'; Lat., Ambrosius Catharinus; 1484–1553), Dominican theologian, polemicist, and bishop. Born and raised in Siena in a prominent family, Politi studied philosophy and law, taking the doctorate in canon and civil law. After teaching briefly at Siena, he toured several Italian universities before settling down to teach civil law at Rome. Leo X sent him to Florence in 1515 to examine the works of the Dominican Girolamo Savonarola; the piety of the Dominicans so moved him that he entered the order in 1517 and took the name Ambrosius Catharinus, which his later publications carried. Doubtless because he was an established scholar, he was allowed to teach himself theology without undergoing the traditional Dominican training. By 1520 he was already serving as prior in his native Siena. Although most of his later life was spent in Italy, Politi spent the years 1532 to 1538 and 1539 to 1544 in France, mainly at Paris, Lyon, and Toulouse.

Politi combined a pugnacious personality with great learning and was willing to take on any scholar whom he felt was straying from the true faith. He was among the first Catholics to attack Martin Luther with his *Apologia pro veritate catholicae etapostolicae fidei* (Florence, 1520), in which he attempted to refute Luther's teachings on indulgences, papal primacy, purgatory, and penance. Luther replied with *Ad Librum eximii Magistri Nostri M. Ambrosii Catharini . . . responsio* (Wittenberg, 1521). Politi answered with *Excusatio disputationis contra Martinum Lutherum* (Florence, 1521). These controversies forced Politi to develop his views on original sin, justification, good works, purgatory, predestination, and the veneration of the saints in several short works that he gathered into his *Opuscula* (Lyon, 1542). He returned to the attack against Lutheranism in his *De Consideratione et iudicio praesentium temporum* (Venice, 1547).

Politi was among the first to detect heretical teaching in Italy's most popular preacher, the Capuchin Bernardino Ochino, against whom he published *Speculum haereticorum contra Bernardinum Ochinum* (Rome, 1537). The work was republished in Italian two years after Ochino fled to Protestant lands in 1542. Some of Politi's early works against Luther were also republished in Italian, and he attacked the immensely popular *Il Beneficio di Christo* in his *Compendio d'errori. . .* (Rome, 1544).

Since Politi was largely self-taught as a theologian, his views and style owed much to his humanist training, and his theology of grace freely mixed elements derived from Augustine, Thomas Aquinas, and Duns Scotus. Perhaps because of his eclectic views, Paul III appointed him one of the papal theologians at the Council of Trent, where Politi served from 1545 to 1547. On several points his writings took stances quite independent of traditional Dominican positions. Thus he defended celebrations honoring Mary's Immaculate Conception. His teaching on predestination had similarities with the views that were later developed in greater depth by the Jesuit Luis de Molina. Politi did not hesitate to write against the two most distinguished Dominican theologians of his time, Cardinal Cajetan, former master general of the order (1508–1518), and Domingo de Soto. His work against Cajetan was *Annotationes in excerpta quaedam . . . Cardinalis Cajetani* (Paris, 1535), which also bitterly attacked Erasmus as the fount of later Protestant errors. Politi wrote several works against Soto, including *Defensio catholicorum pro possibili certitudine gratiae* (Venice, 1547) and *Adversus Apologiam D. Soto . . . de praedestinatione* (Venice, 1547). He also engaged in a controversy with Soto over the right interpretation of the articles on justification decreed by the Council of Trent.

Toward the end of his life his writings turned to Scripture, notably a commentary on all the Pauline epistles (Venice, 1551) and a commentary on the first five chapters of *Genesis* (Venice, 1552). His *Claves duas ad aperiendas Scripturas* (Lyon, 1543) developed his understanding of the relation of scripture to Catholic tradition, which soon became a key issue at the Council of Trent. He argues that it would be unsafe if part of revelation were handed down independent of scripture, which contains all revelation and the Church's traditions. Still, the proper interpretation of scripture requires a special gift from the Holy Spirit and does not rest on subjective conviction but must be in line with Church teaching: "The church and scripture have the same authority." People who ignore the church, which possesses the Holy Spirit, and its teaching also ignore the scripture and the Holy Spirit. Politi was a strong supporter of the papacy and enjoyed papal favor even though his book on the Mass was listed on the Index of Prohibited Books. Paul III nominated him bishop of Minori in 1546, and Julius III elevated him to archbishop of Conza in 1552. Both sees were in the kingdom of Naples.

BIBLIOGRAPHY

Bietenholz, Peter, ed. *Contemporaries of Erasmus.* Toronto, 1974. Vol. 3, pp. 105–106. Short sketch.

Benedetto di Mantova. *Il Beneficio da Christo.* Edited by Salvatore Caponetto. DeKalb, Ill., 1972. Reprints Politi's attack on *Il Beneficio di Christo*, pp. 343–422.

Gorce, M.-M. "Politi, Lancelot." In *Dictionnaire de Théologie catholique*, vol. 12, no. 2, pp. 2418–2434. Paris, 1935. Thin on biography but summarizes Politi's doctrine.

Jedin, Hubert. *A History of the Council of Trent.* London, 1961. Vol. 2, passim, for Politi's activity at Trent.

Lauchert, Friedrich. *Die Polemik des Ambrosius Catharinus gegen Bernardino Ochino.* Innsbruck, 1907.

———. *Die italienischen literarischen Gegner Luthers* (Freiburg, 1912). Reprint, Nieuwkoop, 1972.

Schweizer, Joseph. *Ambrosius Catharinus Politus, 1484–1553: Ein Theologe des Reformations zeitalters; Sein Leben und Seine Schriften.* Münster, 1910. This volume is the most detailed study of Ambrogio Catarino Politi's life.

Verzeichnis der im deutschen Sprachbereich erschienenen Drucke des XVI. Jahrhunderts. Stuttgart, 1983–. See vol. 16, nos. 3983–3986.

JOHN PATRICK DONNELLY

POLITICAL THEORY. *See* Magistracy.

POLITIQUES. Since the eighteenth century the Politiques of the French Wars of Religion (1562–1598) have usually been described as moderate advocates of religious toleration and the priority of secular objectives. They have been supposed to constitute a continuous third party between two rival sets of religious enthusiasts, the Huguenots and the members of the Catholic League. Throughout the period of the wars the word *politique* was used pejoratively for those who would tolerate religious diversity for the sake of civil peace. Uncompromising believers accused Politiques of religious hypocrisy, political expediency, and self-interest. Modern historians generally apply the word to three groups who are thought to have pursued identical forward-looking policies. The first includes the queen mother, Catherine de Médicis, and the chancellor, Michel de L'Hôpital, who pursued a policy of temporarily tolerating heresy while rebuilding royal authority in the years 1560–1568. The second comprises a mixed group of Catholic and Protestant lords who plotted and rebelled against the Crown after it had endorsed the massacre of Huguenots in August 1572. The third is made up of supporters of Henry of Navarre, who was to inherit the crown of France in 1589 and after nine years of struggle with the Catholic League and Spain, its ally, was finally to impose peace. Although these groups have little personal continuity, the ideas of the first and of the third are affiliated.

In the 1560s, when the influence of Catherine de Médicis was at its height, L'Hôpital called for the cessation of religious passions and the institution of administrative and judicial reforms. Associated with him and the queen mother in pursuit of these policies were such trusted members of the royal council as Claude de Laubespine, the principal secretary of state, and his brother Sébastien, bishop of Limoges. An agent of the Crown beginning his administrative career at this time was Pomponne de Bellièvre, who was to inherit the mantle of L'Hôpital when Henry IV appointed him chancellor in 1599. In 1561 a colloquy was held at Poissy to bring about a national religious reconciliation, and in the following year the first edict in favor of toleration was issued. Both these politique measures failed, but the peace edicts that punctuated the Wars of Religion until the Edict of Nantes in 1598 reflected their spirit of compromise.

The noble house most commonly associated with the view of the Politiques as a third party is that of Montmorency, traditionally the rivals of the House of Guise, who espoused the ultra-Catholic cause. After the death in 1567 of Anne de Montmorency, the constable of France, the most powerful members of the family were his sons François de Montmorency and Henri de Damville, who were respectively governors of Îsle-de-France (including Paris) and Languedoc. Early in 1573, some six months after the Saint Bartholomew's Day Massacre, a number of disaffected nobles in the royal army besieging the Huguenot bastion of La Rochelle began a series of discussions culminating in a conspiracy against Charles IX in March of the following year. The Montmorency were included, and their figurehead was the duke of Alençon, the king's youngest brother. At this time the Catholic Damville was in open alliance with the Huguenots in the south. Early in the reign of the next Valois king, Henry III, Alençon linked the Montmorency with the Huguenot lords and their German mercenary allies in an open war against the Crown. At the Peace of Monsieur (1576) Alençon gained the appanage of Anjou and the Huguenots the most favorable terms they ever acquired. To the first Catholic League, formed in protest against this settlement, this was indeed a "politique" peace, but the leaders of Alençon's coalition were not Politiques in the modern sense. They were guided by self-interest and deserved the contemporary title applied to them of "malcontents." One fortuitous circumstance that associated the coalitions of 1573–1576 with more positive Politique concepts was the fact that within Alençon-Anjou's retinue was Jean Bodin, whose *Methodus ad facilem historiarum cognitionem* (Method for the Easy Comprehension of History; 1566) reflected L'Hôpital's thinking, and whose *Six Libres de la république* (Six Books of the Commonwealth; 1576) presented a secular statement of royal authority against both noble faction and the Huguenot justification of resistance.

When Alençon-Anjou died in 1584, Huguenots as well as moderate Catholics came to the defense of the right of the Protestant Henry of Navarre to be acknowledged as heir to the throne. The Catholic League revived in its most militant form to oppose this pretension. Even in the previous phases of the wars there were Huguenots, such as the military memorialist François de la Noue and the magistrate Innocent Gentillet, whose royalism deserved their classification as Politiques in the positive sense. Now some of the foremost advocates of Huguenot resistance theory published Politique propaganda. Philippe Duplessis-Mornay expounded the sanctity of monarchy by divine right, while François Hotman denounced the pope's bull excommunicating and deposing Henry of Navarre. Both writers appealed to Gallican sentiment supporting the independence of the French Catholic church against the ultramontane sympathies of the Catholic League. Defense of the Salic law of succession, by which Navarre was heir presumptive, was given priority over the religious considerations dominating leaguer propaganda. In this way positive Politique tenets prepared the way for the ideology of monarchical absolutism. These included Bodinian legislative sovereignty, the divine right of kings, and royal administrative control of the Gallican church. The most eloquent exponent of these doctrines was a Catholic Jurist from Toulouse named Pierre de Belloy, who composed *Apologie catholique* (A Catholic Apology; 1585) and *De l'authorité du Roy* (On the Authority of the King; 1587). In the next decade the idea of reason of state, whereby morality could be set aside in the interest of the commonwealth, also became explicit in some Politique thinking.

After the assassination of Henry III in 1589, Navarre relied on Politique support in his fight to establish his authority as Henry IV. National sentiment became an increasingly important element in the positive Politique cause as the Catholic League became increasingly dependent on Madrid and Rome. Even that branch of the parlement that remained in Paris felt the pull of patriotic tradition when it defended the Salic law to prevent the choice of a Spanish princess as queen of France. It was at this time (1593) that Henry IV chose to convert to Catholicism, an act that enabled the triumph of Politique thinking in the positive sense but one branded by leaguer extremists as the ultimate in Politique perfidy in the pejorative meaning of the word.

[*See also* Catholic League; Gallicanism; Henry III of France; Henry IV of France; Huguenots; Montmorency, House of; *and* Wars of Religion.]

BIBLIOGRAPHY

Beame, Edmond M. "The Politiques and the Historians." *Journal of the History of Ideas* 54 (1993), 355–379. A revisionist account of the traditional treatment of the subject.

Bettinson, Christopher. "The Politiques and the Politique Party: A Reappraisal." In *From Valois to Bourbon: Dynasty, State and Society in Early Modern France*, edited by Keith Cameron, pp. 35–49. Exeter, 1989. Another revisionist account.

Decrue, Francis. *Le parti des politiques au lendemain de la Saint-Barthélemy*. Paris, 1892. Deals mainly with the malcontents after the Saint Bartholomew's Day Massacre. Asserts continuity of politique sentiment throughout the wars.

Diefendorf, Barbara. *Beneath the Cross: Catholics and Huguenots in Sixteenth-Century Paris*. Oxford, 1991.

Greengrass, Mark. *France in the Age of Henri IV: The Struggle for Stability*. London, 1984.

Holt, Mack P. *The Duke of Anjou and the Politique Struggle during the Wars of Religion*. Cambridge, 1986.

Salmon, J. H. M. *Society in Crisis: France in the Sixteenth Century*. Rev. ed. London, 1979.

Sutherland, N. M. *The Huguenot Struggle for Recognition*. New Haven, 1980.

J. H. M. SALMON

POLITY. *See* Magistracy.

POLYGAMY. The Reformation called into question the elaborate regulations for monogamous marriage established by canon law and seemingly handed marriage over to civil law and temporal government, informed by scripture. According to Luther: "Marriage is an external, worldly thing like clothes, food and shelter"; that marriages between Christians and non-Christians were invalid was a mere papal invention. In 1539–1540 Luther and other Wittenberg theologians gave conditional approval to the bigamy of Philipp of Hesse, citing the precedent of Old Testament concubinage, as they had done earlier when Henry VIII was seeking to free himself from his marriage to Catherine of Aragon. A loosening of marital restrictions, partly justified by the Old Testament, was a blessing that major reformers could extend to sympathetic princes.

Charges of marital irregularities against nonconformist Anabaptists were circulated as early as 1526 by Zwingli and appeared soon afterward in Swiss and south German chronicles. The accusation was that the Anabaptists "held everything in common, including women." In fact, neither "community of women" nor polygamy was practiced or defended by Anabaptists before they assumed power in Münster. But various sexual irregularities, perhaps based on antinomian beliefs, did occur in St. Gall in 1526, where notions of "spiritual marriage" were current. The reality behind the "spiritual marriages" was often the unwillingness of a spouse to adopt Anabaptism. Both the Zollikon Anabaptist Jakob Hottinger and Hans Hut's prominent lieutenant Jorg Volk became practicing bigamists when their wives refused the new baptism. Although the Hutterites in Moravia never went beyond condoning separation from an unbelieving spouse, ample evidence indicates that some Anabaptist refugees in Moravia remarried in the lifetime of their former spouses without formal divorce.

Polygamy in Münster occurred against the background of a massive Anabaptist migration to Münster (about 2,500) and a comparable expulsion of non-Anabaptists (about 2,000) from Münster as the town came under siege. Many non-Anabaptist men left Münster, but their wives often stayed behind to secure the family property; subsequently these wives were forcibly inducted into Anabaptism. The migration of Anabaptists to Münster separated many husbands and wives, often but not always on religious grounds. The wife of John of Leiden was, for instance, an Anabaptist, but she did not accompany him to Münster.

The decision to introduce polygamous marriage in Münster originated with John of Leiden, the town's leading prophet, in July 1534. He needed a week to convince the Anabaptist preachers, on the basis of his exegesis of *Genesis* 1:28: the command that Adam and Eve should be fruitful and multiply and replenish the earth. The Münsterites stressed the significance of the male seed in procreation, eclipsing the maternal function just as their christological doctrine reduced Mary to a mere vessel of the heavenly flesh injected into her by the Father. Reformation teachers held, to a man, that continence was a special gift of God, but one almost never bestowed. Since Christians generally held that the sex act could be justified only by the aim of procreation, it was a grave sin for men to waste their seed on barren women or women otherwise unable to conceive, as they might do in a monogamous marriage. Hence Bernhard Rothmann, the Münsterite spokesman, concluded: "The freedom of the man in marriage is that he can have more than one wife at the same time." Women had no corresponding freedom; indeed, a woman was executed in Anabaptist Münster for proposing polyandry.

The proportion of men to women in Münster was roughly 2,000:5,000; in addition to this great preponderance of women a large number of married persons were separated from their spouses. The object of polygamy was certainly at least partially social control: the potentially explosive relations between the sexes needed to be regulated, and the women, who made an essential, largely noncombatant contribution to the defense of the besieged town, needed to be officered. Rothmann defended Münster polygamy not as the liberation of women but as the triumph of patriarchy: "God wants to create something new on earth, the men shall no longer be to women [effeminate] . . . so here among us he put all women in obedience to men, so that all of them, young and old, must let themselves be ruled by men according to God's word." The immediate response to the introduction of polygamy was an uprising of Münster citizens that came close to destroying the Anabaptist realm from within. Women were imprisoned and some executed for resistance to the polygamous order. Divorce was eventually permitted primarily as a concession to women. Given the explanation of polygamy by Rothmann and the description of its effects in the eyewitness account of Heinrich Gresbeck, it seems implausible to interpret its meaning for the women who lived under it as potentially liberating. The women who lived in Anabaptist Münster were indeed indispensable to its resistance of sixteen months, and many of them were no doubt dedicated to their cause, but they were also its chief victims.

Polygamy was defended at the Bocholt meeting of the Melchiorite factions in August 1536. It was one of the chief subjects of controversy at Bocholt, and the Münster Anabaptists who had taken refuge in Oldenburg upheld it tenaciously. Likewise the Batenburger terrorists in the Netherlands, who split from allegiance to Münster in April 1535, continued to practice polygamy. When large numbers of former Batenburgers accepted David Joris as a messianic prophet in 1538, polygamy entered his following. Although David's teachings on sexuality often developed ideas of Rothmann, the Davidites did not advocate polygamy and their leaders did not practice it. As the leader of the other Melchiorite successor group, Menno Simons regarded any accommodation to Münsterite polygamy as the mark distinguishing the "corrupt sects" from the Christian covenanters. He did, however, continue to uphold Melchior Hoffman's Christology, buttressing it with traditional Aristotelian embryology according to which the male seed determined the character of the offspring. Against the Mennonites the Belgian Calvinist Guy de Brès advocated a Galenic embryology that assigned more importance to women in their children's biological inheritance and more importance to the Virgin in the Virgin Birth. Hence the misogyny of Münsterite polygamy experienced a continuing half-life in the embryological arguments with which Menno defended the Christology that he shared with Münster.

[*See also* Marriage.]

BIBLIOGRAPHY

Brendler, Gerhard. *Das Täuferreich zu Münster, 1534–1535.* Berlin, 1966. A chapter discusses polygamy and regards its accompanying free choice of marriage partner and right of divorce as a revolutionary anticipation of bourgeois society. Brendler holds that women's right of divorce in Münster was "a step towards the emancipation of women."

Dülmen, Richard van, ed. *Das Täuferreich zu Münster, 1534–1535.* Munich, 1974. Anthology of source readings in modern German about Münster Anabaptism.

———. *Reformation als Revolution: Soziale Bewegung und religiöser Radikalismus in der deutschen Reformation.* Rev. ed. Frankfurt a.M., 1987. The treatment of Münster Anabaptism, based on recent scholarship, is a valuable section of an otherwise flawed book.

Hennig, Matthias. "Askese und Ausschweifung: Zum Verständnis der Vielweiberei im Täuferreich zu Münster 1534–1535." *Mennonitische Geschichtsblätter* 40 (1983), 25–45. An interpretation with psychological elements, holding that the Anabaptists tried to realize medieval ascetic goals, and that in Münster repressed sexual energies were released through polygamy.

Irwin, Joyce. "Embryology and the Incarnation: A Sixteenth Century Debate." *The Sixteenth Century Journal* 9.3 (1978), 93–104. Points to the applications and misapplications of the classical embryologies of Aristotle and Galen in christological debates of the Reformation era.

Scribner, Robert. "Konkrete Utopien. Die Täufer und der vormoderne Kommunismus." *Mennonitische Geschichtsblätter* 50 (1993), 7–46. Devotes a special section to accusations of sexual irregularities and "community of women" against the Anabaptists.

Stayer, James M. "Vielweiberei als 'innerweltliche Askese': Neue Eheauffassungen in der Reformationszeit." *Mennonitische Geschichtsblätter* 37 (1980), 24–41. Concentrates on the apologetics of Münsterite polygamy, which are put in the context of the Reformation radicals' preoccupation with *1 Cor.* 7:29 and the widespread misogyny of the period.

JAMES M. STAYER

PONCE DE LA FUENTE, Constantino (1502–1559),

Spanish theologian, preacher, and reformer, onetime courtier to Charles V and Philip II. Of partial Jewish *Converso* ancestry, Constantino studied at the University of Alcalá, from 1524 to 1532; while there he was strongly influenced by Erasmian ideals, not only in his scholarship and piety, but also in his sense of humor and his sarcasm. Like Erasmus, Constantino delighted in unmasking hypocrisy and shallowness in religion and often reserved his sharpest barbs for the regular clergy. Well versed in theology and scripture and proficient in the biblical languages, he left Alcalá to finish his studies at the University of Seville in 1534. After his ordination into the priesthood at Seville in 1535, Constantino was appointed preacher at its cathedral and soon gained renown for his learning, humor, and eloquence, attracting so many people to his sermons that they would begin to fill the church hours before dawn. He also authored several books, including *Suma de la doctrina cristiana* (1543), *Catecismo cristiano para los niños* (1547), *Confesión de un pecador* (1547), and *Doctrina cristiana* (1548), in which he promoted an Erasmian type of devotion focused on Christ and the inner life of the spirit rather than on external observances.

Emperor Charles V requested his services as a preacher; in 1548–1550 he journeyed with the court throughout the Low Countries and Germany, and once again in 1553–1555. Upon returning to Seville, he resumed preaching at the cathedral, writing, and teaching scripture at an orphanage. In addition to associating with a reformist circle that would later form the nucleus of Seville's "Lutheran" community, he also became an ardent opponent of the Society of Jesus and used his pulpit to attack and ridicule them. In 1556, soon after he was awarded a hotly contested appointment as cathedral canon, Constantino found himself suspected of heresy by the Inquisition, particularly for his teachings on justification, which stressed faith in Christ rather than in one's own merits. After his first brush with the inquisitors, he expressed confidence in his own Erasmian ambiguities by joking that he would always be as green firewood for the flames of the Holy Office. Perhaps as a means of deflecting suspicion, he surprised the Jesuits by repenting of his animosity toward them and asking for membership in their order. Rejected by them, he was arrested and jailed by the Inquisition in August 1558. Though at first he denied having written some openly heretical manuscripts found among his possessions, he later owned up to it and died in prison while awaiting sentence. He was condemned as a heretic, and his books were placed on the Index of Prohibited Books in 1559; his remains and his effigy were burnt at an auto da fe in 1560.

While Constantino's detractors in Spain reviled him, exposing him as a bigamist and Nicodemite who committed suicide, Jean Crespin praised him in the *Histoire des Martyrs* (1564), ensuring him a place of honor in Protestant history. Always ready to critique, yet never ready to publicly cross the line into overt heresy, the very embodiment of the complex history of Spanish Erasmianism and religious dissent, Constantino remains an enigmatic figure.

BIBLIOGRAPHY

Aspe Ansa, M. P. *Constantino Ponce de la Fuente: El hombre y su lenguaje.* Madrid, 1975.

Bataillon, Marcel. *Erasme et l'Espagne.* 3rd ed. Geneva, 1991. A concise analysis of Constantino Ponce de la Fuente in the context of Erasmianism and Protestantism in Spain; see vol. 1, especially pp. 555–579, 750–761.

Boehmer, Eduard. *Spanish Reformers of Two Centuries, 1873–1902.* Reprint, New York, 1971. See vol. 2, pp. 3–40.

Guerrero, J. R. *Catecismos españoles del siglo xvi: La obra catequética del Dr. Constant Ponce de la Fuente.* Madrid, 1969.

Jones, William Burwell. *Constantino Ponce de la Fuente: The Problem of Protestant Influence in Sixteenth Century Spain.* Ph.D. diss. 1965.

Schäfer, Ernst. *Sevilla und Valladolid, die evangelischen Gemeinden Spaniens im Reformationszeitalter.* Schriften des Vereins für Reformationsgeschichte, no. 78. Halle, 1903.

Wagner, Klaus. *El Doctor Constantino Ponce de la Fuente: El hombre y su biblioteca.* Seville, 1979.

CARLOS M. N. EIRE

PONET, John (1516?–1556), bishop of Winchester, English reformer and political theorist. Educated at Cambridge, where he was a pupil of the humanist scholar Sir Thomas Smith, Ponet studied Greek and developed an interest in mathematics and astronomy. He advanced his career in the church through ties with Thomas Cromwell, chief minister of Henry VIII, and Thomas Cranmer, archbishop of Canterbury, whose chaplain he became. Ponet made his greatest contribution to the Protestant Reformation during the reign of Edward VI (1547–1553), when he was appointed to the episcopal bench as bishop of Rochester (1550–1551) and bishop of Winchester (1551–1553). Ponet supported efforts to legalize clerical marriage with a vigorous polemical work, *Defence for Marriage of Priestes. . .* (1549). Preaching at Paul's Cross in London, he expounded reformed teaching on the Eucharist in *A Notable Sermon Concerning the Ryght Use of the Lordes Supper. . .* (1550).

Ponet's catechism, published in Latin and English in 1553, is a testimonial to his commitment to Christian education and articulates his views on the great issues of the day. Written as a dialogue between a master and a scholar, the catechism defined the church as a congregation of all who "truly fear, honor and call upon God, wholly applying their mind to holy and godly living." Such individuals were "forechosen, predestinate, and appointed" before the world was created. That Ponet was an activist as well as an intellectual may be seen in his participation in Wyatt's Rebellion in 1554. After the defeat of the rebels by forces loyal to Mary Tudor, Ponet fled into exile, where he produced his great political work, *A Shorte Treatise of Politike Power. . .* (Strasbourg, 1556; reprinted 1639 and 1642). The *Shorte Treatise* is traditionally interpreted as a work advocating limited monarchy and tyrannicide and as such exercised a powerful influence on Puritanism and the political thought of the early seventeenth century.

BIBLIOGRAPHY

Allen, J. W. *A History of Political Thought in the Sixteenth Century.* London, 1928.

Beer, Barrett L. "John Ponet's *Shorte Treatise of Politike Power* Reassessed." *Sixteenth Century Journal* 21.3 (1990), 373–383. Challenges traditional interpretation and suggests that as a consequence of the collapse of Protestantism, Ponet lost faith in mankind and political institutions.

———. "Episcopacy and Reform in Mid-Tudor England." *Albion* 23.2 (1991), 231–252. A study of Ponet and seven other episcopal reformers.

Garrett, Christina H. *The Marian Exiles.* Cambridge, 1938. The major work on the Edwardian Protestant exiles.

Hudson, Winthrop S. *John Ponet, 1516?–1556: Advocate of Limited Monarchy.* Chicago, 1942. The only book-length study of Ponet and the most important work on the subject.

Verzeichnis der im deutschen Sprachbereich erschienenen Drucke des XVI. Jahrhunderts. Stuttgart, 1983–. See vol. 16, nos. 4182–4186.

BARRETT L. BEER

POOR LAWS. *See* Begging; Social Welfare.

POPES. *See* Papacy.

POPULAR RELIGION. [*To consider popular beliefs and practices as they differed from official religion in sixteenth-century Europe, this entry comprises nine articles:*

An Overview
Popular Religion in Germany
Popular Religion in France
Popular Religion in England and Scotland
Popular Religion in Italy
Popular Religion in Spain
Popular Religion in Portugal
Popular Religion in the Low Countries
Popular Religion in Scandinavia

The first provides an overview of the historiographical and methodological problems associated with the study of popular religion and with the term itself, discusses those practices that were common throughout Europe, and considers the impact of both Protestant and Roman Catholic reform. The companion articles focus on popular beliefs and practices that were peculiar to the geographical regions of Europe in the sixteenth century and the effects of reform on them.]

An Overview

The writing of religious history, no less than that of social, political, or cultural history, has been affected by the movement, beginning in the late twentieth century, for history "from below"—in the double sense of the history of the lives of ordinary people and of history seen from their point of view. The interest of "ecclesiastical historians," as they used to call themselves, has shifted from institutional history to the history of religious practice and from the history of theology to that of "piety" (in the sense of mentalities, values, and sentiments). Although not exactly discovering popular religion—which has in fact a lengthy historiography, especially in Germany where popular piety and religion have long been objects of extensive scholarly attention—they have begun to take it seriously instead of dismissing it as had some of their predecessors; they have given it a central rather than a marginal place in the history of religious movements, including the Reformation.

Problems of Definition. As in other fields, it has proved easier to identify specific areas for research that earlier historians neglected than it has to offer a general definition of the "popular." Like other binary models, the one contrasting the "elite" with the "people" is an oversimplification. The fact that some sixteenth-century writers themselves used this model (as in the case of the description of "the blind devotion of the people" by John Hooker of Exeter) is not sufficient cause to guarantee its reliability.

Perhaps the most obvious approach to the problem is to define popular religion as the religion of the laity as opposed to that of the clergy. If the concept of "non-clerical religion" is used, however, there is a risk of ignoring variations within each of the two groups as well as similarities between them. Thus, one might lump together as clerics scholars who knew Latin and villagers who could not read or write, and Catholic villagers might themselves be separated from their parish priests, who—before the Council of Trent and in some places until 1600 or even later—were scarcely distinguishable from their lay neighbors in education or attitudes.

A second possibility is to define popular religion in terms of unofficial beliefs and practices as opposed to those sanctioned or recommended by the religious authorities—or, in other words, by what actually happened as opposed to what was officially supposed to happen. In this case too there are risks involved, notably that of confusing the distinction between precept and practice with that between clergy and laity (or elites and people) and so of assuming that the religion of ordinary people is necessarily unorthodox. A third approach to the problem is to define popular religion as the religion of "the popular classes," the "subordinate classes," or—since the proper use of the term *class* has become controversial among historians—"subordinate groups." The use of the term *groups* in the plural at least avoids any hasty homogenization of the beliefs and practices of men and women or of townspeople and villagers. All the same, the danger remains of translating social distinctions too easily into religious ones and of assuming that the devotion of, say, a weaver's wife was essentially different from that of a noblewoman, despite the fact that they might, in Venice, for example, be members of the same religious association.

No wonder then that some historians, such as William Christian, have abandoned the term *popular religion* altogether, preferring to speak, in his case, of *Local Religion in Sixteenth-Century Spain.* All they have done, however, is to abandon one binary model for another, contrasting the "local" (implicitly or explicitly) with the "central," as if social distinctions were not as relevant to religious practice as geographical ones. The moral of this story seems to be that whether they opt for the local/central model or for that distinguishing the elite from the people, historians need to be aware that they are condemned to simplify the world they study in the course of giving a coherent account of it.

A final problem of definition concerns popular Christianity. The French historian Jean Delumeau has argued that the beliefs of ordinary Europeans in 1500 were pagan rather than Christian and that a process of "christianization" took place between the time of Martin Luther and that of Voltaire, when "dechristianization" became visible. This is, of course, to view the attitudes of ordinary people—including the majority of parish priests—from the point of view of the clerical elite of the day, who also used the term *pagan.* The alternative would be to define Christianity in terms of what people calling themselves Christians actually believe and practice. By this criterion ordinary people were indeed Christian in 1500. Their religion may well have included elements surviving from pre-Christian times, but they identified themselves as Christians.

Problems of Sources. The problems of defining popular religion are equaled by the problems of interpreting the sources, which are for the most part condemnations by the learned of what they regard as the false or silly beliefs of "the people." Johan Huizinga's celebrated description of the pious imagery and symbolism of the late Middle Ages is flawed by the author's uncritical acceptance of the critique of popular beliefs as an exterior, "mechanical" religion to be found in the writings of such reformers as Desiderius Erasmus, Luther, and John Calvin. The historian cannot simply bracket the critique of such writers while accepting their descriptions. Thomas More, for example, claimed to have heard two pilgrims disputing over the relative merits of Our Lady of Ipswich and Our Lady of Walsingham as if they were different people, but can we trust his statement? In the first place, "Our Lady" is a topos, recurrent in many places and times with different names of shrines inserted. In the second place, one cannot afford to forget that More was an imaginative satirical writer.

It is not easy to find records of the voices of ordinary people, and when they are found, as in the case of the registers of interrogations by the Inquisition, the circumstances are so unusual and so terrifying to the accused that the testimony may be distorted. In the case of late medieval heretics, such as the Waldensians (as Euan Cameron has reminded us), the evidence is doubly distorted, overlaid not only by the prejudices of the inquisitors but also by those of the Protestants who saw the Waldensians as their forerunners. Even when the testimony is not distorted, it may be difficult for us to interpret, as in the case of the Englishman on his deathbed being questioned by a minister in the early seventeenth century: "Being demanded what he thought of God, he answers that he was a good old man." Similar problems are raised by the records of blasphemers brought before the Inquisition in various parts of Spain and Italy, because they were heard to say "I deny God" (*reniego en Dios*) or some such phrase. If expressions like these slip out in a moment of anger, are they a clue to the individual's private thoughts, or, on the contrary, is it the inquisitors who blaspheme, precisely because they assume the power of sacred words?

In their attempts to listen to the silent majority, historians of popular religion have been making an increasingly intensive and quantitative study of wills, with the hope that in the expectation that death is near the ordinary testator will reveal something of his or her fundamental values. Sixteenth-century wills have certainly survived in large quantities. The problem of using them to write about religion lies in the fact that wills were drawn up by professional notaries according to set formulas. For this reason wills tell us little about the religious beliefs of individual testators. On the other hand, changes in notarial formulas over the long term probably follow cultural trends and so reveal them to modern historians. In addition, wills often refer to the testator's membership in religious fraternities and so of his or her tastes in piety.

The Protestants and the People. As historians have begun to emphasize, Protestant reformers were much concerned with reaching the people and with freeing them from what they regarded as the "idolatry" and "superstition" encouraged by the Catholic church. Luther, who liked to call attention to his popular origins, was concerned with what he called "the common man." He translated the Bible into the vernacular and wrote many works in German so that his ideas would not be confined to the circle of readers of Latin. Books, however, were expensive and too long for people who were only marginally literate, so it is likely that shorter, cheaper pamphlets reached a wider readership. The abundant pamphlet literature of the German Reformation has been studied as a "mass medium," notably in a collective project headed by H. J. Köhler at the University of Tübingen. Other historians are skeptical of this view of pamphlets, since the majority of German people could not read at all at this time. Robert Scribner, for example, has noted that Luther supported the broadcasting of his message by means of images—such as the woodcuts of the Cranach family—"above all," in Luther's words, "for the sake of children and the simple folk, who are more easily moved by pictures and images to recall divine history than through mere words or doctrines." Scribner agrees with Luther about the centrality of the image in late medieval popular piety.

In the late twentieth century it is the German situation that has been studied most intensively, but the problems discussed in the last paragraph were not, of course, confined to the German-speaking world. In France, for instance, there was an abundant pamphlet literature, especially during the Wars of Religion. Netherlanders were also great consumers of pamphlets.

For a student of the Reformation, the most important question to ask about these media is also the most difficult one—the question of reception. How did ordinary people interpret the messages beamed at them by Luther, Huldrych Zwingli, Calvin, and their followers, whether in sermons, prints, or pamphlets? What difference did their understanding of these messages make to their beliefs and their daily life? Was there a clean break with the religious past?

In one sense there was such a break: the institutional structure of the Catholic church was demolished relatively quickly, religious images smashed or at any rate removed from churches, and traditional rituals abandoned. The more positive side of the Reformation, the conversion of ordinary people to Protestantism, took more time. In other words, the middle to late sixteenth century may be seen as a kind of vacuum, an awkward period of transition between two religious cultures.

A number of historians—among them Gerald Strauss, Robert Kingdon, and Scribner—agree in emphasizing the survival of some traditional Catholic practices in Protestant communities during this period, including Saxony in the late sixteenth century and even Geneva itself in Calvin's day. In the Dutch Republic too, Calvinist synods still found it necessary to denounce divination and other popular practices in 1600 and even later. The "magic of the medieval church" does not seem to have lost its appeal, even for people who at the conscious level mocked the beliefs and ceremonies of the "Papists," from transubstantiation to purgatory. Luther may have told his listeners not to worship saints, but this did not stop him from being turned into a saint by his followers and even represented with a halo. In any case, the creation of a new popular culture in Protestant Europe seems to have been the achievement of the seventeenth century rather than the sixteenth, built on the spread of literacy.

Popular Catholicism. Among the most influential accounts of late medieval popular Catholicism are those that present it as a system of beliefs and rituals of which the main function was the inducement of security or relief from anxiety. Saints were regarded as powerful protectors, many of them with specific functions. Saint Sebastian and Saint Roch offered protection against the plague, Saint Margaret against the dangers of childbirth, Saint Blaise against sore throats, Saint Augustine against bad eyes (in German, *Augenkrankheit*), and so on, while the Virgin Mary was regarded as a "general practitioner." "Patron saints" of cities, guilds, or individuals looked after the safety and the interests of their clients, who sometimes addressed them as if they were godparents. In cases of emergency, such as epidemics, famines, wars, and individual accidents, collective processions would take place and individual vows would be made—to go on pilgrimage to a particular shrine, to light candles, to commission a painted *ex voto*, or to offer gifts, such as a silver hand or foot, in return for a cure of that part of the body. This security system generated anxieties of its own. The saints required propitiation with offerings and if angry might punish their lukewarm devotees.

This explanation of popular religion in terms of the need for reassurance and protection is surely too reductionist, and it seems to be a historiographic legacy of the reformers' complaint that people prayed only for material benefits. In a general description of popular Catholicism, it may be wiser to place the emphasis on the public, collective nature of devotion; the importance of festivals; the expectation of miracles; and finally the ubiquity of the sacred and popular familiarity with it. This familiarity has impressed historians, as well as the sixteenth-century reformers who tried to encourage or impose a more decorous behavior and a more acute sense of the distinction between sacred and profane times, places, people, and actions.

In both the Catholic and Protestant worlds, ordinary people found themselves the objects of a campaign to change their beliefs and practices (or as Jean Delumeau would say, to "christianize" them), especially in the second half of the century. It was relatively easy to teach people to hate the Protestants; the local massacres of Huguenots in France during the Wars of Religion are eloquent testimony of this facility. Some people believed that Protestants (like witches and Jews) sucked the blood of babies and engaged in sexual orgies. They defined themselves in opposition to the Protestants, as the Protestants defined themselves in opposition to the Catholics.

Spreading theological knowledge, on the other hand, was rather more difficult. The seminaries that were supposed to educate the parish clergy took a long time to found and to fund. Meanwhile, the Italian schools of Christian doctrine were set up to teach children the rudiments of the faith on Sundays and holidays. Originally a lay initiative, they were eventually taken over by the clergy. In the southern Netherlands, Sunday schools of a similar type were founded at Lille (1584), Valenciennes (1584), and elsewhere. Catechisms, such as those written by the Jesuits Peter Canisius (1555) and Roberto Bellarmino (1597), were printed in large numbers and in various languages in order to assist this kind of religious instruction.

Most difficult of all was persuading the people to give up what they had held sacred, including unorthodox images and unofficial rituals. The Catholic clergy were themselves divided on this issue; some were more concerned with rooting out what they called "abuses," while others preferred the church to "accommodate" itself to popular beliefs in order not to lose the loyalty of the faithful.

As in the case of the Protestant Reformation, the problem for historians has been to decide how far this campaign of reform was effective. In the late twentieth century historians of Catholicism have tended to suggest that its effectiveness was great. For example, a study of the archbishopric of Toledo based on the records of the Inquisition has shown that the percentage of people interrogated who were able to recite the *Ave Maria*, the *Pater Noster* and the *Credo* doubled in the years 1555–1575. Even if this trend were a general one, however, it would not follow that popular belief or practice changed in essentials. It is more likely that the Catholic Reformation was a process at least as long drawn out as the Protestant one, and probably, given the tendency toward "accommodation," even more protracted.

The Interaction of Popular Religions. In the 1980s Natalie Davis urged historians of sixteenth-century religion to adopt a more comparative approach—that is, to examine what the Catholic, Protestant, and Jewish cultures had in common and how each was diversified according to class, gender, and region. The value of comparing developments within popular Catholicism and Protestantism has become more or less accepted, and subsequent work on the rise of "social discipline" in the second half of the sixteenth century makes the parallels seem even closer than before. On the other hand, only a few scholars have yet extended their analyses to the worlds of Eastern Orthodoxy and Judaism, let alone to that of Islam. It has been argued that the hostility toward popular entertainments expressed by Archpriest Avvakum in mid-seventeenth-century Russia is not unlike that expressed by many Catholic and Protestant clergy at the same time. Again, Jewish beliefs and practices should not be confined to a kind of cultural ghetto. Actually, ghettos were established in Italy only in the course of the sixteenth century (in Rome in 1555, for example, and in Florence in 1571), and in any case their inhabitants spent much of the day outside. It would have been odd if their religion had not been affected by the cultural changes taking place around them, and some historians have offered concrete examples of this. Thomas Cohen, for instance, has pointed out that the Catholic Carnival influenced its Jewish equivalent, Purim, in sixteenth-century Rome, while Elliott Horowitz has noted common trends, such as the "reform of popular culture," among Jews and Christians alike. In the case of Islam, accounts written by sixteenth-century travelers suggest a considerable amount of cultural exchange on the borders between the Habsburg and Ottoman empires, with Muslims frequenting Catholic shrines and vice versa. The comparisons between Calvinism and Islam, often made for polemical purposes in the sixteenth century, ought not to be dismissed but rather examined more coolly and in greater depth. Muslim and Christian "puritanism" have something in common, for example. Again, while looking at the abstract or floral decoration on a pulpit in a Calvinist temple in Transylvania, for example, it is difficult not to be struck by parallels to the decoration of mosques not so many hundreds of miles away. Comparative approaches of this kind are likely to be a continuing concern for scholars.

[*See also* Alchemy; Astrology; Carnival; Devotional Practices; Festivals; Flagellants; Iconoclasm; Magic; Mariology; Miracles; Pilgrimages; Possession and Exorcism; Prodigies and Portents; Religious Riots; Sacramentals; Saints, *article on* Cult of Saints; Social Discipline; *and* Witchcraft.]

BIBLIOGRAPHY

Abray, Lorna Jane. *The People's Reformation: Magistrates, Clergy and Commons in Strasbourg, 1500–1598.* Ithaca, N.Y., 1985.

Benedict, Philip. "The Catholic Response to Protestantism: Church Activity and Popular Piety in Rouen, 1560–1600." In *Religion and the People, 800–1700*, edited by James Obelkevich, pp. 168–190. Chapel Hill, N.C., 1979.

Blickle, Peter, and Johannes Kunisch. *Kommunalisieruung und Christianisierung: Voraussetzungen und Folgen der Reformation.* Baden, 1989.

Bossy, John. "The Counter-Reformation and the People of Catholic Europe." *Past and Present* 47 (1970), 51–70.

Burke, Peter. *Popular Culture in Early Modern Europe.* New York, 1978. A general survey.

———. "Popular Piety." In *Catholicism in Early Modern History: A Guide to Research*, edited by John W. O'Malley, pp. 113–132. Saint Louis, 1988. Focuses on historiography.

Cameron, Euan. *The Reformation of the Heretics: The Waldenses of the Alps, 1480–1580.* Oxford, 1984; corr. ed., 1986. A perspective study by an author unusually conscious of the treacherous nature of the sources.

Christian, William A., Jr. *Local Religion in Sixteenth-Century Spain.* Reprint, Princeton, 1989. An anthropological approach that deliberately avoids the term *popular.*

Collinson, Patrick. *The Birthpangs of Protestant England.* Reprint, London, 1991.

Davis, Natalie Zemon. "Some Tasks and Themes in the Study of Popular Religion." In *The Pursuit of Holiness in Late Medieval and Renaissance Religion*, edited by Charles Trinkhaus and Heiko A. Oberman, pp. 307–336. Leiden, 1974.

———. *Society and Culture in Early Modern France.* Stanford, Calif., 1975. Collected essays with much to say about Catholicism and Calvinism.

———. "From Popular Religion to Religious Cultures." In *Reformation Europe: A Guide to Research*, edited by Steven Ozment, pp. 321–336. Saint Louis, 1982. Discusses conceptual and methodological problems.

Delumeau, Jean. *Catholicism between Luther and Voltaire.* Philadelphia, 1977. Helped launch the debate on "christianization" and "de-christianization."

Frijhoff, Willem. "Official and Popular Religion in Christianity." In *Official and Popular Religion*, edited by Pieter Hendrik Vrijhof and Jacques Waardenburg, pp. 71–100. The Hague, 1979.

Galpern, A. N. *The Religions of the People in Sixteenth-Century Champagne.* Cambridge, Mass., 1976.

Gilmont, Jean-François, ed. *La réforme et le livre.* Paris, 1990. Eighteen essays concerned with the whole of Europe from 1517 to about 1570.

Ginzburg, Carlo. *The Cheese and the Worms: The Cosmos of a Sixteenth-Century Miller.* Reprint, Baltimore 1992. A pioneering and controversial study in history from below, first published in Italian in 1976.

Greyerz, Kaspar von, ed. *Religion and Society in Early Modern Europe.* London, 1984. Includes essays by, among others, Bossy, Davis, Muchembled, Scribner, and Strauss.

Haliczer, Stephen, ed. *Inquisition and Society in Early Modern Europe.* London and Sydney, 1987. Includes five essays on the Inquisition and popular culture in Italy and Spain by Sara Nalle, Mary O'Neil, John Martin, Jean-Pierre Dedieu, and Mary Elizabeth Perry.

Hsia, Ronald Po-Chia. *Social Discipline in the Reformation.* Reprint, London, 1992. Comparative analysis of Catholic and Protestant "confessionalization" in central Europe, 1550–1750.

Muchembled, Robert. *Popular Culture and Elite Culture in France, 1400–1750.* Baton Rouge, 1985. A controversial study emphasizing anxiety and acculturation; first published in French in 1978.

Ozment, Steven. "Pamphlet Literature of the German Reformation." In *Reformation Europe: A Guide to Research*, edited by Steven Ozment, pp. 85–106. Saint Louis, 1982.

Scribner, Robert W. *For the Sake of Simple Folk: Popular Culture Propaganda for the German Reformation.* Cambridge, 1981. Concentrates on images.

———. "Ritual and Popular Religion in Catholic Germany at the Time of the Reformation." *Journal of Ecclesiastical History* 35 (1984), 47–77. Concentrates on sacramentals.

Strauss, Gerald. "Success and Failure in the German Reformation." *Past and Present* 67 (1975), 30–63. Emphasizes the failure, on the basis of visitation records.

Yoder, Don. "Toward a Definition of Folk Religion." *Western Folklore* 33 (1974), 2–15. Opts for a definition in terms of unofficial religion.

PETER BURKE

Popular Religion in Germany

The Reformation deeply affected popular religion in Germany, more noticeably in Calvinist regions, while in the Catholic areas the Catholic reform and Counter-Reformation also brought about important changes in popular piety. In the territories and towns that had become Lutheran, the religious sentiment of the people changed under the influence of increasingly better educated and more numerous ministers, whose actions were both repressive and pedagogical.

Luther and the Lutheran churches were anxious to avoid breaking abruptly with traditional religious sentiment. The changes were few, limited as they were to doing away with Latin, introducing Communion under both kinds, abolishing a range of paraliturgical ceremonies and processions, and discontinuing the veneration of Mary and of the saints and the belief in purgatory. Collective salvation obtained through specific rites developed into concern about individual salvation granted in return for the belief in simple dogmas whose appropriation called for a personal intellectual effort. The individual's direct relationship with God was not incompatible, however, with the continuing mediating function of the pastor. To the faithful, the pastor remained a necessary intermediary whose task was to pronounce the right forms that alone made the ceremony valid and gave dying persons the assurance that they would enter heavenly bliss. The enhanced social status of the pastor gave rise to specifically Protestant forms of anti-clericalism, often directed against pastors' wives, and given impetus by difficulties in maintaining financial support of the clergy without new religious endowments. The continuation of the tithe and the reintroduction of Communion fees and fees for other religious services ensured that clerical-lay tensions remained within the new churches, albeit without the same intensity as in the old church.

Religion on the popular level consisted, first of all, in church going; such activity was encouraged, in addition to the weight of tradition, by the notion of God's reward in the form of earthly blessings and eternal salvation in return for worshiping him. In most parishes the faithful attended the service without excessive eagerness, were sometimes late, and sat in their usual, reserved, and hereditary pews. Although Luther had reduced the status of sacraments such as confession and confirmation, these continued as important religious rituals.

The congregation joined in singing, which was typical of the new service, for hymns helped to propagate the Reformation. After 1650 it became customary to give confirmands a valuable leather-bound hymnbook with a small silver lock. In singing, people found an emotional and sentimental support for their piety. Some hymns seem to have been particularly popular because their tunes were easy to remember and they expressed unwavering faith, confidence in God's help, and the assurance of salvation. These hymns shaped a form of piety based on the religious emotions, the inner life, and a direct relationship with God. They were meant to develop specific traits, such as faithfulness and the need for comfort, and to sustain people through life's hardships. Hymnbooks were ascribed the same sacredness and miraculous power as the Bible, and in popular belief sometimes seemed to have the same miraculous power as Catholic relics.

The Eucharist was of paramount importance in Lutheran churches, so much so that it served as a test when people were confronted with Calvinist proselytizing efforts. They acutely feared profaning the act, for it was the only ceremony that plainly expressed the immediacy of believer and God, who, according to Lutheran teaching, was thought to be truly received in the bread and wine. It is then understandable why, when receiving the elements, the communicant genuflected. Many folklore beliefs in Lutheran areas were associated with the sacredness of the time at which the Lord's Supper was received, and for some Lutherans the bread and wine had sacred power similar to that of the Catholic Eucharist. The three great liturgical festivals were favorite times for receiving Communion, so much so that many pastors called their congregations "Christmas and Easter Christians." Distinctions gradually emerged between women and men, and between married and unmarried adults, the former receiving Communion more frequently than the latter.

Sunday, which was a rest day, was devoted to church going, relaxation, and leisure. It had its place in the cycle of the liturgical year, which culminated in the three great festivals, each a two-day holiday together with a half-day off. After 1600 Christmas began to gain its special significance particularly in Germany. Good Friday became a specific holy day in Lutheranism, and has remained so in Lutheran areas to this day. It developed into a day of penance with the complete reading of the passion story and general Communion.

Although it has been claimed that the Reformation created a religion virtually devoid of ritual elements, popular demand gradually led to many older rituals being retained or reinstated in a Reformed version. Besides confession and confirmation, churching was retained as an important life-cycle ceremony, while evangelical consecrations became a routine part of Lutheran life in the seventeenth century. There were distinctively evangelical forms of Rogation processions, and of May Day, Whitsun, and harvest festivals, while many pious customs grew up around Christmas, such as the dressing and display of a Christ Child.

Books played an important role in forming a distinctly Lutheran piety. The most remarkable of these was Luther's *Kleine Katechismus.* Written in clear rhythmical prose with its sentences easy to understand and to remember, it was a simple, practical, and popular manual, suitable even for children. Of course, remembering easily does not necessarily mean understanding properly. Difficult as it is to evaluate the success of religious instruction, it seems certain that instruction gave some of the population religious grounding and a robust faith. The catechism thus resulted in a reassuring religion and increased group consciousness.

Religious instruction also promoted what might be called a biblical culture related to the growing number of people who were able to read and write. Schools helped to develop a form of popular insight for secularization through a popular culture based on almanacs, printed legendaries, and tales that before long opened even non-Christian horizons.

This biblical culture was also fostered by prayer books, a widespread literary genre. Copies are mentioned in virtually all estate inventories, even among the lowest classes. Daily prayers at home seem to have been fairly common, the family gathering in the evening for Bible reading and prayer. Grace was said before and after every meal. In line with the mentality of the time as found in the prefaces to prayer books, prayers were viewed as comfort in times of distress, danger, or disease. They were especially meaningful in a society that was predominantly rural, with prayers against bad weather replacing the traditional intercessions to the saints before the Reformation. Prayers were also employed to help with psychological problems such as nervous breakdowns. By the end of the seventeenth century, under the influence of Pietism, some devotional objects, which had been suppressed by sixteenth-century Protestantism, reappeared, such as crucifixes, crosses, religious pictures, and "letters of baptism."

An aura of sanctity clung to parish churches and cemeteries, strengthened by the solemn consecration of new churches and cemeteries. The removal of cemeteries from built-up areas after 1550 met with violent opposition, especially in towns. Some evidence suggests that for a long time people clung to some traditional practices but performed them secretly, making the study of their survival nearly impossible. Among these was an attachment to blessings, magical spells, and charms, which were often retained in popular practice despite ecclesiastical disapproval, on the grounds that they used words found in the Bible and were no different from the forms of prayer enjoined by pastors.

It was in shaping the attitude toward death that Lutheran spirituality was particularly pronounced. By making the certainty of Christ's victory over death the center of the doctrine of salvation through faith, the Reformation made death less uncertain through the concepts of resurrection and victory. To prepare their parishioners for death was one of the main responsibilities of the pastors. Parishioners sent for the minister to "settle their accounts" with God since belief in the hereafter was virtually universal. However, the Reformation was unable to abolish fear of the "dangerous dead," those who had died unshriven or in unusual circumstances. Possibly because Lutheranism had deemphasized the importance of rites of separation, the fear of the dangerous dead actually increased in Lutheran areas, especially in times of plague or epidemic, and the sixteenth century saw an intensification of belief in revenants and those able to harm from beyond the grave.

For numerous decades German Protestantism was marked by the intense controversy between Lutheranism and Calvinism, so much so that among Lutherans "rather papist than Calvinist" was a widespread motto. The introduction of Calvinism coincided with the simplification of liturgy and church decoration and, more important still, with the replacement of the Host and paten by bread and ordinary drinking glasses, which was considered by Lutherans to be a form of desecration.

In recent years, some Reformation scholars have painted a somewhat different picture of popular and peasant religion. Using late sixteenth-century sources, especially visitation records, they have noted the extraordinary tenacity of popular resistance to imposed doctrines and observances, new or old. Age-old folk practices, notions, piety, and traditions stood in contrast to the attempts to inculcate the new formulas of creedal orthodoxy. Such resistance to change meant, of course, the vigorous persistence of a religious subculture. The visitation records offer a rich picture of such popular religion, because they probed for soothsayers, casters of spells, witches, wise women, and those who pronounced incantations.

Since the common folk promised to comply with official doctrines when challenged about their practices, it is difficult to ascertain if church teaching was effective. Also, this was a rural phenomenon, which was, to begin with, at odds with the urban churchmen and theologians (and their disdain for things peasant and rural) and intensified by the increased religious fiscal burden, such as the reimposition of the tithe.

Protestantism may be said to have been quintessentially urban; it called for literacy owing to the importance of catechisms, devotional books, and sermon books. A religion of the word was taught and imposed in a remarkably successful way. Indeed, many justifications for popular belief in magic or unofficial rituals emphasized that they were wholly in accordance with the "word of God," or else not directly prohibited by it. Many pastors found themselves frustrated by this popular appropriation of the word, which was often theologically unsophisticated but informed by a pious literalism.

In territories that remained Catholic the Counter-Reformation enhanced popular piety through new approaches to devotion, confession, frequent Communion, processions, pilgrimages, and veneration of Mary. Both the Jesuits and the Capuchins deliberately sought to revive healing shrines as part of a missionizing strategy. This also had the polemically useful effect of wrong-footing Protestants, who were unable to show equivalent evidence of divine favor to miracles or healing saints. Both Reformed and Lutheran controversialists found themselves embarrassed in the consequent debate over miracles, unwilling to admit that miracles were impossible but unable to produce any comparable to those claimed by Catholics. The same occurred with exorcism as a means of dealing with demonic possession, and Catholic polemicists were able to capitalize on several renowned and successful exorcisms. Other manifestations of Catholic vitality were the restoration and renovation of churches, the increasing number of foundations established for decorating and solemnizing the liturgy, and chiefly the numerous charitable religious orders. Books were used in Catholicism no less than in Protestantism to enhance piety, especially Peter Canisius's *Catechism* as well as collections of hymns, devotional books, and books of spiritual exercises inspired by Spanish mysticism and the fifteenth-century Rhenish mystics.

Catholic piety was essentially characterized by the affirmation of devotional practices inherited from the Middle Ages. The renewal brought by Catholic reform influenced the meaning, form, and mode of a more personal religious feeling. Devotions most strongly promoted were those centering on the Passion story and the glorification of the cross, which subsequently found expression in Baroque architecture. Piety became tinged with asceticism because of the importance attached to meditation and contemplation. There was juxtaposition of ascetic discipline and *joie de vivre* (festivals of the Virgin and the saints, numerous processions).

The presence of three religious traditions together with a numerous and efficient clergy contributed to the robust vitality of popular religion and helped these traditions to take root. All three shaped the religious mentalities for nearly two centuries and retained their respective specificities in rural areas well into the twentieth century.

BIBLIOGRAPHY

Châtellier, Louis. *La religion des pauvres: Les missions rurales en Europe et la formation du Catholicisme moderne, XVIe–XIXe siècles.* Paris, 1993.

Forster, Marc. *The Counter-Reformation in the Villages: Religion and Reform in the Bishopric of Speyer, 1560–1720.* Ithaca, N.Y., 1992.

Schürmann, Thomas. *Nachzehrglauben in Mitteleuropa.* Marburg, 1990.

Scribner, R. W. *Popular Culture and Popular Movements in Reformation Germany.* London and Ronceverte, W.Va., 1987.

———. "The Impact of the Reformation on Daily Life." In *Mensch und Objekt im Mittelalter und in der frühen Neuzeit,* pp. 315–343. Österreichische Akademie der Wissenschaften, Philologische-historische. Klasse, Sitzungsberichte, vol. 568. Vienna, 1990.

———. "The Reformation, Popular Magic and the 'Disenchantment of the World.' " *Journal of Interdisciplinary History* 23 (1993), 475–494.

Soergel, Philip M. *Wondrous in His Saints: Counter-Reformation Propaganda in Bavaria.* Berkeley, 1993.

BERNARD VOGLER

Translated from French by Simone Wyss

Popular Religion in France

Lay or popular religion in France was regionally diverse and can best be defined in terms of behavior and practice, not belief. Ordinary Christians expressed their faith through collective devotion rather than theological or credal statements. Doctrine and theology provided a frame within which the religion of the laity developed and responded to changing economic, social, and psychological needs, but they did not impose a straitjacket of narrowly defined behavior. Ideally, parish clergy served the larger ecclesiastical institution as well as the communities in which they worked; popular religion and the official faith were thus connected and their interdependence mediated.

Devolved ecclesiastical authority meant that pre-Tridentine diocesan *rituels* and *processionaux,* guidebooks that the invention of typography had made commonplace parts of many priests' equipment, were not all exactly alike: they suggested different invocatory patterns and proposed a variety of calendars of celebration of saints' days. Likewise, parish clerics, implementing the wishes of bishops (not always their own; in the diocese of Sens, individual parishes had missals from Evreux, Utrecht, Auxerre, and Paris), did not all impose the same devotional norms on their flocks; practices that did not seem to undermine or implicitly challenge episcopal standards were maintained and sometimes extended. A common faith was thus manifested in many distinctive ways. In the dioceses of Chartres and Auxerre traditional interparochial processions on certain feast and saints' days indicated a notion of Christian solidarity that extended well beyond individual villages. In Touraine a relatively greater attachment to name saints than to parish patrons (expressed in wills) and the absence of evidence of religious connections to neighboring parishes imply a concept of religion that was much more individual. Neither of these visions contradicted the official teachings of the church, but each indicates that, collectively, ordinary French people could express considerable religious autonomy, just as individual theologians held differing interpretive positions within the broader confines of officially defined orthodoxy. Local autonomy may sometimes have gone further: Chiffoleau suggests that Communion in both elements, reserved almost exclusively for clerics by church authorities, was available to at least some laypeople in Quercy, Alsace, and perhaps Brittany (Jacques Chiffoleau, in *Histoire de la France religieuse,* vol. 2, *Du christianisme flamboyant à l'aube des Lumières,* Paris, 1988, p. 135).

Much of the religious life of rural communities was managed by members of village elites, acting as churchwardens and as masters of confraternities, which often were indistinguishable from the parish in which they were nested. Poorly paid deputies of nonresident *curés,* many village priests (*vicaires*) had few reasons to feel responsible for the church, its equipment, and its sources of revenue. The late medieval church's toleration of clerical pluralism and nonresidence left it little choice but to accept lay management of local church business; wardens were essential to ecclesiastical administration. Likewise, urban and rural confraternities arranged their activities independently of the clergy, except to pay them for masses they wished to have said. Parish and confraternal celebrations included processions led by clergy but also banquets and dances, which were not seen as contaminants of true religious devotion until the later sixteenth century.

Processions were often less austerely devout than the standards of the Council of Trent required. Pious citizens of Lyon visited a statue each Saint Stephen's Day, wearing their shirts backwards, until forbidden by a priest who destroyed the statue in the early sixteenth century. Other devotions, too, involved behavior less decorous than later church authorities considered acceptable. In Troyes a painted crucifix with a canopy, erected in the main square of the town in 1474, was soon renowned as a curative shrine. By 1500 large numbers of pilgrims caused such congestion that the city council forbade anyone to pray before it for more than thirty minutes at a time and ordered that the entire area around it be cleared completely between 10 P.M. and 3 A.M. Here, too, the close connections between "official" and "popular" religion are manifested. Popular devotion made the crucifix an especially potent object of veneration, but this did not trouble the clergy; it was the council, concerned with trade and traffic, that moved to regulate its use.

Rural devotional norms are more difficult to discover. The sparse records of parochial and confraternal celebrations are mostly laconic account-books, which tell little of what people actually did or thought they were doing. Veneration of some saints prompted local pilgrimages and relic cults as a result of their healing reputations, but except for saints Roch and Sebastian, guardians against plague, few were thought of as specialists. The Virgin, parish patrons, and name saints were people's main connections with the divine, but in their wills some individuals went far beyond this short list in asking for assistance for their souls. Peter, Paul, and the archangel Michael were the most widely venerated additions. Most confraternities were dedicated to various Christ-centered devotions or to the saints already mentioned; but it is always possible to find groups like that at Thiviers, west of Poitiers, which honored Saint Quitterie, a little-known Spanish virgin and martyr. Usually begun in a remote and undocumented past, these manifested local traditions only distantly linked to "official" religion. They were suppressed or fell into disuse as more rigorous priest-centered norms of parish organization were imposed after the Council of Trent, particularly in the seventeenth century.

Despite confraternal autonomy, "a web of paraliturgical ritual accompanied each sacrament and drew the curé into the life of his village" (Philip Hoffman, *Church and Community in the Diocese of Lyon, 1500–1789*, New Haven, 1984, p. 53). After baptisms, bells were rung and mothers were blessed by priests who then attended the post-baptismal banquets. Confession and absolution were communal; priests distributed unconsecrated wine, donated by laypeople, to drink with the sacrament. Everywhere church bells were baptized and given Christian names, but this did not mean that they played no role in the secular life of the community (if, indeed, this could be separated from its religious life). Bells summoned parishioners to prayer and to village assemblies and feasts; they tolled the deaths of neighbors as well as their births and marriages; they served to call people to fight fires, and warned of the appearance of *routiers*, soldiers, and other potential dangers.

Communal religiosity was often extrasacramental. Reception of the Eucharist was infrequent for most; people went to church to see the consecration of the elements more than to receive them. Corpus Christi celebrations reinforced the notion that veneration of Christ's presence in the consecrated host was the central devotional task. The pax board was a nonsacramental means of passing the kiss of peace among a congregation. Distribution of *pain bênit* (bread blessed, but not consecrated, by the priest) provided an alternative for parishioners who did not receive the Host. All these served to create a framework in which religious behavior was less closely tied to participation in the liturgy than it was among Protestants or later Catholics, served by Tridentine clergy (who implemented the reforms of the Council of Trent). Such devotion tied parish and village community in ways that blurred the distinctions modern observers usually expect to find between religious and secular life. For example, although they manifested devotion to Christ's incarnation and his sacrifice for all mankind, Corpus Christi processions were also a means to collective solidarity, undercutting interfamilial animosity, and a method of marking off a community's boundaries. While secular ritual embodied the political and social beliefs of people in much the same way that religious ritual stated their fundamental religious assumptions, the two are often impossible to separate.

Although the French counter-reformers began their work before 1600, they did so only in the cities; in the diocese of Lyon, few ordinary clerics actively imposed new standards in the countryside before 1650. Nowhere were reforming priests an ongoing problem for rural communities before 1614. Even in the cities traditional religious behavior was often actively maintained in the face of attempts by clerical reformers to suppress it. The new standards of the orthodox church, like those of Calvinist reformers, mark the first stage in the creation of a distinction between "popular" and "ecclesiastical" religion in France. Earlier besieged by reformers, the cities were first to fall. By 1625 most towns had abandoned much of what has been called "popular religion," while to reformers and some recent historians the countryside remained mired in superstition.

At the village level, in most regions, lay heresy was either imposed by a noble patron or was individual opinion held by unusually articulate marginal individuals. In parts of Languedoc, particularly where many rural people were involved in migratory labor that took them into towns, whole villages did opt for the Reformation, but this was exceptional. Often individual rural "heretics" seem to have been tolerated or ignored by their neighbors even in the seventeenth century, with what Robert Sauzet calls "l'œcuménisme de cabaret" (*Les visites pastorales dans le diocèse de Chartres pendant la première moitié du 17e siècle*, Rome, 1975, p. 227). When a group of inhabitants of the small town of Illiers, southwest of Chartres, claimed in the middle of the Wars of Religion to support "la religion prétendue reformée" they did not arouse their neighbors' ire. The demands for ecclesiastical reform they made in a separate group *cahier de doléance* (1576) make it clear that their beliefs were not those of John Calvin. Given the nondoctrinal nature of most rural religion in the sixteenth century and the fact that few parish priests in the northern part of the kingdom supported the reform, this is hardly surprising.

Rural practices did not indicate insufficiently Christian community standards or the maintenance of pagan or pre-Christian rituals after a millennium of official Christian orthodoxy. Most popular religious customs were integrated into the life of the community; even when they did not actively involve the priest, there is no evidence that they occurred despite his objections or that episcopal visitations in the pre-Reformation era led to orders that they be terminated. While eight synodal statutes between 1404 and 1583 mentioned and condemned charivaris (loud serenading and taunting of those who some in the community thought should not have married), hundreds of other diocesan assemblies left these community rituals of marital control unmentioned; they were not prohibited in diocesan *rituels* until after 1640. The story of the holy greyhound, Guinefort, an object of veneration discovered in late thirteenth-century Bresse (northeast of Lyon), and evidence of beliefs in the healing powers of his long-disappeared shrine as late as the early twentieth century (Jean-Claude Schmitt, *The Holy Greyhound: Guinefort, Healer of Children Since the Thirteenth Century*, 1979; translated by Michael Thom, New York, 1983), have been alluded to in arguments that popular religion was full of superstition and crypto-paganism. Such stories are both rare and much more ambiguous than they seem in simple recountings. The records of many credulous beliefs and practices published in the late seventeenth century by Jean-Baptiste Thiers have likewise been cited as evidence of rural unbelief, but they derive from research in ancient books and from reports sent to Thiers from all over the kingdom, which makes their witness less than clear-cut. In few communities can more than a couple of problematic beliefs be documented. Lay devotion and behavior usually embodied the same religious and operational assumptions as official ritual and practice.

Marital rituals reflected the relatively late date at which marriage became a fully sacramentalized process and the fact that, apart from insisting on mutual consent and public avowal, the church imposed no universal norms until Trent. The Anglo-Norman tradition of a nuptial rite before the mass, at the church door, spread in the late Middle Ages, but the actual content of services varied greatly. Consent could be given passively or actively and before or after the joining of the spouses' hands: in a few regions it was given twice. The ring was placed on all the bride's fingers before reposing on the third or fourth finger of the right hand (though as early as 1500 Uzès and Autun were prescribing what would become the imposed "Roman" norm). Blessings of the marriage chamber, while the bride and groom stood beside or sat on the bed, reflected the relatively unprudish nature of pre-Tridentine priests' attitudes toward marriage and were common everywhere but in Périgord. Wedding feasts and dances, often in the churchyard, were an integral part of the celebration, as were charivaris in instances of second marriages and of those between partners considered ill-matched. Although need to discover any impediment that might lead to annulment or divorce was used to justify the establishment of priestly control over marriage, the imposition of the uniform Tridentine marriage ritual and the suppression of festivities in or near the church were more the result of a desire to free the sacraments from profanation by secular affairs and of the vision of a church dependent on the clergy, not the laity.

Women's role in ritual and religious life was constrained and limited by both the traditional masculine authority structures of secular society and the teachings and institutional framework of the church. Nonetheless, traditional Catholic piety offered a number of "feminine" supports and rituals: the Virgin, Saint Anne, and other female saints could be called on in specifically feminine crises, like childbirth. It is not known, however, how much or to what extent female religiosity existed independently of clerical and community norms.

In 1500 funerary piety, while it varied greatly by region, usually meant public pomp and display. Testators often laid out detailed instructions for services, with as many priests and friars as they felt they could afford, and wanted at least twelve poor people to pray for their souls. Endowments of perpetual masses were regular parts of bequests; those who could not afford them left money for prayers on specific dates or asked their heirs to pray for them. Often referred to as "flamboyant" piety, by analogy to the ornamented late Gothic architectural style so labeled, the processional and prayer-oriented devotion of many French laypeople has been analyzed as indicating an uncertain and fearful religiosity, in which many people, unsure of their own merits, called on saints, community, and priests to assist in their progression from this life to eternal bliss. The implication that this was but a phase in the history of French religion, a crisis to which both Calvinism and reformed Catholicism provided effective and more emotionally satisfying responses, is belied by evidence that not all regions manifested the same "flamboyance" and that "at the end of the eighteenth century, the 'baroque' testamentary preambles [from Provence] studied by Michel Vovelle did no more than translate the Latin formulas of the 'flamboyant' wills of the age of Charles VII" (Chiffoleau, p. 183). Funerals did change, often becoming more austere, and regional diversity was reduced by the Tridentine clergy; but connections between these alterations and the religious needs and desires of individuals and communities were much more complex than a simple crisis-and-response model suggests. In the sixteenth century traditional funerary piety provided a social frame in which to come to terms with death in addition to serving clerical and ecclesiastical needs. Wakes were extensions of the social elements in funerals. New, austere, clerically controlled models may have worked for literate and semiliterate people with a more individuated sense of their place in the cosmos, but they also undercut the communal piety that had served rural Christians well for many centuries.

Like tax collectors and merchants, later priests and ministers connected towns and villages to the cities; but they were outsiders who judged the religion of their flocks negatively, distinguishing between doctrinal orthodoxy and what some modern researchers have called "popular religion." This dichotomy would not have seemed a useful one to most pre-Reformation observers. To them the practices of the laity were but another mode of religious devotion.

BIBLIOGRAPHY

Chiffoleau, Jacques. *La comptabilité de l'au-delà: Les hommes, la mort et la religion dans la région d'Avignon à la fin du moyen âge, vers 1320–vers 1480*. Rome, 1980. Not, strictly speaking, about the era of the Reformation, but an exemplary work which clearly lays out the "flamboyant" spirituality that continued to typify much popular devotion well into the sixteenth century.

Davis, Natalie Zemon. *Society and Culture in Early Modern France: Eight Essays*. Reprint, Cambridge, 1987. A number of essays in this stimulating collection address lay culture and religion, primarily in the cities.

Diefendorf, Barbara B. *Beneath the Cross: Catholics and Huguenots in Sixteenth-Century Paris*. New York, 1991. The first two chapters show the connections between community and church in the capital and largest city of the kingdom in the first sixty years of the century.

Galpern, A. N. *The Religions of the People in Sixteenth-Century Champagne*. Cambridge, Mass., 1976. A well-presented demonstration of the continuation of "medieval" modes of devotion through the century.

Garrisson-Estèbe, Janine. *Protestants du Midi, 1559–1598*. Paris, 1980. Part 3 focuses on the process of religious change in Huguenot communities and the tensions between the new faith and traditional customs.

Le Roy Ladurie, Emmanuel. *Carnival in Romans*. Translated by Mary Feeney. Reprint, Harmondsworth, 1981. An intriguing study of the connections between popular paraliturgical ritual and sociopolitical discontent.

Luria, Keith. *Cultural Change in the Seventeenth-Century Diocese of Grenoble*. Berkeley, 1991.

Molin, Jean-Baptiste, and Protais Mutembe. *Le rituel du mariage en France du 12e au 16e siècle*. Paris, 1974. Although focused primarily on the church's prescriptions, a clear picture of the diversity of nuptial rites in pre-Tridentine France.

Muchembled, Robert. *Popular Culture and Elite Culture in France, 1400–1750*. Translated by Lydia Cochrane. Baton Rouge, 1985. Interesting and full of examples of rural and urban custom and "superstition," it tends to overstate the conceptual gulf between popular and elite religion.

Reinburg, Virginia. "Liturgy and the Laity in Late Medieval and Reformation France." *Sixteenth Century Journal* 23.3 (Fall 1992), 526–547. A masterful, brief explication of the many paraliturgical elements in Christian devotion.

Vincent, Catherine. *Des charités bien ordonnées: Les confréries normandes de la fin du 13e siècle au début du 16e*. Paris, 1988. The best discussion of the place of confraternities in the religious life of a region.

ALAN G. ARTHUR

Popular Religion in England and Scotland

To study popular religion in sixteenth-century England is to seek answers to two crucial but highly controversial questions. First, on the eve of the official Reformation, did traditional Catholicism still retain the support of the English people? In most respects it continued to enjoy the approval of their government, including Henry VIII himself. Some historians argue that the support of his subjects remained equally strong. Others claim that it was already in substantial decline. Second, how was this support affected by the Reformation itself? The official assault upon traditional practices and institutions was initiated by Henry VIII in 1534–1547 and intensified by Edward VI in 1547–1553. Though temporarily halted in 1553–1558 by Mary Tudor, it was renewed thereafter by Elizabeth I. According to some historians, the assault met considerable popular resistance and only slowly took effect. According to other historians, it encountered general acceptance and rapidly prevailed. In order to suggest even tentative answers to these questions, it is necessary to survey briefly the impact of the Reformation on each major component of traditional religion.

Of traditional religious institutions, the most remote from laypeople on the eve of the official Reformation was the papacy. Nevertheless they seem usually to have dutifully rendered the tax called Peter's Pence to the papal coffers, and often, as in the southwest in 1530, to have happily purchased papal indulgences. Papal authority was rejected only by small groups of Lollards and (from about 1520) of Protestants, particularly in the southeast.

This authority was removed by Henry VIII in 1534 and only temporarily restored by Mary. Apart from some of the northern rebels in 1536, most English people apparently acquiesced in its removal. Significantly, not even the conservative southwestern rebels of 1549 sought its return.

Of greater importance to popular religion before the 1530s were monks and especially friars. As intercessors, confessors, and spiritual guides, these individuals still received bequests from a significant number of testators in areas such as Lincolnshire and the southwest. At the same time, hostility was voiced by southeastern Lollards and Protestants, while in Buckinghamshire and elsewhere bequests were fewer.

The governmental suppression of religious houses in 1536–1540 was reportedly resented by "all the whole [north] country"; here the rebellion of 1536 was raised partly in their defense. But elsewhere resistance was limited. Many laypeople in fact assisted by purchasing monastic property, or even, as in Warwickshire, by plundering dissolved houses. Bequests ceased; seldom would they resume in Mary's reign.

Substantially more important to popular religion on the eve of Reformation were the secular clergy. As performers of the sacraments, particularly baptism, absolution, and the Mass, they seem largely to have retained their traditional status as mediators between lay parishioners and God. In the southwest, some 70 percent of testators still bequeathed to them. The anticlericalism reported by John Colet and Christopher St. German—"now of late," wrote the latter in 1532, "the great multitude of all the lay people have found default as well at priests as religious"—was apparently strongest in the southeast.

After 1530, however, there were apparent signs of a general decline in respect for priests. These included verbal outbursts and physical assaults as well as nonpayment of clerical dues, resistance to ecclesiastical discipline, and falling ordination figures. Bequests to clerics declined—in the southwest, to a mere 3 percent by 1560–1569. Apart from the northern rebels in 1536, the laity showed little inclination to defend "benefit of clergy" or other priestly privileges from official attack.

On the eve of the Reformation, the primary centers of popular devotion were the parish churches. Bequests to these were frequent, appearing, for example, in 76 to 92 percent of wills in the diocese of Lincoln. Moreover, investment in their construction or furnishing remained impressive in many parts of England. It was motivated largely by a desire to honor a saint or to secure prayer for the benefactor's soul.

In the 1530s bequests to parish churches began generally to fall. Statistics from the southwest, Lincoln diocese, and elsewhere indicate that the decline was significant under Henry VIII, rapid under Edward VI, and only temporarily reversed under Mary. Even more drastic was the decline of church building. In a sample from eight counties, the number of parish churches and chapels with evidence of major construction fell from eighty-one in 1520–1529 to only eight in 1560–1569.

After churches, the institutions most vital to popular piety until the 1530s were religious guilds. Composed mainly of laypeople, these parish-based fraternities sometimes maintained images and usually organized prayers or masses on behalf of their dead. In several regions they remained numerous and well supported, receiving bequests, for example, from 57 percent of southwestern testators. Elsewhere, as in Buckinghamshire, they attracted less support.

The late-Henrician years saw a marked decline in bequests to such guilds and the local dissolution of many. They were effectively suppressed by Edward VI and were only rarely revived under Mary, when gifts were few. The destruction was completed under Elizabeth I.

Turning from institutions to practices, on the eve of the Reformation a range of traditional sacraments and ceremonies retained a high degree of popular support. This support is indicated, for example, by frequent attendance at Mass, as observed by an Italian visitor in about 1500, and by substantial individual and parochial expenditure on ritual apparatus, as recorded by many churchwardens' accounts. Lollard and Protestant hostility was again strongest in the southeast.

As the Reformation proceeded, however, there was evidence of increasing attacks (even in Yorkshire) on the Catholic sacraments; of dwindling expenditure upon ritual apparatus, accompanied by frequent sale or embezzlement; and, in some places, of falling attendance at traditional services. These trends were only partially reversed in Mary's reign: for example, expenditure on ritual equipment seldom regained its pre-Reformation level.

One of the most crucial elements of popular religion was intercession. Prayers and masses on behalf of the dead, in order to hasten their souls' passage through purgatory and into heaven, retained substantial support. Chantries continued to be founded, though more frequently in rural areas than in towns, and in the north and west more frequently than in the Midlands, south, and east. The last three areas also heard most Lollard and Protestant hostility to intercession. Bequests to intercessions still appeared in 60 to 70 percent of wills in areas like Devon, Cornwall, and Huntingdonshire; in London, Buckinghamshire, and elsewhere the percentage was significantly lower.

In most areas, including even Yorkshire and Lancashire, the period 1530–1547 saw a marked decline in chantry foundations and also a significant increase in private suppressions. Bequests to intercessions fell—to 33 percent in Devon and Cornwall, and to 18 percent in Huntingdonshire. They collapsed under Edward VI, and recovered only partially under Mary. After Elizabeth's accession they virtually disappeared.

Though attacked by Lollards and Protestants, saint veneration remained widely popular until the 1530s. This is demonstrated by church art, which focused largely on saints, and by wills. Commendation of the soul not only to God or Christ but also to the Virgin Mary or the saints still appeared in some 90 percent of wills throughout the realm.

By the end of Henry's reign, however, this percentage had usually begun to fall—to 76 percent in Yorkshire, and to only 52 percent in Kent. It slumped everywhere under Edward, in most areas revived only partially under Mary, and again collapsed under Elizabeth.

Despite Lollard and Protestant rejection, images continued to perform important functions for the layperson until the 1530s. As aids to prayer they were honored by lights, offerings, and pilgrimages. Substantial expenditure was devoted to their construction and ornamentation, and to the erection of roodlofts for their display.

The most venerated were usually suppressed in response to the royal injunctions of 1536–1538. The remainder were generally removed, and often destroyed, in Edward's reign. Replacement under Mary was no more than partial and was reversed after Elizabeth's accession. Though occasionally resisted, as in Cornwall in 1548, this destruction more often encountered acquiescence. Sometimes, as in Maidstone and London in 1538, it received popular support.

A final component of pre-Reformation popular piety was the veneration of sacred sites and relics. Holy wells, associated with saints, continued to be visited for healing in Cornwall and elsewhere. Pilgrims still honored the shrines of innumerable obscure figures, such as Urith at Chittlehampton in Devon, as well as major saints such as Saint Hugh in Lincoln Cathedral. In the southeast such cults were rejected by Lollards and Protestants, while that of Thomas Becket at Canterbury was already in financial decline.

Shrines were usually destroyed by government order in the Henrician Reformation. They were seldom restored under Mary. Although the northern rebels of 1536 objected to relic violation, the destruction rarely evoked resistance. Wells were more difficult to destroy, but pilgrimages to them were usually in decline by Elizabeth's reign.

What conclusions may one draw? Although evidence is far from complete, it appears that most of the traditional Catholic institutions and practices remained significant components of England's popular religion on the eve of the official Reformation. Enthusiasm for these, however, was generally higher in the north and west than in the southeast. It also seems clear that in the Reformation decades, under governmental assault, they experienced massive and sometimes terminal decline. This seems generally to have proceeded most rapidly in the southeast, but by the 1560s was unmistakable throughout the realm. The "blind devotion of the people," though not yet wholly eradicated, had been to a remarkable extent effectively suppressed.

BIBLIOGRAPHY

Aston, Margaret. *Faith and Fire: Popular and Unpopular Religion, 1350–1600*. London and Rio Grande, Ohio, 1993.

Bowker, Margaret. *The Henrician Reformation: The Diocese of Lincoln Under John Longland, 1521–47*. Cambridge, 1981. Contains useful information relating to England's largest diocese.

Brigden, Susan. *London and the Reformation*. Oxford, 1989. Evaluates the progress of religious change in the capital.

Clark, P. *English Provincial Society from the Reformation to the Revolution: Religion, Politics and Society in Kent, 1500–1640*. Hassocks, England, 1977. Includes material on the reception of the Reformation in a county relatively open to change.

Dickens, A. G. *Lollards and Protestants in the Diocese of York, 1509–1558*. London, 1959. Pioneered the regional approach to English Reformation history.

———. *The English Reformation*. London, 1967. Remains one of the most valuable overviews of the subject.

Duffy, Eamon. *The Stripping of the Altars: Traditional Religion in England, 1400–1580*. New Haven, 1992. Valuable, particularly for its analysis of pre-Reformation religion.

Haigh, Christopher. *Reformation and Resistance in Tudor Lancashire*. Cambridge, 1975. Well-written study of a particularly conservative county.

———. *English Reformations: Religion, Politics, and Society under the Tudors*. Oxford, 1993. A vigorous exposition of the "revisionist" interpretation.

Haigh, Christopher, ed. *The English Reformation Revised*. Cambridge, 1987. Essays reflecting some of the recent research, particularly emphasizing conservatism.

Kreider, Alan. *English Chantries: The Road to Dissolution*. Cambridge, Mass., 1979. Careful study of a crucial element in popular religion.

Mayhew, G. J. "The Progress of the Reformation in East Sussex, 1530–1559: The Evidence From Wills." *Southern History* 5 (1983). Good example of the use of wills to illuminate changes in religious attitude during this period.

Scarisbrick, J. J. *The Reformation and the English People*. Oxford, 1984. Emphasizes the continuing popularity of traditional Catholicism on the eve of the Reformation.

Whiting, R. *The Blind Devotion of the People: Popular Religion and the English Reformation*. Cambridge, 1989. Study of the southwest; argues that the Reformation decades saw a relatively rapid devastation of traditional religion.

ROBERT WHITING

Popular Religion in Italy

For an overview of popular religion in Italy around 1500, the richest sources are literature and art. For example, the printed books that sold most widely in late fifteenth-century Italy included Saint Antoninus's *Confessionale*, a vivid description of Christ's passion attributed to Saint Bonaventure, and an anonymous account of the miracles of the Virgin Mary. The works of the Dominican Girolamo Savonarola, who declared that the millennium was at hand, were bestsellers in the 1490s, and crowds flocked to hear him preach in the cathedral of Florence or the church of San Lorenzo. The many paintings surviving from the time give a graphic impression of the strength of devotion to the Virgin and to the saints, especially John the Baptist (the patron of Florence), Sebastian (believed to offer protection against plague), and Francis of Assisi.

Religious images in general and some of them in particular, such as the statue of the Virgin at Impruneta, a few miles from Florence, were treated as if they possessed supernatural power. When the Florentines needed help, because of too little rain or too much, or because the government was in crisis, the Virgin of Impruneta would be brought to Florence, carried in a solemn procession, and given coats and other gifts. Relics were treated in the same way. In Catania, for instance, the veil of the city's patron, Santa Agata, was taken in procession in order to stop the flow of lava from Mount Etna (in 1536 and 1579) and to counteract the plague (in 1592).

It is not easy to say how widely all these beliefs were shared at this time. To draw sharp distinctions between the beliefs of the clergy and those of the laity, or even between the piety of the elites and that of ordinary people, would probably be misleading. For example, Savonarola had followers among the patriciate of Florence as well as among the artisans, while the Medici gave costly coats to the Virgin of Impruneta. One can say with more confidence that ordinary laypeople, especially in the towns, were no mere passive listeners or spectators but were actively involved in religious practice through a network of lay fraternities that might exclude the clergy altogether. These brotherhoods (which often admitted women but were dominated by men) went in procession and ate together on feast days, attended one another's funerals, and commissioned altarpieces for their chapels. Lay preachers were not uncommon at this time, whether they operated within the framework of a fraternity or spread their message on the piazza. In the 1490s, for instance, laymen preaching the end of the world in the squares of Florence, Rome, and other cities seem to have been common.

Over the next two or three generations, major religious changes took place in Italy as elsewhere in Europe, the result of various attempts at reform. For example, books by Erasmus, Luther, and Calvin were all translated into Italian. An anonymous treatise, the *Beneficio di Cristo* (published in Venice in 1543), which appears to have sold widely before it was suppressed, contains echoes of Luther, together with passages taken unacknowledged from Calvin's *Institutes.* The popularity of this treatise suggests that a shift toward a more interior religion was taking place.

This shift was not a completely new phenomenon. The Venetian *Zardin de oration,* a text that recommended the reader to "go into your chamber" and there, "alone and solitary, excluding every external thought from your mind," to make a systematic attempt to imagine Christ's passion, dates from the late fifteenth century. The spread of printed books like the ones mentioned at the beginning of this article, doubtless encouraged the trend, which was reinforced rather than begun by the *Beneficio* and by clandestine Protestant literature. Some ordinary people, silkweavers in Lucca, for example, converted to Protestantism. Other readers may have been attracted by new ideas without necessarily perceiving them as heretical. Domenico Scandella, the talkative miller of Montereale in Friuli brought back to life by the historian Carlo Ginzburg, was bubbling with unorthodox notions, but he still told the inquisitors that "a Lutheran is one who goes about teaching bad things, and eats meat on Friday and Saturday."

The spread of heterodoxy naturally alarmed the authorities and led to a series of measures to halt it, notably the foundation of local branches of the "Holy Office," or Inquisition, in Milan, Naples, Sicily, Venice, and elsewhere. In Venice, for example, the tribunal concentrated its attention for some forty years on the unorthodox beliefs prevalent among some of the city's artisans, ranging from anticlericalism to Anabaptism and millenarianism. That it made the investigation of witchcraft its highest priority in the 1580s suggests that the inquisitors considered their crusade against heresy to have been successful. The other Italian branches of the Roman Inquisition also shifted their attention from heresy to what they called "superstition."

On the positive side, measures were taken to spread religious knowledge and to introduce new forms of devotion to the laity. One of the most important of these measures was the establishment of Sunday schools, the Schools of Christian Doctrine, which began in 1536 and rapidly spread over north Italy in particular and concentrated on teaching boys and girls the rudiments of the faith. Another was the foundation of sodalities (religious fraternities under clerical control). Also important in the long term was the spread of seminaries, to raise the educational level of parish priests, the members of the clergy who had the most frequent and direct contacts with ordinary members of the laity.

Individual bishops such as Carlo Borromeo at Milan, Gabriele Paleotti at Bologna, and Carlo Bascapè at Novara did their best to ensure that the devotion of the people of their diocese flowed through orthodox channels. They outlawed unorthodox religious practices, however innocent, such as the custom of eating and drinking in cemeteries (denounced at Bologna in 1566), of baptizing dolls on the feast of Saint John (banned in Mazara in Sicily in 1575), and of giving unconsecrated hosts to women making their first visit to the church after childbirth (condemned at Tortona in 1575). They tried to eradicate "popular errors," such as the idea that it is permissible to work on holy days, that fornication is only a venial sin, and that the devil is not as black as he is painted, because images and strict rules are intended to frighten people. They were suspicious of popular festivals, such as the celebration of the first of May, on the grounds that they were survivals from the days of paganism.

These pastors were also concerned with moral reform. For example, Borromeo separated men from women in the churches of Milan. He declared war on Carnival and other "immoral recreations" as occasions of sin, and on plays, even religious ones, on the grounds that they made people laugh. In the place of these performances, he favored sermons, penitential processions, and the Forty Hour's devotion to the blessed sacrament. He tried to turn Milan into what historians have called a "ritual city" marked by the erection of the stations of the cross in the streets. Borromeo also encouraged pilgrimages to the holy mountain near Varallo in Piedmont, with its lifesize polychrome statues enacting scenes from the Bible, especially the Passion. A sign of the success of Borromeo and other bishops of his persuasion is that fraternities founded in the later sixteenth century tended to be dedicated not to the saints but to the Blessed Sacrament and the Blessed Virgin. Despite his hostility to what we think of as "popular religion," Borromeo himself became a popular hero, as witnessed by the more than ten thousand ex-votos offered at his tomb by the year 1610, a quarter of a century after his death.

The new forms of devotion naturally took time to spread beyond the major cities. Toward the end of the sixteenth century, however, the religious orders began a campaign of missions to the countryside. Inspired by accounts of conversion in the Indies, missionaries such as the Jesuits Michele Navarro and Silvestro Landini spread the faith in such mountainous regions as Corsica, central Sicily, and the Abruzzi, areas remote from major urban centers and so from the new religious values. This missionary movement would gather momentum in the seventeenth and eighteenth centuries. One might sum up the changes that took place in the course of the sixteenth century as the more or less successful imposition of a new model of Catholicism marked by increased discipline, more effective clerical control over lay devotion, and a sharper separation of the spheres of the sacred and the profane.

BIBLIOGRAPHY

Black, Christopher F. *Italian Confraternities in the Sixteenth Century.* Cambridge, 1989.

Burke, Peter. "The Bishop's Questions and the People's Religion." In *Historical Anthropology of Early Modern Italy*, pp. 40–47. Cambridge, 1987.

Ginzburg, Carlo. *The Cheese and the Worms: The Cosmos of a Sixteenth-Century Miller.* Baltimore, 1981. A pioneering and controversial study in history from below, first published in Italian in 1976.

Martin, John. "Popular Culture and the Shaping of Popular Heresy in Renaissance Venice." In *Inquisition and Society in Early Modern Europe*, edited by Stephen Haliczer, pp. 115–128. London and Sydney, 1987.

Muir, Edward. *Civic Ritual in Renaissance Venice.* Princeton, 1981.

Niccoli, Ottavia. *Prophecy and People in Renaissance Italy.* Princeton, 1990. A study of sixteenth-century broadsheets, originally published in Italian in 1987.

O'Neil, Mary. "Ecclesiastical and Superstitious Remedies in Sixteenth-Century Italy." In *Understanding Popular Culture*, edited by Steven L. Kaplan, pp. 53–84. Berlin, 1984.

Rozzo, Ugo, and Silvana Seidel Menchi. "Livre et réforme en Italie." In *La réforme et le livre*, edited by Jean-François Gilmont, pp. 327–374. Paris, 1990.

Schutte, Anne J. "Printing, Piety and the People in Italy: The First Thirty Years." *Archiv für Reformationsgeschichte* 71 (1980), 5–19. Analyzes twenty-nine religious best-sellers published between 1465 and 1494.

Trexler, Richard C. *Public Life in Renaissance Florence.* New York, 1980. Discusses religious rituals.

Weinstein, Donald. *Savonarola and Florence.* Princeton, 1970. Emphasizes Savonarola's debt to Florentine popular religious traditions.

PETER BURKE

Popular Religion in Spain

Historians of Spanish Catholicism in the early modern period have been fascinated by the unusual and the heterodox. Many studies focus upon extraordinary individuals, particularly well-known mystics, saints, theologians, and missionaries, on the Inquisition and its victims, or on members of ethnic and sectarian minorities. This orientation tends to ignore the majority of Spaniards, who, for the most part, held to a consensus view of what religion was and how it ought to be practiced. For all their distinctions of wealth and social rank, most Spanish peasants, urban dwellers, nobles, and monarchs were united in their conformity to a (basically) orthodox set of beliefs about the nature of the sacred and the individual and collective obligations owed to God and his saints. They articulated their faith through rituals designed to establish and maintain relations between humans and the divine. For the majority of Spaniards, religious life did not center on abstract tenets of theology, as it did for clerical elites, nor on highly subjective, internalized spiritual experiences, as it did for certain mystics, but rather on a cycle of ceremonies performed on the level of the village, parish, barrio, or brotherhood.

One important way in which this collective and locally based religion of the people manifested itself was through an intense devotion to the saints. Given the harsh realities of life in early modern Spain, where famine, drought, epidemic disease, and infant death were everyday occurrences, it is no wonder that men and women sought protection from higher powers. Typically they bound themselves in a set of mutual obligations, making personal or group vows of devotion and loyalty to a particular patron saint in return for his or her aid against dearth and deprivation.

As William A. Christian, Jr., has shown (*Local Religion in Sixteenth-Century Spain*, Princeton, 1981), by the late sixteenth century the Spanish landscape was dotted with shrines and chapels dedicated to various saints. Sometimes the faithful honored saints known for their intercessory specialties. For example, Saint Sebastian was believed to offer protection against plague, while Saint Gregory of Nazianzus was helpful in the battle against insect pests. Even more frequently, however, Spaniards turned to Christ or, especially, the Virgin Mary in ways that identified these universal protectors of Christians with particular locations. Shrines to, say, the Christ of Urda or Our Lady of Sonsoles affirmed an intimate link between these divine helpers and their devotees in certain villages, neighborhoods, cities, or, in some cases, regions of Spain. Parents often named their children for their local saint or Marian shrine, once again underscoring the close ties of patronage and devotion.

Fundamental to the ritual life of early modern Spanish Catholics were the pilgrimages made to the shrines and chapels dedicated to Christ, Mary, and the saints on their feast days and in times of need. These ceremonial occasions infused certain spaces and times with sacred meaning and gave people an opportunity to make contact with a beloved image or statue, which they carried in solemn processions through village, neighborhood, or fields. While many theologians despaired that "the masses" could not distinguish between the holy personages represented by images and the images themselves, laypeople lovingly adorned and displayed their statues and revered them as artifacts imbued with sacred power. Saints' relics also helped Spaniards to make contact with the divine, and they were enthusiastically collected and exhibited by villages, municipalities, bishops, and King Philip II.

Early modern Spaniards also sought intercession and protection from living persons whose charismatic brand of spirituality distinguished them as exemplars of holiness. During the fifteenth, sixteenth, and seventeenth centuries, the humble and wealthy alike turned to a variety of hermits, prophets, mystics, and faith healers for help and comfort in their daily lives. These spiritual celebrities impressed the faithful with their ascetic practices and extreme mortifications in imitation of Christ's sufferings. Many also claimed to have been endowed by God with the ability to see visions, prophesy the future, and penetrate the mysteries of the faith.

The Spanish faithful frequently experienced religious life as members of collectivities and thus organized themselves in groups for mutual support, the performance of ritual acts, and communal affirmation of the faith. For example, devout lay men and women could affiliate themselves with religious orders by becoming members of third orders, or tertiaries. This option offered adherents occasions for worship with like-minded individuals, a sense of shared identity, and the rights to burial within the precincts of a given monastic house but did not require that they make formal vows as monks or nuns. Closely related to this phenomenon was the decision of many pious women to live together in houses called *beaterios.* This term was used to describe a wide variety of situations, from two or three women living quietly in a private home to institutions that boasted over one hundred residents.

An even more common option for lay Spaniards of all social ranks was membership in one of the thousands of confraternities that proliferated during the late medieval and early modern period. According to Maureen Flynn (*Sacred Charity: Confraternities and Social Welfare in Spain, 1400–1700*, Ithaca, N.Y., 1989), many of these brotherhoods, especially in cities, featured ritualized acts of charity designed to ease the sufferings of the poor and to fulfill the religious obligations of the more well-to-do. Confraternities were commonly dedicated to the Eucharist, to performing acts of penitence, and to reciting prayers for the souls in purgatory, thus reifying those Catholic devotions affirmed with particular intensity by early modern Spaniards. By offering opportunities for group identity and solidarity, staging public ceremonies such as processions and ritual flagellations, and functioning as burial societies, Spain's numerous confraternities responded to their members' most pressing social and spiritual needs.

How did the reform movements of the early modern period affect the religious practices of lay Spaniards? During the late fifteenth century and the early decades of the sixteenth, clerical reformers, notably the powerful prelate Francisco Jiménez de Cisneros, endeavored to raise the moral and educational level of priests, especially on the parish level. Strongly influenced by the writings of Erasmus of Rotterdam, intellectuals such as Cisneros and John of Ávila promoted a more personal and internalized religious style and strove to teach the mass of lay Spaniards the basics of Catholic doctrine through preaching, confession, the publication of devotional books and pictures, and the establishment of schools of religious instruction for both children and adults.

In the second half of the sixteenth century, kindled by fear of Protestantism and energized by the Council of Trent, reformers redoubled their efforts to indoctrinate "el vulgo." Using printed materials, oral instruction, and visual representation, they emphasized strict adherence to those Catholic beliefs and rituals then under attack by Protestants: the cult of the saints, devotion to the Eucharist, prayers for the souls in purgatory, regular attendance at Mass, and confession. At the same time inquisitors, bishops, and parish priests worked to eliminate the "superstitions" and "errors" they routinely encountered among ordinary Spaniards, who committed blasphemy, fornication, and bigamy, and occasionally dabbled in sorcery and witchcraft.

In the seventeenth century, clerical elites continued to extend their authority over many aspects of religious life. They were quite effective at wresting control of confraternities, *beaterios,* and hermitages from lay men and women and in regulating the saint-making process. More frequent parish and diocesan visitations, intensified inquisitorial surveillance, and sustained indoctrination efforts achieved some notable successes, as the common folk learned their basic prayers, acknowledged fornication as a sin, and exhibited greater conformity and decorum during religious services.

However, clerical reformers were never able to completely suppress individual and local religious expression in early modern Spain. Well into the eighteenth century the residents of villages and urban neighborhoods continued to acclaim patron saints not necessarily recognized in the approved church calendars. They continued to celebrate feast days in their customary ways, such as by staging the bullfights much frowned upon by clerics. They persisted in revering charismatic mystics and faith healers, despite increasing official skepticism. Ultimately ordinary Spaniards found that recourse to holy persons, living and dead, sacred spaces and sacred times, and rituals of collective worship helped them to maintain contact with the divine, and thus they continued to embrace these traditional Catholic beliefs and practices.

BIBLIOGRAPHY

Bataillon, Marcel. *Erasmo y España: Estudios sobre la historia espiritual del siglo 16.* Rev. ed. Madrid, 1979. Originally published in French in 1937, this study remains unsurpassed for its analysis of religious movements in Spain.

Bennassar, Bartolomé. *The Spanish Character: Attitudes and Mentalities from the Sixteenth to the Nineteenth Century.* Berkeley, 1979. Some penetrating, if controversial, insights from an important member of the Annales school.

Bilinkoff, Jodi. *The Avila of Saint Teresa: Religious Reform in a Sixteenth-Century City.* Ithaca, N.Y., 1989.

Caro Baroja, Julio. *Las formas complejas de la vida religiosa: Religiòn, sociedad, y caràcter en la España de los siglos 16 y 17.* Madrid, 1978. Detailed study by one of Spain's greatest cultural anthropologists.

Christian, William A., Jr. *Apparitions in Late Medieval and Renaissance Spain.* Princeton, 1981. This and other works by this noted scholar are indispensable to the study of popular religion in Spain.

Cruz, Anne J., and Mary Elizabeth Perry, eds. *Culture and Control in Counter-Reformation Spain.* Minneapolis, 1992. Contains many useful essays by North American, Spanish, and French scholars on topics such as the cult of the saints and clerical efforts to reform morals.

Dedieu, Jean-Pierre. "The Inquisition and Popular Culture in New Castile." In *Inquisition and Society in Early Modern Europe*, edited by Stephen Haliczer, pp. 129–146. Totowa, N.J., 1987.

Deleito y Piñuela, José. *La vida religiosa española bajo el cuarto Felipe.* 2d ed. Madrid, 1963. Offers a wealth of fascinating detail, yet a bit weak on analysis.

Domínguez Ortiz, Antonio. *La sociedad española en el siglo 17.* 2 vols. Madrid, 1963. See especially vol. 2, *El estamento eclesiástico,* for an examination by one of Spain's most highly respected social historians.

Henningsen, Gustav. *The Witches' Advocate: Basque Witchcraft and the Spanish Inquisition, 1609–1614.* Reno, Nev., 1980.

Kagan, Richard L. *Lucrecia's Dreams: Politics and Prophecy in Sixteenth-Century Spain.* Berkeley, 1990. Provides much useful information while narrating the story of an intriguing Madrid prophetess.

McKendrick, Geraldine, and Angus McKay. "The Inquisition, Visionaries, and Affective Spirituality." In *Cultural Encounters: The Impact of the Inquisition in Spain and the New World,* edited by Anne J. Cruz and Mary Elizabeth Perry, pp. 93–104. Berkeley, 1991.

Martz, Linda. *Poverty and Welfare in Hapsburg Spain: The Example of Toledo.* Cambridge, 1983.

Nalle, Sara T. "Literacy and Culture in Early Modern Castile." *Past and Present* 125 (1989), 65–96. Ground-breaking study that closely examines the impact of religious printing and indoctrination on the society of Counter-Reformation Spain.

———. *God in La Mancha: Religious Reform and the People of Cuenca, 1500–1650.* Baltimore, 1993.

JODI BILINKOFF

Popular Religion in Portugal

During the Middle Ages, the Catholic church permitted its parishioners to organize their spiritual lives without interference. By the sixteenth century, however, the church began to play a more active role in the religious lives of its parishioners. Religion in Portugal during the Reformation was conditioned by Portugal's geographic isolation, far from the center of the Protestant activity in Germany. Owing to the negligible influence of Martin Luther on the Iberian peninsula, popular religious practices were much more affected by changes within the Catholic church than by Protestant thought. In the wake of the Protestant upheavals in northern Europe, the Catholic church attempted to define clearly Roman Catholic practice and belief through the doctrines and decrees of the Council of Trent (1547–1563). During the sixteenth and seventeenth centuries, in a movement known as the Catholic Reformation, the Catholic clergy used the decrees of the council in an attempt to impose a degree of religious conformity on all levels of religious participation in Portugal as well as the rest of Christendom.

Scholars have noted that the Catholic Reformation church's singular control of religious activity on the Iberian peninsula created a gulf between the official church and the religion of the people. Probably the most defining components of popular religion in Portugal during the Catholic Reformation were the variety of communal rituals, only some of which were sanctioned by the church. These communal rituals defined life within the parish, or *paroco.* The Catholic Reformation church actively encouraged universal participation in the life-cycle sacraments (baptism, confirmation, marriage, and extreme unction). These religious events were important on both an individual and a communal level. Although participation in the sacraments had always been a part of Catholic theology, parishioners had not always faithfully participated. One of the Catholic Reformation's most important innovations was the annual visitations to the parishes by bishops after the middle of the sixteenth century. Through these visitations the church scrutinized the religious activities of both the individual and the parish. Those who conformed to the expectations of the church by participating in these sacraments were duly recorded in parish registers, while those who did not were denounced to the bishop for admonition and punishment.

Other expressions of popular devotion found less favor with the church hierarchy. Portuguese parishioners focused their religious fervor on local festivals and pilgrimages to local shrines. These *festas* and *clamores* were often as much social as religious affairs and were conducted outside of the rigid liturgical structure of the Catholic church. Most of the local *festas* celebrated the feast day of a local saint, often the patron saint of the village or hamlet. The recitation of mass by the parish priest gave these celebrations a religious element; however, the secular, social nature of these gatherings distressed the church hierarchy. During a *festa* the entire parish attended a day of eating, drinking, music, and revelry.

Local pilgrimages called *romarias* or *clamores* ("shoutings") provided another form of communal religious expression. In these popular pilgrimages, the parish, led by the parish priest, traveled in procession to the country shrine of a local saint. In Portugal the majority of these shrines, and so too the *romarias,* were devoted to the Virgin Mary, worship of whom had proliferated throughout the peninsula during the late Middle Ages. Although the processions were conducted in order to express communal devotion to a particular saint, the records show that the church disapproved of the *clamores* because of the moral laxity, including drunkenness and sexual liaisons, that often accompanied the processions.

Pilgrimage could express individual as well as communal spirituality. Often these expeditions were motivated by a vow. Sometimes parishioners made these vows when they were in need of miraculous intervention owing to ill fortune or poor health; for example, a mother might promise a pilgrimage to a shrine should her child survive an illness. Other times the vows were made in grateful response for such intervention. For the most part, parishioners made special journeys to the shrines of local saints, leaving ex-votos, or symbols of their vows, at the altar. More adventurous people and those with more serious difficulties traveled far from their homes to the major religious sites on the peninsula: the burial site of Saint James at Santiago de Compostela and the site of the appearance of the Virgin at Guadalupe, both in Spain.

In order to have better control over their parishioners and the communal religious activity of the parish, Catholic Reformation clergy encouraged the Portuguese faithful, like their European counterparts, to form *confrarias* ("confraternities"). *Confrarias,* although they existed during the Middle Ages, became a prominent part of sixteenth- and seventeenth-century popular religion. The *confrarias* acted as social welfare organizations for both their members and the community. These organizations tended the sick, buried paupers, organized *festas,* and provided spiritual and financial care for their members. Most of the *confrarias* were dedicated to the Virgin or to local saints, but the influence of the Catholic Reformation is visible in the formation of new confraternities dedicated to important Catholic Reformation devotions such as the Rosary and the Holy Sacrament. The most prestigious and powerful of these lay organizations, in Portugal as well as throughout the Portuguese empire, was the *Misericordia.* This institution was first founded in Lisbon at the close of the fifteenth century, and chapters spread rapidly throughout the Portuguese world. Larger and more prestigious than their local counterparts, *Misericordia* chapters in addition to their other activities became actively involved in the establishment and maintenance of *recolhimentos* ("institutional shelters") such as orphanages and Madaleines (houses for repentant prostitutes).

The Catholic Reformation church and its Portuguese parishioners came into direct conflict over issues of morality. As visitation and Inquisition records clearly demonstrate, Portuguese parishioners saw no contradiction between their religious beliefs and their social/sexual activity. The Catholic Reformation church condemned a wide variety of communally accepted behavior such as extramarital sexuality, drunkenness, and blasphemy. However, parishioners unrepentantly continued to engage in these activities despite clerical admonitions, monetary fines, and even the threat of excommunication.

BIBLIOGRAPHY

Brettell, Caroline B. "The Priest and His People: The Contractual Basis for Religious Practice in Rural Portugal." In *Religious Orthodoxy and Popular Faith in European Society,* edited by Ellen Badone, pp. 55–75. Princeton, 1990. An anthropological perspective on the relationship between the Catholic church and its parishioners.

Johnson, H. B., Jr. "Portrait of a Portuguese Parish: Santa Maria de Alvarenga in 1719." In *Estudos de História de Portugal,* vol. 2, pp. 180–201. Lisbon, 1983. Provides an excellent picture of Portuguese parish activities.

Oliveira Marques, A. H. de. *Daily Life in Portugal in the Late Middle Ages.* Madison, Wis., 1971. The English translation of a seminal Portuguese work that includes an overview of religious attitudes and activities in the period just before the Catholic Reformation.

Riegelhaupt, Joyce. "Festas and Padres: The Organization of Religious Action in a Portuguese Parish." *American Anthropologist* 75 (1973), 835–851.

Sanchis, Pierre. "The Portuguese 'romarias.'" In *Saints and Their Cults: Studies in Religious Sociology, Folklore and History,* edited by Stephen Wilson, pp. 261–289. Cambridge, 1983. A helpful discussion of the meaning of *romarias.*

ALLYSON M. POSKA

Popular Religion in the Low Countries

Historians of popular religion in the Netherlands have faced the same difficulties, in terms of the scarcity, ambiguity of sources, and problems of definition, as their colleagues in other countries; other problems, however, are peculiar to the situation in the Low Countries. If popular religion is defined as "unofficial" religious ideas and activities held widely among the people but not sanctioned and approved by religious authorities, the problem of definition becomes especially acute in the Netherlands because of the exceptionally wide range of religious opinions, both before and after the establishment of the Reformed church as the "public" church. After the first introduction of evangelical ideas in the 1520s, there was never one established body of doctrine against which "unofficial" or "popular" religious ideas could sensibly be measured.

The Reformation in the Netherlands was fed by many streams: there was no single "national" reformer with the stature of a Martin Luther or a Huldrych Zwingli. The Habsburg rulers of the Netherlands strove to maintain the monopoly of the Catholic church; hence, in the absence of a secular ruler imposing the Reformation from above, the religious situation remained in a pliable phase much longer than in Germany or England. After the official introduction of the Reformation, the Reformed Protestant church never achieved a monopoly position, nor did it wish to do so. Along with the public church, Mennonites, Lutherans, Catholics, and Jews enjoyed various degrees of religious liberty. Perhaps as much as 50 percent of the entire population did not officially belong to any church at all. Among them were the so-called *liefhebbers,* or "amateurs," who visited the occasional Reformed sermon without becoming a full *lidmaat* ("member"); the adherents of numerous religious sects; people indifferent to any sort of religion; and possibly full-fledged atheists. In this situation of bewildering plurality, it is hardly meaningful to distinguish ideas between those approved and those unapproved by religious authorities. Religious ideas and activities that in the twentieth century are considered well beyond the pale of Christian dogma were, of course, not confined to the "popular" classes or to the laity. The strictly Reformed Protestant Abel Eppens (1534–1590), a well-to-do gentleman-farmer from the province of Groningen, believed in prognostications, prophecies, pacts with the devil, comets as divine warnings, and astrology. He shared these beliefs with most of his contemporaries, Protestant and Catholic, urban and rural, literate and illiterate, and laity and clergy.

Sources illuminating religious ideas among the population

at large are scarce and notoriously hard to interpret. Although literacy rates were high in the Netherlands (particularly in the numerous cities), pious works and theological tracts, printed in abundance, may not necessarily have reflected the religious opinions of ordinary people. Their readership is not known, nor how they were understood. Some works of the "popular" Reformation survive, but problems of authorship and chronology prevent a reliable assessment of their influence. Preaching was, of course, the most common way in which religious ideas were divulged, but those sermons that were published were probably exceptional, and it is impossible to know what they meant to those who listened to them. As for the religious opinions of those who rarely or never visited the church at all (a large part of the population, both before and after the Reformation), literally nothing is known.

Before the Reformation. Thanks to the seminal work by Abbé Jacques Toussaert, historians are relatively well informed about religious attitudes among the population in Flanders during the period before the impact of the Lutheran Reformation was felt throughout the Low Countries. For the majority of the population, "external" religious activities—such as baptism and the last sacrament or processions and pilgrimages—were more vital than dogmatic religion. The teachings of the church were accepted by all without further reflection, but their faith was "opinion rather than belief, religiosity rather than religion." Credulity and superstition replaced the dogmatic content of religion. The sacrament of penance was little observed; not many attended Mass during the year or even at Easter. Religious life in the Low Countries appears to fit well the model developed by Scribner for sixteenth-century Germany (R. W. Scribner, "Ritual and Popular Belief in Catholic Germany at the Time of the Reformation," in *Popular Culture and Popular Movements in Reformation Germany*, London, 1987, pp. 17–47). Scribner discerns three areas of ritual, which were largely overlapping. First, there was an "official" area, approved by the clergy and based on the celebration of the Mass and the administration of the sacraments. Second, there was a semiofficial area of "para-liturgical" ceremonies, including *functiones sacrae*, in which events in the liturgical year were dramatized, and "sacramentals," including exorcisms and benedictions. Finally, there was an area that had little to do with official religion: "folklorized" ritual, which had attached itself to the sacral functions, and "magical" ritual connected to the sacraments. In sixteenth-century Amsterdam, for example, *kindeke wiegen* ("baby rocking") was observed: during Mass on Christmas day children were allowed to rock small cradles and chime tiny bells brought for the occasion. At *Dommeldemet*, or Tenebrae, schoolboys brought rattles into the church and made as much noise as they could, possibly directed against the traitor Judas. On Easter Saturday a fire was lit and consecrated in the porch of the Old Church and then sold for a small sum to ward off the devil. Palm leaves, consecrated during Mass on Palm Sunday, were taken home and burned as a protection against thunderstorms.

The Early Reformation. For the period of Habsburg rule leading up to the Revolt of the Netherlands, the records of heresy trials are the most important sources, but they should be used carefully. Most religious dissidents were tried before a secular court, which had only to establish whether the antiheresy edicts had been contravened, not what an individual actually believed. On the other hand, these sources often provide a lively picture of how passionately ordinary people discussed religious issues at home or in taverns.

During the early years of the Reformation, many dissidents professed opinions that were quite unrelated to the teachings of Luther or other German and Swiss reformers. In particular, many evangelicals went further than Luther's rejection of transubstantiation and boldly denied the presence of Christ in the elements of the Eucharist. The consecrated host was "mere bread," no better than the corruptible bread in one's larder. Wendelmoet Claesdochter of Monnikendam, questioned during her trial in November 1527 about the holy oil used to anoint the sick, bluntly responded that "oil was good for a salad or for greasing boots." Pieter Floriszoon, a crippled tailor from Gouda, curiously compared the Virgin Mary to "a sack that once held cinnamon, but now only retains the sweet flavor." Other defendants likened the Virgin to a flour bag from which the flour had been emptied or a lantern without a candle. The vicar of the main church at Leeuwarden taught that images in the church are unimportant. "The same wood used to make an image," he said, "could be used for a seat in the shithouse (*tschijdthuys*)." Perhaps the quaintest opinions came from a certain Jelys Vientz of Hoorn, who compared Our Lady to "a chimney or a pisspot," thought that the devil had composed the Apostles' Creed, and believed that Saint Lawrence had been justly put to death on a gridiron for embezzling the treasury of the local congregation. What might be called the materialism of these early Dutch "Sacramentarians" is more reminiscent of English Lollardy than of German and Swiss Reformation theology. Alastair Duke has plausibly advanced the hypothesis that these ideas may be connected to a late medieval oral tradition of dissent.

The Dutch Republic. With the establishment of the Reformed church, the minutes of the consistory meetings begin to provide insight into the religious opinions of ordinary people, but this source is doubly biased. The members of the Reformed congregation subject to ecclesiastical discipline formed only a minority of the population; moreover, they were a religious elite, admitted only after some religious training. Nevertheless, reality did not always match the ideal. Sometimes magical qualities were ascribed to the Lord's Supper. In 1616 a woman asked the ministers and elders of the Reformed community in Amsterdam to be admitted to the table of the Lord just for once in order "to be healed from her sickness." The consistory acted against church members who sought the assistance of fortune-tellers, magicians, and sorcerers when confronted with problems of love and marriage, the loss or theft of property, and the incidence of a serious disease. In general, however, the ministers and elders showed remarkable restraint in such cases. Even when witchcraft was involved, they remained skeptical, although few of them had any doubts about the existence of supernatural phenomena.

It is difficult to establish how successful the consistories were in their struggle against popular beliefs that did not match the Reformed creed. Many believers showed remarkable resistance against any attempts at confessionalization. The consistories repeatedly had to act against church members who believed that salvation could be found in other churches as well. In 1592 a Franciscan friar was surprised at how easily the Hollanders remarked that a deceased person, of whatever religious persuasion, was "with the Lord." As late as 1713 peasants from North Holland, Protestant and Catholic alike, flocked to the site of a well, formerly dedicated to Our Lady, which miraculously had begun to flow again. Its water was said to be singularly effective against the cattle plague.

Catholicism. Catholic missionary clergy in the Dutch Republic appropriated popular religious beliefs and practices and used them as a strategy for confessional identification. The cult of saints, devotional practices, fraternities, and processions became a distinguishing mark of Catholic identity, in sharp contrast to the alleged drabness of Calvinism.

In the southern or "Spanish" Netherlands, however, a triumphant Counter-Reformation wiped out most traces of evangelical sympathies among the population and successfully worked to win their allegiance to post-Tridentine Catholicism. Visitation records illuminate how popular religious attitudes were gradually transformed by the Counter-Reformation. The attitude of religious authorities toward sorcery and witchcraft stands in marked contrast to the moderate stance of the Reformed consistories in the North. The offensive of Catholic authorities against popular religion took the form of a fierce antiwitchcraft campaign.

BIBLIOGRAPHY

Bergsma, Wiebe. *De wereld volgens Abel Eppens: Een Ommelander boer uit de zestiende eeuw.* Groningen, 1988. An attempt to reconstruct from his own writings the world-view of a sixteenth-century gentleman-farmer from the province of Groningen.

Decavele, Johan. *De dageraad van de reformatie in Vlaanderen, 1520–1565.* 2 vols. Brussels, 1975. An excellent work on the Reformation in Flanders.

Deursen, A. Th. van. *Plain Lives in a Golden Age: Popular Culture, Religion and Society in Seventeenth-Century Holland.* Translated by Maarten Ultee. Cambridge, 1991. The best introduction to popular culture and popular religion in the Netherlands. Originally published as *Het kopergeld van de gouden eeuw,* 4 vols., Assen, 1978–1980.

Duke, Alastair. *Reformation and Revolt in the Low Countries.* London and Ronceverte, W.Va., 1990. Among the best works in any language on the Reformation in the Netherlands.

Roodenburg, Herman. *Onder censuur: De kerkelijke tucht in de gereformeerde gemeente van Amsterdam, 1578–1700.* Hilversum, 1990. A study of the activities of the Amsterdam Reformed consistory; sensitive to issues of popular religion and popular culture.

Rooiakkers, Gerard, and Theo van der Zee. *Religieuze volkscultuur: De spanning tussen de voorgeschreven orde en de geleefde praktijk.* Nijmegen, 1986. Contains a bibliography of works on popular religion in the Netherlands.

Toussaert, Jacques. *Le sentiment religieux en Flandre à la fin du moyen âge.* Paris, 1963. A path-breaking work on religious attitudes among the ordinary people at the eve of the Reformation, yet flawed by the author's attempts to measure late medieval religion against a modern yardstick.

Woltjer, J. J. *Friesland in hervormingstijd.* Leiden, 1962. A classic study on the Reformation in Friesland.

HENK VAN NIEROP

Popular Religion in Scandinavia

Because the topic of popular religion in Scandinavia has not been the object of much research, what follows is an outline of the late-medieval background, a presentation of the scattered evidence of sixteenth-century popular religion, and a discussion of the issues. The evidence concerning popular religion in the Nordic countries before the Reformation reveals only those expressions of popular piety and rituals that were sanctioned by the church. Some popular rituals, such as the Yuletide feasts, may have heathen roots, but to distinguish pagan from Christian elements in late-medieval Scandinavia is to set up a false dichotomy. The building of churches and chapels, the payment of tithes, and the donation of land and money to ecclesiastical institutions show that by the high Middle Ages the Nordic peoples had accepted the main tenets of the Christian church and shaped their values and ideals after Christian teachings. By 1500 the Scandinavian countries had been Christian for 400–500 years. Pagan rituals, customs, and figures had been transformed into expressions of Christian piety acceptable to the church and its officials. The feast of Saint John the Baptist (24 June), for example, falls right after the summer solstice, which had always been celebrated. This solstice continued to be celebrated, but in all likelihood people sincerely believed that they were celebrating the saint. Another example is the feast of Saint Lucia (13 December), which fell on the day that was generally believed to be the winter solstice.

Expressions of popular piety were found most clearly in the cult of the saints and of the Virgin Mary, which was common throughout Catholic Europe. In the late Middle Ages the cults of Saint Anne, of the Holy Family, and of the Suffering Christ also flowered in the north and were expressed in art (wall paintings, altarpieces, and statues) and in the founding of religious fraternities (rosary societies and Corpus Christi guilds). In addition to these saints, there were specifically Nordic saints, some known only locally but others more widely, such as the Norwegian Saint Olav (995–1030) and the Swedish saints Erik (d. about 1160) and Birgitta (1303–1373, canonized 1391).

Not until about 1600 was there a consolidation of the Nordic Reformation—that is, the point at which the Lutheran state had been established with politics and religion intertwined under the government of the king, with a well-defined set of doctrines, and with a church organization capable of teaching the people the contents and form of this new church. Throughout this period the kings of Denmark, who also ruled Norway and Iceland, adhered firmly to the Lutheran faith. Among the Swedish kings, who also ruled Finland, some favored Lutheranism and others Catholicism.

The Nordic peoples appear to have found their own compromise between the old and the new faiths, regardless of the faith of their prince. The Virgin Mary and the saints continued to appeal to people, not as a consciously formulated, underground alternative to the Lutheran faith and church, but as a popular addition to the authorized faith.

When masses and feasts for saints and the Virgin Mary were abolished and pilgrim shrines demolished, the artistic expressions of pre-Reformation popular piety remained visible on the walls in the churches. More often than not, the early reformers preferred to use the images of saints as illustrations of their sermons rather than to destroy them. Only when images were openly adored and considered divine did the church interfere.

Some images were hidden in private homes. On isolated Norwegian farms, statues were kept that were offered food and drink every year. Older scholars have proposed a pre-Christian cult origin for this practice, but a more obvious explanation is that these statues had adorned medieval churches and were carried into the safety and privacy of homes after the Reformation. Pictures, jewelry, and textiles bearing images of the Virgin Mary and of the saints appear in private inventories of household objects from the later sixteenth century in Denmark.

Well into the modern period, pregnant and parturient women continued using amulets and rituals connected with female saints and reciting verses and rhymes that had their roots in prayers to the Virgin Mary and Saint Margaret. In Iceland small manuscripts of Margaret's *vita* were produced after the Reformation for use at childbirth.

During the seventeenth and eighteenth centuries, peasants in all Nordic countries regularly organized processions in their fields, with statues of saints or banners bearing their images, in order to insure good weather and bountiful harvest, even though the church prohibited such ceremonies. The yearly fairs held in various towns of the kingdoms also retained their medieval names, taken from the saint whose feast day fell on or near the date of the fair.

The many holy wells that played an important role in popular belief in the early modern period appeared after the Reformation. These wells may have fulfilled a popular demand for miracle-working objects after the major pilgrimage shrines, saints' graves, and miracle-working pictures had been removed or destroyed.

At some point verses, names, and tales changed from being part of popular religion to being part of folklore, completely separate from the church, but it is hard to say when this happened. After 1600 efforts were made to teach the population the proper Lutheran faith; such efforts helped separate elements of folklore and what church authorities considered superstition from proper religious beliefs and customs. This was, however, a long process, which in the more remote areas of Scandinavia was not completed until the late nineteenth century.

While elements of late-medieval popular piety thus continued, albeit transformed, there is no evidence of extensive popular support for the Catholic church and priests after 1550. The popular religion of the Nordic countries during the Reformation period was not an expression of preference for one confession or the other but of the religious beliefs held by ordinary people and by some ministers that were shaped by political events, the rise of the national states, and the organizational and educational abilities of the reformed churches. The discrete features of this popular religion have yet to be described in detail or analyzed.

BIBLIOGRAPHY

Andersen, Susanne. "Helligkilder og valfart." In *Fromhed og verdslighed i middelalder og renaissance: Festskrift til Thelma Jexlev*, edited by Ebba Waaben et al., pp. 32–44. Odense, 1985. Analyzes the appearance of holy wells after the Reformation.

Brohed, Ingmar, ed. *Reformationens konsolidering i de nordiska länderna, 1540–1610*. Oslo, 1990. Several of the articles on the consolidation of the Nordic Reformation touch on popular religion; copious references.

Dahlerup, Troels. "Sin, Crime, Punishment and Absolution: The Disciplinary System of the Danish Church in the Reformation Century." In *Die dänische Reformation vor ihrem internationalen Hintergrund*, edited by Leif Grane and Kai Horby, pp. 277–288. Göttingen, 1990. Abbreviated version of the author's article in *Reformationens konsolidering* that argues that disciplinary measures were successful in reforming the population to the degree that popular religious expressions were believed to be Protestant, not Catholic.

Jacobsen, Grethe. "Pregnancy and Childbirth in the Medieval North: A Typology of Sources and a Preliminary Study." *Scandinavian Journal of History* 9.2 (1984), 9–111. Includes a discussion of popular beliefs during the Middle Ages and the Reformation.

———. "Nordic Women and the Reformation." In *Women in Reformation and Counter-Reformation Europe: Public and Private Worlds*, edited by Sherrin Marshall, pp. 47–67. Bloomington, Ind., 1989. Includes a discussion of popular beliefs held by women.

Jørgensen, Ellen. *Helgendyrkelse i Danmark: Studier over Kirkekultur og kirkeligt Liv fra det llte Aarhundredes Midte til Reformationen*. Copenhagen, 1909. This older dissertaion is still the best overview of medieval saint cults, though some arguments have been disproved by newer research (e.g., see *Kulturhistorisk Leksikon for Nordisk Middelalder*).

Kolsrud, Oluf. "Folket og reformasjonen i Noreg." In *Heidersskrift til Gustav Indrebø på femtiårsdagen 17, november 1939*, pp. 23–53. Bergen, 1939. Argues that the Reformation brought social disorder and, in some cases, led to the murder of ministers by enraged parishioners. The author's sources (primarily folktales) are of dubious value, but the article contains information on popular reaction to the Reformation.

Kulturhistorisk Leksikon for Nordisk Middelalder fra Vikingetid til Reformationstid. 22 vols. Copenhagen, Oslo, and Stockholm, 1956–1978. Includes articles on cults of saints, ceremonies, feast days, and popular rites from c.800 to c.1550.

Semmingsen, Ingrid, et al., eds. *Norges kulturhistorie.* Vol. 2, *Kaupang og katedral.* Oslo, 1979. Good introduction to popular piety during the Middle Ages and the sixteenth century; sparse but useful references.

GRETHE JACOBSEN

POPULATION. During the sixteenth century, Europe's population grew from roughly sixty million to roughly eighty million. Rates of change varied considerably across Europe. For example, England's population nearly doubled, but extensive emigration meant that of Portugal only marked time. Population densities during the period also varied widely. For example, in Lombardy (northern Italy) and the Netherlands it was greater than one hundred per square kilometer in 1550 but less than thirty in much of southern Italy and well below ten in vast tracts of eastern and northern Europe.

Not only did population grow but more people came to inhabit towns and cities. One Dutch person in five lived in a town of five thousand or more inhabitants as early as 1550. By contrast, urbanization in eastern Europe and Scandinavia was negligible: less than 1 percent of the population lived in a large city. Saxony is more typical of European urbanization in 1550: it had just eight cities of five thousand people or more but 133 towns with two thousand or fewer. This is important because the Protestant Reformation of the sixteenth century was primarily, if not exclusively, an urban phenomenon. Relatively extensive urbanization in Germany and the Netherlands helped Protestantism to spread and take hold, but the example of northern Italy—highly urbanized and firmly Catholic—warns us against hasty generalizations. Nor should we exaggerate the extent of urbanization, for even in 1600 more than 90 percent of Europe's people lived in the countryside or in very small towns and villages. Paris, probably the largest city in Europe in 1500 (perhaps 200,000 inhabitants) and again in 1600 (300,000), was small compared with a modern metropolis.

We know that the relatively rapid growth between 1500 and 1600 was unparalleled since the late thirteenth- and early fourteenth-century rise which had been cut short by the Black Death. The reasons for population increase are less certain. Life expectancy at birth rose—from just over thirty years in early sixteenth-century England to roughly forty years by 1600—thanks largely to a reduction in the incidence and virulence of infectious diseases such as plague and influenza. Mortality still sometimes rose to appalling heights but only for brief periods. Fertility also increased because in many parts of Europe women began to marry younger and fewer remained unmarried at the end of their reproductive years. Because there was no widespread use of contraception these changes in marriage practice ("nuptiality") were the most significant influence on fertility. (Whether there was much knowledge of contraceptive techniques in the early modern period is an issue debated by historians; population data indicate, however, that even if people knew something about contraception—the primary means available was coitus interruptus—they rarely practiced it.) Migration, much of it to the New World, helped to ease population pressures in some countries, but rates were generally low. The relative importance of fertility, mortality, and migration varied considerably across Europe, and there is no single explanation of change that fits all countries.

A 30-percent increase in numbers over one hundred years may seem unremarkable from our modern viewpoint. However, population growth took place in relatively "backward" economies with generally low levels of agricultural productivity and limited transportation facilities. It brought in its wake important economic and social consequences. The sixteenth century saw relatively rapid price inflation, fueled partly by monetary forces such as the inflow of bullion from the New World and by devaluations of coinage, but also by growing demand for food, clothing, and housing. Sometimes the demand for food simply could not be met, and the second half of the sixteenth century saw periodic but serious shortages. The French Wars of Religion drew to a close amid a decade marked by famine, disease, and death. European societies filled up from the bottom, and the poor formed a much larger proportion of the population in 1600 than in 1500. From the 1530s and 1540s towns across Europe instituted new measures to deal with poverty, and countries such as England responded to growing inequalities of wealth by implementing national poor laws at the end of the sixteenth century. Religious ideas informed the different approaches to poverty across Europe. Important landmarks in the Reformation derived some of their distinctive character from the results of population growth and social polarization, notably the German Peasants' War of 1525. The development of commerce spurred by the direct and indirect consequences of demographic increase helped the dissemination of Protestantism by creating contacts within Europe and enabled the spread of both Protestantism and Catholicism to the rest of the globe.

Demography formed an important part of the context in which the Reformation took place. However, population structures and trends in the sixteenth century must not be seen as the sole determinants of social and religious change. Indeed, religious developments influenced aspects of demographic behavior. For example, Protestant and Catholic churches began to insist on a closer definition of what constituted wedlock and to curb the sexual anticipation of marriage which had traditionally formed part of popular culture. As with many other aspects of social and cultural life, the relationship between demographic and religious change was a two-way street.

BIBLIOGRAPHY

Dupâquier, J., and J.-P. Bardet, eds. *Histoire de la population européenne.* Vol. 1. Paris, 1992. Comprehensive surveys of both countries and themes to 1700 by leading authorities. Supersedes all earlier surveys of European population. Available in English, French, German, and Italian editions.

Houston, R. A. *The Population History of Britain and Ireland, 1500–1750.* London, 1991. A brief and lucid survey of sources, methodologies, and findings relating to one part of Europe.

R. A. Houston

PORTUGAL. A kingdom on the Iberian Peninsula bordered on the west and south by the Atlantic Ocean and on the north and east by the kingdom of Spain (or, more specifically, Castile and León). Its population was less than two million and chiefly inhabited the coastal plains and river valleys from Lisbon north. Most engaged in agriculture. The southern part of Portugal was semiarid and thinly populated, and the maritime and mercantile communities on which the great explorations depended were of limited size. Lisbon between 1527 and 1620 did grow dramatically from 65,000 to 165,000; the other principal towns—Oporto, Coimbra, Évora, and Elvas—never exceeded 20,000. Portuguese was spoken throughout the kingdom, and the population was remarkably homogenous, save for a few descendants of Moors surviving in the southern countryside and a small but influential urban Jewish population, which was broken up after 1496 through expulsion or conversion to Christianity.

The ruling House of Aviz achieved the throne in 1385 when John I (r. 1385–1433) defeated his rivals and repelled invasion by Castile. He continued the tradition of strong monarchical government that had forged the Portuguese nation-state, and he enjoyed the support of the representative Cortes ("parliaments") and in particular the towns. In 1415 John, moved by crusading zeal and economic interest, captured Ceuta in Morocco, opening the age of Portuguese overseas expansion. His son Prince Henry the Navigator (1394–1460) promoted the colonization of Madeira and the Azores and exploration along the African coast, on which forts and missions were established. While significant conversions were achieved, at the price of considerable syncretism, the Portuguese also entered the slave trade with native rulers and began the export of Africans; some were shipped to Europe, but after 1500 they were sent in ever growing numbers to the New World.

In 1498 an expedition commanded by Vasco da Gama reached India. By the end of the reign of Manuel the Fortunate (r. 1495–1525), Portugal had established dominion over Goa and the Malabar Coast of India, Malacca in Malaya, and Amboina in the Spice Islands (Moluccas), and had begun the colonization of Brazil. Macao was added to its holdings in 1557, and trading and missionary activities spread to Japan.

The Catholic zeal of Ferdinand I and Isabella's Spain affected Portugal, promoting reform in the church and increasing devotion. It also determined the fate of Portugal's Jews, whose number, with the arrival in 1492 of Jews expelled from Spain, increased to nearly 100,000, some 5 percent of the population. Under pressure from the Spanish rulers, Manuel expelled them from Portugal by a series of edicts published in 1496 and 1497. While many left, particularly after a massacre of Jews in Lisbon in 1506, most accepted baptism and became New Christians (*cristoãos novos*).

Despite popular resentment, the New Christians enjoyed full legal rights and were able, through commercial influence, to hinder until 1531 the authorization of an Inquisition that might pry into their religious practices. After an uneven start the Inquisition began in 1547 to hound the New Christian community in search of Judaizers with a zeal that exceeded that of Spain. It is the Portuguese term *auto da fé* that is used in English for the Inquisition's public spectacle of repentance and punishment, not the Spanish *auto de fé.*

Statutes of purity of blood (*limpeza de sangue*), like those of Spain, were also decreed, forbidding important state and church offices to descendants of Jews. Though New Christians wealth, influence, and intermarriage with noble families made the statutes difficult to enforce, they proved a serious nuisance.

The Inquisition, seeking evidence of Protestant heresy, rooted out Erasmian humanists from Portuguese education. In 1547 King John III (r. 1525–1557) had chartered the Colegio das Artes at the University of Coimbra and provided a faculty of distinguished humanist scholars headed by André de Gouveia. Most were Portuguese who had taught in colleges in Paris and Bordeaux, but their number included several Frenchmen and the Scot George Buchanan. On the testimony of academic rivals, the Inquisition indicted Gouveia's successor, João da Costa, as well as Diogo de Teive and Buchanan, on charges of Lutheranism, Judaism, and various other disorders. Despite their denials, they were convicted to terms of confinement. (When released in 1552, Buchanan returned to France, converted to Calvinism, and participated in the Scottish Reformation.) In 1555 the Jesuits, who backed the inquisitors, gained control of the college. They were soon the dominant force everywhere in Portuguese education and opened their own university at Évora.

The Jesuits had established themselves early in Portugal and by the 1550s eclipsed the older orders of Dominicans and Franciscans. John III's grandson and heir, Dom Sebastian (1557–1578), was educated by Jesuits; his widowed mother, Princess Juana, sister of Philip II of Spain, was the only woman ever allowed to take Jesuit scholastic vows. In 1571 the Jesuit provincial Simão Rodrigues fomented the trial by the Inquisition of the last Erasmian—the aged humanist, historian, and sometime diplomat Damião de Góis. His humiliation and conviction to two years in prison dramatized the triumph of strict Tridentine orthodoxy.

In 1578 Dom Sebastian fell while leading a madcap crusade into Morocco. After the brief reign of Sebastian's great-uncle, Henry, a cardinal and grand inquisitor, Philip II of Spain annexed the kingdom in 1580. Portugal retained, however, its separate institutions and in 1640 regained its independence from Spain. Dom Sebastian became a messianic figure in the Portuguese imagination and hero of Portugal's apocalyptic destiny to become the "Fifth Monarchy."

Overseas missionary activity is probably the most remarkable religious achievement of Portugal in the era. Though the evangelization of the Congo and Angola stagnated because of the slave trade, the Christian message was carried, with Jesuits in the forefront, to Portuguese Asia and Brazil. Despite European anxieties and prejudice, natives were often educated and ordained to the clergy. In 1518 Leo X consecrated as a bishop a son of the king of Congo, who in 1521 established his see in his homeland. Goa became Christian, while the indigenous Nestorian Christian community of the Malabar Coast was coerced into orthodoxy. In Japan, after considerable success and a belated decision to form a native clergy, missionaries and thousands of converts were slaughtered or expelled between 1614 and 1639 by the Tokugawa shoguns. In China Portuguese missionaries were prominent in unsuccessful efforts to convert the emperor and court.

BIBLIOGRAPHY

Boxer, C. R. *The Church Militant and Iberian Expansion, 1440–1770.* Baltimore, 1978. Brilliantly summarizes Portuguese missionary activity.

Diffie, Bailey W., and George D. Winius. *Foundations of the Portuguese Empire, 1450–1580.* Minneapolis, 1977.

Herculano, Alexandre. *History of the Origin and Establishment of the Inquisition in Portugal.* Translated by John C. Branner. Reprint, New York, 1972. Remains useful.

Hurst, Elisabeth Feist. *Damião de Gois.* The Hague, 1967. A biography, it introduces Portuguese humanism and lists the essential works.

Silva Dias, José Sebastião da. *Correntes do sentimento religioso em Portugal.* 2 vols. Coimbra, Portugal, 1960. The standard introduction.

PETER O'M. PIERSON

POSSESSION AND EXORCISM. In Christian belief, possession is the process whereby a demonic spirit invades the body of a human being, assumes control of its physical movements, and alters its personality. It is to be distinguished from obsession, in which the body is assaulted externally by demons but not actually inhabited. The recorded symptoms or marks of possession in medieval and early modern Europe were not always the same, but they often included bodily contortions and convulsions, the ability to perform great feats of strength, clairvoyance, the vomiting of foreign objects, insensitivity to pain, knowledge of previously unknown foreign languages, and speaking in strange voices. European demoniacs also exhibited a horror and revulsion of sacred things and the words of scripture, and they frequently uttered obscenities and blasphemies. The number of reported cases of possession increased dramatically throughout Europe in the second half of the sixteenth century. These possessions could be either individual or collective, the latter often involving groups of children and nuns. Although possession was not restricted to persons of any particular age or sex, the majority of victims in all known cases were adult females.

The evident rise in demonic possession in the late sixteenth century coincided with a dramatic increase in the number of witchcraft prosecutions. Both developments reflect the demonization of learned and popular culture that accompanied the Protestant and Catholic Reformations. Witchcraft and possession were often directly linked, since witches were often accused of causing possessions. Contemporary demonological theory acknowledged two methods of possession. Either a demon could enter a person's body directly, with God's permission but without any human agency, or it could enter the person's body as the result of a witch's command. In the latter case, possession became just one of many maleficent deeds of which a witch might be accused. Accusations of witchcraft from demoniacs occurred throughout the early modern period, but they reached their peak in the early seventeenth century. Many of the large group possessions of nuns or children, such as those at Aix-en-Provence (1609–1611), Lille (1613), Loudun (1632–1638), and Louviers (1643–1647), included charges of witchcraft.

Demonologists usually made a sharp distinction between demoniacs and witches on the grounds that possession, unlike witchcraft, was an involuntary condition and was not considered sinful or criminal. The demoniac, unlike the witch, was not held responsible for her actions, which often included unconventional, rebellious, and immoral behavior, although the distinction between witches and demoniacs was occasionally blurred. In Germany some demoniacs were reported to have made pacts with the Devil, even though they were not prosecuted for witchcraft, while in Puritan New England there was a popular fear that demoniacs, if not dispossessed, would become witches.

During the sixteenth century Protestant theologians qualified but never completely rejected the belief in demonic possession. Luther accepted its reality, considering it mainly as punishment for sin, while Melanchthon declared it "most certain that devils enter into the hearts of some men and cause frenzy and torment in them." Calvin did not, as the Jesuit Louis Richeome later claimed, deny the reality of demons and demonic possession, even though he had a more spiritual view of demonic power than did Luther. Calvin did, however, assert that the age of miracles had ceased, and this doctrine led a number of later writers, including the English clerics John Jewel and Samuel Harsnett, to claim that the "miracles" of both possession and dispossession would not recur. At the University of Cambridge the question whether "in these days there is no possession or dispossession of demons" was the subject of a disputation at the turn of the seventeenth century.

Belief in the reality of possession did not preclude skepticism regarding the authenticity of specific cases. Following standard medieval practice, the Catholic church required the administration of a series of tests to determine whether a possession was bona fide, and sixteenth century Catholic demonologists like the Italian Franciscan Girolamo Menghi insisted upon rigorous testing of demoniacs before dispossession. The Synod of Rheims (1583) required that demoniacs be questioned to establish their credibility before an exorcism could be performed. It was common for French, German, and English Protestants to expose counterfeit possessions, especially when their confessional rivals used such cases for political advantage. A number of writers, including the French royal physician Michel Marescot, attributed the afflictions of demoniacs to disease. The Lutheran physician Johann Weyer, while accepting the authenticity of the group possession of nuns at Wertet in 1491, attributed most others to either melancholia or diabolical delusion. In the early seventeenth century the English physician Edward Jorden diagnosed the possession of the fourteen-year-old Mary Glover as hysteria.

The process of exorcising or dispossessing demoniacs was a source of much greater theological controversy than the phenomenon of possession itself. Throughout the early modern period the Catholic church continued to use the ritual of exorcism to expel demons from the persons they inhabited. Exorcism was a ceremony of varying length, performed either publicly or privately, involving the recitation of prayers, blessing with holy water, reading from scripture, and repeated signs of the cross. Occasionally it included the use of the sacraments and relics of the martyrs. The essence of the rite was putting the demon on oath in order to interrogate him and commanding him to depart. The efficacy of an exorcism, unlike that of a sacrament, was considered to be dependent on the moral state of the priest who performed it; hence it could be used to prove the holiness of the exorcist as well as to relieve the afflicted. During the Reformation period Catholics used exorcism to demonstrate the truth of Catholic doctrine and to convert Protestants. In Augsburg, where Catholic priests conducted a series of controversial exorcisms in the 1560s and 1570s, the ritual became a central means by which the Counter-Reformation progressed. In France the highly publicized exorcism of a sixteen-year-old demoniac at Laon in 1566 and the dispossession of four women at Soissons in 1582, both of which involved the use of the Eucharist to expel the demons, served as propaganda against the Huguenots. In England exorcism played a significant role in the efforts of English Catholic missionaries to return the English church to Rome during the reign of Elizabeth I.

Protestants uniformly rejected the Catholic ritual of exorcism as fraudulent magic, but they generally permitted efforts to dispossess demoniacs by means of prayer and fasting. For Melanchthon devils could be expelled by "the prayers of pious men" and by commands for them to depart, but not by the "worshipping of bread," the use of holy water, and the invocation of the saints. The Lutheran writer Johannes Marbach, while condemning the exorcisms conducted by the Jesuit Peter Canisius as collusions with the Devil, admitted that genuine exorcisms could take place. The English church never prohibited exorcisms, although the canons of 1604 required Anglican clergymen to receive episcopal permission to perform the rite "in any fashion." Reports of actual Protestant exorcisms are relatively rare. In 1536 the Protestant clergy of Frankfurt an der Oder, on Luther's recommendation, relieved the symptoms of possession in a sixteen-year-old girl by bringing her to divine service and praying for her. Luther himself attempted one exorcism in 1545, as did at least one Protestant pastor during the 1560s in Augsburg. In the 1580s and 1590s the English Puritan minister John Darrell dispossessed a number of children using only prayer and fasting. Darrell and another exorcist, the minister George More, publicized their success in order to refute the claim made by Roman Catholics that their power to cast out devils proved that theirs was the one true church.

In addition to expelling demons from those who were possessed, exorcism had a prominent place in the ritual of baptism. In the early church exorcism was used to drive away the evil spirits in those about to be baptized, and hence it became part of the baptismal liturgy of the medieval church. In the early years of the Reformation, most Lutherans retained the rite, but since it was considered a nonessential part of the sacrament, some Lutheran churches chose to omit it. Reformed Protestants, however, uniformly eliminated it on the grounds that it was popish and magical. In late sixteenth-century Germany a heated controversy arose between Lutherans and Calvinists over the use of baptismal exorcism. The Calvinists claimed that it implied the exclusion of children from God's covenant of grace, while the Lutherans contended that its omission amounted to a denial of original sin. In England Archbishop Thomas Cranmer retained baptismal exorcism in *The Book of Common Prayer* of 1549, but the second Edwardian book of 1552 omitted it.

Exorcism also formed a part of the blessing ceremonies performed by priests in Catholic parishes. Salt and holy water were exorcised each Sunday, while candles were the subject of the same ritual on Candlemas Day. In addition to serving liturgical purposes, the blessed and exorcised substances were also used by the clergy and the laity to expel demons from persons, places, animals, and inanimate objects. The texts of the liturgical blessings and exorcisms served as models for numerous "magical" charms and invocations, many of which were used for protective or curative purposes. These lesser exorcisms, as well as the charms that derived from them, were condemned by Protestants, especially those in the Reformed tradition, as magical and superstitious.

[*See also* Magic *and* Witchcraft.]

BIBLIOGRAPHY

Goddu, André. "The Failure of Exorcism in the Middle Ages." *Soziale Ordnungen im Selbstverständnis des Mittelalters* 12 (1980), 540–557. Explores changes in theological thought in response to failure of exorcisms.

MacDonald, Michael, ed. *Witchcraft and Hysteria in Elizabethan England: Edward Jorden and the Mary Glover Case.* London, 1991. Contains a valuable introduction and reprints of three contemporary treatises.

Mandrou, Robert. *Magistrats et sorciers en France au XVIIe siècle: Une analyse de psychologie historique.* Reprint, Paris, 1980. Discusses the connection between possession and witch hunting.

Midelfort, H. C. Erik. "The Devil and the German People: Reflections on the Popularity of Demon Possession in Sixteenth-Century Germany." In *Religion and Culture in the Renaissance and Reformation,* edited by Steven Ozment, pp. 99–119. Sixteenth Century Essays and Studies, 11. Kirksville, Mo., 1989. Reveals differences between popular and learned views of possession.

Mora, George, ed. *Witches, Devils, and Doctors in the Renaissance: Johann Weyer, De Praestigiis daemonum.* Medieval and Renaissance Texts and Studies, 73. Binghamton, N.Y., 1991. Contains commentaries on many cases of possession.

Nischan, Bodo. "The Exorcism Controversy and Baptism in the Late Reformation." *Sixteenth Century Journal* 18 (1987), 31–51. Studies the differences between Lutherans and Calvinists regarding the baptismal rite.

Oesterreich, Traugott K. *Possession, Demoniacal, and Other among Primitive Races in Antiquity, the Middle Ages and Modern Times.* Translated by D. Ibberson. New Hyde Park, N.Y., 1966. Places the European phenomenon in a broader context.

Pearl, Jonathan L. "'A School for the Rebel Soul': Politics and Demonic Possession in France." *Historical Reflections* 16 (1989), 286–306. A study of works by Catholic French demonologists in the late sixteenth and early seventeenth century.

Roper, Lyndal. "Magic and Theology of the Body: Exorcism in Sixteenth-Century Augsburg." In *No Gods Except Me: Orthodoxy and Religious Practice in Europe, 1200–1600,* edited by Charles Zika, pp. 84–113. Melbourne, 1991. Reveals differences between Protestants and Catholics regarding the link between the physical and the spiritual.

Thomas, Keith. *Religion and the Decline of Magic.* London, 1971. Deals with possession and exorcism in England within the context of the Reformation.

Walker, Anita M., and Edmund H. Dickerman. "'A Woman under the Influence': A Case of Alleged Possession in Sixteenth-Century France." *Sixteenth Century Journal* 22 (1991), 535–554. An analysis of the famous case of Marthe Brossier in 1598.

Walker, D. P. *Unclean Spirits: Possessions and Exorcism in France and England in the Late Sixteenth and early Seventeenth Centuries.* Philadelphia, 1981. Explores the use of exorcism for religious propaganda and establishes the connections between possession and witchcraft.

BRIAN P. LEVACK

POSSEVINO, Antonio (Fr., Possevin; 1533–1611), Jesuit preacher, diplomat, and writer. Possevino was born at Mantua to a family of goldsmiths. After a humanist education he served as tutor to two Gonzaga princes, both future cardinals. Months after entering the Jesuits in 1559 he was sent to negotiate the establishment of a Jesuit college at Mondovì with Duke Emanuele Filiberto of Savoy. He spent the years 1561 to 1573 in France as preacher, writer, and superior, mainly at Lyon and Avignon. From 1573 to 1577 he was secretary to the Jesuit general in Rome.

Gregory XIII sent Possevino as nuncio (1577–1580) to Sweden, where John III was inclining toward Catholicism. After John III reconsidered, Possevino was sent to Moscow. He mediated a treaty ending the long Livonian War between Ivan IV and King Stephen Báthory of Poland in 1581, but his efforts to open Russia to Catholicism achieved little. He did help establish six papal seminaries in Poland-Lithuania, Moravia, and Transylvania to train priests for work in Scandinavia and eastern Europe. He wrote three books for Gregory XIII that described Moscovia, Livonia, and Transylvania and provided plans to foster Catholicism in them. Possevino had close ties with Stephen Báthory, who died in 1586. He fell into disfavor with the Habsburgs, Sixtus V, and Claudio Acquaviva, the Jesuit general, who exiled him to Padua in 1587.

Possevino's last twenty-three years, spent mainly at Padua, Venice, Bologna, and Ferrara, were largely devoted to writing. His forty books include several polemical works against Protestants. His most lengthy and important books were the *Bibliotheca selecta* (Rome, 1593) and the *Apparatus sacer* (Venice, 1603). The first gives bibliographic advice on education, theology, law, and medicine and presents plans for world evangelization. The second lists and discusses eight thousand writers, mainly theologians. Possevino's lengthy autobiography, now partly lost, remains unpublished.

BIBLIOGRAPHY

Garstein, Oskar. *Rome and the Counter-Reformation in Scandinavia until the Establishment of the S. Congregatio de Propaganda Fide in 1622.* 2

vols. Oslo, 1963 and 1980. Possevino is a major figure in the events described in this scholarly account.

Graham, Hugh F., ed. and trans. *The Moscovia of Antonio Possevino, S.J.* Pittsburgh, 1977. Possevino's account of Russia and his dealings with Ivan the Terrible.

Polcin, Stanislas. *Une tentative d'union au XVIe siècle: La mission religieuse du Père Antoine Possevin S.I. en Moscovie, 1581–1582.* Rome, 1957. Modern account of Possevino's Moscow mission and the Russian-Polish peace he mediated.

Verzeichnis der im deutschen Sprachbereich erschienenen Drucke des XVI. Jahrhunderts. Stuttgart, 1983–. See vol. 16, nos. 4446–4474.

John Patrick Donnelly

POSTEL, Guillaume (1510–1581), French philologist, Cabbalist, missionary enthusiast, and prophet of a new age. Educated at the University of Paris, Postel accompanied a French legation to Constantinople in 1538. Here he first encountered the Arabic language, discovered the existence of Christians within the Ottoman empire, and developed an interest in the expansion of Christianity into the Near East, where he also traveled in later years. When he returned to Europe from Constantinople, this interest resulted in the publication of *Linguarum duodecim characteribus*, the first European comparative study of languages. This book expressed ideas developed in his later works: the derivation of all languages from Hebrew, the danger of Islam and the need for missions, and knowledge of languages as an instrument of world unification; he then published the first Arabic grammar in Europe. He considered *De orbis terrae concordia* (Basel, 1544) his major book; it was a rational justification of Christianity intended for missionaries to the Islamic world.

To promote his missionary projects he also joined the Society of Jesus and became a priest. But his apocalyptic concerns and his radical Gallicanism resulted in his dismissal from the society; and from this point his views became increasingly extreme, nourished by his discovery of Cabbala, whose syncretic mysticism he combined with a conception of himself as the firstborn son of the *restitutio omnium*, a new age of the world. Viewed with increasing suspicion by the church, he was eventually declared insane by the Inquisition and imprisoned in Rome from 1555 to 1559. Once released, he published his *République des Turcs* (1560), a remarkably positive account of Ottoman society. Although he gave up none of his views, his later years were more peaceful, and he collaborated in 1568 on the preparation of the Antwerp polylingual Bible published by Christophe Plantijn.

Postel always considered himself a Catholic, and his universalism made him hostile to much in Protestantism. His comparison of Protestantism with Islam angered Calvin, and he was attacked by Matthias Flacius Illyricus. But in his zeal to win converts to his views, he also sought alliance with Protestant scholar-theologians such as Philipp Melanchthon, Heinrich Bullinger, and Konrad Pellikan, and with the radical sectarians David Joris and Kaspar von Schwenckfeld. In his later years he was also attracted to the Family of Love.

BIBLIOGRAPHY

Bouwsma, William J. *Concordia Mundi: The Career and Thought of Guillaume Postel, 1510–1581.* Cambridge, Mass., 1957. Includes a bibliography of Postel's published writings and a bibliographical note on earlier scholarship.

Kuntz, Marion L. *Guillaume Postel: Prophet of the Restitution of All Things; His Life and Thought.* International Archives of the History of Ideas, vol. 98. The Hague, 1981. Emphasizes the prophetic aspects of Postel's thought, exploiting his unpublished writings.

Verzeichnis der im deutschen Sprachbereich erschienenen Drucke des XVI. Jahrhunderts. Stuttgart, 1983–. See vol. 16, nos. 4475–4484.

William J. Bouwsma

POVERTY. *See* Begging; Social Welfare.

PRAETORIUS, Michael (Ger., Schultheiss, Schulze; c.1571–1621), German composer, church and court musician, and music theorist. Born in Kreuzberg, near Eisenach, Thuringia (hence the frequent appellation Creuzbergensis), he was educated at the Latin school in Torgau, where he was immersed in the musical tradition of Johann Walter, Martin Luther's collaborator. Praetorius's father had been a colleague of Walter, and the young Praetorius was taught music by Walter's immediate successor, Michael Voigt. In 1582 he entered the University of Frankfurt an der Oder, becoming the organist of the Marienkirche in the city in early 1587. Around 1595 he became court organist to Duke Heinrich Julius of Braunschweig-Wolfenbüttel and from 1604 until his death was court Kapellmeister.

Once established as the court Kapellmeister, Praetorius began an astonishing sequence of musical publications, containing more than one thousand compositions and arrangements, mostly of church music, ranging from the diverse settings of the nine volumes of *Musae Sionae* (1605–1610) to the large-scale works of the *Polyhymnia* (1619–1620). These liturgical collections supplied a rich repertory for the Lutheran churches of the early seventeenth century, just as Georg Rhau had done with his musical publications during the first generation of Lutheranism.

His magnum opus, the *Syntagma musicum*, a systematic and encyclopedic exposition of the theory and practice of music, was issued in three volumes (1614–1619). Volume 1 deals with the purpose and function of liturgical music—essentially a valuable anthology of many citations. Volume 2 offers detailed descriptions, as well as illustrations, of musical instruments current around 1600, with a particular emphasis on the organ. Volume 3 expounds the various musical forms then current. A fourth volume, covering music theory, was announced but never published. The prefaces Praetorius wrote for many of his individual compositions, together with his *Syntagma*, provide valuable documentary evidence for the extraordinary richness of early baroque Lutheran church music in its varied use of instrumental, vocal, and choral resources. Praetorius, a contemporary of Heinrich Schütz and Claudio Monteverdi, occupies a pivotal position in the history of Lutheran church music, synthesizing the diversity of the Reformation era and providing much of the basic repertory of church music for the following generation.

BIBLIOGRAPHY

Primary Source

Praetorius, Michael. *Syntagma musicum.* 3 vols. Facsimile ed. Kassel, 1958–1959. Translations of various sections can be found in a number of American doctoral dissertations; a translation of part of vol. 2 has been issued as *De organographia, Parts I and II*, translated and edited by David Z. Crookes, Oxford, 1985.

Secondary Sources

Blankenburg, Walter. "Praetorius, Michael." In *The New Grove Dictionary of Music and Musicians*, edited by Stanley Sadie, vol. 15, pp. 188–192. This is the most up-to-date summary of the life and work of Praetorius in English; even in German there is no really substantial work on this important musician.

Gurlitt, Wilibald. *Michael Praetorius (Creuzbergensis): Sein Leben und seine Werke* (1915). Reprint, Hildesheim, 1968.

Leaver, Robin A. "The Lutheran Reformation." In *The Renaissance from the 1470s to the End of the 16th Century*, edited by I. Fenlon, pp. 263–285. London and New York, 1989.

ROBIN A. LEAVER

PRAYERBOOK REBELLION. *See* Book of Common Prayer.

PŘÁZA, Paul (Lat., Pressius; also Pavel; c.1540–1586), Czech Protestant theologian and humanist of Melanchthonian orientation. Educated at Prague University, he was a pupil of the famous Czech and Latin humanists Petrus Codicillus and Matthaeus Collinus. Subsequently he attended Wittenberg University, where he studied Latin, Greek, and Hebrew and received the degree *magister artium* in 1566. After disputations in 1568 he became a teacher at Prague University and in 1571, provost of the College of Charles IV. He tried to renew theology lectures at this university, where during the sixteenth century only a philosophy faculty existed. His activities, however, were forbidden by university authorities, and he was permitted to teach only Hebrew grammar. In 1572 he obtained his doctorate in theology at Vienna. Přáza had good contacts with the Bohemian and Moravian Protestant nobility, which prepared the way for him to enter high confessional politics. In 1575 Přáza became a leading theologian in the struggle for religious liberty of Bohemian non-Catholics and was one of the coauthors of the Bohemian Confession, a common confession of Bohemian neo-Utraquists, Lutherans, and members of the Unity of Brethren (Bohemian Brethren). He was also a coauthor of the rules for the unified Bohemian Protestant church anticipated by the framers of the confession.

Přáza had to defend himself against the accusations that he was an illegal Calvinist or Zwinglian (in 1575, 1577, and 1584). In 1577, after a short university career (1575–1576 as dean of the philosophy faculty), he left Prague for Kutná Hora, an important town in central-east Bohemia, where he became a preacher. He then moved to Styria, where he served briefly as superintendent, and then to Moravia. Under the patronage of the Moravian Protestant aristocrat Jetřich of Kunovice, he assumed the office of dean of the Lutheran church in Uherský Brod in southeastern Moravia (1581). There he ordained pastors and wrote the *Formula obligationis ordinandorum ad ministerium* (1582), *Agenda*, and *Řád církevní* (1583). His propositions, however, were disapproved because the clergy and nobility from the Unity of Brethren were resistant to the Melanchthonian principles of Přáza's regulations. Přáza had originally taken a liking toward the Bohemian and Moravian Unity of Brethren, but his faithfulness to Melanchthonian theology was accepted neither by the Orthodox Lutherans (Přáza did not accept the Formula of Concord) nor by the Unity of Brethern. Nevertheless, his theological work was very important in the compilation of the Bohemian Confession. It represented the religious thought of the majority of the Czech people (above all that of the burghers) and the long tradition of post-Hussite religious tolerance in sixteenth century Bohemia. Přáza's pedagogical and linguistic work led him to prepare several language handbooks for Czech schools, among them the *Compendium grammatices pro primis tyronibus* (Prague, 1570) and a Latin-Czech-German dictionary, *Vocabularium trilingue pro usum scholarum* (Prague, 1576).

BIBLIOGRAPHY

Burian, Ilja. "Dr. Pavel Pressius." *Křesťanská revue* 42 (1975), 70–77. Brief biography.

Hejnic, Josef, and Jan Martínek. *Rukověť humanistického básnictví Čechách a na Moravě.* 5 vols. Prague 1966–1982. See vol. 4, pp. 240–243, for a good bibliography and commentary on Přáza's Latin works.

Hrejsa, Ferdinand. *Česká konfesse, její vznik, podstata a dějiny* (The Bohemian Confession: Its Origin, Essence and History). Prague, 1912. The most important monograph on the Bohemian Confession to date; also analyzes the theological thought of Přáza.

Wižďálková, Bedřika. "K trojjazyčným vokabulářům Pavla Pressia" (On the Trilingual Dictionaries Edited by Paul Přáza). *Strahovská knihovna* 1 (1966), 39–72.

JAROSLAV PÁNEK

PREACHING AND SERMONS. [*This article comprises four articles that consider the theory and practice of homiletics in four major regions of sixteenth-century Europe: Germany, France, England, and Spain and Portugal.*]

Germany

During the sixteenth century massive changes—ecclesiastical, theological, political, economic—took place across the European landscape. In this transformation sermons played an important role—and not only in Europe, for they caused repercussions as well in parts of the world that had fallen under European domination. For preaching to have attained this profound and virtually unique significance, several factors had to converge and influence one another.

These developments were centered in Germany—specifically, the small town of Wittenberg, which in 1502 had become the seat of a university; the roots of the change, however, could be traced to southern Germany, where the form, content, and sites of medieval preaching were being abandoned and new ways were being explored. The sermons of, for example, Johann Geiler (1445–1510)—born in Schaffhausen, educated in Kaysersberg (Alsace), and subsequently preacher at Strasbourg cathedral—were earthy, direct, and full of humor. Innovative yet still tied to the old ways, Geiler advocated reform, recommended indulgences and good works, and criticized emerging humanism. Throughout southern Germany, both in larger towns such as Nuremberg and in smaller ones such as Schwäbisch-Hall, positions similar to Geiler's were created that permitted theologians (often doctors of theology) to concentrate on preaching. Many of these preachers would later become the reformers of their towns or entire regions.

Luther as Preacher. Although Luther, the first of the three leading Protestant preachers of the sixteenth century—the others being Zwingli and Calvin—preached frequently, only a few of his sermons are extant in the form in which they were delivered. These sermons, collected in so-called postils, were compiled by Luther himself so that less competent preachers could read them aloud to their congregations. In 1522 Luther composed and compiled a series of Christmas and Advent sermons—the *Wartburg Postil*—after having previously written Advent sermons in Latin; in 1525 he published his *Lent Postil.* Most of his approximately two thousand sermons, however, were edited and published by contemporaries. A number are extant in condensed versions, especially those transcribed by Georg Rörer between 1522 and 1546, frequently using Latin phrases in place of German.

Luther's sermons dealt essentially with the themes of reform as he envisioned it: law and gospel, faith and works, justification and obedience, "Christ for us" and "Christ in us." Their content—summarized by the phrases "Nothing if Christ is not preached," and "If you take Christ out of scripture, what will you find?"—was based in the Bible, *sola Scriptura.* Luther preached on biblical texts at the same time that he gave academic lectures on biblical books. In his German Mass (1526) he set forth directions regarding which biblical passages were to be preached at Wittenberg and when. The text of the first Sunday morning service was taken from the Pauline Epistles, that of the next from one of the Gospels; an Old Testament text was used in the afternoon service. On Mondays and Tuesdays sermons were based on the catechism; on Wednesdays, on the Gospel of Matthew; on Thursdays and Fridays, on other New Testament books; on Saturdays, on the Gospel of John. But the decisive innovation of the Lutheran sermon was that the Bible was no longer interpreted according to the notion of the fourfold meaning of scripture. Traditionally, interpreters had queried a biblical passage for its literal, allegorical, moral, and, finally, eschatological meaning, and the dogmatic declarations of the church had been the norm for understanding the Bible. For Luther, however, Christ was the heart of scripture and the key to scriptural interpretation. Thus freed, Luther by 1529 had abandoned the traditional method of exegesis—albeit that occasionally the allegorical interpretation appears, if only for illustrative and playful purposes, even in his late sermons. Regarding exegesis, Luther claimed to be bound only by the text.

The purpose of the sermon was to instruct and exhort, a task that, although it placed heavy demands on the preacher, was limited by the freedom both of God and of the auditor. The scriptural passage that is interpreted in the sermon, and in which Christ is found, exhibits external and internal clarity. The former relates to the sermon and is the task of the preacher; the latter relates to the heart and is due to the spirit of God. Luther pointed to the boundary between the two at a decisive time in his own life and in that of the Reformation: when, in 1521–1522, the Wittenberg reform threatened to fall into the hands of radicals, Luther took to preaching and in his first "Invocative Sermon" noted, "We can shout into one another's ears, but everyone must be prepared for the time of death." Both instruction and exhortation respect the boundaries of human freedom. In accordance with Paul, Luther described teaching as preaching to the ignorant, and he described exhortation as stimulation and confirmation of something that is already known. Each leaves room for the auditor to act and occurs by means of scripture. The auditors of the sermon have the power, as a congregation, to judge the preachers and to appoint and to dismiss them. Auditors are Christians in a state of becoming, those who have not yet fully arrived and who must therefore be instructed. Such instruction must occur in love because the auditors are neighbors of the preachers and each Christian lives in Christ and in his neighbor.

Rather than follow traditional medieval forms, Luther based his sermons on the models found in ancient rhetoric, and particularly on that of the speech in exhortation of the people (*genus deliberativum*) as furnished by Quintilian. Structurally the sermon began with a brief introduction to the text, went on to the exposition, and ended with suggestions pertaining to daily life. The style of Luther's sermons, which were generally given in the vernacular, was straightforward, even austere. Illustrations were taken from daily life. The audience might comprise townspeople of Wittenberg or students and colleagues. Many of Luther's sermons were preached at the university church; at other times he preached in the absence of Johannes Bugenhagen, the town preacher. Luther also preached while on travels and on special occasions, as for example at the consecration of the castle church in Torgau. A clue to his preaching style may be found in his tract on translating, wherein he set forth the principles on which he based his translation of the Bible. Sermons served as the basis for some of his publications, including the catechisms.

Zwingli as Preacher. Although Zwingli preached countless sermons—more than one thousand in the Großmünster in Zurich alone—not one is available in its original form. The transcripts, frequently prepared long after the fact, are more suggestive of tracts than they are of sermons. Zwingli preached on biblical texts, at first on the appointed pericopes and from 1519, as people's priest in Zurich, on biblical books. Between 1518 and 1526 he preached on the New Testament (with the exception of *Revelation*); thereafter he also preached on the Old Testament. Like Luther, Zwingli also took the opportunity to preach during the course of his travels.

As for the content of the sermons—which show evidence of humanist erudition—Zwingli used the biblical texts to examine fundamental questions of the day. Political issues came increasingly under scrutiny, and the laxity of the nobility was criticized. According to Zwingli, the preacher was bound by the word of God and must act without regard to such considerations as family, finances, or rulers. The treatise that he published on this topic was significantly entitled *Der Hirt* (The Shepherd).

In accordance with *I Corinthians* 14:22, Zwingli organized regular gatherings of the theologians in the city. At these meetings, which were held five days a week, consecutive passages from scripture were read and explained; the insights would later be shared with the congregation. The meeting (or *Prophezei*) took the place of the traditional daily offices and was the beginning of the theological faculty in Zurich. It was later echoed in German Pietism and in Lutheran Bible studies.

Calvin as Preacher. Calvin's sermons are extant both in transcripts and in published versions that were edited by others. After 1549 his sermons were recorded by a stenographer and transcribed. Some forty volumes of transcribed sermons would be compiled, some fourteen volumes of which are still extant today. By 1563, twenty-one volumes of Calvin's sermons had been published.

Calvin preached daily and generally twice on Sundays. He meditated on the text and interpreted it extemporaneously, holding the Bible in his hand. Scriptural passages were interpreted consecutively, the New Testament and the Psalms on Sundays, the Old Testament on weekdays, in language that was simple, pedagogical, at times wide-ranging to the point of exhaustiveness, but always comforting and sustaining.

Other Protestant Preachers. Luther's method of preaching served as a powerful example to his evangelical contemporaries. Often, sermons taken from Luther's postils were read from the pulpit. In addition, a new and distinctive literary genre appeared in the form of *summaria* ("summaries"), or homiletic instructions and working materials for pastors. Influential *summaria* were published by Johannes Bugenhagen and Veit Dietrich. Postils were published by Johann Spangenberg (d. 1550), Antonius Corvinus, Johannes Brenz, and Sebastian Fröschel (d. 1570). These collections contained a variety of sermons, even as the goal was more or less to imitate Luther's method.

The theologian, pastor, and school principal Johann Spangenberg composed a postil for young Christians in question-and-answer format, and, for pastors, *Dispositiones für Evangelien und Epistel* (Outlines of Gospels and Epistles). This format was popular in sixteenth-century instruction. Luther mentioned it in his German Mass of 1526 and employed the format himself in his Small Catechism. Spangenberg praised Luther as "Moses, David, Elias, God's chosen tool," and helped to create the image of Luther that lasted until the nineteenth century. The sermons of Johannes Brenz, which displayed both biblical competence and humanist ideals, continued to be published into the nineteenth century. Antonius Corvinus in his postil offered practical applications for pastors, congregations, and heads of families. Sebastian Fröschel, whose sermons were regularly attended by Luther, published children's sermons as well as sermons on Luther's Small Catechism. He was heavily influenced by Melanchthon, whom he acknowledged in the preface to his sermons on the Gospel of Matthew.

Important preachers of the Reformed tradition were Johannes Oecolampadius, preacher and reformer of Basel; Ambrosius Blarer; Théodore de Bèze, who, preaching a Christmas sermon in a field outside Paris in the face of physical threats, was vividly reminded of the fate of Stephen in *Acts of the Apostles*; and Martin Bucer, the reformer of Strasbourg. Heinrich Bullinger, Zwingli's successor at Zurich, published collections of sermons; his *Hausbuch*—partly a postil, partly a collection of sermon materials for pastors—achieved wide circulation and was translated from its original Latin into a number of languages, including English.

Sixteenth-Century Protestant Preaching Theory. Although Luther did not elaborate an explicit theory of preaching, specific comments and casual remarks concerning preaching and its diverse problems are sprinkled throughout his writings. His overall conception is embodied in his sermons, particularly in the sections of his postil that he wrote himself. He probably arrived at his ideas on preaching solely in the course of writing sermons, just as his influence on the formation of New High German owed nothing to theory but was felt through his Bible translation. Zwingli and Calvin likewise developed no theories of preaching.

Melanchthon published theoretical reflections, particularly his *Elementa rhetorices* (Elements of Rhetoric; 1532), *Dissertatio* (Dissertation on Public Preachers; 1535), and *De modo arte concionandi* (Concerning the Art of Speaking; 1537–1539). In 1519 he had recommended the "sophia" teaching of Erasmus, but in the final edition of *Elementa rhetorices* (1542) he deleted any such references. According to Melanchthon, the purpose of the sermon was to instruct, a view that placed him in the medieval tradition as described by the Cistercian Alanus ab Insulis in 1202—"Preaching is the manifest and public instruction in morals and faith"—and one that differed from Luther's notion that the purpose of the sermon was instruction and exhortation. Georg Major appropriated Melanchthon's homiletic reflections and in 1562 published Melanchthon's *Elementa rhetorices* in question-and-answer format. David Chytraeus in *Quaestiones rhetoricae* and Aegidius Hunnius in *Methodus concionandi* also show the influence of Melanchthon. Melanchton's postil, published by Christoph Pezel (d. 1604) in Latin in 1594, was historically influential as well; yet Melanchthon said of himself, "I cannot preach."

The first textbook of homiletics was published in 1533 by Andreas Gerhard Hyperius (d. 1560); a second, enlarged edition appeared in 1562. A number of other homiletic texts were published as well, all of which remained within traditional parameters and marked the transition to the period of orthodoxy. Wilhelm Zepper's *Ars habendi et audiendi conciones sacras* (The Art of Delivering and Listening to Sacred Speech), published in 1598, was indebted to Hyperius and Melanchthon. Zepper distinguished between the preacher and the scholastic speaker, a distinction which until the twentieth century was routinely ignored—especially by preaching university professors.

Catholic Preaching in the Sixteenth Century. Catholic preaching throughout Europe remained linked to rhetoric. Already at the beginning of the century, its achievements were significant. By effectively advertising the sale of indulgences, the sermons of Johann Tetzel, a member of the Order of Preachers, were an important catalyst for Luther's reform. Later, challenged by the reformers, the monastic orders became committed to the sermon as a form of speech. At the opening of the Jesuit school in Coimbra in 1555, Petrus Perpinyá delivered a speech that had far-reaching implications. He returned to themes of this address in 1562 when he published *De perfecta doctoris christiani forma* (Concerning the Perfect Form of Christian Scholars), for which he appropriated both Cicero and Augustine, who in his opinion were complementary. The connection between the ethical and political/oratorical ideals of Cicero, as well as those of Quintilian and Augustine, was also made at the Council of Trent, which in its session of 7 May 1546 promulgated the decree *De lectoribus et praedicatoribus Sacrae Scripturae* (Concerning the Teachers and Preachers of Sacred Scripture). The council upheld the humanism of the fifteenth century whereby medieval teachings had been abandoned in favor of the language and rhetorical ideal of Cicero and Quintilian. In accordance with the conciliar decree Perpinyá sought to exhort the faithful to imitation through speech and set them on a moral, holy walk of life. To the triad of ancient rhetoric—*docere, delectare, movere* ("teach," "delight," "move")—Augustine had already added setting an example by one's actions.

For two hundred years Cyprian Soarez's *Ratio studiorum* (1586), a compilation of Aristotle, Cicero, and Quintilian, was the foundation of Jesuit instruction in rhetoric at secondary schools. Soarez, a teacher at Coimbra, had published in 1560 a textbook entitled *De arte rhetorica libri tres. Ex Aristotele, Cicerone & Quintiliano praecipue deprompti* (Three Books concerning the Art of Rhetoric, Derived Mainly from Aristotle, Cicero, and Quintilian).

The Council of Trent had enjoined all bishops and priests to be attentive to preaching. In Italy, Carlo Borromeo, the archbishop of Milan, assembled a group of teachers who admired Cicero for his literary elegance, his ability to move hearts by means of an unadorned style. Borromeo established an academy for the education of preachers. In Germany, Mainz cathedral witnessed sermons by such eminent preachers as Friedrich Nausea (later bishop of Vienna), Johann Ferus, and Michael Helding. Several Catholic preachers wrote postils in the manner of the Lutheran publications. Johann Eck published interpretations of the Sunday gospel lessons in *Homiliarus contra sectas* (Homily against the Sectarians) as well as five volumes of German sermons. Martin Eisengrein published *Postilla catholica* and numerous other sermons dealing with controversial theological topics. All in all, however, Catholic efforts at reform bore fruit later—as for example in France in the seventeenth century—and much more is known regarding the practice and theory of Catholic preaching during that period.

The End of the Century. The process of preaching reform as undertaken by Protestants and Catholics alike was carried on into the seventeenth century. Although the European map was now divided along confessional lines, this was less the case with regard to the format of sermons. In the age of orthodoxy the dogmatic controversies between the confessions became increasingly important and determined both the theological content and the form of sermons.

[*See also* Clergy.]

BIBLIOGRAPHY

Bauer, Barbara. *Jesuitische "Ars Rhetorica" im Zeitalter der Glaubenskämpfe*. Frankfurt a.M., 1986.

Bruchmann, Gerhard. "Luthers Bibelverdeutschung auf der Wartburg in ihrem Verhältnis zu den mittelalterlichen Übersetzungen." *Luther-Jahrbuch* 18 (1936), 47–82.

Drews, Paul, and Ferdinand Cohrs, eds. "Philipp Melanchthons Schriften zur praktischen Theologie." Pt. 2, "Homiletische Schriften." In *Supplementa Melanchthoni*, pt. 5. Leipzig, 1929.

Luther, Martin. *Kritische Gesamtausgabe*. Weimar, 1883ff.

Müller, Hans Martin. "Homiletik." In *Theologische Realenzyklopädie*, vol. 15, pp. 526–565. Berlin and New York, 1986.

Nembach, Ulrich. *Predigt des Evangeliums: Luther als Prediger, Pädagoge und Rhetor*. Neukirchen-Vluyn, 1972.

Niebergall, Alfred. "Die Geschichte der christlichen Predigt." In *Leiturgia*, vol. 2, pp. 181–353. Kassel, 1955.

———. "Luthers Auffassung von der Predigt." In *Reformation und Gegenwart*, pp. 83–109. Marburg, 1968.

Quintilianus, M. Fabius. *Institutio oratoria, libri XII*. Edited by Ludwig Rademacher. Leipzig, 1959.

Schütz, Werner. *Geschichte der christlichen Predigt*. Berlin and New York, 1972.

ULRICH NEMBACH

Translated from German by Hans J. Hillerbrand

France

On the eve of the Reformation, preaching in France occurred regularly in towns and cities. Local and itinerant friars (primarily Franciscans, Dominicans, and Augustinians) often preached daily, at least during Lent and Advent, and all of the major churches in a town competed for the services of the most gifted preacher. Although preaching was not totally lacking in rural and mountainous regions and inhabitants of these areas often traveled long distances to hear a great preacher, the lack of regular preaching in rural areas was a serious problem facing the Catholic church, one that had engendered heresies in the past. Yet on the whole, France was well served by mendicant preachers in the decades before the Reformation. This was part of an active spirit of reform within the French church after 1450. Pre-Reformation sermons, geared to a largely illiterate audience, were given in the language and idiom of the people, and were peppered with amusing, titillating, and interesting stories designed to make the biblical message meaningful. Although friars drew on church fathers, medieval theologians, and other sources, they overwhelmingly chose the Bible as their primary source. The sermons that have survived, which were usually translated into Latin for printing, are often the shorthand notes of auditors, but they reveal that most preachers before 1530 used the "modern method" of sermon construction based on elaborate divisions and subdivisions. Intended for mnemonic purposes, this artificial structure, combined with the often bawdy or humorous examples, rendered the friars vulnerable to attacks from Catholic humanists and later from Protestants.

Between 1510 and 1520, Guillaume Briçonnet, bishop of Meaux, gathered around him a circle of men devoted to biblical learning. Since his diocese had suffered unusually from the lack of effective or frequent preaching, Briçonnet held synods and instituted regulations to promote the spread of the word of God. The circle of Meaux encompassed a wide range of viewpoints, including those of Jacques Lefèvre d'Étaples and Guillaume Farel. Not surprisingly, these efforts provoked an outburst of mendicant and diocesan rivalry; the Faculty of Theology of Paris moved quickly to suppress the group.

Although Catholic authorities denounced almost all evangelical preaching after 1520 as Lutheran, most early French reformed preaching was a blend of native French mysticism and biblicism, sometimes combined with Swiss Zwinglian theology. François Lambert traveled to Wittenberg to study with Luther, but overall Strasbourg proved more influential for the burgeoning French reform movement. The imperial city soon became a refuge and school for French and Swiss reformers, including Farel and John Calvin. Here the volatile mix of new and radical ideas spurred many of the reformers to take their messages back to France, where they could begin the process of conversion. Large cities and university towns such as Bourges became focal points for the new evangelical preaching.

The Catholic preaching response was generally rapid, at least in major urban areas. As early as 1518, some Paris preachers in their sermons show clear knowledge of Luther's ideas as enunciated in the Ninety-five Theses and his sermons. They objected particularly to the doctrines of justification by faith alone and *sola scriptura*, and were quick to denounce Luther, although they grouped him as simply one in a long line of heretics who had challenged the Church's teachings. Some scholars have questioned the efficacy of the early response, but a decrease in the printing of sermons in these years should not be confused with a lack of preaching. Rather, a glut on the market, censorship problems after 1534, and the priority of preaching rather than printing affected the publication process.

Royal policy during the reign of Francis I, alternating between toleration and repression, influenced both Catholic and Protestant preaching. Several Catholic preachers in the capital, outraged at the king's perceived leniency toward heretics, preached vehemently against the new ideas. Referring to Jerome's praise of ancient Gaul for its lack of heresy, Catholic preachers implicitly criticized the king for allowing heretics to gain a foothold. From 1533 to 1545, while the suspect preaching of Gérard Roussel at the Louvre (at the behest of Marguerite d'Angoulême) attracted large crowds, several Catholic preachers, including François LePicart, were denounced to the king and suffered imprisonment and exile. Not until the reign of Henry II, whose policy on heresy was stronger and more consistently applied, could Catholic preachers deliver sermons without fear of royal reprisals.

Nevertheless, this did not stop most Catholic preachers from preaching against heresy.

Significantly, by 1535 bishops, priests, and canons preached; this had seldom been the case before the Reformation, but under the changed circumstances Catholic churchmen at all levels took to the pulpit. Sermons from the 1530s to the 1550s show a strong awareness of the Protestant threat, with a relatively accurate understanding of both Lutheran and Swiss doctrines. Preachers did differ on how best to respond—some argued that teaching solid Catholic doctrine was essential and insisted that it was better not to give further publicity to the heretics, while others felt that their listeners needed to be warned of the dangers facing them. Most Catholic sermons in these years have a simplified structure with a greater use of the Bible than was found among pre-Reformation preachers. By 1550 some popular sermons display the typically Renaissance interest in the uses of sacred eloquence and are characterized by their use of the ornate style. Both types emphasize God's love and compassion, the need for reform from within in order to remove one of the "causes" of the Reformation, and the falseness of Protestant belief and behavior. By midcentury the funerary sermon, which as a genre had fallen into abeyance at the end of the Middle Ages, experienced a revival both as a vehicle for the display of Renaissance eloquence and as an excuse for anti-Protestant propaganda.

The 1550s and 1560s witnessed the implantation of Calvinist churches throughout France. Often, young men who had traveled to Geneva to study at Calvin's academy would return as pastors to their communities, while others proselytized throughout France. Preaching often took place secretly, at night, usually in private homes or other secluded locations. *Prêches* were often informal assemblies in which the congregation gathered to hear the minister deliver a sermon taken exclusively from the Bible. The sermon was usually a simple exegesis given in the plain style, and the service was punctuated at beginning, middle, and end by the singing of psalms, which had been translated into French by Clément Marot and Théodore de Bèze. Later Protestant preachers, however, often found that like their pre-Reformation counterparts they had to include secular announcements as well as "amuse and delight" their listeners.

After the death of Henry II, as factions formed around the young king Francis II, the tensions that would lead to religious war began to spill over into the sermons. François de Lorraine, duke of Guise, and his brother Charles, cardinal of Lorraine, personally sponsored some of the best Catholic preachers of their generation, who in turn supported the family's interests from the pulpit. Great Catholic preachers such as Pierre d'Ivollé, while retaining many of the themes of earlier sermons, now flirted outright with sedition. The tone of these sermons became increasingly polemical and militant, and in some instances verged on the apocalyptic.

The battle of the pulpits truly began with the outbreak of the Wars of Religion in 1561. For Catholics, the Colloquy of Poissy, organized by Catherine de Médicis in a last-ditch effort to find some means of reconciliation between Catholics and Protestants, represented all that was wrong with royal policy. Bèze's preaching in Paris only exacerbated existing tensions. Increasingly, preachers of both confessions used their sermons to inflame the hearts of their listeners, in the process not only influencing but sometimes causing events. As fear and rumor proliferated, the sway of a preacher's rhetoric was often enough to touch off riots, iconoclasm, murder, and pillage. Catholic preachers now attacked royal policies and persons, urging their listeners to take matters into their own hands. Still, they did not neglect doctrine; an effort truly to educate their listeners on such hotly debated issues as the Eucharist was typical in these sermons. The sermons of the radical preacher Simon Vigor exemplify this combination of basic teaching, political critique, and incitement to violence. But as the war of words heated up, Vigor and other preachers attacked the king and called for the wholesale extermination of the Huguenots.

The newly established Jesuits were not particularly active in the struggle against heresy in these years, at least from the standpoint of preaching. Émond Auger was noted for his fairness to his enemies and despite his own abilities believed that education and catechism were the best means of combating heresy. Ignatius Loyola had argued that the Jesuits should make efforts to avoid controversy with the Protestants, and it was in their writings rather than their sermons that the early Jesuits adopted the most belligerent positions. Unlike the radical preachers of the Catholic League, most Jesuits did not preach sedition; indeed, they were often criticized for working with royal authorities to restore order.

During the period of the Wars of Religion (1561–1598), Catholic and Huguenot preachers alike filled their sermons with political commentaries that often sought either to undermine or to prop up the king's authority or to serve such other groups as the Catholic League or the Sixteen (the Paris radicals named for the sixteen arrondissements of the city). The violent tenor of these sermons increased dramatically during these years, often including calls for regicide. Yet on both sides, the voices of moderation were heard as well. After the assassination of Henry III in 1589, the *politique* position was strengthened, and the radical preachers of earlier years fell into disrepute as the Catholic League itself began to come apart.

Preaching was a fundamental aspect of life in Reformation France. Whether sermons were delivered by mendicants, priests, or bishops, or given in private by wandering Protestant ministers, they were a basic source of religious instruction, civic information, and, in many cases, political critique. In a culture that was still overwhelmingly oral and in which the newspaper was still in its infancy, the pulpit both reflected and molded public opinion. After the Reformation, when religious fanaticism became the norm rather than the exception, preachers often advocated a religion of hate, spurring their listeners on to religious violence with the weapon of their words. But even at the worst of times, there were also voices of moderation from the pulpit, preachers who still felt that gentle persuasion was the only true means of conversion.

[*See also* Clergy.]

BIBLIOGRAPHY

Bayley, Peter. *French Pulpit Oratory, 1598–1650.* Cambridge, 1980. A largely literary discussion of preaching after the Wars of Religion.

Crouzet, Denis. *Les guerriers de Dieu: La violence au temps des troubles de religion.* 2 vols. Paris, 1990. Suggests that a strong undercurrent of apocalyptic thought influenced preaching and writing throughout the sixteenth century.

Delumeau, Jean. *Sin and Fear: The Emergence of a Western Guilt Culture, Thirteenth–Eighteenth Centuries.* New York, 1990. A general overview of attitudes toward guilt with some attention to preachers and sermons.

Diefendorf, Barbara. "Simon Vigor: A Radical Preacher in Sixteenth-Century Paris." *Sixteenth Century Journal* 18 (1987), 399–410.

———. *Beneath the Cross: Catholics and Huguenots in Sixteenth-Century Paris.* New York, 1991. Important discussion of the role of preaching as an incitement to violence during the Wars of Religion.

Farge, James. *Biographical Register of Paris Doctors of Theology, 1500–1536.* Toronto, 1980. Indispensable for the researcher. Gives short biographies and bibliographical information for many preachers who received their doctorates in these years.

Imbart de la Tour, Pierre. *Les origines de la réforme* (1905–1935). 4 vols. Reprint, Geneva, 1978.

Labitte, Charles. *De la démocratie chez les prédicateurs de la Ligue* (1841). Reprint, Geneva, 1971. A dated but still somewhat useful account.

Martin, Hervé. *La métier du prédicateur à la fin du moyen âge, 1350–1520.* Paris, 1988.

Martin, Lynn. *The Jesuit Mind: The Mentality of an Elite in Early Modern France.* Ithaca, N.Y., 1988.

O'Malley, John. *The First Jesuits.* Cambridge, Mass., 1993. Study of the society between 1540 and 1565, including their preaching.

Taylor, Larissa. *Soldiers of Christ: Preaching in Late Medieval and Reformation France.* New York, 1992. Analysis of content and context of 1,657 sermons delivered in France between 1460 and 1560.

LARISSA JULIET TAYLOR

England

The Reformation did not introduce preaching to England, but it gave preachers a new rationale and urgency and increased their political importance. The duties of parish clergy had long included preaching—ideally, the priest would deliver a weekly exposition of that Sunday's gospel or of the Lord's Prayer, perhaps occupying five or ten minutes between the Apostles' Creed and Offertory. But this was subject to the officiant's ability and discretion. Even in the more important churches the weekly Sunday sermon was probably rare. This reflected not the church's official priorities so much as individual priests' lack of training and the pressure of other duties. According to the medieval tradition, hearing sermons was not necessary to salvation. As the English church entered the sixteenth century, the purpose of occasional preaching was mainly moral instruction.

Relatively few sermon manuscripts survive from parish priests of the early sixteenth century, but medieval sermon manuals continued to be popular: Myrk's *Liber Festialis*, or *Festial* (1403?), for example, went through nineteen printings between 1483 and 1532. The sermons included in such collections explained the biblical readings for a particular holy day, distilled the moral lesson, and illustrated it with reference to pious legends of saints' lives. According to later Protestant critics, these collections exemplified the worst shortcomings of pre-Reformation preaching, using far-fetched allegorical interpretation and extrabiblical embellishment. Nevertheless, they fulfilled the traditional purposes of pulpit rhetoric.

Senior clergy and bishops preached more than their parish counterparts: at court; at state funerals such as Lady Margaret Beaufort's in 1508, where Bishop John Fisher of Rochester preached; and at convocations, such as the 1510 assembly where the Erasmian John Colet, dean of Saint Paul's, urged reform upon his colleagues. In London sermons could be heard on Sundays and holy days at traditional meeting places like Paul's Cross. These sermons would sometimes be topical or controversial, as in 1515, when following Richard Hunne's suspicious death in the custody of the bishop of London's chancellor, the abbot of Winchcombe preached against punishment of the clergy by secular courts. Sermons were also frequent at the universities: Colet's lectures on the Pauline epistles at Oxford approximated to demonstration sermons as new college foundations emphasized the professional training of the secular clergy.

As they began to influence university churchmen such as Thomas Bilney, Robert Barnes, John Lambert, and Hugh Latimer in the 1520s, Erasmian humanism and Luther's writings offered a new rationale as well as new content for preaching. These early Protestants, like earlier Lollards, valued individual faith and acceptance, and thus sermons as the incitement to that individual faith, over the church's ministrations in the form of sacraments. Latimer articulated their argument when he cited Paul to Edward VI in 1549: "And howe shal they heare wythout a preacher? I tel you it is the fotesteppes of the ladder of heauen, of oure salvacion. There must be preachers if we loke to be saued." Luther's ideas prompted other sermons, too—official ones at Paul's Cross, such as that by Fisher in 1525 when the German reformer's books were burned and his English admirers humiliated, and at the show trials of heretics, such as Bilney's in 1527, where Bishop John Longland of Lincoln preached.

Henry VIII's "divorce" from Catherine of Aragon and his declaration of royal supremacy over the English church provoked a flood of sermons. Catherine's supporters, such as Edward Bocking, spiritual director to the "holy maid" Elizabeth Barton, preached God's judgment against Henry. Thomas Cromwell responded not only by arranging Barton's public confession of fraud and a sermon against her at Paul's Cross in 1533, but by revoking all preaching licenses in 1534 and assigning Latimer to review new applications. In addition, he issued injunctions to the clergy in 1536 and 1538 that set forth standards for licensure and listed allowable and forbidden sermon themes: sermons were to be biblically based and were not to find fault with the injunctions. Reformist bishops responded by demanding sermons against papal supremacy, conservative bishops by warning their clergy against the preaching of controversial issues of doctrine.

The climate created by subsequent Protestant administrations encouraged preaching to a greater degree than had Henry's. Thomas Becon (a contributor to the official *Book of Homilies*) and Richard Taverner published postils, or explications of the biblical lessons assigned to each Sunday, for the use of nonpreaching clergy, and several volumes of postils by Continental reformers such as Niels Hemmingsen and Antonius Corvinus were translated and published during the reigns of Edward VI and Elizabeth I. Official sermons had always been useful as instruments of statecraft, establishing control over religious life. Under Edward VI and his archbishop of Canterbury, Thomas Cranmer, official sermons were also prepared to encourage the uniformity of emerging doctrinal changes and to help assure a governable populace. Further, sermons could enjoin upon the public the duty of obedience and support for the monarch. This cause was advanced in 1547 with the publication of *Certain Sermons or Homilies*, which provided instructive discourses for each Sunday and holy day (though the priest might instead preach his own sermon). The book reveals its political objective in the preface: hearing the homilies, the common people "maye learne vnfaynedly, and according to the mynde of the holy Ghost, expressed in the scriptures . . . to serue their Kyng, with all humilitie and subiection" (*Certain Sermons*, 55). Homilies entitled "An exhortation to obedience" and "Agaynst strief and contencion" further stressed the point. Decades later, when Elizabeth wished to limit preaching, her bishops, among them Edmund Grindal, archbishop first of York, then of Canterbury, reminded her over and over of the link between frequent preaching and obedient subjects: "where preaching wanteth, obedience faileth." John Jewel's sermon responding to the pope's 1570 excommunication of Elizabeth, *A viewe of a seditiovs Bul*, illustrates the service preachers could provide for their ruler.

Thus routine pulpit messages had an explicitly political purpose. The importance of the preacher in the Protestant paradigm of salvation, however, gave him an independent authority that potentially competed with that of his royal sponsor. Whereas the Catholic priest had derived his authority from his ability to dispense saving sacraments, the preacher began to define his own authority—independently of the government—as resting in his ability to expound the scriptures and point the way to salvation. Edwardian preachers such as Latimer and Thomas Lever and Elizabethan preachers such as Thomas Drant, Edward Dering, and Matthew Hutton used this prerogative to prescribe, challenge, and even criticize publicly the monarch's conduct of ecclesiastical, domestic, and foreign policy. Edward's government, like his sister's, took measures to curb such liberties. In 1548 Edward's administration became the first to require all preachers, even parish priests, to hold licenses—which, of course, the government itself issued. Thus the monarchy's control of church life intensified at the same time as many Protestant preachers began to view their authority in more expansive terms than had their Henrician counterparts.

Upon Edward's death and Mary Tudor's accession in 1553, preaching received less emphasis. Mary's bishops, among them Stephen Gardiner of Winchester, Edmund Bonner of London, and Cardinal and Archbishop of Canterbury Reginald Pole, regarded Protestant heresy as a minor problem and gave priority to the restoration of the Mass. But though they saw no urgent need for Catholic evangelism, they continued to preach at court and at Paul's Cross, and Bonner brought out a new book of homilies presenting Catholic doctrine in 1555. The real presence of Christ in the Sacrament of the Altar was a frequent theme, as for instance in Thomas Watson's Lenten sermons at court in 1554.

Though Elizabeth I was to return the church to the theology and liturgy of the beginning of Edward's time, she herself was not a wholehearted supporter of preachers and preaching. One of her first injunctions concerning religion was to call in all licenses to preach, and she subsequently voiced her wish that she could limit the number of preachers in England to a very few: six or seven for all of England, or (less grudgingly) three or four in each diocese. (She envisioned instead a manageable clergy reading from the 1547 *Homilies*, reissued in 1559, and a second volume of homilies that the bishops brought out in 1563.) But her bishops overruled her, patronizing preaching, supporting promising scholars at the university, and often writing homilies and preaching themselves. Protestant nobility and even private citizens further expanded the English public's opportunities to hear sermons: the wealthy endowed "lectureships," "planting" preachers in London and in the larger market towns, such as Ipswich, where men such as Bartimaeus Andrews and Samuel Ward discharged their responsibilities by preaching an assigned number of sermons per week, without the liturgical and administrative duties of the parish clergy. These "lectures," differing from sermons only in that they were often read, rather than delivered extemporaneously or from notes, were scheduled on weekdays as well as Sundays and became a regular feature of urban life, providing diversion for shoppers and supplementing the education of schoolboys.

The ideal Elizabethan priest was a university-educated theologian who resided in his parish and devoted his time to the care of his flock and the preparation of a weekly sermon. But the actual requirements were less rigorous, at least early in the reign. Licensure as a preacher in 1561 depended not on any educational qualifications or spirituality, but on submission to parliamentary and queenly authority, that is, subscription to the royal supremacy and endorsement of *The Book of Common Prayer* and the ordinal. No homiletic or rhetorical training was required, and published sermons show little evidence of thorough study of the Genevan treatises on the art of preaching, such as Hemmingsen's *Evangelie Postil* (The Preacher, or Method of Preaching; 1561, translated into English in 1574), or Andreas Hyperius's *De formandis Concionibus Sacris* (Practis of Preaching; 1553, translated into English in 1577), handbooks that derived their rules from the conventional classical sources—Cicero and Quintilian—and offered little specifically homiletic advice. Sermons can be classified by style as plain, middling, or ornate, and the overall trend, with many exceptions, was for early and mid-sixteenth century Protestant evangelists such as John Knox and William Perkins to preach plainly, while later, fashionable court preachers such as Drant and William Barlow, bishop of Lincoln, made much use of allegory and rhetorical figures.

By the close of the century, preachers with university degrees were no longer rare, and probably more than half of the parish clergy held preaching licenses. Nonpreaching priests were enjoined to engage the services of a preacher once a month (in remote parts of those dioceses least provided with preachers, four times a year). Most English men and women heard sermons regularly, and many found supplementary sermons, if the parish supply was deemed unsatisfactory, available within walking distance.

[*See also* Clergy.]

BIBLIOGRAPHY

Blench, J. W. *Preaching in England in the Late Fifteenth and Sixteenth Centuries: A Study of English Sermons, 1450–c.1600*. Oxford, 1964. A survey of the sermons' scriptural interpretation, form, style, use of classical allusion, themes, and literary influence. Each topic is treated in its own chronologically ordered chapter. A useful bibliography includes lists of sermon texts, preaching manuals, and works of sermon criticism.

Block, Joseph. "Thomas Cromwell's Patronage of Preaching." *Sixteenth Century Journal* 8.1 (1977), 37–50. A study that illustrates the government's use of the sermon to sway public opinion during the 1520s and 1530s.

Christian, Margaret. "Elizabeth's Preachers and the Government of Women: Defining and Correcting a Queen." *Sixteenth Century Journal* 24 (1993), 561–576. A study of court and accession-day sermons as they reveal the complex relation between preachers and the government.

Collinson, Patrick. *The Religion of Protestants: The Church in English Society, 1559–1625*. Oxford, 1982. Sermons and preachers figure prominently throughout this distillation of a dedicated scholar's thirty years of patient work, as they do in his collection of essays and occasional pieces, *Godly People: Essays on English Protestantism and Puritanism*, London, 1983, and in his *The Elizabethan Puritan Movement*, Oxford, 1990.

———. *Birthpangs of Protestant England: Religious and Cultural Change in the Sixteenth and Seventeenth Centuries*. New York, 1988. This fascinating book mentions many preachers and sermons in its analysis of the popular reaction, favorable and otherwise, to Protestant evangelism.

Dickens, A. G. *The English Reformation*. 2d ed. University Park, Pa., 1991. This classic mentions many preachers and sermons in passing; its contribution is the social and political context it offers for sermon study.

Haigh, Christopher. *English Reformations: Religion, Politics, and Society under the Tudors*. Oxford, 1993. Chapter 16, "Evangelists in Action," focuses on the preaching activity of the Elizabethan church. Preachers and sermons are placed in their political and social context.

Herr, Alan Fager. *The Elizabethan Sermon: A Survey and a Bibliography*. Reprint, New York, 1969. Though dated and at times maddeningly imprecise, flippant, or wrong about issues that have come to be better understood in the half-century since its publication, this doctoral dissertation provides a readable, lively introduction to the subject.

MacLure, Millar. *The Paul's Cross Sermons, 1534–1642*. Toronto, 1958. A comprehensive and scholarly celebration, anthropological, historical, and anecdotal, of this London institution.

———. *Register of Sermons Preached at Paul's Cross, 1534–1642*. Revised and expanded by Peter Pauls and Jackson Campbell Boswell. Occasional Publications, Centre of Reformation and Renaissance Studies, Victoria University, University of Toronto, vol. 6. Ottawa, 1989. A chronological listing of sermons, including available information about the author, biblical text, short-title catalog number, and tidbits of political and theological gossip which place the sermon in its original context.

McCollough, Peter E. *The Sermon at the Courts of Elizabeth I and James I*. Amherst, Mass., 1995.

Seaver, Paul S. *The Puritan Lectureships: The Politics of Religious Dissent, 1560–1662*. Stanford, Calif., 1970. Discusses the importance of preaching and its relationship to politics, and clarifies the types and development of various lectureships.

Stroup, Herbert W., Jr. "John Mirk: Tutor to England's Medieval Preachers." *Lutheran Theological Seminary, Gettysburg, Bulletin* 47.3 (1967), 26–38. Analysis, illustration, and context of the *Festial*.

Wabuda, Susan. *Preaching in the English Reformation*. New York, forthcoming.

MARGARET CHRISTIAN

Spain and Portugal

From 1492 onward, Spain could claim to be united in the Catholic faith, even though compulsory missionary preaching to the Moorish peasantry of Valencia was still being undertaken in 1525 by Fray Antonio de Guevara and Fray Juan de Salamanca. The latent problems of an unintegrated *morisco* population remained unresolved until the seventeenth century. The nominal Christianity and presumed "backsliding" of the forced converts from both Judaism and Islam was a question that would exercise the Inquisition throughout the sixteenth century but one that was not directly addressed by preachers of the period, except for the speech on the statutes of *limpieza de sangre* by the controversial Dominican preacher Fray Augustín Salucio (1523–1601). Andalusia was ripe for evangelization, but the clergy seemed unwilling or unable to undertake it. Preaching within the peninsula was envisaged as a ministry to the faithful rather than to the unconverted, and therefore the missionary endeavors of Spanish and Portuguese mendicant friars and the members of the newly formed Society of Jesus were chiefly directed toward the indigenous peoples of the New World and Asia.

Within Spain the reforms initiated by Cardinal Francisco Jiménez de Cisneros (1436–1517) in the religious orders, particularly his own Observant Franciscan congregation, and his founding in 1508 of the new University of Alcalá, with its particular emphasis on biblical exegesis and the humanistic study of philology, led indirectly to a revival of preaching. Cisneros had instituted the Constitutions of Alcalá and Talavera in 1497 and 1498 to oblige parish priests to explain the gospel to their congregation each Sunday, but these were resisted, and there were repeated complaints throughout the sixteenth century about the theological and rhetorical ignorance of the clergy, regulars and seculars alike. Such criticisms surfaced again in those sessions of the Council of Trent (session 5, chapter 2 [17 June 1546], and session 24, chapter 4 [11 November 1563]) that discussed episcopal residence and the obligation of bishops to preach regularly to their flocks (*praecipuum episcoporum munus*). Bishops were supposed to license substitute preachers and oversee their training in diocesan seminaries, but in practice it was members of religious orders rather than secular priests who carried out the major part of the preaching ministry. Priests tended to prefer the more lucrative town benefices, or the prestige of preaching at court, to the mundane drudgery of attending to the needs of a rural congregation. A distinguished exception was John of Ávila (1499–1569), often called the "Apostle of Andalusia." An account of his life was written in 1588 by the much better known Dominican preacher and spiritual writer Fray Luis de Granada (1504–1588), expressly to provide a role model for the Christian preacher.

The murmurings of Lutheran reform reached Spain only faintly, but Charles V and his entourage of Flemish advisers were reformists of the Erasmian tendency, and his Spanish secretary Alfonso de Valdés and one of the court preachers, Alonso de Virués, were Erasmus's chief supporters in Spain. The writings of Erasmus, especially the *Enchiridion*, translated into Spanish by the archdeacon of Alcor in 1526, were particularly popular in Spain until put on the *Catalogi librorum reprobatorum* of 1551. However, Erasmus's opponents among the friars used the pulpit to attack him, and by 1533 the tide had turned against the supporters of Christian humanism and reform.

Small clusters of quietist *Alumbrados* and lay preachers who were active throughout the first half of the century (for example Pedro Ruíz de Alcaraz, 1488–1555) have been identified as a crypto-Protestant movement, one that seems to have been tolerated at first, being protected by minor aristocrats and *Converso* clergy, before being extinguished in the sterner repression of the reign of Philip II. An important figure, based in Seville, was Constantino Ponce de la Fuente, who was a highly acclaimed preacher for twenty-five years but died in a prison of the Inquisition. The fear of Lutheran heresy provoked the requirement that all preaching be licensed and exercised only by ordained priests. Spain was, however, firmly linked to the rest of Europe at this period; printed works (including sermons) by Spanish authors in both Spanish and Latin would appear in Antwerp, Naples, and Augsburg, and certain authors were swiftly translated into other European languages. Spaniards studied and taught at universities in the Spanish Netherlands and Italy, until forbidden to do so in 1557 except at Bologna, Rome, and Naples. Preaching in Spain, therefore, belongs to a European tradition.

From medieval times, in most European countries, the hard-pressed or poorly educated parish priest would have had recourse to those miscellanies of homiletic material and "ready-made" sermons known generically as *Dormi secure*. In Spain such collections existed and were, from the 1540s onward, supplemented by the printed works of preeminent preachers, either in Latin or, in the last quarter of the century, in Castilian, once the fears about making available scriptural texts in the vernacular had passed. However, a debate about the use of the vulgar tongue in printed sermons was held at the University of Salamanca as late as 1601. (See Pedro Urbano González, "Documentos inéditos acerca del uso de la lengua vulgar en libros espirituales," *Boletín de La Real Academia Española* 12 [1925]). Manuscript sermons also circulated and were reused by members of the same religious community.

Gradually printed collections of sermons took on the character of books of devotion, addressed as much to a lay readership (including women) as to apprentice preachers. They sometimes included an *ars praedicandi* as part of their preface, but they also contained copious indexes of scriptural texts and theological points that could be recombined in different preaching contexts.

These collections were usually organized according to the main preaching seasons of Lent and Advent, when longer sermons (most probably by an invited "celebrity" preacher) would have been delivered on at least three afternoons a week, in addition to the short homily as part of the eucharistic liturgy, which was a Tridentine innovation. Other collections consisted exclusively of sermons to be preached on saints' days, which were in the form of panegyrics. Funeral sermons followed a similar pattern and were sometimes printed in an anthology for preachers, but were more likely to survive as a separate broadsheet when the deceased was a royal personage and the preacher a Court appointee (*Pre-*

dicador del Rey). Sermons on special occasions—natural disasters or the dedication of a church—were also printed separately or accompanied by an account of the proceedings.

One of the most famous court preachers to Charles V was the Augustinian Fray Dionisio Vázquez (c.1480–1539), whose sermons in Spanish were among the earliest to appear in a modern edition (by F. García Olmedo in 1943). Vázquez held a chair in biblical theology at Salamanca and was a strong defender of Erasmus. Others include Alonso de Orozco (1500–1591), Tomás de Villanueva (1488–1555), and Antonio de Guevara (c. 1480–1545), who is better known for his *Libro aúreo del emperador Marco Aurelio* (1529) and his *Reloj de príncipes* (1529). His convoluted style and mannered rhetoric owed much to late medieval preaching techniques.

The Portuguese experience of preaching was very similar to that in Spain. Many Portuguese clergy preached within Spain and published sermons in Spanish, especially after the union of the kingdoms in 1560. The Dominican Frei Bartolomeu dos Martires (1514–1590), archbishop of Braga, was a close friend of Fray Luis de Granada. The sermons of Jeronimo Osorio da Fonseca, the Jesuit bishop of Silves, were widely available; he too was frequently quoted by Granada in his treatise on preaching. The Franciscan Felipe Dias taught theology at Salamanca, where he died in 1601. Another well-known Portuguese preacher of the period was the Trinitarian Frei Alvaro Cabide (1526–1606). Both Spanish and Portuguese bishops took a prominent role at the Council of Trent, and the Latin sermon of Diego Paiva de Andrada to the assembled fathers on the second Sunday of Easter in 1562 is preserved in print.

Formal treatises on preaching that seem to have been influential in the sixteenth century include Fray Luis de Granada's own treatise, *Ecclesiasticae rhetoricae* (Lisbon, 1576). This is a broadly Ciceronian rhetoric, but adapted to the special needs of preachers and illustrated from the church fathers rather than the pagan poets. A more strictly preacherly manual is the *Modus concionandi* (Salamanca, 1576) of the Franciscan Fray Diego de Estella, which is available in a modern edition (by P. Sagüés Azcona, Madrid, 1951) along with Estella's own Spanish version, *Modo de predicar*.

Earlier than either of these, but not readily accessible, is Lorenzo de Villavicencio's *De formandis sacris concionibus* (Antwerp, 1564), which is broadly based on the work of the same title by Hyperius of Marburg, published at Dortmund in 1555. More manuals for preachers in the vernacular appeared from the 1580s and into the early seventeenth century. The best known is Francisco Terrones de Caño's *Instrucción de predicadores*, which was published posthumously in 1617 (edited by F. G. Olmedo, Madrid, 1946). By the end of the sixteenth century the sermon was being treated as a literary exercise as well as a form of religious instruction.

[*See also* Clergy.]

BIBLIOGRAPHY

Andrés Martín, Melquíades. *Historia de la teología en España, 1470–1570*. 2 vols. Madrid, 1976. Quite a comprehensive coverage of the major schools and movements.

Bataillon, Marcel. *Erasme et L'Espagne* (1937). Geneva, 1991. (Also available in Spanish: *Erasmo y España*. 2d ed. Mexico City, 1966.) Still the indispensable work on Spanish sixteenth-century spirituality.

Cerdán, Francis. "Historia de la historia de la Oratoria Sagrada española." In *Criticón* 32 (1985), 55–107. A survey of studies on Spanish preaching from the eighteenth century to the present.

Miguel, Herrero García. *Sermonario clásico*. Madrid and Buenos Aires, 1942. The pioneering overview of the subject with an essay on preaching and an anthology of ten sermons on saints by different seventeenth-century preachers.

Smith, Hilary Dansey. *Preaching in the Spanish Golden Age: A Study of Some Preachers of the Reign of Philip III*. Oxford, 1978. First English-language monograph on this subject. Concentrates mainly on early seventeenth-century theory and practice.

HILARY S. D. SMITH

PREDESTINATION. The doctrine of predestination inherited by the Reformation of the sixteenth century bore the imprint of Augustine's teaching and evidenced many of the fine nuances given to the concept of a divine decree or counsel by the medieval doctors. From the very beginnings of the Reformation, a pronounced doctrine of the entirely gracious predestination of certain individuals to salvation out of the fallen mass of humanity was evident in the writings of major magisterial reformers, such as Luther, Bucer, and Zwingli. This teaching carried over into the thought of second-generation codifiers of Reformation theology and was developed, particularly by Reformed thinkers such as Calvin, Bullinger, Wolfgang Musculus, and Vermigli, while among the Lutherans, a movement away from the most strict Augustinian definitions of the doctrine occurred as Melanchthon's views interacted with those of Luther. By the second half of the sixteenth century, the doctrine had become a major point of controversy among Reformed, Lutheran, and Roman Catholic and had received a substantial elaboration and development in the hands of Reformed theologians and exegetes. Reformed thinkers in particular were responsible for a full, scholastic, and highly variegated development of the doctrine as they defended it against Lutheran and Roman Catholic alternatives and, eventually, against the internal threat of Arminian teaching.

Early Reformation Views. Despite his opposition to many aspects of late medieval scholastic theology, Luther's views on predestination certainly stand in continuity with the strongly Augustinian teaching of his order, as evidenced in such scholastic thinkers as Giles of Rome, Thomas of Strasbourg, Gregory of Rimini, and, above all, his mentor, Johannes von Staupitz. Given this continuity, Luther's assumption that an unconditioned divine will was the foundation of salvation can be viewed as a significant motif in his theology from the very beginning of his opposition to the various aspects of late medieval semi-Pelagianism, whether its doctrine of grace or of free choice or of merit and indulgences. In the *Romans* lectures of 1515–1516, Luther clearly connected predestination with assurance of salvation, noting that were salvation dependent on the human will and human works, it would be utterly uncertain. Our very ability to will and to work the good depends on the grace and mercy of God.

The primary source for Luther's doctrine of predestination is his treatise *De servo arbitrio*, published in December 1525 in response to Erasmus's *De libero arbitrio* of the previous year. Luther's treatise pressed the problem of the fallen will and its inability to perform the good—and, against the background of this problem, drew out a doctrine of the all-determining will of God as the counter to Erasmus's view of human freedom. Luther argues that God wills all things, including human sin and error, yet in such a way that human beings sin by their own fault. Given the encompassing character of the divine causality, all things occur by necessity, although not by compulsion. In this context, salvation belongs entirely to the will of God, which alone can bring about human willing of the good. Luther insists, moreover, that we must not inquire into the secret will of God in an attempt to discern why God chooses some for salvation and leaves others to their own damnation—we must simply accept the revealed will of God and its election of some to salvation by grace alone.

Luther thus juxtaposes almost paradoxically the assumptions that all things come to pass necessarily by the decree of God's eternal will, that all human beings are foreordained to salvation or damnation, that God nonetheless genuinely wills (as scripture states) the salvation of all people, and that those who are rejected by God are rejected for their unbelief. Any attempt to resolve such issues encounters the problem of the secret counsel or inscrutable divine good pleasure: some are elected to salvation, others are rejected, but the causes of the divine decision remain hidden and can never become the subject either of preaching or of legitimate theological speculation.

Melanchthon's views on predestination offer a significant counterpoint to Luther's. Although Melanchthon clearly rested election on the merciful will of God, he balanced his declarations concerning the cause of election with an insistence on the universality of the divine promise of salvation and with an assumption that the cause of reprobation is the sinful and willful rejection of the gospel. In his *Loci communes* (1543), Melanchthon cites Saul as an example of one who "of his own free will fought against the Holy Spirit when the Spirit tried to move him," and argues that, although the beginning of salvation lies with God, human beings must necessarily "hear, learn, and grasp hold of God's promises." The argument clearly echoes Melanchthon's famous dictum from the locus on free choice that good works are caused by "the word of God, the Holy Spirit, and the human will which assents to and does not contend against the Word of God."

The Reformed doctrine of election stands as a clear descendant of the Augustinian theology of the later Middle Ages and represents a spectrum of opinion rather than a monolithic doctrinal perspective: it moves between the concept of a single predestination to life and the concept of a full double predestination to salvation and damnation conceived in the mind of God prior to his permissive willing of the Fall. Nonetheless, despite the emphasis placed on the doctrine by the Reformed, predestination cannot be understood as a "central dogma" or fundamental constructive principle in Reformed theology, whether that of Zwingli and Bucer, that of Calvin and his contemporaries, or that of later Reformed orthodox or scholastic thinkers of the late sixteenth century.

Zwingli and Bucer both developed significant approaches to predestination, the former on a more dogmatic and philosophical level in his treatise *De providentia* (1530) and his *Fidei ratio* (1530), the latter exegetically and doctrinally in his massive *Metaphrases et enarrationes perpetuae Epistolarum D. Pauli Apostoli* (1536). Both adhere to the basic Augustinian pattern of the doctrine, with Zwingli tending more toward the delineation of an overarching divine causality of predestination and providence. Bucer's approach offers the clearer antecedent for the teaching of Calvin and the other second-generation Reformed writers.

Calvin's doctrine of predestination was developed in connection with the second edition of his *Institutes* (1539) and his commentary on *Romans* (1540). Shortly thereafter he engaged in a bitter controversy over the doctrine with Albertus Pighius. Pighius's *De libero hominis arbitrio et divina qratia libri decem* (1542), dedicated to Cardinal Jacopo Sadoleto, Calvin's opponent in debate over the nature of the church, argued the case for a cooperation between the will and grace. Calvin's response came in two parts: in the first treatise, *Defensio sanae et orthodoxae doctrinae de servitute et liberatione humani arbitrii adv. calumnias A. Pighii Campensis* (1543), Calvin addressed the issue of free choice; in the second, *De aeterna praedestinatione qua in salutem alios ex hominibus elegit, alios suo exitio reliquit: item de providentia qua res humanas qubernat, Consensus pastorum Genevensis Ecclesiae a Jo. Calvino expositus* (1552), predestination and providence. As the title of the second treatise indicates, it was signed by the pastors of Geneva and is sometimes identified simply as the *Consensus Genevensis*. The *Consensus* was not received beyond Geneva and, indeed, received a strenuous rebuke for some of its language from Bullinger.

The more politically bitter controversy arose when Jérome

Bolsec, a former Carmelite monk, arrived in Geneva in 1550. Calvin's God, he claimed, was hypocritical and more vile than Satan. Eventually called before the consistory, he argued that God had elected some to salvation, but reprobated no one—a view of election with some parallels to that of Bullinger. Bolsec also maintained that grace was offered equally to all people and that the reason that some are saved and others damned lay entirely in the human faculty of free choice. This point, Calvin argued, was utterly inconsistent with any genuine concept of election. In all of these treatises, as in his *Institutes*, Calvin argued the divine election of some to salvation by sheer grace, apart from any inherent merit, and the divine reprobation of others to their own sinfully merited damnation. His doctrine indicates a strictly defined double decree of predestination, infralapsarian in form, but unmitigated by any concept of divine permission for sin.

Bullinger, who had voiced reservations about Calvin's views in the controversies with Pighius and now argued for moderation in debate with Bolsec, taught a single predestination of the elect only and understood the damnation of the unfaithful as resting on their own sinfulness rather than on a positive will of God. In Bullinger's *Decades* (1549–1551) and *Confessio et expositio simplex orthodoxae fidei* (1566), predestination is synonymous with election. Musculus, like Bullinger, counseled caution in the debate with Bolsec, although he was not opposed to a double decree of election and reprobation. In the definition of election in his *Loci communes* (1560), Musculus identified two related elective wills of God, one concerning the salvation of human beings, the other, God's choice of Israel as the bearer of the promise. The former concept refers strictly to the doctrine of predestination, the latter points toward Musculus's interest in covenant. Musculus indicates that all things predestinated by God are also foreknown, while not all things within the divine foreknowledge are predestined: God foreknows evil but does not cause it directly. In contrast to Calvin, Musculus argues a category of divine permission. He can then hold that all humanity falls justly under the wrath of God and that the election of some to salvation and the reprobation of others to damnation belongs solely to the mercy and justice of God. Like Calvin and Bullinger, Musculus also grounded election fully in Christ who is both the eternal, creative Word of God and the mediator of salvation. For Musculus, this christological ground of election connected God's original creative with his ultimate redemptive purpose, the restoration of human beings in the image and likeness of God.

Yet another significant voice in the framing of the Reformed doctrine was Peter Martyr Vermigli, whose *Loci communes* (1576) were gathered and published posthumously. Against Pighius, Vermigli argued that although God eternally understands and wills without past and without future, creatures are temporal and experience, in their own temporal order, a real foreordination. Even so, scripture teaches a predestination that divides the elect from the nonelect prior to the foundation of the world. Although Vermigli includes all sins in the divine decree permissively and assumes that the wicked are formed by God as "vessels of wrath," he nonetheless argues that the positive act of predestination or election refers to the salvation of fallen human beings. Reprobation is a passing over of the fallen in their sin that is not, properly understood, "predestination." Vermigli echoes his contemporaries in arguing that election is to be understood in Christ, but somewhat more clearly indicates that the Incarnation and Crucifixion rest on the divine counsel and are to be understood, together with the salvation of believers in Christ, as effects of the decree.

Predestination in the Era of Early Scholastic Protestantism. From a confessional perspective, the great difference between the Lutheran and the Reformed churches of the late sixteenth and early seventeenth centuries lies in the contrast between the Lutheran movement through bitter controversy toward confessional synthesis in the Formula of Concord (1577–1579) and the Reformed development of a large-scale confessional synthesis before the rise of internecine controversy on a large scale. Many Reformed theologians of the sixteenth century had, of course, debated key issues like the doctrine of predestination with a variety of adversaries; and there were differences over the definition of predestination among the various Reformed teachers.Théodore de Bèze, Calvin's successor in Geneva, is typically regarded as a major influence in the development of the Calvinist doctrine of predestination. Nonetheless, the document usually identified as the basis of Bèze's "predestinarian system, in the *Tabula praedestinationis* (1555), neither constitutes a full theological system nor indicates the relationship between the doctrine of predestination and the doctrine of God. Rather, the *Tabula* contains a presentation of the homiletical and pastoral use of the doctrine of predestination and a substantive discussion of the relationship of the divine decrees to the work of Christ. This christological emphasis is found also in Bèze's *Confessio christianae fidei* (1558) and *Quaestionum et responsionum christianarum libellus* (1570), and even the *Ad sycophantarum* (1558), written in support of Calvin against Castellion, offers a moderate, not particularly speculative presentation of the doctrine. Like Calvin, Bèze maintains that no doctrine contained in scripture should be hidden away—even the seemingly harsh doctrine of reprobation should be preached if only to teach the elect humility. He insists that the number and identity of the elect and reprobate cannot be a subject of speculation: believers must look to the testimony of scripture that those who have been predestinated from eternity will be effectually called and, in God's own time, be justified, sanctified, and glorified through the grace of God in Christ. Although the elect are no more worthy of salvation than the reprobate and the divine will is the sole reason for both election and reprobation, the human will remains the immediate cause of sin and the basis for damnation.

Although his views are somewhat more patterned, more strictly defined, and more indicative of the direction of later supralapsarianism than Calvin's, Bèze did not argue an "order of the decree" in the manner of later supra- and infralapsarianism; and although one of his later works, the *Catechismus compendarius* (1575), did link knowledge of election to temporal effects of the decree arguing the so-called "practical syllogism," Bèze remained for the most part concerned to ground election and assurance in the work of Christ. Even so, Bèze disappoints those who expect a strong association of the doctrine of predestination with a speculative doctrine of God and with the creation of a deductive, predestinarian system of theology: since the identity of the elect and reprobate is hidden in God, Bèze examines primarily not the decree but its effects, not the absolute will of God but the working-out of election in the world. Bèze does argue a full, double decree of election and reprobation, but he lessens the strict causal sequence of the decree by introducing a category of divine permission or permissive willing to deal with the problem of the Fall, as had Musculus and Vermigli in the previous generation. Bèze also insists that damnation justly results from human wickedness and from the obstinate refusal to accept the blessings of Christ.

More than Bèze, the Reformed theologians of Heidelberg, Zacharias Ursinus and Girolamo Zanchi, were responsible for the transition from the Reformation to early orthodoxy and the development of the Reformed doctrine of predestination in the late sixteenth century. Both followed the infralapsarian definition that would become the confessional norm. Zanchi's Strasbourg controversy with Johannes Marbach, which occurred before his appointment to Heidelberg, provides both the outline of his views and an insight into the disagreement between Lutherans and the Reformed. In 1561 Marbach began to inquire into Zanchi's doctrine, finding that Zanchi stressed the indefectibility of faith as a result of election. Zanchi's doctrine of predestination was distinctly infralapsarian, defining the elect as drawn out of the fallen mass of mankind, but Marbach found even this offensive because it was formulated in an *a priori* and not an *a posteriori* order and because it undermined the declaration of universal grace. Nor would Marbach allow a doctrine of perseverance: the elect, he insisted, could fall from faith.

Marbach accused Zanchi of teaching contrary to the Augsburg Confession. Zanchi countered by arguing that his views accorded with those of Luther, Augustine, and Bucer and proved the point in his *De praedestinatione sanctorum* (1561) with explicit citation, under each thesis, of Luther, Augustine, and Bucer. Marbach was not impressed and insisted that Zanchi had violated the confessional standard of the city not only in his doctrines of predestination and perseverance but also in his opposition to a doctrine of ubiquity. Argument had gone on for nearly two years when the debate was submitted for adjudication to the theologians of Marburg, Heidelberg, Zurich, Basel, Tübingen, and Saxony. The result of this consultation was mixed: Marburg, Heidelberg, and Zurich favored Zanchi; the Saxons divided on the issue, with the Melanchthonians opposing Marbach's ubiquitarianism and Zanchi's predestinarianism; Brenz at Tübingen held precisely opposite views from those of the Melanchthonians but hoped, as did the theologians of Basel, for conciliation. Finally, in 1563, Strasbourg adopted a form of agreement in which predestination was affirmed and indefectible perseverance denied. Zanchi signed the formula but expressed reservations concerning its treatment of perseverance and eventually left Strasbourg for a professorship in Heidelberg.

Ursinus's *Doctrinae christianae compendium* (1584) defined predestination as a part or aspect of providence, but also defined the decrees more as part of his soteriology than as the ground of a generalized metaphysic. His definition of predestination begins with the eternal, most righteous, and immutable counsel of God according to which human beings are to be created, permitted to fall, and then brought to redemption through Christ by grace through faith. Those who are not chosen for this salvation are to be left in their sins and ultimately condemned to eternal death. Zanchi's definition is almost identical. Both theologians assume that the eternal counsel or decree grounds all causality, including (under divine concurrence or permission) all free and contingent acts. Since human beings are locked in sin, election rests entirely on the free mercy of God while damnation arises because of human sin. The concept of a divine permission and concurrence that supports freedom and contingency distinguishes this view from a metaphysical determinism. Election, according to Zanchi's *De praedestinatione sanctorum*, is the special predestination of God: it is God's "eternal, most wise, and immutable decree, constituted by him in eternity, by which certain men in the trap of deepest sin and death, and one with all the fallen are, according to his merciful will, rescued graciously through Christ." This strictly infralapsarian theme resounds still more clearly in Zanchi's *De natura Dei* (1577), where he sets predestination in the context of God's larger work of creation, salvation, and judgment.

In contrast to the Reformed position, the Lutheran doctrine of predestination codified in the Formula of Concord attempted to balance the themes of salvation by grace alone and the universal divine offer of salvation by affirming a divine election or predestination to salvation only, by identifying this election as the "cause of salvation," and by arguing that damnation rests not on a divine decree but in the wickedness of the nonelect, who refuse the grace of the Holy Spirit. Believers ought not, moreover, to seek out the doctrine in the eternal counsel of God, but in the gospel and, thereby, in Christ. The Calvinist concept of a special calling of the elect and an ineffectual calling of the reprobate is explicitly condemned, and the potential paradox of a God who wills the salvation of all, elects some, but permits others to damn themselves is left unresolved by either a use of Luther's own necessitarian language or of Melanchthon's mildly synergistic formulation.

The controversy between Samuel Huber and Aegidius Hunnius was the first trial of the doctrines of the formula against pressure from the synergistic side, the affirmation of universal grace to the point that it negated the *sola gratia* of justification. Huber arrived in Tübingen in 1589, fresh from controversy with the Reformed in Bern, where he had opposed the concepts of the perseverance of the elect and of a limited offer of redemption. It was not long before he began to press upon the Lutheran formulation as not responsive enough to the scriptural doctrine of universal grace. Huber held that God's grace was given freely to all, apart from merit, and therefore that the all-sufficient merit of Christ must be effective for all. The Lutherans objected on the ground that those who reject grace and fall into unbelief are obviously excluded from salvation: election must conjoin with faith, indeed, election referred primarily to that salvation which takes place "with a view to faith" (*intuitu fidei*). The argument against Huber was refined and developed most fully by Hunnius in his *Articulus de Providentia Dei et aeterna praedestinatione seu electio filiorum Dei ad salutem* (1595). Hunnius responded to Huber and at the same time attempted to resolve the tensions in the Formula of Concord by affirming a particular election and by restricting somewhat the gift of grace to coincide with the election—grace is given on the grounds of the foreknowledge of faith (*praevisa fides*). The universal call of the gospel is maintained by this formulation, and damnation rests firmly upon stubborn unbelief. In addition, this formulation permits a doctrine of single predestination and a doctrine of the immutability of the divine will and intention: God wills to save those who come to faith. The will to save all on grounds of faith refers to an immutable *voluntas Dei antecedens* whereas the predestination of some on grounds of faith belongs to the *voluntas Dei conseauens*.

During the same period, debate in England over the Reformed doctrine adumbrated the problems that would lead toward Arminianism and the Synod of Dordrecht. As early as 1581 Lawrence Chaderton had criticized the synergistic view of salvation held by a Huguenot professor of theology at Cambridge, Peter Baro. Controversy began in 1595, when Baro argued in favor of a conditional decree of election. Baro's position also looked suspiciously like the theory of predestination as *ex praevisa fidei* proposed by Hunnius or, indeed, like the views of the synergistic Danish Lutheran Niels Hemmingsen. He was immediately opposed by William Whitaker, the regius professor of divinity at Cambridge, who vowed "to stand for God against the Lutherans." Archbishop Whitgift, who favored Whitaker's position, called a conference of theologians and churchmen at Lambeth in November 1595. A set of nine articles, drawn up by Whitaker against Baro, was debated and modified by the conference. These Lambeth Articles are uncompromisingly predestinarian and look directly toward the Irish Articles (1615) and the *Canons of Dordecht* (1619). The Lambeth conference, moreover, viewed their articles as definitive of the doctrine of the Thirty-nine Articles—a view which would be the source of bitter controversy in the English church after the accession of James I in 1603.

William Perkins's doctrine of predestination, found in his *Golden Chaine* (1590) and *Exposition of the Symbole* (1595), exemplifies the English Reformed view of the doctrine and is reflected in the Lambeth Articles. Perkins's Ramistic version of Reformed scholasticism consistently balances divine and human will, primary and secondary causality, and places emphasis on Christ's work in the believer despite his supralapsarian definition of the decree as an election and reprobation before the creation of the world. His doctrine of predestination is also significant for its elaboration of the divine logic of election in precise causal relation to the *ordo salutis* and for its profoundly negative impact on the thought of Arminius. The logic can be seen in Perkins's discussion of a first and second divine "act" of predestination, each distinguished into several "degrees," extending from the eternal saving purpose of God, to the ordination of Christ as mediator, to the promise of salvation in Christ, to the application of Christ's work to the elect, their salvation, and ultimate glorification.

Perkins's teaching, moreover, paralleled developments in continental Reformed thought. Amandus Polanus and other early orthodox writers such as Francis Junius, Bartholomaus Keckermann, Johannes Scharpius, Lucas Trelcatius, Jr., Antonius Walaeus, Johannes Maccovius, and Franciscus Gomarus used traditional scholastic distinctions concerning the divine essence and attributes far more than the reformers and did use these distinctions to produce a more metaphysical and scholastic statement of the doctrine of predestination, they did not develop the doctrine toward philosophical determinism. According to Polanus's *Syntagma theologiae christianae* (1617), the decree of divine good pleasure (*decretum beneplaciti*) itself remains hidden in eternity and can only be known as it is revealed in the word of God (*decretum siani Dei*), in the work of Christ, and in the order of salvation. While the *decretum beneplaciti* ordains all things to their ends, it does so in such a way as to respect the freedom and contingency of secondary causes. Since the decree is absolute and prior to all things, including the creation of human beings, Polanus moves toward a supralapsarian view of election and reprobation.

The Arminian Controversy and the Synod of Dordecht. The synergistic theology against which the early reformers reacted remained a theological option in sixteenth-century Protestantism not only among the Lutheran followers of Melanchthon and the English, but also among the Dutch Reformed, most notably in the thought of Jacobus Arminius. Arminius's theological training in Leiden and Geneva was strongly Reformed; but it was not, as often stated, so rigidly supralapsarian as to produce a massive reaction against Bèze's form of orthodoxy in the young Arminius. As his *Declaration of Sentiments* delivered to the States of Holland in 1608 indicates, Arminius objected not only to the more speculative supralapsarian definition of the decrees associated with Bèze and his successors but also to the confessional infralapsarian definition. His mature view argues, rather than a single eternal decree and its objects, four decrees and an order of priorities in the mind of God that rests on a distinction between an antecedent, universal will to save and a consequent particular will directed toward believers. In the antecedent divine willing, a first eternal decree appoints Christ as the savior of the human race in general, a second declares the divine intention to save in Christ all who repent and believe, and a third establishes the means of salvation. Then, as the expression of God's consequent will, a fourth decree, resting on divine foreknowledge of belief and perseverance, concludes the salvation of believers and the damnation of unbelievers. From the Reformed perspective, this predestination was fundamentally synergistic and rested salvation on the choice of individuals to believe, rather than solely on the grace of God.

When Arminius died in 1609 his supporters and followers had acquired enough strength to continue the controversy and to see the appointment of a successor in the university, Simon Episcopius, who could carry the debate forward. Whereas Arminius left no full system of theology but only a series of theses for disputation, Episcopius produced both the *Confessio pastorum qui Remonstrantes vocantur* (1622) and a massive, though incomplete, *Institutiones theologicae* (c.1640). Episcopius was also instrumental in the composition of the Remonstrance issued in 1610 to express the views of his party. The Reformed side immediately produced a Contra-Remonstrance. Debate polarized and led to the national Synod of Dordecht (1618–1619), which drew delegates not only from the Netherlands but also from the Swiss cantons and cities (Geneva, Basel, Bern, Zurich), the German Reformed communities (Heidelberg and Bremen), and from Britain—including the bishops of Chichester and Salisbury.

The Arminian Remonstrance is the necessary starting point for understanding the work of the Synod of Dordecht. Article one of the Remonstrance contains a distillate of the doctrine of predestination found in Arminius' *Declaration of Sentiments*: it defines predestination as the eternal purpose of God in Christ to save those who believe and to damn those who reject the gospel and the grace of God in Christ. Here already the implication is synergistic and the will of God is viewed as contingent upon human choice. Next (article two) the Remonstrance speaks of the universality of Christ's death: Christ died for all and the limitation of the efficacy of his death arises out of the choice of some not to believe. The third article argues the necessity of grace if fallen humanity is to choose the good and come to belief. In the fourth article this insistence upon prevenient grace is drawn into relation with the synergism of the first two articles. Prevenient and subsequent assisting grace may be resisted and rejected: ultimately the work of salvation, in its efficacy and application, rests on human choice. The fifth and final article of the Remonstrance argues continuing gracious support of believers by God but refuses to decide on the issue of perseverance.

It was clear from the outset that the Synod of Dordecht would not receive these points for debate with a hope for compromise and the ultimate incorporation of some form of Arminian theology into either the Belgic Confession or a new confessional document. The Remonstrant position was inimical to the confessional stance not only of the Dutch but also of the British, German, and Swiss delegates. No compromise was possible—and in this sense, the synod could only result in the condemnation of Arminianism.

The first canon, "Of Divine Predestination," takes as its point of departure the fallen condition of humanity and the punishment of eternal death that will be visited on sin. In Christ, God has manifested his saving will and his promise of salvation to believers and has also graciously called sinful mankind to repentance and belief. Only those who fail to respond to the call of God receive his wrath. The doctrine of election arises as the answer to the question of how this salvation is possible and why some are able to come to faith and others are not. Against what many of the delegates viewed as Arminian speculation, the canons insist that there is only one divine decree, which includes the entire plan of salvation in both testaments. In a thoroughly infralapsarian fashion, the canons define election as the unchangeable divine purpose, before the foundation of the world, to choose some people for redemption in Christ and to leave the rest in their sins to their own damnation. Since election does not rest on human merit or even on divine foreknowledge of faith but only on the good pleasure of God, it is unalterable.

The *Canons of Dordrecht* mark the full confessional codification of early Reformed orthodoxy, not as an independent systematic statement of doctrine but rather as an interpretive codicil to the Belgic Confession and the Heidelberg Catechism in which the major deviations from the Reformed confessional consensus are outlined and refuted. In the history of the doctrine of predestination, they are the Reformed equivalent of the Formula of Concord, but given the Lutheran development of the doctrine of election in view of faith, far more conclusive. In sum, the doctrine of predestination was a major focus of doctrinal discussion and debate in the sixteenth century and served to ground and explain the concept of salvation by grace alone without ever becoming either a "central dogma" in the nineteenth-century sense or the basis of a necessitarian metaphysic.

[*See also* Free Will; Good Works; Grace; Justification; *and* Sin.]

BIBLIOGRAPHY

Bray, John S. *Theodore Bèze's Doctrine of Predestination.* Nieuwkoop, 1975. A major, balanced work that has done much to place Bèze's teaching in clearer perspective over against descriptions of his thought as rigidly scholastic predestinarianism.

Gründler, Otto. *Die Gotteslehre Girolami Zanchis und ihre Bedeutung für seine Lehre von der Prädestination.* Neukirchen, 1965. A significant study of Zanchi's thought which errs, however, in interpreting his theology as supralapsarian.

Jacobs, Paul. *Prädestination und Verantwortlichkeit bei Calvin.* Reprint, Darmstadt, 1968. A crucial work in the reappraisal of Calvin's theology as not centered on predestination.

Klooster, Fred H. *Calvin's Doctrine of Predestination.* 2d ed. Grand Rapids, Mich., 1977. Perhaps the best exposition in English.

McClelland, J. C. "The Reformed Doctrine of Predestination according to Peter Martyr." *Scottish Journal of Theology* 8 (1955), 255–271.

Muller, Richard A. *Christ and the Decree: Christology and Predestination in Reformed Theology from Calvin to Perkins.* Studies in Historical Theology, vol. 2. Grand Rapids, Mich., 1988. Surveys the development of the doctrine and argues against the idea of a central dogma or predestinarian system.

———. *God, Creation, and Providence in the Thought of Jacob Arminius: Sources and Directions of Scholastic Protestantism in the Era of Early Orthodoxy.* Grand Rapids, Mich., 1991.

Otten, Hans. *Calvins theologische Anschauung von der Prädestination.* Munich, 1938.

Schweizer, Alexander. *Die protestantischen Centraldogmen in ihrer Entwicklung innerhalb der reformierten Kirche.* 2 vols. Zurich, 1854–1856. The positive foundation of the view of predestination as a central dogma—a dogmatic treatise, organized historically, to demonstrate the development of Reformed theology toward the Schleiermacherian concept of absolute or utter dependence.

Walser, Peter. *Die Prädestination bei Heinrich Bullinger im Zusammenhang mit seiner Gotteslehre.* Zurich, 1957.

Weber, Hans Emil. *Reformation, Orthodoxie und Rationalismus.* 2 vols. Reprint, Darmstadt, 1967. The negative presentation of the central thesis that asserts rather than proves the contention that Reformed dogmatics is a metaphysic deduced from the divine decree.

RICHARD A. MULLER

PRESBYTERIANISM can be defined as a system of church government in which a series of ecclesiastical courts, composed of both clergy and lay elders, forms an ascending order of discipline within the church. At the congregational level the minister(s) and elders form a consistory (the Continental Reformed churches' term) or a session (the Scottish term). Above that is a district court made up of representatives from the individual churches, usually called either a classis (Continental term,) or presbytery. At the next level there may be a regional synod to monitor the several presbyteries within its bounds. At the top a national synod or general assembly (Scottish term) will hear problems within the lower courts and establish policy for the whole church. Presbyterianism is usually distinguished from episcopacy, in which bishops oversee the work within the churches, and from congregationalism, a system in which power lies within the local churches (however governed) and higher courts do not exist, or are merely associational.

It was from Calvin that the rudiments of presbyterianism were borrowed by the French Huguenots in their 1559 *Discipline ecclésiastique*, as well as by the Dutch and Scots soon afterward. For Calvin the two marks of the true church were right preaching of the word of God and proper celebration of Holy Communion and baptism, so church polity was not an essential element, nor was the discipline of morals that was soon characteristic of Reformed churches. But polity was not unimportant, and the Genevan model was incorporated and enlarged into a synodical or presbyterian polity in regions where the Reformed churches prevailed over Roman, Lutheran, or Anglican expressions of reform in the sixteenth century.

Calvin's Fourfold Ministry. In his analysis of the church of the New Testament and the early centuries, Calvin found a fourfold order: doctors, *presbyteroi* as pastors, *presbyteroi* as lay elders, and deacons. Neither the first nor the last proved to be essential to presbyterial order, for the doctors (professors) as an order never became a core element, despite their mention in all the earliest polity statements. And, although deacons as collectors and distributors of alms and services were active in all early Reformed churches, they failed to find a place in higher courts and were often later absent from churches otherwise perfectly presbyterian in order. But Calvin insisted on a diaconate, an order of lay men (and, in theory, women) to help the poor and the ill with resources provided by the whole of Christ's body. The church had not recognized "lay" ecclesiastical ministries since the early centuries, so the diaconate represented a sharp break with tradition.

The two orders of *presbyteroi* ("elders" in Greek), the pastors and elders, saw to the moral life of the church, the latter providing a lay representation in the basic court of Calvin's church, the consistory. All Geneva's pastors and the dozen elders—elected annually, but often reelected—met weekly with a layman as moderator. Modern folk might wonder at the consistory's concern about what people did in private, but we can hardly doubt the dedication that motivated laymen to sit on those courts, especially as two of the elders also met on another weekday as members of the city's Small Council. So the consistory was both a church institution and a governmental body, its presiding officer not a pastor, but the elected head of Geneva's Small Council. Most of the penalties it meted out were in the form of admonishment or advice. Often it required public confession at a service of worship. Sometimes it excommunicated stubborn malefactors and then called on the city council to impose further punishment. In the latter case the modern reader will detect an inner contradiction in the Reformed theory of church-state relations: on the one hand Calvin insisted on the church's freedom; but on the other hand, calling on the state to help cleanse the church was a "Constantinian hangover" that often embittered relations between church and government officials.

Recent studies show that Calvin had come to his mature teaching by the 1543 edition of *The Institutes of the Christian Religion.* Based upon his exegesis of *Romans* 12:6–7, *1 Corinthians* 12:28, *Ephesians* 4:11, and *1 Timothy* 5:17 ("elders who rule" and "those who labor in preaching and teaching"), Calvin insisted that the New Testament taught that a senate of nonteaching presbyters was to govern the local church, yoked with the ministerial elder, whose primary calling was to be teacher, preacher, and minister of the sacraments. Again, this is a break from the Roman church, which assigned all church offices to clergy, as well as a break with his friend Heinrich Bullinger in Zurich, who left to the Christian magistrate the role of discipline. It is here that the Calvinist Reformed most clearly refused to identify the church with Christian society, even when the two appeared to coincide. But in the German Palatinate, as well as Swiss towns like Zurich and Basel, Reformed churches tended to leave discipline to the government, a position argued so strongly by Heidelberg physician Thomas Lüber (Lat., Erastus) that "Erastianism" became the byword for placing the church under the Christian magistrate or ruler.

Calvin's teaching about bishops is somewhat ambivalent. On the one hand, he noted the equivalency of *presbyteros* and *episkopos* in the *Acts of the Apostles* and in the pastoral epistles, and argued that the post–New Testament practice of raising the "overseers" above the presbyters signaled a corruption of authority in the early church. He believed it had been practically necessary to appoint some presbyter to be "moderator" over others within urban-rural districts but thought that calling that moderator "bishop" perverted New Testament language, where the two are equivalent. But Calvin did not make polity a mark of the church and was able to accept bishops under certain circumstances. He never argued against episcopacy in his correspondence with Archbishop Thomas Cranmer in England. The Reformed churches in Hungary adopted a modified episcopacy, and Poland might have done so had the Reformation not been riddled by unitarianism and nearly destroyed by Catholic rulers, for Calvin had written the king of Poland recommending that he establish a church run by bishops within a presbyterian, that is, nonhierarchical, system. This "reduced episcopacy," where bishops moderate presbyteries (or classes) and are corrected by their presbyter peers, was later advocated in Great Britain by Calvin's friend Martin Bucer, who had fled there in exile, and in the next century by Irish archbishop James Ussher.

The French and Dutch Reformed Churches. Geneva constituted a tiny urban-rural classis and could not itself be a model for a national church. It was left for the Huguenots to put in place a consistent presbyterial government for the Reformed Christians of France. In 1559 representatives of the churches met in Paris and wrote their *Confession du foy* (or Gallic Confession) and the *Discipline ecclésiastique,* the latter applying the polity principles outlined in the confession. Like Calvin, the Huguenots did not make discipline a mark of the true church—as the Scots did in their Scottish Confession (1560) and the Dutch the year following. They outlined a structure that called for Calvin's four offices and urged that all who served in church offices should be elected, if at all possible. One problem for the historian arises because article 30 of the confession insists that all pastors "have the same authority and equal power under one head . . . Jesus Christ," but article 32 reads "It is desirable and useful that those elected to be superintendents devise among themselves what means should be adopted for the government of the whole body. . . ." Who are these superintendents? They never show up in any form among the churches of France, and both the confession and the discipline explicitly reject any primacy among ministers. The French rotated the moderatorship of their national synod among the pastors of local churches, so even a temporary superintendency was not followed.

Although the discipline does not carefully name the hierarchy of courts above the consistory, it provides for "colloquies" of ministers and elders (or deacons) in small areas, for regional synods, and the national synod, which was to meet once a year. So a four-tiered system was in place. But there were also congregationalist tendencies among the Huguenots, advocated by Jean Morély and Petrus Ramus, who argued for the same democratic principles that gave congregationalism's advocates victory over the presbyterial system among English Puritans. But the 1572 Saint Bartholomew's Day Massacre abruptly terminated that quarrel.

Whereas twenty representatives wrote and approved of the confession of the Huguenot church, the Belgic Confession was basically the work of one man, Guy de Brès, martyred by Philip II in 1567, six years after his confession was penned. War with Spain prevented a national assembly until the (Great) Synod of Dordrecht in 1619, at which the confession, the Heidelberg Catechism, and the articles of the synod itself were adopted as the doctrinal and polity standards of the Dutch churches in the Netherlands, Belgium, and America. There is nothing unusual in the confession for the student of ecclesiastical polity. As noted above, it argues for church discipline as a third mark of the true church. The hierarchy of courts was already operative before Dordrecht.

The only real differences are not found in the statutes, but in the actual practice of church-state relations. That Calvin insisted on the church's freedom from the state has already been highlighted. Gordon Donaldson, the Scottish historian and antipresbyterian, says this two-kingdoms approach is what sets the Calvinist Reformed apart and pits monarchs solidly against the system. But in the Low Countries the Reformed church was not able to make that stick, for after the Synod of Dordrecht, the Dutch States-General would not allow the national church to meet again for two hundred years. So orthodox Calvinists, who cheered the triumph of true Calvinism because Dordrecht so clearly and strongly supported predestinarian doctrine, cannot pretend that Calvin's church survived the synod, for a church dominated and restricted by the state is not the independent church Calvin insisted upon.

A parallel failure within the Dutch church was the comparative inability of the local churches to set up serious consistorial discipline, although they tried hard enough. It is apparent from the Netherlands experience that a consistory that imposes discipline, but without support from the government, will not produce the pure church that the Reformed aimed at. That fewer than forty percent of the population were even nominally Protestant by the middle of the seventeenth century certainly had a cautionary influence on Dutch magistrates.

Scotland. The final establishment of the presbyterian system within the Scots Kirk in 1690 was often in grave doubt during the first 130 years or so of the Reformed church's existence there. It was a government that Scotland's monarchs fought bitterly. James VI (later James I of England) said that "presbytery . . . agreeth with monarchy as God with the devil" because it allows "Tom, Will, and Dick" to censure the king. His grandson remarked that it was "no religion for gentlemen." No doubt both of them recalled that time when young King James had his sleeve pulled by arch-presbyterian Andrew Melville, who called him "God's silly vassal."

Since the 1570s Scottish partisans have disagreed on whether John Knox and his company intended to establish a church without bishops. Both the Scottish Confession and the so-called *First Book of Discipline* call for parity of clergy, but the latter also envisions the election of ten or twelve superintendents, whose role is to visit in their dioceses, plant churches, and generally exercise a ministry of *episkope.* Given that during the Reformation epoch only two of Scotland's thirteen bishops—most of whom had noble patrons, usually relatives, so that imminent dismissals were unlikely—were actively Protestant, it was necessary to get on with the difficult task of reforming a country without help from men in office. So an interpolation was made in the discipline that gives fairly exact directions on the choice of superintendents, the work they do, and how their work will be judged. (In the end, only five were appointed.)

Most of the other accoutrements of presbyterianism are found in the discipline: the education, trial, and election of godly ministers of word and sacrament; the election of elders and deacons, and the moral discipline and relief work for which the two offices are responsible; the annual meeting of the national synod, called the General Assembly; and the rudiments of presbytery, although that body is called, interchangeably, a "diocese" or a "province." The word *presbytery* is not used even in the *Second Book of Discipline* (1578), where the provincial synod is named, as well as the congregational "eldarschip" and the national assembly. But the function of presbytery is in place and actual presbyteries, which replaced ancient diocesan boundaries, began to be established in the Lowlands about 1581; soon the whole ecclesiastical system would be called by that name.

The Scottish Reformation is usually dated at 1560, with the first meeting of ministers and laymen—mostly nobility—to decide national church policy. Whether it can be called a General Assembly or not, it functioned as one in some respects, although the lay representatives excluded the clergy from voting on the *Book of Discipline,* and finally refused to approve it. When Mary departed in 1572, the infant king's regent continued to appoint bishops—against the church's expectations—in order to provide the church's historical representation in Parliament and the Privy Council. Only a turn of fortunes in that regency allowed Andrew Melville's program of presbyterial polity as set forth in the *Second Book of Discipline* to be voted upon by the General Assembly; it was approved unanimously in 1578.

No one denies that the second book established serious presbyterian polity, for it excluded bishops in a typical Reformed argument for parity of ministers. But Parliament rejected that measure and the one that returned ancient church revenues to the national church and local congregations. Both issues touched the nobles in the pocketbook, so there was little chance that ancient titles or the lands and funds attached to them would be given up and used to support a Reformed church. As Donaldson described it: while a new Reformed ecclesiastical structure had been put in place by the national church, the old ecclesiastical structure had the bulk of endowments but was no longer the mechanism by which spiritual functions were performed.

In 1584 presbyteries were proscribed and the bishops were declared to answer only to the king. It was this "Erastian" subordination of church to ruler that James VI wished above all, wedding his personal theological Calvinism to an Anglican theory of church and state. He pursued that policy until he died in 1625, and his son Charles did the same. But presbyteries did not die under the Stuart kings and continued to pull in uneasy tandem with bishops. Royal control over the Scots church was asserted in the strongest fashion between 1618 and 1638, when no General Assembly could be called without royal permission, which was never given. Finally, in 1638, in the famous confrontation between Charles I and the church over the imposition of the modified English prayerbook upon the church, ministers, nobility, burghers, and commoners struck against the whole episcopal system and brought it crashing down with the signing of the National League and Covenant.

The subsequent attempt at the Westminster Assembly (1643–1649) by Puritan presbyterians, nurtured on the writings of Walter Travers and Thomas Cartwright, to establish presbyterianism in England died aborning, despite the best efforts of the four Scots minister commissioners who lobbied and wrote on its behalf. Oliver Cromwell's personal preference for a congregational system without the rigorous discipline and intolerant tendencies of the Scots church session guaranteed a presbyterian defeat.

Through the vicissitudes of Cromwell's Commonwealth and the return of bishops at the restoration of Charles II (1660), church sessions and presbyteries continued to work as the backbone of the Scottish church—despite the rule of bishops—and the presbyterian system without bishops was established in law after the deposition of James II. Unfortunately lay patronage, the election of local pastors, was returned to the lords and lairds and king in 1712 and weakened the presbyterian system. That was, in part, responsible for the Seceder split at the end of the eighteenth century, and was at the heart of the Great Disruption of the national church in the middle of the next century.

[*See also* Anglicanism; Knox, John; *and* Scotland.]

BIBLIOGRAPHY

Armstrong, Brian G. *Calvinism and the Amyraut Heresy*. Madison, Wis., 1969. Fine study of the Reformed church in France as it struggled for self-understanding in theology and church order.

Cameron, James K., ed. *The First Book of Discipline*. Edinburgh, 1972. Text and historical context to the rejected *First Book of Discipline*, written by Scottish Reformation leaders, headed by John Knox.

Cochrane, Arthur C., ed. *Reformed Confessions of the Sixteenth Century*. Philadelphia, 1966. Handiest place to find important confessions, including the French (Gallic), Belgic, and Scottish.

Donaldson, Gordon. *The Scottish Reformation*. Cambridge, 1960. Best statement of view that Knox and others intended a "reduced episcopacy" for Scotland. He admires the "fertile brain of King James VI," an admiration not shared by his one-time student James Kirk.

Henderson, G. D. *Presbyterianism*. Aberdeen, 1954. Often-reprinted history of the presbyterian system by an even-handed presbyterian historian. The discussion of the lay elder needs correcting by way of the work of McKee.

Höpfl, Harro. *The Christian Polity of John Calvin*. Cambridge, 1982. Studies Calvin's understanding of secular and church polity development as he struggles for three decades to create a Christian society.

Kingdon, Robert M. *Geneva and the Consolidation of the French Protestant Movement, 1564–1572*. Geneva and Madison, Wis., 1967. By the dean of Americans who study Geneva and its influence, here—among other topics—is the story of Jean Morély.

Kirk, James, ed. *The Second Book of Discipline*. Edinburgh, 1980. Should be read in tandem with Donaldson, for Kirk not only provides the text for the strongly presbyterian discipline of 1578, but argues that it does not deviate from the first book.

Knox, S. J. *Walter Travers: Paragon of Elizabethan Puritanism*. London, 1962. English clergyman Travers was the fiercest and clearest presbyterian in the English quarrels that escape the encyclopedia article. His views and Andrew Melville's are in agreement and his arguments won the day in foreign Scotland but not in his native England.

McGinn, Donald Joseph. *The Admonition Controversy*. New Brunswick, N. J., 1949. While Travers wrote, Thomas Cartwright involved himself in disputes over bishops. This work chronicles his famous dispute with John Whitgift, the archbishop.

McKee, Elsie Anne. *Elders and the Plural Ministry*. Geneva, 1988. Fullest study of Calvin's teaching on church office, complementing her earlier work on the diaconate, *John Calvin on the Diaconate and Liturgical Almsgiving*, Geneva, 1984.

Melville, James. *Autobiography and Diary of James Melville*. Edited by Robert Pitcairn. Edinburgh, 1842. Indispensable account of church-state struggles in Scotland, written by the nephew of Andrew Melville, architect of presbyterianism in Scotland.

Mullan, David George. *Episcopacy in Scotland: The History of an Idea, 1560–1638*. Edinburgh, 1986. Careful and satisfying study of Scottish episcopacy up to its temporary downfall in 1648.

Sunshine, Glenn. "The French *Discipline ecclésiastique*." In *Later Calvinism*, edited by W. Fred Graham. Kirksville, Mo., 1992. Careful study of Huguenot church order and its roots in Calvin and Bèze. Also includes small studies by Mary Black Verschuur and Michael Graham on the actual effect of session discipline in local churches in Scotland in the sixteenth century.

W. FRED GRAHAM

PRESSIUS, Pavel. *See* Přáza, Paul.

PRIERIAS, Sylvester Mazzolini (1456–1523),

Dominican theologian and early opponent of Luther. Born in the Piedmontese town of Priero, from which he took his surname, Prierias became a Dominican in 1471. He began teaching at Bologna in 1495, and in 1508–1510 served as vicar-general of his order's Lombard congregation. In 1514 he was called to Rome to teach Thomistic theology, and in late 1515 became "Master of the Sacred Palace," the pope's court theologian.

In the first years of the sixteenth century Prierias published vernacular works that encouraged devout souls to advance in tender love of the crucified Jesus, even to mystical marriage with divine wisdom. Prierias gave materials for sermons on the Sunday and feast-day gospels in his *Rosa aurea* of 1503, a work that went through eleven printings. His most successful work was the *Summa summarum de casibus conscientiae*, known as the *Summa Silvestrina*, published in 1514 and reprinted twenty-nine times. This dictionary-style exposition of theological, moral, and canonical topics was intended to be a reference work for confessors but in fact was much more. An ecclesiology accentuating papal authority appears in the sometimes lengthy entries on the canonization of saints, councils, faith, heresy, and the pope.

In late 1517 the archbishop of Mainz, Albert of Brandenburg, wrote to Pope Leo X to denounce Luther's attack on Johann Tetzel's preaching of the Saint Peter's indulgence. In Rome Leo commissioned Prierias to examine Luther's Ninety-five Theses as a preliminary step in the canonical procedure against one accused of heresy. A printed copy of Prierias's critical report, the *Dialogus*, was forwarded to Luther along with the citation to appear in Rome to answer the charges brought against him. Luther immediately composed a *Responsio* to ward off Prierias's accusations of error and heresy. Luther appealed to the freedom of theologians to debate issues not yet decided by council or pope. Where Prierias argued from positions of Thomas Aquinas, Luther urged the authority of scripture, the fathers of the church, and canon law. Especially emblematic of this early Reformation debate are the "four foundations" that Prierias laid down, defining the universal church in strict relation to the pope and the Roman church, the doctrine and practice of which is an infallible rule of orthodoxy. In response Luther stated the Pauline maxim, "Test everything; hold fast to what is good" (*1 Thes.* 5:21), and took scripture as his inerrant norm. He stated that the Roman church had in fact followed this rule of faith, by Christ's special protection, but on indulgences there was as yet no binding teaching to ground Prierias's accusations of heresy.

Prierias appears to express Roman doctrinal norms in a typical manner against Luther. His views do anticipate the dogmatic decisions of the First Vatican Council (1870) on papal primacy and infallibility. But at the time his accentuation of papal authority was one part of a broader spectrum of ecclesiological views, which included residual conciliarist ideas in France, the episcopal emphases of Spanish thinkers, and more spiritual views of ecclesial consensus (e.g., Thomas More). Erasmus judged Prierias's critique of Luther arbitrary and extreme, and saw it occasioning Luther's reactive first step toward his contestation of papal authority at the Leipzig Disputation of 1519 and in his later antipapal polemics.

BIBLIOGRAPHY

Fabisch, Peter. "Silvester Prierias." In *Katholische Theologen der Reformationszeit*, edited by Erwin Iserloh, vol. 1, pp. 26–36. Münster, 1984.

Fabisch, Peter, and Erwin Iserloh, eds. *Dokumente zur Causa Lutheri, 1517–1521*. 2 vols. Münster, 1988–1991. Vol. 1, pp. 33–201, gives Prierias's main texts of 1518 and 1519 against Luther with ample introductions and commentary.

Horst, Ulrich. *Zwischen Konziliarismus und Reformation*. Rome, 1985. A study of developments in ecclesiology among Dominican authors in the early sixteenth century, treating Prierias in chapter 4.

Klaiber, Wilbirgis. *Katholische Kontroverstheologen und Reformer des 16. Jahrhunderts*. Münster, 1978. Prierias's publications are listed on pp. 238–240.

Lindberg, Carter. "Prierias and His Significance for Luther's Development." *Sixteenth Century Journal* 3 (1972), 45–64.

Wicks, Jared. "Roman Reactions to Luther: The First Year, 1518." *Catholic Historical Review* 69 (1983), 521–562. Reprinted in *Luther's Reform: Studies on Conversion and the Church*, Mainz, 1992.

JARED WICKS

PRINTING. The importance of printing for the spread of Martin Luther's ideas has been affirmed since the sixteenth century. As early as 1526 François Lambert of Avignon wrote that it was precisely to make the Reformation possible that God willed the invention of printing. Among other tributes, Luther made this remark: "Printing is the latest of God's gifts and the greatest. Through printing God wills to make the cause of true religion known to the whole world even to the ends of the earth." John Foxe, the author of the *Book of Martyrs*, spoke of printing as a "divine and miraculous invention." It is understandable that historians reiterated that the success of the Reformation owed much to the invention of printing. But should one not step back somewhat from this "Doctrine of Justification by Print Alone," as A. G. Dickens quipped?

As a matter of fact, Luther rarely sang the praises of printing in his writings. More often the reformer expressed a negative opinion about the new invention. For him useless and even harmful books abounded. Many of his contemporaries had the same reservations as did he about the multiplication of books.

To analyze precisely the relationships between printing and the Reformation, one must first recognize the diversity of books and the variety of historical situations. The pamphlet warfare that developed in Germany between 1520 and 1525 and that spread Luther's name everywhere no doubt had an impact on people's thinking both in the sixteenth century and later on. But the phenomenon was limited to a few years within the narrow confines of the empire. What about books elsewhere, at other times, and in Europe as a whole? It is also appropriate to distinguish among literary genres. There is a big difference between a Bible and a liturgical manual, for example, or between a catechism, a theological treatise, and a pamphlet. Finally, since the printed work has an effect on its readers, one must ask about the way in which the books were read.

The Beginnings of Printing. The outbreak of the Reformation coincided with the coming of age of printing. The originality of the invention perfected by Johannes Gutenberg around 1455 became apparent only in the course of a slow maturation process over almost eighty years. At first printed books were modeled on manuscripts, but then gradually they took on a distinctive appearance. The process culminated between 1520 and 1540, shortly after Luther raised his protest against the sale of indulgences. The outward appearance of books was transformed by the addition of a title page. The design of characters was standardized, and numerous abbreviations were discarded. There were especially profound changes in the choice of texts, with more openness to modern authors and languages. Large publishers set up distribution networks to find readers beyond the confines of their own cities. During the years from 1530 to 1540, changes occurred in the makeup of libraries. As a result of the lower price of books, the average size of libraries increased, and manuscripts gave way to printed books. In short, books became commonplace.

The church did not disapprove of Gutenberg's invention. From the time of Innocent VIII's constitution *Inter multiplices* (1487) to the Fifth Lateran Council (1515), the ecclesiastical authorities showed some degree of enthusiasm, even if they also expressed some reservation. Specifically, a large number of the printed works produced served the interests of the church. Alongside scholarly publications intended for theologians and priests, there were manuals of piety intended for the laity. In short, the use of books for religious purposes was widespread by 1517, the year Luther produced his Ninety-five Theses.

The Spread of Printing. Starting in 1460 printing shops quickly multiplied. From Germany they spread to Italy and then France, the Netherlands, and the whole of Europe. Around 1520 the regions on the periphery were still not well equipped, but western Europe already had a dense network of printing houses.

Germany. The situation of printing in Germany was a mirror image of its political organization—extremely scattered. The fragmentation of the empire favored the printers' freedom. It was always possible to find a principality or a city to authorize their publications. Moreover, the mercantile mind-set of certain cities, such as Basel and Strasbourg, brought about a great deal of tolerance in publishing. The diversity of dialects reinforced the diffusion of publishing. Each printer used the spelling of the local dialect.

Around 1500 there were printing shops in about sixty German cities. But there was no great center of printing comparable to Venice, Paris, Lyon, or Antwerp. The printing shops were generally modest in size. Over the course of the century, the publishers became concentrated in the Rhine region (Cologne, Frankfurt am Main, Strasbourg, and Basel) and in the Danube region (Nuremberg, Augsburg, and Ulm). In eastern Germany Leipzig, Erfurt, and Wittenberg became noted for their printing houses.

The outbreak of the Reformation benefited from this situation of freedom. The pamphlets published between 1520 and 1525 often violently attacked the traditional church. The Reformation reinforced the decentralization of printing through the creation of printing houses in numerous small cities.

One of the most significant effects of the Reformation on printing can be seen in Wittenberg. The need to spread the reformer's writings promoted this small provincial city to fifth place among centers of printing in Germany.

In publishing matters, tolerance was not absolute. The semiannual Frankfurt fair came together without any denominational restrictions since the *Meßkataloge* ("fair catalogs"), which appeared starting in 1564, present in turns Protestant and Catholic theological books. Books, even polemical ones, were a commodity to be traded.

France. France, Italy, and the Netherlands had in common a dense network of printing houses, with a heavy concentration in one or two cities. Moreover, the rulers in these countries remained faithful to the Catholic Church, which forced Protestant publishers underground.

During the first decades of the Reformation the Protestant press in France distributed devotional books that steered clear of polemical excesses. Beginning in 1534 a more uncompromising faction formed around refugees who had settled in Switzerland. This group fostered literature of a frankly polemical nature that advocated breaking away from the traditional church.

From 1530 onward, after a few publications had been produced in Paris by some isolated publishers, evangelical publishing took refuge outside of France, particularly in Antwerp. The radical trend then taking hold initially benefited from printing houses established in Neuchâtel (1533–1535) and then, after 1536, in Geneva. The volume of works produced was nevertheless rather limited until 1550. About that time an influx of printers and publishers made Geneva the hub of French-language Reformed publishing. A network of peddlers spread these publications throughout France and in the southern Netherlands. The creation of the Huguenot party and the Wars of Religion somewhat reduced Geneva's monopoly after 1562 in favor of some French cities outside Paris, such as Caen, Rouen, Orléans, La Rochelle, and Lyon.

Netherlands. Printing in the Netherlands was concentrated in the port city of Antwerp. The presence of numerous foreign communities whose activity was necessary for the city's prosperity explains the tolerance of the local authorities, at least until 1545. The publishers, who tended to avoid polemics, produced works not only in Dutch and Latin but also in French, English, and even Danish.

In about 1545 repression became harsher, and this caused many to emigrate to England and Germany. The center of Dutch Reformed publishing shifted to London until 1553. Subsequently Emden in East Friesland became the major producer of Dutch Reformed books at least until 1570. Changes in the political situation led to the temporary opening of some Protestant printing houses in Vianen and Wesel and then in Holland.

Italy. Italian book production was concentrated in Venice. This large port city offered relative freedom of the press until 1550. Some publishers took advantage of this to distribute literature that was discreetly heretical.

From 1540 onward Reformed books of a markedly more polemical nature were published outside of Italy, particularly in Geneva and Basel. As a result of the tightening grip of the Inquisition, the Italian publications produced outside of Italy became scarcer; from this time on they were directed only to Italians who had emigrated to northern Europe.

England. At the beginning of the sixteenth century, the English printing industry was scarcely developed, and most publishing in English was done on the Continent (Paris, Normandy, and particularly Antwerp). As long as Henry VIII maintained an attitude of reservation about the Reformation, protest literature was published on the Continent, particularly in Antwerp. The situation changed under Thomas Cromwell. Protestant publishing houses flourished for the first time under Edward VI, all the more because some heretical publishers from Antwerp found refuge in London.

The reign of Mary Tudor obviously marked a break with this trend and caused many to go into exile. The result was a rash of English publications on the Continent. With the coming of Elizabeth I to the throne, the situation reversed, and this allowed for the return of most of the exiles to England.

From the time of Henry VIII the royal authorities had understood the advantages of establishing an English publishing industry in England itself. Thus, there was systematic encouragement for printing houses to be set up in England. Moreover, to facilitate better oversight of the works published, the printing shops were concentrated in London itself.

Spain. In Spain, where printing was at a rudimentary stage, the authorities, thanks to the Inquisition, succeeded in controlling local publishing and particularly in forbidding the importation of heretical books. The production of Reformed books in Spanish, which was organized in Geneva in the 1550s, was quickly stopped. No other government in the sixteenth century managed so successfully to prevent the importation of forbidden books.

East-central Europe. In central Europe the development of printing occurred later, just as the Reformation spread there later than in western Europe. The fragmentation of authority during the second half of the sixteenth century fostered the multiplication of more radical currents there. The result was a great dispersion of publishing, and its development was linked to religious history. Each denomination needed its publishing house, even if limited in its impact.

Even before Luther the Utraquists of Bohemia and Moravia had made use of printing, producing works in small scattered printing shops. The boom in printing that dates from the end of the century was closely linked to the production of religious literature.

Poland, especially the city of Kraków, already had a humanist publishing tradition. The introduction of the Reformation there increased the volume of printing and led to the setting up of new printing shops. Lutheran works were produced in east Prussia, while Poland had Calvinist printing houses. In the second half of the century the antitrinitarian churches opened printing houses in Lithuania and Poland.

Hungary, which was divided under three different political jurisdictions at the time, saw its first books printed in Vienna and Poland. In about 1540 in Transylvania and then in royal Hungary, some printers were working mainly to respond to religious needs. The denominational divisions of the 1560s brought about a multiplication of small printing houses.

Scandinavia. Printing in Scandinavia was even less developed than in east-central Europe. Until 1530 Denmark, which resorted to German printing presses, was visited by itinerant printers. Only after 1530 did churchmen found some small printing shops.

In Sweden, which had become independent in 1521, there had been some small printing shops since 1510. From 1526 Gustavus Vasa authorized only his own royal publishing house, which was the best way to control all publishing. Norway did not have a printing house until 1643.

Publishing Conditions. The situation under which books were produced varied greatly from country to country. In Germany there were many printing presses, but they were scattered. In France, Italy, and the Netherlands production was concentrated in Paris and Lyon, in Venice, and in Antwerp, respectively. Other countries gradually achieved autonomy. This was done either by setting up a single printing house, as in Sweden, or by encouraging a proliferation of small printing shops with the support of local leaders, as in Poland, Bohemia, and Hungary.

The political situation played a primary role in the setting up of printing houses. Freedom and support by the authorities favored their development. Some printing houses were set up near the borders of Catholic countries in order to ship books into those countries. This was the specialty of Geneva and Emden for several decades. But there were also underground printing shops. Sometimes the authorities ignored such shops as long as the printers remained discreet, as in Antwerp before 1545, in Venice before 1550, and in Basel throughout the century. Other Protestant ventures defied prohibitions in Catholic countries, just as spiritualist and Anabaptist publishers did in Protestant countries.

A printing operation could not function without financial resources. Even in hard times religious books remained good business for a publisher. The pace of re-editions and conflicts between publishers attest to the scale of the financial interests at work. There were also risks involved, as bankruptcies proved. If there was no profit to be made, a patron was the only resort.

Some printers were satisfied with producing for local consumption. Others aimed at wider markets. The publishers in Basel and Geneva worked primarily for export. But capturing a wide market presupposes good commercial networks. Wittenberg's situation is a negative proof of this. With Luther's presence this city could have achieved overwhelming dominance in German evangelical publishing. Instead it achieved no more than a respectable place because it failed to deliver its products to the whole empire.

Literary Genres. The printed works took on various forms. It is dangerous to lump them together by oversimplifying, and so below is a concise overview of the types of Protestant books produced during the sixteenth century.

A good starting point is the pamphlets that brutally condemned the opposing side, as the wave of *Flugschriften* made a profound mark on the beginnings of the Reformation. This was the first time printing was enlisted for a press campaign. The same phenomenon occurred in other crisis situations—in England around 1540 after Cromwell's fall, in France during the Wars of Religion, and in the Netherlands after 1565 during the Revolt of the Netherlands against Spain. Among these pamphlets, fliers or posters that were intended to be posted in public occupied a special place because of their greater use of pictures.

The spread of holy scripture was always a concern for Protestants. They produced scholarly editions to improve the original text or the Latin versions. In particular they increased the number of vernacular translations. Such translations had existed since the fifteenth century in Germany and Italy. But the Reformation accelerated the pace of translations of the Bible throughout Europe. Editions of the Bible might differ from one another in various ways—the format (and thus the handiness), the forewords and annotations (and thus not only the denominational but also the pastoral orientations), and the illustrations. These nuances corresponded to the intended audiences and the types of reading desired. Following Luther's example, all Christian churches published a large number of catechisms to support simple Christian teaching that was imparted from childhood.

The liturgy was a constant concern of the reformers. There was a transition in all Protestant areas to the vernacular languages, and congregational singing was given greater prominence in religious services.

Continuing the tradition of the *Devotio moderna*, the Reformation produced works of devotion and spiritual consolation. These works were also one of the channels through which the Reformation filtered into places where an open battle was too dangerous, such as Italy, the Netherlands, and France during the first half of the century. The sermons spread by printing had a twofold function: they nourished the devotion of isolated Christians and served as a guide for novice pastors.

In addition, scholarly literature was published for theologians and pastors—commentaries on the Bible, as well as doctrinal essays, such as the *Loci communes* of Philipp Melanchthon and the *Institutes* of Calvin. These imposing volumes written in Latin sometimes became best-sellers. The best works were translated for a wider audience.

The texts of scholarly debates between Catholic and Protestant theologians, and even more so between Lutherans and Calvinists, are numerous, but their audience seems to have been limited to specialists. Since the religious conflict invaded all areas of life, religious concerns were also present in poetry, theater, and song.

The Success of the National Languages. The beginnings of the modern era coincided with a strong advance of the vernacular languages. In the religious sphere the choice of a language understood by all the faithful involved the liturgy, pastoral care, theological discourse, and above all the Bible. The factors involved in this evolution were of several kinds.

First, the question arose whether a popular language is capable of expressing the sacred. Some wished to preserve an aura of mystery for religious language in order to make an impression on the worshiper. Moreover, Latin served to guarantee the stability of the texts. On the other hand, the vernacular language was the only means by which to make the evangelical message more widely accessible.

The debate was complicated in the sixteenth century by the fact that the popular languages were in a state of flux. It was not always easy to express in these tongues concepts that had long since been elaborated in Latin. Although by the end of the Middle Ages the church was encouraging the distribution of devotional books and prayer books in modern languages, it maintained theology and the liturgy in Latin. The Reformation overturned this practice.

Reading. In the spread of the Reformation, the written text never supplanted the spoken word. All the reformers were preachers, as well as authors, teachers, and letter writers. Moreover, the spoken word remained preeminent. In the sixteenth century what was novel about books was their proliferation in a world in which communication was essentially oral. Information circulated through many channels—public and private debates, public criers, peddlers, sermons, comic or polemical theater, correspondence, ballads, and also public readings.

Furthermore, a great majority of the population remained illiterate. Therefore, these people did not have direct contact with the written word. Also there are quite different levels in the ability to decode a written message: basic literacy does not automatically bring about ease in reading. Even among the educated public, not all readers necessarily practiced silent reading.

All these factors justify an attempt to outline some of the main features of this diversity in reading. Certain categories of works seem to be closely linked to reading aloud, while others were tied more to silent reading. Some books were sometimes read in groups and sometimes in private. This is at least the hypothesis that emerges from curent research.

The works of popular polemics suggest that they were mainly read aloud. The oral structure of the written discourse, its impact on a society that was largely illiterate, and the frequent use of drawings all point to this conclusion. The influence of press campaigns on the public was doubtlessly largely the result of their being relayed by public speaking.

Catechesis and liturgy were areas in which the oral medium dominated. Therefore, catechisms and liturgical books were primarily aids to memory. They did not reveal any original thought but rather served to recall something already known. In contrast, the technical works intended for theologians and pastors were primarily read silently and individually. They addressed a limited audience who had acquired a solid mastery of reading.

The Bible was read in various ways. A comparison of formats makes this clear. Lutheran printers tended to adopt the folio format for the sake of group reading, either in the liturgy or in the family. Other evidence indicates that the production of Lutheran Bibles was mainly intended for parishes and clergymen. Calvinism, which was more widespread in urban settings, gave more encouragement to individual reading of the Bible. Thus, there was a preference for smaller formats.

Writings of devotion and spiritual consolation also seem to make up a category of works that served several purposes. This is certainly corroborated during the period of the early Reformation, when works having an intentionally ambiguous message served as vehicles for religious protest in Italy, the Netherlands, and France. What scarce evidence there is concerning their influence suggests that they were read in small groups and then discussed afterward.

In any case, the impact of a book goes beyond the individual reader as soon as the reader propagates the ideas discovered in the book. This was a common occurrence at the beginning of the Reformation. For Luther, who considered preaching to be the normal channel for spreading good doctrine, theological works were intended only to make it possible for "the theologian and the bishop to be properly and thoroughly informed so as to be able to teach the doctrine of devotion."

Church of the Spoken Word, Church of the Written Word. The debate over printed books involves values central to Christianity. Indeed, theology uses as its central concepts terms borrowed from the means of communication. It is a religion of the word (*Logos*) and a religion of the book (*Biblos*). A Christian moves from one expression to the other without experiencing any opposition between the two media, which in any case complement one another. In fact, the Christian religion sees itself as combining the properties of both the living presence of the word and the intangible timelessness of the book. Whenever Judaism and Christianity resorted to the written word, the only aim was to preserve the message.

The question of popularization through the written word had not been posed for the church before the end of the Middle Ages. At the end of the fifteenth century, the circulation of the Bible among the laity began to worry church authorities. Ignorant people might stop listening to the word as preached by the priests, wanting instead to interpret it themselves. Printing exacerbated this danger.

The resulting debate revealed two contradictory positions. Some thought it necessary to ensure a wide distribution of the scriptures and free access to it for all. Others feared deviations and wished to reserve the transmission of evangelical truth to the "professionals"—pastors and theologians. The debate over the spread of the divine word did not merely set Catholics and Protestants in opposition to one another. Rather, it divided Christians of all confessions.

As the debates at the Council of Trent demonstrate, the majority of Catholic bishops preferred the divine message be transmitted exclusively by preaching. They therefore refused to permit vernacular translations of the Bible. But they were opposed by a significant minority who thought the holy books were intended for the whole of the people of God. For these bishops the Bible had to be translated.

Similarly among Protestants there were serious reservations about putting the Bible in the hands of all. It was doubtless in the ardor of the first combats that Luther expressed the wish that "each Christian would study for himself the Scriptures and the pure Word of God." But he quickly retreated from that position and instead gave priority to distributing his catechism widely. For him the purpose of school was not to provide access to the Bible for all but rather to raise up an elite charged with leading both civil and religious society.

For his part Calvin did not believe that the Bible should be accessible to everyone. It was bread with a thick crust, and God willed that "the bread be sliced for us and that the pieces be placed in our mouth and that they be chewed for us." Certainly Calvinism encouraged individual reading of the Bible more than Lutheranism, but it strictly monitored editions of the sacred text and its interpretation.

On the subject of recourse to scripture, the radical wing of the Reformation adopted a position best described as a conviction of the priority of the Spirit over the text. As a matter of principle, the spiritualists rejected all mediation by any ecclesiastical authority whatsoever. Christians were capable of consulting the Bible themselves.

Although there was a certain opposition between the church of the spoken word and the church of the printed word, one must avoid overemphasizing this opposition for two reasons. On the one hand, the line of demarcation between the two groups did not coincide with confessional lines. On the other hand, no major confession left its faithful free to interpret the scriptures as they wished.

All confessions and all governments sought to control the circulation of printed materials, and they concurred in their common vigilance for subversive writings. Censorship occurred sometimes in advance and sometimes after the fact. This control, however, was no easy matter. Many authorities managed to prevent the printing of forbidden books in their own territory, but they generally found it impossible to stop the flow of books coming from other countries. There are numerous examples of this throughout the sixteenth century. The Spanish Inquisition was the only institution that managed the feat of imposing effective control.

The general awareness of the impact of printing is confirmed by the persistence of the dissident sects of central Europe in seeking to set up printing presses. They needed them to produce their liturgical, catechetical, and spiritual books and to carry on their proselytizing work in the society that surrounded them.

It is curious that in the case of criminal prosecution, the authorities punished authors more harshly than printers. It is as though the printer were a minor factor whose responsibility was secondary in the production of books. Nonetheless, the role of publishers was all the more significant since authors' copyright did not exist. There were many publications that reprinted earlier texts, modifying and enlarging them and even changing their intent. Whenever certain elements of a written piece appealed to them, publishers did not hesitate to reproduce them and even to change their orientation. Copies, which might be more or less faithful, abounded. In some cases they pose insoluble problems as to authorship. For instance, can it be said that a page from Luther inserted into a devotional work after substantial modification is still Luther's?

A Quiet and Limited Revolution. Can one assert that the movement launched by Luther took advantage of printing? The answer is clear, at least so long as one avoids the oversimplification that would make the Protestant churches the champions of the written word and the Catholics the guardians of a church of the spoken word. By the same token it is unwarranted to credit books with sole responsibility for the Reformation.

From the very beginning Protestants resorted to printed books more spontaneously than did Catholics. They innovated with their war of pamphlets, the first press campaign in history. This also marked the first time that theology was debated in the language of the people. It is true as well that the Protestants spread the text of the Bible in the vernacular on a much larger scale than did the Catholics, and they resorted to printing for liturgy and catechesis. At that time Catholics did not yet use individual missals during Mass. In contrast, however, very early on they did adopt the use of printed catechisms. Curiously, although in the middle of the sixteenth century Catholics and Protestants did not manifest the same confidence in the printed word, they did concur in an identical mistrust of its perverse effects; thus, censorship was universally practiced.

If one reverses the question of the relationship between books and the Reformation, it does seem that the development of printing was fostered on different occasions by Protestants. In Germany, Central Europe, and Scandinavia, many new printing houses were founded to respond to religious needs. The most spectacular instances were Geneva, Wittenberg, and Emden, where printing began to boom thanks to the Reformation.

The role of printing in the Reformation, however, must be nuanced on one essential point. Written works in the sixteenth century circulated in a society engulfed by change. New uses for the printed word were discovered, but the majority of the population remained illiterate. The multiplying effect achieved by the printed word was mainly mediated by public speaking. In its role as an instrument of propaganda, the printed word acted more as a support for oral communication than as a direct medium to be read silently. The printed word was invested with new authority, making an impression on both those who could read and those who were illiterate.

Is it possible that the Reformation awakened a new sensibility in reading? Looking at the short term, it is difficult to conclude anything whatsoever. The idea of free enquiry was completely foreign to the major reformers. Although they did encourage Christians to have direct contact with the Bible, they were far from leaving them free in their interpretation of the sacred text. The principle of *sola scriptura* demanded that theological statements be supported by the texts, but not that every Christian have the right to engage in exegesis. The early attitude of confidence in the written word, with its applied questioning of authority, quickly gave way to control by the new powers.

In the sixteenth century silent reading, it seems, remained limited. Nonetheless, Protestants were encouraged to read. Medieval Christianity hardly encouraged believers to make the sacred text their own, either by hearing or by reading. The followers of Luther, Huldrych Zwingli, and Calvin were able to take the book into their own hands. This direct contact must have compromised the sense of sacredness of the "holy" scriptures. Even more frequently, Protestants leafed through catechisms, the Psalter, and liturgical manuals. Using these works certainly did not represent the shortest road to silent reading, but it was a modest approach. The practice of placing texts already known by heart before the eyes of the faithful steadily increased the number of people who could read.

Silent reading, done in private, nourishes solitary reflection and personal questioning. Fears concerning this kind of reading were not without foundation. The church's control over the interpretation of scripture ran the risk of being questioned once individual reading became widespread. But the reading practices of Protestants led only gradually to silent contact with the texts. More than two centuries had to pass before the freedom to scrutinize and question penetrated the religious domain. But was this development a consequence of Protestantism? The idea has been long accepted that the line that divides the Western world in its relationship to the written word has its roots in the religious divisions of the sixteenth century: in the north Protestants became great consumers of books, while in the south Catholics remained more attached to oral traditions. Historians of culture are nowadays reluctant to attribute the growing literacy of the masses to religious factors alone; analysis of the bulk of works printed is not complete enough to provide reliable figures on trends in the fifteenth and sixteenth centuries. The gaps between the north and the south certainly existed prior to 1517. There also seem to have been significant differences between the more rural societies where Lutheranism became established and the more literate social spheres that were won over by Calvinism. The latter group certainly found itself more in tune with social groups already more familiar with the written word.

But at this point the question shifts. It is not a sufficient explanation to note that Protestantism promoted reading. Its effects have to be nuanced according to the social spheres that welcomed it. Without a doubt there was a circular interplay of reciprocal influences between societies and confessions. In any case, the revolution in printing was quite slow. Its effects became generalized at the time of the Enlightenment and even more in the nineteenth century, which was truly the age of triumph for books.

[*See also* Education; Hymnals; Literacy; *and* Pamphlets.]

BIBLIOGRAPHY

Boehmer, Edward. *Bibliotheca Wiffeniana: Spanish Reformers of Two Centuries* (1874–1904). 3 vols. Reprint, New York, 1962. A classic containing essential documentation on Spanish Protestant books.

Chartier, Roger. "Les pratiques de l'écrit." In *Histoire de la vie privée*, edited by Philippe Ariès and Georges Duby, vol. 3, pp. 113–161. Paris, 1986. The evolution of reading in the ancien régime.

Davis, Nathalie Zemon. "Printing and the People." In *Society and Culture in Early Modern France*, pp. 189–226. Stanford, Calif., 1975. The question is studied in the framework of the Reformation in France.

Duke, Alistair, and C. A. Tamse, eds. *Too Mighty to Be Free: Censorship and the Press in Britain and the Netherlands.* Zutphen, 1987. See the essays by D. M. Loades ("Illicit Presses and Clandestine Printing in England, 1520–1580") and H. F. K. van Nierop ("Censorship, Illicit Printing and the Revolt of the Netherlands").

Eisenstein, Elizabeth. *The Printing Press as an Agent of Change: Communications and Cultural Transformations in Early Modern Europe.* 2 vols. Cambridge and New York, 1979. Questionable thesis (because it is too simplistic) on the influence of printing in the emergence of the modern world.

Febvre, Lucien, and Henri-Jean Martin. *L'apparition du livre.* Paris, 1958. English translation: *The Coming of the Book: The Impact of Printing, 1450–1800*, reprint, London, 1990. A classic on the early days of printing.

Gawthrop, R., and Gerald Strauss. "Protestantism and Literacy in Early Modern Germany." *Past and Present* 104 (1984), 31–55. A fundamental article on the use of the Bible in the Lutheran world.

Gilmont, Jean-François, ed. *La Réforme et le livre: L'Europe de l'imprimé, 1517–v.1570.* Paris, 1990. Only work that explicitly addresses the whole range of questions posed by the present article. Some fifteen authors offer a detailed look at Protestant books throughout sixteenth-century Europe.

Gravier, Maurice. *Luther et l'opinion publique.* Cahiers de l'Institut d'études germaniques. Paris, 1942. Still the best synthesis on the war of pamphlets (1520–1525).

Harline, Craig E. *Pamphlets, Printing and Political Culture in the Early Dutch Republic.* Archives internationales d'histoire des idées 116. Dordrecht, 1987. The pamphlets of the war of independence of the United Provinces.

Heijting, Willem. *De catechismi en confessies in de Nederlandse reformatie tot 1585.* 2 vols. Nieuwkoop, 1989. Catechisms in the Netherlands.

Higman, Francis M. *La diffusion de la Réforme en France, 1520–1565.* Geneva, 1992. The role of printing in the spread of the Reformation.

Köhler, Hans Joachim. "Die Flugschriften der frühen Neuzeit." In *Die Erforschung der Buch- und Bibliotheksgeschichte in Deutschland*, edited by W. Arnold, pp. 307–345. Wiesbaden, 1987.

Lecler, Joseph. "Protestantisme et 'libre examen': Les étapes et le vocabulaire d'une controverse." *Recherches de science religieuse* 57 (1969), 321–374.

Oelke, Harry. *Die Konfessionsbildung des 16. Jahrhunderts im Spiegel illustrierter Flugblätter.* Arbeiten zur Kirchengeschichte 57. Berlin and New York, 1992. The role of pictures in printed propaganda.

Ozment, Steven, ed. *Reformation Europe: A Guide to Research.* Saint Louis, 1982. Articles by Ozment and Kingdon on pamphlets in Germany and France.

Pettegree, Andrew. *Emden and the Dutch Revolt: Exile and the Development of Reformed Protestantism.* Oxford, 1992. This study not only sheds light on the role of Emden; it also contains a good overview of Reformed publishing in the Netherlands.

Prosperi, Adriano, and Albano Biondi, eds. *Libri, idee e sentimenti religiosi nel Cinquecento italiano.* Modena, 1987. A collection of studies on religious books in Italy.

Scribner, Robert W. *For the Sake of Simple Folk: Popular Propaganda for the German Reformation.* Cambridge, 1981. The printed word, pictures, and the spoken word in the spread of the Reformation.

———. *Popular Culture and Popular Movements in Reformation Germany.* London, 1987. A complement to the previous work.

JEAN-FRANÇOIS GILMONT

Translated from French by Robert E. Shillenn

PRODIGIES AND PORTENTS. The Reformation era coincided with a Renaissance explosion of interest in strange or unusual events and experiences. Faced with a crisis of variety, sixteenth-century Europeans sought to discover order partly by focusing on the most rare and remarkable things in creation. They found a world filled with weird phenomena, which they struggled to understand in light of their spiritual, moral, and practical concerns. The term *prodigy* could refer to any event in nature that had a supernatural meaning; it is now used especially for monstrous births and terrestrial freaks. *Portent* can be used more broadly for the whole range of "wonders," including supernatural apparitions and prophetic visions. In an even more general sense, which cannot be discussed here, the portentous could include human, social, and political developments prophetically interpreted.

The ancient world handed down powerful yet confused traditions regarding the meaning of prodigies and portents, which were summarized in key writings such as Cicero's *De divinatione.* The heritage of Augustinian Christianity, while generally dismissing philosophical notions of divination, inculcated a profound sense of nature itself as miraculous. Medieval thinkers had shown constant interest in the marvelous and the fantastic, but in the late fifteenth and early sixteenth century a newly pervasive and urgent concern was emerging. Spurred both by the humanist revival of ancient divinatory arts and by the dissemination of images through popular broadsheets and pamphlets, this new obsession reflected the belief that the signs were above all divine warnings and exhortations to a sinful world. Monsters and other portents, which many observers believed had become more common, were signals of universal corruption and the coming wrath of God. Especially in Italy and Germany the pre-Reformation era saw frequent efforts to gather and interpret reports of meteors, eclipses, monstrous births, floods, hailstorms, epidemics, and other sensational happenings. Such wonders received close attention in humanist "world-chronicles," such as that of Hartmann Schedel. A key progenitor of the "wonder book" genre was Sebastian Brant, whose writings on amazing appearances such as the 1492 "meteor of Ensisheim" were at once political, moral, religious, and natural-scientific. After 1500 such figures as Gaspar Torella, Jacob Mennel, and Joseph Grünpeck contributed to the spread of wonder literature.

The Reformation in Germany opened the floodgates for this sort of thinking. The evangelical movement gave full legitimacy to an apocalyptic vision of history that was also manifest in attitudes toward nature. Martin Luther and Philipp Melanchthon sanctioned the prophetic interpretation of prodigies with their 1523 pamphlet on the monk-calf and papal ass, monsters that revealed not only a host of priestly abominations but also the approaching end of papal power. Luther himself balked at any effort to read natural signs systematically; as a good Augustinian he put little stock in ancient forms of divination, and warned believers about the difficulty of distinguishing divine signs from satanic and misleading ones. Yet in contrast with early Zwinglianism and the radical reform movements, Lutheranism proved remarkably open to the use of visual images to convey prophetic truth; this fact helps to explain why Lutheran Germany saw the most consistent and elaborate efforts to record and announce the significance of natural wonders in particular. Melanchthon's interest in prophetic events of all sorts was typical of an urgent attitude shared by learned and popular cultures throughout Europe but particularly evident among German Protestants.

The decades after 1550 brought the full flowering of this preoccupation, manifest in countless broadsheets, pamphlets, sermons, and above all in a spate of amazing wonder books that presented reports on the whole range of prodigies and portents. Among the best-known collections was the *Prodigiorum ac Ostentorum Chronicon* of Conrad Lycosthenes (Latin edition 1557, followed by many vernacular translations), which left no doubt whatever that the recent multiplication of prodigies and portents pointed to the nearness of divine judgment. Even more popular in Germany were the tomes of Job Fincel, a product of Melanchthonian schooling; these works coupled heated Lutheran polemic against all enemies of the gospel with intense preaching on the universal significance of the wonders now seen everywhere in the heavens and on earth. Some writers specialized; there were large works on monstrous births, meteors, comets, eclipses, and strange forms of precipitation (including the raining of blood, fire, and frogs). The *De spectris* of Ludwig Lavater (1570) devoted particular attention to spectral combats. Virtually all observers assumed that the shocking new star of 1572 had prophetic meaning, and the comet of 1577 brought the discussion of celestial portents to new heights of intensity. Typical of the sensational reports that appeared in a wide range of literature was the celebrated monster of Kraków. A hideous creature covered with the heads of barking dogs, it died a few hours after its birth crying "Watch, the Lord cometh."

In Catholic regions the discourse on divine signs changed rapidly after the early sixteenth century. In Spain a culture in which saintly apparitions had been common was increasingly suppressed by the Inquisition. Yet other sorts of miraculous signs, such as weeping statues of the Virgin and the appearance of crosses, continued into the early modern period, both as warnings of divine anger and as exhortations to imitate Christ. In Italy the intense publicity surrounding visions and prodigious signs disappeared even more quickly as such concerns came to be associated with Protestant heresy. Many French Catholics, on the other hand, channeled apocalyptic fears over prodigies and portents into defense of the traditional church; reading the signs became an aspect of anti-"Lutheran" polemic.

While Catholics tended to see any true wonder as a direct and miraculous act of God, many Protestant thinkers assumed that unusual or noteworthy natural events, even those with explainable physical causes, could be counted as wonders. This was especially true of astronomical events, such as eclipses; understanding the natural causes by no means diminished the prophetic meaning of such occurrences, especially since they appeared to be multiplying ominously. In this regard most prodigies and portents were distinct from what are now typically called miracles—that is, events that violate natural laws. By the end of the sixteenth century, particularly in England and France, this double sense of wonders was allowing for the growth of medical and scientific interest in proximate natural causes, and the use of apocalyptic terms began to wane. This trend is already evident in *Des monstres et Prodiges*, the 1573 work of Ambroise Paré; it would become even clearer in later thinkers such as Francis Bacon. By the early to mid-seventeenth century, educated culture was clearly starting to distance itself from what it increasingly saw as popular superstitions, such as belief in divine portents. Prodigy writing rapidly died out after about 1650, as a new understanding of nature came to prevail. That new conception, however, had important roots in a religious outlook that saw all nature as suffused with divine meaning and crucial messages waiting to be explained.

[*See also* Magic; Miracles; *and* Popular Religion.]

BIBLIOGRAPHY

Barnes, Robin Bruce. *Prophecy and Gnosis: Apocalypticism in the Wake of the Lutheran Reformation.* Stanford, Calif., 1988.

Céard, Jean. *La nature et les prodiges: L'insolite au XVIe siècle, en France.* Geneva, 1977.

Christian, William A., Jr. *Apparitions in Late Medieval and Renaissance Spain.* Princeton, 1981.

Niccoli, Ottavia. *Prophecy and People in Renaissance Italy.* Princeton, 1990.

Park, Katharine, and Lorraine J. Daston. "Unnatural Conceptions: The Study of Monsters in Sixteenth- and Seventeenth-Century France and England." *Past and Present* 92 (August 1981), 20–54.

Schenda, Rudolph. "Die deutschen Prodigiensammlungen des 16. und 17. Jahrhunderts." *Archiv für Geschichte des Buchwesens* 4 (1963), cols. 637–710.

Schilling, Heinz. "Job Fincel und die Zeichen der Endzeit." In *Volkserzählung und Reformation,* edited by Wolfgang Brückner. Berlin, 1974.

Warburg, Aby. *Heidnisch-antike Weissagung in Wort und Bild zu Luthers Zeiten.* Heidelberg, 1920. Reprinted in *Gesammelte Schriften,* vol. 2, pp. 487–558, Nendeln, Germany, 1969.

Weber, Bruno. *Wunderzeichen und Winkeldrucker, 1543–1586: Einblattdrucke aus der Sammlung Wikiana in der Zentralbibliothek Zurich.* Zurich, 1972.

ROBIN B. BARNES

PROSTITUTION. During the late Middle Ages, most major cities in Europe and many of the smaller ones had an official house of prostitution or an area of the city in which prostitutes were permitted. Some of these houses, such as one in Frankfurt am Main and one in Mainz, actually belonged to bishops or religious orders. Cities justified the existence of municipal brothels with the comment that prostitution protected honorable girls and women from the uncontrollable lust of young men, an argument at least as old as Augustine. Visiting prostitutes was associated with achieving manhood in the eyes of young men, though the women themselves thought of prostitution as work. Indeed, in some cases the women had no choice, for they had been traded to the brothel manager by their parents or other people in payment of debt.

In the fifteenth century many cities passed ordinances regulating the municipal brothels, attempting to guard the health and safety of the brothels' customers by forbidding weapons and checking prostitutes for disease; some of these ordinances also protected the women themselves, setting a minimum age limit and prohibiting brothel owners from selling women. Prostitutes appeared often in public at city celebrations, though at the same time cities and private individuals opened "Magdalene houses," small religious endowments for prostitutes who had decided to give up their former lives. The official attitude toward prostitution in the late Middle Ages was thus ambivalent, with the women somewhat protected but still socially marginal.

In the late fifteenth century official attitudes toward prostitution became more negative. Cities began to limit the women's freedom of movement in an attempt to hide them from public view; they required prostitutes to wear distinctive head coverings or bands on their clothing so that they would not be mistaken for "honorable" women and prohibited them from attending events where "honorable" women would be present. They also began to impose harsher penalties on women who did not live in the designated house or section of town.

Restrictions on prostitutes increased dramatically after the Protestant Reformation, in part because most Protestant reformers were unwilling to accept traditional justifications for prostitution. Luther saw prostitution as an abomination and preached and spoke fervently against it, not because it was degrading and harmful to the women involved but because the women corrupted and enticed his students. He described them regularly as "stinking, syphilitic, scabby, seedy, and nasty. Such a whore can poison 10, 20, 30, 100 children of good people, and is therefore to be considered a murderer, worse than a poisoner." In his opinion, they were the tools of the Devil, who had sent them to Wittenberg to bewitch his students. Luther also used the image of the whore symbolically. He equated simony (selling church offices) with prostitution, and so termed Rome a "whore" and called the University of Paris the "pope's whoring chamber." "The Devil's whore" is Luther's favorite epithet for human reason.

Such harsh language, combined with the fear of syphilis that was spreading rapidly in Europe in the sixteenth century and increasing concerns about morality on the part of guilds whose journeymen were often the chief customers of brothels, led many Protestant cities to close their municipal brothels. In England the Bankside brothels, the only legal and protected brothels in the country, were closed by royal statute in 1546. Catholic cities in Germany and France followed, with their leaders arguing that the possible benefits they provided did not outweigh their moral detriments. Closing the official brothels did not end prostitution, of course; many women continued to make their living this way, often combining prostitution with piecework or laundering or with theft and other crimes. What it did end was official ambivalence toward prostitutes, for religious and civic leaders in central and northern Europe increasingly regarded prostitutes as worse than other criminals, seducing citizens from the life of moral order that they regarded as essential to a godly city.

Major Italian cities such as Florence and Venice were more tolerant of prostitution than were those in the north, favoring regulation over suppression and often viewing prostitutes as significant sources of municipal income. From 1559 until the mid-eighteenth century in Florence, for example, all prostitutes were required to contribute an annual tax based on their income that went to support a convent for those women who wished to give up prostitution; payment of extra taxes would allow a woman to live where she wished in the city and wear whatever type of clothes she chose. Convents for repentant prostitutes became more numerous and a more popular type of charity in the late sixteenth century, however, indicating that in Italy as well, prostitution was becoming less acceptable. Such houses also began to admit women who were regarded as in danger of becoming prostitutes, generally poor women with no male relatives who were "pretty or at least acceptable looking"; unattractive women apparently were not admitted because they were not seen as being in danger of losing their honor.

The official contempt of prostitution was not always internalized by the prostitutes themselves, however, particularly in large cities like Rome, where the number of prostitutes remained high despite all attempts to prohibit them. Roman prostitutes often offered their customers music and poetry along with sexual services, and worked independently, living with other prostitutes or with their mothers or children; they often described their occupation in terms of the quality of their clients instead of simply in monetary terms. Their neighbors did not shun them but socialized with them and defended them against verbal and physical attacks. The clear distinction in the minds of civic and religious authorities between "honorable" and "dishonorable" women was not necessarily shared by all segments of the population.

In both Italian cities and the capitals of northern Europe such as Paris or London, a few prostitutes achieved great prominence, wealth, and near-respectability through their connections with state and church officials, nobles, and intellectuals. Such courtesans were often glamorized in plays and poetry, but the lives of most prostitutes were filled with violence, imprisonment, disease, and, by the seventeenth century, deportation. Women who occasionally used prostitution to supplement their incomes as laundresses, spinners, and weavers lived with similar dangers; their numbers went up, as one would expect, during times of war, including the religious wars of the sixteenth and seventeenth centuries. Thus in actual terms, despite the reformers' attempts to eradicate prostitution, the Protestant and Catholic Reformations may have forced more women to turn to prostitution to support themselves and their families while denying them the slight protection that had been offered by the regulated city brothels of the more ambivalent Middle Ages.

[*See also* Celibacy and Virginity *and* Sexuality.]

BIBLIOGRAPHY

Brundage, James A. *Law, Sex, and Christian Society In Medieval Europe.* Reprint, Chicago, 1990. Magisterial and comprehensive survey of legal doctrines in all areas of sexuality from the early Middle Ages through the Catholic Reformation.

Otis, Leah Lydia. *Prostitution in Medieval Society: The History of an Urban Institution in Languedoc.* Chicago, 1985. Traces the institutionalization and then restriction of municipal brothels in southern France; based on extensive archival sources.

Roper, Lyndal. "Discipline and Respectability: Prostitution and the Reformation in Augsburg." *History Workshop* 19 (Spring 1985), 3–28.

Rossiaud, Jacques. *Medieval Prostitution.* Translated by Lydia G. Cochrane. London, 1988. Discusses the social significance of prostitution, and particularly its relation to youth culture, using primarily French examples.

Wiesner, Merry E. "Paternalism in Practice: The Control of Servants and Prostitutes in Early Modern German Cities." In *The Process of Change in Early Modern Europe: Essays in Honor of Miriam Usher Chrisman,* edited by Phillip N. Bebb and Sherrin Marshall, pp. 179–200. Athens, Ohio, 1988.

MERRY E. WIESNER-HANKS

PROTESTANTISM.

[*This entry comprises two articles. The first traces the history of the movement that came to be known as the Protestant Reformation; the second provides a history of the use of the term* Protestantism.]

An Overview

The terms "Protestant" and "Protestantism," as used by historians to indicate the cluster of beliefs and practices associated with the sixteenth-century Reformation, had their origins not in religious or theological considerations as such, but in the politics of the Holy Roman Empire of the German Nation during the 1520s. Following the Diet of Worms in 1521, Emperor Charles V was absent from Germany until the Diet of Augsburg in 1530. During these critical years evangelical church reforms proceeded apace in many cities and territories throughout the empire (as well as in the Swiss Confederation, which in 1499 had become effectively independent of the empire). This development was abetted by the reluctance and, often, the inability of the imperial diet (*Reichstag*), the imperial governing council (*Reichsregiment*), and the imperial supreme court (*Reichskammergericht*) to impede such reforms. Failure to implement the Edict of Worms (dated 8 May 1521) against Martin Luther and his supporters was the result of many factors, including the intensity of popular agitation for reform, the relative strength of the princes vis à vis the emperor, the desire—in the face of the formation of hostile military alliances—to maintain peace and unity in the realm, and the widespread conviction that the "Lutheran" problem could be adjudicated only by means of a general council of the church.

In 1526 at the Diet of Speyer (25 June–27 August), the imperial estates agreed that the edict could not be enforced on a national basis. Pending the calling of a general council by the pope, or at least the convocation of a national assembly on church affairs, the estates unanimously resolved that "each one of us with our subjects will so live, govern, and deport ourselves in the matters treated by the Edict [of Worms] as each hopes and trusts to answer for it before God and his Imperial Majesty." The intent of this recess was to perpetuate the status quo; it did not grant a right of reform (*ius reformandi*) to the estates, a legal warrant for organizing churches on a territorial basis.

At the second Diet of Speyer in 1529 (15 March–22 April), the relatively small number of evangelical estates found themselves in straitened circumstances. The majority of the estates repealed the recess of 1526; ordered the implementation of the Edict of Worms and an end to religious innovations; demanded that the traditional observance of the Mass be permitted everywhere and that all Roman authorities and religious orders be allowed full enjoyment of their former rights, property, and incomes; and called for the suppression of those who debased the sacraments (i.e., Zwinglians and Anabaptists). On 19 April 1529 five territories and fourteen south German cities (many of the latter Zwinglian in orientation) entered their oral *Protestation* (which, on 25 April, was incorporated in a written *Appelation*). Contending that the unanimous recess of 1526 could not be annulled without the unanimous consent of all parties, and acting for the sake of "our souls' salvation and good conscience," these estates declared: "We herewith protest and testify openly before God . . . and likewise before all persons and creatures, that we for ourselves, our subjects and in behalf of all, each and every one, consider null and void the entire transaction and the intended decree." Henceforth the evangelical estates came to be called "protesters" or "protestants."

In modern English "protest" carries largely negative connotations, namely, "to oppose" or "object to" some action, proposal, and so on. This negative meaning first entered the language (and remained comparatively rare) during the seventeenth century. The Latin *protestari*, however, means "to profess," "declare formally," "bear witness openly." It is this meaning that attaches to the Protestation at Speyer, where the evangelicals made their public witness of conscience before God and all creatures.

It is both misleading and anachronistic to speak of distinct groups of "Protestants" ranged against "Catholics" throughout the 1520s or even at Speyer in 1529, not least since all the contending parties at the imperial diets considered themselves "good Christians," that is, "true Catholics." To be sure, the defenders of the traditional faith and practice of the Roman Catholic church denied the legitimacy of this sensibility to their opponents, deeming them heretics and schismatics, especially in view of Luther's excommunication. Hence one can identify, already during the early 1520s, a definite impulse toward the creation not only of "reformed" local congregations but of new, non-Roman ecclesial structures on the part of all who identified themselves with Luther's cause or, more broadly, with the cause of evangelical reform in opposition to "Romanists" and "papists."

In the course of the 1520s, accordingly, new churches began to emerge: a process that may be termed "Protestantization" even though Protestants, explicitly called such, did not arrive on the scene until 1529. These churches were new, in the first instance, because their organization contravened the juridical and doctrinal authority of the papacy and Roman Curia. Such organization, moreover, usually occurred in the face of determined opposition from local prelates, whose authority was circumvented by town councils and territorial princes acting as "emergency bishops" or, in any case, as "godly rulers" duly charged with maintaining public order and serving the common good, including the promotion of true religion. Further, the secular authorities had long claimed and exercised a right to regulate ecclesiastical matters in their own lands (a right that they judged to be upheld at Speyer in 1526). One also speaks of new churches in respect of their distinctive belief, teaching, and confession vis à vis the then regnant traditions of doctrine, ritual, and polity.

Historians have amply demonstrated that the original evangelical message was pluriform and the early evangelical movement polycentric: the former was not simply a set of minor variations on the themes of Luther's teaching and preaching; the latter issued from multiple locations, not Wittenberg alone. Still, both message and movement displayed a common core of affirmations and negations. The movement, which drew upon a long history of lay resentment against the clergy, was animated by a popular demand for the preaching of the "pure word of God," namely, of the biblical gospel, in whose light the egregious failings and false teachings of the contemporary, "unreformed" church would be exposed. Some concluded that this same gospel also disclosed the inequities and injustices of the current ordering of society, especially at a time when feudal overlords and city-states were imposing new fiscal and legal exactions on their peasant subjects and rural dependencies. The cardinal motif of "Christian freedom," so forcefully asserted by Luther, could be applied to the sociopolitical and economic spheres no less than to the directly religious issue of the sinner's standing in the judgment of a righteous God. Popular demand for evangelical preaching was itself set in motion by reforming clerics (and lay supporters), who communicated their message through many and diverse media: sermons, treatises, pamphlets, letters, cartoons and lampoons, vernacular translations of scripture and vernacular liturgies, catechisms, hymns and ballads, poems and plays.

Among the beliefs and teachings of the Roman church that the reformers deemed unbiblical and unevangelical were the following: that the pope possesses supreme authority in the church by divine right, namely, by authority of the gospel itself; that the authority of scripture is dependent on the teaching authority of the Roman church and is to be supplemented by "unwritten traditions" conveyed to the apostles by Christ himself and handed down by the apostles' episcopal successors, above all by the bishop of Rome; that sinful human beings become right with God and attain eternal salvation by performing meritorious works in cooperation with divine grace; that the souls of those who have died in a state of grace must make expiation in purgatory for any unrepented sins and for the temporal punishments still due forgiven sins; that seven sacraments have been instituted by Christ, either directly or through the apostles; that the Mass is a propitiatory sacrifice—an unbloody "repetition" of Christ's passion—offered to God by the priest; that the entire substance of the consecrated elements of bread and wine has been changed into the entire substance of Christ's body and blood ("transubstantiation"), while only the "accidents" (or appearances) of bread and wine remain; that the cup (consecrated wine) is to be withheld from the laity; that, in the sacrament of penance, works of satisfaction are required of penitents, as well as contrition and confession, in order to avoid punishment in purgatory after sin itself has been remitted through priestly absolution; that the pope, drawing on the superabundant merits of Christ and the saints, may grant (or sell) indulgences for the partial or plenary remission of the temporal penalties due forgiven sins, and that the virtue of indulgences extends to all the souls in purgatory; that monastic vows are forever binding and that the monastic life is the true life of Christian perfection, qualitatively superior to the life of the ordinary lay Christian and, hence, especially meritorious of salvation; that celibacy is mandatory for all the clergy.

In addition to focusing critical attention on these fundamental matters of authority in the church, the sinner's justification before God, the sacramental system, and monasticism, the reformers also attacked what they regarded as forms of "self-invented worship" (in Huldrych Zwingli's phrase). These forms included mandatory days and seasons of fasting by all the faithful; the proliferation of holidays for religious observances and celebrations; pilgrimages to shrines; the veneration of saints' images and relics; the invocation of the saints as intercessors for the favors of God and Christ; the exhibition of the eucharistic Host (consecrated bread) in monstrances for purposes of adoration, as in Corpus Christi processions; the buying and selling of masses and indulgences for the dead, which (so charged the reformers) amounted to nothing less than a venal "feeding on the dead" (*Totenfresserei*) by a multitude of priests and prelates who fleeced the flock while enjoying exemption from civic taxation and from the jurisdiction of civil courts.

The reformers' teachings centered on the sovereign authority of the divinely inspired scriptures as the sole source of all binding doctrine and the judge of all teachers and teachings; on God's unmerited forgiveness of sins for Christ's sake alone, declared by the gospel and personally appropriated by faith alone; on the two dominical sacraments (baptism and the Lord's Supper, with confession and absolution sometimes reckoned a third) as bearers of the divine word of forgiveness in connection with outward or visible signs (water, bread, wine); on the church as the assembly of the faithful constituted and sustained by the proclamation of the word and the administration of the sacraments, in which community all believers are equally priests before God though not all have been called and ordained to the church's public ministry; and on the Christian life as one of charitable works in service to the neighbor and in gratitude to God for salvation freely bestowed.

This brief description of shared Protestant doctrine generally holds good for the principal German and Swiss reformers (Luther, Philipp Melanchthon, Zwingli, Martin Bucer, Johannes Oecolampadius, and, later, John Calvin). It does not, however, take adequate account of important differences among them that soon came to light and that served to alienate the "Lutherans" from the Swiss and south German "Zwinglians," thereby preventing the establishment of a united Protestant front. Their respective interpretations of the "pure word," in part influenced by their differing relations to the Augustinian, scholastic, and humanist traditions, generated disagreement on such issues as whether the sacraments actually contain and convey God's grace or, rather, are pledges and memorials of a grace already granted through Christ's atoning death; whether Christ's body and blood are physically present in the Supper (this was the pivotal issue); whether obedience to the law of God revealed in the New Testament no less than in the Old—hence the active imitation of Christ—is more central to the Christian life than "bare trust" in the promise of God's mercy; whether the New Testament prescribes a specific form or order of the church's ministry; and whether traditional ritual uses (e.g., liturgical vestments, images, altars, and organs in churches) may be retained as "free things" even if lacking explicit New Testament sanction, on the assumption that they do not contradict the gospel.

New church orders, in the dual sense and with the diversities indicated above, began to appear in numerous cities and territories of Germany and Switzerland during the mid-1520s (e.g., in electoral Saxony, Hesse, Nuremberg, Strasbourg, Constance, Zurich). This development accelerated during the late 1520s and, in particular, during the 1530s, when Charles V was again absent from Germany from 1532 to 1541. Not until 1555, however, in the aftermath of the Schmalkald War (1546–1547), which proved to be only a temporary victory for the emperor, did Lutherans (i.e., adherents of the Augsburg Confession) gain legal standing in the empire, alongside Roman Catholics, by the terms of the Peace of Augsburg. Such status was still denied to Zwinglians, Calvinists, Anabaptists, and other groups. Of these, only Calvinists ultimately gained legal recognition through the Peace of Westphalia (1648) that terminated the Thirty Years' War. (Calvinism, nonetheless, had long been a significant force in German ecclesiastical and political affairs, beginning in the early 1560s.)

One observes that it was chiefly in the towns and cities—above all in the free imperial cities and the Swiss city-states—that the Reformation message took root and new churches were established during the two decades after the Edict of Worms. By the mid-1540s, however, the German territorial rulers had increasingly come to the fore as sponsors of reform, and the urban Reformation, while continuing, now gave way to what was more decidedly a "princes' Reformation." The great exception continued to be Switzerland, where, by 1560, Geneva had replaced Zurich as the primary leader of the Swiss Protestant cause and as the center from which radiated a "Second" (or Calvinist) Reformation throughout much of continental Europe and the British Isles during the later sixteenth century. (Geneva, in turn, was eventually succeeded by Heidelberg, in the Palatinate, and by the Dutch cities of Herborn and Leiden as centers of international Calvinism.)

A distinguishing feature of the Reformation in England was that it preserved and, in crucial respects, presupposed the traditional system of episcopal government. With but a few notable exceptions, the English bishops (and parish clergy) acquiesced in King Henry VIII's withdrawal of the church from obedience to the Holy See. In March and May 1534 the convocations of the clergy (of Canterbury and York, respectively) formally abjured papal supremacy, and in November 1534 Parliament passed the famous Supremacy Act by which Henry and his successors were declared "the only supreme head on earth of the Church of England." Thus the reform of the English church was at once antipapal and episcopal. Likewise, in Sweden, where the "apostolic succession" of bishops was also maintained, the establishment of antipapal Lutheranism did not involve a break with the traditional episcopate.

Such was the heterogeneity of the early evangelical movement that the German and Swiss "magisterial" reformers—those who, like Luther and Zwingli, carried out reform in cooperation with the magistrates—were soon challenged by individuals and groups who considered them but halfway men: false prophets, in fact, who were unbiblical in their continuing allegiance to inherited patterns of faith and practice, and to the apparatus of state-sponsored religion and religious reform, therefore incapable of effecting a genuine transformation of life in keeping with the "mind of Christ." The representatives of this so-called radical Reformation—commonly identified as Anabaptists, spiritualists, and antitrinitarians—obliged the magisterial reformers to address such theological issues as the following: whether the Holy Spirit works only through outward means or, rather, acts directly on the human spirit through an inner word that alone is properly called "word of God"; whether the baptism of infants has scriptural warrant and whether, in any case, such "water" baptism is necessary (as contrasted with the inward baptism of the Spirit); whether the church is rightly thought of as a visible community of believers (as contrasted with an invisible fellowship of the Spirit); whether various legal prescriptions of the Old Testament (e.g., against graven images) are still binding for Christians; whether the "sword" (secular authority with its coercive power) is necessary for Christians and may be wielded by Christians; and whether the classical doctrines of the Trinity and Christ's two natures are scriptural and, as formulated, even reasonable.

By the late 1520s, scattered throughout continental Europe were sizable groups of evangelical Christians—pejoratively called Anabaptists ("rebaptizers")—whose views of reform entailed a rejection not only of the Roman hierarchy but also of the authority of secular rulers in church affairs. Persuaded that true Christianity in no way depends on magisterial fiat and force, they sought to establish a "gathered church" of "genuine believers," namely, of those who received baptism as adults, in full consciousness of faith, and whose lives displayed the palpable fruits of faith, including a refusal to swear oaths and to undertake any form of military and governmental service. The Anabaptists thus broke with the traditional concept of a unified Christian society, to which persons were admitted by virtue of infant baptism, universally administered, and in which the ecclesiastical and the civil communities were regarded as practically coterminous. For this reason Anabaptists were persecuted as seditionists by Protestants, and as heretics by Roman Catholics.

The old system of inclusive territorial churches was maintained by all the magisterial reformers, albeit not without theological reservations (as in Luther's case) and conflict with the magistrates over the extent of their legitimate role in church affairs (as in Calvin's case). Although joined in opposition to the magisterial reformers as well as to Rome, the Reformation radicals did not constitute a homogeneous movement of dissent and alternative reform. Significant, often profound differences obtained among the several groups, which were also beset by internal controversies and factionalism. Most of the spiritualists and Anabaptists, for example, were orthodox trinitarians, yet the former advocated an interior, essentially individualistic Christianity, the latter a communitarian type that was undergirded by church discipline and use of the ban. The spiritualists, therefore, did not create new churches as such; their stress on inward piety sometimes led, rather, to the formation of "brotherhoods" or conventicles within particular territorial churches.

Anabaptists and antitrinitarians, for their part, established their respective churches only with travail, subject as they were to widespread persecution and thus dependent for their continuing existence on the goodwill of local lords (as in Moravia) or on a climate of relative religious toleration (as in the northern Netherlands and in the eastern European regions outside the empire and Habsburg rule). Beginning in the mid-1550s, antitrinitarianism—fusing itself with some strands of Anabaptism—took root in Poland and the grand duchy of Lithuania, and somewhat later in Transylvania, which was a vassal state of Turkish Hungary. The result was the emergence, by 1565, of the so-called Minor Reformed church in Poland (the Polish Brethren) and, by 1569, of a unitarian Reformed church in Transylvania and Turkish

Hungary, both of which groups had separated from the local orthodox Reformed churches of Swiss-Calvinist orientation. The Racovian Catechism—published at Raków, Poland, in 1605—has been recognized as a classic exposition of early Unitarianism, holding that Christ himself, though a mortal man, was raised by God from the dead and, in the ascension, was accorded an adoptive deity and made co-regent of the world.

The representatives of major manifestations of sixteenth-century Protestantism regarded the Anabaptists, spiritualists, and antitrinitarians as "sectaries" and "heretics," not as fellow Protestants. Mere anti-Romanism, therefore, did not constitute Protestantism nor define Protestant self-understanding. Of fundamental importance for the first Protestants, rather, was the nature of a particular church's public confession of faith—its "protestation" (as in the original sense obtaining at the Second Diet of Speyer). This confession, all acknowledged, must be demonstrably orthodox, that is, in agreement with the teaching of the one church catholic whose sole head is Christ and whose foundation is the apostolic witness to Christ as set forth in the scriptures and summarized in the early Christian creeds. The first Protestants were those who judged that such catholic orthodoxy had not been consistently maintained by the Roman church of the Middle Ages, which had fallen into grievous errors of both doctrine and morals. Hence, for these original Protestants, there was an exigent need for a comprehensive reform of the particular church of which they were members—the Western Catholic church in communion with the bishop of Rome, even if this reformation should require a withdrawal of obedience to the Roman see owing to the latter's intransigent rejection of reform and its excommunication of the reformers. Hence also the parallel need of these Protestants to distance themselves from and to condemn the "radicals" who soon began to appear in their own midst and who, so they concluded, had likewise broken with the orthodox catholic faith.

The gradual organization of Protestant churches, normally ordered on the basis of a particular confession, took place with widely varying degrees of success and permanence. On the Continent, the fate of these churches was closely bound up with the prolonged Wars of Religion in both France and the Low Countries during the last half of the sixteenth century, and with the devastating Thirty Years' War (1618–1648) in Germany and central Europe. In England the growth of Protestantism—which was less dependent on decrees of Crown and Parliament and much more gradual, piecemeal, and contested than traditional accounts allow—was threatened by Mary Tudor's efforts to return the realm to Roman Catholicism and by the plans of King Philip II of Spain to subdue the realm by his great armada (1588). Throughout all of Europe, Protestantism was confronted by a rejuvenated and newly militant Roman Catholicism, following upon the sweeping institutional reforms effected by the Council of Trent. This Roman Catholic Reformation and Counter-Reformation succeeded in restoring to the Roman fold many areas that had earlier undergone extensive Protestantization, notably Bavaria, Silesia, Poland, and the Habsburg lands of Austria, Bohemia, and Hungary. (In Turkish Hungary, however, and especially in Transylvania, Protestant churches, principally Calvinist, maintained themselves.)

In summary, by 1600 (or, at the latest, 1650) Protestantism—in one or more of its several types or confessional traditions—had established itself on a national basis in the Scandinavian lands (Lutheran), England (Anglican), Scotland (Calvinist), the seven northern provinces of the Netherlands, that is, the Dutch Republic (Calvinist), as well as on a semi-national or partial basis in Germany (Lutheran and Calvinist) and Switzerland (Zwinglian and Calvinist). In France, Calvinist Protestants (Huguenots) remained an embattled minority until achieving a limited legal recognition by the Edict of Nantes in 1598 (which was subsequently revoked by King Louis XIV in 1685). The term "Calvinist," as used above, is not altogether apt or accurate. In 1549, meeting at Zurich, Calvin and Heinrich Bullinger (Zwingli's successor) jointly subscribed to the *Consensus Tigurinus*, or Zurich Agreement, on the understanding of the Lord's Supper. This agreement served to create a common "Reformed" tradition, in contrast to which Lutheranism came to be identified as "Evangelical."

The development of a full-blown "confessionalization" within the territorial states of the empire during the last half of the sixteenth century, in the wake of the Peace of Augsburg (with its principle, "Whose the rule, his the religion"), served to militate against the idea of a single Protestantism in united opposition to Roman Catholicism. From the 1560s to the mid-seventeenth century, paramount importance was increasingly ascribed (by rulers and subjects alike) to confessional identity and uniformity as the fundament of society, thus giving rise to intense rivalry and conflict within the Protestant ranks. The churches of the Reformation were not thought of as generically "Protestant" but as specifically "Lutheran" or "Calvinist"—as "Evangelical" or "Reformed" or "Anglican" (though the Church of England did not order itself on the basis of formal subscription to a corpus of doctrines set forth in contemporary "symbols" or confessions). The reemergence of a shared "Protestant" consciousness first occurred, on a wide front, during the course of the nineteenth century, with concerted efforts to join Evangelical and Reformed in a "united church" (as in Prussia and its annexed territories, where such a union was mandated by royal decree in 1817).

This superordination of a common "Protestantism" to a disparate and divisive "confessionalism" was due, in part, to the legacy of Pietism, the European Enlightenment, and theological rationalism, all of which had condemned a doctrinaire Christianity for sanctioning religious warfare through its confessional intolerance and bitter polemic. Still more influential was the growth of a new "sense of history," chiefly indebted to German romanticism and philosophical idealism. This "historicism" (*Historismus*), as it came to be called, construed historical phenomena as organic "wholes," each of which (e.g., the Roman Republic, the Renaissance) emerged and developed—in all its rich individuality and complexity—on the basis of a driving "idea" (*Idee*) or animating "spirit" (*Geist*). Not surprisingly, therefore, the nineteenth century was a time when Protestant theologians and historians produced hundreds of books and essays devoted to a determination and delineation of the unique "essence" or "principle" or "spirit" of Protestantism, which could readily be compared to and contrasted with the "spirit" of Roman Catholicism. To be sure, weighty differences in the identification of Protestantism's essence (*Wesen*) could and did lead to profoundly different estimates of the role of confessional identity and integrity in constituting that essence. Nineteenth-century historicism, in short, promoted a neo-confessionalism as well as a transconfessional and supra-confessional "Protestant" consciousness.

Historians have often asserted that the Reformation era, with its establishment of Protestant churches, witnessed the dissolution of the medieval *corpus christianum*, with its principle of "one baptism, one faith." This generalization, while defensible, requires qualification, not least in order to obviate some stereotyped interpretations of Protestantism.

In withdrawing themselves from obedience to Rome (a phenomenon that itself had notable precedents in the later Middle Ages), Protestant churches did not thereby surrender the consciousness of being "Catholic." This consciousness characterized both Lutheranism and Anglicanism; it was also shared by Calvin and the early Reformed tradition. The Protestant assault on the doctrinal formulations of many of the scholastic theologians of the Middle Ages, as well as on the decrees of medieval popes and church councils, was not understood as an attack on or break with the "one faith" of the universal Christian church, as exhibited in the canonical scriptures, epitomized in the ancient ecumenical creeds, and expounded by the early church fathers. Nor was it denied that this faith had been preserved in the Latin church of the Middle Ages, by not a few of its doctors and by Christians at large. Protestantism, in short, was not thought to be synonymous with anti-Catholicism, even as Catholicism was not thought to be synonymous with Romanism or papalism.

As regards the terms "Protestant" and "Protestantism," it is a clear indication of their immediate political (rather than ecclesiastical) provenance—and, hence, of their limited usefulness—that they do not appear in the voluminous writings of Luther (apart from an occasional reference to "protesting estates"), in the confessional writings of the Lutheran church contained in the *Book of Concord* (1580), in any edition of the Anglican *Book of Common Prayer* (first edition, 1549), in John Jewel's *Apology of the Church of England* (1562, 1564), in Calvin's *Institutes of the Christian Religion* (final Latin edition, 1559), and in two of the most widely used Reformed confessions of the sixteenth century: the Heidelberg Catechism (1563) and the Second Helvetic Confession (1566). The sense of all these texts is one of continuing communion with and membership in the "one holy catholic and apostolic church," not one of membership in particular churches that were both "new" and specifically "Protestant." Whenever engaging in polemic, the authors of these texts did not identify their primary opponents as "Catholics," but rather as "Romanists," "papists," "our adversaries," and so on. Protestants, therefore, continued to maintain, certainly during the Reformation era itself, that they were "Catholics," and that such catholicity did not depend on allegiance to the bishop of Rome as the putative vicar of Christ and supreme head of the earthly church by divine right.

Whether Protestants, past and present, have been correct in holding that catholic orthodoxy (fidelity to the apostolic tradition) can be preserved apart from a Roman primacy and teaching office, and largely apart from age-old institutions, such as monasteries, that nurture the religious life of daily prayer and praise; whether Protestant churches (discounting sheer institutional inertia) still have valid reasons for being after the dramatic reforms of the Roman church enacted at the Second Vatican Council (1962–1965) and during the years since; thus whether the great ecclesiastical schism of the sixteenth century can be ended by a reunion of "protesting" Catholics and "reformed" Roman Catholics—these are questions, plainly, that cannot be answered by recourse to Reformation history alone. Nevertheless, they derive their salience from that history because they emerge from a consideration of Protestantism in its original sixteenth-century sense and self-understanding.

BIBLIOGRAPHY

Aulén, Gustav. *Reformation and Catholicity*. Translated by Eric H. Waldstrom. Edinburgh, 1962. A pioneering investigation of the meaning and legitimacy of the original Protestant claim to apostolicity and catholicity. (Originally appeared as: *Reformation och Katolicitet*, Stockholm, 1959.)

Burgess, Joseph A., ed. *The Role of the Augsburg Confession: Catholic and Lutheran Views*. Philadelphia, 1980. Discusses the possibility of official Roman Catholic recognition of the Augsburg Confession as "a legitimate expression of Christian truth"; representative of the new ecumenical climate since the Second Vatican Council.

Dillenberger, John, and Claude Welch. *Protestant Christianity Interpreted through Its Development*. 2d ed. New York, 1988. Addresses the question "What is Protestantism?" through an exposition and analysis of the term's sixteenth-century origins and overall historical development.

Forell, George W. *The Protestant Faith*. Englewood Cliffs, N.J., 1960. Among the most informative of the many books in this genre, focusing on the Protestant mainstream.

Gerrish, B. A. *The Old Protestantism and the New*. Chicago, 1982. Essays on Reformation thought and its heritage in the modern world, chiefly in nineteenth-century Protestant liberalism.

Kühn, Johannes, ed. *Deutsche Reichstagsakten, Jüngere Reihe: Deutsche Reichstagsakten unter Kaiser Karl V.* Vol. 7, pt. 2. Gotha, 1935. Critical edition of the proceedings at the Second Diet of Speyer, including texts of the "Protest" and "Appeal."

McGrath, Alister. *The Intellectual Origins of the European Reformation.* Oxford, 1987. Analyzes the divergent relations of the Lutheran and Reformed churches to humanism and late medieval scholasticism.

Oberman, Heiko A. *The Dawn of the Reformation.* Edinburgh, 1986.

———. *The Impact of the Reformation.* Grand Rapids, Mich., 1994.

———. *The Reformation: Roots and Ramifications.* Edinburgh and Grand Rapids, Mich., 1994. Three volumes of the author's collected essays that illumine the social and intellectual context of the sixteenth-century reform movements, both Protestant and Roman Catholic.

Ozment, Steven. *Protestants: The Birth of a Revolution.* New York, 1992. This work considers what it meant to be a "Protestant" in the sixteenth century and what role Protestantism has played in shaping the modern world.

Pelikan, Jaroslav. *The Christian Tradition: A History of the Development of Doctrine.* Vol. 4, *Reformation of Church and Dogma, 1300–1700.* Chicago, 1984. Delineates the principal doctrines of the late medieval and Reformation-era churches in the light of the history of church doctrine since the second century.

Raitt, Jill, ed. *Shapers of Religious Traditions in Germany, Switzerland, and Poland, 1560–1600.* New Haven, 1981.

Schilling, Heinz. *Religion, Political Culture and the Emergence of Early Modern Society.* Studies in Medieval and Reformation Thought, vol. 50. Leiden, 1992. Especially valuable for its treatment of "confessionalization" and the "Second Reformation."

Williams, George Huntston. *The Radical Reformation.* 3d ed. Sixteenth Century Essays and Studies, vol. 15. Kirksville, Mo., 1992. Remains the most comprehensive treatment of its subject.

DAVID W. LOTZ

History of the Term

The terms "Protestant" and "Protestantism" are the overarching, generic label for the movement (or, for that matter, movements) of reform in the sixteenth century and its adherents. Literary usage in the English-speaking world has come to embrace these terms as normative for describing the adherents of the Reformation, while in other countries these terms vie with the term "evangelical," which, in English, seems inappropriate for application to the sixteenth century because of a distinct theological meaning.

The question of an overarching term to describe and identify all adherents of the movement of reform in the sixteenth century is exceedingly complicated. Understandably, the different European languages pose different problems, though it is fair to say that the term "Protestant" enjoys the most widespread usage. A close analysis of sixteenth-century realities and usage suggests the complications. The term is anachronistic for the time before 1529, when the "protestation" at the Diet of Speyer gave rise to the term. Even after 1529, the use of the term is not without its difficulties: the adherents of the reform movement did not so designate themselves; they were "Lutheran," for example, or "Zwinglians." Thus the use of the term "the Protestant estates" to refer to the political and theological situation in Germany in the 1530s conjures up the same difficulty. The term is useful for the years after 1529, since the alternatives "Lutheran" or "Zwinglian"—unless used in an artificial, even hyphenated way—do not describe the full phenomenon of the Reformation any better.

There are no studies of the history of the concept of "Protestantism." The reason lies in a lack of interest in the issue and a complicated source situation. The editors of the major series on the Reformation, such as the German Reichstagsakten and the Weimar edition of Luther's works, have preferred to use modern terms, such as "Protestants," instead of attempting to find a contemporary equivalent to the term "protesting," which is, after all, the original meaning of the term as used at Speyer.

In sixteenth-century Germany the terms known to have been used were "the protesting estates/princes/cities," and "those who have protested." One recognizes in those terms the echoes of the legal and confessional statement of Speyer in 1529. This language usage seems to have been influenced by jurists rather than theologians, and it relates to the diplomatic and political sphere (negotiations, treaties, alliances, common action, Schmalkald War). In 1545 Martin Luther viewed the term "the protesting estates" to be part of the anti-Reformation polemic (WA 54.288), and his biographer M. Ratzeberger claimed the same shortly after Luther's death. During the Diet of Speyer in 1529 the representatives of Strasbourg and Constance used the phrase "the protesting cities" as a self-designation. In the correspondence of Ulm regarding the fourth Memmingen meeting of the "protesting" south German cities (15–16 November 1529) the term "the protesting estates" was used several times (Fabian 6.60–61). Subsequently, the terms "protesting estates" and "those who protest" are found as self-designations primarily among the south German cities, for example in the Ulm instructions for the meeting of the Schmalkald League in 1537.

The early recesses of the Schmalkald League have the phrase "evangelical protesting and estates" ("evangelischen protestierenden und recusirenden stenden"). The phrase "Christian protesting estates" ("christlichen protestierenden stenden") was used in the hearings before the imperial camerial court about the religious legislation during 1534/35. The terms "related by unity" ("einungsverwandte") or "estates related through unity" ("einungsverwandte Stände") were the most frequent self-designations of the members of the Schmalkald League, including in its constitution of 1535. The recess of the league on 31 December 1530 had the heading "recess of the evangelical estates." This term, alongside others, was frequently used in official documents of the league, for example, by Philipp of Hesse.

In 1541 Duke Moritz of Saxony referred to the "recess of those who are protesting" ("der protestierenden abschied") in Regensburg, but generally used the term "those related in religion" ("Religionsverwandte") or "those related in unity" ("Einungsverwandte"). At the beginning of the Schmalkald War Justus Jonas solicited the town of Halle to pray for the elector and "all related protesting estates" ("allen mitverwandten protestierenden stenden").

Johannes Sleidanus's history of the Reformation explained the term "protesting ones" by reference to the Protestation of Speyer: "And that is the origin of the term 'Protestant' not only in Germany but also among foreign peoples where it has become widespread" ("et haec quidem est origo nominis protestantum, quod non solum in Germaniae, sed apud exteras quoque gentes pervulgatum est atque celebre"). This formulation influenced subsequent historiography. Sleidanus used the term *protestantes* ("those who protest") exclusively and described with it the political actions of the protesting estates: the diets of Speyer (1529) and Augsburg (1530), the Schmalkald League, and the Schmalkald War. Sleidanus also used the term in conjunction with the Council of Trent in 1552.

The reference to the Schmalkald War as the "war of the protesting ones" ("protestierende Krieg") appeared in the 1573 German translation of the *De bello Germanico* by the Dutch humanist Lambert Hortensius (1560). The contemporary German translations of Sleidanus's commentaries by the Basel historian Heinrich Pantaleon (1556ff.) and the Strasbourg historian Michael Benther (1558ff.) always render *protestantes* as "those who are protesting" ("protestierende"). A French translation of 1558 correctly followed Sleidanus's intent with *protestans* as did the English translation by John Daus (1560) with "Protestauntes." Only in Johann Salomon Semler's translation of 1771 is there the term "Protestants" with the explanation "and this is the origin of the name of the Protestants" (Semler 1.425). Both German and Latin sixteenth-century authors employed the terms *protestantes* or "protesting ones" (Hans Wilhelm Kirchhoff, 1563; Johannes Mathesius, 1566; Heinrich Bullinger, 1567). At the thirteenth session of the Council of Trent (October 1551) *protestantes* (Lat.) was used as the self-designation of the evangelical estates; not until the nineteenth century was that term translated as "Protestants." Toward the end of the sixteenth century the terms *Protestants* and *Protestans* gained usage in England and France, respectively, in order to denote the contrast to the Roman church. The specificities of the English and French languages, in which "the protesting ones" and "those who protest" are awkward, suggested the use of "Protestant" or "protestans," particularly if the root meaning of the word was kept in mind and understood. At any rate, this West European linguistic influence eventually caused "those who protested" ("protestierende") to be replaced by "Protestants" even in German language usage. In the eighteenth century this process was repeated with the abstract noun "Protestantism." In French the term was used in 1623. John Milton used the term "Protestantism" as the opposite of "papist" in his *Eikonoklastes* of 1642. In Italian, *protestantismo* was used in 1677.

In sum, the term "Protestantism" was not used in the sixteenth century. Even the term "Protestant" came to be accepted through a slow process of transition from a legal to a confessional usage. The details of the development still await definitive analysis, and thus the observations in scholarship (about initial use, etc.) all have an element of tentativeness. It is clear that the self-designation as *Protestantes* or *Protestierende* included an element of confession, but in the sixteenth century the main emphasis was on the legal consideration of having protested a legal maneuver. Reformation theologians were not part of this linguistic development. For Lutheran theologians the Augsburg Confession had priority. Friedrich Myconius's *Reformation History* dealt extensively with the Diet of Augsburg of 1530 and the position of those "related in religion"; the Protestation of Speyer was not even mentioned by him. The terms "protesting estates" or "protestants" were not seen as having an integrative content. The acknowledgment of Luther's teaching was considered crucial. Diverging teachings were rejected: the Anabaptists at Speyer in 1529, the Zwinglians at Augsburg in 1530.

Efforts to arrive at substantive criteria for the definition of "Protestants" and "Protestantism" in the sixteenth century (repudiation of papal authority; priority of scripture and faith against tradition, institution, and office; relationship of the word to the Sacrament, etc.) lead to unsatisfactory results because the appropriate differentiation is lacking. The efforts to discern an "essence of Protestantism," a "Protestant principle," or a "spirit of Protestantism" begin in the eighteenth century. They are a consequence of the Enlightenment and grow out of the tendency to minimize or even to ignore theological differences.

The usefulness of the term "Protestantism" as a historical ordering principle must thus be questioned for the sixteenth century. Even the distinction between Old Protestantism and New Protestantism in modern discourse is unsatisfactory. The necessity to distinguish between "official Protestantism" and "unofficial Protestantism" in historiography is further evidence that it makes little sense to retain the concept and terms of Protestantism for the sixteenth century. Accordingly, current research, much influenced by social history, has embraced the term "confessionalization" for the time when the movement of reform (Reformation) was replaced by a legally and confessionally defined social structure.

BIBLIOGRAPHY

Bayle, Pierre. *Dictionnaire historique et critique.* Rotterdam, 1697–1702.

Cortelazzo, Manlio. *Dizionario etimologico della lingua italiana.* Reprint, Bologna, 1988.

Fabian, Ekkehart. *Die Entstehung des Schmalkaldischen Bundes und seiner Verfassung, 1529–1531/33*. Schriften zur Kirchen- und Rechtsgeschichte 1. Tübingen, 1956.

———, ed. *Die schmalkaldischen Bundesabschiede, 1530–1532*. Schriften zur Kirchen- und Rechtsgeschichte 7 and 8. Tübingen, 1958.

———, ed. *Quellen zur Geschichte der Reformationsbündnisse und der Konstanzer Reformationsprozesse, 1529–1548*. Schriften zur Kirchen- und Rechtsgeschichte 34. Tübingen, 1967.

Sleidanus, Johannes. *De statu religionis et rei publicae Carolo Quinto Caesare, commentarii idem de summis imperiis Babylonica, Persico, Graeco, and Romani*. Paris, 1559.

Wrede, A., ed. *Deutsche Reichstagsakten Jüngere Reihe*. Reprint, Göttingen, 1956.

SIEGFRIED BRÄUER
Translated from German by Hans J. Hillerbrand

PROTESTANT LEAGUE. From her accession to the throne of England in 1559, Elizabeth I of England attempted to unite Protestant rulers in a Protestant league to oppose the pope and shortly thereafter to organize assistance to the Huguenots during the Wars of Religion in France. In 1576 Elizabeth's efforts intensified. With the enthusiastic support of his mentor, Hubert Languet, Elizabeth sent Philip Sidney as her envoy to deliver her condolences to Emperor Rudolf II and also to the Palatine princes, Ludwig and Johann Casimir, whose fathers had recently died. Sidney's underlying objective, however, was to explore the possibility of a Protestant league with the German Protestant princes, among them Count Ludwig, a Lutheran, and with more hope of success, Johann Casimir, who was loyal to the Reformed tradition and allied with the Huguenots in the French Wars of Religion. Casimir became Elizabeth's staunchest supporter of a Protestant league and agreed to help persuade other Protestant princes to join it. Casimir's Reformed brand of Protestantism, however, lessened his credibility in the eyes of the German Lutheran princes. Philipp, landgrave of Hesse, also supported Elizabeth's idea and himself wrote to his German Protestant peers. In the meantime, Amias Paulet, Elizabeth's ambassador to France, was also concerned to find support against the Catholic League, which included the pope, the Spanish king, and the increasingly powerful Guise of France.

In 1577 Elizabeth's counsel drew up an outline for the proposed Protestant league. It was entitled "Heads of the Treaty between the Queen of England and the Protestant Princes of Germany." The points of the outline asked the princes who followed the Augsburg Confession to form a defensive league against the pope, setting aside their theological disputes, committing money and troops, and promising to draw in the Protestant Swiss cantons. Again Philipp of Hesse actively supported the idea. He called for a meeting of Protestant theologians at Frankfurt am Main in 1577 to draw up a common confession that would serve not only to unite Protestants against Catholic attacks but to put an end to the persecution of Calvinists by Lutherans and to engage Lutheran support for the French Huguenots in the Wars of Religion.

Elizabeth's next move was to write to Frederick II, king of Denmark, from whom she received an encouraging response. Less encouraging was the response of William of Orange, who accurately predicted that the German princes would never agree to such a league, for both political and theological reasons. William advised Elizabeth to turn her efforts to a political league among the Hanse cities, Holland and Zeeland, some Swiss cantons, and the counts of Wederaw. Meanwhile, Casimir moderated his own enthusiasm for the league with a bit of realism, realizing that the theological differences between Lutherans and Reformed would make such a league extremely difficult to achieve. Nevertheless, Casimir obtained Elizabeth's monetary support for the Huguenots.

Meanwhile, Elizabeth's counselors advised her against such a league for a number of reasons: leagues were often betrayed, such a league might provoke the papal forces to strengthen their own league, the German princes could not agree about religion, and finally, Elizabeth was liable to lose her money. Answers to these objections were forthcoming and centered on the need to allow for freedom of conscience, an interesting proposition given religious conditions in Elizabeth's England.

Although 1577 was a year of hope and hopes dashed, Elizabeth did not give up. By 1585 the position of the Huguenots in France was more perilous as Henry III decreed that France should be Catholic and all who would not conform must leave the country. The Catholic League of the Guise was growing stronger. Casimir wrote to Elizabeth that Henry of Navarre (later Henry IV), leader of the Huguenots, needed immediate assistance. Casimir advised that Elizabeth try again to form a Protestant league and also to send him £100,000 to support the troops he was leading into France. Elizabeth agreed with both requests. She was especially incensed by Casimir's report that Protestant Saxon troops were being sent to the Guise and that the Lutheran ministers incited the troops by inflaming them against the Calvinists.

Meanwhile, in 1585 Elizabeth sent Thomas Bodley to Frederick II of Denmark, who agreed that a Protestant league was not only desirable but necessary. The king, who had rejected the Formula of Concord, told Bodley that the German princes had sent the *Book of Concord* to Henry of Navarre, signifying that their aid depended on Navarre's acceptance of Lutheranism. Denmark was opposed to the princes' notion that differences between Lutherans and Reformed might be settled by a conference of theologians. Philipp of Hesse sent more letters to the German princes, who rejected the idea on the basis of their allegiance to the Holy Roman Emperor and their need to be united within the empire against the Turks. The German princes also appealed to the Peace of Augsburg (1555) as a *modus vivendi* between the followers of the Augsburg Confession and the Roman Catholics. The princes called Elizabeth's idea of a Protestant league a dangerous and destructive plan.

By 1588 even Casimir had despaired of a Protestant league and reduced his requests to Elizabeth for help in the French Wars of Religion. Elizabeth's navy defeated the Spanish Armada, and one year later Henry of Navarre succeeded Henry III, becoming a Catholic in 1593 in order to enter Paris and unite France. After both Elizabeth and Casimir died, Casimir's successor in the Palatinate, Elector Frederick IV, founded a Protestant union in 1608 against the Counter-Reformation in German lands.

BIBLIOGRAPHY

Calendar of State Papers, Foreign Series, of the Reign of Elizabeth. London, 1863ff. See especially vols. 11, 12, and 19–21.

Osborn, James M. *Young Philip Sidney, 1572–1577.* New Haven and London, 1972.

Raitt, Jill. "Elizabeth of England, John Casimir, and the Protestant League." In *Controversy and Conciliation: The Reformation and the Palatinate, 1559–1583,* edited by Derk Visser, pp. 117–145. Allison Park, Pa., 1986.

JILL RAITT

PROTESTANT LITURGY. *See* Liturgy, *article on* Protestant Liturgy.

PROTESTATION OF SPEYER. *See* Speyer, Protestation of.

PRUSSIA.

A territory of the Teutonic Order on the southeastern coast of the Baltic Sea, Prussia became a secularized duchy under Polish suzerainty in 1525, when Albert of Brandenburg-Ansbach, grand master of the order, converted to the new reformed view of religion. The area was bounded on the north by the river Niemen, on the west by the river Vistula, and on the east by Poland. The original inhabitants of the region, the Prussians (also known as Borussi or Prussi) were neither Germans nor Slavs but belonged to the Baltic-speaking Letto-Lithuanians.

The ascendancy of the Teutonic Order dated from 1226, when the Polish duke Conrad of Masovia invited it to combat and Christianize the heathen Prussians. Having received promises from Emperor Frederick II and Pope Gregory IX that it could retain full sovereignty, independent of the Holy Roman Empire, over all the lands that it seized, the order quickly overran the native Prussians and colonized the region with German settlers. Towns were founded at Thorn, Culm, Elbing, Danzig, and Königsberg, and in 1309 the headquarters of the order were moved from Venice to Marienburg on the Vistula.

Teutonic power reached its height in the fourteenth century, after which decline set in. With the Christianization and colonization of the southeastern Baltic completed, the order occupied itself mostly with mundane tasks, thereby losing touch with its original spiritual purpose. Never more than a narrow oligarchy of German knights, it failed to extend membership to any of its subjects in Prussia, treating them with disdain instead; its selfish, monopolistic commercial practices and rumors of widespread corruption among the knights only exacerbated the situation. As the Prussian towns and secular nobility became more alienated, they began to look to neighboring Poland and Lithuania for help. The unification of these two countries into a powerful state (1386) set the stage for a series of military confrontations in the fifteenth century. The knights suffered a humiliating defeat at Tannenberg (1410) and, after protracted hostilities, submitted to the Peace of Thorn (1466), ceding West Prussia (with Danzig and Thorn) to Poland and acknowledging the suzerainty of the Polish king over the rest of their territory.

In 1523 Albert, margrave of Brandenburg-Ansbach (1490–1568), elected grand master of the knights, initiated a series of steps that would lead to the order's secularization in Prussia. At the Diet of Nuremberg in 1523, Albert had listened to the sermons of Andreas Osiander and met several supporters of the evangelical cause. Shortly afterward he requested Martin Luther's confidential advice concerning the reform of the order and, in the fall of 1523, visited the reformer in Wittenberg. Luther responded with his *Exhortation to the Knights of the Teutonic Order,* in which he urged the grand master to convert publicly and to turn his spiritual territory into a secular principality. With Luther's help Albert now began to call preachers to Prussia, (Johann Briessmann, Paul Speratus, Johann Poliander). Briessmann, a former Franciscan from Kottbus, is credited with preaching the first evangelical sermon at the Königsberg cathedral (September 1523) and instructing George von Polentz, bishop of Samland (in whose diocese Königsberg lay), in the new faith. Polentz publicly converted on Christmas Day, 1523, then directed his clergy to read Luther's writings diligently and to preach only the pure gospel. Shortly afterward Prussia's other prelate, Erhard von Queiss, bishop of Pomesia, also embraced the Reformation and ordered the spiritual renewal of his diocese on the basis of the pure gospel (*Themata Episcopi Risenburgensis,* 1 January 1525). In the meantime, Albert had entered into secret negotiations with his Polish overlord and secured his consent to the dissolution of the Teutonic Order. By the Treaty of Kraków (1525), which was approved by the Prussian estates, the order's possessions were transformed into a hereditary secular duchy. Albert took the oath of homage, as duke of Prussia, to King Sigismund I of Poland (10 April 1525). A year later he was married at Königsberg castle to Dorothy, daughter of the Lutheran king Frederick I of Denmark.

As the new duke of Prussia, Albert vigorously promoted the Reformation. A church ordinance (1525), approved by the estates, regulated the appointment and support of ministers and contained detailed provisions for the reform of worship (*Artikel der Zeremonien und anderer Kirchenordnung*, 1526). In agreement with the bishops Albert named a commission in 1526 to visit the duchy's parishes, to investigate the life and teachings of pastors, and, where necessary, to correct existing abuses. Also in 1526 the first evangelical German hymnal was published in Prussia. Translations of Luther's writings were made available in the languages of the Lithuanian and Masurian minorities. The 1525 ordinance, which would remain in force for twenty years, was significant because it made Prussia the first German principality with an established Lutheran territorial church.

Another tour of inspection resulted in a new church order (*Ordnung vom äußerlichen Gottesdienst*, 1544), one based on the Saxon ordinance of 1539. By eliminating the elevation, it provided for a more evangelical celebration of the Eucharist than did the 1525 articles. The University of Königsberg, founded by Albert with the aid of Briessmann and Luther, dated from 1544 as well; George Sabinus, son-in-law of Melanchthon, was the school's first rector. Popularly known as the Albertina, it won a reputation as the "Wittenberg of the East" and would remain an exclusively Protestant institution for more than two hundred years.

From the beginning the Reformation enjoyed widespread popular support, especially in Königsberg. Schwenckfeldian enthusiasts were tolerated until the time of the Anabaptist debacle at Münster (1534), when Albert issued a mandate strictly proscribing all spiritualist and Anabaptist activities in the duchy. Far more divisive than these heterodox minorities, however, was a controversy provoked by Andreas Osiander, the former Nuremberg reformer whose preaching had first attracted Albert to Lutheranism. Osiander's incessant and bitter disputes with colleagues, notably his resolute opposition to the Augsburg Interim, the Catholicizing compromise formula Protestants had been compelled to accept as a result of their defeat in the Schmalkald War, had forced his departure from the imperial city. He had fled to Prussia, where he was received with open arms by Duke Albert, who named him professor of theology at the Albertina (1549). But there too Osiander soon became involved in a fierce dispute, this time over the doctrine of justification. Like other Lutherans he affirmed salvation by grace alone; unlike most, however, he argued for a mystical conception of justification, insisting that the sinner is not simply declared righteous but receives actual righteousness from the indwelling Christ. Albert, who called Osiander his "spiritual father," supported his teaching; he tried to reconcile the opposing parties but instead created only more division. Osiander died in the midst of the strife (1552), yet the controversy only worsened. Johann Funck, his son-in-law and leading supporter, who also was Albert's court preacher, had Osiander's chief critics, notably Joachim Mörlin, the Königsberg cathedral preacher, expelled from the duchy. Relations between the duke and the estates deteriorated when Albert tried to enforce a new church ordinance (1558) that the Junkers, who had not been consulted, promptly condemned as "Osiandrian." The confusion became so great that the Prussians finally called in a Polish commission. Order was restored in 1566 when, at the instigation of the Poles, Funck and two associates were tried and executed as traitors and promoters of the Osiandrian heresy.

The winners in this struggle were, confessionally, the Gnesio-Lutherans and, politically, the Prussian estates, especially the landed aristocracy. In 1542 Albert had conceded to the Junkers that the duchy's *Oberräte* ("superior councillors") would be selected solely from among their ranks; now, in 1566, he also recognized the estates' right of appeal to the Polish king if ever they thought their rights were being violated. By solidifying their power the knights thus were able to remake Prussia into an aristocratic republic. This process went hand in hand with the consolidation of Lutheranism. A new manual of dogma, the *Repetitio Corporis Doctrinae* by Joachim Mörlin and Martin Chemnitz, which was approved by the Synod of Königsberg (1567) and by the estates, endorsed the unaltered Augsburg Confession but repudiated the errors of the Osiandrians, Schwenckfeldians, and Calvinists. Exorcism, which earlier had been deleted from the baptismal service, was restored as an appropriate antidote to Calvinism.

The influence of the estates was also very much in evidence in the revised (Prussia's fourth) church order of 1568. At the deaths of the two bishops—Polentz in 1550 and Paul Speratus, who had succeeded Queiss, in 1551—Duke Albert had suspended the episcopal constitution as he tried to replace the bishops with superintendents who were accountable to him rather than to the estates. The Königsbergers and Junkers objected, noting that the duchy's constitution, the *Regimentsnotel* of 1542, specifically provided for two bishoprics. Albert, afraid of Polish intervention, eventually relented (1566) and allowed representatives of the estates to elect George Venediger (Venetus) as bishop of Pomesia and Joachim Mörlin as bishop of Samland. The two helped prepare the new church ordinance that was published shortly before Albert died in March 1568.

The Junkers were able to solidify their power further during the reign of Albert's son and successor, the demented Albert Frederick (1568–1618). The duke's illness soon necessitated a regency that was ably administered by his cousin Margrave George Frederick of Ansbach (1577–1603) and later by John Sigismund, heir to the Brandenburg electorate.

In 1594 the margrave, a strong proponent of Hohenzollern dynastic interests, arranged the marriage between Anna (daughter of Albert Frederick and Mary Eleanor of Jülich-Cleves) and John Sigismund. This union was important, for it strengthened the Hohenzollerns' rights in Prussia and provided the basis for their dynastic claims in the Rhineland.

Poland's Catholics, ably guided by Stanislaus Hosius, bishop of Ermland (West Prussia), tried to take advantage of the regency and the growing rift between ruler and estates. They sought concessions from the Junkers by guaranteeing their constitutional interests and were able to use the enfeoffment negotiations with the Hohenzollerns (in 1605 and 1608) to gain additional preferences. Margrave George Frederick responded by siding squarely with the supporters of orthodox Lutheran doctrine and tightening his control of the Prussian church. The duchy's estates, equally zealous to protect their interests, both secular and spiritual, reacted by seeing to it that new bishops were selected after Mörlin and Venediger had died.

In 1573 Tilemann Hesshus of Wesel, who had a solid reputation as a Calvinist-hater, was consecrated as bishop of Samland, and two years later Johann Wigand, a former professor of theology from the University of Jena, was installed in the Königsberg cathedral as bishop of Pomesia. The two soon became involved in a bitter feud when Hesshus, overly zealous in his condemnation of Genevan errors, published a book (*Adsertio Sancti Testamenti Jesu Christi contra blasphemam Calvinistarum Exegesin*, 1574) in which he stated that not only is Christ omnipotent and omniscient, "concretely," but that "abstractly" his humanity possesses these attributes as well, on the basis of the unity of the two natures. Hesshus's position provoked a major controversy that involved the pastors as well as their parishioners. Since Hesshus refused to modify his position, he was deposed in 1577. Wigand was entrusted with his diocese; he would administer both Prussian bishoprics until his death in 1587. The "abstract-concrete controversy," meanwhile, lingered into the 1580s.

The Hesshus-Wigand strife was disruptive but did not prevent the Prussian church from moving further toward orthodox Lutheranism. George Frederick, who had fallen under the influence of Jakob Andreae and turned against Melanchthon's teachings, was an enthusiastic backer of the Formula of Concord and had it immediately enforced in Prussia. A segment of the Königsberg professorate, a stronghold of Philippism, was opposed, but the duchy's clergy readily subscribed. The margrave instructed his superior councillors to see to it that the new creedal statement was strictly observed throughout the principality; this order was reinforced by Bishop Wigand, who ordered another visitation in 1585.

Finally, to ensure religious orthodoxy and also to enhance his own position, George Frederick in the 1580s revived a theme that would engender new confrontation with the estates: the administration of the duchy's church. The continuing threat of the Catholic Counter-Reformation and the very real possibility that a future duke, as vassal of the king of Poland, might attempt to restore the old faith, put Prussia's Lutherans in a precarious position. The Junkers maintained that only an administration by bishops whom they elected would ensure the survival of the faith of the Augsburg Confession. George Frederick disagreed, insisting that this could only be guaranteed by a more centralized form of church government. Accordingly, in 1584 he introduced a consistorial organization on the Franconian model. His efforts were not entirely successful, however; when Wigan died three years later, a second consistory had to be created so that there was one for each of the two bishoprics.

By the end of the century the Prussian church thus had been firmly anchored in the camp of Concordianist Lutheranism, while its administration had been restyled to fit the pattern found in most Lutheran territorial churches, with the prince assuming—or better, still trying to assume—the unequivocal supreme episcopate. Events in the early seventeenth century, precipitated largely by the Hohenzollern rulers' conversion to Calvinism (1613), would demonstrate anew the commitment of Prussia's estates to the faith of the Augsburg Confession and their opposition to all centralizing efforts by the ducal government.

[*See also* Brandenburg; Holy Roman Empire; Osiander, Andreas; *and* Religious Orders.]

BIBLIOGRAPHY

Arnold, Undo. "Luther und die Reformation im Preußenland." In *Martin Luther und die Reformation in Ostdeutschland und Südosteuropa*, edited by Ulrich Hutter, pp. 27–44. Sigmaringen, Germany, 1991. Sees Albert's conversion to Lutheranism as politically motivated.

Carsten, Francis L. *The Origins of Prussia.* Reprint, Westport, Conn., 1981. Focuses on the growth and decline of the Junkers and political institutions in early modern Prussia.

Gorski, Karol. "The Teutonic Order in Prussia." *Medievalia et Humanistica*, o.s. 17 (1966), 20–37. Brief survey with useful bibliographical information.

Graßmann, Antjekathrin. "Das Herzogtum Preußen und Habsburg 1525–1568." In *Zur Problematik "Preußen und das Reich,"* edited by Oswald Hauser, pp. 13–34. Cologne, 1984. For a more detailed treatment of this topic, see her *Preußen und Habsburger im 16. Jahrhundert*, Cologne, 1968.

Gundermann, Iselin. "Herzogtum Preußen." In *Die Territorien des Reichs im Zeitalter der Reformation und Konfessionalisierung: Land und Konfession, 1500–1650*, vol. 2, *Der Nordosten*, edited by Anton Schindling and Walter Ziegler, pp. 220–33. Münster, 1990. Concise summary, with bibliography.

Hintze, Otto. "Calvinism and Raison d'État in Early Seventeenth-Century Brandenburg." In *The Historical Essays of Otto Hintze*, edited by Felix Gilbert, pp. 88–154. New York, 1975. Argues that the second, Calvinist Reformation infused a new, more ambitious spirit into early modern Hohenzollern politics.

Hubatsch, Walther. *Geschichte der Evangelischen Kirche Ostpreußens.* 3 vols. Göttingen, 1968. A major work of scholarship describing the history of the Lutheran church in Prussia; with illustrations and selections of documents. Emphasizes religious factors in secularization of Teutonic Order and introduction of Reformation.

———. "Albert of Brandenburg-Ansbach, Grand Master of the Order of Teutonic Knights and Duke in Prussia, 1490–1568." In *Studies in Medieval and Modern German History*, edited by Walther Hubatsch, pp. 41–69. New York, 1985. Excerpts from Walther Hubatsch, *Albrecht von Brandenburg-Ansbach*, Cologne, 1960.

Mallek, Janusz. "Die Politik des Herzogtums Preußens gegenüber Polen zur Zeit Herzog Albrechts, 1525–1568." In *Historisches Jahrbuch* 97/98 (1978), 255–269. Focuses on Duke Albert's diplomatic relations with Poland.

Nischan, Bodo. *Prince, People, and Confession: The Second Reformation in Brandenburg.* Philadelphia, 1994. Emphasizes Lutheran confessionalization resulting in Hohenzollerns' abortive effort to achieve a Calvinist reform in the early seventeenth century.

Stupperich, Martin. *Osiander in Preussen, 1549–1552.* Berlin, 1973. Church historical analysis of Osiander controversy.

Thadden, Rudolf von. "Prussia: What Was Its Church Like?" In *Prussia: The History of a Lost State*, edited by Rudolf von Thadden, pp. 86–117. Cambridge, 1987. General reassessment of state's historical significance; illustrative of current scholarship in Prussian renaissance.

Tschackert, Paul, ed. *Urkundenbuch zur Reformationsgeschichte des Herzogtums Preussen.* 3 vols. Reprint, Osnabrück, Germany, 1965. Collection of source materials; basic for study of Reformation in Prussia.

Williams, George H. "Stanislas Hosius, 1504–1579." In *Shapers of Religious Traditions in Germany, Switzerland, and Poland, 1560–1600*, edited by Jill Raitt, pp. 157–174. New Haven, 1981. Study of life and work of leading Catholic counter-reformer in Polish Prussia.

BODO NISCHAN

PURGATORY. As described by Western theology, purgatory (Lat., *purgatorium*, from the verb *purgare*, meaning to cleanse or purify) refers to the purification process through which one goes after death in order to be cleansed of any blemish and to make heavenly salvation possible. Since the twelfth century the phrase cleansing fire (*ignis purgatorius*) has been used in reference to *1 Corinthians* 3:15, which emphasizes the punitive aspect of the purifying process. The notion of purgatory presupposes an intermediate state (a state of existence of the soul) between death and resurrection in which the soul is separated by death from the body but focused on the resurrection of the body. The fully developed doctrine of purgatory in late Scholasticism (thirteenth century)—in accord with church tradition and such passages as *2 Maccabees* 12:45; *Matthew* 12:32; *Revelation* 22:15; and especially *1 Corinthians* 3:15—defined purgatory as the purification from venial sins or at times from temporal punishment, which remain after the guilt of sin has been forgiven. Most theologians have understood the cleansing fire to be a physical phenomenon, whereby the fire attaches uniquely to the soul freed from the body. This understanding resulted in efforts to fit the idea of purgatory into a unified conception of the physical world, even though no consensus emerged. Differing opinions existed also about the length and intensity of the purification process after death. As a rule, however, the medieval theologians, following Augustine, assumed the punishment in purgatory to be more severe than any punishment endured in this life. At the councils of Lyon (1274) and Florence (1439), the church adopted essential elements of the teaching on purgatory and at the same time sought a compromise with the teaching of the Orthodox church.

The reformers of the sixteenth century accepted the existence of an intermediate stage but rejected the existence of purgatory. Martin Luther, whose teachings have not been uniformly interpreted, understood this intermediate stage to be "a deep, dreamless sleep without consciousness and sensation." The souls sleep "happily in the peace of Christ, even if alive and awake before God." Huldrych Zwingli and John Calvin, together with Protestant orthodoxy, rejected the "sleep of the soul" but accepted an intermediate stage. Early on Luther maintained the belief in the existence of purgatory but understood the pain of fire not as punishment wrought from without but as internal agonies of conscience suffered under God's wrath. This brings the individual close to despair (*prope desperatio*). In the course of further development, Luther came to reject and oppose the teaching of purgatory. He believed that it has no basis in scripture and contradicts the teaching on justification, which was understood as a lifelong process ending only at death. Prayers and acts of penance performed for the souls of the departed are human works and therefore devalue the holy work of Christ. Zwingli and Calvin likewise held that scripture offered no proof for the existence of purgatory. Moreover, Zwingli found purgatory incompatible with *Mark* 16:16: whoever believes and is baptized attains eternal salvation, not a roasting in fire. For Calvin purgatory was a "terrible blasphemy of Christ." Because the blood of Christ is the only satisfaction and atonement for the sins of the faithful, there can be no further satisfaction required of the deceased after death.

At the Council of Trent (1545–1563) the doctrine of purgatory was thorougly discussed by the theologians. Since the reformers had called the scriptural basis for purgatory into question, the council endeavored to find a convincing proof from holy scripture. Among others, *1 Corinthians* 3:11–15 was the foremost reference. Some theologians were of the opinion that purgatory is not expressly attested in scripture. Others spoke of an indirect attestation and referred to the interpretation of scripture by the church. Since no unanimity could be reached after lively debates, it was decided to dispense with any direct citation of a scriptural text and to make a general reference to scripture, the tradition of the Fathers, and the councils. In this sense the final decree on purgatory, dated 3 December 1563, states in a broad and pastorally balanced manner: "Instructed by the Holy Spirit, drawing from Holy Scriptures and the ancient tradition of the Fathers, the Catholic Church has taught in the holy councils and finally in the ecumenical Synod: there is a purgatory and the souls that are detained there are helped by the prayers of the faithful but most especially by the acceptable sacrifice of the altar. . . ." The council expressly required that only sound teaching should be imparted and that hairsplitting questions that do not contribute to the edification of the faithful should be avoided. In the Decree on Justification, dated 13 January 1547, it is stated that, with the exception of baptism, temporal punishment is not always remitted with the forgiveness of guilt; temporal punishment due for sin that remains after forgiveness of guilt can be remitted in this world or in purgatory. Hence, according to the Council of Trent, it is therefore a binding teaching that the possibility of purification in the afterlife must be acknowledged, while any explanation as to the particulars is to be evaluated on the merits of theological argument.

Post-Tridentine theologians based their views on purgatory on scripture and church tradition, while the Protestant churches categorically rejected the doctrine. The Second Vatican Council echoed Tridentine teaching on purgatory and referred to the awareness of the unity of the church in the one love: the church with her members still makes her way toward her Lord, will be purified after death, or already views God as he is.

Catholic theology further developed the teaching on purgatory in various directions, so that it was hardly a burden for the ecumenical dialogue. Of all Christian theology, the notion of an intermediate state, based on tradition, was seen as problematic: the concept of time, known from experience as physically measurable, was transferred to the hereafter. The notion of a resurrection in death was advocated by most late twentieth-century Protestant theologians, and it was also embraced by respected Catholic theologians despite opposition from the Holy Office.

Some Catholic theologians no longer considered the notion of an intermediate stage a relevant church doctrine, viewing it instead as a conceptual model with which medieval theology sought to reconcile collective and individual eschatology. By the late twentieth century the teaching on purgatory had been subjected to major revision in Catholic theology. Purgatory was under no circumstance to be understood as unimaginable anguish or suffering that could not be reconciled with divine mercy. Purification occurs because of the intensification of love toward God, which fills the hearts of people. Some theologians have come to see the ancient doctrine on purgatory as sustainable if viewed as the moment when, in death, the encounter with God and Christ takes place.

BIBLIOGRAPHY

Fleischhack, Erich. *Fegefeuer: Die christlichen Vorstellungen vom Geschick der Verstorbenen geschichtlich dargestellt.* Tübingen, 1969.

Kunz, Erhard. "Protestantische Eschatologie: Von der Reformation bis zur Aufklärung." In *Handbuch der Dogmengeschichte*, edited by M. Schmaus et al., vol. 4, pt. 1. Freiburg, 1980.

Ott, Ludwig, and Erich Naab. "Eschatologie in der Scholastik." In *Handbuch der Dogmengeschichte*, edited by M. Schmaus et al., vol. 4, pt. 7b. Freiburg, 1990.

Schäfer, Philipp. "Eschatologie: Trient und Gegenreformation." In *Handbuch der Dogmengeschichte*, edited by M. Schmaus et al., vol. 4, pt. 2. Freiburg, 1984.

JOSEF FINKENZELLER
Translated from German by Caroline March and Robert E. Shillenn.

PURITANS. The one-word title of this article implies that Puritans actually existed, even that they constituted a creed or ideology known as Puritanism. So many books exist with titles like *The Rise of Puritanism* (William Haller, 1938), *Tudor Puritanism* (M. M. Knappen, 1939), or, more recently, *Puritanism: A Seventeenth-Century Anglo-American Faith* (edited by F. J. Bremer, 1993) that these might seem to be uncontroversial premises. Other books assume a clear-cut polarity in the post-Reformation Church of England and bear titles like *Anglican and Puritan: The Basis of Their Opposition, 1558–1640* (J. F. H. New, 1964). *Society and Religion in Elizabethan England* by R. L. Greaves (1981)—a prodigious dissection of hundreds of literary sources meant to identify prevailing attitudes on a large number of religious, moral, and social issues—searches persistently for distinctively "Anglican" and "Puritan" attitudes. Often Greaves fails to find them, but that does not lead him to question the categories that are the organizing principle of his work. Rather, he remarks that on this and that topic Anglicans and Puritans evidently held very similar views.

An article on the phenomenon of witches or witchcraft in the same period would not, by contrast, assume the existence of witches but would ask why they were thought to exist. Accounts of atheists or atheism proceed along similar lines, resulting from the fact that, although contemporaries never ceased to complain of atheism, it is not easy for the modern historian to identify many individuals prepared to deny the existence of God. Talk of atheism is evidence of some anxiety on the side of those who discussed it rather than of atheism itself.

The term *Puritans* presents us with a definitional situation that is somewhat closer to *witches* and *atheists* than to such expressions as *tall man* or *fat woman*, which are objectively incontrovertible, or even Roman Catholic or Reformed when those descriptions apply to individuals who belong to churches or confessions bearing those names. *Puritan* was never a term of ecclesiological or confessional precision. It is a debilitating naiveté in the historian to suppose that the names and labels he encounters in his sources are simple descriptions of various ideologies and tendencies. Language can, to be sure, serve the function of description, but it is also a polemical weapon, and description itself may consist of concealed polemic. One should be on particular guard against statements (which abound in the early seventeenth century) defining what "a Puritan is," for these belong to the satiric literary genre known as characters, the purpose of which was to construct an identity (not necessarily fictional) for an unfriendly purpose. A student of deviance (Walter Lippman) has remarked, "We do not first see, then define. We define first and then see." If there is a language of politics, there is also a politics of language.

Insofar as Puritans existed to be described, we cannot quarrel with the following statement, written in 1641, of a sympathetic but controversial author: "Those whom we ordinarily call puritans are men of strict life and precise opinions, which cannot be hated for anything but their singularity in zeal and piety" (*A Discourse Concerning Puritans*). The trouble is that such people have always existed in the history of all religions. Such "precise" Christians were the saints and martyrs and, more obscurely, the humble country parson of Geoffrey Chaucer's *Canterbury Tales*. The hint in this definition that Puritans are a social minority ("their singularity") also provides a clue about the nature of Puritanism itself. It is a fair assumption, implicit in countless sources of the period, that Puritans made themselves objectionable by the intrusive nature of their singular zeal and piety. They were sometimes called "busy controllers."

Again, the trouble is that there is nothing new in that reactive and interactive state of affairs apart from the name Puritan. One hears of a young woman in a Wiltshire Village in 1624 who complained of the interference of the parson in her favorite pastimes. "We had a good parson here before but now we have a puritan. . . . A plague or a pox in him that ever he did come hither." "A puritan" makes a syntactic climax to this carefully constructed complaint and serves an invaluable purpose. But in similar circumstances two hundred and fifty years earlier, Chaucer's parson had been called a Lollard for rebuking a fellow Canterbury tourist for swearing ("this man would sowen some difficulty"). In the early fifteenth century Margery Baxter of Norwich, who was a Lollard (or Wycliffite heretic), and Margery Kempe of King's Lynn, who was not, were both accused of Lollardy when they complained of swearing.

The historiography of Puritans and Puritanism, leaving aside the promiscuous and careless use of these terms, suggests that Puritans appeared on the scene during the reign of Elizabeth I, played their parts on the historical stage (especially in New England and in the English Civil Wars), and subsequently went into declension or suffered some other kind of sea change in later seventeenth-century England, passing under new names, such as Nonconformist, Dissenter, and even Fanatic. The English literature on the subject has been much influenced by the conviction of American histories that this minority religious tendency, translated across the Atlantic, created a cluster of "Puritan" commonwealths that were the seedbed of a distinctively American civilization.

The reader should now be sufficiently alert to take none of this for granted. To define an individual as a Puritan is to suggest that this label is the only, or at least the most important, thing to be said about him or her. But the coherence of our concept of Puritanism depends critically upon our knowing as little about such individual Puritans as possible. Such sources as diaries, letters, and criminal proceedings suggest that they may have been quite diverse. When one confronts an ostensibly "godly" Puritan with a tainted reputation (such as Angelo in Shakespeare's *Measure for Measure*), does one conclude that he was not really a Puritan since Puritans do not behave like that or, as anti-Puritan satirists and dramatists insinuate, that this is exactly how Puritans behave? One should also think carefully before describing Massachusetts as a "Puritan" commonwealth.

So the proper questions to ask are why the name Puritan came into play when it did and why it remained an important part of the vocabulary of religion and politics, at least until the collapse of the mid-seventeenth-century Interregnum. Puritans did not, at least at first, call themselves Puritans, and the term is indicative of rancor and division on a scale that had not existed before the Reformation of Henry VIII's reign. Ostensibly the English Reformation carried into schism a national church united as never before in belief, liturgical practice, and obedience to its royal head. In reality only a minority of the population was more than nominally committed to the new religion, and the nation was profoundly divided. Indications of this division were the terms of insult and derision deployed in the street wars of mid-Tudor England—for example, *new-fangled, popish,* and *scripture men*. Some of these "opprobrious" terms such as *pratlingstant,* were too much of a mouthful to stick. But in Elizabethan England *Puritan* joined *Protestant* and *papist* as landmarks on the religious map, together with *neuters,* used to describe those allegedly of no religion. To denote those religious conservatives who still attended Protestant services in the parish church, Elizabethans invented another handy term of reproach, *church papists*.

Elizabethan Puritans: "Further Reformation" and Its Frustration. The substance of Puritanism was rejection of conservative, retrogressive elements in the politically enforced Reformation. There were premonitions in the reign of Edward VI and in the congregations of Marian Exiles. But Puritans had their historical point of departure in the restoration of a carefully moderated form of Protestantism within the terms of the Elizabethan Settlement of 1559. The statutes and royal injunctions that, together with *The Book of Common Prayer* and other formularies, constituted and stabilized the Church of England in something like perpetuity enforced a liturgy that retained many traditional features, thus distinguishing the Elizabethan church from other Reformed churches with which it was in substantial doctrinal agreement. The Anglican church also retained a ministry and a constitution that were substantially reformed. Most importantly, the church kept the office of bishop and all that went with episcopacy. In many distinctive features, from the parish system to the laws of marriage, the Church of England was a kind of ecclesiastical fossil not subject to either Reformed or Tridentine reconstruction.

Traditionally historians of the Church of England have supposed that these arrangements defined an Anglicanism that was resisted on the right by an unreconciled Catholic minority and on the left by dissident Puritans. But it is not easy to identify very many Anglicans who were positively attached to those features of the church that distinguished it from other churches of the Reformation, and it is more realistic to think in terms of a contention between Protestant and Catholic tendencies within a church politically contrived to conceal and, if possible, reconcile their differences. If the Elizabethan Settlement failed to meet many expectations, then the Puritans were those who carried their discontent to the length of conscientious nonconformity and into a literary and political agitation for "further reformation."

It seems to have been Catholics, not Anglicans, who were the first to call such dissidents Puritans, with the motive of suggesting that "papists" were not the greatest threat to religious unity. In the seventeenth century it would be said that the word *Puritan* was an "essential engine" in the work of reconciling England and Rome. Those called Puritans indignantly repudiated the word, since to anyone versed in church history it implied the perfectionist heresy of the third-century Novationists or the Albigensians of the twelfth century. Far from laying claim to purity, Puritans (like Paul) boasted that they were the chiefest sinners.

The issues on which the earliest Nonconformists took up a rejectionist stance were at first confined to certain ceremonies and liturgical gestures, such as the vestment of the white linen surplice and the sign of the cross in baptism, deemed to be "popish" and unlawful. Underlying the so-called Vestiarian Controversy of the 1560s was the justified suspicion that such ceremonies had been retained for the benefit of those many closet papists still concealed in the church and its ministry. In effect, the Nonconformists took exception to sharing the same church with such people and questioned the credentials of such an elastic church. Conformist defenders of what the law said insisted not that the disputed ceremonies were beneficial, nor that they were essential, but that they were adiaphora—things indifferent—on which the lawful authority of the Christian prince could legitimately legislate for individual consciences. Nonconformists either denied the indifference of the things in dispute or held that their imposition robbed them of their indifference. The imposed ceremonies were incompatible with the principle of Christian liberty, which in its turn was connected to the Pauline notion of "edification"—a church composed of lively stones rather than artificially constructed by laws and ceremonies that were not scriptural.

Late Elizabethan apologists for the Church of England against Puritanism, such as Richard Bancroft and Richard Hooker, told a story of progressive degenerative radicalization, with which the accounts of modern historians are in essential agreement, though not always agreeing on the causes of radicalization. In the early 1570s a new generation of mostly younger Nonconformists emerged, with its intellectual leadership at the University of Cambridge and its organizational nerve center in London. Reacting to the episcopal "persecution" of the first Nonconformists and to a new and more narrowly scriptural ecclesiology propagated from Geneva and associated with Calvin's successor, Théodore de Bèze, this generation announced a more drastic diagnosis of the ills of the Elizabethan church.

It was no longer a matter of mere "shells and chippings of popery," but of a fundamentally flawed form of worship and of a ministry and discipline that was unscriptural and actually anti-Christian. This new and harder line was announced in 1572 in the anonymous pamphlet *An Admonition to the Parliament* (the work of two young London preachers, John Field and Thomas Wilcox) and in other ephemeral publications, which led to a major and definitive drafting of battle lines. John Whitgift, a future archbishop of Canterbury, published an *Answer* to the *Admonition,* provoking from the Cambridge Puritan ideologue Thomas Cartwright a series of *Replies*. The new radicals have been called, at the risk of a wild anachronism, Presbyterians. By no means, however, were all Nonconformists (or those not content with all features of the Elizabethan church) Presbyterians in the sense that they repudiated government by bishops or advocated an alternative hierarchy based on the authority over local congregations of representative synods.

The *Admonition* announced that "we in England are so far off from having a church rightly reformed that as yet we are not come to the outward face of the same." The authors had second thoughts and altered "not" to "scarce." The essence of Elizabethan Puritanism consisted in the afterthought of that "scarce." The Church of England, according to the Elizabethan Settlement, left much to be desired, though not everything. It was so far a true church, in spite of its blemished liturgy and unreformed discipline, that it was possible, indeed mandatory, to remain within its communion, which most Puritans did, forming a kind of church within the church.

Those who stayed with the "not" were bound to abandon the legally established church, as Protestants had earlier left the Roman church (both were "Babylon"), and to find another scriptural space in which to lay the foundations of a true church, a gathered and covenanted body. This was the course taken from the 1560s onward by a succession of small groups of Separatists, who consciously departed from both Puritanism and the Church of England. The East Anglian followers of Robert Brown (who would give their name to generations of Brownists) believed that the true church should be composed of "the godly, be they never so few," "without tarrying for the magistrate." Separatism, which was subject to severe repression and prone to internal disintegration, found a new leadership in the later 1580s in the pugnacious lawyer Henry Barrow. His followers formed a church that was to have a continuous if complex and fissiparous history in a diaspora that took the Separatists first to Holland and later to the Plymouth plantation in New England.

The history of Elizabethan Puritanism has to be reconstructed from unstable materials. Nonseparatist Puritans were blood brothers of the Separatists but maintained a principled stand against Separatism. Many Separatists, including Brown himself, returned to the Church of England and its opportunities for employment. So-called Puritans shared many of their aspirations with powerful forces within the Elizabethan establishment (bishops, privy councillors, and local magistrates). Contemporaries called these elements "forward" in their outlook on politico-religious issues, which in an age of religious wars were international in scope and seemed to concern the very survival of England as a Protestant state. (Queen Elizabeth I, by contrast, was conspicuously "backward.") At times and especially with the archiepiscopate of Edmund Grindal (r. 1576–1583), it may have seemed that many of these aspirations would be realized within and by the Elizabethan establishment, thus eliminating or reducing the need for Puritan Nonconformity. The effective deprivation of Grindal for softness toward Puritanism (if not for adopting Puritanism itself) was consequently a watershed of some significance.

The subsequent hardening of attitudes on the Conformist side, the queen's ticket, stimulated a radical response. This happened under Whitgift (r. 1583–1604), Grindal's successor as archbishop and Cartwright's old opponent, who attempted to impose a total conformity by suspending hundreds of ministers who could not or would not subscribe to an exacting test of conformity. The broad coalition of ministers, magistrates, and people ("gospellers" or "private Christians") that formed Elizabethan Puritanism fought back in a campaign of petitioning, pamphleteering, and parliamentary lobbying, which for a time found Whitgift and his few allies in such an exposed position that the future of episcopacy may have seemed in doubt. Insofar as Puritanism was the cause of "forwardness," it was espoused by such powerful figures in the Elizabethan state as Robert Dudley, earl of Leicester, and the secretary of state, Francis Walsingham, politicians who believed, with some reason, that the real enemy was international Catholicism. In their perception "the godly ministers" were providers and promoters of a preaching ministry, a commodity as necessary for security as salvation and still in desperately short supply. The archbishop, by contrast, was silencing the preachers and barring them from their pulpits.

Whitgift, however, had the only ally who mattered, the queen herself. By the early 1590s the cause of "further reformation" had been defeated politically, the victim of its own provoked radicalization. The Puritan church within the church was now presented as a dangerous conspiracy, especially by Bancroft, the head of ecclesiastical intelligence and a churchman destined to succeed Whitgift as primate. In 1593 the Separatist leaders—Henry Harrow, John Greenwood, and John Penry—were hanged, an act of Parliament was passed under which Protestant "sectaries" could be banished from the realm, and Puritan ministers of the stature of Cartwright were placed in peril of some of the law's harshest penalties.

All this time those on the wrong side of the ecclesiastical law and of Whitgift's and Bancroft's repressiveness were not called Puritans with consistency and almost never by Bancroft in his furious polemics against "our pretended reformers." The crystallizing of the Puritan stereotype seems to have begun in 1588–1589, when an anonymous author calling himself Martin Marprelate (almost certainly the radically Puritan member of Parliament Job Throckmorton) published a series of clandestine and viciously satiric antiepiscopal pamphlets known to English literature as the Marprelate Tracts. It was Bancroft's strategy to answer Martin "in his own vein," not only by means of anti-Martinist printed pamphlets but by lampooning the Martinists in the public theaters. This was how the "stage Puritan" originated. In 1600 Shakespeare's *Twelfth Night* would present Malvolio as "a kind of puritan" (a variation on a theme already familiar to his audience), and in 1610 and 1614 Ben Jonson would stage the most famous of anti-Puritan and anti-Separatist dramatic pieces, *The Alchemist* and *Bartholomew Fair*, which retained its polemical popularity into the 1670s. The stage Puritan helped to fix in the public mind for seventy-five years the character of the Puritan who seeks financial, political, and sexual advantage under the cloak of hypocrisy. "Marry," says one actor to another in a jestbook, "I have so naturally played the Puritan that many took me to be one."

Epigrams, characters, and satiric verses all helped. These genres would reach their apotheosis in the 1650s in Samuel Butler's mock-heroic poem *Hudibras*, a bitter verdict on the civil wars and revolutions that royalists and Anglicans blamed on Puritan "fanaticism." In many provincial towns and rural communities of early seventeenth-century England, those rancors had been anticipated in the antagonism to Puritans expressed in libelous ballads, "ballading" being a recognized form of direct political action. There was substance in the provincial politics of anti-Puritanism—resentment of ambitious ruling cliques that promoted a "severe" public morality and were suspected of self-interest. In the country Puritans campaigned against maypoles and alehouse disorders. In London they opposed the newly institutionalized theaters. But these cultural conflicts were indebted to the affair of Martin Marprelate and were anti-Martinist in finding a voice and a name.

The Seventeenth Century: Transformations and Contradictions. It is ironic that just when the stereotype of the Puritans became firmly established in the public mind and especially the sophisticated public mind, the issues contested between Nonconformists and Conformists for much of Elizabeth's reign appear to have run their course. If a drastically presbyterian restructuring of the church had ever been a serious option, it now lost all credibility. In 1593 Hooker had completed, at least in draft, the most admired and philosophically magisterial confutation of Puritanism, *The Laws of Ecclesiastical Polity*. But these matters no longer attracted much interest, and Hooker was published only with the aid of a private subvention. There is no evidence that his book had any immediate impact.

After the publication of the fifth book of *The Laws* in 1597, Hooker was subjected to a hostile review, *A Christian Letter*. The argument of this critic has been endorsed by a modern historian (Peter Lake, *Anglicans and Puritans?*, 1988). Under cover of attacking the Puritan platform, Hooker had called in question fundamental tenets of the Church of England as a Reformed church and for the first time had located the church somewhere between Geneva and Rome, acknowledging it to be a true if defective church. Hooker did not so much defend Anglicanism as invent it. The response of some Puritans was to abandon old positions and to roll up their sleeves in defense of the fundamental bulwarks that were now declared to be in danger—Reformed doctrine (in crude shorthand, "Calvinism") and a robust confutation of Catholicism as anti-Christian. At the Hampton Court Conference, summoned by James I in 1604 as a means of resettling the church, the agenda of the "plaintiffs" retained some of the more moderate concerns of the Elizabethan Puritans but betrayed a new anxiety to underwrite the church's fundamentally Reformed credentials.

James I, the victor in notable battles against his own Puritans in Scotland, perpetuated the Tudor tradition of equating religious conformity with simple obedience, uttering at Hampton Court the memorable aphorism "no bishop, no king." In the aftermath of the conference, as many as eighty ministers were deprived for Nonconformity or refusal to subscribe, which tended to perpetuate the good old cause. There were now further eruptions into Separatism, as well as strategies perfected to enjoy all the benefits of a gathered, covenanted church without separating. These devices were christened by the late Perry Miller as "non-separating Congregationalism," and their manifest destiny was realized in the colonies of New England, where Miller encountered them.

James, however, took to a fine art the distinction between moderate and more radical Puritan tendencies, looked with a tolerant eye on the former, and, instead of reconstructing the church along the reactive lines of what might be called "provocative Conformism," promoted an episcopate that balanced divergent tendencies in the upper echelons of the church. Many of his bishops—including Bancroft's successor as archbishop of Canterbury, George Abbot, and the archbishop of York, Tobie Matthew—were enthusiastic patrons of the preaching ministry and dedicated preachers themselves, sharing the essentials of a Reformed, evangelical, and anti-Catholic faith with the old but by now often conforming Nonconformists.

The consequence was that Puritanism was increasingly absorbed into the establishment or parts of the establishment. The first priority of many Elizabethan Puritans had always been the promotion of a converting, evangelical experience through the preaching and pastoral ministry and the "godly" reformation of both individuals and society. Some had felt the tension, if not a conflict, between these aspirations and a more legalistic preoccupation with ceremonies and forms. Under James I Puritanism as a program of practical religion came into its own. Its concerns were at once public and private: publicly to purge the nation and the local community of such "land-destroying sins" as swearing, neglect of the sabbath, and drunkenness; and privately to prove the salvation of the elect Christian through the strenuous exercise of those spiritual disciplines characteristic of what has been called "experimental" Calvinism.

At this point Puritanism, if it means anything, means a distinctive style of piety and religious culture, with extensive implications for the society that cultivated it or suffered its intrusive influence. These implications have included (for some scholars) capitalism, radical politics, individualism, the rise of the new science, and the invention of the modern family. How far this was a nationally distinctive religious culture, distinct from that of other Reformed communities, is a question still neglected by historians whose approach has been linguistically and theologically limited, or who have read back into Colonial America impressions of the "exceptionality" of the Puritan culture of New England. Was that form of Reformed divinity called covenant theology a distinctively Anglo-American deviation from orthodox Calvinism, as Miller thought? Was Sabbatarianism something peculiarly English? The English/New English Puritan model provided Max Weber with the paradigm of the "Protestant ethic," which he made the midwife of capitalist and bureaucratic rationality. But it was a preoccupation of late nineteenth-century German politics that directed Weber along this road.

How far one should extend the blanket cover of Puritan in any description of early seventeenth-century English civilization remains problematic. A Puritan bishop seems like a contradiction in terms. Not all "severe" magistrates who cracked down on sexual crimes and country disorders were motivated by Puritanism. On the other hand, it is certain that early Stuart society contained a kind of sub-culture of godly people whose exemplary and prodigious piety was recognized both within their own circles and to outsiders and who, if they were still from time to time called Puritans, now acknowledged the name and used it for themselves with some pride, understanding it pragmatically if not literally and presumptuously to correspond to the elect within the Calvinist scheme of things. Their semiprivate, semipublic meetings, or "conventicles," were also self-identifying, as well as symptomatic of what one may call semi-Separatism. The historian, too, knows who many of these people were—gentlemen like the Herefordshire knight Robert Harley, ministers like Harley's great friend William Gouge, and tradesmen like London furniture maker Nehemiah Wallington. If these Puritans shared many consensual convictions about the reform of society and its manners, they held them more decisively and energetically.

After about 1620 Puritanism was progressively reconstructed and repoliticized until it became a force capable of resisting Charles I and of ideologically sustaining a civil war. That was the achievement of Charles I and his archbishop William Laud, but the new anti-Puritan reaction can be traced from the later years of James I, when the king was incensed by the widespread opposition to those philo-Hispanic policies that culminated in the abortive "match" with the Spanish Infanta (1622–1623). As a consequence, the fortunes improved for the anti-Calvinist churchmen whom Peter Lake calls "avant-garde conformists" (deriving intellectually from Hooker), who were increasingly accused of the Dutch heresy of Arminianism by their enemies. Puritanism was now reconstructed and confronted by a Conformist religious style as distinctive and self-conscious as Puritanism itself. If, according to an extreme view, all Calvinists (those "of the religion") were Puritans, their ranks had swelled.

The anti-Puritan party, headed by Archbishop Laud, was in charge in the 1630s. At the level of the Court and the episcopate, it was checked only by its own internal contradictions. But in the country at large its efforts to impose new liturgical standards and fashions, widely perceived as "popish" and unorthodox, met with massive resistance. With the benefit of hindsight, it appears the Laudian program was certain to fail or to succeed only in creating a new and more broadly based Puritan opposition, which after 1640 called Laud to account and provided the religious ammunition for civil war.

In a sense all that has now been covered amounts to the pre-history of the Puritans, for it is with the winning of the civil war, the destruction of the episcopal Church of England, and the setting up of a republican commonwealth that one reaches what a famous historian called *The Rule of the Puritans in England* (C. H. Firth, 1900), a rule anticipated in Massachusetts. Now most of what had been demanded since the 1570s came to pass, at least on paper. Bishops ceased to exist, and the cathedrals were dissolved, just as the monasteries had been under Henry VIII. *The Book of Common Prayer* was replaced by a Puritan Directory of Public Worship. The sabbath was upheld as never before, and "popish" holidays, such as Christmas, were abolished. Rural sports and pastimes were disrupted, and the London theaters were closed.

Puritanism, however, had now succumbed to its own internal contradictions, with consequences that ultimately contributed to the downfall of the interregnal regime and the restoration of both the monarchy and the Church of England. Not all antiepiscopal Puritans were presbyterians. In the Westminster Assembly non-presbyterian models of a decentralized church, worked out in the laboratory of the Puritan colonies of New England, found significant support among the Independents and those of "the Congregational way." The removal of royal and episcopal constraint and censorship led to an explosion of more or less radical sects, some as radical as the Quakers, who persist as a major religious force to this day and represent a post-Puritan phase in English religious history.

The deepest contradiction of all was that between two contrary principles, always held together in tension within English Puritanism—the principle of a godly and imposed rule and discipline and the contrary principle of religious liberty, requiring the toleration of sincerely held religious differences. Such a toleration was dear to the heart of Oliver Cromwell, England's ruler in the 1650s, although such a toleration had its limits, beyond which were placed, in principle, Catholics, Anglicans, and many Quakers.

While this profoundly principled contention was continuing, the Puritans were overtaken by events and—whatever their inclination, whether to dominate or tolerate—were reduced to relative impotence as an alternately repressed and tolerated religious minority, now deeply unpopular in many quarters for its fatal association with rebellion and regicide. As Dissenters, never again to be accommodated within the national and established church and eventually no longer called Puritans, the Puritans continued to make a signal contribution to English social, political, and religious life, not only through the continued pursuit of Puritan interests and concerns (to be taken up in the eighteenth century by the Methodists and never absent from the established church itself) but also by the fact of their separated presence, making England a pluralistic and ultimately liberal rather than a monolithic and repressive society.

BIBLIOGRAPHY

Bozeman, T. D. *To Live Ancient Lives: The Primitivist Dimension in Puritanism.* Chapel Hill, N.C., 1968. A recent study which, like Foster's *The Long Argument,* bridges a gap between English and American studies.

Bremer, Francis J., ed. *Puritanism: Transatlantic Perspectives on a Seventeenth-Century Anglo-American Faith.* Boston, 1993. With reference to this article, see especially Peter Lake, "Defining Puritanism—Again?"

Cohen, C. L. *God's Caress: The Psychology of Puritan Religious Experience.* New York, 1986. The best of a number of recent accounts of this subject.

Collinson, Patrick. *The Religion of Protestants: The Church in English Society, 1559–1625.* Oxford, 1982. Emphasizes, perhaps excessively, the absorption of Puritanism into the ecclesiastical mainstream.

———. *Godly People: Essays on English Protestantism and Puritanism.* London, 1983. A variety of essays, written over a period of twenty years.

———. *English Puritanism*. Reprint, with revised bibliography, London, 1987. A more comprehensive bibliography than this short list.

———. *The Puritan Character: Polemics and Polarities in Early Seventeenth-Century English Culture*. Los Angeles, 1989. A rather extreme exposition of the nominalist line on Puritans and Puritanism.

———. *The Elizabethan Puritan Movement*. Reprint, Oxford, 1990. The standard politico-religious account of Elizabethan Puritanism.

Coolidge, John S. *The Pauline Renaissance in England: Puritanism and the Bible*. Oxford, 1970. In some ways, the most important book on the subject.

Fincham, Kenneth, ed. *The Early Stuart Church, 1603–1642*. London, 1993. An invaluable conspectus of what the younger historians of early seventeenth-century religion are saying.

Foster, Stephen. *The Long Argument: English Puritanism and the Shaping of New England Culture, 1570–1700*. Chapel Hill, N.C., 1991.

Haller, William. *The Rise of Puritanism*. New York, 1938. A historical classic, deriving the rise of Puritanism from the beginnings (in the early seventeenth century) of a literary tradition devoted to its pious memorialization.

Hill, Christopher. *Society and Puritanism in Pre-Revolutionary England*. London, 1964. Of all the author's many books which concern Puritans, the one most relevant to matters discussed in this article.

Knappen, M. M. *Tudor Puritanism: A Chapter in the History of Idealism*. Chicago, 1939. Essential reading. The subtitle accurately indicates the nature of the author's interest in the subject. It should be supplemented by a reading of Collinson, *The Elizabethan Puritan Movement*.

Lake, Peter. *Moderate Puritans and the Elizabethan Church*. Cambridge, 1982. An account of how high-ranking Cambridge academics, Puritans, reconciled their higher aspirations to the reality of their situations and to their careers.

———. *Anglicans and Puritans? Presbyterian and English Conformist Thought from Whitgift to Hooker*. London, 1988. Explains what the Admonition Controversy was "really" about, and how Richard Hooker was a milestone.

Miller, Perry. *The New England Mind: The Seventeenth Century*. New York, 1939. Holy writ, and like holy writ, subject to higher criticism.

Seaver, Paul S. *Wallington's World: A Puritan Artisan in Seventeenth-Century London*. Stanford, Calif., 1985. The inner life and religious traffic of a Puritan furniture maker, revealed by his own compulsive record keeping.

Tyacke, Nicholas. *The Fortunes of English Puritanism, 1603–1640*. London, 1990. Shows that accounts of the old Elizabethan Puritan cause as dead by the early seventeenth century (see Collinson, *The Religion of Protestants*) have been somewhat exaggerated.

Underdown, David. *Fire from Heaven: Life in an English Town in the Seventeenth Century*. London, 1992. The town is Dorchester, the shire town of Dorset. The story Underdown tells could be replicated, with variations, for many other Puritan towns.

Weber, Max. *The Protestant Ethic and the Spirit of Capitalism*. Translated by Talcott Parsons. London, 1991. A seminal work, to say the least.

PATRICK COLLINSON

PUTS, Johannes. *See* Fontanus, Johannes.

Q

QABBALAH. *See* Cabbala, Christian; Christian Hebraica; Mysticism.

QUERINI, Vincenzo (Lat., Quirinus; Eng., Quirini; 1479–1514), Venetian patrician, humanist, and diplomat, proponent of monastic and church reform after joining the Camaldolese branch of the Benedictine order and taking the name Pietro. Querini's stellar career began with his education at the University of Padua. At the age of twenty-three, he maintained forty-five hundred propositions in philosophy and theology, subsequently printed as *Conclusiones Vincentii Quirini Patritii Veneti Romae disputatae* (probably 1503), leading to the conferral of a doctorate by Pope Alexander VI. Despite his youth he was chosen Venetian ambassador to Philip I (the Fair) of Spain and Joan I of Castile in 1506, and to the emperor Maximilian I one year later. In September 1511 he changed the course of his life by entering the hermitage of Camaldoli near Florence, to which his friend Tommaso Giustiniani had preceded him. On 22 February 1512 Querini made his monastic profession.

A complex and open-minded man, Querini even as a monk maintained that salvation depended on one's closeness to God rather than on the choice of a particular vocation. He joined Giustiniani in efforts to reform the Camaldolese and in writing the famous *Libellus ad Leonem X* of 1513, a visionary and radical proposal for the revitalization of the entire church. The two Camaldolese minced no words in calling for a thorough cleansing of abuses at all levels of the hierarchy, the revision of the code of canon law, liturgical uniformity, and the tightening of discipline in religious orders. Most remarkable were their sweeping recommendations for missions to the newly discovered lands in America and for union with Eastern Christians. Querini's sudden death thwarted Pope Leo X's plan to appoint him a cardinal and therefore a proponent of reform at the highest levels of the church on the eve of the Reformation.

BIBLIOGRAPHY

Brunetti, M. "Alla vigilia di Cambrai: La legazione di Vincenzo Quirini all'Imperatore Massimiliano, 1507." *Archivio Veneto-Tridentino* 10 (1926), 1–108. Querini's diplomatic activity.

Jedin, Hubert. "Vincenzo Quirini und Pietro Bembo." In *Miscellanea Giovanni Mercati,* vol. 4, pp. 407–424. Vatican City, 1946.

Minnich, Nelson, and Elisabeth G. Gleason. "Vocational Choices: An Unknown Letter of Pietro Querini to Gasparo Contarini and Niccolo Tiepolo, April, 1512." *Catholic Historical Review* 75 (1989), 1–20. Useful bibliography.

Elisabeth G. Gleason

QUIÑONES, Francisco de los Angeles (1475–1540), Spanish cardinal, theologian, liturgist, and diplomat. The son of the count of Luna, Quiñones was related to Emperor Charles V. He studied at the University of Salamanca and joined the Franciscans in 1491. Quiñones rose to the summit in the administration of his order, serving as definitor general (1517), provincial vicar (1521), commissary general (1522), and minister general (1523).

Despite his preference for the eremitical life—which he encouraged among the Spanish Franciscans through the establishment of hermitages—Quiñones became involved in weighty civil and ecclesiastical affairs. During the Revolt of the Comuneros in Castile (1520–1521), Quiñones acted as a mediator between the rebels and the monarch, Charles V. In 1526, when Charles V alienated the papacy by pursuing war in Italy, Quiñones mediated between pope and emperor; and when the Sack of Rome made the pope Charles V's prisoner in 1527, it was Quiñones who helped gain his release and draw up a peace treaty. As a reward, Pope Clement VII made him a cardinal.

Pope Clement also asked Quiñones to produce a new breviary, the liturgical book containing the psalms, hymns, prayers, and lessons to be recited in the Divine Office of the Roman Catholic church, which, owing to various evolutions, was in need of revision. Initially designed for the private use of the clergy, Quiñones's *Breviarium Sanctae Crucis* rapidly gained popularity, even for use in the public offices of certain religious orders. Though a hundred editions were printed between 1535 and 1556, the changes made by Quiñones displeased some within the church, including the faculty of the Sorbonne; its use was prohibited by Rome in 1556, and it was finally replaced by Pope Pius V's *Breviarium Romanum* in 1568. Ironically, the breviary prepared by Quiñones, who defended the interests of Catherine of Aragon at Rome in Henry VIII's annulment case, had a profound influence on Thomas Cranmer and helped shape *The Book of Common Prayer* used by the Church of England.

BIBLIOGRAPHY

d'Alcedo, Fernando. *Le Cardinal Quiñones et la Sainte Ligue*. Bayonne, France, 1910.

Jungmann, J. A. "Warum ist das Reformbrevier des Kardinal Quiñones gescheitert?" *Zeitschrift für Katholische Theologie* 78 (1956), 98–107.

Legg, J. Wickham, ed. *The Second Recension of the Quignon Breviary*. 2 vols. London, 1908–1912. The text of the *Breviarium Sanctae Crucis*, along with a life of Quiñones and a brief liturgical history.

Meseguer Fernández, Juan. "El Padre Francisco de los Angeles Quiñones, OFM, al servicio del Emperador y del Papa." *Hispania* 73 (1958), 651–689.

Salmon, Pierre. *The Breviary through the Centuries*. Translated by D. Mary. Collegeville, Minn., 1962.

CARLOS M. N. EIRE

QUIRINUS, Vincenzo. *See* Querini, Vincenzo.

QUIROGA, Gaspar de (1499–1593), Spanish cardinal and reformer. Born at Madrigal de las Altas Torres in 1499, Quiroga studied canon law at Salamanca and Valladolid and was eventually appointed canon of Toledo by Archbishop Juan Pardo de Tavera. From 1554 to 1556 he served as auditor of the Roman Rota, where his regalism brought him to the attention of the Spanish court. In 1558 he was named inspector of monasteries in Naples and Sicily and a member of the Council of Castile. Though he was already an old man, his preferment thereafter was rapid—president of the Council of Italy (1567), bishop of Cuenca (1572), inquisitor general (1573), archbishop of Toledo (1577), and cardinal (1578).

As primate of Spain, Quiroga's greatest achievement was to implement the decrees of the Council of Trent. His primary concern was for lay education and for the reform of popular piety, which he sought to achieve through an extensive program of catechization. To separate the sacred from the profane, he reduced the number of festivals and banned bullfights and other secular pastimes from religious celebrations. In 1581 he directed the publication of a new *Manual de los sacramentos* that would standardize their administration throughout the country. In the following year Quiroga convened a special synod at Toledo to establish minimum standards for ordination, condemn absenteeism, and introduce a system for imposing clerical discipline.

Quiroga was not an intellectual but rather a skilled and cautious ecclesiastical statesman who sought reform by consensus. Though he encouraged the establishment of seminaries, he agreed with his own diocesan clergy that Toledo could not afford one. As inquisitor general he extended the tribunal's jurisdiction but was generally fair-minded and concerned less with formal heresy than with the correction of popular errors. He patronized the arts as an aid to faith and supported El Greco (Doménikos Theotokópoulos), who painted his portrait.

BIBLIOGRAPHY

Boyd, Maurice. *Cardinal Quiroga, Inquisitor-General of Spain*. Dubuque, 1954.

WILLIAM S. MALTBY

R

RABELAIS, François

RABELAIS, François (1483?–1553), French writer. Although more commonly known as a comic writer and satirist, Rabelais was also a bold humanist and a prudently fierce champion of religious reform in an Erasmian spirit. As a novice caught learning Greek, he was expelled from the Franciscan order and was then admitted to the Benedictine; he was now in fact able to initiate a correspondence with Erasmus. He further broadened his horizons by obtaining a medical degree from the University of Montpellier while also participating in one of the first sanctioned human dissections. He was thus ready to practice medicine at the Hôtel Dieu in Lyon (1532) and to travel to Rome (1534, 1535, 1547) as the private secretary and physician to Cardinal Jean du Bellay, the ambassador to the Vatican, and in the same capacity later sojourned in Turin (1540, 1542) with the cardinal's brother, Guillaume. He would have to flee Paris for Metz after his *Tiers Livre* (1546) was censured by the Sorbonne, just as his *Pantagruel* (1532) and *Gargantua* (1534) had been and as his *Quart Livre* (1552) would be.

Indeed, Rabelais challenged the dogmatism of the Sorbonne theologians because he advocated broader access to the scriptures, hence to its recent translation into French by Jacques Lefèvre d'Étaples (1523, 1528), protected by Marguerite d'Angoulême, to whom he dedicated his *Tiers Livre*. Marguerite was at the center of a reform movement known as evangelism, and Rabelais was certainly in its orbit. This movement had no schismatic aim but intended rather more textual, exegetical readings of the scriptures, while excising scholastic commentaries and bringing more to the fore the Old Testament. This reform movement soon had to go underground as a result of the Affaire des Placards (1534).

The dangers of continuing to adhere to censored opinions did not deter Rabelais from maintaining his beliefs before 1534, in *Pantagruel*, and he did not hesitate to do so afterward in his *Tiers Livre* and *Quart Livre*; nor did he refrain from lashing out at the dogmatism of Luther and Calvin. Thus staying his course, for example in the *Quart Livre*, he has his heroic travelers start on their journey under the aegis and blessing of "When Israel came out of Egypt."

Rabelais was a reformist, not a reformer; he never left or even intended to leave the church. Like Dante and others, he took to task those in Rome and those he considered deceivers and abusers of the word, but not the institution of the church. Among his many barbs toward the church, he questioned the desirability of pilgrimages and even of celibacy to some degree; he also sneered, for example, at the doctrinaire status of the decretals that were assuming an ascendancy over the scriptures. In a sense, he was an idealist who wished to have people read his own text and the scriptures without prejudice, namely not reductively; this would assume at all times a natural goodness of humanity, of which laughter is an integral and therapeutic part.

BIBLIOGRAPHY

Febvre, Lucien. *The Problem of Unbelief in the Sixteenth Century: The Religion of Rabelais.* Translated by Beatrice Gottlieb. Cambridge, 1982. A basic study of the subject.

Frame, Donald M., trans. *The Complete Works of François Rabelais.* Berkeley, 1991. One of the most readable translations.

Higman, Francis M. *Censorship and the Sorbonne, 1520–1551.* Geneva, 1979. The standard work for Rabelais's period.

———. *La Diffusion de la Réforme en France, 1520–1565.* Geneva, 1992. A basic study for background material and primary texts.

Krailsheimer, A. J. *Rabelais and the Franciscans.* Oxford, 1963. Valuable study for the impact of the Franciscan world on Rabelais's humanistic and religious thought.

Screech, M. A. *L'Evangélisme de Rabelais.* Geneva, 1959. The standard work on this issue.

MARCEL TETEL

RACOVIAN CATECHISM

RACOVIAN CATECHISM. When the Polish Reformed church split into two movements in 1565, the new movement that came into existence was the Minor Reformed church of Poland, popularly known as the Polish Brethren. The Racovian Catechism, an antitrinitarian publication first issued in 1605, served as a statement of belief for the Polish Brethren.

Although the Polish Brethren at first embraced a variety of religious views including tritheism, ditheism, and the strict monotheism that would eventually be called Unitarianism, some coherence soon developed under the leadership of Simon Ronemberg, who led the community that was established at Racow (Raków), Poland, in 1569. George Schomann, one of the leaders of the Polish Brethren, prepared a short catechism, *Catechesis et confessio fidei, coetus per Poloniam congregati . . .* (Kraków, 1574), for the use of members of his family and others. This catechism reflected the faith of the Polish Brethren before the advent of Fausto Sozzini in 1579.

Sozzini, whose influence from 1579 to his death in 1604 was great, advocated the strict unity of God; the threefold office of prophet, king, and priest of the strictly human Jesus of Nazareth, whom God resurrected and to whom God gave a divine office (divinity by office, not by nature); and the suppression of the Anabaptist theme of regenerative adult baptism. From about 1590 until his death, Sozzini exercised dominant leadership among the Polish Brethren, and he sought to ensure his influence with them by his *Praelectiones Theologicae* (Theological Lectures; written in 1592 and published in 1609), his Racow lectures to his closest followers of 1601 and 1602, and his *Christianae Religionis brevissima institutio, per interrogationes et responsiones, quam Catechismum vocant* (Instruction in the Christian Religion through Questions and Answers, Called a Catechism; begun in 1603 and published in 1611). He did not live to complete this last work.

The task then fell to his followers, four of whom undertook the responsibility of collating and preserving Sozzini's theological legacy in a book that became well known as the *Racovian Catechism.* The name was drawn from Racow, the intellectual and spiritual center of their movement. The first edition was published in 1605 under the long Polish title *Katechism zbory tych ludzi, który w Królestwie Polskim, y w Wielkim Xiéstwie Litewskim, y w innych Pańśtwach do Korony nalezących, twierdzą y wyznawaią, ze nikt inszy, jedno Ociec Pana naszego Jezusa Christusa, iest onym iedynym Bogiem Izraelskim, a on człowiek Jezus Nazaránski który sie z Panny narodził, a nie zaden inszy oprócz niego, abo przed nim, iest iednorodzonym Synem Bozym* (Catechism of the Assembly of Those People Who in the Kingdom of Poland, and in the Grand Duchy of Lithuania, and in the Other Dominions Belonging to the Crown, Affirm and Confess, That No Other than the One Father of Our Lord Jesus Christ is the Only God of Israel; and the Man Jesus of Nazareth, Who Was Born of a Virgin, and No Other Besides Him is the Only Begotten Son of God). There is a unique copy of this first edition in the Polish National Library at Warsaw.

The work was intended not so much for internal use by the Polish Brethren themselves as for proclaiming their beliefs to others in the hope of winning converts. Peter Statorius Stoinski, minister of the Polish Brethren's congregation at Sozzini's final residence, Lucławice (and later at Racow), organized the project. After his death on 9 May 1605, Valentine Schmalz (Smalcius) appears to have guided the project and was aided by Jerome Moskorzowski (Moscorovius) and John Völkel, Sozzini's secretary for many years.

Other editions were later published. A second Polish edition, appeared in 1619; in 1608 Schmalz prepared a German translation, reprinted in 1612; and Moskorzowski prepared a Latin translation in 1609. A generation later, when the Polish Brethren were in exile, they published several other editions and translations.

Schomann's *Catechesis* of 1574 contributed a number of features to the *Racovian Catechism,* particularly the structural organization of the threefold office of Christ as prophet, king, and priest. In general, however, the two catechisms are marked more by their differences than by their similarities, owing to the influence of Sozzini.

The central theme of the *Racovian Catechism* is that God revealed through Jesus Christ the way to attain to eternal life. There are short discussions of the authority of holy scripture. A discussion of the way of salvation is followed by chapters on the importance of knowledge of God and knowledge of Christ. Knowledge of God's nature and will centers on knowing that God is one, not three-in-one, and that Jesus was a real human, born of a virgin, resurrected by God, and given the divine office of guardianship over the church in the Father's behalf.

There is also an extensive, detailed discussion of Christ's prophetic office—the longest section of the book—which includes considerations of Christ's commands that were added to the Law; the Lord's Supper (a memorial ceremony commanded by Christ); baptism; promises of eternal life and of the Holy Spirit; confirmation of the divine will; the death of Christ; faith; free will; and justification. The book concludes with short sections on the kingly office of Christ as judge of all and rewarder of those who are righteous; his priestly office, in which he makes intercession for us; and the church of Christ.

The entire organization of the book, was influenced by Sozzini's view of the authority of scripture and his concept of humanity as mortal by nature. Eternal life comes only through divine resurrection. Christ's resurrection, not his death, is the central event in the scheme of salvation. The catechism emphasizes human free will, opposing doctrines of predestination and original sin.

The *Racovian Catechism* effectively made known the beliefs of the Polish Brethren and therefore was received with hostility by more conservative Christians. It was attacked repeatedly. Later editions of the catechism bear evidence of the Polish Brethren's exile in the Netherlands, and of the criticism by Hugo Grotius of Sozzini's doctrine of the atonement.

BIBLIOGRAPHY

Primary Sources

Catechesis Racoviensis, seu, Liber Socinianorum Primarius, ex Fidem Editionis Anno MDCIX. 1739 "refutation" with full text.

Catechism of the Churches of Poland. Stauropolis, 1680.

The Racovian Catechism, with Notes and Illustrations, translated from the Latin: To which is Prefixed a Sketch of the History of Unitarianism in Poland and the Adjacent Countries. Translated by Thomas Rees. Reprint, London and Lexington, Ky., 1962. Contains lengthy historical introduction.

The Racovian Catechisme. Amsterdam, 1652.

Secondary Sources

Kawecka-Gryczowa, Alodia. *Ariańskie oficyny wydawnicze Rodeckiego I Sternackiego: Dzieje i bibliografia; Les imprimeurs des antitrinitaires polonais Rodecki et Sternacki, Histoire et bibliographie.* Kraków, 1974. Detailed information on editions of the Catechism published in Poland and in exile (Amsterdam, London). Text in Polish and French.

Wilbur, Earl Morse. *A History of Unitarianism, Socinianism, and its Antecedents.* Reprint, Boston, 1977. The standard source for the historical context, with a chapter on the Catechism.

Williams, George H. "The Polish Brethren: Documentation of the History and Thought of Unitarianism in the Polish-Lithuanian Commonwealth and in the Diaspora, 1601–1685." In *Proceedings of the Unitarian Historical Society* 18, pts. 1 and 2 (1976–1977, 1978–1979); also in *Harvard Theological Studies* 30, pts. 1 and 2 (1980). Important, detailed information on different editions of the Catechism.

———. *The Radical Reformation.* 3d ed. Kirksville, Mo., 1992. Authoritative on the historical context and theological issues involved.

Wrzecionko, Paul. "Die Theologie des Rakower Katechismus." *Kirche im Osten* 6 (1963), 73–116. A careful philosophical and theological analysis.

JOHN C. GODBEY

RADAŠÍN, Michael (also Radácsi, Radaschinus, Radašovský, surname Liburnus; 1510?–1566), pastor, theologian, and ecclesiastical administrator in Upper Hungary (Slovakia). Born in Liburnia (in Dalmatia), Radašín, a Croat, matriculated at the University of Wittenberg in 1529. Upon his return to Austria he briefly served as pastor in Hainburg (1539–1540) and then moved to nearby Bratislava, where he lived until 1544. Although he had ben recommended for a pastorate in the wealthy mining city of Banská Bystrica in central Slovakia, he accepted the pastorate in Bardejov in eastern Slovakia.

Two years after taking up his post, Radašín was elected the first evangelical senior of Šariš county and of the five free royal cities (Bardejov, Prešov, Košice, Levoča, and Sabinov) at the synod of 1546, which adopted the Augsburg Confession and the *Loci communes* of Philipp Melanchthon as their doctrinal standard. The synod also accepted sixteen articles concerning the teaching and practices of their Lutheran congregations.

Radašín compiled a collection of sixty-eight liturgical prayers that was used throughout the region (*Gebethe nach der Summa der Evangelien*), two meditations on the nativity of Jesus, and notes for a commentary on the letters to Timothy, which he never completed. He also probably collaborated with or at least edited the *Confessio Pentapolitana,* prepared by Leonard Stöckel (1549). Although he received calls in 1556 from both Levoča and Košice to serve as pastor, he remained in Bardejov until his death in October 1566.

As senior, Radašín was expected to regularly visit the congregations of the region, including those in the towns belonging to the free cities, in order to supervise the life and doctrine of the clergy. Together with Stöckel, the rector of the "humanist" school of Bardejov, Radašín helped to foster the spread and the consolidation of Lutheranism throughout the entire region and engaged in theological controversies with Matthias Lauterwald, Paul Thury, Francis Stancarus, and others.

BIBLIOGRAPHY

Hajduk, Andrej "Michal Radašín, ná prvý senior." *Cirkevné listy* 91 (1978), 186–189.

———. "Literárne dielo Michala Radaina." *Cirkevné listy* 104 (1991), 151–152.

ANDREJ HAJDUK

RADICAL REFORMATION. Outwardly this movement was formed by congeries of reforming and actively or passively separatist churches, communes, sects, itinerant evangelists, prophets, and brooders that left or did not join the territorial churches of the three major confessions—Lutheran, Calvinist, and Anglican. Also called the Left Wing of the Reformation, the radical Reformation clashed with Protestant reformers, who in one way or another were allied with the established order or state—that is, the magisterial Reformation ordained by kings, princes, and city-states and their often university and theologically trained advisers, masters (*magistri*), and holders of theological doctorates (*doctores*).

This sociologically radical and theologically primitivist movement shared with the magisterial Reformation the yearning for divine immediacy, the recovery of the scriptures, and the ardent impulse to renovate society at large. The radical Reformation followed Andreas Bodenstein von Karlstadt and then Martin Luther in eliminating the intercessory role of the saints, including *Maria Mediatrix*, and in accepting as "the sole Mediator between God and men, the *man* Christ Jesus" (*1 Tm.* 2:5). Like the magisterial Reformation, the radical Reformation accepted a clergy committed to family life.

In sharp contrast with classical Protestantism, even the many clerically and humanistically trained teachers among the radicals disparaged humanist learning and trilingual classical education. They espoused the simpler life of the peasants and artisans, dressed plainly, and preferred vernacular Bibles. Radical reformers spurned tradition when they refuted or ignored the doctrine of original sin, the belief that the first trespass of Adam and Eve universally caused sin and death, which was vanquished only by the death and resurrection of the Second Adam, Jesus Christ. Most radicals also quietly abandoned or marginalized the dogmatic medieval view of a three-tiered afterlife of heaven, purgatory, and hell.

Not until the Fifth Lateran Council (1517) had the church authoritatively defined the human soul as naturally immortal, and most of the radicals embraced a primitive and scriptural eschatology, believing in the sleep of the soul until the general resurrection of the dead. Like the young Luther, most radicals (and even a Lutheran like William Tyndale) were Christian mortalists, awaiting the imminent resurrection of all reanimated flesh before the second advent of Christ and the Last Judgment. The radicals, accepting natural death, eschewed divinely predetermined election of only a few from all the mass of humanity assigned to purgatory or doomed to hell. By various strategies the radicals, mostly inconspicuously, abandoned exceptionalism by grace. Almost all believed that upon the resurrection of the body God would reward the righteous with eternal life and punish the unrighteous or, more mercifully, consign them to eternal oblivion. The radical Reformation in all its three subgroupings was eschatologically intense.

When one distinguishes *reform* from *reformation*, the radicals can be called the "separatist reform" or the "radical restitution" (Franklin Littell) for aiming to restore primitive Christianity. But "radical Reform*ation*" properly links these disparate movements in the Reformation era, sharing with the classical reformers the basic intent to return to the scriptures without the intermediation of sacerdotal authority.

Radical Reformation suggests a return to the roots of Christianity—a motif also shared with magisterial Protestants—but linked to a final break with the established church, the repudiation of baptism in infancy, and usually the insistence on believers' baptism. Radicals often reordained their ministers, engaged in extensive missionary campaigns, and even faced martyrdom in confrontation with established authorities. As part of a Christian renaissance, radicals tried to liberate Christianity from Constantinian and medieval incrustations. Persecution by state-church authorities or even the populace was to the radicals often interpreted as the seal of the authenticity of their mission to restore the pure church and recover the assignments of the apostolic age.

Since they usually practiced rebaptism, the radicals were pilloried by outsiders as Anabaptists. Rebaptism was a capital offense in the ancient Christian world in the codes of Theodosius II and Justinian I, and Emperor Charles V resurrected these codes against Anabaptism with the consent of Lutherans and Catholics alike at the Diet of Speyer (1529).

With the removal of external authority—such as the papacy, hierarchy, and regulated cultus—and the repudiation of religious coercion on the part of the Inquisition and of the new magistracy, the original diversity of scriptures (the radicals' solely acknowledged authority) reasserted itself and could no longer be contained, not even by the new authorities like Luther and Calvin. Thus, the variegated radical Reformation reflects a similarly variegated biblical legacy. Still, historians in identifying individuals or movements must stress the unique or peculiar, while traditional polemics stressed distinctions, concealing common premises. Typology is used here to rectify some distortions and to identify basic historical commonalities.

The radical Reformation includes three major intertwined subgroupings—the Anabaptists, the spiritualists, and the evangelical rationalists—all with regional and ecclesio-theological variants, reflecting their uneven distribution from Spain to Ukraine and from Sicily and the kingdom of Naples to southern England and the Low Countries. As the third force of the Reformation era, the other being the Counter-Reformation, the radical Reformation was an interrelated religio-social entity and dynamic, not a merely conceptual aggregate of opponents of the three main Protestant churches.

The historiography that separates the radical Reformation as a conceptual unity distinct from magisterial Protestantism was, ironically, inaugurated in the comprehensive but polemical treatment of "Anabaptism" by the Reformed divine Heinrich Bullinger (1504–1575) of Zurich. To him the radical Reformation was a many-headed monster reared up against the true Reformation, and the unitive principle was demonic. Though an anti-Remonstrant in Holland disparaged the heirs there of the radical Reformation as "the garbage wagon of the Reformation," Polish Brother and chronicler, Stanislas Lubeniecki (d. 1675) regarded Socinianism as "the climax of the Reformation" begun by Luther. Modern historians have, in the meantime, joined to help differentiate and define the three sixteenth-century radical thrusts.

Alfred Hegler, in his *Geschichte des Spiritualismus in der Reformationszeit* (1892), identified a distinctive spirituality that he called spiritualism, eventually susceptible to expanded meanings. Sebastian Franck (1499–1542)—sometime Lutheran pastor, geographer, and chronicler—was to Hegler the archetypical spiritualist, a term going back to the Spiritual Franciscans and unrelated to occultism. Franck, a quasi-mystical seeker and proponent of religious toleration, sympathetically described many forms of Anabaptism and spiritualism.

Franck relied heavily on Deutero-Taulerian mysticism, popularized in Luther's editions of *Theologia Deutsch* (1516 f.) and Bodenstein's treatises on renunciation (*Gelassenheit*) of 1520 and 1523. Thus, in the typology of Ernst Troeltsch in *Die Soziallehren der christlichen Kirchen und Gruppen* (1912; The Social Teachings of the Christian Churches, 1931), Franck, on the basis of Hegler's monograph, became the paradigm of the mystic-type in his socio-religious scheme, which also included the church-type and the sect-type of religious community. Troeltsch (1865–1923), with the input of Max Weber (1864–1920), recognized that almost any modern state church in Europe and almost all disestablished state churches in the United States and elsewhere, along with many denominations of "sectarian" antecedents, converge in morphology as "churches" (and eventually as "denominations"), distinct from the programmatically separatist and otherworldly "sects." Troeltsch freed the term *church* for broader typological usage over against both the gathered sect and the self-disciplining and spiritualizing or mystical fellowship (the spiritual *ecclesiola* in or outside the public church.)

Troeltsch's work lies behind the conceptualization of this article. Besides several Anabaptist subgroups, historiographers, in still shifting nomenclature, now increasingly distinguish from them the spiritualists (spiritualizers) and the evangelical rationalists. The latter were latently present in the early Reformation but did not surface as the third distinct subgrouping until the Catholic Counter-Reformation provoked the flight of many reform-minded Italians or failed to halt their "inner migration" while they conformed as quietistic Nicodemites.

During the early Reformation the figure who singularly embodied radicality in several potential directions was Bodenstein (1486–1541). All along Bodenstein deviated from Luther in softening the doctrine of predestination, leaving all human beings free to choose their destiny on the basis of universal prevenient grace.

Having taught at the University of Wittenberg longer than Luther, Bodenstein—indirectly challenging the Saxon elector Frederick—celebrated the first publicly "Protestant" Communion on Christmas 1521, doing so without vestments and omitting the fixed prayer of eucharistic consecration and the elevation of the elements. His service was conducted in German with the lay communicants taking the bread in their hands and sharing the wine. In Orlamünde Bodenstein encouraged lay participation in common worship, renounced his degrees as "Brother Andrew," and introduced the congregational singing of psalms in the vernacular. He also restored foot washing after Communion.

Bodenstein did not resort to rebaptism but did abolish infant baptism in Orlamünde in 1524; in his treatises on the Lord's Supper, printed in Basel with the support of Felix Mantz and other radicals from Zurich, Bodenstein encouraged a total break with sacramentalism. Bodenstein's brother-in-law, Gerhard Westerburg, became the first Bodensteinian to entertain rebaptism, but the first to put it in practice in the Reformation-era context were Mantz and Conrad Grebel (c.1498–1526) on 21 January 1525, followed by a Communion service among themselves. Mantz became the first Anabaptist martyr when he was drowned in Zurich on 5 January 1527. In 1525, sympathetic with the social outrage of the peasants, Bodenstein preached among them during their uprising.

Chafing under Luther's restrictions, Bodenstein left Saxony for the last time in 1528. Although Bodenstein ultimately conformed in the emerging Swiss Reformed—rather than Lutheran—context, he provided biblical and theological grounding for separatist spiritualism, as well as Anabaptism, if not so much for the still inchoate evangelical rationalism, though Bodenstein, like many among the evangelical rationalists, was an alienated and egalitarian intellectual who cast aside his doctoral degrees, wore plain clothing, and tried to become a peasant. From 1521 to 1528 in Saxony and during his final Reformed phase, 1528–1542, in Switzerland, Bodenstein had embodied or anticipated many features of sixteenth-century radicality in his convictions, thought, strategy, and even temperament and passion. Complex Bodenstein had freely used moral and rationalistic arguments to uphold personal responsibility, to define the human nature of Christ, and to attack convention and tradition concerning baptism and the Lord's Supper.

Spiritualists and Spiritualizers. Some separatist spiritualists abstained from Communion in the local parish and broke with the organized church or sect, maintaining personal piety in new fellowships of seekers. Spiritualizers of suspended sacraments and spiritualists driven by the Spirit ranged from the eschatological and learnedly contemplative like Kaspar von Schwenckfeld (d. 1561), to the eschatological and angrily prophetic like Bodenstein and Thomas Müntzer (d. 1525). Often they criticized the rigidities that develop in any religion and the often oppressive social consequences.

Socioreligious typology recognizes among the contemplative spiritualists and spiritualizers a distinct piety of the disciplined, devout, charismatic, and prophetic and sees their modality of spiritualism at the core of many a new sect or church (as an *ecclesiola in ecclesia*) or even as escaping all the structures of church or sect in favor of eclectic spiritual freedom (not unlike some scholarly liberal Christians who first identified this type of spirituality). This modality of spiritualism was embodied in prayer and preaching circles in Spain, Italy, and France, as well as in Germany and eastward.

Spiritualists—of varying temperaments and divergent in theology, especially on the sacraments (ordinances) and eschatology—were often intellectuals with or without higher education. In different eras and locales they acquired distinctive and circumstantial labels that often keep them from being recognized generically as spiritualists or spiritualizers. They all had been nurtured by a church or sect, but became dissatisfied with ecclesial organizations and cultus. Eclectic and often headstrong, they often tactically or devoutly favored religious toleration.

In the lands that, amid socioreligious upheaval, settled down as territorially Catholic or Protestant, spiritualists were dissatisfied with any form of magisterial Protestantism and particularly with Catholicism in Romance lands, often feigning nominal conformity to the gradually more exacting standards of public adhesion and practice. During their inward migration of loyalties, they were sustained by a network of friends and correspondents and by prayer-group pieties. In contrast, prophetic spiritualism was often angry, fiercely evangelical, and iconoclastic toward perceived idolatry, as with many scorned Sacramentarians and other spiritualizers in Germany, the Netherlands, England, Silesia, Moravia, Poland, and Palatinate Lithuania. Spiritualists, like many Anabaptists, often adhered to variants of the originally Valentinian Gnostic doctrine of the celestial flesh of Christ that protected his human nature from original sin and was thought to sanction their perfectionism.

Spiritualism sometimes became manifest as a final phase of disciplined Anabaptism, as with Hans Denck (c.1500–1527), who abandoned its originating asperities on becoming a spiritualizer. A tolerant unitarianizing spirituality was, indeed, often the final stage of several former Anabaptists. A sometimes outwardly conforming spiritualism was evident among unitarianizing Anabaptists such as the Adam Pastorians, the Gabrielites (Gabriel Ascherham), the Obbenites (Obbe Philips), and some David Jorists.

Almost paradigmatic for Troeltsch and Weber's definition of contemplative spiritualism was the community led by Kaspar von Schwenckfeld (1489–1561). Schwenckfeld, early a reformer in Silesia, sadly imposed here and elsewhere in Germany the suspension (*Stillstand*) of the Lord's Supper (1529) pending ecumenical clarification of the meaning of this "feast of love and reconciliation" because it had provoked such bitter strife. In his views on spiritualizing baptism and the Eucharist, Schwenckfeld resembled the Dutch Sacramentarian Wessel Gansfort (d. 1489) and anticipated the seventeenth-century nonsacramental Quakers.

Another spiritual trajectory led to a comparable spirituality among the (Sebastian) Franckists, the Loists (Loy Pruystinck [d. 1544]), the Familists (Family of Love, followers of Hendrik Niclaes [1502–1582]), and speculative brooders of often creative intellect. They, too, were a disparate company, often reviled as notorious heresiarchs. Their distinctive personalities easily escape the net of typology. For example, Michael Servetus (1509–1553), a practitioner of baptism by immersion at age thirty—the presumed moment of Jesus' own immersion by John the Baptist—is seldom classed among the Anabaptists or the other subgroupings, partly because he was born in Navarre, distant from their homelands, and partly because of his idiosyncratic theological system, which included an economic (dispensational) doctrine of the Trinity. Servetus also believed in the celestial flesh of Christ without human insemination. A physician, he discovered the pulmonary circulation of the blood while trying to identify the specific work of the Holy Spirit. Condemned to death in Geneva as an antitrinitarian at the instigation of Calvin, but then burned at the stake despite Calvin's objections to this form of execution, Servetus was *sui generis* an eschatological spiritualist who sought a pansophist understanding of body, mind, and soul.

A learned scriptural spiritualist, the Christian Hebraist Matthias Vehe-Glirius (d. 1590) was widely influential from the Rhineland to Poland and Transylvania. He became a Judaizer as a consequence of his trilingual scholarship and held, as did many early Christians, that believers should live communally disciplined lives while awaiting the final return of Jesus. There were enough Christian Hebraists who became in effect ethnically gentile Jews in a primitive Christian modality to constitute almost a fourth subtype of sixteenth-century radicalism. Vestigially they were Christian in awaiting the return of the human Jesus as messiah and celebrating in his memory a simple supper. Francis (Ferencz) Dávid (1520–1579)—the Unitarian Reformed superintendent in Transylvania and sponsor of Vehe-Glirius—before his own imprisonment and death approached this extreme reductionism in the final stage of his Unitarianism, refusing to regard Jesus as other than a great prophet but fervently foreseeing as imminent his return for the Last Judgment.

Anabaptists. In the pre-Constantinian era rebaptizing "rigorists" contended with the "laxists." The division persisted between Donatists and Catholics in North Africa. They had their medieval analogue in the monks and friars with the monastic vow and rigorous communal life apart from the world. Rebaptism was practiced by the Czech Brethren (Bohemian Brethren, heirs of the Hussites) for all recruits from beyond their own birthright community. Their baptismally immersed counterparts in Poland and Lithuania, resolved to avoid the notoriety of the bellicose Anabaptists of Münster (1535), always called themselves simply brethren and sisters. Rebaptism constituted a common bond among most radicals, including the Polish Brethren (except Fausto Sozzini). Anabaptists, baptized on profession of faith, saw themselves as recruits in the company of Christ and his apostles, and spoke of baptism of believers and hence eventually of "believers baptism" and thought of themselves as the "baptist-minded" reformers

German, Dutch, and English Anabaptists. Centuries of controversy having abated, and with the ecumenical benevolence of others, the descendants of the first Germanic rebaptizers vindicated themselves in the public domain, calling themselves in German simply *Taüfer* ("baptists") or in Dutch *Doopsgezinden* ("people of the baptizing persuasion"), terms, however, largely limited to these languages. In English *Anabaptists* continues to be used for those who practiced adult baptism in the Reformation era, whether or not they used the term themselves. The term is best used primarily for the Reformation era.

The most important variants of Anabaptism were found in the German and Netherlandish realms. This includes the Anabaptism of southeastern England, introduced by Dutch and Flemish refugees, although some new traits developed as the movement became Anglicized. About two-thirds of the Germanic Anabaptists (not the Swiss Brethren) appropriated the doctrine of Christ's celestial flesh, which sets Jesus apart even in his human nature. This doctrine was introduced into Anabaptism by Melchior Hoffman (1495?–

1543) and slightly modified by Menno Simons (c.1496–1561) among Mennonites.

Three subgroupings, located in three main regions, are emphasized in studies of Germanic Anabaptism. The first—separatism in Zurich—overflowed into German territory from the border of the Swiss and Rhaetian confederations northward. This movement, including Michael Sattler, embodied recoil in chagrin at the bloody failure of the peasant uprisings for social justice (1524–1525). The second hearth was Nuremberg in 1526, when the humanist Denck rebaptized Hans Hut, a fiery preacher of apocalyptic fervor. Because of the final shift of trilingual Denck toward spiritualization and also his premature death (1527), his more analogous than derivative movement has not until recently been clearly distinguished. Not so commonly included here are the university humanist Balthasar Hubmaier and his stalwart wife, who preceded him in their execution as Anabaptists (1528). Hubmaier accepted the role of magistracy and the temporal sword. The third subgrouping centered in Emden, East Frisia, where Hoffman, a furrier and roving preacher of Schwäbisch-Hall, baptized Jan Matthijs in 1530 and initiated the Lower German–Dutch phase of what became increasingly bellicose Anabaptism. This led to the mass conversion of Münster and dependent towns and insurrection in 1534–1535 in a popular movement that would be called Hoffmanite or, in its violent phase, Melchiorite or Münsterite.

Recoiling from the unexpected violence, the survivors of Münster and allied communes such as Amsterdam took the name of Mennonites in reference to Menno Simons (1496–1561), a former priest, who in 1536 shepherded the stricken followers of a social revolution into separatist, pacifist communities, highly disciplined by the frequent imposition of the ban, even between spouses. His own missionizing extended from the Netherlands to the mouth of the Vistula. His main ideas were embodied in his *Foundation Book* (in Low German, 1539), successively revised and translated. In another, less widespread version, Germanic Anabaptism took the name of another mentor, Jacob Hutter (1500?–1536), who was in effect the posthumous founder of all the related communes of Hutterites from the Rhineland to Moravia. With the Mennonites they survive to the present.

Since the German, Dutch, and English subgroupings are set forth in the article on Anabaptism, the less-known Anabaptists in Italy and Slavic lands will be covered further. None of the Italian and Slavic Anabaptists went through an insurrectionary phase. The various Slavic Brethren, as they called themselves, were, in fact, reacting against accommodations to "worldly" means on the part of the first philo-Protestant leadership in their lands, while the Italians did the same in a Catholic context.

Italian Anabaptists. Numerous conventicles of Italian Anabaptists extended from Sicily and Calabria to the French, German, and Slavic frontiers. Many members fled to Moravia for refuge among the Hutterites. They were of two strands—those Italian sectaries who were converted by contagion or by Germanic Anabaptists during their missions abroad and those who were former Marranos, often long-Christianized Jews who may have known of Jewish proselyte baptismal cleansing. They were drawn to Anabaptism out of their yearning for a purified Christianity. The two Italianate strands were not everywhere entirely distinct. Because of their common desire to return to scriptural sources, pious and often learned Marranos who became Anabaptists were highly esteemed by converts of non-Jewish stock because of their knowledge of the biblical languages and because of their courageous espousal of evangelical Christianity. Both types of Italian Anabaptists were drawn to the spirituality of the Castilian humanist Juan de Valdés (1500/10–1541) and his twin brother, Alfonso (c.1500–1533).

It was Pietro Manelfi who first distinguished the "old" strand of the Tirolese-Venetian type from the "new" strand of the Neapolitan-Sicilian type, which had evangelical Marranist antecedents. Distinctive features of all Italian Anabaptists were their sustained pacifism, discipline, devotion to scripture study, devotional prayer, preaching, prophecy, and evangelization through sustained missions in Italy and abroad. To both types the Lord's Supper was a solemn commemoration of Christ's suffering and a joyful anticipation of Christ's final return and vindication.

The first references to Italian Anabaptists, beginning in 1526, include people of all classes and motivations. As Anabaptists they were not explicitly credal, merely traditional and scriptural, never expressly challenging the Nicene or the Chalcedonian formularies, but content with the Apostles' Creed.

The first recorded Italian Anabaptist was the Tirolean master Antonio Marangone, a Venetian carpenter, who was tried in 1533 and sentenced to life imprisonment in 1535. His testimony documents the transition in Italy from "Lutheranism" to Anabaptism. Antonio's Lutheran legacy included predestination, salvation by faith alone, and the priesthood of all believers. Antonio also regarded Saint Peter as the only pope. He avoided infant baptism and then espoused adult rebaptism as a disavowal of Roman jurisdiction. He believed in spiritual Communion—without reception—at the parish Mass, which he otherwise found idolatrous. He denied purgatory and eschewed the doctrine of the Trinity.

Giacometto (the Stringer) Stingaro, a haberdasher of Vicenza, rebaptized many and became the first Italian Anabaptist to produce his own writings as "bishop of his church." In 1547 he addressed his "brethren in Christ" in a semiliterate but profoundly biblical tract entitled *La rivelatione*, wherein he clarified his doctrine on the basis of scripture, notably the New Testament. He distinguished Christ's common humanity from Christ's Spirit and held that the flesh of Christ was not generated by God at conception or even during gestation but that Jesus was infused with the Spirit at baptismal regeneration and was then "generated" definitively at the Resurrection (*Acts* 13:33, *Rom.* 8). Giacometto suggested that in the church, as resurrection community, Christ and the Spirit might well be one, but in the age to come this Christ would be subject to God, and God, in turn, would place all earthly things under Christ (*1 Cor.* 15:27).

A former Franciscan from southern Italy, Camillo Renato (1500?–1575?) espoused believers' baptism in the lost Latin tract *Adversus baptismum . . . sub regno papae atque Antichristi* (1548). There Renato also defended his "rite of Caspano" (Rhaetia), which included an ample agapetic meal for the poor. Some at the time regarded Renato as the "father of Italian Anabaptism."

Il Tiziano (not the Anabaptist Lorenzo Tizzano), a cleric in the court of a cardinal in Rome, fled to Geneva "and some other Lutheran places," returning to Italy as a messenger sent by God. After he established himself as an "Anabaptist minister" in Rhaetia, the federal government expelled him from its Reformed synod in 1549. Il Tiziano organized several conventicles in northern Italy between 1549 and 1553. In his most fateful action, Il Tiziano converted Pietro Manelfi in Florence and rebaptized him in Ferrara around 1549. Manelfi, as a priest in Ancona, a Marranist center, had been drawn to Protestantism by Bernardino Ochino around 1540. Having read works of Luther and Philipp Melanchthon, Manelfi gave up his priestly duties. Lutherans instituted him as a minister in Padua, and he traveled extensively. In Florence Manelfi espoused both rebaptism and pacifism and held that it was Il Tiziano who first introduced Anabaptism into Italy.

Some Neapolitan-Sicilian Anabaptists became antitrinitarians. They were Josephites, regarding Jesus as the son of Joseph and Mary, and were inspired especially by the Hebrew prophets, interpreting them in the light of the Reformation. During the pan-Italian Anabaptist Synod of Venice in 1550—in which both evangelical Marranos and old-stock sectaries participated—the Ten Articles were adopted, consolidating the Josephite strand of Italian Anabaptism. Josephites became even more programmatically antitrinitarian, humanizing Jesus sometimes as the adoptive Son of God, or as the hidden and prospective Messiah, or as the greatest of the prophets, and always as the son of Mary and Joseph.

On his defection in 1551 Manelfi revealed numerous Anabaptist names at Inquisitorial hearings in Bologna and Rome. This delation almost killed the movement in Italy, though a distinctly evangelical Anabaptism continued for three more decades in ebbing strength. Survivors of the first wave of persecution of 1551 were the Venetians Giulio Gherlandi, Francesco della Sega, and Antonio Rizzetto. They had moved toward antitrinitarianism but remained moderates. The three and their followers found asylum with the Hutterites in Moravia.

In 1550 the university-educated Gherlandi (b. 1520) left the Roman church to join the Anabaptists and was baptized with della Sega in Padua. In 1559 Gherlandi, having renounced the more extreme of the Ten Articles, arrived in Venice with two Hutterites bearing a letter from della Sega, which described Hutterites as communitarian, and welcomed Italian Anabaptists only if uncontaminated with Josephitism or with the tenet that the Resurrection applied only to the persevering saints. Gherlandi's comprehensive confession of faith recounted why he joined the Hutterites, who for him exemplified the peculiar people (*1 Pt.* 2:9), reborn in the Spirit and in Christ overcoming the sin of Adam.

Della Sega (b. 1528) studied civil law in Padua. Stricken with illness, he turned to the New Testament determined to model his life after Christ. He gave up law, became a tailor, and joined the Anabaptist movement, another of many instances of highly educated people seeking the simple disciplined Anabaptist life. Della Sega recognized the mystery of Communion but feared participating to one's detriment, like a Judas. Della Sega and Gherlandi wrote on religious toleration, recognizing the God-ordained role of magistracy but contending that the Roman church was now a rival worldly kingdom. Theological Inquisitors should be servants, not masters. Christians should never condone capital punishment for heresy. In Venice Jews and Muslims rightly enjoyed religious toleration, he said; but those who follow Christ's commands deserve equal treatment. Della Sega visited the Hutterites, and in 1562 he and two friends led twenty-one members of the Cittadella conventicle to Moravia. Della Sega was arrested, tried by the Inquisition at Venice, and sentenced to be drowned.

Antonio Rizzetto, having been rebaptized (1551) in Vicenza by the apostle Marc Antonio of Asolo, a companion of Manelfi, visited the Hutterites and was with della Sega's group when they were imprisoned. Both della Sega and Rizzetto appealed to scripture and the rights of conscience. They reserved baptism for believers who had received the Holy Spirit, noting that Christ bade children come to him but without baptizing them. Christ's sacrifice wiped out the guilt of Adam (Original Sin) for all; thus, Christ cleansed all infants universally. Confession of sin and acceptance of group discipline qualified one for believers' baptism.

Silesian and Slavic Anabaptists. In the vastness of the Polish-Lithuanian commonwealth—a royal republic of the lesser and middle nobles (*szlachta*) and the princes and three city-states—the synodal church of the Reformed spawned a three-way schism of the Polish and Lithuanian Brethren. One grouping became implicitly Unitarian and, in effect, Anabaptist while steadfastly upholding the Apostles' Creed and scorning the Münsterites. In a rigoristic fellowship of peasants, burghers, and especially the *szlachta*, many of whom were inclined to pacifism and the liberation of their serfs, these nobiliary brethren and articulate sisters would endure as the synodal Minor Reformed church until the banishment of the Polish Brethren in 1660.

The origins of this Anabaptist movement in the Polish-Lithuanian commonwealth are obscure. Slavic Anabaptism developed in Poland and the Polish-speaking part of Lithuania partly through the influence of refugees and partly through the inner dynamics of their delayed Reformation movement. In Silesia as early as 1528 mass adult baptisms by immersion occurred at the confluence of the Neisse and Weistritt among Germanic evangelicals, the earliest such usage documented in the Reformation era. The immersed were "initiated" (*eingeweiht*) as "covenanters" (*Bundesgenossen*). In 1535 two hundred Germanic Anabaptists moved from Silesia to Toruń (Thorn), Grudziądz, and Chełmno (Culm). In the same year six hundred Anabaptist refugees from Hungary (Slovakia) settled near Lublin, and a year later (1536) others settled near Poznań, while Dutch and Flemish Mennonites settled around Gdańsk (Danzig), from which the peaceful Mennonite diaspora would much later overflow into Russia. These Polish Anabaptists were fortified by a large contingent of Moravian Brethren (Unitas Fratrum), who settled in Great Poland (1548).

The diets in the commonwealth (1552–1553) urged the king to call a national synod to reform the traditional church, including its prelates. In 1555, after the Peace of Augsburg, the nobility demanded that King Sigismund Augustus establish a national church on the English (Edwardian) model.

In 1550 the first evangelical synod in Minor Poland convened in Pińczów, attended by, among others, Francis Stancarus (Stancaro) and Hieronym (Jerome) Filipowski, soon spokesmen of two of the three main Reformed schisms in the commonwealth alongside the Lutherans and the eventually Polonized Czech Brethren. The Reformed attempted to set forth a creed and organization for their church in Minor Poland in their first synod held at Słomniki (1554).

At their synod of Krzcięcice in 1555 Felix Cruciger was appointed as the first superintendent of the Reformed churches in Poland-Lithuania. The Czech Unity of Brethren, with their Slavic liturgy and exemplary discipline, federated with the Polish Reformed at Koźminek in 1556. Jan Łaski was invited to return from Germany to lead the native pan-Protestant Reformation. The synod of Książ (1560) cemented the union between the Minor Poland Calvinists with their Lithuanian counterparts. From them would arise the (Unitarian) Polish Brethren (1565), radical reformers in Poland and Lithuania who regularly rebaptized and immersed their offspring only after a disciplined catechumenate.

Reformed radicalism moved from rejecting the Athanasian Creed to the sole use of the Apostles' Creed, considered binding, ancient, and free from philosophical constructs. Scruples about infant baptism preceded the widespread practice of believers' baptism by immersion; and an increasingly radical social agenda led the nobiliary brethren to question or disavow their ancestral right to the sword (*ius gladii*).

Unintentionally decisive in the transformation of socially radical Calvinism into Anabaptist Unitarianism was Stancarus, formerly lecturer of Hebrew at the Jagiellonian University in Kraków, who taught that Christ was the mediator only in his human nature, which is, in fact, the orthodox postulate. But for many among the Polish Reformed, Stancarus's formulation derogated from the plenary dignity of the Savior, and this anxiety precipitated the first schism in Polish Calvinism—that of the Stancarists (1561–1570). Stancarus had been the scholarly founder of the Polish Reformed church (1550), but because of his prickly personality and preeminent biblical, perhaps Marranist, scholarship, he drove the also well-educated native leadership into compromising formularies. In the end they would recite in their churches only the Apostles' Creed, which the Polish Brethren continued to uphold until their banishment from the Polish commonwealth on pain of death in 1660.

Among the Polish and Lithuanian Brethren, believers' (re)baptism and explicit Christocentric Unitarianism had evolved by several stages: (1) doubts about infant baptism, notably by Peter Gonesius (Piotr z Goniąza) and Marcin Czechowic (1558–1562/63); (2) theoretical rejection of infant baptism (antipedobaptism) by the groups around Gonesius and Szymon Budny in Lithuania and by Jerzy (George) Schomann in Minor Poland (1558–1563/64); (3) theoretical advocacy of believers' baptism (mainly by Gonesius and Czechowic in 1558); (4) widespread refusal to have infants baptized, beginning with the general postponing of baptism in Lithuania until 1563, when the Reformed pastors Czechowic, Mikolaj (Nicholas) Wędrogowski, and Albrecht Kościeński refused to baptize infants, and with Schomann's withholding of his daughter from pedobaptism in 1564; (5) the theoretical justification of rebaptism by Czechowic after 1563/64 and by Stanisław Paklepka; (6) the institution of believers' baptism for the progeny of the communities and rebaptism of converts and most ministers and lay patrons (as with the Czech Brethren) after 1566; and (7) the sole use of the Apostles' Creed for catechized baptizands at their nocturnal immersion in pond or stream, followed by first Communion.

Before these final stages, however, there had been a balancing act between lay patrons and ministers in the local and regional presbyteries of the Reformed churches of Poland-Lithuania, during which the adroit royal physician and lay archpresbyter Giorgio Biandrata, active in both Poland and Transylvania, had only temporarily preserved the presbyterial-synodal polity by compromising on doctrine. As a distinguished lay leader in both lands, Biandrata took most of the Reformed church over into New Testament Unitarianism, although he himself in the Transylvanian context declined believers' baptism.

The separate Unitarian baptist (neither term used by the sixteenth-century brethren) Minor Reformed church in the commonwealth had emerged amid controversy over the Trinity, baptism, and the social gospel. In January 1556 the Reformed church of Minor Poland, at the synod of Secemin, rebuffed the learned Gonesius, who, in an unscheduled speech, spoke against the doctrine of the Trinity. Gonesius had early on proclaimed his Anabaptist and antitrinitarian theme and again in 1558 before the Lithuanian Synod of Brest Litovsk.

Biandrata was a wily but earnest compromiser and spokesman for the Polish Reformed in rapid transition. As a theological "liberal" but a social conservative, Biandrata was indifferent to, or conventional on, the issue of baptism. After the Swiss Reformed attacked him, Biandrata had to present at the synod of Pińczów (1561) a written confession of faith, which was still nominally Catholic (orthodox) but omitted "one God in three persons." The synod's acceptance of Biandrata's compromise confession encouraged other theological radicals at the synod of Pińczów (1562) to resolve "to teach about the Lord God in simple terms and solely according to the scriptures and the Apostles' Creed."

In the same year, Gregory Pauli (Grzegorz Paweł) of Brzeziny published his *Tabula de Trinitate* (lost), the first antitrinitarian baptist book in the Polish-Lithuanian commonwealth. Soon afterward, the synod discussed it, with inconclusive results that reflected the mounting schism. Francis (Francesco) Lismanino, formerly superior of the Franciscans, a moderate, mediating follower of Catholicism, identified three theological groupings among the Reformed as of 1563—a few followers in Poland of Giovanni Valentino Gentile (tritheists), a grouping following Gregory Pauli (the proto-Unitarians), and a small party of Calvinists under his own equivocal leadership. Calvin angrily responded with *Brevis admonitio ad fratres Polonos* and *Epistola* (1563), which attacked Pauli as a heretic worse than Stancarus, but the Reformed synods everywhere became dominated by the ecclesio-theological radicals (1562–1565).

The general Synod of Pińczów (1563), under the influence of Pauli, elected as the now schismatic superintendent Stanisław Lutomirski, who opposed the already schismatic and theologically and socially more conservative Stancarus. This unitarianizing synod ended with Communion and the signing of the confession of faith: "in one God the Father, and in the Son of God, a true God from God, who died, was raised, and ascended to heaven, and in the Holy Spirit, who proceeds from the Father." It acknowledged only the Apostles' Creed.

Theological and sacramental radicalism was most explicit in Pauli, Gonesius, and Schomann. After 1563 the diminishing hope for royal support had freed the Reformed from any ideal of a nationally united Polish Reformed church and prepared the way for the separatist Minor Reformed church in both Major Poland and especially Minor. It was this grouping of antitrinitarian Anabaptists, at first few in number but counting well-educated leaders, who separated from the Nicene Reformed, as had the earlier credally conservative Stancarists.

Following the synodal schism of 1563–1565, the unitarianizing separatists, at their first synod in Brzeziny in Lithuania (1565), described themselves as "the Brethren from Poland and Lithuania who have rejected the Trinity." The official title of their church, Ecclesia Poloniae Minor Reformata, implied separation from the (Major) Reformed church of Minor Poland. The Minor church held that it was called by God to finish the work of Luther, Huldrych Zwingli, and Calvin (as did Fausto Sozzini, who would assume leadership in 1579). By 1566 congregations (*zbory*) of the Minor church were swiftly founded in more than sixty towns and villages of Latinate Lithuania, Great Poland, Kujawy, Minor Poland, and Ruthenia. This pre-Socinian Minor church of Poland and Lithuania received political backing from *szlachta* and even from Lithuanian magnates like princes Mikolaj Radziwiłł and Jan Kiszka.

Instantly accused of Arianism, but inexactly, the Minor Reformed church was thus transitionally divided over the doctrine of God, passing through tritheistic and ditheistic phases before ending up as a largely pacifistic, otherworldly, Christocentric Unitarian church based on believers' baptism by immersion and a renunciation of worldly means. Among its members, Jan Niemojewski, an early exponent of social equality, freed his serfs.

Szymon Budny, a trilingual biblical scholar who published in both Polish and Ruthenian, moved from ditheism to Unitarianism. He upheld the restrained use of the sword and postponed his own rebaptism until 1578. Czechowic held to doctrines that ranged from ditheism to baptist Unitarianism. Pauli moved from tritheism and ditheism to baptist Unitarianism. Gonesius, a nominal ditheist, did not reject the divinity of the Holy Spirit but was at odds with ditheists like Stanisław Farnowski, who presided over his own (fourth separate) Reformed synod, absorbed by the Polish Brethren in 1615. The biblicism of the emergent Polish and Lithuanian Brethren constrained them from "twisting and changing the Word of God." They countered charges of Arianism and Anabaptism by reaffirming the Apostles' Creed and building their own simple meeting houses close to streams and occasionally in chartered communes, such as Raków (1567). For the instruction of catechumens and converts, the *Catechesis* of Schomann was synodally authorized for publication (1574), based upon the threefold office of Christ as prophet, priest, and king. This *triplex munus Christi* was carried over into the Racovian Catechism (Polish, 1605; German, 1608; Latin, 1609), which was a substantial systematic reconception of the piety and practice of the Polish Brethren on the part of Fausto Sozzini, renowned Florentine refugee among them, whom they had befriended but who, for his part, had come to regard any mode or theology of baptism as vestigial or superseded and who instead emphasized the Eucharist, while vastly nuancing and upholding their pacifism and opposition to warfare as state policy.

Evangelical Rationalists. The evangelical rationalists from Lelio Sozzini (1525–1562) and Camillo Renato to the nephew of Lelio, Fausto Sozzini (1539–1604), were Renaissance humanists commonly of trilingual prowess who criticized ecclesiasticism no less in Protestant than in Catholic guise. Often individualistic in their Christianity, they were, like the evangelical spiritualists, distressed by the division and strife that accompanied organized religion. These humanist reformers and their lay patrons sought a rational, nonmystical, sober church of the informed and the pious. Some may have preferred the half-enunciated ideal of Desiderius Erasmus—a "Third Church," neither Protestant nor Catholic, devout but not doctrinaire.

In Poland, Lithuania, and Transylvania the evangelical rationalist ferment in the local Reformed churches created three well-integrated ecclesiastical bodies, one of them still surviving as the Unitarian church in Romania (Transylvania) and Hungary. But its ecclesial survival in those regions should not obscure the earlier geographical and societal scope of this mostly tolerant, yet disciplined, modality of reform. It was, in fact, international in terms of epistolary correspondence, visitation, and irenic ecumenism.

To these evangelical rationalists the Holy Spirit was not so much mystically experienced as aglow in reason itself, perhaps reflective of the Logos as the mind of God, a view fundamental to their piety and their stalwart courage in national debate. They were evangelical in exalting Jesus' moral teachings, especially the Sermon on the Mount. Those in Transylvania were stronger than the late Socinians in valorizing the Old Testament. Evangelical rationalists were morally perfectionist, like the later Pietists, but without the intense mystical resonance. Divine immediacy was experienced in understanding the scriptural text with philological expertise and even in religious wonder before the original or carefully translated text. Had not Erasmus remained nominally Catholic, he could have been counted "an evangelical rationalist" in emphasizing evangelical precepts and counsels of tolerance. The Castilian Marrano Juan de Valdés (1500/10–1541), as much a Catholic evangelical as a moderate spiritualist, was a forerunner of evangelical rationalism.

Evangelical rationalism was, in a sense, the aborted humanist Italian spirit of reform reconstituted abroad. Yet the evangelical rationalists shared with the other radicals an intense eschatological expectation. The most notable exponents of this were Lelio and Fausto Sozzini, who were content with a doctrine of the Resurrection and the reanimation of the scripturally righteous *only*, opting for sheer oblivion as the benign punishment of the wicked and unbelievers in Christ as the Virgin-born Son of God.

The radical Reformation produced three lasting denominational forms of evangelical rationalism. The antitrinitarianism and immersionist Anabaptism of the Polish Brethren evolved under Fausto Sozzini into the evangelical rationalism, eventually called Socinianism, of the Racovian Catechism (Raków, 1605). Realistically dealing with the state, the antipedobaptist scriptural Unitarianism of multi-confessional establishmentarian Transylvania had Erastian features. Lithuanian biblical Unitarianism, nonadorant of Christ and immersionist as to baptism, similarly linked philological with supernatural rationalism under pluralistically tolerant princely patronage. Transylvanian Unitarians even set aside the Apostles' Creed. The Socinians, the Hebraist Budny and his Lithuanian followers, and Transylvanian Unitarians all adhered to scripture as the sole source of revelation and salvific truth. Only in the seventeenth century did Andrzy Wiszowaty (grandson of Fausto Sozzini) endorse natural theology in his *Religio rationalis* (Amsterdam, 1685).

Unlike later proponents of Reformed and Lutheran rational orthodoxy—and inspired by Socinian methodology—the three evangelical rationalist synods of east-central Europe embraced mutual toleration and irenicism and intrepidly defended public and ecumenical exchanges, which in Transylvania occasionally included Jewish, Karaite, and Muslim spokesmen. In contrast to variegated evangelical rationalism, much of Anabaptism and spiritualism all along had mystical components and left some room for a natural theology prior to biblical revelation, except for Socinianism. The mystical is evident in their understanding of Christ's suffering descent into hell to save the worthy of all traditions prior to his first advent; in the quasi-mystical teaching about the gospel of all creatures; and in the conviction that Christ had died to save all infants, absolving Original Sin.

"Radical Reformation," a handy conceptual aggregate term for most of the regional opponents of, or secessionists from, any of the three main classical (magisterial) Protestant churches, was something of a loosely coherent entity and dynamic in the Reformation century, with processes and persons often closely interconnected, partly by derivation or appropriation, partly by recurrent analogy or imitation, joining and separating—all with reformatory or restorationist agendas and often sharply held eschatological convictions.

A variegated movement during the Reformation and Counter-Reformation, the radical Reformation appears to have extended from 1516—the year of Erasmus's edition of the Greek New Testament—to a cluster of events around 1578 and 1579. These include the death of Peter Walpot, who led the Hutterites in their golden age; the death of Francis (Ferencz) Dávid, who led the Transylvanian Unitarians; the arrival of Fausto Sozzini in Poland and his only partially successful conversion of Racovian, antitrinitarian Anabaptism in the direction of what became known later as Socinianism; the official toleration of Mennonites in the Netherlands by William of Orange; and the Emden Disputation between the Mennonites and the Reformed.

By then the radical Reformation had eliminated its most

obvious excesses and had softened its asperities. Its own disparate impulses were crystallized in diverse and geographically isolated synodal churches, sects, and fellowships. The way had been opened for a deepened appreciation of the individual conscience and the value of religious toleration, with many radical groups reappropriating elements inherent in the theologies of classical Protestantism as they evolved into strong, mission-minded, peace-loving denominations. Slowly gathering strength, bearers of radical ideas and strategies, as well as analogous groupings, became once again involved in general history, notably in the restructuring of English Christendom during the civil wars and the Cromwellian commonwealth and in the consolidation of several new, eventually denominational forms of independency—the Baptists and the Quakers. The socio-religious dynamic of the sixteenth century would replicate itself in ever new configurations.

[*See also* Anabaptists; Antitrinitarianism; Bohemian Brethren; Hutterites; Melchiorites; Mennonites; Polish Brethren; Socinianism; *and* Unitarianism.]

BIBLIOGRAPHY

Baylor, Michael G., *The Radical Reformation.* Cambridge Texts in the History of Political Thought. Cambridge and New York, 1991.

Dán, Róbert. *Matthias Vehe-Glirus: Life and Work of a Radical Antitrinitarian.* Leiden, 1982.

Friedmann, Robert. "Spiritualism." In *Mennonite Encyclopedia,* vol. 4, pp. 596–599. Scottdale, Pa., 1959.

Hillerbrand, Hans J. ed. *Anabaptist Bibliography, 1520–1630.* Saint Louis, 1991.

Horst, Irvin B. *The Radical Brethren: Anabaptism and the English Reformation to 1559.* Nieuwkoop, 1972.

Kot, Stanislas. *Socinianism in Poland.* Boston, 1957.

Lubieniecki, Stanislas. *History of the Polish Reformation and Nine Related Documents.* Translated, annotated, and illustrated by George Huntston Williams. Harvard Theological Studies, 34. Minneapolis, 1995.

McLaughlin, R. Emmet. *Caspar Schwenckfeld, Reluctant Radical: His Life to 1540.* New Haven, 1986.

Menno Simons. *The Complete Writings.* Scottdale, Pa., 1956.

Miller, James. "The Origins of Polish Arianism." *Sixteenth Century Journal* 16.2 (1985), 221–256.

Pater, Calvin A. *Karlstadt as the Father of the Anabaptist Movements: The Emergence of Lay Protestantism.* Reprint, Lewiston, N.Y., 1993.

Szczucki, Lech. "The Beginnings of Antitrinitarian Anabaptism in Lithuania and Poland in the Light of an Unknown Source." In *Anabaptistes et dissidents au XVIe siècle,* edited by Jean-Georges Rott and Simon L. Verheus. Baden-Baden, 1987.

Toth, William. "Unitarianism versus Antitrinitarianism in the Hungarian Reformation." *Church History* 13 (1944), 255–268.

Troeltsch, Ernst. *The Social Teachings of the Christian Churches.* London, 1931.

Wilbur, Earl Morse. *A History of Unitarianism: Socinianism and Its Antecedents.* 2 vols. Reprint, Boston, 1977.

Williams, George Huntston. "Camillo Renato, c. 1500–1575." In *Italian Reformation Studies in Honor of Laelius Socinus,* edited by John Tedeschi. Florence, 1965.

———. "The Two Social Strands in Italian Anabaptism." In *The Social History of the Reformation,* edited by Lawrence P. Buck and Jonathan W. Zophy. Columbus, Ohio, 1972.

———. "Francis Stancaro's Schismatic Reformed Church in Ruthenia, 1559/61–1570." *Harvard Ukrainian Studies* (1979–1980), 267–277.

———. *The Radical Reformation.* 3d ed. Kirksville, Mo., 1992.

———. "The Polish Brethren [of Stanislas Lubieniecki]." In *The Earl Morse Wilbur History Colloquium,* edited by Warren R. Ross, pp. 34–41. Berkeley, 1994.

Williams, George Huntston., ed. and trans. *The Polish Brethren, 1601–1685.* 2 vols. Harvard Theological Studies, 30. Missoula, Mont., 1980.

Williams, George Huntston, and Angel M. Mergal, eds. *Spiritual and Anabaptist Writers: Documents Illustrative of the Radical Reformation.* Library of Christian Classics, 25. Philadelphia, 1957.

GEORGE HUNTSTON WILLIAMS

RADICS, Caspar. *See* Károlyi, Gáspár.

RAEMOND, Florimond de (1540–1601) of Agen, French Catholic polemical historian and member of the Bordeaux Parlement. Raemond wrote three popular works—on the myth of Pope Joan (*Erreur populaire de la Papesse Jane,* 1587), on the Antichrist (*L'Anti-christ,* 1597), and on the Protestant Reformation (*Histoire de la naissance: Progrez et décadence de l'hérésie de ce siècle,* posthumously published 1605)—to disprove the Protestant interpretation of history and vindicate Rome. He edited the first edition of Blaise de Lasseran Massencôme's *Commentaires* on the French civil wars and of the Protestant apostate Jean de Sponde's rebuttal of Théodore de Bèze's (1578) treatise on the true church. Raemond wrote of the "demise" of Protestantism with a feigned confidence shared by not a few co-religionists who were equally uncertain how far to trust the conversion of Henry IV or the ultimate end toward which the Edict of Nantes tended.

His works, he said, "are common and popular books," but learned and unlearned read them nonetheless, for his methodology was respectable, if not always accurate or unbiased, and his prose style was (and still is) eminently readable French, a rarity for historical works in his day. His *Histoire* focused on doctrine and ritual in the lives of Protestants, with much attention given to Lutherans, Calvinists, and, more innovatively, to Anabaptists and radical sectarians. He was one of the first to note the significance of religion to psychological well-being. He described the mentality of the *menu peuple* using pamphlets, anecdotes, and oral history. He was thus an early historian of *mentalité.*

His chapter on Calvin, composed largely of testimony from people who had known him before he fled to Switzerland, offers valuable information on the first forms of French Calvinism. His treatment of the radicals' relationship to Lutheranism displayed an anthropologist's understanding of the importance of linguistic elements in spiritual life. He recognized the seriousness of religious affiliation collectively and individually. He was original because he pursued all varieties of religious experience, showing how it related to social institutions, and how people were easily manipulated by their spiritual leaders. Raemond regarded Luther as educated if deluded, but acknowledged that he salvaged some of the essence of Catholicism. This point and his insistence that Anabaptists and Sacramentarians were inspired by Luther's spiritualism are ideas favorably received by recent historical scholarship.

Raemond was a demythologizer, and, like Étienne Pasquier and others, sought to retrieve history from legend. His most innovative contribution to historiography was his portrait of reform on a European-sized canvas, for his *Histoire* was an example of comparative history, although, because his subject was limited to religion, not of universal history.

The Counter-Reformation encouraged dynamic history, since truth was fought for on two fronts: scriptural and historical. Catholic practice was not always provable by scripture, so both history and tradition were used to justify many church practices. Raemond defended Catholic interpretation on both fronts, a cold warrior for his faith when the religious wars in France had not yet cooled.

BIBLIOGRAPHY

Boase, Alan. *The Fortunes of Montaigne.* Reprint, New York, 1970.

Busch, Martin. *Florimond de Raemond (vers 1540–1601) et l'Anabaptisme.* Ph.D. diss., Université des Sciences Humaines, Faculté de Théologie Protestante, Strasbourg, 1981.

Darricau, Raymond. "La vie et l'oeuvre d'un parlementaire aquitain Florimond de Raemond, 1540–1601." *Revue française d'histoire du livre* (1971), 109–128.

Dubois, Claude-Gilbert. *La conception de l'histoire en France au 16e siècle.* Paris, 1977.

Larroque, Philippe Tamizey de. *Essai sur la vie et les ouvrages de Florimond de Raymond.* Paris, 1867.

Tinsley, Barbara Sher. *History and Polemics in the French Reformation: Florimond de Raemond, Defender of the Church.* Selinsgrove, Pa., and London, 1992.

BARBARA SHER TINSLEY

RAKÓW. A small town in Poland situated on the river Czarna fifty miles to the west of Sandomierz, Raków was founded in 1567 by Jan Sienieński, a rich Calvinist landlord from Zarnów, as a cultural and administrative center for the antitrinitarian movement. The name seems to be derived from the word for crayfish (*rak* in Polish), an element of the coat of arms of his wife, Jadwiga Gnoińska, an ardent antitrinitarian. The town charter, dated 27 March 1567, guaranteed liberty of conscience for all confessions, though only Arians and Jews actually set up places of worship; Catholics applied in vain for the right to build a church.

The town's history is inextricably bound up with that of the Polish antitrinitarian movement, which historians have tended to divide into two main periods. The first three years following the arrival of the antitrinitarian brethren in 1569 was characterized by Stanisław Kot (*Socinianism in Poland,* p. 29) as that of "the simple stormy synod." The town attracted the most radical antitrinitarians, many of plebeian origin. Under the leadership of Gregory Paul, the issues discussed included the abolition of serfdom and the distribution of the property of the landed nobility for the benefit of the poor, as well as pacifism and the right to exercise civic office. Some theologians argued that ministers should earn their livelihood through manual labor. This was a religious vision that combined antitrinitarian ideas with a number of Anabaptist practices, such as the repudiation of infant baptism. Soon all forms of the institutional church were rejected, and the town was brought to the brink of anarchy.

Among the leading theologians associated with Gregory Paul were Jan Niemojewski, Georg Szoman, Marcin Czechowic, Daniel Bieliński, and, in all probability, Piotr of Goniadz. The Judaistic strain of Polish antitrinitarianism was probably developed by Bieliński, who maintained a close relationship with Rabbi Jakub from Bełżyce. It seems probable that he and Gregory Paul established contacts on behalf of the town with the Hutterite community of Moravia. In any case, representatives of the Moravians came to visit Raków in 1569. It is clear from the ensuing *Traktat przeciwko komunistom morawskim. . .* (A Treatise Not Opposed to the Apostolic Community Such as That in Jerusalem . . . but against Such a One as That Proposed by the Sect Called Communist in Moravia), whose author was probably Stanisław Budzyński, that this meeting was a disappointment to the Poles. Far from presenting a model of apostolic purity, the Moravian community was accused of maintaining the principle of hierarchy, with the consequent evils of avarice and social exploitation. The idea of unifying the two communities had to be abandoned. Despite the oft-voiced criticism of the Calvinist party from Kraków, it would seem that the Poles themselves never established any real community of goods.

The bitter confrontation between partisans of ditheism, tritheism, and the Judaizing elements of the community died down around 1570, when the religious doctrine had become essentially unitarian. The social climate also improved as a number of the most vociferous of the radical leaders left town. Another reason for this changed atmosphere was, after 1572, the work of Kraków pharmacist Szymon Ronemberg and Marcin Czechowic, who had opposed the proposal to abolish the office of minister. Replacing Gregory Paul, who in many ways was responsible for the anarchy, Czechowic was able to impose some theological order, and he was commissioned to prepare a catechism. This work that appeared under the title *Rozmowy chrześcijańskie . . .* (Kraków, 1575) was one of the most important documents of

Polish antitrinitarianism before the appearance of Fausto Sozzini.

The original democratic and pacific ideals were rediscovered and became characteristic of the community. The real economic and cultural development of Raków, however, occurred between 1602 and 1638, when the town was able to justify its reputation as the "Sarmatian Athens." The great synods, where Sozzini established his reputation, were held in Raków. These theological debates were further developed in Valentin Smalcius's *Exercitationes theologicæ* and subsequently defended, in somewhat modified form, by Johann Crell.

Many foreign visitors were drawn to Raków, as much by the publications of the press established by Sebastian Sternacki as by the town's growing intellectual reputation. The press at Raków produced some two hundred theological and scientific works in Latin, German, and Polish. The most famous of these was the *Catechism*, which first appeared in Polish in 1605, before being printed in Latin and German. The Latin edition was dedicated to King James I of England, who took umbrage and ordered the work to be burned. Notwithstanding, by 1614 at least one or two secret editions of the work had been produced by Humphrey Lownes of London. In addition to the various editions of the work in Polish, eight Latin, three Dutch, and two German impressions are known. The catechism, which presented antitrinitarian teachings, was probably undertaken by Sozzini and later revised and adapted by Smalcius, Hieronymus Moscorovius (Moskorzewski), and Johann Völkel. This work replaced Czechowic's *Rozmowy*, which did not present the unitarian views of Sozzini.

The production of the Raków press, which was of a high technical level, enabled the Polish Brethren to spread their ideas abroad. Representatives of the community and Polish students were to be found at the universities of Tübingen, Leipzig, Basel, and Strasbourg, where they helped to disseminate Socinian books and ideas. Some of those recruited to the cause later took on posts of responsibility within the community.

Undoubtedly one of the most significant institutions in Raków at this time was its school. While other Protestant academies in Poland followed the model of Johannes Sturm's school in Strasbourg or the academy in Lausanne, the school in Raków conformed to the pedagogical principles of the Polish Brethren. The curriculum emphasized a general education as a preparation for exercising public office and stressed the importance of logic, mathematics, and the sciences. Its success was such that many pupils from other confessional groups, notably the Catholic and Calvinist traditions, attended the school. At its apogee it enrolled about one thousand pupils and had a professorial staff of about thirty. The list of rectors includes Italian Joannes Baptista Celtis, German Völkel, and Silesian Simon Pistorius, as well as the theologians of antitrinitarianism Crell, Martin Ruar, and Joachim Stegman. The school was closed by royal injunction on 19 April 1638, probably because the loyalty of the community to the essentially Catholic state was more and more doubted.

At the same time as the school was closed, the press was forbidden to function, and the community was suppressed. The majority of members then left the town, selling their goods to the Jews and Catholics who remained. Part of the professorial corps moved to Kisielin in the Volhynia (Ruthenia), where another school had been established, although they were unable to recreate the scholarly accomplishments of the old academy. Likewise, the attempt to transfer the center of the Polish Brethren's activity to Lusławice (where Sozzini had lived and died) ended in failure. Following the death of Sieniénski, the proprietor of the town, his children converted to Catholicism. His library, together with that of the school, eventually became part of the library of Prince Czartoryski in Kraków. The library has yet to be properly cataloged. After the suppression of the school, Raków later lost its corporate privileges and returned to the status of a village in 1869.

BIBLIOGRAPHY

Cynarski, Stanisław, ed. *Raków ognisko arianizmu.* Kraków, 1968. A collection of seven papers by the leading Polish authorities on various aspects of the social and intellectual life of Raków.

Kawecka-Gryczowa, Alodia. "Prasy Rakówa i Krakowa w służbie antitrinitaryzmu." In *Studia nad arianizmem,* edited by L. Chmaj, pp. 263–330. Warsaw, 1959. An important study on the antitrinitarian press.

Kot, Stanisław. *Socinianism in Poland: The Social and Political Ideas of the Polish Antitrinitarians.* Translated by E. M. Wilbur. Boston, 1957. Several chapters are devoted to Raków, especially to the social and political ideas of its leading theologians.

Urban, Wacław. "Losy Braci Polskich od założenia Rakówa do wygnania z Polski." In *Ordrodzenie i Reformacja,* vol. 1, pp. 103–139. Warsaw, 1956.

Wilbur, Earl Morse. *A History of Unitarianism: Socinianism and Its Antecedents.* Reprint, Boston, 1977. Still the best work on the general history of antitrinitarianism. The history of Raków (pp. 356–419) is placed in this context. A study based on the original sources.

André Séguenny

Translated from French by Christopher J. Burchill

RAMUS, Petrus (Fr., Pierre de la Ramée; 1515–1572), French humanist philosopher and logician. Ramus was educated at the University of Paris and lectured on philosophy at the Collège de l'Ave Maria, where he befriended Audomarus Talaeus (Omer Talon; 1510–1562). In 1543 he published *Dialecticae partitiones* (The Structure of Dialectic); a second edition, *Dialecticae institutiones* (Training in Dialectic); and *Aristotelicae animadversiones* (Remarks on Aristotle). Ramus's revision of *Dialecticae institutiones* as *Dialectici commentarii tres authore Audomaro Talaeo* (Three Commentaries on Dialectic by Omer Talon; 1546)—despite the title, largely Ramus's work—was his first treatment of "method" in dialectic as a separate subject.

In his master's thesis at the Collège de Navarre in 1536, Ramus vehemently attacked Aristotle's logic as basically misleading. In 1544 Ramus was accused of assaulting the foundations of religion and philosophy, and his books and teaching were banned by King Francis I of France. Nevertheless, in 1545 Ramus was appointed president of the Collège de Presles, and in 1547 Henry II revoked the ban. In 1551 Ramus became a regius professor and then dean at the Collège Royal, later known as the Collège de France. Ramus had become a prominent and widely influential orator and author.

In 1561/62 Ramus converted to Protestantism, and in 1568 he fled France. He sought a teaching position in European universities and studied Protestant theology in Basel. His attacks on Aristotelian logic displeased Théodore de Bèze, who informed Ramus that there was no academic position available in Geneva for which he was suitable. In 1571 Ramus, critical of the actions of the Synod of the Reformed Church of France held at La Rochelle, tried to persuade Bullinger to reject them; in May 1572 the synod met at Nîmes, where it rejected Ramus's advocacy of a congregationalist form of church government. Shortly thereafter Ramus was a victim of the Saint Bartholomew's Day Massacre of 23 August 1572.

Ramus sought to reorganize and reform dialectic. He proposed a "logic" and "method" to simplify all academic subjects and as an alternative to what he considered the intricacies of the Aristotelian system then current in many universities. Drawing on the works of humanist scholars such as Rudolph Agricola, Ramus proposed a single logic for both dialectic and rhetoric. The task of the logician was to classify concepts in order to make them understandable and memorable. This was done by method, the orderly presentation of a subject.

Ramus's method is deductive; it moves from "universals" to "singulars," the general to the specific. It proceeds by a series of divisions into component parts so that as one diagrams these successive divisions, a branching chart emerges. This visualized logic shows the relation of each part to the others and gives an instant perception of the interior logic that constitutes what is being analyzed.

Instead of relying on syllogisms to derive truth (as in Aristotelianism), Ramus sought the self-evidencing axioms inherent in a topic. The logician classifies these and breaks them into constitutive parts through method. For Ramus, the goal of all dialectic is discourse—composed not of a series of syllogisms correctly joined, but of a series of axioms that can be perceived directly once they are uncovered; they can then be arranged in an intelligible order through method.

Ramism spread throughout Europe, achieving particular strength in Germany, Switzerland, and the Low Countries. Ramist logic was especially attractive to English, and later, American Puritans. A Ramist tradition emerged at the University of Cambridge through Lawrence Chaderton, William Perkins, William Ames, and others.

With its emphasis on practicality, Ramism gave Puritanism a view of theology that closely linked theology with ethics ("cases of conscience"). Theological beliefs had practical applications; ethical decisions should be rooted in theological beliefs. With its emphasis on simplicity and accessibility, Ramism provided Puritanism with a powerful educational tool for teaching the scriptures. Puritan "plain-style" preaching owed much to Ramist method. Through a series of clear divisions, a biblical text gradually could be applied to the lives of a congregation. The clarity of the Ramist approach also helped Puritan preachers remember their sermons in the tradition of the classical "art of memory." Applied to the Bible, Ramist tools for "analysis" and "resolution" assisted Puritans in interpreting scripture. Since Ramists believed their method unlocked the metaphysical reality of a subject by laying open the component "arguments" that constituted it, Puritans saw in this a metaphysical grounding for all knowledge in the mind of God. Puritan Ramists such as Ames developed a system called "technometria" or "encyclopedia" to show the interrelationships of all arts by laying out the rules established by God by which all human learning proceeds. The mind of God was revealed supremely in scripture, according to the Puritans. For some Puritans the tools of the Ramist philosophy therefore helped make God's mind known.

BIBLIOGRAPHY

Primary Source

Ramus, Petrus. *A Fresh Suit against Human Ceremonies in God's Worship* (1633). Farnborough, 1971.

Secondary Sources

Ames, William. *Technometry.* Translated by Lee W. Gibbs. Philadelphia, 1979. Translation of William Ames' *Technometria* with introduction and commentary displaying the Ramist influences.

Howell, Wilbur Samuel. *Logic and Rhetoric in England, 1500–1700.* Reprint, New York, 1961. A full and important study of the development of logic and rhetoric in England, with special attention given to the spread of Ramism.

Jardine, Lisa. "The Place of Dialectic Teaching in Sixteenth-Century Cambridge." *Studies in the Renaissance* 21 (1974), 31–62. Valuable examination of the developments in the teaching of dialectic at Cambridge during the Puritan period.

McKim, Donald K. "The Functions of Ramism in William Perkins' Theology." *Sixteenth Century Journal* 16.4 (1985), 503–517. Focuses on the implications of Ramism for William Perkins and English Puritanism.

———. *Ramism in William Perkins' Theology.* New York, 1987. Study of the influence of Ramism in the writings and theological method of William Perkins.

Miller, Perry. *The New England Mind: The Seventeenth Century.* Reprint, Cambridge, Mass., 1983. The early important study that initially drew attention to the pervasiveness of Ramism among New England Puritans.

Ong, Walter J. *Ramus and Talon Inventory.* Cambridge, Mass., 1983. Full catalog inventory of all works and editions of Ramus's and Talon's writings.

———. *Ramus, Method, and the Decay of Dialogue.* Reprint, Cambridge, Mass., 1983. Most extensive and authoritative study of Ramus and Ramism.

Sprunger, Keith L. *The Learned Doctor William Ames.* Urbana, Ill., 1972. Excellent examination of the appropriation of Ramism by William Ames.

Verzeichnis der im deutschen Sprachbereich erschienenen Drucke des XVI. Jahrhunderts. Stuttgart, 1983–. See vol. 11, nos. 446–537.

DONALD K. MCKIM

RATISBON, BOOK OF. *See* Colloquies.

RATISBON, COLLOQUY OF. *See* Colloquies.

REALISM. *See* Scholasticism.

RECUSANCY. A term derived from the Latin *recusare*, recusancy was the refusal to attend the services of the established church as commanded by English law. This and other religious sentiments expressed by the English people on the eve of the Elizabethan Reformation have been a source of much scholarly attention. Scholars such as A. G. Dickens have stressed the role played by Lollardy in generating dissatisfaction with ecclesiastical doctrines and practices and in creating a demand for reform that was independent of the "political" reformation initiated in Parliament. Other historians, such as Christopher Haigh and J. J. Scarisbrick, deny significant desire for reform from the people ("from below"). Indeed, they contend that the average English man or woman was satisfied with the pre-reformed church and that little would have been altered if it had not been for the reformation "from above." Both interpretations admit that those with strong Protestant views were in the minority in 1559, a minority albeit strong enough to effect the changes. Convincing the populace to accept the changes, however, would be more difficult. Positively, it required a serious process of evangelization through preaching. Negatively, it demanded that the people be prevented from practicing their preferred religious services and obliged to attend the established services, where they would be subject to official harangues from the pulpit. The winning of the people demanded the full thrust of the Elizabethan government. Progress was slow.

The first parliamentary act of Elizabeth's reign, the Act of Supremacy (1 Eliz. c. 1), repealed the legislation from the brief reign of Mary Tudor (r. 1553–1558) that reunited the English church with the papacy, and it also reestablished the English monarch as the head of the church in England. The recognition of the spiritual and ecclesiastical authority of the pope was forbidden with graduated penalties that culminated in the charge of high treason for the third offense. The second act of Parliament, the Act of Uniformity (1 Eliz. c. 2), was rooted in the power granted to the monarch in the Act of Supremacy. It imposed a new prayer book, based on a revised version of *The Second Book of Common Prayer* (1552), to be used in every church and chapel after the Feast of the Nativity of Saint John the Baptist (24 June 1559). Ministers who refused could be deprived of their livings and imprisoned. Members of the congregation who mocked or interfered with the service or forced the minister to use a different ritual risked heavy fines and life imprisonment. Those who were absent from the new services were fined one shilling. An amendment in 1563 (5 Eliz. c. 1) made these laws even stricter.

Throughout the first decade of Elizabeth's reign (1559–1569), there were few signs of active Catholic resistance to the new religion, but, beyond the pale of the major towns and cathedral cities, Protestantism's growth was slow. Official records recount the frustrations of various bishops as they attempted to wean their flocks from the habits and superstitions of popery. Some pastors adapted the established rite so that it bore a strong resemblance to the accustomed ritual. Others celebrated the official and the proscribed rite on the same day. Many of the laity were passively present: they said their prayers or socialized as the official service took place around them. They manifested their displeasure in various ways but rarely through refusal to attend the services. Perhaps in the expectation of yet another change, the opponents were not yet ready for a complete break with their traditional community of worship but sought to retain as much of the traditional religion as they could. An aspect of the debate between Dickens and Haigh concerns the importance of this "survivalism" for the subsequent history of post-Reformation Catholicism. The former sees it as negligible, the latter as essential.

Attendance at these services troubled some English Catholics enough to make them seek clarification from Rome. By 1564 both the Holy Office in Rome and a committee at the Council of Trent had condemned the practice. Henceforth even passive attendance was forbidden, and anyone who attended ("church papists") had to be reconciled for full communion with the Roman Church. Catholics were required to separate themselves from the established church. As more and more clergy and laity refused to cooperate, recusancy proper was born.

Elizabethan policy was relatively lenient during the first fifteen years of the reign. This leniency resulted both from Elizabethan fears that severe persecution would drive the Catholics to a despair that would lead to rebellion and from the lack of an efficient mechanism for the enforcement of the legislation. There were not enough sufficiently Protestantized clergy to staff the positions, and the justices of the peace and the churchwardens, on whom the implementation of the laws depended, placed greater emphasis on local communal and familial ties than on distant parliamentary decisions. Time, however, was the queen's ally. The Marian priests would die eventually, and those persons whose recusancy had been encouraged by them would be forced to conform. A series of events in the late 1560s altered the policy.

In May 1568 Mary Stuart, whom many regarded not simply as Elizabeth's legitimate successor but as rightful queen in her place, fled her native Scotland for sanctuary in England. Almost immediately she became the center of numerous conspiracies real and feigned (e.g., the Ridolfi Plot of 1571). Later the same year William Allen founded an English college at Douai in the Spanish Netherlands to train priests to strengthen the resolve of English Catholics. The rebellion of the northern earls in November 1569 confirmed official fears of the disloyalty of the Catholics. Pope Pius V's *Regnans in Excelsis* (February 1570) declared Elizabeth a heretic, deprived her of the throne, and ordered all Catholics to forsake their allegiance. In the face of the spiritual and temporal weapons newly employed by Catholicism, there was a greater danger in forbearance than there was in strict enforcement. Subsequent parliaments demanded stricter legislation and tighter enforcement. In 1571 a new law made it high treason to claim that Elizabeth was either a heretic or a schismatic and not the rightful sovereign (13 Eliz. c. 1). The same Parliament forbade reconciliation with the Roman Catholic church because the rejection of the religious authority of the queen was tantamount to political disloyalty (13 Eliz. c. 2). Renewed vigilance and stricter investigation, introduced because of the threat that Catholicism posed to the established order, revealed the increasing numbers of recusants.

In the spring of 1580 Robert Parsons and Edmund Campion inaugurated the Jesuit mission to England. Although their instructions specifically directed them to work among the Catholics, shortly after their arrival they were obliged to deal with the issue of the schismatics, the occasional conformists who, though Catholic in sentiment, passively attended the established services either in deference to their monarch or out of fear of punishment. The so-called Synod of Southwark (July 1580), a meeting of Marian and seminary priests working in London, was convened by the Jesuits. A few months earlier Alban Langdale, deprived archdeacon of Chichester and chaplain to Anthony Browne, viscount of Montague, had circulated a defense of occasional conformity and a rejection of recusancy. Mere physical attendance, according to Langdale, was not forbidden by divine law because the reluctant conformist neither scandalized other Catholics nor participated in heretical worship. As evidence he cited the pertinent example of Naaman the Syrian, who was allowed by the prophet Elisha to worship at a pagan temple because of allegiance to his king (*2 Kgs.* 5). The assembled clergy rejected Langdale's arguments and agreed that attendance was the greatest iniquity that could be committed. Parsons attacked Langdale's position more forcefully in his first book, *A Brief Discours Contayning Certayne Reasons Why Catholiques Refuse to Go to Church* (Doway [actually London], 1580). According to Parsons, Elisha did not approve of Naaman's attendance: he simply tolerated it. The example demonstrated that a Catholic might accompany his king to a secular service held in a church, but it did not establish a precedent for conformity.

Fears of more joint papal-Spanish ventures similar to the invasion of Ireland in 1579 and doubts regarding the loyalty of the Catholic subjects in the event of such an invasion intensified the pressure on recusants to conform. Offenses that would have been ignored earlier in Elizabeth's reign were now punished severely. The old religion was clearly not going to die a slow death of attrition because there was now a new supply of seminary priests to administer it; it would have to be crushed. In 1581 Parliament passed the Act to Retain the Queen's Majesty's Subjects in Their Due Obedience (23 Eliz. c. 1), which demanded that all recusants conform at least once a month. Failure to do so could result in financial ruin: a £20 fine for each month's absence. Ambiguities regarding the collection of the fine were resolved in 1587 (29 Eliz. c. 6). Anyone convicted of persuading any of the queen's subjects to abandon the established church in favor of the church of Rome would be guilty of high treason, as would anyone so reconciled. Penalties against both saying and attending Mass were increased. In order to enforce these laws more effectively, all who had knowledge of any reconciliations had to report the fact to the justice of the peace within twenty days or be charged with misprision of treason for withholding the information. Common informers were encouraged with promises of a third of the fines of all recusants discovered. A statute of 1585 (27 Eliz. c. 2) sought to curb recusancy by eliminating the priests needed for the preservation of Catholicism. All priests who had been ordained since 1559 were given forty days to leave the kingdom. Those who remained after that date would be charged with high treason. All English subjects currently studying in a Jesuit college or seminary were to return home within six months and, upon arrival, report either to the bishop or to two justices of the peace to pronounce the oath of supremacy. Failure to observe any of these demands could result in the charge of treason. Anyone who continued to support students or seminaries abroad with funds and gifts could be charged with praemunire and the money forfeited to the Crown. Moreover, those convicted of harboring or assisting priests could lose their estates and their lives.

Throughout this period the government consistently explained the intensified persecution as attempts to secure the allegiance of its subjects. Official apologists, such as William

Cecil, claimed that the laws had nothing to do with religion; they were concerned with loyalty. Recusancy was a political offense because it denied the queen jurisdiction within the spiritual realm; it curtailed a subject's loyalty by acknowledging the authority of a foreign prince over an area claimed by the queen. Thus, the government did not prosecute religious dissidents but political traitors. Recusants, such as William Allen, denied that the laws had nothing to do with religion. If that were the case, why were all penalties dismissed if one conformed and attended the established church? Serious attempts by Sir Thomas Tresham and other Catholic nobles and gentry in 1585 to assure the queen of their political allegiance and yet obtain limited religious tolerance failed.

The coming of the Spanish Armada in 1588 resulted in a further intensification of the persecution. The Privy Council ordered that the more obstinate recusants be placed under tight security; more moderate ones were placed in the custody of private individuals. In June 1588 the more prominent recusants were imprisoned either in the Tower of London or in various castles throughout the realm. They were allowed to leave prison after October if they either conformed or demonstrated their loyalty to the queen. Because each was asked to swear that he acknowledged Elizabeth as his queen "notwithstanding any excommunication or past deposition of the Pope, or any present or future such," he was obliged to deny the pope's deposing power. Later in an oath he had to deny the spiritual power of the pope in England. In an attempt to reach a compromise, some Catholics drafted a version of the oath that recognized Elizabeth as lawful queen and offered to her the obedience shown to any prince by a Catholic. Attempts to reach a compromise, however, were fruitless: the demonstration of loyalty demanded either attendance at Protestant services or an explicit repudiation of the pope's deposing power.

The situation deteriorated even more as Spain intervened in the French religious struggles and continued to threaten English security with proposals of another armada directed at Scotland, Ireland, or England itself. Fear of Spain, which bordered on panic, led to the proclamation of 18 October 1591 (but published some time after 21 November), that sought to destroy suspected Spanish supporters through the establishment of commissions to search out seminary priests and Jesuits. The escalation of persecution was periodically fueled by the confessions of priests captured shortly after their arrival. During this period of increased vigilance, Cardinal Allen wrote his last letter to the English Catholics (12 December 1592). Sympathizing with the extreme pain that they suffered, he encouraged them to remain strong and faithful. Despite his repetition of the now traditional prohibition against frequenting Protestant churches, Allen also asked the Catholics to be compassionate and merciful to those who had attended Protestant services. Although this was the first time that a religious leader had publicly expressed any sympathy for the occasional conformists, Allen's position was the customary one espoused in the courses on "cases of conscience" at both English colleges in Douai and Rome: each condemned the sin of frequenting the churches but forgave the contrite sinner.

The secular priest Thomas Bell resuscitated the question of occasional conformity. Like Langdale, he defended Catholic attendance at Anglican services as long as they neither prayed nor received Communion, but entered the church out of obedience to the queen. Lest such attendance, however, give scandal, Bell suggested that all Catholics make some declaration that their attendance stemmed from obedience to their monarch and not from acceptance of the church. Bell's views were seized upon by some of the English Catholics as an acceptable way out of their difficult position, and Allen's letter was cited as corroboration, but to defenders of recusancy, such as Henry Garnet, S.J., any frequenting of Protestant churches was an act of betrayal comparable to the kiss of Judas. A prior declaration that such attendance stemmed from obedience to the sovereign was not sufficient because no protestation could make an evil act good. Regardless of the consequent difficulties, the laws of God had to take priority over those of Caesar. Certain of the secular clergy, the so-called Appellants, who were dissatisfied with the apparently uncompromisingly pro-Spanish policies of the English Jesuits, sought to find some accommodation between the laws of God and the demands of Caesar during the final years of Elizabeth's reign. The Appellants were willing to acknowledge Elizabeth as queen despite her excommunication; nevertheless, all attempts at compromise floundered over the refusal to deny the spiritual jurisdiction of the pope.

Recusancy was the English Catholic version of a universal problem that followed the fragmentation of Christendom: the relationship between a ruler and a religious minority. Could a prince impose a religion upon a reluctant people? Could Catholics be loyal subjects when their monarch was an excommunicated heretic? Would Catholics participate in any rebellions or invasions? Catholic apologists produced treatises on renunciation and domestic martyrologies to strengthen the faith of their co-religionists. They condemned occasional conformity, a practice as odious to the majority of English clergy as Nicodemism was to the Continental Protestants. Other Catholics progressed from recusancy to resistance. Nonetheless, the dilemma was not resolved: all attempts at a negotiated settlement failed. The anti-Catholic laws remained in force, and the loyalty of the Catholics remained in doubt.

BIBLIOGRAPHY

Bayne, C. G. *Anglo-Roman Relations, 1558–1565.* Reprint, Oxford, 1968. This remains an important study of the complex relationship between Rome and England during the opening years of Elizabeth's reign.

Bossy, John. *The English Catholic Community, 1570–1850.* London, 1976. Although Bossy's interpretation is now challenged by many, his remains the most important study of post-Reformation English Catholicism published over the past twenty years.

Caraman, Philip. *Henry Garnet, 1555–1606, and the Gunpowder Plot.* London, 1964. Even though Caraman practically ignores Garnet's debate with Bell over occasional conformity, this is a vibrant portrayal of one of the most important Jesuits of the period.

Clancy, Thomas H. *Papist Pamphleteers: The Allen-Persons Party and the Political Thought of the Counter-Reformation in England, 1572–1615.* Chicago, 1964. This is a good, readable introduction to the writings of the Allen/Persons party on such issues as rebellion and toleration.

Dickens, A. G. *Reformation Studies.* London, 1982. A collection of a number of Dickens's articles; those on recusancy are especially important.

———. *The English Reformation.* 2d rev. ed. London, 1989. The clearest presentation of Dickens's interpretation of the English Reformation, this edition revises the original (1964) to rebut the recent criticisms of Haigh et al.

Duffy, Eamon. *The Stripping of the Altars: Traditional Religion in England, 1400–1580.* New Haven, 1992. Well documented and clearly written, this work corroborates the "revisionist" approach.

Haigh, Christopher. *Reformation and Resistance in Tudor Lancashire.* Cambridge, 1975. This study of Lancashire Catholicism has provided the foundation for Haigh's subsequent interpretation of recusancy.

———. *English Reformation: Religion, Politics, and Society under the Tudors.* Oxford, 1993. This is the first comprehensive "revisionist" history of the Tudor period.

Haigh, Christopher, ed. *The Reign of Elizabeth I.* Reprint, Athens, Ga., 1987. Different aspects of Elizabeth's reign are studied by various "revisionist" historians. Haigh's article on recusancy is important.

———. *The English Reformation Revised.* Cambridge, 1987. Among the important "revisionist" articles included in this volume are three by Haigh.

Holmes, Peter. *Resistance and Compromise: The Political Thought of the Elizabethan Catholics.* Cambridge, 1982. A flaw of this work is an attempt to impose a structure on the writings of the recusants. Nonetheless this is an important study, especially on the debate about occasional conformity, with a good bibliography of primary sources.

Holmes, Peter, ed. *Elizabethan Casuistry.* Catholic Record Society, no. 67. London, 1981. Holmes has edited a few of the important tracts used in "cases of conscience" courses at the English seminaries on the Continent.

Knox, Thomas Francis, ed. *The Letters and Memorials of William Cardinal Allen, 1532–1594.* London, 1882; reprint, Ridgewood, N.J., 1965. Unfortunately there is no modern biography of this important figure. Although the introduction is rather tendentious, it is an important collection of material.

McGrath, Patrick. *Papists and Puritans under Elizabeth I.* London, 1967. This remains one of the best narrative accounts of Roman Catholicism during the period.

O'Day, Rosemary. *The Debate on the English Reformation.* London and New York, 1986. All aspects of the current debates on the English Reformation are handled clearly and judiciously. The bibliography is especially helpful.

Pritchard, Arnold. *Catholic Loyalism in Elizabethan England.* London, 1979. Pritchard studies not the more militant Allen/Persons party but the clergy and laity within England who sought to demonstrate their loyalty without compromising their allegiance to the pope.

Scarisbrick, J. J. *The Reformation and the English People.* Oxford, 1984. Originally given as the Ford Lectures at the University of Oxford, this is probably the clearest exposition of the "revisionist" position.

Walsham, Alexandra. *Church Papists: Catholicism, Conformity, and Confessional Polemic in Early Modern England.* London, 1993. Walsham's study is the first to explore the significant role played by "Church Papists" in the preservation of Catholicism.

Thomas M. McCoog, s.j.

REFERENCE WORKS. The large number of reference works on the sixteenth century is an indication of the extensive scope of Reformation studies, both geographically and thematically. These reference works help facilitate the scholarly studies of the Reformation, as they provide a convenient and instructive overview of sixteenth-century topics and sources.

A survey of historiography is found in *Reformation Europe: A Guide to Research* (S. E. Ozment, ed., Saint Louis, 1982) and *Reformation Europe: A Guide to Research II* (W. S. Maltby, ed., Saint Louis, 1992). There are also numerous encyclopedias and dictionaries covering Reformation topics. Among the standard works are the *Oxford Dictionary of the Christian Church, Die Religion in Geschichte und Gegenwart* (Tübingen, 1955–), and *Theologische Realenzyklopädie,* with its detailed articles on the German scene. Also important are *The Mennonite Encyclopedia,* the *Lutheran Cyclopedia,* the *Handbuch der europäischen Geschichte* (Stuttgart, 1973), and the *Handbuch der Kirchengeschichte* (Freiburg, 1962–). The recent *Handbook of Late Medieval and Early Modern History* (Leiden, 1994) should also be mentioned, though it is a bit idiosyncratic in emphases.

Listed below are some of the most important bibliographies and bibliographic surveys covering the Reformation. Excellent for primary sources is *Verzeichnis der im deutschen Sprachbereich erschienenen Drucke des XVI. Jahrhunderts* (I. Bessel, ed., Stuttgart, 1983–). Though restricted to Germany, *Bibliographie zur deutschen Geschichte im Zeitalter der Glaubensspaltung* (Karl Schottenloher, ed., 6 vols.) is monumental. The *Archive for Reformation History* includes a bibliographic survey of all facets of the sixteenth century.

Bibliography of the Continental Reformation: Materials Available in English (Roland H. Bainton and Eric W. Gritsch, eds., 2d rev. & enl. ed., Hamden, Conn., 1972) provides good coverage with a topical arrangement. Although it has no indexes, there is a detailed table of contents. Most entries have brief annotations. Included are many periodical articles and a large section on the individual reformers.

Bibliographie de la Refórme, 1450–1648 (International Committee of Historical Sciences, Commission internationale d'histoire ecclésiastique comparée, Leiden, 1958–), listing books, dissertations, and articles published between 1940 and 1955 (1960 for fascicles 6 and 7), is divided into fascicles by the country where the material was published. Each fascicle includes indexes of authors, subjects, and other categories, but no overall index exists. Fascicle 8, published in

1982, lists additional materials published in 1956–1975 (Belgium and Luxembourg) and in 1956–1976 (Netherlands). The Netherlands portion (1,526 items) continues the policy of listing materials about the Reformation published in that country, regardless of the specific topic addressed, while the Belgium and Luxembourg portion (1,527 items) lists only materials about the Reformation in those countries, regardless of where the material was published.

The *Center for Reformation Research Microform Holdings from All Periods: A General Finding List* (8 vols., Saint Louis, 1977–1979) is a list of the center's some 10,000 printed works from the Reformation period. The center lends microform copies of its holdings to researchers. This finding list contains all the center's printed works except for the Newberry French political pamphlets (indexed elsewhere) and works listed in earlier numbers (2, 3, 6, and 7) of the series *Sixteenth Century Bibliography.* Entries are arranged by author and subarranged by title and then by publication date. This is a particularly valuable bibliographic tool for Reformation research since copies of works listed here can generally be borrowed from the center.

Contemporaries of Erasmus: A Biographical Register of the Renaissance and Reformation (Peter G. Bietenholz, ed., Thomas B. Deutscher, assoc. ed., 3 vols., Toronto, 1985–) is an ambitious project containing biographic sketches of the more than 1,900 persons referred to in the collected works of Desiderius Erasmus (University of Toronto Press edition). For some obscure persons no additional information is given beyond what is found in the writings of Erasmus. Included with each entry is a partial list of where the individuals are mentioned in Erasmus's works.

Early Sixteenth Century Roman Catholic Theologians and the German Reformation; A Finding List of CRR Holdings (Saint Louis, 1975) lists the microfilm holdings at the Center for Reformation Research of early (1520–1550) anti-Reformation writings by twenty-one Catholic theologians. For each theologian a brief vita is given, followed by a listing of available writings (in the order of publication date). The center also lends copies of these holdings to researchers.

Bibliography of British History, Tudor Period, 1485–1603 (Conyers Read, ed., 2d ed., Oxford, 1959) is a selective 6,543-item bibliography of pamphlets, books, periodical articles, and other sources up to January 1957. Though strong on church history, it covers all aspects of the history of the period and stresses English-language materials. The bibliography includes some annotations, and there is a detailed table of contents and an author/subject index.

Bibliography of British History, Stuart Period, 1603–1714 (Godfrey Davies and Mary F. Keeler, eds., 2d ed., Oxford, 1970) complements the bibliography above, covering another century. This work includes 4,350 items, arranged topically. It contains a detailed table of contents and an author/subject index. Some annotations are included.

The *Bibliography of the Reform, 1450–1648, Relating to the United Kingdom and Ireland for the Years 1955–1970* (Derek Baker, ed., Oxford, 1975)—sponsored by the Commission internationale d'histoire ecclésiastique comparée, British subcommission of the International Committee of Historical Sciences—serves as a complement to *Bibliographie de la Refórme, 1450–1648* for materials on the Reformation in Great Britain. It has three major sections (England and Wales, Scotland, and Ireland) and is subdivided by type of material (book, periodical article, review, and thesis). Sources are also listed alphabetically by author. Given this arrangement and because there is no subject index, subject access is difficult. Also notable is *The Contemporary Printed Literature of the English Counter-Reformation between 1558 and1640* (A. F. Allison and D. M. Rogers, eds., 2 vols., 1989 and 1994).

HANS J. HILLERBRAND

REFORM. In the sixteenth century the term *reform* was used positively in both secular and ecclesiastical contexts with a broad spectrum of meaning that was not tied to any specific religious tradition. It also was a legal term in its own right. Today the related term *Reformation* is, in English- and German-speaking countries, a specialized historical term that designates the emergence of the Protestant confessions and churches; used as an adjective, *reformed* refers to the basic stance that led to the formation of these churches.

The narrowing of the concept of *reform* from its general to its ecclesiastical meaning began in the late seventeenth century; in this narrower meaning, from the late eighteenth century on, the *Reformation* was interpreted from the perspective of universal history as the most significant event of the sixteenth century. Thus in 1839 Leopold von Ranke in his classic *Deutsche Geschichte im Zeitalter der Reformation* (German History in the Age of the Reformation) employed the term as a concept for dividing history into periods. Thereafter the term quickly began to be used as a designation for the period itself and even today is still used as a benchmark for the entire history of Germany, both ecclesiastical and secular, and even for sixteenth-century world history. For example, the relevant volumes of the Cambridge and the New Cambridge Modern History have the title *The Reformation.* During the last few decades the terms *confession* and *Age of Confession* (Konfession and konfessionelles Zeitalter) have been used alongside the term *Reformation,* with varying approaches to marking off that period. More recently the term *Second Reformation* has also been brought into the discussion (Heinz Schilling), more as a term for specifying the type of reform rather than the period; this term may not win general acceptance.

The equivalent for *reform* in French is *réforme* (Ital., *riforma*; Span., *reforma*), which covers an expandable range of meanings. The German *Reform* is, of course, identical to the English term.

Concept of *Reformatio* in the High and Late Middle Ages. Both nouns, *reformatio* and *réforme*, stem from the Latin verb *reformare*, which occurs only twice in the Vulgate translation of the Bible. Thus it does not occur in every instance where the text deals with the basic elements of the Christian life (i.e., baptism, sanctification, and repentance as expressed in *Rom.* 12:2).

From the late classical period the European Middle Ages inherited the concept of *reformatio* with three different shades of meaning: change, renewal, and improvement. Specifically, these concepts were seen as: (1) Correction of a present situation considered inadequate through a return to some earlier model considered a standard and a norm, including the view of the *ecclesia primitiva* as the ideal. Here lies the root of all the medieval and modern Renaissance movements. (2) Correction of some deficient present situation (with or without a predominant reference to the past) with the goal of bringing men and women closer to the image and likeness of God as proclaimed in salvation history while consciously seeking to bring about the divinely ordained world order. This concept of *reform* is primarily marked by its orientation to the future. (3) Without reference to the past or future, as a technical term of Roman law (e.g., the determination of a tax or the amendment of a judgment).

Although the numerous specific elaborations of these three basic meanings will not be described here, for a long time the Middle Ages did not add anything substantially new to the scope of the concept even though numerous terms were used (*corrigere, emendare, meliorare, recreare, reducere ad regularem normam, regenerare, renovare, reparare, restaurare, restituere*). The general appeal for renewal contained in the *reformatio* concept was extended to the secular realm after the Interregnum.

In the late Middle Ages the programmatic content of the idea of *reformatio* became broader and deeper. With the Gregorian reform of the eleventh and twelfth centuries, the papacy succeeded in establishing the essential independence of the hierarchically ordered clergy from the secular powers (*libertas ecclesiae*). At the same time, as a primary duty of their office, the popes were entrusted with the task of interior and exterior "reform" of the church that was constantly necessary. Thus Pope Innocent III convened the Fourth Lateran Council for two purposes: *ad recuperationem terrae sanctae* ("for the reclaiming of the holy land") and *ad reformationem universalis ecclesiae* ("for the reformation of the universal church"). In this context he gave a precise description of the aspects of the church that were in need of reform.

In the course of the thirteenth century, the idea of the need for a general reform not only of individuals but also of the church as an institution became a topic of critical debate, which did not spare even the papacy. Criticism sometimes went far beyond denouncing the misconduct of individuals. Accordingly Duranti the Younger demanded in his *De modo generalis concilii celebrandi* that the Council of Vienne (1311/12) undertake a *reformatio tam in capite quam membris* ("reformation of the head as well as of the members"). This notion of a reform from top to bottom caught people's imagination and was open to interpretation in episcopal, conciliar, and papal terms. There has hardly been another ecclesiastical slogan that made such a lasting impression over such a long time on the minds and hearts of people who wanted to take the message of Christ seriously. On 27 June 1611 a papal nuncio in Cologne still described the program of church reform in similar terms: "si dovrebbono primicramente riformare i superiori, poi gl'altri dell'ordine ecclesiastico cosí regolare come secolare, ultimamente il popolo" (first those who are higher should be reformed, then the other levels of both the regular and secular clergy, and finally the people). In other words, reform must start at the top so that it can finally be realized at the grass roots.

In the fourteenth century the popes were in no position to undertake a reform program that would go to the heart of the religious issue. They were hampered both by their fiscal and financial system and by their political dependence on the French monarchy in Avignon. In the Great Schism that began in 1378 the papacy itself became an ongoing source of scandal. The Council of Constance (1414–1418) finally succeeded in ending the schism in 1417 but was unable to achieve a general reform of the church in head and members. The Council of Basel (1431–1437) likewise failed in this respect. But the papacy also showed itself unable to make the radical changes in the central organization of the church that were imperative if some excesses (such as the accumulation of benefices, the separation of the income attached to a church office from its exercise, and the abuse of ecclesiastical censures) were to be eliminated and if better pastoral care were to made possible. Even popes (such as Nicholas V and Pius II) who acknowledged the urgency of an effective reform of the system accomplished little. The Fifth Lateran Council (1512–1517), hailed as a "reform" council, brought about only scant successes. No abuse was attacked at the root; no reform decree was consistently enforced.

Almost everywhere in Europe during the late Middle Ages individual regions, orders, groups, and centers began with a reform from the bottom up, since no way for a reform from the top down had opened up. This *reformatio in membris* sought to bring about a church that was intellectually more alive and committed to pastoral care, in order to meet the devotional needs of the people, who were apparently more devout than previously. These numerous efforts at reform did not change the church as a whole, but they also went beyond being a mere agenda item. Today many historians classify these initiatives as part of the "Catholic Reformation" to distinguish them from the later Protestant "Reformation." A basic clarification of the concept was offered by Hubert Jedin in his *Katholischer Reformation oder Gegenre-*

formation? Ein Versuch zur Klärung der Begriffe. Until then Catholic historians had refused to use the term *Reformation* with its positive connotation of events on the Protestant side. More recent attempts to use only the term *Counter-Reformation* for the Catholic events (Wolfgang Reinhard) or else to refer exclusively to the "Catholic Reform" (Konrad Repgen) do not seem to have won universal acceptance. That this "reform" had been set in motion well before Luther is no longer disputed today. Its existence, for example, contributed significantly to Spain's remaining Catholic. To what extent Catholic reform would have become more widespread without the challenge posed by Luther's and later Calvin's "Reformation" and whether the papacy would have then taken up reform on its own, as it did after 1534 and 1563, is a matter of speculation. No possible answer can be either proved or disproved. People of that time were thoroughly familiar with the term *reformatio* in speaking of the attempts at Catholic reform in the fifteenth and sixteenth centuries.

Alongside the ecclesiastical concept of *reformatio* with its reference to the *ecclesia primitiva* as an ideal and the use of *reformatio* as a legal term, particularly as a term of courtroom procedure by jurists, the word *reformatio* took on a specialized meaning in the fifteenth century in the sense of a "set of regulations," "determination," or a "presentation of customary law" with validity for a given city, a territory, or the entire Holy Roman Empire. Compilations in the form of a "corpus" of the laws of individual German cities between 1499 and 1578 were called "Reformatio" (of the city of Frankfurt, for example); the important law on public order of the empire from the year 1442 was promulgated under the title *Königliche Reformation* or *König Friedrichs Reformation*, and the officials who were to enforce the law were called *Reformierer.* A similar situation obtained for the improvement of university bylaws; it was in this sense that in 1520 Luther demanded a *"gute Reformation"* and that the new imperial *polizei* ("general law and order") regulations of 1548 were labeled *"Reformation."*

Thus the range of meanings attached to the term *reformatio* had broadened significantly by the early sixteenth century. The term was used in the ecclesiastical, legal, and political spheres and could mean the need to return to the ideal past. It could also carry the meaning of renewal without any reference to the past, purely goal oriented in the sense of improvement through establishing norms that would be generally binding.

The Concept of *Reformatio* in the Early Modern Era. It is difficult to determine which of the late medieval meanings of *reformatio* was the most widely used in the early sixteenth century. What is certain is that the broad range of meanings of the term had not yet narrowed during this period. Eike Wolgast has suggested that a trend had become more widespread to distinguish the content of the *reformatio* concept in the ecclesiastical and secular spheres.

It is undisputed that Luther initially had no intention of splitting the church, but of renewing the entire church. His leadership quickly evolved first into a theological and then into an ecclesiastical revolution. But it had begun with "reform," with a cry for a greater correspondence between claims and reality, for pastoral care, for better theology and a deeper piety. This could be called (in today's language) an incipient "Catholic reform" from below, since Luther the reformer in 1517/18 did not see himself as a "reformer" in the later, narrower sense, motivated as he was by what had been traditionally understood as reform. He used the word *reformatio* only rarely, although he did use it in the sense of an overall renewal of the church from within, for example, in his *Resolutiones* of 1518.

As for the Lutheran churches that emerged starting in the 1520s, no collective name derived from the verb *reformare* was used either by those churches themselves or by their opponents. In juridical language, from 1529 on, there are references to "those who protest" (*protestierende*), and from 1530 on to "adherents/followers of the Augsburg Confession." *Reformation* as an all-encompassing term for what is today called the "Reformation movement and formation of churches" and the official documents that accompanied them or made them possible in a given community, city, or territory was not in common use at that time. Only in 1580 was the new Lutheran tradition first officially defined with the word *reformare* in the *Solida declaratio.* This did not reflect any predominant self-understanding by the Lutherans. Consequently, Roman Catholics continued to use the word as they had before. The term is found, for example, in a polemical theological writing by Hieronymus Emser against Luther in 1521 and as an official title in the imperial laws, for example, Charles V's "Formula Reformationis" of June 1548. The Council of Trent, along with decrees *de fide*, also regularly adopted a *decretum super reformatione* between 1546 and 1563. These "reformation/reform articles" were normative for church life until the Second Vatican Council (1962–1965).

Beginning in the 1540s Calvinist communities emerged in western Switzerland, later in France, and then in the Netherlands. These communities called themselves *églises réformées* or *ceux de la religion réformée* ("reformed churches" or "those of the reformed religion"); thus their designation was derived from the word *reformare.* The high degree of prestige attached to this word was something Roman Catholics and finally the French state preferred to deny to the Protestants. Thus the Protestant movement was referred to as the *religion prétendue réformée* ("religion that claims to be reformed"), and in 1576 this term was adopted as the legal ecclesiastical designation.

When the Lutheran estates of the empire and the Lutheran members of the empire received permanent legal recognition as an ecclesial body in Germany in 1555, there were as yet no Calvinist territories. Consequently, the Peace of

Augsburg contains no mention of the Calvinist ("Reformed") ecclesial entity. In 1566 this problem came before the imperial diet. The diet avoided either recognizing the Calvinists as belonging to the Augsburg Confession or rejecting them formally. The juridical clarification of the matter was delayed with compromises on the wording of the confession until the Thirty Years' War. Although the Edict of Restitution (1629) declared that imperial protection was valid only for the Augsburg Confession in its 1530 version, this could not be enforced. In the Peace of Westphalia the imperial juridical provisions on religion that applied to Roman Catholics and Lutherans were extended to Calvinists, who were now formally designated as *"reformati."* A legal protest against this granting of equal status to the Calvinists was filed by Saxony, the leader of the Corpus Evangelicorum.

In contrast to a widespread opinion among systematic theologians, the formula *ecclesia semper reformanda* is not attested in Protestant theology of the sixteenth century. It is most likely that the idea that the Reformation should not remain simply a one-time event, but that it is an ongoing duty of the church, goes back to those Dutch pastors who should be placed in the context of the prehistory of Pietism.

BIBLIOGRAPHY

Bori, Pier Cesare. *Chiesa primitiva: L'immagine della communità delle origini (Atti 2,42–47; 4,32–37) nella storia della chiesa antica.* Brescia, 1974.

Chaunu, Pierre. *Les temps des Réformes: Histoire religieuse et système de la civilisation; La crise de la chrétienté: l'éclatement, 1250–1550.* Paris, 1975.

Delumeau, Jean. *Naissance et affirmation de la Réforme.* Paris, 1965.

Die Bekenntnisschriften der evangelisch-lutherischen Kirche. Göttingen, 1979.

Ditsche, Magnus. "Die *ecclesia primitiva* im Kirchenbild des hohen und späten Mittelalters." Ph.D. diss., Universität Bonn, 1958.

Goeters, Wilhelm. *Die Vorbereitung des Pietismus in der Reformierten Kirche der Niederlande bis zur labadistischen Krisis, 1670.* Leipzig, 1911.

Heckel, Martin. *Deutsche Geschichte.* Vol. 5, *Deutschland im konfessionellen Zeitalter.* Göttingen, 1983.

Jedin, Hubert. *Katholische Reformation oder Gegenreformation?: Ein Versuch zur Klärung der Begriffe nebst einer Jubiläumsbetrachtung über das Trienter Konzil.* Lucerne, 1946.

———. *Geschichte des Konzils von Trient.* Vol. 1. Freiburg, 1949.

———. "Die historischen Begriffe." In *Handbuch der Kirchengeschichte,* edited by Hubert Jedin, vol. 4, pp. 449–450. Freiburg,1967.

Kaiser, Karl V. "Der Römisch-Kayserlichen Majestät Ordnung und Reformation guter Policey, zu Beförderung des gemeinen Nutzens auff dem Reichstag zu Augspug, Anno Domini 1548 auffgericht." In *Neue und vollständigere Sammlung der Reichs-Abschiede,* edited by Johann Jakob Schmauß and Christian Heinrich Senckenberg, vol. 2, p. 587. Frankfurt a.M., 1747.

Klueting, Harm. *Das konfessionelle Zeitalter, 1525–1648.* Stuttgart, 1989.

Knemeyer, Ludwig. "Polizei." In *Geschichtliche Grundbegriffe,* vol. 4, pp. 875–888. Stuttgart, 1978.

Ladner, Gerhart B. "Die mittelalterliche Reform-Idee und ihr Verhältnis zur Renaissance." *Mitteilungen des Instituts für Österreichische Geschichtsforschung* 60 (1953), 31–59.

———. *The Idea of Reform: Its Impact on Christian Thought and Action in the Age of the Fathers.* New York, 1959.

Lepp, Friedrich. *Schlagwörter des Reformationszeitalters.* Leipzig, 1908.

Leuschner, Joachim, ed. *Deutsche Geschichte.* Vol. 4, *Deutschland im Späten Mittelalter.* Göttingen, 1983.

Miethke, Jürgen. "Reform, Reformation." In *Lexikon des Mittelalters,* vol. 7, cols. 543–550. Munich, 1994.

Moeller, Bernd. *Deutsche Geschichte.* Vol. 4, *Deutschland im Zeitalter der Reformation.* Göttingen, 1988.

Ozment, Steven E. *The Age of Reform, 1250–1550: An Intellectual and Religious History of Late Medieval and Reformation Europe.* New Haven, 1980.

"Reformation." In *Wetzer und Welte's Kirchenlexikon,* vol. 10, pp. 881–891. Freiburg, 1897.

Reinhard, Wolfgang, ed. *Nuntiaturberichte aus Deutschland: Die Kölner Nuntiatur.* Vol. 5. Munich, 1972.

Repgen, Konrad. "Reform als Leitidee kirchlicher Vergangenheit und Zukunft." *Römische Quartalschrift für christliche Altertumskunde und Kirchengeschichte* 84 (1989), 5–30.

Richard, Willy. *Untersuchungen zur Genesis der reformierten Kirchenterminologie der Westschweiz und Frankreichs, mit besonderer Berücksichtigung der Namengebung.* Bern, 1959.

Schindling, Anton, Karl Amon, and Walter Ziegler, eds. *Die Territorien des Reiches im Zeitalter der Reformation und Konfessionalisierung: Land und Konfession, 1500–1650.* Münster, 1991.

Seckendorf, Veit Ludwig von. *Historia lutheranismi, Commentarius historicus et apologeticus de lutheranismo: Sive de reformatione religionis ductu D. Martini Lutheri in magna Germaniae parte aliisque regionibus.* Leipzig, 1694.

Venard, Marc, ed. *Histoire du christianisme.* Vol. 8, *Le temp des confessions, 1530–1620/30.* Paris 1992.

Wolgast, Eike. "Reform, Reformation." In *Geschichtliche Grundbegriffe,* vol. 5, pp. 313–360. Stuttgart, 1984.

Konrad Repgen

Translated from German by Robert E. Shillenn

REFORMATIO LEGUM ECCLESIASTICARUM.

This document, written in 1551–1552, was a proposed revision of traditional canon law in the wake of England's break from the Roman Catholic church. In 1532 Parliament provided for a royal commission that would bring ecclesiastical law into conformity with English common law. Not until 1551, however, during the reign of Edward VI (r. 1547–1553) and under the leadership of Thomas Cranmer, archbishop of Canterbury, was this committee of thirty-two people established. Bishops, theologians, civil law experts, and civil lawyers were equally represented, and members included such well-known figures as Nicholas Ridley, John Ponet, Matthew Parker, John Hooper, William Cecil, Thomas Smith, Peter Martyr Vermigli, and Jan Łaski.

Completed during the winter of 1551–1552, the *Reformatio legum ecclesiasticarum* came before Parliament in March 1553, but its progress was blocked by John Dudley, duke of Northumberland, then head of the government. Edward died soon thereafter, and further action was postponed until the reign of his half sister, Elizabeth I (r. 1558–1603). Working from Parker's manuscript, John Foxe, the martyrologist, first published an edition of the *Reformatio legum ecclesiasticarum* in 1571 after the queen thwarted attempts in 1559 and 1563 to revive the project. Individual laws and injunctions were passed by Parliament in piecemeal fashion to deal with particular aspects of canon law that needed reform while the comprehensive *Reformatio legum ecclesiasticarum* languished in continued obscurity. Only with the *Canons and Constitutions of 1604* were more thorough and decisive amendments officially made to the ecclesiastical law.

The proposed reform of 1552 covered a wide range of topics, including heresy, qualifications for clergy, church government and organization, marriage and divorce, discipline, crimes and punishments, and court procedures. The *Reformatio legum ecclesiasticarum* would have liberalized divorce laws, expanded diaconate duties, and probably eliminated heresy as a capital crime. A potential for conflict existed in the document's positing separate claims for supreme authority in the sovereign and scripture, even as the new canons themselves clearly fell under the civil law as expressed through king-in-parliament.

BIBLIOGRAPHY

Logan, F. Donald. "The Henrician Canons." *Bulletin of the Institute of Historical Research* 47 (1974), 99–103. Reveals new evidence of an earlier collection of canon law reforms compiled as early as 1535.

Sachs, Leslie Raymond. "Thomas Cranmer's 'Reformatio legum ecclesiasticarum' of 1553 in the Context of English Church Law from the Later Middle Ages to the Canons of 1603." J.C.D. diss., Catholic University of America, 1982. Places the *Reformatio* within a broad context of long-standing church-state issues.

Spalding, James C. "The *Reformatio Legum Ecclesiasticarum* of 1552 and the Furthering of Discipline in England." *Church History* 39 (1970), 162–71. Discusses some possible outcomes had the *Reformatio* become law.

———. *The Reformation of the Ecclesiastical Laws of England, 1552.* Kirksville, Mo., 1992. An edited edition of the original manuscript with a detailed history provided in the introduction.

BEN LOWE

REFORMATION. In modern historiography the term *Reformation* is customarily applied to a series of religious protests and reforms that swept Europe during the sixteenth century. To speak of the Reformation, then, is not to speak of a single, coherent movement with a single leader and a unified program. At the same time, the term encompasses more than a disparate collection of movements unrelated to one another and sharing few or no common characteristics. Collectively, these parallel movements sought to reform the Western church in ways that went well beyond previous reform movements within Western Christendom in both degree and kind. Using scripture as their primary authority and the early church as a model (and with some, as a norm), these movements rejected the authority of the papacy and, to varying degrees, much of traditional belief and practice that had grown up within medieval Catholicism. They also attempted to reestablish the church (and sometimes society) in accord with their often varying understandings of scripture and early Christianity. They shared certain ideological tenets, which engaged and motivated to varying degrees the larger population. Except for some sectarian groups, they relied ultimately upon the governing authorities to institutionalize and preserve the desired reforms. Primarily a religious phenomenon, the Reformation also had profound political and social implications.

Substantial Reformation movements developed in most of the imperial cities and many of the princely territories of the Holy Roman Empire, in several cantons of the Swiss Confederation, and in the duchy of Austria and its dependencies. The Scandinavian kingdoms of Denmark and Sweden and their dependencies (Iceland, Norway, Finland, and Schleswig-Holstein) also experienced Reformation movements, as did England, Scotland, France, and parts of eastern Europe, especially the fragmented kingdoms of Poland and Hungary. In some of these territories, such as parts of the Holy Roman Empire, Switzerland, England, Scotland, and Scandinavia, the Reformation movements were successfully institutionalized; in others, such as France, Poland, and parts of Hungary, the Holy Roman Empire, and the Austrian lands, initial success was later reversed by a resurgent Catholicism.

The Reformation as a Historical Concept. In the course of the sixteenth century, "reformation" and "reform" became confessionalized, distinguishing first Lutherans from Catholics and then Lutherans from Reformed. In France, the Netherlands, England, and the Holy Roman Empire the term *Reformed* came gradually to be applied to Protestants of a Calvinist character, who claimed to be "reformed according to Scripture."

In the literature of the first centennial of the posting of the Ninety-five Theses (1617), the term *Reformation* was applied by Lutherans specifically to the religious and ecclesiastical events surrounding Martin Luther. In an attempt to defend Luther from the charge that he had preached new teachings, these writers of the centennial characterized this narrowly defined Reformation as a necessary and singular divine intervention intended to save the church and reestablish true doctrine. This one-time correction needed now only to be maintained.

In his defense of Lutheranism against Jesuit attack at the end of the seventeenth century, the Lutheran historian Veit Ludwig von Seckendorf (1626–1692) took this confessional and personal concept of the Reformation and employed it as a historic designation. Although Seckendorf paid some attention to political factors, the Reformation remained for him largely the history of Luther's criticism of the Catholic church and his involvement in the formation of a new church; the history of Calvinism, Seckendorf expressly argued, did not belong to the history of the Reformation. This conception of the Reformation, limiting the term to the life and work of Martin Luther, is sometimes still encountered in modern treatments, especially those by theologians. But whatever its theological justification, such use of the term ignores the complex historical situation in which Luther lived and had his influence.

It was in the course of the eighteenth century that the term *Reformation* was first used in the modern sense by Protestant historians to characterize an epoch or period in European history. The historiographic designation of this period as the "Age of Reformation" was given definitive formulation by the great German historian Leopold von Ranke (1795–1886). In treating the Reformation as the product of interacting spiritual and political factors with European-wide significance, Ranke broadened the concept of Reformation beyond the theological and church-historical limits exemplified in Seckendorf's work.

Influenced by confessional conflict that continued well into the twentieth century, Catholic historians challenged both the Protestant conception of the Reformation and the use of the term itself, preferring alternatives such as the "Age of Schism" (*Glaubenspaltung*). It was only in the mid-twentieth century that Catholic historians such as Joseph Lortz inaugurated from the Catholic side a more sympathetic view of the Reformation movements. Modern historians—Protestant, Catholic, and secular—have widened the term *Reformation* even further to encompass not only the political and religious elements of Ranke's characterization but also the social and cultural components of the Reformation movements.

The Ideology of the Reformation Movements. Without ignoring the profound political and social content of the Reformation movements of the sixteenth century, historians generally agree that they were first and foremost religious in their motivation and articulated goals. While the leaders of the movements shared through the medium of the press a relatively coherent set of beliefs centered around the authority of scripture and justification by grace through faith, their followers were more likely to acquire their own often quite various understandings of these beliefs through preaching and other forms of oral communication.

Although there were considerable differences in detail and emphasis, certain central convictions were widespread. The movements shared an insistence on scripture as the sole authority for deciding matters of religious belief and, to a lesser extent, practice. To varying degrees these movements all harked back to the ideal of earlier belief and practice—and in this respect, at least, accorded with the late medieval notion of reformation. The movements frequently diverged with respect to the articulation of this ideal, and, because they were relying largely on scripture as their authority, they often disagreed as to the right understanding of scripture. The influence of humanism, especially of an Erasmian bent, was evident in the general desire to reduce "externalities" and promote a more inward and "spiritual" form of religion. "Human laws" were widely held to be inapplicable within the spiritual realm, but differences arose over what should take their place, whether the "law of Christ," or justification by faith alone, or some (occasionally uneasy) combination of the two.

These various Reformation movements advocated simplified ceremonies and practices, which they based on their understanding of the ceremonies and practices of early Christianity as depicted in the New Testament. Accordingly, they rejected monastic vows, the veneration of saints, pilgrimages, indulgences, and much else of the devotional practice that had grown up within Western Catholicism during the Middle Ages. With some few exceptions these movements also generally reduced the number of sacraments from the traditional seven to two or three (baptism, Eucharist, and sometimes penance). While they disagreed among themselves on matters such as images and music in church, they all agreed that services should be held in the vernacular language and should involve significant lay participation.

Most of these movements at some stage generated fairly widespread popular support and lay involvement, but these varied in timing and degree from movement to movement. This popular support reflected a variety of motives predominantly of a religious nature, but political, economic, and social motives influenced and shaped, and on occasion even dominated, issues of religious conviction. While Reformation movements drew adherents from all segments of sixteenth-century society, conflict between different social groups played an important role and accounts in part for the varied directions the movements took. Generally speaking, Reformation movements tended to be more urban than rural in nature, although rural society also occasionally became involved, sometimes with violent consequences, as in the German Peasants' War.

The Institutionalization of the Reformation and Government Involvement. At some point in the history of each movement, ideological goals buttressed by popular support needed to take institutional form. Except in the case of certain sectarian movements, such as most forms of Anabaptism, the ruling authorities became at some point part of the Reformation. In some cases, such as the reform in many German imperial cities, the involvement of the governing authorities in institutionalizing the reforms came late in the history of the movement; in others, such as England and Scandinavia, the authorities were involved early in its promotion or perhaps even initiated the Reformation movement itself. But whenever the authorities became involved, they often came to dominate the movement, shaping it to their own ends.

Catholic Reform and Counter-Reformation. The term *Counter-Reformation* (*Gegenreformation*) was first employed in the middle of the seventeenth century to describe attempts by secular authorities to return a territory to Catholicism. In the course of the late eighteenth and early nineteenth century, it came in German historiography to describe, often in the plural (*Gegenreformationen*), the forcible attempts to return territories to Catholicism during the period up to the Treaty of Westphalia in 1648. Finally, Leopold von Ranke and Moriz Ritter (1840–1923) used it to designate, now in the singular (*Gegenreformation*), the period in German history from 1555 to 1648.

Not surprisingly, Catholic historians took issue with this terminology as being too negative and ignoring the continuity between late medieval reforms and Catholic reforms of the sixteenth century. In a famous essay in 1946, the Catholic historian Hubert Jedin suggested the paired terms *Catholic Reform* and *Counter-Reformation* to describe the dual phenomena of continuing ecclesiastical reform and specific actions taken against the Reformation on the basis of the decrees of the Council of Trent (1545–1563). The term and its alternatives continue to be debated.

Extensions of the Term *Reformation*. In the twentieth-century various attempts have been made to identify specific "reformations" within the larger constellation of Reformation movements. For example, historians of Anabaptism and related dissident movements have applied the term *Radical Reformation* to their field of study, thereby suggesting that these movements were in some sense more fundamental ("getting back to the roots") or politically and socially radical. Marxist historians have distinguished between the "People's Reformation" (*Volksreformation*) that allegedly came to an end with the German Peasants' War and the "Princes' Reformation" (*Fürstenreformation*), which followed; Peter Blickle has coined both the concept and terminology of the Communal Reformation (*Gemeindereformation*). Historians investigating the process of "confessionalization" and state-building in the Holy Roman Empire in the late sixteenth and early seventeenth century have employed the term *Second Reformation* (*Zweite Reformation*) to describe the confessionalization process within German Reformed (Calvinist and Philippist) Christianity. Many of these attempts at subdivision and distinction have proved useful to historians but have also generated controversy and disagreement. Historians have reached no consensus on the appropriateness of these subsidiary designations.

[*See also* Catholic Reformation; Reform; *and* Reformation Studies.]

BIBLIOGRAPHY

Cameron, Euan. *The European Reformation.* Oxford, 1991. Attempts to define and explore the Reformation as a European-wide phenomenon.

Dickens, A. G., and John Tonkin. *The Reformation in Historical Thought.* Cambridge, Mass., 1985. The best-survey of the historiography.

Jedin, Hubert. *Katholische Reformation oder Gegenreformation? Ein Versuch zur Klärung der Begriffe nebst einer Jubiläumsbetrachtung über das Trienter Konzil.* Lucerne, 1946. Classic statement on the problems of the terms "Counter-Reformation" and "Catholic Reformation."

Lohse, Bernhard. "Luthers Selbsteinschätzung." In *Evangelium in der Geschichte: Studien zu Luther und der Reformation,* edited by Leif Grane, Bernd Moeller, and Otto Pesch, pp. 158–175. Göttingen, 1988. Best survey of what Luther thought of himself and his "Reformation."

O'Malley, John, ed. *Catholicism in Early Modern History: A Guide to Research.* Saint Louis, 1988. Group of distinguished scholars surveys current historiography on the "Catholic Reformation" and "Counter-Reformation."

Ozment, Steven. *The Age of Reform. 1250–1550: An Intellectual and Religious History of Late Medieval and Reformation Europe.* New Haven, 1980. Sets the Reformation within the larger reform tradition of western Christendom.

Ozment, Steven, ed. *Reformation Europe: A Guide to Research.* Saint Louis, 1982. Distinguished scholars survey current historiography on the Reformation, concentrating largely on Protestant movements and their context.

Schilling, Heinz, ed. *Die reformierte Konfessionalisierung in Deutschland: Das Problem der "Zweiten Reformation."* Gütersloh, 1986. Group of German scholars discusses the "Second Reformation" and debate the merits of the term.

Spitz, Lewis W. *The Protestant Reformation, 1517–1559.* New York, 1985. The best recent consideration of the "Age of Reformation" in European history.

Strauss, Gerald. *Law, Resistance, and the State: The Opposition to Roman Law in Reformation Germany.* Princeton, 1986. Discusses the "reformation" of German law and its relation to the Reformation.

Wohlfeil, Rainer. *Einführung in die Geschicte der deutschen Reformation.* Munich, 1982. Offers a social-historical introduction to the German Reformation with an overview of the term "Reformation" and a survey of the relevant historiography.

Wolgast, Eike. "Reform, Reformation." In *Geschichtliche Grundbegriffe: Historisches Lexikon zur politisch-sozialen Sprache in Deutschland,* edited by Otto Brunner, Werner Conze, and Reinhart Koselleck, vol. 5, pp. 313–360. Stuttgart, 1972–1984. Definitive article on the term "Reformation" and its history and usage in Germany and German historiography.

Mark U. Edwards, Jr.

REFORMATION STUDIES. The scholarly study of the Reformation is virtually as old as the Reformation itself. While the key doctrinal battles were still being fought and the issues remained fluid and unresolved, early chroniclers and historians were already seeking to define the historical contexts of these struggles.

Characteristically they interpreted the material of their time in terms of preexistent historical patterns, of which two were predominant. The first was a schema of ecclesiastical history covering six thousand years, divided into three equal periods, and culminating in the yet-to-be-completed time of the gospel. The second reflected the book of Daniel's prophetic vision of a succession of world empires culminating in Rome. Both patterns appeared in Johann Carion's *Chronica* (1532), which owed much of its final form to Philipp Melanchthon's revisions. Nourished by traditions of patriotic humanism and antipapal sentiment, early Protestants identified a tragic deviation from the true faith of the early

Christian era and saw their own history as a revival of the true church that had remained hidden during centuries of papal rule.

The Reformation Interprets Itself: The Sixteenth Century. Despite a certain preoccupation with earlier Christianity, what we call "contemporary history" was very much the norm, as historical assessments of the Reformation were published even before Martin Luther's death. The framework of such histories was largely circumscribed by Luther's original revolt, on the one hand, and the establishment of the evangelical church, on the other, with the politico-religious conflicts of the diets as the central theme.

From midcentury a broader historical perspective entered through the work of Johannes Sleidanus (1506–1566), whose *De Statu Religionis et Reipublica Carolo Quinto Caesare Commentarii* (Commentaries on Religion and the State in the Reign of the Emperor Charles V; 1555) remains the most accomplished contemporary Reformation history. Through his training in Liège, Louvain, Paris, and Orléans and his sustained correspondence with major reformers, Sleidanus brought a genuinely international perspective to his task, while his translations into Latin of French historical classics had sharpened his own historical techniques.

Sleidanus's insistence on solid evidence and his sustained attempt at maintaining impartiality pleased neither Romanists, who judged his work heretical and unscholarly, nor Protestants, who regarded him as too moderate toward Rome. His understanding of the Reformation as a miraculous work of God rendered his impartiality more a matter of style than substance, yet it was a significant advance on the polemical writings of his day. Notable, too, was his awareness of the secular context of religious disputes, yet the converse of this was a slight interest in defining the theological and religious issues, so that the Reformation in the end was seen too exclusively in terms of the actions of princes, diets and councils.

Sleidanus's career was in some ways symptomatic of a significant academic shift originating in the Italian Renaissance, which had seen history achieving increasing prominence as an academic discipline through the establishment of chairs in universities and appointments of civic historians. Initially geared toward practical politics and propaganda, these appointments accentuated a trend toward an appeal to history rather than theological and philosophical speculation as the basis for dealing with problems in both church and society.

Sleidanus's work provides an interesting contrast with that of Heinrich Bullinger (1504–1575), whose academic preparation was not dissimilar but who, in the wake of Huldrych Zwingli's untimely death, was called to assume a position of leadership in a world dominated by clerical controversy rather than lay diplomacy. In his narrative history of the Swiss Reformation from 1519 to 1532, Bullinger portrayed Zurich as the pioneer of true religion for the whole confederation and idealized Zwingli to the point of supporting the reformer's dubious claim to total independence from Luther. Nevertheless, his methodological principles closely resembled those of Sleidanus, and he presented accounts of the process of the Reformation in the various cities with due care for factual detail, even showing a concern, almost unknown elsewhere among evangelicals, for discovering what radical sectarians actually believed.

Catholic opponents of the Reformation lost little time in entering the field. Six years before Sleidanus's work appeared, Johannes Cochlaeus (1479–1552) published his *Commentaria de actis et scriptis Lutheri* (Commentaries on the Acts and Writings of Luther; 1549), a year-by-year record of events and controversies from the initial revolt until Luther's death. A zealous reformer in the humanist and conciliar mold, Cochlaeus combined a concern for cleansing the institutional church of abuses with a total refusal to countenance any doctrinal reassessment. Whereas other Catholic writers were denouncing Desiderius Erasmus as a crypto-Protestant, Cochlaeus used the humanist against Luther. Sharply critical of the religious orders, he interpreted the indulgence affair as a quarrel between Augustinians and Dominicans. He became notorious as the purveyor of numerous unjustified calumnies against Luther, whom he portrayed as the offspring and instrument of Satan, as well as both a product and an expression of the moral decline of the church. Consequently, though he perceived the Reformation as a battle of ideas, he failed utterly to recognize Luther's deep religious passion.

Other Catholic writers showed strong dependence on Cochlaeus's view of Luther without sharing his positive attitude toward Erasmus. The Frenchman Simon Fontaine, in *Histoire catholique de nostre temps* (A Catholic History of Our Times; 1558), while recognizing Erasmus's differences from Luther, identified his departure from the Vulgate text as partly responsible for the spread of Luther's ideas; while the *Commentarius brevis* (Short Commentary) of the German Lorenz Sauer (also Surius; 1522–1578) attacked Erasmus for his failure to combat Luther earlier. Intended as a counterattack to Sleidanus, this work rarely rose above abusive polemic.

On the Protestant side a team of Lutheran scholars under Matthias Flacius Illyricus (1520–1575) produced, in the *Ecclesia Historia* (generally known as the *Magdeburg Centuries*; 1559–1574), the first Protestant church history, a backward-looking survey that impeded the development of mature historiography. Its narrative extended only to the thirteenth century, and its contribution to the Reformation was therefore limited to providing an arsenal of weapons against papal claims. By contrast, Friedrich Myconius (1490–1546), a pastor at Gotha who had been present at Marburg and Schmalkalden and who was sent on an embassy to Henry VIII in 1535, provided a lively contemporary sketch of German history from 1517 to 1542 (*Historia reformationis*, published 1718) based on his original personal experiences as one of Luther's lieutenants. His last nine chapters amount to an "urban history" of Gotha in the process of reform.

Another historian with tenacious local roots—this time in Saxony—was Mattäus Ratzeberger (1501–1559), a medical student who became attached to Luther. Ratzeberger's position in court enabled him to record more confidential episodes, and his staunch loyalty led to his being entrusted with ecclesiastical negotiations. Though a partisan work, Ratzeberger's *Luther und seine Zeit* (Luther and His Times; 1704) revealed shrewd observation of unusual integrity but in an anecdotal rather than analytical mode. It focused on the close relations of religion and politics, and the intra-Lutheran conflicts were starkly evident in its critique of Melanchthon for ambivalence and weakness.

In an age dominated by eminent leaders, the prominence of biographical writings was not surprising. Most of these works were rooted in academic humanism rather than dogmatic theology, owing much to the classical tradition of Plutarch and in some cases to the traditional pattern of the funeral encomium. Biographies by Beatus Rhenanus on Erasmus, by Melanchthon and Johannes Mathesius on Luther, and by Théodore de Bèze on John Calvin have remained influential over time, but the genre was extensive and included a host of relatively minor figures. Often slight and superficial in factual content, these biographies were nevertheless valuable for their evocation of authentic atmosphere and their coverage of background detail neglected in later works.

Another genre of works prominent in the early period was the martyrology, of which those by the Frenchman Jean Crespin, the German Ludwig Rabus, the Netherlander Adriaan Corneliszoon van Haemstede, and the Englishman John Foxe stand out. Contemporary with Sleidanus's histories, these works made no claim to impartiality, their explicit purpose being to inspire, to proselytize, and to strengthen faith in an age of religious turmoil. Yet their propagandist style did not prevent them from providing, like the biographies, an authentic reflection of their age, and their particular merit was to illuminate the world of popular religion that was absent from Sleidanus. The appearance of Catholic works of the same genre provides a measure of their effectiveness.

Outside the German-Swiss heartland of the early Reformation, distinctive patterns of reform were reflected in diverse historiographic traditions. The English Reformation's cultivation of a "middle way" between Romanist superstition and reckless innovation, coupled with the doctrine of adiaphora, soon found its literary advocacy in Thomas Starkey (c.1495–1538), whose *An Exhortation to the People* (1535) combined both concepts. On the other hand, John Bale (1495–1563) offered an ultra-Protestant version of church history, a chronicle of a true church surviving amidst a pattern of corruption that had set in soon after apostolic times, reached its apogee in Gregory VII's manipulation of political and ecclesiastical power, and was evident also in England's enthrallment to superstitious monasticism since the days of Augustine of Canterbury.

In England Erasmus maintained an honored place even among Protestant sympathizers, and after the Marian interlude the Elizabethan settlement reasserted a middle course between Tridentine Catholicism and Puritanism. The *Apologia* (1562) of John Jewel (1522–1571), bishop of Salisbury, stressed the novelties and errors of the Roman church, while the *Laws of Ecclesiastical Polity* by Richard Hooker (1554–1600) was more clearly directed at keeping Puritanism at bay. For Hooker the law of reason emanating from the mind of God and the revealed religion of scripture were faithfully mirrored in the belief and practice of the Anglican church, which was both a church of the Reformation and a continuation of the *ecclesia anglicana* of earlier centuries. One for whom that middle way had no appeal, however, was John Knox (1513–1572), whose *History of the Reformation in Scotland*, written between 1559 and 1567, presented an uncompromising Calvinist perspective on the turmoil of his day and on the unique outcome of reform in the northern kingdom.

In France the Reformation created a different range of problems from those in the Holy Roman Empire. France had an effective monarchy that could persecute on a large scale, and the urban citadels of Protestantism were much more vulnerable than their German equivalents. On the other hand, the geographical situation and the intellectual leadership of Geneva had created the possibility of undermining Catholicism in areas of France remote from Paris, and there was no possibility of solving problems of religious divergence through territorial division, since France was a political unity. Accordingly, there was every reason to reexamine the relations between religion and civil authority amidst the competing claims of toleration and social stability.

In this most historically minded nation, which saw more than 650 historical works published in the sixty years after 1550, there remained a deep chasm between moderates and extremists, both in Catholic circles and among Huguenots. The *Historia sui temporis* by Jacques-Auguste de Thou (1553–1617) was a massive work of a Catholic moderate, yet it was placed on the Index of Prohibited Books. Some Huguenots were avid partisans, while others, such as Philippe de Mornay, envisaged a "true church" comprising all Christian churches.

For those predominant shapers of public opinion known as the politiques, internal tranquillity took precedence over support for established religion, but as the 1572 Saint Bartholomew's Day Massacre showed, French monarchs could not be relied on to maintain this posture. During the civil wars of 1572–1580, politique Catholics assessed the Reformation from the standpoint of state and society and tended to treat the rival claims of Catholics and Protestants skeptically. No less significant was the impact of intellectual influences from outside France, especially the discovery of new cultures overseas and the influx of rationalist ideas from Italian sources, both of which reinforced a sense of detachment from the polemical struggles of the Reformation.

That sense of detachment was clearly evident in reassessments of the Reformation by leading men of letters. Jean Bodin (1529/30–1596) saw the Reformation as an opportunity for discovering a natural religion that could appeal to all and unite the human race. The essayist Michel Eyquem de Montaigne (1533–1592), outwardly a devout Catholic but intellectually at home in pagan Greece, criticized the Reformation for disturbing esthetic life. A more substantial and original historian, La Popelinière (Lancelot du Voisin, 1541–1608), published in 1581 his *Histoire de France,* which surpassed even Sleidanus in its remarkable impartiality and was consequently neglected by both sides. Aiming at evenhandedness, he totally avoided discussion of theological issues, resulting in a strangely remote perspective on his subject.

Studied detachment among leading French scholars, however, was only half the story, for there were many who remained deeply involved in the confessional commitments of earlier generations. A fascinating insight into the early history of the scattered Huguenot communities emerges from the *Histoire ecclésiastique des églises reformées au royaume de France* (Antwerp, 1580), assembled by Calvin's successor, Théodore de Bèze, from reports sent to him by many congregations throughout France up until 1577 and edited (but not radically revised) for publication. Lacking for this reason any analytical or literary qualities, it is valued for its detailed survey of actual Protestant communities in their formative stages, including their rivalries and doctrinal quarrels, and for its sense of immediacy and authenticity, which no single author could convey.

A Legacy of Problems: The Seventeenth Century. The Reformation's legacy of unresolved problems in religious allegiance and political organization provided much of the agenda for seventeenth-century scholars. Moreover, the questioning of tradition on an unprecedented scale at the end of the century brought with it a fundamental reexamination of the Reformation heritage.

In the part of Germany that subscribed to the Augsburg Confession, this was a time not for fresh initiatives but for guarding the inheritance of sacred dogma. Johann Gerhard (1582–1637), the dominant figure in early seventeenth-century Lutheranism and leader of the revival of Aristotelian metaphysics in German universities, ignored the historical Luther to emphasize instead the reformer's pure doctrine and his extraordinary divine appointment to carry out church reform. For Johann Müller (1598–1672) Luther was less a subject for historical investigation than an object of faith, and the Reformation was interpreted as a supernatural act in the history of salvation.

France was experiencing a time of rebuilding and consolidation following the religious wars. While Armand-Jean du Plessis, cardinal and duke of Richelieu, addressed the Huguenot problem by statecraft and while Francis de Sales and Vincent de Paul did so by peaceful persuasion and practical Christianity, the polemical spirit was kept alive by Florimond de Raemond (c.1540–1602), a reconvert to Rome whose account of the heresies of his time dealt predominantly with Calvin and his relationship to France.

In Italy and Spain, Rome's spokesmen displayed renewed confidence. The Catholic tradition of saints' lives received a new lease on life in Pedro de Ribadeneira's *Vita Ignatti Loyola* (Life of Ignatius Loyola; 1569, published 1572), while Niccolò Orlandini (d. 1606) and Francesco Sacchini (1570–1625) wrote accounts of the Society of Jesus that showed concern for historical accuracy. Cesare Baronio (1538–1607) provided the official Catholic counterblast to the *Magdeburg Centuries* in his *Annales ecclesiastici* (Ecclesiastical Annals; Rome, 1598–1607), whose twelve volumes to the year 1198 were extended to 1565 by Oderico Rinaldi. Though pioneering many fields and discovering new documents, these two were selective partisans and contributed more to polemics than historiography.

The most original perspective emerging from Italy at this time was from Paolo Sarpi (1552–1623), a "universal man" of encyclopedic learning and chief theologian and canonist to Venice during that city's period under papal interdict. A man of tolerant and rational outlook and a harsh critic of the papacy, he approved of some Protestant ideas and looked forward to the "advance of the Reformation." His *Istoria del concilio Tridentino* (History of the Council of Trent; 1619), based on Sleidanus, documentary studies, and oral recollections, including some from Protestants, ran against the dominant Roman understanding and highlighted outcomes at odds with Trent's aims—the consolidation of schism rather than unity, total submission to the papacy rather than a recovery of episcopal authority, and the emergence through clever intrigues of an increasingly powerful Curia Romana. Pietro Sforza Pallavicino's own *Istoria del concilio di Trento* (1656–1657) provided a Jesuit counterblast to Sarpi, refuting him point by point.

The United Provinces, independent since 1609, were chiefly preoccupied with Holland's struggle for hegemony over the others and with tensions between Calvinist Orangists and a more liberal Arminian burgher party. Accordingly, this was a period marked by fierce party loyalties rather than considered historical reflection.

England, on the other hand, saw a rich and varied development in historical writing about the Reformation. Here was a nation not merely wrestling with the Reformation legacy but still undergoing the Reformation process, whose outcome was not assured.

Reform contended with Rome, Anglican with Puritan, and Calvinist with Arminian. In this second phase of reform, commentators were unable to take a detached view of the first phase but used to it to substantiate their own positions. Preoccupied with their own conflicts, they retreated into insularity, ignoring their heavy debt to Continental sources. Moreover, the interaction of religious controversy with political conflict caused most historians of the Stuart period to see the Reformation in political rather than social and religious terms.

Yet their outlook and methodology was not on that account slavish, static, or monothematic. Thomas Cartwright (1535–1603), leader of the moderate Presbyterians, identified a succession of reformers from John Wycliffe to Luther, praised Henry VIII for his part in disseminating the Bible, and saw Elizabeth as a providential instrument. William Camden (1551–1623), interpreting Elizabeth's role in more political terms, showed in his *Annals* the pervasive influence of Sleidanus and some connection with de Thou. Elizabeth's *via media* was admired as a prudent attempt to create political stability rather than finalize religious truth—that is, to support the religious outcome that functioned as a prop of sound government.

Puritan interpreters, on the other hand, saw the English Reformation as a movement cut off before full fruition. Their greatest spokesman, by no means typical, was John Milton (1608–1674), whose tracts *Of Reformation Touching Church Discipline in England and the Causes that Hitherto Have Hindered It* (1641), and *Areopagitica* (1644), accord a fundamental role to Wycliffe in the restoration of the gospel. Only the perverseness of prelates had prevented Wycliffe's reformation from matching purity of doctrine with purity of discipline and thereby leading the way for all Europe, which might never then have heard of Jan Hus, Luther, or Calvin. Milton opposed the erection of a new orthodoxy to replace the old and saw the Reformation as a continuous unending process. The task was "reforming the Reformation," with toleration of all sects the key to a decline in sectarianism.

The 1660 Restoration brought no immediate resolution of the religious issues, while the Great Ejectment of 1662 permanently institutionalized dissent. After the Glorious Revolution of 1688–1689 resolved the political issue by making the throne securely Protestant, religious comprehension became the key issue and toleration a tacit necessity. This new situation provided the framework for two major histories of the Reformation, one by John Strype (1643–1737) and the other by Gilbert Burnet (1643–1715).

A low churchman who welcomed the 1688 deliverance from popery but detested Puritanism, Strype portrayed Thomas Cranmer as the great instrument of God in reforming the Church of England. His *Annals of the Reformation* (1708–1709), covering the reign of Elizabeth, and his *Ecclesiastical Memorials* (1721), dealing with Henry VIII, Edward VI, and Mary Tudor, relied heavily on documentary sources. Burnet, a courtier, politician, and Whig bishop, argued in his *History of the Reformation* (1679, 1681, 1714) that the principles of the Reformation were being endangered not only by Romanism and dissent but by high church toryism and called for an invigoration of the church on Reformation principles. An advocate of Anglicanism for its combination of unity, comprehensiveness, and latitude, he nevertheless restrained his partisanship, while his portrayal of the Reformation as a developing historical movement represented a major advance from the annalistic method and a step away from English insularity toward a greater awareness of Continental historiography.

On the continent of Europe the late seventeenth century revealed a bewildering pattern of continuity and change. Controversial writings continued but showed increasing distance from the original battles, with harsh invective giving way to more sophisticated presentation of the issues. The Catholic writer Louis Maimbourg (1610–1686), while identifying Luther's pride and presumption as the root problem, nevertheless sharply criticized Pope Leo X and gave due recognition to Luther's outstanding gifts and achievements. Jacques Bénigne Bossuet (1627–1704) avoided libelous legends and scandalous muckraking, highlighting instead in his *Histoire des variations des églises protestantes* (History of the Variations of the Protestant Churches; 1688) Protestantism's inherent tendency toward creating a multiplicity of sects. For Bossuet true faith spoke with a single voice, while variation was a mark of inconsistency and falseness. The Reformation was a chapter in the history of heresy as old as the church itself. But while Bossuet traced the roots of the Reformation to medieval heresies, he provided no historical analysis of the connections.

Bossuet played a leading role in international debates about reunion of the churches, arguing that variety of opinion was possible on matters not defined by the church. He exchanged letters on the subject with the German scholar Gottfried Wilhelm Leibniz (1646–1716), whose replies projected a genuinely historical understanding of the Reformation in the framework of Germany's and Europe's problems and indicated an unexpected degree of rapprochement.

Ambivalent Responses: The Enlightenment. Although increasing historical distance from the Reformation had brought a certain attenuation of polemical fury and a willingness to address the urgent issues of comprehension, toleration, and even reunion, Reformation scholarship was still dealing essentially with a legacy of unresolved problems. As the seventeenth century yielded to the eighteenth, however, a fundamental reassessment of the Reformation inheritance became inescapable as a result of major shifts in European intellectual life. Cartesian philosophy, Newtonian science, and the political theories of Thomas Hobbes and John Locke amounted to a radical questioning of all tradition and implied a relativizing of the European religious experience. What had appeared to be transcendent and self-evident truth was increasingly understood as circumstantial cultural variation.

Two writers who expressed this new spirit were Pierre Bayle (1647–1706) and Jean Le Clerc (1657–1736), who looked to reason rather than authority yet nevertheless saw the Reformation in highly positive terms. For Le Clerc the turbulence and disorder that had accompanied the Reformation were part of the onward movement of history, while Bayle stressed the liberating quality of the Reformation, despite its ambiguities and contradictions. Bayle's *Dictionnaire historique et critique* (Historical and Critical Dictionary; 1697), one of the vital books of the Enlightenment, provided a moderate and judicious study of the Reformation, defending Luther from two centuries of lies and misplaced censures.

The two most significant contributions of this period to Reformation studies, however, originated in the movement of Pietism, which rejected authoritarian religion not on the basis of reason but rather by appeal to religious experience. Philipp Jacob Spener (1635–1705) articulated a dynamic view of the Reformation that shifted the balance from dogma to ethics, identifying Luther as a faithful messenger to his own age rather than God's final word, and called for the Reformation to be advanced in new directions, in particular toward moral reformation. Veit Ludwig von Seckendorff (1626–1692), while deeply committed to Lutheran ideals, looked beyond doctrine to the man behind the image projected by orthodoxy. His *Historia Lutheranismi* (1692), based on genuine sources, portrayed Luther as a flawed human being chosen by God to lead the church to reform. Seckendorff stressed the liberating spiritual quality of the Reformation, implicitly contrasting the early creative years with the years of state-church consolidation. Though clearly a partisan, he showed an unusual openness to Rome and acknowledged improvements since the Reformation.

More directly a product of Pietism, Gottfried Arnold's *Unpartheneyische Kirchen- und Ketzerhistoire* (Non Partisan History of Churches and Heresies; 1699) was controversial in Lutheran circles, amounting to a celebration of religious variety and therefore of heresy. Arnold (1666–1714) drew a radical contrast between vital living piety and dogmatically regulated religion. The Reformation was an act of God because it renewed vital piety and practical religion, but orthodoxy had betrayed that impulse. No less than Catholicism, Lutheranism had violated the free conscience and subjected piety to dogma, so that true Christianity was likely to be found among heretics. Yet Arnold showed a warm regard for Luther as a man of piety, appealing to him against institutionalized religion. More explicitly than Seckendorff, he exalted Luther the young liberator against the conservative middle-aged statesman and church builder.

There are few ages, if any, in European history in which scholars have been so acutely aware of their own distinctiveness and importance as the age of Enlightenment, and perhaps none that betrayed in the end such an inability to understand the Reformation. The famous *Encyclopédie* project, based on the notion of an accessible body of rational truths, was a bold attempt to give a complete account of human knowledge and promote its diffusion to a wider public. Yet its editor, Denis Diderot (1713–1784), presented in it a cautious survey of the Reformation written very much from the standpoint of the Catholic church and echoing Bossuet.

In his *Essai sur les moeurs* (1756) Voltaire (1694–1778) focussed on Europe from Charlemagne to Louis XIII, devoting only a short chapter to the sixteenth century, which portrays the papacy under Leo X as a veritable Roman rebirth and a civilizing force and Luther's attack on the papacy as a triumph of barbarism over Roman civility. More memorable for witty aphorisms than sustained historical argument, Voltaire was unable to recognize the spiritual dimensions of the Reformation conflict, regarding its theological disputes as stupid and irrelevant and the indulgences affair as no more than "a monks' squabble." Religious war and civil strife were in his view too high a price to pay for marginal improvements in the Catholic church.

Marie-Jean-Antoine-Nicolas de Caritat, marquis de Condorcet (1743–1794), expressed a more negative view of the Catholic church and a more positive assessment of Luther, whose crucial historical function was to show the distinction between Christianity and priestly religion. In this sense the Reformation was a stage in mankind's progress toward perfection until it became enmeshed in the political ambitions of secular rulers. While valuing the progress toward freedom of thought and toleration, he regarded the Reformation's contribution to that progress as an accidental by-product of doctrinal variety.

During this time Germany, organically linked with Reformation traditions in a way not true of France, reflected more authentic Reformation accents, though refracted through the intellectual preoccupations of their time. Johann Georg Walch (1693–1749), a convinced Lutheran influenced by both orthodoxy and pietism, portrayed Luther as an extraordinarily gifted individual and the Reformation as a movement understood in natural terms against a background of centuries of preparation by other reformers, the revival of learning, and the advent of printing. Not justification by faith but the elimination of Roman tyranny was the heart of the Reformation, while princely authority over religion was one of its principal benefits, since faith validated itself through civic utility. Johann Salomo Semler (1725–1791) also bypassed the issue of justification and saw the Reformation as the overthrow of a corrupt and tyrannical papacy. Intellectually it stood for the freedom of each man to think for himself, and its variety was evidence of positive and lasting achievement.

Despite its rediscovery of aspects of the Reformation tradition overlooked by orthodoxy, Pietism lacked theological power. Its deep impact in early Enlightenment Germany was evident rather in a pervasive emphasis on inwardness and liberation and a critique of dogma that placed no limits on individual subjectivity and relativism in religious thought. Part of Luther's legacy was the freedom to dissent from his doctrinal formulations. In the absence of uniform doctrine, the focus of identity moved to the church, held together externally by civil community and internally by a common religious purpose.

By the late eighteenth century these tendencies were being expressed in more extreme ways. Gotthold Ephraim Lessing (1729–1781) combined a genuine enthusiasm for Luther's person with deistic and pantheistic religious views verging on disbelief and a faith in human improvement that could scarcely have been more remote from Luther's views. Johann Gottfried von Herder (1744–1803) portrayed Luther as a German hero, the herald of both the Enlightenment and freedom.

Among the historians, Johann Lorenz von Mosheim (1694–1755) devoted the third volume of his heavily documented *Institutiones historiae ecclesiasticae* (Ecclesiastical Institutes; 1737–1741) to the Reformation and its antecedents. An overwhelming concentration on the deep moral corruption of the pre-Reformation church led him to an interpretation of the Reformation that largely ignored Luther's piety and personal anguish and focused on his heroic onslaught on a corrupt system. Divorced from Luther's theological concerns, the Reformation became a series of political events leading to the establishment of a state church.

Despite this narrowing of focus, Mosheim's work had many virtues, being highly comprehensive in tracing the detailed history of major groups and reasonable and moderate in its judgments, including those of Rome. The English edition of 1764 became a major source for English historians, including Edward Gibbon (1737–1794), though with largely unimpressive results. Gibbon's doctrinal interpretation of the Reformation as a Manichaean movement linked with the Cathars and the Paulicians was bizarre in the extreme, while his general perception never moved beyond the standard Enlightenment cliché that accorded it the role of demolishing superstition, breaking the chains of authority, and establishing freedom of conscience and private judgment far in excess of its intentions. The influential Scottish philosopher David Hume (1711–1776) was so fundamentally hostile to religion, in both its Catholic form ("superstition") and its Protestant counterpart ("enthusiasm"), that he saw no further than the political imperative of state maintenance of religion as vital to the interests of society.

In this largely barren field the Scottish historian William Robertson (1721–1793), an active and committed Presbyterian leader, stood against the trend. His *History of Scotland* was the first reasonably objective account of the Scottish Reformation and was an international rather than parochial work, set in the context of Reformation Europe. Its Enlightenment provenance was clear in the strong connection made with the "revival of letters." Robertson's *History of the Reign of the Emperor Charles V* (1769) was a comprehensive political history of which the Reformation was only one part and was clearly the best work in the field until Leopold von Ranke. Against a background of papal tyranny and ecclesiastical abuses, on the one hand, and, on the other hand, such positive developments as printing, the revival of learning, and the preparatory work of Erasmus, Luther's success could be readily understood since he appeared at a critical juncture when all the signs were propitious.

Robertson's work was especially interesting for its unusual attempt at reconciling Enlightenment ideals with institutional Christianity. The achievement of the Reformation was to rescue one part of Europe from the papal yoke, to mitigate its rigor in another, and to produce "a revolution in the sentiments of mankind." Although this notion of a revolution in sentiments might have led him toward a serious encounter with the intellectual inheritance of the Reformation, he remained reticent about discussing doctrinal issues, which he regarded as the province of ecclesiastical historians, and chose to commend the Reformation in terms most likely to win acceptance. Unlike most of his Enlightenment contemporaries, however, he saw emancipation as a direct rather than unintended result of the Reformation.

Although the characteristic intellectual postures adopted by Enlightenment scholars—optimistic notions of progress and emancipation—were bound to inhibit a sound historical grasp of Reformation theological concerns, there were significant exceptions when, for one reason or another, direct contact was established with the Reformation inheritance. In Germany, for example, Johann Georg Hamman (1730–1788) rejected Enlightenment notions of reason and natural religion as a result of a deep appreciation of Luther as interpreter of the Christian gospel and theologian of the human heart. In England the Evangelical Revival rediscovered some forgotten themes of Reformation Christianity, not least in John Wesley (1703–1791), whose conversion was directly associated with a reading of Luther's preface to *Romans*.

The achievement of the Enlightenment with respect to the understanding of the Reformation was in the end profoundly ambivalent. The efforts of scholars to break from tired and unproductive polemical debates, to gain reliable information about the past free from the pervasive domination of myth, and to free history from theological presuppositions and the parochialism of Christian scholars were integrally related to the durable achievements of nineteenth-century scholars. On the other hand, their intellectual postures and presuppositions, no less dogmatic than those they rejected, made it difficult for them to enter with empathy into a world so different from their own and restricted their ability to evaluate soundly the sixteenth century. Their intellectual verve and literary skill were in the end rarely matched with profound insight into idioms of Reformation thought.

Toward Professional Historiography: The Early Nineteenth Century. If the eighteenth century had enlarged the scope of Reformation history, the nineteenth extended it even more dramatically. Enlightenment perceptions strongly persisted in the Romantic historian Jules Michelet (1798–1874), whose *Histoire de France* (1833–1867) celebrated the Reformation as a victory over clerical autocracy and as the forerunner of the French Enlightenment, and in the Genevan François-Pierre-Guillaume Guizot (1787–1874), who had retained his family's Calvinist religious tradition yet, in *Histoire de la civilisation en Europe* (1828), largely ignored the religious beliefs of the reformers and viewed the Reformation as a campaign for the enfranchisement of the human mind against clerical control.

In England a similar perspective was presented by Thomas Babington Macaulay (1800–1859), who betrayed no sense of the importance of theological debates but saw Luther's revolt as the "third and most memorable struggle for spiritual freedom" after the Albigensians and Jan Hus, a struggle based on the Renaissance of letters and the invention of printing, which together had broken the ecclesiastical monopoly on learning. A more individual perspective was presented by Thomas Carlyle (1795–1881), whose direct references to the Reformation should be evaluated in the context of his radical perspective on culture and society. For Carlyle cultural phenomena, modes of social order, and belief systems were transient symbols that needed to be broken and renewed as they outlived their significance. In his series of lectures *On Heroes, Hero-Worship and the Heroic in History* (1841), Carlyle asked how the shells of dead cultures could be broken to recover a living moral and spiritual life and looked to exceptional individuals as the source of hope. In a chapter entitled "The Hero as Priest," he provided an extended sketch of Luther, a "breaker of idols" whose stand at Worms was the greatest moment in modern history, delivering the European world from "stagnant putrescence" and containing within it the germ of the great achievements of modern times, among which he lists Puritanism, the English Parliament, the discovery of the Americas, and the French Revolution. Highly subjective and at times bizarre in his judgments, Carlyle at least had the virtue of restoring to Reformation history the element of religious passion that had been as foreign to its Enlightenment supporters as to its detractors.

Carlyle's close personal friend and biographer James Anthony Froude (1818–1894) wrote a twelve-volume *History of England from the Fall of Wolsey to the Defeat of the Spanish Armada,* which presented the English Reformation as a victory over the powers of darkness, personified in Philip II and the popes. Its achievement was to have "untwisted slowly the grasp of the theological fingers from the human throat." Divorcing the Reformation in this way from dogma clearly required a highly selective approach, while a distrust of popular expressions of religion and a scant recognition of social and economic forces tended to leave his story, for all of its grand style, marooned in a world of high politics and diplomacy. An altogether different perspective emerged in *The History of England* (1819–1830) by the Catholic John Lingard (1771–1851). Trained at Douai and influenced by Gallicanism, Lingard wrote a fair-minded account of the late medieval church that included a strong critique of the papacy and a recognition of Luther's admirable qualities, though he dismissed him ultimately as a self-seeking opportunist and the father of sectarian division.

Whatever contribution these nineteenth-century historians made to the study of the Reformation must be regarded as marginal by comparison with the seminal influence of Leopold von Ranke (1795–1886), who exemplified as no other historian of his time a truly professional standard of historiography. Ranke's claims to have based all his work on archival studies have been significantly qualified as his immense debt to massive printed compilations of historical material has become clearer, yet his imagination and creativity in the use of all his sources remain unchallenged.

A product of an evangelical family and a student of theology and classics, Ranke nevertheless avoided a narrow confessional stance. A political conservative with an abiding respect for Prussia, he remained remote from the chauvinism of some of his younger contemporaries. In later life he ascribed his development to three diverse influences—Thucydides, Barthold Georg Niebuhr, and Luther, "the three spirits to whom I owe the basic elements upon which my later historical studies have been built."

Ranke's so-called Luther Fragment, written in 1817, was a romantic piece that has little in common with the mature writings on which his reputation finally rests. His *Die römischen Päpste* (History of the Popes; 1834–1839), which was focused for obvious reasons more on the Counter-Reformation—a term Ranke seems to have invented—was notable for its fair and balanced assessments, though his personal commitment is clear in the claim that Germany had restored Christianity to its purest form since the time of the early church.

Ranke's six-volume *Deutsche Geschichte im Zeitalter der Reformation* (German History in the Age of the Reformation; 1839–1847) belies the common assumption that his interests were restricted to high politics and diplomacy. His account of the causes of the early Reformation was remarkable in its time for the breadth of its analysis of interlocking social, intellectual, religious, and educational factors, and he expanded his sources to pioneer the use of popular pamphlet literature. His study of the social protests of the 1520s can justly be called the first "modern" account of the crisis because of its heavy dependence on printed sources and local histories.

Ranke was committed to a standard of historical "objectivity" for which his name was to become a byword, but his personal sympathies are nevertheless always clear. Germany, in his view, had given birth to a religious movement of far deeper significance for mankind than the Italian Renaissance. Luther emerges from the narrative as a man of great spiritual power and passion, a reforming Catholic whose wish was not to found a new church, but to restore early Christian doctrine. Beside him Zwingli, though assessed with scrupulous fairness, seems plodding and limited. As for the English Reformation, the subject of a later work, Ranke appeared unable to see beyond the state Reformation to a broader movement encompassing the same elements of theological concern and popular support that he had found in the German movement.

Confessionalism Restated and Reassessed (c.1850–1914). Throughout the nineteenth and early twentieth century, the great majority of Reformation studies fell into the genre of "church history" and indeed "confessional history," being the work of scholars who saw their primary task as historical analysis of the Christian tradition and whose confessional commitment remained a crucial element. Yet this was no mere replication of an earlier age of confessional orthodoxy, for these studies, whether Catholic or Protestant in origin, showed the unmistakable influence of major cultural and intellectual movements of the previous century—Enlightenment perceptions of the superiority of reason to dogmatic revelation, the Hegelian challenge to the idea of unchangeable truth, and Rankean principles of historical writing.

Catholic studies. Catholic writers endorsed Rankean principles while perceiving Ranke himself as a Protestant apologist and their own work as a corrective. But while serious historical scholarship might at times mitigate polemic, in practice it often accentuated it, and much of Catholic writing on the Reformation from Johann Joseph Ignaz von Döllinger (1799–1890) in the mid-nineteenth century to Heinrich Seuse Denifle (1844–1905) and Hartmann Grisar (1845–1932) in the early twentieth represented a grand finale to earlier polemical traditions.

Döllinger's writings reveal a fascinating interplay between historical and polemic interests. In his *Die Reformation* (History of the Reformation; 1846–1848) and his 1851 "Sketch" of Luther, one can trace the beginnings of the intense psychobiographical preoccupation with the reformer that was to become so prominent in modern Catholic Luther studies. For Döllinger the key to Luther's thought was nothing external, but rather his inward dispositions and motives—pride, an innate violence, and a morbid preoccupation with evil, all plausibly related to major tenets of Luther's thought. Döllinger's views underwent significant change, owing to the immense length of his career and his disillusionment with the papacy over the doctrine of infallibility. In his later writings Luther the tortured spirit who caused the Reformation yielded to Luther the catalyst of reform in a church unable to bring about the changes it so desperately needed.

Given Döllinger's estrangement from the papacy, it was another historian, Johannes Janssen (1829–1891), who provided the dominant historical framework for Roman Catholic interpretation of the Reformation for subsequent generations. His *Geschichte des deutschen Volkes seit dem Ausgang des Mittelalters* (History of the German People at the Close of the Middle Ages; 1876–1894), based on extensive use of archival sources, was less preoccupied with the person of Luther, for Janssen's subject was the German people. He presented the picture of a late medieval church, fundamentally flourishing and healthy, that needed reform but that had within itself the means to carry it out. Luther's failure to recognize this cast him in the role of destroyer, despite his genuine spiritual gifts.

The complex relationship between polemics and history was demonstrated in the early twentieth century by the writings of Denifle and Grisar, whose unparalleled attack on Luther gained much of its impact from reliance on genuine historical sources. In *Luther und Luthertum* (1904), Denifle made extensive use of sources previously unavailable, including a recently discovered copy of Luther's lectures on *Romans.* Rejecting Janssen's idyllic picture of the fifteenth-century church, Denifle identified a current of evil in the late medieval church, of which Luther—morally corrupted by his personal submission to sensuality and theologically incompetent—was the personal incarnation.

Denifle's work exposed the massive ignorance of many of Luther's admirers and forced Protestant scholars to reexamine their whole approach to Luther. He was also criticized by Catholics, especially Grisar, whose three-volume study *Luther* (1911–1912) aimed to correct Denifle. Immensely erudite and consciously aiming at a Rankean objectivity, Grisar could not conceal a deep hostility and partiality, and if in some respects he softened the picture of Luther by portraying him as a diseased soul rather than a moral degenerate, his condescending pity proved less acceptable to many than Denifle's outright contempt.

Protestant studies. Two Protestant studies of wide influence well beyond their place of origin were the Reformation history by Swiss evangelical Jean-Henri Merle d'Aubigné (1794–1872) and the studies of Luther's theology, life, and writings by Julius Köstlin (1826–1902), founder of the Verein für Reformationsgeschichte. Both authors were widely translated and especially influential in English-speaking countries.

A more fundamental reassessment of the Reformation was taking place, however, among liberal Protestants who worked on the borderlands of theology and undertook a thorough reexamination of the Reformation heritage in the light of major shifts in philosophical thought. Orthodox theology was effectively challenged by both Kantian and idealist philosophy, and Protestant thinkers were faced with the choice of adapting to current philosophy or striking out in new directions. Among those who took the second option, Friedrich Schleiermacher (1768–1834) looked to religious experience as a new basis for theology and in that context appealed to the experiential dimension of Luther's thought, while Søren Kierkegaard (1813–1855) explored Luther's understanding of faith as a key element in an "existential" response. Both effectively subordinated historical analysis to a philosophical-theological agenda.

Other Protestant scholars showed a wholehearted commitment to genuine historical research as the pathway to intellectual understanding. Albrecht Ritschl (1822–1889) opposed dogmatism of all kinds and approached dogmatics through history. This enabled him to reveal Luther's essential catholicity, an unusual perception at the time, yet he showed no understanding of the reformer's significant inheritance from late medieval thought. Adolf von Harnack (1851–1930), a patristic scholar and son of the leading conservative Lutheran scholar of his day, ended his massive *Dogmengeschichte* (History of Dogma) with Luther, to whom he attributed the paradoxical achievement of having liberated religion from ecclesiasticism and moralism while at the same time strengthening the structures of Catholic dogma, thus leaving the task of the critique of dogma to his successors.

In Britain historical scholarship was inextricably linked with continuing theological debate about the nation's unique inheritance from the Reformation period. Anglicans not only confronted Rome, on the one hand, and Dissent on the other, but differed sharply among themselves as to whether the Church of England was a legitimate child of the Reformation and whether its Reformation was a renewal or a perversion of the true faith.

Tractarians preserved their estimate of Anglican integrity by driving a wedge between the English and Continental reformations. The concept of the *via media* received a new lease on life, and though there were different views on Luther's intentions, there was broad agreement that the outcome of his work was doctrinal error and loss of the apostolic succession. The confidence of John Henry Newman and his associates in dismissing the reformer's fundamental errors seemed in no way inhibited by minimal firsthand acquaintance with his works.

Evangelicals, on the other hand, saw themselves as spiritual heirs of the Reformation. Though divided ecclesiastically between the established church and Dissent, and theologically between Calvinists and Arminians, they maintained a cohesive view of an evangelical succession of true faith, which found substantial expression in the composite historical works of Joseph and Isaac Milner and John Scott.

Among liberal Protestants, who emphasized scriptural religion and ethics over dogma, Erasmus and Zwingli fared better than Luther or Calvin, who had remained dogmatic in spirit. In his *History of Latin Christianity* (1855) Henry Hart Milman (1791–1868) portrayed the reformers as men of destiny who set the church on course but had remained burdened with the legacy of the past. On the other hand, Frederick Denison Maurice (1805–1872) responded warmly to Luther's spiritual depth and his striving for inwardness, regreting only that he had neglected the imperative of social renewal.

Such ecclesiastical controversies generated major scholarly achievements, including the Parker Society edition of the English reformers, intended to remind the English church of its Reformation origins, and the Calvin Translation Society's fifty-two-volume edition of Calvin's works. Yet few English writers of any group knew the reformers' works firsthand. One exception was Julius Charles Hare (1795–1855), an admirer of Ranke, whose *Vindication of Luther against His Recent English Assailants* (1852) was a systematic refutation of attacks from various quarters, based on detailed familiarity with Luther's works and expounded in the context of broad historical thinking about the Reformation.

The 1883 Luther jubilee stimulated a resurgence of interest in the Continental Reformation across a wide range of scholars, from the Unitarian Charles Beard (1827–1888) to the Scottish Free Churchman Thomas M. Lindsay (1843–1914). Beard interpreted the Reformation as an antiauthoritarian movement for free rational inquiry that had stopped short of its goal and admired Luther's profound spirituality while arguing that the way to the future lay with Erasmus. Lindsay not only summed up the best of nineteenth-century scholarship but his *History of the Reformation in Europe* (1906–1907) broke new ground in the detail with which it explored the social and economic context of reform and in the wide sympathies its author displayed with Reformation sectarians and fringe groups.

Despite its geographic remoteness, the United States had retained a more intimate, though not particularly scholarly, connection with the European Reformation through its immigrant communities. As in England, the 1883 jubilee had a major impact, and though Köstlin's works in translation were influential, it was Phillip Schaff (1819–1893) who made the most enduring contribution through his founding of the American Society for Church History, his broad ecumenical and scholarly contacts, and his six-volume *History of the Christian Church* (1892), which remained for many years the most substantial account of the Reformation in English.

New Directions: The Twentieth Century. For Reformation church history the celebration of the 1917 jubilee represented a significant turning point on both sides of the religious divide. The theological movement of neo-orthodoxy, associated in particular with Karl Barth (1886–1968), launched a radical critique of the liberal Protestant theology of the previous generation, in so doing recapturing many authentic Reformation accents and restoring them to doctrinal prominence. In this revival of Reformation thought, however, history remained clearly subordinate to dogmatics.

Church history. More significant for historical scholarship was the so-called Luther Renaissance of the twentieth century, effectively inaugurated by the seminal essay of Karl Holl (1866–1926) on Luther's understanding of religion. In part a response to the polemics of Denifle and Grisar, this essay helped to counteract excessively doctrinal and political perceptions of the Reformation by opening up again to Protestant scholars a direct encounter with the historical Luther and in particular with that religious inwardness that was so central to his being.

A comparable achievement from the Catholic side was the pioneering essay of Franz Xaver Kiefl (1869–1928) on Luther's "religious psyche," which firmly established the perception of the reformer as *homo religiosus.* This perception became fundamental to a new generation of Roman Catholic scholars and culminated in the magisterial history *Die Reformation in Deutschland* by Joseph Lortz (1887–1975). For Lortz, Luther remained a heretic, but his heresy arose not out of moral corruption or psychological sickness but a one-sidedness born of an earnest and godly spirit. In exploring the Reformation background, Lortz identified a lack of doctrinal clarity in the late medieval church as a far more serious problem than moral corruption and declared that Luther had rejected a Catholicism that was not fully Catholic.

Lortz's positive work was usefully supplemented by Adolf Herte (b. 1887), who launched a devastating critique of Roman Catholic Reformation scholarship, exposing its thorough dependence on the polemic of Johannes Cochlaeus. Later generations of Catholic scholars have in many cases shed Lortz's reservations and embarked on major explorations of Luther's thought that are still recognizably Catholic and judiciously critical yet fundamentally appreciative of Luther as a self-consciously loyal son of the church seeking redress for the sake of the gospel.

Throughout this period and in line with the fading of the partisan spirit among Catholic scholars, histories by Protestant scholars have tended to become more ecumenical, more interdisciplinary, and more interconnected with other studies. Explorations of areas barely touched before by Reformation research—above all the vast and complex world of the radical Reformation—have enriched the field and rendered anachronistic the simple dichotomies of the past. The systematic analysis of the intellectual background of the Reformation in late medieval Scholasticism, spearheaded in Germany by Heiko Oberman (b. 1930), has transformed simplistic understandings of the relationship between the Reformation and the medieval Catholic inheritance, while the massive growth of social history has irrevocably ended the isolation of religious issues from the broader setting of historical experience.

The social sciences. Although the bulk of writing about the Reformation has continued to emerge from church historical circles, new perspectives from other sources have expanded and immeasurably enriched the field. The materialist perspective emerging from the philosophy of Karl Marx and directly applied to the study of the Reformation from Friedrich Engels on challenged all interpreters of the Reformation to broaden the scope of their inquiries, and even the unconvinced were obliged to take account of the Marxist view.

The sophisticated development of the social sciences, especially from the early twentieth century, added another perspective. In the field of sociology a preoccupation with the relationship between capitalism and the Reformation focused on the work of Max Weber and Richard Henry Tawney. Working from a closer knowledge of the historical materials than either of these, Ernst Troeltsch (1865–1923), in his *Die Soziallehren der christlichen Kirchen und Gruppen* (The Social Teachings of the Christian Churches; 1912) developed a typology of "church-type" and "sect-type" Christianity ranging across twenty centuries. On the basis of this typology Troeltsch challenged the assumption that Protestantism represented the dawn of the modern era and saw it rather as a reshaping of the medieval idea, extending the authoritarian ecclesiastical culture of the Middle Ages for two centuries longer.

Among those stimulated by Troeltsch's views were Americans H. Richard Niebuhr (1894–1962), whose *Christ and Culture* (1952) comparatively explored alternative conceptions of the relationship between Christianity and culture, illuminating in the process major differences of social outlook among the Protestant reformers; and Werner Stark (b. 1909), whose massive five-volume study of Christendom put forward an alternative threefold model comprising "established religion" (Lutheran or Anglican), "universal church" (Catholic or Calvinist), and "sectarian religion." More directly influenced by Émile Durkheim and Weber, Guy Swanson's *Religion and Regime* (1967) tried to establish along a continuum connections between differing religious traditions and types of political structures.

Given the tendency of church historians to categorize Reformation traditions too rigidly in terms of confessional divisions, such fresh perspectives have been valuable in revealing complexities that would likely otherwise be ignored—specifically, the striking differences between Protestant traditions with similar doctrinal bases and the unexpected likenesses across confessional boundaries. Unfortunately their value has in many cases been limited by inadequate primary historical research.

Another social science whose application to the study of

the Reformation has been received with some skepticism is psychology and in particular psychoanalysis. Analyses of the Reformation through psychoanalysis had begun in a decidedly unscientific way with Catholic writers like Döllinger, Denifle, and Grisar, who attempted to discredit Luther and his work by exposing his personal depravity or psychic illness. A more plausible and professional approach was made by Danish Catholic psychiatrist Paul Reiter (1895–1973), whose massive study diagnosed Luther as a manic-depressive psychotic; from a more sympathetic viewpoint the Swiss pastor Oscar Pfister (1873–1956) analyzed the reformer's career in terms of religious fear and its resolution. The full impact of this approach was not felt, however, until the American neo-Freudian Erik Erikson (1902–1982) produced his study *Young Man Luther* (1962), which has remained influential for three decades as a specific study of Luther and as a test case for the psychoanalytic approach to history. Focusing on the young Luther's "identity-crisis," it was a provocative challenge to conventional ways of explaining Luther's development, and though at times it exhibited a profound empathy with its subject, its manifest defects in the use of historical evidence made it vulnerable to attack.

Historians have shown a decided ambivalence toward the application of the social sciences to the study of the Reformation. Some have welcomed it as a desirable widening of the field of Reformation studies with which historians should be willing to collaborate, while others have remained fundamentally skeptical of the inadequate historical research evident in many such works and the consequent tendency for the particularities of history to be surrendered to the tyranny of models.

Social history. The social contextualization of the Reformation, however, does not necessarily depend on the application of abstract models. Probably the major development in Reformation studies in the second half of the twentieth century has been the overwhelming impact of social history in its many forms. The novelty of this approach should not be overestimated. Clear signposts of it were evident among earlier commentators, sometimes in unexpected places, and its origins in some respects go back to the Reformation itself. On the other hand, modern research has applied its insights in a more sustained and systematic way and pursued research in new directions.

Movements in scholarship can rarely be precisely dated, but the foundation of the historical journal *Annales* in 1929 by Lucien Febvre (1878–1956) and medievalist Marc Bloch provides a symbolic starting point for the Reformation's encounter with modern social history. In a major seminal essay in 1928 on the origins of the French Reformation, Febvre turned away from institutional church history to focus instead on the mental attitudes of individuals and communities in the context of intellectual, social, and economic factors in society. In his view the Reformation was the outward sign of a profound revolution in religious sentiment—more specifically, an attempt to satisfy the spiritual aspirations of the rising middle class.

The value of Febvre's approach in breaking from a pattern of scholarship too much dominated by doctrinal and institutional concerns is evident in the ongoing exploration of "mentalities" through the work of such scholars as Janine Garrisson-Estèbe and Natalie Davis. Nevertheless, critics have rightly questioned whether one can so easily distinguish "right" from "wrong" questions and why the opening of new areas of inquiry should in itself invalidate the continuing quest to understand doctrines and institutions that were so manifestly vital to the individuals and communities whose "mentalities" Febvre wanted to understand.

English social history is rooted in a long tradition of local and regional studies going back as far as the sixteenth century and impressively institutionalized in the *Victoria History of the Counties of England*, founded in 1901 and still being published. There is little in this tradition, however, to reflect the questions and preoccupations of Febvre's manifesto, as the English Reformation, under the strong influence of the monarchy, lacked the complex connections of its Continental counterpart with peasant revolts and municipal politics. The social history of the Reformation in the English context has been largely concerned with examining the Reformation at the grass roots level and on a regional basis as a prelude to any meaningful generalizations.

In Germany social history of the Reformation has primarily concerned itself with local and regional studies and in particular with the role of cities, as the urban communities of Germany and Switzerland had overwhelming importance in determining the fate of the Reformation. Bernd Moeller's 1962 essay "Reichstadt und Reformation" (Imperial Cities and the Reformation) was the catalyst for an ongoing series of studies of individual cities and also for a stimulating debate on the reasons for the prominence of the city as the unit of reform. In this respect Moeller emphasized the role of the late medieval city as a *corpus christianum* and argued that the Reformation was most successful where it drew on and strengthened the inherited ideal of the city as a sacred community. This conclusion, implying that the Reformation was most successful where it challenged existing practice least, was strongly disputed by Steven Ozment, who argued in *The Reformation in the Cities* (1975) that the success of the urban Reformation was based rather in Protestantism's religious message—its simplification of spiritual life and its enhancement of secular life.

Since the 1970s efforts have been made to remedy the almost comprehensive past neglect of the role of women in the Reformation, which can be explained partly by a scarcity of detailed information and partly by a sheer lack of interest. Roland Bainton's three volumes of studies on individual women did something to remedy the former problem, while the growing field of women's history and feminist studies has embraced the Reformation as it has all other fields. The result has been an increasing number of analytical studies of individual women and a systematic analysis of the gains and losses accruing to women as a result of the Reformation.

Another major growth area in recent years has been the rich area of popular culture and folk religion. Building on earlier studies, such as Keith Thomas's *Religion and the Decline of Magic* (1971), these inquiries have sought to illuminate the vast penumbra of magic, witchcraft, and popular superstition surrounding the ministrations of the church and to ask, among other things, how far both Protestant reform and Tridentine Catholicism managed to draw the masses away from these primitive folk traditions toward a "purer" Christian piety. According to French scholars Jean Delumeau and Pierre Chaunu, this was the common and avowed aim of "orthodox" Catholics and Protestants. Inquiries in this area have led in turn to significant general debates about the phenomenon of acculturation and to research into new areas, among which Robert W. Scribner's research into the social iconography of Reformation pamphlets has proved especially illuminating.

Avant-garde studies of recent years have expanded knowledge of the Reformation and added an element of freshness and excitement to the process of research as new questions have enlarged understanding. Suggestions that they should displace the more traditional studies reflected here, however, seem not only premature but misguided. The field of Reformation studies is broad and populous enough to accommodate a balanced and pluralist approach to the ongoing task of illuminating this rich area of history.

BIBLIOGRAPHY

Dickens, A. G., and John Tonkin. *The Reformation in Historical Thought.* Cambridge, Mass., and Oxford, 1985. The most comprehensive study available of the historiography of the Reformation over nearly five centuries.

Hazard, Paul. *The European Mind, 1680–1715.* London, 1953. An innovative intellectual history still of considerable value. Little directly related to the Reformation, but its analysis of the European "crisis of conscience" of the late seventeenth and early eighteenth centuries illuminates the shifting intellectual framework within which Reformation studies developed.

Maltby, William S., ed. *Reformation Europe: A Guide to Research II.* Saint Louis, 1992. A sequel to the earlier volume edited by Ozment, summarizing research over the 1980s in various subdisciplines of Reformation history and suggesting future projects.

Mansfield, Bruce. *Phoenix of His Age: Interpretations of Erasmus, c.1550–1750.* Toronto, 1979.

———. *Man on His Own: Interpretations of Erasmus, 1750–1920.* Toronto, 1992. Mansfield's two volumes are exhaustively detailed studies of the changing historical reputation of Erasmus, which at the same time provide a window on the changing interpretation of the Reformation.

O'Day, Rosemary. *The Debate on the English Reformation.* London, 1986. A detailed historiographical study of the English Reformation, including coverage of the lively revisionist discussions of recent decades.

Ozment, Steven, ed. *Reformation Europe: A Guide to Research.* Saint Louis, 1982. A collection of essays by fifteen scholars covering major areas and aspects of Reformation research, each with a bibliography for further research.

Scribner, Robert. *The German Reformation.* London, 1986. A short but densely packed survey of Reformation research to the mid-1980s with an emphasis on social history and helpful guidance for additional reading.

Zeeden, E. W. *The Legacy of Luther.* Westminster, Md., 1954. A shortened translation of a major two-volume study of changing views of Luther within the German Lutheran tradition.

JOHN TONKIN

REFUGEES. The sixteenth century, like our own, was an age of refugees. All of western and central Europe recorded great numbers of persons with "no fixed abode." Many, though certainly not all, of these were refugees, a term that is neither clearly defined nor widely used for the sixteenth century. Even dictionary definitions of a refugee—such as "one who flees in search of refuge from war or from religious or political persecution"—fail to include those forced to migrate by famines and disabling economic conditions. Broadly, a refugee flees an established habitation in order to preserve life. The reasons for flight may be religious, political, or social persecution; war; such economic conditions as famine or lack of employment; or even exile by magistrates for various crimes. Removed from their cocoon of customs and laws, refugees were often considered "outlaws." Those excluded from legitimate work depended upon alms; others, fortunate indeed, were able to establish or join agricultural or industrial communities in a new land. Because conformity in both the political and religious spheres was thought essential for maintaining society, dissension led easily to persecution and dislocation. Toleration of dissenting views was rare.

Religious Refugees. The variety and number of religious refugees was great; Catholics, Lutherans, Calvinists, Zwinglians, and Anabaptists all expelled dissidents, quite apart from those displaced for other reasons. Catholic refugees (monks, nuns, and secular clergy displaced by reform, and private individuals during the religious wars) could usually find nearby shelter or protection. Calvinists scattered to various parts of France and as far as Poland and Hungary, as well as to favored Geneva. The 1555 Peace of Augsburg excluded Calvinists from the Holy Roman Empire, but drew Lutherans from other countries and from Catholic territories within the empire. Lutherans also sought brethren in Scandinavia, Poland, and Hungary. Spiritualists, who often claimed all men as their brothers, discovered few of them anywhere. Anabaptists at first found some imperial cities open to them, but after the Mandate of 1529, which stipulated the death penalty for rebaptizing, and after the backlash against the Münster rebellion in 1534–1535 closed most cities, they moved to Frisia and ducal Prussia or to eastern Europe (Poland, Silesia, Moravia, and Hungary). After 1577 Holland protected them and indeed people of all religions except Catholicism. Cities almost everywhere, though with increasing reluctance, temporarily supplied food and shelter for vagrants of all sorts. Expectably, key figures have been studied, while little is known about lesser persons displaced by wars, dissolutions of monasteries, famines, economic crises, and legal decisions.

Many famous persons, known for their publications or outstanding activities, were refugees, though often not identified as such. Among them were Martin Luther at the Wartburg castle; John Calvin at the court of Navarre and Ferrara and later at Strasbourg when forced to leave Geneva temporarily; Martin Bucer after 1548 in England; several members of the Sozzini (Socinus) family, including Fausto, who was to found the Unitarian church in Poland; outsiders like Bernardino Ochino, Andreas Bodenstein Karlstadt, Thomas Müntzer, Balthasar Hubmaier, Conrad Grebel, Hans Denck, Kaspar von Schwenckfeld, Sebastian Franck, Michael Servetus, Melchior Hoffman, Jacob Hutter, and Sébastien Castellion; and famous women including Charlotte de Bourbon at Heidelberg and Louise de Coligny at Geneva, Bern, and Basel after the murder of her husband, Admiral Gaspard II de Coligny, in the Saint Bartholomew's Day Massacre. In the twenty-one years before his death in 1563, Ochino moved from Italy to Geneva, and then to Strasbourg, Augsburg, and England, and finally to Zurich after Mary Tudor's accession; exiled from Zurich, he died in Moravia. Though usually only the male is mentioned, many refugees traveled as families. The Interim of 1548–1552 in Germany caused the exile of many non-Catholic clergy; Francis I's occasional persecutions and the frightful Wars of Religion in France, culminating in the Saint Bartholomew's Day Massacre of 1572, as well as the activities of the Inquisition in Spain and Italy, led to flight and exile for thousands.

Most of the estimated 100,000 Jews expelled from Spain in 1492 went to the eastern Mediterranean, some to North Africa and to Navarre. A thousand families from the Papal States in Italy migrated to Turkey when expelled by Pius V (r. 1566–1572). The *Moriscos* were not expelled from all of Spain until 1609, but more than 100,000 migrated from Granada into Castile after a failed uprising in 1568, while the general expulsion of 1609–1614 resulted in the migration, chiefly to North Africa, of three or more times that number. Some French Waldensians, persecuted in 1534–1535 and again in 1555–1559 escaped to northern Italy and eastern Europe.

Anabaptist refugees, among the best documented, fled persecutions in Germany, while the activities of Fernando Álvarez de Toledo, duke of Alba, in the Netherlands (1567–1573) drove out perhaps fifty thousand dissidents, chiefly Anabaptists. Since few places in western Europe offered shelter for extended periods, northern Anabaptists moved in large numbers to Poland, to Turkish-controlled Transylvania, and especially to Moravia. Already in 1530 Poland welcomed Anabaptists from the Netherlands to the lands along the Vistula River near Danzig (Gdánsk), where their ability to control the marshes made wastelands profitable. After the Münster rebellion in 1534–1535, Dutch Mennonites moved there in great numbers, while other groups from Silesia and Slovakia also settled in Poland. Bohemian Brethren expelled from their homeland arrived after 1548. South German and Swiss Anabaptists fled to Moravia. Scattered in 1534–1535 and again in 1547–1551, the Moravian Anabaptists, chiefly Hutterites, enjoyed peace during the rest of the century. After about 1551 a large number of refugees from Germany, Switzerland, and Austria arrived in Moravia, some 1,600 at Nikolsburg (Mikulov) alone in 1587. Isolated in eastern Europe, the Anabaptists' tendency toward communal society was reinforced when surrounded by customs and languages very different from their own.

Calvinist refugees from Alba's regime in the Netherlands tended to flee toward northern France, including Paris, and some even went to Poland. Fear and haste caused their destinations to vary greatly. The Saint Bartholomew's Day Massacre in 1572 generated massive flights to such southern Huguenot strongholds as La Rochelle, Montauban, and Nîmes, as well as Geneva.

Non-religious Refugees. Exclusionary social and political practices, which accelerated in the sixteenth century, acted in concert with worsening economic conditions to marginalize members of the lower classes. Those marginalized either conformed to increasingly harsh conditions of welfare (e.g., wearing badges or symbols that advertised one's poverty, following restrictions on gaming and drinking, and eventually being forced into workhouses) or took to the roads. Economic dislocations, characterized by rising or fluctuating prices, stable or declining wages, and frequent famines, were the most important factors in driving workers and peasants to flee from almost certain starvation. Nameless, these unfortunates are known only from the expenditure records kept by the towns they visited while seeking food and shelter. Unable to support themselves, hundreds of thousands lived in wretched conditions of homelessness.

Following the German Peasants' War of 1524–1525, many townspeople who had supported the revolt and many rebellious peasants fled from harsh reprisals. Their destinations are seldom known, though local archives may reveal much more about them. Switzerland was a key destination. James Stayer has shown that these refugees provided fertile ground for Anabaptism, whose origins lay in the same years. Many or even most of them, however, simply melted into obscurity.

Tribunals frequently banished persons for lesser crimes, adding them to the hordes of refugees. Save for trial records, not fully exploited, they left little trace during these periods of exile. Branding or mutilation made them unacceptable as workers anywhere and therefore permanent refugees. The German 1559 *Polizeiordnung* ("social regulations") prescribed exile for journeymen who refused work or changed masters illegally. Unhirable, they inevitably became refugee-vagabonds. Similar exclusionary policies elsewhere had the same results. A history of the nonreligious refugees of the sixteenth century remains to be written, though the immense problems they created for government at all levels, especially municipal, are generally well known.

Economic and Social Impacts. One can only generalize about economic and social impacts of refugees in the sixteenth century, great as they were. The economic drain on financial and food resources of towns across Europe was itself enormous in order to care even minimally for the hordes begging for help. How can one estimate the damage to local economies caused by the exodus of skilled people? The Jews had formed an important commercial and financial segment of Spanish society, and the *Moriscos* were perhaps its most productive agricultural portion. The final cost of their expulsion is debatable but must have been large; also, their skills could be applied in foreign lands to the detriment of Spanish aims. Hardworking Anabaptists enriched their new homelands at the expense of the old. Lutheran weavers who settled in Wesel and Hamburg received help in establishing a manufacture that benefited those towns, though their competition hurt the already depressed south German weavers. Geneva accepted more than five thousand refugees from France, England, Scotland, Italy, Spain, and the Holy Roman Empire. Forming about a third of the city's population late in the century, they dominated its printing industry, and the merchants and workers among them, especially in the new silk industry, drove Geneva's commerce to new heights. Many economic and political refugees entered the ranks of mercenary armies, and many were forced into the workhouses which sprang up everywhere. Though many religious refugees apparently traveled as families, families were often broken, with wives and children left to make their way in a harsh world.

[*See also* Marian Exiles; Persecution; *and* Toleration.]

BIBLIOGRAPHY

Clasen, Claus-Peter. *Anabaptism: A Social History, 1525–1618*. Ithaca, N.Y., 1972.

Germek, Bronislaw. "Criminalité, vagabondage, pauperisme: La marginalité à l'aube des temps modernes." *Revue d'Histoire moderne et contemporaine* 21 (1974), 337–375.

———. "Men without Masters: Marginal Society during the Preindustrial Era." *Diogenes* 98 (1977), 28–54.

Monter, William. *Calvin's Geneva*. Reprint, Huntington, N.Y., 1975. Contains a model chapter on refugees.

Norwood, Frank A. *Strangers and Exiles: A History of Religious Refugees*. Nashville and New York, 1969.

Oberman, Heiko. "*Europa afflicta*: The Reformation of the Refugees." *Archiv für Reformationsgeschichte* 83 (1992), 91–111.

Stayer, James. *The German Peasants' War and the Anabaptist Community of Goods*. Montreal, 1991.

Williams, George H. *The Radical Reformation*. 3d ed. Kirksville, Mo., 1992.

PHILIP L. KINTNER

REGENSBURG, BOOK OF. *See* Colloquies.

REGENSBURG, COLLOQUY OF. *See* Colloquies.

REIGER, Urban. *See* Rhegius, Urbanus.

REINA, Casiodoro de (Lat., Cassiodorus Reinius; c.1520–1594), converted Spanish monk and priest, irenic Calvinist, and Lutheran minister. Inquisition records place Reina's birth in Montemolín, near Seville; the date can be estimated only from his own later statements. He had a humanist education at the University of Seville and was ordained. He became an observantine Hieronymite in San Isidro del Campo and was strongly affected by the evangelical movement in Seville, becoming one of the leading propagators of Protestant ideas. When the Inquisition got wind of Protestants in the city in 1557, he fled, arriving in Geneva at the time of difficulties for the Italian Protestants. He felt obliged to move to London as soon as Elizabeth I's reign began and gathered a congregation of exiled Spaniards. Recognition by the other stranger churches was slow, owing to suspicion of his theological views, which was not surprising, in view of his known interest in heterodox writers and his defense of Michael Servetus and the Anabaptists. Jacob Acontius helped Reina to compose the Spanish Confession of Faith of London (1560/61), which is strongly irenic in tone, condemning no group of Christians outright. Boldly the confession states that the Bible does not mention the Trinity, its persons, or infant baptism.

Spanish agents in London engineered moral and doctrinal charges against Reina, prompting him to flee to Antwerp, where he was hidden by Marcos Pérez. He escaped to visit Antonio del Corro in France in order to discuss a project dear to both, the translation of the Bible into Spanish from the original languages. Life was difficult for foreign ministers, and both were saved by being given shelter by Renée of France in Montargis.

Reina left to rejoin his wife, by now in Frankfurt am Main, where he continued what had become his overriding interest, the preparation of his Bible translation. He kept looking for a pastorate and in 1565 was offered the oversight of the French congregation of Strasbourg. After moving to that city and waiting for several years for the city council to ratify his appointment, the unresolved matter of the accusations against him in London prevented his taking the post. He continued the Bible translation, however, but after several crises, illness, and financial difficulties caused by the death of the original printer, pressure of time led him to borrow almost word for word the last five or six books of the New Testament from Juan Pérez's version; it was finally published in Basel in 1569. There is evidence that Reina was also connected with the production of *Sanctae Inquisitionis Hispanicae artes* (1567).

Reina returned to live in Frankfurt am Main, ceaselessly badgered by the church council of the French congregation to get himself cleared of the London charges. The intransigence of these and of Théodore de Bèze concerning these allegations of moral and doctrinal lapses, contrasted with the friendship of Matthias Ritter the Younger, finally caused him to join the Lutheran church. In 1573 he published two Latin commentaries, one on *Matthew* 4 and the other on John's gospel, the latter apparently to establish definitively his trinitarian orthodoxy. In 1577 he issued the first printed version of his Spanish Confession of Faith of London. Resolution of the charges against him became imperative when the chance arose to become pastor of the French-speaking Lutheran congregation of Antwerp. He returned to England in 1578 to be cleared in the consistory court of the archbishop of Canterbury, Edmund Grindal, and was free to take up his post. Calvinists in Antwerp attempted to discredit him by publishing the text of his declarations before the court, where he proclaimed his Calvinist orthodoxy in an Anglican setting so that he could minister to Lutherans. His diligence and irenic spirit, however, soon brought Calvinist respect. He collaborated in the publication of the Antwerp Lutheran catechism in 1580.

After the Spanish attack on Antwerp in 1585, Reina led his congregation into exile in Frankfurt am Main, where he set up an exiled French-language Lutheran church and a charitable fund for indigent refugees from the Low Countries. His ministry was not ratified by the city council until 1592, two years before he died.

From his days in Spain Reina was dominated by a desire to produce a Spanish translation of the Bible for the purpose of evangelizing in Spain. It would later serve as a support for his fellow exiles. It was the first complete Bible translated into Castilian directly from the original languages and, with revisions, remains standard among Spanish Protestants.

Reina was an open-minded Christian, who, while remaining firmly Protestant, was willing to consider all points of view in the Reformation field, even those seen as unacceptable. He was reluctant to condemn anyone for doctrinal reasons. His theology could be described as pragmatic and biblical rather than dogmatic. A major influence on his attitude seems to have been the liberal Italians and Sébastien Castellion. An assessment of his caliber can be obtained from the knowledge that, besides his Bible, the Dutch Lutheran catechism and his charitable foundation in Frankfurt am Main have stood the test of time, and the church he founded there existed until World War II.

BIBLIOGRAPHY

Primary Sources

Reina, Casiodoro de. *Confessioñ de fe Christiana.* London, 1560–1561.

———. *The Spanish Protestant Confession of Faith London, 1560/61.* Edited by A. Gordon Kinder. Exeter, England 1988.

Secondary Sources

Boehmer, Eduard. *Bibliotheca Wiffeniana: Spanish Reformers of Two Centuries.* Vol. 2. London, 1883. See especially pp. 163–313.

Kinder, A. Gordon. *Casiodoro de Reina, Spanish Reformer of the Sixteenth Century.* London, 1975.

———. "Casiodoro de Reina." In *Bibliotheca Dissidentium,* edited by André Séguenny, vol. 4, pp. 99–153. Baden-Baden, 1984.

A. Gordon Kinder

REIS, Hans de.

See Ries, Hans de.

RELICS.

See Saints, *article on* Cult of Saints.

RELIGIOUS ORDERS.

On the eve of the Reformation most of the religious orders were subject to a wide range of criticism. Many humanists, above all Desiderius Erasmus, derided their formalism, sloth, and attachment to pettifogging scholasticism. Vernacular writers from Boccaccio and Chaucer to Sebastian Brant and Marguerite d'Angoulême made the friars the butts of jokes. The criticism sometimes reflected prejudice but often rested on solid ground and was shared by bishops, who resented the papal exemptions from ordinary church jurisdiction that the orders enjoyed. In 1537 the famous reform commission set up by Paul III argued that all the conventual orders had become so deformed that they should be done away with by prohibiting the admission of novices. Other cardinals urged the amalgamation of the existing orders into a few basic types.

Pressure to reform sometimes came from the outside. Thus Ferdinand and Isabella, urged on by the austere Franciscan Cardinal Francisco Jiménez de Cisneros, attempted to reform the Spanish church and especially the orders. Their efforts rested on mixed motives—religious idealism and the desire to bring the orders under greater royal control. While generally successful, their efforts met resistance. Hundreds of Franciscans refused to give up their concubines, fled to Africa, embraced Islam, and married. Most efforts at reform came from within the orders and centered not on the vow of chastity but on that of poverty. The food and drink allowed in most religious houses were generous by contemporary standards. Many monks and friars enjoyed a small private purse. When reformers insisted that they return to the full rigor of their rules, the result was friction that frequently split religious orders into conventual and observant (reformed) observances. The extreme example was the male Franciscans, who split into six observances. Efforts to encourage or block reform often involved lobbying at the papal Curia, Martin Luther's trip to Rome as a young Augustinian being but one example.

Italy was the scene of several reform efforts on the eve of the Reformation. The Venetian aristocrat Tommaso Giustiniani tried to reform the Camaldolese. The Augustinian friars had a reforming general in the gifted humanist Giles of Viterbo, who as prior-general (1507–1518) improved their educational standards and insisted on common life, sending around visitors with broad powers to enforce reform and dismiss lax superiors. Cajetan, the leading theologian of his day, was Dominican master general (1508–1518) and tried to reform the Dominicans by stressing studies and common life. Lack of support from the papacy limited the effectiveness of these early reforms. More lasting were reform efforts of the Italian Benedictines, who linked monasteries together with a common membership in the Cassinese Congregation (1515); a general chapter elected their abbots so that they escaped the curse of abbots *in commendam*—absentee laymen who siphoned off revenues. There were parallel developments among the Spanish and German Benedictines.

The Franciscans were easily the largest religious order, but efforts in Italy to return to their demanding original rule resulted in the split of the Franciscans into the Conventual and the Observant branches in 1517. There were some 25,000 Conventuals and 30,000 Observants. The desire of many for a still stricter observance of the rule, especially regarding poverty, led to the establishment of the Capuchins in 1528. The Capuchins can be regarded as either reformed Franciscans or, perhaps better, as a new order. Aside from the Jesuits, they were the most influential new order. The papacy approved the Capuchins in 1536 but restricted them to Italy until 1574; thereafter they spread rapidly in France, Germany, Spain, and Poland. Linked to the Observant Franciscans were the Reformed Franciscans, who began in Italy in 1532. Parallel reform movements in Spain resulted in the Discalced Franciscans and the Recollects (1570). By 1700 there were 15,000 Conventuals, 34,900 Observants, 6,200 Discalced, 9,600 Recollects, 12,000 Reformed, and 27,300 Capuchins.

Impact of the Protestant and Catholic Reformations. In Protestant countries the orders were either driven out or forced to carry on a clandestine existence, but in Catholic countries their numbers gradually rose through the period 1550–1700. Many orders reached an all-time high about 1700, when decline again set in. By 1700 there were some 30,000 Dominicans, 19,000 Jesuits, 17,000 Augustinian hermits, 17,000 Benedictines, 14,000 Carmelites, plus many smaller orders. Most of the new male orders of the Catholic Reformation counted fewer than a thousand members. These statistics suggest that reform movements in the older orders contributed more to the Catholic Reformation than did the foundation of new orders. After the Council of Trent, reformers consistently enjoyed the support of the papacy, and the mendicant orders generally enjoyed a silver age of fervor and influence. Efforts at reform sometimes ran into determined resistance. For example, some members of the Humiliati in Milan tried to kill the reforming Cardinal Carlo Borromeo.

The military religious order largely disappeared during the period 1517–1650. The Spanish and Portuguese crusading orders lost much of their purpose after the fall of Granada in 1492. The popes allowed the Iberian kings to become grand masters and transformed them into honorary societies of noblemen. The grand master of the Teutonic Knights converted to Lutheranism and secularized their Prussian lands. The heroism of the Knights of Malta in defending Malta from the Turks in 1565 increased their popularity and prolonged their life.

The New Male Orders. Both the Capuchins and the Discalced Carmelites can be regarded as new orders. The Capuchins have already been discussed. The Spanish Discalced Carmelites secured independent status in 1593 and established many convents in France and Italy, where they spread the mysticism of Teresa of Ávila and Juan Álvarez.

The most important and innovative of the new orders were the Jesuits, founded at Rome by Ignatius Loyola in 1540. His first companions were mainly Spaniards but included others from France, Portugal, and Savoy. The Jesuits spread rapidly outside Italy, in contrast to several other new orders. The most important Jesuit ministry was education, followed by missionary work. During the sixteenth century their growth was most rapid in Spain, Italy, and Portugal. During the seventeenth century they grew strong in France, Germany, and Poland. Several characteristics set the Jesuits apart from the friars: they did not sing or recite the Divine Office in common; they had different grades of membership, with only an elite being admitted to solemn vows; the superior general was elected for life and appointed lesser officials; and their training was usually long and demanding.

Italy was the birthplace of several other new orders of clerics regular; their numbers remained small, and their ministries were often specialized, but they all shared with the Jesuits a reorientation of the religious life toward a more active ministry with less emphasis on prolonged prayer. Thus the Somaschi, founded by Girolamo Emiliani in 1528, devoted themselves to the care of orphans, while the Camillans, founded by Camillo de Lellis in 1586, undertook the care of the sick. The Theatines were founded at Rome in 1524 by Cajetan of Thiene and the learned aristocrat Gian Pietro Carafa (later Paul IV). The Theatines fled Rome during the sack of 1527 and settled in Venice and Naples before returning to Rome in 1555. Devoted exclusively to parish work, they furnished the church with many reforming bishops. The Clerics Regular of the Pious Schools (Piarists), founded in 1597 at Rome by José Calasanz, taught boys. The Clerics Regular of Saint Paul were founded by Antonio Maria Zaccaria at Milan in 1530 and won papal approval in 1533; they were popularly known as the Barnabites from their mother church of Saint Barnabas in Milan. Carlo Borromeo encouraged their efforts to raise the level of morals and devotion in Lombardy and the Veneto by preaching and encouraging frequent Communion and various devotions. A parallel women's order, the Angelics, was approved two years after the male branch. Francesco Caracciolo founded the Minor Clerks Regular in Naples, who won papal approval in 1588 and spread to Rome and Spain. They engaged in works of charity and spread the perpetual adoration of the Eucharist.

The Oratorians, begun at Rome by Filippo Neri in 1564, were not technically a religious congregation because they did not take religious vows, but they did live in community under a superior and adopted constitutions (1588). Later communities were only loosely linked to the Roman Oratory. The flourishing French branch founded by Cardinal Pierre de Bérulle in 1611 edged closer to religious congregations. The Italian Oratorians worked in parishes; the French staffed colleges and seminaries.

The Catholic Reformation in France flourished only after the Wars of Religion ended. The most important French male congregation was the Congregation of the Mission (Vincentians, Lazarists) founded by Vincent de Paul in 1625. The Vincentians were technically not an order, but secular priests living in community with simple, private vows. Their main work was giving parish missions to the peasantry, but they staffed fifteen seminaries by 1660. They spread quickly to Italy and Poland. Much smaller than the Vincentians were the Eudists (Congregation of Jesus and Mary) founded by Jean Eudes. A popular preacher of parish missions, Eudes left the Oratorians in 1643 and began his new society of priests without vows; they were devoted to giving parish missions and running seminaries in western France.

The Work of the Male Orders. The ministries of the orders partly overlapped with those of parish priests, who sometimes regarded the religious as archrivals and sometimes as valued helpers. Many of the new orders engaged in ministries for which the secular clergy were unsuited. In the Americas the first missionaries were the friars, later helped by the Jesuits. The Jesuit role in the Asian missions was larger still. The Jesuits, French Oratorians, and Piarists ran schools for boys and young men. Religious often staffed the new seminaries. The Jesuits, Capuchins, and Vincentians preached parish missions in rural areas. The Somaschi ran orphanages, and the Camillans ran hospitals. When plague swept the land, religious were expected to volunteer to help the stricken; the Capuchins showed outstanding heroism in this dangerous work. The orders were uniquely able to provide chaplains for Catholic armies and fleets. The medieval Trinitarians and Mercedarians continued their traditional work of ransoming and ministering to Catholic slaves in Muslim countries. The Dominicans supplied most of the Inquisitors, helped by the other friars. The Spanish kings usually took a Dominican as confessor; the kings of France and the emperors usually chose Jesuit confessors. Members of the orders served occasionally on papal commissions or as papal diplomats. Three important popes (Paul IV, Pius V, and Sixtus V) of the late sixteenth century belonged to religious orders.

The orders ran many of the confraternities that were central to Catholic social and devotional life. The Jesuits gave retreats based on Ignatius's *Spiritual Exercises.* The Jesuits, Theatines, Oratorians, and Barnabites urged frequent Communion for the laity. Certain orders encouraged particular devotions: Jesuits and Capuchins encouraged the Forty Hours devotion to the Eucharist. All the new orders were devoted to preaching, as were the friars. The majority of Catholic philosophical, theological, and polemical works of the sixteenth century came from the friars or the Jesuits. The sixteenth century was rich in spiritual classics; here Jesuit and Capuchin writers were the most popular, but the Carmelites were the most profound. Members of the orders encouraged Catholic publishers; some, notably the Cologne Carthusians, ran their own presses.

The orders traditionally provided the church with scholars and theologians. Here the Dominicans and the Jesuits took the lead, but relative to their numbers the Oratorians were even richer in distinguished scholars. The Oratorian schools in France were more innovative than the numerous Jesuit colleges, whose curriculum was tied to their *Ratio studiorum,* which continued the tradition of Renaissance humanism. The Jesuits and Dominicans, with help from the other friars, were the leading representatives of the scholastic revival, which climaxed in late sixteenth-century Spain. There was a notable shift back to the *via antiqua* and especially to Thomas Aquinas. The Dominicans had always taken Thomas as their guide, but the Jesuits also embraced Thomism, a bit more flexibly. The Capuchins continued the shift from the *via moderna* by following the pious Bonaventure rather than the more subtle John Duns Scotus and William of Ockham within the Franciscan tradition. These developments muted but did not remove rivalry among the orders. The Dominicans and the Jesuits fought fierce theological battles over free will and the primacy of grace. The Jesuits in mission lands tended to be more accommodating to non-Christian cultures than the friars.

Orders and Congregations of Women. Both churchmen and secular elites felt that the breakdown of discipline among female religious flowed from contact with the world. The Council of Trent insisted that cloister be enforced and that semireligious lifestyles (Beguines in Germany and the

Netherlands, *beatas* in Spain) be gradually abolished, thereby restricting religious women to prayer and personal sanctification.

Nevertheless, several semiactive congregations sprang up, chiefly in Italy and France. The first and largest congregation was the Ursulines, started by Angela Merici in 1535 at Brescia. She and her followers lived at first in their own families without formal vows. Cardinal Borromeo organized the Ursulines into a community under episcopal control. By 1700 there were 11,000 Ursulines in France alone, where they were gradually converted into a semicloistered order with formal vows, but they continued to teach girls in their convents.

The Filles de Notre Dame won papal approval in 1607; concentrated in southern France, they were devoted to both contemplation and teaching. They were paralleled in northern France by the Congrégation de Notre Dame, begun in 1597. The Spanish Discalced Carmelites took their inspiration from Teresa of Ávila and remained strictly cloistered; they spread rapidly in France after 1601. The Visitation order, begun in 1610 in Savoy by Francis de Sales and Jeanne-François de Chantal, stressed simplicity rather than austerity and was semicloistered. By 1700 there were 6,500 Visitandines in France. A more radical innovator was Mary Ward, who modeled her English Ladies on the Jesuits. They were uncloistered and did not wear distinctive garb. Their first community was set up in Belgium in 1612, followed by others in Germany and Italy, until the congregation was suppressed in 1631. More successful were the Daughters of Charity, who helped the poor and the sick. They began taking private vows in 1640 and continued to wear secular garb so that their informality saved them from paternalistic regulations. Today they are the largest of all religious orders.

[*See also* Augustinians; Barnabites; Capuchins; Carmelites; Jesuits; Monasticism; Theatines; *and* Ursulines.]

BIBLIOGRAPHY

Bangert, William. *A History of the Society of Jesus.* Saint Louis, 1986.

Collett, Barry. *Italian Benedictine Scholars and the Reformation: The Congregation of Santa Giustina of Padua.* Oxford, 1985.

Cuthbert of Brighton. *The Capuchins: A Contribution to the History of the Counter-Reformation* (1929). 2 vols. Reprint, Port Washington, N.Y., 1971.

Demolen, Richard L., ed. *Essays on the Religious Orders of the Catholic Reformation.* New York, 1995. Essays by specialists on the major new male and female orders of the Counter-Reformation.

Dizionario degli istituti di perfezione. Rome, 1974–. This multivolume encyclopedia is the most important single source for information about religious orders and congregations (i.e., institutes of perfection in canonical terminology).

Knowles, David. *From Pachomius to Ignatius: A Study in the Constitutional History of the Religious Orders.* Oxford, 1966.

Lekai, Louis I. *The Rise of the Cistercians of the Strict Observance in Seventeenth-Century France.* Washington, D.C., 1968.

Lunn, David. *The English Benedictines, 1540–1688.* London, 1980.

Nimmo, Duncan. *Reform and Division in the Medieval Franciscan Order from Saint Francis to the Foundation of the Capuchins.* Rome, 1987.

O'Malley, John, ed. *Catholicism in Early Modern History: A Guide to Research.* Saint Louis, 1988. See the essays on male and female orders, spirituality, missionary work, and theology.

———. *The First Jesuits.* Cambridge, Mass., 1993.

Peters, Henriette. *Mary Ward: Ihre Persönlichkeit und ihr Institut.* Innsbruck, 1991. Studies Mary Ward's frustrated efforts to found a female parallel to the Jesuits.

Polgár, László. *Bibliographie sur l'histoire de la Compagnie de Jésus, 1900–1980.* 6 vols. Rome, 1980–1990.

Rapley, Elizabeth. *The Dévotes: Women and Church in Seventeenth-Century France.* Montreal, 1990.

Ravier, André. *Ignatius of Loyola and the Founding of the Society of Jesus.* Translated by Maura Daly et al. San Francisco, 1987.

Schmitz, Philibert. *Histoire de l'ordre de Saint-Benoît.* 7 vols. Maredesous, Belgium, 1948–1956.

Smet, Joachim. *The Carmelites: A History of the Brothers of Our Lady of Mount Carmel.* 4 vols. Darien, Ill., 1975–1982.

JOHN PATRICK DONNELLY, S.J.

RELIGIOUS RIOTS. *See* Riots, Religious.

REMONSTRANCE OF 1610.

A petition of Dutch Reformed clergy in the province of Holland asking its civil government to maintain the rights of the Arminians in the church, the *Remonstrantie ende Vertooch* (Remonstrance and Representation) provided the name by which the Arminian party would henceforth be commonly known; by extension the Calvinists came to be known as Contra-Remonstrants. The Remonstrance was but one episode in an ongoing struggle over the interpretation, authority, and possible revision of the Belgic Confession and Heidelberg Catechism in the Dutch church. The Calvinists upheld the documents as unchangeable standards. In November 1608 the States of Holland and West Friesland had invited the Arminians to present their alternative views. Upon the death of the Leiden theologian Jacobus Arminius on 19 October 1609, his party felt pressed to act. They met, probably in Gouda, and on 14 January 1610 fourty-four ministers signed the Remonstrance, which is believed to have been composed by Johannes Wtenbogaert, court chaplain at The Hague and a longtime intimate friend of the late Arminius.

The signatures, although from only one province, provide insight into the makeup of the Arminian movement. Seven signatories had studied at Geneva while Théodore de Bèze was there, three of them, including Wtenbogaert, as fellow students with Arminius. Five of the Geneva alumni were also alumni of the University of Leiden, and sixteen others were Leiden alumni from the six years that Arminius taught there. There were also signatories of greater age: three who had been Roman Catholic priests before Holland opted for the Reformation and at least one who had been an early clandestine hedge preacher. The presence of these veterans of the Dutch Reformed ministry suggests that Arminianism was not the innovation it was said to be by the Calvinists.

The list represents a high-water mark of Arminian strength in the Dutch church. One signer repudiated the document even before it was presented to the States in July. Several others vacillated or recanted, avoiding censure when the Synod of Dordrecht condemned Arminianism in 1619. Some died, and by 1619 only thirty-four signatories were left. They were deposed from their offices. Ten of them, to avoid deportation or imprisonment, agreed to be silent. By the time the Remonstrants could regroup a decade later as a separate church, only a handful of the signatories of 1610 remained with them.

The Remonstrance renewed the Arminian insistence that the States call a national synod that would revise the confession and catechism, favored by the Calvinists, to bring these formulas "in harmony with the word of God." It presented five alleged errors of the Calvinists to be corrected by such a revision, with five corresponding tenets of the petitioners, which, they felt, would be supported by such a revision.

The Remonstrance affirmed (1) that God by an eternal decree has elected those who will believe in Christ and persevere in that faith; (2) that Christ by his death on the cross gained reconciliation for all, although none but believers may enjoy this forgiveness; (3) that sinners cannot turn from their original state of rebellion without being reborn by God in Christ through the Holy Spirit in order to think, will, and perform the true good; (4) that apart from this preventing, awakening, and following grace no good can be willed, but that such grace is not irresistible; and (5) that those who have been engrafted into Christ by true faith will be aided to persevere in that faith, although scripture should be examined carefully to determine whether they can neglect grace and lose a good conscience. In August the States responded with a somewhat ambiguous resolution granting tolerance to the Arminians and refusing to make the five points the means of excluding either Arminian or Calvinist candidates from the ministry.

The public perception of Arminianism formed by the Remonstrance was modified by two other Remonstrant tracts in 1610. Peter Bertius in his *Hymenaeus desertor* . . . went beyond the fifth point by asserting baldly, to the dismay of other Remonstrants, the doctrine of falling from grace. Wtenbogaert's *Tractaet* . . . , which made explicit the Arminians' Erastian views of the supremacy of lay magistrates in the government of the church, has been called "the sixth point of the Remonstrance."

[*See also* Arminius, Jacobus; Dordrecht, Synod of; Episcopius, Simon; Gomarus, Franciscus; *and* Remonstrants.]

BIBLIOGRAPHY

Primary Sources

Schaaf, Philip. *The Creeds of Christendom.* 6th ed. Grand Rapids, Mich., 1990. See vol. 3, pp. 545–549, for a translation into English.

Tideman, J. *De Remonstrantie en het Remonstrantisme.* Haarlem, 1851. See pp. 17–20.

Secondary Sources

Groenewegen, H. IJ. *De Remonstrantie op haren Driehonderdsten Gedenkdag. . . .* Leiden, 1910. The best single work in Dutch.

Harrison, A. W. *The Beginnings of Arminianism to the Synod of Dort.* London, 1926. Perhaps the best work in English.

CARL BANGS

REMONSTRANTS. The term *Remonstrants* refers in the first instance to the forty-four signatories of a petition, or "remonstrance," to the States of Holland and West Friesland asking for toleration in the Dutch Reformed church of those who dissented from a narrowly fashioned Calvinism. They had met at Gouda in January 1610, about three months after the death of Jacobus Arminius, whose views they found acceptable. Their remonstrance immediately became a party label; the Calvinists thus came to be known as the "Contra-Remonstrants." In addition, there were other Dutch Remonstrant partisans outside the province of Holland.

During the decade, which had opened with a ten-year truce with Spain, the term could apply also to circles in government and commerce. In Amsterdam many of the merchant oligarchy, including Arminius's wife's family (the Reaels) and the family of Simon Episcopius (the Bisschops), had regarded Arminius as "one of their own," but under the influence of Petrus Plancius and other Calvinists, power in the city government shifted early in the decade to Calvinists. The tightly drawn lines found parallels in other Dutch cities, especially The Hague, Leiden, Alkmaar, and Oudewater.

At the provincial level, lines were drawn between the pro-peace party of Johan van Oldenbarnevelt and the pro-war party of Prince Maurits van Nassau. Calvinist clergy generally supported Maurits's hopes of continuing the war for independence against the Spanish "papal" power. The Arminians found support among merchants of the new Dutch East India Company, who wanted to get on with world trade. The factionalism became international when King James I of England intervened in the selection of a successor to Arminius in the Leiden faculty, hoping to get a Calvinist in place of the invited Conradus Vorstius.

The conflict issued in a decade of pamphleteering. Among the chief Remonstrant writers were Simon Episcopius and Johannes Wtenbogaert, the presumed author of the Remonstrance itself but also of another tract advocating an Erastian doctrine of lay control of the call of pastors. When ministers and theologians finally met at the Synod of Dordrecht (1618–1619), the larger stage was political, economic, military, and also diplomatic.

The Remonstrant party itself, however, was no longer that of the Remonstrance of 1610. Ten of the forty-four signatories had recanted, retired, or died. Of the remaining thirty-four, only one was seated in the synod, along with another minister and a layman. The real Remonstrant leaders, thirteen in all, were refused seats along with their fellow ministers and were instead cited to appear before the synod as the accused.

The Remonstrants then chose three of the signatories and one other minister to represent them. The synod made no concessions, demanding that the Remonstrants choose between silence or confiscation of goods with imprisonment or exile unless they would sign "without coercion" an act of cessation. Ten, mostly elderly, signed the act; the others were deprived of their livings. Some, including the jurist Hugo Grotius, were imprisoned in the Loevestein castle, where one minister died.

Two groups went into exile. Episcopius and other ministers went first to Antwerp and then to Rouen and Paris. Another group was given a site in Holstein, where they built a substantial Dutch-style town that they named Friedrichstadt, after their protector Duke Frederick III. There is still a Remonstrant church there (long since German-speaking except for the recitation of the Lord's Prayer in Dutch).

The synod had purged the Dutch Reformed Church of dissent. It was a low point for the Remonstrants. With the death of Maurits in 1625, however, many Remonstrants returned to organize local churches and establish a theological school in Amsterdam with Episcopius as its rector.

With a friendly Prince Frederick Henry succeeding Maurits, Amsterdam Remonstrants protested openly against Calvinist domination. In 1628 nearly 250 of them signed a petition asking for redress. Wide espousal of the Remonstrant cause came from both old families of inherited status and the newer merchant oligarchy. The Remonstrants were soon back in power and became the prime promoters of Amsterdam's golden age. Rembrandt had numerous commissions from the interlocking Remonstrant regent families, including the Reael family and the Wtenbogaerts. Rembrandt's etching of Johan Wtenbogaert is well known. The earliest known purchase of a Rembrandt painting was by a Remonstrant.

The church that emerged was known variously as the Remonstrant-Reformed church, the Remonstrant Society, or, chiefly, the Remonstrant Brotherhood. It had two foci: laity drawn largely from the regents of Amsterdam and of other towns, and scholars with their commitment to toleration and openness to new intellectual currents.

Remonstrants are perhaps unique in tracing their history through their professors. Episcopius broadened the foundation laid by Arminius. Stephan Curcellaeus (1588–1659) introduced the rationalism of Descartes, as did Jean Le Clerc (1657–1736). Other noteworthy Remonstrant professors include A. Poelenburg (1628–1688), known for his study of rabbinic literature; Philip van Limborch (1632–1712), whose *Christian Theology* was adapted into an English translation for use in the Church of England, and who along with Le Clerc, welcomed Descartes philosophy in Holland. J. J. Wetstein (1693–1754), a noted biblical scholar; Paul van Hemert (1765–1825), who introduced Kant's philosophy to Holland; C. P. Tiele (1830–1902), a pioneer of comparative religion; and J. H. Scholten (1811–1885), who was a modernist and moved the Remonstrant seminary to the University of Leiden.

[*See also* Arminius, Jacobus; Dordrecht, Synod of; Episcopius, Simon; Gomarus, Franciscus; *and* Remonstrance of 1610.]

BIBLIOGRAPHY

Bangs, Carl. "Regents and Remonstrants in Amsterdam." In *In het Spoor van Arminius.* Nieuwkoop, 1975.

Brandt, Gerard. *The History of the Reformation and Other Ecclesiastical Transactions in and about the Low Countries . . .* (1720–1721). 4 vols. Translated by John Chamberlayne. Reprint, New York, 1979. See vols. 2–4.

Calder, Frederick. *Memoirs of Simon Episcopius . . . .* London, 1838.

Colie, Rosalie L. *Light and Enlightenment: A Study of the Cambridge Platonists and the Dutch Arminians.* Reprint, Cambridge, 1987.

Harrison, A. W. *Arminianism.* London, 1937. See pp. 43–121.

Heering, G. J., and G. J. Sirks. *Het Seminarium der Remonstranten driechonderd jaar, 1634–1934.* Amsterdam, 1934.

Hoenderdaal, G. J. "Arminius en Episcopius." *Nederlands Archief voor Kerkgeschiedenis* 40.2 (1980), 203–235.

Holk, L. J. van. "From Arminius to Arminianism in Dutch Theology." In *Man's Faith and Freedom: The Theological Influence of Jacobus Arminius,* edited by G. O. McCulloh, pp. 27–45. New York, 1962.

Platt, John. *Reformed Thought and Scholasticism: The Arguments for the Existence of God in Dutch Theology, 1575–1650.* Leiden, 1982.

Rogge, H. C., and J. Tideman. *De Remonstrantsche Broederschap: Biographische Naamlijst.* 2d ed. Amsterdam, 1905.

Schwartz, Gary. *Rembrandt: His Life, His Paintings.* Reprint, London and New York, 1991.

CARL BANGS

RENAISSANCE. The Renaissance evokes a world of images rich and enigmatic. Yet scholars differ on whether, where, when, and how *a* Renaissance happened. Thus, the term requires some precision as a historian's tool. By custom, *Renaissance* refers either to a historical period or to distinctive features of social reality and human consciousness discernible in some but not all contexts during a given period. The term always bears reference to Italy between at least 1370 (the diffusion of Petrarch's and Giovanni Boccaccio's writings) and 1527 (the Sack of Rome), although dates slightly earlier and considerably later (mid-1300s to early 1600s) can easily be defended. Outside Italy the term *Renaissance* calls attention to a network of historical changes occurring in different parts of Europe with varying degrees of effectiveness and different patterns of temporal sequence. In such cases the time frame shifts to a distinctly later period for one or both of two reasons: first, because some interpreters view the Renaissance outside Italy as a delayed diffusion from Italian centers to other areas; second, because interpreters discover only in later generations those cultural transformations and attitudes that they consider essential to a definition of the Renaissance. Thus, when referring to affairs outside Italy, the Renaissance period usually begins in the later 1400s and lasts at least until Lutheran Germany breaks from Rome in the 1520s. But for many historians the Renaissance overlaps, unfolds simultaneously, or blends imperceptibly with the Reformation so that it can be traced through the 1500s to as late as the outbreak of the Thirty Years' War (1618).

Renaissance is a French word meaning rebirth. The image of this period as one of rebirth derives from writers at that time who used rebirth or renewal as metaphors to speak of the ideals and accomplishments of the age. The metaphor occurs as early as the poet Petrarch (Francesco Petrarca; 1304–1374) and as late as the artist and historian Giorgio Vasari (1511–1574). The rebirth first connoted a literary recovery, or at least a reevaluation, of classical Latin and Greek antiquity. Beyond incentives to write in purified classical style and advances in the philological study of ancient texts, Italian men of letters considered the educational models and moral wisdom reflected in the ancient texts as better suited than the Scholasticism of the universities to the needs of an emerging class of self-confident lay leaders and reformed clergy. A simultaneous flowering of innovations in painting, sculpture, and architecture was regarded also as an imitation of ancient classical models. Indeed, this artistic creativity is often popularly treated as synonymous with the Renaissance. The pioneering example of litterateurs and artists from Florence—such as Dante (1265–1321), Giotto (1267–1337), Petrarch, Boccaccio (1313–1375), Leonardo Bruni (1378–1444), and Filippo Brunelleschi (1377–1446)—early established the sense that the Renaissance fanned out from Tuscany to the other centers of Italy and thence to Spain and trans-Alpine lands.

Two significant points marked these literary and artistic awakenings. First, wherever they struck root, they usually bore fruit for several generations. They found patronage apart from traditional academic institutions, often in privately endowed academies, princely courts, and elite coteries. Gradually, the new models of education influenced universities as well. Second, these awakenings were widely viewed as the causes or the effects of a new political vitality. The mutual reinforcement of classical literature, educational renewal, aesthetic refinement, and politics was expected to yield rulers adept at maintaining order, counselors equipped to analyze strategies, diplomats and officials quick to persuade others to their princes' policies, and courtiers and citizens skilled in a new gentility.

Thus, while historians may debate whether *Renaissance* is a legitimate term for the age, three points are clear. First, contemporaries of that age for more than two centuries used terms and images of rebirth for a range of endeavors. As a description of their consciousness, *Renaissance* is a documentably accurate term. Second, however, beyond the sense of a re-birth, re-awakening, or re-discovery of something ancient, common usage has often broadened the meaning to include newly emerging historical realities—that is, things being born, not reborn. Third, therefore, whether one allows the term *Renaissance* or prefers some neutral designation such as "early modern Europe," several other real transitions make the period in question different from the previous and subsequent ones. These other transitions, customarily counted as Renaissance phenomena, can be briefly summarized. In the political and economic spheres the period marks a prolonged transition from a system of power based on feudal relations and agricultural economy to a network of monarchies, principalities, and city-states based increasingly on an economy of banking and commerce and a political assumption of personal or state sovereignty. Some would call the economic facets of this change nascent capitalism. After 1492 the discoveries of new parts of the world opened horizons of trading and material resources; these were immediately seized upon to enhance the new economies and the new monarchies. Diplomacy was altered in this period by the establishment of permanent embassies to deal with political and commercial matters. Mercenary armies played increasingly significant roles in warfare. Even before and apart from the Protestant reforms, the papacy curtailed its power over regional churches, conceding much practical control to Catholic princes in a series of concordats and sanctions. Above all else, the invention of movable print in the second half of the 1400s immeasurably transformed this world, accelerating and widening the effect of almost all the other transitions just noted. For all these reasons the age from roughly 1400 to 1600 has the qualities of a distinct historical period: it has real transitions interconnected in their causes and effects, and the age is related to but discernibly different from the configuration of reality fifty years before and after the dates proposed.

Even if the term *Renaissance* is allowed, the identity of the age remains problematic because of the overlapping changes associated with the Reformation, not to mention the chronic dispute about the nature of the "middle" and "late Middle Ages." Obviously much that is claimed for the Renaissance derives from the Middle Ages, and much becomes inseparably tied to the Reformation. For example, Renaissance and Reformation realities go hand in hand in some areas, notably England, even to the point that certain "Renaissance" impulses—such as the consolidation of a princely court, the establishment of permanent foreign ambassadors, and the flourishing of artistic and literary innovation—developed only after church reform was underway. Any formula must further allow for differences among localities: it probably makes little sense to speak of Renaissance Zurich or Reformation Venice. Ultimately one can use these terms only with a judicious sense of their interpretive function.

The interplay of the distinctive and the overlapping elements of the Renaissance and Reformation becomes clear in those Protestant and Catholic reformers of the sixteenth century who hailed some of the changes summarized above as preparations for their work. Most Protestant and some Catholic reformers shared with "Renaissance" thinkers a conviction that they had reawakened a nobler antiquity and thus made a sharp break with an age of error and darkness. Yet the rebirth they prized was that of authentic Christianity, and so they focused on certain aspects of rebirth (and new birth) rather than others, notably the philological progress in understanding holy scripture, the humanists' emphasis on the Greek and Latin fathers as guides to Christian life and doctrine, the new educational models adaptable to the training of a reformed clergy, the miraculous benefits of printing, and the princes' resistance to papal authority. Of course, the reformers deplored or ignored other matters that would later seem central to the Renaissance. In any case, by 1600 the notion of three separate ages—ancient, middle, and new—was widely held, inevitably with a negative value assigned to the middle one. In turn, Enlightenment thinkers also saw themselves descending from a historical development that they traced from around 1400, although they played down the religious elements once important to the reformers. Voltaire (1694–1778) even spoke of that earlier age as a renaissance that broke away from barbarism and ignorance.

The idea of the Renaissance held renewed fascination for the nineteenth and twentieth centuries thanks to the rich prose of historians in the grand manner such as Jules Michelet (1798–1874) and John Addington Symonds (1840–1893). The Swiss Jacob Burckhardt (1818–1897) excels all others, however, for the imaginative power and enduring authority of his historical synthesis *Die Kultur der Renaissance in Italien* (The Civilization of the Renaissance in Italy), first published in 1860. Apart from Burckhardt's narrative skill, which may prove the most lasting aspect of his legacy, his initial appeal lay in his thesis that the Renaissance had given birth to the modern world. His argument also drew strength from its compatibility with nineteenth-century liberalism, individualism, nationalism, and the conviction popular since Hegel about the distinctive spirit of each age (*Zeitgeist*) and people (*Volksgeist*).

The six sections of Burckhardt's work offered major points for subsequent discussion and merit review here. Part 1, "The State as a Work of Art," depicts the Italians' ongoing reconstruction of their political reality as an activity like that of an artist creating an artifact. Burckhardt dwells on their political inventiveness amidst the harrowing instability of their tyrannies and city-states. Part 2, "The Development of the Individual," a popular and influential section, describes the Renaissance sense of individuality and pursuit of fame, which Burckhardt considers a key to modern identity. Part 3, "The Revival of Antiquity," reviews the Renaissance uses of the classical heritage. In Part 3 and again in part 4, "The Discovery of the World and of Man," Burckhardt adapts themes explored by earlier historians. Part 4 glorifies both the Italians' skill as observers of reality, whether in nature, society, or the person, and their gift for depicting it in historical writing, scientific treatises, travelogues, and the arts. As part 5, "Society and Festivals," discusses social structures, it celebrates the refinement of Renaissance life and manners. Part 6, "Morality and Religion," surveys the paganism, ecclesiastical corruption, and moral anarchy that sharpened the stark contrasts of the age between decadence and nobility.

Burckhardt's study determined the interpretations of the Renaissance, as well as reactions against them, for virtually a century. Although numerous features of his work have been corrected or rejected and although his interpretation is no longer tenable as a whole, his vision still influences historical reflection.

From Burckhardt until World War II two issues dominated the discussion of the Renaissance and the Protestant Reformation. The first was the conviction that both epochs had distinctively shaped the modern world. The second was the notion of specific Italian and German national characters and destinies. One equation, typified by Michelet, saw the Reformation as the German version of a Renaissance. A variation on this theme, popular with German writers, held humanism to be the principal legacy of Italy to the northern countries, where it was soon absorbed into the tasks of the Reformation. A different equation treated the Renaissance and the Reformation as parallel movements, either as separate expressions of the Italian and German spirits or, in the synthesis of Wilhelm Dilthey (1833–1911), as compatible features of a heroic European quest for spiritual liberation. All these views proposed some measure of harmony between the Renaissance and the Reformation. At the turn of the century, that perspective was challenged by the liberal Protestant theologian Ernst Troeltsch (1865–1923). Echoing Burckhardt's view but doing so within church circles, Troeltsch hailed the Renaissance as the harbinger of a noble modernity, but he reviled early Protestantism (reaching into the 1700s) as a revival of the authoritarian and irrational elements of the Middle Ages, unlike his own rational, liberal Protestantism. Crucial to Troeltsch's still influential view is the assertion that the Enlightenment, not the Reformation, introduced the modern age. The reaction against Protestant liberalism by such theologians as Karl Barth (1886–1968) and Reinhold Niebuhr (1892–1971) held Renaissance classicism incompatible with Reformation principles of biblical revelation and unmerited grace. Since the 1950s ongoing historical study has recast these questions and their answers, especially as historians probe late medieval nominalism, the religious substance of Italian and northern humanism, and the details of social history. Building on much of that work,

William Bouwsma, Charles Trinkaus, and others have freshly articulated the affinities and differences between the Renaissance and the Reformation.

To the extent that Burckhardt's views prevailed, the traditional Roman Catholic position on the Renaissance and Catholic reforms interpreted the Counter-Reformation as a repudiation of such Renaissance features as secularism, pagan classicism, and moral anarchy, although it allowed for great religious artists like Fra Angelico (Guido di Pietro) and Michelangelo. This view was readily seconded by secular historians, who treated Catholic reform as an authoritarian regression from the heights of the Renaissance. Both these views drew strength from a Catholic tendency to glorify certain medieval movements and thinkers as norms for Catholic identity. An alternative Catholic view emphasized continuity between the Middle Ages and the Renaissance, even at one point tracing Renaissance origins to figures like Francis of Assisi (1181–1226). More recently, as scholars appreciated the religious energies and the reforming tendencies of many Renaissance figures, they have argued for greater continuity between the Renaissance and the Catholic reforms.

As the twentieth century draws to its close, relationships between the Renaissance and the Reformation, like the meaning of the Renaissance itself, are open to continuing revision. Yet the perennial fascination with the idea of the Renaissance guarantees its future in our imagination of the past.

[*See also* Humanism.]

BIBLIOGRAPHY

Bouwsma, William J. "Renaissance and Reformation: An Essay in Their Affinities and Connections." In *Luther and the Dawn of the Modern Era*, edited by Heiko A. Oberman, pp. 127–149. Leiden, 1974. An authoritative step toward a new synthesis of the question.

Burckhardt, Jacob. *The Civilization of the Renaissance in Italy*. Translated by S. G. C. Middlemore. Reprint, London and New York, 1990. The classic synthesis of 1860 which set the terms for discussion of the Renaissance for at least a century.

Ferguson, Wallace K. *The Renaissance in Historical Thought: Five Centuries of Interpretation.* Cambridge, Mass., 1948. Masterful study of the shifting understandings of the Renaissance.

Goodman, Anthony, and Angus MacKay. *The Impact of Humanism on Western Europe.* London and New York, 1990. Focused on intellectual history but helpful to understand the European dimension of the Renaissance.

Hay, Denys. *The Italian Renaissance in Its Historical Background.* 2d ed. Cambridge, 1977. One of many useful modern introductions to the facts and issues of the Renaissance, with a chapter on the Renaissance in the north.

Kerrigan, William, and Gordon Braden. *The Idea of the Renaissance.* Baltimore and London, 1989. A new examination of the relevance of Burckhardt's views to a vision of a European literary and philosophical renaissance reaching from Petrarch to Descartes and Milton.

O'Malley, John W. *Rome in the Renaissance: Studies in Culture and Religion.* London, 1981. Essays on the affinity between Renaissance and Catholic reform.

O'Malley, John W., Thomas Izbicki, and Gerald Christianson. *Humanity and Divinity in Renaissance and Reformation: Essays in Honor of Charles Trinkaus.* Leiden, 1993.

Panofsky, Erwin. *Renaissance and Renascences in Western Art.* 2d ed. London, 1970. Although concerned with art history, these essays make distinctions essential to the understanding of the Renaissance as an epoch and the related rebirth and imitation of antiquity.

JAMES MICHAEL WEISS

RENATO, Camillo (also Paul Ricci, Lisia Phileno; c.1500–1575), Italian Anabaptist, spiritualist, and antitrinitarian. Renato superbly illustrates the complexity of various strands of the radical Reformation: he was sentenced to death as a heretic by the Roman Inquisition. Agostino Meinardo, his great Reformed antagonist in his later years, called him "pestis ecclesiae et magnus hereticus" ("a pest of the church and a great heretic"), thus indicating that it was the fate of some sixteenth-century reformers to be haunted from diverse ends of the religious spectrum. His life span suggests that in the sixteenth century even radicals could have long lives.

Not much is known of Renato's early life. Born Paul Ricci, according to his own account he was Sicilian. Probably in the early 1520s, he appeared in Naples as a Franciscan monk. He seems to have been an eloquent preacher as well as a person of remarkable erudition and great diplomatic and social skills. By 1525 he had moved northward to Padua, then to Venice. By that time he had evidently come into contact with the rich but unorthodox theological discussion in Italy, involving such figures as Benedetto da Mantova, Juan de Valdés, and others. Renato (at that time still Paul Ricci) gained the attention of the ecclesiastical authorities and was charged with heresy but acquitted. It is not altogether clear if his acquittal resulted from his theological orthodoxy or his skillful defense. In 1538 he was in Bologna, where he again gained a reputation for his learning and eloquence. A lengthy written defense of various charges reveals a theological moderate, acquainted with radical Anabaptist thought.

On his way to his native Sicily for a visit in 1540, illness detained him in Modena, where the duke of Ferrara had him arrested under suspicion of heresy. A number of charges were brought against him (faith must be based solely on scripture; salvation is based solely on divine election; the soul dies at death and is not reified until the Last Judgment; all ecclesiastical practices based on the notion of purgatory are an abomination). Renato's *Apologia* (1540) is one of the most courageous defenses of an accused before the Inquisition in the sixteenth century. But in the end Renato abjured, promising to give up his opinions. He was led in solemn procession through Ferrara, and his sentence was commuted to life imprisonment. After having been transferred to Bologna, he escaped from prison in the spring of 1541.

On that occassion he changed his name to Camillo Renato—both the first and second name had symbolic significance—Renato standing for the "reborn." He moved north to the Raetian Republic, which comprised roughly the area of the present-day Swiss canton of Graubünden (Grisons). Because of the influences of Huldrych Zwingli, Heinrich Bullinger, and John Calvin, Protestantism had taken hold. At the same time, this area also had become, because of its geopolitical location, a haven for Protestant thinkers of all persuasions from Italy who moved north to escape the Inquisition. Renato sought to move the Raetian Reformed church in the more radical direction that he thought biblical. He developed an intriguing understanding of the Last Supper, namely, that Christians should reenact it the way it had been held by Jesus and his disciples—including a real meal. In 1548 he wrote his treatise *Adversus baptismum quem sub regno Papae Antichristo acceperamus*, which expressed the Anabaptist notion that baptism received under the rule of the Antichrist was invalid. Thus his Anabaptist leanings were clear.

His chief antagonist was Agostino Meinardo, an important and influential Reformed pastor. In his controversy with Meinardo he composed a defense of no less than 125 articles, entitled *Errores, ineptiae, scandala*, which sought to summarize the errors, blasphemies, and mistakes of his opponent. But Meinardo enjoyed the support of Bullinger, and he succeeded in having Renato eventually excommunicated in July 1550. Renato promptly proceeded to establish an Anabaptist congregation. Within the year, Renato had abjured, this time his Anabaptist beliefs.

On a sally south into northern Italy in the fall of 1552, he was captured in Bergamo. Brought to trial, he abjured all of his heretical beliefs and returned to Raetia, much to the dismay both of Bullinger, who called him a "poisonous bladder," and of the Inquisition, which called him "the Sicilian heresiarch." Back in relative security, Renato was dismayed by the burning of Michael Servetus in Geneva and wrote his *Carmen in Johannem Calvinum de iniusto Michaelis Serveti incendio*, a deeply emotional indictment of Calvin for his involvement in the burning of Servetus. Renato was still active in Graubünden in the 1570s and he died in 1575. He was a major theological influence on Lelio Sozzini, and his historical significance derives both from that influence and from the paradigmatic quality of his complex career.

BIBLIOGRAPHY

Primary Sources

Renato, Camillo. *Opere: Documenti e testimonianze.* Edited by Antonio Rotondo. Corpus Reformatorum Italicorum, vol. 1. De Kalb, Ill., 1968.

———. "Carmen against John Calvin on the Unjust Burning of Michael Servetus (Carmen o Professo)" (1554). Translated by Dorothy Rounds. In *Italian Reformation Studies in Honor of Laelius Socinus* edited by John A. Tedeschi, pp. 187–195. Florence, 1965. The only writing of Renato available in English.

Secondary Sources

Calvani, Simona. "Camillo Renato." In *Bibliotheca Dissidentium*, vol. 4, pp. 155–190. Baden-Baden, 1984. Brief biographical sketch with full bibliography of primary and secondary works.

Williams, George H. "Camillo Renato, 1500–1575." In *Italian Reformation Studies in Honor of Laelius Socinus*, edited by John A. Tedeschi, pp. 103–183. Florence, 1965. Well-done biographical sketch.

HANS J. HILLERBRAND

RENÉE OF FRANCE (1510–1575), Calvinist sympathizer and patroness of the Italian and French reform movements. The second daughter of Louis XII and Anne of Brittany, she was raised at the court of Francis I during the "liberal" years of his reign and was influenced by Marguerite d'Angoulême, the popularity of *évangélique* preaching, and her Calvinist governess, Madame de Soubise. In 1528 Renée married Hercule d'Este, the duke of Ferrara. There she championed French culture and to the stream of Lutheran and *évangéliste* ideas already flooding northern Italy, added Calvinism in particular. Although the details are sketchy, John Calvin, who recognized the value of French aristocratic support for the reform, visited Renée's court briefly in 1536 on his way from the court of Marguerite of Navarre in Nérac. From then until his death, Calvin and Renée exchanged letters whose major subject was Renée's reluctance to support his movement publicly. Yet, Calvinists such as Francesco Porto, her personal secretary and adviser, always had the most influence at her court. Inquisitorial proceedings confirmed rumors that Renée secretly protected Italian heretics and French fugitives. Forced to abjure publicly in 1555, she defied her husband and church authorities by persisting in sponsoring secret Calvinist worship and corresponding with Calvin.

Her husband's death freed her to return to France in 1560. Although she appeared occasionally at court, which was then dominated by Catherine de Médicis, she preferred to live apart from political and religious controversies. At her château at Montargis, she protected Calvinist pastors and laymen, established Calvinist worship with the help of a Genevan-trained pastor, and sponsored a Protestant school while resisting Calvin's entreaties to take a more public stand. She was a friend of Gaspard II de Coligny, commander of the Huguenot army, and mother-in-law to Francis, duke of Guise, the leader of the Catholic forces. She never resolved two major conflicting ideals: loyalty to the Crown and public commitment to Calvinism.

Renée died at Montargis, where she was buried as a Calvinist without ceremony or ostentation. Although she was not a leader of the Huguenot movement, maintained a position of neutrality during the French Civil Wars, and lacked visible influence on the fate of nations, she nevertheless played a significant role in Reformation history as a victim of the Inquisition, a friend and correspondent of John Calvin, and a royal patroness and protector of leaders of Italian and French reformers. Her beliefs have been interpreted variously as Erasmian, Calvinist, and crypto-Calvinist.

BIBLIOGRAPHY

Blaisdell, Charmarie J. "Renée de France between Reform and Counter-Reform." *Archiv für Reformationsgeschichte* 63 (1972), 196–226.

———. "Heresy and Politics in Ferrara, 1534–1559." *Sixteenth Century Journal* 6.1 (April 1975), 68–93.

Fontana, Bartolomeo. *Renata di Francia Duchessa di Ferrara.* 3 vols. Rome, 1889–1899. Valuable because of extensive use of documents in the Vatican Archives, but author made little use of documents in French, Swiss archives. Purpose is to prove that Renée was a Catholic and Erasmian.

Rodocanachi, Emmanuel. *Une Protectorice de la réforme, Renée de France, Duchesse de Ferrare.* Paris, 1896. Biography based on research in French, Swiss, and Italian archives it is nevertheless a superficial and sentimental attempt to prove Renée was a Calvinist.

CHARMARIE J. BLAISDELL

RESISTANCE THEORY. The period of the Reformation witnessed an important flowering of resistance theory, which was caused by the bitter split in the religious unity of western Europe. Governments reacted with violence against the creation of church structures that were alternatives to official ones and used force to root out their members. These targets of persecution often reacted with similar violence. The resulting confrontations might be limited to minor riots and uprisings but often escalated into full-scale religious wars and could even descend to licensed assassinations of political leaders and general massacres. It was to justify and control these differing forms of resistance to religious persecution that this body of theory grew.

Resistance began early in the Reformation in its German homeland, when Lutherans defied edicts making their form of worship illegal throughout the Holy Roman Empire, between 1521, when Luther was placed under the imperial ban, and 1555, when the Peace of Augsburg was adopted. It continued in France, where the Calvinist brand of Protestantism was illegal and was subjected to ferocious persecution most of the time from its early formation until the promulgation of the Edict of Nantes in 1598. Resistance took a similar form in the northern provinces of the Netherlands, which formed a loose confederation that turned Calvinist in a revolt against the Spanish monarchy, a confederation not universally recognized as a legitimate government until the Peace of Westphalia in 1648. It developed yet another form in England, where the government of Elizabeth I, soon after reestablishing an Anglican church in 1558, sought to preserve a middle way by force, persecuting both Roman Catholic conservatives and Puritan radicals. Similar processes in other countries evoked similar reactions. Many of them produced resistance theories, often linked in interesting ways.

Although the basic reason for these bloody controversies was religious, it was difficult for resistance thinkers of the period to build their arguments on Christian foundations. In its beginnings Christianity had been pacifist, eschewing all forms of violent resistance. Jesus of Nazareth had refused to incite his followers to resistance and had meekly accepted execution by the Roman government. The apostle Paul had taught early Christians that they had a religious duty to obey the governments under which they lived, even if those governments mistreated them. The early Christian church had gloried in its martyrs. Protestant religious leaders like Luther and Calvin were good enough students of the Bible and of early church history to be well aware of this tradition and thus reluctant to adopt theories of resistance, even when the movements to which they were devoted seemed to face annihilation. Thus most resistance theory of the period was developed by laypeople, often by lawyers, using arguments derived from nonreligious sources. They included appeals to ancient Greek ideas and institutions. One favorite was to note that most good governments possessed institutions like the ephors in ancient Sparta, charged with checking and controlling the chief executive. These arguments also included use of the codified Roman law, particularly passages from civil or private law. It was often pointed out, for example, that the law permitted any private citizen to resist force with force (*vim vi repellere licet*). In addition they appealed to arguments developed by scholastic theologians concerned to limit the powers over the medieval church claimed by medieval governments. They also included arguments developed during the Middle Ages by parliamentary and conciliar theorists contending for institutions that asserted the right to limit the plenary powers claimed by ruling monarchs, whether of secular governments or of the church. Some versions of resistance theory did add sacred sources, most commonly the Old Testament.

The first significant resistance theories of the Reformation period were developed in the chanceries of Saxony and Hesse, following a decision of the imperial government to suppress all forms of Protestantism by force; they were ratified by the Imperial Diet (*Reichstag*) in 1530. The theories were developed in conjunction with the formation of the Schmalkald League of Protestant principalities and cities, created to resist repression. The Hessians argued that the imperial government could be resisted on constitutional grounds: the constitution of the Holy Roman Empire had not made the emperor an absolute sovereign. His powers were limited by the seven great prince-electors, who elected him, and by the lesser princes and cities who were represented in the diet. These "inferior magistrates" reserved to themselves many of the powers to control local government, including the powers to provide for "true" religious worship. Since the emperor now proposed to overturn these local arrangements by force, he could be resisted by force. The Saxons argued from principles of Roman civil and canon law that the emperor was like a judge who was required to make his decisions in accordance with an agreed-upon body of law. If rather than simply enforcing existing law he tried to act arbitrarily, he became an "unjust judge" who could be ignored or actively resisted, with force if necessary.

These theories did not lead to immediate violence, since the emperor was distracted by responsibilities in other parts of the world. But they did help justify open revolt a number of years later in the Schmalkald Wars of 1546–1547 and 1552–1555. The first of those wars ended in a smashing Catholic triumph and the imposition on most of Germany of a settlement that made a few temporary concessions to Protestants but looked forward to general reunification of the Christian church. This settlement quickly unraveled, however, thanks in part to a group of conservative Lutherans in the city of Magdeburg. They issued a number of confessions and manifestos insisting on the powers of local governments to establish the true form of Christian worship and defying imperial attempts to impose uniformity. These pronouncements helped ignite another round of war, ending in the Peace of Augsburg of 1555, which permitted local governments, both Catholic and Lutheran, to establish whichever form of worship they preferred. Once that had been accomplished, resistance theory began to shrivel among Lutherans.

It was soon picked up, however, by Calvinists. The Lutheran experience of resistance was widely publicized in Calvinist communities by the histories of Johannes Sleidanus. A version of the Hessian theory, justifying resistance if led by constitutionally privileged "inferior magistrates" such as the electors of the Holy Roman Empire, was adopted by the Reformed theologian Peter Martyr Vermigli and worked into his commentaries on scripture. When the Wars of Religion began in France in 1562, the leaders of the Calvinist party at first limited their resistance theory to claims that they were only trying to rescue the royal family from wicked advisers. But after the Saint Bartholomew's Day Massacre, when thousands of Protestants were killed (1572), for which the royal family openly claimed responsibility, elaborate resistance theories developed, theories that could be applied in France, the Netherlands, and elsewhere.

These theories took several forms. In *Franco-Gallia* the Calvinist jurisconsult François Hotman based his theory on a history of the French constitution, claiming that from the beginning royal power in France had depended on a council of elite advisers, a precursor to the present Estates-General, and that this council gave each king his royal power and had the right to take it away if the king became a tyrant. The theologian Théodore de Bèze, Calvin's successor as leader of the entire movement, argued in an anonymous tract entitled *Du droit des magistrats* that two types of "inferior magistrates," those entitled to advise the king because of their social rank and those charged with administering local governments, had the right to disobey and resist a monarch turned tyrant. The anonymous authors of the *Vindiciae contra tyrannos* developed an elaborate legal argument for the rights of "inferior magistrates" to lead resistance. It asserted that all government is created and regulated by two contracts, a first between God and the general population, both ruler and ruled, and a second between a ruler and his or her subjects. Any ruler who broke these contracts, such as the Catholic kings of contemporary France or the Spanish ruler of the Netherlands, lost both divine support and the right to expect human obedience. The *Vindiciae* fleshed out this argument with examples drawn from Roman law. It cited the Roman civil law of co-guardianship, for example, that provided that if one guardian of the property of a minor misused it, his fellow guardians were obliged to take over control. It argued that the king and the main "inferior magistrates" shared the powers of guardians over the general population and thus had the legal responsibility to watch over and check each other. The *Vindiciae* further argued that foreign powers had the right to intervene in support of citizens abused by a ruler who had turned tyrant.

At later stages in the French Wars of Religion, the tables were temporarily turned when Henry III moved in a religiously neutral direction and then was succeeded by the Protestant Henry IV. French Catholic thinkers now began advancing theories of resistance. So did Catholics in England, faced with growing persecution from the government of Elizabeth I. In doing so they adopted some features directly from Protestant thinkers but added new ones of their own. One was to provide a role for the pope in the process of resistance. William Allen elaborated such an argument in *A True, Sincere, and Modest Defense of English Catholics.* He insisted that to resolve any political dispute of real significance, the parties had to have recourse to some supranational neutral arbiter. But the only institution in all of Europe at that time that was really supranational was the papacy. Thus the papacy had the right and obligation to resolve major political disputes, if necessary even deposing rulers whose oppression of their subjects made them intolerable.

Then an argument arose among Catholics as to how the pope could depose a ruler. Some, like Cardinal Roberto Bellarmino, argued that since the pope was a spiritual leader and not a temporal ruler, his power of deposition was indirect, that he simply had the right to license Catholic "inferior magistrates" or Catholic neighboring rulers to intervene and overthrow a tyrant. This theory was used in support of a number of attempts to organize factions of English or Irish noblemen to overthrow the government of Elizabeth I from within, and to support the sailing of the Spanish Armada to overthrow with external help her government. But others, most notably Pope Sixtus V, insisted that the pope had a direct power to intervene in any government and could on his own authority simply order the subjects of a heretical ruler to rise up in revolt against him or her. He tried unsuccessfully to use this power to dispose of both Elizabeth I of England and Henry IV of France.

Another Catholic version of resistance theory focused on the coronation oaths monarchs in western Europe took at the time they assumed office. This oath often included a solemn promise to maintain and protect the true Catholic faith by eliminating heresy. Catholic theorists insisted that the coronation oath had the force of a contract, and that if any ruler ignored its religious clause he or she violated a fundamental law of the kingdom and forfeited the right to expect obedience. Some extremists even argued that since monarchs swore to eliminate heretics, the first act of heretic monarchs faithful to their promises would have to be to commit suicide.

One should note that the most prominent resistance theories of the Reformation period were constitutional. They all preserved the existing structures of governments, limiting the right to organize armed resistance to existing institutions. Those institutions might be representative bodies such as the Imperial Diet, or the French Estates-General, or the Estates of the United Netherlands. They might be aristocrats entitled to positions of special importance in governments, such as the electors of the Holy Roman Empire or the princes of the blood royal in France. They might be local governments such as those controlling the cities of Magdeburg in Germany and La Rochelle in France. They might be ecclesiastical, such as the papacy.

Most of these resistance theories were not democratic. They did not seek to justify or encourage resistance undertaken by private individuals or by the people in general. They were informed by a profound fear of anarchy, which intensified every time a revolt, such as that of the Peasants' War in Germany during the 1520s, threatened governments at every level. Furthermore, most of these theories reflected a semireligious reverence for the persons of rulers. Their authors tended to be deeply shocked by occasional assassinations of political leaders, even if justified as "tyrannicide." One can find, however, extremists at the fringes of most of these groups. For examples of proto-democratic theory, one can look to groups of religious radicals in Germany who advocated a more popular form of resistance led by simple artisans and farmers. Or one can recall a fervently Catholic group of middle-class people called the "Sixteen" who, after seizing control of Paris during the later stages of the French Wars of Religion, sponsored a pamphlet entitled *Dialogue d'entre le maheustre et le manant* that attacked hereditary nobles as well as the monarch, arguing instead for a government representing the common people. For a theory of tyrannicide, one can cite John Ponet's *A Shorte Treatise of Politike Power*, a slashing attack on the Catholic government of Mary Tudor of England that formally supported the deposition and killing of tyrants. Or one can point to a passage in *De Rege*, an otherwise sober analysis of government by the Spanish Jesuit Juan de Mariana, which supported strongly the assassination of Henry III of France by a Catholic fanatic. But most of sixteenth-century European society clearly regarded positions of this sort as extremist, and most leaders of public opinion repudiated these positions with some vehemence.

The constitutional resistance theories of the Reformation period persisted for centuries. They were adapted for important use in seventeenth-century Germany (e.g., Althusius) and England (e.g., John Locke). Versions of them helped support the American and French Revolutions of the eighteenth century. Traces of them linger to the present.

[*See also* Bodin, Jean.]

BIBLIOGRAPHY

Baumgartner, Frederic J. *Radical Reactionaries: The Political Thought of the French Catholic League.* Geneva, 1976. Analyzes French Catholic resistance theories.

Burns, J. H., and Mark Goldie, eds. *The Cambridge History of Political Thought, 1450–1700.* Cambridge, 1991. A general survey of political thought in the period by several authors. See particularly the chapters by Robert M. Kingdon on Calvinist resistance theory and by J. H. M. Salmon on Catholic resistance theory. Contains a useful bibliography.

Clancy, Thomas H. *Papist Pamphleteers: The Allen-Persons Party and the Political Thought of the Counter-Reformation in England, 1572–1615.* Chicago, 1964. Analyzes English Catholic resistance theories.

Kingdon, Robert M. *Myths about the St. Bartholomew's Day Massacres, 1572–1576.* Cambridge, Mass., 1988. Analyzes several classic statements of Calvinist resistance theory.

Skinner, Quentin. *The Foundations of Modern Political Thought.* Vol. 2, *The Age of Reformation.* Cambridge, 1978. A brilliant and somewhat personal overview of political thought in the period, with extended discussion of resistance theory. Contains another useful bibliography.

ROBERT M. KINGDON

REUCHLIN, Johannes (also Capnio Phorcensis; 1455–1522), German humanist, jurist, writer, and translator. Born in Pforzheim on 29 January 1455, Reuchlin studied in the south German city of Freiburg im Breisgau (from 1470) and Basel (from 1474), receiving a master of arts degree in Basel in 1477. After a stay in Paris (1478), he studied Roman law in Orléans (from 1479) and Poitiers (from 1480), where he received the licenciate in law in 1481. According to his own account, he received the degree of doctor of imperial law (*inn Kayserlichen Rechten Doctor*), probably in 1484.

It was as a jurist that Reuchlin earned his livelihood and the means for his humanist studies. It is uncertain whether at the end of 1482 or the beginning of 1483 he accepted a short-term position teaching law at the University of Tübingen. From 1485 on he was associate judge at the court of the dukes of Württemberg. From 1502 until 1509 he sat on the Supreme Court in Speyer, and from 1502 until 1512 he was one of the three judges of the Swabian League.

With the publication of his Latin dictionary (*Vocabularius breviloquus,* Basel, 1478) and his Greek *Micropædia* (no longer extant), Reuchlin established himself as a scholar of Latin and Greek. This was before he turned to the Hebrew language and Jewish literature in the 1480s and especially in the 1490s. Through his encounter in Basel or Paris with Wessel Gansfort (d. 1489), the first Christian Hebraist north of the Alps, Reuchlin became aware of the importance of the Hebrew language for Christian theology. His travels in Italy as adviser and interpreter to his sovereign, Duke Eberhard V of Württemberg, also influenced him. On his first trip in 1482 he became acquainted with Lorenzo de' Medici and his library in Florence; the second trip brought him the acquaintance of Pico della Mirandola, who introduced him to the Cabbala. At the court in Linz he was introduced in 1492 to Jakob ben Jehiel Loans, the physician of Frederick III, from whom Reuchlin was said to have received thorough language instruction and knowledge of Hebrew literature. As a result of his studies, his first Cabbalistic work, *De verbo mirifico* (The Miraculous Word), was published. There he asserted the Hebrew language and the Cabbala to be the sustainer of divine powers. The Hebrew grammar *De rudimenti hebraicis,* published in 1506, was the second preparatory step for the work *De Arte cabalistica,* published in 1517, in which Reuchlin pointed out the way to decipher the Cabbala. It represented, from his own point of view, his main scholarly work.

Nevertheless, Reuchlin's attitude toward Judaism remained ambivalent. He was not a friend or supporter of the Jews, as the liberal Reuchlin reception of the nineteenth century and the post-1945 historiography have portrayed him. He pleaded for the christianization of the Jews but opposed forced baptism as well as expulsion of the Jews. Referring to Roman law, he conceded to them as *concives imperii Romani* the right to exist and also the right to their sacred works and sacral property (*Tütsch missive, warumb die Juden so lang im ellend sind,* Pforzheim, 1505). This was made clear in Reuchlin's correspondence, as well as in the controversy caused by the publication of his 1510 report and reflected in *Augenspiegel* (Tübingen, 1511) and *Clarorum virorum epistolae* (Tübingen, 1514). This report, provided on the order of Emperor Maximilian I, was on the toleration of the Jews and the nonblasphemous part of their literature as the bearer of divine wisdom. With this the humanist found himself again between two fronts—a controversy with the Jewish convert Johannes Pfefferkorn, and a second controversy with the Dominicans of Cologne and their leader Jakob Hochstraten.

The polarization of the "Reuchlinists" and their polemical adversaries, described as "Obscure Men," in the so-called Pfefferkorn controversy led to the portrayal of Martin Luther, Urlich von Hutten, and Reuchlin in the picture propaganda of the time as the three opponents of Rome and champions of the Reformation. This view does not apply to Reuchlin. From 1517 until his death in Stuttgart on 30 June 1522, he remained with the old church. Still, through his discussion with the inquisitors of Cologne and the condemnation by Rome, he prepared the intellectual climate for the Reformation in Germany. Beyond that, through the support of his relative Philipp Melanchthon, he contributed indirectly to the advancement of the Reformation.

BIBLIOGRAPHY

Geiger, Ludwig. *Johann Reuchlin: Sein Leben und seine Werke* (1871). Reprint, Nieuwkoop, 1964.

———. *Johann Reuchlins Briefwechsel* (1875). Bibliothek des Litterarischen Vereins in Stuttgart, 126. Reprint, Hildesheim, 1962.

Herzig, Arno, and Julius H. Schoeps with Saskia Rohde, eds. *Reuchlin und die Juden.* Sigmaringen, 1993.

Kisch, Guido. *Zasius und Reuchlin: Eine rechtsgeschichtlich-vergleichende Studie zum Toleranzproblem im 16. Jahrhundert.* Pforzheimer Reuchlinschriften, 1. Constance, 1961.

Krebs, Manfred. *Johannes Reuchlin, 1455–1522: Festgabe seiner Vaterstadt Pforzheim zur 500. Wiederkehr seines Geburtstages.* Sigmaringen, 1993.

Oberman, Heiko A. *The Roots of Anti-Semitism in the Age of Renaissance and Reformation.* Philadelphia, 1984.

ARNO HERZIG and SASKIA ROHDE

Translated from German by Susan M. Sisler

REVOLT OF THE NETHERLANDS. In the middle of the sixteenth century the seventeen provinces of the Netherlands, joined together by the dukes of Burgundy and their Habsburg heirs, had many of the same problems as other western European states: tensions between the pretensions of the sovereign and the ancient privileges of corporate bodies like the provincial states and the towns; among the high nobility who owed their position largely to birth and the new officials of the king; and between the growing financial needs of the monarchy—war was becoming increasingly expensive—and reluctance of the states to grant new taxes. The unity of the church was strained by the presence of all sorts of new ideas, commonly called the Reformation but which in fact could more accurately be called the reformations (in the plural). All these familiar problems acquired a distinctive character in the Netherlands because the Low Countries had been linked with Spain through a personal union since the beginning of the sixteenth century. When Philip II left the Netherlands for Spain in 1559, he appointed his half sister, Margaret of Parma, governess-general of the Low Countries.

In the midst of all these problems, the question of the persecution of Protestants soon became the overriding issue. Charles V had tried to suppress all heretical opinions and had given the political authorities a central role in this process. A new, comprehensive, and uncompromising edict (1550) that required the death penalty even for the possession of heretical books continued in force under Philip II; nonetheless, both the Anabaptist and the Calvinist congregations grew in the 1550s. Only a small minority of Netherlanders supported this policy of harsh persecution. As more victims fell, the opposition to the bloody persecutions grew stronger and came to include the town magistrates and even the courts of justice. Persecution was in fact abandoned or significantly curtailed in some provinces but continued apace in others, including Flanders and Brabant. Provincial governors voicing criticism of this religious policy included Egmond (Flanders), William of Orange (Holland), Bergen (Hainaut and Valenciennes), and Montigny (Tournai), of whom the first three were also members of the Council of State. Their oral and written remonstrances to the king met, however, with no success. In October 1565 Philip II's "letters from the Segovia Wood" demanded continued strict enforcement of the heresy edicts.

In response several governors refused to carry out the king's orders and attempted to resign. Many lesser nobility joined together late in 1565 in a confederation (the "Compromise") and on 5 April 1566 they presented a petition (the "Request") to Margaret of Parma pleading for a mitigation of the persecution. The less-than-firm reply of Margaret gave many people hope that better times had come. Exiles returned home. Clandestine gatherings turned into open-air Protestant services—hedge-preaching—and no one put a stop to them. More radical Protestants began to attack the images in churches and monasteries; the iconoclasm began on 10 August 1566 in West Flanders (now northern France), moved on to Antwerp on 20 August, and then spread to many other parts of the country. At times the activity of the iconoclasts began with the freeing of imprisoned heretics.

This iconoclasm brought the division in the government to a climax: Margaret demanded a vigorous response to the Protestants, but William of Orange, Egmond, and others in her council refused to take action without the assurance that the Protestant services would be tolerated. Only under heavy pressure did Margaret give way on 23–25 August: preaching was to be permitted where it had so far occurred, but action would have to be taken against the iconoclasts. On this basis order was successfully restored, although in some cases William of Orange and Egmond gave the Protestants more concessions than Margaret had intended. It appeared to be a victory for the moderates.

Margaret, however, did not consider herself bound by the concessions that had been forced out of her. With money from Spain she was able to recruit troops, while at the same time sympathy for the Protestants had diminished because of the iconoclasm. Egmond supported her now. At the end of November she laid siege to the city of Valenciennes, which was in Protestant hands, and in March 1567 it had to capitulate. By April she was again in control of the situation and was able to put an end to all preaching. William of Orange and many others went into exile.

It would have been advisable at this stage for the king to cultivate carefully the loyalty of moderates like Egmond, who after the iconoclasm were prepared to support him. But Philip II, deeply shaken by the desecration, believed that strong action was necessary. He appointed the duke of Alba, Fernando Álvarez de Toledo, governor of the Low Countries and dispatched him with a Spanish army to punish his rebellious subjects and to establish a powerful royal authority. In August 1567 Álvarez arrived in Brussels. He arrested Egmond and another leading nobleman, Filips van Montmorency, Count of Horne, ignored normal judicial procedures, and condemned them to death because of their actions in 1566. Many more convictions followed, and the fires designed for heretics were lit once again. In addition, in order to rebuild the financial structure of the Netherlands and to pay for his army, Alba tried to impose heavy taxes, among them a "tenth penny" on the sale of all merchandise. Thus he was blamed for the high prices in 1571–1572, when in actuality they were primarily the consequence of poor harvests and the activities of the Sea Beggars.

In 1568 and 1572 William of Orange attempted, in conjunction with the Huguenots, to organize a large-scale assault against Alba. In 1568 this effort failed, although some exiles and other adventurers—the Sea Beggars—continued on with the resistance, at times as privateers under William's command, at times simply for their own profit. By 1572 Álvarez's regime was so hated that the rebels managed to get a firm hold in the provinces of Holland (although not in Amsterdam) and Zeeland. After a lengthy siege Álvarez was able to reconquer Haarlem (12 July 1573), but the Spanish army failed at Alkmaar (October 1573) and Leiden (October 1574). In 1573 Don Luis de Requeséns y Zúñiga succeeded Álvarez as governor of the Low Countries.

The war also weighed heavily on the regions that remained loyal to the king. The rebels controlled the important sea routes and the poorly paid royal troops often mutinied. With the opportunity that resulted from Requeséns's death (5 March 1576), the moderates again attempted to seize power. The States-General met on its own authority and concluded a peace with Holland and Zeeland—the Pacification of Ghent (8 November 1576) but the king refused to recognize this accord, and in the latter part of 1577 the war began again. In 1581 the rebels declared Philip II deposed from his office as king. Only Luxembourg and Namur remained initially under the control of the king, but in the space of eight years his regent (since 1578 Alessandro Farnese, duke of Parma) managed to reconquer almost all the territory south of the Meuse River, including Antwerp in 1585, and large areas in the north and the east as well.

The revolt in Holland and Zeeland in 1572 at first had the support of a broad range of groups, including moderate Catholics, and in the rebel provinces both Protestants and

Catholics were accorded equal rights. But this policy failed almost immediately. Many Catholics, especially the priests, were suspected of supporting the king, and Catholic worship was soon forbidden. After the Pacification of Ghent this pattern repeated itself elsewhere. The Catholic provinces were initially willing to work together with Protestant Holland and Zeeland. In Flanders and Brabant Protestant exiles returned. When the war effort fared badly, however, Catholics once again became suspect. This situation turned into a self-fulfilling prophecy because as Catholics increasingly fell under suspicion, they were more inclined to look to the king for their well-being and safety. Protestants then would seize power, and before long Catholic worship was forbidden in one city after another. From 1581 on this situation applied in all the territory controlled by the rebels.

But Protestants themselves were never a unified front. Spiritualists like Sebastian Franck and Kaspar von Schwenkfeld—as well as the Family of Love movement—all had their supporters. Mennonites (strict and less strict) were numerous, as were Erasmian humanists, among the learned. Of course, there were also many who were indifferent to Protestantism but strongly anticlerical. Only the Calvinists knew exactly what they wanted, and that gave them an advantage. In refugee churches and the "churches under the cross" in Catholic areas Calvinists increasingly took a stronger leadership role in the 1560s. At a synod convened in Emden in October 1571 Calvinists secured adoption of a blueprint for a presbyterian-synodal form of church organization; it would turn out to be a powerful tool in the hands of those who championed a strict supervision over the doctrine and morals of ministers and believers alike.

After 1572 the strict Calvinists of Holland, with the support of the ecclesiastical structure, succeeded at forcing the non-Calvinist ministers out of the church, but only through a series of fierce battles with the town magistracies. In Flanders and Brabant the grip of the Calvinists on the church had been firm since the time of the "churches under the cross" in the 1560s. An intense controversy within the Reformed church over predestination in the early seventeenth century led to the victory of the strict predestinarians at the Synod of Dordrecht (1619).

Because of the sharply cut features of the Calvinist church, it remained relatively small for a long time. In 1620 it probably did not include more than twenty percent of the population. In its new role as the official church, the Reformed church continued to baptize the children of many who were not professing members, and it also performed marriages for this same group. In most regions, however, it was also possible to marry before the civil authorities.

William of Orange and the States of Holland accepted the right of the church to exercise discipline over doctrine (especially of its ministers) and morals, but only for those who had willingly joined the Reformed church. This rule also applied outside Holland. The secular authorities thus did not use the church as a means to discipline the general populace; on the contrary, they protected individuals with different beliefs from efforts by the Calvinists to impose their doctrine and discipline on them. In the course of time more possibilities opened up for Catholics as well. The reality of a public church that maintained a strict orthodoxy but included only a minority of the population made Dutch society, under its Calvinist exterior, extremely variegated.

The advance of the king's army stalled after 1585. In 1588 the attempt to end the conflict with the armada failed, and in the 1590s Philip II committed his troops to the civil war in France. Under the leadership of Johan van Oldenbarnevelt and Maurits van Nassau, the republic managed to recover all of the territory north of the Meuse River and a few areas to the south of it. With the Twelve Years' Truce in 1609 the king of Spain had to recognize—at least provisionally—the independence of the new republic. After the expiration of the truce, the conflict resumed, and it continued for another quarter of a century, during which time the republic reconquered parts of Brabant and the Meuse valley. Permanent recognition of the Dutch Republic came with the Peace of Münster in 1648.

BIBLIOGRAPHY

Decavele, Johan. *De Dageraad van de Reformatie in Vlaanderen, 1520–1565.* 2 vols. Brussels, 1975.

Duke, Alastair. *Reformation and Revolt in the Low Countries.* London, 1990.

Gelderen, Martin van. *The Political Thought of the Dutch Revolt, 1555–1590.* Cambridge, 1992.

Kossmann, E. H., and A. F. Mellink, eds. *Texts Concerning the Revolt of the Netherlands.* Cambridge, 1974.

Maltby, William S. *Alba: A Biography of Fernando Álvarez de Toledo, Third Duke of Alba, 1507–1582.* Berkeley, 1983.

Nierop, H. F. K. van. *The Nobility of Holland: From Knights to Regents. 1500–1650.* Cambridge, 1993.

Parker, Geoffrey. *The Army of Flanders and the Spanish Road, 1567–1659.* Cambridge, 1972.

———. *The Dutch Revolt.* Ithaca, N.Y., 1977.

Rowen, Herbert H. *The Princes of Orange: The Stadholders in the Dutch Republic.* Cambridge, 1988.

Spaans, Joke. *Haarlem na de Reformatie: Stedelijke Cultuur en Kerkelijk Leven, 1577–1620.* The Hague, 1989.

Tex, Jan den. *Oldenbarnevelt.* 2 vols. Cambridge, 1973.

Tracy, James. *Holland Under Habsburg Rule, 1506–1566: The Formation of a Body Politic.* Berkeley, 1990.

JULIAAN WOLTJER

Translated from Dutch by Michael A. Hakkenberg

RHAU, Georg (1488–1548), German scholar, teacher, musician, composer, printer, and publisher. The premier printer of the Wittenberg reform movement, he published numerous works of Martin Luther and other reformers. His great significance is, as editor and publisher, to have shaped the theology and practice of the music of the Wittenberg reformation into a liturgically conservative, musically traditional, and theologically evangelical form.

Rhau received the baccalaureate from Wittenberg University in 1514. In 1518 he was appointed tutor at Leipzig University and also cantor at the Thomas school and church. He is credited with composing *Missa de Sancto Spiritu* (now lost) in twelve voices, which was sung at the opening exercises of the Leipzig Disputation in 1519. Perhaps drawn to Luther's reform by the debate, he left Leipzig within a year, traveling by 1523 to Wittenberg. There he opened the printing office that was his career until death. He acquired great esteem, was elected to the city council in 1541, and was accorded full civic and academic ceremonies at his funeral.

No known compositions are attributed to Rhau. His stature in Reformation music derives from publishing. His most substantial achievement was the publication of fifteen comprehensive collections of music between 1538 and 1545. These volumes are arranged into three categories, directly reflecting Lutheran uses of sacred music. The first is four cycles of motets for the Mass, arranged seasonally. Representative is *Officia paschalia de resurrectione et ascensione domini* (1539), containing, among others, a through-composed Easter mass by Johannes Galliculus. The second is six volumes of music for Vespers collected from numerous composers and arranged for use in schools. One is *Novum ac insigne opus musicum triginta sex antiphonarum* (1541) by Sixt Dietrich. The third group comprises four volumes mostly of sacred songs in a variety of formats for occasional use in worship, school, and home. Prominent among them are his own hymn collection, *Neue Deudsche Geistliche Gesenge* (1544), containing 123 compositions drawn from nineteen named composers and representing the state of German polyphonic choral art.

Rhau's prestige in Reformation music is confirmed in the prefaces to several of these volumes, written by himself and Johannes Bugenhagen, Philipp Melanchthon, and Luther. They affirmed soundly the theological triad of Reformation music: Music is divine in origin, glorifies God, and propagates the word. Rhau combined musical ability and knowledge, religious intellect, educational purpose, and publishing sense to conceive, organize, and produce a publishing program that guided the music of the Wittenberg reformation (in traditional, eclectic, and conservative but evangelical directions) through the sixteenth century. He thus substantially founded the musical heritage of the Lutheran church.

BIBLIOGRAPHY

Primary Sources

Rhau, Georg. *Enchiridion utriusque musicae practicae* (1517). Facsimile ed. Edited by Hans Albrecht. Kassel, 1951.

———. *Enchiridion musicae mensuralis* (1520). 10th ed. Wittenberg, 1555. Early Rhau school music manuals that became curriculum standards in Lutheran Germany.

———. *Musikdrucke aus den Jahren 1538 bis 1545 in praktischer Neuausgabe.* Kassel and Saint Louis, 1955. Modern edition of his seminal publications in Lutheran church music.

Secondary Sources

Mattfeld, Victor H. "Rhau, Georg." In *The New Grove Dictionary of Music and Musicians*, edited by Stanley Sadie, vol. 15, pp. 787–789. London, 1980. Accessible; contains bibliography.

Schrade, Leo. "The Editorial Practice of George Rhau." In *The Musical Heritage of the Church*, edited by Theodore Hoelty-Nickel, vol. 4, pp. 31–42. Saint Louis, 1954. Significance of Rhau's publishing achievement.

KYLE C. SESSIONS

RHEGIUS, Urbanus (Ger., Urban Rieger, or König; 1489–1541), German Lutheran pastor and reformer. Rhegius was born in Langenargen, a town on Lake Constance between Switzerland and Germany. His father was probably the priest Conrad Rieger, and his mother was presumably the concubine of Rieger, who might have borne the name König. Although at the time many priests had children, Rhegius was known as the son of a priest. Occasionally it made him the object of ridicule, but it also inspired him to work for education and reform of the clergy.

Rhegius never became a university professor, but as a young man he was a well-known humanist who delivered lectures and corresponded with the likes of Desiderius Erasmus. He studied the liberal arts and theology at Freiburg (1508–1512), Ingolstadt (1512–1518), and Basel (1520). In Freiburg, he met two men who later would become his vigorous Catholic opponents: Johann Eck (1486–1543), a brilliant teacher whom he admired and followed to Ingolstadt, and Johann Fabri (1478–1541), with whom Rhegius lived in Constance in 1519 and who later became bishop of Vienna. While in Ingolstadt Rhegius earned a master's degree and was also honored by Emperor Maximilian I with the title of poet laureate; in Basel he received a doctorate in theology or its equivalent. By 1520 the young scholar had become proficient in both Greek and Hebrew, and he had written two books on the clergy: a treatise on the dignity of the priesthood and a textbook of pastoral care.

Under the influence of Fabri, Rhegius had been ordained to the priesthood in 1519, and in late 1520 he accepted a call to become the cathedral preacher in Augsburg. One of his first duties was to read from the pulpit the papal bull that threatened Martin Luther with excommunication. A year later Rhegius wrote a polemical pamphlet in which he argued that the bull itself, and not Luther's writings, posed the real religious danger. After he began to criticize indulgences and to preach on Protestant themes, he was replaced as cathedral preacher in 1522 and retreated to the Tirol to examine his religious allegiance.

In 1523 the council in Augsburg invited Rhegius to return, and he remained a Lutheran preacher in the city until 1530.

On Christmas Day 1525 he presided at the first public Protestant celebration of the Lord's Supper in Augsburg. In the controversy between Zwingli and Luther over how Christ was present in that sacrament, Rhegius strongly supported the mediatory efforts of Philipp of Hesse though he was unable to attend the Colloquy of Marburg. He remained in contact with Zwingli and Luther and represented the Protestant clergy in debates with Anabaptists in 1527 and 1528.

While in Augsburg, Rhegius published pamphlets on almost every religious issue of the 1520s. His most popular works were a defense of Protestant theology against the charge that it was a new (and thus heretical) teaching (*Nova Doctrina*, 1526) and a treatise for the consolation of the sick and dying (*Seelenartznei*, 1529). The latter was published in ninety editions and appeared in ten languages. In June 1525, three days after Luther himself was wed in Wittenberg, Rhegius married Anna Weissbrucker, an Augsburg citizen. The couple had eleven children, four sons and seven daughters.

At the imperial diet of 1530 in his city, Rhegius was an active member of the Lutheran party that produced the Augsburg Confession. He was then invited by Duke Ernst of Lüneburg, a signer of the confession, to return with him to consolidate the Reformation in the north. In late 1530 Rhegius moved with his family to the town of Celle in Lüneburg, stopping on the way to meet Luther in person for the first time.

For the next ten years (1531–1541) Rhegius worked tirelessly for the new Protestant churches in north-central Germany. As superintendent of the church in Lüneburg, he assisted Duke Ernst in his efforts to reform the monasteries, especially the cloisters of women that resisted Lutheranism. Rhegius also strove to build a skilled Lutheran clergy. He lectured and preached to the pastors and wrote one of his most enduring works on their behalf, a homiletical handbook entitled *Formulae quaedam caute et citra scandalum loquendi de praecipuis Christianae doctrinae locis* (How to Speak Cautiously and without Giving Offense about the Chief Articles of Christian Doctrine). Published in Latin in 1535 and in German in 1536, and reprinted many times thereafter, this guide stressed the need of teaching repentance and good works so that people would not take the gospel for granted. The practical concern was typical of Rhegius's theology: it provided resources for the clergy to use in presenting a balanced Lutheran message to the laity.

Rhegius also worked directly with clergy and laity to complete the process of reform in the cities of Lüneburg and Hannover. To that end he visited each city several times and wrote church orders (1531 and 1536) for both of them. Moreover, through letters, treatises, and in person, Rhegius supported the Reformation in other north German towns such as Minden, Soest, Hildesheim, and Hamburg. In 1540 he urged the Lutheran pastors in Braunschweig to endorse the toleration of that city's Jewish community.

Until declining health curtailed his travel, Rhegius accompanied Duke Ernst to meetings of the Protestant Schmalkald League. In 1537 he was present in Schmalkalden itself and added his signature to Luther's Schmalkald Articles and to Melanchthon's *Tractus de potestate et primatu papae* (Treatise on the Power and Primacy of the Pope). In the political and theological negotiations of the 1530s, Rhegius defended the distinctive Lutheran emphasis on justification by faith while insisting that Lutheran theology was compatible with the best of early Christian thought. After his death in Celle in 1541, his wife found a thick compendium of citations from the church fathers (*Loci theologici*, 1545) that had served Rhegius in advocating the historical orthodoxy of Lutheranism. The German and Latin works of Rhegius were collected by his son Ernst and published in two large volumes in Nuremberg in 1562. They illustrate the rich legacy of the reformer whom Luther hailed as the bishop of Lower Saxony.

BIBLIOGRAPHY

Primary Source

Rhegius, Urbanus. *Wie man fursichtiglich und ohne argerniss Reden soll* (1536). Leipzig, 1908.

Secondary Sources

Gerecke, Richard. 'Studien zu Urbanus Rhegius' kirchenregimentlicher Tätigkeit in Norddeutschland." *Jahrbuch der Gesellschaft für niedersächsische Kirchengeschichte* 74 (1976), 131–177. One of several studies by this author of Rhegius's activity in north Germany; demonstrates Rhegius's importance to the Protestant movement in the 1530s.

Hampton, Douglas B. *Urbanus Rhegius and the Spread of the German Reformation.* Ph.D. diss., Ohio State University, 1973. The longest study of Rhegius in English; focuses on his years in Augsburg.

Hendrix, Scott H. "Toleration of the Jews in the German Reformation: Urbanus Rhegius and Braunschweig, 1535–1540." *Archive for Reformation History* 81 (1990), 189–215. Text and analysis of Rhegius's letter to the clergy of Braunschweig; argues that Rhegius took a more tolerant stance than other Protestant reformers.

———. "The Use of Scripture in Establishing Protestantism: The Case of Urbanus Rhegius." In *The Bible in the Sixteenth Century*, edited by David C. Steinmetz, pp. 36–49, 202–209. Durham, N.C., and London, 1990. Illustrates how Rhegius taught Protestant clergy to interpret scripture in the light of early Christian doctrine.

Jacobs, C. M. "Sources for Lutheran History II: Sixteenth Century Preaching." *Lutheran Church Quarterly* (July 1928), 350–361. English translation of the preface to Rhegius' guide for preachers (*Formulae quaedam caute. . .*, 1535).

Liebmann, Maximilian. *Urbanus Rhegius und die Anfänge der Reformation.* Münster, 1980. Very detailed biography of Rhegius to 1530; most valuable for the bibliography of Rhegius's works.

Uhlhorn, Gerhard. *Urbanus Rhegius: Leben und Ausgewählte Schriften* (1861). 2d ed. Nieuwkoop, 1968. This old standard biography is still useful.

Verzeichnis der im deutschen Sprachbereich erschienenen Drucke des XVI. Jahrhunderts. Stuttgart, 1983–. See vol. 17, nos. 1722–2058.

Vinke, Rainer. "Urbanus Rhegius." In *Contemporaries of Erasmus*, vol. 3, pp. 151–153. Toronto, 1987. Focuses on the humanism of Rhegius.

Scott H. Hendrix

RICHARDOT, François (1507–1574), French bishop. Born at Morey in Franche-Comté to a family of lower nobility, Richardot studied with and, at an early age, joined the Augustinians of Champlitte in Haute-Saône. Having received his doctorate in theology from the University of Paris, Richardot displayed excellent skills in Latin and Greek, though he was a mediocre Hebraist. He revealed his talents as an orator beginning in 1525 while publicly teaching the holy scriptures at Paris. Suspected of heresy, he hurriedly left Paris for Italy, where he received a papal dispensation from his religious vows and then became chaplain of Renée of France at Ferrara. In 1541 Calvin wrote to her that Richardot was a man who sought "his own profit and ambition" and had his "renunciation ready" in order to escape from persecutions. Imprisoned by order of the duke of Ferrara in 1545, perhaps for heresy, he returned to Champlitte.

Quickly chosen as provost of the local chapter of canons, he began a brilliant career in the service of Antoine Perrenot de Granvelle, bishop of Arras from 1538 and son of the celebrated chancellor of Charles V. As a canon at Besançon beginning in 1546, Richardot became suffragan bishop in 1554 with the title of bishop of Nicopolis; he was then called to Arras as suffragan bishop of Granvelle. In addition he became canon of the cathedral in 1557 and schoolmaster of the school of Sainte-Gudule at Brussels, which permitted him to gain fame as the preacher at the memorial observances for such great personages as Charles V, Mary of Hungary, Mary Tudor, Henry II, and so on.

Promoted to archbishop of Malines in 1559, Granvelle arranged for Richardot to succeed him as bishop at Arras. On 11 November 1561 he assumed responsibility for a diocese that had been little affected by Protestantism, to the point that Philip II founded the Douai College with a view to consolidating royal power and Catholicism in the south of the Low Countries. Richardot dedicated himself with enthusiasm to the establishment of this prestigious university, solemnly inaugurating the courses of study on 5 October 1562 and himself assuming responsibility for the instruction in the holy scriptures.

His reputation reached a peak on 11 November 1563, when he delivered the opening discourse at the twenty-fourth session of the Council of Trent. He was a zealous propagator of the Tridentine decisions to the provincial council of Cambrai in 1565. He faced a relatively moderate inconoclastic revolt in Artois in 1566 (with the exception of the region of Lalleu). Until his death on 26 July 1574, he imposed the principles of the Counter-Reformation in his diocese with a relative measure of ease: he stabilized the clergy, published synodal statutes in 1570, and the following year created the small seminary of Arras. A partisan of the use of education and persuasion as means for combating heresy, he also attempted to moderate the use of excessive repression by Fernando Álvarez de Toledo, duke of Alba, which finally contributed to his recall. On 6 June 1574 he was accorded the honor at Brussels of delivering the discourse on the general pardon accorded by Philip II.

Richardot was down to earth but also an ambitious courtier who knew how to capitalize on his position to emphasize his own worth in all circumstances. He was renowned as the greatest orator of the Low Countries of his time, though his learned eloquence might rather appear as exaggeratedly complicated to the twentieth-century reader. His career bears witness to the complexity of his personality. Tempted by heresy in his youth, he was able to distance himself vigorously from Protestantism by means of his *Apology* in 1556. Protection accorded to him by powers in high places then allowed him to make a place of eminence for himself at the princely court. He consolidated his place by embracing with ever greater ardor the cause of the Counter-Reformation, which he had adopted at a late date. Worldly, "a bit impetuous and yet fearful," according to Morillon, vicar-general of the diocese of Malines, he was typical of the bishops who served as a transition between the prelates of previous generations, who were themselves feudal lords, and those who would entirely dedicate themselves to the apostolic ministry and to the spirituality characteristic of the time of the archdukes.

BIBLIOGRAPHY

Duflot, Léon (Abbé). *Un orateur du XVIe siècle: François Richardot, évêque d'Arras* (1898). Reprint, Geneva, 1971. Although somewhat difficult and apologetic, contains numerous texts and extracts from sermons by Richardot.

ROBERT MUCHEMBLED

Translated from French by Paul D. Leslie

RICHE, Hans le. *See* Ries, Hans de.

RIDEMAN, Peter. *See* Riedemann, Peter.

RIDLEY, Nicholas (1502?–1555), one of the ablest English theologians of his generation. He was a learned and quick-witted scholar rather than an original thinker, having a sure touch in both oral and written controversy. He wrote no major systematic treatise. He is supposed to have been responsible for converting Cranmer to the Reformed doctrine of the Eucharist.

Ridley was born in about 1502, the second son of Christopher Ridley of Willimoteswick, a minor Northumberland gentleman. He entered Pembroke Hall, Cambridge, in 1518 under the patronage of his uncle, Richard Ridley, and soon made his mark as an able scholar. He graduated with a B.A. in 1521 and an M.A. in 1526, becoming a fellow of his college between those dates. After periods of study in Paris and Louvain, Ridley returned to Cambridge in about 1530 and resumed his academic career, proceeding with a B.D. in 1537 and a D.D. in 1540. In the latter year he was also elected master of Pembroke, despite the fact that he had left Cambridge to become Cranmer's chaplain, and named rector of Herne (in Kent). By the end of Henry's VIII's reign he had quietly embraced many reforming doctrines, but partly because of his own discretion and partly because of the archbishop's protection, he was not seriously troubled by the government.

After 1547 he quickly emerged as a convinced Protestant whose sympathies were with the Reformed rather than the Lutheran tradition. In September 1547 he was appointed to the see of Rochester, but in April 1550 he was transferred to the key bishopric of London, where Edmund Bonner had just been deprived of the position. It was as bishop of London that he made his main contribution to the English Reformation, strongly defending the ecclesiastical authority of the Crown both against the Catholics and against those reformers, such as John Hooper, who wished to place their own interpretation of the scriptures above the commands of the supreme head. He took a leading part in the campaign against idolatry, being particularly responsible for the destruction of altars throughout his diocese in 1551. Like Cranmer, he was a thoroughgoing Erastian and was the only bishop to emerge strongly in support of Lady Jane Grey in 1553. This stand ensured his swift imprisonment by Mary, but unlike Cranmer, he did not allow his Erastian principles to confuse his defense of Reformed doctrine. He disputed forcefully but unavailingly against the prelates of the restored Catholic church and died at the stake without hesitation or bravado in October 1555.

BIBLIOGRAPHY

Primary Source

Christmas, Henry, ed. *The Works of Nicholas Ridley* (1841). Reprint, New York, 1968.

Secondary Sources

Jones, N. L. "A Bill Confirming Bishop Bonner's Deprivation and Reinstating Bishop Ridley As the Legal Bishop of London, from the Parliament of 1559." *Journal of Ecclesiastical History* 33 (1982), 580–585.

Loades, D. M. *The Oxford Martyrs*. London, 1970.

Ridley, J. G. *Nicholas Ridley*. London, 1954.

DAVID LOADES

RIEDEMANN, Peter (also Rideman, Rydeman, Ryedeman; 1506–1556), one of the few Anabaptist leaders to bridge the first and second generations of Anabaptism. At twenty-three, Riedemann was already a leader among the first-generation Austrian Anabaptists. In 1532 he joined the incipient Hutterian Anabaptist movement in Moravia, becoming *Vorsteher* ("head elder") and leading theologian within Hutterian Anabaptism (1542–1556), thereby earning the title "second founder of Hutterianism."

Born in Hirschberg, Silesia, Riedemann learned the shoemaker's trade. As a traveling journeyman he apparently came into contact with Austrian Anabaptism, joined the movement in the Linz area of upper Austria, and by 1529 was called to be minister. Whether he had met Hans Hut (d. 1527 as a martyr), a central figure in upper German Anabaptism who introduced Anabaptism wherever he traveled, is unknown; but he certainly soon caught the vision of Hut, indirectly, through Hut's disciples Leonhard Schiemer and Hans Schlaffer (both d. 1528 as martyrs), and more directly through Wolfgang Brandhuber. (Brandhuber was influenced not only by Hut but also by Hans Denck of Nuremberg and his emphasis on following in the way of Christ's love; Brandhuber also laid the foundation within Austria for religious communism—that is, community of goods—which became a primary motif for Moravian Hutterianism.) Upon Brandhuber's martyrdom in 1529, Riedemann became his acknowledged successor. In 1529 Riedemann was captured and imprisoned in Gmunden (upper Austria) for three years. While in prison he wrote his first known treatise, focused largely on the theme of Christian love, showing the probable influence of Brandhuber and Denck.

In 1532 Riedemann regained his freedom and made his way to the communal (Hutterian) Anabaptists at Auspitz (Hustopece) in Moravia, remaining with this group for the rest of his life. He married Catherine (calling her his "marital sister, Treindl"), and soon was elected minister and missioner. During his travels he was apprehended a second time and imprisoned in the city tower of Nuremberg (1533–1537) but was eventually released.

In 1539 Riedemann again traveled, this time to the landgraviate of Hesse, where through his missionary efforts many people emigrated to Moravia as Hutterites. Within a year, Riedemann was again apprehended and chained in the Hundsturm jail in Marburg, the capital of Hesse. Later he was transferred to the nearby Wolkersdorf Castle, where he gained the respect of the castle *Vogt* ("steward"), ate at the *Vogt's* table, and was given almost full freedom of movement. During this time Riedemann not only wrote many letters to his people in Moravia but also composed a confession of faith, *Rechenschaft unserer Religion, Lehr und Glaubens. . .* (Account of our Religion, Doctrine and Faith. . .), intended for Landgrave Philipp. The Hutterites would soon recognize this work as programmatic, lying at the very heart of the Hutterian idea both in theory and practice. The volume was published about 1542 and reprinted in 1565—the only volume the Hutterites published in the sixteenth century.

During this time, the Hutterian leader, Hans Amon, died,

and Leonhard Lanzenstiel was chosen as successor. His strengths lay primarily in the day-to-day economic administration of a growing Hutterian society. There was a need for a strong leader who would complement Lanzenstiel in the spiritual dimensions of Hutterian life, and Riedemann was called on to meet this need. He found the means to return to his people, occupying the leadership position from 1542 to his death in 1556.

That the Hutterites survived this stormy era of social upheaval and persecution and have persisted through the centuries when all other such communal groups disappeared is certainly in part because of the wisdom and fortitude of Riedemann, whose spirit and substance, conveyed in his writings, became the definitive expression of the Hutterian way of Christian community. Much of this character is captured in the tribute of the Hutterian chronicler to Riedemann's legacy: "The gift of God's Word flowed from him like running water and brimmed over. All who heard him were filled with joy."

Riedemann composed over forty hymns, among them the best of Anabaptist hymnody. Some three dozen of his epistles and letters also survive, which radiate the human warmth and empathy of a sincere, spiritual leader.

In a unique manner Reidemann spans the formative decades of Upper German Anabaptism. He began as something of a spiritualist, in line with Denck (holding to a quasi-individualistic, caring discipleship) and Hut (as charismatic missioner). This aspect may be seen in his first written treatise (c.1529) on Christian love. When Riedemann entered the way of Hutterian community, however, his spiritualism was transformed into a more concrete expression of Christianity, which he believed could find ultimate fulfillment only within a voluntary, gathered church. By 1542 his earlier, more loosely defined views on discipleship were thus transformed into a view of discipleship tied firmly to a visible community of faith. In his confession of faith, Riedemann attempted to define the Hutterian understanding of living out God's kingdom on this earth, as established by Christ. Part one demonstrates his keen ability to express the Hutterian view, in this regard, of how faith and life intersect. Part two, an extended summary of the Bible, is in itself a serious hermeneutical interpretation from an Anabaptist perspective.

Apart from his strong, magnetic leadership, perhaps the greatest contribution of Riedemann to ongoing Reformation history lies in his having bridged the first and second generations of upper German Anabaptism, both intellectually (from spiritualism to communalism), as well as in his having outlived the persecution of the 1520s that took the lives of so many Anabaptist leaders, and which in turn generally impelled the new movement to go underground. In contrast, the sum and substance of Riedemann's life-long influence upon a growing, quasi-tolerated Hutterian movement in itself demonstrates how a strong continuity of leadership in this instance meshed with a congregational dynamic, within an emerging group that was permitted to take its own natural course within sixteenth-century Europe.

BIBLIOGRAPHY

Primary Sources

Riedemann, Peter. "Ein Rechenschafft und Bekanndtnus des Glaubens." In *Glaubenszeugnisse oberdeutscher Taufgesinnter,* edited by Robert Friedmann, vol. 2, pp. 4–47. Quellen zur Geschichte der Täufer, vol. 12. Gütersloh, 1967.

Walter, Elias, ed. *Die Lieder der Hutterischen Brüder.* Scottdale, Pa., 1914. Contains hymns by Riedemann.

Secondary Sources

The Chronicle of the Hutterian Brethren, vol. 1. Translated and edited by the Hutterian Brethren. Rifton, N.Y., 1987. Covers Hutterian history from the 1520s to 1665.

Friedmann, Robert, ed. *Die Schriften der huterischen Täufergemeinschaften: Gesamtkatalog ihrer Manuskriptbücher, ihrer Schreiber und ihrer Literatur, 1529–1667.* Vienna, 1965. Description and location of Hutterian codices containing Riedemann's works.

———. "Peter Riedemann: Early Anabaptist Leader." *Mennonite Quarterly Review* 44 (1970), 5–44. Most comprehensive treatise on Riedemann to date.

Hillerbrand, Hans J., ed. *Anabaptist Bibliography, 1520–1630.* 2d. ed., rev. & enl. Saint Louis, 1991. See Riedemann listings, pp. 293–294.

Hofer, Joshua, and Elisabeth Kliewer, eds. *Die Hutterischen Episteln, 1527 bis 1767.* 4 vols. Elie, Manit., 1986–.

Mennonite Encyclopedia, vols. 1–4, 1955–1959; vol. 5, 1990. See "Riedemann, Peter," "Rechenschafft unserer Religion, Leer und Glaubens" (Account of our Religion, Doctrine and Faith), and other articles on Amon, Brandhuber, Denck, Hut, Lanzenstiel, Schiemer, Schlaffer.

LEONARD GROSS

RIEMENSCHNEIDER, Tilman (c.1460–1531),

German sculptor in wood and stone active in Würzburg. Expressing primarily religious themes, Riemenschneider's sculpture is characteristic of the idealizing trend of late Gothic art in Germany. Limited to a few figure types, it aims for spiritual expression and partly omits polychromy and gilding.

Born in Heiligenstadt in the Eichsfeld, Thuringia, Riemenschneider is thought to have been trained in stonemasonry at Erfurt and in wood carving in the workshop of Michel Erhart at Ulm. His sculpture also shows the influence of upper Rhenish art, especially the engravings of the Alsatian artist Martin Schongauer. Riemenschneider spent most of his life in Würzburg, where he joined the guild of Saint Luke's as a journeyman in 1483, became a master and burgher of the city, and established his own workshop in 1485. His earliest dated work is the Münnerstadt altarpiece of 1490–1492. Known are at least twelve large carved-wood altarpieces or fragments thereof, of which only two are preserved intact, the altar of the Holy Blood in Rothenburg ob der Tauber (1501–1505) and the altarpiece of the Virgin in Creglingen (c.1505–1510). His most famous work in marble is the grave monument of Emperor Henry II and his wife, Kunigunde, in Bamberg cathedral (executed 1499–1513). Riemenschneider's workshop was large and productive, with fourteen apprentices recorded there through 1531.

Like many German artists of his time, Riemenschneider held a number of offices in the city council of Würzburg (beginning in 1505), and he was elected burgomaster in 1520–1521. He was in charge of municipal building, fishing, taxes, hospitals, and the chapel (Marienkapelle), for whose portal he had carved the stone figures of Adam and Eve in 1491–1493 (today at Mainfränkisches Museum, Würzburg) and fourteen figures of apostles with Salvator Mundi and John the Baptist in 1500–1506. In 1525, when the Peasants' War spread to Franconia, he was implicated in the Würzburg burghers' refusal actively to support the bishop against the revolting Franconian peasants. He was expelled from the council, fined, and imprisoned for two months. No major work after 1525 is known; he died in 1531. His support of the Reformation, often presumed, has not been proved; his grave relief shows Riemenschneider holding a rosary.

BIBLIOGRAPHY

Baxandall, Michael. *The Limewood Sculptors of Renaissance Germany.* New Haven and London, 1980.

Bier, Justus. *Tilmann Riemenschneider: Die frühen Werke.* Edited by R. Sedlmaier. Würzburg, 1925.

———. *Tilmann Riemenschneider: Die reifen Werke.* Edited by R. Sedlmaier. Augsburg, 1930.

———. *Tilmann Riemenschneider: Die späten Werke in Stein.* Vienna, 1973.

———. *Tilmann Riemenschneider: Die späten Werke in Holz.* Vienna, 1978. Bier's well-illustrated books are still the basic reference.

———. *Tilmann Riemenschneider: His Life and Work.* Lexington, Ky., 1982. Gives special attention to his works now located in the United States and Canada.

Kalden, Iris. *Tilman Riemenschneider: Werkstattleiter in Würzburg; Beiträge zur Organisation einer Bildschnitzer- und Steinbildhauerwerkstatt im ausgehenden Mittelalter.* Ammersbek bei Hamburg, 1990. The most recent scholarly work on the artist and his workshop; provides a summary of the earlier literature.

CHRISTIANE ANDERSSON

RIES, Hans de (also de Rys, de Reis, de Rycke; Fr., le Riche; 1553–1638), Dutch Mennonite leader. He was a spiritualistic and irenic churchman who stressed the inner over the outer religion and worked for Mennonite unity. He was born to Catholic parents in 1553 in Antwerp, but little else is known of his early years and education before he joined the Reformed church in Antwerp in his early twenties. He was asked to train as pastor, but he found the dogmatism of the Reformed not to his liking, and he was soon attracted by the ideas and practices of Antwerp Mennonites. The conservatism of the Antwerp Mennonites as well as their factiousness and internal divisions caused de Ries to look elsewhere, however, and after hearing of the more liberal and peaceful Waterlander Mennonites of north Holland, he traveled to the island of De Ryp, where he was baptized into the congregation in late 1575 or early 1576.

After joining the Mennonites de Ries traveled widely. In 1577 he was in Alkmaar, where he worked with other Waterlander leaders to draw up a twenty-five-article confession of faith, the first written confession known among Dutch Mennonites. After stays in Aachen, Middelburg, and Emden, he returned to Alkmaar in 1600 as leader of the Waterlander congregation. He was acquainted with the Dutch humanist Dirk Volkertszoon Coornhert and probably influenced by his doctrine of perfectionism: according to de Ries, God did not command humans to do the impossible, so humans could obey God perfectly. Because Christ made the souls of believers his temple, he wiped out all evil from the lives of his followers so he would not live in an impure temple. Those born out of God did not sin, de Ries believed.

Under the influence of the ideas of Kaspar von Schwenckfeld, de Ries stressed the indispensable nature of an inner personal relationship to Christ. Without the living word of the Holy Spirit, all externals of religion—even the Bible—were but empty forms. This spiritualistic approach to religion led de Ries to work hard for unity among the various Mennonite groups in Holland. He felt that toleration and love could overcome differences on doctrinal matters. Stimulated by the union in 1591 of the High German Mennonites with some Waterlander and Frisian Mennonites, de Ries worked for a more complete union of the three groups, which took place in 1601 under the name of the Brotherhood of Peace. In 1615 an Amsterdam group of English Brownists united with the local Mennonites, and de Ries and Waterlander leader Lubbert Gerritszoon wrote a confession of thirty-eight articles for the new group. Later, with two added articles, this document became known as the Confession of Hans de Ries.

De Ries served several times as arbiter of disputes within different Mennonite groups. He wrote a new and expanded history of Anabaptist martyrs (1615) and a hymnbook for Mennonite congregations (1582), both of which he saw as tools to promote Mennonite unity. He died in Alkmaar in 1638 at the age of 85 after making a boat trip to preach to Mennonites in Zaandam.

BIBLOGRAPHY

Primary Sources

Ries, Hans de. *Lietboeck inhoudende Schriftuurlijcke Vermaen Liederen der Ghemeenten Christi.* Rotterdam, 1582. De Ries wrote many of the hymns in this hymnbook himself and included some of the Psalms, the first time they had been introduced for singing in Mennonite services.

———. *Klaer bewys van de eeuwigheydt ende godheyt Jesu Christi.* Haarlem, 1672. Defense of the divinity of Christ written in approximately 1600 against Socinian ideas. De Ries wrote this work to show his lack of sympathy for antitrinitarianism and his concern for doctrine.

———. *Historie der martelaren ofte waerachtighe getuygen Jesu Christi.* Haarlem, 1615. Nine-hundred-page history of Anabaptist martyrs calling on Mennonites to set aside their differences and fight for their common beliefs as their forefathers had. Used by T. J. van Braght as basis for *Martyrs Mirror* of 1680 and 1685.

Secondary Sources

Coggins, James R. "A Short Confession of Hans de Ries: Union and Separation in Early Seventeenth Century Holland." *Mennonite Quarterly Review* 60 (1986), 128–138.

Dyck, C. J. "The Middelburg Confession of Hans de Ries, 1578." *Mennonite Quarterly Review* 36 (1962), 147–154.

———. "Hans de Ries." In *Biografisch Lexicon voor de Geschiedenis van het Nederlandse Protestantisme.* Vol. 2, pp. 308–310. Kampen, 1988.

"Hans de Ries." In *The Mennonite Encyclopedia,* vol. 4, pp. 330–331. Scottdale, Pa., 1955.

ANDREW C. FIX

RIETHOVEN, Maarten van (Lat., Riethovius, Rythovius; 1511–1583), Catholic theologian and first bishop of Ieper (Ypres). Born near Riethoven (Brabant) into a modest family and christened Bauwens, Riethoven made his mark as one of the earliest reforming bishops in the Low Countries after Trent. He distinguished himself first not by his family connections but by his training. So good was his academic work at Louvain that he joined the faculty of philosophy in 1535, followed by ordination, then "licentiaat" and doctoral degrees in theology (1550, 1556). None of his lectures, most of which were delivered at Louvain, were published, though his *Tractatus de Controversis Fidei* was meant to be. Riethoven was also rector magnificus in 1558, vice-chancellor of the university in 1559, and part of a delegation to meet with Protestants at Worms, where he greatly impressed Philipp Melanchthon.

Riethoven also distinguished himself by devotion and service. Though he was inclined to privacy (he considered becoming a Carthusian), his life became unavoidably dramatic after his appointment in 1559 to the newly created diocese of Ieper. Besides the problem of building a diocese from scratch, his pastoral efforts were hampered by the usual arguments with canons, competition from Protestants, political turmoil, and big assignments. In 1563, Margaret of Parma asked Riethoven, Michaël Baius, and two other Louvain theologians to travel immediately to the Council of Trent, where during the last three sessions Riethoven spoke on clandestine marriage and sat on the committee that reviewed the decrees on purgatory. Back in Ieper by February 1564, Riethoven renewed his efforts at reform, including the establishment of the first seminary in the new dioceses (1566), endless visitations and sermons, and the conversion of Protestants. Again he was interrupted, this time by the Iconoclastic Fury of 15–16 August 1566, when he escaped the mob's wrath by hiding at a ropemaker's. After only two weeks in exile, Riethoven returned to Ieper, celebrating mass almost immediately and determined to maintain Catholicism. More drama came in 1568, when he was summoned to Brussels by Fernando Álvarez de Toledo, duke of Alba, and ordered to break the news to the Count of Egmont that the sentence of execution against him would be carried out the following day. Riethoven, heartbroken, consented, waking the count at midnight, spending the night and next morning with him, and standing close enough to the scaffold, said one witness, to get blood on his cassock. He subsequently pleaded with Philip II to be merciful toward Egmont's family.

Once again turning his attention to reform, Riethoven threw himself into the provincial synods of 1570 and 1574 and his diocesan synods. Then, as a member of the States-General of Flanders, Riethoven helped urge the duke of Alba to rescind the famous Tenth Penny, wrote to Philip II to report on the brutality of Alba's soldiers, and boldly defended Catholic rights in the face of the growing Calvinist majority, which contributed to a final dramatic event: his imprisonment from 1577 to 1581. Upon release, Riethoven found his diocese a Calvinist stronghold and was forced to live on its fringes, reconsecrating altars and churches as possible. In October 1583 he fell ill with the plague in Saint-Omer, then died at the hospital of the Gray Sisters. His remains were returned to Ieper from Saint-Omer only in 1607 and were destroyed with almost everything else during World War I.

BIBLIOGRAPHY

Declerck, P. "De priesteropleiding in het bisdom Ieper, 1565–1626." *Handelingen van het Genootschap voor Geschiedenis* 50 (1963), 7–67. Has much to say about the role of Riethoven in establishing the first seminary, which set a pattern for so many others in the Low Countries.

Schrevel, A. de. "Rythovius." In *Biographie Nationale,* vol. 20, cols. 725–763. Brussels, 1908–1910. A relatively lengthy, informative sketch, in French.

Verhoeven, P. H. *Maarten van Riethoven, eerste bisschop van Ieper: Geschiedkundige levensschets.* Wetteren, Belgium, 1961. The major biography of Riethoven, but it is hampered, as are all other studies of the old diocese, by the destruction of so many records during the world wars.

CRAIG HARLINE

RINCK, Melchior (also Rink; c.1493–1553?), a central/south German Anabaptist leader. Educated at the University of Leipzig, he likely excelled in languages, as suggested by court records that sometimes identify him as the Greek. He appeared in 1523 as an evangelical chaplain in the Hessian village of Hersfeld, working with Heinrich Fuchs. Their preaching aroused the ire of the local monastery and brought about their dismissal, thereby generating a revolt by the townspeople and prompting Landgrave Philipp of Hesse to order their expulsion. With the assistance of Jakob Strauss, Rinck emerged as pastor in early 1524 at Eckardtshausen in Thuringia. He married Anna, the daughter of Hans Eckhardt. He eventually came under the influence of Thomas Müntzer and participated in the Peasants' War. He escaped with his life, surfacing in 1527 in Landau, where he became friends with the Reformed pastor Johannes Bader and also the Anabaptist Hans Denck. Rinck became an Anabaptist while Bader, who did not, attacked Denck, thereby inducing Rinck to respond to Bader in his *Widderlegung* (Refutation), a strong antipedobaptist statement. Not long after, he wrote *Vermanung* (Admonition), a short treatise on government.

In 1528 Rinck appeared in Hersfeld and petitioned for permission to preach in the Hersfeld congregation. Philipp of Hesse summoned Rinck and gave him the option of recanting publicly or debating his views before the University of Marburg. A disputation was held at Marburg on 17–18 August based on twelve allegations made by the Hersfeld pastor Balthasar Raidt. Rinck responded with "Berechnung meines Glaubens" (Account of my Faith), covering five points that suggest the influence of Denck as well as Rinck's continuing concern with the issue of adult believers' baptism, which views led to his exile. He was arrested again in Hesse in 1529 and held in Haina. A visit by his father-in-law prompted a letter by Rinck in which he refused to consent to a marriage annulment. After a short time of freedom, Rinck was once again arrested in November 1531. He was to remain incarcerated until his death. Attempts to convert Rinck back to the Reformed church by the former Anabaptist Peter Tasch and the Reformed theologian Martin Bucer failed. He likely died in prison sometime after 1553.

BIBLIOGRAPHY

Franz, Günther. *Urkundliche Quellen zur hessischen Reformationgeschichte*. Vol. 4, *Wiedertäuferakten, 1527–1626*. Marburg, 1951. The standard collection of materials related to Hessian Anabaptists; contains among other materials the articles of Balthasar Raidt, Rinck's testimony at Marburg, his account of his faith for that disputation, and his defense of his refusal to consent to an annulment of his marriage to Anna.

Geldbach, Erich. "Toward a More Ample Biography of the Hessian Anabaptist Leader Melchior Rinck." *Mennonite Quarterly Review* 48 (1974), 371–384. Based on competent research, provides a concise overview of the most important elements in the life and work of Rinck.

Neumann, Gerhard J. "A Newly Discovered Manuscript of Melchior Rinck." *Mennonite Quarterly Review* 35 (1961), 197–217. Provides an introduction to and transcription of two works by Rinck, the *Widderlegung* (Refutation) and *Vermanung* (Admonition).

Oyer, John S. *Lutheran Reformers against Anabaptists*. The Hague, 1964. Contains a useful overview of the rise, spread, faith, and life of the Anabaptists of central Europe. Should be used in conjunction with Geldbach.

Schowalter, Paul. "Rink, Melchior." In *The Mennonite Encyclopedia*, edited by Cornelius Krahn, vol. 4, pp. 336–338. Scottdale, Pa., 1955. Overview of the known biographical details of the life of Rinck.

H. Wayne Pipkin

RIO, Martin del (1551–1608), Spanish Jesuit theologian. He contributed significantly to Dutch humanism, served and chronicled the beleaguered Spanish regime in the Low Countries, and composed the most authoritative Counter-Reformation demonology. Educated at Paris before taking his B.A. in civil law at Louvain (1570) and his licentiate at Salamanca (1574), this precocious Antwerp native was called by his mentor, Justus Lipsius, the "prodigy of his century" after completing a major study of Seneca at nineteen and publishing an edition of the obscure polyhistor Solinus at twenty. Scion of wealthy Spanish and Flemish merchants (his father owned the castle and lordship of Aertselaer) and kinsman to Louis del Rio, one of the most trusted Dutch collaborators of Fernando Álvarez de Toledo, duke of Alba, the young Martin rose quickly in the government of the Spanish Netherlands; he was appointed a councillor of Brabant in 1575, and gained rapid promotions after John of Austria (Don Juan) became governor-general, becoming vice-chancellor of Brabant in 1578 and provincial fiscal auditor. Devastated by the sudden deaths of both his patrons, John of Austria and Louis del Rio, he resigned late in 1578. Sometime before 1585 he composed a lengthy memoir of John of Austria's era under the anagram Rolandi Myrte Onatini; claiming to write "without eloquence or oratory" and "without any hatred of persons or flattery," del Rio emphasized "the evils that the old Catholic religion has endured among the Belgians." An abridged Spanish translation appeared at Madrid in 1601, but del Rio's Latin text remained unpublished until 1869.

After withdrawing from public service, del Rio moved to Spain and became a Jesuit in 1580. Finishing his studies by 1585, he returned to the Low Countries; taught at Douai, Louvain, Liège, and Mainz before going to the University of Graz in 1600; and then moved to Spain and back again to his native land, where he died in 1608. As a Jesuit, he converted Justus Lipsius to Catholicism in 1592 while continuing his humanist publications, now combined with theological subjects. His work on Seneca, published without his consent in 1576, was revised and incorporated into his thousand-page *Syntagma Tragediae Latinae* (1593–1594). Among other projects del Rio published a commentary (1602) on the *Song of Songs* and compiled a two-volume edition of commentaries on civil law (1606).

Del Rio's most significant and enduring work, however, was his three-volume *Disquisitionum Magicarum Libri Sex* (1599), which he revised and updated until he died. Composed by an expert in both law and theology, it became the most influential Counter-Reformation demonology, reprinted two dozen times before 1760. Just as plague follows famine, asserted del Rio, witchcraft follows heresy. Del Rio's work, including a "Confutation of various superstitions," condemned many excesses of witch hunting: he insisted on strict limits to the employment of torture, described many "natural" remedies for witches' spells, and claimed that lycanthrophy was pure illusion. Nonetheless, Bayle's opinion that he was a dangerous fanatic also has substance; when the duke of Bavaria requested his advice on a perplexing case in 1602, del Rio urged strict and full torture.

His first and only biography, *Martini Antoni Del Rii L.L. Lic. S. Th. Docotoris Vita Brevi Commentariolo expressa*, composed pseudonymously by a fellow Jesuit, appeared in 1609. A champion of lost causes, del Rio has fallen into complete oblivion since the eighteenth century.

BIBLIOGRAPHY

Dréano, Maturin. *Humanisme chrétien: La tragédie latine commentée . . . par Martin Antoine Del Rio*. Paris, 1936.

Fischer, E. "Die *Disquisitionum Magicarum libri sex* von Martin Delrio als gegenreformatorische Exampel-Quelle." Ph.D. diss., Johann Wolfgang Goethe-Universität Frankfurt, 1975.

E. WILLIAM MONTER

RIOTS, RELIGIOUS. Urban and agrarian riots were a familiar pattern of European social behavior long before the Reformation. Many of these violent outbursts involved religion in one way or another, for socioeconomic and political grievances were often linked to anticlericalism and theological dissent in the Middle Ages. The religious crisis of the sixteenth century intensified this behavior: for well over a century, beginning around 1520, religious rioting proliferated wherever Catholics confronted Protestants. In speaking of "religious" rioting one must think broadly, for in an age when religion touched on virtually all aspects of life, those who rioted did not distinguish clearly among theological, political, economic, and social discontent. What is meant here by "religious riot" is any public act of violence in which religion was explicitly invoked, as legitimation or objective, and in which the participants acted independent from—or against—their political or ecclesiastical authorities.

It is unlikely that a comprehensive inventory of Reformation rioting will be compiled before the end of the twentieth century, for this phenomenon strains the boundaries of geography, chronology, and typology. Riots could be local affairs involving as few as three individuals, or regional and national events involving hundreds, even thousands, of people; they could be limited to specific grievances but could also be closely linked to rebellion and revolution, as in the cases of the German Peasants' War (1524–1525) and the Dutch challenge to Spanish authority (1566–1619), or to civil war, as in the case of France (1561–1598). Rioting could involve both men and women, rich and poor, young and old in various combinations according to time and place, but many contemporary accounts single out male youths as those most frequently involved. While in some instances accounts simply state that "common people" caused the rioting (Stralsund, 1525), in many cases it is possible to identify a preponderance of burghers, merchants, and artisans (Pernau, 1526; the Netherlands, 1566; and Orleans, 1572), or even to narrow it down to specific guilds (Bern, 1528; Dieppe, 1562). In other places (Geneva, 1532–1535), nobles and rich merchants assumed leadership roles.

Religious rioting took place throughout all of western and central Europe in the sixteenth and seventeenth centuries with varied intensity and for different reasons. Though much of this violence stemmed from the tensions caused by Catholic-Protestant conflict in urban settings, there were also instances of agrarian riots and of intra-Catholic and intra-Protestant violence (for example, the Catholic peasant riots of the Cilento in southern Italy, 1647, in which churches were attacked; the "bread or peace" riots against the Catholic League in Paris, 1590; and the Anabaptist uprising at Münster, 1534–1536), and even of non-Christian rioting (involving Muslims in southern Spain, 1499–1500, 1519–1523, and 1568–1570). Nonetheless, some areas were more heavily scarred by riots than others: those that bore the brunt of such violence over this long period were Germany, Switzerland, the Netherlands, and France.

The taxomony of religious rioting is as complex and varied as the Reformation itself, but one can identify some common elements in regard to the goals and targets of violence. In a pioneering article on "The Rites of Violence" in the French religious wars, Natalie Zemon Davis identified three principal motives on the part of rioting crowds: (1) they acted to defend truth as they perceived it and to combat false doctrine; (2) they acted to rid the community of a feared pollution; and (3) they acted in place of magistrates perceived to have failed in defending the faith (*Society and Culture in Early Modern France*, Stanford, Calif., 1975, pp. 152–187). These motives could overlap or exist at different levels of consciousness; they nevertheless offer a useful framework for analysis of the behavior of religious rioters. They also underscore two further points in Davis's argument: participants in crowd violence see their actions in terms of the defense of a cause and therefore as somehow legitimate, and their behavior has some underlying dramatic and ritual structure.

The assertion of doctrinal truth could be as simple as the interruption of religious services with shouted words or tolling bells; it could also take the form of iconoclasm and sacrilege, or of direct aggression against representatives of the opposing faith. Religious rioting could serve as a form of protest against religious changes introduced too rapidly by government fiat, as in Cornwall, Devon, and Norfolk in England (1548–1549) and the Upper Palatinate in Germany (1581–1589). It could also serve as a means of challenging the status quo. For instance, in Memmingen, Germany, a mob of Protestant men and women forced a public debate and ensured the triumph of their cause by storming Our Lady's church on Christmas Day 1524, overturning the altar, smashing some images and windows, and roughing up a prominent Catholic priest. Similarly, in many Hanseatic towns in the Baltic region (1524–1529) and in numerous Swiss cities (1528–1530), iconoclastic rioting both prompted and marked the abolition of Catholicism. In France and the Netherlands, by contrast, iconoclastic rioting was most characteristic of the early stages of clashes that intensified into prolonged and bitter war. In the Netherlands, the wave of iconoclastic fury that resulted in the sacking of hundreds of Catholic churches in the summer of 1566 provoked a brutal repression that in turn helped push the Spanish king's already restive subjects into overt rebellion.

Iconoclasm—the destruction of religious images and artifacts—has been identified as a characteristically Protestant form of religious violence, intended to demonstrate the nullity of objects the Catholics revered and the superstitious nature of their faith. But Catholics too attacked the objects—books, pulpits, assembly halls—associated with their opponents' worship, and members of both faiths attacked the persons of their enemies. In many of these attacks one can see an inversion of the sacred/profane dichotomies held by the "other" through deliberate acts of desecration. Thus Protestant youths publicly mocked images before destroying them (as in Wesen, Switzerland, 1528), and Catholic children urinated on Protestant corpses (Geneva, 1535). It was, moreover, no coincidence that religious tensions commonly reached their peak during the period between Easter and Corpus Christi celebrations, when the calendar was most crowded with processions and other public demonstrations of faith.

If rioting was a means of defending doctrinal truth, it was also a means of purifying the community by attacking persons and practices seen as sources of pollution within it. Protestant iconoclasm can be cast in this light—as attempts to purge practices that spoiled the purity of the Christian faith; so can Protestant attacks on the priests who propagated these rituals and claimed a special role in them. For Catholics, however, the "heretics" themselves were a dangerous source of pollution, which threatened to bring down on the entire community the wrath of an angry God; hence their predilection for physical attacks on Protestants and the books that might spread their teachings.

Rioting thus derived from inner convictions and fear of the "other." It was often instigated by preaching and by rumor of impending violence. In Geneva (1532), a mob nearly lynched the first Protestant preachers before forcibly expelling them from the city. Three years later, deadly riots involving men, women, and children erupted when both Protestants and Catholics suspected attacks from one another. Situations that involved competition for ritual and sacred space could also be trigger riots. Most often, it was dissatisfaction or impatience with the way in which secular and religious authorities were handling the religious crisis that caused tension between rivals to explode into violence. Rioting thus resulted from unresolved tensions and could itself be the cutting edge of change. As rioters in Basel boasted to their magistrates on Ash Wednesday 1529, after having illegally destroyed all of the city's religious images: "All that you failed to effect in three years of deliberation we have completed within this hour."

The Basel rioters clearly saw themselves as acting in place of a magistracy that had been too slow to accept religious change. In other situations, the tendency of rioting crowds to take on the role of magistrates emerged as a distorted mimicking of rituals of justice. Crowds in Paris (1562 and 1563) and Rouen (1563) snatched condemned heretics from their official executioners to force upon them even more humiliating, painful, and elaborately symbolic punishments. Youths who seized the dead body of Admiral Gaspard II de Coligny, the first victim of the Saint Bartholomew's Day Massacre in 1572, reenacted a parody of the trial conducted against him in absentia in 1569 and dragged his mutilated corpse through the streets just as a straw effigy had been dragged in 1569. Indeed, even if originating in a government-ordered coup, the events of Saint Bartholomew's Day display the same underlying patterns as other religious riots. Denis Crouzet has argued (*Les guerriers de Dieu*, 2 vols., Paris, 1990) that the scale of violence evinced in these events shocked both Catholics and Protestants to such an extent that the subsequent stages of the French Wars of Religion witnessed an internalization of violence, which henceforth was expressed more in violent polemics than in direct physical attacks. Similar reactions may have occurred in other areas that witnessed particularly violent religious conflicts, but Crouzet's thesis has not yet been tested in comparative studies.

[*See also* Anticlericalism; Common Man; Iconoclasm; *and* Peasants' War.]

BIBLIOGRAPHY

Bak, János M., and Gerhard Benecke, eds. *Religion and Rural Revolt.* Manchester, 1984.

Beer, Barrett L. *Rebellion and Riot: Popular Disorder in England during the Reign of Edward VI.* Kent, Ohio, 1982.

Crew, Phyllis Mack. *Calvinist Preaching and Iconoclasm in the Netherlands, 1544–1569.* Cambridge and New York, 1978. Attempts to define the relationships between Calvinist ideology, popular religious violence, and political authority in the Netherlands.

Deyon, Solange, and Alain Lottin. *Les casseurs de l'été 1566: L'iconoclasme dans le nord de la France.* Paris, 1981. Focuses on areas now part of France but surveys more broadly the iconoclastic fury of 1566.

Diefendorf, Barbara B. *Beneath the Cross: Catholics and Huguenots in Sixteenth-Century Paris.* Oxford and New York, 1991. See especially chapters 3–6 on religious violence before and including the Saint Bartholomew's Day Massacre and chapter 9 on the provocative role of radical preachers.

Eire, Carlos M. N. *War Against the Idols: The Reformation of Worship from Erasmus to Calvin.* Cambridge and New York, 1986. See chapters 3 and 4 on iconoclastic rioting in the early Reformation.

Goldstone, Jack. *Revolution and Rebellion in the Early Modern World.* Berkeley, 1991.

Heller, Henry. *Iron and Blood: Civil Wars in Sixteenth-Century France.* Montreal, 1991. A not-entirely-convincing attempt to recast the French religious wars as a reaction to underlying social tensions.

Zagorin, Perez. *Rebels and Rulers, 1500–1600.* 2 vols. Cambridge and New York, 1982. See especially vol. 1.

CARLOS M. N. EIRE AND BARBARA B. DIEFENDORF

RITUAL. *See* Liturgy.

ROGGENDORF, Hans Wilhelm (1533–1591), Lutheran nobleman in lower Austria. Roggendorf was born 4 July 1533 and, because of his father's early death, was raised by his mother and guardians. The family was relatively wealthy and owned extensive estates. Roggendorf received the education traditional for a young nobleman, including a European grand tour. In 1554 he took part in the division of his family property and efficiently managed his inheritance, which he administered from the castle at Sitzendorf near Eggenburg in Lower Austria. He married twice. His first wife was Baroness Margarete Herberstein from Styria. A year after her death he married Countess Anna von Wied-Runkel. In all he had nineteen children, only a few of whom survived him. He was named the marshall of Lower Austria in 1565 and as such both administered the courts and served as the president of the diet of Lower Austria. He died on 13 September 1591 in Baden. Nicholas Rink's funeral sermon characterized him as a faithful member of the church and a supporter of Lutheranism.

Influenced by Matthias Flacius Illyricus, he was uncompromising in his views and opposed Calvinists, "accidentalists," and the introduction of the Gregorian revision of the calendar in 1585. He was one of the four religious deputies in 1569 to supervise the Protestant churches in Lower Austria, and he took part in the visitation of 1580. He also invited Josua Opitz to serve as the minister of the Lower Austrian *Landhaus* in Vienna. Despite his efforts on behalf of Lutheranism in Lower Austria, he was unable to obtain for it legal recognition before his death.

BIBLIOGRAPHY

Neidhart, Herbert. "Aus der Geschichte Pöggstalls: Die Herren von Roggendorf." *Das Waldviertel* 42 (1993).

DAVID P. DANIEL

ROMAN CATHOLICISM. At the end of the sixteenth century, Cardinal Roberto Bellarmino (1542–1621), the Jesuit theologian and controversialist, described the one true church in his apology *Disputationes de Controversiis* (1593) as "the community of men brought together by the profession of the same Christian faith and conjoined in the communion of the same sacraments, under the government of the legitimate pastors and especially the one vicar of Christ on earth, the Roman pontiff." He thereby expressed a belief shaped by both the development of papal primacy and the long confessional struggle with emergent Protestantism. Bellarmino's ideal of the Roman Catholic church—the institution—was shaped by his experience of Catholicism—the culture that embodied it. His description of the church also suggests that community and sacramental life supersede hierarchy and institution. Catholicism in the sixteenth century was far more than parish, bishop, or pope. Above all Catholicism was an organism composed of many of the peoples of Europe and those of other areas of the world where Europeans had planted themselves.

As a consequence, Catholicism was profoundly local, shaped by relentless pressures such as the emergence of the nation-state, language, economy, folklore, and custom. Certainly Catholicism was structured by such familiar characteristics as the traditions and innovations of Petrine primacy and scholasticism, but it was also structured by political, social, and economic pressures at the local, national, and international levels. To speak of Roman Catholicism one must speak in concrete local and social contexts if what is said is to be meaningful.

At the beginning of the sixteenth century most of the 80 million or so people of western Europe called themselves Christians without reflection. They were less likely to be divided into Catholics and non-Catholics than into good Christians or bad Christians, or perhaps unrepentant sinners and repentant sinners, that is, those parishioners who had made peace with their neighbors and fulfilled their Easter sacramental obligations and those who had not.

In addition to this self-identity, western European Christians had access to a well-articulated schema for describing the "other." There were schismatic Christians, heretics, unbelievers, infidels, and pagans. All of these groups had been identified and put into relationships in theory and practice with Roman Catholics for centuries. Neither theory nor practice, however, was static. Jews in Catholic countries, for example, went from a shaky protection by princes to isolation, persecution, pogrom, and expulsion. Formerly tolerant Spain developed such a pitch of xenophobia that not only were Jews and later Muslims expelled, but "New Christians" (*Conversos*) whose ancestors had been Muslims or Jews were harassed by the Inquisition and forced into second-class status. By mid-century, when Ignatius Loyola refused to discriminate against New Christians in the Society of Jesus, he was an exception to a pernicious bigotry. In Rome, where popes had protected the Jewish community, relations grew increasingly strained. Concerted efforts were made to convert the local Jewish community, and after 1555 all Jews in papal territory were forced into ghettos.

The Catholic tradition was not, however, in agreement on the fundamentals of these relationships between community and other. As a result of the Thomist synthesis of the Aristotelian concept of natural slavery and the Augustinian concept of just war and beneficial coercion, the Spanish conquistadors—temporal and spiritual—found that they possessed an ideological language that allowed them to subordinate pagan peoples encountered in the New World. The humanist historian and courtier Juan Ginés de Sepúlveda (1490–1573) gave comfort to the Spanish *encomenderos* with his assertions that Spanish conquerors and conquests were legitimate; former *encomendero* and Dominican friar Bartolomé de Las Casas (1484–1566), bishop of Chiapas in Mexico, and Dominican canonist Francisco de Vitoria (1483/86–1546) of Salamanca used the traditions to judge the Spanish conquests and find them immoral and illegal. The ecclesiastical preoccupation with the connection between Christianity and conquest was not a fluke. The sixteenth century witnessed an explosion of missionary activity under Catholic auspices. While Martin Luther was setting up the evangelical church in electoral Saxony and John Calvin was struggling to reform Geneva, Catholic missionaries in the wake of Spanish and Portuguese conquistadors were converting thousands of pagans each day to the faith with a zeal fired by the glory of God and the need to save souls. Nor were these spiritual conquests carried out only at the point of the sword. The Jesuits Francis Xavier (1506–1552) and Matteo Ricci (1552–1610) labored in hostile or indifferent mission fields in Japan and China and won converts as a result of their preaching and way of life. Far from wrenching the native population from its way of life by violence, Ricci accommodated Catholicism to Chinese society so well that his successors were severely reined in by the papacy for syncretism.

A far more important conflict in the experience of early modern Catholics than that between community and other, however, was that between laity and clergy. The great majority of Catholics belonged to the laity and lived in the countryside. Throughout the sixteenth century most of these people experienced Catholicism as a religion of practices rather than of dogma. Learned understanding of the faith was rudimentary for these rural populations. When dogmatic teaching appeared in pastoral ministry, it often consisted of little more than memorization of the *Pater Noster*, the *Ave Maria*, the *Credo*, and possibly the Ten Commandments. Sometimes there was practical catechesis directed toward informed participation in the sacramental system. The most important sacrament about which lay people received instruction was that of penance. They were encouraged to order their sins according to the categories determined by the late medieval canonists and penitential theologians as preparation for a good confession. Thus the sacraments were central to official Catholicism. Of the seven canonical sacraments, the Eucharist and its rituals and devotions, including the Forty Hours veneration, the processions, and frequent reception of the Sacrament loomed largest in the experience of the faith. The Mass was so central to Catholic ritual experience that reformers stated that they were abolishing Catholicism by abolishing the Mass. The distinction between official and unofficial Catholicism is important in view of the local quality of Catholicism. Even a great city such as Milan clung tenaciously to its own Ambrosian liturgy and its abbreviated Lenten season. Besides the liturgy and the sacraments, every village had its own ritual places, practices, and patron saints. Local cults existed in relationship to the orthodox cult, and the critical link between local and universal was often the parish pastor.

Notwithstanding the centrality of eucharistic piety and the apparatus of confession, penance, and penitential practices, Catholic pastoral ministry focused as much attention on preaching as did its Protestant counterpart. The major innovation in sixteenth-century Catholic preaching was not that preaching became important in response to the Protestant stimulus, but rather that in addition to the indefatigable efforts of the Catholic religious orders, the diocesan clergy began to preach more frequently and more effectively. As a result the period witnessed an explosion of preaching pedagogy in the form of instructions, handbooks, sermon collections, and even pastoral congregations for training new parish preachers. The sixteenth century was a golden age of Catholic preaching.

Bellarmino's concept of the church asserted an emphatically hierarchical relationship in which the laity were subordinated to the clergy. The social reality experienced by laity and clergy, however, was more complicated. The laity were structured by sharp class distinctions, while the clergy were divided into two broad groups. The secular clergy were those who were ordained in one of the seven orders of clergy and who labored in the world (*saeculum*). They included university students and archdeacons, pastors of parishes and bishops, exorcists and popes. The upper echelons of the secular clergy lived in the glittering realms of the rulers of states and territories. The humblest of the secular clergy, the massing priests, curates, and pastors, were often scarcely distinguishable from those among whom they practiced their particular craft. They labored in the world and were subject to its vicissitudes.

The other broad category of Catholic clergy consisted of those clerics who belonged to one of the religious orders. They were called the regular clergy because they took vows and were bound by a rule of life, or *regula*. In offering to society institutions and structures predicated on the assumption that there was a value to seeking to live according to the "counsels of perfection," they offered to the Catholic world a dimension aggressively rejected by the reformers. The regular clergy included not only the great monastic orders such as the Benedictines, the Cistercians, and the Carthusians, but also the mendicant orders such as the Dominicans, the Franciscans, the Augustinians, the Carmelites, and the Servites. Part of the stimulating variety of regular clergy derived from the histories of the various orders. Most orders had long since developed not only second orders that included women, but even third orders that functioned at the boundary between laity and clergy.

The histories of the orders also fostered characteristic institutional developments that enriched the experience of Roman Catholics. Most orders split into suborders distinguished by the severity with which they observed their rules of life. Much to the dismay of monastic reformers such as Teresa of Ávila and the young Martin Luther, "conventuals" generally interpreted their rules of life in the context of a host of mitigating traditions, interpretations, and exemptions. By contrast, "observants" sought to return to the pristine rule of their founder before their order slipped into a worldliness typical of the secular clergy.

For example, the Franciscan order revealed a particular tendency to handle reform by subdivision. Besides medieval schismatic and heretical filiations, such as the "spirituals" and the "fraticelli," the Franciscan universe included a conventual branch, an observant branch, and admirers such as the Minims; in addition to the friars themselves, there was a tertiary order that lived in the world and a second order of nuns (the Poor Clares). In 1529 the observant friar Matteo di Bassi (1495–1552) initiated yet another Franciscan reform when he received permission to begin following a reformed rule that provided the basis for a severely observant branch of the order; they came to be known as "Capuchins" because of the shape of their characteristic hoods. By their ministry, their piety, and their example, the Capuchins played a fundamental role in the support and spread of the ideals of reform Catholicism.

The religious orders also provided institutions that structured the experience of specific kinds of spirituality. The Carthusians, for example, practiced rigorous asceticism and contemplation. Carmelite Teresa of Ávila (1515–1582) and her disciple John of the Cross (1542–1591) integrated the ecstatic self-annihilation of mystical experience with the rituals and practices of traditional worship in a synthesis that would play a critical role in shaping seventeenth-century Catholic spirituality, especially in France. Female monasticism also provided women with opportunities for autonomy, spiritual development, and community denied them both in Roman Catholic and Protestant lay communities.

The sixteenth century witnessed the advent of new religious orders that both shaped and were shaped by the needs of the new century. Angela Merici of Brescia (1474–1540) intended the Ursulines to have an active apostolic ministry in the world and deliberately eschewed the rigid rules of cloister that were characteristic of female religious orders but that would have prevented the social ministries envisioned for the new order. The Ursulines represented, therefore, both a response to the needs of the world and a challenge to established gender relations that dictated that women—lay or secular—needed protection by males of their families, whether of blood or order. Despite a struggle throughout the sixteenth century, the Ursulines were finally subordinated and cloistered by powerful bishops who were troubled by their apostolic independence. The resulting order, which was instrumental for Catholic education in succeeding centuries, conformed little to the original vision of Merici but was acceptable to a church enmeshed in the structures and the ideology of the world around it.

By contrast, the Society of Jesus, which embraced a similar impulse to offer a wide range of chosen "customary ministries," developed new structures, such as a fourth vow placing the order at the disposal of the pope to be sent wherever most needed, freedom from singing the canonical hours in choir, and a framework of governing constitutions. As with the Ursulines, the advantages for pastoral ministry of the new order were not always recognized. During the pontificate of Paul IV (r. 1555–1559), the Jesuits were obliged to modify their characteristic "way of proceeding" and recite the canonical hours in common. This might have thwarted the effectiveness of the order had not the mandate been reversed by Paul IV's successor.

This panoply of religious orders did not always coexist peacefully. Indeed, rivalry and competition within and among the orders was so notorious that Cardinal Gian Pietro Carafa (the future Paul IV) recommended that many of them be abolished and that no new orders be permitted. Desiderius Erasmus mercilessly satirized the regular and the secular clergy in "The Funeral." His satire captures the selfish jockeying that sometimes characterized relations among the orders as well as between the orders and the secular clergy; it also hints at some of the more substantive areas of competition. A fundamental conflict centered on the provision of pastoral care. The *cura animarum*, or "care of souls," was the canonical prerogative and responsibility of the secular clergy. Some religious orders, however, had been integrated into the hierarchy of pastoral ministry almost from their founding. As a result, in the sixteenth century the regular orders were deeply involved in such aspects of the care of souls as preaching and the administration of the sacraments, particularly the sacrament of penance. One consequence of this pastoral situation was that the religious orders were a major feature of Catholicism for Christians not only in the cities but also in the Christian countryside.

Another consequence was an ongoing jurisdictional conflict between the local bishop, who was often able to enlist the support of his fellow bishops at diocesan synods and church councils, and the orders, which proved effective at obtaining papal exemptions from control by the bishops. This confusion over who provided what services under whose jurisdiction was not particularly serious where the local bishop was lax in fulfilling his responsibilities. After all, as papal legate, Cardinal Giovan Maria de' Ciocci del Monte (later Julius III, 1487–1555) asked at the Council of Trent in connection with the reform of preaching: if the regulars are prevented from preaching, then who would preach? After the movement to reform pastoral ministry under the aegis of the local bishop culminated with the reform decrees of the final phase of the Council of Trent, however, this conflict became more serious. Trent gave the committed bishop more control over the religious orders in his diocese. Bishops like Gabriele Paleotti (1522–1597) in Bologna, Carlo Borromeo (1538–1584) in Milan, and Carlo Bascapè in Novara insisted that regulars laboring within the bounds of their dioceses pass stringent examinations of their preaching ability, their knowledge of penitential theology, and especially their knowledge of cases of conscience; they also insisted that their mendicant colleagues respect the obligation to reserve certain sins to the bishop alone for absolution. At the end of the sixteenth century the religious orders still played an important role in the provision of pastoral care and in the laity's experience of Catholicism; they did so, however, in more clearly defined and more closely regulated contexts.

The triumph of the Tridentine bishops over their rivals in the religious orders was but one aspect of an overall campaign to reform Christian life that affected the secular clergy and the laity as well. Diocesan priests were ordered to shun the company of lay people lest they give occasion for scandal or ridicule. Pastors were expected to meet monthly in church in their vicariate to practice preaching and discuss difficult cases of conscience. In accordance with the Tridentine decree, Carlo Borromeo established a seminary in Milan within the first year of his archiepiscopate for the instruction of his secular clergy. While these institutions did not provide the university-level theological education characteristic of the emerging Protestant ideal of the learned ministry, they provided candidates with a solid basis in elementary education, theology, and basic skills.

The seminary and examination proved important instruments by which bishops might impose conformity and obedience on their subordinates. Far-flung congregations in the archdiocese of Milan were accustomed to electing their own parish priests and seeking confirmation of their decisions from the archbishop in Milan. Borromeo accepted this practice but insisted that the candidate repair to Milan within a given time to submit to an examination. Hence by a letter of 15 July 1568 he notified the community of Creciano that he could not confirm their choice of curate until the latter be examined in Milan. The archbishop gave the candidate a month to come at his convenience. That same summer Borromeo notified the community of Chironico that their elected curate had failed his examination and would be detained in Milan for "one or two months" while he studied up on "the things that pertain to the cure of souls." Despite these efforts, the reform of the secular clergy was a drawn out and ultimately generational process. By the end of the sixteenth century there were often two corps of mutually suspicious priests. Young priests trained in the seminaries and imbued with reforming zeal looked askance at old veterans who were scarcely distinguishable from their parishioners and were more tolerant of their customs and foibles.

This episcopal effort to impose doctrinal and devotional conformity did not neglect the laity. Priests banned scores of old and suspect practices, relentlessly emphasized new devotions, kept detailed records, and watched vigilantly for heresy, contumacy, and, of course, sin in all its colorful variety. The messages promulgated by Trent and by the local councils and synods were preached from the pulpit, emphasized in the confessional, taught in the school of Christian doctrine, offered in a profusion of catechisms, and modeled by the pastor himself. So much of pastoral ministry was devoted to forming the practices and the doctrinal understanding of the layperson that the second half of the sixteenth century may be seen as the era of the Catholic "Formation," rather than the Catholic Reformation.

Catholic lay people were not, however, passive recipients of clerical instruction. Just as the religious orders offered the clergy a variety of self-consciously elite religious organizations, so the ubiquitous confraternities and sodalities offered Catholic lay people a thick skein of affinities that defined group identity in various ways. These associations of corporate Catholic devotion and social identity did not wane through the sixteenth century; indeed, they grew stronger. Although many confraternities came increasingly under clerical supervision if not control, they remained vehicles for the expression of Catholic piety and became instruments for the inculcation of a reformed and disciplined piety more consonant with post-Tridentine ideals of religiosity. Many communities saw the rise of confraternities devoted to the cult of the Eucharist. In France during the Wars of Religion such confraternities deployed themselves to defend the Eucharist as it was being carried to the sick or in processions against Huguenots bent on disgracing the "Paste God." Other confraternities grew up around the performance of specific works of mercy such as ministry to prisoners and the sick.

Preexisting confraternities were enlisted in the service of the Catholic Reformation. Carlo Borromeo integrated the schools of Christian doctrine, established in Milan by Castellino da Castello in 1535, into his overarching reform of Christian life in the archdiocese after 1565. The Society of Jesus was particularly active in exploiting the omnipresent Catholic urge to confraternity for expressing its characteristic ministries. Hence the Jesuit Jan Leunis set up a new confraternity for boys at the Collegio Romano in 1563, under the patronage of the Virgin Mary, that encouraged the boys to attend daily mass, confess regularly, take Communion monthly, and undertake corporal acts of mercy. Leunis himself directed this "Marian congregation," and the confraternity was institutionalized by Gregory XIII and spread rapidly through the worldwide network of Jesuit schools. In the same way that Catholicism undertook world missions, so too resources, personnel, and a common educational agenda contributed to the establishment of an educational empire by the end of the sixteenth century. Jesuit schools—using the most modern pedagogy, charging no fees, and organizing their students into disciplined communities—could be found wherever Jesuits were found; the Piarists undertook the education of boys from lower social classes, and the redirected Ursulines extended educational opportunities to women.

If Bellarmino's model of the true church emphasized community and sacraments, one cannot deny that there was a factual basis for supposing that the structure of the church mattered. The second most characteristic of Catholic institutions (after the confraternity), the papacy, enjoyed a peculiar renaissance of its own at the beginning of the sixteenth century. The fifteenth century had been difficult for the authority of the successors of Saint Peter. Had the impulses behind the reform decrees of the Council of Constance (1414–1418) been sustained, the papacy might have devolved into a constitutional figurehead of a parliamentary church. Rather than throwing down the gauntlet to the church in council assembled, however, the papal successors to Martin V spent the rest of the fifteenth century in a series of political maneuvers that profited from the localism of the late medieval church. By cultivating and encouraging increasing control of the church by local lay elites, the popes were able to evade the controls so earnestly sought by the conciliarists.

By the beginning of the sixteenth century, the papacy had been largely successful in escaping from the gravity of the Council of Constance. Pope Julius II (r. 1503–1513) in armor before the walls of the contumacious city of Bologna demonstrated that the papacy was reestablishing itself as an autonomous power in central Italy, as the Fifth Lateran Council he summoned to Rome (1512–1517) demonstrated that the papacy was once again taking control of doctrine and reform from both the council and the princes. Both victories, however, were more seeming than real. As a political power the papacy was quickly eclipsed in the conflict between the Habsburg dynasty and their French rivals, the Valois. Papal autonomy was rudely concluded when an army of Charles V (1500–1558) subjected Rome to one of its most ferocious sackings. Pope Clement VII (r. 1523–1534) barely escaped to the Castel Sant' Angelo, where he watched the advance of new hegemonic power in Italy.

By the same token, the triumph of papal power inherent in the Fifth Lateran Council proved illusory as well. Important reforms dealing with abuses and doctrine were debated and decreed but not implemented. The decrees promulgated by Pope Leo X (r. 1513–1521) revealed the tenuousness of the papal claim to be able to reform the church "in head and members." Nowhere is this clearer than in the Concordat of Bologna (1516), according to which Leo X ceded to Francis I of France (r. 1515–1547) the power to nominate the bishops of France subject to confirmation by the Holy See. As a result, Francis I obtained the right to nominate candidates to ten archbishoprics, eighty-two bishoprics, and hundreds of abbeys—and to control their vast financial resources. In return, the king allowed to lapse the Pragmatic Sanction of Bourges (1438), which had denied the papacy any jurisdiction whatsoever in the kingdom of France.

Similar developments in Spain and England reveal the extent to which lay control of the ecclesiastical hierarchy set limits on the papacy's capacity to carry out reform on its own, as well as the importance of the bishops in that enterprise. Using the justification of crusading fervor, Ferdinand and Isabella, "the Catholic monarchs," reformed and dominated the church from the Spanish *reconquista* on. Their grandchild, Charles V, and his son, Philip II, did not fail to follow in their ancestors' footsteps. Ferdinand and Isabella enlisted ecclesiastical advisers committed to reform, such as Hernando Talavera and Francisco Jiménez de Cisneros (1436–1517), and began a systematic reform of the Spanish clergy, both secular and regular. They were aided in their efforts to control the clergy by several particularly supple instruments of the central state. They won the prerogative of the Patronato Real (the royal prerogative of appointing bishops) over the churches brought back to the faith as a result of the conquest of Granada (1492). In 1508 Pope Julius II extended to Ferdinand a universal patronato in the Spanish dominions in the New World. By 1523 Charles V had obtained from his former tutor, Pope Adrian VI (r. 1522–1523), the prerogative of presenting candidates to all the benefices of the Spanish kingdoms. In addition to putting their own candidates into church offices, the Spanish Crown also collected one third of the tithes paid to the church—the so-called *tercias reales*—after 1494, and the revenues of a crusade indulgence were also funneled to the Crown long after the final conquest of Granada.

Finally, Ferdinand and Isabella persuaded Pope Sixtus IV (r. 1471–1484) to permit them to establish the Spanish Inquisition (1478) to deal with the problem of apostasy and later, heresy. Carried from the kingdom of Castile to the other Spanish kingdoms with difficulty and resistance, the Inquisition nevertheless became a critical means for the Spanish monarchs to unite their domains and suppress their aristocratic and urban rivals. Although originally sanctioned by the pope, the Spanish Inquisition soon operated independently. Through the sixteenth century it was an inescapable part of Spanish life: such important figures as Ignatius

Loyola and Bartolomé de Carranza (1503–1576), archbishop of Toledo, fell afoul of it.

The trend toward royal domination of national churches so evident in France and the Spanish kingdoms was manifest in England as well, where Henry VIII's minister, Cardinal Thomas Wolsey (1474–1530), exercised such wide legatine powers under his monarch's control that he was virtually pope in England. Moreover, with the medieval punitive statutes of *Provisors* and *Praemunire* (medieval parliamentary decrees prohibiting, respectively, papal provision to benefices and appeals to the papacy), the Tudor monarchs could compel the papacy to accommodate royal interests in appointments to benefices and in revenues.

Long before the Diet of Augsburg (1555) and its programmatic formula for practical religious concord in Germany, different formulas applied in France, Spain, and England. By or before 1525, the "Defender of the Faith," the "Most Christian King," and the "Most Catholic King" had won from the papacy tacit acknowledgments of their control of the church patronage and revenues. The power to reform the church that the papacy seized with one hand, it ceded with the other when it surrendered control over the appointments of the bishops who would be responsible for bridging the gap between theory and practice, between center and the periphery. Notwithstanding later threats to princely hegemony, such as Cardinal Giovanni Morone's ominous proposal during the final phase of the Council of Trent that the prelates should take up a "reform of the princes" to address secular interference with the church, the papacy had conceded before the Reformation began the link between center and periphery that would be fundamental for implementing reform.

Bishops were, therefore, critical links in the reform enterprise, and yet in case after case they were either deeply entangled in local political and dynastic pursuits or absent altogether, pursuing their ambitions or their leisure in the royal or the papal court. The best intentioned reform would remain void until the bishops themselves recognized their pastoral responsibilities, eschewed multiple benefices, resided in their sees, and made the transition from secular princes to pastors. The hierarchical challenge for the church was whether the papacy would implement and preside over this necessary reformation according to the medieval aphorism "Reform Rome and Rome reforms the world," or whether the bishops, in council assembled and in their own dioceses, would take control of reform.

The Sack of Rome (1527) was a watershed event for Catholic reform efforts. First, it greatly moderated papal political ambitions. For the rest of the sixteenth century the popes chafed or flourished under the domination of the Habsburgs. Second, the sack put a temporary end to the practical possibility of reform from above. The papal curia was in disarray. Curialists who had voiced reform sentiments scattered to the safety of their dioceses. Jacopo Sadoleto (1477–1547), humanist, curialist, and papal secretary, left Rome for his diocese in Carpentras, where he began to experience the challenges and opportunities of pastoral ministry. Gian Matteo Giberti (1495–1543) made his way to his diocese in Verona and began reforms of all aspects of life in his diocese. Both men represented an important development. Sincere prelates and absentee pastors who saw Rome as the center and the pope as the head of the church and its hope for reform and who had shaped their careers in accordance with these convictions, both Sadoleto and Giberti were thrust out of Rome into their dioceses. There they became pastors and began to articulate both a critique of the church and a vision for its repair.

It was a council of bishops rather than papal fiat that crafted and imposed the necessary reforms. In spite of the threat of conciliarism that any council of bishops represented for the early modern papacy, Paul III (r. 1534–1549) reversed the obstruction of his predecessors—Clement VII's policy had been "Never offer a council, never refuse it directly"—and held out for a council that would do more than simply ease Emperor Charles V's relations with his Protestant subjects. The realization of this council, which was originally summoned to the city of Mantua in 1535, proved difficult indeed, and the opening rituals were celebrated in the compromise imperial city of Trent only in December 1545. Three papal legates, four archbishops, twenty-one bishops, and five generals of religious orders arrived in Trent to open the ecumenical council. Italians dominated the attendees, and papal legate Girolamo Seripando later said that the first phase seemed more like a diocesan synod than an ecumenical council.

If the council was difficult to assemble, it was also difficult to keep in session. A variety of factors conspired to disrupt the council on several occasions. The outbreak of plague in the winter of 1547 led to the transfer of the council to Bologna and its eventual suspension early in 1548 in order to avoid schism between papalists and imperialists. In November 1550 the council was summoned back to Trent, where the bishops, now augmented by several bishops from Germany, including the three imperial electors, labored on in their twin enterprise of doctrinal definition and reform until the menacing approach of the Protestant army induced them to adjourn in April 1552.

After a gap during the reign of Paul IV, the council was convened for its final phase in November 1560 by Paul IV's successor, Pius IV (r. 1559–1565). The final phase was the best attended of the three, opening with 109 cardinals and bishops, eventually including a French delegation of thirteen led by Charles of Guise, cardinal of Lorraine. The final phase represented the new contours of the church better than had the first phase, with its preponderance of Italians; if more ecumenical, however, it was not more irenic. By the fall of 1562 the council was seriously divided over a new version of the old and vexing issue of episcopal residence and the abuse of absenteeism. Zealous defenders of papal primacy asserted that the obligation of episcopal residence derived from human law and thus could be dispensed with by the pope. A stubborn minority of reform-minded bishops, many of them belonging to the French and Spanish delegations, insisted that episcopal residence was mandated by divine law—*ius divinum*—rather than human law. The issue turned on two matters critical for the perception and reality of reform: first, how serious were the bishops about empowering themselves to take control of reform, and, second, what was the relation between the papacy and the episcopacy?

Despite expectations, neither the papacy nor the ecumenical council was able to seize the decisive advantage. Although the popes tried to manage the council through their legates, no pope ever controlled it. The endless maneuvers by the legates to keep the peace and to keep the agenda on track, and the correspondence of the young Carlo Borromeo, who tried to persuade the prelates to agree with his papal uncle's positions, make clear that the papacy most effectively controlled the council with political negotiation rather than absolutist decree. For their part, the prelates assembled were not particularly fearful of the papacy. During the final phase of the council Juan Alonso de Polanco, who was at Trent in his capacity as secretary to Diego Laínez, general of the Society of Jesus, drafted a proposal for the reform of the curia that threatened the pope with deposition if he failed to reform the church. Nevertheless, no powerful antipapal front emerged, and the prelates were not able to draft an acceptable decree defining the role of the papacy.

In spite of the enormous amount of positive work done by the council, two potentially insuperable obstacles threatened its reform agenda. First, the bishops assembled at Trent could set in motion a reform of the church in its members, not least by educating and inspiring themselves as models for those members; what the council could not easily do was reform the papal curia itself. Second, while this reform could not become operative unless implemented and facilitated by the papacy, the council's efforts were for naught unless the bishops brought the spirit and the letter of Trent to their dioceses.

The papacy enjoyed a series of vigorous administrators who worked to establish and amplify the decisions of Trent and to reform the curia in Rome. The first impulses toward curial reform began to surface during the pontificate of Paul III (r. 1534–1549) as advocates of reform began to assume positions of authority. If he lavished preferment upon the members of his own family, he also elevated a number of distinguished and active reformers to the college of cardinals. Far from advancing a common program for curial and ecclesial reform, however, these new cardinals differed widely in prescriptions for reform. Indeed, in the persons of several of the cardinals the various and sometimes mutually hostile factions of the Counter-Reformation were represented. Perhaps the best example of this diversity can be seen in the conflict between the conciliatory Gasparo Contarini (1483–1542) and the zealous Gian Pietro Carafa (1476–1559), the future Pope Paul IV. The former's vision of reform led him to seek compromise and reunion with the Protestants at the Colloquy of Regensburg (1541); the latter's vision demanded extirpation of the heretics and all their works and sympathizers.

These new cardinals began seriously to make reform rather than obstruction the business of the curia. This was important because a reformation of the papacy presupposed a reformation of the college that elected the pope. Yet the impact of the introduction of a critical mass of reformers into the college of cardinals was more far-reaching. As a consequence of the consistories of Paul III and like-minded successors, a number of curial reformers were brought into positions of power and encouraged to articulate their respective visions of reform. Nowhere is the cumulative impact of Paul III's reform of the college of cardinals clearer than in the *Consilium de emendanda ecclesia*. This consensus document, drafted by a committee of hard-liners, moderates, and radicals and submitted to Paul III on 9 March 1537, detailed the vices of the curia, their impact on the church, and the pope's responsibility for them. The committee's final document was a disturbing litany of abuses that spared neither pope nor bishop, neither teacher nor lay person. In addition to castigating such familiar vices as simony, abuse of benefices, pluralism, and absenteeism, the drafters took to task the *Colloquies* of Erasmus, criticized indulgence hawkers, identified abuses in "dispensing in the case of marriages between those related by blood or by marriage," and even recommended the abolition of the conventual religious orders, "for many have become so deformed that they are a great scandal to the laity and do grave harm by their example." The changes proposed in the document would have had an impact at all levels of Christian life and could have been a call to arms against many of the problems that the bishops at Trent would later address. The pope, however, failed to undertake most of the reforms demanded by the document. In particular, efforts to reform the corrupt agencies of the curia were thwarted by entrenched interests and by the pope's own reservations; when the pope attempted to send home some eighty bishops tarrying in Rome, his effort met a storm of protest from bishops for whom there was no lack of precedent for such absenteeism.

Although he failed to reform the curia, Paul III was much more effective in recognizing and encouraging the reform activities of others. His judicious appointments to the college of cardinals allowed him to build a core of like-minded supporters and so escape the isolation and insulation that rendered the short-lived Pope Hadrian VI (r. 1522–1523) impotent. He gave his approval to the Society of Jesus in the bull *Regimini militantis ecclesiae* (1540) and endorsed the aggressive orthodoxy of the curial hard-liners by establishing the papal Inquisition (1542). Perhaps most important, Paul III managed the intricate political choreography necessary to convene the council that met in Trent in 1545. As a consequence of these competing instincts, the pontificate of Paul III was a strange and volatile blend of old problems and the promise of new solutions; new shoots of reform grew up with old strains of abuse. Only time would tell whether the hoped-for reform of the head of the church would be accomplished.

The difference between the opportunities of episcopal and papal reform is clear in the papal career of Paul IV. Elected between the second and third phases of the Council of Trent, he resolutely turned his back on it and focused his considerable energies on reforming the church not only in its head but from its head. He attacked with all of his characteristic rigor those aspects of unorthodoxy that came under his direct control. He published the first papal *Index librorum prohibitorum* by both withdrawing all licenses to read the materials and by including the writings of the reformers and the complete works of Erasmus. He also greatly strengthened the papal Inquisition by putting its head, the Dominican Michele Ghislieri (the future Pope Pius V and saint), on the same level as the cardinals and by encouraging him to strike at all manner of lapses. If Erasmus was the most famous victim of Paul IV's Index, the highly respected reform cardinal and former Tridentine legate Giovanni Morone (1509–1580) was one of the most famous victims of the Pauline Inquisition. Morone was imprisoned for suspicion of heresy and was released from prison in the Castel Sant' Angelo only upon the pope's death. He immediately became an important adviser to Pope Pius IV (r. 1559–1565).

Paul IV did not restrict his reforming impulses to the Curia or to Rome. He knew the importance of reforming the episcopate and took his responsibility for naming appropriate candidates to vacant sees so seriously that upon his death there were more than fifty vacancies still unfilled. The experience of Paul IV, however, showed the limitations of the fantasy that the church could be reformed from Rome and by the papacy. The papacy had neither the practical authority nor the power and mechanisms necessary to oversee a comprehensive reform of the church. Papal power could be projected effectively in central Italy and elsewhere along certain lines of authority (for example, where the papacy still had the prerogative of naming bishops and through the Inquisition), but elsewhere the papacy could most help by setting the best example and by facilitating the work of reformers at the local level.

Both of these characteristics may be recognized in the activities of Paul IV's successors. Pius IV brought the Council of Trent to a close, promulgated its decrees, and began publishing the Roman catechism as a way of bringing those decrees to the level of the average Catholic. Pius V (r. 1566–1572) oversaw the completion of the Roman catechism, reformed such crucial liturgical works as the breviary and the missal, and reformed the papal household. Sixtus V (r. 1585–1590) inaugurated a new edition of the Vulgate and decisively reformed the Curia. He turned it into a precocious state bureaucracy by setting up fifteen departments of government called congregations headed by cardinals; he also deployed the formidable resources of papal patronage to support an artistic celebration of Catholic reform, so that the city of Rome, previously scorned as a sinkhole of corruption, became itself a model of reform.

Notwithstanding the powerful administrative support of the papacy and moral example of the physical and spiritual reform of Rome, at best the papacy in the sixteenth century could reform itself and its own but not the church as a whole. Reform fell to the local authorities, lay and clerical, and increasingly to the bishops. Within the context of law and pastoral practice, the Council of Trent greatly increased the instruments available to bishops. What remained was for the post-Tridentine episcopate to rise to the challenge. A series of exemplary and effective bishops such as Carlo Borromeo took the initiative and worked the pastoral implications of the Tridentine decrees into concrete regulations and instructions. There had been precedents for the bishop as reformer rather than feudal potentate. Gian Matteo Giberti had prefigured in his diocese of Verona many of the pastoral reforms that would later be embraced by the prelates of Trent. Borromeo himself was attentive to the reform legislation of Trent when he was papal secretary. Biographer Gian Pietro Giussano reported that Borromeo studied the decrees of the council "with the utmost minuteness in order that he might have every detail carried out." He was also a disciple of the exemplary reformer Bartolomeo de Martyribus, archbishop of Braga. In his archdiocese Borromeo restored the practice of convening regional councils and diocesan synods in order to restore clerical discipline. He also conducted annual pastoral visitations throughout his archdiocese, which allowed him to test directly whether his pastors and flocks were conforming to his expectations. Whether he was successful in reforming the archdiocese of Milan is less important than that his life, his institutions, and even his prompt canonization (1610) indicate that the Catholic episcopate was on the road toward epochal renewal.

Carlo Borromeo's reform program was codified in a monument of regulation called the *Acta Ecclesiae Mediolanensis*, first compiled in 1582. The *Acta* proved such a fruitful model for fashioning the Tridentine diocese, the Tridentine clergy, and the Tridentine lay person that from its compilation it was forwarded whole to harried bishops in Poland and Germany. In 1592 Carlo Bascapé, one of Borromeo's earliest biographers, claimed that "the *Acta* were now being sought with unbelievable eagerness by all parts of the Christian world." In France, where the publication of the decrees of the Council of Trent were long delayed for political reasons, the *Acta* provided a means to smuggle in the decrees of Trent via Milan. In the seventeenth century, when formation and Counter-Reformation battled Protestantism, sloth, and indifference for supremacy in every diocese of Catholic Europe, Carlo Borromeo was both the ideal and the practical model to whom the Tridentine bishops turned.

The differences in theology, liturgy, and practices that set Catholicism apart from Protestantism by 1600 are critical for understanding both confessional trajectories. In addition to unresolvable differences over justification, grace, predestination, the Mass, veneration of the saints, and the efficacy of indulgences, there were other more subtle but equally important differences. Catholic Christians retained a host of structures within which laity and clergy could express their faiths. Religious orders and confraternities allowed a variety of experiences eliminated by emergent Protestantism. In the same way, Catholicism permitted women more variety of expression within the constraints of a patriarchal and often misogynistic society. The balance created by local practices and global institutions permitted enough flexibility to dampen sectarian divisions of the sort that shattered Protestant communities. With access to long-standing independent political structures in the hierarchy, local Catholic churches were better able to withstand absorption though not cooptation by burgeoning absolutist states than were the Protestant churches. The keystone of Catholic political independence, the papacy, should have been decisively weakened by the assault of the Reformation and the stern internal measures necessary to combat it. Instead, it emerged stronger than ever at the end of the sixteenth century, secure and authoritative in its new role of doctrinal and administrative leadership.

There were certainly similarities between the Catholic and Protestant faiths. Protestants and Catholics alike considered the Bible authoritative. Both stressed the importance of the ministries of the word for the communication of the faith. Both Catholic and Protestant clerical elites catalyzed a shift in emphasis from orthopraxis to orthodoxy by availing themselves of the catechism. Mired as they were in what would be centuries of conflict, Roman Catholicism and the varieties of Protestantism too easily stressed the differences that separated the confessions and ignored their common traditions and assumptions. It would be centuries before the two confessions, forged in this crucible of polemic and hatred, could soften enough to share the name of Christian.

[*See also* Catholic Reformation; Papacy; *and* Trent, Council of.]

BIBLIOGRAPHY

Alberigo, Giuseppe. *I vescovi italiani al Concilio di Trento, 1545–47.* Florence, 1959.

Black, Christopher F. *Italian Confraternities in the Sixteenth Century.* Cambridge, 1989.

Bossy, John. *Christianity in the West, 1400–1700.* Oxford and New York, 1985.

Burke, Peter. *Popular Culture in Early Modern Europe.* New York, 1978.

Carroll, Michael P. *Madonnas That Maim: Popular Catholicism in Italy since the Fifteenth Century.* Baltimore and London, 1992.

Christian, William A., Jr. *Local Religion in Sixteenth-Century Spain.* Princeton, N.J., 1981.

Delumeau, Jean. *Catholicism between Luther and Voltaire: A New View of the Counter-Reformation.* Introduced by John Bossy. London, 1977.

DeMolen, Richard L., ed. *Religious Orders of the Catholic Reformation.* New York, 1994.

Duffy, Eamon. *The Stripping of the Altars: Traditional Religion in England, 1400–1580.* New Haven and London, 1992.

Evennett, H. Outram. *The Spirit of the Counter-Reformation.* Edited with postscript by John Bossy. Notre Dame, Ind., 1970.

Gleason, Elisabeth G. *Reform Thought in Sixteenth-Century Italy.* Texts and Translations Series, American Academy of Religion. Ann Arbor, Mich., 1987.

Hallman, Barbara McClung. *Italian Cardinals, Reform and the Church as Property.* Berkeley, Calif., 1985.

Headley, John, and John B. Tomaro, eds. *San Carlo Borromeo: Catholic Reform and Ecclesiastical Politics in the Second Half of the Sixteenth Century.* Washington, D.C., 1988.

Hoffman, Philip. *Church and Community in the Diocese of Lyon.* New Haven, 1959.

Iserloh, Erwin, Joseph Glazik, and Hubert Jedin. *History of the Church.* Vol. 5, *Reformation and Counter Reformation.* Edited by Hubert Jedin and John Dolan, translated by Anselm Biggs and Peter W. Becker. New York, 1980.

Jedin, Hubert. *Geschichte des Konzils von Trient.* 4 vols. in 5. Freiburg im Breisgau, 1948–1975.

McHugh, John A., and Charles J. Callan, trans. *Catechism of the Council of Trent for Parish Priests.* South Bend, Ind., 1976.

Olin, John C., ed. *The Catholic Reformation: Savonarola to Ignatius Loyola.* New York, 1992.

O'Malley, John W. *The First Jesuits.* Cambridge, Mass., 1993.

O'Malley, John W., ed. *Reformation Guides to Research.* Vol. 2, *Catholicism in Early Modern Europe: A Guide to Research.* Saint Louis, 1988.

Pastor, Ludwig von. *History of the Popes.* Edited by R. F. Kerr et al. 40 vols. London, 1938–1953.

Pelikan, Jaroslav. *The Christian Tradition: A History of the Development of Doctrine.* Vol. 4, *Reformation of the Church and Dogma, 1300–1700.* Chicago, 1984.

Prodi, Paolo. *Il cardinale Gabriele Paleotti, 1522–1597.* 2 vols. Rome, 1959–1967.

———. *The Papal Prince: One Body and Two Souls: The Papal Monarchy in Early Modern Europe.* Translated by Susan Haskins. Cambridge, 1987.

Prosperi, Adriano. *Tra evangelismo e controriforma: G. M. Giberti, 1495–1543.* Rome, 1969.

Schroeder, H. J., trans. *Canons and Decrees of the Council of Trent.* Rockford, Ill., 1978.

Schurhammer, Georg. *Francis Xavier: His Life, His Times.* 4 vols. Translated by J. Costelloe. Rome, 1973–1982.

Wright, A. D. *The Counter-Reformation: Catholic Europe and the Non-Christian World.* New York, 1982.

BENJAMIN WOOD WESTERVELT

ROMAN COLLEGE. *See* Seminaries.

ROMAN CURIA. *See* Curia Romana.

ROMAN LAW. *See* Law, *article on* Roman Law.

ROME. In the first quarter of the sixteenth century, Rome, capital of the papal states and the seat of the papacy, was one of the brightest cultural and artistic centers of Europe. Donato Bramante worked on the reconstruction of Saint Peter's basilica under Julius II (elected in 1503), and Raphael painted the famous *Stanze* ("apartments") of the Apostolic Palace under Leo X (elected in 1513), who numbered among his secretaries two famous humanists and men of letters, Jacopo Sadoleto and Pietro Bembo. The wealthier cardinals were not to be outdone, as evidenced by the grandiose palace that was begun by the future Paul III, cardinal Alessandro Farnese (elected in 1534); Michelangelo Buonarroti also later worked on it. Overall, the life of Roman high society, both lay and clerical, was marked by a spirit of worldliness, moral laxity, and ostentatious luxury in an unending round of banquets, parties, and hunts. It is thus easy to understand how people involved in the world of the German Reformation might have looked on Rome as a modern Babylon.

With all this the situation of the Roman clergy did not appear to be any better or worse than that of other Italian cities of the time. More than a few priests led immoral lives, and in general most were poorly prepared; some were so uneducated that they were not even capable of celebrating the Mass correctly. Others, instead of tending the churches entrusted to them, preferred to hold jobs in the Curia Romana or to work in the service of some powerful cardinal. Jurisdiction over the clergy was delegated by the pope as the bishop of Rome and was exercised by a cardinal or a bishop in the Curia with the title of vicar, who was in turn assisted by a viceregent. The powers of the vicar, which were clearly delineated only in 1559, were in fact limited by the exemptions and privileges enjoyed by many ecclesiastics as well as by the concurrent jurisdiction exercised by individual cardinals over the churches connected to their respective offices as cardinals.

Neither the reform decrees of the Fifth Lateran Council (1512–1517) nor the timid attempts at reform made by Clement VII (elected in 1523) were to lead to any improvement in the overall situation, because all these measures aimed at eliminating specific abuses without removing the root causes. Not even the terrifying Sack of Rome in 1527, during which rampaging soldiers of the imperial army laid waste to the city, changed this sad state of affairs, although it appeared to some more delicate consciences as divine retribution visited on a corrupt and dissolute city. The truth is that before the pontificate of Paul III, the popes were too caught up with their political and temporal interests to devote themselves in earnest to the spiritual reform of the city as well as of the church in general.

Meanwhile yearnings for renewal took concrete form in the spontaneous initiatives of what has been customarily referred to as the Catholic Reformation. The most notable of these initiatives was the foundation of the Oratory of Divine Love, which originated before 1515 in imitation of a similar initiative promoted in Genoa by the layman E. Vernazza. The oratory was composed of laymen and ecclesiastics who committed themselves to prayer, devotional practices, and aid to the sick and infirm.

A notable contribution to spiritual awakening was also to come from the new religious orders. As early as 1524, some ecclesiastics who were members of the Oratory of Divine Love, including Cajetan and Gian Pietro Carafa (the future Paul IV, elected in 1555), founded the order of clerics regular called the Theatines, after the Latin name of the diocese of Chieti, of which Carafa was bishop. But the Theatines became permanently established in the Eternal City only in 1555. At that time the Jesuits were already active in Rome. Ignatius Loyola and his first companions had arrived in the city about 1537; their presence made itself quickly felt because of their devotional and charitable foundations, but also especially because of their educational institutions after the opening of the Roman College in 1551 and the Germanic College in 1552.

The urgency of a radical religious renewal had also been felt within a circle of people who soon became known as the *spirituali* because they strove to become detached from worldly honors so as to embrace a more intense and internalized spiritual life. Some of these ended up adopting doctrinal positions that were questionable, if not outright heretical. This occurred chiefly through the spread of the writings of the Spaniard Juan de Valdés, whose works show traces of the spirituality of the *Alumbrados* and also of Erasmian thought, as well as of Luther's teachings. The influence of Valdés made itself felt particularly in Naples, where he lived from 1535 until his death. But he also had followers in Rome, both among the aristocracy, as in the case of Vittoria Colonna, the greatest female poet of her time, and in the Curia, as in the case of the prothonotary Pietro Carnesecchi.

Starting with Paul III, the initiative for reform was in the hands of the pope, who became convinced of the necessity of calling a general council, which was to open in Trent in 1545. With Paul III, the new course of papal policy expressed itself not only in measures that aimed at making the clergy respect their duties but also in a greater commitment to the fight against heresy. This is reflected in the creation of the Sacred Congregation of the Inquisition in 1542. The repression or heresy became particularly harsh under Paul IV, and its severity did not spare even some high-ranking officials, such as Cardinal Giovanni Morone. He was imprisoned in Castel Sant'Angelo and was subsequently cleared of charges only in 1560, after the pope's death. In those years several prelates were imprisoned, including the bishop of Modena, Egidio Foscarari, but he too was later declared innocent. A different fate befell Carnesecchi; he was condemned to death as a follower of Valdés and Luther and was executed in the square at the bridge to Castel Sant'Angelo in Rome in 1567, where Aonio Paleario was to suffer the same penalty in 1570. The truth is that the spread of heretical teachings at no time represented a real danger in Rome itself, since the majority of the subsequent condemnations involved non-Italians or Italians sent to the Eternal City by tribunals of the Inquisition in other cities. This was the case of Giordano Bruno, who was condemned to the stake in 1600.

Immediately after the close of the Council of Trent at the end of 1563, the conciliar decrees were implemented in Rome. In 1564 Pius IV ordered the cardinal vicar to conduct a pastoral visitation of the parishes, while in February 1565 the Roman Seminary was opened and its administration was entrusted to the Jesuits. This marked a first affirmation of the principle whereby Rome, as the seat of the papacy, was to serve as an example and model for the rest of Christendom. This was so much the case that Pius V (elected in 1566) and later Clement VIII (elected in 1592) did not hesitate to conduct the pastoral visitation personally.

Although implementation of the Tridentine reform was slow and met with some resistance, the educational and moral level of the clergy improved markedly. Comparable efforts were also made to improve the Christian education of the laity through the teaching of the Roman Catechism, whose first edition was published in Rome in 1566. In a more general way the popes of the Counter-Reformation issued decrees aimed at restoring public morality by combating the excessive power and extravagant excesses of the nobility, striving to curb the spread of prostitution, and fighting crime.

The new thrust given to religious life was also a result of the activity of the new religious orders, which, in addition to the Theatines and the Jesuits, included the Capuchins, established in Rome in 1529; the Somaschians, who in 1570 had taken over the administration of the orphanage of Santa Maria in Aquiro; and the Barnabites who had been present in the city since 1551 but who set up permanent headquarters at San Biagio all'Anello only in 1575. Of singular importance for the city of Rome was the canonical approbation of the Congregation of the Oratory that same year. This approbation formally raised to the status of a religious order the community of ecclesiastics that had formed around the charismatic figure of Filippo Neri and that had already been active for about twenty years. At the center of the activity of the new order, established at Santa Maria della Vallicella, stood the oratory, the most distinctive expression of Neri's apostolate: a company of laity, both youths and adults, who gathered in daily meetings in which moments of prayer alternated with spiritual readings and edifying sermons along with the singing of religious songs.

The renewal of religious fervor was also fostered by the activity of lay confraternities: in the mid-sixteenth century there were sixty-two, although not all of them were active, while by the end of the century some forty-seven more had been established. The goals pursued by the confraternities varied, ranging from devotional and penitential purposes to charitable works and assistance to the needy. Particularly significant as an instrument of Christian education, but also as a factor in spreading literacy, was the Archconfraternity of Christian Doctrine, founded in 1560. Its mission, following a model already in operation in other parts of Italy, was to create in the city approved schools in which, in addition to receiving basic primary instruction, children were taught the catechism.

Although the records of the pastoral visitation conducted by Clement VIII at the end of the sixteenth century reveal that not all the objectives of the reform had been met, there can be no doubt that the pilgrims who came from everywhere for the celebration of the Holy Year of 1600 found a city that, in its ecclesiastical and religious profile, differed profoundly from that of a century earlier.

[*See also* Papacy *and* Papal States.]

BIBLIOGRAPHY

Beggiao Cavani, Diego. *La visita pastoral di Clemente VIII, 1592–1600: Aspetti di riforma post-tridentina a Roma.* Corona Lateranensis 23. Rome, 1978.

Caponetto, Salvatore. *La riforma protestante nell'Italia del Cinquecento.* Rome, 1992.

Delumeau, Jean. *Vie économique et sociale de Rome dans la seconde moitié du XVIe siècle.* 2 vols. Paris, 1957–1959. See vol. 1, pp. 165–188. Deals with the theme of the presence of pilgrims in the city.

Fagiolo, Marcello, and Maria Luisa Madonna, eds. *Roma Sancta: La città delle basiliche.* Rome, 1985. A collection of essays on various aspects of religious life in Rome in the sixteenth and seventeenth centuries, especially in relation to the Holy Years.

Fiorani, Luigi. "Discussioni e ricerche sulle confraternite romane negli ultimi cento anni." *Ricerche per la storia religiosa di Roma* 6 (1985), 11–105.

Monticone, Alberto. "L'applicazione a Roma del Concilio di Trento: Le visite del 1564–1566." *Rivista di storia della Chiesa in Italia* 7 (1953), 225–250.

———. "L'applicazione a Roma del Concilio di Trento: I "Riformatori" e l'Oratorio, 1566–1572." *Rivista di storia della Chiesa in Italia* 8 (1954), 23–48.

Partner, Peter. *Renaissance Rome, 1500–1559: A Portrait of a Society.* Berkeley and London, 1976. See pp. 204–226. An effective outline of the religious history of Rome in the first half of the sixteenth century.

Pecchiai, Pio. *Roma nel Cinquecento.* Storia di Roma 13. Bologna, 1948. See pp. 361–386.

Pelliccia, Guerino. "Seminari e centri di formazione del prete romao nel Cinque-Seicento." *Ricerche per la storia religiosa di Roma* 7 (1988), 95–134.

Rivabene, Serio. "L'insegnamento catechetico dell'Arciconfraternità della Dottrina Cristiana a Roma nei secoli XVI-XVIII." *Archivio della Società romana di storia patria* 105 (1982), 295–313.

Agostino Borromeo

Translated from Italian by Robert E. Shillenn

RÖRER, Georg (1492–1557), transcriber, collector, and editor of many of the works of Martin Luther. Rörer was born in the Bavarian town of Deggendorf and in 1511 entered the University of Leipzig, where he met and became friends with the future evangelicals Stephan Roth and Caspar Cruciger. He received his bachelor of arts in 1515 and his master of arts in 1520. He entered the University of Wittenberg in 1522 and shortly thereafter began to record Luther's sermons and lectures, using his own method of shorthand. Rörer's notes constitute the only source for many of Luther's sermons and lectures. In 1525 he became deacon of the town church in Wittenberg and was the first person to be ordained by Luther through the laying on of hands. Later that year he was the liturgist for the first mass celebrated by Luther in German. Rörer was highly regarded as a preacher and was active in pastoral work, especially during the time of the plague. He lost his first wife, the sister of Johannes Bugenhagen, to the plague in 1527. He remarried the following year.

Rörer received his doctorate in theology in 1535 and in 1537 resigned from the diaconate in order to devote himself full time to copying, editing, and proofreading Luther's works. As proofreader, he was intensely involved in the various revisions of the Bible translation culminating in the final edition of 1546. His protocols of the many meetings of Luther and his associates offer a detailed picture of the arduous task of translation. Luther also entrusted Rörer with preparing the collections of his works in German and Latin.

The Schmalkald War forced Rörer to flee Wittenberg in 1551. For a time he received refuge from the king of Denmark, but in 1553, at the request of Elector John Frederick, he returned to Saxony and spent his remaining years in Jena, continuing his labors on the collected edition of Luther's works.

BIBLIOGRAPHY

Albrecht, Otto. "Quellenkritisches zu Aurifabers und Rörers Sammlungen der Buch- und Bibeleinzeichnungen Luthers." *Theologische Studien und Kritiken* 21 (1919), 279–306. A discussion of the reliability of Aurifaber and Rörer as sources for Luther's works.

Bornkamm, Heinrich. *Luther in Mid-Career, 1521–1530*. Translated by E. Theodore Bachmann. Philadelphia, 1983. Notes Rörer's role as recorder of Luther's sermons and letters.

Brecht, Martin. *Martin Luther: Shaping and Defining the Reformation, 1521–1531*. Translated by James L. Schaff. Minneapolis. 1990.

———. *Martin Luther: The Preservation of the Church, 1532–1546*. Translated by James L. Schaff. Minneapolis, 1993. Brecht's two volumes discuss Rörer's activity as transcriber of Luther's sermons and lectures, as well as his friendship with Luther.

Buchwald, Georg. *Zur Wittenberger Stadt- und Universitätsgeschichte in der Reformationszeit: Briefe aus Wittenberg an M. Stephan Roth in Zwickau*. Leipzig, 1893. Includes various letters by Rörer to Roth.

Schwiebert, E. G. *Luther and His Times: The Reformation from a New Perspective*. Saint Louis, 1950. Describes Rörer's role in the several revisions of Luther's and his colleagues' translation of the Bible.

MARILYN J. HARRAN

ROSENBERG, Vilém and Peter. *See* Rožmberk, Vilém and Petr Vok.

ROTHENBURG OB DER TAUBER. Located in southern Germany, Rothenburg ob der Tauber was an imperial free city from 1274 to 1803. Even before the Reformation the ecclesiastical policies of its city council had sought to limit the special privileges of the monastic orders and clergy and to regulate strictly all of ecclesiastical life. Beginning in 1522 this conservative, patrician council of staunch Catholic orientation had to confront a growing movement for reform, which resulted in Lutheran ideas being combined with the social demands of artisans and peasants. Among these ideas were the dissolution of monasteries; the repudiation of celibacy, ecclesiastical jurisdiction, and the clergy's immunity from taxation; the establishment of a common chest with the resources of church endowments and confraternities; the adoption of Communion under both kinds; the rejection of images of the saints, the cult of relics, pilgrimages, and oral confession; and the introduction of the Mass and baptism in German.

In 1522 Johannes Teuschlein began to preach the message of reform in Rothenburg. Between December 1524 and May 1525 Andreas Bodenstein von Karlstadt stayed in the city, and his radical preaching caused a division in the Lutheran reform movement. Centers of reform agitation were the Franciscan monastery and the Order of the Teutonic Knights, commanded by Kaspar Christian. The schoolmasters Wilhelm Besmeier and Valentin Ickelshamer also supported the cause. From the end of March 1525 an elected committee of citizens ruled alongside the city council and became responsible for church reform. Negotiations with the peasants of the surrounding areas (Heidingsfeld) led in May 1525 to an alliance with the peasants of the Taubertal.

After the defeat of the peasants, Rothenburg was subjected to the punishment of the Swabian League. Teuschlein was executed in July 1525, and the Catholic liturgy was reintroduced. A second attempt at ecclesiastical reform in Rothenburg occurred about 1530. Ten years later the prebendal property of the parishes was confiscated, and its management was placed under the jurisdiction of the administrators. The first evangelical sermon was preached at Saint James' Church in 1544, and one year later the Mass was prohibited. After the Schmalkald War (1545–1546) and the Interim (1548–1552), Rothenburg finally and definitively adopted the Protestant faith. The property of the monasteries and the religious orders was confiscated and redirected for purposes of worship, education, and charity. A new church order was promulgated in 1559. A consistory, headed by a superintendent, was in charge of ecclesiastical affairs. As one of the consequences of this development, the Formula of Concord was signed in Augsburg in 1580.

BIBLIOGRAPHY

Borchardt, Karl. "Die geistlichen Institutionen in der Reichsstadt Rothenburg ob der Tauber und dem zugehörigen Landgebiet von der Anfängen bis zur Reformation." In *Darstellungen aus der fränkischen Geschichte.* Veröffentlichungen der Gesellschaft für fränkische Geschichte, vol. 37, no. 1. Neustadt-Aisch, Germany, 1988. Latest account of church history of and around Rothenburg, based on pertinent archival material and current literature on the history of the Reformation and social history. See especially pp. 725–739.

Schattenmann, Paul. *Die Einführung der Reformation in der ehemaligen Reichsstadt Rothenburg ob der Tauber, 1520–1580.* Munich, 1928. Comprehensive but slightly dated account based on research of primary sources from an orthodox Lutheran perspective.

SIGRID LOOß

Translated from German by Wolfgang Katenz

ROTHMANN, Bernhard (also Bernd; 1495?–1535), Catholic priest, founder in 1532 of the Protestant congregation in Münster, and author of Anabaptist writings (1534–1535). He was born the son of a blacksmith on a farm between Stadtlohn and Gescher in the western part of the diocese of Münster. After Rothmann attended schools in Deventer, Münster, and Alkmar (before 1517), a vicar at the Foundation of Saint Moritz near Münster arranged a position for him as choir singer. Afterward he was a teacher (*ludi magister*) in Warendorf and completed studies in Mainz by earning the title *Magister artium* in 1524. He later became a priest (1529) and chaplain at the church of Saint Moritz.

He was sent to Cologne to study theology but during 1529–1530 stayed in unknown places. After his return to Münster, he began to preach according to Reformation thought and won followers from among the merchants in Münster, who financed for him a trip to Wittenberg (by way of Marburg) during April and May 1531. Since he did not meet Martin Luther, he continued to Strasbourg, where he met with Zwinglians and Sacramentarians. After his return in July 1531, he criticized the ceremonies of the Catholic church. He refused to say Mass for the dead or to hold processions. In September 1531 he protested to the city council of Münster against the preaching of purgatory by Johann of Deventer, a Franciscan preacher in the cathedral of Saint Paul. Rothmann ignored several bans on his own preaching issued by Bishop Friedrich, earl of Wied (1522–1532). At the beginning of January 1532, some of the citizens of Münster requested the authorities to persuade the bishop to lift the ban and permit Rothmann to preach in Münster. This written request, which was the first collection of the teachings of Rothmann on repentance, faith, and works, was printed in Lübeck by Johannes Bugenhagen ("Christlike unde erbare Erthöginge der Börgere tho Münster der evangelischen lere halven," 25 January 1532). Because an imperial mandate had charged the bishop to maintain strictness, Rothmann sought refuge in Münster and was taken into the house of the merchants guild (Kramer). Here he completed his first written confession of faith on 23 January ("Confessionis doctrinae Bernardi Rothmanni polimisthaei Epitome"), which was printed in Cologne (Greek: *polimisthaeum,* "Stadtlohn"). A translation into Low German by city council member Johann Langermann was printed immediately in Münster ("Eyn kortte bekantnisse der lere, so H. Berndt Rothman van Statloen tho Sant Mauritius vör der stat Münster prediget hefft"). Rothmann drew upon a work of Zwingli's for a few passages; otherwise he represented Luther's doctrine.

After a successful public disputation (19 May) with Catholic clerics, Rothmann was supported by the city council, because, as Rothmann often emphasized, it was the duty of civil authorities to protect the proclamation of the true faith in the city. With the help of Protestant preachers sent to Münster by Philipp of Hesse, Lutheran preaching was introduced into six parish churches in August 1532. Rothmann published sixteen articles that designated the ceremonies of the Catholic church to reject. This tract ("Korte anwisunge der missbruch der romischen kerken," August 1532) was printed in German and was distributed outside the city. The list included the Mass, the consecration of water, candles, herbs, images, salt, and oil; the honoring of images of saints; intercession to the saints; processions; and pilgrimages. The Lord's Supper was to be a memorial celebration of the congregation. Because Rothmann distributed wheat bread (commonly called *Stuten*) in place of the host, his opponents called him *Stutenbernd.*

The city council and citizens protected Rothmann's followers during the winter of 1532–1533 in the power struggle with the new bishop, Franz von Waldeck (r. 1532–1553), who had been elected in June. The Treaty of Dülmen (14 February 1533) guaranteed the existence of the Protestant church in Münster. Under assignment by the council, Rothmann drafted a church ordinance, which was introduced in April. The text, which has been only partially preserved, reveals that Rothmann used examples from the ordinances of Basel (1529) and Ulm (1531). Rothmann's ordinance put special value on the doctrines of the Sacrament and baptism, as well as on the free election of pastors by the congregation.

If this form of the church had endured, the Protestantism of Münster would have been adopted in the smaller neighboring cities of the diocese (Warendorf, Coesfeld, Dülmen, Ahlen, and Beckum), which maintained close connections with Rothmann. But the so-called Wassenberg preachers arrived in Münster after having been recently expelled from Jülich. Already in July Rothmann had called on their help as he formulated his answer to the misgivings of the Marburg theologians against his church ordinance ("Wydder antwurt der diener des Evangelii zu Münster," 24 July 1533).

A public disputation in the city hall (August 1533) made

the separation from Luther even clearer, because the five Wassenberg preachers polemicized against infant baptism and a little later refused to administer it. The preachers also placed their signatures under the tract on the sacraments, written by Rothmann in October ("Bekenntnisse van beyden Sacramenten, Doepe unde Nacht-maele, der Predicanten tho Munster," 8 November 1533). In this first clear Anabaptist tract, Rothmann calls infant baptism an idolatry, a cause for the desolation and downfall of the holy church. The date of this "downfall" became important a few years later for establishing the beginning of the restitution.

The prophecies of Melchior Hoffmann, who expected the Last Judgment to occur at the end of 1533, spread from Strasbourg and were known in Münster. Rothmann accepted them. After early November 1533 he was considered no longer Lutheran, and his followers were designated as Anabaptists (*Wedderdoeper*). On 5 January 1534 Rothmann and the Wassenberg preachers received baptism from apostles of Jan Matthijs from Amsterdam, thereby founding the true Church of Christ (*Gemeinde Christi*) at Münster.

During the first weeks of the siege of the city, begun by the bishop in February, Rothmann laid down the basis of the faith in a long tract ("Bekentones des globens und lebens der Gemein Christe zu Monster," March 1534). Afterward Rothmann faded into the background, as the charismatic prophets Jan Matthijs and John of Leiden did not need his theological support. Only when internal difficulties arose as a result of the formidable innovations in the city did the preachers need to explain to the people the introduction of polygyny (summer 1534) and of the Anabaptist kingdom (September). Rothmann now occupied a high position as the keeper of the word in the "court ordinance" of the king. In several voluminous tracts Rothmann established the progressive development of Münster theology, which led from the pacifist Church of Christ, to a monarchical theocracy, and from there to the dictatorial rule of the "New David."

Rothmann's last writings were "Eyne Restitution edder eine wedderstellinge rechter unde gesunder christliker leer, gelovens unde levens uth Gades genaden durch die gemeinte Christi tho Munster an den dach gegeven" (A Restitution or a Restoring of Right and Healthy Christian Doctrine, Faith and Life, Brought to Light from God's Grace through the Church of Christ at Münster; 10 October 1534); "Eyn gantz troestlick bericht van der wrake unde straffe des babilonischen gruwels" (A Thoroughly Comforting Account of the Penalty and Punishment of the Babylonian Horror; December 1534); "Van verborgenheit der schrift des Rykes Christi unde van dem daghe des Heren, durch die gemeinte Christi tho Munster" (Concerning the Hiddenness of the Scripture of the Kingdom of Christ and Concerning the Day of the Lord, through the Church of Christ at Münster; 9 February 1535); and "Van erdesscher unde tytliker gewalt. Bericht uith Gotlyker Schryfft" (Concerning Earthly and Temporal Force. An Account from Divine Scripture; June 1535). This last writing was adressed to Landgrave Philipp of Hesse and was not printed. On 24 June 1535 mercenaries penetrated the city. In battle during the night, Rothmann was probably killed, although his body was never found.

BIBLIOGRAPHY

Primary Source

Stupperich, Robert, ed. *Die Schriften der münsterischen Täufer und ihrer Gegner.* Part 1, *Die Schriften Bernhard Rothmanns.* Münster, 1970. Reprints surviving letters, sermons, disputations, church ordinances, tracts, and broadsides. Further volumes contain opposing writings from the Catholic side (Part 2, 1980) and the Protestant side (Part 3, 1983).

Secondary Sources

Brecht, Martin. "Die Theologie Bernhard Rothmanns." *Jahrbuch für Westfälische Kirchengeschichte* 78 (1985), pp. 49–82. Content and development of Münster theology are presented and analyzed, old partisan and incorrect expositions corrected.

Detmer, Heinrich. *Bilder aus den religiösen und sozialen Unruhen in Münster während des 16. Jahrhunderts.* Vol. 2, *Bernhard Rothmann.* Münster, 1904. Explanatory presentation based on Detmer's earlier writings.

Haller, Bertram. "Bernhard Rothmanns gedruckte Schriften: Ein Bestandsverzeichnis." *Jahrbuch für Westfälische Kirchengeschichte* 78 (1985), pp. 82–102.

Porter, Jack Wallace. *Bernhard Rothmann 1495–1535: Royal Orator of the Munster Anabaptist Kingdom.* Ph.D. diss., University of Wisconsin, 1964. Porter worked with George L. Mosse (Wisconsin) and Robert Stupperich.

Rothert, Hugo. "Bernhard Rothmann." In *Westfälische Lebensbilder,* vol. 1, pp. 384–399. Münster, 1930. The bibliographical account tries especially to explain the character of Rothmann and his transformations.

Verzeichnis der im deutschen Sprachbereich erschienenen Drucke des XVI. Jahrhunderts. Stuttgart, 1983–. See vol. 17, nos. 3300–3308.

Wray, J. "Bernhard Rothmann's Views on the Early Church." In *Reformation Studies: Essays in Honor of Roland H. Bainton,* edited by F. H. Littell, pp. 229–238. Richmond, 1962.

Karl-Heinz Kirchhoff

Translated from German by Jeff Bach

ROUSSEL, Gérard (also Girard; d. 1555), French reformist, chaplain to Marguerite d'Angoulême, and later bishop of Oloron. Born at Vaquerie in northern France, Roussel studied at Paris under Jacques Lefèvre d'Étaples, was a teacher at the College of Cardinal Lemoine (c.1512), and published translations of Aristotle's *Ethics* (c.1516) and Boethius' *Arithmetica* (1521). He joined Lefèvre in the reform movement at Meaux in 1521–1525, becoming a canon of Meaux Cathedral. On the suppression of the Meaux movement in 1525 and facing an arrest warrant, Lefèvre and Roussel fled to Strasbourg, where they admired the Reformed liturgy and teachings. Returning to France after

Francis I's release from captivity in Madrid, Roussel became preacher, confessor, and subsequently chaplain to Marguerite d'Angoulême, the king's sister. From 1530 he was abbot of Clairac. His highly evangelical sermons at the Louvre during Lent 1533 caused a scandal in the Faculty of Theology of Paris, but royal intervention protected him, and it was the leading theologians who were exiled from Paris. Roussel himself, however, was imprisoned for three months for his evangelism.

In 1536 he became bishop of Oloron, in southwest France, and within the realm of Marguerite, now queen of Navarre. This provoked Calvin to publish an open letter of rebuke (the second of *Duae Epistolae*, 1537) to his former friend for not having drawn the right conclusions from his evangelical faith and breaking with Rome. But Roussel was not the self-seeking "nicodemite" Calvin claimed; he was sincerely concerned with reforming the church from within, preached frequently in his diocese, distributed both bread and wine to the laity in the Eucharist, and was much concerned with education. His religious ideas, formulated in his *Familière exposition du simbole, de la loy et oraison dominicale* (c.1549), are close to those of the Reformation: justification by faith, Christ as sole mediator, scripture as supreme authority in the church. The *Exposition* was condemned by the Paris Faculty of Theology in October 1550 and was never published. Roussel's death in 1555 (not 1550 as earlier believed; his will is dated 8 July 1555) was the result of an absurd act of violence: a mad nobleman hacked down the pulpit in which Roussel was preaching, and he died of the injuries he sustained.

BIBLIOGRAPHY

Roussel, Gerard. *Familière exposition du simbole, de la loy et oraison dominicale* (c.1549). Unpubl. manuscript. Bibliothèque Nationale, Paris.

Schmidt, Charles. *Gérard Roussel, prédicateur de la reine Marguerite de Navarre* (1845). Reprint, Geneva, 1970. Still the only published study of Roussel.

FRANCIS HIGMAN

ROVENIUS, Philip (1572–1651), second apostolic vicar of the Holland Mission. Born in 1572 in Deventer, Overijssel, the son of a school rector, Rovenius matriculated in the theology faculty at Louvain in 1592 and subsequently received his ordination as a priest in 1599. Three years later Rovenius was appointed professor in theology and president of the Collegium Atticollense, the seminary for Dutch priests at Cologne. In 1606 he was called to Oldenzaal to become vicar-general of the bishopric of Deventer. After the death of Sasbout Vosmeer, Rovenius was appointed apostolic vicar of the Holland Mission in 1614 and subsequently ordained archbishop of Philippi i.p.i. (1620). With Vosmeer's title, Rovenius also inherited the continuing hostility of the Dutch authorities—which culminated in a trial and verdict of lifelong banishment in 1640—and the ongoing jurisdictional disputes with the Haarlem chapter and the Jesuits. Whereas the conflict with the Haarlem canons was definitely settled in 1616, the jurisdictional struggle with the Society of Jesus continued to drag on despite the *Articuli* of 1610, the foundation of the Congregation de Propaganda Fide in 1622, and the conclusion of a new *Concordia* at Brussels in 1624. These ongoing disputes and his relentless efforts gradually undermined the health of the aging Rovenius. Following the appointment (1640) of the nobleman-priest Jacobus de la Torre (1608?–1661) as coadjutor with the right of succession and consecration as archbishop of Ephesus i.p.i. (1647), Rovenius died in Utrecht on 1 October 1651 at the house of Jvr. Hendrika van Duivenvoorden.

Rovenius was more of a pragmatist than an original thinker. His devotional works, *Het Gulden Wieroockvat* (1620) and *Institutionum Christianae Pietatis Libri Quattor* (1635), were influenced by the Spanish and French devotional tradition represented by Jesuit theologian Diego Alvaraz de Paz (1560–1620) and the Genevan bishop François de Sales (1567–1622). Both works provide practical guidelines for the exercise of virtue in everyday life, including affective prayers and confession, all aimed at the imitation of Christ. The works dealing with jurisdictional issues, *Tractatus de Missionibus* (1624) and *Reipublicae christianae libri duo* (1648), reflect the ideas of the French canonists François Hallier (1595–1659) and Nicolas Lemaitre. Apart from stressing the dignity of Rovenius's position as deputy of the pope, the tracts emphasize the primacy of the pope and the authority of the bishops and priests over the members of the religious orders, who have been incorporated in the hierarchy only *ex commissione*. Finally, other volumes on instruction, liturgy, and discipline, influenced by the bishop of Milan Carlo Borromeo (1538–1584), deal with such reforms as the introduction of a Roman ritual and new catechism (1622), the intensification of the worship of national saints, in particular Boniface and Willbrord, and the creation of vicariate in reaction to the gradual Protestantization of the Utrecht chapter (1633). Building on the pioneering work of Vosmeer. Rovenius was the great organizer of the *Missio Hollandica* and his reforms had lasting effect on the Holland Mission until its dissolution in 1853. Rovenius's works, however, characteristic of the first generation of post-Tridentine reformers, were soon forgotten because of the increasing influence of French pietistic literature in the second half of the seventeenth century.

BIBLIOGRAPHY

Primary Sources

Rovenius, Philip. *Het Gulden Wieroockvat eenen ieghelycken nut ende oorbaar om syn gebeden Godt op te dragen.* Brussels, 1620.

———. *Tractatus de Missionibus ad propagandam fidem et conversionem Infidelium et hereticorum.* Louvain, 1624.

———. *Institutionum Christianae Pietatis Libri Quattor*. Antwerp, 1635.
———. *Officia Sanctorum Archiepiscopatus Ultrajectensis et Episcopatuum suffraganeorum*. Cologne, 1640.
———. *Reipublicae christianae libri duo*. Antwerp, 1648.

Secondary Sources

Cornelissen, J. D. M., ed. *Romeinsche bronnen voor den Kerkelijken Toestand der Nederlanden onder de apostolische vicarissen, 1592–1727: Deel I, 1592–1651*. Rijks Geschiedkundige Publicatien, no. 77. The Hague, 1932. Collection of documents relating to the religious situation in the Netherlands under Vosmeer and Rovenius.

Fruin, R. "De wederopluiking van het katholicisme in Noord-Nederland, omstreeks den aanvang der XVIIe eeuw." In *Verspreide Geschriften*, edited by P. J. Blok, P. L. Muller, and S. Muller, vol. 3, pp. 249–344. The Hague, 1901. Thorough analysis of the Catholic renewal in the northern Netherlands in the early seventeenth century.

Janssen, J. A. M. M., and M. G. Spiertz. *Gids voor de studie van reformatie en katholieke herleving in Nederland, 1520–1650*. The Hague, 1982. Contains a list of the *Relations* (reports) sent to Rome by Vosmeer and Rovenius between 1602 and 1648, as published in modern works and journals; see pp. 114–121.

Jong, J. de. "Het Utrechtsche vicariaat en de strijd over de hierarchische orde in de 17de eeuw." *De Katholiek* 164 (1924), 73–103. Deals with the ambiguous legal position of the apostolic vicar in the church hierarchy.

Jong, J. de, and W. L. S. Knuif. "Rovenius en zijn bestuur der Hollandsche zending." *Archief voor de geschiedenis van het aartsbisdom Utrecht* 50 (1925), 1–410. First, somewhat dated, biography of Rovenius and his administration of the Holland mission.

Rogier, L. J. *Geschiedenis van het katholicisme in Noord-Nederland in de 16e en 17e eeuw*. 2 vols. Amsterdam 1947. Classic, rather biased, general history of Catholicism in the northern Netherlands.

Tracy, James D. "With and Without the Counter-Reformation: The Catholic Church in the Spanish Netherlands and the Dutch Republic, 1580–1650." *Catholic Historical Review* 71 (1985), 547–575. Excellent overview of the historiographical literature since World War II.

Visser, J. *Rovenius und seine Werke: Beitrag zur Geschichte der Nordniederländischen Katholischen Frömmigkeit in der Ersten Hälfte des 17. Jahrhunderts*. Assen, 1966. Thorough study of the works of Rovenius, includes a short biography.

MARCUS P. M. VINK

ROVERE, Giuliano della. *See* Julius II.

ROŽĎALOVSKÝ, Jiřík. *See* Melantrich of Aventin, George.

ROŽMBERK, Vilém and Petr Vok (Ger., Wilhelm Rosenberg; Lat., a Rosis; 1535–1592; also Peter Wok; 1539–1611), Czech statesmen in the Kingdom of Bohemia and protectors of the Catholic clergy (Vilém) and the Czech Unity of Brethren, or Bohemian Brethren (Petr Vok). They were brothers, sons of the Czech lord Jošt III of Rožmberk and the Austrian noblewoman Anna of Rogendorf. As the last "rulers of the House of Rožmberk," they were the most important and wealthiest magnate family in medieval and early modern Bohemia.

Vilém continued the anti-Hussite religious policy of the family, tempered in his case by his partly Protestant education and his political aims. Seeking to restore the preeminence of the Rožmberks in the Bohemian estates against the Lutheran princes of Plauen (1551–1556), Vilém created a powerful group of lords and knights from both Catholic and Utraquist noble families. This group secured the confessional-political stability of Bohemia until 1592 and made it possible for Vilém to obtain the highest offices in the Kingdom of Bohemia and become a rival of Maximilian II in internal and foreign policy. Vilém was an unsuccessful candidate for the throne of Poland in 1572–1575, despite the support of the Polish Protestant nobility. The anti-Habsburg activities of the Bohemian Protestant estates and their goal to legalize the Augsburg or the Bohemian Confession of 1575 threatened Vilém's privileged position and brought him closer to the Habsburgs. He personally made impossible the acceptance of the Bohemian Confession by the Prague diet in 1575 and the reorganization of the confessional-political structure of the kingdom. Vilém's later orientation was more pro-Habsburg (he became a prominent member of the powerful Privy Council in 1577) and pro-Catholic. He supported the Jesuits, especially in his residence at Český Krumlov, and began the re-Catholicization of his serfs. Nevertheless, Vilém became a symbol of tolerant Catholic lordship both for contemporaries and for historiographers of the seventeenth century.

Overshadowed by his elder brother, Petr Vok was the twelfth and last ruler of the Rožmberk house (1592–1611). He was extraordinarily interested in religious questions and had wide contacts with Protestant sovereigns and aristocrats in Austria, Germany, the Netherlands, and England. He described his travels to western Europe in "Die niederlendische raiss," his unpublished diary of 1563, which is stored in the archives of Třeboň. His interest in and extended knowledge of religion was expressed in his personal conversion from Catholicism to Lutheranism, then to Czech Neo-Utraquism, and finally to the Bohemian Brethren. In the 1580s and especially after 1592, he became the most powerful protector of this small but very important pro-Calvinist church. At the beginning of the seventeenth century, Petr Vok supported the Protestant opposition of Bohemian, Moravian, Austrian, Hungarian, and German aristocrats against Rudolf II and Matthias of Habsburg and held secret meetings at his residence at Třeboň. He was elected president of the Estates of Bohemia in 1609. With his political and financial support, the opposition of the estates forced Emperor Rudolf II to recognize the religious liberty of Protestants in Bohemia (Letter of Majesty, 1609). Petr Vok's great legacy to Bohemia was his financial contribution to the pacification of the kingdom and to the foundation of the Protestant gymnasium in the south Bohemian town of Soběslav. Petr Vok supported the publication of theological, historical, and other books in Czech and created at Třeboň castle the largest library in late Renaissance Bohemia (approximately eleven thousand volumes), including a large collection of theological literature. Remnants of the collection can be found at Stockholm, Rome, Prague, and elsewhere.

BIBLIOGRAPHY

Březan, Václav. *Životy posledních Rožmberků* (Biographies of the Last Lords of Rožmberk). 2 vols. Edited by Jaroslav Pánek. Prague, 1985. Critical edition of two biographical works on Vilém and Petr Vok of Rožmberk, compiled by the Rožmberk archivist V. Březan in 1610–1615.

Kavka, František. *Zlatý věk Růží* (The Golden Age of Roses). České Budějovice, 1966. A historical outline of the Rožmberk family in the context of the south Bohemian nobility of the sixteenth century.

Míka, Alois. *Osud slavného domu* (The History of a Famous House). České Budějovice, 1970. A study of the economic and social background of the Rožmberks' religious policies.

Pánek, Jaroslav. "Zwei Arten böhmischen Adelsmäzenatentums in der Zeit Rudolfs II." In *Prag um 1600: Beiträge zur Kunst und Kultur am Hofe Rudolfs II*, pp. 218–231. Freren, Germany, 1988. A summary of the author's studies of the cultural and religious history of the last Rožmberks.

———. *Poslední Rožmberkové: Velmoži České renesance* (The Last Lords of Rožmberk: Magnates of the Bohemian Renaissance). Prague, 1989. The only modern comparative biography of Vilém and Petr Vok of Rožmberk, with a complete bibliography.

JAROSLAV PÁNEK

RUDOLF II

RUDOLF II (1552–1612), Holy Roman Emperor, king of Hungary and Bohemia. The eldest surviving son of Emperor Maximilian II (r. 1564–1576), Rudolf received much of his education in Spain at the court of his second cousin, Philip II, between 1563 and 1571. After he became emperor in 1576, he grew increasingly preoccupied with artistic, scientific, and occult concerns. His court in Prague, where he resided almost continually after 1583, was a center for these activities, drawing to it such figures as the Italian Mannerist Giuseppe Arcimboldo and the mathematician and astronomer Johannes Kepler.

Though Rudolf's religious views were less controversial than those of his father, he was careful not to associate too closely with either papal or Spanish policy. His confessional stance, which combined support for Catholic orthodoxy and receptiveness to Protestant concerns, created mistrust and hostility on both sides in the empire and the Habsburg lands. By 1600 Rudolf had become casual in his observance of Catholic ceremonies. Like his father, he died without receiving the last rites of the church.

Rudolf's inclination to turn the business of government over to local subordinates had serious consequences in Hungary. The efforts of prelates there to suppress Protestantism during the so-called Long Turkish War (1593–1606) provoked an uprising led by the Calvinist nobleman Stephen Bocskay. The 1606 Peace of Vienna, negotiated on Rudolf's behalf by his ambitious younger brother, Archduke Matthias, virtually assured freedom of religion in Hungary. It was the threat of a coup d'état from Matthias, not religious conviction, that led Rudolf to issue the Bohemian Letter of Majesty in 1609. Though assuring primarily the position of the Utraquist faith, the declaration effectively granted religious liberty throughout Bohemia. Similar concessions were made in Silesia, though not in Moravia. Eventually driven by Matthias from all his thrones save in Bohemia, Rudolf died a virtual prisoner in Prague.

BIBLIOGRAPHY

Evans, Robert J. W. *Rudolf II and His World: A Study in Intellectual History, 1576–1612.* Oxford, 1984. Stresses the emperor's cultural environment.

Kaufmann, Thomas DaCosta. *The School of Prague: Painting at the Court of Rudolf II.* Chicago and London, 1988. Scholarly treatment of an important side of Rudolf's reign.

Vocelka, Karl. *Rudolf II und seine Zeit.* Vienna, 1985. Topical introduction, beautifully illustrated, with an excellent bibliography.

PAULA SUTTER FICHTNER

RUIZ DE VIRUÉS, Alonso

RUIZ DE VIRUÉS, Alonso. *See* Virués, Alonso Ruiz de.

RUSSIA

RUSSIA. During the sixteenth and seventeenth centuries "Russia" was synonymous with "Moscovia," or "Muscovy." Although the term *Czardom of All Russia* was officially recognized with the crowning of Ivan IV (1553–1584), it was not the case in practice. Outlying settlements of the eastern Slavs/ethnic Russians extended beyond the borders of Muscovy, reaching well into the kingdom of Poland-Lithuania. Until the Union of Brest in 1596, the eastern Slavs universally belonged to the Russian Orthodox church, which was divided into the metropolis of Moscow (which became a patriarchate after 1589) and the metropolis of Kiev (which had jurisdiction over the Orthodox churches in Poland-Lithuania). To the north and east of the Muscovite czardom lived substantial Finno-Ugric and Turkish-Tatar populations, comprising both Muslims and semi-Christianized pagans.

Given the quickness with which it had spread throughout the neighboring states to the west, it might be considered surprising that the Reformation made little headway into Russia. (The Marxist historian Aleksandr Il'ich Klibanov [*Reformatsionnye dvizheniia v Rossii*, Moscow, 1960] argued that there were indeed "reform movements" in Muscovy—albeit that he presents as evidence any and all religious dissent and criticism directed against the official church from the fourteenth century onward.) Reformist ideas provoked little reaction among the Orthodox hierarchy—the exception being the prosecution of Feodosij Kosoj and others on the grounds of heresy during the mid-1550s—and there are no extant writings on the Reformation by Orthodox theologians. The young Czar Ivan IV was reputed to be open-minded regarding religion, however, and therefore in 1552 King Christian III of Denmark sent along to Moscow a Bible and two other books, presumably the Augsburg Confession and Luther's Small Catechism, for translation into Russian. The conservative Moscow leadership was opposed to tampering with the state church; Ivan IV, meanwhile, in an effort to learn more about the new faith, in 1557 sought to arrange a disputation between the Russian patriarch and the Lutheran archbishop of Uppsala. Those talks ultimately failed, but Ivan IV pursued private religious discussions with numerous foreigners, including the Englishman Jerome Horsey (his personal physician) and the preacher Humphry Cole, who made the articles of faith of the Calvinist church of England accessible to the czar.

Among the public hearings sponsored by the czar, that of 1570 involving Jan Rokyta merits attention. Rokyta, a prominent theologian and the consenior of the Bohemian Brethren in Poland, had accompanied a Polish delegation as preacher. His hope of lecturing in Moscow on his teachings was fulfilled spectacularly in two disputations. At the conclusion, the czar gave Rokyta a written statement that was soon translated into Latin, Polish, and German and that brought on anti-Reformation polemic in Russia.

The marriage of Czar Ivan IV's niece to his Danish vassal Duke Magnus of Oesel marked the first such Lutheran-Orthodox union in Russia. In the meantime, many Russians must have been exposed to Protestantism—apparently without being much affected by it—as a result of the Livonian War (1558–1582) and the arrival of tens of thousands of Protestant prisoners (particularly in 1558 and 1565, when the German population of Dorpat/Tartu [Estonia] was deported en masse, chiefly to Moscow and Nizhnii-Novgorod). Lutheran preachers certainly entered Russia during this period, including Tilman Brakel, who published his Russian experiences in 1579, and Johann Wettermann, who was close to the czar. German Lutherans were among Czar Ivan IV's political advisers, and for a time, mindful of his religious interests, they hoped to win him over to the Reformation. There was a Protestant parish—temporarily granted the use of its own church by the czar—in the "German suburb" of Moscow. The Protestant colony in Moscow prospered under czars Feodor (r. 1584–1598) and Boris (r. 1598–1605) and experienced setbacks under the Romanovs (r. from 1613); finally, however, it inspired the young Peter the Great (r. 1689–1725) to Europeanize Russia.

The one Russian who might be termed a reformer was Feodosij (called Kosoj, "the cross-eyed"), a serf from Moscow who escaped from his Boyar master and entered a monastery. He was condemned as a heretic in 1554 and was placed under confinement. Around 1555 he fled to Vitebsk in White Russia, where he married and from which he spread his "new teachings." Because he published nothing, the content and influence of his message are known only at second hand. According to Andreas Wengerscius (*Libri Quatuor Slavoniae reformatae*, Amsterdam, 1679, p. 262), Feodosij preached the "invocation of the one God through Christ and with the help of the Holy Spirit." The Orthodox polemic directed against him suggested that Feodosij disseminated Calvinist, even antitrinitarian ideas. He rejected the official church, with all its rituals, ecclesiastical traditions, and its hierarchical teaching profession. The learned monk Zinovij, who in 1566 wrote the long "Explanation of Truth"—a theological refutation of Feodosij from the Orthodox standpoint—claimed that "the entire Orient has been ruined by Muhammad, the West by Martin the German; Lithuania, however, by Kosoj" (*Istiny pokazanie k voprosivshim o novom utchenii*, Kazan, 1863, p. 49). Feodosij's "new teachings" rested upon written proof from the "pillar books" (*stolpovye knigi*), as he called them. Contrary to Orthodox custom, "he carries the books in his hand, opens them and provides the scripture for each to read himself—he interprets these books" (Zinovij, p. 42). In the kingdom of Poland-Lithuania, the monolingual Feodosij could reach only the Russian population, yet the breadth of his influence must not be underestimated. Zinovij polemicized against Feodosij's followers in northwestern Russia, and in the 1560s he wrote (probably from the northeastern Russian city of Suzdal) an "epistle against the Lutherans" that was in fact an attack on the teachings of Feodosij. In Lithuania, meanwhile, Prince Andrej Kurbskij polemicized against Feodosij's followers among the White Russian nobility. It should be borne in mind, however, that the isolated world of the Russian villages and small towns offered no public on the scale of the middle European urban landscape, not least because of the absence of printing presses.

BIBLIOGRAPHY

Amburger, Erik. *Geschichte des Protestantismus in Rußland.* Stuttgart, 1961.

Fechner, J. W. *Chronik der evangelischen Gemeinden in Moskau: Zum dreihundertjährigen Jubiläum der evangelisch-lutherischen St. Michaelis-Gemeinde zusammengestellt.* Moscow, 1876. See vol. 1. Still the basic chronological collection of sources, with critical commentary.

Mainka, Rudolf M. *Zinovij von Oten': Ein russischer Polemiker und Theologe der Mitte des 16. Jahrhunderts.* Rome, 1961. Pointed Catholic perspective. Emphasizes the theology of Zinovij rather than the teachings of Feodosij.

Müller, Ludolf. *Die Kritik des Protestantismus in der russischen Theologie vom 16. bis zum 18. Jahrhundert.* Wiesbaden, 1951.

Tumins, Valerie A. *Tsar Ivan IV's Reply to Jan Rokyta.* The Hague, 1971. Supplements the author's dissertation on the same topic, Cambridge, 1959. Russian and Polish texts with English translation and bibliography.

Wegierski, Andrej. *Libri Quattuor Slavoniae Reformatae.* Biblioteka Pisarzy reformacyjnych, no. 11. Warsaw, 1973.

Frank Kaempfer

Translated from German by Susan M. Sisler

RYCKE, Hans de. *See* Ries, Hans de.

RYDEMAN, Peter. *See* Riedemann, Peter.

RYS, Hans de. *See* Ries, Hans de.

RYTHOVIUS, Maarten van. *See* Riethoven, Maarten.

S

SABBATARIANISM. Those who rejected the Christian Sunday in favor of the Jewish Sabbath (Saturday) were part of a movement whose significance lies in the fact that while the major reformers were calling for persecution of the Jewish faith, Sabbatarians were seeking positive interaction between Christianity and Judaism. There were two manifestations of this teaching in the sixteenth century. The earliest appeared as a radical faction of Anabaptism in Silesia and Moravia between 1527 and about 1540, against which Martin Luther wrote his *Wider die Sabbather* in 1538. Led by Oswald Glaidt and Andreas Fischer, this small group was heavily influenced by a chiliastic interpretation of Anabaptism. We do not know much about the inner life of these Sabbatarians. We may speculate that they carried on an active, joyful, and loud style of worship. There are some cryptic hints that marital scandal was present in the group. Mentioned scornfully in this regard is Fischer's attempt to institute the Mosaic *Scheidtbrief*, that is, the letter of divorcement. Some Anabaptist groups taught that one ought not to be "unequally yoked." Therefore, divorce from unbelieving spouses was not only permitted but encouraged. In certain instances, particularly those in which chiliastic excesses became the norm, marital irregularities occurred. If these Anabaptists believed Hans Hut's predictions of the apocalypse for Pentecost 1528, we have a good basis for suggesting that marital irregularities became trivialized in eschatological expectation. When the world did not end, they were left with a problem. Fischer stepped into this crisis. He not only formulated a foundational defense of Sabbatarian practice that was not dependent on chiliastic speculation, but he also used Mosaic customs to help bring order to a community that had been moved beyond the boundaries of acceptable Christian marital practices.

A second manifestation of Sabbatarianism occurred as a radical wing of the Unitarian movement in Transylvania beginning in 1588. These Sabbatarians believed that they continued the spirit of the Unitarian bishop Francis Dávid, who had been condemned to life in prison for rejecting the adoration of Christ. Led by the Szekler nobleman Andreas Eőssi, these Sabbatarians taught that the Christian New Testament, like the Jewish Talmud, is commentary on the law of God, which is eternal. "Law" meant the Ten Commandments and some dietary proscriptions. In obedience to the law and by faith in Christ, gentiles became "adopted" Hebrews, enjoying the same relationship with God as is enjoyed by the chosen people, the Jews.

For some thirty years these Sabbatarians remained within the Unitarian church and carried on their Sabbath services at various locations. By 1623 the Unitarians were forced to expel them, and from that point on they suffered extreme persecution. Eőssi's adopted son, Simon Péchi, translated Jewish prayer books and other sources and led these Sabbatarians into increasingly Jewish beliefs and practices. By 1640 the Sabbatarians were supposedly wiped out altogether. Yet they carried on their practices in secret, outwardly adhering to one of the four officially recognized religions, Unitarianism, Catholicism, Lutheranism, and Reformed. When detected, they "recanted" and carried on as before, or fled to Muslim lands. Laws and edicts against Judaizers and Sabbatarians appeared regularly every generation or two.

At long last, in 1867, the emancipation of the Jews was proclaimed in the Austro-Hungarian empire. Jews were to have full citizenship rights and the Jewish religion was legally recognized. Against all odds, and after some 230 years of secrecy, some 40 Hungarian families, about 180 people, stepped forward from each of the four accepted Christian religions and asked to be legally recognized as "of the Jewish faith." This status was granted them, and in the town of Bözödujfálu a "proselyte" Jewish synagogue was erected.

This lasted only until the German occupation in 1941. The Nazis offered these "Jews" the choice to reconvert to Christianity or face deportation with the rest of Transylvania's Jews. About half chose deportation. To "prove" the sincerity of the rest, the Germans demanded that they burn down their synagogue. Thus ended one of the most unusual chapters among Reformation religious movements.

BIBLIOGRAPHY

Kohn, Samuel. *A Szómbatosók: Történetük, Dógmatikajük és Irodálmük* (The Sabbatarians: Their History, Dogmas and Writings). Budapest, 1889. Because very little has been written on Sabbatarians of the Reformation period, this book remains the definitive secondary source for the Transylvanian group. Although long out of print, it was widely distributed at the time of its publication and is available from most European research libraries.

Liechty, Daniel. *Andreas Fischer and the Sabbatarian Anabaptists*. Scottdale, Pa., 1988. The best source, extensively documented, for Sabbatarian Anabaptism.

———. *Sabbatarianism in the Sixteenth Century*. Berrien Springs,

Mich., 1993. The only comprehensive treatment of continental Sabbatarianism in English.

Pakózday, Lászlo. *Der siebenbürgische Sabbatismus*. Stuttgart, 1973. This small booklet presents a series of lectures for which Kohn's book was the main source. By no means as extensive as Kohn's work, it is more accessible in North America and written in German.

DANIEL LIECHTY

SACHS, Hans (1494–1576), shoemaker-poet of Nuremberg, prolific versifier, leading Meistersinger, and popular propagandist for the Lutheran Reformation. Born into an artisan family, he had eight years of Latin school before being apprenticed at age fifteen to the shoemaker's trade. At the same time, he was introduced by the weaver Lienhard Nunnenbeck to the art of mastersinging, a craftlike method for writing and performing verse and melody, the tradesmen-practitioners of which formed associations in German cities. From 1511 to 1516 Sachs traveled through Germany as a journeyman. He then settled in his hometown, married, had seven children (none survived him), became master (in 1520), and began an astonishing literary production that, in his own preliminary reckoning in 1567 (*Summa all meiner gedicht*), included over four thousand mastersongs, more than two hundred dramas and carnival plays, and some two thousand didactic poems in rhyming couplets, in addition to prose dialogues, tales, fables, and assorted verses.

Essentially an autodidact, Sachs processed an enormous amount of reading into his writings. Principally aimed at his fellow artisans—the majority of Nuremberg's population—these writings adapted the "high" culture of the Bible, Roman classics, history, and the Italian Renaissance to the reality of common experience, stressing in a heavily didactic manner the correct moral choices to be made for the sake of social peace and fairness in people's private dealings. They excoriate self-interest, envy, greed, social climbing, and the desire for power over others and praise moderation, equity, faithfulness, and devotion to the common weal.

In 1520 Sachs discovered Martin Luther, and from then on he made the reformer's cause his own. His first publication as an advocate of the Reformation was *The Wittenberg Nightingale*, a long didactic poem with a rousing opening line, "Sleepers awake! A new day is dawning." Written in 1523 after several years of apparently intense study (he owned forty Lutheran books and tracts by 1522), it was his most famous work, reprinted many times as a popular summary of Reformation teachings and a call for conversion to them. There followed church hymns, psalms, poems, plays, and entertainments based on the Old and New Testaments, as well as several dialogues in prose, an untried form in the vernacular literature at the time but a powerful tool for disseminating ideas and opinions. Unhesitatingly accepting Luther's *sola fide* and *sola scriptura*, Sachs was inventive in finding ways of popularizing and dramatizing these and other Lutheran doctrines.

To the extent that his partisanship touched political issues, Sachs's was not always a welcome voice to the Lutheran, but highly cautious, authorities of his city. Frequently in trouble with them, he was put under a publication ban in 1527 for having written some viciously antipapal verses. His public acclaim, on the other hand, was solid. Critics have pointed to the lack of artistic development in his huge output over a long life, but this is precisely what assured him of his popularity among his own kind. He was a purveyor of simple messages, steadfastly repeated and often preachy, but always conveyed through lifelike situations and in plain and vivid language.

BIBLIOGRAPHY

Balzer, Bernd. *Bürgerliche Reformationspropaganda: Die Flugschriften des Hans Sachs in den Jahren 1523–1525*. Stuttgart, 1973.

Bernstein, Eckhard. *Hans Sachs*. Reinbeck, 1993.

Brunner, Horst, et al., eds. *Hans Sachs und Nürnberg: Bedingungen und Probleme reichsstädtischer Literatur*. Nuremberg, 1976.

Könneker, Barbara. *Hans Sachs*. Stuttgart, 1971.

Strauss, Gerald. *Nuremberg in the Sixteenth Century*. Bloomington, Ind., 1976.

GERALD STRAUSS

SACK OF ROME. This event began with the storming of the city's walls by the troops of Emperor Charles V shortly after dawn on 6 May 1527. Seven months later, when Pope Clement VII was finally able to ransom himself and flee to Orvieto (7 December), Rome had been reduced to a depopulated shell, despoiled of its treasures, decimated by famine and disease, and repeatedly ravaged by soldiers. Nothing was spared, least of all convents and churches. At the height of the sack the Venetian ambassador had grimly reported that hell itself must have been a prettier sight.

Charles V laid the blame on the pope for joining with France and Venice in the League of Cognac (1526), whose real purpose was to expel the imperial forces from Lombardy. His view was advanced in the *das en Roma* Dipolemic written by his Latin secretary, Alfonso de Valdés, the *Diálogo de Lactancio y un arcediano* (Dialogue of Lactancio and an Archdeacon). While the emperor may not have authorized an attack on Rome, his habitual disposition to let warfare in Italy pay for itself certainly aggravated the course of events. On 13 March 1527, after eight months of desultory fighting with the army of the league, the unpaid, famished, and mutinous imperial troops under the command of Charles, duke of Bourbon, demanded their pay, or at least an opportunity to sack Florence. Foiled by the timely arrival of the league's forces in Florence, the troops were persuaded by their leaders to make a dash for poorly defended Rome. Charles himself was killed by the ball of an arquebus during the assault (a shot later claimed by Benvenuto Cellini) and replaced in nominal command by Philibert, prince of Orange. It became clear, however, when the pope relinquished the castle of Sant' Ángelo on 7 June, that he was the prisoner not of the emperor or his commanders but of the soldiers.

Luther had often predicted Rome's destruction, and for the many Lutherans among the *Landsknechts* in the imperial army the sack represented a religious mission. They had been recruited and led to Italy by Georg von Frundsberg, who often displayed a golden cord with which he boasted he would hang the pope. Quartered in the Vatican, the Lutherans took particular satisfaction in deriding and destroying relics. Nonetheless contemporaries observed that the cruelest of the troops were not the Germans but the Spanish regulars. Although many Protestants and not a few Catholics, including the pope himself, saw in Rome's ordeal a punishment for its sins, most of Europe adopted Erasmus's attitude that the sack was a catastrophe for civilization. It heralded the end of the high Renaissance in Rome. Despite the pope's Palm Sunday (1528) sermon stressing the need for reform, however, the sack did not bring to an end the ecclesiastical abuses denounced by the reformers. Nor were the diplomatic consequences lasting. Pope and emperor soon entered into an alliance formalized by the Treaty of Barcelona (1529).

[*See also* Clement VII.]

BIBLIOGRAPHY

Chastel, André. *The Sack of Rome, 1527*. Translated by Beth Archer. A. W. Mellon Lectures in the Fine Arts. Princeton, 1983. Traces impact of the sack on the arts.

Hook, Judith. *The Sack of Rome, 1527*. London, 1972.

Guicciardini, Luigi. *The Sack of Rome*. Edited and translated by McGregor. New York, 1993. A contemporary account by a brother of the famous historian.

Longhurst, John E., ed. and trans. *Alfonso de Valdés and the Sack of Rome: Dialogue of Lactancio and an Archdeacon*. Albuquerque, 1952.

T. C. Price Zimmermann

SACRAMENTALS.

As used in the late medieval and early modern Catholic church, sacramentals encompassed a variety of sacred signs, rites, blessings, prayers, symbolic gestures, ceremonies, and objects. Those most commonly encountered in the daily life of most late medieval Christians were various forms of blessed water and salt, the *Agnus Dei* (a small wax wafer bearing the insignia of the Lamb of God), and objects blessed on appropriate feast days: palms on Palm Sunday; ashes on Ash Wednesday; candles and herbs, respectively, on the feasts of the Purification and Assumption of the Virgin; and bread on Saint Agatha's Day and sometimes during the Mass. In a more restricted sense the term was applied to objects consecrated for use in the liturgy, especially in connection with the administration of the sacraments, such as an altar or a chalice, or the chrism used for consecration in conferring confirmation, holy orders, or the last rites. The conferral of a clerical tonsure as a form of consecration was also considered a sacramental.

The notion of a sacramental emerged only gradually in the twelfth and thirteenth centuries as theologians, such as Hugh of St. Victor and Peter Abelard, began to give closer attention to the understanding of what constituted a sacrament. Until that time the term *sacrament* was applied indiscriminately to designate both sacraments and sacramentals. Gradually a distinction emerged between those religious ceremonies that were held to be necessary to human salvation (*sacramenta*) and those that were not (*sacramentalia*). A further differentiation followed between objects and actions linked to the preparation and administration of the sacraments and those merely relating to veneration and piety. It was in this last category that sacramentals began to proliferate in the late Middle Ages. The peculiar character of sacramentals derived from the power of the church to consecrate or bless, and the term was often applied both to the acts of blessing and to the persons or objects so blessed. A further dimension derived from the power of the church to exorcise demonic spirits, and most sacramentals were created through a twofold rite of exorcism and blessing.

Sacramentals provide a major example of the difficult relations between official and popular belief. Theological imprecision about their definition, as well as popular demand for an instrumental application of the church's powers to bless and exorcise, enabled them to fall into a shadowy area between approved religious practices and magic. That the clergy often gave in to such demands can be seen in the wide range of persons, actions, and objects blessed as sacramentals. Besides those mentioned above, one can find in ritual books blessings of cattle, homes, granaries, threshing floors, hearths, wine, grain, beer, seed, and even radishes. When pious images (especially the crucifix) were blessed, they became sacramentals. Much of the ambiguity of sacramentals flowed from problems in understanding their efficacy. Unlike the sacraments, which contributed to human salvation, sacramentals were an aid only to this-worldly spiritual formation; yet, like the sacraments, they could also bring temporal benefits. In theory sacraments were automatically efficacious, working *ex opere operato*, by virtue of the ritual itself; sacramentals worked *ex opere operandis*, by virtue of the pious dispositions of those using them. Thus, they were not thought to be automatically efficacious, but ordinary Christians (and often the clergy) regarded them as if they were. Theologically, part of this difficulty flowed from the notion that temporal benefits were conferred by the power of the church to expel demonic forces (which caused disorder in the natural world) and to bless objects such that they were safe and beneficial for human use. Thus, ordinary believers were able to treat such blessed objects as forms of protection against material harm and the demonic and to hope for material benefits from them. Usually the sacraments, especially the Eucharist, were carefully policed against magical misuse, but once sacramental objects had been blessed by a priest, there was really no control over the uses to which they were put. They became, in effect, a do-it-yourself form of appropriation of sacred power, used most frequently as a form of protective magic for the good of humans, animals, and valued property.

For the reformers sacramentals embodied all the crassness and false belief (*superstitio*) of late medieval religion. They held that Christ's unique act of redemption had blessed everything in creation and that further blessing was unnecessary, indeed a denial of faith. Martin Luther directed his attack against blessed water, most commonly used as a form of magical protection, but this was merely representative of the whole class of sacramentals. It did not take long before such blessings were stigmatized as a form of magic; in 1543 the Württemberg pastor Johann Spreter classified them as "magic on the right hand," as opposed to magical incantations, which were "magic on the left hand." The Counter-Reformation attempted to provide closer definition of sacramentals and to remove some of their theological ambiguity but without great success, and their undoubted popularity was such that their use was impossible to eradicate. Indeed, the range and number of sacramentals even increased, and the ambivalence about their efficacy has lasted into the modern Catholic church. They clearly fulfilled an important function—a means of coping with the anxieties of daily life by the instrumental application of sacred power. It was this aspect that even led convinced Protestants to regard them with a certain nostalgia, and some Protestants sought to gain access to Catholic sacramentals, especially holy water. The desire for some form of sacred blessing even led to the emergence in the Lutheran church of a range of consecrated objects, which could be said to represent a weak echo of Catholic sacramentals. These forms of consecration or blessing provided items or actions accorded especial veneration and therefore were susceptible to "superstitious" uses. Such practices in popular Protestantism proved an embarrassment for Protestant commentators, even into the nineteenth century, who admitted that evangelical notions of benediction were permeated with Catholic presuppositions.

[*See also* Devotional Practices; Piety; Popular Religion; *and* Sacraments.]

BIBLIOGRAPHY

Achelis, E. Ch. "Benediktionen." In *Realencyklopädie für protestantische Theologie und Kirche,* edited by A. Hauck, vol. 2, pp. 588–591. Leipzig, 1897.

Davies, John Gordon. "Benediktionen III." In *Theologische Realenzyklopädie,* vol. 5, pp. 564–573. Berlin and New York, 1980.

Duffy, Eamon. *The Stripping of the Altars: Traditional Religion in England.* New Haven, 1992. See pp. 281–282 on the importance for late-medieval popular religion.

Franz, Adolf. *Die kirchliche Benediktionen im Mittelalter* (1909). 2 vols. Reprint, Graz, 1960. Contains the most detailed discussion.

Kawerau, G. "Exorcisme." In *Realencyklopädie für protestantische Theologie und Kirche,* edited by A. Hauck, vol. 5. pp. 695–700. Leipzig, 1898.

Löhrer, M. "Sakramentalien." In *Sacramentum Mundi. Theologisches Lexikon für die Praxis,* edited by K. Rahner, vol. 4, pp. 342—347. Freiburg i.B., 1969. For the modern position.

Neidhart, Walter. "Exorzismus III." In *Theologische Realenzyklopädie,* vol. 10, pp. 756–760. Berlin and New York, 1982.

Quinn, J. R. "Blessings, liturgical." In *New Catholic Encyclopedia,* vol. 2, pp. 613–615. New York, 1967.

———. "Sacramentals." In *New Catholic Encyclopedia,* vol. 12, pp. 790–793. New York, 1967. For the modern position.

Reifenberg, Hermann. *Sakramente, Sakramentalien und Ritualien im Bistum Mainz seit dem Spätmittelalter.* 2 vols. Münster, 1971–1972.

Scribner, Robert W. "Ritual and Popular Religion in Catholic Germany at the Time of the Reformation." In *Popular Culture and Popular Movements in Reformation Germany,* pp. 19–49. London and Ronceverte, W.Va., 1987.

Thomas, Keith. *Religion and the Decline of Magic.* London, 1971. Emphasizes importance for late-medieval religion.

ROBERT W. SCRIBNER

SACRAMENTARIANS. The term *Sacramentarian* refers to a person who denies the salvific significance of any of the sacraments of the church. It was widely used during the Reformation as a designation especially for those who denied the corporeal presence of Christ in the eucharistic elements or who belittled the Eucharist in any way. Martin Luther, therefore, branded Andreas Bodenstein von Karlstadt, Martin Bucer, Huldrych Zwingli, and Johannes Oecolampadius, among others, as Sacramentarians for their interpretation of the Eucharist as a symbol. While Luther rejected the medieval view of transubstantiation, his view retained the essence of the real presence of Christ in the Eucharist. In using the term *Sacramentarian* for his Protestant opponents, Luther was drawing on a medieval theological tradition that had discredited the symbolic interpretation of the Eucharist as heresy. Nevertheless, the sacramental view was incorporated into the Helvetic Confessions and has been an integral element in Reformed Protestantism.

In the Netherlands a spiritual teaching concerning the sacraments, and especially the Eucharist, reached back to at least the thirteenth century. It was strongly present in the environment before the Reformation, and this clearly had an influence on the Dutch acceptance of Reformed theology over Lutheranism. Sacramentarianism was most often represented by a humanistic spirituality to which even reform-minded Catholics, such as Desiderius Erasmus, were attracted. When coupled with apocalyptic spirituality, however, the teaching would sometimes issue in iconoclastic attacks on the symbols of the church. Between 1524 and 1530 many of those who would later become involved in Anabaptism were numbered among the Sacramentarians. Most well known of these was David Joris, who in 1528 led an attack on the image of the Virgin in Delft. For this he was scourged, had his tongue bored, and was sent into exile. Dutch Anabaptism retained a strongly sacramentarian spirit that was not confined to the Eucharist. Most Sacramentarians, however, found their way into more politically conservative expressions of religion. Sacramentarianism remained a focal issue in the divisions within Protestantism for centuries to come.

BIBLIOGRAPHY

Bainton, Roland H. *Studies on the Reformation.* Boston, 1963. Remains an excellent source for an overview of the "Swiss" Sacramentarians and the issues involved in their opposition to Luther.

Williams, George H. *The Radical Reformation.* 3d ed. Kirksville, Mo., 1992. Encyclopedic survey of radical movements within the Reformation. Chapters 2, 3, and 12 are especially informative concerning Sacramentarians.

DANIEL LIECHTY

SACRAMENTS.

Reformation controversies over the sacraments were rooted in a common medieval heritage of theology and liturgy. The diversity in this heritage became church-dividing, as each reform movement reread the tradition in light of its own theological and pastoral commitments. Thus, Reformation understandings of the sacraments cannot be isolated from the complex interplay of the received tradition with late medieval social and political developments. The received tradition included the trinitarian and christological dogmas of the early church, the influence of Arianism, and the controversy between Nestorius (d. about 451) and Cyril of Alexandria (d. 444). Also important were the responses of Augustine (d. 430) to the Donatists and Pelagians. Throughout these early controversies the guiding motif for the orthodox was that salvation is not achieved but received. In terms of sacramental theology this meant that the sacraments are primarily God's gifts, not human works. What made the sixteenth-century controversies so bitter was the universal conviction that to be right about the sacraments was to be right about God and salvation. Hence, Reformation understandings of the sacraments included not only the vocabulary of theology but the vocabulary of theological actions. In the words of R. W. Scribner (*Popular Culture and Popular Movements in Reformation Germany*, London, 1987), "The Reformation was in this sense fundamentally a ritual process."

The Medieval Heritage. The early Christian community initiated members through baptism and centered its worship in the celebration of the Eucharist (Greek: *eucharistia*, "thanksgiving") but only gradually classified these and other ritual activities under the general concept of sacrament. The concept of sacrament developed from the Latin translation of the Greek *mysterion* ("mystery") by *sacramentum.* In classical Latin this meant a soldier's oath of allegiance (*sacramentum militare*) accompanied by the concrete symbol (*signum*) of a tattoo. Hence, Tertullian (d. about 225) spoke of baptism as the beginning of the *militia Christi* and the early church referred to baptism as the "Lord's seal." From Augustine through Thomas Aquinas (d. 1274) the particular sacraments of baptism, confirmation, and ordination were understood to imprint an indelible character (*character indelebilis*) on the soul. Since this character remains in spite of the gravest sins, these sacraments are received only once.

Liturgical activity, the context for the sacraments as signs of holy things, stimulated the theological drive to define the sacraments. This relation of praxis to theory is indicated already in the fifth-century axiom that prayer establishes belief (*lex orandi lex credendi*).

Augustine provided two important premises to Western sacramental theology: Christian rituals are forms of God's word of promise ("The word comes to the element; and so there is a sacrament, that is, a sort of visible word"), and the validity of the sacrament does not depend upon the administrant. The latter countered the Donatist (a North African church renewal movement) claim that sacraments administered by unworthy priests were invalid. Augustine emphasized that the grace of God is independent of the subjective attitudes and holiness of the minister. By the early thirteenth century this objective action of the sacraments would be expressed in the phrase *ex opere operato*—that is, the sacraments are effective through the operation of the rite itself. From a pastoral perspective, later shared by Martin Luther, this indicates the certainty of sacramental grace in spite of the communicant's doubts of worthiness.

The understanding of sacraments as "signs of holy things" included a number of ritual actions, which the medieval church gradually reduced to seven sacraments. As late as the twelfth century there were varying lists of sacraments. The Gregorian reformer Peter Damian (d. 1072) counted twelve (baptism, confirmation, anointing of the sick, consecration of bishops, anointing of kings, consecration of churches, confession, marriage and the consecrations of canonists, monks, hermits, and nuns) but omitted the Eucharist and penance. Hugh of Saint Victor (d. 1141), author of a major work on the sacraments, listed as many as thirty. Peter Lombard (d. 1160), author of the *Four Books of Sentences*, which became the standard textbook of theology in the Middle Ages, fixed the number of sacraments at the seven still recognized within the Roman Catholic communion. His list of baptism, confirmation, Eucharist, penance, extreme unction, orders, and marriage, accepted by Thomas from the perspective that they reflect the stages of life, was formally affirmed in the "Instruction for the Armenians" (Council of Florence, 1439). It was reaffirmed at the Council of Trent (1545–1563) from the perspective that these seven had been divinely instituted by Christ.

Medieval life and doctrine consistently focused on the sacraments of baptism, penance, and the Eucharist. These became controversial to the extent of church-dividing in the Reformation, but during the medieval period it was the Eucharist that sparked controversies. These controversies were intertwined with diverse theologies from the early church and developing liturgical practices.

Augustine defined sacrament as the "visible word." In relation to baptism he said, "Take away the word, and the water is neither more nor less than water." In the Eucharist the word was the institution attributed to Jesus in the New Testament accounts of the Last Supper, while the elements were the bread and wine. Influenced by neoplatonic philosophy, Augustine could refer to the bread as the "sign" or "image" of the body of Christ. This symbolic theology of the sacrament was influential in the development of the Roman liturgy.

Realist or "metabolic" (Greek: *metabolé*, "transmutation") theology stemming from Ambrose (d. 397) was influential in the liturgical developments in Spain and Gaul. Ambrose wrote of the "transmutation" of the elements of bread and wine into the flesh and blood of Christ, by virtue of the words of consecration. This foreshadowed later scholastic developments toward transubstantiation. From the time of Isidore of Seville (d. 636), the understanding of the Eucharist shifted from community in union with Christ who gives thanks to the Father for salvation, to the real presence of Christ, who in the consecration descends from heaven. The focus upon the real presence was burdened by the tension between the metabolism of Ambrose and the symbolism of Augustine. This tension increased as Germanic thinking was less and less able to understand the platonic relation between symbol and reality and as the dramatic action of the congregation was being displaced by a dramatic spectacle for the congregation.

The Carolingian introduction of the Roman liturgy into the Frankish kingdom, as well as the imperial interest in liturgical uniformity and education, raised awareness of the tensions between the liturgies influenced by the theologies of Augustine and Ambrose. The first doctrinal treatment of the Eucharist in this context was by the Benedictine monk Paschasius Radbertus (d. 865) of Corbie. A version of his *De Corpore et Sanguine Domini* (831) was presented to emperor Charles II ("the Bald") in 844. Paschasius emphasized the identity of the body and blood of the Lord in the Sacrament with the earthly and risen body of Christ.

Charles then requested an intepretation from another monk of Corbie, Ratramnus (d. 868). Ratramnus took the more Augustinian emphasis of the Eucharist as an effective sign of Christ's presence and did not identify the elements of bread and wine with the risen, earthly body of Christ. Indeed, Ratramnus foreshadowed the sacramentarian and Zwinglian concerns of the sixteenth century when he contested the corporeal eating with the arguments that Christ has ascended to heaven and that it is the Holy Spirit, not the flesh, that gives life (*Jn.* 6:63). His Latin treatise influenced Berengar of Tours (d. 1008) and was reprinted under the name Bertram by Swiss and English reformers of Zwinglian and Calvinist persuasion.

The controversy that erupted over the eucharistic theology of Berengar provided the framework for subsequent medieval and Reformation discussions of the Sacrament. Berengar's claim that the reception of Christ in the Eucharist can be only a spiritual reception, a faithful recollection of the mystery of Christ's passion and resurrection, is similar to the later memorial theologies of the Sacrament advanced by Andreas Bodenstein von Karlstadt (d. 1541), Huldrych Zwingli (d. 1531), and the Sacramentarians.

Berengar's position was widely opposed and condemned. In 1059 at Rome he was forced to sign a formula by Cardinal Humbert (d. 1061) that "the bread and wine placed on the altar are, after consecration, not only a sacrament, but also the true body and blood of our Lord Jesus Christ, . . . are sensibly, not only sacramentally but in truth, handled by the hands of the priests and crushed by the teeth of the faithful."

The opposition to Berengar was not only led by the most powerful theologians and ecclesiastics of the time but also reflected popular piety and liturgical practice. Theologically, Berengar's view that Christ was not substantially present in the Eucharist was perceived to undermine salvation. Furthermore, Berengar's understanding of the Eucharist as a symbolic meal in which the believer through his willful memory unites with Christ was the sacramental analogy to the Arian claim that Christ unites with the Father through his will. Against this Humbert affirmed that the believer is united with Christ because Christ's substantial presence is mediated in the Eucharist. The imagery used here has been termed metabolic because, as Paschasius stated, "we become part of Christ because we eat him."

The Berengar controversy raised the question of how the bread and wine become the actual body and blood of Christ. This question led to the doctrine of transubstantiation (Fourth Lateran Council, 1215), focused the theology of the Eucharist increasingly on Christ, and encouraged the view that the Sacrament contained grace as a bottle contains medicine. These developments contributed to the phenomenon, beginning in the twelfth century, of popular devotion to Christ in the Eucharist.

Visions and miracle stories surrounding the Sacrament proliferated; for example, the stolen Host (Latin: *hostia*, "a sacrificial victim") became bloody flesh, and Christ as he existed in the Sacrament became the greatest of all relics. Popular piety influenced liturgical practices, such as burning a perpetual light before the reserved species, ringing bells to signal the consecration and elevation of the Host. In 1264 the Feast of Corpus Christi, the commemoration of the institution of the Eucharist, was commanded by Pope Urban IV, largely owing to the influence of the visions of Juliana (d. 1258), a nun of Liège. By the eve of the Reformation, Corpus Christi processions had become popular ritual reaffirmations of community solidarity to the extent of displacing the early church's sense of communion in the Eucharist.

People adored the Host and brought their petitions to it. The Sacrament was so revered that frequency of reception declined drastically; the sight of the Host alone was a devotional substitute for reception. In response to the laity's fears of spilling God's blood, the doctrine of concomitance (Council of Constance, 1415) legitimated lay communion with only the bread by affirming the presence of the whole Christ in one specie; the Hussite (from Jan Hus, d. 1415) movement's protest against this practice was reiterated by the sixteenth-century reformers. Since Latin was of little use to the uneducated laity, they no longer "heard" the Mass but saw the elevation of the Host as the reenactment of the Passion that the priest, by virtue of the sacrament of orders, "offered" to God. Such sacerdotal offerings increased in value as they increased in number. The English reformer Thomas Cranmer (d. 1556) described people running about from altar to altar in order to see and worship God in the Host. These practices were scathingly denounced by the sixteenth-century reformers as superstitious at best and idolatrous at worst.

Thomas emphasized that the sacraments contain grace. He introduced Aristotelian causality and its corresponding concepts of matter and form into reflection on the sacraments (the word is the form of the sacrament, and the material elements are the matter), as well as the concepts of *opus operatum* and *opus operantis.* The former affirmed that the sacraments are effective independently of the piety and morality of the recipient or the priest when he intends to do what the church does. The latter affirmed that the right disposition of the recipient is necessary if the received grace is to be really effectual.

According to Gregory Dix (*The Shape of the Liturgy*, 9th ed., London, 1964), the medieval preoccupation with relating the Eucharist to the Passion led to the sixteenth-century controversy over whether the Mass is a repetition or a remembrance of the Passion. If the church is to enter into the past action of the Passion, it can do so either by the willful mental activity of remembering it or, if there is to be an objective reality outside the mind, by some sort of repetition of the redeeming act of Christ. In the sixteenth century these would become church-dividing alternatives, which in the polemics of the time were presented, respectively, as the spiritual dissolution of sacramental means of grace into mental voluntarism or as the mechanistic manipulation of sacramental grace.

The Sixteenth Century. The Reformation was initiated by Luther's attack on the abuse of indulgences in relation to the sacrament of penance (Ninety-five Theses, 1517). Luther's critique, based on his theology of justification by grace alone, expanded into an attack on the entire medieval understanding of sacraments (*The Babylonian Captivity of the Church,* 1520). God's promise of salvation, he insisted, is unconditional because it is not based on an inner change in the hearer but on a change outside the person (*extra nos*) in his or her standing before God. The reality of word and sacraments, as God's self-communication, does not depend on faith. "Faith does not constitute Baptism but receives it. Baptism. . . is bound not to our faith but to the Word" (Large Catechism, 1529). Like Augustine, Luther coordinated word (*sacramentum audibile*) and sacrament (*verbum visibile*); their focus is God's action instead of human actions.

A consequence of this focus was to reduce the number of sacraments from seven to two. Augustine had defined a sacrament as the word added to the element. Thus, a visible sign was necessary, and since, moreover, only baptism and Eucharist had a dominical institution in the New Testament, the other sacraments were eliminated. All the Protestant reformers accepted this, although Luther continued to view confession as a means of grace.

In reducing the number of sacraments, the reformers claimed the church did not have authority to institute sacraments without biblical warrant. This displacement of the church as hierarchical institution (*Kirche*) by the church as community (*Gemeine*) is expressed by the Eucharist as a "communion," a communal meal celebrating God's promise, instead of a meritorious sacrifice offered by the priest to God. Calvin stressed the pastoral aspect of this shift: "The most serious matter of all is under discussion: namely, forgiveness of sins" (*Institutes*, 1559). Since Communion involves communication and participation, the reformers translated the Mass into the vernacular and distributed Communion in both kinds (bread and wine); they rejected transubstantiation, withholding the cup from the laity, the Mass as a sacrifice, and private masses. Furthermore, all the reformers, in spite of their differences, understood that Communion has ethical significance for community.

To the reformers transubstantiation shifted the focus from the proclamation *that* God communicates himself in the Eucharist to speculation about *how* that communication takes place. Theologically transubstantiation appears to give priests power to make Christ in the Mass, thereby usurping Christ and positing the infallibility of grace upon correct performance of the rite (*ex opere operato*). Salvation thus appeared as a human work dependent upon a clerical class, rather than as a divine gift. Ironically transubstantiation was the culmination of the post-Berengarian medieval efforts to express the gift character of salvation and to deny that the sacraments depend on what persons bring to them. Luther retained this intentionality in his emphasis on the real presence of Christ in the Eucharist but rejected the metaphysical tradition that had expressed it.

Unhappy with this perceived papist remnant in Luther's theology and aided by linguistic tools borrowed from the humanists, Zwingli insisted that the "is" in "this is my body" means "signify." Thus, when Jesus says, "this is my body," he means "this signifies my body," just as a wedding ring signifies a marriage but is not the relationship itself. A favorite biblical verse used in support of this symbolic understanding was *John* 6:63: "It is the spirit that gives life, the flesh is of no avail." This text was read in light of Augustine's well-known comment on spiritual eating in his *Exposition of the Gospel of John*: "Believe, and you have already eaten." The more radical reformers questioned and, in extreme cases such as Kaspar von Schwenckfeld (d. 1561), even rejected the need for sacraments altogether. This is the logical consequence of the Sacramentarians' divorce of the reception of the Holy Spirit from such external means as the sacraments. In contrast, Luther insisted that God "deals with us in a twofold manner, first outwardly, then inwardly. . . . The inward experience follows and is effected by the outward. God has determined to give the inward to no one except through the outward (Word and sign instituted by him)" (*Against the Heavenly Prophets in the Matter of Images and Sacraments*, 1525).

These Sacramentarians argued that the sacraments do not give faith but presume it. Thus, water baptism and participation in the Lord's Supper are outer expressions or disclosures of an inner change. Zwingli, for example, retained the sacraments of baptism and the Eucharist, but only as signs and symbols aiding the believer's spiritual exercise of recalling God's grace and as acts of the community to confess its faith. The focus is thus not so much God's self-communication but the spiritual-psychological activity of the believers, a kind of reverse Donatism. According to B. A. Gerrish ("The Lord's Supper in the Reformed Confessions," in *Major Themes in the Reformed Tradition*, edited by Donald K. McKim, Grand Rapids, Mich., 1992, pp. 245–358) this perspective continued in Zwingli's successor, Heinrich Bullinger (d. 1575), who wrote, "Believers therefore bring Christ *to* the Supper in their hearts; they do not receive him *in* the Supper." This is why, as David Steinmetz remarks (*Luther in Context*, Bloomington, Ind., 1986), "Modern Zwingli scholarship has spoken of a transubstantiation of the worshipping congregation into the body of Christ through the invisible activity of the Spirit."

W. P. Stephens (*Zwingli: An Introduction to His Thought*, Oxford, 1992) suggests that the operative motifs in Zwingli's theology of the sacraments were his stress on the sovereignty of God and his Platonism. With regard to God's sovereignty, Zwingli wrote that a "channel or vehicle is not necessary to the Spirit, for he himself is the virtue and energy whereby all things are borne and has no need of being borne" (*An Account of the Faith*, 1530). This conviction dovetailed with a Platonic metaphysics that posited a spiritual-material dualism wherein outward things, such as sacraments, cannot affect what is inward. A sacrament, then, does not communicate grace but commemorates it. Sacraments are "signs by which a man proves to the church that he either aims to be, or is, a soldier of Christ, and which inform the whole church rather than yourself of your faith" (*A Commentary*, 1525).

To Luther this vitiated the gospel by making it dependent upon faith and personal piety, thereby releasing once more all the medieval insecurities attendant upon introspection as the prerequisite for the Sacrament. The "because . . . therefore" grammar of God's promise shifted to the "if . . . then" grammar of human achievement: *If* you have a heartfelt remembrance of Christ's passion, *then* you may participate in the Eucharist as an outward and visible sign of an inward and spiritual grace already present. Beyond such a commemorative view of the Lord's Supper as a devotional exercise, both Luther and John Calvin asserted divine self-communication in the Sacrament.

In the polemical exchanges over the Eucharist at the Colloquy of Marburg (1529), Luther and Zwingli rang all the historical and theological changes available to them. Luther accused Zwingli of a Nestorian separation of the natures of Christ (since Christ's body has ascended to heaven, it cannot be in the Eucharist) and took up Cyril of Alexandria's *communicatio idiomatum* (the communication of natures) as an affirmation that, where Christ's divine nature is, so also is his human nature. In other words, the finite is capable of the infinite (*finitum capax inifiniti est*). The practical consequences of these differing Christologies are evident in Luther's opposition to iconoclasm and his preservation of art in the church and in Zwingli's denuding of the church of art and organ music. The ecclesial and political consequences were evident in the subsequent divisions among the reformers.

Both Luther and Zwingli retained the sacrament of infant baptism, but their stress on faith as the constitutive element suggested logically that baptism ought to be administered only to those who possessed faith. Both Andreas Bodenstein von Karlstadt and Thomas Müntzer questioned infant baptism, while a group of Zwingli's followers made the move to adult baptism. Led by Conrad Grebel (d. 1526) and George Blaurock (d. 1529), these dissidents performed the first recorded believers' baptisms. Since all present had been baptized as infants, this reforming movement was labeled Anabaptist ("re-baptist").

The geographical and theological diversity of the Anabaptist movements precludes a simple all-encompassing description, but it seems they desired a spirituality renewed Christendom that would outwardly conform to Christ. Water baptism and the Lord's Supper, therefore, outwardly expressed an inwardly renewed life; the true sacraments are interior, or spiritual. It was clear to these reformers that the sacramental practice of the *corpus Christianum* could not univocally lead to conformity to Christ; after all, Judas had also shared in the Last Supper. Thus, Thomas Müntzer (d. 1525) asserted that because true inner baptism by the Holy Spirit was not understood, Christendom had become a "crude monkey business." The Grebel circle claimed that infant baptism had created a church of "Mr. Everyman," where people remain in their old vices. If a degenerate Christendom is to be restored, baptism must be a sign that the faithful publicly obligate themselves to better their lives. Believers' baptism marked an exclusive church in contrast to the inclusive church signified by infant baptism.

At the Council of Trent Roman Catholicism sealed its basic acceptance of the medieval development of the sacraments and rejected Protestant interpretations. Transubstantiation, lay Communion with bread only, and the seven sacraments were reaffirmed as objectively efficacious. Since all the reformers were convinced that erroneous sacramental theology jeopardized salvation, their diverse convictions about baptism and the Eucharist—sacraments of unity—provided endless possibilities for division both between and within the various Reformation movements. The sixteenth-century understandings of the sacraments remained church-dividing until their reconsideration in the modern ecumenical movement.

[*See also* Baptism, *article on* Theological Views; Eucharist; Ordination; *and* Penance.]

BIBLIOGRAPHY

Armour, Rollin. *Anabaptist Baptism.* Scottdale, Pa., 1966.

Bakhuizen, J. N. van den Brink. "Ratramn's Eucharistic Doctrine and Its Influence in Sixteenth-Century England." In *Studies in Church History*, edited by G. J. Cuming, vol. 2, pp. 54–77. London, 1965. Discussion of the context and theology of Ratramnus's understanding of the Eucharist and its influence in the sixteenth century.

Bossy, John. "The Mass as a Social Institution, 1200–1700." *Past and Present* 100 (1983),29–61. Places the late medieval celebration of the Mass in its social and cultural settings.

Braaten, Carl E., and Robert W. Jenson, eds. *Christian Dogmatics.* 2 vols. Philadelphia, 1984. "The Sacraments" (vol. 2, pp. 291–389) provides definition and discussion from a Lutheran perspective.

Empie, Paul C., and T. Austin Murphy, eds. *Lutherans and Catholics in Dialogue, III: The Eucharist as Sacrifice.* Minneapolis, 1974.

———. *Lutherans and Catholics in Dialogue, IV: Eucharist and Ministry.* Minneapolis, 1979. Both volumes contain sound historical-theological studies of the sacraments by medievalists and Reformation scholars.

Fiorenza, Francis Schüssler, and John P. Galvin, eds. *Systematic Theology. Roman Catholic Perspectives.* 2 vols. Minneapolis, 1991. The articles under the heading "Sacraments" (vol. 2, pp. 181–346) provide historical-theological expositions of the concept of sacrament and discussions of all seven sacraments.

Gerrish, B. A. "Gospel and Eucharist: John Calvin on the Lord's Supper." In *The Old Protestantism and the New, Essays on the Reformation Heritage*, edited by B. A. Gerrish, pp. 106–117. Chicago, 1982.

———. *Grace and Gratitude: The Eucharist Theology of John Calvin.* Minneapolis, 1992. Exposition of Calvin's theology from the perspective of his doctrine of the Lord's Supper.

Klaasen, Walter, ed. *Anabaptism in Outline: Selected Primary Sources.* Waterloo, Ont., 1981.

Lehmann, Karl, and Wolfhart Pannenberg, eds. *The Condemnations of the Reformation Era: Do They Still Divide?* Minneapolis, 1990. Chapter 3 discusses scholastic and Reformation understandings of the sacraments in light of contemporary ecumenical discussions.

Lindberg, Carter. "Karlstadt's *Dialogue* on the Lord's Supper." *Mennonite Quarterly Review* 53 (January 1979),35–77. Introduction to and translation of one of Karlstadt's major writings.

———. "The Conception of the Eucharist according to Erasmus and Karlstadt." In *Les dissidents du 16e siècle entre l'humanisme et le Catholicisme*, edited by Marc Lienhard, pp. 79–94. Baden-Baden, 1983. Discusses the influence of Erasmus on Karlstadt and Zwingli.

———. *The Third Reformation? Charismatic Movements and the Lutheran Tradition.* Macon, Ga., 1983. Chapter 2 focuses on Luther's controversies with the spiritualists over the sacraments.

Macy, Gary. *The Theologies of the Eucharist in the Early Scholastic Period: A Study of the Salvific Function of the Sacrament according to the Theologians, c.1080–c.1220.* Oxford, 1984. Argues for a diversity of sacramental views in the early scholastic period.

McDonnell, Kilian. *John Calvin, the Church, and the Eucharist.* Princeton, 1967. Comprehensive analysis of Calvin and his contemporaries in their historical context.

McLaughlin, R. Emmet. "Schwenckfeld and the South German Eucharist Controversy, 1526–1529." In *Schwenckfeld and Early Schwenckfeldianism*, edited by Peter C. Erb, pp. 181–210. Pennsburg, Pa., 1986.

Palmer, Paul F., ed. *Sacraments and Forgiveness: History and Doctrinal Development of Penance, Extreme Unction and Indulgences.* London and Westminster, Md., 1959.

———. *Sacraments and Worship: Liturgy and Doctrinal Development of Baptism, Confirmation, and the Eucharist.* Westminster, Md., 1963. Both Palmer volumes provide good collections of primary texts on the sacraments from the early church to the modern period.

Pater, Calvin Augustine. *Karlstadt as the Father of the Baptist Movements.* Reprint, Toronto, 1986.

Payne, John B. *Erasmus: His Theology of the Sacraments.* Richmond, 1970.

Pelikan, Jaroslav. *The Christian Tradition, 3: The Growth of Medieval Theology (600–1300).* Chicago, 1978.

———. *The Christian Tradition, 4: Reformation of Church and Dogma (1300–1700).* Chicago, 1984. Both Pelikan volumes are strong on the history of theological ideas; excellent bibliographies.

Raitt, Jill. *The Eucharistic Doctrine of Theodore Beza: Development of the Reformed Doctrine.* Chambersburg, Pa., 1972.

Rempel, John D. *The Lord's Supper in Anabaptism.* Waterloo, Ont., 1993.

Rorem, Paul. *Calvin and Bullinger on the Lord's Supper.* Bramcote, England, 1989. First published in *Lutheran Quarterly* 2.2 (Summer 1988),155–184, and 2.3 (Autumn 1988),357–389.

Rubin, Miri. *Corpus Christi: The Eucharist in Late Medieval Culture.* Cambridge, 1991. Relates development of Eucharist devotion and practice to cultural contexts.

Steinmetz, David C. "Calvin and His Lutheran Critics." *Lutheran Quarterly* 4 (1990), 179–194.

Strayer, Joseph R., ed. *Dictionary of the Middle Ages.* 13 vols. New York, 1982. Entries for specific sacraments.

Williams, George H. *The Radical Reformation.* 3d ed. Kirksville, Mo., 1992. Comprehensive and exhaustive resource with useful indexes.

CARTER LINDBERG

SADOLETO, Jacopo (1477–1547), humanist scholar, curialist, and reform cardinal, the only one of seven Sadoletos in two generations whose vocation drew him to letters rather than the law in service to the dukes of Ferrara. The course of his career in Rome and the church was set in 1513, when he and Pietro Bembo were appointed to the Apostolic Secretariat by Leo X—two gifted Latinists drawn abruptly into Medicean patronage and politics, and then into the prosecution of Luther, who once described Sadoleto as "able and learned, but crafty in the Italian manner." To the twelve benefices he received in 1513, the pope added the Provencal diocese of Carpentras in 1517, where Sadoleto claimed he could best serve the church through his literary and episcopal commitments.

Following the death of Leo X in 1521, Sadoleto went briefly to Carpentras before being recalled by Clement VII to resume his position as domestic secretary, finding himself a troubled participant in the confusion and disastrous diplomacy of the Medici court. He returned to Carpentras in May 1527, two weeks before the Sack of Rome.

Between 1527 and 1536 Sadoleto produced three works of exegesis and three long treatises, dividing his efforts between the defense of Christian orthodoxy and the cause of good letters. The elegant *De pueris instituendis* (1530) was his most frequently published book and *In Pauli epistolam ad Romanos commentariorium libri* (1535) the most controversial—a Pelagianizing commentary on justification that alarmed Erasmus (whose cautions went unheeded), was disapproved by the Faculty of Theology of Paris, and was later placed under the ban in Rome.

Following a nine-year absence, Sadoleto was summoned to Rome again in 1536, this time by Paul III, to serve on Gasparo Contarini's commission on reform. Sadoleto immediately emerged as the radical critic on the commission in a written dissent from the majority report in the ill-fated *Consilium de emendanda ecclesia.* Nonetheless, at the end of the year he was one of the three reform prelates among the nine cardinals nominated in December 1536: "called anew," he said, "from the harbor into the storm."

While strongly supporting the convocation of the council, Sadoleto undertook his own efforts at conciliation with the Protestants, hoping, like Erasmus, to promote rapprochement through moderates on both sides. But his conciliatory letters to Melanchthon, Rupert Mosheim, and Johannes Sturm went unanswered and had only the effect of enraging the hard-core Catholic conservatives in Germany: Johann Eck, Johannes Cochlaeus, Friedrich Nausea, and Johannes Fabri. His ambitious *Epistola ad senatum populemque Genevensem* (1539), an appeal for preserving the unity of the historical church, not only provoked a brilliant response from Calvin but opened up serious differences between Sadoleto and Contarini.

Recalled to Rome in 1545 to serve on commissions dealing with matters of the council, Sadoleto died two years later. He was buried in the basilica of Saint Peter in Chains.

To an anticurical Venetian ambassador, Sadoleto was "the very model of sound learning, high principles, and innocence in this court." Although unyielding in his defense of Catholic doctrine, he was also unmatched in the Sacred College for his attacks on abuses in the church and for his belief that institutional reform could serve as the basis of reconciliation with the north.

BIBLIOGRAPHY

Primary Sources

Calvin, John, and Jacopo Sadoleto. *A Reformation Debate.* Edited with an introduction by John C. Olin. New York, 1966.

Sadoleto, Jacopo. *Epistolarum libri secdeim, nunc multo quam antehac umquam diligentius recogniti, atque in lucem aediti.* Cologne, 1590.

———. *Jacopi Sadoleti Cardinalis et Episcopi Carpentoractensis viri disertissimi, Opera quae extunt omnia.* (1737). 4 vols. Reprint, Ridgewood, N.J., 1964.

———. *Jacobi Sadoleti S.R.E. Cardinalis Epistolae Leonis X, Clementis VII, Pauli III, nomine scriptae.* Edited by V.A. Costanzi. Rome, 1759.

Secondary Sources

Douglas, Richard M. *Jacopo Sadoleto, 1477–1547: Humanist and Reformer.* Cambridge, 1959.

Reinhard, Wolfgang. *Die Reform in der Diözese Carpentras unter den Bishöfen Jacopo Sadoleto, Paolo Sadoleto, Jacopo Sacrati, und Francesco Sadoleto, 1517–1596.* Münster, 1966.

Verzeichnis der im deutschen Sprachbereich erschienenen Drucke des XVI. Jahrhunderts. Stuttgart, 1983–. See vol. 18, nos. 1239–1271.

RICHARD M. DOUGLAS

SADOLIN, Jørgen Jensen (c.1499–1559), Danish reformer and bishop. Nothing certain is known about Sadolin's childhood and youth—according to reform-Catholic Paul Helie's polemic *Skibykrønike* (Chronicle of Skiby; c.1530), he was the son of a Catholic priest—but from 1526 he was active as a master of arts and an eager Lutheran (together with Hans Tausen) in Viborg, the most important city in western Denmark. Under King Frederick I's protection he established a sort of evangelical ministers' school. In 1529 he was ordained by Tausen and became the parish minister at the newly established evangelical Dominican monastery church. When Tausen moved to Copenhagen shortly thereafter, Sadolin led the introduction of the Reformation into the city, and he translated and published (1529–1530) Martin Luther's *Vom Abendmahl: Bekenntnis* (The Last Supper: Confession; 1528) and *Daß Eltern die Kinder zur Ehe nicht zwingen* (Parents Must Not Force Their Children into Marriage; 1524), as well as Johannes Bugenhagen's *Summa der Seligkeit* (Sum of Blessedness; 1524) and *Eyn Underricht deren, so yn kranckheyten . . . ligen* (A Lecture to Those Who Lie Sick; 1527). Only the latter, published in 1970, has been preserved.

In 1530 he was to participate in the planned (but never carried out) religious colloquy in Copenhagen, and he left an interesting report on the confessional clash there, *Danmarks christelige prædikanters gensvar på prælaternes klager* (Denmark's Christian Ministers' Reply to the Prelates' Complaints; 1530), republished in 1885. As *coadjutor in verbo* for the Catholic bishop in Odense, Knud Gyldenstjerne, who showed sympathy for the Reformation movement, he worked from 1532 for the reeducation of the priesthood. He was able to introduce Luther's *Lille Katekismus*

(Small Catechism) and the Augsburg Confession, which he himself translated and published (1532 and 1533); the Eucharist *sub utraque*; and church visitations. He became a member of the commission that wrote the proposal for the church ordinance (1537) and was ordained bishop of Fyn's diocese (Odense) by Bugenhagen in 1537. In this office he expressed his continued pastoral-theological interest in a failed plan for a Lutheran cathedral chapter and a reorganization of Odense's clerical conference.

The extant sources are hardly sufficient to evaluate his theological position completely. As a co-author of the *Confessio Hafniensis* (1530), he has been considered to be a biblical humanist, but his many publications on the writings of the Wittenberg reformers indicate that he saw himself as a Lutheran theologian of the Wittenberg persuasion.

BIBLIOGRAPHY

Andersen, Niels Knud. *Confessio Hafniensis: Den københavnske bekendelse af 1530*. Copenhagen, 1954.

Andersen, Niels Knud, and J. Oskar Andersen. "Jørgen Jensen Sadolin." In *Dansk Biografisk Leksikon*, 3d ed., vol. 12, pp. 565–566. Copenhagen, 1982.

Lausten, Martin Schwarz. *Reformationen i Danmark*. 2d ed. Copenhagen, 1992.

Lausten, Martin Schwarz, and Inger Bom, eds. *Skrifter fra Reformationstiden*. Vol. 1. Copenhagen, 1970.

Rørdam, Holger Fr., ed. *Skrifter fra Reformationstiden*. Copenhagen, 1885–1890.

MARTIN SCHWARZ LAUSTEN

Translated from Danish by Walter D. Morris

SAINT BARTHOLOMEW'S DAY MASSACRE.

Begun in Paris on 24 August 1572, the Saint Bartholomew's Day Massacre was one of the most horrifying episodes of violence that accompanied the Reformation. This massacre, which continued for weeks in various parts of France, was particularly shocking because it occurred during a period of truce after a decade of increasingly bloody wars between the country's Protestant and Catholic factions. The French government at that time was vested in the hereditary rule of the Valois family of kings, but the authority of the Crown had been considerably weakened, beginning in 1559, with the premature death of King Henry II. He was succeeded in turn by three young sons—Francis II, Charles IX, and Henry III, all under the influence of their mother, Catherine de Médicis, and other relatives. It is a structural problem in any hereditary monarchy that government becomes fragile during the rule of a minor. This extended period of rule by minors was further complicated in sixteenth-century France by bitter religious controversy. Two religious factions, Protestant and Roman Catholic, took advantage of this period of prolonged weakness to wage war for their form of belief and for control of the apparatus of government. The Protestant faction, demanding toleration for their new form of religion, was led by princes of the blood royal from the House of Bourbon, who were in line to inherit the throne of France should the reigning Valois family die out. The Catholic faction, demanding the complete extirpation of the Protestant heresy, was led by nobles of the Guise family, including cardinals with close ties to the international Roman Catholic establishment.

In August 1572 the king of France was Charles IX, who at the age of twenty-two was no longer a minor but nevertheless remained very much under the influence of his mother, Catherine de Médicis, and her Italian advisers. The titular head of the Protestant faction was eighteen-year-old Henry of Bourbon, King of Navarre (later Henry IV of France). Particularly important in the retinue of powerful nobles who supported his faction were members of the Chatillon family, of whom the most prominent was Admiral Gaspard II de Coligny, at that time the principal political and military commander of the Protestant forces. The titular leader of the Catholic faction was twenty-one-year-old Henry, duke of Guise, deeply influenced by his uncle, the cardinal of Lorraine.

To end a full decade of wars and make the truce permanent, the royal government had invited leaders of both factions to Paris for the lavish celebration of a royal wedding, which was designed to bring together permanently leaders from both sides. The Protestant Henry of Navarre was married to the Catholic Marguerite of Valois, sister to King Charles IX. Some, most notably Admiral Coligny, hoped that once this alliance had bound all Frenchmen together they could unite in fighting a foreign foe, specifically the Spanish, who were then launching a vigorous campaign against the Protestant Dutch on the northern frontiers of France.

Analysis of public opinion in these years, however, makes it clear that the royal policy of conciliation and truce was very fragile. There was bitter resentment among large segments of the general population directed at any policy designed to tolerate more than one form of religion in the nation. This resentment had frequently erupted into violence. Mobs of Protestants would riot against the use in religious ceremonies of objects they believed to be "idols." They felt the "worship" of these objects was blasphemy and bound to bring down the wrath of God upon the country. Their attempts to cleanse their communities of these objects led to iconoclastic riots. They also led to acts of violence directed against the custodians of these objects, members of the Roman Catholic clergy, sometimes descending to murders. Mobs of Catholics would riot against religious services organized by people they believed to be heretics and polluters of sacred places and rituals, who by this pollution threatened to bring down the wrath of God upon the country. If Protestant violence tended to be directed more against property and Catholic violence more against people, there was still plenty of both in each camp. The resentments of both factions, furthermore, were increasingly directed against the government for permitting idolatry, blasphemy, or pollution, which, they thought, was bound to incur divine punishment of the entire community.

It was during the festivities organized to celebrate the grand wedding of alliance between the Bourbon and Valois families that the Saint Bartholomew's Day Massacre began. It thus marked a particularly brutal switch from celebration to killing, from high hopes for peace to pure horror. The massacre was touched off on Saint Bartholomew's Day, 24 August, by the assassinations of Admiral Gaspard II de Coligny and several other aristocratic Protestant leaders. These assassinations were ordered in the name of King Charles IX by the royal privy council. Fears of the consequences of a policy that would lead to war with Spain on the part of the queen mother, Catherine de Médicis—as well as a desire to appear as a champion of Catholicism on the part of the king's younger brother Henri—seemed to have played an important part in the debate that led to this brutal decision. The first assassinations were personally supervised by the duke of Guise, who believed Coligny to be responsible for the assassination of his father at the end of the first War of Religion and was thus seeking revenge.

Bloodshed did not stop, however, with these political assassinations of aristocrats ordered by the Crown. They were immediately followed by a general massacre in Paris of thousands of Protestants from all walks of life by mobs of religious fanatics. These mobs went on the rampage following a signal from leaders in the city government, who had been tipped off with news of the impending assassinations. This general massacre was a culmination of several years of episodic violence in Paris that civic authorities had found increasingly difficult to control. The massacre in Paris was then followed by violence in about a dozen French provincial cities, in each case by mobs of fanatics on signals from civic authorities. Altogether thousands of Protestants were killed in the space of a few weeks, and thousands more went into hiding or fled the kingdom. Large groups of Protestant refugees poured over French borders into England, Germany, and Switzerland.

This widespread bloodshed upset many moderate Catholics and profoundly shocked the international Protestant community. Of the French Protestants who were unable to flee, many, in terror at the violence and seeing in it evidence that God did not support their cause, promptly converted to Catholicism. Roman Catholic authorities, led by the papacy, immediately took energetic measures to welcome these new converts back to the traditional church.

In the succeeding months, however, other French Protestants defied both the Catholic faction and the royal government and returned to religious war. They ejected royal garrisons in a number of cities, most notably La Rochelle, and withstood long and bitter sieges. They raised entire armies in other areas, primarily in the south of France, and moved in the direction of secession from the kingdom. They sought and gained moral, financial, and military help from Protestant powers elsewhere, particularly from certain German principalities and England, in support of this revolt. Some of these resisting Protestants even went so far as to attack the very form of monarchical government that had permitted these atrocities, calling it a tyranny that had forfeited all right to be obeyed. They justified their armed resistance, led not by formless mobs but by duly constituted "inferior magistrates" (subordinate officials in government), as a defense of basic human rights. This case was developed in eloquent pamphlets that were widely circulated at the time and that have been used again in similar circumstances over the centuries. Among the most influential of these pamphlets were François Hotman's *Francogallia*, Théodore de Bèze's *Du droit des magistrats*, and the anonymous *Vindiciae contra tyrannos*.

The Saint Bartholomew's Day Massacre deeply scarred the French Protestant movement. Never again did it possess any realistic hope of winning the entire kingdom, and repeatedly it feared the possibility of a renewal of persecution with an intensity that sometimes approached paranoia but that all too often proved to be justified. More generally this massacre remains perhaps the most traumatic single reminder of the depths to which confessional hatreds could descend during the period of the Reformation.

[*See also* Catherine de Médicis; Charles IX of France; Coligny, Gaspard II de; Henry IV of France; Lorraine-Guise, House of; *and* Wars of Religion.]

BIBLIOGRAPHY

Crouzet, Denis. *Les guerriers de Dieu: La violence au temps des troubles de religion (vers 1525–vers 1610)*. Seyssel, France, 1990. Massive study of religious violence in the period, setting the episode in its full context.

———. *La Nuit de la Saint-Bartélemy: Un rêve perdu de le Renaissance.* Paris, 1994. A psychological interpretation.

Diefendorf, Barbara B. *Beneath the Cross: Catholics and Huguenots in Sixteenth-Century Paris.* New York, 1991. Provides a fine analysis of the growth of urban violence that culminated in the Saint Bartholomew's Day Massacre.

Garrison, Janine. *La Saint-Barthélemy.* Brussels, 1987. Useful and authoritative recent overview of the episode.

Kingdon, Robert M. *Myths About the Saint Bartholomew's Day Massacres, 1572–1576.* Cambridge, Mass., 1988. Explores the stories of martyrdom provoked immediately by the massacres and how they were used by Protestant propagandists to keep their movement alive.

Sutherland, N. M. *The Massacre of Saint Bartholomew and the European Conflict, 1559–1572.* New York, 1973. Analyzes closely the diplomacy leading up to the massacres.

ROBERT M. KINGDON

SAINT-GERMAIN, COLLOQUY OF. An unsuccessful attempt at dialogue between Catholic and Reformed theologians in France, this colloquy was held at the royal chateau of Saint-Germain-en-Laye in January and February 1562. It was sponsored by the queen mother Catherine de Médicis, after the failure of the Colloquy of Poissy (September and October 1561) and included many of the same participants.

Catherine was desperate to avoid civil war. She hoped that both sides would compromise, but most French Catholics rejected toleration, and Calvinists held similarly absolute views. The royal family was present at the opening session, where Chancellor Michel de l'Hôpital appealed for reconciliation and set the agenda—images, baptism, the Eucharist, the Mass, ordination, and doctrine. Only the first topic was actually discussed. Speaking for the Calvinists, Théodore de Bèze denounced images as idolatry, as specifically prohibited by the Decalogue, and as condemned by the church fathers and councils. Bèze rejected the veneration of images as unknown to the early church. Jean Pelletier and the Jesuit general Diego Laínez defended the Catholic position by distinguishing between the image and the thing represented; they also cited paintings in the Roman catacombs as evidence of early Christian usage.

Despite some divisions among the Catholics, Catherine recognized that prospects for compromise were slight. Discussions were soon suspended, and the parties submitted written reports. French bishops were then ordered to attend the Council of Trent, whose authority the Calvinists did not accept. At the same time, there was a rash of iconoclasm in France. The Catholic report from the Colloquy of Saint-Germain did influence the statements of the Council of Trent, but the failure to achieve compromise led to greater polarization and the outbreak of the Wars of Religion, which began with the Massacre of Wassy on 1 March 1562.

BIBLIOGRAPHY

Baum, G., and E. Cunitz, eds. *Histoire ecclésiastique des églises réformées au royaume de France.* 3 vols. Reprint, Nieuwkoop, 1974. The principal Calvinist source; contains notes referring to the correspondence of Bèze and Calvin.

Nugent, Donald. *Ecumenism in the Age of the Reformation: The Colloquy of Poissy.* Cambridge, Mass., 1974. The best and most detailed account in English; judicious and fair.

Salmon, J. H. M. *Society in Crisis: France in the Sixteenth Century.* New York and London, 1975. Good overview of the French Wars of Religion.

MAARTEN ULTEE

SAINT-GERMAIN, EDICTS OF.

Royal proclamations on the spread of Protestantism in France, the Edicts of Saint-Germain were issued at the chateau of Saint-Germain-en-Laye in 1561–1562. Particularly important were two edicts of the regent Catherine de Médicis issued during the minority of Charles IX just prior to the outbreak of the Wars of Religion.

The first of these, the "Edict on religion, on the means of keeping the people at peace, and repressing seditious elements," was promulgated on 31 July 1561. This edict prohibited all Protestant *conventicules*, or assemblies, from preaching and administering the sacraments. It confirmed the earlier measures against heresy announced in the Edict of Romarantin (May 1560) but ordered secular judges not to impose the death penalty. Banishment and confiscation of property were recommended punishments. The edict also pardoned all persons charged with crimes of religion or sedition since the death of Henry II (July 1559). Neither Catholics nor Protestants found these terms satisfactory. The edict was ineffective and signaled the weakness of the monarchy.

The second edict, the "Declaration on the repression of the troubles associated with the Reformed religion," was issued on 17 January 1562. After the failure of the Colloquy of Poissy (September and October 1561), Catherine tried again to find a moderate solution to religious conflicts. She called deputies from the superior courts (parlements) to Saint-Germain and drafted a new edict. Reformers were ordered to return churches and other properties they had taken from the Catholics. Destruction of religious images was prohibited, as was Reformed preaching in towns. Yet the penalties of the July edict were suspended, and Protestants were allowed to hold assemblies in the countryside. There they could meet with the permission and presence of royal officials. Limits were placed on preaching and membership in the Reformed faith, which could receive only voluntary contributions. Reformed ministers had to swear their obedience to the edict. Severe punishments were set for printers of placards and libels, and the courts were ordered not to interfere with officers in the performance of their duties. Extreme Catholics responded to the edict with predictable anger, resistance, and violence. As Jean Delumeau has written (*Naissance et affirmation de la Réforme*, Paris, 1965), "this measure of pacification unleashed war."

BIBLIOGRAPHY

Baum, G., and E. Cunitz, eds. *Histoire ecclésiastique des églises réformées au royaume de France.* 3 vols. Reprint, Nieuwkoop, 1974. Vol. 1 contains texts of the edicts.

Isambert, F. A., et al., eds. *Recueil général des anciennes lois françaises.* 29 vols. Paris, 1822–1833. Vol. 14 contains texts of the edicts.

Keller, Abraham Charles. "Michel de l'Hospital and the Edict of Toleration of 1562." *Bibliothèque d'humanisme et renaissance* 14 (1952), 301–310. Discusses the changing role of the chancellor.

Knecht, Robert Jean. *The French Wars of Religion, 1559–1598.* London and New York, 1989. Good introduction with selected documents in English for students.

MAARTEN ULTEE

SAINT-GERMAIN-DES-PRÉS.

A Benedictine monastery and site of two important reform movements, the abbey of Saint Germain-des-Prés was founded by the Merovingian king Childebert in the sixth century in fields outside Paris. The surrounding neighborhood, Faubourg Saint-Germain, included the parish of Saint-Sulpice and was under the abbey's jurisdiction (and so exempt from the authority of the bishops of Paris). The abbot and monks became powerful lords with vast landholdings. By the sixteenth century their privileges were well established and included an annual fair. The abbey's income was divided between the monks and commendatory abbots, courtiers who regarded the abbey as a lucrative benefice but seldom participated in its religious life.

In 1507 Guillaume Briçonnet (c.1470–1534), bishop of Lodève, received the abbey from his father, Cardinal Guillaume Briçonnet. The younger Briçonnet overcame opposition from the monks and displayed an interest in reform. He supported the humanist Jacques Lefèvre d'Étaples (Faber Stapulensis), who lived at the abbey while writing his *Quincumplex Psalterium* (1509) and commentaries on the Pauline epistles (1512). These works—dedicated to the Briçonnets, father and son, respectively—were important to the evangelism of the proto-reformers at Meaux, where the younger Guillaume became bishop in 1515. Already in 1512 he had invited the congregation of Chezal-Benoît to reform Saint-Germain-des-Prés, but considerable effort was required to persuade the monks to accept stricter observance (1513–1515). Royal and papal approval were sought for a return to regular abbots, although this provision became a dead letter after the Concordat of Bologna (1516). As French ambassador to Rome, Guillaume Briçonnet obtained bulls confirming the privileges of Saint-Germain-des-Prés.

For nearly a century after Briçonnet's death in 1534, his successors Cardinal François de Tournon, Cardinal Charles de Bourbon, and Prince François of Conti and his wife, used abbatial revenues only to increase their personal income. Buildings and estates were not maintained, and lands were alienated during the Wars of Religion. Monastic observance became lax as the congregation of Chezal-Benoît lacked resources and discipline. The queen mother, Marie de Médicis, in 1614 proposed a national reform with the abbey of Saint-Germain as its center, but the project failed. More lasting reform was achieved in Lorraine by the Congregation of Saint-Vannes, whose French sympathizers founded the Congregation of Saint-Maur in 1618 with the support of Louis XIII. His half-brother Henri de Verneuil, commendatory abbot of Saint-Germain-des-Prés, accepted the Maurist reform in 1631. The Maurists made Saint-Germain their national headquarters and a model house of monastic learning, reaching a peak of activity in the reign of Louis XIV. They established classes in theology and philosophy for young monks and assigned capable scholars to work in teams on publishing projects. The Maurists edited works of the church fathers, pioneered techniques of medieval scholarship, and wrote religious and civil histories. Among the most prominent scholar-monks were Jean Mabillon and Bernard de Montfaucon. The French Revolution of 1789 dissolved the community and severely damaged the buildings, yet the writings survive as testimony to the learning and faith of the monks of Saint-Germain-des-Prés.

BIBLIOGRAPHY

Chaussy, Yves. *Les Bénédictins de Saint-Maur.* Vol. 1, *Aperçu historique sur la Congrégation.* Paris, 1989. History of the parent congregation, with particular attention to religious observance.

Ultee, Maarten. *The Abbey of St. Germain des Prés in the Seventeenth Century.* New Haven and London, 1981. Social and economic study of the abbey during the Maurist period.

Veissière, Michel. *L'évêque Guillaume Briçonnet, 1470–1534.* Provins, France, 1986. The most detailed study of the reforming bishop.

MAARTEN ULTEE

SAINTS. [*This entry comprises two articles on saints in sixteenth-century Europe. The first considers the principal figures and institutions associated with saints and sainthood and discusses the impact of the Reformation on the tradition; the second focuses on popular devotion to the cult of saints, the Protestant rejection of the cult of saints, and the Roman Catholic reaction evidenced by changes in the types of individual canonized. For related discussions, see* Books of Martyrs, Devotional Practices, Pilgrimages, *and* Sanctification.]

Sainthood

Late medieval veneration of the saints left its impression on the young Martin Luther: in 1503, as a twenty-year-old law student, he called on Mary for help when he was critically wounded in an accident on his way home from Erfurt; elsewhere, caught in a thunderstorm, he prayed, "Help, Saint Anne, I want to become a monk." Saint Anne, the legendary mother of Mary and the object of Luther's special veneration, was widely esteemed by ordinary people as well as by the German humanists. Her popularity during the late Middle Ages is confirmed by legends, pictures and statues, churches and chapels, pious associations, foundations and pilgrimages—forms of veneration of the saints that were characteristic of the epoch and that were quite different from those of the patristic church.

For the church fathers, saints were all those, in heaven and on earth, who participated in the life of Christ, who followed him in his suffering and resurrection; after a good death, preferably as a martyr, the saint entered fully into the union with Christ that had begun on earth. Saints were venerated for having attained their final goal, and veneration was understood as a memorial of their love of God and neighbor, as an invitation to imitate their heroic example, and as a call for their intercession in order to help the members of the pilgrim church to experience, in communion with them, perfect union with Christ. By the late Middle Ages, however, such conceptions had given way to an object-centered piety and the belief that prayers were answered directly. The Middle Ages saw the rise of relic collections, among the most famous of which was that of Frederick III of Saxony (1463–1525); invocation of the saints came to be seen as more important than imitation. Individual saints were perceived as having been endowed by God with particular protective powers, and their protection was to be sought for particular needs. Such specialized patronage had little foundation in theological reflection, but was connected with events or motifs, legendary or otherwise, in the life of the saint. Thus fishermen and seafarers had Saint Peter as intercessor in heaven; tent makers and weavers had Saint Paul; Saint Barbara, according to legend a young Christian woman incarcerated in a tower by her pagan father, was patron saint of miners and architects. Philosophers and theologians, meanwhile, had Saint Catherine of Alexandria as their protectress. From this kind of piety arose the veneration of the "Fourteen Holy Helpers," which, as reflected in many pictures and statues, was widely practiced in southern Germany during the late Middle Ages. By the time of the Reformation, then, intercessory prayer was no longer Christocentric as in the hagiology of the patristic period; instead the goal seems to have been to receive assistance directly from the saint.

Popular forms of piety such as these, however, found no support in the writings of the Scholastics. Thomas Aquinas (1225/26–1274) himself developed an integrated hagiology, grounding it in Paul's image of the church as a spiritual body in which one shares everything with everyone else. Thomas considered the uniting bond of the sacraments of Christ and the gifts of the Holy Spirit to be the essential elements of the *communio sanctorum.* All Christians are saints, according to Thomas. Christ is their head and they are all part of his body; all share the same final goal and are in communion with the Father through the love given by the Holy Spirit. This applies both to those who have finished their journey and have reached the final communion with God and to the saints on earth who are still on their way to their final goal. In this context intercession of the saints means the assistance that helps all to reach the final communion in God's love. According to Thomas, those people have to be reprimanded "qui sperant in homine sicut in principali auctore salutis: non autem qui sperant in homine sicut in adjuvante ministerialiter sub Deo" (who place their hope in a human as in the primary author of salvation: not, however, those who place their hope in a human as a helping minister under God; *Summa theologiae* II–II, q. 25, a.1 ad 3); similarly, in his treatise on hope Thomas rejects "sperare de aliquo homine, vel de aliqua creatura, sicut de prima causa movente in beatitudinem licet autem sperare de aliquo homine, vel de aliqua creatura, sicut de agente secundario et instrumentali, per quod aliquis adiuvatur ad quaecumque bona consequenta in beatitudinem ordinata. Et hoc modo ad sanctos convertimur" (to place hope for blessedness in any human, or any creature, as in the prime moving cause. It is permitted, however, to place hope in a human or in a creature, as a secondary and instrumental agent, through which one is helped toward blessedness and whatever good things are ordained. And it is in this way that we are turned toward the saints; *Summa theologiae* II–II, q. 17, a.4 resp.).

Theological Renewal. Veneration of the saints as practiced in the late Middle Ages was, in Luther's view, fundamentally beyond renewal. His Christocentrism and related understanding of soteriology were guided by the old Christian perspective and by the Pauline theory of the body of Christ as presented by Thomas. According to Luther, the *communio sanctorum* is based on community with Christ in faith and life. Human sanctity is gratuitous participation in the sanctity of Christ; saints are all those who are in living communion with Christ regardless of whether they have already died in communion with him or are still on their journey of faith. From union with Christ comes union with others—that is, the *communio sanctorum*—which is entered into through faith and the sacraments, and which is actualized and represented in the Eucharist. Mutual assistance among the saints is possible, and such help is neither outside of nor in competition with Christ's actions because he is the reason for those actions, which extend his power into time. When, because of their union with Christ, the saints, whether in heaven or on earth, offer help to their brethren, they witness to the unique mediation of Christ, and the actions of the saints are the fruit of his life. This applies also to their general intercessions on our behalf. Luther's positive contribution was that he anchored the foundations of hagiology in the mystery of Christ. Like Thomas before him, he admonishes that one not put trust in man, but in Christ alone.

It is noteworthy that these conceptions did not lead to a Lutheran hagiology and a corresponding veneration of the saints. As the reform movement progressed, the focal point became the question of direct invocation. Saints were not to be invoked individually, according to Luther, for that would be to look to them as special and direct helpers who, in their particular area of competence, come through their own power to the aid of the petitioner. Above all, there is no biblical foundation. In the absence of these questionable practices and with the saints not being called as special helpers, Luther wrote in his Schmalkald Articles, "I can honor you, love you, and thank you in Christ." "In Christ" is the essential element when we honor the saints in heaven or on earth. Inspired and guided by these thoughts, Melanchthon in the Augsburg Confession (art. 21) states that God deserves our gratitude for having presented the saints as examples of his grace who, in turn, strengthen Christians in their faith and encourage the imitation of the saints. Invocation was rejected, as was their intercession and, *a fortiori*, their mediating or redeeming function. This narrow interpretation of Luther's legacy was expressed even more radically by Zwingli and Calvin, who, in consideration of Christ's unique role as mediator, denied that human beings have function.

Response at Trent. In responding to the arguments of the reformers, the Council of Trent did not prepare a comprehensive hagiology taking into consideration all christological and ecclesiological aspects, but rather addressed and clarified particular issues. In the view of the council, the saints who reigned with Christ directed their prayers for the people to God, and therefore to ask for their intercessions was good and beneficial, and not idolatrous. Relics deserved to be honored because the saints were living members of the body of Christ and temples of the Holy Spirit, destined for resurrection; so too for images of Christ, Mary, and the saints, because they represented and pointed to the original. In addition to such doctrinal statements the council issued disciplinary directives, stating that bishops had the right and the duty to evaluate reports of miracles and to supervise the veneration of pictures and relics.

The saints of the Counter-Reformation were people who represented in a special way the church's determination to effect renewal, including Teresa of Ávila (1515–1582), Juan Álvarez (1542–1591), Carlo Borromeo (1538–1584), and Ignatius Loyola (1491?-1556) and his Jesuit confreres Francis Xavier (1506–1552), Peter Faber (1506–1546), and Peter Canisius (1521–1597). The theological controversy continued to be dominated by a hagiology that was hardly receptive to the *communio* concept of the old church, but rather emphasized ethical and eschatological aspects. Centuries later, the Second Vatican Council revitalized the biblical-patristic legacy of the communion of the saints and the appropriate veneration of the saints.

The sixteenth-century controversy furnishes new insights for Christian hagiology: it is situated at the point where a christologically conceived ecclesiology and eschatology are interwoven. This means that the importance of the saints to the communion in Christ must be understood before their role as examples can be considered. The central theme in today's ecumenical dialogue concerns the efficacious unity and active solidarity between the pilgrim church and the heavenly church. Can, in reference to classical tradition as well as Luther, Lutheran and Catholic Christians agree that there is a living unity of all those who are gathered under the headship of Christ and are open to the workings of the Holy Spirit? If that were the case, the ministry of the saints could be understood by both Lutheran and Catholic Christians as a service offered to the body of Christ. The invocation of the saints would, in this context, be an exchange in, before, and through Christ.

BIBLIOGRAPHY

Anderson, H. George, J. Francis Stafford, and Joseph A. Burgess, eds. *The One Mediator, the Saints, and Mary.* Lutherans and Catholics in Dialog, vol. 8. Augsburg and Minneapolis, 1992.

Benko, Stephen. *The Meaning of Sanctorum Communio.* Studies in Historical Theology, 3. London, 1964.

Brown, Peter. *The Cult of the Saints: Its Rise and Function in Latin Christianity.* Reprint, London, 1983.

Kolb, Robert. *For All the Saints: Changing Perceptions of Martyrdom and Sainthood in the Lutheran Reformation.* Macon, Ga., 1987.

Lackmann, Max. *Verehrung der Heiligen: Versuch einer lutherischen Lehre von den Heiligen.* Stuttgart, 1958.

Manns, Peter. "Luther und die Heiligen." In *Reformatio Ecclesiae: Festgabe für E. Iserloh*, edited by Remigius Bäumer, pp. 535–580. Paderborn, 1980.

Molinari, Paolo. *Saints: Their Place in the Church.* New York, 1965.

Moeller, Bernd. "Piety in Germany around 1500." In *The Reformation in Medieval Perspective*, edited by Steven E. Ozment. Chicago, 1971.

Müller, Gerhard Ludwig. *Gemeinschaft und Verehrung der Heiligen: Geschichtlich-systematische Grundlegung der Hagiologie.* Freiburg, 1986.

Oberman, Heiko A. *Masters of the Reformation.* Cambridge, 1981.

———. *The Harvest of Medieval Theology.* Durham, N.C., 1983.

Rahner, Karl. "Der eine Mittler und die Vielfalt der Vermittlungen." In *Schriften zur Theologie VIII*, pp. 218–235. Einsiedeln, 1967.

———. "Gemeinschaft der Heiligen." In *Ich glaube: Vierzehn Betrachtungen zum Apostolischen Glaubensbekenntnis*, pp. 129–138. Einsiedeln, 1968.

Scharfe, Martin. "Der Heilige in der protestantischen Volksfrömmigkeit." *Hessische Blätter für Volkskunde* 60 (1969), 93–106.

Vajta, Vilmos. "Die Kirche als geistlich-sakramentale communio mit Christus und seinen Heiligen bei Luther." *Lutherjahrbuch* 51 (1984), 10–62.

FRANZ COURTH

Cult of Saints

The cult of saints played a central role in medieval Catholicism and was a major target for attack by religious reformers of both the pre-Reformation and Reformation periods. For evangelical reformers, devotion to the saints distracted the Christian believer from Christ as the only source of salvation and distorted the gospel message by its implication that salvation could be mediated by mere human beings. For those persuaded by the Reformation message, the saints became theologically marginal, repudiation of their cult only incidental to the main purpose of restoring the word of God to the center of Christian worship. Indeed, Luther was not opposed to veneration of the saints within a proper evangelical perspective. Attacks on the cult of the saints acquired a major polemical importance during the Reformation, however, because they effectively demonstrated the stark difference between the two forms of religion. The Catholic saints were a major casualty wherever the Reformation was introduced, and a waning of devotion to them was always a sure sign of reception of evangelical ideas. The subject long evoked confessional discord, the heat of Protestant condemnation being countered by the fervor of Catholic apologetics, but recent scholarship enables one to describe the complexities of the historical phenomenon more dispassionately.

It arose from devotion to persons of exceptional holiness and from a desire to honor their memory as bearers of sanctity. This sanctity was held to have inhered in their bodily presence as an inner-worldly manifestation of sacred power, a divine gift that attested their saintliness. Devotion to the saints thus included veneration of their bodily remains and, by further extension, of all material objects or places with which they had come into contact. The cult of the saints thus became inextricably tied to veneration of relics and pilgrimages to holy shrines. It led to a restless search for ever more relics and eventually to their proliferation and falsification. Because relics transmitted the sacrality of the holy person, they were believed to have the power to heal, so that the cult of the saints became a preeminent example of attempts at inner-worldly appropriation of sacred power. This linked it closely to the functional aspects of medieval religion, to the ways in which medieval Catholicism offered succor for inner-worldly distress, whether spiritual or material. Quintessentially, the saints were helpers to whom the believer could turn for assistance in coping with the exigencies of daily life, the most commonly invoked late medieval saints being the "Fourteen Helpers in Emergency," who between them covered every form of human need. It was, perhaps, this kind of role that also led the saints to be perceived as capable of influencing the believer's eternal salvation, interceding before God for their devotees as they helped in dealing with anxiety, sickness, and suffering. Equally the notion of the saint as reformed sinner or as manifestations of "another Christ" (such as the stigmatized Saint Francis) presented them as models for imitation for the earnest seeker after salvation.

The cult of the saints could thus be regarded as a preeminent manifestation of "popular belief," of laypeople's initiative and creativity in shaping religion to suit their own perceived needs. Formally, it was the institutional church that declared a holy person to be a saint, a process reserved to the papacy from 1234 and the result of a rigorous and complex judicial procedure that sought cast-iron proof of both sanctity and miraculous intervention. Saints were also created out of local religion, however, through local forms of devotion that grew into cults and were then officially sanctioned and controlled by the church, or else discouraged and repressed. The nexus of such local veneration was virtually a contract between saint and devotee, the latter taking a vow of devotion to which the saint was obliged to respond. Because of this inherently popular aspect, the number of saints and their individual cults was virtually unlimited. At the core of the phenomenon were universal figures such as the Virgin Mary, the apostles, the early martyrs, eminent leaders of the early church, persons of exemplary piety such as ascetics, hermits, and missionaries, and those who manifested heroic virtue. But the number proliferated beyond count thanks to the vast body of local figures venerated in any country or territory, their status as saints developing out of folk memory, local traditions, pious histories, and retrospective legitimation (for example, of a church, abbey, chapel, or pilgrimage place). In this way the saints came to include a good many fictitious figures alongside historical persons, their numbers sometimes seeming to multiply like a mutating virus. The canonization process provided a major means of control, however, as did the liturgical calendar that cataloged feast days and gave them a firm place within the annual cycle of Christian worship.

Much research since the mid-twentieth century has emphasized the sociological dimensions of saints' cults, that is, that they were made in the image of the society in which they arose. Saints were constructed by power relationships, on the one hand, and by their devotees, on the other. The predominance of Latin and especially Italian saints mirrored the power of Rome as the seat of canonization, but officially recognized sainthood was decidedly skewed in other ways as well. One was more likely to become a canonized saint if one was male rather than female, a cleric or member of a religious order rather than a layperson. Bishops and members of the higher clergy dominated, followed by royal saints, the last often promoted by a conscious politics of dynastic sanctity that also accounted for many women saints, since canonized princesses helped establish charismatic legitimation for a princely house. Distribution of social power was further mirrored by a discernible structure by social class. Some saints appealed more to noble and clerical elites, some to military aristocratic groups, and some to urban and peasant strata.

The official church attempted to present saints as ideal models for imitation, but in effect they represented an extrapolation by their devotees of certain social ideals. The power of saints to punish those who offended them reflected a fundamental belief in immanent justice, while the willingness of many devotees to punish saints who had failed them was clearly a result of applying contractual notions of the feudal relationship to relations with the saint. The idea of patronage, so important for many forms of protection or advancement in medieval and early modern society, was very pronounced in saints' cults, which were undeniably constructed to mirror relations of patronage present in the inner-worldly sphere. Local, regional, and national patron saints thus provided a universal protection perhaps more reassuring than that of the secular variant. From such relationships of sacred clientage flowed the late medieval efflorescence of confraternities.

Sainthood was also gender specific in complex ways. The number of female saints never rose above 20 percent, and these were overwhelmingly highborn women. But women also participated in cults of male saints in gender-specific ways that have yet to be explored. The cult of the Virgin was a complex phenomenon, since she found devotion from both women and men, although in terms appropriate to each gender. The importance of female saints for women can be seen in the remarkable growth of the cult of Saint Anne in the late Middle Ages as an image both of idealized motherhood and of matriarchy, although this cult was also appropriated for male purposes. Saint Margaret was an important women's saint because of belief in her power to help female illnesses and to assist in childbirth.

The medieval cult of the saints did not escape criticism before the Reformation, not only from evangelical reformers such as the Lollards and Hussites but also from reformers within the institutional church—both Jean de Gerson (Charlier) and Nicholas of Cusa attacked observation of dubious saints' days. A more searching critique was offered by humanists whose rational and historical bent made them skeptical of claims made for relics, pilgrimages, and some of the more excessive cults. Desiderius Erasmus's devastating attack on the cult of Saint Thomas of Canterbury undoubtedly contributed to the complete uprooting of that shrine during the Reformation (admittedly helped by royal determination to erase a figure who stood for saintly opposition to overweening royal authority). Saints' cults quickly became a major casualty of the Reformation, undermined by both its theological reorientation and by evangelical condemnation of the cash nexus that had permeated them. It was difficult, however, to eradicate overnight something with so strong a popular foundation, and there may have been many like the parishioners in Erfurt, who enquired of Luther why their new-found evangelical convictions meant that they must give up veneration of the saints. In keeping with Luther's general principles of slow reform that did not offend "weak consciences," many Lutheran areas retained a substantial number of saints' days. But more radical forms of reform—Zwinglian, Calvinist, and Anabaptist—removed them in one fell swoop.

The saints' days that remained, detached from the former manifestations, were largely Marian feasts, those of the apostles, major saints of the early church, and local saints or patrons. In Protestant England the fictitious Saint George managed to survive because of his role as national patron. There is some indirect evidence, especially for Scandinavian countries, however, that the role of the saints as bearers of thaumaturgic aid may not have been as easily or as thoroughly uprooted as was their public cult. This can also be seen in the continued use of baptismal names such as Maria, Anna, Margaret, Barbara, and Katharine for women, and George and Christopher for men. In Hesse, the bestowal of the name Margaret became a surrogate form of continuation of this popular women's cult for at least a generation after the introduction of reform.

The Counter-Reformation church did not feel the least embarrassed about promoting the cult of the saints as a means of winning or retaining popular support. In a world (Protestant as well as Catholic) that still believed firmly in the power of divine intervention in human affairs to help and to heal as well as to punish, the miracle-working saint was a potent weapon in the propagandist armory, and bodies of saints who were preserved in their graves without corruption (such as Saint Filippo Neri) made a profound impression, especially on Lutherans, who felt a deep discomfort that they were unable to cite similar miraculous signs of divine favor as proof of the rightness of their faith. Such considerations undoubtedly encouraged the growth of a saintlike cult of Luther, with miraculous images and even claims that his body had also proved incorruptible, a cult promoted by eminent Lutheran churchmen well into the eighteenth century.

Catholic missionary activity into Protestantized areas sought to revive miraculous shrines as a conscious strategy of reconversion, and with some apparent success. But the papacy hesitated for some years before beginning a new wave of canonization. New Counter-Reformation canonizations continued the emphasis on male saints from the ecclesiastical hierarchy and the religious orders, with occasional female and lay figures. The church also promoted existing saints such as Saint Joseph as part of an idealization of the family and the role of the pious paterfamilias. At a popular level, saints played a continuing role as healers, and the power of "living saints" to heal was still a major means of attracting local veneration in Counter-Reformation Italy well into the eighteenth century. Indeed, the cult of the saints has survived in the Catholic world without significant check into the twentieth century, undoubtedly because it fulfills the same or similar needs to those of pre-Reformation times.

BIBLIOGRAPHY

Ashley, Kathleen M., and Pamela Scheingorn, eds. *Interpreting Cultural Symbols: St. Anne in Late Medieval Society.* Athens, Ga., 1990.

Burke, Peter. "How to Become a Counter-Reformation Saint." In *Religion and Society in Early Modern Europe*, edited by Kaspar von Greyerz. London, 1984.

Christian, William A. *Local Religion in Sixteenth-Century Spain.* Reprint, Princeton, 1989.

Delooz, Pierre. *Sociologie et canonisations.* Liège, 1969.

Gentilcore, David. *From Bishop to Witch: The System of the Sacred in Early Modern Terra d'Otranto.* Manchester, 1992.

Opitz, Claudia, et al., eds. *Maria in der Welt: Marienverehrung im Kontext der Sozialgeschichte 10.–18. Jahrhundert.* Zurich, 1993.

Soergel, Philip M. *Wondrous in His Saints: Counter-Reformation Propaganda in Bavaria.* Berkeley, 1993.

Vauchez, André. *La Sainteté en Occident aux derniers siècles du Moyen Age: D'après les procès de canonisation et les documents hagiographiques.* Rome, 1981.

Weinstein, Donald, and Rudolph M. Bell. *Saints and Society: The Two Worlds of Western Christendom, 1000–1700.* Chicago, 1982.

Wilson, Stephen, ed. *Saints and Their Cults: Studies in Religious Sociology, Folklore, and History.* Reprint, Cambridge, 1985. Includes extensive annotated bibliography.

Robert W. Scribner

SALMERÓN, Alfonso (1515–1585), Jesuit exegete, educator, papal emissary, and delegate to the Council of Trent. Born in Toledo on 6 September 1515, Salmerón studied literature and philosophy at the University of Alcalá before joining the small band of followers of Ignatius Loyola at the University of Paris. In 1534 he was among those who, with Ignatius, took the vow of service and loyalty to church and pope which led to the founding of the Society of Jesus in 1540. Salmerón's contribution to sixteenth-century Catholic renewal was substantial, mainly in doctrinal and educational reform.

Both before and after his ordination to the priesthood in 1537, Salmerón traveled through northern Italy preaching, caring for the sick, and giving pastoral care. From 1538 he held lectures on the Bible in Rome and worked with Ignatius on the Jesuit constitution. In 1549 Salmerón received a doctorate in theology from the University of Bologna. He then went on to lecture on the letter to the Romans at the University of Ingolstadt.

Salmerón traveled throughout Europe as a papal emissary with missions to Scotland, Ireland, Poland, and Belgium, and to the Diet of Augsburg in 1555. He was a notable theological adviser to all three sessions of the Council of Trent, contributing briefs on justification, sacramental teaching, confession, the Eucharist, the orders, and marriage. In 1561–1562 he served as interim head of the Jesuits while the vicar general, Diego Laínez, was traveling in France.

In 1551 Salmerón went to Naples to establish one of the first Jesuit colleges. In addition to teaching and writing, he served as superior of the Jesuits in Naples from 1558 to 1576. In 1562 he was appointed theological adviser to the papal commission on the Index of Prohibited Books. Salmerón spent the last years of his life working on his commentaries on the New Testament. These were published posthumously in sixteen volumes, four of them devoted to the Pauline letters, between 1598 and 1602.

BIBLIOGRAPHY

Primary Sources

Salmerón, Alfonso. *Commentarii in Evangelicam historiam.* 11 vols. Milan, 1597–1601.

———. *Commentarii in Acta Apostolorum.* Milan, 1601.

———. *Commentarii in omnes Epistolas B. Pauli.* 3 vols. Milan, 1602.

———. *Commentarii in epistolas Canonicas et in Apocalypsim.* Milan, 1602.

———. *Epistolae P. A. Salmeronis.* Edited by F. Cervés. 2 vols. Milan, 1906–1907.

Secondary Sources

Bangert, William V. *Claude Jay and Alfonso Salmerón: Two Early Jesuits.* Chicago, 1985. With extensive bibliography.

Guitiérrez, C. *Españoles en Trento.* Valladolid, 1951.

Koch, Ludwig. "Salmeron, Alphons." In *Jesuiten-Lexicon,* p. 1585. Paderborn, Germany, 1934.

O'Malley, John. *The First Jesuits.* Cambridge, Mass., 1993.

"Salmerón, Alfonso." In *Bibliothèque de la Compagnie de Jésus,* vol. 7, pp. 478–483. Paris, 1896. A comprehensive list of Salmerón's sermons, letters, and other writings, published and unpublished.

Schneider, B. "Salmerón, Alfonso." In *Lexicon für Theologie und Kirche,* vol. 9, pp. 270–271. Freiburg, 1964.

Schottenloher, Karl, ed. *Bibliographie zur deutschen Geschichte im Zeitalter der Glaubensspaltung, 1517–1585.* Stuttgart, 1956. See vol. 2, p. 216.

Willis, John D. "A Case Study in Early Jesuit Scholarship: Alfonso Salmerón, S.J., and the Study of Sacred Scripture. In *The Jesuit Tradition in Education and Missions,* edited by C. Chapple, pp. 52–80. Scranton, Pa., 1993.

KAREN BRINKMANN BROWN

SALVARD, Jean-François (also du Palmier; d. 1585), Reformed pastor from the Val d'Aoste notable for collecting Protestant confessions that eventually resulted in the *Harmony of Confessions.* There is no record of the date of his birth; the earliest record concerning him is his matriculation in 1559 into the new academy of Geneva. Two years later, he was sent as pastor to the church of Nevers in spite of the French royal decree against the return to France of those who had left because of religion. Salvard had not been in Nevers a full year before he and his fellow pastor, Isaac de la Barre, were imprisoned. De la Barre died in prison, and Salvard was released only in May 1563. In 1564, Salvard returned to Geneva, where, in November, he was asked to join the Compagnie des Pasteurs. On the grounds that if he accepted their invitation, his Roman Catholic father would be even more enraged, Salvard asked to be excused and shortly thereafter joined Pierre Viret in Lyon. Viret was expelled the following year, while Salvard was enjoined not to exercise his ministry. By 1568 Salvard was driven out of Lyon by the Wars of Religion and took refuge at Lausanne. In 1571 he was sent to the French church at Frankfurt am Main. This pastorate was also troubled, but not because of Roman Catholic opposition: from 1561 the Lutherans had been vexing the French Calvinists at Frankfurt. Nevertheless, Salvard remained there until 1576.

In 1577 Count Palatine Johann Casimir convoked in Frankfurt a meeting of the Reformed churches, and the French Reformed churches named Salvard as a delegate. The purpose of the convocation was to address the renewed attacks of those Lutherans who subscribed to the Formula of Concord of 1577. During the meeting, Philipp, landgrave of Hesse, said that he would convoke a synod of all the churches, while Salvard agreed to collect Protestant confessions of faith. Casimir suggested drawing up a new confession of faith that might serve not only for the Reformed but for all Protestants, a task assigned to Girolamo Zanchi.

In 1578 the French national synod of Sainte-Foy named Salvard among those assigned to the study commission for the new confession of faith, but, with the support of the Geneva pastors, Salvard preferred to continue to gather confessions. Working with him were Théodore de Bèze, Antoine de la Roche Chandieu, Lambert Daneau, and Simon Goulart. On 23 March 1581 Salvard sent his list for the *Harmony of Confessions* to Rudolf Gwalther in Zurich. On the following day, Bèze wrote to the Zurich pastors explaining the document in detail. Gwalther answered on 4 April for the Zurich pastors, correcting two errors but approving in principle and saying that they awaited the approval of other German Swiss towns. The *Harmony of Confessions* was published in August 1581.

In early 1582 Salvard was called to the church of Castres, but his departure was delayed by illness. He arrived in Castres only in June 1582. Two years later he traveled to Geneva, where he died in 1585.

BIBLIOGRAPHY

Primary Source

Salvard, Jean-François. *The Harmony of Protestant Confessions* (1842). Translated by Peter Hall. Reprint, Edmonton, 1992.

Secondary Sources

Bernus, A. "Jean-François Sallvard." *Bulletin historique et littéraire de la Société de l'histoire du protestantisme français* 36 (1887), 498–503.

Registres de la Compagnie des Pasteurs de Genève. Vol. 4, 1575–1582. Edited by Olivier Labarthe and Bernard Lescaze. Geneva, 1974.

JILL RAITT

SALZBURG. An ecclesiastical principality of the Holy Roman Empire since the twelfth century, Salzburg definitively separated from the Duchy of Bavaria about 1340. The regions in the foothills of the Alps along with Salzburg were easily controlled. The so-called *Land inner Gebirg* (mountains districts), including Pongau, Pinzgau, Lungau, Zillertal, and Brixental, remained relatively inaccessible and difficult to govern. Just as uprisings and civil unrest started in the mountainous areas, so too the evangelical movement found its staunchest support there.

An early connection between Salzburg and Wittenberg was Johann von Staupitz, a fatherly friend of Luther and, at one time, Luther's superior. Staupitz often worked in Salzburg from 1512, and on a continuing basis from 1516. In a letter dated 15 September 1518, Staupitz went so far as to urge Luther to come to Salzburg "to live and die there" with him. Staupitz, the abbot of Saint Peter's monastery in Salzburg from 1522 to 1524, believed that to his end there could be a reconciliation between Luther and the Catholic Church. Reformation writings found their way to the monks of Saint Peter's and to the city of Salzburg. Among the students from the Salzburg region who studied in Wittenberg were Georg Brenner from Werfen and Georg Führer from Salzburg. The most prominent was Christoph Weitmoser, who enrolled at Wittenberg in 1523 and later became an entrepreneur in the mining industry of Gastein and Rauris. Owing to the close commercial ties with Nuremberg, Reformation writings and thought filtered into the city of Salzburg.

The archbishop of Salzburg, Cardinal Matthäus Lang, attempted to remedy the sad state of the diocesan clergy and to prevent the spread of Reformation writings. However, neither the Regensburg Accord as concluded with the dukes of Bavaria in 1524 nor the diocesan synod of Salzburg of 1525 met with much success. The execution of two young peasants who had freed a convicted evangelical preacher touched off the Salzburg Peasants' War in 1525. This uprising was organized by mine operators from Gastein, with miners making up the core of the fighting units. Every list of demands presented by the insurgents, particularly the *24 Artikel Gemeiner Landschaft Salzburg*, contained harsh criticism of the Catholic church. Two demands stood at the forefront: freedom to preach the gospel and the right of parishioners to elect their parish priest. In addition they demanded the abolition of serfdom and the repeal of the small tithe (on cattle) on the grounds that neither could be justified from the Bible. After a treaty was concluded with the leaders of the first uprising on 31 August 1525, a new rebellion organized by the Tyrolian peasant leader Michael Gaismaier broke out in the spring of 1526. It was brutally crushed by the troops of the Swabian League and more than one hundred peasants were executed. With the failure of the peasant wars the focus shifted from the political and economic arena to the religious sphere.

Cardinal Matthäus Lang proved to be a relentless opponent of the new doctrine at the imperial diets at Worms (1521), Speyer (1529), and Augsburg (1530). A visitation he ordered in 1528 showed Pongau and parts of Pinzgau around Rauris and Taxenbach to be the hub of the evangelical movement. It also revealed great abuses among the diocesan clergy. The bishop of Chiemsee, Berthold Pürstinger, had already sharply criticized the state of affairs in the Catholic church, especially in Rome, in *Onus Ecclesiae* (1524). In 1526–1527 he wrote a reformist work entitled *Teutsche Theologey.* But Lang and his successors were frustrated in their attempts to carry out full-scale reform because of the shortage of priests. Under the administration of Ernst von Bayern (1540–1556), four canons left the cathedral chapter, married, and became Protestants. A visitation made in 1555 showed that the Protestant movement had gained further ground, particularly in the mountain districts.

Several decades earlier Martin Lodinger of Gastein had written to Luther complaining that he was unable to celebrate the Lord's Supper under both species. On the advice of the reformer, he left his native land. Now the demand that the chalice be offered to the laity became more insistent. This practice was authorized by Archbishop Johann Jakob of Kuen-Belasy in 1565, but was again forbidden in 1571. The Salzburg provincial synod of 1569, which sought to implement the decrees of the Council of Trent, and the founding of a seminary to train priests in 1582 marked the start of the Counter-Reformation. In 1588 the youthful archbishop of Raitenau, Wolf Dietrich, ordered that all residents who would not profess the Catholic faith were to leave the city. Many members of such prosperous Salzburg families as the Alt, Thenn, Praun, Unterholzer, Füller, and Klanner families moved either to Upper Austria (Linz, Wels, Vöcklabruck), to Protestant cities in the Empire such as Augsburg, Nuremberg and Heidelberg, or even to Silesia.

In the countryside, and particularly in the mountain districts, Archbishop Markus Sittikus (1613–1617) had Capuchin friars, accompanied by soldiers, conduct the most rigorous visitation to that date. More than 1,000 people, including 954 from the Pongau district, were ordered to leave the territory of Salzburg. To all outward appearances the resistance of the Protestants had been broken, but the evangelical movement survived among the people as a kind of underground Protestantism. Many Salzburg residents who disagreed with Melanchthon's more moderate course had turned to the teachings of Matthias Flacius Illyricus. The Großarl, St. Johann, and Radstadt districts of Pongau emerged as centers of the Flacian movement. Many of Flacius's followers "ran off" to towns over the border in Carinthia and Styria to receive Communion under both species. At the time of the expulsion ordered by Markus Sittikus, a large number of the Flacians, who were frequently suspected of being Anabaptists, went into exile in Moravia.

In the Peace of Westphalia of 1648 the local sovereigns were given the power to decide which religion would be followed in their territory. At the same time, religious dissidents were granted a three-year grace period to move away. In Salzburg, however, harsh Counter-Reformation-style measures were taken belatedly under Archbishop Max Gandolf von Kuenburg. In the spring of 1684, on the basis of an allegation of heresy, Capuchins were sent to the Defereggental region (eastern Tirol), where many of the residents wandered far and wide because they were engaged in peddling. On 10 October an order was issued for all Protestants to depart within four weeks and for them to leave their children under the age of 15 with Catholic families. Beginning on 10 December almost 1,000 people left the Defereggental region in small groups in the middle of winter. The exiles were portrayed as rebels and sectarians and under this pretext were granted no grace period for leaving their homes. Not until five years later were the 298 children who had been left behind allowed to join their families, thanks to the mediation of the *Corpus Evangelicorum* in Regensburg. Between 1686 and 1691 some seventy miners from the salt mines left their homes on account of their religious beliefs. One of these expatriates, Joseph Schaitberger, exerted great influence from his exile in Nuremberg over his fellow believers who had remained back in Salzburg through his song "Ich bin ein armer Exulant" (I Am a Poor Exile), his "circular letter," and other widely disseminated writings.

In an attempt to restore religious unity, Archbishop Leopold von Firmian brought Bavarian Jesuits to Salzburg in 1728. In reaction to the increasing pressure of this mission, ever larger numbers of the population openly converted to Protestantism. On 16 June 1731 a petition in the name of 19,000 believers was represented to the *Corpus Evangelicorum* in Regensburg, which had already come to the assistance of Protestants in Defereggental and Dürrnberg. This petition, however, incorrectly alluded to an "oppressed church" and simply demanded freedom to emigrate for those who so desired, without insisting on the usual three-year grace period. A series of unauthorized gatherings served as a pretext for the archiepiscopal government of Chancellor Hieronymus Cristani di Rallo to claim that a "rebellion of the mountain peasants" was at hand.

On 11 November 1731, the Authorization for Emigration was officially promulgated and stipulated that all Protestants must leave the country—residents who were not landowners (servants and maids) within eight days, propertied residents in both smaller cities and the country within three months. During the course of the winter of 1731–1732 almost 5,000 non-landowning residents left the country; little is known about their fate. King Frederick William I of Prussia offered to take in the peasants who began their emigration on 24 April 1732. Overall, 20,694 people reached east Prussia (Prussian Lithuania) in sixteen convoys. Two smaller groups of emigrants numbering 135 persons altogether reached Georgia (in what is now the United States), where they founded the settlement of Ebenezer in the territory of the Uchee Indians. However, the harshest fate befell the approximately 780 Protestant miners from Dürrnberg near the city of Hallein who accepted an invitation to settle in Holland in the winter of 1732–1733. The settlement on the Cadzand Peninsula met with such unfavorable conditions that a large number of the emigrants fell victim to an epidemic, while another portion of the group left Holland after a few months.

As for the settlement of property rights, which dragged on for years, the Prussian envoy Erich Christoph von Plotho and the *Corpus Evangelicorum* intervened on behalf of those who had emigrated. With the emigration of 1731–1732 Salzburg had lost over a fifth of its population. In certain districts of Pongau three-fourths of all the inhabitants had left; in the village of St. Johann the number of those who had emigrated represented 84.2 percent of the population.

Only with the *Protestantenpatent* (a decree authorizing Protestants to reside in the area) of 1861 was Protestantism once again able to gain a foothold in Salzburg (which had in 1816 become part of the Austro-Hungarian Empire). In 1863 an autonomous evangelical parish was established in Salzburg that at first encompassed all of Tirol and parts of

Upper Austria. The evangelical Friedenskirche (today Christuskirche) in the city of Salzburg was dedicated in 1867. Salzburg is today the seat of superintendent for the diocese of Salzburg/Tirol, which numbers almost thirty thousand Lutherans.

BIBLIOGRAPHY

Dopsch, Heinz, and Hans Spatzenegger, eds. *Geschichte Salzburgs: Stadt und Land.* 2 vols. in 8 pts. Salzburg, 1981–1991. See especially vol. 2, pt. 1, pp. 1–324; vol. 2, pt. 3. pp. 1521–1550.

Florey, Gerhard. *Geschichte der Salzburger Protestanten und ihrer Emigration, 1731/32.* Studien und Texte zur Kirchengeschichte und Geschichte 1/2. Vienna, 1977.

Jones, George Fenwick. *The Salzburger Saga: Religious Exiles and Other Germans along the Savannah.* Athens, Ga., 1984.

———. *Detailed Reports on the Salzburger Emigrants Who Settled in America . . . Edited by Samuel Urlsperger.* 8 vols. Athens, Ga., 1993.

Langer, Hermann. *Joseph Schaitberger: Ein evangelischer Glaubenskämpfer des 17. Jahrhunderts.* Mitteilungen der Gesellschaft für Salzburger Landeskunde, Ergänzungsband 10. Salzburg, 1985.

Marsch, Angelika. *Die Salzburger Emigration in Bildern.* Weissenhorn, 1977.

Marx, Gerhard. *Glaube, Werke und Sakramente im Dienste der Rechtfertigung in den Schriften von Berthold Pürstinger, Bischof von Chiemsee.* Erfurter Theologische Studien 45. Leipzig, 1982.

Ortner, Franz. *Reformation, katholische Reform und Gegenreformation im Erzstift Salzburg.* Salzburg, 1981.

Sallaberger, Johann. "Johann von Staupitz: Luthers Vorgesetzter und Freund und seine Beziehungen zu Salzburg." *Mitteilungen der Gesellschaft für Salzburger Landeskunde* 117 (1977), 159–200.

Zaisberger, Friederike, ed. *Reformation, Emigration, Protestanten in Salzburg.* Exhibition catalog, 2. Salzburger Landesausstellung auf Schloß Goldegg. Salzburg, 1981.

HEINZ DOPSCH

Translated from German by Robert E. Shillenn

SAN CRISTOBAL, Diego de. *See* Estella, Diego de.

SANCTIFICATION. The most natural interpretation of the Vulgate term *sanctification* is *sanctus facere,* or "to make holy." Although the notions of "setting apart" and "consecration" are generally regarded as integral to the Hebraic root underlying the biblical term, there are indications that these were not fully appreciated during the sixteenth century.

Semantic Aspects of Sanctification. The term *sanctificatio* is by no means restricted to the writings of the Protestant wing of the Reformation. Nevertheless, it has a particular association with this wing, apparently on account of a semantic issue that should be noted. In the writings of Augustine, which served as a seminal resource to much medieval and Reformation theological reflection, the term *iustificatio* was understood to possess the basic sense of "making righteous." The ideas of regeneration, renewal, and sanctification were thus embraced in this complex and highly nuanced concept, making it unnecessary (indeed, problematic) to draw a distinction between the dual divine actions of initiating the Christian life and sustaining it through spiritual and moral growth.

From the 1520s it became commonplace for Protestant writers to draw a distinction between the event of justification, taking place outside the believer and affecting his or her status *coram Deo,* and the process of regeneration or sanctification, taking place within the believer and effecting his or her renewal through the Holy Spirit. Yet Catholic writers regarded both these as being subsumed under the aegis of justification. Where Philipp Melanchthon introduced a notional distinction, with its accompanying vocabulary, between "declaring to be righteous" and "making righteous," the Catholic tradition regarded both of these as being comprehended by the overall concept of "justification." This inevitably led to considerable terminological confusion and misunderstanding, especially in the polemical literature of the late sixteenth century.

Luther and Melanchthon. In his early period Martin Luther declined to distinguish justification and sanctification. In part this reflects his eschatological understanding of justification, in which the renewal of the sinner is understood proleptically as an aspect of the *promissio Dei* that undergirds the Christian hope. (This consideration is also thought to underlie Luther's early hesitations in making extensive use of the anagogic sense of scripture.) Another consideration, however, underlies Luther's reluctance to employ any form of terminology that suggested "a growth in holiness" or "being made righteous." Luther was concerned that this would lead to introspection, in which believers would be encouraged to look within themselves for signs of spiritual growth or development instead of looking outside themselves to the gracious promises of God. Luther's conception of fallen human nature as *incurvatus in se* led him to avoid any soteriological strategies that might encourage such introspection. For Luther the Christian life is a process of *semper a novo incipere,* "always beginning all over again," in which believers become aware of their lack of holiness and are thus forced to return to the cross in order to receive forgiveness.

This suspicion of the concern for personal holiness was understood by at least some of Luther's colleagues and opponents alike to imply that good works had no real place in the Christian life or that there was no obligation on the part of the believer to be concerned about spiritual growth or moral improvement. Luther's celebrated concern with distinguishing law and gospel—linked with his fear that any hint of obligation on the part of the Christian to perform good works could lead to justification being seen as the consequence of human achievement—led to both personal and social sanctification being given low priority at Wittenberg.

This would be the cause of some friction between Luther and Andreas Bodenstein von Karlstadt. Perhaps the issue at stake can be seen as ultimately verbal rather than substantive; nevertheless, there was a body of opinion that held that Luther was not interested in holiness.

Yet Luther's aversion to the language of renewal and spiritual growth was not universally shared. In fact, there are reasons to suppose that it was an aspect of Luther's thought that even his colleagues at Wittenberg found puzzling. Melanchthon found it natural to draw a distinction between being granted the status of righteous through a judicial pronouncement (as when the people of Rome declared Scipio to be free) and the internal process of renewal. Melanchthon did not make any significant usage of the terminology of sanctification; nevertheless, the language of regeneration abounds in his writings of the 1520s.

Reformed Theology. A much more positive estimation of the significance of sanctification may be discerned in the Reformed tradition. The early Reformation writings of Huldrych Zwingli emphasized the need for believers to lead "blameless lives wrought after the pattern of Christ." In some ways Zwingli's emphasis on the need for moral renewal within the believer reflects the moralist ethos of the humanist sodalities of eastern Switzerland, with which he was familiar. The life of a Christian ought to be about "building a life in holiness and innocence according to the example of Christ." It would be incorrect to see this as a doctrine of justification by works; Zwingli's concern was to ensure that those who were Christians demonstrate their calling in their public and private lives.

Martin Bucer also emphasized the need for moral and spiritual regeneration. In his *Berner Predigt* Bucer affirms that one of the central purposes of the death of Christ is to "make people holy" (*selig zu machen*). The terminology of sanctification is firmly established in Bucer's vernacular and Latin writings. In common with the emerging reformational consensus, Bucer stressed that sanctification is not a human achievement but the work of the Holy Spirit: *Spiritus est, quia a sancto venit, et sanctificat.* For Bucer the chief means of the sanctifying work of the Spirit are the word of God, the ministers of the church, the sacraments, and the discipline of the church:

> [The Spirit] still works this holiness day by day in those who believe in Christ, but not without intermediaries. In this, the Spirit makes use of the word and the holy sacraments. . . . Thus through the ministry of Paul, the Corinthians were sanctified, born again, and became Christians. So great is the honor that God gives to his own people, poor worms that we are, whom he raises up and appoints as his own instruments.

Bucer's concern with sanctification is expressed clearly in his distinction between *iustificatio impii* and *iustificatio pii,* both of which he regarded as fundamental to the Christian life. Believers are initially justified in the sight of God through faith; they are subsequently justified publicly by their good works. Sanctification is thus understood as an integral element of the soteriological trajectory from election to final glorification.

With Calvin the theology and terminology of sanctification receives its definitive statement. The term *sanctificatio* is firmly established and comes to take precedence over such alternatives as *renovatio* and *regeneratio.* The relation between justification and sanctification is defined and clarified in terms of the controlling image of "union with Christ," which is understood to act as the foundation of both. Acceptance in the sight of God (justification) is not dependent upon moral improvement or regeneration (sanctification), nor does justification render sanctification superfluous. For Calvin justification and sanctification are both direct consequences of the believer's incorporation into Christ. If the believer has been united with Christ through faith, he or she is at one and the same time made acceptable in the sight of God (justification) and launched on the path to moral improvement (sanctification). By treating these two elements, which had hitherto been regarded as independent entities requiring correlation, as subordinate to the believer's union with Christ, Calvin was able to uphold both the total gratuitousness of acceptance before God and the subsequent demands of obedience.

The location of the discussion of sanctification in the 1559 edition of the *Christianae religionis Institutio* has been the subject of some puzzlement. A discussion of sanctification precedes that of justification even though the reverse order would appear to make more theological sense. The most elegant explanation of this would appear to be a desire to preempt the criticism that the doctrine of justification by faith alone leads to moral laxity or antinomianism. It must be noted, however, that no totally convincing explanation of this point has yet emerged.

The Radical Reformation. From its outset the radical Reformation was concerned with personal holiness. The emphasis placed upon personal and social sanctification by Karlstadt during his time at Orlamünde led to a degree of alienation between him and Luther. Karlstadt incorporated the mystical notion of *Gelassenheit* into his thought in this context, which seemed to reduce faith to merely one aspect of a general surrender to God. Similarly, Kaspar von Schwenckfeld sought to defend the doctrine of justification by faith during the 1520s; however, he shared the general perception that this doctrine, at least as stated by Luther, was detrimental to personal ethics. Probably more in a desire to safeguard rather than to modify the doctrine, Schwenckfeld emphasized the progressive nature of sanctification. This emphasis, however, would lead him to regard Luther's solifidianism as deficient in its moral aspects.

Underlying this can be seen a general Anabaptist trend to retain the traditional Catholic understanding of justification in terms of sanctification, or "making righteous." Converts to Anabaptism were expected, as a matter of course, to demonstrate regeneration in their lives, partly as a public manifestation of their break with the fallen temporal order. The separatist tendencies within the radical Reformation appear to have given rise to expectations of immediate and tangible spiritual and moral transformation as a consequence of separation from the world; the magisterial Reformation did not experience comparable pressures for public signs of change within their memberships.

The Catholic Reformation. As noted above, the Catholic Reformation proceeded on the assumption that sanctification was an integral aspect of justification. This was given formal expression by the Council of Trent's decree on justification, the seventh chapter of which affirms that justification "is not only a remission of sins, but also the sanctification and renewal of the inward person." This statement represents a consensual summary of the main lines of interpretation of sanctification within the medieval tradition, which were affirmed and defended in the light of the early Reformation controversies. Trent formulated an essentially Augustinian conception of justification, closer to Luther's understanding than is often realized, in which sanctification is subsumed under justification.

[*See also* Books of Martyrs; Justification; *and* Saints, *article on* Sainthood.]

BIBLIOGRAPHY

Beachy, Alvin J. *The Concept of Grace in the Radical Reformers.* Nieuwkoop, 1978.

Greschat, Martin. *Melanchthon neben Luther: Studien zur Gestalt der Rechtfertigungslehre zwischen 1528 und 1537.* Witten, 1965.

Hefner, Joseph. *Die Entstehungsgeschichte des Trienter Rechtfertigungsdekretes.* Paderborn, 1909.

Kolb, Robert. *Nikolaus von Amsdorf: Popular Polemics in the Preservation of Luther's Legacy.* Nieuwkoop, 1978. Excellent analysis of aspects of early Lutheran controversies, including the antinomian debate.

McGrath, Alister E. *Iustitia Dei: A History of the Christian Doctrine of Justification.* 2 vols. Cambridge, 1986. Follows the development of the doctrine of justification, including its relation to sanctification, from its biblical origins through to the modern period.

Stadtland, T. *Rechtfertigung und Heiligung bei Calvin.* Neukirchen-Vluyn, Germany, 1972.

Stephens, W. P. *The Holy Spirit in the Theology of Martin Bucer.* Cambridge, 1970.

Williams, George H. "Sanctification in the Testimony of Several So-Called *Schwärmer.*" *Mennonite Quarterly Review* 42 (1968), 5–25.

Zimmermann, G. "Calvins Auseinandersetzung mit Osianders Rechtfertigungslehre." *Kerygma und Dogma* 35 (1989), 236–256.

ALISTER E. MCGRATH

SÁNTA, Martin Kálmáncsehi. *See* Kálmáncsehi, Márton.

SARAVIA, Adrianus (c.1532–1613), Reformed theologian and minister. An influential figure with a long and varied career, Saravia made significant contributions both to the upbuilding of the Reformed church in the Netherlands and to the theological justification of episcopacy in England. Born in Saint-Omer, France, he was the son of a Spanish father and Flemish mother. Originally intended for a career in the priesthood, he spent his formative years in the Franciscan monastery at Hesdin, interspersed with a period of study in Paris.

In 1557 he abandoned the religious life and shortly after fled to England, where in 1559 he joined the newly regathered refugee church in London. Over the next years the services of this highly regarded young scholar were much in demand, and Saravia spent short periods in the Netherlands ministering to secret congregations in Antwerp and Brussels before accepting in 1563 a new position as headmaster of the Elizabeth College on the island of Guernsey. His time in Antwerp was notable principally for an important if shadowy role in the drafting of the Belgic Confession. With the outbreak of the Revolt of the Netherlands in 1566, Saravia was again called back to the Netherlands: he appeared briefly as a minister in Antwerp in the summer but returned to Guernsey after the outbreak of iconoclasm. Nevertheless, Saravia was again in the Netherlands in 1568, when he joined William of Orange on his first abortive campaign against Fernando Álvarez de Toledo, duke of Alba, and wrote a pamphlet in justification of Orange's proceedings. In 1571, having returned once more to England, Saravia was appointed headmaster of the King Edward VI school in Southampton, a post that would occupy him for the next seven years.

Only with the greatest reluctance was he persuaded to accept a new call from his homeland, first to Ghent and then to Leiden, where he served briefly as minister before taking up a post as professor of divinity in the new university. Saravia was now a person of some influence in the councils of the church, frequently called upon for an opinion in disputes between ministers or in clashes of jurisdiction with the lay power. His superior command of English also made him an ideal choice for negotiations with the English allied forces then stationed in the Netherlands. It was this association which would bring a sudden reversal in Saravia's fortunes and necessitate his final departure from the Netherlands, as Saravia soon identified himself wholeheartedly with the policies of Robert Dudley, earl of Leicester, leader of the English forces and briefly a figure of great influence in the formulation of policy in the new state. In 1587 a plot was discovered aimed at increasing the influence of Leicester and those Dutchmen who shared his political aims; Saravia was implicated and consequently stripped of his posts and forced to flee.

He settled for the final time in England, where he quickly accumulated ecclesiastical patronage and influence. Rector of Tattenhill in Staffordshire from 1588, he was appointed in 1595 a prebendary of Canterbury and vicar of Lewisham in Kent. Here he became an intimate friend of Richard Hooker, with whose views on episcopacy and church government he became closely associated. His first important work from this period (1590) was a defense of episcopacy and became sufficiently well enough known to merit a reply from Théodore de Bèze. Saravia was not intimidated, and published his own response two year later (1594). His powerful writings in defense of the English establishment secured him in his last years a variety of valuable preferments, including prebends in both Westminster and Worcester. In 1607 he was nominated to the committee charged with the production of a new authorized translation of the scriptures. He died in 1613 at the age of 81 and was buried in Canterbury Cathedral. His long and distinguished career is a monument to the permeability of international frontiers in this period and to the close ecclesiastical connections between England and the Low Countries, which allowed Saravia to build a career that spanned both Dutch Reformed and Anglican churches.

BIBLIOGRAPHY

Bakhuizen van den Brink, J. N., ed. *De Nederlandse belijdenisgeschriften.* 2d ed. Amsterdam, 1976.

Grave, J. W. de. "Notes on the Register of the Walloon Church of Southampton and the Church of the Channel Islands." *Proceedings of the Huguenot Society* 5 (1894–1896), 125–178.

Hodges, G. F. "Adrian Saravia: Headmaster of Elizabeth College." *Société guerniaise: Reports and Transactions* 12 (1933), 57–72.

Nijenhuis, Willem. *Adrianus Saravia, c.1532–1613.* Leiden, 1980.

Verzeichnis der im deutschen Sprachbereich erschienenen Drucke des XVI. Jahrhunderts. Stuttgart, 1983–. See vol. 18, nos. 1663–1665.

ANDREW PETTEGREE

SARCERIUS, Erasmus (Ger., Sorck, Schürer; 1501–1559), Lutheran educator, clergyman, and publicist. Sarcerius taught in several places before Saint Catherine's in Lübeck. In 1536 William, Count of Nassau, appointed him head of the school in Siegen. He became superintendent of the Nassau churches and court preacher. He was one of the first to establish moral discipline as a mark of the Reformed church, enforcing it through synods and consistories, but he stressed the household as a nucleus of the evangelical life. His *Methodos in praecipous scripturae locos* (Commonplaces) was translated into English (1538), and Melanchthon praised his church order as a worthy model.

After the Reformation was introduced in Albertine Saxony, Sarcerius was invited to become professor of theology in Leipzig, but he remained in Nassau until 1548. He left then because he could not work under the conditions imposed by the Augsburg Interim, though he soon became pastor in Leipzig, which was then widely known for the so-called Leipzig Interim, Elector Moritz of Saxony's compromising response to Charles V. In 1552 he joined Melanchthon as a delegate to the Council of Trent, but the delegation was recalled as the elector engaged in an anti-imperial conspiracy.

Appointed general superintendent of the Mansfelt churches, Sarcerius was once again influential in formulating the disciplinary codes of regional churches. He also became a critic of the Majorist thesis that good works are necessary for salvation. George Major, one of Sarcerius's predecessors in Mansfelt, then taught at Wittenberg.

Asked to evaluate one of Sarcerius's books, Melanchthon sought to assuage Sarcerius in private before he sent his critique to the elector. In 1557, at the Colloquy of Worms, Sarcerius joined the adversaries of Melanchthon. There Melanchthon strongly rejected Sarcerius's question whether Christ's body remained in the consecrated bread after Communion so that Christ might descend into the stomach of a mouse. He died soon after being appointed pastor in Magdeburg.

BIBLIOGRAPHY

Primary Source

Sarcerius, Erasmus. *Conciones annuae pro iis qui in Ecclesia docent. . . .* Frankfurt a.M., 1983.

Secondary Sources

Bundschuh, Benno von. *Das Wormser Religionsgespräch von 1557.* Münster, 1988. Discusses Sarcerius's (minor) role at Worms and provides a brief biographical sketch.

Eskuche, Gerhard. *Sarcerius als Erzieher und Schulmann.* Siegen, 1901. Contains some biographical information; useful about Sarcerius as educator.

Spalding, James G. "Discipline as a Mark of the True Church in Its Sixteenth Century Lutheran Context." In *Piety, Politics and Ethics,* edited by Carter Lindberg, pp. 119–139. Kirksville, Mo., 1984. Suggests that Sarcerius's emphasis on moral discipline may have inspired Bucer and others. Corrects many biographical data in the nineteenth century works.

Verzeichnis der im deutschen Sprachbereich erschienenen Drucke des XVI. Jahrhunderts. Stuttgart, 1983–. See vol. 18, nos. 1669–1791.

DERK VISSER

SARPI, Paolo (1552–1623), Venetian friar, scholar, and antipapal polemicist; author of the first history of the Council of Trent. Born to modest circumstances in Venice, Sarpi joined the Servite order in 1565, rising to become provincial head and, in 1585, procurator general of the order. Of brilliant intellect and wide-ranging erudition, he was proficient in classical languages, history, mathematics, and canon law as well as natural science. Sarpi's mastery of theological disputation brought him a professorship in Mantua at the age of eighteen, but his evident independence of mind provoked the Inquisition to question his orthodoxy. On three occasions between 1593 and 1601 he was denied a bishopric. He rejected confession as unscriptural and demoralizing, opposed the veneration of Mary as promoted by the Jesuits, and questioned papal authority over any council of bishops.

In 1606 Sarpi became embroiled in a controversy between Rome and the Venetian Republic over church property rights, clerical immunity, and other matters touching on church-state relations. As state theologian, he directed the republic's assault on papal authority, declaring it null and void in secular matters. In supporting Venice in its conflict with Rome, Sarpi was instrumental in the Venetian Senate's decision to expel the Jesuits and ignore the interdict issued by Paul V in what proved to be a futile attempt to command the obedience of the republic.

Sarpi corresponded with French Huguenots and had close relations with the Protestant community in Venice, particularly the English ambassador, Sir Henry Wotton, leading to speculation that he might lead Venice away from the Catholic church altogether. While his ultimate motives remain unclear, the Venetians were, in any case, too conservative to effect a permanent break with Rome. Still, the Senate held its ground, and the final resolution of the dispute, with the pope yielding on virtually all points, proved a landmark in the struggle of Catholic states for dominion over their national churches.

In 1607 Sarpi survived an assassination attempt believed to have been initiated in Rome after Venice refused to deliver its chief theologian to the Inquisition for questioning. Sarpi proceeded to write a history of the Council of Trent which, although based on interviews with participants and documents collected over a lifetime, was flawed by its strong antipapal bias and deliberate intent to discredit the post-Tridentine church as a tool of the Curia Romana.

BIBLIOGRAPHY

Primary Sources

Sarpi, Paolo. *Opere.* Edited by Gaetano Cozzi and Luisa Cozzi. Milan, 1969. A one-volume edition of Sarpi's works including his *Lettere ai gallicani e protestanti* and *Istoria del Concilio Tridentino* as well as his theological and philosophical writings.

———. *Pensieri.* Turin, 1976.

———. *Istoria del Concilia Tridentino.* Florence, 1982.

Secondary Sources

Bautz, Friedrich Wilhelm, ed. *Biographisch-bibliographisches kirchenlexikon.* Hamm, Germany, 1970–. See vol. 8, nos. 1254–1260.

Fra Paolo Sarpi dei Servi di Maria. Venice, 1986. Papers from a congress celebrating the 750th anniversary of the founding of the Servites bibliography.

Frajese, Vittorio. *Sarpi scettico: Stato e chiesa a Venezia tra Cinque e Seicento.* Bologna, 1994. The most recent work. Useful modern bibliography.

Guaragnella, Pasquale. *La prosa e il mondo: "Avvisi" del moderno in Sarpi, Galilei e la nuova scienza.* Bari, 1986.

Hitchcock, Maxine C. "From Anathema to Aggiornamento: The Contest between Sarpi and Pallencino over the Council of Trent." Ph.D. diss., University of California, Santa Cruz, 1980.

Lievsay, John L. *Venetian Phoenix: Paolo Sarpi and Some of His English Friends.* Lawrence, Kans. 1973. Scholarly examination of Sarpi's English connections. Extensive bibliography of primary sources and modern studies.

Peusieri, G., and L. Cozzi, eds. *Paolo Sarpi.* Turin, 1976.

Wootton, David. *Paulo Sarpi: Between Renaissance and Enlightenment.* Cambridge, 1983.

KARIN BRINKMANN BROWN

SARTORIUS, Jan (also Tosarrius; 1500?–1557?), Dutch Christian humanist with strong evangelical sympathies. Serious gaps in the record and the apparent contradictions in the sources make the course of his career hard to reconstruct. He was probably born at Amsterdam, where by 1525 he held the post of rector of a school. In the autumn of that year the authorities detained him for several months on account of heretical opinions, which he evidently abjured. According to a later, if unsubstantiated, account, Sartorius had earlier belonged to a circle of evangelically inclined clerics and schoolmasters that met at Delft under the guidance of a mysterious "Lutheran monk." Whatever the truth of this report, Sartorius certainly remained in correspondence with other members of this alleged group, including Willem Gnapheus (1493–1568), the evangelical and neo-Latinist schoolmaster in The Hague. Despite these doubts about his orthodoxy, Sartorius was apparently appointed to teach Latin by the magistrates of Amsterdam, where his advocacy of justification by faith alone prompted the conservative humanist Cornelius Crocus (1500?–1550?) to reprimand him by open letter on this subject in 1531. Sartorius's influence extended to his pupils, who expressed their anticlerical opinions in the tolerant religious climate then prevailing in Amsterdam. But the apocalyptic enthusiasm of the Münsterite Anabaptism in Holland and, especially, the attempt by religious radicals to seize control of Amsterdam in May 1535 compelled the town government to bow to demands from Brussels and conservatives to deal rigorously with heretics. Evangelically minded clerics and schoolmasters were dismissed and many Anabaptists executed. Though he took no part in the disturbances, Sartorius was suspected of familiarity with the leaders, and in December 1535 he was banished from the city for having flouted an earlier prohibition on his teaching. Sartorius withdrew to the coastal village of Noordwijk, for which reason he dubbed himself Aquilovias (i.e., from Noordwijk). Here in 1537 he again fell afoul of the authorities for having concealed a suspected heretic. Here too he seems to have spent much of the rest of his career as a schoolmaster, though he made excursions in 1544 to east Friesland and, probably, to Basel, where he had connections with the publisher Oporinus.

Only five works of Sartorius's considerable literary output have apparently survived. As a schoolmaster-humanist and a fervent admirer of Erasmus, Sartorius was concerned to ensure that his pupils acquire a fluent command of classical Latin, and his four pedagogical works include collections of proverbs, the best known being *Adagiorum chiliades tres*, published posthumously in 1561. By also providing Dutch translations or equivalents Sartorius helped to awaken interest among humanists for the vernacular language. Sartorius also discussed religious issues in his textbooks, especially his *Exercitus*, which was often reprinted. He betrays his Erasmian sympathies in the distinction he makes between letter and spirit and in his attack on clerical celibacy. Trapman, however, has demonstrated that Sartorius also drew extensively on the writings of Sebastian Franck when he composed *Paraphrases in omnes Prophetas*, and he has suggested that as Sartorius grew more disillusioned with the rampant sectarianism, he took refuge in the individualistic spiritualism advocated by Franck. Unlike Gnapheus and Wouter Delenus, evangelical schoolmasters of his acquaintance, Sartorius saw no benefit in leaving the Roman church; true Christians were everywhere few in number.

BIBLIOGRAPHY

Primary Sources

Sartorius, Ioannes. *Selectissimarum orationum germanice redditarum delectissimus adversus barbariem exercitus.* 1540?; Antwerp, 1543; Antwerp, 1545; Antwerp, 1556; Antwerp and Leiden 1563; Antwerp, 1565; Antwerp, 1573.

———. *Paraphrases in omnes Prophetas, tam Maiores, quam Minores duodecim ... Item in Sapentiam Salomonis.* Basel, 1558.

———. *Adagiorum chiliades tres, quae Ioannes Sartorius in Batavicum sermonem proprie ac eleganter convertit, et brevi ac perspicua interpretatione illustravit.* Antwerp, 1561.

Secondary Sources

Grosheide, D. "Enige opmerkingen over de reformatie en het humanisme in de noordelijke Nederlanden." *Serta historica* 2 (1970), 72–93. Minimizes the impact of Christian humanism on the Reformation in the northern Netherlands.

Kölker, A. J. *Alardus Aemstelredamus en Cornelius Crocus. Twee Amsterdamse priester-humanisten.* Nijmegen, 1963. Detailed study of two Catholic opponents of Sartorius at Amsterdam.

Schoockius, Martinus. *Liber de bonis vulgo ecclesiasticis dictis.* Groningen, 1651. Uses letters of Sartorius since lost.

Spruyt, Bart Jan. "Humanisme, evangelisme en reformatie in de Nederlanden, 1520–1530." In *Reformatie in meervoud: Congresbundel 1990*, edited by W. de Greef et al., pp. 26–54. Kampen, 1991. A sensitive discussion of the various reform movements in the first decade of the Reformation. Forthcoming in English in *Archiv für Reformationsgeschichte.*

Trapman, Johannes. "Ioannes Sartorius (ca. 1500–1577), gymnasiarch te Amsterdam en Noordwijk, als erasmiaan en spiritualist." *Nederlands archief voor kerkgeschiedenis* 70 (1990), 30–51. The fullest account of his career and the most satisfactory treatment of Sartorius's religious development, with a summary in English.

Alastair C. Duke

SATTLER, Michael (c.1490–1527), Benedictine monk, then Anabaptist martyr, author of the Schleitheim Articles (1527). Before becoming an Anabaptist, Sattler had been prior of Saint Peter's of the Black Forest, near Freiburg im Breisgau. In 1519 Saint Peter's of the Black Forest initiated a process of monastic reform through the Bursfeld Union. This reform was never fully instituted, and the influence of Benedictine reform on Sattler, while possible, remains a matter of inference.

Subjects of Saint Peter's participated in the Peasants' War of 1525. On 12 May 1525 the monastery was taken by the Black Forest troop, which included Anabaptist volunteers from Waldshut and Hallau. This event may have provided the occasion for Sattler's departure from the monastery, for he appears subsequently in the company of Anabaptists of the Waldshut/Hallau region. That fundamental grievances championed by the peasants found their way into the Schleitheim Articles suggests that Schleitheim is in some significant ways a continuation of, rather than a total break with, the movement of the common people.

Sattler's earliest documented missionary activity as an Anabaptist dates from June 1526, when he made Anabaptist converts in the Zurich Unterland and later in the town of Lahr, near Strasbourg. Early in 1527 he met with Martin Bucer and Wolfgang Capito, reformers in Strasbourg; he pleaded with them for the release of imprisoned Anabaptists and discussed doctrinal disagreements. Bucer and Capito held Sattler in high regard; after Austrian authorities put him to death they described him as "a martyr of Christ." But Jakob Ottelinus, Reformed pastor in Lahr, described Sattler and his work in that city in more disparaging terms.

Following a February 1527 meeting of Anabaptists in the Swiss village of Schleitheim, which resulted in the adoption of seven articles, Sattler traveled to Württemberg to become pastor at an Anabaptist congregation in the town of Horb. He was arrested there sometime before 18 March 1527 along with his wife, Margaretha, a former Beguine sister whom he married at an unknown date. The official charges read at the trial (which mention Margaretha by name), as well as a record of Sattler's pretrial questioning, are extant, as are three independent trial accounts. Following particularly cruel and grisly torture, Sattler was burned at the stake on 20 May 1527 at Rottenburg am Neckar. Margaretha was executed by drowning two days after Sattler's death, declining all offers of mercy in return for her recantation.

Given Sattler's brief tenure as an Anabaptist leader, his influence on the Swiss Anabaptist movement and on the larger Reformation was posthumous, carried out primarily through his authorship of the Schleitheim Articles and published accounts of his steadfastness unto death. The articles were the first systematic articulation of Swiss Anabaptist principles and played a crucial role in consolidating the movement. They dealt with adult baptism, the Lord's Supper of baptized believers, the ban, separation from the world, election of pastors, and the refusal to wield the sword or to swear oaths. These principles came to define Swiss Anabaptism and distinguish it from the Zwinglian and Lutheran reforms. The articles circulated widely in print for at least two decades, printed together with accounts of Sattler's martyrdom and his prison letter to the Horb congregation. But the articles were fully accepted only by the Swiss Anabaptists and the Hutterites. They had no discernible impact on important Anabaptist leaders such as Balthasar Hubmaier, Hans Hut, Pilgram Marpeck, Melchior Hoffman, or Menno Simons.

The Reformed clergy in Switzerland soon engaged the Schleitheim Articles directly. Reformed pastors Johannes Oecolampadius in Basel and Berchtold Haller in Bern had copies in hand only a few months following the Schleitheim meeting. By the time Huldrych Zwingli prepared a Latin translation and refutation of the articles in the summer of 1527 (the *Elenchus*) he had before him four separate copies of the articles. Since the articles set the theological agenda for Swiss Anabaptists, they indirectly provided the basis for several formal disputations between them and Reformed clergy (Zofingen, 1532; Bern, 1538). A French translation of the articles (no longer extant) came into Calvin's hands in 1544; he cited portions of this text in the process of writing a refutation ("Briève instruction pour armer tous bons fidèles . . .").

By 1600 the Schleitheim Articles were no longer being printed. Sattler's memory was kept alive among descendants of the Anabaptists primarily through continued printings of the account of his trial and martyrdom, his pastoral letter to the Horb congregation, and one hymn attributed to him in the *Ausbund* (the Swiss Brethren hymnal). The full significance of Sattler and Schleitheim for Anabaptism and the Reformation has come to be recognized again only in the modern period, as a result of critical historical studies.

BIBLIOGRAPHY

Fast, Heinold. "Michael Sattler's Baptism: Some Comments." *Mennonite Quarterly Review* 60 (1986), 364–373. Fast questions Snyder's dating of Sattler's acceptance of adult baptism.

Haas, Martin. "Michael Sattler: On the Way to Anabaptist Separation." In *Profiles of Radical Reformers,* edited by Hans-Jügen Goertz, pp. 132–143. Scottdale, Pa., 1982. Although superseded in some details by subsequent scholarship, remains a useful, brief biography.

Jackson, S. M., ed. *Selected Works of Huldreich Zwingli.* Philadelphia, 1901. See pp. 123–258 for the *Elenchus.*

Martin, Dennis. "Monks, Mendicants and Anabaptists: Michael Sattler and the Benedictines Reconsidered." *Mennonite Quarterly Review* 60 (1986), 139–164. Martin questions Snyder's thesis concerning Benedictine influences on Swiss Anabaptism.

Snyder, C. Arnold. "Rottenburg Revisited: New Evidence Concerning the Trial of Michael Sattler." *Mennonite Quarterly Review* 54 (1980), 208–228. A critical examination of extant textual evidence documenting the trial and martyrdom of Michael Sattler.

———. *The Life and Thought of Michael Sattler.* Scottdale, Pa., 1984. The most complete biographical work on Sattler, a critical monograph that collates the recent scholarship. Snyder argues for a significant Benedictine influence on Sattler and, through him, on Swiss Anabaptism. This thesis has been contested (see D. Martin and C. A. Snyder) as have some of Snyder's other conclusions (see H. Fast and C. A. Snyder).

———. "The Schleitheim Articles in Light of the Revolution of the Common Man: Continuation or Departure?" *Sixteenth Century Journal* 16 (1985), 419–430. Snyder concludes that there was a closer relationship between Sattler/Schleitheim and the Peasants' Revolt of 1525 than has sometimes been assumed.

———. "Michael Sattler, Benedictine: Dennis Martin's Objections Reconsidered." *Mennonite Quarterly Review* 61 (1987), 262–279.

———. "Michael Sattler's Baptism: Some Comments in Reply to Heinold Fast." *Mennonite Quarterly Review* 62 (1988), 496–506.

———. "The Influence of the Schleitheim Articles on the Anabaptist Movement: An Historical Evaluation." *Mennonite Quarterly Review* 63 (1989), 323–344. Snyder concludes that Schleitheim was not a universally accepted "Anabaptist" confession of faith, but rather its influence was limited to the Swiss Anabaptists and the Hutterites.

Verzeichnis der im deutschen Sprachbereich erschienenen Drucke des XVI. Jahrhunderts. Stuttgart, 1983–. See vol. 18, nos. 1881–1885.

Yoder, John H. *The Legacy of Michael Sattler.* Scottdale, Pa., 1973. Source edition containing all of Sattler's known writings, in English translation.

C. ARNOLD SNYDER

SAVONAROLA, Girolamo (1452–1498), Dominican preacher, religious and political reformer, polemicist, and prophet. Born in Ferrara, in northeastern Italy, he studied medicine and liberal arts at the University of Ferrara. Possibly as the result of a disappointment in love, Savonarola underwent a long spiritual crisis and decided to become a Dominican friar, entering the convent of Saint Domenico at Bologna. On the completion of his novitiate in 1476, he was professed; he received his sacerdotal ordination in late 1477.

Savonarola early acquired a reputation as a biblical scholar. He was appointed master of novices to the convent of Santa Maria degli Angeli, Ferrara, in 1479 and then in 1482 reader to the convent of San Marco, Florence, where his primary duty was the exposition of scripture. In Florence he composed philosophical and spiritual treatises and preached both in the city and countryside. His surviving works from this period are heavily influenced by Thomism in approach and in method of exposition.

At San Gimignano in the Florentine countryside in 1485, he was moved to preach that the church would soon be scourged and then reformed. In 1487, he was appointed dean of studies (*Magister studiorum*) at the Studium in Bologna and continued to preach his apocalyptic message, now to the cities of northern Italy.

In 1490, at the behest of Lorenzo de' Medici, the *de facto* ruler of Florence, he was reappointed reader to the convent of San Marco. Claims to the contrary notwithstanding, relations between Savonarola and the Medici were close. He was elected prior in 1491. By 1493, with the active support of the Florentine government, he succeeded in creating a new Dominican observant congregation centered on the convent of San Marco and controlled by him.

Savonarola's learning won him acceptance in the circle of *literati,* humanists, Neoplatonist philosophers, and religious thinkers that gathered around Lorenzo de' Medici. Exposure to the ideas of such eminent figures as Giovanni Pico della Mirandola, Marsilio Ficino, Angelo Ambrogini (Poliziano), and the brothers Girolamo and Domenico Benivieni wrought important changes upon his doctrines and their presentation. He evolved a more personal style for his sermons, which drew praise for their directness and force. Stylistic innovation was accompanied by more varied doctrinal content. Neoplatonic, Scotist, and Ockhamist themes were now presented in both his sermons and spiritual treatises.

His apocalyptic message was further elaborated by means of a revelation that the process of scourging and renewal would be heralded by the invasion of a mighty king, who, like Cyrus of Persia, would act as God's instrument and wreak divine vengeance upon the sinful peoples of Italy. He enjoined the Florentines to repent and to strive for their own salvation by imitating the life of Christ and seeking spiritual union with him. He also ensured that the convent of San Marco and the congregation he headed would be reformed so as to serve as a guide to the laity.

When the invasion of Italy in 1494 by Charles VIII of France seemed to confirm all Savonarola's predictions, his popularity knew no bounds. Following the expulsion of Piero de' Medici, he played a primary role in Florentine politics, contributing to the political settlement of December 1494, whereby a great council on the Venetian model was instituted. Not only the settlement itself but the terms of the debate leading up to it were conditioned by a new religious message. Almost overnight Savonarola transformed himself from a preacher of doom into the prophet of the Florentine millennium. Florence, he declared, was divinely appointed to lead Christianity into the new age, benefiting thereby from untold spiritual and material gifts.

For the next three years Savonarola sought to prepare Florence for its destiny. He called for the reform of children and of women, for the regulation of lay brotherhoods, for harsher penalties against homosexuals and blasphemers, and for the expulsion of Jews from Florence, the New Jerusalem. Opposition in government and from clerics meant that few of his proposals became law. Much resented were his campaigns against secular festivals, gamblers, prostitutes, and transgressors of sumptuary laws. These campaigns, organized from the convent of San Marco, mobilized youthful enforcers. They were characterized by processions, public prayer, and bonfires of "vanities." Savonarola's most enduring achievement, however, was the creation of a system of public welfare in which existing and newly founded institutions, such as the Monte di Pietà, were organized to relieve the lot of the city's poor and sick.

Opposition against Savonarola began to mount. His pro-French policy isolated Florence and turned Pope Alexander VI against him. Savonarola's refusal either to obey a summons to Rome or to stop preaching led to his excommunication and eventually to the threat of an interdict over Florence. Abandoned by the Florentine government, Savonarola and two of his brethren were arrested, tortured, forced to confess to the crimes of false prophecy and political conspiracy, and executed on 23 May 1498. Savonarola's ideology nonetheless influenced the next fifty years of Florentine history. The last Florentine republic (1527–1530) may be viewed as the embodiment of this ideology at its most fanatical.

Savonarola's religious thought proved most adaptable, inspiring groups and individuals throughout Western Christendom. His call for a root and branch reform of the church was taken up by numerous reformers, among them Giovanfrancesco Pico and Gasparo Contarini, who incorporated it into their own influential programs. Italian evangelism—the complex and widespread spiritual movement of the mid-sixteenth century, which stressed personal religious renewal and accommodation with Protestantism, especially over justification—was deeply influenced by Savonarola's message of salvation. Well-known figures outside Italy also came under Savonarola's spell, Marguerite d'Angoulême being the most eminent of his French "converts." Through her, his message was circulated in the courtly spiritual circles over which she presided. Luther himself praised Savonarola for his righteousness and may have been partly indebted to him for his own teaching on justification.

Equally profound was Savonarola's influence on biblical and patristic studies. Theologians trained at San Marco made important contributions to both fields by translating texts from the original Hebrew and Greek and by ensuring their circulation in humanist circles in Italy and elsewhere. The Catholic and Protestant reforms alike benefited from these scholarly advances. Close contacts were established by Savonarolans with France and in particular with Lyon, where a much imitated system of poor relief on the Florentine model was established.

BIBLIOGRAPHY

Cattin, Giulio. *Il primo Savonarola: Poesie e prediche autografe dal Codice Borromeo.* Florence, 1973. Publishes some of the earliest works of Savonarola drawn from the Borromeo Codex, long presumed lost.

Cordero, Franco. *Savonarola.* 4 vols. Bari, Italy, 1986–1988. A huge, somewhat chaotic, and very critical treatment of Savonarola; useful, nonetheless, for the wealth of information it provides and for serving as a corrective to the devotional current in Savonarolan studies.

Nolte, Josef. *"Evangelicae doctrinae purum exemplum*: Savonarolas Gefängnis meditationen im Hinblick auf Luthers Theologische Anfänge." In *Kontinuität und Umbruch,* edited by J. Nolte et al., pp. 59–92. Stuttgart, 1978. A detailed treatment of the influence of Savonarola's theory of justification on Luther.

Polizzotto, Lorenzo. *The Elect Nation: The Savonrolan Movement in Florence, 1494–1545.* Oxford, 1994. The first extended treatment of the follwers of Savonarola and of their influence on Florentine society.

Polizzotto, Lorenzo, and Caroline Elam. "*La unione de' gigli con gigli*: Two Documents on Florence, France and the Savonarolan Millenarian Tradition." *Rinascimento* 31 (1991), 239–259. Opinions of Savonarola on the French court and the "conversion" of Marguerite d'Angoulême to the Savonarolan cause are discussed on the basis of two newly discovered documents.

Ridolfi, Roberto. *The Life of Girolamo Savonarola.* Translated by Cecil Grayson. Reprint, Westport, Conn., 1976. Its devotional slant is often too marked, nonetheless still the best biography of Savonarola.

Schnitzer, Joseph. *Savonarola: Ein Kulturbild aus der Zeit der Renaissance.* 2 vols. Munich, 1924. Italian edition, revised and extended, Milan, 1930. Despite its age and its hagiographic tone, an invaluable discussion of Savonarola and of his apostolate. Particularly useful on theological issues.

Simoncelli, Paolo. *Evangelismo italiano del Cinquecento.* Rome, 1979. Discusses Savonarola's influence on Italian evangelism and on other non-Italian reformers connected with it.

Weinstein, Donald. *Savonarola and Florence: Prophecy and Patriotism in the Renaissance.* Princeton, 1970. A milestone in Savonarola historiography in which the complex relationship between Savonarola and Florence is discussed and in which, for the first time, Savonarola's message is analyzed historically and the shift from an apocalyptic to a millenarian content is identified and explained.

LORENZO POLIZZOTTO

SAVOY. A duchy since 1416, Savoy was one of Europe's most important buffer states, controlling a large block of territories, including the main Alpine passes between Italy and France. Its first duke, Amadeus VIII, had been elected pope by the Council of Basel, while all three of its sixteenth-century rulers married royal princesses from Portugal, France, and Spain. Its political destiny, however, shifted dramatically during the Reformation era. When Charles III (1504–1553) inherited it, Savoy's territories and interests lay primarily on the northwestern side of the Alps, and political control of Geneva, the natural capital of this region, seemed within his grasp. By the time his son Emmanuel-Philibert (r. 1553–1580) recovered a smaller duchy in the 1560s, its northeastern zones had been permanently lost to the Swiss confederation, primarily to the Protestant canton of Bern. By the time Charles Emmanuel (r. 1580–1630) died, all his lands northwest of the Rhone had been permanently lost to France; however, the marquessate of Saluzzo had been added in the south, solidifying his control of the western Italian Alps from Piedmont south to the Mediterranean at Nice. Although Savoy still retained control of the French side of major alpine passes, its political center had become Italian. Its capital had been fixed at Turin by Emmanuel Philibert in 1564. The ducal House of Savoy was well on its way toward becoming kings of Italian territories (1714) and ultimately of all Italy, when they ceded their remaining French-speaking territories west of the Alps in 1860.

No event did more to make the duchy of Savoy into an essentially Italian state than the disastrous invasion and occupation by allied French and Swiss forces in 1536. At the same time, no event so decisively marked the religious history of Charles III's hereditary lands. This brief war, which erased the duchy from Europe's political map for over twenty years, began in order to protect the precarious independence of the city of Geneva, ruled by a prince-bishop usually related to the House of Savoy. As Henri Naef remarked, Geneva around 1500 "knew that she . . . rotated about the Savoyard sun" and "neither sought nor felt the need to escape from it." Yet the fortuitous selection of a Genevan bishop who was not a vassal of Savoy invigorated a civic rebellion which allied the city's burghers with the Swiss by 1526 and effectively expelled him. (Geneva's most famous bishop, Francis de Sales, observed in 1602 that he was the city's only legitimate sovereign: the dukes of Savoy held a few minor offices, but the citizens' independence was based on sheer usurpation.) When Charles III finally began to besiege Geneva in 1535, he fatally alienated the Swiss, who struck a quick deal with their French ally; both declared war on Savoy in 1536, overran it with little resistance, and divided its territories between them.

The Swiss annexed everything north and east of Lake Geneva, along with the French-speaking territories around its southern shore; Francis I of France controlled virtually all of the remaining Savoyard territories, except Nice and one Italian fortress. Savoy became a French province and remained under Valois rule until the Treaty of Cateau-Cambrésis (1559) ended the Italian wars and restored most of the territories to Emmanuel Philibert, who had commanded the army of Philip II at its decisive victory over the French at Saint-Quentin in 1557. The reinstated duke conducted separate negotiations with the Bernese, which ultimately resulted in the Treaty of Lausanne (1564), under which Bern kept the Pays de Vaud while returning three *bailliages* (Gex, Ternier, and Thonon), located around the southwestern portion of Lake Geneva, to Savoy. Emmanuel Philibert negotiated another treaty with Valais (1569), which returned to him the remaining south shore of Lake Geneva west of the Rhone. This famous soldier carefully avoided further wars after recovering most of his lands, and even reached a *modus vivendi* with the Republic of Geneva in 1570.

The next duke, Charles Emmanuel, was an indefatigable schemer but an unlucky warrior. His persistent pursuit of territorial objectives, first in France and later in Italy, produced chronic warfare after 1588, often on his own soil: twice, in 1600 and 1630, the French occupied his lands. He proved equally tireless and equally unsuccessful in his attempts to acquire Geneva, to whose inhabitants he always promised freedom of religion if they would accept his sovereignty. The failure of his great surprise attack, the Escalade of December 1602, is still celebrated annually in Geneva. The subsequent Treaty of Saint-Julien (1603) ratified the republic's *de facto* independence, which endured until 1798.

The religious history of the Savoyard lands during the Reformation provides extensive variations on the theme of *cuius regio, eius religio.* Geneva became Protestant in the process of expelling its prince-bishop and allying with Protestant Bern. Protestantism was forcibly introduced in all territories conquered by the Bernese in 1536, and Emmanuel Philibert guaranteed freedom of Protestant worship in those districts surrounding Geneva that he recovered after the Treaty of Lausanne. Elsewhere, apart from a few Waldensian communities in the Piedmontese Alps which adopted a Reformed confession of faith in 1532, heresy was not a serious problem, either for the French rulers before 1560 or the Savoyards afterward. Protestantism in these territories, however, proved impossible to uproot wherever it had been organized before 1560 so long as the Bernese continued to protect their fellow Protestants—which they ceased to do after negotiating a new treaty with Savoy in 1590.

The Catholic reconversion of the lands around Lake Geneva became the great work of Geneva's most famous absentee bishop, Francis de Sales (1567–1622). In 1594 he began his missionary work in the Chablais, a district on the southern side of the lake, which had changed rulers four times during the previous sixty years. Without significant assistance from Charles Emmanuel, Francis's remarkably gentle methods (he believed and practiced the proverb about catching flies with honey instead of vinegar) netted a few hundred converts after three difficult years. Once the Chablais mission was entrusted to more combative Capuchins, and especially when the duke prohibited Protestant worship after signing a peace treaty with France, the vast majority of the inhabitants of the region rapidly accepted Catholicism: a list of more than two thousand newly converted heads of household, representing nearly the entire population of Chablais, was sent to Rome in 1598. Three years later Francis complained that a few stubborn Huguenots had not yet been banished.

North of Geneva lay the Pays de Gex, another Protestant part of the diocese that Francis acquired in 1602. Savoy, however, had ceded it to France in 1601; despite many missions to Paris, Francis never gained adequate support to underwrite Catholic missionary work there. After the Edict of Nantes was extended to Gex in 1612, nearly all of its two dozen churches were formally returned to Catholic worship, but most of its ecclesiastical revenues remained in Protestant hands. Without funds or state support, Francis accomplished little. Gex remained overwhelmingly Protestant until Louis XIV withdrew the provisions of the Edict of Nantes from this district in 1662. Twenty years later his minions demolished its Protestant temples and expelled its ministers, thereby provoking a mass exodus and an insincere conversion.

[*See also* Bern *and* Geneva.]

BIBLIOGRAPHY

Devos, Roger, and Bernard Grosperrin. *Histoire de la Savoie.* Vol. 3, *La Savoie de la réforme à la révolution française.* Rennes, 1985.

Kleinman, Ruth. *Saint Francis de Sales and the Protestants.* Travaux d'Humanisme et Renaissance, 52. Geneva, 1962.

Monter, E. William. *Calvin's Geneva.* Reprint, Huntington, N.Y., 1975.

E. William Monter

SAXONY. In 929 Henry I built the fortress of Meissen as a base of German dominance in the region that had been settled by Sorbs. The diocese of Meissen was founded in 968. The enfeoffment of Henry of Eilenburg with the Meissen March marked the beginning of the dominant presence of the Wettiners in the Elb region. In 1247 the House of Wettin acquired Thuringia and in 1423 received the office of elector along with the dukedom of Saxony-Wittenberg. The name Saxony was thereby applied to the Meissen territories of the House of Wettin. At the same time the rise of the House of Wettin in the Holy Roman Empire began and was to reach its first peak toward the end of the fifteenth century.

After the territory of the Habsburgs, the lands of the House of Wettin represented the most important sovereign entity in the empire. In 1476 Ernest of Saxony received the archiepiscopal see of Magdeburg and in 1479 the diocese of Halberstadt. The House of Wettin was unable to exploit these new possibilities for expanding its power, however, since both these benefices fell to Albert of Brandenburg in 1510. Only from 1482 to 1484 was the archbishop of Mainz installed by the House of Wettin, while Frederick of Saxony led the fortunes of the Teutonic order in Prussia from 1498 to 1510. The year 1485 witnessed the "partition of Leipzig" between Prince Elector Ernest and his brother Albert. The partition into Ernestine and Albertine territories was to have significant repercussions and endured until 1918. Ernest received the district connected to the office of elector, parts of Vogtland as well as central and southern Thuringia with Wittenberg, Torgau, Weimar, Gotha, and Coburg as major centers. Northern Thuringia, Leipzig, and Meissen along with the residence of Dresden fell to the Albertines. This created the framework within which an important segment of the history of Saxony was played out with the Reformation. The rivalry between the two Saxonies had existed from the beginning, but as it steadily increased, this rivalry determined the course of events between the Oder and the Werra rivers in the decades that followed. On the one hand, Elector Frederick III (the Wise), who succeeded his father in 1486 and ruled until 1525, pushed for a reform of the empire and for the strengthening of the estates of the empire over against the emperor, acting prudently and deliberately but without energy or drive. On the other hand, Albert rendered invaluable service to Austria and the Habsburgs as field commander. He had already entrusted the administration of his lands to his son George in 1488. George put his fifty-year rule to good use and worked successfully at consolidating the Albertine portion from within.

While agriculture was dominant in the Ernestine territories, economic development in the more densely populated Albertine territories was influenced by the expansion of the ore-mining industry. There trade and industry played a larger role. Agents of the Fugger and Welser banks appeared in Leipzig and Zwickau. Textile production developed in Vogtland and in the foothills of the Erzgebirge. The economic productivity fostered increasing construction activity as well as the fine arts. As a result of the Leipzig partition the University of Wittenberg was founded. This university quickly overshadowed Leipzig as a center of humanistic scholarship and thereby provided the Reformation with its scientific and theological foundations.

This territorial duality defined the terms of the relationship between the Ernestines and the Albertines and by 1539 included religious and ecclesiastical policy. While Elector Frederick protected the Reformation movement and ensured Luther the freedom of action he needed, his brother and successor, John the Constant, consciously supported the renewal and systematically built up a new ecclesiastical order. In 1532 his son John Frederick continued this path with determination. He took advantage of the political situation in the empire and carried out an aggressive domestic and imperial policy that was beholden to the Reformation. After 1525 the Ernestine electors succeeded in becoming the leading Protestant power in the empire with the support of Hesse and the Schmalkald League, and they also became the model for religious renewal and the establishment of evangelical territorial churches. In the conflict between the emperor and estates adhering to the old faith and those who favored the Reformation, the Ernestines assumed the influence that the House of Wettin had partially lost in 1485. On the one hand, the Wittenberg Reformation strengthened the position of the House of Wettin within the empire. On the other hand, it led Duke George to become a staunch opponent of Luther and to combat actively the evangelical movement like no other imperial prince.

The introduction of the Reformation on the Wittenberg model in Albertine Saxony in 1539 bridged the tensions within the House of Wettin only for a short time. Duke Henry, who was succeeded by Duke Moritz in 1541, did not join the Schmalkald League and pursued the pro-Habsburg policy of the Dresden court. In the Schmalkald War (1546/47) the potential for conflict that had been building up between the Albertines and Ernestines exploded on the level of imperial and religious politics. The Wittenberg surrender of May 1547 sealed the defeat of John Frederick and his aggressive pro-Protestant policy, while it won for Moritz the office of elector and considerable territorial gain, but it did not put an end to the Leipzig partition of 1485. From now on the Ernestines were limited to Thuringia, and only the Albertine territories were considered to be Saxony. The enhanced position the Ernestines had gained with the Lutheran Reformation shifted to the Albertines. After 1550 the Albertines increasingly took advantage of this shift. The desire for restoration shaped Ernestine policy for a long time. Through his loyalty to the emperor, Moritz helped to bring about the Augsburg Interim of 1548 and plunged the evangelical estates of the empire into a profound political crisis after Luther's death.

The controversies over the Interim led to a serious theological struggle. With the Treaty of Passau in 1552 Moritz prepared the way for the Peace of Augsburg, which was achieved in 1555 by his brother August, who succeeded him in 1553. The legal recognition of the adherents to the Augsburg Confession led to the coexistence of two confessions in the empire and strengthened the estates of the empire over against the emperor. But this recognition did not lead to a lasting balance between the confessions throughout the empire.

Elector August pursued a pro-evangelical policy. He had clearly dissociated himself from the Interim. He purposefully proceeded with the establishment of the evangelical territorial church. On 8 May 1557 August ordered the publication of the General Articles as the keystone in the formation of an Albertine territorial church and the completion of the Reformation. The establishment of the evangelical ecclesiastical order was followed by its consolidation and theological grounding. But the territorial church became part of the state. An outward sign of this was the issuing of the church and school regulations of 1580 that encompassed the whole of public and church life and endured in part into the nineteenth century.

[*See also* Diet; Holy Roman Empire; Interims; Schmalkald League; *and* Schmalkald War.]

BIBLIOGRAPHY

Blaschke, Karlheinz. *Sachsen im Zeitalter der Reformation.* Gütersloh, 1970.

Junghans, Helmar, ed. *Das Jahrhundert der Reformation in Sachsen.* Berlin, 1989. Bibliography.

Kötzschke, Rudolf, and Hellmut Kretzschmar. *Sächsische Geschichte* (1935). Reprint, Frankfurt a.M., 1965.

GÜNTER WARTENBERG

Translated from German by Robert E. Shillenn

SCALIGER, Joseph Justus (1540–1609), Italian Protestant scholar. Scaliger was the son of Julius Caesar Scaliger, a natural philosopher, doctor, and humanist, originally named Bordone, who settled in Agen and pretended to be a last survivor of the della Scala of Verona. Joseph attended the Collège de Guyenne for three years and acted as his father's secretary until the latter's death in 1558. But he basically educated himself, mastering Greek, Hebrew, Aramaic, and many other languages without the help of teachers. As a young man in the 1560s, he converted to Calvinism, joined the learned circles that centered on the Collège Royal in Paris, and traveled in Italy with a nobleman, Louis Chasteigner de la Roche Posay. Later he studied Roman law with the great historical scholar Jacques Cujas and taught briefly in Geneva (1572–1574). Commentaries on Latin texts—Varro's *De lingua latina,* the *Appendix Virgiliana,* Ausonius, Festus, the elegists, and Manilius—established his reputation as a brilliant textual critic.

But the work that definitively made his name was his study of the calendars and dates of ancient and medieval, Eastern and Western history. A first installment of this study reached print in 1583 as the *Opus novum de emendatione temporum.* Though so technical as to repel most readers, this work addressed issues of vital concern to both Catholic and Protestant scholars: how to establish a single skeleton of dates to which one could attach the main events of biblical and classical history, starting from the Creation and including the Flood, the Exodus, the Babylonian Exile, and dates of the life of Christ. These problems had already spawned a massive technical literature when Scaliger first addressed them. He drew freely on his predecessors—especially the Germans Johannes Funck and Paulus Crusius—who argued, in the tradition of Melanchthon, that the historian must use astronomical data and pagan texts as well as the Bible. He rebutted the influential thesis of the Calvinist chronologer Matthieu Béroalde, his successor at the Genevan academy, who held that the Bible was in itself a sufficient basis for writing the history of the world. Scaliger's work had innovative and iconoclastic components. He attacked the *Historia Ecclesiastica* of Eusebius as partly unreliable and used the Passover Haggada to explicate the account of the Last Supper in Mark's gospel.

Though Scaliger met some opposition in Geneva and enraged Catholic scholars by his (largely unjustified) attack on the Gregorian calendar reform, he became the most famous chronologer in an age when biblical and classical chronology ranked among the most fashionable scholarly studies. In 1593 the innovative University of Leiden appointed him to a permanent and highly paid research post, for which he reluctantly left France. For the next decade and a half he devoted himself to compiling new editions of his earlier works and to composing the vast *Thesaurus temporum,* the most ambitious of his books. Here he reconstructed the lost Greek text of the *Chronicle* of Eusebius from Byzantine chroniclers who had drawn on it, showing that the original had had two books, though the surviving Latin adaptation by Jerome had only one. He also assembled and commented on many of Eusebius's lost sources, the works of such Hellenistic writers as Manetho and Berossus. In this book Scaliger not only attacked a vast range of technical problems but also brought to light much evidence for the great antiquity of the pagan kingdoms, such as the Egyptian dynasty lists of Manetho, which would prove crucial in the seventeenth-century debates about the authority of the Bible.

Scaliger had no teaching duties at Leiden, but he gathered the most talented young men in the Low Countries—Hugo Grotius and Daniël Heinsius, for example—around him, helping them to study the classics and imparting to them his scholarly method. He had a powerful impact on the philological study of the New Testament and its context, which preoccupied many seventeenth-century scholars—as opposed to the theological study of the text, which his insights did not affect. Scaliger became one of the first scholars to grasp the vast size and historical importance of the communities of Hellenized Jews in the centuries before and after the beginning of the Christian era, a lesson he passed on to his pupil Heinsius, who would argue that the New Testament was written in a special "Hellenistic" Greek. He did pioneering work on the Jewish sects of the time of Jesus. His studies in the Talmud and other Jewish sources—which a Jewish convert, Philippus Ferdinandus, helped him to read—enabled him to show how much that was characteristic of the Judaism of the time of Jesus had passed into Christianity.

Though Scaliger's reputation became enormous, his last years were ruined by the attacks of Protestant chronologers and Catholic polemicists; the latter revealed his true family origins, a heavy blow to a man who had his portrait painted in the purple robes appropriate to a prince. Scaliger died in 1609, having given an example of erudition, independence of thought, and Christian humanism that would be admired and imitated by such men as John Selden and Leibniz.

BIBLIOGRAPHY

Bernays, Jacob. *Joseph Justus Scaliger.* Reprint, New York, 1965.

Grafton, Anthony. *Joseph Scaliger.* 2 vols. Oxford, 1983–1993.

Jonge, H. J. de. "The Study of the New Testament." In *Leiden University in the Seventeenth Century: An Exchange of Learning,* edited by Th. H. Lunsingh Scheurleer et al. Leiden, 1975.

Pattison, Mark. *Essays.* Edited by Henry Nettleship. Oxford, 1889.

Verzeichnis der im deutschen Sprachbereich erschienenen Drucke des XVI. Jahrhunderts. Stuttgart, 1983–. See vol. 18, nos. 2077–2078.

Anthony Grafton

SCANDINAVIA. *See* Denmark; Finland; Iceland; Norway; Sweden.